WORDS AND PHRASES
legally defined

Volume 3: K–Q

WORDS AND PHRASES
legally defined

THIRD EDITION

under the General Editorship of
John B Saunders
of Lincoln's Inn, Barrister

Volume 3: K–Q

London
Butterworths
1989

United Kingdom	Butterworth & Co (Publishers) Ltd, 88 Kingsway, LONDON WC2B 6AB and 4 Hill Street, EDINBURGH EH2 3JZ
Australia	Butterworths Pty Ltd, SYDNEY, MELBOURNE, BRISBANE, ADELAIDE, PERTH, CANBERRA and HOBART
Canada	Butterworths Canada Ltd, TORONTO and VANCOUVER
Ireland	Butterworth (Ireland) Ltd, DUBLIN
New Zealand	Butterworths of New Zealand Ltd, WELLINGTON and AUCKLAND
Puerto Rico	Equity de Puerto Rico Inc, HATO REY
Singapore	Malayan Law Journal Pte Ltd, SINGAPORE
USA	Butterworth Legal Publishers, AUSTIN, Texas; BOSTON, Massachusetts; CLEARWATER, Florida (D & S Publishers); ORFORD, New Hampshire (Equity Publishing); ST PAUL, Minnesota; and SEATTLE, Washington

First published 1989

British Library Cataloguing in Publication Data

Words and phrases legally defined.—3rd ed/edited by John B Saunders
1. Commonwealth countries. Common law countries. Law—Encyclopaedias
I., Saunders, John B (John Beecroft), *1911*—
342.009171′241

ISBN 0 406 08040 2 (set)
0 406 08041 0 (vol 1)
0 406 08042 9 (vol 2)
0 406 08043 7 (vol 3)
0 406 08044 5 (vol 4)

Typeset by Phoenix Photosetting, Chatham, Kent
Printed and bound in Great Britain by
Mackays of Chatham Ltd, Kent

OVERSEAS REVISING EDITORS

Australia
Arthur E Garcia LLB(NSW), LLM(Syd)

Canada
Heather Probert LLB
of the Ontario Bar

New Zealand
Hellen Papadopoulos LLB
Barrister and Solicitor of the High Court of New Zealand

USA
Michael G Walsh
Assistant Professor in Business Law at the College of Commerce and Finance, Villanova University, Villanova, Pennsylvania

EDITORIAL MANAGER

Margaret Cherry LLB

The United Kingdom material in this volume states the law as at 30 June 1989. Material from jurisdictions outside the United Kingdom is up-to-date to 31 March 1989.

K

KANGAROO COURT

Australia [The defendant was charged with wilfully insulting a Royal Commission by describing its procedures as a 'kangaroo court'.] 'To describe the inquiry as a "kangaroo court" was to pour scorn upon the inquiry. The Macquarie Dictionary defines "a kangaroo court" as "an unauthorised or irregular court conducted with disregard for or perversion of legal procedure. . . ." To describe either a court or an inquiry pursuant to a commission as "a kangaroo court" is to be contemptuous of it.' *R v O'Dea* [1983] 72 FLR 436 at 445–446, per Davies J

KEEP *See also* HAVE OR KEEP

[The Mines and Quarries Act 1954, s 48(1) imposes a duty on the manager of every mine to take such steps as may be necessary for 'keeping' the road or working place secure.] ' "Keeping" the road secure does not mean that the manager must ensure there shall never be a fall, however unforeseeable. He can only "take steps" against foreseeable dangers.' *Brown v National Coal Board* [1962] 1 All ER 81 at 91, HL, per Lord Denning

[The Vehicles (Excise) Act 1962, s 7 (repealed; see now the Vehicles (Excise) Act 1971, s 8 made it an offence to use or 'keep' on a public road any mechanically propelled vehicle for which a licence under the Act was not in force. An unlicensed car was moved into a public road from a motor showroom whilst the showroom was rearranged.] 'I approach the word "keeps" in what seems to me the ordinary meaning of some continuing process; not a mere isolated moment, but a keeping of the car there, at any rate for some interval of time. It is no doubt a matter of degree and fact in every case. So far as this case is concerned, the point left for the decision of the court is whether the mere presence, albeit for a moment of time, of the vehicle on the road amounts to a keeping of that vehicle on the road. In my judgment, keeping means something more than that, both according to its ordinary meaning and when it appears in conjunction with the other word "uses".' *Dudley v Holland* [1963] 3 All ER 732 at 734, per Lord Parker CJ

Australia [The Vermin and Noxious Weeds Act 1958–1986 (Vic), s 13 provides that where an inspector finds that noxious weeds are growing upon any land he may give notice to any owner to effectually destroy all noxious weeds and to 'keep' the land clear.] 'The word "keep", I think, is wide enough to do duty in s 13(2) as a word involving an obligation to bring the land to a state where weeds are absent, as well as an obligation to maintain the land in that state.' *McNeill v O'Keeffe* [1962] VR 680 at 681, 682, per Sholl J

Canada 'In the case at bar the gasoline was not "kept" in the garage [within a statutory condition of a policy]. The gasoline did not remain in the garage continuously for an extended period. On the contrary a small quantity was brought into the garage occasionally for a particular purpose, and when this purpose was served, as it was in the course of one or two hours, the gasoline was taken out of the garage. I am of opinion that on these facts gasoline was not "kept" or "stored" in the garage. Nor, in my opinion, should this view be altered because of the fact that on one occasion, by mistake, the can containing gasoline remained in the garage over night. If, despite the insured's settled practice as to the use of gasoline in the garage and despite his regular nightly inspection to see that the gasoline was removed, the can by some oversight escaped attention and remained all night in the garage, that single instance would not, in the circumstances, constitute "keeping" gasoline in the garage.' *Blue v Pearl Assurance Co Ltd* [1940] 3 WWR 13 at 19, 20, Alta SC, per Ewing J

New Zealand 'Subsection 1 of s 37 [of the Licensing Amendment Act 1910 (repealed; see now the Sale of Liquor Act 1962, s 264)] makes it illegal to keep or use any building, room, or other premises in any no-licence district as a place of resort for the consumption thereon of intoxicating liquor. A room in the defendant's hotel is, with his knowledge and consent, habitually used by a number of persons as a place of resort for the consumption of intoxicating liquor therein, or, in the language of the section, "thereon". The defendant supplies these persons with glasses. . . . They can also be supplied with soda-water or other beverage (non-intoxicating, of course). . . . Obviously but for the facilities thus afforded for the consumption of intoxicating liquor these persons would not resort to this room and bar. A person keeps or uses a room for the purpose or purposes for which he knows it is resorted to. It is immaterial, on the question of keeping or using, that he may also keep it for the sale of non-intoxicating beverages.' *Bingham v Coleman* (1914) 33 NZLR 989 at 991, 992, per Denniston J; also reported 16 GLR 652 at 653

New Zealand [The Crimes Act 1961, s 147(1)(a) makes it an offence to 'keep' a brothel.] 'The word "keep" in ordinary parlance has many differing connotations, including to retain, to maintain, and also in a global sense to keep business premises and to conduct the business accommodated therein, as in the "keeping of a boarding-house", or a store, or a common gaming house, etc. In my view, it is in this sense that the word is used in para (a) of s 147(1).' *R v Mickle* [1978] 1 NZLR 720 at 723, SC, per Bain J

New Zealand 'In short, control or a share of control over the brothel is essential to constitute a person a keeper. Similarly a person does not "manage" the brothel unless he or she takes part in its control. The shade of difference between keeping and managing is that the former term is more apt for the owner of the business and the latter for a delegate conducting it for him.' *R v Barrie* [1978] 2 NZLR 78 at 81, CA, per Cooke J

Ordinarily keep

Australia 'To take the word "ordinarily" first, that word connotes in this context [Dog Act 1966–1986 (NSW), s 4(2) (see now s 6(2)(a)(ii))] some degree of continuity. I now turn to the word "kept". The words "kept" or "keep" can bear a very wide variety of meanings according to the subject matter of that which is alleged to be kept. When used in the context of a person ordinarily keeping a dog on any land or premises, and in relation to the occupier of that land or those premises who is entitled to occupy that land or those premises in one of the capacities mentioned in sub-s (4) of s 4 of the Act, I think that the phrase "ordinarily kept" can include the meaning of the act of so treating the dog with some degree of continuity that the animal becomes attached to that land or those premises for the time being.' *Porter v Cook* [1971] 1 NSWR 318 at 319, CA, per cur.

KEEP IN REPAIR *See* REPAIR

KEEP OPEN

Canada [A deed reserved a right of way at the rear of property as long as the owners of the property adjoining 'kept open' an equal width of land for a similar purpose.] 'I think that the words "shall *keep open*" in the condition in question, imply that the transferor regarded the way as either already open or that he had reason to believe that its opening was imminent. I think further that the same words involve a continuing act, which imply a question of time.' *Re Winters and McLaren* [1960] OR 479 at 485, Ont SC, per Thompson J; reversed on other grounds [1962] OR 402, Ont CA

KEEP UP

'To keep up a policy is to pay the premiums thereon as they fall due, and the person who pays the premiums is the person who keeps up the policy.' *Barclays Bank Ltd v A-G* [1944] AC 372 at 377, HL, per Lord Macmillan

KEEPER *See also* KEEP

Of animal

A person is a keeper of an animal if—

(a) he owns the animal or has it in his possession; or
(b) he is the head of a household of which a member under the age of sixteen owns the animal or has it in his possession;

and if at any time an animal ceases to be owned by or to be in the possession of a person, any person who immediately before that time was a keeper thereof by virtue of the preceding provisions of this subsection continues to be a keeper of the animal until another person becomes a keeper thereof by virtue of those provisions. (Animals Act 1971, s 6(3))

[But a person is not a keeper where he has only taken and kept an animal in possession to prevent it causing damage or in order to restore it to its owner (Ibid, s 6(4)).]

Of disorderly house

'I do not assent at all to Mr O'Connor's argument [for the defendants] that nobody can ever be dealt with as keeper of a disorderly house [under the Sunday Observance Act 1780] unless he is found on the premises when the acts complained of are being committed. Such a doctrine would be most pernicious, as it seems to me, and I see no foundation for it whatever. It is difficult to find any stronger evidence, as I think, that a man is appearing, acting, and behaving himself as a person having the management of a place than that he permits his name to appear on all advertisements as that of the person having the management of the place, and is in fact cognisant of what is going on.' *Green v Berliner* [1936] 2 KB 477 at 489, per du Parcq J

KIDNAP

'A composite word made up of two colloquial expressions which together denote child-snatching . . . but in common parlance it is used to describe the carrying away of anybody, child or adult.' *People (AG) v Edge* [1943] IR 115 at 146, per Black J

' "Kidnapping" may include any case of a child being taken out of this country by some person against the wishes of the parents, or by one parent against the wishes of the other parent, at any rate where some element of force or deception or secrecy is involved.' *Re P (G E) (an infant)* [1964] 3 All ER 977 at 984, CA, per Pearson LJ; also reported [1965] Ch 568

'Kidnapping is much in the air at the moment; one sees stories about it in the newspapers every day and it is sometimes carried out with dreadful results. But in this court "kidnapping" has a rather different meaning; there has been a series of at least four cases of what is called the kidnapping variety, which really consist of this: that when a child, or children, have a settled home in one jurisdiction—anyhow any foreign jurisdiction—and one of the parents, by fraud or stealth, removes them from this jurisdiction and makes them wards of court, the court will not countenance that procedure and will, if it is satisfied that no harm will come to the children if they are returned to the jurisdiction where they belong, send them back there without further investigating the matter.' *Re A (Infants)* [1970] 3 All ER 184 at 186, CA, per Harman LJ

'It is convenient to take first the question of whether some secreting or concealment of the victim is necessary to constitute the offence of kidnapping. Counsel for the appellant referred to Archbold [37th edn, p 889] which under the heading "kidnapping" has the sentence: "The stealing and carrying away, a secreting of any person of any age or either sex against the will of such person . . . is an offence at common law . . ." It is, however, quite clear that the word "a" in that sentence is a misprint for "or". That this is so is evident because the authority cited is Russell on Crime, where the wording is exactly the same except that the word "or" and not "a" is used. Russell cites East, where the statement is: "The most aggravated species of false imprisonment is the stealing and carrying away, or secreting of any person, sometimes called kidnapping, which is an offence at common law . . ." We can find no reason in authority or in principle why the crime should not be complete when the person is seized and carried away, or why kidnapping should be regarded, as was urged by counsel, as a continuing offence involving the concealment of the person seized.' *R v Reid* [1972] 2 All ER 1350 at 1351, 1352, CA, per cur.

'There are many old cases in which consenting minors have been removed from their homes and parents, in the context of subsequent forced or fraudulent marriages, or unlawful sexual intercourse, but these cases all appear to have been dealt with as offences of conspiracy against public morals or, in the case of females, of abduction or conspiracies to abduct. The present case has none of these features. There are also older authorities which deal with offences of "kidnapping", either as a common law misdemeanour or as crimes against old statutes, no longer in force. These appear to present an element of removing a person from this country. That is why they are "kidnapping" cases, and "kidnapping" is used in these cases in the sense in which Robert Louis Stevenson used the word in the title to his book. It is worthy of note that in Blackstone's *Commentaries*, under the rubric "Kidnapping", the only cases which are dealt with are cases of taking young people out of the country. Similarly, the offence of "kidnapping" is mentioned in East's *Pleas of the Crown* where the cases are cases of taking people out of the country. The kidnapping cases to which I have referred also present elements of force or fraud and, as far as I have been able to discover, in the absence of one or other of those elements the case of a consenting victim does not seem to have been adjudicated on by the English courts. The vital point in the present case is that [the] count does not allege that the named girl was taken or secreted by force or fraud or against her will. The only modern authority which seems to bear on the question I had to decide is a decision of the Supreme Court of Ireland, *People (A-G) v Edge* [supra], in which that court by a majority of four to one held that the offence of kidnapping a 14½-year-old boy by—I quote—"unlawfully carrying him away and secreting him against the will of his guardian" was not an offence at common law.' *R v Hale* [1974] 1 All ER 1107 at 1108, 1109, per Lawson J

'There is surprisingly little authority in the books about the crime of kidnapping. The authority which has been referred to in the fairly recent past comes from the definition of kidnapping which is set out in East's *Pleas of the Crown* [1803 edn, pp 429–430]. There the learned author said: "The most aggravated species of false imprisonment is the stealing and carrying away, or secreting of any person, sometimes called kidnapping, which is an offence at common law punishable by fine, imprisonment and pillory." . . . In our judgment . . . all that has to be proved is the false imprisonment, the deprivation of liberty coupled with a carrying away from the place where the victim wants to be. It may be that in some circumstances the movement would not be sufficient in the estimation of the jury to amount to carrying away. Every case has to be considered on its own facts.' *R v Wellard* [1978] 3 All ER 161 at 162, 163, CA, per cur.

'From [a] wide body of authority six matters relating to the offence of kidnapping clearly emerge. First, the nature of the offence is an attack on, and infringement of, the personal liberty of an individual. Second, the offence contains four ingredients as follows: (1) the taking or carrying away of one person by another, (2) by force or by fraud, (3) without the consent of the person so taken or carried away and (4) without lawful excuse. Third, until the comparatively recent abolition by statute of the division of criminal offences into the two categories of felonies and misdemeanours (see s 1 of the Criminal Law Act 1967), the offence of kidnapping was categorised by the common law as a misdemeanour only. Fourth, despite that, kidnapping was always regarded, by reason of its nature, as a grave and (to use the language of an earlier age) heinous offence. Fifth, in earlier days the offence contained a further ingredient, namely that the taking or carrying away should be from a place within the jurisdiction to another place outside it; this further ingredient has, however, long been obsolete and forms no necessary part of the offence today, Sixth, the offence was in former days described not merely as taking or carrying away a person but further or alternatively as secreting him; this element of secretion has, however, also become obsolete, so that, although it may be present in a particular case, it adds nothing to the basic ingredient of taking or carrying away.' *R v D* [1984] 2 All ER 449 at 453, HL, per Lord Brandon of Oakbrook

Canada 'The Criminal Code gives no definition of the word "kidnap". The Dictionary of English Law—Earl Jowitt, defines it thus: "Kidnapping (Dut *kind*, a child, *nap*, to steal), the forceable abduction or stealing away of a person, whether man, woman, or child, from his own country, and sending him into another." . . . It has been held in Canada that kidnapping does not necessarily mean sending or taking the person stolen out of the country: *Cornwall v The Queen* [(1872) 33 UCQB 106 at 117]. The actus reus [of the offence of kidnapping] includes "intent to cause him (or her) to be secretly confined within Canada against his (or her) will".' *R v Leech* (1972) 10 CCC (2d) 149 at 154, 155, Alta, per MacDonald J

KIN *See* NEXT OF KIN

KIND

'To identify the "kind" to which a particular article belongs, you must ascertain first what is the common characteristic which turns a collection of individual articles into a "kind".' *Customs & Excise Comrs v Mechanical Services (Trailer Engineers) Ltd* [1979] 1 All ER 501 at 511, CA, per Megaw LJ

KINDRED

[By the Marriage Act 1949, s 1 marriages between certain degrees of kindred and affinity are prohibited. The prohibited degrees of relationship are set out in Sch 1 of that Act.]

KING'S ENEMIES *See* ADHERENT

KNACKER

The expression 'knacker' means a person whose trade or business it is to kill any cattle not killed for the purpose of the flesh being used as butcher's meat, and the expression 'knacker's yard' means any building or place used for the purpose, or partly for the purpose, of such trade or business, and the expression 'cattle' includes any horse, ass, mule, bull, sheep, goat, or pig. (Protection of Animals Act 1911, s 15)

KNACKER'S YARD

In this Part of this Act [Part I: slaughterhouses and knackers' yards] . . . 'knacker's yard' means any premises used in connection with the business of slaughtering, flaying or cutting up animals whose flesh is not intended for human consumption. (Slaughterhouses Act 1974, s 34)

In this Part of this Act [Part II: slaughter of animals] . . . 'knacker's yard' means any building, premises or place used in connection with the business of killing animals whose flesh is not intended for sale for human consumption. (Slaughterhouses Act 1974, s 45)

'Knacker's yard' means any premises used in connection with the business of slaughtering, flaying or cutting up animals the flesh of which is not intended for human consumption. (Food Act 1984, s 132(1))

KNIGHT

Knighthood is a personal dignity conferred for life. It is not of a particular kingdom, like a peerage or a baronetcy, but is an order of chivalry recognisable in every part of the Queen's dominions.

An individual of the male sex is now legally entitled to be addressed with the prefix 'Sir' and to rank before untitled persons, only if the Queen or her especially appointed lieutenant, who must be a knight, has directed him to kneel before her and has struck his shoulder with a naked sword or has created him a knight by letters patent. (35 Halsbury's Laws (4th edn) para 867)

Orders of knighthood

The age of chivalry engendered societies whose membership was restricted to knights. Of these the earliest in England was a society, founded by Edward III in or about 1348, of knights under the name of the Order of the Garter. It is limited to twenty-five knights in addition to the Sovereign, who is head of the order but the Sovereign has power to create additional royal knights and may appoint foreign Sovereigns as extra knights. Although usually bestowed upon a peer, the recipient of the honour need not necessarily belong to the peerage. Knights of the Garter take precedence in England before Privy Councillors and baronets.

Another society of knights in England, the precise origin of which is not clear, is that of the Order of the Bath. However, the Order has been so altered by its conversion into a military order by George II, and by a subsequent division into grades of companionship by George III that it has lost the medieval character preserved by the Garter. The order is now divided into two branches, military and civil.

Other orders of knighthood are the following:

Knights of St Andrew or the Thistle, founded or revived in Scotland by James II in 1687, and re-established on 31st December 1703;

Knights of St Patrick, founded in Ireland by George III on 5th February 1783, and revived in 1833;

Knights of the Order of the Star of India, founded in 1861, and used to reward service in connection with India;

Knights of St Michael and St George, founded in 1818 to reward service in the Mediterranean, chiefly Maltese and Ionic, but now used to reward all colonial or diplomatic service;

Knights of the Order of the Indian Empire, founded to commemorate the title of Emperor or Empress of India in 1878;

Knights of the Royal Victorian Order, founded in 1896;

Knights of the Order of the British Empire, founded in 1917.

Knights bachelor, or ordinary knights, are those who are merely created knights but belong to no particular Order. (35 Halsbury's Laws (4th edn) paras 868, 869)

KNOCK-FOR-KNOCK

The essence of a knock-for-knock agreement is that, in the event of an accident involving more than one insured vehicle, each insurer carries the risk so far as concerns the damage to the car he has insured, whoever may be legally responsible for causing the damage. It is, however, an arrangement operative only between insurers, and there is no means of enforcing it against the individual assured. Therefore, if an assured, minded perhaps to avoid losing a no-claims bonus, pursues on his own a claim for damage to his car, it is no answer that he is entitled to receive or has already received indemnity for the damage from his own insurers. The fact that the claimant has insurance rights against his own insurers is irrelevant so far as the tortfeasor is concerned. (25 Halsbury's Laws (4th edn) para 753)

'This appeal from a judgment of His Honour Judge Konstam raises an interesting point which, as far as I know, is a matter of first impression, at any rate so far as the Court of Appeal is concerned. The plaintiff, in a running-down action before the county court judge, had in respect of the damage to his own motor-car a claim for the sum of £33 2*s* 8*d*. He was insured on the terms that he himself was his own insurer for the first £5 of the risk, and was paid the balance, £28 2*s* 8*d*, by this insurance company. He then brought this action against the defendant, and no question arises but that the defendant was liable for this damage. The defendant was also insured, and we are informed, as the county court judge was informed, that there was between these two insurance companies what I am informed is known as a "knock-for-knock" agreement. We have not before us, nor had the county court judge before him, the terms of this agreement, but again we are informed that the purpose of this agreement is that each insurance company pays its own assured, without question, that which the assured is entitled to receive under the particular policy and that both of them do their utmost to discourage either of their own assureds from making claims against the other, or, putting it in another way, the insurance companies amongst themselves do not insist upon their assured bringing such action as they may be entitled to bring against the party insured by the other insurance company.' *Morley v Moore* [1936] 2 KB 359 at 361, 362, CA, per Sir Boyd Merriman P

[For form of 'knock for knock' agreement and comments thereon, see *Hobbs v Marlow* [1977] 2 All ER 249 at 252 et seq, HL, per Lord Diplock]

KNOW

Australia [Where a person injured by an unidentified motor vehicle sues a nominal defendant under the Motor Car Act 1951, s 47(1) [see now Motor Car Act 1958–1986, s 49(1)(a)] (Vic) the burden of proof lies on him to show that he has complied with the proviso to that section, which stipulates that he must as soon as possible after he 'knew' that the identity of the vehicle could not be established give notice of his intention to make claim.] 'The word "know" is used in the provision in an ordinary sense, without any intention that it should be analysed or refined upon. But of course there are gradations of knowledge or belief upon such a matter. The gradations extend from a slight inclination of opinion to complete assurance. Here it seems to amount to an awareness or consciousness that no reasonable probability exists of ascertaining the identity of the car satisfactorily or with any certainty. Complete assurance is by no means necessary. When the plaintiff has come to think that the identity cannot be established that is enough. If the expression "think" must be refined upon, it may be said to mean that the steady preponderance of his opinion of belief is that it cannot be done.' *Vines v Djordjevitch* [1955] ALR 431 at 435, per cur.

Australia 'A claimant "knows" a material fact, within the meaning of s 23A(2)(a)(i) of the Limitation of Actions Act (Vic) [see now s 23A(3)(e)] 1958–1986, when he receives information of the existence of that fact from a person, who, to the knowledge of the claimant, is in a position to have direct knowledge of the fact. Further, the claimant cannot prove ignorance of the material fact by proving his belief that the information is incorrect.' *Loveday v IND* [1980] VR 346 at 352, per Southwell J

Canada 'The verb "know" has a positive connotation requiring a bare awareness, the act of receiving information without more. The act of appreciating, on the other hand, is a second stage in a mental process requiring the analysis of knowledge or experience in one manner or another.' *R v Barnier* [1980] 1 SCR 1124 at 1136, 1137, SCC, per Estey J

Canada 'To "know" the nature and quality of an act may mean merely to be aware of the physical act, while to "appreciate" may involve estimation and understanding of the consequences of that act.' *Cooper v R* [1980] 1 SCR 1149 at 1161, SCC, per Dickson J

KNOW-HOW

In sections 530 and 531 [disposal of know-how] 'know-how' means any industrial information and techniques likely to assist in the manufacture or processing of goods or materials, or in the working of a mine, oil-well or other source of mineral deposits (including the searching for, discovery or testing of deposits or the winning of access thereto), or in the carrying out of any agricultural, forestry or fishing operations. (Income and Corporation Taxes 1988, s 533(7))

[See also a similar definition in the Aircraft and Shipbuilding Industries Act 1977, s 56(1).]

KNOWINGLY

'"Knowingly" must mean with a design.' *R v Bannen* (1844) 1 Car & Kir 295 at 299, CCR, per Tindal CJ

'Section 5 [of the Companies Act 1900 (repealed; see now Companies Act 1985, s 85)] . . . says this: "An allotment made by a company to an applicant in contravention of the foregoing provisions of this Act shall be voidable at the instance of the applicant within one month after the holding of the statutory meeting of the company and not later, and shall be so voidable notwithstanding that the company is in course of being wound up". . . . Under that section not only is the applicant entitled to void his contract, but if he suffers any loss in consequence of it he is entitled to bring his action against the directors or any director of the company who knowingly contravenes or permits or authorises the contravention of any of the foregoing provisions of the Act with respect to allotment. . . . I think that "knowingly" means with knowledge of the facts upon which the contravention depends. I think it is immaterial whether the director had knowledge of the law or not. I think he is bound to know what the law is, and the only question is, did he know the facts which made the act complained of a contravention of the statute?' *Burton v Bevan* [1908] 2 Ch 240 at 246, 247, per Neville J

[The Children Act 1908, s 17(2) (repealed; *cf* now Sexual Offences Act 1956, s 28) provided that any person having the custody of a girl under the age of sixteen should be guilty of an offence if he 'knowingly' allowed her to consort with a prostitute or person of known immoral character.] 'There is a wide difference between allowing and "knowingly allowing" within the meaning of this enactment. There are many cases upon the meaning of "allowing", "permitting", or "suffering" in other statutes, but they do not give much assistance in this case, because it is clear that the "knowingly allowing" which is contemplated in s 17, sub-s 2 of the Act of 1908, must be such a permission as can be deemed to be causing or encouraging.' *R v Chainey* [1914] 1 KB 137 at 142, per cur.

'When one finds put up as a danger signal or a signpost . . . the words "If any person knowingly" does certain things, it seems to me that discussions about mens rea are of something less than academic interest. The knowledge on the part of the alleged offender is described prominently as an essential ingredient of the offence.' *Gaumont British Distributors Ltd v Henry* [1939] 2 KB 711 at 716, per Lord Hewart CJ

'The point that is raised is purely a matter of construction of s 4(1) of the Explosive Substances Act 1883, which is in these terms: "Any person who . . . knowingly has in his possession or under his control any explosive substance, under such circumstances as to give rise to a reasonable suspicion that he . . . does not have it in his possession or under his control for a lawful object, shall unless he can shew that he . . . had it in his possession or under his control for a lawful object, be guilty of felony. . . ." The question is whether the word "knowingly" means that he must know not only that he has a parcel or a substance in his possession but also that it is an explosive. The words, I repeat, are "knowingly has in his possession any explosive substance". Having given the best consideration that we can to this case, we think that the words must mean that he must know that it is an explosive substance.' *R v Hallam* [1957] 1 All ER 665 at 665, CCA, per cur. (Also reported in [1957] 1 QB 569 at 571, 572)

Canada [The Insurance Act, RSO 1937, c 256, s 191 (see now Insurance Act, RSO 1980, c 218, s 206) provided that where an applicant for insurance 'knowingly' mis-represented, any claim should be invalid.] 'I do not think that a person making a proposal for insurance can avoid the effect of the section when the proposal is untrue, by saying that while he signed, he was not aware of the contents of the application. I think "knowingly" in the statute is used in the sense that the applicant is in possession of information that what is in fact stated in the application is untrue or does not disclose the truth.' *Sleigh v Stevenson* [1943] 4 DLR 433 at 441, Ont CA, per Kellock JA

New Zealand 'Due effect must . . . be given to the word "knowingly" in s 170 of the Companies Act 1908 [(NZ) (repealed; see now Companies Act 1955 (NZ), s 364(1))], where the proceeding is under the section; but, in my opinion, all that it means is that, before an order can be made, it has to be shown that the member of the company sought to be mulcted knew that the particular debts were being incurred and also had a knowledge generally of the company's affairs, so that, as a reasonable person, he should have known that, at the time when the particular debts were contracted, the company should not have had any reasonable or probable expectation of being able to pay the same as well as all its other debts. That construction places the member in the same position as if he were conducting the company's business as his own private business and had become bankrupt, and that, I think, is what the Legislature intended.' *Re J & E Hurdley & Son Ltd* [1941] NZLR 686 at 734, CA, per Myers CJ; also reported [1941] GLR 260 at 285

KNOWLEDGE *See also* COMMON KNOWLEDGE

[The Road Traffic Act 1930, s 112(3) (repealed; see now the Road Traffic Act 1988, s 175(2), as prospectively substituted by the Transport Act 1982, s 24(1), as substituted by the Road Traffic (Consequential Provisions) Act 1988, s 3, Sch 2, para 13) enacted that any person who issued a certificate of insurance or security, which was 'to his knowledge' false in any material particular committed an offence.] 'I do not think that "knowledge" in the subsection under which this conviction took place has any relation to any presumptions as to knowledge of law. I think that the subsection requires in order to support a conviction, knowledge in fact of the falsity of the statement under consideration.' *Ocean Accident & Guarantee Corpn Ltd v Cole* [1932] 2 KB 100 at 106, 107, DC, per Hawke J

United States A person has 'knowledge' of a fact within the meaning of this Act not only when he has actual knowledge thereof, but also when he has knowledge of such other facts as in the circumstances shows bad faith. (Uniform Partnership Act 1914, s 3(1))

KNOWLEDGE AND CONSENT

Canada 'Speaking for myself, I think "knowledge and consent" in s 5(2) [see now the Criminal Code 1970, c C–34, s 3(4)] of the Criminal Code does not include situations where the association, interest or participation of the accused, cannot reasonably be regarded as an exercise of a power or of a right to some measure of control over the subject-matter. No doubt, inferences of "possession" may be drawn in opium cases from circumstances rarely paralleled in cases of stolen goods. But if consorting with one who is in physical possession of opium, or who has it in his control or has the right to its custody, is sought to be regarded *eo ipso* and "knowledge and consent" within s 5(2), supra sufficient to constitute joint possession, then one would expect inequivocal authority for it in the Opium and Narcotic Drug Act. The "knowledge and consent" which is an integral element of joint possession in s 5(2) must be related to and read with the definition of possession in the previous s 5(1). It follows that "knowledge and consent" cannot exist without the co-existence of some measure of control over the subject-matter. If there is the power to consent there is equally the power to refuse and vice versa. They each signify the existence of some power or authority which is here called control, without which the need for their exercise could not arise or be invoked. The principle of "sufficient reason" applies. For example it would be an irrational act for A to attempt to consent to or refuse B the use of C's motor car unless A has some measure of control over it.' *R v Colvin & Gladue* [1943] 1 DLR 20 at 24, BCCA, per O'Halloran JA

L

LABEL *See also* CONTAINER

'Label' includes any band or ticket. (Agricultural Produce (Grading and Marking) Act 1928, s 7)

'Label' includes any device for conveying information by written characters or other symbols, and any characters or symbols stamped or otherwise placed directly on to any produce or container, and references to the affixing of a label shall be construed accordingly. (Agriculture and Horticulture Act 1964, s 24)

'Labelling', in relation to a container or package of medicinal products, means affixing to or otherwise displaying on it a notice describing or otherwise relating to the contents, and 'label' has a corresponding meaning. (Medicines Act 1968, s 132(1))

LABOUR DISPUTE

United States 'Labor dispute' includes any controversy concerning terms, tenure, or conditions of employment, or concerning the association or representation of persons in negotiating, fixing, maintaining, changing, or seeking to arrange terms or conditions of employment, regardless of whether the disputants stand in the proximate relation of employer and employee. (Labor-Management Reporting and Disclosure Act 1959, s 3(g))

LABOUR ORGANISATION

United States 'Labor organization' means a labour organisation engaged in an industry affecting commerce and includes any organization of any kind, any agency, or employee representation committee, group, association, or plan so engaged in which employees participate and which exists for the purpose, in whole or in part, of dealing with employers concerning grievances, labor disputes, wages, rates of pay, hours, or other terms or conditions of employment, and any conference, general committee, joint or system board, or joint council so engaged which is subordinate to a national or international labor organisation, other than a State or local central body. (Labor-Management Reporting and Disclosure Act 1959, s 3(i))

LABOURER *See also* DAILY

[By the Sunday Observance Act 1677, s 1 (repealed) no tradesman, artificer, workman, 'labourer', or other person whatsoever, might do or exercise any worldly labour upon the Lord's Day.] 'I agree with the Lord Chief Justice that "labourer" means a person labouring for another, and "farmer" a person who may work or not as he likes: if he sometimes takes up a spade or a rake he cannot on that account be called a labourer.' *R v Cleworth* (1864) 4 B & S 927 at 933, per Crompton J

'Neither a carpenter, a bailiff nor the clerk of a parish can be described as a "labourer", but a man employed to dig the ground is a "servant in husbandry": a stevedore may be a person "engaged in manual labour". As to the conductor of an omnibus, I cannot think that he falls within any of the classes enumerated: he is not "engaged in manual labour", he does not lift the passengers into and out of the omnibus; . . . his real and substantial business is to invite persons to enter the omnibus and to take and keep for his employers the money paid by the passengers as their fares: in fact, he earns the wages becoming due to him through the confidence reposed in his honesty.' *Morgan v London General Omnibus Co* (1884) 13 QBD 832 at 833, 834, CA, per Brett MR

Australia [A clause in an industrial award prescribed a weekly wage for 'labourers'.] 'A common meaning of that term, according to the New English Dictionary, is "one who performs physical labour, as a service, or for a livelihood, specially one who does work requiring, chiefly, bodily strength, or aptitude, and little skill, or training, as distinguished, e.g., from an artisan." While according to the Concise Oxford Dictionary, "labourer" is a word of variable meaning, but "used especially as one who does, for wages, work requiring strength or patience, rather than skill or training." What degree of skill is sufficient to raise a manual worker out of the labouring class is a question upon which widely varying opinions may be, and frequently are, held; but a man with a recognised trade or profession, or an artisan in "any art, trade, or mystery" [see Lord Ellenborough's remarks in *Lewther v Radnor* (1806) 8 East 124], is not in relation to that trade, profession, art, or mystery properly styled a labourer.' *Hume Pipe (Australia) Ltd v Lawson* [1925] SASR 385 at 389, per cur.

LACHES

A plaintiff in equity is bound to prosecute his claim without undue delay. This is in pursuance of the principle which has underlain the Statutes of Limitation, *vigilantibus et non dormientibus lex succurit*. A court of equity refuses its aid to stale demands, where the plaintiff has slept upon his right and acquiesced for a great length of time. He is then said to be barred by his laches. The defence of laches, however, is only allowed where there is no statutory bar. If there is a statutory bar, operating either expressly or by way of analogy, the plaintiff is entitled to the full statutory period before his claim becomes unenforceable; and an injunction in aid of a legal right is not barred till the legal right is barred, although laches may be a bar to an interlocutory injunction.

In enacting a statute of limitation the legislature specifies fixed periods after which claims are barred; equity does not fix a specific limit, but considers the circumstances of each case.

In determining whether there has been such delay as to amount to laches, the chief points to be considered are (1) acquiescence on the plaintiff's part, and (2) any change of position that has occurred on the defendant's part. Acquiescence in this sense does not mean standing by while the violation of a right is in progress, but assent after the violation has been completed and the plaintiff has become aware of it. It is unjust to give the plaintiff a remedy where, by his conduct, he has done that which might fairly be regarded as equivalent to a waiver of it; or where by his conduct and neglect, though not waiving the remedy, he has put the other party in a position in which it would not be reasonable to place him if the remedy were afterwards to be asserted. In such cases lapse of time and delay are most material. Upon these considerations rests the doctrine of laches. (16 Halsbury's Laws (4th edn) paras 1476, 1477)

'Laches is a neglect to do something which by law a man is obliged to do.' *Sebag v Abitbol* (1816) 4 M & S 462 at 463, per Lord Ellenborough CJ

'The doctrine of laches in Courts of Equity is not an arbitrary or a technical doctrine. Where it would be practically unjust to give a remedy, either because the party has, by his conduct, done that which might fairly be regarded as equivalent to a waiver of it, or where by his conduct and neglect he has, though perhaps not waiving that remedy, yet put the other party in a situation in which it would not be reasonable to place him if the remedy were afterwards to be asserted, in either of these cases, lapse of time and delay are most material. But in every case, if an argument against relief, which otherwise would be just, is founded upon mere delay, that delay of course not amounting to a bar by any Statute of Limitations, the validity of that defence must be tried upon principles substantially equitable. Two circumstances, always important in such cases, are, the length of the delay and the nature of the acts done during the interval, which might affect either party and cause a balance of justice or injustice in taking the one course or the other, so far as relates to the remedy.' *Lindsay Petroleum Co v Hurd* (1874) LR 5 PC 221 at 239, 240, PC, per cur.

LAID UP

[A policy of insurance on a ship provided for the return of part of the premiums if the ship should be sold or 'laid up'.] 'I am of opinion that the words laid up being in company with the word sold, must mean a permanent laying up, similar to that which would take place if the ship had been sold; that is, such a laying up as would put a final end to the policy.' *Hunter v Wright* (1830) 10 B & C 714 at 716, per Lord Tenderden CJ

LAKE

Canada 'Black's Law Dictionary defines lake as, inter alia, a considerable body of standing water in a depression of land but it also defines lake as meaning a widened portion of a river. . . . Anyone who has grown up in the prairie provinces of Canada has a preconceived notion of what is a lake and what is a slough. A lake, to that person, is a body of water of considerable depth surrounded by a well-defined beach or bank and with a reasonably permanent nature where one can swim if the water is not too cold. On the other hand, a slough is a shallow body of dirty water usually full of weeds and insects or aquatic life where one would not consider swimming. Sometimes there is water present in the slough and sometimes there is not. To describe the latter body of water in the manner set forth in Black would be to stretch the definition of lake as such word has become known in this part of the country.' *Re R in right of Alberta and Very* (1983) 149 DLR (3d) 688 at 701, 703, Alta QB, per Egbert J

LAMMAS LANDS

These are open arable and meadow lands held in severalty during a portion of the year, but which, after the severalty crop or hay has been removed, are commonable not only to the parties who have the severalty right but also to some other classes of commoners. (6 Halsbury's Laws (4th edn) para 517)

These are so called because Lammas Day (1st August), or old Lammas Day (12th August), was the usual day on which they were thrown open. They usually remained open till the following Lady Day (25th March). (Ibid, 517*n*)

'These are lammas lands, that is, lands which, as I understand the meaning of the term, belong to a person who is absolutely the owner in fee simple, to all intents and purposes, for half the year, and the other half of the year he is still the owner in fee simple, subject to a right of pasturage over the lands by other people.' *Baylis v Tyssen-Amhurst* (1877) 6 Ch D 500 at 507, per Jessel MR

LAND *See also* COMMON

The term 'land' in its legal signification, includes any ground, soil or earth, such as meadows, pastures, woods, moors, waters, marshes and heath; houses and other buildings upon it; the air space above it, and all mines and minerals beneath it. It also includes anything fixed to the land, as well as growing trees and crops, except those which, broadly speaking, are produced in the year by the labour of the year. A grant of all the profits of land passes the whole land, herbage, trees, mines and whatever is parcel of the land; but a grant of a particular profit of or right in the land does not extend beyond such profit or right. For the purposes of ownership, land may be divided horizontally, vertically or otherwise, and either below or above the ground. Thus separate ownership may exist in strata of minerals, in the space occupied by a tunnel, or in different storeys of a building.

The meaning of 'land' may be extended for the purpose of a particular instrument when this is required by the context and it is extended for the purpose of statutes. In statutes generally, passed after 1850 and before 1st January 1979, 'land' includes messuages, tenements and hereditaments, houses and buildings of any tenure. In statutes generally, passed on and after 1st January 1979, 'land' includes buildings and other structures, land covered with water, and any estate, interest, easement, servitude or right in or over land. In the Lands Clauses Consolidation Act 1845 it includes messuages, lands, tenements, and hereditaments of any tenure; in the Law of Property Act 1925, it includes land of any tenure, and mines and minerals, whether or not held apart from the surface, buildings or parts of buildings (whether the division is horizontal, vertical or made in any other way), and other corporeal hereditaments; also a manor, an advowson, and a rent and other incorporeal hereditaments, and an easement, right, privilege, or benefit in, over, or derived from land; but not an undivided share in land. Thus, under statutory definitions, the word 'land' is usually extended to include not only land in the physical sense, with all that is above it or underneath it, but also all rights in the land. The phrase 'interest in land' has an even wider meaning, and may include an interest in the proceeds of sale of land held on trust for sale. (39 Halsbury's Laws (4th edn) paras 377, 378)

The word 'lands' shall extend to manors, advowsons, rectories, messuages, lands, tenements, tithes, rents, and hereditaments of any tenure (except copy of court roll), and whether corporeal or incorporeal, and any undivided share thereof, but when accompanied by some expression including or denoting the tenure by copy of court roll, shall extend to manors, messuages, lands, tenements, and hereditaments of that tenure, and any undivided share thereof. (Fines and Recoveries Act 1833, s 1)

Land, unless a contrary intention appears, includes land of any tenure, and tenements and hereditaments, corporeal or incorporeal, and houses and other buildings, also an undivided share in land. (Conveyancing Act 1881, s 2)

'Land' includes land of any tenure, and mines and minerals whether or not held apart from the surface, buildings or parts of buildings (whether the division is horizontal, vertical or made in any other way) and other corporeal hereditaments; also a manor, an advowson, and a rent and other incorporeal hereditaments, and an easement, right, privilege, or benefit in, over, or derived from land; but not an undivided share in land; and 'mines and minerals' include any strata or seam of minerals or substances in or under any land, and powers of working and getting the same but not an undivided share thereof; and 'manor' includes a lordship, and reputed manor or lordship; and 'hereditament' means any real property which on an intestacy occurring before the commencement of this Act might have devolved upon an heir. (Law of Property Act 1925, s 205)

[A similar definition is to be found in the Land Charges Act 1972, s 17(1).]

'Land' includes land covered by water and as respects Scotland includes salmon fishings. (National Parks and Access to the Countryside Act 1949, s 114)

'Land' means any corporeal hereditament, including a building as defined by this section, and includes any interest or right in or over land and any right to water. (Land Compensation Act 1961, s 39).

[As defined by the section, building includes any structure or erection, but not plant or machinery.]

'Land' includes land covered by water. (Harbours Act 1964, s 57)

'Land' includes any interest in or right over land. (Countryside Act 1968, s 49)

'Land' includes land covered with water and also includes any part of the seashore whether above or below high water mark. (Deposit of Poisonous Waste Act 1972, s 7)

In this Part of this Act [Part I: compensation for depreciation caused by use of public works] . . . land in relation to Scotland, includes salmon fishings. (Land Compensation Act 1973, s 19(1))

'Land' includes mines and minerals, whether or not severed from the surface, buildings or parts of buildings (whether the division is horizontal, vertical or made in any other way) and other corporeal hereditaments. (Local Land Charges Act 1975, s 16)

'Land' includes water and any interests in land or water and any easement or right in, to, or over water. (Land Drainage Act 1976, s 116(1))

'Land' includes buildings and other structures, land covered with water, and any estate interest, easement, servitude or right in or over land. (Interpretation Act 1978, Sch 1)

'Land' includes messuages, tenements and hereditaments, house and buildings of any tenure. (Agricultural Statistics Act 1979, s 6(1); Capital Gains Tax Act 1979, s 155(1))

'Wood will passe by the name of land, if there be no other land whereby the words may be otherwise supplied.' *Dockwray & Beal's Case* (1614) Godb 256 at 256, per cur

'In common acceptation . . . lands are often taken for all a man's estate, or annual revenue. If the question be put, How much land hath he? Resp. £400 a year; that is a proper answer; and yet the value is answered, not the quantity or the quality of his estate. But in this computation we shall reckon tithes, rents, profits, à prendre or render, anything whereof he hath a freehold or fee simple estate.' *Meredith v Webber* (1666) O Bridg 560 at 562, per Bridgman CJ

'The word land properly means corporeal hereditaments, and shall be so taken, unless there be an express intent to extend the meaning.' *Smith d Jerdon v Milward* (1782) 3 Doug KB 70 at 73, per Buller J

'Nobody will doubt that if the word "land" merely is used, without any qualification, it would be sufficient to pass meadow and pasture land, and land covered with water; but when we find that in this instrument twelve messuages are mentioned, and when we find also, not merely that twenty acres of land are mentioned, but also twenty acres of meadow, twenty acres of pasture, five acres of wood, and five acres of land, covered with water; it is impossible not to see that the term 'land' was not intended to comprise meadow and pasture; and if it be clearly intended not to comprise meadow and pasture, *a multo fortiori* we must say that it was not intended to pass houses.' *Denn d Bulkley v Wilford* (1826) 8 Dow & Ry KB 549 at 554, per Abbot CJ

'Lord Coke has said, "*terra est nomen generalissimum*, and comprehends all species of land as meadow pasture", etc. Although the distinction [between the words 'land' and 'meadow'] is taken in *Silly v Silly* [(1648) Vent 260], the decision in that case does not turn upon it; the distinction, indeed, is so absurd, that no man of sense can accede to it.' *Cooke v Yates* (1827) 4 Bing 90 at 90, 91, per Best CJ

'A vein of coal is land, unless distinguished from the land by the deed of conveyance.' *Wilkinson v Proud* (1843) 11 M & W 33 at 39, per Lord Abinger CB

'In the present case, the subject of the devise is described as the testator's "manors or lordships, rectories, advowsons, messuages, lands, tenements, tithes, and hereditaments" situate as in the will mentioned. It is as if the testator had devised all his land, or all his lands, farms, and messuages and other real estate; and in such a case, I conceive, that the word "land" (which may be thought ambiguous, and without qualifying expressions may be deemed to include lands in which the testator had only a leasehold interest), would have its ambiguity removed, and by reason of the words "other real estate" would be limited to its original and proper legal meaning [of real estate].' *Wilson v Eden* (1848) 11 Beav 237 at 250, 252, per Lord Langdale MR

'Now "land", according to English law, includes everything on or under the soil; all buildings that you may erect on it; all mines that you may sink under it.' *Newcomer v Coulson* (1877) 5 Ch D 133 at 142, 143, CA, per Jessel MR

'The expression "the land" cannot be restricted to vegetable mould or to cultivated clay; but . . . it naturally includes, and must be held to include, the upper soil including the subsoil, whether it be clay, sand, or gravel.' *Glasgow Corpn v Farie* (1888) 13 App Cas 657 at 679, HL, per Lord Watson

'The word "land" would be variously understood by different persons. To a farmer the word "land" would not mean his farm buildings; to a lawyer the word would include everything that was upon the land fixed immovably upon it.' *Smith v Richmond* [1899] AC 448 at 448, per Lord Halsbury LC

'The section of the present Settled Land Act, that of 1925 . . . is s 75, sub-s 5, and it provides as follows: "Capital money arising under this Act while remaining uninvested or unapplied, and securities on which an investment of any such capital money is made shall for all purposes of disposition, transmission, and devolution be treated as land. It seems to me . . . that the word "land" must be construed and given effect to in relation to the particular facts of the case, and, where you are dealing with a settled freehold which is sold, the capital money would be treated as freehold, and, where you have a settled leasehold which is sold, the capital money would be treated as leasehold and so forth.' *Re Cartwright, Cartwright v Smith* [1939] Ch 90 at 104, CA, per Greene MR

'I think that it is plain that the word "land" when used in s 1 of this Act [Landlord and Tenant (Requisitioned Land) Act 1944] will include buildings, and would also include any machinery which was so affixed to the freehold as to become part of it.' *Jordan v May* [1947] KB 427 at 432, CA, per Morton LJ

Australia 'The word "land" comprehends in law any ground, soil or earth whatsoever: Coke on Littleton, 4a: even though it originally meant only arable land: Sheppard's Touchstone, 92. Coke further says that land "legally includes also all castles, houses and other buildings. . . ." Thus, primarily, the ownership of land carries with it everything both above and below the surface, the maxim being "*cujus est solum, ejus est usque ad coelum et ad inferos*". This maxim, however, is not a presumption of law applicable in all cases and under all circumstances; hence the possibility of a freehold in an upper chamber; but at common law it is the presumption. If there is found the word "land" and no statutory definition governs the context, the word "land" includes all buildings on the land and the maxim applies. To say this, however, is different from saying that an upper floor of a building, even though capable of being the subject of an estate in fee and the subject of separate holding as realty, can properly be described as land. To describe the upper floor as land would be to deny the application of the presumption that prima facie land includes buildings. My conclusion is that the word "land" at common law prima facie includes buildings on the soil, but is not appropriate to describe the building alone or any part thereof, even if it be the subject of an interest in realty separate from the soil itself.' *Re Lehrer and the Real Property Act* 1900 [1960] NSWR 570 at 574, per Jacobs J

New Zealand 'The words of the exception in the definition of rateable property in s 2 of the Act [Rating Act 1908 (repealed; see now the

Rating Act 1967, Sch 1(12))] are "lands occupied by churches and chapels". . . . It seems to me . . . that in this exception the word "land" is used in its primary sense of part of the material forming the surface of the earth on which is erected a building used as a church or chapel.' *Perpetual Trustees, Estate & Agency Co of New Zealand v Dunedin Corpn* (1915) 34 NZLR 877 at 879, 880, per Sim J; also reported 17 GLR 667 at 668

In lease

When used in a lease or other assurance, 'land' includes, if there is nothing to restrict its technical meaning, all kinds of land, whether arable, meadow or otherwise, and also everything on or under the soil, all buildings erected on it, and all mines and minerals beneath it and the air space above it to such height as is necessary for the ordinary use and enjoyment of it and the structures on it. A lease of woods includes not only the trees, but the land on which they grow. Words which are appropriate for granting part of the profits of the land do not carry the land itself, for instance a grant to dig turves, or a grant of water, which ordinarily gives only the fishery in the water. Where the soil under the water is intended to pass the expression 'land covered with water' should be used. However, a grant of all the profits of land is equivalent to a grant of the land itself. (27 Halsbury's Laws (4th edn) para 129)

In mining law

Prima facie 'land' or 'lands' includes everything on or under the surface although this meaning has in some cases been held to have been restricted by the context. 'Soil' is apt to denote the surface and everything above and below it, but similarly its meaning may be restricted by the context so as to exclude the mines. 'Subsoil' includes everything from the surface to the centre of the earth; and 'surface' may include, in addition to the actual plane surface, all the land except the mines, or the soil overlying the minerals. 'Close', 'tenement', and 'hereditament' are sufficiently wide to include the mines. (31 Halsbury's Laws (4th edn) para 15)

LAND (verb)

[A local Act entitled the defendant corporation to levy tolls on ships and on all goods 'landed' within the local harbour. Stones were shot from the plaintiff's boats below high-water mark, where they remained until shipped for exportation from the harbour.] 'What is landing? It is putting on the land. Where does the land begin? Where the sea ends. Where does the sea end? At high-water mark; above the place where the goods were deposited. We must say that the goods were landed in the sea. It would certainly be strange if the captain of a steamboat were to say that he had landed his passengers, if he made them get out in three feet of water. Yet I do not say that the goods might not be said to be landed, if they were put there with the means and right of taking them up on to the land. As a matter of good sense it might perhaps be, that though goods would not be landed in the usual sense of the word until they had got to the land, yet as soon as in any manner they had reached what might be considered as the end of their transit, that might be called a landing. Suppose, however, the goods were taken out of the lighter within the harbour where the water never left the ground, for the purpose of being taken to the land, would they be landed, though below the limits of the lowest low-water mark? I say again, if they were so placed that they could be fetched thence by the owner into the country, it might perhaps be a landing within the spirit of the Act; but not otherwise. But the present case is neither within the spirit and intent, nor within the words of the Act; it is no more a landing than a transhipment would be.' *Harvey v Lyme Regis Corpn* (1869) LR 4 Exch 260 at 264, 265, per Bramwell B

'The policy in question includes all risk of craft until the said goods or merchandise be discharged and "safely landed". . . . Landing goods means putting them upon the land, or upon that which by custom of the port is its equivalent. In the present case, instead of placing the goods on lighters to carry them to the shore, the goods were placed upon lighters which were to take them to an export vessel and there to load them as soon as she was ready to receive them. . . . Nobody, in commercial or business language, can say that goods are landed which are transhipped without land, or that goods which are placed in lighters for transhipment are placed in lighters to be landed.' *Houlder v Merchants Marine Insurance Co Ltd* (1886) 17 QBD 354 at 355, 356, CA, per cur.

[The plaintiffs imported bunker coal, insuring the cargo until the goods were (in the words of the policy) 'discharged and safely landed'. Their practice was to have the coal discharged into barges, leave it there until a vessel required bunkers, and then supply the vessel direct from the barges.] 'The material words are "until the goods are discharged and safely landed". The defendants contend that the word "landed" must be construed in a business sense, and that in a case like the present goods must be held to be landed when they have been loaded into the barge and the barge has been towed to her mooring berth and is at rest there, but not till then. The third party contends that the word "landed" must be construed strictly and can have no application where a process is used which is expressly designed to avoid putting the goods on land. This contention is . . . right.' *Lindsay Blee Depots Ltd v Motor Union Insurance Co Ltd* (1930) 46 TLR 572 at 573, per Talbot J

Landing place

'The words "landing place" are nowhere defined in the section of the Act [the Merchant Shipping (Liability of Shipowners and Others) Act 1900, s 2], and I think, in those circumstances, their meaning has to be arrived at on commonsense principles. Therefore, I ask myself whether the front of a warehouse which is so built as to have an aperture through it for the admission of goods from craft, and which has alongside it a prepared berth in which craft can lie for the purpose of landing and loading goods, can properly be described as a "landing place". It seems to me that if that is not a "landing place" it is very difficult to see what a "landing place" could be. The place in question is a place adjacent to the plaintiffs' warehouse, where craft are, in fact, invited to come and lie for the purpose of landing their goods. I therefore hold that this is a "landing place".' *Nicholson (J & W) & Co Ltd v Humorist (Owners), The 'Humorist'* [1946] P 198 at 201, per Willmer J

LAND COVERED WITH WATER

'The statute [a local Act] imposes a rate of one-fourth part only of the net annual value on the occupiers of "land covered with water", and it is impossible to say that a reservoir does not come within that description.' *R v Birmingham Waterworks Co* (1861) 1 B & S 84 at 93, 94, per Cockburn CJ

'It is plain common sense to say that a pipe which may or may not have water in it, cannot be looked on as "land" really "covered with water". It might as well be contended that a gas pipe is a pipe covered with gas.' Ibid at 94, per Crompton J

LAND DRAINAGE

'Land drainage' includes defence against water (including sea water), irrigation other than spray irrigation, warping and the provision of flood warning systems. (Water Resources Act 1963, s 135 as substituted by the Water Act 1973, Sch 8, para 85)

'Land drainage' means the drainage of land and the provision of flood warning systems. (Land Drainage Act 1976, s 116(1))

LAND TAX

Australia 'By the covenant now in question, which is contained in a lease . . . the lessees covenanted to pay all taxes, rates, charges, assessments, impositions, both municipal and Government . . ., except land tax. The point for determination is the meaning of this exception. . . . I am unable to see any reason for thinking that the term "land tax" has ever been used in New South Wales, or indeed in any part of Australia, in any other sense than a tax on land directly imposed by the State. . . . The suggestion that a tax on unimproved capital value is in principle a land tax, while a tax on annual value is not, is quite untenable.' *Solomon v New South Wales Sports Club Ltd* (1915) 19 CLR 698 at 702, 705, per Griffith CJ

Australia 'The parties [to a lease] made . . . an agreement as to "any future land tax or municipal tax upon the unimproved capital value". . . . What then is a land tax? A yearly impost laid upon real property by parliamentary enactment for the provision of public revenue appears to be within the description. . . . As matters are the definition of "a land tax" which is given by the learned Chief Justice [Griffith CJ, in *Solomon v New South Wales Sports Club Ltd* (supra)] may well be applied here.' *Leventhal v David Jones Ltd* (1930) 30 SRNSW 123 at 129, 130, PC, per Lord Merrivale

LAND WITHOUT BUILDINGS

Australia [A planning scheme Ordinance classified land into certain categories. User of land was determined by the category in which it fell. In the Ordinance, 'vacant land' was defined as being land upon which, before the appointed date, there were no buildings or only buildings of a subsidiary or minor nature specified.] 'What is meant by land upon which there were no buildings? Except in city streets it is usual for buildings to stand on land greater in area than the actual building. It is seldom that there is not at least a curtilage to a building. . . . One thing only seems certain about the meaning of the phrase "land upon which, immediately before the appointed day, there were no buildings" and that is that it cannot refer only to the exact area on the earth's surface on which buildings literally stand. And yet if that meaning must be rejected what criterion must be adopted to define the area of land which is sufficiently connected with the building to be land on which there is a building? Many suggestions to solve this problem have been made but perhaps the least unsatisfactory is one that makes the existing buildings the cardinal factor and inquires what land really belongs to them in the sense to be explained. Any building, whether it is a habitation or has some other use, may stand within a larger area of land which subserves the purposes of the building. The land surrounds the building because it actually or supposedly contributes to the enjoyment of the building or the fulfilment of its purpose. A garden, however large, belonging to a dwelling house is there as an amenity contributing to the use of the building as an abode. But if you find a caretaker's or a gardener's cottage in a park, it is evident that it is put there for the better care, management and use of the park. The park is not an incident of the cottage, the cottage is an incident of the park. No one would say that the cottage made the park built-up land. In the same way no one would regard a farm as built-up land because the farmer's house stood on some part of it. If anyone were required to say how much of the land was built-up because of the farm-house he would do his best to fix upon an area which was seen to comprise all that was really devoted to the better use or enjoyment of the house as a dwelling or place of residence, what was incidental to it.' *Royal Sydney Golf Club v Federal Comr of Taxation* (1955) 91 CLR 610 at 625, 626, per cur.

LANDLORD

The expression 'landlord' means in relation to any land the person for the time being entitled to receive the rents and profits of the land. (Allotments Act 1922, s 22)

The expression 'landlord' means any person who under a lease is, as between himself and the tenant or other lessee, for the time being entitled to the rents and profits of the demised premises payable under the lease. (Landlord and Tenant Act 1927, s 25)

'Landlord', in relation to a lease, means the person who under the lease is, as between himself and the tenant, for the time being entitled to the rents and profits of the demised premises payable under the lease, and, in a case where the reversion immediately expectant on the lease is mortgaged and the mortgagee is in possession thereof or has appointed a receiver of the rents and profits thereof, means that mortgagee. (Landlord and Tenant (Requisitioned Land) Act 1942, s 13)

Subject to the provisions of this section, in this Part of this Act [Part I, as to security of tenure for residential tenants] the expression 'the landlord', in relation to a tenancy (in this section referred to as 'the relevant tenancy'), means the person (whether or not he is the immediate landlord) who is the owner of that interest in the property comprised in the relevant tenancy which for the time being fulfils the following conditions, that is to say—

(a) that it is an interest in reversion expectant (whether immediately or not) on the termination of the relevant tenancy, and
(b) that it is either the fee simple or a tenancy the duration of which is at least five years longer than that of the relevant tenancy,

and is not itself in reversion expectant (whether immediately or not) on an interest which fulfils those conditions. (Landlord and Tenant Act 1954, s 21)

Subject to the next following subsection, in this Part of this Act [Part II, as to security of tenure for business, professional and other tenants] the expression 'the landlord', in relation to a tenancy (in this section referred to as 'the relevant tenancy'), means the person (whether or not he is the immediate landlord) who is the owner of that interest in the property comprised in the relevant tenancy which for the time being fulfils the following conditions, that is to say—

(a) that it is an interest in reversion expectant (whether immediately or not) on the termination of the relevant tenancy, and
(b) that it is either the fee simple or a tenancy which will not come to an end within fourteen months by effluxion of time and, if it is such a tenancy, that no notice has been given by virtue of which it will come to an

end within fourteen months or any further time by which it may be contained under s 36(2) or s 64 of this Act,

and is not itself in reversion expectant (whether immediately or not) on an interest which fulfils those conditions. (Landlord and Tenant Act 1954, s 44, as amended by Law of Property Act 1969, s 14(1)).

[Section 36 of the Act deals with the carrying out of an order for a new tenancy; s 64 with interim continuation of tenancies pending determination by the court.]

'Landlord' includes any person from time to time deriving title under the original landlord and also includes, in relation to any dwelling-house, any person other than the tenant who is, or but for Part VII of this Act would be, entitled to possession of the dwelling-house. (Rent Act 1977, s 152(1)).

[Part VII of the Act relates to security of tenure. As for a dwelling-house being reasonably required by a landlord for occupation, see now Rent Act 1977, Sch 15, Cases 8, 9]

'Landlord' in relation to any land means the person entitled to the immediate reversion or, if the property therein is held in joint tenancy, any of the persons entitled to the immediate reversion. (County Courts Act 1984, s 147(1))

'The word "landlord" does not mean the lord of the soil, but the person between whom and the tenant the relation of landlord and tenant exists.' *Churchward v Ford* (1857) 2 H & N 446 at 450, per Bramwell B

'"Landlord" is defined by s 48, sub-s 1 of the Act of 1908 [Agricultural Holdings Act 1908 (repealed; see now Agricultural Holdings Act 1986, s 96(1))] as being "Any person for the time being entitled to receive the rents and profits of any land." That, of course, means the person entitled as between landlord and the tenant, and, of course, it is obvious that, as dealings and transactions in the land take place from time to time, the same person is not necessarily at all times the landlord; one person may be landlord at one moment, and after transactions have taken place with reference to the land, another person may become landlord at some subsequent moment, but the question under the statute is always the same, namely, whether the person claiming to be landlord is the person entitled as against the tenant to receive the rents and profits.' *Tombs v Turvey* (1923) 93 LJKB 785 at 787, per Bankes LJ

'The relation of landlord and tenant in its ordinary legal significance arises whenever one party confers on another the right to exclusive possession of premises, e.g. a dwelling-house, for a time which is either subject to a definite limit originally, as in the case of a lease for a term of years, or which though originally indefinite can be made subject to a definite limit by either party, as in the case of a tenancy from year to year, or a quarterly, monthly, or weekly tenancy. This relation is created by contract to which there is usually, though not necessarily incident, a right on the part of the landlord to receive from the tenant payment for the use of the premises in the shape of rent. "The word 'landlord' does not mean the lord of the soil, but the person between whom and the tenant the relation of landlord and tenant exists": per Bramwell B in *Churchward v Ford* [supra]. The relation of landlord and tenant is of course fully established only when the tenant has entered on the premises let. If that has happened pursuant to a contract of the kind indicated the parties to such a contract are accurately described as the landlord and the tenant.' *Oakley v Wilson* [1927] 2 KB 279 at 288–290, DC, per cur.

New Zealand [The Fair Rents Act 1936 (NZ), s 13 (repealed), provided in part as follows: '(1) An order for the recovery of possession of any dwelling-house to which this Act applies, or for the ejectment of the tenant therefrom, may, subject to the next succeeding subsection, be made on one or more of the grounds following, but shall not be made on any other ground: . . . (d) That the premises are reasonably required by the landlord for his own occupation as a dwelling-house; (e) That the premises are reasonably required for occupation as a dwelling-house by any person in the regular employment of the landlord.'] 'The first question raised is as to the meaning of the word "landlord" as used in the Fair Rents Act 1936. The word is not defined in the Act. The object of the Act is plain from its words. It is to protect poor tenants of small houses from the exercise of their rights as property owners by their landlords. Among other objects it was designed to restrict the power of landlords to eject such tenants so long as they paid the rent and performed the conditions of the lease. The Act is *in pari materia* with ss 180 to 192 of the Magistrates' Courts Act 1928 (NZ), which are under the heading "Recovery of Possession of Tenements". It contains stringent restrictions on the rights given by those sections of the

Magistrates' Courts Act to landlords. The word "landlord" is defined in s 2 of the Magistrates' Courts Act as "the person entitled to the immediate reversion", etc. The two Acts being *in pari materia*, prima facie the word "landlord" would have the same meaning in both Acts. But I think there can be no doubt that the draftsman of the Fair Rents Act must have had the provisions of the Magistrates' Courts Act and the definition of "landlord" in mind, and must have intended the word to have the same meaning in the Fair Rents Act as in the Magistrates' Courts Act. If the Fair Rents Act is carefully perused, it will, I think, be seen that it deals throughout with the relations between the landlord in this sense and his tenant in respect of dwelling-houses which come within the purview of the Act, and it recognises that there may be from time to time different landlords of the same tenant even within a period of six months. . . . The purchaser qua purchaser has no *locus standi* at all; but if he has become landlord—that is to say, if he has become entitled to the possession of the premises subject to the lease—then, of course, he can apply for possession under any one of the grounds as stated in the section. The Act discloses no intention whatever of altering the law which was so well established before its enactment—viz that a purchaser of a dwelling-house subject to a tenancy becomes the landlord of that tenant as soon as he is given possession of the premises subject to the lease by his vendor, inasmuch as the purchaser then becomes entitled to the immediate reversion, and, therefore, to the receipt of the rents. I have no doubt that the word "landlord" was intended by Parliament to have this meaning in the Fair Rents Act, and that this is its true construction.' *Stable Securities Ltd v Cooper* [1941] NZLR 879 at 886, 887, per Ostler J; also reported [1941] GLR 469 at 472

Superior landlord

In this Act 'superior landlord' shall be deemed to include a landlord in cases where the goods seized are not those of an under tenant or lodger; and the words 'tenant' and 'under tenant' do not include a lodger. (Law of Distress Amendment Act 1908, s 9)

LANDOWNER

The word 'landowner' shall mean herein, as to lands in England, the person who shall be in the actual possession or receipt of the rents or profits of any land, whether of freehold, copyhold, customary, or other tenure, except where such person shall be a tenant for life or lives holding under a lease for life or lives not renewable, or shall be a tenant for years holding under a lease or an agreement for a lease, for a term of years not renewable, whereof less than twenty-five years shall be unexpired at the time of making any application to the Commissioners, without regard to the real amount of the interest of any person so excepted; and in the case where the person in the actual possession or receipt of the rents or profits of any land shall fall within the above exceptions, then the person who for the time being shall be in the actual receipt of the rent payable by the person so excepted, unless he shall also fall within the above exceptions, shall, jointly with the person who shall be liable to the payment thereof, be deemed for the purposes of this Act to be the owner of such lands. (Improvement of Land Act 1864, s 8)

LANE

'A "lane" usually means a minor road leading between one main road and another main road.' *A-G v Woolwich Metropolitan Borough Council* (1929) 93 JP 173 at 174, per Shearman J

Canada 'The learned judge [in the Court below] said: ". . . A lane, being a narrow road, is not generally used in connection with a highway." In the charge he is quite plain: "a lane . . . not really a highway." . . . The learned trial judge quite properly assumed the role of a lexicographer; it is for the Court not the dictionaries to state the meaning of words. In this instance I think he was wrong; it is, I think, quite clear that "lane" may be a perfectly correct designation for a public highway.' *Nixon v O'Callaghan* (1926) 60 OLR 76 at 91, Ont CA, per cur.

LAPSE

Ecclesiastical law

[A species of forfeiture whereby the right of presentation to a benefice accrues to the bishop, by neglect of the patron to present. If the bishop also neglects to present, the right accrues to the archbishop, or in the final resort, to the Crown. Similar in effect to ESCHEAT (qv).]

Of interest on land

'The word "lapse" seems an apt expression for the loss of any interest in land by reason of an omission to renew, or the non-performance of a condition, such as the payment of money.' *O'Keefe v Malone* [1903] AC 365 at 377, per cur.

Of testamentary gift

The term 'lapse' is applied to the failure of a testamentary gift owing to the death of the devisee or legatee in the testator's lifetime, whether before or after the date of the will, or, in the case of a gift to a spouse, owing to the dissolution or annulment of the marriage, but the testator may indicate in his will that he is using the word in a wider sense. As a rule a devisee or legatee must survive the testator in order that he or his estate may have the benefit of the gift, and a confirmation by codicil of a gift in a will to a legatee who has died since the date of the will does not prevent a lapse. (50 Halsbury's Laws (4th edn) para 347)

'The will is very short. I will read the relevant portions of it: "I give to my executors all my substance upon trust as to one-fourth part thereof for my daughter Fanny Sarah Fox for her separate use as to one other fourth part for my daughter Anna Charlotte Perry for her sole use for her life, and after her decease for her children if she shall leave children equally as to one other fourth part of the children of my deceased son George John Fox in equal shares and as to the remainder one-fourth part for Thomas William Spinney and Tiny Spinney now living with me and I declare that benefit hereunder shall become vested on the coming of age of the legatee and that any legacy which by the death of any person shall lapse shall go to my said daughter Fanny Sarah." . . . The real argument which was put forward here was to this effect: that, having regard to the language used in this sentence, it is not legitimate to say that, by necessary implication, the contingency of no children having come into existence must be imported. The ground for that argument is that the testator, by the phrase "by the death of any person shall lapse", has indicated one event, and one event only, upon which the gift over is to take effect—namely, lapse in the strict sense by the death of the legatee during the testator's lifetime. I am unable to take the view that the word "lapse" has in this will such a strict meaning. I cannot accept the proposition that in this will the words "death of any person" are to be construed as referring and referring only, to the death in the lifetime of the testator. The testator has not said "by the death in my lifetime", but simply "by the death"; and his dispositions include not merely immediate gifts, with reference to which the argument is a forcible one, but also a settled legacy. Further, the sentence comes immediately after a provision to the effect that vesting is to take place only on the coming of age of the legatee. Having regard to all these circumstances, particularly to the fact that the testator has not added any point of time to the words "the death", I have come to the conclusion that the words "by the death of any person" there include the case of death not merely in the lifetime of the testator, but before the legacy vests in possession. If that be the true meaning, it seems to me that the word "lapse" cannot be construed in its strict technical sense.' *Re Fox's Estate, Dawes v Druitt, Phoenix Assurance Co Ltd v Fox* [1937] 4 All ER 664 at 665, 667, CA, per Greene MR

'First . . . it must be and is accepted that the word "lapse" is, in an appropriate context, perfectly apt to cover the happening of any event in a testator's lifetime which prevents the intended legatee from being entitled to the legacy, and thus to mean nothing more than "fail".' *Re Sinclair (dcd), Lloyd's Bank plc v Imperial Cancer Research Fund* [1985] 1 All ER 1066 at 1070, CA, per Slade LJ

LARGE-SCALE

'Large-scale' means, with reference to a map, a scale not less than that of twenty-five inches to the mile. (Harbours Act 1964, s 57)

LARGEST

[A condition of sale provided that the purchasers of the 'largest lot' should be entitled to the possession of the title deeds.] 'In the simple case of a sale of land lotted out I can have no hesitation in saying, that the purchaser of the largest lot must mean the largest in superficial extent. The lot is the land, and the largest lot is that which includes the largest quantity of land. The condition does not refer to the largest in value.' *Griffiths v Hatchard* (1854) 1 K & J 17 at 18, per Page Wood V-C

LAST WILL *See* WILL

LATE NIGHT REFRESHMENT HOUSE *See* REFRESHMENT HOUSE

LATELY

'The question which I have to decide now is, whether a garden, which is marked "G" on the plan before me, and which did not, until a late period, attach to, belong to, or form part of any particular house which is marked on the plan, passed by the specific devise (because it is strictly a specific devise) contained in a codicil of the testator in the action, which for all purposes we may treat as his will. . . . The codicil, or will as I may call it, is dated August 24, 1867. . . . The devise is, in the first instance—that is to say, the governing words of the devise are—"all those three freehold cottages", which I take for granted (there is no dispute about it) mean 105, 106 and 107. It is impossible to suppose that the garden was intended to pass, or would pass, by the description of those freehold cottages, at any rate at that time. He adds the words, "and premises thereunto belonging, situate in Exeter Street aforesaid"—"situate in Exeter Street aforesaid" of course referring to the cottages, and not to "the premises thereunto belonging". . . . Then come these words which apply to the whole question, "which I have lately purchased", a statement which was perfectly true in 1867, but was only true in 1883 on the hypothesis that "lately" is a flexible word, and might mean at any time in the testator's lifetime. . . . Not only does he [the testator] specify three freehold cottages, but he refers to them as those which he had lately purchased. I must look at the will as at the date, for the purpose of ascertaining his intention and what he meant, and though I must read it as at the date of the death, for the purpose of ascertaining what property was comprised therein, I am bound to look at the will for the purpose of ascertaining what he meant. The words seem to me to deal with this specific property specified by reference to a purchase then lately made. I do not think that any alteration really would be made in the sense if I construed it at the date of the will.' *Cave v Harris* (1887) 57 LJ Ch 62 at 62–64, per Kekewich J

[A restrictive covenant described certain land as part of or 'lately' part of a certain estate.] 'Counsel for the defendant . . . founded his uncertainty argument on the word "lately", but in my judgment it merely means "formerly" or "heretofore" and does not import uncertainty as to how long lately may be.' *Re Selwyn's Conveyance, Hayman v Soorle* [1967] 1 All ER 339 at 344, per Goff J

LATENT AMBIGUITY *See* AMBIGUITY

LAW *See also* COMMON LAW; EQUITY; INTERNAL LAW; STATUTE

[The Local Government Act 1858, s 73 (repealed; see now Public Health Act 1936, ss 333 et seq) prohibited a local authority from doing any act injuriously affecting any reservoir, river, or stream, etc, in cases where any company or individuals would, if the Act had not been passed, have been entitled by 'law' to prevent or be relieved against the injuriously affecting such reservoir, river, stream, etc, without their consent in writing.] 'I take "law" here, in its widest sense, as equivalent to all proceedings for protecting civil rights equitable as well as legal. . . . I prefer putting the question on that ground to saying that the prohibition in the section is confined to cases where relief may be had in equity.' *R v Darlington Local Board of Health* (1865) 6 B & S 562 at 569, per Erle CJ

LAW MERCHANT

The term 'law merchant' may be defined as a number of usages, each of which exist among merchants and persons engaged in mercantile transactions, not only in one particular country, but throughout the civilised world, and each of which has acquired such notoriety, not only amongst those persons, but also in the mercantile world at large, that the courts of this country will take judicial notice of it.

A usage of the law merchant has therefore two characteristics—it must in the first place amount to *jus gentium*, that is to say, it must be in vogue beyond the limits of this country and its notoriety must be cosmopolitan rather than national; and in the second place it must be of such a nature that it will receive judicial notice in our courts. It does not follow, however, that every mercantile usage of which the courts take judicial notice forms part of the law merchant. The law merchant is composed of those usages of merchants and traders in the different departments of trade which have been ratified by the decisions of courts of law and adopted as settled law with a view to the interests of trade and the public convenience. (12 Halsbury's Laws (4th edn) para 460)

'The law merchant is sometimes spoken of as a fixed body of law, forming part of the common law, and as it were coeval with it. But as a matter of legal history, this view is altogether incorrect. The law merchant thus spoken of with reference to bills of exchange and other negotiable securities, though forming part of the general body of the *lex mercatoria*, is of comparatively recent origin. It is neither more nor less than the usages of merchants and traders in the different departments of trade, ratified by the decisions of courts of law, which, upon such usages being proved before them, have adopted them as settled law with a view to the interests of trade and the public convenience, the court proceeding herein on the well-known principle of law that, with reference to transactions in the different departments of trade, courts of law, in giving effect to the contracts and dealings of the parties, will assume that the latter have dealt with one another on the footing of any custom or usage prevailing generally in the particular department. By this process, what before was usage only, unsanctioned by legal decision, has become engrafted upon, or incorporated into, the common law, and may thus be said to form part of it. "When a general usage has been judicially ascertained and established", says Lord Campbell, in *Brandao v Barnett* [(1846) 12 Cl & F 787 at 805] "it becomes a part of the law merchant, which courts of justice are bound to know and recognise".' *Goodwin v Robarts* (1875) LR 10 Exch 337 at 346, per cur.

'This was an action in trover to recover the value of certain bearer bonds alleged to have been converted by the defendants to their own use. . . . A body of evidence was called at the trial to shew that all these bonds pass from hand to hand among the people who deal in them, and that they are treated as negotiable in the same way as the bonds of foreign governments. No serious attempt was made to refute this evidence, and it quite satisfied me that all the bonds in question belong to a class which bankers, stockbrokers, and others whose business it is to deal in such securities treat, rightly or wrongly, as negotiable and as passing from hand to hand by mere delivery. . . . It is no doubt true that negotiability can only be attached to a contract by the law merchant or by a statute; and it is also true that, in determining whether a usage has become so well established as to be binding on the courts of law, the length of time during which the usage has existed is an important circumstance to take into consideration; but it is to be remembered that in these days usage is established much more quickly than it was in days gone by; more depends on the number of the transactions which help to create it than on the time over which the transactions are spread; and it is probably no exaggeration to say that nowadays there are more business transactions in an hour than there were in a week a century ago. Therefore the comparatively recent origin of this class of securities in my view creates no difficulty in the way of holding that they are negotiable by virtue of the law merchant; they are dealt in as negotiable instruments in every minute of a working day, and to the extent of many thousands of pounds. It is also to be remembered that the law merchant is not fixed and stereotyped; it has not yet been arrested in its growth by being moulded into a code; it is, to use the words of Cockburn CJ in *Goodwin v Robarts* [supra], capable of being expanded and enlarged so as to meet the wants and requirements of trade in the varying circumstances of commerce, the effect of which is that it approves and adopts from time to time those usages of merchants which are found necessary for the convenience of trade; our common law, of which the law merchant is but a branch, has in the hands of the judges the same facility for adapting itself to the changing needs of the general public; principles do not alter, but old rules of applying them change, and new rules spring into existence. Thus it has been found convenient to treat securities like those in question in this action as negotiable, and the Courts of law, recognising the wisdom of the usage, have incorporated it in what is called the law merchant, and have made it part of the common law of the country.' *Edelstein v Schuler & Co* [1902] 2 KB 144 at 153–155, per Bingham J

LAWFUL

[The master of a ship insured in any 'lawful trade' engaged in smuggling, with the result that the ship was seized, and the underwriters refused to make good the loss.] 'In the present case the owner has not engaged in any unlawful trade; for the words "lawful trade" in the policy mean the trade in which the ship is sent by the owners. It is stated correctly [in the pleadings] that the ship was sent on a lawful voyage: but owing to the misconduct of the master she was lost; for he in defiance of his duty took on board certain commodities which subjected the ship to seizure.' *Havelock v Hancill* (1789) 3 Term Rep 277 at 278, per Lord Kenyon CJ

'The words "it shall be lawful", in a statute are obligatory or not, according to the subject matter.' *Castelli v Groom* (1852) 18 QB 490 at 495, per Crompton J

[A testator by his will devised land to his daughter and her 'lawful' heirs.] 'The word "heirs" is, in no degree, qualified or affected by the word "lawful" which precedes it, just as it makes no difference if you prefix the word "legitimate" to children or "credible" to witness. It is no more than is implied in the simple word "heirs".' *Mathews v Gardiner* (1853) 17 Beav 254 at 257, per Romilly MR

'"It shall be lawful" means, in substance, that it shall not be lawful to do otherwise.' *Re Neath & Brecon Rly Co* (1874) 9 Ch App 263 at 264, per James LJ

'The words "it shall be lawful" [in a statute] are distinctly words of permission only—they are enabling and empowering words. They confer a legislative right and power on the individual named to do a particular thing, and the true question is not whether they mean something different, but whether, regard being had to the person so enabled—to the subject-matter, to the general objects of the statute, and to the person or class of persons for whose benefit the power may be intended to have been conferred—they do, or do not, create a duty in the person on whom it is conferred, to exercise it.' *Julius v Oxford (Bp)* (1880) 5 App Cas 214 at 229, 230, per Lord Penzance

[A testator by his will made it a condition on a devisee of his estate that within twelve months after having become entitled he should 'lawfully' assume the testator's name and arms.] 'The practical difficulty arises from the use by the testator of the word "lawfully". Strike that word out of the will, and there still would be a very difficult question, perhaps even a more difficult one, than the one which I have to decide here. There is some authority for saying that you cannot "assume" arms, according to the directions of the will, except by getting a proper grant of the arms, which may be either from the Herald's College, or by Royal warrant, or, of course, by Act of Parliament. There are many dicta in cases in favour of that view, and something certainly against it on the mere etymological reading of the word "assume". . . . I must take it for granted that by the use of the word "lawfully" he has meant something more than mere assumption—whatever that may mean—although I do not credit the testator with the knowledge of the dicta to which I have referred. Otherwise the word is mere surplusage, and, according to the most ordinary rules of construction, it is not right to disregard any word unless there is some very obvious reason for so doing. . . . I come to the word "lawfully". It is extremely difficult to say exactly what the word "lawfully" means. I have referred to a dictionary, and according to that it really comes to this—that anything is lawful which is not forbidden by law. No doubt a man may lawfully assume a coat of arms in that sense. . . . To my mind "lawfully" cannot be construed as not doing anything which is improper—that is, taking the coat of arms in such a way that no court in this country would interfere with it. I think the testator must be taken to have intended that something should be done to give a legal title to the arms which were assumed. Unless you give some sense of that kind to it, I fail to see how the word can give any additional force to the word "assume".' *Re Croxon, Croxon v Ferrers* (1904) 73 LJ Ch 170 at 171, 172, per Kekewich J

[The Merchandise Marks Act 1887, s 18 (repealed; see now the Trade Descriptions Act 1968, s 34) provided that the provision of the Act with respect to false trade descriptions should not apply to trade descriptions 'lawfully' and generally applied at the time of the passing of the Act.] 'The conclusion that an act is done "lawfully" within the meaning of s 18 if it does not involve the commission of a criminal offence . . . is giving too restricted a meaning to the word "lawfully". I do not think it was intended by the use of that term that the adoption of any conventional meaning should be protected provided that its use does not constitute an infringement of the criminal law and that the term has been generally applied. In my opinion the word "lawfully" means that the use of the conventional trade description must have been lawful in the widest sense of the term, and that it is not restricted merely to implying that there has been no infringement of the criminal law.' *Lemy v Watson* [1915] 3 KB 731 at 750, 751, per Lord Reading CJ

'It is clear that, if any real meaning is to be given to the words "lawful merchandise", which are, of course, inserted into the charterparty for the protection of the owners, the goods loaded must be such as can be loaded without breach of the law in force at the port of loading. Inasmuch as the master is under the general orders of the charterer as to where a cargo shall be carried within the charter limits, it is at least logical to suppose that the charterer undertakes that the cargo shall also be the type of cargo which can be lawfully carried and discharged at the port to which he has ordered the vessel to proceed. The purpose of the provision that only "lawful merchandise" shall be carried by the charterers would be largely nullified if all that was necessary was that the cargo could be loaded without breaking the laws of the country where it was loaded.' *Leolga Compania de Navigacion v John Glynn & Sons Ltd* [1953] 2 All ER 327 at 332, per Pilcher J (also reported in [1953] 2 QB 374 at 386)

Australia [The Primary Producers Debts Act 1935–1986 (SA), s 39 provides that a person authorised by the Board may require any person to attend and give evidence and may require answers to enquiries made by him. If any person 'refuses to answer any lawful question', he is guilty of an offence.] ' "Lawful" question in my view, connotes one which calls for an answer according to law, one that the witness is compellable to answering according to the established usage of the law.' *Crafter v Kelly* [1941] SASR 237 at 242, per Angas Parsons J

Australia 'The natural meaning of "lawful" depends on the context in which the word is used. It may mean, simply, "permitted". In this sense an act is lawful, when it can be done without any infraction of the law, and so of a lawful trade or purpose. Another use is in the sense of supported by the law, e.g., lawful authority, excuse, or impediment; but it seems to me that, in some connections, the word implies the quality of being "legally enforceable". A lawful owner or heir is one whose rights are recognised and enforceable by law, and a claim or demand is "lawful" in the sense that the law compels the debtor to satisfy it.' *Crafter v Kelly* [1941] SASR 237 at 243, per Napier J

Australia [The defendant was charged of being found in a dwelling for an unlawful purpose or without excuse.] 'What then, will constitute a "lawful excuse"? An exhaustive definition is impossible, but some illustrations may be given. First, there will be a lawful excuse if the defendant had the leave and licence, express or implied, of the occupier, or, if there is no occupier, of the owner, to be in the house. Secondly, there will be a lawful excuse if the defendant entered under superior authority, as, for instance, under a lawfully issued search warrant, or a warrant of execution, or a warrant to distrain. Thirdly, in my opinion, there will be a lawful excuse if the defendant is able to prove, or if it can be proved on his behalf, that he had no mens rea. Thus, if it can be shewn [sic] that he was in such a mental state from disease or otherwise that he was not responsible for his actions, or that he was forcibly taken to the house by some other person and left there in a helpless condition, or that he entered the house in the honest and reasonable belief that the house was his own dwelling, and that he was discovered before he found out his mistake, there would, in my judgment, be an answer to the charge. Mistake of law can never be pleaded, but an honest and reasonable belief in the existence of a state of facts which, if true, would make the act charged against the accused innocent would, I think, be sufficient defence (I Russell on Crimes 8th edn at 104).' *Crafter v O'Reilly* [1934] SASR 20 at 23, per Murray CJ

LAWFUL EXCUSE

New Zealand [Concerning the various offences of being found on premises without lawful excuse.] 'While an attempt to define "lawful excuse" rigidly is not desirable . . . we think that an intention to commit an offence is usually inconsistent with a lawful excuse.' *Police v Carter* [1978] 2 NZLR 29 at 33, CA, per Cooke J

LAWFUL ISSUE *See* ISSUE

LAWFULLY MADE

Canada [The accused alleged that interceptions of private communications under Criminal Code, RSC 1970, cc-34, were not 'lawfully made', having involved entry into designated premises.] 'The term "lawfully made", when it appears in a codification of criminal law, favours the conclusion that it means "not contrary to criminal law". It would not be construed without something more in the phrase, as meaning "made in conformity with all laws". For example, it would be an extension of the ordinary meaning of those words in their context in the *Criminal Code* to adopt an interpretation ruling the interception to be unlawfully made because it contravened the laws of copyright; or because it invaded a civil right such as the right to privacy; or indeed, because the act of interception constituted a tort such as deceit or trespass where the tort in question has no presence in the *Criminal Code* in the form in which the tort in question was committed.' *Lyons v R* [1984] 2 SCR 633 at 674, SCC, per Estey, J

LAY

Laying of information

[Magistrates, in their criminal jurisdiction, may try summarily an information that has been laid before them; in their civil jurisdiction, a complaint that has been made to them. The question was whether the 'laying' of an information (or making of a complaint) should be personally to a justice of the peace or a clerk to the justices, or whether other persons could be authorised to receive it.] 'The laying of an information before, or the making of a complaint to, a justice of the peace or the clerk to the justices to my mind means (in reference to a written information or complaint) procuring the delivery of the document to a person authorised to receive it on behalf of the justice of the peace and the clerk to the justices. The acts of delivery and receipt are ministerial and I see no reason why the justices of the peace or the clerks to the justices should not delegate to an appropriate subordinate authority to receive the information which the prosecutor desires to deliver. It can sensibly be inferred that any member of the staff in the office of the clerk to the justices authorised to handle incoming post has such authority. Accordingly, once the information has been received at the office of the clerk to the justices, which today in most cases is likely to be at the magistrates' court house, the information will, in my view, have been laid. No more is required of the prosecutor to launch the intended criminal proceedings. Similarly with a complaint; once the complaint is received at the office of the clerk to the justices no more is required of the complainant.' *Hill v Anderton* [1982] 2 All ER 963 at 971, per Lord Roskill

Australia 'The word "lay", like the word "exhibit", is well known in law as meaning to present or put forward an accusation or charge (usually in the form of an information or indictment) or some other relevant allegation as in "lay the damages" or "lay the venue". An information is not laid by handing a document to a justice and misleading him as to its nature. Such misinformation is not an information. A written information is only duly laid before a justice when he receives it as information for his attention.' *Electronic Rentals Pty Ltd v Anderson* (1971) 124 CLR 27 at 39, per Windeyer J

LAY DAYS

A charterparty may stipulate that the cargo is to be loaded within a specified number of days, usually called 'lay days'. According to the ordinary form of stipulation, this period begins when written notice of readiness to load is given to the charterer. Sometimes it may be stipulated that the period is not to begin before a certain date, unless the charterer begins loading sooner. It is a condition of the charterparty that the charterer is to tender a cargo within the specified period or within a reasonable period if none is specified, and his failure to do so entitles the shipowner to treat the contract as at an end, and also to sue for damages except in certain exceptional cases. Except in these cases and subject to any express provisions of the charterparty the cause of the charterer's failure is immaterial, whether it is attributable to his own default or to circumstances beyond his control. Failure to complete the loading, as distinct from tendering a cargo, within the specified period will not of itself entitle the shipowner to treat the contract as repudiated, but, in the absence of stipulation to the contrary, will entitle him to damages or demurrage even if the failure is not due to the charterer's default.

However, the charterparty may contain exceptions applying to the charterer's duty to tender a cargo, and will usually contain exceptions in favour of the charterer applying to the actual loading.

Where the detention of the ship at the port of loading beyond the specified time is attributable to the default of the shipowner or of persons for whom he is responsible, the charterer is not liable to pay demurrage. (43 Halsbury's Laws (4th edn) para 466)

'Now I come to another clause which is commonly inserted in charterparties. There must be a stipulation as to the time to be occupied in the loading and in the unloading of the cargo. There must be a time, either expressly stipulated, or implied. If it is not expressly stipulated, then it is a reasonable time which is implied by the law; but either the law or the parties fix a time. Now, when they do fix a time, how do they fix it? Why, they allow a certain number of days, during which, although the ship is at the disposal of the charterer to load or to unload the cargo, he does not pay for the use of the ship. That is the meaning of "lay days". It is a stipulation always of the charterer. Now the days, which are given to the charterer in a charterparty, either to load or to unload without paying for the use of the ship, are "lay days". Other days are sometimes given also in favour of the charterer, which are called "demurrage days". Those are days beyond the lay days, but during which the amount that he has to pay for the use of the ship is a fixed sum, not necessarily what it costs the owner to keep his ship, but a fixed sum, which is usually about what it is supposed it costs the owner to keep the ship. This stipulation also is in favour of the charterer, because instead of being involved in a dispute as to what he would have to pay for the days during which the ship is kept idle, a sum is fixed, and he knows what he has to pay if he keeps the ship beyond the lay days. Those are the "demurrage days". If he keeps the ship beyond the lay days, when he pays nothing, and only the number of demurrage days, he pays a fixed sum for demurrage. If he keeps the ship after that, it is a question of damages, and he does not know what he has to pay until the question is settled by a tribunal or by agreement. We have here to deal with lay days. "Lay days" are described in a charterparty in various ways; sometimes certain days are fixed for loading or unloading. If these days are described simply as "days", then, although they are not so called when they are said to be for loading or unloading, nevertheless they are "lay days". "Days" and "lay days" are really the same in a charter-party. "Days" or "lay days" may be calculated in a different manner. They may be described, and sometimes they are described, in a charter-party as days of so many working hours. Then the number of days is fixed, but the length of each day is also fixed. The days may be described as "working days".' *Nielsen v Wait* (1885) 16 QBD 67 at 70, 71, CA, per Lord Esher MR

'What "laytime" and "demurrage" mean was stated succinctly by Lord Guest (with the substitution of "lay days" for "laytime") in *Compania Naviera Aeolus SA v Union of India* [[1962] 3 All ER 670]: "Lay days are the days which parties have stipulated for the loading or discharge of the cargo and, if they are exceeded, the charterers are in breach; demurrage is the agreed damages to be paid for delay if the ship is delayed in loading or discharging beyond the agreed period." For the purposes of the adventure in four stages contemplated by a voyage charter-party, laytime is that period of time, paid for by the charterer in the freight, for which the shipowner agrees to place the ship at the disposition of the charterer for carrying out the loading operation or the discharging operation. Laytime for discharging is generally based on an estimate of the time which will be needed to carry out the operation with reasonable diligence if everything else goes well.' *Dias Compania Naviera SA v Louis Dreyfus Corpn* [1978] 1 All ER 724 at 726, HL, per Lord Diplock

LAY-OFF

Canada [The employers temporarily reduced number of working hours during shortage of work.] 'The Union's case rests in large measure on the submission that there is no difference between a reduction in the hours of work and a lay-off and the moment one reduces the hours of work of an individual that individual is laid off (*mise à pied*). "Lay-off" is not defined in the Quebec Labour Code, RSQ 1964, c 141. However, the Shorter Oxford English Dictionary defines "lay-off" as follows: "Lay-off, a period during which a workman is temporarily discharged." and Nouveau Larousse Universel, Tome 2 "Mise à pied": "retrait temporaire d'emploi". In my opinion none of the employees of Air-Care Ltd was laid off on the occasions in respect of which the grievance was raised. There was no reduction in the working force and the status of the employees as employees was unaffected.' *Air-Care Ltd v United Steel Workers of America* [1976] 1 SCR 2 at 6, SCC, per Dickson J

LAY OUT

'I do not think that if a person merely puts up a boarding, or leaves the way without any fence, or leaves the old fence untouched while he is building, he can be said to have laid out the road; but as soon as he begins to put up fences, and marks out the boundary which he intends to be the permanent boundary between his building and the road, then he may be said to have begun to lay out the road for the forming of the street.' *Taylor v Metropolitan Board of Works* (1867) LR 2 QB 213 at 221, per Blackburn J

LAY UP

[By a policy of insurance on ship for a year, the underwriter stipulated to return a part of the premium, if sold or 'laid up', for every uncommenced month.] 'I am of opinion, that the words laid up being in company with the word sold, must mean a permanent laying up, similar to that which would take place if the ship had been sold; that is, such a laying up as would put a final end to the policy.' *Hunter v Wright* (1830) 10 B & C 714 at 716, per Lord Tenterden CJ

'The parties might undoubtedly stipulate in the manner it is contended they did stipulate on the behalf of the defendant, but I think the true construction of the words "laying up" must be such a laying up as would put an end altogether to the policy.' Ibid at 716, per Parke J

LEAFLET

'Leaflet' includes any written information. (Medicines Act 1968, s 132(1))

LEAKAGE

'Oil had been carried from Leghorn to Liverpool. When the ship arrived there many of the casks were partially empty, and this action was brought to recover damages for this leakage of the oil. . . . By the Memorandum in the margin of the bill of lading, the shipowners are not to be accountable for leakage. On the argument different views were suggested by counsel as to the meaning of this word "leakage". For the respondents it was contended that the word means only ordinary leakage (which, according to the evidence, amounts to 1 per cent), and does not extend to extraordinary leakage, such as that in question, amounting to an alleged deficiency of 2,000 gallons. On the part of the appellants it was denied that, according to the natural and ordinary meaning of the words employed, the amount of leakage was at all limited in quantity. . . . It may be observed that the learned judge of the Admiralty Court appears to have adopted the construction of the word "leakage", contended for by the respondents, viz. that it means "ordinary leakage" only. . . . But we do not think such a construction allowable. The condition that the shipowners are not to be accountable for leakage does not, in its ordinary and grammatical sense, put any limit to the quantity of leakage; and on principle, therefore, we do not think it would be justifiable to add any such limit to its terms. Nor are we aware of any authority for doing so.' *Ohrloff v Briscall, The Helene* (1866) LR 1 PC 231 at 237, 238, 240, PC, per cur.

'The agents in Rotterdam for an American company . . . sold by cable authority to Messrs De Monchy, the respondents in this appeal, 100 barrels of spirits of turpentine at a certain price. The contract was a c.i.f. contract; it need not be quoted in full. It contained (inter alia, . . . the following clause: "Insurance documents to include risk of leakage in excess of 1 per cent upon the basis of the above reduction of weight." . . . Leakage I take to mean any stealthy escape either through a small hole which might be discernible or through the pores of the material of which the cask is composed.' *Phoenix Insurance Co of Hartford v De Monchy* (1929) 141 LT 439 at 440, 441, per Lord Dunedin

Australia 'I consider it [leakage] means the passing or seeping of a fluid through a crack or crevice or leak; a passing or dripping away by gradual waste through a crevice or hole.' *Nicholson v Fremantle Port Authority* [1969] WAR 27 at 28, per Wolff J

LEARNING

[A testator gave to trustees funds to be applied by them according to their discretion for the advancement and propagation of 'learning' all over the world.] 'The word "learning" is a word which is susceptible of various meanings. It is rather extraordinary that in Archbishop Whateley's work upon logic, it is placed among the equivocal words, that is words which have two significations. He says, " 'learning' signifies either the act of acquiring knowledge, or the knowledge itself. *Exempli gratia*, he neglects his learning; Johnson was a man of learning." Now the question is, in what sense did the testator use this expression? I apprehend that if there are two meanings of a word, one of which will effectuate and the other will defeat a testator's object, the court is bound to select that meaning of the word which will carry out the intention and objects of the testator; and I think that your Lordships are not without aid in giving the particular limited interpretation (if I may use the expression), to the word "learning" which is required for the purpose of establishing the validity of his bequest, because when you find that the testator associates with the word "learning" the word "education", I think that from the society itself in which you find the word, your Lordships may gather the meaning which it is necessary to put upon it, and that he means the word "learning" in the sense of imparting knowledge by instruction or teaching. . . . Under these circumstances, my Lords, without going into the different authorities that have been cited, because I do not think it is at all necessary, it appears to me, that giving that interpretation to the word "learning", which, I think, we are entitled to give to it, and to which its association with the word "education" seems to me necessarily to point, this, according to all the authorities, is a valid charitable bequest.' *Whicker v Hume* (1858) 7 HL Cas 124 at 154, 155, per Lord Chelmsford LC

[The Obscene Publications Act 1959, s 4(1) provides that a person shall not be guilty of publishing an obscene article if it is proved that such publication is justified on the ground that it is in the interests of (inter alia) art or 'learning'.] 'The first question to consider, no doubt, is the meaning of the word "learning" in s 4(1). . . . It seems to us that the fundamental question is whether "learning" in this context is a noun, in which case (as it seems to me) it must mean the product of scholarship. The only possible meaning of "learning" as a noun I would have thought would have been something whose inherent excellence is gained by the work of the scholar.' *A-G's Reference (No 3 of 1977)* [1978] 3 All ER 1166 at 1169, CA, per cur.

LEASE *See also* CONDITION

An instrument in proper form by which the conditions of a contract of letting are finally ascertained, and which is intended to vest the right of exclusive possession in the lessee, either at once, if the term is to commence immediately, or at a future date, if the term is to commence subsequently, is a lease which takes effect from the date fixed for the commencement of the term without the necessity of actual entry by the lessee.

An instrument is usually construed as a lease if it contains words of present demise. Even where the instrument is called an 'agreement', and contains a stipulation for the subsequent granting of a formal lease, it may be construed as a lease if the essential terms are fixed, especially if possession is to be taken under it and if the covenants which would be inserted in the lease are to be binding at once. (27 Halsbury's Laws (4th edn) para 51)

'Lease' includes an agreement for a lease where the term to be covered by the lease has begun, and any tenancy, but does not include a mortgage and 'lessee', 'lessor' and 'leasehold interest' shall be construed accordingly. (Capital Allowances Act 1968, s 87)

'Lease' includes an underlease and an agreement for a lease or underlease, but does not include an option to take a lease or a mortgage, and 'leasehold interest' means the interest of the tenant under a lease as so defined. (Town and Country Planning Act 1971, s 290(1))

'If the owner of land consents by deed that another person shall occupy the land for a certain time, that is a lease.' *St Germains (Earl) v Willan* (1823) 2 B & C 216 at 220, per Bayley J

'The word "lease" in law is a well-known legal term of well-defined import. No lawyer has ever suggested that the title of the lessor makes any difference in the description of the instrument, whether the lease is granted by a freeholder or a copyholder with the licence of the lord or by a man who himself is a leaseholder. It being well granted for a term of years it is called a lease. It is quite true that where the grantor of the lease holds for a term the second instrument is called either an underlease or a derivative lease, but it is still a lease.' *Camberwell & South London Building Society v Holloway* (1879) 13 Ch D 754 at 759, per Jessel MR

'The lessee covenants that he shall not have any interest in the lease either directly or indirectly and shall not have any interest in any company or firm interested in the lease. Those are rather vague expressions. A lease may be regarded from various points of view. It may be regarded as a piece of paper, as a lease and counterpart, or a piece of parchment, or it may be regarded merely as the label or compendious evidence of title for the property which it includes. I should be inclined to read the expression "have any interest in" the lease as really meaning have any interest in the demised premises, because I cannot see very much sense, if any (and I cannot attribute nonsense to the parties) in treating the lease as being merely a piece of paper or parchment. I think that the same construction must be applied when we have references to "company or firm interested in" the lease. I see very little difference between that expression, read, as I think, sensibly, and "interested in the demised premises".' *Lewin v American & Colonial*

Distributors Ltd [1945] Ch 225 at 231, 232, per Vaisey J; affirmed ibid at 236, CA

Agreement for lease

An instrument which only binds one party to create and the other to accept a lease in the future is an agreement for a lease. Moreover, an instrument is construed as an agreement for a lease and not as a lease, notwithstanding that it contains words of present demise, if the provisions to be inserted in the lease are not finally ascertained; or if from other indications it appears that it was not intended to take effect as a lease. . . . The essential terms of an agreement for a lease are (1) the identification of the lessor and lessee; (2) the premises to be leased; (3) the commencement and duration of the term; and (4) the rent or other consideration to be paid. (27 Halsbury's Laws (4th edn) paras 53, 57)

Building lease

'Building lease' means a lease granted in pursuance or in consideration of an agreement for the erection or the substantial rebuilding or reconstruction of the whole or part of the house in question or a building comprising it. (Leasehold Reform Act 1967, s 4(1)(d))

For purpose of residence

Australia [The Landlord and Tenant (Amendment) Act 1948–1986 (NSW), s 8(1) provided (inter alia) that 'dwelling house' meant any prescribed premises leased for the purposes of residence.] 'The definition . . . must . . . be taken to mean what it says. There is no justification for reading into it a qualification which would confine its application to cases where residence is considered of greater importance than other uses which also are within the actual or presumed contemplation of the parties. The purpose or combination of purposes to which the parties must be held to have contemplated that the premises would be put by the tenant must be ascertained by considering the provisions of the contract as it stands at the date when the notice to quit is given and any facts which at that date affect their mutual rights and duties in relation to the user of the premises; and if the inquiry is not thereby answered, then by considering the nature of the premises and all the circumstances existing at the date of the original lease. If the conclusion be that residence was either the sole purpose or one of several purposes which the parties should be held to have contemplated, the premises must be held to be "leased for the purposes of residence"; but a conclusion that residence was a purpose of the letting is not open where the parties are considered to have had in view no residence except as part of the enjoyment of the entire premises for non-residential purposes. An illustration may be found in the case of a large city store which contains caretaker's quarters. Residence by a caretaker is one of the uses which the parties to a lease of such a building may well be found to have contemplated, yet the building could not on that account alone be held to be leased for the purposes of residence, for residence by a caretaker merely forms part of the use of the building for the purposes of a store.' *Thompson v Easterbrook* (1951) 83 CLR 467 at 485, per cur.

Consumer lease

United States The term 'consumer lease' means a contract in the form of a lease or bailment for the use of personal property by a natural person for a period of time exceeding four months, and for a total contractual obligation not exceeding $25,000, primarily for personal, family, or household purposes, whether or not the lessee has the option to purchase or otherwise become the owner of the property at the expiration of the lease, except that such term shall not include any credit sale as defined in section 1602(g) of this title. Such term does not include a lease for agricultural, business, or commercial purposes, or to a government or governmental agency or instrumentality, or to an organization. (Truth in Lending Act 1968, s 181(1))

Full restoring lease

'Full restoring lease' means a mining lease imposing on the lessee an obligation to restore to a condition suitable for the purposes of agriculture all land excavated under the lease in the course of winning and working ironstone by opencast operations and containing no provision for the payment of sums in lieu of compliance with that obligation in respect of any of the land or by way of liquidated damages for failure to comply with it. (Mineral Workings Act 1951, s 41)

Ground lease

'Ground lease' means a lease at a rent (or, where the rent varies, at a maximum rent) which does not substantially exceed the rent which a tenant might reasonably have been expected, at the commencement of the term created by the lease, to pay for the land comprised in the lease, excluding any buildings, for a term equal to the term created by the lease. (Landlord and Tenant (War Damage) Act 1939, s 24)

'Ground lease' means a lease for building purposes at a rent (or, where the rent varies, at a maximum rent) which does not substantially exceed the rent which a tenant might reasonably have been expected, at the date when the lease was granted, to pay for the land comprised in the lease, excluding any buildings, for a term equal to the term created by the lease. (Coal-Mining (Subsidence) Act 1957, s 17(1))

Long and short leases

'Long lease' means a lease in the case of which the portion of the term for which it was granted remaining unexpired at the end of the financial year is not less than fifty years, the expression 'short lease' means a lease which is not a long lease and the expression 'lease' includes an agreement for a lease. (Companies Act 1985, Sch 9, para 34)

Mining lease

A lease may be granted of land or any part of land, and since minerals are a part of the land it follows that a lease can be granted of the surface of the land and the minerals below, or of the surface alone, or of the minerals alone. It has been said that a contract for the working and getting of minerals, although for convenience called a mining lease, is not in reality a lease at all in the sense in which one speaks of an agricultural lease, and that such a contract, properly considered, is really a sale of a portion of the land at a price payable by instalments, that is, by way of rent or royalty, spread over a number of years. (31 Halsbury's Laws (4th edn) para 222)

The expression 'mining lease' means a lease for any mining purpose or purposes connected therewith, and 'mining purposes' include the sinking and searching for, winning, working, getting, making merchantable, smelting or otherwise converting or working for the purposes of any manufacture, carrying away, and disposing of mines and minerals, in or under land, and the erection of buildings, and the execution of engineering and other works suitable for those purposes. (Landlord and Tenant Act 1927, s 25)

'Mining lease' means a lease for the purpose of working and getting minerals, whether by underground or by surface working; and in this definition 'lease' includes an underlease and an agreement for a lease or underlease and a tenancy agreement, and also includes a licence, but does not include an option to take a lease, underlease or tenancy agreement, and does not include a mortgage. (Opencast Coal Act 1958, s 51(1))

Multiple lease

'Multiple lease' means a lease comprising buildings which are used or adapted for use as two or more separate tenements (Landlord and Tenant (War Damage) Act 1939, s 24)

[The Landlord and Tenant (War Damage) Act 1939, s 15 contains special provisions where the lease is a 'multiple lease', which is defined by the Act (see supra).] 'A multiple lease is in its very nature granted as one, not as a number of leases. To constitute it there must be premises used or adapted for use as two or more tenements, but the lease must be one. There may possibly be leases whose terms are so clear as to shew that they cannot be multiple, though I find it difficult to envisage such a result, inasmuch as the buildings comprised in the lease might still be adapted for use as separate tenements, and I do not see how a court could reach a conclusion upon this point without evidence.' *Westminster Bank Ltd v Edwards* [1942] 1 All ER 470 at 476, per Lord Porter

Repairing lease

'The only question raised, whether this lease is authorised by the power contained in the will of the testator; that is, whether it is a "repairing lease" within the meaning of the clause in the will which empowers the tenants for life to grant "building or repairing leases for the term of sixty-one years". . . . Looking at the circumstances, and the finding of the arbitrator that the greater part of the premises were, at the time when the lease was granted, in a very dilapidated state, I think that this is a good "repairing lease" within the meaning of the power. I do not find that the term "repairing lease" has a meaning as a term of art; nor do I find that the Court of Chancery has defined what is a "repairing lease". There is therefore no authority which compels us to say that this is not a repairing lease, and I think that nothing could be added to the words of this covenant which would render it the more a "repairing lease". The lessee covenants well and sufficiently to repair, uphold, support, maintain, amend, and keep, not only the demised premises, but all buildings thereafter erected, and to deliver them up well and sufficiently repaired, upheld, supported, amended, and kept together. That seems to me to fall within the requirements of the testator. I am at a loss to know what stronger words could be used, for to satisfy that covenant it would not be sufficient merely to prevent the premises from falling down.' *Easton v Pratt* (1864) 2 H & C 676 at 686, 687, per Erle CJ

LEASEHOLD INTEREST

'The ordinary meaning of leasehold interest is an interest in land of leasehold tenure.' *Sheffield Waggon Co v Stratton* (1878) 48 LJQB 35 at 36, CA, per Cotton LJ

LEAVE

'In common understanding the word *leave* must be taken to apply to that sense of it in which a person making his will would naturally use it, namely, by a testamentary disposition.' *Doe d Thorley v Thorley* (1809) 10 East 438 at 442, 443, per Lord Ellenborough CJ

[A testator by his will made a gift to the child or children of a daughter, with a gift over in the event of the daughter dying without 'leaving' children.] 'In this case a clear vested interest is in the first place given to the children of a daughter attaining twenty-one. If in the clause which gives the property over on failure of children of the daughter, the word "having" be read for "leaving", the whole Will will express a consistent intention to that effect.' *Maitland v Chalie* (1822) 6 Madd 243 at 250, per Leach V-C

'Upon the whole instrument [a marriage settlement], the construction is, that the word "leave" [in the phrase "leave issue"] is to be construed "have"; and that accords with the leaning of the courts to favour such a construction as will not leave the children of the marriage unprovided for.' *Wynne v Brady* (1843) 5 I Eq R 239 at 242, 243, per Pennefather B

'The gift contained in the will . . . is, that, after the death of the tenant for life, the fund shall be equally divided between all the children of the tenant for life who should be living at the time of her death, and the lawful issue of any child then dead leaving issue. As to the children living at the death of the tenant for life no question arises. But as to the issue of any child then dead two constructions have been contended for; one is, that the issue of a deceased child who are to take, are a class to be ascertained at the death of the tenant for life. The other construction would include a child of a child surviving his parent, but dying in the lifetime of the tenant for life. . . . After a careful consideration of the words in this will, I think "leaving issue" means at the death of the child whose death is contemplated, and not at the death of the tenant for life; and that, consequently, the time for ascertaining the class is the death of such child.' *Barker v Barker* (1852) 5 De G & Sm 753 at 758, 759, per Parker V-C

[The testatrix by her will gave her residuary estate to A, and after his decease in case he should 'leave any child or children' of his body lawfully begotten, in trust for all and every such child or children equally at twenty-one. A had one child who attained twenty-one and died in his father's lifetime.] 'Prima facie, leaving children means leaving children at the period of death. . . . For the plaintiff . . . it was contended that . . . "leaving" must be construed as "having children". . . . The answer to this is that the words of the will are clear and unambiguous. . . . The fact may be, that the testatrix did not contemplate the event which has happened; but if she had, it does not follow she would have done what is now contended for, namely, substituted the word "have" for "leave"; for in that case a child dying an hour after its birth would have taken the whole.' *Bythesea v Bythesea* (1854) 23 LJ Ch 1004 at 1005, per Lord Cranworth LC

[A testator by his will bequeathed the residue of his personal estate upon trust to be divided equally amongst the children of his daughter Elizabeth when the youngest of such children should attain twenty-one, followed by a gift over in case of the death of his daughter without 'leaving' any child or children.] 'There being a gift of the residue under which all the children of Elizabeth have acquired vested interests, the gift over in case of the death of Elizabeth without leaving any child is contradictory, if the word "leaving" be read literally; and . . . the word "leaving" must be read as equivalent to "having".' *Kennedy v Sedgwick* (1857) 3 K & J 540 at 541, 542, per Page Wood V-C

[A testator devised certain property to his daughter for life, and afterwards to her children; and in case she died without 'leaving children', then to his son.] 'In this case, the gift is followed by the words, "In case she shall die under the age of twenty-one, or afterwards, without leaving any child or children of her body"; and then there is a gift over. . . . "Leaving" is a word that may be construed, in its primary sense, as leaving on the decease of the person to whom the word applies; but it has been construed as "having", rather than that a child shall be deprived of a vested interest which seems to have been made as a provision for it.' *White v Hill* (1867) LR 4 Eq 265 at 269, 270, per Page Wood V-C

'"Leaving issue male" prima facie means "leaving issue male living at his [the reversioner's] death".' *Re Ball, Slattery v Ball* (1888) 40 Ch D 11 at 13, CA, per Cotton LJ

'The first question raised by the will under consideration is one of construction. The critical words are found in the two phrases: "In the event of such child of mine leaving any issue him or her surviving" and "in the event of such child of mine not leaving any issue him or her surviving". I cannot think that upon the true construction of these words a posthumous child of a child of the testatrix is issue left by the parent him surviving. The expression "leaving any issue him or her surviving" is not in its ordinary and natural meaning appropriate to include a posthumous child, and there is nothing in my opinion in the context to justify extending the meaning.' *Elliot v Joicey (Lord)* [1935] AC 209 at 214, per Lord Tomlin

LEAVE WITHOUT MEANS OF SUPPORT

Australia [Section 63 of the Maintenance Act 1928 (Vic) (repealed; see now Maintenance Act 1965–1986, s 6(b)), provided, inter alia, that whenever in Victoria any husband 'left his wife without adequate means of support', and went to reside temporarily or permanently in another State, any justice of the State of Victoria might issue a summons on behalf of the wife.] 'We are of the opinion that, on the proper construction of s 63, the words "leaves his wife without adequate means of support" mean wrongly lets his wife be without adequate means of support and have no denotation or connotation of physical movement.' *Zacher v Zacher* [1954] VLR 204 at 207, per cur

LEGACY *See also* ABATEMENT

Legacies are ordinarily divided into two classes, specific legacies and general legacies, general legacies also being described as legacies of quantity or number.

A specific legacy must be of some thing or of some interest, legal or equitable, forming part of the testator's estate; it must be a part as distinguished from the whole of his personal property or from the whole of the general residue of his personal estate; it must be identified by a sufficient description, and separated in favour of the particular legatee from the general mass of the testator's personal estate. The forgiveness of a debt by will is a specific legacy of the debt.

A general legacy may or may not be part of the testator's property: it has no reference to the actual state of his property, and is a gift of something which, if the testator leaves sufficient assets, must be raised by his executors out of his general personal estate. Whether or not a particular thing forms part of the testator's personal estate is a pure question of fact; so long as it is the testator's at his death it is capable of being specifically bequeathed. Whether or not it has been separated from the general personal estate depends upon the true construction of the will. In the case of real estate a devise, whether of a specific property or by way of residue, is specific.

There is a third kind of legacy, called a demonstrative legacy, which consists of a pecuniary legacy payable out of a particular fund. Such a legacy has the following advantages: (1) it is not adeemed by the total or partial failure at the testator's death of the fund out of which it was directed to be paid, but becomes payable out of the general personal estate to the extent of such failure, pari passu with ordinary general legacies; and (2) it does not abate with the general legacies until after the particular fund is exhausted. (17 Halsbury's Laws (4th edn) paras 1228–1230)

'Though the word (legacy) be usually taken for the bequest of a personal thing and on the contrary a gift of land by will be commonly (and more properly) called a devise, yet the word (legacy) may, in an extensive sense, be understood to comprehend any kind of estate, real as well as personal, left by the testator's will to any person.' *Beckley v Newland* (1723) 2 P Wms 182 at 185, 186, per Lord Macclesfield LC

'It has been said, that the word legacy will include a devise of land as well as a bequest of personal estate; . . . and it is indeed true, that the word legacy will include a devise of real estate, as well as a bequest of personal.' *Griffyn v Griffyn* (1740) Barn Ch 391 at 395, per Hardwicke LC

'The word legacy is, in general, applicable to every testamentary disposition, and used in contradistinction to a general devise to the *haeres factus*, who, in the rule of construction, stands foremost, and the legatees come in by way of exception, out of the general devise to him. . . . The word legacy, by our law, as well as the Roman law, is applicable to every particular testamentary donation, though the word devise is more commonly used, among lawyers, to denote a gift of land.' *Hope d Brown v Taylor* (1757) 2 Keny 9 at 13, per Lord Mansfield CJ

'The word "legacy" in its ordinary signification is applied to money, but it may signify a devise of land, and may here comprehend the devise to the university, which the testator calls a gift.' *Brady v Cubitt* (1778) 1 Doug KB 31 at 40, per Lord Mansfield CJ

'Even if there were no decision to warrant us in saying that the word "legacy" may be applied to a real estate, if the context required it, I should have had no difficulty in making such a determination for the first time. But that construction has already been put on the word "legacy". . . . We fully subscribe to the doctrine . . . laid down.' *Hardacre v Nash* (1794) 5 Term Rep 716 at 721, per Lord Kenyon CJ

'I should think . . . it is perfectly clear that the term "legacy", meaning any legacy payable out of the personal estate of the party deceased, would not only extend to a legacy properly payable out of the personal estate, but a legacy payable out of any property which the party had the power of disposing of by will.' *Re Cholmondeley* (1832) 1 Cr & M 149 at 170, per cur.

'The word "legacies" is a proper word to designate legacies given in the shape of annuities as well as those given in the shape of a bequest of a sum payable at once.' *Heath v Weston* (1853) 3 De G M & G 601 at 606, per Knight Bruce LJ

'The words "legacy" and "residuary legatee" prima facie have reference to personal estate only. There is indeed no magic in the words themselves, and if they are so used by a testator they may no doubt be construed as referring to real estate. Any man may use his own nomenclature if he only expresses what he means. I have not, however, been able to discover any case which satisfies my mind that independently of context you can understand "legacy" or "legatee" or "residuary legatee" as applying to anything but personal estate. I think that in that case in the House of Lords of *Kellet v Kellett* [(1815) 3 Dow 248] we must understand Lord Eldon and Lord Redesdale to have been of opinion that, if there is nothing to qualify them, the words "legatee" or "residuary legatee" have reference to personal property only. I need not refer to the words used by Lord Eldon (they were very characteristic of his mode of expression) from which I think we may come to the conclusion that that was his opinion, and that the only question he had there was whether there were or were not circumstances that would enable him to put a construction, or rather to say that the testator had put a construction, on those words different from that which they ordinarily import; and he thought there were not. The general rule therefore I take to be, that if you constitute a person residuary legatee or if you speak of him in reference to his character of legatee, you refer only to a gift of personalty or are speaking of him only with reference to some gift of personal property.' *Windus v Windus* (1856) 6 De G M & G 549 at 557, 558, per Lord Cranworth LC

'What is the extent of the meaning of the word "legacies"? . . . According to the plain import of the word it includes specific as well as pecuniary legacies. . . . It is true that "residue" is not a "legacy" in the ordinary sense of the term. . . . "Residue" is what remains after payment of legacies.' *Ward v Grey* (1859) 26 Beav 485 at 489, 491, 492, per Romilly MR

'The testator gives certain legacies of stock, and then says, that if he has no such stock at his decease, then he gives the value in money. . . . As the testator had stock to answer the bequest at his decease, those legacies were specific; but if he had had no such stock at his decease, then the bequest of the money would have been, not specific, but general legacies. These legacies of stock are specific legacies, in contradistinction to general and to demonstrative legacies. They are not money legacies payable out of a particular property (which would be demonstrative legacies); but they are legacies of specific portions of a particular property, which he contemplated his being in possession of at his death (which are specific legacies). . . . The points of difference between specific and demonstrative legacies are these:—A specific legacy is not liable to abatement for the payment of debts, but a demonstrative legacy is liable to abate when it becomes a general legacy by reason of the failure of the fund out of which it is payable. A specific legacy is liable to ademption, but a demonstrative legacy is not. A specific legacy, if of stock, carries with it the dividends which accrue from the death of the testator; while a demonstrative legacy does not carry interest from the testator's death.' *Mullins v Smith* (1860) 1 Dr & Sm 204 at 209–211, per Kindersley V-C

'If you find simply the word "legacy" used, and a direction to apportion the property amongst the legatees, unless there be something apparent on the face of the will which shews that the testator has not used the word in its ordinary legal signification, it will include annuitants.' *Gaskin v Rogers* (1866) LR 2 Eq 284 at 291, per Page Wood V-C

'No doubt, the word "legacies" may include annuities, but whether it does or does not depends on the context, and in its ordinary use probably it would apply rather to gifts of a sum or specific chattel.' *Weldon v Bradshaw* (1873) 7 IR Eq 168 at 173, per Chatterton V-C

'There is no doubt that the word "legacy" is sufficient to include an annuity, but it is a word *ancipitis usus*, which sometimes may include an annuity, and sometimes may not; whether it does or not depends upon the context.' *Cunningham v Foot* (1878) 3 App Cas 974 at 989, per Lord Cairns LC

'A thing which is claimed under a will, being the gift of the testator, is a legacy. . . . I am unable to see the difference between a legacy of a lump sum to a man upon condition that he shall perform services to the testator's estate, and a legacy of an annuity to a man upon the same condition. Each seems to me to be distinctly and plainly a legacy.' *Re Thorley, Thorley v Massam* [1891] 2 Ch 613 at 628, 629, CA, per Kay LJ

'Here a solicitor is allowed by a testator, under a clause which is very common, to charge profit costs notwithstanding that he is appointed executor and trustee. . . . It is the same thing as a gift of, say, £100: there is no difference whatever between a gift of profit charges and a gift of £100. In my opinion it is a legacy. . . . This is certainly not a "debt": it is bounty.' *Re White, Pennell v Franklin* [1898] 1 Ch 297 at 299, 300, per Kekewich J; affirmed [1898] 2 Ch 217, CA

'Of course, "legacy" is a word of art, and apart from any context its strict meaning confines its application to gifts to personalty, but like any other word it has a flexible meaning and yields to a sufficient context so as to include a gift of realty.' *Re Previté, Sturges v Previté* [1931] 1 Ch 447 at 453, per Luxmoore J

'It is quite a mistake, in my judgment, to say that the interest payable to a legatee is in any sense a legacy given by the testator. It is a sum given in the course of administration to the legatee because justice requires that owing to the failure to pay his legacy in due time he should be put in the position in which he would have been had it been so paid.' *Re Wyles, Foster v Wyles* [1938] Ch 313 at 316, per Farwell J

Demonstrative legacy

'A demonstrative legacy . . . is simply a general legacy, with the quality attached to it that it is directed to be paid out of a specific fund, and, if there is a shortage of assets, and that fund remains, is paid out of that fund without abating. On the other hand, if the fund does disappear, then it has this advantage over a specific legacy, that it is still payable, in virtue of its quality of a general legacy, out of the testators' residue along with other general legacies.' *Walford v Walford* [1912] AC 658 at 663, HL, per Lord Haldane LC

See, generally, 17 Halsbury's Laws (4th edn) para 1230.

Pecuniary legacy

'Pecuniary legacy' includes an annuity, a general legacy, a demonstrative legacy so far as it is not discharged out of the designated property, and any other general direction by a testator for the payment of money, including all death duties free from which any devise, bequest, or payment is made to take effect. (Administration of Estates Act 1925, s 55(1))

Specific legacy

'This question, as has been truly said, entirely depends on the intention of the testator, as expressed or to be collected from the words of the will. Here the words, "If I shall not have so much stock", have no reference certainly to the stock which he may have actually had at that time, but, on the contrary, refer to some future time; and the most appropriate period which we can assign, is the time of the testator's death. Now, as I understand, he had at his death £10,000 in one or other, or both stocks: and it appears to me to have been the manifest intention of the testator, in the event of his leaving sufficient in the stocks specified, that £10,000, part of such stock, should be held on his death by the trustees, for the use of the legatees. What is that but a gift of so much stock specifically? I consider it as much a specific legacy, as if he had said—"If I shall have a particular horse, I desire that it may be given to the legatee." The reference to the corpus is clear and direct; and if that corpus shall be found amongst his assets, he gives a certain portion of it, referring clearly to his possession of the thing at the time of his death. It is not necessary, in considering this question, to inquire what would have been the effect of this bequest, if the testator had not had £10,000 in the stocks specified, at the time of his death. Having given it thereout, and it being found in his possession, it is clearly a specific legacy, and must go immediately to the legatees upon the testator's death.' *Fontaine v Tyler* (1821) 9 Price 94 at 103, 104, per Richards CB

'If I give £10,000 consols standing in my name, that is specific; and if I sell the stock in my lifetime, the legacy fails. If I give £10,000 stock, that is general, because the executors must buy stock to meet it, in case I do not leave stock for the purpose.' *Oliver v Oliver* (1871) LR 11 Eq 506 at 510, 511, per Malins V-C

'The first point to consider is, what a specific bequest means. . . . In the first place it is a part of the testator's property. A general bequest may or may not be a part of the testator's property. A man who gives £100 money or £100 stock may not have either—the money or the stock, in which case the testator's executors must raise the money or buy the stock. . . . In the case of a general legacy it has no reference to the actual state of the testator's property, it being only supposed that the testator has sufficient property which on being realised will procure for the legatee that which is given to him, while in the case of a specific bequest it must be of a part of the testator's property itself. That is the first thing. In the next place, it must be a part emphatically, as distinguished from the whole. It must be what has been sometimes called a severed or distinguished part. It must not be the whole, in the meaning of being the totality of the testator's property, or the totality of the general residue of his property after having given legacies out of it. But if it satisfy both conditions, that it is a part of the testator's property itself, and is a part as distinguished . . . from the whole, or from the whole of the residue, then it appears to me to satisfy everything that is required to treat it as a specific legacy.' *Bothamley v Sherson* (1875) LR 20 Eq 304 at 308, 309, per Jessel MR

'If the bequest is of a particular chattel, such as a horse or a ship, it is manifest that the testator intended the thing itself to pass unconditionally, and in status quo, to the legatee; which could not be if it were subject to the payment of funeral and testamentary expenses, debts, and pecuniary legacies. As against creditors, the testator cannot wholly release it from liability for his debts; but as against all persons taking benefits under his will he may. The same principle applies to everything which a testator, identifying it by a sufficient description, and manifesting an intention that it should be enjoyed or taken in the state and condition indicated by that description, separates in favour of a particular legatee, from the general mass of his personal estate, the fund out of which pecuniary legacies are in the ordinary course payable.' *Robertson v Broadbent* (1883) 8 App Cas 812 at 815, per Lord Selborne LC

See, generally, 17 Halsbury's Laws (4th edn) paras 1228–1230.

LEGAL *See also* LAWFUL

[A policy of insurance provided that it should be void in certain events, except it should have been 'legally assigned'.] 'The only question is, whether the policy has been "legally assigned"? That depends upon the meaning of the word "legal". . . . The word "legal" cannot have been used in a technical sense as opposed to the word "equitable". Any one not a lawyer would be shocked at the word "legal" being confined to the sense as distinguished from the word "equitable". With reference to the ordinary dealings of mankind, the word "legal" means "lawful", that is, something effectual and proper and which the courts of judicature of the country will recognise and enforce. . . . I am satisfied that those who prepared this policy used the word "legal" in its popular sense. In any other view the word would have been merely inoperative, because a policy cannot be assigned at law. The words "legally assigned" must therefore mean "validity and effectually assigned".' *Dufaur v Professional Life Assurance Co* (1858) 25 Beav 599 at 603, 604, per Romilly MR

As distinguished from equitable

'Much difficulty has sometimes arisen in determining the precise distinction between legal and equitable assets. The general proposition is clear enough, that when assets may be made available in a court of law, they are legal assets; and when they can only be made available through a court of equity, they are equitable assets. This proposition does not, however, refer to the question whether the assets can be recovered by the executor in a court of law or in a court of equity. The distinction refers to the remedies of the creditor, and not to the nature of the property.' *Cook v Gregson* (1856) 3 Drew 547 at 549, 556, per Kindersley V-C

'The question whether assets are legal or equitable depends on this, whether, if the case were before a court of law that Court would treat the property as assets; if it would, then it is legal assets in this Court. And the principle on which a court of law proceeds is this,—to inquire whether the property came to the hands of the executor, *virtute officii*. If it did, the court of law regards it as assets of the testator applicable to the payment of his debts, and then this Court treats it as legal assets.' *Shee v French, French v French* (1857) 3 Drew 716 at 717, per Kindersley V-C

LEGAL CUSTODY *See* CUSTODY

LEGAL ESTATE *See* ESTATE

LEGAL MEMORY *See* PRESCRIPTION; TIME IMMEMORIAL

LEGAL OFFICER

Australia 'The argument most strongly relied upon by the appellant is that the use by an unqualified person of the words "legal officer" . . . would be in breach of s 40 [of the Legal Practitioners Act 1898–1986 (NSW)] because it is contended that these words imply that the person using them is, in the words of the section, "qualified or recognised by law as qualified to act as a Solicitor". We cannot agree with this submission, for it seems to us that these words can be merely a statement of an official position held in a corporation or association and that the phrase could merely imply that the person using it is the officer of the corporation or the association responsible for such of its business as is related to legal affairs.' *Law Society of New South Wales v Goodwin* [1972] 2 NSWLR 462 at 464, CCA, per cur.

LEGAL PERSONAL REPRESENTATIVES *See* PERSONAL REPRESENTATIVES

LEGAL TENDER

(1) Gold coins shall be legal tender for payment of any amount, but shall not be legal tender if their weight has become less than that specified in Schedule 1 to this Act [e.g. in the case of a sovereign, 7.93787 grams], or in the proclamation under which they are made, as the least current weight.

(1A) Subject to any provision made by proclamation under section 3 of this Act, coins of cupro-nickel, silver or bronze shall be legal tender as follows—

(a) coins of cupro-nickel or silver of denominations of more than 10 pence, for payment of any amount not exceeding £10;
(b) coins of cupro-nickel or silver of denominations of not more than 10 pence, for payment of any amount not exceeding £5;
(c) coins of bronze, for payment of any amount not exceeding 20 pence;

Other coins, if made current by a proclamation made under s 3 of this Act, shall be legal tender in accordance with the provision made by that proclamation or by any later proclamation made under that section. (Coinage Act 1971, s 2(1), as substituted by Currency Act 1983, s 1(1))

[Section 3 of the Act enables changes in the coinage to be made by Royal proclamation.

By s 2(2) silver coins of the Queen's Maundy money issued before 15 February 1971 are to be treated as being denominated in the same number of the present pence as the number of pence in which they were denominated.]

LEGATEE *See also* RESIDUARY LEGATEE

In this Act, unless the context otherwise requires, 'legatee' includes any person taking under a testamentary disposition or on an intestacy or partial intestacy, whether he takes beneficially or as trustee, and a person taking under a *donatio mortis causa* shall be treated (except for the purposes of s 49 below (death)) as a legatee and his acquisition as made at the time of the donor's death.

For the purposes of the definition of 'legatee' above, and of any reference in this Act to a person acquiring an asset 'as legatee', property taken under a testamentary disposition or on an intestacy or partial intestacy includes any asset appropriated by the personal representatives in or towards satisfaction of a pecuniary legacy or any other interest or share in the property devolving under the disposition or intestacy. (Capital Gains Tax Act 1979, s 47(2), (3))

LEGITIMATE

[A testator by his will devised his whole estate to his nephew and his 'legitimate' heirs.] 'The proper construction of legitimate heirs is heirs of his body lawfully begotten.' *Barret v Beckford* (1750) 1 Ves Sen 519 at 521, per Lord Hardwicke LC

'In contrast to adoption the meaning of legitimation is plain and unambiguous. When a person is said to have been "legitimated" there is little, if any, room for doubt as to what is intended: it means that he has been placed in the position of one born in lawful wedlock. Adoption, on the other hand, is the creation of a purely artificial relationship with characteristics which are quite undefined.' *Re Wilson, decd, Grace v Lucas* [1954] 1 All ER 997 at 1000, per Vaisey J; see also [1954] Ch 733

'Legitimacy is a status: it is the condition of belonging to a class in society the members of which are regarded as having been begotten in lawful matrimony by the men whom the law regards as their fathers. Motherhood, although also a legal relationship, is based on a fact, being proved demonstrably by parturition. Fatherhood, by contrast, is a presumption. A woman can have sexual intercourse with a number of men any of whom may be the father of her child; though it is true that modern serology can sometimes enable the presumption to be rebutted as regards some of these men. The status of legitimacy gives the child certain rights both against the man whom the law regards as his father and generally in society.' *Ampthill Peerage Case* [1976] 2 All ER 411 at 424, HL (Committee for Privileges), per Lord Simon of Glaisdale

Australia 'I cannot attribute any other meaning in the language of a lawyer to the word "legitimate" than a meaning which expresses the concept of entitlement or recognition by law.' *Salemi v Minister for Immigration and Ethnic Affairs (No 2)* (1977) 14 ALR 1 at 7, per Barwick CJ

New Zealand [The concept of illegitimacy has been abolished in New Zealand by the Status of Children Act 1969 (NZ). Under s 3(1) of this Act, for all purposes of the law of New Zealand the relationship between every person and his father and mother shall be determined irrespective of whether the father and mother are or have been married to each other, and all other relationships are to be determined accordingly.]

LEND

[A treaty between Britain and Sweden prohibited the subjects of either country from selling or 'lending' their ships for the use and advantage of the enemies of the other.] 'To let a ship on freight to go to the ports of the enemy, cannot be termed lending, but in a very loose sense: and I apprehend the true meaning to have been, that they should not give up the use and management of their ships directly to the enemy, or put them under his absolute power and direction.' *The Ringende Jacob* (1798) 1 Ch Rob 89 at 90, per Sir William Scott

LESSEE

'Lessee' means the person to whom is granted, under a restricted contract, the right to occupy the dwelling in question as a residence and any person directly or indirectly deriving title from the grantee. (Rent Act 1977, s 85(1))

LESSOR

'Lessor' means the person who, under a restricted contract, grants to another the right to occupy the dwelling in question as a residence and any person directly or indirectly deriving title from the grantor. (Rent Act 1977, s 85(1))

LET

New Zealand 'One of the conditions, and a fundamental condition, of a residence being a "dwelling-house" within the meaning of the section [s 2 of the Fair Rents Act 1936 (NZ)

(repealed)] is that it should be *let* as a separate dwelling-house. That means that there should be an agreement for letting. That provision, I think, meets the argument . . . that there is no provision in the Act requiring that, in order to constitute a tenancy, rental should be paid. By the use of the word "let" that is implied, because letting creates something in the nature of a tenancy, and, as the cases . . . show, that confers on the tenant what, in legal terms, is called "an estate in the land"—i.e. a distinct and definite interest, ownership or occupation, or possession of the land which is conferred on the tenant as a legal right, existing irrespective of other considerations.' *Betts v Brookfield* [1947] NZLR 170 at 192, per Fair J; also reported [1946] GLR 438

LETHAL WEAPON *See* FIREARM

LETTER OF CREDIT

A letter of credit is in principle an undertaking by a banker to meet drafts drawn under the credit by the beneficiary of the credit in accordance with the conditions laid down therein. A letter of credit may be addressed (1), as in a traveller's letter of credit, to all the issuing banker's correspondents throughout the world, or (2) where the credit is designed to facilitate trade (generally, but not always, foreign trade), to another specified banker (called the intermediary banker) or to the beneficiary. (3 Halsbury's Laws (4th edn) para 131)

United States 'Credit' or 'letter of credit' means an engagement by a bank or other person made at the request of a customer and of a kind within the scope of this Article [Letters of Credit] (Section 5–102) that the issuer will honor drafts or other demands for payment upon compliance with the conditions specified in the credit. A credit may be either revocable or irrevocable. The engagement may be either an agreement to honor or a statement that the bank or other person is authorised to honor. (Uniform Commercial Code 1978, 5–103(1)(a))

Sale of goods

United States Unless otherwise agreed the term 'letter of credit' or 'banker's credit' in a contract for sale means an irrevocable credit issued by a financing agency of good repute and, where the shipment is overseas, of good international repute. The term 'confirmed credit' means that the credit must also carry the direct obligation of such an agency which does business in the seller's financial market. (Uniform Commercial Code 1978, s 2–325(3))

LETTERS OF MART

Letters of mart (or marque) were commissions issued by governments in time of war entitling privately-owned vessels to cruise in search for, and to attack, the shipping of a hostile power without being guilty of piracy. Such cruising amounted to a deviation. The Declaration of Paris respecting Maritime Law of 1856 prohibited privateering and letters of mart have long since ceased to be issued. (25 Halsbury's Laws (4th edn) para 164)

LETTERS PATENT

In Theatres Acts

[Section 2 of the Theatres Act 1843 (repealed; see now the Theatres Act 1968, s 17(1)) made it unlawful for a person to have or keep a house or other place of public resort for the public performance of stage plays without authority by virtue of 'letters patent' from the Crown.] 'I . . . hold that those words mean letters patent directed to the holding of a particular place as a theatre and do not include charters which, like the present [the Royal Albert Hall charters], although they may be called and properly called "letters patent", include a great many other objects besides, and are more to be regarded as the permission of Her Majesty to use the theatre for this purpose [of holding theatrical performances] subject to the other public authorities who may have jurisdiction in the matter, and whose consent, authority, or licence may be required.' *Royal Albert Hall v London County Council* (1911) 104 LT 894 at 898, DC, per Ridley J

LETTING BEDROOM

In this Part of this Act [Part II: financial assistance for hotel development] . . . 'Letting bedroom' means a private bedroom which—

(a) if booked in advance, does not have to be so booked for more than seven consecutive nights; and
(b) if not so booked, can be taken, if desired, for a single night;

and which is not normally in the same occupation for more than twenty-one consecutive nights. (Development of Tourism Act 1969, s 16(1))

LEVEL CROSSING

'The railway was, at the place where it crossed each of the highways in question, made at a considerably higher level than that of the highway as it originally existed at that place; and, inasmuch as the railway would otherwise have formed an impassable barrier to the passage of traffic along the highway, inclines had to be made on each side of the line extending back for some distance, in order that the roadway might be carried up to the level of the railway. Therefore, although there was in the railway sense of the term a "level crossing", the roadway had to be raised in order to cross the railway on the level.' *Hertfordshire County Council v Great Eastern Rly Co* [1909] 2 KB 403 at 407, 408, CA, per Lord Alverstone CJ

LEVY

Canada 'The word "levying", the equivalent of "imposing" signifies the execution of legislative power which charges on person or property the obligation of or liability for a tax.' *City of Vancouver v BC Telephone Co* [1951] SCR 3 at 6, SCC, per Rand J

Levy distress

[The common law remedy of distress damage feasant as applicable to animals was replaced by the Animals Act 1971, s 7]

'Distress is the substantive expressing the process indicated by the verb "distrain". "Distrain" meant originally "to constrain a person by the seizure and detention of his property." That was all it meant as to any sort of distraining until 1689, in which year a landlord was given the right to sell the property of his tenant which he had seized in order thereby to exact the rent due from him. In that sort of distraining, therefore, the landlord, exercising the right, did more than seize and detain. He paid himself by selling the property seized. Hence came naturally the phrase, on such action by the landlord, "levy distress" and the word "levy", means "to raise a sum by legal execution or process".' *Watkinson v Hollington* [1944] 1 KB 16 at 21, 22, CA, per Mackinnon LJ

Levy rate

'To "levy" a rate would imply the taking legal proceedings, if necessary, to enforce payment of the rate by recusant ratepayers.' *R v Southampton Port & Harbour Comrs* (1861) 30 LJQB 244 at 251, per Cockburn CJ

'The word "levy" is to be found in one of the earliest rating Acts, the Poor Relief Act 1601, and is there used in a very narrow sense. But the word is frequently used in the multifarious rating Acts, and often bears a wide meaning. In my judgment, the phrase "the making and levying of rates" is here [in the Rating and Valuation (Miscellaneous Provisions) Act 1955, s 8(2) (repealed)] used to describe the whole statutory process of raising money by means of a rate from start to finish.' *Westminster City Council v University of London King's College* [1958] 3 All ER 25 at 29, per Roxburgh J

Levy war

The treason of levying war against the Sovereign in her realm may be of two kinds: (1) express and direct, as where war is raised against the Sovereign or her forces with a view to injure her person or to imprison her or to force her to remove any of her ministers or counsellors; or (2) constructive, as where there is a rising for some general public purpose. A rising for a limited or local purpose or directed against private persons, does not amount to a levying of war.

A bare conspiracy or consultation with a view to a levying of war is not a levying of war. To constitute a levying of war it is not, however, necessary that there should be an engagement; it is sufficient if there is arming, enlisting and marching, or if large numbers assemble with warlike intent, or if a small number use sufficiently violent means in carrying out their treasonable intent.

In an actual insurrection it is a levying of war to join with rebels in any act of rebellion. A person who takes part in a constructive levying of war, even though he had not previously any formal intention of doing so, is guilty of treason. Service in war under the Sovereign de facto is not an act of treason against the Sovereign de jure. (11 Halsbury's Laws (4th edn) para 814)

[Section 3 of the Treason Felony Act 1848 makes it a felony to 'levy war' against the King within the United Kingdom in order (inter alia) by force or constraint to compel him to change his measures or counsels, or to overawe

Parliament.] 'The term "levying war" is, in the profession at least, well understood and settled by a long train of decisions. . . . There is no necessity that an army should be formed; the legality or illegality of an assembly under this Act depends upon its object. If a number of people assemble to burn a particular mill, it is not levying war; but if the object of such assembly was to raise an insurrection, to gain by force from the Government what could not otherwise be obtained, it is war. In a word, to excite a hostile insurrection against the Government is levying war.' *R v Cuffey* (1848) 12 JP 807 at 809, per Platt B

LIABILITY—LIABLE *See also* CONTINGENT LIABILITY

[Sections 32, 33 of the Settled Land Act 1882 (repealed; see now Settled Land Act 1925, ss 76, 77), contained provisions as to the application of money in court under the Lands Clauses and other Acts, and in the hands of trustees under settlements, and 'liable' to be laid out in the purchase of land.] 'I agree . . . that the expression "is liable to be laid out in the purchase of land" does not mean "has to be laid out in the purchase of land", but means money subject to some disposition under which it may be laid out in the purchase of land.' *Re Soltau's Trust* [1898] 2 Ch 629 at 632, per North J

'The 1st section [of the Maritime Conventions Act 1911] is in these terms: "Where, by the fault of two or more vessels, damage or loss is caused to one or more of those vessels, to their cargoes or freight, or to any property on board, the liability to make good the damage or loss shall be in proportion to the degree in which each vessel was in fault." . . . What is it that is to be in proportion to the degree of fault? It is described as the "liability to make good the damage or loss". This cannot, in my opinion, mean simply the liability in a court of law to be ordered to make it good, for that which is to be made good includes the damage or loss which has to be borne by the injured vessel herself, and she cannot properly be said to make good her own damage or loss. It seems to me that the expression must be read as equivalent to "the burden of the damage or loss", or some such expression.' *The Cairnbahn* [1914] P 25 at 36, 37, CA, per Warrington J

See, generally, 43 Halsbury's Laws (4th edn) paras 964 et seq.

'At the outset it is necessary to construe the word "liable" as used in s 2, sub-s 3 [of the Chancel Repairs Act 1932]. It is I think used in that sub-section in a sense different from that in which it is used in s 2, sub-s 1. In s 2, sub-s 1, the words "any person, who appears to them to be liable to repair the chancel" connote a liability that imports a duty resting on that person for which he is answerable in law. In the latter sub-section it intends a peril of being admonished, to which he is exposed and subject, or from which he is likely to suffer.' *Wickhambrook Parochial Church Council v Croxford* [1935] 2 KB 417 at 428–430, CA, per Lord Hanworth MR

See, generally, 14 Halsbury's Laws (4th edn) para 1106.

'In my opinion, the ordinary meaning of the word "liable" in a legal context is to denote the fact that a person is responsible at law.' *Littlewood v George Wimpey & Co Ltd* [1953] 2 All ER 915 at 921, CA, per Denning LJ (also reported in [1953] 2 QB 501 at 515)

'It is said that, under the Companies Act 1948, s 302 [repealed; see now Companies Act 1985, s 596] the "liabilities" which the liquidator in a voluntary winding-up is bound to discharge include an obligation to pay tax due to a foreign state. All turns on the meaning of the word "liabilities" in this section. On the one hand, it is said by the respondent, that it means only those obligations which are enforceable in an English court, and on the other hand, that its meaning is extended—I do not know how far—but at least so far as to cover liabilities for foreign tax in respect of which the company might have been sued in the courts of the country imposing it. My Lords, I have no hesitation in adopting the former of these meanings. I conceive that it is the duty of the liquidator to discharge out of the assets in his hands those claims which are legally enforceable, and to hand over any surplus to the contributories. I find no words which vest in him a discretion to meet claims which are not legally enforceable.' *Government of India, Ministry of Finance (Revenue Division) v Taylor* [1955] 1 All ER 292 at 298, HL, per Viscount Simonds; see also [1955] AC 491

'No doubt the words "liability" and "contingent liability" are more often used in connexion with obligations arising from contract than with statutory obligations. But I cannot doubt that if a statute says that a person who has done something must pay tax, that tax is a "liability" of that person.' *Winter v Inland*

Revenue Comrs [1961] 3 All ER 855 at 858, HL, per Lord Reid

'A great many unlikely results are reasonably foreseeable. . . . Liable is a very vague word, but I think that one would usually say that when a person foresees a very improbable result he foresees that it is liable to happen.' *The Heron II, Koufos v Czarnikow, (C) Ltd* [1967] 3 All ER 686 at 694, HL, per Lord Reid

'The phrase "liable to" when used otherwise than in relation to legal obligations has an ordinary and well-understood meaning, namely "subject to the possibility of".' *Squibb United Kingdom Staff Assocn v Certification Officer* [1979] 2 All ER 452 at 459, CA, per Shaw LJ

Australia 'The ordinary natural grammatical meaning of a person being liable to some penalty or prohibition is that the event has occurred which will enable the penalty or prohibition to be enforced, but that it still lies within the discretion of some authorised person to decide whether or not to proceed with the enforcement—cf. *James v Young* (1884) 27 Ch Div 652; *Re Loftus Otway* [1895] 2 Ch 235. The word "liable" is sometimes used in the sense of exposure to liability, but this is not the ordinary natural grammatical meaning of the word. It would require a context to give the word this meaning.' *O'Keefe v Calwell* [1949] ALR 381 at 401, per Williams J

Australia [Section 25 of the Wrongs Act 1936–1986 (SA), provides, inter alia, that where damage is suffered by any person as the result of a tort any tortfeasor 'liable' in respect of such damage may recover contribution from a joint tortfeasor.] 'The dictionaries do not agree on the derivation of "liable" (or "lyable") from "*ligabilis*" (cf. the Oxford English Dictionary with the Shorter Oxford Dictionary), but we think that they agree that the primary meaning (in law) is "that can be bound". In this context, however, where the legislature is dealing with "proceedings against and contributions between tortfeasors", the meaning is rather narrower than that. A person "liable" is one "who can be compelled to pay by using the due process of law". In other words, as "vulnerable" means, "who can be wounded *if attacked*", so "liable" means "who can be bound *if sued*", or, to speak more accurately, "who can be compelled to pay by taking such steps as may be *or remain* necessary to obtain and enforce the judgment of a court of justice". In this sense it seems to us that "liable" comprehends the state of a wrong-doer from the time of the fault committed to the point at which his liability is established and quantified by the judgment, and, beyond that, to the point at which it is discharged whether by release or payment or otherwise, as by lapse of time. The context may show that some other meaning is intended, but this is, we think, the natural meaning.' *Hall v Bonnet* [1956] SASR 10 at 15, per Napier CJ and Abbott J

LIBEL *See also* BLASPHEMY; DEFAMATION; INNUENDO; SEDITION

A libel for which an action will lie is a defamatory statement made or conveyed by written or printed words or in some other permanent form, published of and concerning the plaintiff, to a person other than the plaintiff. (28 Halsbury's Laws (4th edn) para 11)

'Scandalous matter is not necessary to make a libel, it is enough if the defendant induces an ill opinion to be had of the plaintiff, or to make him contemptible and ridiculous.' *Cropp v Tilney* (1693) 3 Salk 225 at 226, per Holt CJ

'There is a distinction between libels and words: a libel is punishable both criminally, and by action, when speaking the words would not be punishable in either way; for speaking the words rogue and rascal of any one action will not lie; but if those words were written and published of any one, I doubt not an action would lie; if one man should say of another that he has the itch, without more, an action would not lie; but if he should write these words of another, and publish them maliciously, as in the present case, I have no doubt at all but the action well lies: that is the reason why saying a man has the leprosy or plague is actionable; it is because the having of either cuts a man off from society: so the writing and publishing maliciously that a man has the itch and stinks of brimstone cuts him off from society. I think the publishing any thing of a man that renders him ridiculous is a libel and actionable.' *Villers v Monsley* (1769) 2 Wils 403 at 404, per Gould J

'Any publication which exposes an individual to hatred and contempt or ridicule, being published without lawful excuse, is a libel.' *Wilson v Reed* (1860) 2 F & F 149 at 150, per Hill J

'In order to justify a libel the justification must justify in the sense attributed by the innuendo. It is not the mere words of a written statement being true, or the accuracy of fact in a model or scene represented which will render it justifiable. The circumstances of time or play may raise such inferences as will render either libellous, though the words may be true and the model exact. Lord Blackburn, in giving judgment in the *Capital and Counties Bank v Henty* [(1882) 7 App Cas 741 at 786] deals with this very question. After expressing his reluctance to express his opinion on cases not before him, he continues: "I think I may safely say that in a time of panic a statement published in a City article of one of our newspapers that such an one had withdrawn his account from such a bank might have a tendency to shake the credit of that bank, and would very probably be understood by such persons as came for information as conveying an imputation upon the credit of that bank." In the same case it was laid down that the test as to whether a writing is a libel or not is whether, under the circumstances in which the writing was published, reasonable men would be likely to understand it in a libellous sense.' *Monson v Tussauds Ltd, Monson v Tussaud (Louis)* [1894] 1 QB 671 at 685, 686, CA, per Lord Halsbury

'The essence of libel is the publication of written words to a person or persons by whom they would be reasonably understood to be defamatory of the plaintiff. But those words may give rise to two separate and distinct causes of action. . . . First, the cause of action based on a *popular* innuendo. If the plaintiff relies on the natural meaning of the words (pleading what is called a "popular" innuendo so as to show what, in his view, is the natural and ordinary meaning) he must, in his statement of claim, specify the person or persons to whom they were published, save in the case of a newspaper or periodical which is published to the world at large, when the persons are so numerous as to go without saying—or book, I would add. Secondly, the cause of action based on a *legal* innuendo. If the plaintiff relies on some special circumstances which convey (*to some particular person or persons knowing these circumstances*) a special defamatory meaning other than the natural and ordinary meaning of the words (pleading what is called a "legal" innuendo so as to show what is that special defamatory meaning), then he must in his statement of claim specify the particular person or persons to whom they were published and the special circumstances known to that person or persons, for the simple reason that these are the "material facts" on which he relies, and must rely, for this cause of action.' *Fullam v Newcastle Journal & Chronicle Ltd* [1977] 3 All ER 32 at 35, CA, per Lord Denning MR

LIBERTY

[Section 62 of the Law of Property Act 1925 provides that a conveyance of land includes and operates to convey, with the land, all 'liberties, privileges, easements, rights, and advantages' whatsoever appertaining or reputed to appertain to the land at the time of conveyance.] 'The material words of the section appear to be "liberties, privileges, easements, rights, and advantages". First, what do these words mean? A "liberty" must, I think, be something which results from a permission given to, or something enjoyed under sufferance by, a particular person or body of persons, as distinguished from something enjoyed by sufferance by all and sundry, while a "privilege" describes some advantage to an individual or group of individuals, a right enjoyed by a few as opposed to a right enjoyed by all. "Easement" and "right" are obviously words not appropriate to universal enjoyment nor is the word "advantage", for it necessarily connotes the enjoyment of something which is denied to others. It seems to me that something which by sufferance no one is prevented from doing or enjoying cannot properly be described by any of the words "liberty, privilege, easement, right, or advantage", for each connotes something which is the subject of individual or class enjoyment as opposed to general enjoyment.' *Le Strange v Pettefar* (1939) 161 LT 300 at 301, per Luxmoore LJ

Canada 'Proponents of a broad interpretation of the right to liberty, look primarily to the decisions of American courts, which have often directed attention to the meaning of the right to liberty as guaranteed by the Fifth and Fourteenth Amendments to the Constitution of the United States. In that country the courts have generally given the concept of liberty a broad and comprehensive interpretation. They have not limited it to matters of arrest, detention, restraint or physical interference. Specifically, American courts have for many years held that "liberty" includes the right to live and work and pursue such business as a person may choose, subject only to restrictions necessary to secure the protection of the public.' *Re Gershman Produce Co Ltd & Motor Transport Board* (1984) 14 DLR (4th) 722 at 730, Man QB, per Kroft J

Liberty to apply

'The petitioning wife obtained a decree nisi for the dissolution of her marriage on the ground of the adultery of the respondent husband. . . . In due course the petitioner presented a petition for permanent maintenance. . . . When the matter came before the President [in the court below] the question which arose was whether the words "liberty to apply" which had been inserted in the registrar's order should be deleted. . . . Those words meant that the summons could be restored for consideration afresh by the tribunal seised of the matter without the taking of fresh proceedings, and perhaps thereby saving time, expense, and trouble. But where a party has a right to apply to the court that right is not lost or diminished by the failure to add the words "liberty to apply", which only refer to procedure.' *Stephen v Stephen* [1931] P 197 at 203, CA, per Lord Hanworth MR

[The terms of settlement of an action were approved by a judge, who added the words 'liberty to apply' to a note of the terms signed by counsel.] 'When the learned judge added "Liberty to apply", that was that the court sanctioned what in fact occurred, namely that the action was not finally determined upon the day on which it came in the judge's paper, on December 11, 1939, but remained undetermined in order that, if necessary, at some moment it should be completely determined by the judgment being given which would then be found to be the right judgment to give having regard to the arrangement that the parties had entered into. . . . In the Chancery Division it is not uncommon to say to the learned judge when the action is coming on: "We have settled this action; will you please stay all proceedings and put an end to the action, but with this limitation, that it is the desire of all parties that if a question arises on the construction, or the working out of the enforcement, of the terms of settlement, it should be dealt with as though the action were for that purpose still alive?" The object thus to be attained is effected by an order staying proceedings on the terms of the settlement—and they are usually scheduled to the order—with liberty to apply to the judge. It is not liberty to apply to the judge to give judgment in the action, but liberty to apply to the judge to make such order as, having regard to the terms of the settlement, the parties consensually agree should be made in order to enforce their intentions.' *Page v Skelt* [1940] 1 KB 778 at 784, 785, CA, per Clauson LJ

'I think, with respect, that Langton J [in *Abbott v Abbott* (1931) 47 TLR 207 at 209], in dealing with these words "liberty to apply", used language which went beyond what was necessary for the decision of the case. He said: "The expression 'liberty to apply' means what it says, namely, that leave was reserved to both parties to make any application concerning any part of the order at any subsequent time." I think that is too wide a statement. Prima facie, the words "liberty to apply" refer to the working out of the actual terms of the order.' *Cristel v Cristel* [1951] 2 All ER 574 at 577, CA, per Somervell LJ; [1951] 2 KB 725

Liberty to shift

'The subject matter of this time policy is the houseboat *Dorothy*, however, though not wherever employed, for she is covered only "whilst anchored in a creek off Netley", with liberty to shift and with such other liberty as is involved in the "docking clause". . . . When the *Dorothy* sustained the loss sued for she was off Messrs Camper and Nicholson's yard on the River Itchen and was still in tow, that is, she was too far from Netley to be "off Netley" or "in a creek off Netley", and further, was not at anchor. Was she then exercising her liberty to shift? I think not. Whatever the area be within which she was laid up, it is within that area that she can shift, and not beyond it. Liberty to shift is not unlimited liberty to cruise or to anchor wherever the owner likes. The liberty must be confined to the limits of the lying up to which the liberty to shift is ancillary.' *Mountain v Whittle* [1921] 1 AC 615 at 627, 628, per Lord Sumner

LIBRARY

'The view which presents itself to my mind is this: that a library is a perfectly well-known thing, and is essentially different from a hall, which is generally a place that is used for some business purposes connected with the general objects of the society, company, or corporation which possesses it, whereas a library is a place devoted to books, reading, and study; and I cannot help thinking that if anybody were asked to describe the buildings constituting either the buildings of the Middle Temple, or of Lincoln's Inn, or of any college or university in the United Kingdom, he would say that they consisted, amongst other things, of lecture-rooms, a hall, and a library; and I do not think that any person would describe a building which contained a library without the specific use of the expression. I cannot think that it is less a library because it happens to be structurally such a building as, if it stood without the books in it and were used for a totally different purpose, would be naturally described as a hall.' *Styles v Middle Temple Treasurer* (1898) 68 LJQB 157 at 161, DC, per Wills J

[A barrister by his will bequeathed the contents of his room in the Temple including all the 'law library' therein.] 'The words used were "all the law library therein" and I cannot help thinking that the testator must have had in his mind what might be called the "peripatetic tendencies" of a law library in a set of chambers and meant that all the books which he had put in the room should be re-assembled there.' *Re Nielson, Cumming v Clyde* (1929) 73 Sol Jo 765 at 766, per Eve J

LICENCE—LICENSE *See also* EXCISE DUTIES

A licence is normally created where a person is granted the right to use premises without becoming entitled to exclusive possession of them, or the circumstances and conduct of the parties show that all that was intended was that the grantee should be granted a personal privilege with no interest in the land. If the agreement is merely for the use of the property in a certain way and on certain terms while the property remains in the owner's possession and control, the agreement will operate as a licence, even though the agreement may employ words appropriate to a lease.

A mere licence does not create any estate or interest in the property to which it relates; it only makes an act lawful which without it would be unlawful.

A right to enter on land and enjoy a profit à prendre or other incorporeal hereditament is a licence coupled with an interest, and is irrevocable. (27 Halsbury's Laws (4th edn) paras 8, 9, 12)

'The word licence has a well recognised signification in English law. According to our law a licence properly so called is merely a permission granted to a person to do some act which but for such permission it would be unlawful for him to do. Being in its nature a mere personal privilege and nothing more than a mere personal privilege—a privilege personal to the individual licensee—such a licence cannot be transferred by him to anyone else and it dies with the person to whom it was given. . . . There are, of course, different types of licence. A man may grant another a licence to use the grantor's property in some particular way. Or a statute may authorise the granting of a licence to carry on some trade or business which the statute does not allow to be carried on without such a licence. But whatever may be the type of licence, the presumption is that it is purely personal privilege, that it is not capable of being assigned or transferred by the licensee to anyone else, and that it comes to an end on the death of the licensee. No doubt one frequently hears the phrase "transfer of a licence" especially in connection with the law relating to the sale of intoxicating liquors. But it is well established that even in this connection the phrase, though convenient, is nevertheless quite inaccurate and misleading. What is referred to as a transfer of a publican's licence is not in strict law a transfer at all. A licence to sell intoxicating liquors is a personal privilege granted to a named individual. And what the assignee of licensed premises gets is a new licence and not the old licence transferred. . . . When one finds the word "licence" used in a statute the presumption is that it is intended to designate a purely personal privilege, a privilege not capable of being assigned or transferred by the licensee to anyone else and which comes to an end on the death of the licensee.' *Russel v Ministry of Commerce for Northern Ireland* [1945] NI 184 at 188, 193, per Black J

'A licence created by a contract is not an interest. It creates a contractual right to do certain things which otherwise would be a trespass. It seems to me that, in considering the nature of such a licence and the mutual rights and obligations which arise under it, the first thing to do is to construe the contract according to ordinary principles. There is the question whether or not the particular licence is revocable at all and, if so, whether by both parties or by only one. There is the question whether it is revocable immediately or only after the giving of some notice. Those are questions of construction of the contract. It seems to me quite inadmissible to say that the question whether a licence is revocable at all can be, so to speak, segregated and treated by itself, leaving only the other questions to be decided by reference to the true construction of the contract. As I understand the law, rightly or wrongly, the answers to all these questions must depend on the terms of the contract when properly construed in the light of any relevant and admissible circumstances.' *Millennium Productions Ltd v Winter Garden Theatre (London) Ltd* [1946] 1 All ER 678 at 680, CA, per Lord Greene MR

Australia 'A licence provides an excuse for an act which would otherwise be unlawful as, for example, an entry upon a person's land, or the infringement of a patent or copyright. It is an authority to do something which would otherwise be wrongful or illegal or inoperative.' *Federal Comr of Taxation v United Aircraft Corpn* (1943) 68 CLR 525 at 533, per Latham CJ

Australia 'Prima facie, a licence is a mere permission to a person to do something which would otherwise be wrongful, and is therefore not exclusive in character. If it is expressed to be exclusive, then, of course, it is exclusive. If it is not so expressed, it should not be held to be exclusive unless the subject-matter is such as to show that it was the intention of the parties that it should be exclusive.' *Reid v Moreland Timber Co Pty Ltd* [1947] ALR 1 at 2, per Latham CJ

LICENSED PREMISES

Unless the context of a particular provision of the Licensing Act 1964 otherwise requires, 'licensed premises' means premises for which a justices' licence or occasional licence is in force and also includes any theatre premises in respect of which a notice has been given by the proprietor of his intention to sell liquor, and has not been withdrawn. (26 Halsbury's Laws (4th edn) para 382)

[Section 12 of the Licensing Act 1872 imposes a penalty upon persons found drunk on 'licensed premises'. An information was laid against the appellant, an innkeeper, for being found drunk on 'licensed premises' in his own occupation.] ' "Licensed premises", for the purposes of the section must mean premises open to the public during licensed hours, or during the time when the premises are a quasi public place. It seems to me that the innkeeper, if drunk on his own premises while they are open, is as much amenable to the penalty as if he was found drunk on the highway. It is clear, however, that the section does not apply to a person, not being an innkeeper, found drunk in his own private house. If the innkeeper lived next door to the licensed premises, he might be drunk in his own house without being liable. Why should he be liable if he lives on the licensed premises and gets drunk at a time when they are not open, because during certain hours of the day they are open to the public? When they are closed they are as much his private house as a house in which he lives next door. It is contended that the Act applies to licensed premises at all times of the day. This would have the effect of making an innkeeper who gets drunk in his own bedroom liable. It cannot have been intended that the section should produce such an extraordinary result. The section must apply only to licensed premises, meaning premises used for the time being as licensed premises, and so open to the public.' *Lester v Torrens* (1877) 2 QBD 403 at 405, 406, DC, per Lush J

'In this case it is clear that the premises at the material time were a public place, a place to which the public had access, for the justices have found that the front door was open and that the hotel was open for the public to come in and purchase anything in the shape of food or drink other than intoxicating drink. It is clear that the respondent could have been apprehended for being found drunk in a public place [under the Licensing Act 1872, s 12 (see supra)], and she was liable to be fined for this offence. The justices were therefore wrong in holding that because the premises were not open for the sale of intoxicating liquor they ceased to be licensed premises and ceased to be a public place.' *Lewis v Dodd* [1919] 1 KB 1 at 5, DC, per Avory J

'I think the words "any licensed premises" mean licensed premises open to the public.' Ibid at 6, per Salter J

LICENSED VICTUALLER

'In ordinary and colloquial language a licensed victualler means a publican, one who keeps a place where people can go to drink and for no other purpose.' *Lorden v Brooke-Hitching* [1927] 2 KB 237 at 251, per Salter J

LICENSEE

[The distinction between the duty owed to invitees and that owed to licensees was abolished by the Occupiers Liability Act 1957, which imposed a 'common duty of care' to all visitors. The common law rules continue, however, to determine who is an occupier and to whom the duty of care is owed, and 'visitors' in the Act of 1957 include only those categories who would at common law be treated as invitees or licensees.]

'A bare or mere licensee, one who has no common interest with the owner of the premises but is there by the owner's permission, takes the premises as he finds them, with all their dangers and traps, a trap being a danger which a person who does not know the premises could not avoid by reasonable care and skill. The owner is under no liability as to existing traps unless he intentionally set them for the licensee, but must not create new traps without taking precautions to protect licensees against them.' *Sutcliffe v Clients Investment Co* [1924] 2 KB 746 at 756, 757, per Scrutton LJ

LIE *See* LOITER

LIE (Falsehood)

'An action cannot be supported for telling a bare naked lie; but that I define to be, saying a thing which is false, knowing or not knowing it to be so, and without any design to injure, cheat, or deceive, another person. Every deceit comprehends a lie; but a deceit is more than a lie on account of the view with which it is practised, its being coupled with some dealing, and the injury which it is calculated to occasion, and does occasion, to another person.' *Pasley v Freeman* (1789) 3 Term Rep 51 at 56, per Buller J

LIEN

In its primary or legal sense 'lien' means a right at common law in one man to retain that which is rightfully and continuously in his possession belonging to another until the present and accrued claims of the person in possession are satisfied. In this primary sense it is given by law and not by contract. A written agreement to give a lien is not a bill of sale, for a legal lien does not as a rule arise until possession of the property is obtained. However, in exceptional cases, possession is not essential to constitute a legal lien, as for instance in the cases of liens of seamen's wages and bottomry bonds.

In its secondary sense, 'lien' may be applied to a right subsisting in a person who has no possession of the property concerned but who nevertheless has a right against the owner analogous to a legal lien. Such a right may arise in equity, by statute or under a court order. Thus, a trustee has an equitable lien on the trust estate or fund for money properly expended on it and a solicitor, in addition to his legal lien on the client's documents in his possession, has a statutory right to ask the court to direct that property recovered is to stand security for his costs. A trustee's lien on the trust estate or fund for money properly expended on it seems to extend to the payment of costs of proceedings authorised by the court, but where a beneficiary or minority shareholder is entitled to a similar indemnity there can be no legal lien because there is no possession. It is not clear whether an equitable or judicial lien could be said to arise in such a case, or whether such a proposition could have any useful effect. A trustee's equitable and statutory rights to impound a beneficiary's interest, where the trustee has committed a breach of trust at the instigation of the beneficiary, do not depend on the trustee's actual possession of the trust fund. (28 Halsbury's Laws (4th edn) paras 502, 503)

'A lien is a right in one man to retain that which is in his possession belonging to another, till certain demands of him the person in possession are satisfied.' *Hammonds v Barclay* (1802) 2 East 227 at 235, per Grose J

'A "lien", in the strict sense of the word, can only exist where the person claiming the lien has the property which he claims to be subject to the lien in his possession. An artificer has a lien on property on which he has spent time, labour and trouble in making repairs or other work because he has that property in his possession and can refuse to give it up until he is paid. . . . A solicitor has a lien on papers of his clients which are in his possession; he can refuse to give up those papers so long as his costs are not paid. He is also commonly said to have a lien on a sum of money which comes into existence owing to his exertion, but in that case the term "lien" is really a misnomer. . . . It is the solicitor's right to go to the Court and ask the Court to charge property in his favour; until that is done he has no right in it.' *James Bibby Ltd v Woods and Howard* [1949] 2 KB 449 at 453, 454, per Lord Goddard CJ

Canada 'The definition of "lien", at law, and in equity, and in admiralty, is well and succinctly set out in Hall on Possessory Liens (1917) Ch 1, and at p 16 it is said: "The word is derived directly from the French *lien*, and further back from the Latin *ligamen*, which signifies 'a tie' or 'something binding'. As will be seen, the right in its fullest and widest application means a charge upon property—that is to say, something which is binding upon it.' And at p 17: "Perhaps the widest and most satisfactory definition is that adopted by Whitaker in his Treatise of the Law of Lien, published in 1812—namely, 'Any charge of a payment of debt or duty upon either real or personal property'. This is lien in its most extensive sense.' And at p 18: "A lien, therefore, is 'any charge of a payment of debt or duty upon either real or personal property', whilst a possessory lien is 'a right in one man to retain that which is in his possession belonging to another, till certain demands of him, the person in possession, are satisfied'.".' *Chassey v May* [1925] 2 WWR 199 at 201, 203, per Martin JA

Bankruptcy

United States '[L]ien' means charge against or interest in property to secure payment of a debt or performance of an obligation. . . . (Bankruptcy Act 1978, s 101(28))

Equitable lien

'Equitable lien' means an equitable right, conferred by law upon one person, to a charge upon the real or personal property of another, until certain specific claims have been satisfied. To the extent that it operates by law and not by contract, an equitable lien is not a 'security' within the Consumer Credit Act 1974. An equitable lien is founded on the principle of equity that he who has obtained possession of property under a contract for payment of its value will not be allowed to keep it without payment. Like an equitable charge, an equitable lien is liable to be defeated under the Limitation Act [1980].

An equitable lien differs from a common law lien in that a common law lien is founded on possession and, except as modified by statute, merely confers a right to detain the property until payment, whereas an equitable lien, which exists quite irrespective of possession, confers on the holder the right to a judicial sale. (28 Halsbury's Law (4th edn) para 551)

Innkeeper's lien

The proprietor of a hotel, as an innkeeper, may detain, and thus he has a lien upon, any property, other than that excluded by statute, brought by a guest into the hospitium of the inn in respect of the guest's unpaid bill. He is not, however, entitled to detain the guest himself or take clothes from his person.

At common law, the innkeeper's lien extended to all property a guest brought to the inn, including his horse and vehicle, and the harness and other equipment. The extent of the innkeeper's lien has been restricted by statute; it now extends only to those goods of a guest in respect of which the hotel proprietor is strictly liable in the event of their being lost or damaged. Without prejudice to any other right of his with respect to it, the proprietor of a hotel has not, as an innkeeper, any lien on any vehicle or any property left in the hotel, or any horse or other live animal or its harness or other equipment. (24 Halsbury's Laws (4th edn) paras 1245, 1246)

Lien creditor

United States A 'lien creditor' means a creditor who has acquired a lien on the property involved by attachment, levy or the like and includes an assignment for benefit of creditors from the time of assignment, and a trustee in bankruptcy from the date of the filing of the petition or a receiver in equity from the time of appointment. (Uniform Commercial Code 1978, s 9–301(3))

Maritime lien

A maritime lien is a claim or privilege upon a maritime res in respect of service done to it or injury caused by it. Such lien does not import or require possession of the res, for it is a claim or privilege on the res to be carried into effect by legal process. A maritime lien travels with the res into whosesoever possession it may come, even though res may have been purchased without notice of the lien or may have been seized by the sheriff under a writ of fieri facias issued at the instance of execution creditors. A maritime lien is inchoate from the moment the claim or privilege attaches, and, when called into effect by the legal process of a proceeding in rem, relates back to the period when it first attached. (43 Halsbury's Laws (4th edn) para 1131)

'A maritime lien does not include or require possession. The word is used in Maritime Law not in the strict legal sense in which we understand it in Courts of Common Law, in which case there could be no lien where there was no possession, actual or constructive; but to express, as if by analogy, the nature of claims which neither presuppose nor originate in possession. This was well understood in the Civil Law, by which there might be a pledge with possession, and a hypothecation without possession, and by which in either case the right travelled with the thing into whosesoever possesssion it came. Having its origin in this rule of the Civil Law, a maritime lien is well defined by Lord Tenterden, to mean a claim or privilege upon a thing to be carried into effect by legal process; and Mr Justice Story (1 Summer 78) explains that process to be a proceeding in rem, and adds, that wherever a lien or claim is given upon the thing, then the Admiralty forces it by a proceeding in rem, and indeed is the only Court competent to enforce it. A maritime lien is the foundation of the proceeding in rem, a process to make perfect a right inchoate from the moment the lien attaches; and whilst it must be admitted that where such a lien exists, a proceeding in rem may be had, it will be found to be equally true, that in all cases where a proceeding in rem is the proper course, there a maritime lien exists, which gives a privilege or claim upon the thing, to be carried into effect by legal process. This claim or privilege travels with the thing, into whosesoever possession it may come. It is inchoate from the moment the claim or privilege attaches and when carried into effect by legal process, by a proceeding in rem, relates back to the period when it first attached. This simple rule, which, in our opinion, must govern this case, and which is deduced from the Civil Law, cannot be better illustrated than by reference to the circumstances of *The Aline* [(1839) 1 Wm Rob 111], referred to in the argument, and decided in conformity with this rule, although apparently upon other grounds. In that case, there was a bottomry bond before and after the collision, and the Court held, that the claim for damage in a proceeding in rem, must be preferred to the first bondholder, but was not entitled against the second bondholder to the increased value of the vessel by reason of repairs effected at his cost. The interest of the first bondholder taking effect from the period when his lien attached, he was, so to speak, a part owner in interest at the date of the collision, and the ship in which he and others were interested was liable to its value at that date for the injury done, without reference to his claim. So by the collision the interest of the claimant attached, and dating from that event, the ship in which he was interested having been repaired, was put in bottomry by the master acting for all parties, and he would be bound by that transaction. This rule, which is simple and intelligible, is, in our opinion, applicable to all cases. It is not necessary to say that the lien is indelible, and may not be lost by negligence or delay where the rights of third parties may be compromised; but where reasonable diligence is used, and the proceedings are had in good faith, the lien may be enforced, into whosesoever possession the thing may come.' *Harmer v Bell, The Bold Buccleugh* (1852) 7 Moo PCC 267 at 284, 285, PC, per Sir John Jervis

Solicitor's lien

At common law a solicitor has two rights which are termed liens. The first is a right to retain property already in his possession until he is paid costs due to him in his professional capacity and the second is a right to ask the court to direct that personal property recovered under a judgment obtained by his exertions stand as security for his costs of such recovery. In addition, a solicitor has by statute a right to apply to the court for a charging order on property recovered or preserved through his instrumentality in respect of his taxed costs of the suit, matter or proceeding prosecuted or defended by him. (44 Halsbury's Laws (4th edn) para 226)

LIFE ANNUITY *See* ANNUITY

LIFE ASSURANCE *See* INSURANCE

LIFE ASSURANCE COMPANY

The expression 'life assurance company' means any corporation, company, or society carrying on the business of life assurance, not being a society registered under the Acts relating to friendly societies. (Life Assurance Companies (Payment into Court) Act 1896, s 2)

LIFE IMPRISONMENT

'Life imprisonment means imprisonment for life. No doubt many people come out while they are still alive, but, when they do come out, it is only on licence, and the sentence of life imprisonment remains on them until they die.' *R v Foy* [1962] 2 All ER 246 at 247, per cur.

LIFE INTEREST

An estate for life, when it could exist as a legal estate, was an estate of mere freehold as distinguished from an estate of inheritance. It can now exist only as an equitable interest, but the legal estate in fee simple is usually in the tenant for life in possession in addition to his equitable life interest. The estate may be for the life of the tenant or for the life or lives of other persons. These estates are known as an estate or interest for life and an estate or interest pur autre vie respectively.

An interest for the life of the tenant arises (1) by express or implied limitation; (2) formerly by operation of law, as in the case of tenancy by the curtesy or in dower; and (3) by a tenant in tail being reduced to the position of tenant for life in consequence of the possibility of issue in tail becoming extinct. (39 Halsbury's Laws (4th edn) paras 459, 460)

LIFE-JACKET

In this Article the expression 'life-jacket' includes any appliance capable of being fitted on the body, having the same buoyancy as a life-jacket. (Merchant Shipping (Safety and Load Line Conventions) Act 1932, Sch 1)

LIFE PEER *See* PEERAGE

LIFE POLICY

The expression 'life policy' includes any policy not foreign to the business of life assurance. (Life Assurance Companies (Payment into Court) Act 1896, s 2)

'Life policy' means any instrument by which the payment of money is assured on death (except death by accident only) or the happening of any contingency dependent on human life, or any instrument evidencing a contract which is subject to payment of premiums for a term dependent on human life. (Insurance Companies Act 1982, s 96(1))

LIFETIME

[A testator by his will directed that the residue of his estate should be divided equally between his brother and his four sisters during their 'lifetime' but after their death it should be divided equally between his nephews and nieces.] 'In this case I should, unaided by authority, come to the conclusion that on the true construction of the testator's residuary disposition the gift to the nephews and nieces was not intended to take effect until the death of the survivor of the testator's brother and four sisters, and that until that event occurred the brother and sisters for the time being alive would share the income equally between them, and that the survivor would take the whole income for the remainder of his or her life. The reasons that would lead me to this conclusion are as follows: It is clear in the first place that, as each brother and sister dies, his or her interest in the estate ceases. It is equally clear that the interest of all of them does not cease with the death of one. Accordingly I read "during their lifetime" as meaning "during their respective lives".' *Re Foster, Coomber v Hospital for Maintenance & Education of Exposed & Deserted Young Children (Governors & Guardians)* [1946] Ch 135 at 136, 137, per Romer J

LIFTING MACHINE

In this section 'lifting machine' means a crane, crab, winch, teagle, pulley block, gin wheel, transporter or runway. (Factories Act 1961, s 27(9))

LIFTING TACKLE

In this section 'lifting tackle' means chain slings, rope slings, rings, hooks, shackles and swivels. (Factories Act 1961, s 26(3))

LIGAN

'*Lagan (vel potius ligan)* is when the goods which are so cast into the sea, and afterwards the ship perishes, and such goods cast are so heavy that they sink to the bottom, and the mariners, to the intent to have them again, tie to them a buoy, or cork, or such other thing that will not sink, so that they may find them again.' *Constable's Case* (1601) 5 Co Rep 106a at 106b, per cur.

LIGHT *See also* ACCESS

Ancient light

'Great injury may in reality be done by an interference with property, at present not attended with that amount of injury, but which amount of injury may be consequent upon a very probable future application and use of that property. Of course, in speaking of the future use of the property, I assume a use where the aperture of the window would remain the same as it is now, because any future complaint must still be founded upon the existence of the ancient light. The words "ancient light", however, do not in the smallest degree import that the window itself shall remain of the same construction and shape; for example, the windows of this court, which are the old-fashioned casements, may be replaced by large sashes consisting of one piece of plate glass, and of course therefore affording a much greater and more abundant supply of light; but the aperture must remain the same.' *Jackson v Newcastle (Duke)* (1864) 3 De G J & Sm 275 at 291, per Lord Westbury LC

Right to light

The easement of light is a negative easement or a species of negative easement. It is a right acquired in augmentation of the ordinary rights incident to the ownership and enjoyment of land, and may be defined as a right which a person may acquire, as the owner or occupier of a building with windows or apertures, to prevent the owner or occupier of an adjoining piece of land from building or placing upon the latter's land anything which has the effect of 'illegally' obstructing or obscuring the light coming to the building of the owner of the easement. (14 Halsbury's Laws (4th edn) para 211)

'The right of a person who is owner or occupier of a building with windows, privileged as ancient lights, in regard to the protection of the light coming to those windows, is a purely legal right. It is an easement belonging to the class known as negative easements. It is nothing more or less than the right to prevent the owner or occupier of an adjoining tenement from building or placing on his own land anything which has the effect of illegally obstructing or obscuring the light of the dominant tenement.' *Colls v Home & Colonial Stores Ltd* [1904] AC 179 at 185, 186, per Lord Macnaghten

LIGHT LOCOMOTIVE *See* LOCOMOTIVE

LIGHTER

'A lighter is defined in the definition clause [of the Port of London River By-laws 1914–26] as "any dumb barge or other like craft for carrying goods . . .". and the only reason why it could be said that the phrase about lighters does not include this hopper barge is that it might be said that it is not a craft for carrying goods. But I should accept the word "goods" in its widest possible sense, as including spoil from dredging.' *The Dagmar* (1929) 141 LT 271 at 273, per Hill J

LIGHTHOUSE

'Lighthouse' shall in addition to the ordinary meaning of the word include any floating and other light exhibited for the guidance of ships, and also any sirens and any other description of fog signals, and also any addition to a lighthouse of any improved light, or any siren, or any description of fog signal. (Merchant Shipping Act 1894, s 742)

LIKE

[An equality clause in a railway Act provided that charges should be made equally to all persons in respect of all goods, wares, merchandise, articles, matters, and things 'of a like description' and quantity, and conveyed in or propelled by a like carriage or engine, passing only over the same portion and the same distance along the railways, and under the like circumstances.] 'The question what is the meaning of the equality clause when it speaks of things of "like description" conveyed under "the like circumstances" ought, I think, to be answered by saying that things are of a "like description" when, although their composition and structure are not "identical" which would be expressed by "the same description", not "like description", they are similar in those qualities which affect the risk and expense of carriage.' *Great Western Rly Co v Sutton* (1869) LR 4 HL 226 at 247, per Willes J

'"Like" may not import identity of amount as definitely as the use of the word "same" would have done. But at least it connotes resemblance in main features.' *Lumsden v*

Inland Revenue Comr [1914] AC 877 at 894, per Lord Haldane LC

'When one speaks of a written instrument and then of some other instrument "to the like effect", I should have thought that, as a matter of ordinary English, what was meant was that, according to the natural construction of the words used in the second agreement, it was one which was intended to operate in substantially the same way as the first. I do not suggest that that should be taken as an exhaustive statement of what this phrase means, but I do say that, in the ordinary case, the duty of the court is to look at the new agreement in order to see what, according to the language used, its terms, if made effective, will do or achieve, and then ask the question: Are those things done or achieved the same as those which the old agreement, if operative, would have done or achieved?' *Re Black Bolt and Nut Association of Great Britain's Agreement (No 2)* [1962] 1 All ER 139 at 145, CA, per Lord Evershed MR

'The word "like" requires not identity but similarity; and similarity in substances suffices, without the need of similarity in form or detail or wording.' *Re Wallace's Settlements* [1968] 2 All ER 209 at 212, per Megarry J

Australia '"Like" (in the phrase "the like trusts") may be used in contradistinction to the "same" trust (*Brigg v Brigg* [(1885) 54 LJ Ch 464]). It means primarily, *mutatis mutandis*, as regards both subject matter and beneficiaries. . . . "Like" connotes . . . changes in point of detail.' *Re Barnett, Public Trustee v Dilks* [1942] SASR 69 at 72, per Mayo J

LIKELY

Australia 'The ordinary and natural meaning of the word is synonymous with the ordinary and natural meaning of the word "probable" and both words mean . . . that there is an odds-on chance of the thing happening.' *Australian Telecommunications Commission v Krieg Enterprises Pty Ltd* (1976) 27 FLR 400 at 410, per Bray CJ

Australia 'The word "likely" is one which has various shades of meaning. It may mean "probable" in the sense of "more probable than not"—"more than a fifty per cent chance". It may mean "material risk" as seen by a reasonable man "such as might happen". It may mean "some possibility"—more than a remote or bare chance. Or, it may mean that the conduct engaged in is inherently of such a character that it would ordinarily cause the effect specified.' *Tillmanns Butcheries Pty Ltd v Australasian Meat Industry Employees' Union* (1979) 42 FLR 331 at 339, per Bowen CJ

Australia 'In my opinion the word "likely" in [s 157(1)] of the Criminal Code Act (Tas) means "probable" and not "possible". That is its natural meaning.' *Boughey v R* (1986) 65 ALR 609 at 611, per Gibbs CJ

New Zealand 'A tree is likely to cause damage when the reasonable probabilities are that it will cause damage unless it gets timeous attention. The question is: Has the time arrived when a reasonable person, considering the probabilities of growth and space, would conclude that removal of the tree or part or parts thereof is a proper precaution for the protection of [an] electric line from damage.' *Dowling v South Canterbury Electric Power Board* [1966] NZLR 676 at 678, per Henry J

New Zealand 'The Shorter Oxford English Dictionary gives one meaning of the word "likely" as being "probable", but it also gives as another "such as might well happen". That "likely" may mean something less than "probable" is suggested by the fact that very often it is accompanied by the use of "very", "most" or "more". In my view the meaning to be given to the word "likely" where it is used in a statute or regulation will depend upon the statute or regulation and the context in which the word is used. An event which is likely may be an event which is probable but it may also be an event which, while not probable, could well happen. But it must be more than a bare possibility.' *Transport Ministry v Simmonds* [1973] 1 NZLR 359 at 363, per McMullin J

New Zealand [The police summarily charged the defendant with certain offences. Before the trial the police refused to supply the defendant with written briefs of prosecution witnesses' evidence. The test to be applied when deciding whether to make available the information was whether it would be 'likely' to prejudice the maintenance of the law including the right to a fair trial in terms of the Official Information Act 1982, s 6(c).] 'The words "would be likely" in s 6(c) of the Act mean that there is a distinct or significant possibility the result may occur, but no higher than that. On the scale of probability it is above a slight chance and below an expectation . . . It is not as high on the probability scale as "more likely than not".' *Comr of Police v Ombudsman* [1985] 1 NZLR 578 at 589, 593, per Jeffries J

New Zealand 'In some dictionaries "likely" is regarded as synonymous with "probably". It is difficult to differentiate clearly between them in any sensible degree. On a graduated scale one might place expressions of likelihood in the following order of certainty—possible, distinct or significant possibility, reasonably probable, probable, highly probable.' *Air New Zealand Ltd v Commerce Commission* [1985] 2 NZLR 338 at 342, HC, (Admin Division), per Davison CJ

New Zealand 'In my view . . . a proposal is likely to be contrary to the public interest in a case where the [Commerce] Commission, even though it is unable to form the view that a proposal is in fact contrary to the public interest, is yet left in a state of mind where there is a probability that it is so.' Ibid at 342, per Davison CJ

LIKEWISE

[A testator devised an estate to his son. This devise was followed by a gift of the produce of the estate to his nephews, the gift commencing with the word 'likewise'.] 'My principal reason for wishing to look into the authorities on the subject, was with relation to the case which was cited of *Boosey v Gardener* [(1854) 5 De G M & G 122], in which it is said the Lords Justices have laid down, that where the word "likewise" began the sentence, it constituted a separate and independent gift, which was not to be connected at all with that which preceded. It may be, that their opinion may bear that construction, but I think it is only to be taken with reference to that particular will, and that they did not intend to lay that down as the general law or as a general rule. In that particular case, I did not think that to be the proper construction; their Lordships thought otherwise, but I feel satisfied, that it was not their intention to establish this proposition:—that wherever the word "likewise" occurs, the contingency which governs the previous gift is not to govern that which follows, if the subject-matter is clearly connected as, for instance, where one part is dealing with a life estate, and the other with the reversion.' *Paylor v Pegg* (1857) 24 Beav 105 at 111, per Romilly MR

LIMITATION OF ACTIONS

For most actions, periods of limitation are prescribed by statute with the consequence that an action begun after the period of limitation has expired is not maintainable.

The statutes which impose periods of limitation for classes of actions are called statutes of limitation. The principal statutes of limiation in force at the present time are [the Limitation (Enemies and War Prisoners) Act 1945, the Limitation Act 1980, the Foreign Limitation Periods Act 1984 and the Latent Damage Act 1986.]

In the Limitation (Enemies and War Prisoners) Act 1945 'statute of limitation' means in addition to the Limitation Act 1939 [repealed; see now the Limitation Act 1980] a number of other enactments, but it is doubtful whether these enactments would all be regarded as statutes of limitation except for the purposes of the Act which so defines them.

All statutes of limitation are analogous and should receive a uniform construction; they are beneficial statutes, and are to be construed liberally and not strictly. Besides the general statutes relating to the limitation of actions there are special statutes fixing special periods of limitation in particular cases. (28 Halsbury's Laws (4th edn) para 601)

'Statutory provisions imposing periods of limitation within which actions must be instituted seek to serve several aims. In the first place, they protect defendants from being vexed by stale claims relating to long-past incidents about which their records may no longer be in existence and as to which their witnesses, even if they are still available, may well have no accurate recollection. Secondly, the law of limitation is designed to encourage plaintiffs to institute proceedings as soon as it is reasonably possible for them to do so. . . . Thirdly, the law is intended to ensure that a person may with confidence feel that after a given time he may regard as finally closed an incident which might have led to a claim against him, and it was for this reason that Lord Kenyon described statutes of limitation as "statutes of repose".' *Burkett v James* [1977] 2 All ER 801 at 815, 816, HL, per Lord Edmund-Davies

[See the Limitation Act 1980.]

LINEAL

'Whatever may be the range of the word "lineal" considered by Mr Collyer in his note to *Craik v Lamb* [(1844) 1 Coll 489] to speak of a man's collateral kindred as related to him in any line is not an improper use of language, but equally allowable with the genealogical "*transversa linea*" of the civil lawyers.' *Boys v Bradley* (1853) 22 LJ Ch 617 at 623, per Knight Bruce LJ

LIQUIDATED DAMAGES *See* DAMAGES

LIQUIDATED DEMAND

[A contract for the construction of a ship provided for payment of the contract price by instalments as the work proceeded. The plaintiff brought an action for an instalment which was due according to the terms of the contract.] 'The question is whether this is an action which comes within the purview of Ord 14, r 1 [see now RSC 1965, Ord 14]. That depends on whether it is an action for "a debt or liquidated demand in money" within the meaning of Ord 3, r 6. There is nothing . . . in the nature of the claim, apart from its being a claim for an instalment forming part of a larger sum contracted to be paid, to prevent its coming with the before-mentioned rules. . . . I have heard nothing . . . which satisfies me that the provisions of Ord 14 cannot be applied in the case of an action to recover an instalment of money, such as that here sued for. . . . The conclusion at which . . . I arrive is that this claim is for a liquidated demand in money within the meaning of the rule.' *Workman, Clark & Co Ltd v Lloyd Brazileño* [1908] 1 KB 968 at 979–981, CA, per Kennedy LJ

New Zealand 'In my opinion there can be no doubt that, in deciding whether a demand is liquidated, important factors are that it be capable of arithmetical calculation and that no investigation of the amount claimed should be necessary other than inquiry as to well-established scales of charges, etc. Thus a claim by a land agent for commission may require investigation of the scale of charges adopted by the Real Estate Institute of New Zealand from which the amount of the commission could readily be ascertained by a mere arithmetical process. Similarly in the case of doctors' fees for regular visits to patients or of legal charges for ordinary conveyancing work. On the authorities such claims would be liquidated demands. But the case would ordinarily be on the other side of the line if the investigation was of a more extensive kind.' *Paterson v Wellington Free Kindergarten Association Inc* [1966] NZLR 468 at 471; per Barrowclough CJ; on appeal [1966] NZLR 975, CA

LIQUIDATOR

There are three kinds of liquidators in a winding up by order of the court: (1) a provisional liquidator, who may be appointed at any time after the winding-up petition has been presented and before the winding-up order has been made; (2) the official receiver acting as liquidator *ex officio* from the time the winding-up order is made until he is displaced by the appointment of some other person as liquidator; and (3) the liquidator appointed by the creditors and contributories, by the court or by the Secretary of State instead of, or to replace, the official receiver. (7 Halsbury's Laws (4th edn) para 1552)

LIQUOR *See* INTOXICATING LIQUOR

LIS

'*Lis* . . . implies the conception of an issue joined between two parties. The decision of a *lis*, in the ordinary use of legal language, is the decision of that issue.' *Johnson & Co (Builders) Ltd v Minister of Health* [1947] 2 All ER 395 at 399, CA, per Lord Greene MR

LITERARY WORK

The copyright protection under the Copyright Act 1956 [repealed; see now the Copyright Designs and Patents Act 1988] extends to all original literary works, and to adaptations of them. The expression 'literary work' covers work which is expressed in print or writing, irrespective of whether the quality or style is high, and is used in the sense of written or printed matter. 'Writing' includes any form of notation, whether by hand, or by printing or by any similar process. 'Manuscript' in relation to a work means the original document embodying the work, whether written by hand or not. The expression 'literary work' in the Copyright Act 1956 [repealed] includes any written table or compilation, but (unlike the corresponding expression in the Copyright Act 1911) does not include maps, charts, or plans. Maps, charts and plans come within the definition of 'drawing' in the Act of 1956 and hence are subject to the provisions protecting the copyright in 'artistic' works. There is no copyright in a mere collection of words, which is not a compilation and the collection of which has not involved any literary skill. (9 Halsbury's Laws (4th edn) para 835)

'Literary work' means any work, other than a dramatic or musical work, which is written, spoken or sung, and accordingly includes—
(a) a table or compilation, and
(b) a computer program.
(Copyright, Designs and Patents Act 1988, s 3(1))

'A literary work is intended to afford either information and instruction, or pleasure, in the form of literary enjoyment. The sleeve chart before us gives no information or instruction. It does not add to the stock of human knowledge or give, and is not designed to give, any instruction by way of description or otherwise; and it certainly is not calculated to afford literary enjoyment or pleasure. It is a representation of the shape of a lady's arm, or more probably of a sleeve designed for a lady's arm, with certain scales for measurement upon it. It is intended, not for the purpose of giving information or pleasure, but for practical use in the art of dressmaking. It is, in fact, a mechanical contrivance, appliance, or tool, for the better enabling a dressmaker to make her measurements for the purpose of cutting out the sleeve of a lady's dress, and is intended to be used for that purpose. In my opinion it is no more entitled to copyright as a literary work than the scale attached to the barometer in *Davis v Comitti* [(1885) 52 LT 539].' *Hollinrake v Truswell* [1894] 3 Ch 420 at 428, CA, per Davey LJ

[The plaintiff invented an outfit which consisted of a box in which coloured cards with different headings were inserted, the object being to enable an employer to find easily the insurance cards of his employees.] 'The question which I have to determine is whether the alleged subject matter of copyright is or is not a "literary work" within the meaning of s 1 of the Copyright Act 1911 [repealed; see now Copyright, Designs and Patents Act 1988, s 1]. By s 35 of that Act [see s 3(1) of the 1988 Act supra] "literary work" includes maps, charts, plans, tables, and compilations. It is clear that a card, if the matter written on it was capable of copyright, might be a "literary work"—the mere fact that it was a card would not prevent its being the subject of copyright. Is this an original literary work? In my opinion it is impossible to hold that it is. It is part of an outfit, and by itself useless and conveys no meaning. There is no unusual arrangement of words on the card; simply the words "name", "address", and other words which might be used by anybody. It is subject to the same objections as were stated by Lord Herschell in *Hollinrake v Truswell* [supra]. It is impossible to say that the card is an original "literary work".' *Libraco Ltd v Shaw Walker Ltd* (1913) 30 TLR 22 at 22, per Warrington J

[The question for decision was whether a translation from a foreign language could be said to be an 'original literary work', and thus the subject of copyright under the Copyright Act 1911, s 1 (repealed; see supra).] 'To ascertain whether the plaintiff had the copyright he claims, one must turn to the Copyright Act 1911. By s 1 copyright subsists in every original work first published in England, and by s 5 [repealed] the author of a work shall be the owner of the first copyright therein. No question arises about publication. The plaintiff's translation was first published in England. The remaining questions upon these sections are: Was the plaintiff's translation an original literary work? and was the plaintiff the author of it? These are questions of fact. The translation was, I think, certainly literary work. Was it original and was the plaintiff the author? These are, I think, in effect but one question. I think the words "original literary work" mean a literary work of which the person in whom the copyright is laid, or through whom the title to the copyright is traced, is the author. A translator of a literary work has for many years been held to be the author of his translation, and the House of Lords, in *Walter v Lane* [[1900] AC 539], went so far as to hold that a shorthand writer who reported a speech verbatim was the author of his report. I answer these questions, therefore, in the plaintiff's favour.' *Burne v Statist Co* [1914] 1 KB 622 at 627, per Bailhache J

'Section 1(1) of the Copyright Act of 1911 [repealed; see supra], provides for copyright in "every original literary dramatic musical and artistic work", subject to certain conditions. . . . Although a literary work is not defined in the Act, s 35 states what the phrase includes; the definition is not a completely comprehensive one, but the section is intended to show what, amongst other things, is included in the description "literary work", and the words are "'literary work' includes maps, charts, plans, tables, and compilations." . . . In my view the words "literary work" cover work which is expressed in print or writing, irrespective of the question whether the quality or style is high. The word "literary" seems to be used in a sense somewhat similar to the use of the word "literature" in political or electioneering literature and refers to written or printed matter. Papers set by examiners are, in my opinion, "literary work" within the meaning of the present Act.' *University of London Press Ltd v University Tutorial Press Ltd* [1916] 2 Ch 601 at 608, per Peterson J

[The plaintiffs published a code of made-up words considered suitable for cabling purposes. Each word, which in itself was meaningless, consisted of five letters only, and differed from every other word in the code in at least two out of the five letters. The question was whether this was an 'original literary work' within the Copyright Act 1911, s 1 (repealed; see supra).] 'The plaintiffs say that their code is a compilation which is an "original literary work" within the meaning of that expression in the Act. On behalf of the defendants it is contended that it is not a literary work, either original or otherwise, and the ground upon which this contention is based is that the words in the code are not words in the ordinary sense at all, but are merely collections of letters which are in themselves meaningless and are made up in a merely mechanical way. I cannot accede to that argument. The words—I call them so for want of a better name—are for use for telegraphic purposes, and to each of them a meaning can be attached by the person sending the message and also by the addressee, provided, of course, he is informed of the meaning attached to it by the sender. They are telegraphic words or ciphers. . . . I come, therefore, to the conclusion that the plaintiffs are right in saying that their code is a proper subject of copyright.' *Anderson (D P) & Co Ltd v Lieber Code Co* [1917] 2 KB 460 at 471, 472, per Bailhache J

'There is copyright in every original literary work, which by definition includes compilation, so that there can be copyright in such productions as timetables and directories, provided always they are "original". The requirement of originality means that the product must originate from the author in the sense that it is the result of a substantial degree of skill, industry or experience employed by him.' *Ladbroke (Football) Ltd v William Hill (Football) Ltd* [1964] 1 All ER 465 at 478, per Lord Devlin

'The words "literary work" include a compilation. They are used to describe work which is expressed in print or writing irrespective of whether it has any excellence of quality or style of writing. . . . The word "original" does not demand original or inventive thought, but only that the work should not be copied and should originate from the author.' Ibid at 479, per Lord Pearce

'The mere fact that a single word is invented and that research or labour was involved in its invention does not in itself in my judgment necessarily enable it to qualify as an original literary work within s 2 of the 1956 Act.' *Exxon Corpn v Exxon Insurance Consultants International Ltd* [1981] 2 All ER 495 at 634, 635, per Graham J; affirmed [1981] 3 All ER 241, CA

Australia 'In my opinion, none of the [computer] programs are literary works within the meaning of the statute [Copyright Act 1968 (Cth), ss 10, 37, 38]. In my view, a literary work for this purpose is something which was intended to afford "either information or instruction or pleasure in the form of literary enjoyment". . . . The function of a computer program is to control the sequence of operations carried out by a computer. In this sense, as [was] submitted on behalf of the respondents, a contrast may properly be drawn between something which is merely intended to assist the functioning of a mechanical device and literary work so called. . . . Support for the conclusion I have formed may, I think, be found in the circumstance that the legislature has decided to extend the protection afforded by statutory copyright to literary works in the form of cinematograph films, sound recordings and the like. This was done at a time when computers had been developed and were well known. In my view, the omission by the Parliament to make any reference to computers or computer equipment when it determined to extend the scope of copyright protection should be treated as an indication on its part that this field was not to be afforded the significant privilege given by copyright, but intended rather to leave such matters to be dealt with by other legislation dealing with patents and industrial designs.' *Apple Computer Inc v Computer Edge Pty Ltd* (1983) 50 ALR 581 at 591, per Beaumont J

[See, however, as to English law, the Copyright, Designs and Patents Act 1988, s 3(1), supra.]

United States 'Literary works' are works, other than audiovisual works, expressed in words, numbers, or other verbal or numerical symbols or indicia, regardless of the nature of the material objects, such as books, periodicals, manuscripts, phonorecords, film, tapes, disks, or cards, in which they are embodied. (Copyright Act of 1976, s 101)

LITTER (Bedding)

'Litter' means straw or other substance commonly used for bedding or otherwise for or about animals. (Animal Health Act 1981, s 89(1))

LITTER (Rubbish)

[Litter, under the Litter Act 1958, s 1(1) (repealed; see now the Litter Act 1983, s 1(1)) can consist of 'any thing whatsoever' if it is thrown down, dropped or otherwise deposited in, into or from any place in the open air to which the public are entitled or permitted to have access without payment, and left there, unless authorised by law or done with the consent of the owner, etc, of the place.] 'It is quite clear that not only the depositing but also the leaving is necessary, because it was not intended that an offence should be committed if somebody deposited litter and immediately cleared it up. Accordingly, although the act constituting the offence consists of throwing down, dropping or otherwise depositing, it is only an offence if it is not removed. The offence is not committed unless both of these things, the depositing and the leaving, occur. Depositing is an act fixed in point of time and not a continuing matter, and accordingly, I am quite satisfied that this cannot be treated as a continuing offence.' *Vaughan v Biggs* [1960] 2 All ER 473 at 474, per Lord Parker CJ

LIVE *See also* LIVING

Australia 'The natural meaning of the word "live" is to abide or reside with some degree of permanency, or for an indefinite period.' *Hughes v Hughes* [1941] SASR 281 at 282, per Napier J

New Zealand 'The distinction between the word "live" and the word "reside" relates to the social status of the person referred to. The poor "live" in cottages, the wealthy build residences in which they "reside". They are both doing the same thing. Both words denote some degree of permanency, and in that respect differ from such words as "sojourn" or "abide" which connote a mere temporary abode. Although the words "live" and "reside" suggest some degree of permanency, nevertheless they are apt to any abode which constitutes the residence or home for the time being. A person possessed of a town and also a country house "resides" in each while he is actually living there, although that term would be inapt to a mere visit of a day or two. A school-girl boarding at a boarding-school, while a boarder, is in residence at the school, and here absence on holidays constitutes a mere interval in her residence.' *Avery v University of New Zealand* [1934] NZLR 95 at 101, 102, per Blair J; also reported [1934] GLR 136 at 138

Live apart

'The husband having married without any arrangement securing to him a portion of his wife's fortune, and unhappy differences having arisen between them, it was agreed that they should live apart on her paying to him £400 a year. He refused to sign an agreement on those terms, but he did live separate from his wife, and although the arrangement was that they were to see one another, this was in my opinion an arrangement to live apart on the terms agreed on. To suggest that they were not living apart, because occasionally they paid short visits to one another, there being at the same time an entire absence of mutual affection, is absurd.' *Re Rogers* (1865) Har & Ruth 85 at 88, per Erle CJ

Live in

'If a legacy had been given to a person, with a condition expressed that he should be "living in Suffolk", and his abode had been in that county, but he had been at the time taking a drive, or making an excursion in the county of Norfolk, the latter circumstance would not have deprived him of the benefit of the legacy. The testatrix has varied the words from being in England to living in England, but there is no reason to suppose that she did not mean the same thing by the different expressions. The words were used rather in apposition than in opposition.' *Woods v Townley* (1853) 11 Hare 314 at 319, per Page Wood V-C

Australia 'In 1869 the appellant applied to the Government for some agricultural and pastoral land, then open to selection by conditional purchasers, under the Crown Lands Alienation Act of 1868. . . . The form [of application] is as follows, "I . . . do hereby state my desire to become the lessee of the Crown lands hereunder described. . . . I declare that I live in Queensland. . . ." The first question to be considered is the meaning of the word "live". It is not a technical word, and was evidently used by the Legislature in a popular sense. So reading it, no one can reasonably doubt that the word implies something different from the transient presence in the colony of the applicant for land, and that it imports that the applicant is dwelling in Queensland having made it, for the time at least, his home.' *Fisher v Tully* (1878) 3 App Cas 627 at 630, 631, 635, PC, per cur.

Live together

A man and his wife shall not be deemed to be living otherwise than together unless—
(a) they are permanently living in separation either by agreement or under an order of the court, or
(b) one of them has deserted the other and the separation incident to the desertion has not come to an end.
(Social Security Act 1975, Sch 20)

'A husband and wife are living together, not only when they are residing together in the same house, but also when they are living in different places, even if they are separated by the high seas, provided the consortium has not been determined.' *R v Creamer* [1919] 1 KB 564 at 569, CCA, per cur.

'In the present case the appellant and his wife entered into a very peculiar deed dated 9th December 1912, by which they were to occupy or . . . have the right of occupying together a house called Rigby Hall, not that they might live there together as husband and wife, but merely as having a joint establishment arranged for them. . . . In February, 1913, the appellant ceased to reside at or to visit Rigby Hall, and took a residence for himself in London. . . . In these circumstances I should have thought that it was perfectly clear that the appellant's wife was not a married woman living with her husband. She had her residence and he had his residence. His home was not her home, and her home was not his home. They had two separate addresses; two separate residences; two separate homes; and therefore I think they were not living together.' *Eadie v Inland Revenue Comrs* [1924] 2 KB 198 at 206, 207, per Rowlatt J

Live with

[A testator by his will bequeathed a year's wages to each of the servants 'living with' him at his decease, who should then have lived three years in his service.] 'It was argued upon the words of the will, that the expression "living with me", imports living in my house, and therefore, that no servant who was not living in the house could be entitled under the bequest; but I cannot adopt that construction. The words "living with me", as applied to servants, may, I think, well be understood to mean living in my service; and this, I am much disposed to think, is the ordinary import of the words: but it is not necessary to go so far in the present case, for here the plaintiff was actually living in a cottage belonging to the testator, on the grounds adjoining to the testator's mansion; and it cannot, I think, reasonably be held that he was not living with the testator in the sense in which servants live with their masters, because he was not actually in the same house with his master.' *Blackwell v Pennant* (1852) 9 Hare 551 at 553, per Turner V-C

'"Living with a person" implies personal association with that person and is not satisfied by mere proximity or by anything short of personal contact.' *Re Paskin's Will Trusts, Paskins v Underwood* [1948] 2 All ER 156 at 158, 159, per Vaisey J

LIVELIHOOD

'On behalf of the defendant in this case, reliance is placed on the words "seeking a livelihood". But I think those words must be construed with reference to the preceding and subsequent words [in a local Court of Requests Act]. The whole stands thus,—"keeping any house, warehouse, shop, shed, stall, stand, or seeking a livelihood, or trading or dealing, within the same city or liberties". When I see the words, "seeking a livelihood", so associated with those other words, it appears to me that the expression must be taken to point to a person who is carrying on some business on his own account, and not in the subordinate situation of a clerk, which does not answer to the description of "keeping a shop", or "trading or dealing".' *Smith v Hurrell* (1830) 10 B & C 542 at 545, 546, per Lord Tenterden CJ

LIVESTOCK

'Livestock' includes any creature kept for the production of food, wool, skins or fur, or for the purpose of its use in the farming of land. (Agricultural Act 1947, s 109)

'Livestock' means cattle, sheep, goats, swine, horses, or poultry, and for the purposes of this definition 'cattle' means bulls, cows, oxen, heifers or calves, 'horses' includes asses and mules, and 'poultry' means domestic fowls, turkeys, geese or ducks. (Dogs (Protection of Livestock) Act 1953, s 3)

In this section livestock includes the carcases of livestock. (Agriculture Act 1957, s 6(6))

'Livestock' means cattle, sheep and pigs. (Agriculture Act 1967, s 25(2))

'Livestock' means any creature kept for the production of food, wool, skin or fur or for use in the farming of land or for such purpose as the Minister [of Agriculture, Fisheries and Food] may by order specify. (Agriculture (Miscellaneous Provisions) Act 1968, s 8)

'Livestock' means cattle, horses, asses, mules, hinnies, sheep, pigs, goats and poultry, and also deer not in the wild state and, in sections 3 [liability for injury done by dogs to livestock] and 9 [killing of or injury to dogs worrying livestock], also, while in captivity, pheasants, partridges and grouse. (Animals Act 1971, s 11)

'Livestock' means creatures kept for any purpose. (Agricultural Statistics Act 1979, s 6(1))

'Livestock' includes any creature kept for the production of food, wool, skins or fur or for the purpose of its use in the farming of land or the carrying on in relation to land of any agricultural activity. (Agricultural Holdings Act 1986, s 96(2))

[A testator gave a legacy which included the use of his house, with all his furniture and stock of carriages and horses, and other 'live and dead stock'.] 'I do not mean to say, what "live and dead stock" might mean, if it stood independent of everything else: but upon the whole of this will taken together, I cannot by any fair inference deduce, that the testator did intend under the words "live and dead stock", as they stand here, his books and wine. Consider first what would be the interpretation of these words, if nothing was said of furniture at all. No person could have conceived that those words preceded by "carriage and horses", would have meant in-door stock, furniture, etc.; which, though dead, could not be coupled and enjoyed with carriages and horses. Therefore it is clear, if those words stood alone, the interpretation would be out-of-door stock. They would mean corn, hay, straw, carts, etc . . . In *Lady Gower v Lord Gower* [(1763) Amb 612], the words were "which should be in and about his dwelling-house and outhouses". These words differ from those in this respect: it was perfectly clear the testator meant to make a general gift of every thing within doors and without; and if this testator meant the same thing, he would have used some such words as "all my live and dead stock in doors and out". If he had meant to add any thing more in-doors to the bequest of the furniture, he would have said "all my stock of wines". But the word "furniture" is decided not to include books or wine. By that word he disposed of every thing he meant to dispose of in the house; and by the other words he meant out-of-door stock. This must never be quoted as a governing case; because it does not determine what "live and dead stock" may mean, not coupled with other words.' *Porter v Tournay* (1797) 3 Ves 311 at 313, 314, per Arden MR

'"Livestock" generally means live animals. If the live and dead stock on a farm are advertised for sale, everybody knows what that means. The dead stock are the implements; the live stock are the animals on the farm, and I should think that in the great majority of cases at any rate it would include, and would be thought to include, the poultry on the farm.' *Wardhaugh (A F) Ltd v Mace* [1952] 2 All ER 28 at 31, per Lord Goddard CJ

[The Town and Country Planning Act 1947, s 119(1) (repealed; see now the Town and Country Planning Act 1971, s 290(1)) defined 'agriculture' as including (inter alia) 'the breeding and keeping of livestock (including any creature kept for the production of food, wool, skins or fur, or for the purpose of its use in the farming of land'.] 'Of course, on one view "livestock" can be said to be used in contradiction to dead stock, and to include any animal whatsoever. In some contexts that might be so, but it seems to me that in the context of agriculture, as here, it has some less extensive meaning. What exact meaning should be given to it if it stood alone in this agriculture context, I do not propose to determine. I think that it is sufficient to say that there must be a limitation in that context on what I may call the wide dictionary meaning. I find it unnecessary to decide what it would mean if it stood alone because it does not stand alone, and the words in brackets that follow assist in determining what is meant by "livestock". The words are "including any creature kept for the production of food, wool, skins or fur". Pausing there, that is clearly an extension to cover, no doubt, an argument that, for instance, bees, possibly pheasants and fish are not livestock. It covers any creature kept for this purpose, and it then goes on to say "including any creature kept for the purpose of its use in the farming of land". Granting that the word "including" has been used in an extensive sense, it seems to me nonsense for the draftsmen to use these words "any creature kept for the production of food, wool, skins or fur, or for the purpose of its use in the farming of land", if the word "livestock" was intended to cover the keeping of any creature whether for its use in farming land or not. It seems to me that those words shew a clear intention that "livestock", however it is interpreted, does not extend to the breeding and keeping of horses unless it is for the purpose of their use in the farming of land.' *Belmont Farm Ltd v Minister of Housing and Local Government* (1962) 60 LGR 319 at 322, per Lord Parker of Waddington CJ

'The definition of "livestock", which is quite clearly intended to extend the meaning of "livestock" in the definition of "agriculture" [in a statute (repealed)], is itself an inclusive definition and [counsel] would say that the extension is not limited to the words which follow "kept for the production of food, wool, skins or fur, or for the purpose of its use in the farming of land". It may be that it has some extended meaning slightly beyond the words used: I know not, but it seems to me quite clear that whatever extension is provided under the definition of "livestock" it must be an activity which can properly be brought within the general meaning of "agriculture". I find it quite impossible to hold that this activity [the breeding of cats and dogs for research purposes] comes within that extended meaning.' *Minister of Agriculture, Fisheries and Food v Appleton* [1969] 3 All ER 1051 at 1054, per Lord Parker CJ

'I do not think that pheasants kept and reared for shooting, and which when sufficiently grown are released from captivity, can properly be regarded as "domestic animals" or as being kept for use or profit. They cease to be kept when they are let go free. I do not therefore consider that the pheasants looked after by Mr Giles [a gamekeeper] were within the definition of livestock in the dictionary and consequently the rearing and keeping of them does not come within the definition in the dictionary of agriculture.' *Normanton (Earl) v Giles* [1980] 1 All ER 106 at 112, HL, per Viscount Dilhorne

'It is noteworthy that in the Rating Act 1971 there is no reference whatsoever to "creatures", to "furs" or to "skins". All that appears in association with the word "livestock" are "mammal" and "bird", which seems to indicate an intention to give a more restricted meaning to the word than has been given in previous legislation. It can in my opinion properly be said that, so far as the 1971 Act is concerned "livestock" is restricted in its meaning so as to include only something which is either a mammal or a bird. Accordingly, I see no reason for including fish within the category of the "livestock" referred to in the Act, whether they be bred or farmed in tanks, ponds, lakes or reservoirs.' *Cresswell (Valuation Officer) v BOC Ltd* [1980] 3 All ER 443 at 477, CA, per Watkins LJ

Australia 'Dogs are "live stock" within the meaning of the term as used in s 514A [of the Local Government Act 1919–1986 (NSW)].' *Halliday v Hornsby Shire Council* (1979) 1 NSWLR 391 at 394, per Mahoney JA

Livestock industry

'Livestock industry' means all the activities comprised in the production, marketing and distribution of livestock in Great Britain, including the carrying on of slaughterhouses and livestock auctions and markets. (Agriculture Act 1967, s 25)

Livestock product

'Livestock product' means any product for human consumption which is derived to any substantial extent, with or without any process of manufacture, from livestock, but excluding milk and milk products, so, however, that references to the production or processing or manufacture of livestock products include references to the production or processing or manufacture in slaughterhouses of any inedible products obtained from the slaughter of livestock in slaughterhouses. (Agriculture Act 1967, s 25)

Livestock products industry

'Livestock products industry' means the activities comprised in the production, processing, manufacture, marketing and distribution of livestock products in Great Britain, including the carrying on of livestock product auctions and markets. (Agriculture Act 1967, s 25)

LIVING (Alive) *See also* EN VENTRE SA MERE

'Whatever may be the meaning of the word "born" in ordinary parlance, a rule of construction has been established which was stated forty-four years ago by Mr Vaughan Hawkins, in my opinion with absolute accuracy, in his admirable treatise on Wills, in these terms . . .: "*Rule*. A devise or bequest to children '*born*' or to children '*living*' at a given period, includes a child *en ventre* at that period, and born afterwards".' *Re Salaman, De Pass v Sonnenthal* [1908] 1 Ch 4 at 8, CA, per Farwell LJ

LIVING (Benefice)

'The devise is in these terms: "I give to my great nephew Henry Webb Byng the livings of Quendon and Chickney, should he like the profession and be qualified for them, or to William Cranmer Byng". Now, the word "living" is ambiguous. It is sufficient to pass the advowson. On the other hand, it may be restricted to a single presentation: the law does not determine which is its meaning, and the point must be ascertained from the context. Referring in this will to the context, it is clear that, by the word "livings", the testatrix intended to pass not the advowson, but only a single presentation. The words "should he like the profession and be qualified for them", show an intention to confer on the devisee a personal benefit; and that could only be effected by the devisee being himself presented to the livings. I must, therefore, hold that the devise of the livings is confined to a single presentation, and does not extend to the advowson.' *Webb v Byng* (1856) 2 K & J 669 at 674, 675, per Page Wood V-C

LIVING ACCOMMODATION

'Living accommodation is something in which somebody resides and therefore it is the dwelling-house and it is something distinct from entertainment, domestic or other services or other benefits or facilities of whatsoever nature, and also it is distinct from supplies or services.' *Butter (Inspector of Taxes) v Bennett* [1962] 3 All ER 204 at 209, CA, per Pearson LJ

LIVING ROOM

'It cannot always be clear what ought to be treated as a "living room". . . . The complexities of individual situations and requirements are infinitely various, since patterns of living themselves vary so much, and what is important or even essential for one occupant of rooms separately let may be unimportant or unnecessary for another. I cannot, myself, frame any formula which, in this context, necessarily embraces a kitchen but necessarily excludes a bathroom. The difficulty has led to attempts to speak of "essential living rooms" or "essential manifestations of living"; but I am bound to say that these glosses seem to me either to beg the question or to confuse the issue. And I am afraid that I cannot see anything more satisfying in the definition offered during the course of argument in this case: "a living room is a room wherein you cook, eat, sleep and put your feet on the fender". Why ever should courts of law tie themselves down in this way? As I see it, the truth is that a living room is not something which can be identified objectively without regard to the situation of its particular occupant, occupants or users. What, indeed, may be a living room if in single occupation, as for instance a kitchen, is not necessarily a living room if it has to be made available for the use of several distinct households; and I should say the same of a bathroom and, again, of a spare bedroom.' *Goodrich v Paisner* [1956] 2 All ER 176 at 187, HL, per Lord Radcliffe; also reported in [1957] AC 65 at 91, 92)

'Various cases have dealt with what is a living room and in particular it has been said that a kitchen is a living room. In the present case the kitchen is so small that it is only possible to use it for cooking. There is no furniture in it, I understand, and I myself think that it does not constitute a living room in the proper meaning of that term.' *Marsh Ltd v Cooper* [1969] 2 All ER 498 at 500, CA, per Danckwerts LJ

LOAD

[The Merchant Shipping Act 1862, s 41 (repealed; see now the Pilotage Act 1983), provided that a ship should employ a pilot when calling at a port for the purposes of 'loading'.] 'It is unnecessary . . . to decide various suggested questions as to what would or would not be a loading within the meaning of the section, it is sufficient to say that we are of opinion that loading coals for the purposes of the voyage does fall within its operation.' *The Winston* (1884) 9 PD 85 at 86, CA, per Brett MR

[A railway company's special Act provided maximum charges for the conveyance of goods, which charges were to include every expense incidental to such conveyance except a reasonable charge for 'loading and unloading'.] 'We do not think they [the words loading and unloading] mean anything more than the labour of packing or unpacking a goods train or a goods truck, whether done by hand or by machinery.' *Berry v London, Chatham & Dover Rly Co* (1884) 4 Ry & Can Tr Cas 310 at 320, per cur.

'The question we have to decide arises on a clause in a charterparty providing for cesser of the liability of the charterer, and giving a lien to the shipowner for, among other things, demurrage. The charterparty must be construed so as to make the application of the cesser and lien clauses co-extensive, and the question is whether the lien for demurrage applies to unreasonable detention at the port of loading. The clause obviously divides itself into two parts. The first of these relates to the loading of the ship, which is to be "as customary", which has been held to be equivalent to saying "in the customary manner". In this clause nothing is said as to the time within which the loading is to be effected; and in this particular case the absence of a reference to time is more marked than usual, because the first part of the clause is followed by another clause containing words limiting the time for unloading; so that it is obvious, that this interpretation of the words "as customary" is applicable to this case. This part of the clause then is silent as to time, and leaves the loading to be done in a reasonable time.' *Dunlop & Sons v Balfour, Williamson & Co* [1892] 1 QB 507 at 520, CA, per Fry LJ

[It was provided by a clause in a charterparty that if any dispute arose 'in the loading' of a vessel it should be settled by arbitration.] 'It seems to me that the dispute arises "in the loading" within the meaning of the clause if the loading is claimed by one party and denied by the other to have been delayed by one of the causes named in the clause, and none the less because the extent of the delay cannot be ascertained until the loading has been completed.' *Temperley Steam Shipping Co v Smyth & Co* [1905] 2 KB 791 at 800, CA, per Collins MR

[A ship was chartered to 'load' pit props for delivery at an English port. On loading, when the last part of the cargo was on deck, but before it had been stowed, the ship listed, and a large part of the cargo went overboard and was lost.] 'It has been contended very strenuously that . . . loading . . . means simply the reception of the goods on board, and the moment the last parcel of cargo which it is intended to load is placed on the vessel the loading is completed notwithstanding the fact that some stowage may be necessary and may commonly be done. I do not think that that is the law. I think that in a case like this, and, indeed, in most cases, the mere reception or dumping down of the cargo on the ship does not involve the completion of the loading, because I think the operation of loading involves all that is required to put the cargo in a condition in which it can be carried.' *Svenssons (C Wilh) Travaruaktiebolag v Cliffe SS Co Ltd* [1932] 1 KB 490 at 494, 495, per Wright J

'In the early operative part of the charterparty I find this provision: "Vessel to load under inspection of underwriters' agents, at her expense, and to comply with their rules, not exceeding what she can reasonably stow and carry over and above her cabin, tackle, apparel, provisions, fuel and furniture, and being so loaded shall therewith proceed to one safe port in the United Kingdom". It seems to me quite plain that in that clause the expression "loaded" means not only shipped but stowed.' *Argonaut Navigation Co Ltd v Ministry of Food, Argobec Steamship* [1949] 1 KB 572 at 583, 584, CA, per Cohen LJ

LOADED *See also* FIREARM

A shotgun or an air weapon shall be deemed to be loaded if there is ammunition in the chamber or barrel or in any magazine or other device which is in such a position that the ammunition can be fed into the chamber or barrel by the manual or automatic operation of some part of the gun or weapon. (Firearms Act 1968, s 57(5)(b))

New Zealand [The Crimes Act 1908, s 197(b) (NZ) (repealed) imposed penalties for discharging or attempting to discharge at any person any arms 'loaded' with destructive materials, whether otherwise properly prepared for being discharged or not.] 'A rifle may be said to be "loaded" when there are cartridges in the magazine, one of which, by simple movement of the bolt, would slide into the barrel ready for discharge. I think it would be absurd to regard a rifle with a full magazine but no cartridge in the barrel as unloaded.' *R v Lacey* [1953] NZLR 431 at 431, per Gresson J

LOAN

[The Building Societies Act 1874, s 15(1) (repealed; see now the Building Societies Act 1962, s 39(1)) empowered societies to receive deposits or 'loans', and otherwise to borrow money.] 'The words of s 15, sub-s 1 are general, covering any sort of "deposit on loan at interest from members or other persons. . . ." There is nothing in the Act to distinguish loans by bankers from loans by other persons.' *Looker v Wrigley, Leigh v Wrigley* (1882) 9 QBD 397 at 402, per Denman J

United States 'Loan' includes (1) the creation of debt by the lender's payment of or agreement to pay money to the debtor or to a third party for the account of the debtor; (2) the creation of debt by a credit to an account with the lender upon which the debtor is entitled to draw immediately; (3) the creation of debt pursuant to a lender credit card or similar arrangement; and (4) the forbearance of debt arising from a loan. (Uniform Consumer Credit Code 1969, s 3.106)

LOCAL ACT *See* STATUTE

LOCAL AUTHORITY

'Local authority' means a county council, . . . a district council, a London borough council or a parish or community council. (Local Government Act 1972, s 270(1) as amended by the Local Government Act 1985, s 84, Sch 14)

New Zealand 'We venture to say that "local authority" and "local body" has a popular meaning which is well understood. In common understanding a local authority is a corporate body created for a particular purpose to administer some local undertaking or undertakings. The distinguishing feature of such bodies is that they act for the public good as regards some facet of regional activity. They are distinguishable by the nature of their work and constitution from ordinary trading corporations, charitable institutions, or Government or quasi-Government bodies (we would place education authorities in the last category). In the sense that I have described we are of the opinion that the [Auckland Harbour] Bridge Authority clearly falls in the category of a "local authority".' *Northern & Taranaki Labourers' & Industrial Union of Workers v Auckland Harbour Bridge Authority* [1971] NZLR 988 at 994, per cur.

LOCAL CHARITY *See* CHARITY

LOCAL CONNECTION

References in this Part [III] to a person having a local connection with the district of a local housing authority are to his having a connection with that district—

(a) because he is or in the past was normally resident in that district and that residence is or was of his own choice; or
(b) because he is employed in that district; or
(c) because of family associations; or
(d) because of special circumstances.

(Housing Act 1985, s 61(1))

LOCAL EDUCATION AUTHORITY *See* EDUCATION

LOCAL INQUIRY

[The Highways Act 1959, Sch 1, para 9 (repealed) provided for the lodging of objections to motorway schemes and for 'local inquiries' to be held.] 'The essential characteristics of a "local inquiry", an expression which when appearing in a statute has by now acquired a special meaning as a term of legal art, are that it is held in public in the locality in which the works that are the subject of the proposed scheme are situated by a person appointed by the minister on whom the statute has conferred the power in his administrative discretion to decide whether to confirm the scheme. The subject matter of the inquiry is the objections to the proposed scheme that have been received by the minister from local authorities and from private persons in the vicinity of the proposed stretch of motorway whose interests may be adversely affected, and in consequence of which he is required by Sch 1, para 9, to hold the inquiry. The purpose of the inquiry is to provide the minister with as much information about those objections as will ensure that in reaching his decision he will have weighed the harm to local interests and private persons who may be adversely affected by the scheme against the public benefit which the scheme is likely to achieve and will not have failed to take into consideration any matters which he ought to have taken into consideration.' *Bushell v Secretary of State for the Environment* [1980] 2 All ER 608 at 612, HL, per Lord Diplock

[See now, as to inquiries, the Highways Act 1980, s 302.]

LOCAL RATE *See* RATE

LOCK-OUT

'Lock-out' has been defined as the closing of a place of employment or the suspension of work or the refusal by an employer to continue to employ any number of persons employed by him in consequence of a dispute, done with a view to compelling those persons, or to aid another employer in compelling persons employed by him, to accept terms and conditions of or affecting employment. A lock-out is lawful if the employer first gives due notice to terminate the contracts of the workers concerned. Otherwise a lock-out is likely to be a breach of contract and hence unlawful. A lock-out by several employers acting in combination may involve criminal or tortious liabilities. (47 Halsbury's Laws (4th edn) para 568)

In this Schedule, unless the context otherwise requires, 'lock-out' means the closing of a place of employment, or the suspension of work or the refusal by an employer to continue to employ any number of persons employed by him in consequence of a dispute, done with a view to compelling those persons, or to aid another employer in compelling persons employed by him, to accept terms or conditions of or affecting employment. (Employment Protection (Consolidation) Act 1978, Sch 13, para 24(1))

Australia 'A complaint was preferred . . . "For that on or about 18th March, 1907, at Yarloop and elsewhere in the said State, Millars' Karri and Jarrah Co took part in or did or was concerned in doing a matter or thing in the nature of a lock-out. . . ." In an earlier case of *The W A Supply Co Ltd v The Registrar of Friendly Societies* [(1904) 6 WALR 108], and in the course of the judgment I said this, "A strike may be defined as a refusal by the workers to continue to work for their employer unless he will give them more wages or better conditions of labour; a lock-out is the converse of a strike; it is the refusal by an employer to allow his workmen to work unless they will accept his rate of wages or the conditions of labour he imposes. In neither case is the employment finally determined, the intention of the workman in the one case and of the employer in the other being that the employment should be continued as soon as a satisfactory settlement of the matter in dispute can be arrived at".' *Amalgamated Society of Engineers (Perth Branch) v Millars' Karri & Jarrah Co* (1902) *Ltd* (1907) 9 WALR 207 at 208–211, per McMillan J

LOCOMOTIVE

In this Act 'light locomotive' and 'heavy locomotive' means a mechanically propelled vehicle which is not constructed itself to carry a load, other than excepted articles, and of which the weight unladen—

(a) in the case of a light locomotive, exceeds 7,370 but does not exceed 11,690 kilograms, and
(b) in the case of a heavy locomotive, exceeds 11,690 kilograms. (Road Traffic Regulation Act 1984, s 136)

['Excepted articles' means water, fuel, accumulators and other equipment used for the purpose of propulsion, loose tools and loose equipment.]

LOCOMOTIVE ENGINE

'The term "locomotive engine" has a well-known significance, and is used generally for an engine to draw a train of trucks or cars along a permanent or temporary set of rails.' *Murphy v Wilson & Son* (1883) 52 LJQB 524 at 525, per Pollock B

LODGER *See also* GUEST

'The landlord of the house gives only a limited enjoyment therein to the claimant. The door of the house has a lock to it, of which the claimant has not the key; his right of access therefore to the rooms in his occupation is merely permissive. It is not an occupation as owner or tenant. He is strictly an inmate or lodger.' *Pitts v Smedley* (1845) 7 Man & G 85 at 87, per Tindal CJ

'Where the owner of a house takes in a person to reside in a part of it, though such person has the exclusive possession of the rooms appropriated to him, and the uncontrolled right of ingress and egress, yet, if the owner retains his character of master of the house, the individual so occupying a part of it, occupies it as a lodger only. . . . The fact of the party having or not having a key of the outer door is not decisive of the question. If he has a key, I cannot conceive that the circumstances of other persons enjoying the same privilege, can make any difference,—he having only a right of way, which would be in no degree affected by his having it in common with others. But the question depends upon whether or not the owner of the house resides upon the premises, retaining his quality of master, and reserving to himself the general control and dominion over the whole. If he does, the inmate is a mere lodger.' *Toms v Luckett* (1847) 5 CB 23 at 38, 39, per Maule J

'Where a landlord resides in part of a house, and there is an outer door from the street, and he by himself or his servants has the control of this outer door, and undertakes the care or control of rooms let to other persons and the access to them, and those rooms themselves have not anything in the nature of an outer door, and are not structurally severed from the rest of the house, there could be little hesitation in saying that an occupier of those rooms, being part of the house, is only a lodger. On the other hand, if there be no real outer door to the street, and neither the landlord nor his servants, nor any one representing him, occupies any part of the premises, or exercises any control over any part of them, and the rooms occupied by another person are structurally severed from the rest of the house, and have an outer door to the general landing or staircase, and no one but such tenant has to exercise any care or control over the rooms or that outer door, as a general proposition, the person so occupying those rooms could not properly be said to be a lodger. It is always important, in determining whether a man is a lodger, to see whether the owner of the house retains his character of master of the house, and whether he occupies a part of it by himself or his servants, and at the same time retains the general control and dominion over the whole house; and this he may do, though he do not personally reside on the premises.' *Thompson v Ward, Ellis v Burch* (1871) LR 6 CP 327 at 360, 361, per Bovill CJ

[The Lodgers' Goods Protection Act 1871, s 1 (repealed; see now the Law of Distress Amendment Act 1908, ss 1, 9) conferred immunity from distress in respect of a lodger's property.] 'Looking at the main object of the Act, I am not satisfied that an undertenant who resides with his family and servants in certain rooms of a house other rooms of which are at the same time occupied by the tenant and his family, cannot be a lodger; though probably the Act would not apply to an undertenant who has the exclusive possession and occupation of an entire house.' *Phillips v Henson* (1877) 3 CPD 26 at 32, per Lindley J

'What . . . is the difference between the modes of occupying a room as a lodger, or as a householder? To occupy the room as a lodger, you must lodge in another man's house. There cannot be an exhaustive definition of what will make a man a lodger, but the matter has been considered very much in three cases. . . . In those cases, the distinction was made to turn upon the ownership of the key of the outer door. In one case the owner of the house had the key of the outer door, and he resided in the house [*Pitts v Smedley* (supra)]:—Held, that a person who occupied the rooms in that house was a lodger with him. In another of those cases, the owner had let part of the house, reserving no actual control over it, and he did not keep for himself the key of the outer door [*Score v Huggett* (1845) 7 Man & G 95]:—Held, that the person occupying the part of the house occupied it as a householder and not as a lodger. And the third was a case where the owner had the key of the outer door, but the person who occupied part of the house had a key also [*Wansey v Perkins* (1845) 7 Man & G 151]:—Held, that such person was a lodger.' *Bradley v Baylis* (1881) 8 QBD 195 at 234, 235, CA, per Brett LJ

'The person who takes in another to lodge [within the Lodgers' Goods Protection Act 1871 (repealed; see supra)] must retain power in and dominion over the house, as the master of a house usually does in this country. It is not absolutely necessary that he should live in or sleep in the house: he may live elsewhere, and yet reserve power in and dominion over the house, such as a master of a house does in this country usually have. If, however, he goes away, if he gives up all power of dealing with the house as master, then I do not think it is possible to say that he takes another person in to lodge with him.' *Morton v Palmer* (1881) 51 LJQB 7 at 10, CA, per Brett LJ

'It is difficult to define the difference between a tenant and a lodger; but probably it may be said with accuracy that where the landlord himself resides in the house the other inmates are lodgers because they submit themselves to his control; but where the landlord does not reside in the house, or where he occupies a separate set of rooms in the basement, or where the house is divided into separate and independent dwellings . . . the separate occupation exists which is necessary to constitute a tenancy.' *Ancketill v Baylis* (1882) 10 QBD 577 at 586, per Hannen P

'We have . . . to say what upon the whole we think the statute [Lodgers' Goods Protection Act 1871 (repealed; see supra)] meant by the term "lodger". I come to the conclusion that it meant a "lodger" in the popular sense of the word, that is, one who sleeps upon the premises. In the ordinary use of language a person of average education would not call the appellant a "lodger" because lodging in the common acceptation means living and residing at a place; and if you went further and asked what was meant by living and residence, in general the answer would be that the person fulfilled the description if he slept there, that is, if he undressed and went to bed, staying there until he rose the next morning in the usual way.' *Heawood v Bone* (1884) 13 QBD 179 at 183, DC, per Stephen J

'Lord Collins [in *Kent v Fittall* [1906] 1 KB 60] . . . says this: "It is not disputed"—by which he means that it cannot be disputed—"that in dealing with the occupation of part of a dwelling-house, if the landlord is living in the house, that fact creates a presumption that the occupation of the other part is that of a lodger rather than that of an inhabitant occupier".' *Douglas v Smith* [1907] 2 KB 568 at 575, CA, per Cozens-Hardy MR

'The general test, which has been laid down for many years, is that if the owner of a house who allows other people to live in it lives on the premises and manages the premises himself, or if the owner has a servant resident on the premises to manage them on his behalf, the other people living in the house are lodgers, whereas if he does not live in the house but lets the whole house out to various people it is a letting out of the house in tenements and the persons occupying the tenements are not lodgers but tenants.' *Honig v Redfern* [1949] 2 All ER 15 at 17, per Lord Goddard CJ

'An occupier of residential accommodation at a rent for a term is either a lodger or a tenant. The occupier is a lodger if the landlord provides attendance or services which require the landlord or his servants to exercise unrestricted access to and use of the premises. A lodger is entitled to live in the premises but cannot call the place his own. In *Allan v Liverpool Overseers* [(1874) LR 9 QB 180] Blackburn J said: "A lodger in a house, although he has the exclusive use of rooms in the house, in the sense that nobody else is to be there, and though his goods are stowed there, yet he is not in exclusive occupation in that sense, because the landlord is there for the purpose of being able, as landlords commonly do in the case of lodgings, to have his own servants to look after the house and the furniture, and has retained to himself the occupation, though he has agreed to give the exclusive enjoyment of the occupation to the lodger." If on the other hand residential accommodation is granted for a term at a rent with exclusive possession, the landlord providing neither attendance nor services, the grant is a tenancy; any express reservation to the landlord of limited rights to enter and view the state of the premises and to repair and maintain the premises only serves to emphasise the fact that the grantee is entitled to exclusive possession and is a tenant.' *Street v Mountford* [1985] 2 All ER 289 at 293, per Lord Templeman

Australia 'The general rule, that is to say in the absence of indications to the contrary, is that words are to be given their literal and grammatical meaning. . . . To ascertain the use that words receive we turn to a dictionary. . . . The primary and usual meaning of "lodger", as so defined, is "one who resides as an inmate in another person's house, paying a certain sum periodically for the accommodation" or "one who occupies an hired room in another person's house". . . . In ordinary circumstances with . . . [a] lodger . . . legal possession remains in the person who provides room or rooms. . . . He retains possession and control over rooms and means of ingress and egress, but grants licence to guests who pay, or give consideration for the privilege.' *Noblett & Mansfield v Manley* [1952] SASR 155 at 157–158, per Mayo J

LODGING HOUSE *See also* COMMON LODGING HOUSE

The keeper of a lodging house makes a previous contract for lodging for a set time, usually a week or a month, with each lodger who comes, and does not hold himself out to receive all persons in the same way as does an innkeeper. A mere lodging house keeper, therefore, is not an innkeeper. (24 Halsbury's Laws (4th edn) para 1210)

LOITER

[The Street Betting Act 1906, s 1 (repealed; see now the Betting, Gaming and Lotteries Act 1963, s 8(1)), makes the frequenting or 'loitering' in streets or public places, for the purpose of betting, an offence.] 'The term "loitering" is, perhaps, most appropriately applied with reference to a pedestrian. . . . Loitering is just travelling indolently and with frequent pauses. . . . Speaking for myself, I am quite clear that a person may loiter in a motor car.' *Williamson v Wright* 1924 SC(J) 57 at 60, per Lord Anderson

'Loitering, in my view, connotes the idea of lingering.' Ibid at 61, per Lord Alness, Lord Justice-Clerk

[A local Act made it lawful for a police constable to arrest any person whom he found between sunset and the hour of eight o'clock in the morning lying or 'loitering' in a street, etc, and not giving a satisfactory account of himself.] '"Lying" differs from "loitering" as it seems to me only in that whilst the latter word imports movement the former imports absence of movement, with perhaps a hint of attempted concealment. The Oxford Dictionary defines "loitering" in its early use as "vagrancy, vagabondage, or leading a vagabond's life"; and "loiterer" as "a vagabond or sturdy beggar".' *Ledwith v Roberts* [1937] 1 KB 232 at 268, 269, per Scott LJ

Australia 'In this setting [Police Offences Act 1953 (SA) (repealed). See now Summary Offences Act 1953–1986, s 18(2), (3)] it seems to me that the word "loiter" means no more than "tarrying", or, to use a phrase that has received judicial recognition, "hanging about". . . . I consider that, without any context, the word "loiters" does ordinarily carry the meaning lingering idly or aimlessly, and not merely lingering.' *Samuels v Stokes* [1973–4] 2 ALR 269 at 275, per Menzies J

'The word "loiter" in its ordinary sense does not connote remaining without a lawful reason. Dictionary meanings of the word include "to linger idly about a place" and "to hang about in an idle manner"; it has other senses not relevant in the present context [Police Offences Act 1953–1972 (SA), s 18]. In its natural meaning the word may suggest indolence or inactivity but it does not connote either legality or illegality; a person may loiter for a legitimate reason . . . and an unlawful purpose will not cause activity to become "loitering" if it could not otherwise be so described.' Ibid at 279, per Gibbs J

Australia 'In my opinion . . . the word "loiters" in s 7 of the Vagrancy Act 1966 [Vic] should be construed in its ordinary sense of lingering idly or hanging about idly, subject to the qualification that conduct which in some persons would not properly be described as loitering, may become loitering in the case of other persons where their conduct is accompanied by the existence of an unlawful purpose.' *Wynne v Lockyer* [1978] VR 279 at 286, per Harris J

Canada [The Criminal Code 1953–54, c 51, s 162 (see now RSC 1970, c C–34, s 173) makes it an offence to 'loiter' or prowl at night upon the property of another person, without lawful excuse.] 'After carefully considering the authorities upon the meaning of the word "loiters" in other contexts, the learned judge [in the court below] concluded that in s 162 the word means hanging around or lingering about, and in that sense the appellants were loitering upon the wife's property. The appellants challenge that interpretation and submit that standard dictionaries show the word "loiters" means to linger idly along the way or about a place, or to spend time idly; consequently since the appellants were spending their time on the property for a lawful purpose [surveillance by private detectives], they cannot be said to have been loitering; that their actions are best described by the word "watching". In my opinion the existence or absence of a real purpose is irrelevant to the question of whether there is loitering in fact under s 162 [and therefore the appellants' object was not a lawful excuse within the sections].' *R v Andston and Petrie* (1960) 32 WWR 329 at 330, BCCA, per Davey JA

New Zealand 'The bye-law in question—No 113 of Bye-laws No 1—is in these words: "No person shall loiter, stand, or remain in or upon any street, private street, footpath, or footway, or use the same for such time or in such manner as shall have the effect of obstructing or disturbing the free use thereof, or the access to any house or building in or near thereto." . . . Mr Martin [counsel for the applicant] contends that the bye-law is uncertain, because no definition is given of the word "loiter". Like many other words, this word has several meanings, according to the subject to which it is applied. Applied to street traffic, and used in conjunction with the words "stand or remain", there can be no doubt, in my opinion, that the dictionary definition applicable to the word is "to be slow in moving". In my opinion, therefore, it cannot be said that this meaning in this bye-law is uncertain.' *Davidson v Auckland Corpn* (1904) 24 NZLR 250 at 252–254, per Edwards J; also reported 7 GLR 357 at 358

LONDON

The area comprising the areas of the London boroughs, the City and the Temples shall constitute an administrative area to be known as Greater London (London Government Act 1963, s 2)

[By ibid, s 89 'the City' means the City of London, and 'the Temples' means the Inner Temple and the Middle Temple.]

'The question turns upon the construction of the articles of agreement of December, 1835, by which the defendant stipulated that he would not carry on the business of a surgeon-dentist in London, or any of the towns or places in England or Scotland, where the plaintiffs might have been practising before the expiration of his term of service; and the point to be decided is, whether Great Russell Street, in the county of Middlesex, be within London, as it is to be understood in this indenture. . . . We find nothing in the context to prevent us from construing the word "London" in its proper sense, as the city of London.' *Mallan v May* (1844) 13 M & W 511 at 517, 518, per Pollock CB

LONG LEASE

For the purposes aforesaid [i.e. the interpretation of Sch 9], the expression 'long lease' means a lease in the case of which the portion of the term for which it was granted remaining unexpired at the end of the financial year is not less than fifty years, the expression 'short lease' means a lease which is not a long lease and the expression 'lease' includes an agreement for a lease. (Companies Act 1985, Sch 9, Part V, para 34)

LONG TENANCY

In this Part [Part I] of this Act [rights as to enfranchisement and extension of long leaseholds] 'long tenancy' means, subject to the provisions of this section, a tenancy granted for a term of years certain exceeding twenty-one years, whether or not the tenancy is (or may become) terminable before the end of that term by notice given by or to the tenant or by re-entry, forfeiture or otherwise, and includes a tenancy for a term fixed by law under a grant with a covenant or obligation for perpetual renewal unless it is a tenancy by sub-demise from one which is not a long tenancy. (Leasehold Reform Act 1967, s 3)

LOOTING

Any person subject to military law who—

(a) steals from, or with intent to steal, searches the person of anyone killed, wounded or captured in the course of warlike operations or killed, injured or detained in the course of operations undertaken by Her Majesty's forces for the preservation of law and order or otherwise in aid of the civil authorities, or

(b) steals any property which has been left exposed or unprotected in consequence of any such operations as are mentioned in paragraph (a) above, or

(c) takes otherwise than for the public service any vehicle, equipment or stores abandoned by the enemy,

shall be guilty of looting and liable to imprisonment or any less punishment authorised by this Act. (Army Act 1955, s 30, as amended by Armed Forces Act 1971, s 6)

[Similar definitions will be found in the Air Force Act 1955 and the Naval Discipline Act 1957.]

LOP

[The Highway Act 1835 (repealed; see now the Highways Act 1980, s 136(1)) empowered justices to order that trees prejudicing a highway should be 'lopped'.] I think it would be mere pedantry in the present case not to take notice of the well-known meaning which persons in the country conversant with the cutting of trees would attach to the word used in this Act of Parliament. . . . Two words, "lopping" and "topping", which mean different things, are used in the country with respect to the cutting of trees. The Act gives directions with respect to cutting trees near a highway to the person who has to cut them, and to the magistrates who may order them to be cut, and uses only one of those words, namely "lop". That word is well known in the country to mean cutting off the branches of a tree; "topping" is the cutting off its top.' *Unwin v Hanson* [1891] 2 QB 115 at 119, 120, CA, per Lord Esher MR

LORD OF THE MANOR *See* MANOR

LORDS *See* PARLIAMENT; PEERAGE

LORRY *See* MOTOR CAR; VEHICLE

LOSS

'Gain' and 'loss' are to be construed as extending only to gain or loss in money or other property, but as extending to any such gain or loss whether temporary or permanent; and—
(i) 'gain' includes a gain by keeping what one has, as well as a gain by getting what one has not; and
(ii) 'loss' includes a loss by not getting what one might get, as well as a loss by parting with what one has.
(Theft Act 1968, s 34(2)(a))

Canada '"Loss" may mean the being deprived of, or the failure to keep something or the fact that something can no longer be found or, on the other hand, it may mean the detriment or disadvantage involved in being deprived of something, or simply pecuniary detriment or disadvantage. I am giving in substance the pertinent dictionary definitions from the Oxford Dictionary.

Now it is quite clear that "loss" here [for purposes of bill of lading conditions] means loss of the goods; it does not mean loss in the sense of pecuniary disadvantage sustained by the shipper by reason of the carrier's default. I do not see any reason why it should not be read in the sense of "being deprived of"; and I see no reason why the scope of the phrase should be so restricted as to exclude "loss" in that sense by reason of misdelivery.' *Premier Lumber Co v Grand Trunk Pacific Railway Co* [1923] SCR 84 at 91, SCC, per Duff J

By fire *See* FIRE

By trustee

[The Trustee Act 1925, s 30 provides that a trustee shall not be answerable for the acts, receipts, neglects, or defaults of any other trustee, etc, nor for any other 'loss' unless the same happens through his own wilful default.] 'As regards s 30 of the Act of 1925, the only words upon which Mr Topham [counsel] relied were the concluding words of the section: "Nor for any other loss, unless the same happens through his own wilful default." In my opinion, those words in s 30 are not intended to apply and do not apply to the case of a trustee paying money away to the wrong *cestui que trust*.' *Re Windsor Steam Coal Co (1901) Ltd* [1929] 1 Ch 151 at 169, 170, CA, per Russell LJ

In contract

[A condition on a railway station cloak-room ticket provided that the railway company should not be answerable for 'loss' or detention of any article or property exceeding the value of £5 unless the true value was declared at the time of the deposit and a special charge paid.] '"Loss" must mean "loss by the company", and if the company deliver an article to a wrong person, they, in the ordinary acceptation of the term, lose it.' *Skipwith v Great Western Rly Co* (1888) 59 LT 520 at 522, DC, per Wills J

Loss or damage

'Loss or damage' includes, in relation to persons, loss of life and personal injury. (Civil Aviation Act 1982, s 105(1))

[Goods were loaded on a barge under a contract for carriage by which the barge owner was exempt from liability for any 'loss or damage to goods which can be covered by insurance.'] 'When a clause in such a contract as this is capable of two constructions, one of which will make it applicable where there is no negligence on the part of the carrier or his servants, and the other will make it applicable where there is such negligence, it requires special words to make the clause cover non-liability in case of negligence. . . . There are a number of cases in which the words of a clause of exemption have had to be construed in their ordinary commercial and business sense, and where no other construction could be put upon them, as, for instance, the case of *The Teutonia* [(1872) LR 4 PC 171] though that decision may have hereafter to be considered, where the words were "however occasioned", which were held to include every cause of loss. . . . We have to consider whether the words "we will not be liable for any loss or damage to goods which can be covered by insurance" bring the case within the class in which the negligence of the carrier or his servants is so clearly referred to that we ought to hold that there is a sufficient statement of an intention to exempt the carrier from liability for negligence. . . . It is of course quite possible to construe the words "any loss of or damage to goods which can be covered by insurance" as including everything, because practically everything can be so covered, and . . . a great many policies of insurance would include such a loss as that which arose in this case. The question, however, is not whether these words could be made to cover such a loss, but whether in a contract for carriage they include, on a reasonable construction, an exemption from negligence on the part of the carrier. We have only to look at the case to which I have referred, and in particular to *Sutton v Ciceri* [(1890) 15 App Cas 144] to see that the words of this contract can receive a contractual and businesslike construction and have effect without including in the exemption the consequences of the negligence of the carrier. That being so, the principle that to exempt the carrier from liability for the consequences of his negligence there must be words that make it clear that the parties intended that there should be such an exemption is applicable to this case, and the learned judge was right in holding that the contract does not exempt the defendants from liability for their own negligence.' *Price & Co v Union Lighterage Co* [1904] 1 KB 412 at 414–416, CA, per Lord Alverstone CJ

[A bond entered into by a company required it (the company) to make good any 'loss or damage' occasioned to the estate of a bankrupt by any default in the performance of his duties by the trustee in bankruptcy.] 'In my opinion the loss or damage of the estate of the bankrupt means the difference between the amount of the estate if there had been no default and the amount having regard to the default.' *Board of Trade v Employers' Liability Assurance Corpn Ltd* [1910] 2 KB 649 at 656, CA, per Buckley LJ

[The plaintiffs, the owners of the steam-barge *Millie*, sought a decree of limitation or liability for 'loss or damage', within the Merchant Shipping (Liability of Shipowners and Others) Act 1900, in respect of a collision in which the *Millie* was sunk, obstructing the fairway of the Manchester Ship Canal.] 'It is evidently arguable that, although expenses may not be loss or damage strictly so called, equally the right of the canal company to an unobstructed fairway has in this case been interfered with, and it is no great stretch of language to describe the price of restoring that right as a form of a loss or damage.' *The Millie* [1940] P 2 at 8, per Langton J

Loss or forfeiture

[The lessee of a public-house covenanted to insure against the licence being 'lost or forfeited'. The justices refused to renew the licence on the ground of redundancy.] 'In the absence of any further context the words "lost or forfeited" do not meet this case. "Forfeited" plainly does not. "Forfeited" is used in the sense that the tenant shall not do anything to forfeit the licence, and "lost" may mean lost by reason of the state of the premises. "Lost or forfeited" does not seem to me to meet the case of non-renewal on the ground of redundancy.' *Wootton v Lichfield Brewery Co* [1916] 1 Ch 44 at 55, CA, per Lord Cozens-Hardy MR

Of ship *See also* TOTAL LOSS

[The Merchant Shipping Act 1894, s 158 (repealed; see now Merchant Shipping Act 1970, s 15) provided that where the service of a seaman terminated before the date contemplated in his agreement, by reason of the wreck or 'loss' of the ship, etc, he should be entitled to wages up to the time of such termination, but not for any longer period.] 'I think that the word "loss" in s 158 is not used in any technical sense, but as meaning loss by perils of the seas. In the present case, the ship having been violently seized, and never having been returned to her owner, there is present every element essential to such a loss. If the vessel had been arrested and in some way held in suspense and subsequently returned to her owner, I should not go so far as to say that that would constitute a loss within this section; but having regard to all the facts, that the seizure was unlawful, was final, and was by force, I am of opinion that there was a loss within s 158, irrespective of whether the ship was subsequently destroyed or not.' *Sivewright v Allen* [1906] 2 KB 81 at 90, per Darling J

'The owners of the *Cairnbahn* suffered "damage" because their ship ran into the hopper which was in tow of the tug *Nunthorpe*. They suffered "loss" because the owners of the hopper sued them for her injuries and won. They suffered both by the fault of the two vessels, the *Cairnbahn* and the *Nunthorpe* or rather by the faulty navigation of those in command of them. Why does not s 1(1) of the

Maritime Conventions Act 1911 [which lays down the rule as to division of loss where, by the fault of two or more vessels, damage or loss is caused to one or more of those vessels], apply to this case? Though damage may be caused to a vessel, loss cannot be, nor is the phrase "damage is caused to a vessel" apt to express simply that the vessel is damaged. Loss is caused to the owners and charterers of the vessel, and damage is caused to them too when the vessel is damaged. I think the section regulates rights and liabilities between parties in fault and extends to pecuniary prejudice, which may accrue, legally and not too remotely, to persons interested in vessels by reason of the faulty navigation of persons for whom they are responsible. The word "loss" is wide enough to include that form of pecuniary prejudice which consists in compensating third parties for wrong done to them by the fault of persons for whose misconduct the party prejudiced must answer. It covers the sum recovered by the owners of the hopper against the owners of the *Cairnbahn*. To say that damage to the hopper is not loss to the *Cairnbahn* so as to be loss or damage caused to one or more of "those vessels", namely, those vessels which are in fault, is to make this remedial legislation unexpectedly onesided.' *The Cairnbahn* [1914] P 25 at 32, 33, CA, per Lord Sumner

See, generally, 43 Halsbury's Laws (4th edn) paras 964 et seq.

'I think that the loss referred to in this section [the Merchant Shipping Act 1894, s 158 (see supra)] does not mean merely the loss of the use of the ship, but physical loss. Physical loss, however, is not to be confined to the foundering of the ship, or such like, but physical loss as defined in the judgment of Maule J in *Moss v Smith* [(1850) 9 CB 94 at 103] applicable generally to mercantile contracts, and approved of by Lord Blackburn in *Dahl v Nelson, Donkin & Co* [(1881) 6 App Cas 38 at 52], Maule J said: "It may be physically possible to repair the ship, but at an enormous cost: and there also the loss would be total; for, in matters of business, a thing is said to be impossible when it is not practicable; and a thing is impracticable when it can only be done at an excessive or unreasonable cost. . . . If a ship sustains such extensive damage, that it would not be reasonably practicable to repair her—seeing that the expense of repairs would be such that no man of common sense would incur the outlay—the ship is said to be totally lost".' *Horlock v Beal* [1916] 1 AC 486 at 499, per Lord Atkinson

Proved loss

New Zealand 'Proved losses fall within s 121(1) [of the Accident Compensation Act 1972, consolidated by Accident Compensation Act 1982, see s 20], as a head of claim distinct from actual and reasonable expenses, provided of course that they meet the strict criteria. Read as a whole the subsection is plainly concerned to impose what counsel for the respondent called a stern test. It is a more stringent test than has ever prevailed as to remoteness of damage at common law in either tort or contract. *Directness* of causation is not enough. As well the loss must *necessarily* result from the injury. . . . Section 121(1) also stipulates that the losses must be proved, thereby indicating that prospective or hypothetical losses are not enough. It must be proved that the loss has actually been suffered; the adjective harmonises with *actual* and reasonable expenses. If the strict criteria laid down in the subsection are brought to bear, the question in any given case is one of fact and degree.' *Accident Compensation Commission v Nelson* [1979] 2 NZLR 464 at 466, per Richmond P and Cooke J

Under policy of insurance

[Under a policy of insurance underwriters agreed to indemnify a bank against all losses sustained by reason of securities of a specified description, currency and coin being lost, stolen, mislaid, misappropriated, or made away with. The bank sustained a loss through being put into a position of debtor to a customer by reason of the customer's fraud.] 'The action is brought by a bank against an underwriter under a policy, and the bank's claim, when looked at, really amounts to a contention that, under this policy, they are entitled to an indemnity against all banking losses which may occur to them in respect of any contracts they may have been induced to enter into by the fraud of a third person. I cannot so read the policy. It seems to me to contemplate, and to contemplate solely, a loss or abstraction of physical things taken away from the bank. . . . The policy contemplates certain known or specific securities being taken away from the plaintiffs by fraud, and . . . it does not cover a case where the bankers are induced by fraud to enter into a contract with somebody else.' *Century Bank of City of New*

York v Young (1914) 84 LJKB 385 at 386, 387, CA, per Lord Cozens-Hardy MR

'Mere temporary deprivation would not under ordinary circumstances constitute a loss [under a policy of insurance]. On the other hand complete deprivation amounting to a certainty that the goods could never be recovered is not necessary to constitute a loss. It is between these two extremes that the difficult cases lie, and no assistance can be derived from putting cases which are clearly on the one side or the other of the dividing line between the two.' *Moore v Evans* [1917] 1 KB 458 at 471, CA, per Bankes LJ; on appeal, [1918] AC 185, HL

'Uncertainty as to recovery of the thing insured is, in my opinion, in non-marine matters the main consideration on the question of loss. In this connection it is, of course, true that a thing may be mislaid and yet not lost, but, in my opinion, if a thing has been mislaid and is missing or has disappeared and a reasonable time has elapsed to allow of diligent search and of recovery, and such diligent search has been made and has been fruitless, then the thing may properly be said to be lost.' *Holmes v Payne* [1930] 2 KB 301 at 310, per Roche J

LOSS LEADER

The reference in this section to the use of goods as loss leaders is a reference to a resale of the goods effected by the dealer, not for the purpose of making a profit on the sale of those goods, but for the purpose of attracting to the establishment at which the goods are sold customers likely to purchase other goods or otherwise for the purpose of advertising the business of the dealer.

A sale of goods shall not be treated for the purposes of this section as the use of those goods as loss leaders—

(a) where the goods are sold by the dealer at a genuine seasonal or clearance sale, not having been acquired by the dealer for the purpose of being resold as mentioned in this section; or
(b) where the goods are resold as mentioned in this section with the consent of the manufacturer of the goods or, in the case of goods made to the design of a supplier or to the order and bearing the trade mark of a supplier, of that supplier.

(Resale Price Act 1976, s 13(2), (3))

LOST MODERN GRANT

The method of claiming easements under the doctrine of a lost modern grant was the outcome of the facility with which claims under the common law doctrine of prescription were capable of being defeated merely by showing that the right did not or could not exist at any one point of time since the commencement of legal memory. By founding a claim on the presumption of a grant at some comparatively modern date, this ready method of defence is evaded, since proof of the non-existence of the right prior to the date of the alleged modern grant is *ex hypothesi* immaterial. The courts, following their usual rule in favour of the presumption that an alleged right had a legal origin when proof of long enjoyment can be shown, have readily adopted this convenient fiction. (14 Halsbury's Laws (4th edn) para 89)

LOST OR NOT LOST

'The simple question is, whether it is any answer to an action on a policy on goods lost or not lost, that the interest in them was not acquired until after the loss. We are of opinion that it is not. Such a policy is clearly a contract of indemnity against all past, as well as all future losses sustained by the assured, in respect of the interest insured, by the perils named in the policy.' *Sutherland v Pratt* (1843) 12 LJ Ex 235 at 240, per cur.

LOT

In this Act 'lot to which this Act applies' means a lot consisting of or including one or more prescribed articles; and 'prescribed articles' means any plate, plated articles, linen, china, glass, books, pictures, prints, furniture, jewellery, articles of household or personal use or ornament or any musical or scientific instrument or apparatus. (Mock Auctions Act 1961, s 3)

United States 'Lot' means a parcel or a single article which is the subject matter of a separate sale or delivery, whether or not it is sufficient to perform the contract. (Uniform Commercial Code 1978, s 2-105(5))

LOTTERY

A lottery has been described as a scheme for distributing prizes by lot or chance. In its simplest form the adventurers contribute to a fund which they agree among themselves shall be unequally divided upon the happening of an agreed event. The organiser of such a scheme may or may not himself be an adventurer, and, in considering whether a lottery is set up or maintained, it is unnecessary to consider whether or not the organiser is to make a profit out of the subscriptions. As between the adventurers, the agreement, when the lottery takes this simple form, seems to contain an element of gambling, for all stand to lose the amount of their subscriptions in favour of the winner. This gambling element does not appear ever to be wholly absent, but it need not be common to all the adventurers; it is enough that some of them stand to lose. Therefore, if some of the adventurers have, however indirectly, contributed to the fund out of which the prizes are to be paid, they risk the amount of their contributions, and in such a case it is immaterial that others who have contributed nothing may win the prize. To constitute a lottery, it is not essential that there should be a prize fund provided the scheme has the overall object of the distribution of money by chance.

Conversely, it is not essential that the fund out of which the prizes are provided should consist only or at all of sums contributed by the adventurers; nor does the fact that every adventurer in any event obtains some or even full value for his subscription prevent the scheme from being a lottery. When the chances of a prize are obtained wholly gratuitously, and when, therefore, none of the adventurers risks anything, the scheme is not a lottery. However, a free competition, success in which does not depend to a substantial degree upon the exercise of skill, may constitute an unlawful prize competition, although it would not be a lottery. (4 Halsbury's Laws (4th edn) para 4)

'A lottery has been compendiously defined as a scheme for the distribution of money by chance. It usually, if not always, takes the form of the creation of a fund by the participants in the lottery, who buy tickets or pay subscriptions in consideration of an offer by the promoters to award them a prize on some contingency the happening whereof depends on chance.' *Barnes v Strathern* 1929 SC(J) 41 at 46, per Lord Clyde, Lord Justice-General

'In my opinion a scheme which is a lottery if the prizes are in the hands of the promoters for them to give to the winners does not cease to be a lottery if the scheme provides that each participant shall send a contribution direct to the winner, a contribution to his prize. I entirely agree with the conclusion of Griffiths J who delivered the judgment of the Divisional Court with which the other members of the court agreed, when he said: "Whereas it is true that most lotteries involve a scheme which creates an identifiable prize fund, I can find no reason to conclude that this is an essential feature of a lottery, provided the scheme achieves the overall object of the distribution of money by chance".' *Atkinson v Murrell* [1972] 2 All ER 1131 at 1134, HL, per Viscount Dilhorne

'A lottery is the distribution of prizes by chance where the persons taking part in the operation, or a substantial number of them, make a payment or consideration in return for obtaining their chance of a prize. There are really three points one must look for in deciding whether a lottery has been established; first of all, the distribution of prizes; secondly, the fact that this was to be done by means of a chance; and thirdly, that there must be some actual contribution made by the participants in return for them obtaining a chance to take part in the lottery. It must not be entirely forgotten in the construction of these Acts of Parliament [see now the Lotteries and Amusements Act 1976] that the evil which the lottery law has sought to prevent was the evil which existed where poor people with only a few pence to feed their children would go and put these few pence into a lottery and lose them, and this sociologically was a bad thing. It is for that reason—the reason that that is the mischief aimed at—that the lotteries have always required the third factor to which I have referred, namely that there should be some contribution from the participant, or from a substantial number of the participants, in return for obtaining a chance.' *Reader's Digest Assocn Ltd v Williams* [1976] 3 All ER 737 at 739, per Lord Widgery CJ

[A scheme was devised by a tobacco company whereby purchasers of a certain brand of cigarettes would find in every packet a card which might give entitlement to a cash prize. No charge was made beyond the normal price of the cigarettes.] 'The Act [Lotteries and Amusements Act 1976] provides no definition of lotteries. The draftsman would, however, choose his words against the background of decided cases, of which there is no shortage. There is no dispute between the parties as to the elements broadly speaking which have to be proved. First, there must be a distribution of prizes; secondly, that distribution must depend on chance; thirdly, the customer or participant must give some form of payment or consideration for the chance. The word "contribution" is sometimes used. That is equally correct if it is used simply as a synonym for payment. What is not required is that there should be any contribution by the participant to the prize-fund: see *Atkinson v Murrell* [supra]. The only point at issue is what may constitute the necessary payment, consideration or contribution . . . The whole object of the scheme was to induce him [the purchaser] to ask for a special packet of the respondents' King Size cigarettes and hand over 57p to the tobacconist. The fact that it may not be possible to ascribe any part of that price to the value of the chance so obtained does not affect the matter. Whether one calls it payment or contribution or consideration it seems to me as a matter of first impression at least that the purchase of the cigarettes is indeed the consideration in return for which the card changes hands. That makes the scheme a lottery.' *Imperial Tobacco Ltd v A-G* [1980] 1 All ER 866 at 880, HL, per Lord Lane

Canada 'The sufficiency of the information [that the accused unlawfully sold "lottery" tickets contrary to the Criminal Code, s 236(b)] depends upon the significance or connotation of the word "lottery". As used in the information it is an adjective—it narrows or defines the class of tickets and might properly be converted into a phrase—tickets for a lottery. I have consulted several dictionaries and find the definition of the word "lottery" to be fairly uniform and includes: (1) A scheme for the distribution of prizes by lot or chance; especially a scheme by which one or more prizes are distributed by chance among persons who have paid or promised a consideration for a chance to win them, usually as determined by the numbers on tickets as drawn from a lottery wheel; (2) allotment or distribution of anything by fate or chance; a procedure or scheme for distribution of prizes by lot; (3) the drawing of lots.' *R v Hing Lee Yen* [1947] 1 WWR 611 at 614, Sask KB, per McNiven J

[The word 'lottery' is not used in the present section, s 179 (b) of 1953–54 (Can.) c 51.]

New Zealand 'The only point to which we think it necessary to refer is [counsel's] contention [for the appellant] that the word "lottery" is not properly applicable to any scheme in which prizes are gained independently of and without reference to the contributions of those taking part in it. No such distinction was attempted to be made in any of the cases [previously cited], nor is it apparent in any of the definitions of lotteries in cases and statutes, a number of which are given in the American and English Encyclopædia of Law [2nd edn, IX, p 588].' *Joe Gee v Williams* (1907) 26 NZLR 1016 at 1023; per cur.; also reported 9 GLR 658 at 661

New Zealand [A competition was carried on by customers of a hotel. Each competitor selected the names of eight horses running in the eight races at a race meeting, and paid a contribution in money. Prizes were awarded on a points system and were based on the total amount available for distribution.] 'Though in a sense it could be said that the distribution of the money was dependent upon the results of the races run, strictly and actually the event or contingency in respect of which the money was to be distributed was not the horse-race, but the competitor's ability to forecast the results. . . . It has been held that the word "lottery" denotes a distribution of money by chance and nothing but chance, that is, by doing that which is equivalent to drawing lots; that if merit or skill play any part in determining the distribution it is not a lottery; *Hall v Cox* [[1899] 1 QB 198]; *Scott v Director of Public Prosecutions* [[1914] 2 KB 868]. . . . In my opinion, it is impossible, in the present case, to affirm that the distribution of the money to the successful competitors was determined purely by chance.' *McComish v Alty* [1955] NZLR 172 at 174, per Gresson J

Local lottery

In this Act 'local lottery' means a lottery promoted by a local authority. (Lotteries and Amusements Act 1976, s 6(1))

[Such lotteries must be promoted in Great Britain in accordance with a scheme approved by the local authority, and the scheme is registered with the Gaming Board for Great Britain before any tickets or chances are sold: ibid, s 6(2)]

Private lottery

In this Act 'private lottery' means a lottery in Great Britain which is promoted for, and in which the sale of tickets or chances by the promoters, is confined to, either—

(a) members of one society established and conducted for purposes not connected with gaming, betting or lotteries; or

(b) persons all of whom work on the same premises; or
(c) persons all of whom reside on the same premises and which is promoted by persons each of whom is a person to whom under the foregoing provisions of this subsection tickets or chances may be sold by the promoters and, in the case of a lottery promoted for the members of a society is a person authorised in writing by the governing body of the society to promote the lottery.

(Lotteries and Amusements Act 1976, s 4(1))

[Private lotteries are subject to conditions, as e.g. that the price of every ticket shall be the same and that no tickets shall be sent through the post: ibid, s 4(3).]

Small lottery

[A lottery promoted as an incident of a bazaar, sale of work, fete, dinner, dance, sporting or athletic event, etc, subject to certain conditions, as e.g. that the whole proceeds of the entertainment (after deducting permissible expenses) shall be devoted to purposes other than private gain; and that none of the prizes shall be money prizes. See the Lotteries and Amusement Act 1976, s 3.]

Society's lottery

In this Act 'society's lottery' means a lottery promoted on behalf of a society which is established and conducted wholly or mainly for one or more of the following purposes, that is to say—
(a) charitable purposes;
(b) participation in support of athletic sports or games or cultural activities;
(c) purposes which are not described in paragraph (a) or (b) above but are neither purposes of private gain nor purposes of any commercial undertaking.

(Lotteries and Amusements Act 1976, s 5(1))

LOUDSPEAKER

[A local Act provided that no person should use a 'loudspeaker' for the purpose of advertising in the streets.] 'What is a loudspeaker? A loudspeaker is, in my view, an apparatus which is electrically driven for the purpose of reproducing sound over a wide area. It was suggested at one time in the course of the case that "loudspeaker" is, by inference, limited to an apparatus which reproduces speech, but I have no doubt that that limited construction is wrong. . . . The loudspeaker does not cease to be a loudspeaker because it is used for the reproduction of music.' *Reynolds v John* [1956] 1 All ER 306 at 309, per Ashworth J

LOW RENT

For purposes of this Part [Part I] of this Act [Enfranchisement and Extension of Long Leaseholds] a tenancy of any property is a tenancy at a low rent at any time when rent is not payable under the tenancy in respect of the property at a yearly rate equal to or more than two-thirds of the rateable value of the property on the appropriate day or, if later, the first day of the term. (Leasehold Reform Act 1967, s 4)

LOYALTY

'Attachment to the person of the reigning Sovereign does not complete the idea of loyalty. That comprehensive term includes within its meaning, not only affection to the person, but also to the office, of the King; not only attachment to royalty, but as the word itself imports, attachment to the law and to the constitution of the realm; and he who would by force or by fraud endeavour to prostrate that law and constitution (though he may retain his affection for its head), can boast but an imperfect and spurious species of loyalty.' *R v O'Connell* (1844) 7 ILR 261 at 300, per Crampton J

LUGGAGE

Ordinary luggage

'The obligation of a railway company, or other carrier of passengers, to carry the luggage of a passenger being limited to personal luggage, it follows that it is only in respect of what properly falls under the denomination of personal luggage, or has been accepted by the carrier as such, that the liability to carry safely, irrespective of negligence, attaches. . . . The term "ordinary luggage" being thus confined to that which is personal to the passenger, and carried for his use and convenience, it follows that what is carried for the purposes of business, such as merchandise or the like, or for larger or ulterior purposes, such as articles of furniture or household goods, would not come within the description of ordinary luggage unless accepted as such by the carrier.'

Macrow v Great Western Rly Co (1871) LR 6 QB 612 at 616, 618, 619, 622, per cur.

[A passenger sought to have a bicycle carried free of charge as 'ordinary luggage' within the meaning of a railway company's Act.] 'I am clearly of opinion that a bicycle cannot be considered to be "ordinary luggage" within the meaning of this definition. . . . I think there are certain requirements which must exist in order that the thing may be ordinary luggage; first of all, that it must be for the passenger's personal use; and next, that it must be for use in connection with the journey, which, I understand, means that it must be something that is habitually taken by the person when he is travelling, for use, not merely during the actual journey, but for use during the time he is away from home.' *Britten v Great Northern Rly Co* [1899] 1 QB 243 at 247, 248, per Channell J

'The question raised is whether a violoncello carried by a violoncello player by train, for his professional and not personal use, comes within the words "personal or ordinary luggage". I am not going to give a definition of "personal or ordinary luggage", but I am going to take the definition of Chief Justice Cockburn that "ordinary luggage is that which is personal to the passenger and carried for his use or convenience"—*Macrow v Great Western Rly Company* [supra]. I do not say that a violoncello could never be "ordinary luggage", but in this case it clearly is not.' *Great Western Rly Co v Evans* (1921) 38 TLR 166 at 167, per Horridge J

See, generally, 5 Halsbury's Laws (4th edn) paras 390–392.

Personal luggage

'I think we must confine the definition of personal luggage . . . to that description of goods which passengers usually carry as part of their luggage.' *Hudston v Midland Rly Co* (1869) LR 4 QB 366 at 371, per Lush J

[The plaintiff signed a railway company's receipt, which exempted the company from damage to 'personal luggage' arising through negligence or delay.] 'The plaintiff has signed the receipt, and must therefore be taken to have agreed as therein stated. Next, the unpacked invalid chair is not personal luggage any more than a carriage or a horse could be considered personal luggage.' *Cusack v London & North Western Rly Co* (1891) 7 TLR 452 at 453, DC, per A L Smith J

[The question was whether theatrical clothing belonging to an actor was 'personal luggage'.] 'It is . . . suggested that these articles are personal luggage, and that personal luggage is whatever a passenger takes with him for his personal use or convenience according to the habits or wants of the particular class to which he belongs. I . . . accept that definition, which is laid down by Chief Justice Cockburn in *Macrow v Great Western Railway Company* [supra], and followed in *Jenkyns v Southampton Steam Packet Company* [[1919] 2 KB 135]; but the definition does not include commercial luggage. These theatrical properties are intended for the plaintiff's business and not for his personal convenience.' *Gilbey v Great Northern Rly Co* (1920) 36 TLR 562 at 562, per Shearman J

'In my judgment, the word "pleasure" is used in this policy in contradistinction to "business", and the words "personal luggage" in contradistinction to "merchandise".' *Piddington v Co-operative Insurance Society Ltd* [1934] 2 KB 236 at 238, per Lawrence J

'I can find nothing which shows that, where a guest comes with an article of jewellery to a hotel, and has it in his possession at the hotel, the innkeeper's lien does not attach to that property. It seems to me that, if a person takes jewellery to the hotel, or acquires it during his residence there and takes it to the hotel, there is no more reason why the lien of an innkeeper should not attach to that property than to the clothes which the guest takes with him. It is not a question whether it is "baggage" or "luggage" in the sense in which those words are generally used. The lien attaches to the property or the chattels which the guest brings to the hotel in his character as a guest. . . . I want to say one thing about the view which was taken by the Divisional Court. . . . The Lord Chief Justice, apparently, considered the handing over of the ring as an entirely separate and independent transaction amounting to a pledge. With all respect I am unable to agree. The lien attaches to property, contained in luggage, although the innkeeper does not know what goods are contained in the luggage, and it attaches although the occasion for exercising it does not arise until the guest has incurred a debt, and has been presented with a bill, and seeks to leave the hotel without paying the bill. It seems clear in this case, that the justices could find that this ring was brought into the hotel by the guest in his capacity and character as a guest, and, therefore, whether the innkeepers knew it was there or not, does not matter. The lien attached to it and, as soon as the innkeepers knew of the existence of the ring, they could exercise their lien on it. It makes no difference in law whether the guest produced the ring and said: "There you are. I owe you a debt and you can exercise your lien on this"; or whether the innkeeper laid his hand on it and said: "I am going to exercise my lien on this".' *Marsh v Police Comr* [1945] KB 43 at 46, 47, CA, per Lord Goddard

'I agree. Lord Caldecote CJ [in the court below] said: "I base my judgment on the view which I take that the ring had never been received as part of the guest's luggage." On the facts . . . it was open to the justices to find that the ring was received as part of the guest's luggage. Nobody doubts—as certainly it was not doubted by the learned judges in the Divisional Court—that a ring may be part of a guest's luggage. A woman's ring may be part of a male guest's luggage.' Ibid at 48, per du Parcq LJ

[*See* now the Hotel Proprietors Act 1956, s 2(2).]

LUNACY *See* MENTAL DISORDER

LYING DAYS

[A charterparty contained the following clause: 'Freight to be paid in cash, loading and discharging the ship as fast as the steamer can work, but a minimum of seven days to be allowed merchants, and ten days on demurrage, over and above the said lying days, at £25 per day.'] 'Reading the whole clause together, "loading and discharging as fast as the steamer can work, but a minimum of seven days to be allowed merchants", the lying days must mean working days.' *Commercial SS Co v Boulton* (1875) LR 10 QB 346 at 347, per Lush J

M

MACHINERY *See also* DANGEROUS MACHINERY

'Machinery' includes any driving-belt. (Factories Act 1961, s 176)

'The case turns substantially on the construction of the words "any machinery" in the first line of s 14(1) of the Act [Factories Act] of 1937 [repealed; see now the Factories Act 1961, s 14(1)]. Construed quite literally, these words would, no doubt, include almost anything, for instance, a bicycle or motor car casually left on any premises. But the Act applies only to factories (s 149 [see now s 172 of the Act of 1961]). A "factory" connotes a place in which things are made, and by the definition in s 151 of the present Act [see s 175 of the Act of 1961] it includes a place where they are "repaired", "adapted for sale", and the like. When in such a statute "machinery" of, or in, such a factory is spoken of, prima facie the expression surely relates to the machinery by which the things in question are made, repaired, or adapted for sale, and not to the things themselves, even if those things themselves consist also of machinery.' *Parvin v Morton Machine Co Ltd* [1952] 1 All ER 670 at 673, HL, per Lord Asquith of Bishopstone (also reported in [1952] AC 515 at 523, 524)

'It is not, in my opinion, to be assumed that every part of a machine is a part of machinery. That word is not defined in the Factories Act, and its ordinary meaning must be given to it. A crane can be described as a machine but no one would say that the seat on which the crane driver sits was part of the machinery of the crane; nor would it be right to describe the body of a motor car as part of the machinery of a car.' *British Railways Board v Liptrot* [1967] 2 All ER 1072 at 1077, HL, per Viscount Dilhorne

New Zealand [The Rating Act 1908, s 2 (repealed; see now the Rating Act 1967 (NZ), Sch I(18)) defined 'rateable property' as 'all lands, tenements, or hereditaments with the buildings and improvements thereon', with twelve exceptions, one being 'machinery, whether fixed to the soil or not'.] 'It may be that it [the above section] only had in contemplation machines fixed and movable, but machines in a popular sense—that is to say, appliances for transmitting, regulating, or modifying power, and not further including all kinds of appliances used in transmitting the products of factories, though such appliances are connected with machinery. In such a case a popular test is a fair test, and I feel myself unable to say that such fixed things as the mains laid and used for supplying gas are parts of a machine or are properly included under the term "machinery".' *Auckland City Corpn v Auckland Gas Co Ltd* [1919] NZLR 561 at 584, CA, per Chapman J; also reported [1919] GLR 321 at 332

'The word "machinery" has no definite legal meaning and . . . the general rule is, in dealing with matters relating to the general public, that statutes are presumed to use words in their popular sense. . . . The Rating Act is such a statute, and, as there is no context to suggest any other meaning, the term "machinery" ought to be treated as having been used therein in its popular sense. In that sense, apart from any metaphorical use thereof, it means primarily a number of machines taken collectively, and a machine in its popular sense is a piece of mechanism which, by means of its inter-related parts, serves to utilise or apply power, but does not include anything that is merely a reservoir or conduit, although connected with something which is without doubt a machine.' Ibid at 586, ibid at 333 per Sim J

New Zealand 'I think that, whether it is energy or matter that is made available at, or conveyed to, a distance from the point at which it is generated, it would be using the word "machinery" in a figurative or metaphorical sense, and not in an ordinary or popular sense, to describe as machinery the means by which it is so made available or conveyed, where that means itself contains no element of motion or action.' *Hutt Valley Electric Power Board v Lower Hutt City Corpn* [1949] NZLR 611 at 636, 637, CA, per Hutchison J; also reported [1949] GLR 395 at 407

Machinery or plant

In this Part [Part II: regional development grants] of this Act, unless the context otherwise requires . . . 'machinery or plant' includes part of any machinery or plant, but does not include anything forming part of mining works or any vehicle except—

(a) a vehicle constructed or adapted for the conveyance of a machine incorporated in or permanently attached to it, or
(b) a vehicle constructed or adapted for the conveyance or haulage of loads,

but a vehicle shall not be eligible for grant under this Part of this Act unless its use for the conveyance or haulage of loads is exclusively in or about private premises, including the site of building or civil engineering operations. (Industrial Development Act 1982, s 6(2))

Operative machinery

[A covenant provided that no 'operative machinery' should be fixed on certain premises. The defendant erected a switchback railway thereon.] 'This railway is . . . "operative machinery" . . . within the covenant. A railway impelled by steam must be admitted to be machinery, and on this point I think no distinction can be drawn between the cases of the motive power being steam and being gravitation. Then it was argued that the railway is not "operative". Operative means no more than active, and this railway acts by conveying people.' *Chamberlayne v Collins* (1894) 70 LT 217 at 218, CA, per Lopes LJ

'There is always greater danger in giving definitions, but I think I may say that "machinery" implies the application of mechanical means to the attainment of some particular end by the help of natural forces, and the addition of the world "operative" means "with the potentiality of operating or doing work".' Ibid at 218, per Davey LJ

Trade machinery

For the purposes of this Act—

'Trade machinery' means the machinery used in or attached to any factory or workshop;

1st Exclusive of the fixed motive-powers, such as the waterwheels and steam-engines, and the steam-boilers, donkey-engines, and other fixed appurtenances of the said motive-powers; and
2nd Exclusive of the fixed power machinery, such as the shafts, wheels, drums, and their fixed appurtenances, which transmit the action of the motive-powers to the other machinery, fixed and loose; and,
3rd Exclusive of the pipes for steam gas and water in the factory or workshop.

The machinery or effects excluded by this section from the definition of trade machinery shall not be deemed to be personal chattels within the meaning of this Act. (Bills of Sale Act 1878, s 5)

Transmission machinery

'Transmission machinery' means every shaft, wheel, drum, pulley, system of fast and loose pulleys, coupling, clutch, driving-belt or other device by which the motion of a prime mover is transmitted to or received by any machine or appliance. (Factories Act 1961, s 176)

MAGAZINE (Explosive store)

'Factory magazine' means a building for keeping the finished explosive made in the factory, and includes, if such explosive is not gunpowder, any building for keeping the partly manufactured explosive or the ingredients of such explosive which is mentioned in that behalf in the licence. (Explosives Act 1875, s 108)

'Magazine' includes any ship or other vessel used for the purpose of keeping any explosive. (Explosives Act 1875, s 108)

MAGAZINE (Publication)

Australia 'A publication which has all the other features of a magazine will be called a magazine in New South Wales despite the fact that it has, and is intended to have only one single issue.' *R v Bacon* [1973] 1 NSWLR 87 at 97, per cur.

Canada 'No doubt a publication, containing nothing but puffings and praising of the goods of the publishers, and invitations to purchase those goods, would not in accordance with ordinary usage come under the denomination "magazine". On the other hand, the fact that a magazine was published by a firm of publishers with the deliberate intention of encouraging an interest in literature and incidentally in books published by themselves, would not be a ground for saying that it was not a magazine according to ordinary parlance. Nor could I conceive, if a firm engaged in publishing and selling, as its sole business, books dealing with various subjects of applied science, were to publish a periodical devoted exclusively to such subjects, and very largely to the reviews of books upon them, that it could successfully be argued that such a periodical would not fall within the category of "magazine" according to the ordinary notions of men. The same may be said with regard to what are called "trade journals" which are media for information in relation to their respective trades.' *Miln-Bingham Printing Co Ltd v R* [1930] SCR 282 at 283, SCC, per Duff J

MAGISTRATE

The name 'justice of the peace' was first given to the office of magistrate by the Justices of the Peace Act 1361. 'Magistrate' is the common denomination under which are included all those who are entrusted, whether by commission or appointment, or by virtue of their office, with the conservation of the peace and the hearing and determination of charges in respect of offences against it. (29 Halsbury's Laws (4th edn) para 201)

'Magistrate', in relation to a county, a London commission area or the City of London, means a justice of the peace for the county, London commission area or the City, as the case may be, other than a justice whose name is for the time being entered in the supplemental list and, in relation to a part of a county or of a London commission area, means a person who (in accordance with the preceding provisions of this definition) is a magistrate for that county or area and ordinarily acts in and for that part of it. (Justices of the Peace Act 1979, s 70)

MAIL

'Mail' includes every conveyance by which postal packets are carried, whether it be a ship, aircraft, vehicle, horse or any other conveyance, and also a person employed in conveying or delivering postal packets. (Post Office Act 1953, s 87)

MAIL BAG

'Mail bag' includes . . . any form of container or covering in which postal packets in course of transmission by post are conveyed, whether or not it contains any such packets. (Post Office Act 1953, s 87, as amended by the Post Office Act 1969, Sch 11)

For the purposes of this section [which deals with thefts from mails outside England and Wales] 'mail bag' includes any article serving the purpose of a mail bag. (Theft Act 1968, s 14(3))

In this Part of this Act [Part III: authority for conduct of postal and telegraphic business] 'mail-bag' includes any container in which articles are enclosed by the Post Office or a foreign administration for the purpose of the conveyance thereof by post. (Post Office Act 1969, s 86(1))

MAIM

[Section 2 of Stat (1823) 4 Geo 4, c 54 (repealed), made it a felony to 'maim or wound' any cattle.] 'This is not an offence at common law, and is only made so by a statute, and I am of opinion, that injuring a sheep by setting a dog to worry it, is not a maiming or wounding within the meaning of the statute.' *R v Hughes* (1826) 2 C & P 420 at 420, per Park J

[In this case it was contended that to constitute 'maiming' an injury must be permanent.]

'I have consulted with my brother Patterson, and he agrees with me in thinking that the last objection . . . is a good one. There is no such permanent injury inflicted on the animal in this case as will support the count for maiming.' *R v Jeans* (1844) 1 Car & Kir 539 at 540, per Wightman J

MAIN

'Main' means a pipe laid by the undertakers for the purpose of giving a general supply of water as distinct from a supply to individual consumers and includes any apparatus used in connection with such a pipe. (Water Act 1945, Sch 3, s 1)

MAIN OBJECTS *See* OBJECTS

MAIN TRANSMISSION LINES

The expression 'main transmission lines' means all extra high-pressure cables and overhead lines (not being an essential part of an authorised undertaker's distribution system or the distribution system of a railway company or the owners of a dock undertaking) transmitting electricity from a generating station to any other generating station, or to a substation, together with any step-up and step-down transformers and switch-gear necessary to, and used for, the control of such cables or overhead lines, and the buildings or such part thereof as may be required to accommodate such transformers and switch-gear. (Electricity (Supply) Act 1919, s 36)

MAINLY

[A town planning authority granted permission to develop an area subject to a condition that occupation of the houses built thereon should be limited to certain classes of persons, including those employed in an industry 'mainly'. dependent on agriculture.] 'The word "mainly" at once gives rise to difficulties. Probably it means "more than half" and this was the meaning which this House gave to the phrase "the bulk thereof" in *Bromley v Tryon* [[1952] AC 265].' *Fawcett Properties Ltd v Buckingham County Council* [1961] AC 636 at 669, HL, per Lord Morton of Henryton

MAINTAIN—MAINTENANCE *See also* REPAIR

The duty of a local education authority to maintain a school . . . shall include the duty of defraying all the expenses of maintaining the school . . . except, in the case of an aided school or a special agreement school, any expenses that by virtue of any provision of this Act or of any special agreement made thereunder are payable by the . . . governors of the school. . . . (Education Act 1944, s 114(2))

'Works of maintenance' include minor renewals, minor improvements and minor extensions. (Local Authorities (Goods and Services) Act 1970, s 1(4))

'Maintenance' includes repair, and 'maintain' and 'maintainable' are to be construed accordingly. (Highways Act 1980, s 329(1))

'It is very difficult to define what works of maintenance are. It is a very large term, and useful or reasonable ameliorations are not excluded by it. For instance, if a company had power to maintain the banks of a river which were faced in a particular way, could it be supposed that they were restricted under the words of maintenance to keeping up the banks in precisely the same way, when the mode which might have been very good when the banks were originally formed had been very much improved on by the subsequent advance of science? So where a railway company have to maintain a railway, I should not at all doubt that in maintaining it they might use any reasonable improvement. If, for instance, the railway were originally fenced with wooden palings, and it were sought when they decayed to replace them by an iron fence, I should say that was fully within their powers. If the railway originally was made in a deep cutting, and it was thought desirable to face the cutting with brick to make it more secure, I should say that was fair maintenance. And if a railway station were found inconvenient, and it was desirable when it required repairs to alter the arrangement of the rooms, or to alter the access or form of access, and so ameliorate it at the same time that it was put in repair, I should say all that was within the powers of maintenance given by the legislature; that is, you may maintain by keeping in the same state or you may maintain by keeping in the same state and improving the state, always bearing in mind that it must be maintenance as distinguished from alteration of purpose.' *Sevenoaks, Maidstone & Tonbridge Rly Co v London, Chatham & Dover Rly Co* (1879) 11 Ch D 625 at 634, 635, per Jessel MR

'A hire company which owned, say ten cars, five years ago and still owns ten (either the same or of a similar character) may be said to have maintained its fleet of cars, but if it now owns twenty cars, while it would certainly be true to say that it had maintained its fleet, it had plainly done something else as well, namely, it had added to the fleet. In my judgment, by no reasonable interpretation of the word "maintain" when used in relation to omnibuses, can it include the conception of increase.' *A-G v West Monmouthshire Omnibus Board* [1947] 1 All ER 248 at 252, per Romer J

'It is clear that, because a man who owns a wasting asset may choose wisely to take out an insurance to replace the capital, he cannot claim that the premium he has paid in respect of such a policy be treated as a "maintenance" expense.' *Pearce v Doulton (Inspector of Taxes)* [1947] 1 All ER 378 at 379, per Atkinson J

'The word "maintain" when used in relation to the state or condition of things is not always used in the same sense. It may be used to indicate the continuance of a particular state or condition, as when one says of someone that "he maintains his buildings just as they were". But on occasion it takes colour from the work of maintenance and is used in reference to the acts done or requisite to be done in the course of maintenance, as when one says of another that "he maintains his buildings methodically". This latter use gives the word "maintained" in relation to machinery rather the meaning of "serviced" or "looked after" or "attended to".' *Galashiels Gas Co Ltd v O'Donnell* [1949] AC 275 at 286, per Lord MacDermott

'"Maintenance" is a vague word. It is not necessarily distinguished from "repair". It may in some contexts be the same as "repair", and it may in some contexts have a wider meaning which includes repairing as well as other operations.' *Day v Harland and Wolff Ltd* [1953] 2 All ER 387 at 389, per Pearson J

'The question whether there has been a breach of statutory duty turns on the true construction of s 25(1) of the Factories Act 1937 [repealed; see now the Factories Act 1961, s 28(1)]. That sub-section provides that "All floors, steps, stairs, passages and gangways shall be of sound construction and properly maintained" and s 152(1) [see now s 176(1) of the Act of 1961] defines "maintained" as meaning "maintained in an efficient state, in efficient working order, and in good repair". . . . To be efficient, the appellant contended, the floor must be fit for any of the purposes for which it is intended, e.g. for support and for passing over in safety. The difficulty of such a view is that it puts an excessive obligation on the employer. Indeed, it was conceded that it could not be carried to the length of saying that a temporary obstruction, such as a piece of orange peel or the like, would make it inefficient. Once this concession is made it becomes a question of the degree of temporary inefficiency which constitutes a breach of the employer's obligation. Primarily, in my opinion, the section is aimed at some general condition of the gangway, e.g. a dangerously polished surface, or the like, or possibly some permanent fitment which makes it unsafe. But I cannot think the provision was meant to, or does, apply to a transient and exceptional condition.' *Latimer v AEC Ltd* [1953] 2 All ER 449 at 451, 452, HL, per Lord Porter (also reported in [1953] AC 643 at 653, 654)

[The Factories Act 1937, s 26(1) (repealed; see now the Factories Act 1961, s 29(1)), provided that there should, so far as was reasonably practicable, be provided and 'maintained' safe means of access to every place at which any person had at any time to work.] 'Section 26(1) has given rise to some difficulty because of the close collocation of the words "maintain" and "safe". It has often been read as meaning that the occupier must maintain the safety of the access, or, in other words, must keep it safe. It seems to me that since *Latimer*'s case [supra] that is no longer a correct reading of the section. The proper interpretation is to read "safe" with "provided" so that the section reads in this way: "There shall be provided a safe means of access (such as scaffolding, staging, or so forth) and, such a means having been provided, it must thereafter be "maintained", i.e. maintained in the way defined in s 152(1) [see now s 176(1) of the Act of 1961], viz maintained in an efficient state, in efficient working order, and in good repair. . . . The obligation is not an absolute obligation to maintain safety, but a relative obligation to maintain efficiently.' *Levesley v Thomas Firth and John Brown Ltd* [1953] 2 All ER 866 at 868, 869, CA, per Denning LJ

'"Maintenance" is an ordinary word of the English language, and, if it includes doing a few repairs at one time and then a few more at another time, I do not see how the operation could cease to be maintenance if it is found convenient to do a large number of repairs at the same time. Nor do I see any proper distinction between different kinds of repairs, or between repairs which are done with simple equipment and repairs which are more conveniently done in a fully equipped workshop.' *London Transport Executive v Betts (Valuation Officer)* [1958] 2 All ER 636 at 645, 646, HL, per Lord Reid

[The Mines and Quarries Act 1954, s 81(1) provides for the machinery in mines to be properly 'maintained'.] '"Maintain" may be a word of ambiguous import but ambiguity may disappear in the context in which the word is used. Looking to what is one, if not the main, object of the legislation, namely, to safeguard the workman in the performance of his duties, and having regard to the context in which the words "shall be properly maintained" appear in s 81, I think they should be construed as meaning to keep in proper order by acts of maintenance before the thing to be maintained falls out of condition. To construe the words as covering the restoration of the thing to be maintained to a proper condition by acts of maintenance after it has fallen out of condition would greatly lessen the protection afforded to the workman. Further, the employer is under an absolute obligation of sufficiency in respect of the provision of the things to be properly maintained and keeping them in that condition is but a continuation of his initial obligation.' *Hamilton v National Coal Board* 1960 SLT 24 at 28, HL, per Lord Keith of Avonholm; [1960] AC 633

'Applying the primary canons of construction to what is an ordinary phrase, the ordinary meaning of "to maintain" is to keep something in existence in a state which enables it to serve the purpose for which it exists.' *Haydon v Kent County Council* [1978] 2 All ER 97 at 108, 109, CA, per Shaw LJ

'It is possible to take up two extreme positions on the meaning of the expression "maintenance" in note 2 [to Group 8 in the Value Added Tax (Consolidation) Order 1978]. One extreme position is to say that, if the work done involves an improvement to the building, it can never be maintenance. The other extreme position is to say that, if the work has the purpose of remedying an existing defect in the building or preventing a future defect from developing, it must always be maintenance. In my view, neither of these extreme positions is correct. The expression "maintenance" should be given its ordinary and natural meaning. In regard to the first extreme position, there may well be cases where the work done, although it involves some degree of improvement (for instance, because of the use of modern or better materials or methods), is nevertheless maintenance in the ordinary and natural meaning of that word. For example, if metal gutters, which are liable to decay in time, are replaced with plastic gutters which are not liable to decay however long they remain there, that is an improvement to the building, but I would still regard that work as maintenance. With regard to the second extreme position, there may well be cases where, although the purpose of the work is to remedy existing or to prevent future defects in the building, it is nevertheless not within the expression "maintenance" in the ordinary and natural meaning of that word. For example, if a building has a flat roof which leaks continuously and the owner decides to replace the flat roof with a pitched roof so as to eliminate that defect, then, although that work was designed to eliminate a defect, it would not in my view be maintenance in the ordinary and natural meaning of that word.' *ACT Construction Ltd v Customs and Excise Comrs* [1981] 1 All ER 324 at 329, 330, CA, per Brandon J; affirmed [1982] 1 All ER 84, HL

Canada [The Companies Act, RSM 1954, s 410(1) (see now RSM 1970, c C160) provides that a foreign corporation shall not be capable of commencing or 'maintaining' an action, etc, in respect of any contract made without being licensed; and by s 410(3), that upon the granting of a licence such action may be 'maintained' as if the licence had been granted before the institution of the action.] 'It seems to me that no matter what is "questioned" the action may, upon a licence being obtained, be "maintained", i.e. "not to suffer to fail or decline".' *United Agencies Ltd v Winnipeg Graphic Arts Engravers Ltd* (1961) 34 WWR 49 at 74, Man QB, per Ferguson J

MAINTENANCE (Matrimonial)

'"Maintenance" is a very wide word, and, in my view, it should be read as covering everything which a wife may in reason want to do with the income which she enjoys. It includes much more than food, lodging, clothes, travelling, and so on. It includes, for instance, charity and making arrangements for the future, thus incurring various liabilities in her discretion, and it is wrong to limit it to any particular form of expenditure.' *Acworth v Acworth* [1943] P 21 at 22, CA, per Scott LJ

'Maintenance does not only mean the food a wife puts in her mouth. It also means her clothes, the house in which she lives, and the money which she is to have in her pocket, all of which vary according to the means of her husband. Maintenance cannot mean only mere subsistence.' *Re Borthwick, Borthwick v Beauvais* [1949] 1 All ER 472 at 475, 476, per Harman J; [1949] Ch 395

Australia '"Maintenance" means the act of maintaining, and denotes the regular supply of food, clothing and lodging; the provision of the necessaries and of the conveniences of life. The quality and quantity of wearing-apparel, and to a less degree the amount and nature of food, as well as the size, situation and furnishing of the place of abode, will in each case depend in part on the standing of the parties, their wealth, and the environment to which they in their married state have been accustomed. These factors to provide for existence and comfort in ordinary circumstances, where people live in amity together, are supplied partly *in specie* and partly by money wherewith other such things wanted may be acquired. But maintenance may also be lawfully provided for either wholly in kind, house furnishings, clothing, food, recreation and entertainment, or entirely by the payment to a "dependant" of moneys with which to procure what is necessary. The jurisdiction, whereby monetary contribution for maintenance is ordered, is of course in constant use. But the enforcement of support by the provision of other media is less familiar. This may be expected to be in the form of preventing some right of maintenance presently enjoyed from being interrupted or precluding the wife or husband as the case may be from being molested in the enjoyment of the "right". Where the question concerns the occupation of the matrimonial home pending proceedings, apart from rights as owner or tenant neither spouse has "an absolute right" to remain, or to be suffered to remain, in possession.' *Kallin v Kallin* [1944] SASR 73 at 75, per Mayo J

Canada 'My understanding of the words "alimony" and "maintenance" has always been that they are technical and terms of art. "Alimony" strictly refers to an allowance made while the marriage continues to subsist and "maintenance" strictly refers to the allowance made when the marriage is dissolved. Thus an order nisi provision for payment of an interim allowance pending the order absolute is "alimony" and a like order after dissolution of the marriage is "maintenance". An allowance ordered to be paid on the grant of a divorce *a mensa et thoro* (less technically known as a judicial separation) is alimony as are payments agreed upon between the parties to a marriage in a written separation agreement.' *R v Burgess* [1982] 1 FC 849 at 853, FCTD, per Cattanach J

MAINTENANCE (Of action)

[The offence of maintenance (including champerty but not embracery) has been abolished in England; see the Criminal Law Act 1967, s 13. The first extract below is retained in summarising the former law.]

'There are many definitions of maintenance, all seeming to express the same idea. Blackstone calls it "an officious intermeddling in a suit which no way belongs to one by maintaining or assisting either party with money or otherwise to prosecute or defend it": Bl Com Book iv, c 10, s 12. "Maintenance", says Lord Coke, "signifieth in law a taking in hand, bearing up, or upholding of a quarrel, or side, to the disturbance or hindrance of common right': Co Litt 368b. These definitions are repeated in substance in Bacon's Abridgment, in Viner, and in Comyns, under the head of maintenance. To the same effect, though somewhat differing in words, is the language of Lord Coke in the 2nd Institute in his commentary on the Statute of Westminster the First, c xxviii. There is, perhaps, the fullest and completest of all to be found in Termes de la Ley, "Maintenance is when any man gives or delivers to another that is plaintiff or defendant in any action any sum of money or other thing to maintain his plea, or takes great pains for him when he hath nothing therewith to do; then the party grieved shall have a writ against him called a writ of maintenance". Chancellor Kent, adopting Blackstone's definition, which definition itself is founded on a passage in Hawkins, says that it is "a principle common to the laws of all well governed countries that no encouragement should be given to litigation by the introduction of parties to enforce those rights which others are not disposed to enforce": part vi lect 67. I quote from the excellent edition of Kent's Commentaries, published by Mr O W Holmes at Boston in 1873. To the same effect is another American authority, Mr Story. "Maintenance is the officious assistance by money or otherwise, proffered by a third person to either party to a suit, in which he himself has no legal interest, to enable them to prosecute or defend it": Story on Contract, ch vii, s 578. Jacob's Law Dictionary is to the same effect as the other authorities I have quoted.' *Bradlaugh v Newdegate* (1883) 11 QBD 1 at 5, 6, per Lord Coleridge CJ

New Zealand 'In the case of simple maintenance an interest in the subject-matter or a bona fide belief in such interest, is sufficient for the purpose. . . . The appellant . . . had no direct pecuniary interest in the result of the action [which had been commenced by the respondent against a neighbour], and the mere circumstance that in the action a question of fact would arise in the determination of which he had an interest did not constitute a common interest sufficient to justify maintenance. . . . The action, in point of law, concerned only the parties to it, and it is clear that the existence of a mere business interest in the result of such an action is not sufficient to save interference from being maintenance.' *Duthie v Duthie* (1915) 34 NZLR 897 at 899, 900, per Sim J; also reported 17 GLR 673

MAINTENANCE (Of infant)

A . . . trust instrument may contain express powers for providing maintenance or education for, or otherwise benefiting, a beneficiary who is a minor. Apart from any such express powers and subject to any contrary intention expressed in the trust instrument, where a trustee holds property in trust for any person for any interest whatsoever, whether vested or contingent, he has statutory power during the minority of that person, subject to any prior interests or charges affecting that property, at his discretion to pay to that person's parent or guardian, if any, or otherwise apply for or towards his maintenance, education or benefit the whole or such part, if any, of the income of the property as may in all the circumstances be reasonable, and must accumulate any surplus income. Once the beneficiary attains his majority, the trustees must pay a beneficiary's share of income to him even if his interest is still contingent under the terms of the trust. (48 Halsbury's Laws (4th edn) para 900)

MAINTENANCE AGREEMENT

In this [and the next following] section—

'maintenance agreement' means any agreement in writing made, whether before or after the commencement of this Act, between the parties of a marriage, being—

(a) an agreement containing financial arrangements, whether made during the continuance or after the dissolution or annulment of the marriage; or
(b) a separation agreement which contains no financial arrangement in a case where no other agreement in writing between the same parties contains such arrangements.

(Matrimonial Causes Act 1973, s 34(2)).

[The section goes on to explain what is meant by 'financial arrangements'.]

MAINTENANCE ORDER

In this Part of this Act [Part I: reciprocal enforcement of maintenance orders] . . . 'maintenance order' means an order (however described) of any of the following descriptions, that is to say—

(a) an order (including an affiliation order or order consequent upon an affiliation order) which provides for the periodical payment of sums of money towards the maintenance of any person, being a person whom the person liable to make payments under the order is, according to the law applied in the place where the order was made, liable to maintain; and
(b) an affiliation order or order consequent upon an affiliation order, being an order which provides for the payment by a person adjudged, found or declared to be a child's father of expenses incidental to the child's birth or, where the child has died, of his funeral expenses,

and, in the case of a maintenance order which has been varied, means that order is varied. (Maintenance Orders (Reciprocal Enforcement) Act 1972, s 21(1))

MAJORITY *See also* MINORITY

[The age of majority has been reduced from 21 to 18. *See* generally the Family Law Reform Act 1969, s 1.]

MAJORITY VERDICT *See* VERDICT

MAKE

[The Rag Flock Act 1911, s 1 (repealed; cf now the Rag Flock and other Filling Materials Act 1951) prohibited the sale and use of unclean flock manufactured from rags for the purpose of 'making' articles of upholstery, cushions, or bedding flock.] 'A man who picks to pieces a manufactured article and puts it together again does not make it. Therefore the appellant was not making, and did not have flock in his possession for the purpose of making bedding. . . . If he were to add anything it would be quite another matter. But the mere act of removing the contents of a mattress and then replacing them is not making or manufacturing a mattress.' *Gamble v Jordan* [1913] 3 KB 149 at 152, per Phillimore J

[The Wills Act 1837, s 34 enacts that the Act shall not extend to any will 'made' before the first day of January, 1838.] 'The legislature referred to the date of the making of a will in enacting that that Act should not extend to any will made before 1st of January 1838. What was the date on which a will was made within the meaning of that provision? I think quite clearly the date at the end of the will where the testator says: "In witness whereof I have set my hand on" the date of signing the will.' *Re Waring, Westminster Bank Ltd v Awdry* [1942] Ch 426 at 433, 434, CA, per MacKinnon LJ

'Rates are "made" when the rating authority passes the appropriate resolution, and this . . . is required by statute to be done before the beginning of the rating year in question. But, in my judgment, the process of "making" necessarily starts much earlier, in fact not later than 1st February, when the rating authority has to comply with its statutory duty of estimating the product of a penny in the pound rate in the next rating year.' *Westminster City Council v University of London King's College* [1958] 3 All ER 25 at 29, per Roxburgh J

'As a matter of the ordinary meaning of English words a statement is made when, if oral, it is uttered and if in writing when it is published. . . . The fact that a statement when made was communicated to two or more million people does not affect the act of making it. There was still only one act even though its effect might be felt over a wide area and for a long time.' *R v Thomson Holidays Ltd* [1974] 1 All ER 823 at 827, CA, per cur.

'In my judgment . . . a written acknowledgment cannot be said to be "made to" a creditor or his agent, within the meaning of s 24(2) [of the Limitation Act 1939 (repealed; see now the Limitation Act 1980, s 30)] unless either (i) it is delivered to the creditor or his agent by or with the authority of the debtor or his agent or (ii) it is expressly or implicitly addressed to and is actually received by the creditor or his agent. In my judgment, in case (i) it would not matter that the acknowledgment was not, according to its terms, expressly or implicitly addressed to the recipient. In case (ii) it would not matter that the acknowledgment reached the hands of the creditor otherwise than by or with the authority of the debtor. In either case, however, it would be necessary that the creditor should actually receive the acknowledgment before he could rely on it.' *Re Compania de Electricidad de la Provincia de Buenos Aires Ltd* [1978] 3 All ER 668 at 702, per Slade J

United States The term 'made' when used in relation to any invention means the conception or first actual reduction to practice of such invention. (Act of July 19, 1952, as amended, 1980, s 6(a), (g))

In Rules of Supreme Court

[RSC Ord 11, r 1(e) (revoked; see now RSC 1965 Ord 11, r 1(f)) provided for service of a writ out of the jurisdiction in cases where the action was brought to enforce, etc, contracts 'made' within the jurisdiction or 'made' by or through an agent trading or residing within the jurisdiction.] 'If . . . one must treat a quasi-contract . . . as coming within the terms of such a rule as RSC Ord 11, r 1(e), one must treat the word "made" as being equivalent, in the case of a quasi-contract or other obligation of that kind, to "arising"; that is to say that it is a quasi-contract or other obligation arising within the jurisdiction, or, it may be, is one which by its terms or by its implication should be governed by English law. One must not pay too much attention to the literal meaning of the word "made".' *Rousou (Trustee) v Rousou* [1955] 3 All ER 486 at 492, per Danckwerts J

In Town Planning Act

[The Town Planning Act 1925, s 10 (repealed; cf now Town and Country Planning Act 1971, s 170) provided that any person whose property was injuriously affected by the 'making' of a town planning scheme should, if he made a claim within the time limited by the scheme, be entitled to compensation.] 'Section 10 . . ., as I understand it, says quite plainly, "find the date when a town planning scheme is made; if at that date there is a person whose property is injuriously affected, that person, by virtue of his ownership of the property which is injuriously affected, is entitled to obtain compensation in respect of the injurious affection sustained by his property by reason of the town planning scheme being made". . . . In my view the only way of making the Act work is to construe it as enacting that the date of "the making of" the scheme is the date when the scheme becomes a binding scheme, having effect as it were enacted by the Act. I cannot treat the scheme as made when the period has not arrived at which it is to have effect by reason of the approval of the Minister having been placed upon it.' *Markham v Derby Corpn* [1935] Ch 320 at 323, 325, per Clauson J

Make decree

New Zealand 'I think the expression "on making a decree of divorce" means "on the occasion of the making of a decree of divorce" which would, as good sense demands, include the time just before or just after the pronouncement of the decree. I see nothing in authority or in principle however to extend it to include some unspecified later occasion perhaps days, weeks or months later.' *Duncan v Duncan* [1973] 1 NZLR 344 at 346, per Quilliam J

Make provision

'Though a man might, not doubt, say, in ordinary conversation, during his life, that he had "made provision" for his wife by his will, that in truth is not an accurate use of words: it only means, more strictly construed, that he has executed a will which, if unrevoked, will make provision for his wife on his death.' *Re Westminster (Duke), Kerr v Westminster (Duchess)* [1959] 1 All ER 442 at 444, CA, per Lord Evershed MR; also reported [1959] Ch 265 at 271

Make use of

[A, to secure payment of a debt, assigned all his goods and farming stock to the plaintiff, with a proviso that it should be lawful for him, his executors or administrators to 'make use of' his household goods.] 'The only word that raises a doubt is "make" use of; for that, applied to perishable articles, must mean consume. But the most that can be made of it is, that the stipulation in question may amount to a licence to consume such articles; they are still conveyed to the plaintiff: there are no words defeating the original grant, nor any power of selling and disposing of them, or dealing with them generally as if they had not been conveyed.' *Gale v Burnell* (1845) 7 QB 850 at 862, per cur.

'There remain . . . to be considered the words "use, exercise", in the granting of the patent, and the expression "make use of or put in practice" in the prohibitory part. . . . The first meaning assigned to the word "use" in Johnson's Dictionary is "to employ to any purpose"; it is, therefore, a word of wide signification. It seems to me that the terms "use" and "make use of" are intended to have a wider application than "exercise" and "put in practice", and, without saying that no limit is to be placed on the two former expressions in the patent, I think, on the best consideration that I can give, that they are confined to the use of a patented article for the purpose for which it is patented.' *British Motor Syndicate Ltd v Taylor & Son* [1900] 1 Ch 577 at 581, 583, per Stirling J; affirmed [1901] 1 Ch 122, CA

[The Pilotage Act 1983, s 31(1) makes pilotage compulsory in the case of certain ships while navigating in a pilotage district for the purpose of entering, leaving, or 'making use of any port in the district'.] 'Did the *Anglo-Colombian* make use of the commercial port of Dover? What is "making use" of the port? It appears to be conceded that if she had slowed down . . . for the purpose of putting something or some one on shore at the port of Dover she would have been making use of the port, and personally I see no difference between a case like that and the present case where she altered her course for the purpose of approaching the port, not to put something or some one on shore, but for the purpose of receiving something or some one from the shore. . . . The words "making use" of any port in the district clearly include such a use of the port of Dover as the vessel made on the occasion in question.' *Cannell & Trinity House Corpn v Lawther, Latta & Co* [1914] 3 KB 1135 at 1139, 1140, per Bailhache J

MALE

'Now, upon the best consideration that I can give this case, it does appear to me that "male lineal descendant" must mean a male descendant in the male line; "lineal" is otherwise altogether surplusage, and it is not only surplusage introduced into the clause, but in every word of this will where the male descendant is mentioned. If the person meant was a male descendant, whether of the male or female line, that intent would have been quite sufficiently expressed by the words "male descendant" only, without the word "lineal", and yet that word is, as I have said, used in every clause of the will; and I do not think myself at liberty to hold that that word was not intended to have some additional meaning: if it is to have an additional meaning, it must be a distinct additional meaning, and the testator must have used it in order to express what the words "male descendant" alone would not have expressed. It is not sufficient to say here that "male lineal descendant" may mean nothing more than what "male descendant" would express, because the question is whether a testator who uses both words is not (if the context and provisions, and nature of the will require you to suppose he did) to be taken to mean something more than by the other words.' *Oddie v Woodford* (1821) 3 My & Cr 584 at 618, 619, per Lord Eldon LC

'In speaking of a man and his male descendants as a class, no one would conceive the son of a female descendant as included; and such is the construction which our law has put upon the words; as "issue male", which is, in fact, the same thing as male descendants.' *Bernal v Bernal* (1838) 3 My & Cr 559 at 582, per Cottenham LC

'When a correct speaker says that one person is related to another in the male line, we understand him to mean that they are the *agnati* of the Roman law; that is, *cognati per virilis sexus personas cognatione conjuncti*. A man, therefore, is not necessarily related in the male line to all his father's relations; and I am not satisfied that in the present testator's dispositions it would, either on the ground that he has used also the term "female line", or otherwise, be safe to construe the words "in the male line" as equivalent to "*ex parte paterna*"; that is, as importing more than agnation in the strict sense.' *Boys v Bradley* (1853) 22 LJ Ch 617 at 621, 622, per Knight Bruce LJ

'It has been long settled, that where a testator devises lands to his heir male, he must be held to mean his heir male at common law.' *Thorp v Owen* (1854) 2 Sm & G 90, at 94, per Sir John Stuart V-C

'"Male lineal" has been construed to mean as though it were one word, signifying "male in a line of males". With this construction I entirely agree; and I agree that it may be read as though it were a compound word "male line".' *Thellusson v Rendlesham (Lord), Thellusson v Thellusson, Hare v Roberts* (1859) 7 HL Cas 429 at 455, per Bramwell B

'In this case I am bound to give effect to every word the will contains, and, as it is impossible to give effect to the word "male" by holding that it merely expresses the same thing as nephews, with which it is coupled, I am driven to look about and see if I can give it any other reasonable interpretation. There is another reasonable interpretation, namely, that "male nephews" means the sons of the testator's male relatives, that is to say, of his brothers as distinguished from his sisters.' *Lucas* v *Cuday* (1876) 10 IR Eq 514 at 515, per Chatterton V-C.

'The prima facie meaning of the expression "issue male" will, of course, yield to a context in which the testator or settlor shows that he intended to use the words in a different sense; but in the absence of a context there is no question that the expression "issue male" has a recognised meaning as a term of art, and means male descendants through the exclusively male line. I do not think that it would be legitimate to make any distinction for this purpose between the expression "issue male" and the expression contained in this settlement: "male issue". Nor can I find anything in the context of this settlement which affords an indication that the settlors intended by the expression "male issue" anything other than descendants through the exclusively male line.' *Re Du Cros' Settlement, Du Cros Family Trustee Co Ltd v Du Cros* [1961] 3 All ER 193 at 197, per Pennycuick J

MALICE

Express or actual malice is ill will or spite towards the plaintiff or any indirect or improper motive in the defendant's mind at the time of . . . publication, which is his sole or dominant motive for publishing the words complained of. This must be distinguished from legal malice or malice in law which means publication without lawful excuse and does not depend upon the defendant's state of mind.

The defences of both fair comment and qualified privilege are defeated by proof that the defendant published the words complained of maliciously. In both cases proof that the defendant's sole or dominant motive in publishing the words was improper will establish malice. (28 Halsbury's Laws (4th edn) para 145)

A plaintiff in an action for damages for malicious prosecution or other abuse of legal proceedings has to prove malice in fact indicating that the defendant was actuated either by spite or ill-will against the plaintiff, or by indirect or improper motives. If the defendant had any purpose other than that of bringing a person to justice, that is malice.

The plaintiff has the burden of proving malice. In a jury trial the question of malice or no malice is for the jury not for the judge, and if there is any evidence on which the jury could find malice, the judge must leave the question to it. A plaintiff who proves malice but not want of reasonable and probable cause still fails. (45 Halsbury's Laws (4th edn) para 1351)

'Malice, as is commonly said, is a good prosecutor, and where there is just ground of prosecution, malice against the person is often the true cause of laying hold of it, and yet is not made the ground of an action. To this I say, that this is not the meaning of the word *maliciose* in its proper or legal sense, which the words malice, malicious, or maliciously, bear in common speech. Malice in common acceptation is a desire of revenge, or a settled anger against a particular person, and in like manner the words malicious and maliciously are applied; this is by the vulgar use of the words in English. But it is not the legal sense, taking them as law terms, nor the proper sense as they are Latin words. *Malitia* is the abstract of malice, there it imports directly wickedness, and is the circumstance of an ill action, which cuts off all excuses. A man may do an ill thing ignorantly, which may be an excuse, or rashly, which is an alleviation, or wickedly, which is not excusable. *Malitia*, according to its etymology speaks the last; amongst the Romans it imported a mixture of fraud and of that which is opposite to simplicity and honesty, and so it does in the civil law. . . . Where it is not possible to understand malice in any sense, that has the least relation to the vulgar notion of malice, for here is no anger or desire of revenge against another, but an evidence to prevent his own condemnation; but it being in defiance of the publick justice, it is said to be of malice, or, as that seems to be explained by the next word, of the froward mind, and plainly stands in opposition to such case where some just cause can be assigned, as that it proceeded from madness, distemper, or other disabilities, which in our books are called the acts of God, otherwise it is wickedness and frowardness of mind, refusing to submit to the Court of Justice, which is called malice. In short malice and maliciously I take to be terms of law which in the legal sense always exclude a just cause.' *Jones v Givin* (1713) Gilb 185 at 190, 191, 193, per cur.

'Malice in common acceptation means ill will against a person, but in its legal sense it means a wrongful act, done intentionally, without just cause or excuse. If I give a perfect stranger a blow likely to produce death, I do it of malice, because I do it intentionally and without just cause or excuse. If I maim cattle, without knowing whose they are, if I poison a fishery, without knowing the owner, I do it for malice, because it is a wrongful act, and done intentionally. If I am arraigned of felony, and wilfully stand mute, I am said to do it of malice, because it is intentional and without just cause or excuse. And if I traduce a man, whether I know him or not, and whether I intend to do him an injury or not, I apprehend the law considers it as done of malice, because it is wrongful and intentional. It equally works an injury, whether I meant to produce an injury or not, and if I had no legal excuse for the slander, why is he not to have a remedy against me for the injury it produces? And I apprehend the law recognises the distinction between these two descriptions of malice, malice in fact and malice in law, in actions of slander.' *Bromage v Prosser* (1825) 4 B & C 247 at 255, per cur.

'To satisfy the term "maliciously" . . . it is not necessary that there should have been any spite or revenge in the defendant towards the plaintiff. If from any indirect motive as to extort money to which he was not fairly entitled, the defendant acted as is here complained of, that will be sufficient.' *Clark v Mansford* (1858) 1 F & F 362 at 363, per Watson B

[The plaintiff, a clergyman, had been engaged in a controversy with a brother clergyman, and published a pamphlet concerning his point of view. The editor of a newspaper published a commentary on the pamphlet which the plaintiff maintained was libellous.] 'This is an action which is not maintainable without malice; which means, in law, any wrong motive. . . . If you are of opinion, upon the whole of this inquiry, that the defendant wrote what he did for the purpose of maintaining the truth, sincerely having that object in view, without any corrupt motive, and that the language he used, even although it may be exaggerated, was prompted by the desire to maintain the truth, and that the exaggerated language was provoked by similar language on the other side, and which might well have accounted for the use of strong expressions, then you are at liberty to find the defendant not guilty.' *Hibbs v Wilkinson* (1859) 1 F & F 608 at 610, per Erle CJ

'The word "malice" in law means any corrupt motive, any wrong motive, or any departure from duty.' *Turnbull v Bird* (1861) 2 F & F 508 at 524, per Erle CJ

'Malice does not mean merely spite, but an improper motive; and to do or assist another in doing what one knows to be wrong and wicked is to act maliciously.' *Hall v Semple* (1862) 3 F & F 337 at 357, per Crompton J

'"Malice" in law means not merely personal ill-will, but any undue or indirect object—that is, any intention to gain an undue advantage; and therefore, if the object of the proceeding here was to threaten and intimidate the plaintiff, and then drive him to pay the money claimed from him, and not really from an apprehension that he would be away from the country so as not to be answerable in the action, that would be an indirect motive and an endeavour to obtain an undue advantage, which would in law be malice, even without any personal spite or ill-will.' *Melia v Neate* (1863) 3 F & F 757 at 763, 764, per Bramwell B

'It is common knowledge that a man who has an unlawful and malicious intent against another, and, in attempting to carry it out, injures a third person, is guilty of what the law deems malice against the person injured, because the offender is doing an unlawful act, and has that which the judges call general malice.' *R v Latimer* (1886) 17 QBD 359 at 361, per Lord Coleridge CJ

'We were invited by the plaintiffs' counsel to accept the position from which their argument started—that an action will lie if a man maliciously and wrongfully conducts himself so as to injure another in that other's trade. Obscurity resides in the language used to state this proposition. The terms "maliciously", "wrongfully", and "injure" are words all of which have accurate meanings, well known to the law, but which also have a popular and less precise signification, into which it is necessary to see that the argument does not imperceptibly slide. An intent to "injure" in strictness means more than an intent to harm. It connotes an intent to do wrongful harm. "Maliciously", in like manner, means and implies an intention to do an act which is wrongful, to the detriment of another. The term "wrongful" imports in its turn the infringement of some right.' *Mogul SS Co Ltd v McGregor, Gow & Co* (1889) 23 QBD 598 at 612, CA, per Bowen LJ; affirmed [1892] AC 25

'Between malice in fact and malice in law there is a broad distinction which is not peculiar to any particular system of jurisprudence. A person who inflicts an injury upon another person in contravention of the law is not allowed to say that he did so with an innocent mind; he is taken to know the law, and he must act within the law. He may, therefore, be guilty of malice in law, although so far as the state of his mind is concerned, he acts ignorantly, and in that sense innocently. Malice in fact is quite a different thing; it means an actual malicious intention on the part of the person who has done the wrongful act.' *Shearer v Shields* [1914] AC 808 at 813, 814, HL, per Viscount Haldane LC

'Malice in law means the doing of a wrongful act intentionally without just cause or excuse—*Bromage v Prosser* [supra]. "Intentionally" refers to the doing of the act; it does not mean that the defendant meant to be spiteful, though sometimes, as for instance to rebut a plea of privilege in defamation, malice in fact has to be proved.' *Jones Bros (Huntstanton) Ltd v Stevens* [1954] 3 All ER 677 at 680, CA, per cur.; see also [1955] 1 QB 275

'In our opinion, the word "maliciously" in a statutory crime postulates foresight of consequence. . . . We think it is incorrect to say that the word "malicious" in a statutory offence merely means wicked.' *R v Cunningham* [1957] 2 All ER 412 at 414, CCA, per Byrne J (also reported in [1957] 2 QB 396 at 400, 401).

'The . . . point . . . raises an interesting question as to the true meaning of the word "maliciously" in s 16 of the Offences against the Person Act 1861. The material part of this section provides as follows: "Whosoever shall maliciously send, deliver, or utter, or directly or indirectly cause to be received, knowing the contents thereof, any letter or writing threatening to kill or murder any person, shall be guilty of felony. . . ." This court does not find it strange that the legislature considered that for a man to send or cause a letter to be received which he knows to contain a threat to murder is a wrongful act and so wicked and inherently likely to harass the recipient that it should be made a crime. In these circumstances, it is difficult to see why any meaning should be attributed to the word "maliciously" other than its ordinary meaning in Acts creating a criminal offence, namely wilfully or intentionally and without lawful excuse. And that is the meaning which this court does attribute to that word.' *R v Solanke* [1969] 3 All ER 1383 at 1384, CA, per cur.

[A new s 16, not containing the word 'maliciously', was substituted by the Criminal Law Act 1977, s 65, Sch 12.]

[A person whose convictions are to be treated as spent by virtue of the Rehabilitation of Offenders Act 1974, s 1(1) can recover damages for libel if he can show (see also sub-s (5)) that the publication of those convictions was made with 'malice'.] 'I take malice in this subsection to mean published with some irrelevant spiteful or improper motive.' *Herbage v Preisdram Ltd* [1984] 2 All ER 769 at 772, CA, per Griffiths LJ

Australia [The Police Act 1892–1986 (WA), s 138 provides, inter alia, that no action shall lie against any policeman unless there is direct proof of corruption or 'malice' within the meaning of para H of Interpretation Act 1918–1986 (WA), Sch 2.] 'With regard to what is meant by "malice" in the statute, I think that . . . it was used in the sense, familiar in cases of malicious prosecution, of personal spleen or ill-will, or some motive other than that of bringing a wrongdoer to justice.' *Trobridge v Hardy* (1955) 94 CLR 147 at 155, per Fullager J

Australia 'Malice is an ambiguous term. In its general colloquial significance it means spite or ill-will; in law it may have that meaning as well as several others, one of which is a wrongful act done intentionally.' *Luetich v Walton* [1960] WAR 109 at 112, per Wolff CJ

Canada 'I have read with care, not only all of the authorities to which the court were referred, but many more. The description in those authorities of what constitutes malice is by no means uniform. In some instances reference is made to an "indirect motive"; in others to an "improper motive"; in others to a "sinister motive" and in still others these various descriptions are linked together by describing malice, for example, as "an indirect or improper motive" or again "an indirect and improper motive". . . . I have been unable to find any decision anywhere wherein a plaintiff in an action for malicious prosecution succeeded in his suit unless there was evidence before the jury upon which they could find not merely an indirect motive but an improper motive in the sense of a motive to injure the plaintiff or to benefit the defendant or some other party other than the plaintiff.' *Williams v Webb* [1961] OR 353 at 364, Ont CA, per Aylesworth JA

Canada 'A malicious act is an act characterised by a pre-existing or an accompanying malicious state of mind. That malicious state of mind involves the intentional doing of a wrongful act without legal justification or excuse.' *Reliable Distributors Ltd v Royal Insurance Co of Canada* [1984] 6 WWR 83 at 87, BCSC, per Wood J

Express malice

Canada ' "Express malice" are words of legal distinction differentiating between malice which the law implies from the mere publication of defamatory words and the malice which must be proved where by reason of the occasion being one of qualified privilege, the presumption of malice is thereby rebutted.' *Taylor v Despard* [1956] OR 963 at 973, Ont CA, per Roach JA

Malice aforethought

The mental element of murder, traditionally called malice aforethought, may take any of the following forms: (1) an intention to kill; (2) an intention to cause grievous bodily harm; or (3) an intention to do an act knowing it to be highly probable that the act will cause death or grievous bodily harm. (11 Halsbury's Laws (4th edn) para 1157)

'Malice aforethought has always been defined in English law as either an express intention to kill such as could be inferred when a person having uttered threats against another, produced a lethal weapon and used it on him, or an implied intention to kill, as where the prisoner inflicted grievous bodily harm, that is to say, harmed the victim by a voluntary act intended to harm him and the victim died as the result of that grievous bodily harm. If a person does an act on another which amounts to the infliction of grievous bodily harm he cannot say that he did not intend to go so far. It is put as *malum in se* in the old cases and he must take the consequences. If he intends to inflict grievous bodily harm and that person dies, that has always been held in English law, and was at the time when the Act of 1957 [Homicide Act 1957] was passed, sufficient to imply the malice aforethought which is a necessary constituent of murder.' *R v Vickers* [1957] 2 All ER 741 at 743, CCA, per cur. (also reported in [1957] 2 QB 664 at 670)

'My Lords, the distinction between murder and manslaughter, both felonies at common law, appears to derive from the statutes of Henry VIII and Edward VI by which benefit of clergy was withdrawn from murder committed *ex malitia praecogitata*, which in the form "malice prepense" or "prepensed" and "malice aforethought" has continued in common use in legal circles to the present date. The precise value of this phrase is open to doubt. As long ago as 1883 Stephen [History of the Criminal Law] described it as "a phrase which is never used except to mislead or to be explained away" and advised its abolition as a term of art and the substitution for it of a "definite enumeration of the states of mind intended to be taken as constituent elements of murder." In the present case Cairns LJ, in delivering the judgment now appealed from, said: "There is no doubt that murder is killing 'with malice aforethought', and there is no doubt that neither the word 'malice' nor the word 'aforethought' is to be construed in any ordinary sense." I agree with this latter observation, and would myself think that the sooner the phrase is consigned to the limbo of legal history the better for precision and lucidity in the interpretation of our criminal law. However, "malice aforethought" was and is part of our criminal jurisprudence.' *Hyam v Director of Public Prosecutions* [1974] 2 All ER 41 at 45, per Lord Hailsham of St Marylebone

MALICIOUS ACT

Canada 'A malicious act is an act characterised by a pre-existing or an accompanying malicious state of mind. That malicious state of mind involves the intentional doing of a wrongful act without legal justification or excuse.' *Reliable Distributors Ltd v Royal Insurance Co of Canada* [1984] 6 WWR 83 at 87, BCSC, per Wood J

MALICIOUS PROSECUTION

A malicious prosecution is an abuse of the process of the court by wrongfully setting the law in motion on a criminal charge. To be actionable as a tort the process must have been without reasonable and probable cause, and must have been instituted or carried on maliciously and must have terminated in the plaintiff's favour. The plaintiff must also prove damage. (45 Halsbury's Laws (4th edn) para 1340)

'There is no similitude or analogy between an action of trespass, or false imprisonment, and this kind of action. An action of trespass is for the defendant's having done that, which, upon the stating of it, is manifestly illegal. This kind of action is for a prosecution, which, upon the stating of it, is manifestly legal. The essential ground of this action is, that a legal prosecution was carried on *without a probable cause*. We say this is emphatically the essential ground; because every other allegation may be implied from this; but this must be substantively and expressly proved, and cannot be implied. From the want of probable cause, malice may be, and most commonly is, implied. The knowledge of the defendant is also implied. From the most express malice, the want of probable cause cannot be implied. A man, from a malicious motive, may take up a prosecution for real guilt, or he may, from circumstances which he really believes, proceed upon apparent guilt; and in neither case is he liable to this kind of action.' *Johnstone v Sutton* (1786) 1 Term Rep 510 at 544, 545, per cur.

'To prosecute a person is not prima facie tortious, but to do so dishonestly or unreasonably is. Malicious prosecution thus differs from wrongful arrest and detention, in that the onus of proving that the prosecutor did not act honestly or reasonably, lies on the person prosecuted. A person, whether or not he is a police officer, acts reasonably in prosecuting a suspected felon if the credible evidence of which he knows raises a case fit to go to a jury that the suspect is guilty of the felony charged. This is what in law constitutes reasonable and probable cause for the prosecution.' *Dallison v Caffery* [1964] 2 All ER 610 at 619, CA, per Diplock LJ; also reported [1965] 1 QB 348

MALINGERING

Any person subject to military [*or* air-force] law who—

(a) falsely pretends to be suffering from sickness or disability, or
(b) injures himself with intent thereby to render himself unfit for service, or causes

himself to be injured by any person with that intent, or

(c) injures another person subject to service law, at the instance of that person, with intent thereby to render that person unfit for service, or

(d) with intent to render or keep himself unfit for service, does or fails to do any thing (whether at the time of the act or omission he is in hospital or not) whereby he produces, or prolongs or aggravates, any sickness or disability,

shall be guilty of malingering. (Army Act 1955, s 42(1), as amended by the Armed Forces Act 1971, s 14; Air Force Act 1955, s 42(1), as similarly amended)

A person is guilty of malingering within the meaning of this section if he falsely pretends to be suffering from sickness or disability, if he injures himself with intent thereby to render himself unfit for service, or causes himself to be injured by any person with that intent, if he injures another person subject to service law at the instance of that other person and with intent thereby to render that other person unfit for service, or if, with intent to render or keep himself unfit for service, he does or fails to do anything (whether at the time of the act or omission he is in hospital or not) whereby he produces, or prolongs or aggravates, any sickness or disability; and for the purpose of this subsection the expression 'unfit' includes temporarily unfit. (Naval Discipline Act 1957, s 27(1), as amended by the Armed Forces Act 1971, s 14)

MALPRACTICE

Canada 'The action is for contract and not negligence. But either or both ways it is for malpractice. The key word is "malpractice" which is defined in Mozley and Whiteley's Law Dictionary, 9th edn, at p 200, as follows: "Mala Praxis is improper or unskilful management of a case by a surgeon, physician, or apothecary, whereby a patient is injured; whether it be by neglect, or for curiosity and experiment." A breach of duty whether imposed by law or arising from contract to fully inform a patient of the risks or hazards of a surgical procedure is malpractice.' *Fishman v Waters* (1983) 4 DLR (4th) 760 at 762, Man CA, per Hall JA

MAN

'Man' includes a male of any age. (Sex Discrimination Act 1975, s 5(2))

In the preceding subsection [which makes incitement of a young girl to incest an offence] 'man' includes boy, 'sister' includes half-sister, and for the purpose of that subsection any expression importing a relationship between two people shall be taken to apply notwithstanding that the relationship is not traced through lawful wedlock. (Criminal Law Act 1977, s 54(2))

'No doubt, the word "man", in a scientific treatise on zoology or fossil organic remains, would include men, women and children, as constituting the highest order of vertebrate animals. It is also used in an abstract and general sense in philosophical or religious disquisitions. But, in almost every other connection, the word "man" is used in contradistinction to "woman". Certainly this restricted sense is its ordinary and popular sense.' *Chorlton v Lings* (1868) LR 4 CP 374 at 392, per Byles J

Australia 'The problem for decision is whether the words "officers and/or men" include members of the Royal Australian Naval Nursing Service and the Women's Royal Australian Naval Service. . . . It is argued that the term "men" must be construed in its ordinary sense to include males only. But if the word "officers" includes women officers, it would produce an incongruous result if the "Wrans", as they are called in the Regulations, were excluded. The argument in favour of the women is that "officers and men" is a composite phrase used to embrace all the members of the Royal Australian Navy, and is equivalent to a phrase such as "officers and non-officers". The word "man" is not always used to denote a male member of the human race. It is sometimes used, e.g. in contradistinction to youth, and in a phrase such as this it may be used in contrast to the word "officer". This in my opinion is the true meaning of the expression "officers and men" in the deeds, namely that it denotes all members of the Royal Australian Navy, and the answer to the question asked in the summons therefore turns on whether members of the women's services are members of the Royal Australian Navy.' *Re Royal Australian Navy Relief Fund, Showers v O'Leary* [1946] VLR 285 at 286, 287, per O'Bryan J

MANAGE *See also* KEEP

'By the common law a landlord is entitled to distrain upon goods upon the demised premises without reference to the ownership of the goods. This is the general rule; but it is subject to certain exceptions, which are as well established as the rule itself. Any man claiming the benefit of one of these exceptions must satisfy the court that his case falls within the exception. No considerations of hardship can avail the man whose goods are thus taken to satisfy a debt which he has not contracted to pay. The rights of the landlord are purely legal, and so are the exceptions. Now in the leading case of *Simpson v Hartopp* [(1744) Willes 512] decided in the year 1744, Willes CJ laid down the exceptions with great accuracy, and the words used by him must be taken to define and limit the exceptions precisely. The only one material for this appeal is the second—namely, "things delivered to a person exercising a public trade, to be carried, wrought, worked up, or managed in the way of his trade or employ". . . . What is the meaning of "managed"? . . . It is sufficient to say, in favour of the appellant, that according to a long course of decisions the word "managed" must be taken in a wide sense so as to include, if not to be equivalent to, "disposed of".' *Challoner v Robinson* [1908] 1 Ch 49 at 58, 59, CA, per cur.

MANAGEMENT

Concerned in

'The words [in the Dangerous Drugs Act 1965, s 5(b) (repealed; see now the Misuse of Drugs Act 1971, s 8)] "concerned in the management" are not, on the face of them, very clear, but at least they suggest some technical or acquired meaning, some meaning other than one which refers merely to such common transactions as letting or licensing the occupation of premises. For if it had been intended to penalise anyone who lets or licenses premises on which cannabis comes to be smoked, it would have been easy to do so in simple language. This impression is strengthened when the following words of the paragraph are read. They reflect what I would think to be logically correct, namely, that one does not "manage" premises, the inert subject of a conveyance or a lease, but rather some human activity on the premises which the manager has an interest in directing. And so, when the paragraph speaks of management of premises, and for a purpose, I would expect the purpose for which the premises are used to be that of the manager, otherwise, what would be the nature and object of the management?' *Sweet v Parsley* [1969] 1 All ER 347 at 359, HL, per Lord Wilberforce

New Zealand [By the Companies Act 1955, s 188(1) it is an offence for an undischarged bankrupt to act as a director of, or directly or indirectly take part in or be 'concerned in the management' of, any company.] 'It is not . . . an offence for an undischarged bankrupt to be employed by a company in a minor capacity, for instance as typist or clerk or on routine duties, but I think the section prohibits such a person from taking any hand in the real business affairs of the company. . . . It is irrelevant whether, in the final analysis, what the accused did was given the seal of approval by someone else or not.' *R v Newth* [1974] 2 NZLR 760 at 761, per Quilliam J

Of camp

'Management', in relation to a camp, includes the arrangement and supervision of all matters connected with the use of the camp, and the provision of facilities for recreation for the persons using it. (Camps Act 1939, s 6)

Of property

[The Trustee Act 1925, s 57 enables the court to confer powers of sale, etc, upon trustees responsible for the 'management or administration' of property.] 'It is clear, in our judgment, that the subject-matter both of "management" and "administration" in s 57 is trust property which is vested in trustees, and, in our opinion, "trust property" cannot by any legitimate stretch of the language include the equitable interests which a settlor has created in that property. We think that the reason for the appearance of the word "administration" as an alternative to "management" in the section is that, although the words do largely overlap, it was thought possible that an unduly narrow interpretation might be adopted if only one word were to be used without the other. Be that as it may, we are satisfied that the application of both words is confined to the managerial supervision and control of trust property on behalf of beneficiaries.' *Re Downshire's Settled Estates, Downshire (Marquis) v Royal Bank of Scotland* [1953] 1 All ER 103 at 118, CA, per Evershed MR and Romer LJ (also reported in [1953] Ch 218 at 247)

Of ship *See also* NAVIGATION

'I think it is desirable . . . to express the view which I hold about the question turning on the construction of the words "management of the ship". I am not satisfied that they go much, if at all, beyond the word "navigation". Some things may be suggested, to which the word "management" is perhaps applicable beyond that of "navigation", but I feel that it is not such clear and expressive language as to include within it the words "improper stowage". It seems to me a perversion of terms to say that the management of a ship has anything to do with the stowage of the cargo.' *The Ferro* [1893] P 38 at 46, DC, per Gorell Barnes J

[A bill of lading provided that the shipowner was to be subject to the Act of Congress of the United States approved on 13 February 1893, and known as the Harter Act. By s 3 of that Act, and subject to the conditions therein named, neither the vessel, her owner or owners, or charterers were responsible for damage or loss resulting from faults or errors in navigation or in the 'management' of the said vessel.] 'It seems to me clear that the word "management" goes somewhat beyond—perhaps not much beyond—navigation, but far enough to take in this very class of acts which do not affect the sailing or movement of the vessel, but do affect the vessel itself. . . . I see no reason for limiting the word "management" to the period of the vessel being actually at sea.' *The Glenochil* [1896] P 10 at 15, 16, per Jeune P

[Failure to prosecute a voyage with the utmost dispatch, as required by a charterparty, was found to be due to lack of speed owing to insufficient coal consumption.] 'It is not pretended that the ship was handled in an unseamanlike manner or that either ship or cargo were imperilled by the navigation which took place. The word "management" may better fit the present case, but it is not a term of art; it has no precise legal meaning and its application depends on the facts, as appreciated by persons experienced in dealing with steamers. There is a management, which is of the shore, and a management which is of the sea.' *Suzuki & Co v T Benyon & Co* (1926) 95 LJKB 397 at 404, per Lord Sumner

[Under the Sea Carriage of Goods (Australia) Act 1924, a carrier was not liable for damage arising from neglect in the navigation and 'management' of a ship.] 'The word "navigation" is clearly only applicable to the ship as such, and I think the more general word "management" should be read as *ejusdem generis*, and the word "ship" should receive the same connotation with each of the substantives on which it is dependent, the word "management" covering many acts directly affecting the ship which could not well be covered by "navigation".' *Foreman & Ellams Ltd v Federal Steam Navigation Co Ltd* [1928] 2 KB 424 at 439, per Wright J

'In the case of *The Glenochil* [supra] . . . Gorell Barnes J says . . . "I think that where the act done in the management of the ship is one which is necessarily done in the proper handling of the vessel, though in the particular case the handling is not properly done, but is done for the safety of the ship herself, and is not primarily done at all in connection with the cargo, that must be a matter which falls within the words 'management of the said vessel'." . . . My Lords, in my judgment, the principle laid down in *The Glenochil* . . . is the correct one to apply . . . if the principle is clearly borne in mind of distinguishing between want of care of cargo and want of care of vessel indirectly affecting the cargo. . . . There ought not to be any great difficulty in arriving at a proper conclusion.' *Gosse Millerd Ltd v Canadian Government Merchant Marine Ltd, The Canadian Highlander* [1929] AC 223 at 231–233, per Lord Hailsham LC

See, generally, 43 Halsbury's Laws (4th edn) para 779.

MANAGER

'In a joint stock and in a private bank, every one employed, whether he is called manager or secretary, in reality is nothing more than clerk, and heads of the separate departments may properly be called chief clerks. The prisoner, although called manager, was still a chief clerk.' *R v Greenland* (1867) LR 1 CCR 65 at 69, per Kelly CB

'The word "manager" it is admitted on all hands, will not apply to a man who acts once or twice, but he must be a delegate having the control of all the affairs of the company. I do not find any evidence that these directors have delegated their affairs to any person. The fact that the appellant, being a promoter, writes that he will call a meeting of the company and professes to enter into contracts for the company in the hope that the directors will acknowledge and ratify those contracts, does not make him in any sense the universal delegate of all their affairs, or manager de facto.'

Gibson v Barton (1875) LR 10 QB 329 at 344, per Quain J

[The Larceny Act 1861, s 84 (repealed; see now Theft Act 1968, s 18), made it a misdemeanour for a director, 'manager', or public officer of a corporate body or public company to publish false statements with intent to deceive or defraud, etc] 'It is necessary under this section both to charge in the indictment that the man was manager, and to prove it to the satisfaction of the jury. . . . The learned judge says that the jury must find that the defendant was a person who in fact managed the affairs of the company; the direction does not say "managed the company". . . . The direction to the jury meant, as I think, if you find that the defendant was the person who did the acts in the management of the company as managing its business—"its affairs" is what is said in the direction—if you find that he did that, then it does not signify that there was no appointment of him as manager. It seems to me that upon a fair interpretation of it that is what the direction must have meant. and I think therefore it is correct.' *R v Lawson* [1905] 1 KB 541 at 550, 551, CCR, per Channell J

'The phrase "manager of the company", prima facie, according to the ordinary meaning of the words, connotes a person holding, whether de jure or de facto, a post in or with the company of a nature charging him with the duty of managing the affairs of the company for the company's benefit; whereas a receiver and manager for debenture-holders is a person appointed by the debenture-holders to whom the company has given powers of management pursuant to the contract of loan constituted by the debenture and as a condition of obtaining the loan, to enable him to preserve and realise the assets comprised in the security for the benefit of the debenture-holders. The company gets the loan on terms that the lenders shall be entitled, for the purpose of making their security effective, to appoint a receiver with powers of sale and of management pending sale, and with full discretion as to the exercise and mode of exercising those powers. The primary duty of the receiver is to the debenture-holders and not to the company. He is receiver and manager of the property of the company for the debenture-holders, not manager of the company. The company is entitled to any surplus of assets remaining after the debenture debt has been discharged, and is entitled to proper accounts. The whole purpose of the receiver and manager's appointment would obviously be stultified if the company could claim that a receiver and manager owes it any duty comparable to the duty owed to a company by its own directors or managers.' *Re Johnson (B) & Co (Builders) Ltd* [1955] 2 All ER 775 at 790, CA, per Jenkins L; see also [1955] Ch 634.

'There is an accepted meaning of the word "manager" in the Companies Acts. In *Gibson v Barton* [supra] Blackburn J said: "We have to say who is to be considered a manager. A manager would be, in ordinary talk, a person who has the management of the whole affairs of the company; not an agent who is to do a particular thing, or a servant who is to obey orders, but a person who is intrusted with power to transact the whole of the affairs of the company." That passage was no doubt in the mind of Jenkins LJ, in *Re B Johnson & Co (Builders) Ltd* [supra], where he said: ". . . the phrase 'manager of the company', prima facie, according to the ordinary meaning of the words, connotes a person holding, whether de jure or de facto, a post in or with the company of a nature charging him with the duty of managing the affairs of the company for the company's benefit. . . ." That is the meaning of the word "manager" in the Companies Acts and we should apply it here also. The word "manager" means a person who is managing the affairs of the company as a whole. The word "officer" has a similar connotation. "Officer" may include, of course, a person who is not a manager. It includes a secretary. It would also include an auditor, and some others. But the only relevant "officer" here is an officer who is a "manager". In this context it means a person who is managing in a governing role the affairs of the company itself.' *Registrar of Restrictive Trading Agreements v W H Smith & Son Ltd* [1969] 3 All ER 1065 at 1069, CA, per Lord Denning MR

[The question was whether an employee had committed an offence in connection with the 'management' of a company's affairs within the Companies Act 1948, s 441 (repealed; see now the Companies Act 1985, s 721(1))]. 'The expression "manager" should not be too narrowly construed. It is not to be equated with a managing or other director or a general manager. As I see it, any person who in the affairs of the company exercises a supervisory control which reflects a general policy of the company for the time being or which is related to the general administration of the company is in the sphere of management. He need not be a member of the board of directors. He need not be subject to specific instructions from the board. If he fulfils a function which touches the central administration of the company, that in my view is sufficient to constitute him an officer or manager of the company for the purposes of s 441 of the 1948 Act.' *Re a Company* [1980] 1 All ER 284 at 287, CA, per Lord Denning MR

Canada 'We were not informed as to Mar Leung's duties in the bank, or, for example, if he had a private office. Clearly, however, he must have been something more than a teller or clerk, else why describe him as "Chinese Manager"? The term "Manager" in itself implies certain control and authority. That he had no subordinates does not imply he had not certain control and authority in respect to Chinese business. That he was subordinate to the branch manager and the accountant is not inconsistent with the possession of certain control and authority in respect to Chinese business. For example, the chief trader in *Johnson v Solloway Mills Co Ltd* [(1931) 45 BCR 35] would naturally be subordinate to the manager; and vide *Hyslop v New Westminster Trustees* [[1930] 3 WWR 227]. Mar Leung's apparent authority should be regarded as his real authority, at least for the purpose of determining whether he may be examined for discovery as a former "officer" of the bank.' *Shou Yin Mar v Royal Bank of Canada* [1940] 2 WWR 330 at 332, BCCA, per O'Halloran JA

Canada 'It is obvious, I think, that "managerial" [in the Labour Relations Act, RSO 1950, c 194 (see now RSO 1980, c 228)] means something pertaining to or characteristic of a manager and it is equally obvious that the word "manager" means one who manages. . . . It [manage] apparently includes the action or manner of conducting affairs or administering and directing or controlling any matter. It is obvious, I think, that the essential meaning of the word is to control and direct and that must obviously include not only administration but direction of planning for any particular enterprise. That obviously involves not only planning but the collecting and collating of information from which plans may be evolved.' *Re Canadian General Electric Co Ltd and Ontario Labour Relations Board* [1956] OR 437 at 443, Ont SC, per Wells J; reversed on other grounds, [1957] OR 316

MANAGING DIRECTOR

'The law does not prescribe the duties of a managing director, the parties are left to define his duties, and I can see nothing inconsistent in an agreement that a person shall be a managing director of a company, but shall devote his attention to managing subsidiary companies.' *Holdsworth (Harold) & Co (Wakefield) Ltd v Caddies* [1955] 1 All ER 725 at 738, HL, per Lord Reid

MANDAMUS

The order of mandamus is of a most extensive remedial nature, and is, in form, a command issuing from the High Court of Justice, directed to any person, corporation, or inferior tribunal, requiring him or them to do some particular thing therein specified which appertains to his or their office and is in the nature of a public duty. Its purpose is to remedy defects of justice; and accordingly it will issue, to the end that justice may be done, in all cases where there is a specific legal right and no specific legal remedy for enforcing that right; and it may issue in cases where, although there is an alternative legal remedy, yet that mode of redress is less convenient, beneficial and effectual. (1 Halsbury's Laws (4th edn) para 89)

The order of mandamus is, in form, a command issuing from the High Court and directed to any person, corporation, or inferior tribunal, requiring him or it to do some particular thing specified in it which appertains to his or its office and is in the nature of a public duty. (11 Halsbury's Laws (4th edn) para 1521)

A writ [now order] of mandamus is, in general, a command issuing in the king's name from the court of king's bench, and directed to any person, corporation, or inferior court of judicature, within the king's dominions; requiring them to do some *particular* thing therein specified, which appertains to their office and duty, and which the court of king's bench has previously determined, or at least supposes, to be consonant to right and justice. It is a high prerogative writ, of a most extensively remedial nature: and may be issued in some cases where the injured party has also another more tedious method of redress, as in the case of admission or restitution to an office; but it issues in all cases where the party hath a right to have any thing done, and hath no other specific means of compelling its performance. (3 Bl Com 110)

'A writ [now order] of mandamus is a prerogative writ and not a writ of right, and it is in this sense in the discretion of the court whether it shall be granted or not. The court may refuse to grant the writ not only upon the merits, but upon some delay, or other matter personal to the party applying for it; in this the court exercises a discretion which cannot be questioned. So in cases where the right, in respect of which a rule for a mandamus has been granted, upon showing cause appears to be doubtful, the court frequently grants a mandamus in order that the right may be tried upon the return; this also is a matter of discretion. But where the judges grant a peremptory mandamus, which is a determination of the right, and not a mere dealing with the writ, they decide according to the merits of the case, and not upon their own discretion, and their judgment must be subject to review, as in every other decision in actions before them.' *R v All Saints, Wigan (Churchwardens)* (1876) 1 App Cas 611 at 620, per Lord Chelmsford

[See now the Supreme Court Act 1981, s 29.]

MANDATE

Mandate . . . may be defined as a bailment of a specific chattel in regard to which the bailee engages to do some act without reward. (2 Halsbury's Laws (4th edn) para 1520)

MANDATORY INJUNCTION *See* INJUNCTION

MANIPULATION

'The word "manipulation" is a wide and comprehensive term, defined generally as handling or treating, especially with skill, and I am unable to read it so as to exclude the work of a dresser of stone. According to the ordinary use of language such dressing, whether it be rough-dressing or fine-dressing, can properly be described as manipulation.' *Milne (Alexander) & Son v Maclean & Son* (1935) 28 BWCC Supp 44 at 52, per the Lord Justice-Clerk

MANNER

New Zealand 'The meaning of the word "manner" [in the Estate and Gift Duties Act 1968, s 23] is primarily the way in which something is done or takes place; mode of action or procedure, while the meaning of the word "terms" is conditions or stipulations limiting what is proposed to be granted or done. These meanings have been extracted from the Shorter Oxford Dictionary, To my mind the "manner" of the dealing is the way in which the parties have conducted themselves during the course of negotiations, including a consideration as to the basis from which each party is negotiating. That will include a consideration as to whether they are negotiating on equal terms and at arm's length or as one would expect in a normal commercial transaction.' *Re Peale, Hooper and Milne v CIR* (1984) 7 TRNZ 23 at 31, per Sinclair J

MANOR *See also* WASTE LAND

Manors were not abolished by the Law of Property Act 1922 or the Law of Property Act 1925, and the provisions of the latter Act relating to freehold land were expressly applied to manors, reputed manors and lordships; but since the enfranchisement of copyholds and customary freeholds on 1st January 1926 and the subsequent extinguishment of manorial incidents, the existence, extent and transmission of manors is of considerably less importance than before 1926. Nevertheless, the lordship of a manor may still carry some or all of the manorial rights expressly preserved in 1926, of which the most important are the rights of mines and minerals and the sporting rights; it may carry certain appendant franchises and the theoretical right to hold courts; and certain manors held in grand serjeanty are said to carry the right to perform services at the coronation of the Sovereign. (9 Halsbury's Laws (4th edn) para 753)

Manors are in substance as ancient as the Saxon constitution, though perhaps differing a little, in some immaterial circumstances, from those that exist at this day. . . . A manor, *manerium, a manendo*, because the usual residence of the owner, seems to have been a district of ground, held by lords or great personages; who kept in their own hands so much land as was necessary for the use of their families, which were called *terrae dominicales*, or *demesne* lands; being occupied by the lord, or *dominus manerii*, and his servants. The other *tenemental* lands they distributed among their tenants. (2 Bl Com 90)

'Manor' shall extend to and include any hundred, honor, or lordship. (Inclosure Act 1845, s 167)

In this section 'manorial documents' mean court rolls, surveys, maps, terriers, documents, and books of every description relating to the boundaries, franchises, wastes, customs or courts of a manor, but do not include the deeds and other instruments required for evidencing the title to a manor; 'manor' includes a lordship and a reputed lordship; and 'lord of the manor' includes any person entitled to manorial documents. (Law of Property Act 1922, s 144(6))

'Manor' includes a lordship, and reputed manor or lordship. (Law of Property Act 1925, s 205(1)(ix); Settled Land Act 1925, s 117(1)(xiv))

'In medieval times the manor was the nucleus of English rural life. It was an administrative unit of an extensive area of land. The whole of it was owned originally by the lord of the manor. He lived in the big house called the manor house. Attached to it were many acres of grassland and woodlands called the park. These were the "demesne lands" which were for the personal use of the lord of the manor. Dotted all round were the inclosed homes and land occupied by the "tenants of the manor". They held them by copyhold tenure. Their titles were entered in the court rolls of the manor. They were nearly equivalent to freehold, but the tenants were described as "tenants of the manor". The rest of the manorial lands were the "waste lands of the manor". The tenants of the manor had the right to graze their animals on the waste lands of the manor. Although the demesne land was personal to the lord of the manor, nevertheless he sometimes granted to the tenants of the manor the right to graze their animals on it, or they acquired it by custom. In such case their right to graze on the demesne land was indistinguishable from their right to graze on the waste lands of the manor, so long as it remained open to them and uncultivated, although there might be hedges and gates to keep the cattle from straying. So much so that their rights over it became known as a "right of common" and the land became known as "common land". In the course of time, however, the lordship of the manor became severed from the lands of the manor. This was where the lord of the manor sold off parcels of the land to purchasers. He might, for instance, sell off the demesne lands and convey them as a distinct property. . . . Nowadays there are few, if any, manors left intact. The lords of the manor have sold off the house and lands to strangers. Nothing remains in the lordship except the title of lord of the manor and the right to hold the manorial documents. This bare title and right is sometimes put on the market and sold for a nominal figure of £200 or £300. The one point of principle of all this is that no lord of the manor could, by selling the manorial lands, deprive the tenants of the manor of their rights of common over them, no matter whether those lands were originally part of the demesne lands or the waste land of the manor.' *Corpus Christi College, Oxford v Gloucestershire County Council* [1982] 3 All ER 995 at 998, 999, CA, per Lord Denning MR

MANSE *See* GLEBE

MANSION-HOUSE

[A testator directed by his will that his trustees should erect a 'mansion-house' with suitable offices for the owner of his estates.] 'It would be absurd to hold that the testator intended merely a mansion-house and offices to be erected in a field; and the reasonable construction of the direction in his will, is that he meant the mansion-house to be made suitable, in every respect, for the residence of the owner of an estate worth £15,000 a year; which it would not be without the appendages of a garden, lawns, and pleasure grounds, nor unless proper approaches were made to it.' *Lombe v Stoughton* (1849) 17 Sim 84 at 84, 85, per Shadwell V-C

Principal mansion-house

[The Settled Land Act 1890, s 10 (repealed; see now the Settled Land Act 1925, s 65), provided that the 'principal mansion-house' on settled land should not be leased by the tenant for life without the consent of the trustees of the settlement or an order of the court.] 'I am not prepared to say there may not be more than one principal mansion-house on land settled to the same uses by one and the same instrument. Probably it will be found that there are many cases in which on large estates there are several mansion houses, which might equally be styled principal mansion houses, and that all these lands are settled by one and the same instrument, or at any rate, fall within that which we are familiar with now, a compound settlement. It seems to me it is impossible to say that there cannot be two principal mansion-houses on the same settled land in that sense—on lands which are held by the same tenant for life under the same title. It must be a question in every case, and it is easy, I think, to put a case where there would be two mansion houses, and yet one would be distinctly the principal mansion-house.' *Gilbey v Rush* [1906] 1 Ch 11 at 20, 21, per Kekewich J

'It appears to me . . . that I must form my judgment upon the footing that the testator has died leaving things as they are today, with the land in Essex and this land in Kent settled under one settlement upon the same trusts. . . . But on the land so settled there are two residences, the one Copt Hall and the other this hall at Bickley. Now in that state of things one would have to ask oneself this:—"Are both of these houses the principal mansion-houses on the settled land, or is one of them the principal mansion-house and the other of secondary importance?" Copt Hall is a purely residential property, situate within some 5,000 acres of land, and at present occupied by the tenant for life. Bickley Hall, on the other hand, is situate in a neighbourhood somewhat nearer London, and is on an estate originally containing some 200 acres, of which about 103 acres were formerly pleasure grounds and park land. . . . At the particular moment . . . Bickley Hall has been converted from a purely residential house into a house adapted for the carrying on of the business or profession of a schoolmaster. I cannot help thinking that if the testator had died yesterday, and we were determining today which of these two houses constituted the principal mansion-house, there would be only one answer to the question. The answer . . . would be that the principal mansion-house is the hall on the Copt Hall estate.' *Re Wythes' Settled Estates* [1908] 1 Ch 593 at 598, per Eve J

'In this case, I have this position. I have a house which was undoubtedly the principal mansion-house [within the Settled Land Act 1925 (see supra)] but which, having regard to the circumstances of the present day, it is quite impossible for the limited owner of the property to use as the principal mansion-house. The evidence, apart from one's own knowledge in cases of this sort, is quite plain that such a house as Duncombe Park, having regard to the income of the estate as a whole, is out of the question for the person who is the limited owner of the estate. It is a wholly impracticable proposition, and the only thing to be done, if the sale of it is not possible, is to find a tenant who will take it over, and save the limited owner some part, at any rate, of the expense of its upkeep and maintenance. For the next thirty years, Duncombe Park cannot be treated as the principal mansion-house, in the sense that it cannot be occupied by the owner for the time being of the estate, so that, at any rate for a period of time, it will cease to be the principal mansion-house, in the sense that it can no longer be the house that was adapted for, and intended to be used as, the house of the owner of the estate. The difficulty I have felt in this case is this. Can a limited owner, in circumstances such as these, when a house which was the principal mansion-house ceases to be that principal mansion-house, make some other house on his property the principal mansion-house? . . . On the whole, I have come to the conclusion that I am not precluded from giving effect to what I think, in this particular case, are the true facts. The house itself, Duncombe Park, for all purposes has ceased to be the principal mansion-house of this estate, and will continue in that position—not to be the principal mansion-house—for, at any rate, some thirty years. Meanwhile, the present owner has found a house which, by expenditure of money upon it, has been adapted for use by him, as the owner of the estate, and is intended to be used by him when he is in residence on the estate. Looking at the matter from a purely practical point of view, the result of that, in my judgment, is that Duncombe Park is no longer to be treated as the principal mansion-house of the estate, and, in all the circumstances, I have come to the conclusion that I can properly say that this [the second] house, which has now been adapted for use by the tenant for life, is, and should be treated as, the principal mansion-house of the estate.' *Re Feversham Settled Estate* [1938] 2 All ER 210 at 213, 214, per Farwell J

See, generally, 42 Halsbury's Laws (4th edn) paras 585 et seq.

MANSLAUGHTER *See also* SUICIDE

Manslaughter differs from murder only in relation to the mental element necessary to support the charge. Manslaughter may be classified as voluntary or involuntary, the distinction being that in cases of voluntary manslaughter a person may be convicted of the offence notwithstanding that he may have the mens rea of murder. Voluntary manslaughter takes the forms of (1) killing under provocation; (2) killing by a person who, by reason of abnormality of mind, suffers from diminished responsibility; and (3) killing in pursuance of a suicide pact. Involuntary manslaughter is committed (1) where death results from an unlawful act which any reasonable person would recognise as likely to expose another to the risk of injury; and (2) where death is caused by gross negligence. (11 Halsbury's Laws (4th edn) para 1161)

'A man is guilty of involuntary manslaughter when he intends an unlawful act and one likely to do harm to the person and death results which was neither foreseen nor intended. It is the accident of death resulting which makes him guilty of manslaughter as opposed to some lesser offence, such as assault or, in the present case, abortion.' *R v Creamer* [1965] 3 All ER 257 at 262, CCA, per cur.

'In *R v Larkin* [[1943] 1 All ER 217] Humphreys J said: "Where the act which a person is engaged in performing is unlawful, then if at the same time it is a dangerous act, that is, an act which is likely to injure another person, and quite inadvertently he causes the death of that other person by that act, then he is guilty of manslaughter." . . . That is an admirably clear statement of the law which has been applied many times. It makes it plain (a) that an accused is guilty of manslaughter if it is proved that he intentionally did an act which was unlawful and dangerous and that that act inadvertently caused death and (b) that it is unnecessary to prove that the accused knew that the act was unlawful or dangerous. This is one of the reasons why cases of manslaughter vary so infinitely in their gravity. They may amount to little more than pure inadvertence and sometimes to little less than murder.' *Director of Public Prosecutions v Newbury* [1976] 2 All ER 365 at 367, HL, per Lord Salmon.

[Lord Salmon went on to disapprove a dictum of Lord Denning MR in *Gray v Barr* [1971] 2 All ER 956 which had appeared to suggest that for an act to constitute manslaughter there must be mens rea.]

[The appellant became involved in an altercation with A. He struck A, who fell against B. Both fell to the ground and B later died in hospital from his injuries.] 'Both counsel were agreed that there are four elements in this class of manslaughter, as follows: first, there must be an act which is unlawful; second, it must be a dangerous act, in the sense that a sober and reasonable person would inevitably recognise that it carried some risk of harm, albeit not serious harm (that being an objective test); third, the act must be a substantial cause of death; fourth, the act itself must be intentional.' *R v Mitchell* [1983] 2 All ER 427 at 429, CA, per cur.

Australia 'The correct statement of law is that a man is prima facie guilty of manslaughter if he, without having any intention to kill or do grievous bodily harm, kills another by an act which is both unlawful and dangerous. If, however, he raises by evidence a defence that he had a lawful justification or excuse for his act, he is not guilty of manslaughter unless the Crown establishes beyond reasonable doubt that he had none such. In other words, the act causing death must first be shown to be prima facie unlawful, but it may cease to be unlawful if it can in the particular circumstances be justified or excused.' *R v Turner* [1962] VR 30 at 34, per cur.

MANSUETAE NATURAE *See* ANIMAL

MANUAL LABOUR

'It seems to me that "manual labour" can only mean "labour performed by hand".' *Morgan v London General Omnibus Co* (1884) 13 QBD 832 at 834, CA, per Bowen LJ

'The appellant was employed as a grocer's assistant in a shop, and his business was to take orders from the customers and to carry them out. In doing this he may have to show goods, and if the customers take away the goods he has to make up the parcels. In doing this he has to use his hands, and the question is whether that makes him a manual labourer. There can be no manual labour without user of the hands; but it does not at all follow that every user of the hands is manual labour, so as to make the person who does it a manual labourer.' *Bound v Lawrence* [1892] 1 QB 226 at 228, CA, per Lord Esher MR

'It is difficult to imagine any work done by man so purely intellectual as to require no kind of work with the hands; and the converse is equally true, that there can hardly be work with the hands that requires no intellectual effort. If, then, the words "manual labour" are to have the full significance which could be put on them, they would be extended to every kind of employment. . . . The determination of what is substantial and what accessory may be a question of difficulty; but, in my view of this case, the appellant was not engaged in manual labour. In his occupation the knowledge and skill required in selling the goods to customers is more important than the manual work that he does, and the latter is an incident of his employment.' Ibid at 229, per Fry LJ

[The Factory and Workshop Act 1901, s 149(1)

(repealed; cf now the Factories Act 1961, s 175(1)), defined the expression 'workshop' as being any room in which 'manual labour' was exercised by way of trade in or incidental to certain purposes.] 'I do not think that manual labour need be labour requiring a great exertion of strength, and it seems to me that the kind of labour indicated by this particular Act of Parliament may be very light labour indeed, for the Act appears to contemplate that even the plaiting of straw, which is a thing that one would do with one's finger and thumb, may be properly described as manual labour.' *Hoare v Green (Robert) Ltd* [1907] 2 KB 315 at 321, DC, per Darling J

'No one could say that the work of an artist who painted an original picture, whether in oils or in water colours, was manual labour. It involves manual work—namely, the placing by the artist of the colours upon the canvas, or the paper, or whatever may be the material on which he is painting his picture. So in the present case, the employee [a lithographer] has to deal in a particular way with a particular surface which is ultimately to be used in the production of a picture. In doing this he necessarily uses his hands, but the use to which he puts them is not labour, because it involves no strenuous exercise of the muscles of his hand or his arm. The real labour involved is labour of the brain and the intelligence. A lithographic artist can no more be said to be engaged in manual labour than a Royal Academician who paints a portrait or landscape can be said to be engaged in manual labour. . . . The case of the engravers is that of persons engaged in correcting and improving half-tone plates. That is even an *a fortiori* case. All the employee has to do is to take a graver's tool and make certain corrections in the plate submitted by way of approval, or tentatively submitted, for the reproduction by engraving of a picture or some other object. I think in this case also that the engraver is not employed in manual labour.' *Re National Insurance Act 1911, Re Lithographic Artists, Re Engravers* (1913) 108 LT 894 at 895, 896, per Warrington J

[The Factories Act 1961, s 175(1) defines 'factory' as any premises in which, or within the close or curtilage or precincts of which, persons are employed in 'manual labour' in any process for or incidental to certain specified purposes, amongst which are included the making, altering, repairing, etc, of any article for gain. An electrical engineer worked in a room behind a shop repairing television and radio sets.] 'It has been conceded that manual labour no longer involves any idea of the necessary exercise of the sinews and muscles of the limbs wielding the hammer or pickaxe or shouldering heavy loads and in these days, in my opinion, almost every process involves some mental direction by the brain to the hand. The fact that the employee is doing a technical and skilled job does not, in my view, prevent the operation from being one properly described as being an employment in manual labour.' *Stone (J & F) Lighting & Radio Ltd v Haygarth* [1966] 3 All ER 539 at 552, HL, per Lord Upjohn

'A person is not employed in "manual labour" for the purposes of any of the Acts, if his occupation is primarily or substantially an activity of a different kind and the manual work that he does is merely ancillary or accessory to that activity. . . . Examples of activities which are primarily non-manual, though involving some manual work, are (i) the work of a painter, sculptor or lithographic artist; (ii) managerial or supervisory work; (iii) selling in a shop; (iv) clerical work; (v) driving a vehicle or acting as conductor of a public service vehicle. In the sphere of repairing there seems to be no decided case, but it can be suggested with, at any rate, plausibility, that an artist restoring or even cleaning a picture, an expert in oriental ceramics repairing a Ming vase, or an archaeologist piecing together fragments of an Egyptian papyrus or Linea B script, would not be held to be employed in manual labour.' Ibid at 555, per Lord Pearson

[On the facts of the above case, the repairer was held to be 'employed in manual labour', and the premises therefore to be a factory.]

New Zealand ' "Manual labour" is a popular phrase, and, like most popular phrases, is incapable of precise definition, and hence it is not a matter for surprise that it has been the task of the courts not infrequently to explain its purport and meaning. It is now settled that there is a distinction between "manual work" and "manual labour" since, though every employee necessarily must do some manual work, it does not follow that he was employed by way of manual labour. To be so employed manual labour must have been the dominant feature of his employment.' *Tansey v Renown Collieries Ltd* [1945] NZLR 568 at 572, 573, per O'Regan J; also reported [1945] GLR 254 at 255

MANUFACTORY

In Lands Clauses Consolidation Act

In determining whether premises are a 'manufactory', regard must be had to the main use to which they are put. If the main business is manufacturing, the undertakers [for purposes of compulsory acquisition] may be required to take the whole of the premises, even though part may be used for other purposes, or may be temporarily let to another occupier. If a manufactory is partly worked by water power, and undertakers desire to take the water and the arrangements for storing and conveying the power, they may be required to take the whole manufactory. However, where the main business carried on upon premises is not manufacture, it is immaterial that some manufacture should be carried on incidentally to it. In such a case the undertakers may take the whole of the part used for manufacture without being required to take the other parts, and, similarly, they may take the part not used as the manufactory without taking the part so used. (8 Halsbury's Laws (4th edn) para 131)

[The Lands Clauses Consolidation Act 1845, s 92 provides that no party shall be required to sell or convey to promoters of an undertaking a part only of any house or other building or 'manufactory' if such party be willing and able to sell the whole thereof.] 'One of the meanings of the word "manufactory" is, I suppose, a place where a manufacture is carried on.' *Barker v North Staffordshire Rly Co* (1848) 2 De G & Sm 55 at 68, per Knight Bruce V-C

'The chief point for doubt is, whether the cottages and dwelling-house proposed to be taken for the railway are part of the manufactory [within the Lands Clauses Consolidation Act 1845, s 92 (see supra)] or not. I cannot doubt that the cottages are at all events. I am not sure as to the dwelling-house. But the cottages are the only warehouses attached to the manufactory—the place where all the goods are stored. There must be some place of that sort. And the circumstances of the road separating them from the main workshops is not, in my view, enough to make them a distinct property.' *Spackman v Great Western Rly Co* (1855) 26 LTOS 22 at 22, per Wood V-C

'The words in the 92nd section [of the Lands Clauses Consolidation Act 1845 (see supra)] are "any house, or other building, or manufactory". This is a manufactory beyond all question; it is not actually in work, but that makes no difference; it is in a condition to be worked at any time, and it cannot be said, either in popular or technical language, that this manufactory at Hammersmith consists simply of the land, and the bricks and mortar comprising the buildings, and not of the engines which are now affixed to the freehold.' *Gibson v Hammersmith & City Rly Co* (1862) 2 Drew & Sm 603 at 612, per Kindersley V-C

[A railway company desired to take over, under the Lands Clauses Consolidation Act 1845, s 92 (see supra), part of a goit (being land covered with water) over which they wanted to carry their line, also the shuttles, bridge, and mill house, without this being regarded as taking the 'manufactory'. The reservoir of which was fed by means of the goit.] 'The sole question I have to consider is, whether the land . . . intended to be taken is part of the manufactory within the meaning of the 92nd section. . . . Let us consider for a moment what the nature of the property is. First of all, there is the house of the man who looks after the shuttles; there are the shuttles by which the supply of water is regulated; and then there is the goit; the whole of them as far as I can see, connected with the reservoir, and the reservoir connected with the manufactory. The waterpower is, in fact, part of the motive power of the manufactory, and is sworn to be essential to the manufactory. That being so, the conclusion I have come to is, that what is proposed to be taken is part of the manufactory within the meaning of the 92nd section.' *Furniss v Midland Rly Co* (1868) LR 6 Eq 473 at 477, per Giffard V-C

'There are three words used [in the Lands Clauses Consolidation Act 1845, s 92 (see supra)]—"part only of any house or other building or manufactory". In my opinion those must be considered as three things, that is to say, there may be a manufactory which is not a building, there may be a building which could not properly be described as a house, and a house includes more than mere building, and I am of opinion that although a house or other building is read together in this sense, that a house involves the notion of building, yet that a manufactory does not involve necessarily the idea of building. Manufactory is put in there, in my opinion, to provide for the case of a manufacture being carried on on premises where there was no house or building, but yet it is a manufactory in the sense of its being premises appropriate for the carrying on of what may be called a manufacture, and is a manufactory in that sense.' *Richards v Swansea Improvement & Tramways Co* (1878) 9 Ch D 425 at 437, per Cotton LJ

'The question is whether Postern House is part of the manufactory. The 92nd section of the Lands Clauses [Lands Clauses Consolidation Act 1845 (see supra)] speaks of a house or other building or manufactory". A manufactory (which is not defined in the Act) must be a place where a manufacture is carried on.' *Benington & Sons v Metropolitan Board of Works* (1886) 54 LT 837 at 838, per Chitty J

'To ascertain what is a manufactory [within the Lands Clauses Consolidation Act 1845, s 92 (see supra)], regard must be had, and perhaps principally, to the user at the time of the notice to treat. It would not be necessary that every part of what would be reasonably called a manufactory should actually be in use at the time for the purpose of manufacture; for instance, there might be a large manufactory, and some part of it, say a large room, might not be required for the purpose of the business. Still, as it was all within the walls, although it was not then in use for the purpose of the business, . . . in my opinion that makes no difference as to that part being part of the manufactory.' *Brook v Manchester, Sheffield & Lincolnshire Rly Co* [1895] 2 Ch 571 at 574, per Chitty J

MANUFACTURE

'Manufacturing purposes' includes the carrying out of building operations and works of construction or civil engineering and the treatment of products by any process. (Iron and Steel Act 1967, Sch 4)

'Manufacture' includes construction by any method and the assembly of component parts. (Wireless Telegraphy Act 1967, s 7(12) as substituted by the Telecommunications Act 1984, s 177(1))

'Manufacture', in relation to a medicinal product, includes any process carried out in the course of making the product, but does not include dissolving or dispersing the product in, or diluting or mixing it with, some other substance used as a vehicle for the purpose of administering it and does not include the incorporation of the product in any animal feeding stuff. (Medicines Act 1968, s 132(1))

'Let us resort to the statute itself, 21 Jac 1, c 3 [Statute of Monopolies 1623]. We shall there find a monopoly defined to be "the privilege of the sole buying, selling, making, working, or using any thing within this realm'; and this is generally condemned as contrary to the fundamental law of the land. But the 5th and 6th sections of that statute save letters patent, and grants of privileges of the sole working or making of any manner of new manufacture within this realm, to the first and true inventor or inventors of such manufactures, with this qualification, "so they be not contrary to the law, nor mischievous to the state", in these three respects: first, "by raising the prices of commodities at home"; secondly, "by being hurtful to trade"; or, thirdly, by being "generally inconvenient". According to the letter of the statute, the saving goes only to the sole working and making; the sole buying, selling, and using, remain under the general prohibition; and with apparent good reason for so remaining, for the exclusive privilege of buying, selling, and using, could hardly be brought within the qualification of not being contrary to law, and mischievous to the state, in the respects which I have mentioned. I observe also, that according to the letter of the statute, the words "any manner of new manufacture" in the saving, fall very short of the words "any thing" in the first section. But most certainly the exposition of the statute, as far as usage will expound it, has gone very much beyond the letter. In the case in Salkeld [*Edgeberry v Stephens* (1693) 2 Salk 447], the words "new devices" are substituted and used as synonymous with the words "new manufacture". It was admitted in the argument at the bar, that the word "manufacture" in the statute was of extensive signification, that it applied not only to things made, but to the practice of making, to principles carried into practice in a new manner, to new results of principles carried into practice. Let us pursue this admission. Under things made, we may class, in the first place, new compositions of things, such as manufactures in the most ordinary sense of the word; secondly, all mechanical inventions, whether made to produce old or new effects, for a new piece of mechanism is certainly a thing made. Under the practice of making we may class all new artificial manners of operating with the hand, or with instruments in common use, new processes in any art producing effects useful to the public.' *Boulton v Bull* (1795) 2 Hy Bl 463 at 492, 493, per Eyre CJ

'The word "manufacture" has been generally understood to denote either a thing made, which is useful for its own sake, and vendible as such, as a medicine, a stove, a telescope, and many others, or to mean an engine or instrument, or some part of an engine or instrument, to be employed, either in the making of some previously known article, or in some other useful purpose, as a stocking-frame, or a steam-engine for raising water from mines. Or it may perhaps extend also to a new process to be carried on by known implements, or elements, acting upon known substances, and ultimately producing some other known substance, but producing it in a cheaper or more expeditious manner, or of a better and more useful kind. But no merely philosophical or abstract principle can answer to the word manufactures. Something of a corporeal and substantial nature, something that can be made by man from the matters subjected to his art and skill, or at least some new mode of employing practically his art and skill, is requisite to satisfy this word. A person, therefore, who applies to the Crown for a patent, may represent himself to be the inventor of some new thing, or of some new engine or instrument. And in the latter case he may represent himself to be the inventor of a new method of accomplishing that object, which is to be accomplished by his new engine or instrument, as was the case of Watt's patent [*Hornblower v Boulton* (1799) 8 Term Rep 95] in which he represented himself to be the inventor of a new method of lessening the consumption of steam and fuel in fire engines, and by his specification he described certain parts to be used in the construction of fire engines.' *R v Wheeler* (1819) 2 B & Ald 345 at 349, 350, per cur.

'. . . we think that the term "manufactured goods" must be understood in a popular sense, and must mean not merely goods produced from the raw state by manual skill and labour, but such as are ordinarily produced in manufactories; and we should therefore exclude stationery and include shoes, ironmongery, glass, and drapery. It should be observed, however, that having given what we conceive to be the meaning of the term, the application of that meaning to particular articles is a question of fact, not of law; and what we have suggested in this respect is not to be taken as conclusive.' *Parker v Great Western Rly Co* (1856) 6 E & B 77 at 109, per Coleridge J

'Your Lordships are well aware that by the large interpretation given to the word "manufacture", it not only comprehends productions, but it also comprehends the means of producing them. Therefore, in addition to the thing produced, it will comprehend a new machine, or a new combination of machinery: it will comprehend a new process, or an improvement of an old process.' *Ralston v Smith* (1865) 11 HL Cas 223 at 246, per Westbury LC

'If the proprietor of a quarry converts its soil into some manufactured article, it must be taken that he is a manufacturer *quoad* that article.' *Kent v Astley* (1869) LR 5 QB 19 at 22, 23, per Cockburn CJ

'I think . . . that it is manufacturing a mattress if you take flock out of an old and put it into a new cover.' *Guildford Corpn v Brown* [1915] 1 KB 256 at 258, per Ridley J

'It seems to me that when a person makes a machine, by getting component parts from elsewhere and assembling them together himself, he can properly be said to be "manufacturing" that machine. Take some of the large works where motor cars and aircraft are assembled. Those establishments are engaged in "manufacturing" the machines even though all the components come from other places.' *Prestcold (Central) Ltd v Minister of Labour* [1969] 1 All ER 69 at 71, 72, CA, per Lord Denning MR

Australia 'The ordinary meaning of the verb manufacture is to work up materials into forms suitable for use. . . . Where old materials are supplied there would only be such a manufacture if the work done was more than a mere repair or modification of the old materials and was such as to change the old goods into goods of a different character.' *Federal Comr of Taxation v Zinader* (1949) 78 CLR 336 at 350, per Williams J

Australia 'The primary meaning of the word "manufacture" when used as a verb is to make something by hand; but since the industrial revolution the word has come to mean manufacture by machinery, often on a large scale and with a division of labour. This accords with the dictionary definition. As Windeyer J said in *Ready Mixed Concrete (WA) Pty Ltd v FC of T* (1971) 2 ATR 305 at 308: "All that can perhaps be said of the word manufacture is that its derivative and etymological sense no longer determines its meaning. No longer is it restricted to the handiwork of individual craftsmen." To manufacture an article necessarily involves producing a different article from the articles, materials or ingredients from which it was made. As Darling J said in *McNicol v Pinch* [1906] 2 KB 352 at 361: "I think the essence of making or of manufacturing is that what is made shall be a different thing from that out of which it is made." That passage was approved and applied by Dixon J in *FC of T v Jack Zinader Pty Ltd* (1949) 78 CLR 336—the leading case in this field. Whether the article which results from the process of manufacturing is a different article from the constituents or ingredients from which it was made is a question of fact: the *Jack Zinader* case. "Production" . . . is a word of wide import; but it still involves the element of producing something different from the materials from which it was made.' *Federal Comr of Taxation v Jax Tyres Pty Ltd* (1984) 58 ALR 138 at 141–142, per Lockhart J

Canada 'The term "manufacture" as used in the language today no doubt includes the word "make"; and the converse is likewise doubtless true in modern usage, but it does not follow that "manufacture" and "make" invariably have the same meaning. For example, in the Shorter Oxford English Dictionary, the term "manufacture" is defined as: "The making of articles of material (now, on a large scale) by physical labour or mechanical power. . . . A branch of productive industry." The same dictionary indicates that in earlier times, the word had a connotation of "working with the hands; a manual occupation, handicraft", perhaps by reason of the Latin root, *manu facere*, which refers to making by hand.' *Compo Co Ltd v Blue Crest Music* [1980] 1 SCR 357 at 377, SCC, per Estey J

Product safety

United States The term 'manufacture' means to manufacture, produce, or assemble. (Consumer Product Safety Act 1972, s 3(a)(8))

MAP

'A map is a picture or representation of external objects with their relative positions, and if of two adjoining objects one is laid down incorrectly, the whole of the relative description of the two is incorrect.' *Lyle v Richards* (1866) LR 1 HL 222 at 240, per Lord Westbury

MARE

'Foals and fillies are within the statutes 2 & 3 Edw 6 [c 33 (repealed)], and are included in the words "horse, gelding, or mare", and therefore . . . the evidence of stealing a mare filly would support this indictment for stealing a mare.' *R v Welland* (1822) Russ & Ry 494 at 494, CCR, per cur.

MARINE *See* SEAMAN

MARINE ADVENTURE

(1) Subject to the provisions of this Act, every lawful marine adventure may be the subject of a contract of marine insurance.

(2) In particular there is a marine adventure where—

(a) Any ship goods or other moveables are exposed to maritime perils. Such property is in this Act referred to as 'insurable property';
(b) The earning or acquisition of any freight, passage money, commission, profit, or other pecuniary benefit, or the security for any advances, loan, or disbursements, is endangered by the exposure of insurable property to maritime perils;
(c) Any liability to a third party may be incurred by the owner of, or other person interested in or responsible for, insurable property, by reason of maritime perils.

(Marine Insurance Act 1906, s 3)

MARINE INSURANCE *See* INSURANCE

MARINE WATERS

In this section . . . 'marine waters' means waters (other than inland waters) within the seaward limits of the territorial sea adjacent to Great Britain. (Diseases of Fish Act 1983, s 7(8))

MARITIME LIEN *See* LIEN

MARITIME PERILS

'Maritime perils' means the perils consequent on, or incidental to, the navigation of the sea, that is to say, perils of the seas, fire, war perils, pirates, rovers, thieves, captures, seisures, restraints, and detainments of princes and peoples, jettisons, barratry, and any other perils, either of the like kind or which may be designated by the policy. (Marine Insurance Act 1906, s 3)

MARK

'Mark' includes a device, . . . label, . . . name, signature, word, letter, numeral, or any combination thereof. (Trade Marks Act 1938, s 68, as amended by the Trade Marks Act 1984, s 1(2), Sch 1)

'Mark' includes label. (Weights and Measures Act 1985, s 94(1))

'I do not consider that the ordinary meaning of "mark" in relation to goods extends to something which amounts to an entire and complete description or representation of the external appearance of the goods in question—the entire get-up. A mark, to be registered as a trade mark in respect of goods, must be something which can be represented or described separately from the goods in relation to which it is to be used in the sense that it is not merely a description of the goods as they appear to the eye.' *Re Smith Kline & French Laboratories Ltd's Applications* [1974] 2 All ER 826 at 835, CA, per Russell LJ

'The word "mark" has many meanings: Murray's Oxford Dictionary has nearly five pages dealing with them. In relation to "trade mark", the relevant meanings given in Murray's Dictionary are—"a device, stamp, seal, label, or the like, placed upon an article as an indication of ownership or origin, as an attestation of quality, as a means of identification, etc." The appearance of an article is something different from a mark on it. A mark on an article may be large or small; but if it becomes so large that it represents the appearance of the article, it is no longer a mark. To attempt to state in words when a mark on an article ceases to be such and becomes the appearance of the article itself is to attempt to solve the semantic problem which is typified by the question when does a heap become a pile.' Ibid at 839, per Buckley LJ

MARK OUT

'The lease speaks of a piece of ground which is marked out by a line, and according to the ordinary meaning of those words, and their reasonable interpretation in respect to a lease of land so circumstanced, we should understand them to refer to the operation of marking out by line actually made and completed before the execution of the lease.' *Doe d Mence v Hadley* (1849) 14 LTOS 102 at 103, per cur.

MARKET *See also* AVAILABLE MARKET; FAIR

At common law a market is a franchise conferring a right to hold a concourse of buyers and sellers to dispose of the commodities in respect of which the franchise is given. It is also applied to the same right when conferred by Act of Parliament. Although strictly applicable to the right itself, 'market' is often applied to the concourse of buyers and sellers, or to the market-place, or to the time of holding the market. A gathering of buyers and sellers, although held at regular intervals in a fixed place, if it is not held by virtue of a franchise or under statutory authority, is not in law a market and cannot enjoy the privileges of a franchise market or fair. (29 Halsbury's Laws (4th edn) para 601)

[Section 5 of Stat (1810) 50 Geo 3, c 41 (repealed) enacted that nothing in the Act should hinder any person from selling or exposing for sale goods in any 'market' or fair 'legally established'.] 'Upon the whole, I think, we are driven to give the words their ordinary and natural construction, and to hold that a market legally established must be a legal market, and that those words are not satisfied by showing a market *de facto*.' *Benjamin v Andrews* (1858) 5 CBNS 299 at 304, 305, per Williams J

'No person has a right, without a grant from the Crown, to set up a market or fair. Such a right is a prerogative right, which can only be granted by the Crown, and the Crown itself could not grant the right until there had been a preliminary investigation under the writ *ad quod damnum*. . . . A market is, properly speaking, the franchise right of having a concourse of buyers and sellers to dispose of commodities in respect of which the franchise is given; a market-place is the locality in which such concourse is held, and the grantee has the right, in the absence of anything in the grant to the contrary, to appoint the place in which the market is to be held.' *Downshire (Marquis) v O'Brien* (1887) 19 LR Ir 380 at 389, 390, per Chatterton V-C

'A market is a place to which sellers who have

not found buyers take their goods in the hope of finding buyers, and to which buyers resort in the hope of finding the goods they want.' *Scottish Co-operative Wholesale Society Ltd v Ulster Farmers' Mart Co Ltd* [1959] 2 All ER 486 at 495, HL, per Lord Somervell of Harrow

Canada 'Although the word "market" [in respect of securities offences] is . . . difficult to define in a concise manner, it is none the less essentially the action or business of buying and selling commodities.' *Re Bluestein and R* (1981) 121 DLR (3d) 345 at 350, Que SC, per Malouf J; reversed without affecting definition (1982) 142 DLR (3d) 71, Que CA

Temporary market

In this section 'temporary market' means a concourse of buyers and sellers of articles held otherwise than in a building or on a highway, and comprising not less than five stalls, stands, vehicles (whether movable or not) or pitches from which articles are sold, but does not include—
(a) a market or fair the right to hold which was acquired by virtue of a grant (including a presumed grant) or acquired or established by virtue of an enactment or order; or
(b) a sale by auction of farm livestock or deadstock.
(Local Government (Miscellaneous Provisions) Act 1982, s 37(6))

MARKET GARDEN

[The Public Health Act 1875, s 211(1)(b) (repealed) provided that the occupier of land used as 'market gardens' or nursery grounds should be assessed at one-quarter only of the net annual value thereof.] 'I cannot entertain a doubt that this ground is within the exemption created by the Act and that it ought to be assessed at one-fourth of its net annual value; it is used for gardening, that is, for the production of fruit and vegetables on a more or less small scale, as distinguished from agricultural use on a large scale; and in my judgment it is a market garden. . . . This ground is clearly used, not as a farm, but for the growing of those products for which market gardens and nursery grounds are ordinarily used. . . . It is a garden whether it contains one greenhouse or twelve.' *Purser v Worthing Local Board of Health* (1887) 18 QBD 818 at 820, per Day J

MARKET MAKER

United States The term 'market maker' means any specialist permitted to act as a dealer, any dealer acting in the capacity of block positioner, and any dealer who, with respect to a security, holds himself out (by entering quotations in an inter-dealer communications system or otherwise) as being willing to buy and sell such security for his own account on a regular or continuous basis. (Securities Exchange Act of 1934, s 3(a)(38))

MARKET OVERT

Where goods, other than goods belonging to the Crown, are sold in market overt according to the usage of the market, the buyer acquires a good title to the goods, provided he buys them in good faith and without notice of any defect or want of title on the part of the seller. However, the title is liable to be defeated in the case of stolen goods. The rule is for the protection of the buyer, and the seller is not protected by it and an action for wrongful interference with goods lies in conversion against one who wrongfully sells and delivers the goods of another in market overt. If, after a sale in market overt, the seller becomes again the owner of the goods, the title in the original owner revives. The rule of market overt does not apply in Scotland or Wales.

By the custom of the City of London, of which judicial notice is taken, that part of every shop within the City to which the public is admitted without special invitation is market overt, between sunrise and sunset on all days except Sundays and holidays, for the sale by the shopkeeper of such goods as he professes to trade in.

The place where the goods are sold must be a public and legally constituted market or fair, and a modern statutory market is within the rule as to sale in market overt. (29 Halsbury's Laws (4th edn) paras 624–626)

Where goods are sold in market overt, according to the usage of the market, the buyer acquires a good title to the goods, provided he buys them in good faith and without notice of any defect or want of title on the part of the seller. (Sale of Goods Act 1979, s 22(1))

[Jewels were sold to a jeweller in the City of London in a show-room over his shop, to which customers were only admitted by special invitation.] 'The market to be a market overt must be an "open public and legally constituted one"; *Lee v Bayes* [(1856) 18 CB 599], per Jervis CJ. The shop in London must be one in which goods are openly sold; that is, as I take it, when they are sold in the presence and sight of any one of the public who may come into the shop upon legitimate occasion. The keeping shop is an invitation to anyone who chooses to come to deal with the shopkeeper to enter. . . . In the case of a showroom situated as that in the present case there is no such invitation.' *Hargreave v Spink* [1892] 1 QB 25 at 26, 27, per Wills J

'It has been held that when a tradesman in the City of London displayed goods in his window or on his counter for sale, and there was a sale by that tradesman to a person resorting to the shop for the purpose of buying, that was a sale in market overt. No one would suppose, however, that, if one took goods to sell to a tradesman in his shop, the custom extended to that. I agree that the custom applies to the goods displayed and sold by the tradesman and not to goods sold to the tradesman. In my opinion this was not a sale in market overt because, even if it was a sale in a shop in the City of London, it was not a sale by the shopkeeper but a sale to him.' *Ardath Tobacco Co Ltd v Ocker* (1930) 47 TLR 177 at 178, per Finlay J

MARKET PRICE *See also* MARKET VALUE

'The plaintiffs are brewers and spirit merchants and the defendant holds from them certain licensed premises under leases which bind the defendant to take from the plaintiffs the liquors which he requires in his trade and bind the plaintiffs to supply him at "the fair current market price". . . . The expression "the fair current market price" is not, as it seems to me, equivalent to the expression "the lowest price at which the tenant could buy". The word "fair" and the word "current" seem to import some reference to the general conditions of the particular trade and to the nature of the relations between the parties, and to mean in substance what is current and fair in the case of tied houses and not in excess of the general market rate. The landlord would not establish his case merely by showing that his charges were the same as those of other brewers, if it appeared that the brewers generally were maintaining an excessive scale of prices; but if he shows that his prices are the prices usual and general under the circumstances, and if it is not made to appear that those prices are such as to leave an unreasonable profit or to be in excess of the prices charged in the general course of the trade, I do not think that he ought to be held to have broken his contract merely because there are some cases in which persons exceptionally circumstanced may as matter of special bargain obtain lower prices.' *Perrett & Co Ltd v Radford* (1901) 17 TLR 301 at 301, 302, per Wright J

'What is the fair market price must depend on what is meant by the market, and this must be ascertained by reference to the facts proved. The great bulk of the business of the London brewers is transacted with the tenants of their tied houses. These tenants bid for these houses, and they know that the terms on which they get the right to be supplied with malt liquor are that they should take it exclusively from the owning brewer at the standard price less certain discounts, the variation of which was to be limited by the prevailing practice. This seems to me to be the well understood meaning of the term "market" in this connection, and I do not believe that the respondent when he entered into his contract understood it in any other sense. "Market" is a word covering a variety of possible forms, and the evidence appears to me to establish that it had a special significance in the trade done in tied houses with the London brewers.' *Charrington & Co Ltd v Wooder* [1914] AC 71 at 79, per Lord Haldane LC

'I am unable to accept the contention that the term "market price" has a fixed and definite meaning which must attach to it invariably, in whatever contract it may occur, irrespectively of the context or the surrounding circumstances. The argument was rested chiefly on the force which, it is said, must be given to the word "market". In a different connection this may be a technical term, but in the covenant in question it is not used in any technical sense, and in ordinary language it is a common word of the most general import. It may mean a place set apart for trading, it may mean simply purchase and sale; and in either sense, there are innumerable markets each with its own customs and conditions. Words of this kind must vary in their signification with the particular objects to which the language is directed; and it follows that a contract about a market price cannot be correctly interpreted or applied without reference to the facts to which the contract relates.' Ibid at 80, per Lord Kinnear

'A market is a place where there is sufficient trade to enable a market price at a particular time to be recognisable and where a trader can buy or sell almost immediately at that price, so that a seller can put in his pocket the full price less expenses, which can be neglected as we are not seeking mathematical accuracy. Then market price can fairly be taken to be the value of marketable goods which a trader holds in stock either for sale or consumption in his business.' *BSC Footwear Ltd v Ridgway (Inspector of Taxes)* [1971] 2 All ER 534 at 536, 537, HL, per Lord Reid (dissenting)

MARKET RESEARCH EXPERIMENT

In this section 'market research experiment' means any activities conducted for the purpose of ascertaining the opinion of persons (in this section referred to as 'participants') of—
(a) any goods; or
(b) anything in, on or with which the goods are supplied; or
(c) the appearance or any other characteristic of the goods or of any such thing; or
(d) the name or description under which the goods are supplied.
(Trade Descriptions Act 1968, s 37(1))

MARKET SELLING VALUE

Australia [The Income Tax Assessment Act 1936–1986 (Cth), s 31 [see now s 31(1)] provided that the value of each article of trading stock to be taken into account at the end of the year of income should be, at the option of the taxpayer, its cost price or 'market selling value' or price at which it could be replaced.] 'It was said that the company sold during each year as much of its jams and canned fruits as it could sell, and that the stock which was left on hand at the end of the year represented a "surplus", the "market selling value" of which could only be ascertained by supposing the whole to be offered for sale en bloc on the last day of the accounting period. If one supposes such a sale—by auction or otherwise—I am quite prepared to accept the evidence that much lower values than those taken by the Commissioner would have been realised. But it is not to be supposed that the expression "market selling value" contemplates a sale on the most disadvantageous terms conceivable. It contemplates, in my opinion, a sale or sales in the ordinary course of the company's business—such sales as are in fact effected.' *Australasian Jam Co Pty Ltd v Federal Comr of Taxation* (1953) 88 CLR 23 at 31, per Fullagar J

MARKET VALUE *See also* MARKET PRICE

In this subsection [of a section dealing with writing-down allowances for mineral depletion] 'market value', in relation to an asset, means the price which it might reasonably be expected to fetch on a sale in the open market . . . (Capital Allowances Act 1968, s 60(5))

[A contract was entered into between the plaintiff and the defendant for the making of a tent, the canvas to be of a certain 'market value'.] 'We think the words "market value" in this contract must be taken to mean the price of the commodity in the market as between the manufacturer and an ordinary purchaser; and that those words are not to receive a different interpretation, because a person requiring so large a quantity as was wanted in this case, might . . . have purchased the canvas at a lower rate. We think the contract is only to be construed to mean, the ordinary price in the market, irrespective of the particular contract.' *Orchard v Simpson* (1857) 2 CBNS 299 at 305, per cur.

[The following question was submitted for the opinion of the court, viz whether the claimant was entitled at law to be paid compensation in respect only of the 'ordinary market value of the land' scheduled as an open space.] 'To the . . . question the answer is Yes. With regard to that answer, I will add only that it is agreed at the bar that the words "ordinary market value of the land" mean precisely what is meant by the words in the Acquisition of Land (Assessment of Compensation) Act 1919, s 2 (repealed; see now the Land Compensation Act 1961, s 5); that is to say, "The amount which the land if sold in the open market by a willing seller might be expected to realise". It is common ground that the introduction of the epithet "ordinary" does not in the smallest degree vary the provisions of s 2(2) of the statute.' *Collins v Feltham Urban District Council* [1937] 4 All ER 189 at 190, 191, DC, per Lord Hewart CJ

'No one using ordinary language would say that a liability had a market value of minus something. That is not the meaning of "market value". "Market value" assumes that the thing which is said to have the market value is something which somebody will buy and that there is a market in which it can be sold, and that what the purchaser will pay for it on the average is the market value. I have never heard of the suggestion before today that something which has no value at all and which nobody will have because it would cost him money if he took it can be described as having a market value of minus so many pounds.' *Gibson v Norfolk County Council* [1941] 1 KB 191 at 195, DC, per Humphreys J

[The appellant repaired his damaged car at a cost exceeding the 'market value', and claimed from the defendant the amount in excess of that paid by his insurance company.] 'There is no complete definition of the expression "market value" in the evidence or the judgment [in the court below], but I understand it as meaning standard replacement market value, that is to say the retail price which a customer would have to pay . . ., on a purchase of an average vehicle of the same make, type and age, or a comparable vehicle. It is not the price for a sale to a dealer or between dealers. It appears from a passage in the judgment that the "market value" does not include any allowance for the good maintenance and reliability of the plaintiff's vehicle.' *Darbishire v Warran* [1963] 3 All ER 310 at 314, CA per Pearson LJ

'By "market value" in this connection is meant the price at which the article before damage, or a comparable article, could be purchased.' Ibid at 317, per Pennycuick J

Australia 'In the case of many commodities the current market value thereof may be properly expressed as a range. For example, it is probably correct to say that, in the case of many foodstuffs, the current market value on any particular day may range from 1*s* to 2*s*, from 2*s* 3*d* to 5*s*, or between other limits. . . . Nor, I think, does the expression "current market value" exclude a case where one shopkeeper may be having a "sale", in the course of which he is selling below what other establishments in the relevant neighbourhood are charging. In that case, a purchase at the price affixed by the particular shopkeeper is enough. In that shop, at that time, the "sale" price is within the range of the current market value of the product.' *Stock v W Angliss & Co (Aust) Pty Ltd* [1964] VR 502 at 505, 506, per Sholl J

Australia 'In my opinion the ordinary meaning of the term "market value" is the best price which may reasonably be obtained for the property to be valued, if sold in the general market. The cases cited indicate that where the "value" of an item of property is to be ascertained, this means its value in the general market with three qualifications. Firstly, if there is no general market, as in the case of shares in a private company, such a market is to be assumed. Secondly, all possible purchasers are to be taken into account, even a purchaser prepared for his own reasons to pay a fancy price. Thirdly, the value to be ascertained is the value to the seller.' *Brisbane Water County Council v Commissioner of Stamp Duties* (1979) 1 NSWLR 320 at 324, per Waddell J

MARKETABLE SECURITY

'The question . . . is . . . whether there is upon the face of this document something which brings it within the definition of a marketable security. There can be no doubt that it is a promissory note; it contains an unconditional promise to pay money, and it is given in respect of money advanced. . . . But it may be a promissory note and something more, and that something more, if it is to affect the liability to stamp duty, must be on its face. What . . . is that additional matter? . . . It is in my opinion a representation made to the person who is to lend the money, and is intended to induce him to rely upon it as a statement that he will have the security contained in the trust deed. . . . I have no doubt that this instrument is a marketable security.' *Brown, Shipley & Co v Inland Revenue Comrs* [1895] 2 QB 598 at 600, 601, CA, per Lord Esher MR

[The question in this case was whether a foreign government gold bond, with coupons attached for the payment of interest, was a 'marketable security'.] 'If the plain man conversant with business were asked to describe this instrument, I think he would call it a foreign government security. It is found as matter of fact that the thing is marketable. It is therefore a marketable security.' *Speyer Brothers v Inland Revenue Comrs* [1908] AC 92 at 96, per Lord Robertson

MARQUESS *See* PEERAGE

MARRIAGE *See also* REMARRIAGE

The best known description of marriage as a legal concept is that it is the fulfilment of a contract satisfied by the solemnisation of the marriage, but marriage, directly it exists, creates by law a relation between the parties and what is called a status of each. The status of an individual, used as a legal term, means the legal position of the individual in or with regard to the rest of a community. . . . The requisites of a valid marriage according to English law are (1) that each of the parties should as regards age and mental and physical capacity be capable of contracting marriage; (2) that they should not by reason of kindred or affinity be prohibited from marrying one another; (3) that except where a second or subsequent polygamous marriage has been entered into under a law that permits polygamy, there should not be a valid subsisting marriage of either of the parties with any other person; (4) that the parties, understanding the nature of the contract, should freely consent to marry one another; and (5) that certain forms and ceremonies should be observed. (22 Halsbury's Laws (4th.edn) paras 905, 907)

'In some countries only one form of contracting marriage is acknowledged, as in our own, with the exception of particular indulgences to persons of certain religious persuasions; saving those exceptions, all marriages not celebrated according to the prescribed form, are mere nullities; there is and can be no such thing in this country as an irregular marriage. In some other countries, all modes of exchanging consent being equally legal, all marriages are on that account equally regular. . . . Marriage, being a contract, is of course consensual . . . for it is of the essence of all contracts, to be constituted by the consent of parties. *Consensus non concubitus facit matrimonium*, the maxim of the Roman civil law, is, in truth, the maxim of all law upon the subject; for the *concubitus* may take place, for the mere gratification of present appetite, without a view to anything further; but a marriage must be something more; it must be an agreement of the parties looking to the *consortium vitae*; an agreement indeed of parties capable of the *concubitus*, for though the *concubitus* itself will not constitute marriage, yet it is so far one of the essential duties, for which the parties stipulate, the incapacity of either party to satisfy that duty nullifies the contract.—Marriage, in its origin, is a contract of natural law; it may exist between two individuals of different sexes, although no third person existed in the world, as happened in the case of the common ancestors of mankind: It is the parent, not the child, of civil society. . . . In civil society it becomes a civil contract, regulated and prescribed by law, and endowed with civil consequences. In most civilised countries, acting under a sense of the force of sacred obligations, it has had the sanctions of religion superadded: It then becomes a religious, as well as a natural, and civil contract; for it is a great mistake to suppose that, because it is the one, therefore it may not likewise be the other. Heaven itself is made a party to the contract, and the consent of the individuals, pledged to each other, is ratified and consecrated by a vow to God.' *Dalrymple v Dalrymple* (1811) 2 Hag Con 54 at 61–63, per Sir William Scott

'What is the nature of the marital duty? I say most distinctly that persons who choose to enter the sacred bonds of marriage not only undertake to conduct themselves to one another so that they shall fulfil the vows which they have taken at the altar, but also take upon themselves a responsibility towards such children as they may have so to live that those children shall have that to which they are entitled, the benefit of the joint care and affection of both father and mother, and neither of them is entitled so to act as to deprive the children of that which they have thus guaranteed to them.' *Re Elderton* (1883) 25 Ch D 220 at 229, per Pearson J

'I am bound to hold that a union formed between a man and a woman in a foreign country, although it may there bear the name of a marriage, and the parties to it may there be designated husband and wife, is not a valid marriage according to the law of England unless it be formed on the same basis as marriages throughout Christendom, and be in its essence "the voluntary union for life of one man and one woman to the exclusion of all others".' *Re Bethell, Bethell v Hildyard* (1888) 38 Ch D 220 at 232–234, per Stirling J

'The English law of the validity of marriage is clearly defined. There must be the voluntary consent of both parties. There must be compliance with the legal requirements of publication and solemnisation, so far as the law deems it essential. There must not be incapacity in the parties to marry either as respects age or physical capability or as respects relationship by blood or marriage. Failure in these respects, but I believe in no others (I omit reference to the peculiar statutory position of the descendants of George II) renders the marriage void or voidable.' *Moss v Moss*. [1897] P 263 at 268, per cur.

[Marriages of the descendants of George II require the prior consent of the Sovereign: see the Royal Marriages Act 1772.]

'Lord Hannan in *Sottomayer v De Barros* [(1879) 5 P D 94] said: "Very many and serious difficulties arise if a marriage be regarded only in the light of a contract. It is indeed based on the contract of the parties, but it is a status arising out of a contract." These two terms "relationship" (or "status") and "contract"—both of them essential to the understanding of marriage—are the subjects of two bodies of law: the law of divorce, which concerns the relationship, and the law of nullity, which concerns the contract. In countries which permit of divorce the relationship can be examined, and, if necessary, interfered with, and in countries in which divorce is not permitted only the contract can be inquired into. Divorce may mean the breaking up of a marriage actually in being: nullity (if decreed) means that the marriage never came into being: it is the declaration by competent authority that the contract did not exist. Marriage is not to be considered merely as a contract: regard must be had to the peculiar and unique relationship that results from the contract, and if there is no proper contract, no such relationship can exist. The question of nullity of marriage is best understood as part of the law of contract. A particular country may, or may not, permit of divorce; but in every country that treats of marriage, and that is ruled by law, there must be a law of nullity, i.e. a law laying down the conditions under which the marriage contract is valid and binding.' *Griffith v Griffith* [1944] IR 35 at 41, per Haugh J

'In England it is now not so difficult in certain circumstances to dissolve a marriage. That fact does not alter the fundamental conception that marriage still is a union for life of one man and one woman to the exclusion of all others. The parties enter into matrimony in that state of mind.' *Kenward v Kenward* [1950] 2 All ER 297 at 303, CA, per Evershed MR; [1951] P 124

'It must be borne in mind, as Sir James Hannen P reminded himself in *Durham v Durham* [(1885) 10 PD 80], that a mere comprehension of the words of the promises exchanged is not sufficient. The minds of the parties must also be capable of understanding the nature of the contract into which they were entering. The precise nature of that contract may vary with the religious beliefs which the parties practise or profess. Some people may regard marriage as a sacrament; others, whilst still regarding marriage as a sacred and solemn obligation, do not believe in its sacramental nature. But, as Sir James Hannen P pointed out, the essence of the contract is an engagement between a man and a woman to live together, and to love one another as husband and wife to the exclusion of all others. It may be, in the present times, that submission on the part of the woman is no longer, as it was in 1885, an essential part of the contract, but so far as the husband is concerned there remains the duty to maintain her, which is, I think, implicit in what Sir James Hannen P described as the duty to protect. In recent times Willmer J in *In the Estate of Spier* [*Spier v Bengen* [1947] WN 46] stated the proposition in these terms. "There must be a capacity to understand the nature of the contract and the duties and responsibilities which it created, and . . . there must also be a capacity to take care of his or her own person and property." I was told that this decision was subsequently reversed by the Court of Appeal on the facts, but that the statement of the law made by Willmer J was not criticised. The decision of the Court of Appeal is not reported. It is clear, then, that marriage is in its essence a simple contract which any person of either sex of normal intelligence should readily be able to comprehend.' *In the Estate of Park, Park v Park* [1953] 2 All ER 408 at 414, per Karminski J; affirmed [1953] 2 All ER 1411, CA

'Marriage is, of course, far more than mere legal contract and legal relationship, and even legal status; but it includes legal contract and relationship. . . . It is basically a contract to be and, according to our Christian conception of marriage, to live as a man and wife. It has been said that the legal consideration of marriage—that is the promise to become and to remain man and wife—is the highest legal consideration which there is. And there could hardly be anything more intimate or confidential than is involved in that relationship, or than in the mutual trust and confidences which are shared between husband and wife. The confidential nature of the relationship is of its very essence and so obviously and necessarily implicit in it that there is no need for it to be expressed.' *Argyll (Duchess) v Argyll (Duke)* [1965] 1 All ER 611 at 619, per Ungoed-Thomas J

Australia 'The expression "Christian marriage" does not connote in this context that the parties are Christians, or that the rites observed are Christian rites. It is possible to have a "Christian marriage" in the relevant sense to which neither party is a Christian and which is not celebrated according to the observances of any Christian denomination. The expression means, rather, a marriage in the sense in which that relationship is understood in Christendom. This is a reference to the character of the marriage—to its being, in the words which Lord Penzance used in *Hyde v*

Hyde and Woodmansee [(1866) LRP&D 130], "the voluntary union for life of one man and one woman to the exclusion of all others". Unions of a polygamous character are, of necessity, outside this concept of marriage. Their exclusion therefrom depends, not upon the husband's having taken more than one wife in fact, but upon the character of the marriage—upon whether by the very terms of the marriage compact, a second marriage is a thing allowed to the husband and no cause of complaint to her who had acquiesced in that compact. Marriages, not as yet polygamous in fact and perhaps not likely to become so, but polygamous in character, in that they admit of the taking of further wives, are generally referred to as potentially polygamous, and it is on this ground that they are to be distinguished from Christian marriages in the sense earlier mentioned. A marriage once "Non-Christian" is always Non-Christian; it takes its character at the time when it is contracted under the law according to which it is contracted, and that character remains unaffected by subsequent events.' *Ng Ping On v Ng Choy Fung Kam* [1964] NSWR 953 at 954, 955, per Sugerman J

Contemplation of *See* CONTEMPLATION (of marriage)

De facto marriage

'The expressions to be found in some of the text-books and cases "de facto marriage" or "de facto wife" mean, in our opinion, no more than that, while the parties may have appeared to be, and even have believed that they were, husband and wife, they were not, either because there was an impediment which prevented their marriage or that the marriage was not celebrated according to law.' *R v Algar* [1953] 2 All ER 1381 at 1383, 1384, CCA, per Lord Goddard CJ

In marriage settlement

[By a marriage settlement dated 8 October 1868 the intended wife covenanted to settle all real and personal property to which she should at any time during the said intended 'marriage' become beneficially entitled in possession or reversion except articles not exceeding £100 in value.] 'On 20th November, 1875, the lady obtained against her husband a decree of judicial separation. . . . She . . . became entitled on the death of her mother, who died in 1900, to one-half of her residuary personal estate. She was not entitled to that at the date of the judicial separation, but she became entitled to it afterwards. The question is whether that is property to which she became entitled "during the said intended marriage". In one sense it is. The result of the decree was not to dissolve the marriage. The husband and wife may come together again, and the marriage has not come to an end. But I have to determine what in this settlement is the meaning of the expression "during the said intended marriage". . . . Properly construed, that means during the marriage, in which the usual marital relations subsist, and does not apply to a case where the husband is by reason of a judicial separation deprived of rights in respect of his wife's property. I therefore hold that the property acquired after the separation is not within the covenant.' *Davenport v Marshall* [1902] 1 Ch 82 at 84–86, per Buckley J

Void and voidable *See also* NULLITY

[The grounds on which a marriage is void or voidable are codified by the Matrimonial Causes Act 1973, ss 11–16.

The Matrimonial Causes Act 1965, s 9 was also repealed by the Act of 1973.]

A marriage celebrated after 31st July 1971 is void (1) where it is not a valid marriage under the provisions of the Marriages Acts 1949 to 1970; or (2) where at the time of the marriage either party was already lawfully married; or (3) where the parties are not respectively male and female, or (4) where in the case of a polygamous marriage entered into outside England and Wales, either party was at the time of the marriage domiciled in England and Wales.

A marriage celebrated after 31st July 1971 is voidable (1) if the marriage has not been consummated owing to the incapacity of either party to consummate it or owing to the wilful refusal of the respondent to consummate it; or (2) where either party to the marriage did not validly consent to it; or (3) if, at the time of the marriage (a) either party, though capable of giving a valid consent, was suffering (whether continuously or intermittently) from mental disorder within the meaning of the Mental Health Act 1959 [repealed; see now the Mental Health Act 1983] of such a kind or to such an extent as to be unfitted for marriage, or (b) the respondent was suffering from venereal disease in a communicable form, or (c) the respondent was pregnant by some person other than the petitioner. (13 Halsbury's Laws (4th edn) paras 534, 535)

'Void marriage' means a marriage, not being voidable only, in respect of which the High

Court has or had jurisdiction to grant a decree of nullity, or would have or would have had such jurisdiction if the parties were domiciled in England and Wales. (Legitimacy Act 1976, s 10(1))

MARRIAGE ARTICLES *See* ARTICLES

MARRIAGE SETTLEMENT *See* SETTLEMENT

MARSHALLING

Where one claimant, A, has two funds, X and Y, to which he can resort for satisfaction of his claim, whether legal or equitable, and another claimant, B, can resort to only one of these funds, Y, equity interposes so as to secure that A shall not by resorting to Y disappoint B. Consequently, if the matter is under the court's control, A will be required in the first place to satisfy himself out of X, and only to resort to Y in case of deficiency; and if A has already been paid out of Y, it will allow B to stand in his place as against X. This is known as the doctrine of marshalling, and is adopted in order to prevent one claimant depriving another claimant of his security. The doctrine is applied chiefly in regard to securities and to the administration of assets. (16 Halsbury's Laws (4th edn) para 1426)

MASTER

Of ship

The word 'master' when used in relation to any vessel, shall be understood to mean the person having the command or charge of the vessel for the time being. (Harbours, Docks, and Piers Clauses Act 1847, s 3; cf Dockyard Ports Regulations Act 1865, s 2; Fisheries Act 1981, s 30(3))

'Master' shall include any person having the charge or command of a ship. (Foreign Enlistment Act 1870, s 30)

'Master' includes every person (except a pilot) having command or charge of a ship, and in reference to any boat belonging to a ship, means the master of the ship; and when used in reference to any other boat, includes every person having command or charge of such boat. (Explosives Act 1875, s 108)

'Master' includes every person (except a pilot) having command or charge of any ship. (Merchant Shipping Act 1894, s 742; cf Marine, &c, Broadcasting (Offences) Act 1967, s 1)

'Master', in relation to a ship, includes every person (except a pilot) having command or charge of the ship, whether the ship is a ship of war or other ship. (Post Office Act 1953, s 87)

MASTER AND SERVANT *See* SERVANT

MATERIAL

A representation is material when its tendency, or its natural and probable result, is to induce the representee to act on the faith of it in the kind of way in which he is proved to have in fact acted. (31 Halsbury's Laws (4th edn) para 1075)

Canada 'Every fact is material which would, if known, reasonably affect the minds of prudent, experienced insurers in deciding whether they will accept the risk.' *Stroschein v Wawanesa Mutual Insurance Co* [1943] 3 WWR 509 at 512, Alta SC, per Macdonald J

Material alteration

'Any alteration of any instrument seems to me to be material which would alter the business effect of the instrument if used for any ordinary business purpose.' *Suffell v Bank of England* (1892) 9 QBD 555 at 568, per Brett LJ

Material circumstance

[The Marine Insurance Act 1906, s 18 enacts that, subject to certain provisions, the assured must disclose to the insurer, before the contract is concluded, every 'material circumstance' which is known to him.] 'The duty of disclosure (now found by way of codification in the statute) must be discharged. If the shipowner knows any material circumstance within the meaning of the Act of Parliament he must disclose it in obtaining the assent of the underwriter to the contract, and none the less because it contains as it does the condition "seaworthiness admitted": *Brownlie v Campbell* [(1880) 5 App Cas 925]. I will endeavour to state the disclosure which the assured was bound to make and to see whether he has made it. Before the contract was concluded he owed the duty of disclosing every material circumstance which he knew and every material circumstance which in the ordinary course of business he ought to have known. This duty extended to every such circumstance as was material and was not confined to such as he knew or thought to be material. Whatever was the character of the vessel which he desired to insure he was bound to disclose any specific defect which he knew or in the ordinary course of business ought to have known. But by material circumstance is I think meant a material circumstance of fact to the exclusion of a material circumstance of opinion.' *Cantiere Meccanico Brindisino v Janson* [1912] 3 KB 452 at 470, 471, CA, per Buckley LJ

Material concealment

'The question is, whether there has been a material concealment of facts which the plaintiff knew, and which the underwriter would require to enable him to decide. A material concealment is a concealment of facts, which, if communicated to the party who underwrites, would induce him either to refuse the insurance altogether, or not to effect it except at a larger premium than the ordinary premium.' *Elton v Larkins* (1832) 5 C & P 385 at 392, per Tindal CJ

Material facts

[By Order XIX, r 4 (revoked; see now RSC 1965, Ord 18, r 7), every pleading had to contain as concisely as might be a statement of the 'material facts' on which the party pleading relied.] 'If those words "material facts" are to be confined to matters which are material to the cause of action, that is to say, facts which must be proved in order to establish the existence of the cause of action, then no doubt the facts in this paragraph were not properly pleaded. But in my opinion those words are not so confined, and must be taken to include any facts which the party pleading is entitled to prove at the trial.' *Millington v Loring* (1880) 6 QBD 190 at 194, CA, per Lord Selborne LC

Material interest

[The Companies Act 1948, s 207(1)(a) (repealed; see now the Companies Act 1985, s 426(2)) provided that the 'material interests' of the directors should be disclosed where a scheme of arrangement was proposed.] 'The reference to "material interests" doubtless exempts from the necessity of disclosure a nominal holding for the purposes of a director's qualification in a company with substantial issued capital, or a holding by a director in trust for independent beneficiaries; but the only safe rule is that in doubtful cases it is wiser to disclose than to refrain from so doing, for the effect of the section is to emphasise the fiduciary duty of a director and to compel disclosure of every type of "interest" which in a business sense might be regarded as influencing his judgment. Moreover I would stress that the section would not be satisfied by a disclosure limited to the shares or other interests registered or held in the director's own name, but extends to shares and other interests registered in the names of banks as nominee companies, or otherwise concealed, the essence of the matter being that any kind of personal interest which is "material", in the sense of not being insignificant, must be revealed.' *Re Coltness Iron Co Ltd* 1951 SLT 344 at 346, per the Lord President (Cooper)

MATERIALS *See also* AIRCRAFT MATERIAL

New Zealand [In the Wages Protection and Contractors' Liens Act 1939 (NZ), s 20(1) (repealed) 'work' was defined as including 'any work of labour, whether scheduled or unscheduled, done or commenced by any person of any occupation in connection with . . . (c) the placing, fixing or erection of any material . . . used or intended to be used for any of the purposes aforesaid'.] 'In my opinion the word "material" as used in the Act means some substance which in some form or another is incorporated in the work, and I do not consider that it includes substances like petrol and oil which were merely used by the contractor in the course of the work to supply the motive power for his vehicles and plant.' *Motor Rebuilds Ltd v Bollard* [1956] NZLR 954 at 958, per North J

MATERNITY HOME *See also* NURSING HOME

. . . any premises used, or intended to be used, for the reception of pregnant women or of women immediately after childbirth (in this Act referred to as a 'maternity home'). (Registered Homes Act 1984, s 21(1)(b))

MATRIMONIAL HOME

'The phrase "matrimonial home" extends, in relation to jurisdiction, to the husband's residence here [in England] in such circumstances that any husband similarly circumstanced and not estranged from his wife would set up his home here.' *Milligan v Milligan* [1941] P 78 at 84, per Henn Collins J

See, generally, 22 Halsbury's Laws (4th edn) paras 1046 et seq.

New Zealand 'The matrimonial home of the parties is the dwelling house that was used at the date the parties separated as the only or principal family residence.' *Giles v Giles* [1985] 1 NZLR 760 at 765, per Richardson J

MATRIMONIAL OFFENCE

'It is said by the one side that "matrimonial offence" means only such a breach of matrimonial duty as will entitle and, perhaps, require the Divorce Court to grant a decree to the aggrieved spouse, and that no degree of matrimonial breach of duty, short of what calls for such a decree, can constitute a "matrimonial offence" within the meaning of the decisions. Their argument is based on the contention that the word "offence" correctly construed carries their meaning. The other side reply that the word "offence" has no statutory force, and is merely a word used compendiously in the cases to cover any matrimonial wrongdoing, whether any decree could or could not be based on the particular wrongdoing in fact established. The dispute has thus seemed to turn on a problem of interpreting a judicial phrase. I think the broader viewpoint is the sounder and that it would be fallacious to limit the argument of principle by any such verbal and restrictive interpretation of a convenient judicial phrase.' *Beard* v *Beard* [1946] P 8 at 11, CA, per Scott LJ.

'A matrimonial offence seems to me to mean an offence against the vows of marriage. The vows of marriage are well known. Desertion is certainly one offence, and cruelty as defined by the law is another.' *Richardson* v *Richardson* [1949] 2 All ER 330 at 332, CA, per Bucknill LJ; [1950] P 16.

MATTER

'Matter' means any proceedings in court not in a cause. (Supreme Court Act 1981, s 151(1))

'Matter' means every proceeding in a county court which may be commenced as prescribed otherwise than by plaint. (County Courts Act 1984, s 147(1))

Australia 'Section 75 of the Constitution [Commonwealth of Australia Constitution Act 1901–1986] enacts that the High Court shall have original jurisdiction in "all matters between States". The analogous words in the Constitution of the United States of America are "controversies between States", and it is the settled law of the Republic that the Supreme Court of the United States has under these words jurisdiction to entertain questions of boundaries between States. . . . The word "matters" was in 1900 in common use as the widest term to denote controversies which might come before a Court of Justice. Instances of such controversies which would clearly be justiciable are questions arising under mail contracts, contracts for the construction and maintenance of telegraph lines at joint expense, and running agreements over railways. In my opinion a matter between States, in order to be justiciable, must be such that a controversy of like nature could arise between individual persons, and must be such that it can be determined upon principles of law. This definition includes all controversies relating to the ownership of property or arising out of contracts.' *South Australia v Victoria* (1911) 12 CLR 667 at 674, 675, per Griffith CJ

Australia 'Section 75 [of the Commonwealth of Australia Constitution Act 1901] confers original jurisdiction on the High Court in certain matters, and s 76 enables Parliament to confer original jurisdiction on it in other matters. . . . We do not think that the word "matter" in s 76 means a legal proceeding, but rather the subject-matter for determination in a legal proceeding. In our opinion there can be no matter within the meaning of the section unless there is some immediate right, duty, or liability to be established by the determination of the Court. If the matter exists, the legislature may no doubt prescribe the means by which the determination of the Court is to be obtained, and for that purpose may, we think, adopt any existing method of legal procedure or invent a new one. But it cannot authorise this Court to make a declaration of the law divorced from any attempt to administer that law.' *Re Judiciary Act 1903* (1921) 29 CLR 257 at 264–266, per Knox CJ and Gavan Duffy Powers Rich and Starke JJ

Australia [The Trade Practices Act 1974–1986 (Cth), s 155(1) empowers the Trade Practices Commission and certain officials to require information, documents or evidence to be furnished, produced or given relating to a 'matter' that constitutes, or may constitute, a contravention of the Act.] '"Matter", said Franki and Northrop JJ [in *Melbourne Home of Ford Pty Ltd v Trade Practices Commission* (1979) 5 TPC 26 at 47] "is to be construed in its ordinary sense of an affair or a thing". It refers to a body of facts, a body of facts which "constitute" or "may constitute" a contravention. A contravention is constituted by the conduct of persons (whether corporate or natural) and the factual circumstances attendant upon conduct, so the "matter" to which s 155(1) refers comprehends the conduct of persons and the circumstances attendant upon it.' *WA Pines Pty Ltd v Bannerman* (1980) 30 ALR 559 at 565, per Brennan J

MATTERS IN DIFFERENCE

'It is clear that an arbitrator on a reference of [all] matters in difference has power over all matters down to the period of the submission but cannot award on future and contingent claims. The parties, however, may give him such a power if they think fit; and the arbitrator will then award what is due on each account.' *Re Brown & Croydon Canal Co* (1839) 9 Ad & El 522 at 529, per Littledale J

'I am of opinion that a reference of "all matters in difference" does not mean a reference of all possible matters, but of all matters which are brought before the arbitrator. And if the parties omit to solicit his attention to a matter not being one of the questions in the proceedings themselves, no objection can be made to the award for not adjudicating on it.' *Rees v Waters* (1847) 16 M & W 263 at 269, 270, per Pollock CB

See, generally, 2 Halsbury's Laws (4th edn) para 610.

MATTERS OF SEX

Australia [The Objectionable Literature Act 1954–1986 (Qld) s 5 defines 'objectionable' as including, inter alia, undue emphasis on 'matters of sex'.] 'Every distinction between man and woman may be said to be a matter of sex but obviously it is in no such general sense that the expression is used. No doubt direct references to the physiological distinctions or to actual physical relations are in the contemplation of the phrase as it occurs in the provision, wherever the purpose or effect is immoral or perverted or implies some other aberration.' *Transport Publishing Co Pty Ltd v Literature Board of Review* [1957] St R Qd 19 at 25, per Dixon CJ, Kitto and Taylor JJ

MATURE

[The Bills of Exchange Act 1882, s 62 which is, by s 89, made applicable to promissory notes, enacts that when the holder of a bill at or after its 'maturity' absolutely and unconditionally renounces his rights against the acceptor, the bill is discharged.] 'A promissory note payable on demand is payable at once without any demand, and may be sued upon accordingly. Such a note, therefore, "matures" within the meaning of s 62 as soon as the note is made and delivered to the payee.' *Edwards v Walters* [1896] 2 Ch 157 at 166, CA, per Lindley LJ

Australia 'The use of the word "maturing" in the phrase "maturing only at his death" . . . suggests something brought gradually to a complete state of development rather than a sudden and uncertain happening.' *Re Corteen, National Trustees Executors & Agency Co Ltd v Corteen* [1941] VLR 254 at 261, per Martin J

MATURITY (Age)

Australia [A testator by his will gave to his children and to their children in succession upon the death of the parent one-fifth each of the nett income arising from his estate. Such portion was to be payable to his grandchildren collectively in each family who had not reached 'maturity' and was to cease to be payable upon the youngest reaching 'maturity'.] 'The . . . question is whether, upon the true construction of the will the testator's grandchildren reach or have reached maturity at the age of twenty-one years respectively, or at some other and what age, and by reference to some other and what event. 'Maturity' is a word whose meaning depends on the context in which it occurs. Here it is used in relation to human beings as recipients of benefits under a will, and I may assume that the testator was aware of the two stages of development that are ordinarily recognised by the law. The line is drawn at the age of twenty-one, before which a human being is subject to certain legal disabilities, and after which those disabilities are removed. When the latter condition is attained a child has reached "maturity" in the matter of legal status, and that I take it is the meaning in which the testator has used the word in his will.' *Re Wyld* [1912] SALR 190 at 198, 199, per Murray J

MAY

Generally

'"May" always means may. "May" is a permissive or enabling expression; but there are cases in which, for various reasons, as soon as the person who is within the statute is entrusted with the power it becomes his duty to exercise it. One of those cases is where he has applied to use the power which the Act gives him in order to enforce the legal right of the applicant.' *Sheffield Corpn v Luxford, Sheffield Corpn v Morrell* [1929] 2 KB 180 at 183, 184, DC, per Talbot J

Australia 'The ordinary rule for the construction of statutes containing the word "may" or the word "shall" I think is very well expressed in Halsbury [4th edn, vol 44, para 932]. . . . The use of the word "may" prima facie conveys that the authority which has power to do such an act has an option either to do it or not to do it.' *Massy v Council of the Municipality of Yass* (1922) 22 SR (NSW) 494 at 497, 499, per Cullen CJ

Australia '"May", unlike "shall", is not a mandatory but a permissive word although it may acquire a mandatory meaning from the context in which it is used, just as "shall" which is a mandatory word may be deprived of the obligatory force and become permissive in the context in which it appears.' *Johnson's Tyne Foundry Pty Ltd v Shire of Maffra* [1949] ALR 89 at 101, per Williams J

New Zealand [The Summary Proceedings Act 1957, s 147(1) provides that when an information has been laid, any district court judge, justice or registrar (not being a constable) 'may' issue a summons to the defendant, in the prescribed form.] 'The word "may" where it appears in s 147 of the Summary Proceedings Act 1957 does confer a discretion upon the district court judge, justice or registrar (as the case may be) as to whether or not he will issue a summons upon the information which has been laid. It is also our opinion that the nature of that discretion is . . . a discretion which must be exercised in a judicial manner.' *Daemar v Soper* [1981] 1 NZLR 66 at 70, per Richmond P

New Zealand 'The word "may" is clearly empowering in contradistinction to "shall" which is mandatory. "May" means "entitled to"; it is facultative. It confers on an enforcement officer [under the Transport Act 1962] the right to do something which he might otherwise not be entitled to do. But it does not impose a duty positively requiring the enforcement officer to take the next step and admitting of no exceptions to it.' *Parker v MOT* [1982] 1 NZLR 209 at 211, CA, per McMullin J

Mandatory

'Where a statute directs the doing of a thing for the sake of justice or the public good, the word may is the same as the word shall; thus 23 Hen 6 [Stat (1444–5) Hen 6, c 9 (repealed)] says, the sheriff may take bail; this is construed, he shall; for he is compellable so to do.' *R v Barlow* (1693) 2 Salk 609 at 609, per cur.

[The Arbitration Act 1889, s 5 (repealed; see now the Arbitration Act 1950, s 10), provided that if the appointment of an arbitrator was not made within seven days after the service of a notice by one of the parties in a case where differences had arisen with regard to such appointment, the court or a judge 'may', on application, make the appointment.] 'The parties have agreed with regard to certain matters to substitute arbitration by a single arbitrator for a trial in court; it is admitted that there is a dispute within the submission; the parties have failed to concur in the appintment of an arbitrator; and there has been a proper notice given which has not been complied with. What under these circumstances does the section provide that the court is to do? It says that the court "may" appoint an arbitrator. . . . I think that in such a case as this "may" means "must", and that the court is bound to appoint an arbitrator.' *Re Eyre & Leicester Corpn* [1892] 1 QB 136 at 142, 143, CA, per Lord Esher MR

Permissive

'The words of s 25(8) of the Supreme Court of Judicature Act 1873 [repealed; see now the Supreme Court Act 1981, s 37] are, "A mandamus or an injunction may be granted or a receiver appointed by an interlocutory order of the court in all cases in which it shall appear to the court to be just or convenient that such an order should be made; and any such order may be made either unconditionally or upon such terms and conditions as the court shall think just; and if an injunction is asked, . . . such injunction may be granted, if the court shall think fit", etc. Now no doubt there are Acts of Parliament in which the word "may" has been construed as if it were imperative, but that cannot be so here. The words that follow show that the matter is entirely in the discretion of the court; that is, of course, a judicial not an arbitrary discretion. Looking at the permissive word "may", and the other words "in all cases in which", etc, I think it is necessary that the party applying for a mandamus should make out a case for granting it.' *Widnes Alkali Co Ltd v Sheffield & Midland Rly Co's Committee* (1877), 37 LT 131 at 132, DC, per Grove J

See, generally, 44 Halsbury's Laws (4th edn) para 932.

Australia [The Conveyancing Act 1919–1986 (NSW), s 66G, provides that where any property (other than chattels) is held in co-ownership the court 'may' appoint trustees of the property and vest the same in such trustees to be held by them on the statutory trust for sale.] 'In my view, the word "may", as used in the section, has its ordinary meaning, i.e. it is used in the faculative or permissive sense. I accordingly hold that I have a discretion as to whether or not I should make an order.' *Re Jackson and the Conveyancing Act* (1952) 52 SR (NSW) 42 at 44, per Hardie AJ

Australia 'The authorities show that the word "may" imports a discretion and must be so construed unless there is a sufficiently clearly expressed intention to the contrary. . . . It lies upon those who contend that an obligation exists to exercise the power, to show in the circumstances of the case something which, according to the above principles, creates that obligation.' *Oser v Felton* [1966] ALR 1086 at 1092, per Jenkyn J

MAY BE

'The question for our decision in this case is this: what is the meaning of a certain writing by which the defendant agreed to guarantee the payment of "bills of exchange, and any balance" creating a debt from one Joseph Edge to the plaintiff? Is the guarantee confined to bills running at the date of the guarantee and to the balance then due, or does it extend to bills and balances arising thereafter? In order to interpret the document, the court may, no doubt, be informed by the evidence given in the cause of every circumstance between the parties calculated to throw any light upon what they intended by the language used. Here there had been former dealings, and future dealings were contemplated. It may be well to consider what is the meaning of the first part of the guarantee without reference to the second part, which states what it is to include. The expression "in consideration of the credit given I hereby agree to guarantee the payment of all bills drawn by Broom, and accepted by Edge also, I hereby agree to guarantee the payment of any balance that may be due", in my judgment relates prima facie to future transactions. The word "given" is indefinite in point of time. It is no doubt the perfect, but it may mean past, present, or future. The word "drawn" is also equivocal; but the expression "may be" is, in my judgment, clearly future. I have been unable to find any authority in any dictionary; but in Cruden's Concordance of the Bible from sixty to eighty references are given to the expression "may be", nine out of ten of which have manifestly a reference to the future, and not one is necessarily future. The Concordance of Shakespeare gives no references to words so common as "may" and "be". But as far as I can bring my knowledge of the English language to bear upon the subject, "may be" is much oftener used with references to the future than the past or the present. It does not mean the balance now due. If that was intended nothing was more easy and obvious than to say so. It does not in my judgment mean the balance which, upon an investigation of the accounts, may turn out to be due at this moment. The period is indefinite, and, according to all the authorities I can find, "may be" relates to the future rather than the past. If this be true, then the ambiguous expression "drawn", which no doubt may mean already drawn, or to be drawn, must be expounded in like manner and must receive a construction relating to the future.' *Broom v Batchelor* (1856) 1 H & N 255 at 264, 265, per Pollock CB

[By an ante-nuptial settlement the husband agreed to settle all his 'share, property or interest, as well vested or accruing, to which I may be entitled under any will or settlement'.] 'In my judgment this agreement to settle does not extend to or include the property to which the husband ultimately became entitled under the will of his father, nor does it extend to any property to which he might become entitled in the future. In fact, it does not include what is, in my judgment, a mere *spes successionis*.' *Re Ridley's Agreement, Ridley v Ridley* (1911) 55 Sol Jo 838 at 838, per Swinfen Eady J

MEAN (Average)

[An agreement to fix prices for a marketing scheme by reference to market quotations contained the phrase 'the average of the mean prices for the two kinds of cheese'.] 'Taking the mean price in the case of each cheese, I think the word "mean" has its ordinary significance, that is to say, the middle term between two extremes.' *United Dairies (Wholesale) Ltd v Lemon* [1937] 2 All ER 618 at 625, CA, per Lord Wright MR

MEAN (Verb)

Australia 'It will be noticed that the words "means and includes" are used; and we think that these words imply that the definition . . . is exhaustive.' *In the Will of Jeannie McFie* [1944] St R Qd 130 at 132, per Philp J

Australia 'The general rule is that prima facie when expressions such as "mean" or "include" or "mean and include" are used they must be given their ordinary and precise meaning and be treated as exhaustive, but that they are not necessarily to be given such a rigid construction nor to be taken as substituting one set of words for another, nor as strictly defining what the meaning of a word must be under all circumstances. Rather they should be regarded as declaring what should be comprehended within the particular expressions where the circumstances require that they should.' *Ex p Perry, Re Murdoch* (1948) 48 NSWSR 393 at 399, per Davidson J

Canada '"Means" [in a statutory definition of 'public place'] is restricted to that which is specifically described or defined. When used in contrast to "means" the word "includes" is not restrictive; it signifies that that which is "included" is in addition to something else that is not specifically stated to be so included. In the result in every case which is not "included" in the statutory interpretation clause it becomes a question of fact to determine whether the characteristics of "public place" are present in the sense that comprehensive term is understood among the people at large.' *R v McLeod* [1950] 2 WWR 456 at 462, BCCA, per O'Halloran JA

New Zealand 'The general rule of interpretation is that where a statute declares a certain word or expression to "mean" so-and-so, the definition is explanatory and restrictive in contradistinction to the use of the word "includes", which is extensive.' *R v Webb & McLauchlan* [1924] NZLR 934 at 941, CA, per Stringer J; also reported [1924] GLR 224 at 227

MEANS (Noun)

'What has to be looked at is the means of the husband, and by "means" is meant what he is in fact getting or can fairly be assumed to be likely to get.' *Howard v Howard* [1945] P 1 at 4, CA, per Lord Greene MR

Australia 'The words used throughout the will are "my means and estate". Admittedly, the word "estate" would include realty unless a contrary meaning was to be gathered from the context. The word "means" I have never met with, nor am I aware that it has ever received judicial interpretation, but in common parlance it is a word of very wide significance, and certainly would not narrow the interpretation of the word "estate".' *Robison v Stuart* (1891) 12 NSWLR Eq 47 at 51, 52, per Owen CJ in Eq

Canada [Relief on divorce depended on the consideration of, inter alia, the 'means' of the parties.] '"Means" refers to the pecuniary resources of the person which, in my opinion, also includes his or her potential earning capacity.' *Schartner v Schartner* (1970) 10 DLR (3d) 61 at 67, Sask QB, per Disbery J

MEANS OF ACCESS *See also* ACCESS

Australia [Regulation 73(2) of the regulations made under the Scaffolding and Lifts Act 1912 [see now Construction and Safety Act 1912–1986], as amended, refers, inter alia, to 'means of access'.] 'I agree with the learned presiding judge that it does not mean that in a building where there is a place at which the person entitled to the protection of the Regulation has to work there could not also be places which might properly be described as "means of access", and I would apprehend that in certain cases stairways, passages, gangways, perhaps lifts, all could be considered to be "means of access".' *Trimp v SA Butler Pty Ltd* [1964–5] NSWR 1031 at 1037, per Collins J

Australia [The Factories, Shops and Industries Act 1962–1986 (NSW), s 40 [see now s 40(1)], provides that each factory shall contain safe 'means of access' to every place at which any person has at any time to work.] 'As an abstract proposition the place of a man's work at one time may be the means of access to another place where he has work at another time. I understand that, but I cannot think that it can be said of this case. Originally a means of access to a place ordinarily meant I suppose some thing, like a ladder, a staircase, a gangplank, by which the worker got to his workplace. Doubtless it can be a passageway or a particular part of the factory floor which he must traverse to get to his work. But it must be identifiable as a place distinct from the place where he has to work.' *Australian Iron & Steel Pty Ltd v Luna* (1969) 123 CLR 305 at 322–323, per Windeyer J

MEANS OF GAMING

Australia 'In the Macquarie Dictionary the word "means" is defined as "an agency, instrumentality, method, etc, used to attain an end". In the Shorter Oxford Dictionary the relevant definition is: "That by which some object is or may be attained, or which is concerned in bringing about some result." In both these definitions the emphasis is on use or capability of use rather than on design or adaptation. In my view a member of the police force executing [a] warrant may seize not only money and securities for money, but all articles adapted to or used for the purpose of gaming.' *Walker v West* [1981] 2 NSWLR 570 at 583, per Rath J

MEANS OF SUPPORT

Australia 'The complaint of the wife alleged that her husband had left her without adequate means of support. The evidence at the hearing established that she had apparently been deserted by her husband, and, in effect, had been turned out of the matrimonial home. . . . The contention for the husband is that the furniture was her property, at least on the day when the complaint was heard, and so she had "means" because she could by a sale of it obtain money to support herself. But . . . even on the assumption that the furniture had become hers, that fact did not alter her description of being without adequate means of support. No doubt "means of support" may include property convertible into money which may be applied for subsistence, as Piper J held in *Ashby v Ashby* [[1935] SASR 119]. I do not, however, understand that judgment as being intended to apply to all convertible property, and in all circumstances, and it seems to me that no such general rule should be adopted. A wife who owns a few pieces of furniture which are no more than are required for everyday use, and which may be wanted if she is to occupy a house, should not on that account be regarded as having adequate means of support because she could turn them into money.' *Hampel v Hampel* [1946] SASR 317 at 320, 321, per Reed J

MEASURE (Legislative)

The General Synod of the Church of England may frame and pass legislative proposals, termed Measures, concerning the Church of England. A Measure agreed to by the General Synod is submitted by its Legislative Committee to the Ecclesiastical Committee of members of both Houses whose duty it is to report to Parliament upon the nature and legal effect and expediency of the Measure. The report and the text of the Measure are laid before Parliament, and a resolution is submitted to each House directing that the Measure, in the form laid before Parliament, be presented to Her Majesty. When this resolution has been passed by each House and the royal assent signified, the Measure has the force and effect of an Act of Parliament. Parliament has thus no power to amend a Measure, but either House, by declining to agree to the resolution, is able to effect its rejection. (34 Halsbury's Laws (4th edn) para 1226)

A General Synod Measure is not a statute. However, if such a Measure is laid before Parliament and is then presented to the Queen in pursuance of a resolution of each House of Parliament, it has the force and effect of an Act of Parliament on the royal assent being given to it. (44 Halsbury's Laws (4th edn) para 802)

'Measure' means a legislative measure intended to receive the Royal Assent and to have effect as an Act of Parliament in accordance with the provisions of this Act. (Church of England Assembly (Powers) Act 1919, s 1)

MEASUREMENT

[*See*, generally, as to definitions of units of measurement of length, area, volume, capacity, weight, trade terms and electricity, the Weights and Measures Act 1985, Sch 1]

MEASURING EQUIPMENT *See* EQUIPMENT

MEAT

'Meat' means—
(a) carcase meat and offal obtained from livestock and intended for human consumption, and
(b) bacon and ham.
(Agriculture Act 1967, s 25)

MECHANICAL

Mechanical construction

New Zealand [The Dentists Act 1936 (NZ), s 26 (repealed; see now the Dental Act 1963, (NZ), s 2(1)) provided that no person, unless he held certain qualifications, might hold himself out as practising dentistry. Section 2(1) defined the 'practice of dentistry' as including: '(c) The mechanical construction or the renewal of artificial dentures'.] 'The evil which the statute tried to cure was the practice of dentistry by mechanics and other unqualified persons, and the "mechanical construction" of dentures which it forbids is consequently found to be nothing more or less than the kind of construction which is ordinarily or normally entrusted to and carried out by a dental mechanic, as distinct from the work in making and fitting a denture which a qualified dentist does—this latter is, of course, specifically forbidden to unqualified persons under another subsection. . . . Such work may be properly carried out by a dental mechanic duly working under his qualified employer: but the same work is prohibited to the same unqualified mechanic if he does that work without the prescribed supervision. It is the total of the above considerations which has convinced me that the learned Magistrate misdirected himself when he held that the word "mechanical" restricted the "construction" forbidden by para (c) of the definition of the "practice of dentistry" in the subsection to a construction proved to be effected by the use of tools or machinery, and that he should have concluded that the word "mechanical" had its origin in the functions of the dental mechanic, and that it indicated the construction of a denture by the process normally used by such persons.' *Hoskin v McGee* [1957] NZLR 731 at 733, 734, per Turner J

Mechanical engineering

'The term "mechanical engineering", in our judgment includes something more than the science of mechanical engineering. At least it includes the practice and technique of engineering.' *Institution of Mechanical Engineers v Cane (Valuation Officer)* [1960] 1 All ER 129 at 133, per cur.

Mechanical haulage

[The Coal Mines Act 1911, s 46(4) (repealed; but see now the Mines and Quarries Act 1954, s 41) enacted that on every haulage road where 'mechanical haulage', not being endless-rope or endless-chain haulage, was used, and where the gradient exceeded one in twelve, there should be provided and attached to an ascending tub or set of tubs a backstay or other suitable contrivance for preventing the tub running back.] 'Haulage is the action or process of hauling. It requires power to effect it. That power must be developed, as distinguished from applied. It may be developed . . . by means of mechanical contrivance. . . . But the expression "where mechanical haulage is used" is only another way of saying where the haulage is "worked by" mechanical contrivance.' *Soutar v Reid* 1913 SC(J) 84 at 89, per Lord Johnston

Mechanical power

[The Factory and Workshop Act 1878, s 93 (repealed; see now the Factories Act 1961, ss 135(6), 176(3)) enacted that a factory meant textile factory and non-textile factory, and that a textile factory meant any premises wherein steam, water, or other 'mechanical power' was used to move or work any machinery employed in certain processes.] 'If the use of any instrument worked by hand-power constitutes the premises a place where machinery is worked by steam, water, or other mechanical power, then every place in which a pulley or a crowbar is used to impart motion falls within the definition. I do not think that the expression "mechanical power" is fairly capable of such an extended meaning.' *Willmott v Paton* [1902] 1 KB 237 at 241, CA, per Stirling LJ

MECHANICALLY PROPELLED VEHICLE

'The question is whether this vehicle [a bicycle with an auxiliary motor which, on the day in question, was not in working order] was a mechanically propelled vehicle within the meaning of s 1 of the Road Traffic Act 1930, [repealed; see now the Road Traffic Act 1960, s 253] and that section is one of a group of sections which is headed "Classification of motor vehicles". I am, therefore, satisfied, that the words "mechanically propelled" are intended as words of classification and prima facie do not refer to the way in which a vehicle is being propelled at any given moment. A motor car is a mechanically propelled vehicle. It is designed so that it has only a mechanical means of propulsion, and, therefore, I should hold that, whatever its use might be at any given moment, whether it was in working order or whether it was being driven on a free-wheel or driven downhill with the engine disengaged, it still was being used as a mechanically propelled vehicle. Where, however, a vehicle is designed to have two means of propulsion, one mechanical and the other non-mechanical, different questions are raised, and to see into which classification it comes regard must be had to its working condition and the use to which it is being put at the material time. I agree also that to some extent it is a question of fact and of degree, but in view of the justices' finding of fact that the auxiliary motor was not in a working condition at the material time and that the appellant was riding the machine simply as a pedal cycle, I think the conclusion is irresistible that the cycle did not fall within the classification of a mechanically propelled vehicle.' *Lawrence v Howlett* [1952] 2 All ER 74 at 75, per Devlin J

'The definition of motor cycles in the Road Traffic Act 1930, s 2(1)(f) [repealed; see now the Road Traffic Act 1960, s 253] is ". . . mechanically propelled vehicles . . . with less than four wheels and the weight of which unladen does not exceed eight hundredweight". I think the only sensible construction of "mechanically propelled vehicles" is vehicles constructed so that they can be mechanically propelled.' [The respondent was therefore held guilty of an offence under the Act although he had made no attempt to start or use the engine of a motor-assisted pedal cycle, but had simply pedalled it along the highway.] *Floyd v Bush* [1953] 1 All ER 265 at 266, per Lord Goddard CJ

'We are . . . satisfied that a motor car does not cease to be a mechanically propelled vehicle on the mere removal of the engine if the evidence admits the possibility that the engine may shortly be replaced and the motive power restored.' *Newberry v Simmonds* [1961] 2 All ER 318 at 320, per cur.; also reported [1961] 2 QB 345 at 350

'Where, as in the present case, and unlike *Newberry v Simmonds* [supra], there is no reasonable prospect of the vehicle ever being made mobile again, it seems to me that, at any rate at that stage, a vehicle has ceased to be a mechanically propelled vehicle'. *Smart v Allen* [1962] 3 All ER 893 at 896, per Lord Parker, CJ

MEDAL

[A testatrix by her will left her jewels, plate, pictures, 'medals', and furniture, to her two executors, to be equally divided.] 'Mr Clarke, for the executors, has insisted that under the word furniture, books will pass, and that under the word medals, pieces of current coin kept with them will pass. If current coin are curious pieces, and kept with medals, I am of opinion, notwithstanding they are current coin, yet, as they are kept with medals, they will pass as such, for even medals themselves were once current coin.' *Bridgman v Dove* (1744) 3 Atk 201 at 202, per Lord Hardwicke LC

'What is a medal? It is defined in the Oxford English Dictionary as: "a piece of metal, usually in the form of a coin, struck or cast, with an inscription, a head or effigy of a person, or other device or figure to commemorate a person, action or event; also as a distinction awarded to a soldier. . . ." Counsel for the defendants suggests that this article [a coronation medallion] was not a medal within the meaning of that definition, so far as the definition can be applied to r 26 of the Designs Rules 1949 [see now the Designs Rules 1984, SI 1984/1989]. I do not know why it is not. It is obviously a piece of metal in the form of a coin.

There can be no doubt that it bears an inscription, a head or effigy, and other devices or figures to commemorate an event, namely, the year of the coronation of Her Majesty. Whether the main purpose of the exclusion was to apply to service medals, I cannot say. It may be that that was the primary intention, but I think that it is exceedingly difficult to exclude these and similar objects from the definition of "a medal" in the dictionary and from the conception of a medal in the minds of ordinary people.' *Reliance (Nameplates) Ltd v Art Jewels Ltd* [1953] 1 All ER 759 at 761, per Vaisey J

MEDICAL EXAMINATION

The expression includes bacteriological and radiographical tests and similar investigations. (Social Security Act 1975, Sch 20)

MEDICAL OFFICER

'Medical officer' means, in relation to any local education authority, a duly qualified medical practitioner employed, or engaged, whether regularly or for the purposes of any particular case, by that authority or whose services are made available to that authority by the Secretary of State. (Education Act 1944, s 114(1), as amended by the National Health Service Reorganisation Act 1973)

MEDICAL PRACTITIONER *See also* DOCTOR

'Practitioner' (except where that word occurs as part of the expression 'veterinary practitioner') means a doctor, dentist, veterinary surgeon or veterinary practitioner. (Medicines Act 1968, s 132(1))

A registered medical practitioner. The expression includes a person outside the United Kingdom who is not a registered medical practitioner, but has qualifications corresponding (in the Secretary of State's opinion) to those of a registered medical practitioner. (Social Security Act 1975, Sch 20)

General medical practitioner

'Here the plaintiff's activity was that of general medical practitioner. There is no evidence of what that phrase comprises. The definition which counsel for the plaintiff asks us to accept he formulated in this way: A general medical practitioner is one who holds himself out as prepared to treat any patient for any disease, ailment or injury normally to be met with in the country where he practises. I cannot accept that in the absence of evidence, and counsel invited us to apply our own personal knowledge of what a general medical practitioner is normally thought to be. I think it very inconvenient that the court, on a question of that kind, should have to fall back on some knowledge which may not necessarily be the same for each member of the court, but I should have thought it is notorious that the phrase "general medical practitioner" by itself excludes a consultant. It may also exclude a specialist in some particular treatment, but is not a consultant in that he accepts patients who come to him direct, whereas a consultant, in the strict sense of the term, only accepts a patient who is brought to him for consultation with the patient's own medical attendant.' *Routh v Jones* [1947] 1 All ER 758 at 761, CA, per Lord Greene MR

Physician

'The question . . . is whether a person holding a certificate or diploma from the Society of Apothecaries, by which he is entitled to practise medicine, surgery and midwifery as well as to act as an apothecary, is entitled to describe himself as a physician—whether in so doing he is contravening the provisions of s 40 of the Medical Act 1858 [repealed; see now Medical Act 1983, s 49]. . . . The question arises as to the meaning with which the description "physician" was used; whether it was used in a general and colloquial sense as being equivalent to the expression "medical man", or whether it was used in a more definite sense—a sense which would import to most people that he held a medical degree of one of the universities or a diploma entitling him to call himself a physician. I think the latter was the real meaning of the word; it was the meaning which would ordinarily be conveyed to anybody who saw the word on a brass plate.' *Hunter v Clare* [1899] 1 QB 635 at 638, 639, DC, per Lawrence J

See, generally, 30 Halsbury's Laws (4th edn) paras 3, 4.

Surgeon

'A surgeon formerly was a mere operator, who joined his practice to that of a barber. In latter times all that has been changed, and the profession has risen into great and deserved eminence. But the business of a surgeon is, properly speaking, with external ailments and injuries of the limbs. With a view to the recovery of a patient in a case of that description, he may perhaps, prescribe and dispense medicine.' *Allison v Haydon* (1828) 4 Bing 619 at 621, per Best CJ

'It was contended on behalf of the respondent, that, as he alleged, and the allegation depended upon his sole testimony, the words "manipulative surgeon" had been for upwards of twenty years publicly and generally used to mean, and were generally understood to mean, a person not registered under the Medical Act of 1858 [repealed; see now Medical Act 1983, s 49], and not recognised by law as a surgeon carrying on the occupation in which he was engaged. He contended that those words had been publicly and generally used, by members of the medical profession and others, to distinguish unqualified persons and their occupation, from qualified and registered surgeons and their profession. He even went so far as to contend that the word "surgeon" being used in conjunction with the word "manipulative" qualified and defined the word "manipulative", or, in other words, that the substantive qualified the adjective, and he further contended that the statute contained a prohibition against the wilful and false use of the word "surgeon" by itself, or the wilful and false use of any name, title, or description implying that a person is registered under the Act, or that he is recognised by law as a surgeon, or licentiate in surgery. Indeed, it is apparent that having persuaded himself, it is to be supposed, of the truth of his contention, he said that he used these words "manipulative surgeon" for the very purpose of directing attention to the fact that he was not a surgeon within the meaning of the statute. It was contended on the part of the appellant that the statute contained an absolute prohibition against the use of the title "surgeon" by an unregistered person, and that the use of the word "manipulative" could not justify or legalise the use by the respondent of the word "surgeon". . . . In my opinion, the effect of this section is to prohibit the use of any of these named and well-known descriptions except in cases where they are lawfully employed, those descriptions being physician, doctor of medicine, licentiate in medicine and surgery, bachelor of medicine, surgeon, general practitioner or apothecary. If one of those well-known professional descriptions is employed, I think a defendant cannot be heard to say, borrowing the latter words of the section which are applicable to names and descriptions of a different character, that the name which he employed did not imply that he was registered or recognised in the sense described by the statute. If he is not a surgeon, he must not call himself a surgeon, and it seems to me to be quite idle to say that in this context the word "surgeon" is used to qualify or modify the word "manipulative". It is perfectly clear as a matter of grammar that the word "manipulative" is the adjective and the word "surgeon" the substantive. What this respondent is asserting is: "I am a surgeon, and if you ask me what kind of surgeon I am, I am a manipulative surgeon". It is a curious epithet to apply to the word "surgeon". By its very name the profession of surgeon points to a person who does that which he does by means of his hands, and to say that he is a manipulative surgeon is the same as saying that he is a surgeon surgeon. . . . To suggest to us that the term "manipulative surgeon" does not come within the mischief of s 40 of the Act of 1858 because a man may lawfully call himself a "dental surgeon" or a "veterinary surgeon", is obviously nothing to the point when one remembers that those persons are expressly protected in each case by a statute. I am not inquiring into the frame of mind of this respondent. I take it that he is sincere, but if he desires to represent to the public that he is not a qualified surgeon it is a very unfortunate thing that he should choose the description "surgeon" preceded though it be by the word "manipulative". . . . Apparently he does not like the name "bone-setter". Counsel seemed to be a little reconciled to the description "manipulative healer". But what does all that class of consideration involve except this, that the use of the word "surgeon" is and is thought to be desirable because of the well known and particular connotation and association of that word? The thing which makes the name "surgeon" appear to be attractive and useful is precisely the thing which this section was enacted to prevent. If the respondent is, as we must take him to be, sincere, there are many ways open to him of telling the public that he is not a surgeon other than the way of telling the public that he is a surgeon. It seems to me that this case is really beyond argument. The respondent has chosen to use the word "surgeon", the meaning of which is and is intended to be clear to the man in the street, and it matters not that he has chosen to attach to it the tautologous epithet "manipulative".' *Jutson v Barrow* [1936] 1 KB 236 at 239, 240, 243–245, per Lord Hewart CJ

MEDICAL TREATMENT

Medical, surgical or rehabilitative treatment (including any course of diet or other regimen). (Social Security Act 1975, Sch 20)

'Medical treatment' includes nursing, and also includes care, habilitation and rehabilitation under medical supervision. (Mental Health Act 1983, s 145(1))

MEDICINAL PRODUCT

(1) Subject to the following provisions of this section, in this Act 'medicinal product' means any substance or article (not being an instrument, apparatus or appliance) which is manufactured, sold, supplied, imported or exported for use wholly or mainly in either or both of the following ways, that is to say—

(a) use by being administered to one or more human beings or animals for a medicinal purpose;

(b) use, in circumstances to which this paragraph applies, as an ingredient in the preparation of a substance or article which is to be administered to one or more human beings or animals for a medicinal purpose. . . .

(4) Notwithstanding anything in subsection (1) of this section, in this Act 'medicinal product' does not include any substance or article which is manufactured for use wholly or mainly by being administered to one or more human beings or animals, where it is to be administered to them—

(a) in the course of the business of the person who has manufactured it (in this subsection referred to as 'the manufacturer'), or on behalf of the manufacturer in the course of the business of a laboratory or research establishment carried on by another person, and

(b) solely by way of a test for ascertaining what effects it has when so administered, and

(c) in circumstances where the manufacturer has no knowledge of any evidence that those effects are likely to be beneficial to those human beings, or beneficial to, or otherwise advantageous in relation to, those animals, as the case may be,

and which (having been so manufactured) is not sold, supplied or exported for use wholly or mainly in any way not fulfilling all the conditions specified in paragraphs (a) to (c) of this subsection.

(5) In this Act 'medicinal product' shall also be taken not to include—

(a) substances used in dental surgery for filling dental cavities;

(b) bandages and other surgical dressings, except medicated dressings where the medication has a curative function which is not limited to sterilising the dressing;

(c) substances and articles of such other descriptions or classes as may be specified by an order made by the Ministers, the Health Ministers or the Agriculture Ministers for the purpose of this subsection. . . .

(Medicines Act 1968, s 130)

MEDICINAL PURPOSE

In this Act 'a medicinal purpose' means any one or more of the following purposes, that is to say—

(a) treating or preventing disease;

(b) diagnosing disease or ascertaining the existence, degree or extent of a physiological condition;

(c) contraception;

(d) inducing anaesthesia;

(e) otherwise preventing or interfering with the normal operation of a physiological function, whether permanently or temporarily, and whether by way of terminating, reducing or postponing, or increasing or accelerating, the operation of that function or in any other way.

(Medicines Act 1968, s 130(2))

MEDICINAL TEST ON ANIMALS

In this Act 'medicinal test on animals' means an investigation or series of investigations consisting of any of the following, that is to say—

(a) the administration of a medicinal product of a particular description to one or more animals, where there is evidence that medicinal products of that description have effects which may be beneficial to, or otherwise advantageous in relation to, that animal or those animals, and the product is administered for the purpose of ascertaining whether, or to what extent, it has those or any other effects, whether advantageous or otherwise;

(b) the administration of a medicinal product to one or more animals in circumstances where there is no such evidence as is mentioned in the preceding paragraph, and the product is administered for the purpose of ascertaining whether, or to what extent, it has any effects relevant to a medicinal purpose;

(c) the administration of any substance or article, other than a medicinal product, to one or more animals for the purpose of ascertaining whether it has any effects relevant to a medicinal purpose, whether there is evidence that is has effects which may be beneficial to, or otherwise advantageous in relation to, that animal or those animals or not.

(Medicines Act 1968, s 32(6))

MEDICINE *See also* DRUGS

'The word "medicine" is comprehensive enough to include everything which is to be applied for the purpose of healing, whether externally or internally.' *Berry v Henderson* (1870) LR 5 QB 296 at 304, DC, per Lush J

'The word *medicina* . . . in English is equivalent to the word physic.' *Royal College of Physicians of London v General Medical Council* (1893) 68 LT 496 at 499, per Smith LJ

'A medical witness stated that by "medicine" is meant anything which will influence the functions of the body. The definition of "medicine" in Webster's Dictionary is: "Any substance administered in the treatment of disease; a remedial agent; a remedy"; and the definition of "disease" is: "An alteration in the state of the body or of some of its organs, interrupting or disturbing the performance of the vital functions and causing or threatening pain and weakness". The two definitions seem to coincide if disease is the failure of some function to operate normally and medicine is something which is intended to restore the normal working of the affected function.' *Nairne v Stephen Smith & Co Ltd & Pharmaceutical Society of Great Britain* [1943] 1 KB 17 at 21, per Atkinson J

Canada 'A perusal of dictionary definitions, judicial decisions and text book authorities leads to the conclusion that there is both a restricted definition and a broad definition of "medicine" commonly and generally understood and used. The method by which this conclusion is reached may be stated briefly: A "medicine" in modern parlance has come to mean, inter alia, a drug, a therapeutic agent, a biological agent, and a pharmaceutical speciality. . . . Some of these medical drugs or medical agents are used to cure or heal a patient per se, and are sometimes referred to as therapeutic agents (even though there are many therapeutic agents which do not cure or heal per se, but are used for a particular purpose in the treatment of a patient), while others are used in the course of the whole treatment of the patient. In this connection, for instance in the case of the former kind of medical drugs or medical agents, an antibiotic, say, e.g., penicillin, comes closest perhaps, but even then, it often happens that other medical drugs or agents are necessary as supportive therapy when the antibiotic appears to be specific for a particular type of infection. The former kind of medical drugs or agents are "medicines" in a restricted meaning, while the latter kind are "medicines" in the broad meaning.' *Imperial Chemical Industries Ltd v Commissioner of Patents* [1967] Ex CR 57 at 61, 62, Ex Ct, per Gibson J

MEDIUM

'In the absence of evidence all parties relied without objection on definitions contained in dictionaries and other works, and from these I learn that in connection with what is known as spiritualism the primary meaning of the word "medium" is (I am using my own language) an individual who professes to act as an intermediate for communication between the living and the spirits of persons now dead.' *Re Hummeltenberg, Beatty v London Spiritualistic Alliance Ltd* [1923] 1 Ch 237 at 240, per Russell J

MEETING

'Meeting' means a meeting held for the purpose of the discussion of matters of public interest or for the purpose of the expression of views on such matters. (Public Order Act 1936, s 9)

Public meeting

'Public meeting' includes any meeting in a public place and any meeting which the public or any section thereof are permitted to attend, whether on payment or otherwise. (Public Order Act 1936, s 9)

Australia [The Defamation Act 1974 (NSW), s 24(2) provides a defence for the publication of a fair protected report. Section 24(1) defines 'protected report' as meaning a report of proceedings specified in Sch 2, cl 2 which proceedings (cl 2(9)) include those in a 'public meeting' open to the public.] 'The point of law . . . is whether or not the proceedings of a local council can constitute a "public meeting" within cl 2(9) of the schedule. . . . It was argued that the words "being a meeting which is open to the public" provide the definition of a "public meeting" and include a council which "meets" in public, even though the meeting is confined to elected representatives, and presumably also to council officers. In my opinion, this is the correct view and I do not think that there is any ambiguity in the expression which calls for the application of any artificial rule of construction.' *Cassell v Gold Coast Publications Pty Ltd* [1984] 1 NSWLR 11 at 12–13, per Yeldham J

Race meeting

'Meeting' means any occasion on any one day on which events take place on any track. (Betting and Gaming Duties Act 1981, s 12(4))

Sports meeting

[Underwriters agreed to insure the amount to be received at a cycle 'meeting' provided that the expenses attaching to the meeting should not be less than a certain named sum.] 'I think that the word "meeting" must be read to mean not merely the actual meeting while in progress, but the whole adventure. In my opinion the cost of insurance may be properly construed as being included in the expenses attaching to the adventure.' *London County Cycling & Athletic Club Ltd v Beck* (1897) 3 Com Cas 49 at 50, per Bigham J

MEETING (of company)

Annual general meeting

(1) Every company shall in each year hold a general meeting as its annual general meeting in addition to any other meetings in that year, and shall specify the meeting as such in the notices calling it.

(2) However, so long as a company holds its first annual general meeting within 18 months of its incorporation, it need not hold it in the year of its incorporation or in the following year.

(3) Not more than 15 months shall elapse between the date of one annual general meeting of a company and that of the next. (Companies Act 1985, s 366)

General meeting

The general meetings of the company's members are either ordinary or extraordinary. An ordinary meeting is any meeting which by statute or the articles of the company must be held periodically, and generally means the annual general meeting of the company. An extraordinary meeting is any meeting which is not an ordinary meeting and not the annual general meeting. (7 Halsbury's Laws (4th edn) para 685)

Single preference shareholder

[Under the memorandum of association of a company it was necessary, before the issue of new preference shares, that a 'meeting' of the preference shareholders should be held. There was only one holder of preference shares.] 'In an ordinary case I think it is quite clear that a meeting must consist of more than one person. . . . One must regard the memorandum as far as possible as providing for circumstances which in the ordinary course may arise. That being so, I think I may very fairly say that where one person only is the holder of all the shares of a particular class, and as that person cannot meet himself, or form a meeting with himself in the ordinary sense, the persons who framed this memorandum having such a position in contemplation must be taken to have used the word "meeting", not in the strict sense in which it is usually used, but as including the case of one single shareholder. . . . I think on the whole that I may give effect to obvious common sense by holding that in this particular case, where there is only one shareholder of the class, on the true construction of the memorandum, the expression "meeting" may be held to include that case.' *East v Bennett Brothers Ltd* [1911] 1 Ch 163 at 168, 170, per Warrington J

Usual meaning

[The Stannaries Act 1869, s 10 enacts that a call may be made upon the shareholders at any 'meeting' with special notice.] 'The Act says that a call may be made at a meeting of a company with special notice, and we must ascertain what within the meaning of the Act is a meeting, and whether one person alone can constitute such a meeting. . . . The word "meeting" prima facie means a coming together of more than one person. It is, of course, possible to show that the word "meeting" has a meaning different from the ordinary meaning, but there is nothing here to show this to be the case.' *Sharp v Dawes* (1876) 2 QBD 26 at 28, 29 CA, per Lord Coleridge CJ

MEETING ROOM

The expression 'meeting room' means any room which it is the practice to let for public meetings. (Representation of the People Act 1983, s 95(7)(a))

MELIORATING WASTE *See* WASTE

MEMBER

Of company

The members of a company are those persons (including corporations, if any) who collectively constitute the company, or, in other words, are its corporators. A member is not necessarily a shareholder, for an unlimited company or a company limited by guarantee may exist without a share capital. (7 Halsbury's Laws (4th edn) para 338)

'Member' means, in relation to a company, a holder in his own right of any share in or debenture of the company, and a person interested in any share in or debenture of the company held, whether by himself or another, otherwise than in the holder's own right. (Finance Act 1940, s 59)

(1) The subscribers of a company's memorandum are deemed to have agreed to become members of the company, and on its registration shall be entered as such in its registers of members.

(2) Every other person who agrees to become a member of a company, and whose name is entered in its register of members, is a member of the company. (Companies Act 1985, s 22)

Of household *See* HOUSEHOLD

Of institution

For the purposes of this Act, a member of an institution shall be a person who, having been admitted therein according to the rules and regulations thereof, shall have paid a subscription, or shall have signed the roll or list of members thereof; but in all proceedings under this Act no person shall be entitled to vote or be counted as a member whose current subscription shall be in arrear at the time. (Literary and Scientific Institutions Act 1854, s 31)

MEMBERS' CLUB *See* CLUB

MEMORANDUM OF ASSOCIATION

(1) The memorandum of every company must state—

(a) the name of the company;

(b) whether the registered office of the company is to be situated in England and Wales, or in Scotland;

(c) the objects of the company.

(2) Alternatively to subsection (1)(b), the memorandum may contain a statement that the company's registered office is to be situated in Wales; and a company whose registered office is situated in Wales may by special resolution alter its memorandum so as to provide that its registered office is to be so situated.

(3) The memorandum of a company limited by shares or by guarantee must also state that the liability of its members is limited.

(4) The memorandum of a company limited by guarantee must also state that each member undertakes to contribute to the assets of the company if it should be wound up while he is a member, or within one year after he ceases to be a member, for payment of the debts and liabilities of the company contracted before he ceases to be a member, and of the costs, charges and expenses of winding up, and for adjustment of the rights of the contributories among themselves, such amount as may be required, not exceeding a specified amount.

(5) In the case of a company having a share capital—

(a) the memorandum must also (unless it is an unlimited company) state the amount of the share capital with which the company proposes to be registered and the division of the share capital into shares of a fixed amount;

(b) no subscriber of the memorandum may take less than one share; and

(c) there must be shown in the memorandum against the name of each subscriber the number of shares he takes.

(6) The memorandum must be signed by each subscriber in the presence of at least one

witness, who must attest the signature; and that attestation is sufficient in Scotland as well as in England and Wales.

(7) A company may not alter the conditions contained in its memorandum except in the cases, in the mode and to the extent, for which express provision is made by this Act. (Companies Act 1985, s 2)

Articles of association distinguished

'I will ask your lordships to observe . . . the marked and entire difference there is between the two documents which form the title deeds of companies of this description—I mean the memorandum of association on the one hand, and the articles of association on the other hand. With regard to the memorandum of association, your lordships will find, as has often already been pointed out, although it appears somewhat to have been overlooked in the present case, that that is, as it were, the charter, and defines the limitation of the powers of a company to be established under the Act. With regard to the articles of association, those articles play a part subsidiary to the memorandum of association. They accept the memorandum of association as the charter of incorporation of the company, and so accepting it, the articles proceed to define the duties, the rights and the powers of the governing body as between themselves and the company at large, and the mode and form in which the business of the company is to be carried on, and the mode and form in which the changes in the internal regulations of the company may from time to time be made. With regard, therefore, to the memorandum of association, if you find anything which goes beyond that memorandum, or is not warranted by it, the question will arise whether that which is so done is ultra vires, not only of the directors of the company, but of the company itself. With regard to the articles of association, if you find anything which, still keeping within the memorandum of association, is a violation of the articles of association, or in excess of them, the question will arise whether that is anything more than an act extra vires the directors, but intra vires the company.' *Ashbury Railway Carriage & Iron Co v Riche* (1875) LR 7 HL 653 at 667, 668, per Lord Cairns LC

'There is an essential difference between the memorandum and the articles. The memorandum contains the fundamental conditions upon which alone the company is allowed to be incorporated. They are conditions introduced for the benefit of the creditors, and the outside public, as well as of the shareholders. The articles of association are the internal regulations of the company.' *Guinness v Land Corporation of Ireland* (1882) 22 Ch D 349 at 381, CA, per Bowen LJ

See, generally, 7 Halsbury's Laws (4th edn) para 197.

MEMORY

Legal *See* TIME IMMEMORIAL

MENACES *See also* BLACKMAIL; THREAT

[The Larceny Act 1861, ss 44, 45 (subsequently replaced by the Larceny Act 1916, ss 29, 30) made it a criminal offence to demand money with 'menaces', or to demand with menaces with intent to steal. Both Larceny Acts were repealed by the Theft Act 1968. See now s 21 of the latter Act, which enacts that a person is guilty of blackmail if, with a view to gain for himself or another or with intent to cause loss to another, he makes any unwarranted demand with 'menaces'.]

'If a policeman states that he means to act upon an authority which he professes to have, and to lock a man up, that is a menace. . . . A threat to imprison a man upon a fictitious charge is a menace.' *R v Robertson* (1864) Le & Ca 483 at 488, 489, per Pollock CB

'I think that the word "menace" [in the Larceny Act 1916, s 44 (repealed; see supra)] . . . may well be held . . . to include menaces or threats of a danger by an accusation of misconduct, though of misconduct not amounting to a crime, and that it is not confined to a threat of injury to the person or property of the person threatened.' *R v Tomlinson* [1895] 1 QB 706 at 708, 709, CCR, per Lord Russell CJ

'We think it would be unwise to attempt to lay down any exhaustive definition of the words of the section [the Larceny Act 1861, s 45 (repealed; see supra)]. The degree of fear or alarm which a threat may be calculated to produce upon the mind of the person on whom it is intended to operate may vary in different cases and in different circumstances. . . . When there is evidence of such a threat as is calculated to operate upon the mind of a person of ordinarily firm mind, and the jury have been properly directed, it is for them to determine whether in fact the conduct of the accused has brought them within the section, and whether in the particular case the "menace" is established. If the threat is of such a character that it is not calculated to deprive any person of reasonably sound and ordinarily firm mind of the free and voluntary action of his mind it would not be a menace within the meaning of the section. In our judgment when a man, with intent to steal, threatens either to do violence to the person of another, or to commit acts calculated to injure the property or character of another, it is a menace within the meaning of the section.' *R v Boyle & Merchant* [1914] 3 KB 339 at 344, 345, CCA, per cur.

'When the case of *Rex v Robinson* [(1796) 2 Leach 749] is looked at, it is clear that there was evidence of a demand. The language used may be only a request; it need not necessarily be an explicit demand. A mere request without conditions would not amount to a demand within the Larceny Act 1861, s 45 [repealed; see supra], but in the present case there was ample evidence of a demand. With regard to the question of menace, obviously the appellant acted with the intention of frightening the prosecutor, and there was evidence from which the jury could say that the steps taken by the appellant amounted to a menace.' *R v Studer* (1915) 85 LJKB 1017 at 1017, 1018, CA, per Lord Reading CJ

'I think the word "menace" is to be liberally construed and not as limited to threats of violence but as including threats of any action detrimental to or unpleasant to the person addressed. In may also include a warning that in certain events such action is intended.' *Thorne v Motor Trade Association* [1937] AC 797 at 817, HL, per Lord Wright

'In our opinion, the offence under s 30 [of the Larceny Act 1916 (repealed; see supra)] relates to the acts and the intent of the accused. The intent to steal must be derived from the whole of the circumstances. Words or conduct which would not intimidate or influence anyone to respond to the demand would not be menaces and might negative any intent to steal, but threats and conduct of such a nature and extent that the mind of an ordinary person of normal stability and courage might be influenced or made apprehensive so as to accede unwillingly to the demand would be sufficient for a jury's consideration. The demand must be accompanied both by menaces and by an intent to steal, and there is no intent to steal unless there is an intent to take without the true consent of the person to whom the demand is made. But there can be such an intent without that person being in fact deprived of "that element of free voluntary action which alone constitutes consent" in the words used by Wilde B in *R v Walton and Ogden* [(1863) Le & Ca 288 at 298]. There may be special circumstances unknown to an accused which would make the threats innocuous and unavailing for the accused's demand, but such circumstances would have no bearing on the accused's state of mind and of his intention. If an accused knew that what he threatened would have no effect on the victim it might be different.' *R v Clear* [1968] 1 All ER 74 at 80, CA, per cur.

New Zealand [The Crimes Act 1908, s 268 (repealed; see now the Crimes Act 1961, s 239) was concerned with the crime of demanding the payment of money by 'menaces'. The prisoner had picked up a letter containing confidential information, and had demanded money, which demand had been accompanied by threats of injury.] 'The word "menace" means "a threat to enforce". It may mean not only to accuse a person of a crime, but also to injure him in his position, whatever that may be; and the case of *R v Tomlinson* [supra] shows that the word may be construed quite widely. The prisoner made a threat to injure the owner of the letter, and such a threat can be conveyed by letter just as readily as personally by word of mouth. We have no power to limit the word "menace" to the latter kind of threat only. The word is used in s 268 in the widest sense, and includes a threat by letter, and therefore it cannot possibly be said that the act of the prisoner does not come within the very words of the section.' *R v Hare* (1910) 29 NZLR 641 at 643, 644; CA, per Stout CJ; 12 GLR 605, 606

MENIAL SERVANT *See also* DOMESTIC SERVANT

'The word menial is not explained by our law. . . . A menial servant may be employed out of the house or household affairs, a domestick in or about the house only. A person hired as a clerk is no domestick servant.' *Toms v Hammond* (1733) Barnes 370 at 370, per cur.

'I should have been inclined to have told the jury, that the plaintiff [a gardener] was a menial servant; for, though he did not live in the defendant's house, or within the curtilage (*intra maenia* [but see infra]), he lived in the grounds within the domain.' *Nowlan v Ablett* (1835) 2 Cr M & R 54 at 59, per Lord Abinger CB

'The point reserved was, whether a governess is within the rule by which a menial or domestic servant may be discharged with a month's notice or a month's wages. We are of opinion that she is not. The position which she holds, the station she occupies in a family, and the manner in which such a person is usually treated in society, certainly place her in a very different situation from that which mere menial and domestic servants hold. So far, therefore, as the question is to be treated as a matter of law, a governess does not fall within that rule.' *Todd v Kerrich* (1852) 8 Exch 151 at 152, 153, per cur.

'I can find no better suggested explanation of the term "menial" or statement of the position of a domestic servant than that given in Roberts and Wallace on the Employers' Liability Act (3rd edn), p 214. It is as follows: "It is submitted that the term 'menial servant' may be best explained in accordance with all the authorities and the ordinary use of the word as denoting those persons whose main duty is to do actual bodily work as servants for the personal comfort, convenience, or luxury of the master, his family, and his guests, and who for this purpose become part of the master's residential or quasi-residential establishment". . . . The learned authors also reject the derivation to be found in the older textbooks of the word "menial" from *intra maenia*. In this they are borne out by Mr Justice Lawson in *Lawler v Linden* [(1876) IR 10 CL 188], whose view expressed in his judgment was that "maenia" had nothing to do with it. The word, . . . being originally spelt "meyneall", may well be derived from the Saxon *meine, mesnie*, a household family.' *Pearce v Lansdowne* (1893) 62 LJQB 441 at 444, DC, per Collins J

See, generally, 16 Halsbury's Laws (4th edn) para 508.

MENS REA *See also* ACTUS REUS

A person is not to be convicted of a crime unless he has, by voluntary conduct, brought about those elements which by common law or statute constitute that crime. In general a person does not incur criminal liability unless he intended to bring about, or recklessly brought about, those elements which constitute the crime. The foregoing concepts are traditionally expressed in the maxim 'actus non facit reum nisi mens sit rea'. (11 Halsbury's Laws (4th edn) para 4)

'This is one of the many cases where confusion has arisen by the loose use of the expression mens rea. The true translation of that phrase is criminal intention, or an intention to do the act which is made penal by statute or by the common law. It is true that under the old common law breaches of the laws of morality and crime were much the same. In a mass of cases mens rea involved moral blame, and the result is that people have got into the habit of translating the words mens rea as meaning guilty mind, and thinking that a person is not guilty of a penal act unless in doing what he did he had a wicked mind. That to my mind is wrong.' *Allard v Selfridge & Co Ltd* [1925] 1 KB 129 at 136, 137, per Shearman J

'It has frequently been affirmed and should unhesitatingly be recognised that it is a cardinal principle of our law that mens rea, an evil intention or a knowledge of the wrongfulness of the act, is in all ordinary cases an essential ingredient of guilt of a criminal offence. It follows from this that there will not be guilt of an offence created by statute unless there is mens rea or unless Parliament has by the statute enacted that guilt may be established in cases where there is no mens rea.' *Sweet v Parsley* [1969] 1 All ER 347 at 352, HL, per Lord Morris of Borth-y-Gest

'The beginning of wisdom in all the "mens rea" cases to which our attention was called is . . . that "mens rea" means a number of quite different things in relation to different crimes. Sometimes it means an intention, e.g. in murder, "to kill or to inflict really serious injury." Sometimes it means a state of mind or knowledge, e.g. in receiving or handling goods "knowing them to be stolen". Sometimes it means both an intention and a state of mind, e.g. "Dishonestly and without a claim of right made in good faith with intent permanently to deprive the owner thereof". Sometimes it forms part of the essential ingredients of the crime without proof of which the prosecution, as it were, withers on the bough. Sometimes it is a matter of which, though the "probative" burden may be on the Crown, normally the "evidential" burden may usually (though not always) rest on the defence, e.g. "self-defence" and "provocation" in murder, though it must be noted that if there is material making the issue a live one, the matter must be left to the jury even if the defence do not raise it. In statutory offences the range is even wider since, owing to the difficulty of proving a negative, Parliament quite often expressly puts the burden on the defendant to negative a guilty state . . . or inserts words like "fraudulently", "negligently", "knowingly", "wilfully", "maliciously", which import special types of guilty mind, or even imports them by implication by importing such words as "permit" . . . or . . . prohibit the "possession" of a particular substance, or . . . leaves the courts to decide whether a particular prohibition makes a new "absolute" offence or provides an escape by means of an honest, or an honest and reasonable belief. Moreover of course, a statute can, and often does, create an absolute offence without any degree of mens rea at all.' *Director of Public Prosecutions v Morgan* [1975] 2 All ER 347 at 361, HL, per Lord Hailsham of St Marylebone

[The defendant was charged with being knowingly concerned in the fraudulent evasion of a prohibition on the import of goods under the Customs and Excise Management Act 1979, s 170(2).] 'It is plain, from the use of the word "knowingly" in s 170(2), that the prosecution have the task of proving the existence of mens rea, the mental element of guilt. Mens rea in this context means the mental element required by the particular statute on the part of the defendant before the prosecution can succeed.' *R v Taafe* [1983] 2 All ER 625 at 627, CA, per cur.

Australia 'The general rule as to mens rea is clear and plain. It is a well established rule of the common law that an act is not criminal unless it is the product of a guilty mind. Thus, mens rea has two elements: (1) a mind; (2) which is guilty. The first is always essential. . . . Assuming his mind to be sufficiently normal for him to be capable of criminal responsibility, it is also necessary at common law for the prosecution to prove that he knew that he was doing the criminal act which is charged against him, that is, that he knew all the facts constituting the ingredients necessary to make the act criminal were involved in what he was doing. If this be established, it is no defence that he did not know that the act which he was consciously doing was forbidden by law. Ignorance of the law is no excuse. But it is a good defence if he displaces the evidence relied upon as establishing his knowledge of the presence of some essential factual ingredient of the crime charged. In principle, the rule of the common law is just as applicable to acts which are criminal because prohibited by statute, as to those which are offences at common law; and it was said by Cave J in *R v Tolson* [(1889) 23 QBD 168 at 181] that it is so applicable unless excluded expressly or by necessary implication.' *R v Turnbull* [1944] NSWSR 108 at 109, per Jordan J

New Zealand 'If the offence created by s 5(1)(a) of the Immigration Act 1964 is one of strict liability, then it is not disputed on the appellant's part that he was properly convicted. But in my view, even if the offence be one to which an absence of mens rea is a defence, the result would be no different. The appellant's argument amounts to an assertion that, because the appellant did not know that he was a prohibited immigrant and did not intend to commit a breach of the law, he had no guilty mind and therefore no criminal liability. This argument treats morality of motive and lack of knowledge of illegality as equivalent to a lack of mens rea. With respect, this is an incorrect approach. It is not necessary in demonstrating whether an accused person has mens rea to show that he knew that what he was doing was immoral or contrary to the law, nor is it any defence for him to show that his motives in doing a particular act may have been entirely laudable. Nor does it matter that the accused may have thought that his act was legal because, both at common law and under the Crimes Act 1961, save in a very few exceptional cases, ignorance of the law is no defence. . . . In the present case the appellant was a person who had previous convictions for which he had been sentenced to terms of imprisonment. In that situation he intended to land in New Zealand. It was the landing in New Zealand in those circumstances that the legislature intended to prohibit and it was the appellant's intention to land in New Zealand and his landing there which constituted the mens rea. It is no answer to the charge under this particular section to say that the appellant did not intend to break the law or that he had no ready means of discovering the law. That is no more than a plea of ignorance of the law which is no excuse.' *Labour Department v Green* [1973] 1 NZLR 412 at 414, 415, per McMullin J

MENTAL DISORDER *See also*

ABNORMALITY OF MIND; DEFECTIVE; DELUSION; IDIOT; MENTAL IMPAIRMENT; PSYCHOPATHIC DISORDER; SEVERE MENTAL IMPAIRMENT

'Mental disorder' is defined by statute [see infra] for the purposes of the statutory provisions for the treatment and care of mentally disordered persons and in respect of their property and affairs. The definition and the legislation for which it is designed do not affect the general law regarding criminal possibility or civil capacity for which the ordinary tests of legal responsibility apply. 'Mental disorder' is defined, for the purposes stated, as mental illness, arrested or incomplete development of mind, psychopathic disorder and any other disorder or disability of mind. The statutory classification of persons mentally disordered is subdivided by the use of the terms 'severe subnormality', 'subnormality' and 'psychopathic disorder'. However, no one may be dealt with under the Mental Health Act 1959 [repealed; see now the Mental Health Act 1983] as suffering from mental disorder by reason only of promiscuity or other immoral conduct. . . .

Since early times a distinction has been recognised in the law between idiots, that is to say natural fools who were incurable and whose lack of capacity was from birth, and lunatics, who became insane after birth and whose incapacity was or might be temporary or intermittent. The expression 'non compos mentis' [see infra] was used in an old statute of limitation as a general term, and was approved by Sir Edward Coke as being 'most sure and legal'. The term 'lunatic' was used in the Lunacy Act 1890, under which the issue on an inquisition was whether the person alleged to be mentally disordered was incapable of managing himself or his affairs. The term 'person of unsound mind' was given statutory preference in 1930, and was applied to persons formerly described as lunatics. However, the term 'person of unsound mind' was not statutorily defined, and the courts were loth to attempt to define it. Following the Mental Health Act 1959, the use of this term has been superseded in the treatment of persons suffering from mental disorder and the management of their affairs. (30 Halsbury's Laws (4th edn) paras 1001, 1003)

'Mental disorder' means mental illness, arrested or incomplete development of mind, psychopathic disorder and any other disorder or disability of mind and 'mentally disordered' shall be construed accordingly. (Mental Health Act 1983, s 1(2))

Insane delusion

'Insane delusions are of two kinds; the belief in things impossible; the belief in things possible, but so improbable, under the surrounding circumstances, that no man of sound mind would give them credit; to which we may add, the carrying to an insane extent impressions not in their nature irrational.' *Prinsep & East India Co v Dyce Sombre* (1856) 10 Moo PCC 232 at 247, per cur.

Insanity

'The true criterion—the true test—of the absence or presence of insanity, I take to be the absence or presence of what, used in a certain sense of it, is comprisable in a single term, namely—delusion. Wherever the patient once conceives something extravagant to exist, which has, still, no existence whatever but in his own heated imagination; and wherever, at the same time, having once so conceived, he is incapable of being, or, at least, of being permanently, reasoned out of that conception; such a patient is said to be under a delusion, in a peculiar, half-technical sense of the term; and the absence, or presence, of delusion, so understood, forms, in my judgment, the true, and only test, or criterion, of absent, or present, insanity.' *Dew v Clark & Clark* (1826) 3 Add 79 at 90, 91, per Sir John Nicholl

'To establish a defence on the ground of insanity, it must be clearly proved that, at the time of the committing of the act, the party accused was labouring under a defect of reason, from disease of the mind, as not to know the nature and quality of the act he was doing; or, if he did know it, that he did not know he was doing what was wrong.' *M'Naghten's Case* (1843) 10 Cl & Fin 200 at 210, per Tindal CJ

'The question being, whether the will was duly made by a person of sound mind or not, our inquiry, of course, is whether or not the party possessed his faculties, and possessed them in a healthy state. His mental powers may be still subsisting; no disease may have taken them away; and yet they may have been affected with disease, and thus may not have entitled their possessor to the appellation of a person whose mind was sound. . . . We . . . cannot, in any correctness of language, speak of general or partial insanity; but we may most accurately speak of the mind exerting itself in consciousness without cloud or imperfection, but being morbid when it fancies; and so its owner may have a diseased imagination, or the imagination may not be diseased, and yet the memory may be impaired, and its owner be said to have lost his memory. . . . No confidence can be placed in the acts, or in any act, of a diseased mind, however apparently rational that act may appear to be, or may in reality be. The act in question may be exactly such as a person without mental infirmity may well do. But there is this difference between the two cases; the person uniformly and always sound of mind, could not, at the moment of the act done, be the prey of morbid delusion, whatever subject was presented to his mind; whereas the person called partially insane—that is to say, sometimes appearing to be of sound, sometimes of unsound mind—would inevitably show his subjection to the disease the instant its topic was suggested. Therefore, we can, with perfect confidence, rely on the act done by the former, because we are sure that no lurking insanity, no particular, or partial, or occasional delusion, does mingle itself with the person's act, and materially affect it. But we never can rely on the act, however rational in appearance, done by the latter, because we have no security that the lurking delusion, the real unsoundness, does not mingle itself with, or occasion, the act.' *Waring v Waring* (1848) 6 Moo PCC 341 at 348, 349, 351, PC, per cur.

Non compos mentis

'There are four manners of non compos mentis: (1) Idiot or fool natural. (2) He who was of good and sound memory, and by the visitation of God has lost it. (3) *Lunaticus, qui gaudet lucidis intervallis*, and sometimes is of good and sound memory, and sometimes non compos mentis. (4) By his own act, as a drunkard; and it has been said, that there is a great difference between an idiot *a nativitate*, and he who was of sound memory, and becomes, by the visitation of God, of unsound memory; for an idiot is known by his perpetual infirmity of nature, *a nativitate*, for he never had any sense or understanding to contract with any man; but he who was of good memory and understanding, and able to make a contract, and afterwards becomes by infirmity or casualty of unsound memory, is not so well known to the world as an idiot natural.' *Beverley's Case* (1603) 4 Co Rep 123b at 124b, per cur.

'Lord Coke in his commentary upon Littleton states what embraces every possible case: "Here Littleton explaineth a man of no sound memory to be non compos mentis. Many times (as it here appeareth) the Latin word explaineth the true sense; and calleth him not *amens, demens, furiosus, lunaticus, fatuus, stultus*, or the like; for 'non compos mentis' is most sure and legal." Lord Coke there considers the word '*lunaticus*' as by no means material; only classing it with '*amens, demens*', etc.; but he says, "non compos mentis" is the sure term. The commentary proceeds thus: "Non compos mentis, is of four sorts: 1st, *idiota*; which from his nativity by a perpetual infirmity is non compos mentis; 2ndly he, that by sickness, grief, or other accident, wholly loseth his memory and understanding." Here is the very man: not born without reason; but who has lost it from sickness, grief, or other accident; for you cannot enter into the mind; to know, by what means it is disorganised: but you find it disorganised; and who can say, I have not a jurisdiction? There is no doubt, the moon has no influence; and there are many persons, who never have lucid intervals that come within this second description. But they must have lost their understanding to this extent; that they are not capable of the management of themselves and their affairs. Lord Coke is so far from putting the person he describes by the term "*lunaticus*" in the class, that I have just noticed, that he puts that person by himself; describing him to be a man, who hath sometimes his understanding, and sometimes not; and this is the ancient law of the country. This is not a man, who has sometimes understanding, and sometimes not; his understanding is defunct: he has survived the period, that providence has assigned to the stability of his mind. In the remainder of this part of the commentary Lord Coke continues to use the phrase "non compos mentis".' *Ex p Cranmer* (1806) 12 Ves 445 at 450–452, per Lord Erskine LC

Unsound mind

'We must keep always in view that which the inaccuracy of ordinary language inclines us to forget, that the mind is one and indivisible; that when we speak of its different powers, or faculties, as memory, imagination, consciousness, we speak metaphorically, likening the mind of the body, as if it had members or compartments, whereas, in all accuracy of speech, we mean to speak of the mind acting variously, that is remembering, fancying, reflecting, the same mind in all these operations being the agent. We, therefore, cannot in any correctness of language, speak of general or partial insanity; but we may most accurately speak of the mind exerting itself in consciousness without cloud or imperfection, but being morbid when it fancies; and so its owner may have a diseased imagination, or the imagination may not be diseased, and yet the memory may be impaired, and its owner be said to have lost his memory. In these cases, we do not mean that the mind has one faculty, as consciousness, sound; while another, as memory or imagination, is diseased; but that the mind is sound when reflecting on its own operations, and diseased when exercising the combination termed imagining, or casting the retrospect, called recollecting. This view of the subject, though apparently simple, and almost too unquestionable to require, or even to justify, a formal statement, is of considerable importance, when we come to examine cases of what are called, incorrectly, "partial insanity", which would be better described by the phrase "insanity" or "unsoundness" always existing, though only occasionally manifest. Nothing is more certain than the existence of mental disease of this description. Nay; by far the greater number of morbid cases belong to this class. They have acquired a name, the disease called familiarly, as well as by physicians, "monomania", on the supposition of its being confined, which it rarely is, to a single faculty, or exercise of the mind: a person shall be of sound mind, to all appearance, upon all subjects save one or two; and on these he shall be subject to delusions, mistaking for realities, the suggestions of his imagination. The disease here is said to be in the imagination; that is, the patient's mind is morbid or unsound, when it imagines; healthy and sound when it remembers. Nay; he may be of unsound mind when his imagination is employed on some subjects, in making some combinations; and sound when making others, or making one single kind of combination. Thus, he may not believe all his fancies to be realities, but only some, or one; of such a person we usually predicate, that he is of unsound mind only upon certain points. I have qualified the proposition thus on purpose, because, if the being, or essence, which we term the mind, is unsound on one subject, provided that unsoundness is at all times existing upon that subject, it is quite erroneous to suppose such a mind really sound on other subjects. It is only sound in appearance; for if the subject of the delusion is presented to it, the unsoundness which is manifested, by believing in the suggestions of fancy as if they were realities, would break out; consequently, it is as absurd to speak of this as a really sound mind (a mind sound when the subject of the delusion is not presented); as it would be to say, that a person had not the gout, because his attention being diverted from the pain, by some more powerful sensation by which the person was affected, he, for the moment, was unconscious of his visitation.' *Waring v Waring* (1848) 6 Moo PCC 341 at 349–351, PC, per cur.

'It is impossible to distinguish between unsoundness of mind and insanity.' *Smith v Smith (otherwise Hand)* [1940] P 179 at 180, per Merriman P

'I am not going to attempt a definition of just what is meant by unsound mind, an expression which the Act [Mental Treatment Act 1930 (repealed; see now the Mental Health Act 1983)] itself leaves undefined, nor am I going to search for equivalent language. It is enough to say that unsoundness of mind is plainly something more radical than an emotional disturbance requiring psychiatric treatment. The unsoundness of mind, whose presence is essential to justify a compulsory order, manifestly means something more than mental illness which qualifies a person to be a voluntary patient. No doubt, the phrase "unsound mind" is not one which is in ordinary use; in ordinary language "certifiable" is perhaps more likely to be used to express the same idea. The word originally used in the Lunacy Act 1890, was "lunatic". The Mental Treatment Act 1930, s 20(5), required the use of that word to be discontinued and substituted for it "person of unsound mind". The language of s 20 does not suggest an intent to alter the sense of the Lunacy Act 1890, but rather to substitute a word with less disagreeable associations.' *Re Buxton v Jayne* [1960] 2 All ER 688 at 697, CA, per Devlin LJ

'Any attempt to define insanity is likely to be defeated by the constant search which goes on from generation to generation to discover euphemisms for that condition. The word "lunatic", for example, is now out of fashion, and "medical recommendation" has been found to lack the sinister connotation of "medical certificate". If I were to be asked to interpret the word "insane" where it is used in the Act [Divorce (Scotland) Act] of 1938 I think I would prefer the short word "mad" to any more compendious definition, though no doubt the phrase "of unsound mind" conveys the same meaning.' *Ramsay v Ramsay* 1964 SLT 108 at 112, per Lord Hunter

MENTAL IMPAIRMENT *See also* SEVERE MENTAL IMPAIRMENT

'Mental impairment' means a state of arrested or incomplete development of mind (not amounting to severe mental impairment) which includes significant impairment of intelligence and social functioning and is associated with abnormally aggressive or seriously irresponsible conduct on the part of the person concerned and 'mentally impaired' shall be construed accordingly. (Mental Health Act 1983, s 1(1))

MENTAL NURSING HOME *See* NURSING HOME

MENTION

Australia 'It may be conceded that the word "mentioned", when applied to persons or objects, usually imports or implies some reference which identifies them by name or designation.' *Tooheys Ltd v Comr of Stamp Duties (NSW)* (1961) 105 CLR 602 at 612, per Dixon CJ

MERCANTILE AGENT

'Mercantile agent' shall mean a mercantile agent having in the customary course of his business as such agent authority either to sell goods, or to consign goods for the purpose of sale, or to buy goods, or to raise money on the security of goods. (Factors Act 1889, s 1)

See, generally, 1 Halsbury's Laws (4th edn) para 712.

MERCHANDISE

'Merchandise' includes goods, fish, livestock and animals of all descriptions, and minerals. (Transport Act 1962, s 50)

'The charterparty contemplates that the charterer shall load a "complete cargo of wool, tallow, bark, hides, or other legal merchandise", and I certainly cannot find anything in this instrument which constrains the court to narrow the large meaning which is naturally ascribable to the terms "other legal merchandise". I think for the purpose of considering what is an unobjectionable cargo, it is impossible to narrow that phrase by construing it to mean other legal merchandise *ejusdem generis* as the articles enumerated. For example, when the charter defines the limits within which certain enumerated articles are to be loaded, those articles include hides (which are there mentioned), and if we hold that hides fall within the expression "other legal merchandise", is is very difficult to say they are *ejusdem generis* with tallow or bark, when the stipulated freight is different for hides and the other enumerated kinds of merchandise. Therefore it seems to me upon the true construction of this charterparty that the defendant would not have incurred any breach of it if he had loaded the ship with a full and complete cargo of any legal merchandise other than wool, tallow, hides, and bark, and therefore if he had brought the ship home full of cotton, there is nothing in this charterparty, as it seems to me, to have made that a non-compliance with it.' *Cockburn v Alexander* (1848) 18 LJCP 74 at 84, per Williams J

'I think . . . that the defendants have succeeded in their contention that usage has established a meaning to the word "merchandise" of "articles shipped from the port with reference to which the contract of carriage is made", or "goods ordinarily shipped from port of shipment".' *Vanderspar & Co v Duncan & Co* (1891) 8 TLR 30 at 30, per Charles J

MERCHANT

'One understands a merchant of or in any merchandise, to be a merchant of that merchandise generally. A wine merchant deals in wine generally, port, sherry, claret, champagne, etc. He need not deal in every wine, for though he sold no Hungarian, he could well call himself a wine merchant. But if he sold port only, he should properly call himself a port wine merchant. So of a spirit merchant, he sells gin, brandy, rum, whisky, etc., and if he sold brandy only, should call himself a brandy merchant. A porter merchant, in the same way, sells porter generally, London porter, Dublin porter, Cork porter; but if he sold one sort only, he should describe himself accordingly as a Dublin porter merchant, or, as they commonly say, agent for the sale of Dublin porter. . . . A merchant of or in an article is one who buys and sells it, and not the manufacturer selling. A wine grower is not a wine merchant; even a wine importer is not called a wine merchant, but a wine importer. So of distillers, and so of a brewer.' *Josselyn v Parson* (1872) LR 7 Exch 127 at 129, per Bramwell B

'Dictionaries of different date that I have examined are by no means uniform in their interpretation of the term "merchant". Dr Johnson in 1755 defined a merchant as "one who trafficks to remote countries". Webster's Dictionary, of North American origin, as reprinted in London in 1832, has the following entry: "1 A man who trafficks or carries on trade with foreign countries, or who exports and imports goods, and sells them by wholesale. 2 In *popular usage*, any trader, or one who deals in the purchase and sale of goods.' Skeat's Dictionary of 1882, a great favourite in its day, says simply: "Merchant, a trader", but it is fair to remark that Professor Skeat was much more interested in the derivation than in the meaning of words. A later edition of Webster in 1890 contains the following definition: "1 One who traffics on a large scale, especially with foreign countries; a trafficker; a trader. . . . 3 One who keeps a store or shop for the sale of goods; a shopkeeper. *(US & Scot)*" Finally, Chambers' Dictionary in the edition of 1972 defines a merchant as "a trader, esp wholesale: a shopkeeper". Chambers may be suspect because of its Scottish origins, but the current edition is careful to distinguish Doricisms where they occur and does not qualify the definition that I have just read. In my own experience, the word "merchant" is now rarely used without qualification, except in the economic sense . . . where it distinguishes the trader from any other species of entrepreneur, for example, a manufacturer. Where it is qualified it may signify, according to the qualification, either a wholesale or a retail trader. Thus coal merchants and wine merchants, as the New English Dictionary recognises, are commonly retailers. A provision merchant may be a wholesaler but frequently is, or at any rate was in my youth much the same as a retail grocer. A paper merchant on the other hand is commonly a wholesaler; paper is sold retail by a stationer. Sometimes it is necessary to indicate expressly the limits of the term by the word "wholesale" or "retail". For example, in the London Yellow Pages Classified telephone directory I find a heading of "Fish Merchants—Wholesale," the retailers being classed as "Fishmongers". There are other groups, such as builders' merchants who are in a sense retailers, but retailers to a special section of the public carrying on a particular trade.' *Re New Finance & Mortgage Co Ltd* [1975] 1 All ER 684 at 686, 687, per Goulding J

Canada 'A merchant is one who buys and sells commodities as a business and for profit; who has a place of sale and stock of goods; and is generally a trader in a large way. The term "trader" is generally used in connection with a specialised mercantile business. The essential thing is the same in both cases, the purchase and sale of goods as a business. The goods bought in bulk are sold in retail, but, save for breaking bulk, are passed on unchanged to the customer.' *R v Wells* (1911) 24 OLR 77 at 78, 80, Ont SC, per Middleton J

United States 'Merchant' means a person who deals in goods of the kind or otherwise by his occupation holds himself out as having knowledge or skill peculiar to the practices or goods involved in the transaction or to whom such knowledge or skill may be attributed by his employment of an agent or broker or other intermediary who by his occupation holds himself out as having such knowledge or skill. (Uniform Commercial Code 1978, s 2–104(1))

MERCHANT SEAMAN

For this purpose [entitlement to residential qualification] 'merchant seaman' means any person not having a service qualification whose employment or the greater part of it is carried out on board seagoing ships, and includes any such person while temporarily without employment. (Representation of the People Act 1983, s 6).

In this Part [Part I: Secret ballots for trade union elections] 'merchant seaman' means a person whose employment, or the greater part of it, is carried out on board sea-going ships. (Trade Union Act 1984, s 10]

MERCHANT SHIP

'If the *Germania* is not "*un navire de commerce*", it is not within the protection of art 2 [of the Sixth Hague Convention]. . . . Article 2 protects under the specified conditions "*le navire de commerce*", or, to use the English translation "a merchant ship". A vessel which is described in the claim as a vessel of no value or utility for any commercial purpose, nor adaptable for such purpose, and not any part of the commercial resources of the enemy, is not in any sense a merchant ship.' *The Germania* [1917] AC 375 at 378, 379, PC, per cur.

MERCHANTABLE

Canada [A contract was for the purchase of "good merchantable timber" suitable for the buyer's purpose.] 'What he purchased he should be obliged to take and pay for, even if it did not suit his other contract. If he wanted quality or grade number one, he should not have bargained for number two, and in this case, when selling "merchantable," it was not the business of the seller but of the purchaser to contract in the one case for what would suit in the other. The contract for "merchantable" cannot be turned into "first-class," for that would be contrary to the written contract. The words "suitable for his purpose" cannot raise the class, but would characterise the description of "merchantable" timber, if the respondent and appellant had, when the contract was entered into, agreed upon the application of those words so to characterise the particular "merchantable" timber, the former was to cut and remove.' *Clarke v White* (1879) 3 SCR 309 at 323, SCC, per Henry J

United States Goods to be merchantable must at least be such as (a) pass without objection in the trade under the contract description; and (b) in the case of fungible goods, are of fair average quality within the description; and (c) are fit for the ordinary purposes for which such goods are used; and (d) run, within the variations permitted by the agreement, of even kind, quality and quantity within each unit and among all units involved; and (e) are adequately contained, packaged, and labeled as the agreement may require; and (f) conform to the promises or affirmations of fact made on the container or label if any. (Uniform Commercial Code 1978, s 2–314(2))

MERCHANTABLE QUALITY *See also* QUALITY

Goods of any kind are of merchantable quality within the meaning of subsection (2) above if they are as fit for the purpose or purposes for which goods of that kind are commonly bought as it is reasonable to expect having regard to any description applied to them, the price (if relevant) and all the other relevant circumstances. (Sale of Goods Act 1979, s 14(6))

[Subsection (2) of the above section provides that, in general, there is an implied condition that the goods supplied under a contract are of 'merchantable quality.']

[The Sale of Goods Act 1893, s 14(2) (repealed; see now the Sale of Goods Act 1979, s 14(6)) provided that where goods were bought by description from a seller who dealt in goods of that description there was an implied condition that the goods should be of 'merchantable quality'.] 'The phrase "merchantable quality" seems more appropriate to a retail purchaser buying from a wholesale firm than to private buyers, and to natural products, such as grain, wool, or flour, than to a complicated machine, but it is clear that it extends to both. . . . This is in accordance with the older cases, e.g. in *Laing v Fridgeon* [(1815) 6 Taunt 108] where it was held that in every contract to furnish manufactured goods, however low the price, it is an implied term that the goods shall be merchantable. In *Gardiner v Gray* [(1815) 4 Camp 144], Lord Ellenborough says: "The intention of both parties must be taken to be that it shall be saleable in the market under the denomination mentioned in the contract between them; the purchaser cannot be supposed to buy goods to lay them on the dunghill." The phrase in s 14, sub-s 2 is, in my opinion, used as meaning that the article is of such quality and in such condition that a reasonable man acting reasonably would after a full examination accept it under the circumstances of the case in performance of his offer to buy that article whether he buys for his own use or to sell again." *Bristol Tramways etc, 2 Carriage Co Ltd v Fiat Motors Ltd* [1910] KB 831 at 840, 841, CA, per Farwell LJ

'The defendants sold f.o.b. in England to the plaintiffs a large quantity of "Webb's Indian Tonic" of which the defendants were the manufacturers, and which they knew was intended to be sent out to the Argentine where the plaintiffs carry on business. Unknown to the plaintiffs, the defendants' tonic contained a small proportion of salicylic acid, a fact which by reason of a certain law of the Argentine rendered it legally unsaleable in that country. The plaintiffs now contend that the impossibility of legally selling it in the market for which it was intended constitutes a breach of the implied condition that the goods should be of merchantable quality. . . . In my view "merchantable quality" means that the goods comply with the description in the contract, so that to a purchaser buying goods of that description the goods would be good tender. It does not mean that there shall in fact be persons ready to buy the goods. For instance take the case that I put during the argument; if you sell "vestings" of a particular fancy pattern for sale in China, you do not warrant that the Chinese buyer will like that pattern and will buy it when it goes out there; if the goods are vestings of the pattern contracted for, they are merchantable though nobody likes the pattern or is willing to buy. Similarly I do not think "merchantable quality" means that there can legally be buyers of that article. If the goods are of the contract description the possibility of legally making a sale of them does not in my view come within the expression "merchantable quality".' *Sumner, Permain & Co v Webb & Co* [1922] 1 KB 55 at 62, 63, per Scrutton LJ

'Whatever else "merchantable" may mean, it does mean that the article sold, if only meant for one particular use in ordinary course, is fit for that use; "merchantable" does not mean that the thing is saleable in the market simply because it looks all right; it is not merchantable in that event if it has defects unfitting it for its only proper use but not apparent on ordinary examination' *Grant v Australian Knitting Mills Ltd* [1936] AC 85 at 99, 100, HL, per Lord Wright

'Merchantable can only mean commercially saleable. If the description is a familiar one, it may be that in practice only one quality of goods answers that description—then that quality and only that quality is merchantable quality. Or it may be that various qualities of goods are commonly sold under that description—then it is not disputed that the lowest quality commonly so sold is what is meant by merchantable quality; it is commercially saleable under that description.' *Kendall (Henry) & Sons v Lillico (William) & Sons Ltd* [1968] 2 All ER 444 at 449, 450, per Lord Reid

'The first matter to be considered is the meaning to be attached to the words "merchantable quality". Views on that have been expressed in a number of reported cases. In *Cammell Laird & Co Ltd v Manganese Bronze and Brass Co Ltd* [[1934] AC 402] Lord Wright gave his opinion of their meaning. As my noble and learned friend, Lord Reid, said in *Henry Kendall & Sons (a firm) v William Lillico & Sons Ltd* [supra] Lord Wright must have meant that goods were not of merchantable quality if, in the form in which they were tendered, they were of no use for any purpose for which goods which complied with the description would normally be used.' *Brown (BS) & Son Ltd v Craiks Ltd* [1970] 1 All ER 823 at 829, HL, per Viscount Dilhorne

Australia 'The expression "merchantable quality", in relation to goods the subject of a contract of sale, must, obviously, constitute a reference to their condition or quality. Consequently, goods are said to be of merchantable quality "if they are of such a quality and in such a condition that a reasonable man, acting reasonably, would, after a full examination, accept them under the circumstances of the case in performance of his offer to buy them, whether he buys them for his own use or to sell again".' *George Wills & Co Ltd v Davids Pty Ltd* (1957) 98 CLR 77 at 89, per Dixon CJ, McTiernan, Williams, Fullagar and Taylor JJ

New Zealand 'The sale of a specific article by description . . . imports, under s 16(b) [of the Sale of Goods Act 1908], an implied condition that the article is of merchantable quality under the description so given. What, then, does the term "merchantable quality" mean? It is clear, in the first place, that "merchantable" does not mean merely "saleable". Goods may be saleable yet not of merchantable quality. . . . In the second place, goods are not necessarily merchantable merely because they conform accurately to the description under which they are sold. . . . On the other hand, goods are not to be classed as unmerchantable merely because they are not fit for the particular purpose for which the buyer requires them. . . . Goods may be fit for the particular purpose and yet unmerchantable; or may not be of merchantable quality yet fit for the particular purpose for which they are bought in the individual instance. Furthermore, the term "merchantable" does not mean of good, or fair, or average quality. Goods may be of inferior or even bad quality but yet fulfil the legal requirement of merchantable quality. . . . I think that goods sold by description are merchantable in the legal sense when they are of such quality as to be saleable under that description to a buyer who has full and accurate knowledge of that quality, and who is buying for the ordinary and normal purposes for which goods are bought under that description in the market.' *Taylor v Combined Buyers Ltd* [1924] NZLR 627 at 644, 645; per Salmond J; also reported [1924] GLR 51 at 60

MERGER

Merger is an act of law, and, prior to the alteration effected by statute [see now Law of Property Act 1925, s 185, infra], took place when a particular estate in land and a subsequent estate both became vested in the same person without any intervening estate in another person. The particular estate was then at law merged or drowned in the subsequent estate. Generally, it was essential that the particular estate should not be greater than the subsequent estate. However, the principle of merger was subject to two exceptions. There was no merger at law if the person in whom the two interests united held them in different rights, where, for instance, he held a term of years as executor and the reversion in his own right; and an estate tail in freeholds has always been exempt from merger, and consequently cannot be destroyed by coming in contact with another estate tail or a remainder in fee simple in the same person.

In equity, the question of merger does not depend upon the mere fact of the union of the estates in the same person, but upon the intention of the parties concerned, and where no intention is expressed or can be implied from the surrounding circumstances, it may be presumed from a consideration of the interests or the duty of the person concerned. In this respect the same principles apply to the merger of estates and to the merger of charges on the land. There can be no merger by operation of law only of any estate the beneficial interest in which would not be deemed to be merged or extinguished in equity. Consequently, in questions of merger, whether arising in reference to legal or equitable estates, the equitable rule now prevails, and merger is not recognised as having taken place contrary to the express or implied intention of the parties. (39 Halsbury's Laws (4th edn) paras 598, 599)

There is no merger by operation of law only of any estate the beneficial interest in which would not be deemed to be merged or extinguished in equity. (Law of Property Act 1925, s 185)

MESH

'The ordinary definition of "mesh" is the space from thread to thread.' *Thomas v Evans* (1858) E B & E 171 at 174, per Wightman J

MESNE PROFITS

The landlord may recover in an action for mesne profits the damages which he has suffered through being out of possession of the land or, if he can prove no actual damage caused to him by the defendant's trespass, the landlord may recover as mesne profits the amount of the open market value of the premises for the period of the defendant's wrongful occupation. In most cases the rent paid under any expired tenancy will be strong evidence as to the open market value. Mesne profits, being a type of damages for trespass, can only be recovered in respect of the defendant's continued occupation after the expiry of his legal right to occupy the premises. The landlord is not limited to a claim for the profits which the defendant has received from the land, or those which he himself has lost. (27 Halsbury's Laws (4th edn) para 255)

'A claim for mesne profits can be joined with an action for the recovery of the land, and mesne profits is only another term for damages for trespass, damages which arise from the particular relationship of landlord and tenant.' *Bramwell v Bramwell* [1942] 1 All ER 137 at 138, CA, per Goddard LJ

Australia 'Mesne profits are the pecuniary benefits deemed to be lost to the person entitled to possession of land, or to rents and profits, by reason of his being wrongly excluded therefrom. The wrongful occupant is a trespasser, and the remedy rests on that fact. It may be a claim for mesne profits implies a waiver of the trespass, the claimant seeking to recover for use and occupation. The action is based on the claimant's possession, or right to possession, which has been interfered with.' *Williams & Bradley v Tobiasen* [1955] SASR 50 at 52, per Mayo J

MESSUAGE

'It appears to me that the term messuage denotes all that is occupied together at one and the same time, and no more.' *Kerslake v White* (1819) 2 Stark 508 at 509, per Abbott CJ

'We think, that although the word messuage may, there is no necessity that it must, import more than the word dwelling-house; with which word it is frequently put in apposition and used synonymously. The ordinary language of conveyances is sufficient proof of this, in which "all that messuage or dwelling-house" occurs as a constant description. . . . If the word messuage is referred to in the old book called Termes de la Ley, it will be found that "a house and a messuage differ, in that a house cannot be intended other than the matter of building; but a messuage shall be said, all the mansion place, and the curtilage shall be taken as parcel of the messuage"; showing only that it is more comprehensive where there is any thing besides the building.' *Fenn v Grafton* (1836) 2 Bing NC 617 at 618, 619, per Tindal CJ

Australia 'In conveyancing the expression "messuage" means not only the house itself but the outbuildings, courtyard, garden and adjacent land used and occupied with it.' *Royal Sydney Golf Club v Federal Comr of Taxation* (1955) 91 CLR 610 at 625, per cur.

In will

[A testator devised to trustees all his 'messuages or tenements', etc, and all other his freehold lands and tenements, in trust for his wife.] 'If the word "messuages" were found alone, there might be some ground for saying that the words of the devise would not be satisfied without including the fifteen acres of leasehold land upon which the messuage stood: but the words are messuages or tenements, and not messuages only. . . . In my opinion . . . the fair construction of those general words: "all my messuages or tenements, farms, lands, hereditaments and premises", is to make them applicable to freehold estates alone.' *Arkell v Fletcher* (1839) 10 Sim 299 at 308, 309, per Shadwell V-C

[A testator by his will devised a 'messuage' or dwelling-house 'wherein my son now resides' with the stables or appurtenances thereto belonging and therewith occupied. After the date of the will he bought a piece of land which he converted into a garden and attached to the house.] 'The question is, whether this copyhold garden passed under the devise, and I am of opinion that it did. . . . The burthen of proof lies, therefore, to show that it did not pass, and this from the will itself. I think the word "now" is solely descriptive of the messuage, exactly as if he had said "I give my farm Whiteacre, now in the occupation of J Smith". It is merely descriptive of the subject matter of the devise, and not used as confining the extent of the devise; the devise means the house, and in my opinion the words "messuage or dwelling-house" includes the garden. . . . Here, if the devise had been of the messuage or dwelling-house as it now stands, and the lands now held therewith . . . it would not have included the after-acquired garden but he leaves the messuage and dwelling-house, merely pointing out by the description what messuage he means, the consequence is, that all the additions he makes to it, and which properly belong to the messuage as it stood at his death, pass by the word messuage, and these additions include the garden.' *Re Midland Rly Co, Re Otley & Ilkey Branch* (1865) 34 Beav 525 at 526, 527, per Romilly MR

METAL

[A former statute of 1825, imposed duties on copper, iron, lead, brass, pewter, tin, and on all other 'metals' not enumerated.] 'I think the words "all other metals" in this Act of Parliament must be understood in their ordinary and proper sense; and in that sense they certainly do not include gold and silver. They are never spoken of in popular language as metals, but as the precious metals.' *Casher v Holmes* (1831) 2 B & Ad 592 at 596, per Lord Tenterden CJ

METHOD

'Engine and method mean the same thing, and may be the subject of a patent. "Method", properly speaking, is only placing several things and performing several operations in the most convenient order: but it may signify a contrivance or device.' *Hornblower v Boulton* (1799) 8 Term Rep 95 at 106, per Lawrence J

METROPOLITICAL *See* ARCHBISHOP

MID-CHANNEL *See* FAIRWAY

MIDDLEMAN

'A "middleman" is a person intervening between supplier and consumer with an interest independent of both, be it only to secure a commission on the formation or carrying out of the contract between them.' *Perth Assessor v Shields Motor Car Co Ltd* 1956 SC 186 at 193, per Lord Patrick

'The ratepayers say that the insurer is a "middleman", . . . and, by way of definition, it is said that the word "middleman" covers anyone who stands in a separate legal relationship from the owner of the article, on the one hand, and the . . . manufacturer or repairer on the other. No doubt that is a fair definition of the word "middleman" at least in some contexts.' *Meriden Rural District Council v Standard Motor Co Ltd* [1957] 3 All ER 222 at 226, CA, per Lord Evershed MR

MILE

[The County Courts Act 1846, s 128 (repealed), provided that actions might be brought in the superior courts of record instead of in the county court, where the plaintiff dwelt more than twenty 'miles' from the defendant.] 'I think the true construction to be put upon the 128th section . . . as to the twenty miles, is that which was adopted by my Brother Parke, in

Leigh v Hind [(1829) B & C 774], viz "to take a straight line from house to house, in common parlance, as the crow flies", without any reference to the modes of communication. The words to be construed there were, that the defendant would not exercise the trade of a victualler within the distance of half a mile from the premises assigned: and my Brother Parke says, with his usual accuracy,—"The plain and ordinary sense of these words is, the actual distance; and I think they ought to be so understood, unless we can collect from the context that they were meant to be used in a different sense; and here the context raises no such inference". The phrase "as the crow flies" is a popular and picturesque expression, to denote a straight line, which I think is clearly the proper mode of measuring the distance from one given point to another.' *Stokes v Grissell* (1854) 14 CB 678 at 688, 689, per Maule J

'I am of opinion that the distance is to be measured in a straight line along the horizontal plane from point to point. The words of the Act [County Courts Act 1846, s 128 (repealed; see supra)], "where the plaintiff dwells more than twenty miles from the defendant", are general, and do not specify how that distance is to be measured. We are therefore to consider what is the meaning of the legislature. And I think that we must suppose that the legislature intended by the words to express the meaning that would be most convenient and most capable of being ascertained. Now, if the distance is to be measured by the nearest practicable way, see how uncertain it is. The nearest mode of access may be by boat, by a route varying every day according to the state of the tide; or, if it be by land, it may be rendered longer or shorter by changes in the road. But if the straight line measurement be adopted there can be no uncertainty.' *Lake v Butler* (1855) 5 E & B 92 at 96, 97, per Lord Campbell CJ

[A local turnpike Act enacted that no toll was to be taken within three 'miles' of a certain point.] 'I am of opinion that the mode of measurement in this case is along the straight line on the horizontal plane. In *Lake v Butler* [supra], this court held that such was in general to be considered the mode of measurement. I think it is very inexpedient to act upon nice distinctions, thereby encouraging litigation; and that, unless there appear in the Act a clear indication that there was a contrary intention, this mode of measurement should be adopted.' *Jewel v Stead* (1856) 6 E & B 350 at 353, 354, per Lord Campbell CJ

[The above method of measurement has been confirmed by statute. See the Interpretation Act 1978, s 8, which enacts that in the measurement of any distance for the purposes of an Act that distance shall, unless the contrary intention appears, be measured in a straight line on a horizontal plane.]

Nautical mile

'Nautical mile' means a distance of 1,852 metres. (Customs and Excise Management Act 1979, s 1)

MILEAGE

[A railway company agreed to make a siding up to certain warehouses, which in computing the amount of 'mileage' to be paid to the company was to be considered a terminal station in regard to all goods, wares, merchandises, or other things conveyed to or from the warehouses on the main line.] 'The amount of mileage means . . . that what you are entitled to is in respect of the charge per mile and no other meaning can be given to it. The amount of mileage is a sum calculated . . . by the distance traversed.' *Weaver & Co Ltd v Great Western Rly* (1911) 15 Ry & Can Tr Cas 1 at 11, CA, per Cozens-Hardy MR

MILITARY AIRCRAFT *See* AIRCRAFT

MILITARY POWER

[A policy of insurance contained a clause excepting damage from insurrection, riots, civil commotion, or 'military or usurped power'.] 'The words "military or usurped power" . . . are certainly of a more serious significance than is implied by the "civil commotion" immediately preceding them. This seems a more natural interpretation, and obviates any suggestion of redundancy which might possibly arise from a construction which makes the last words "military or usurped power" only mean, or partly mean over again, the domestic incidents referred to by the first words "insurrection, riot, and civil commotion", especially when, as above pointed out, civil commotion seems to be the last and least of the domestic incidents. Nor can it be properly contended that the words "military power" do not refer to military power of a Government lawfully exercised. The disjunctive "or" is used between and contrasts the words "military" and "usurped". The words are not "usurped military power". Without using words of rigorous accuracy, military and usurped power suggest something more in the nature of war and civil war than riot and tumult. To sum up, in my view this clause is not merely a riot clause from beginning to end, but it is a riot clause and a war clause combined.' *Rogers v Whittaker* [1917] 1 KB 942 at 944, 945, per Sankey J

[A policy of insurance on property situated in Dublin covered loss or damage to the property directly caused by war, bombardment, 'military' or usurped 'power', etc, and fire. The property was destroyed by fire during a rebellion, when a fire caused by bombardment by the military forces of the Crown spread to the premises in question.] 'The plaintiffs claim to be entitled to recover a loss under the war and bombardment policy. . . . The plaintiffs' buildings and their contents were, according to the defendant's submission, destroyed by the Government of the country in which they were situate. . . . I am satisfied that the real and immediate cause of the fire in the General Post Office was bombardment and that the fire spread directly and naturally from the General Post Office to the plaintiff's premises. . . . The argument was that, assuming a shell fired by the forces of the Crown was the cause of the fire, this was not within the policy, because on the true construction of this particular clause "bombardment and military power" meant the bombardment and power, not of the forces of the Crown, but of enemies. . . . I hold that military power in the present clause includes the military power of the Crown as well as that of its enemies.' *Curtis & Sons v Mathews* [1918] 2 KB 825 at 827, 829, 830, CA, per Roche J

MILITARY PRISON *See* PRISON

MILITARY SERVICE

'Military service' includes not only compulsory military service, but also military service of a voluntary and contractual nature. (18 Halsbury's Laws (4th edn) para 1664*n*)

'Military service' shall include military telecommunications and any other employment whatever, in or in connection with any military operation. (Foreign Enlistment Act 1870, s 30, as amended by the Telecommunications Act 1984, s 109(1), Sch 4, para 5)

'Being of opinion from the result of the investigation of the authorities, that the principle of the exemption, contained in the 11th section of the Act, was adopted from the Roman law: I think it was adopted with the limitations to which I have adverted, and that, by the insertion of the words *actual military service*, the privilege, as respects the British soldier, is confined to those who are *on an expedition*.' *Drummond v Parish* (1843) 3 Curt 522 at 542, per Sir Herbert Jenner Fust

'What is the meaning of the words "*in expeditione*", or, as the Wills Act [1837, s 11] puts it, "in actual military service"? . . . I think it must be assumed, in the first place, that a state of war exists, with which the soldier is, or may be connected. . . . Then there is the other test, . . . namely, had the soldier . . . taken some step at the time when he made his will, to bring himself within the words of the section. This brings us very close, if, indeed, not actually, to the same point as what the Romans meant by "*in expeditione*", for when a Roman soldier did anything towards fighting the enemy, he would have been considered, under the law of his time, as being "*in expeditione*". . . . He [the deceased] went into barracks as a first step towards embarcation, and as I hold, as a first step towards joining the field forces. I am, therefore, of opinion that, by taking that first step of going into barracks with a view of being drafted to the front, he brought himself within the words and meaning of the 11th section of the Wills Act, and that he was then engaged "in actual military service".' *In the Goods of Hiscock* [1901] P 78 at 82–84, per Jeune P

'I have no doubt myself that mobilisation . . . may be fairly taken as a commencement of that which in Roman law was expressed by the words *in expeditione*. . . . If the order for mobilisation has been received, although the man himself may have done nothing under it, yet that order so alters his position as practically to place him *in expeditione*.' *Gattward v Knee* [1902] P 99 at 102, per Jeune P

'The commencement of the military service is the time when the mobilisation takes place. In the same way it seems to me that the actual military service does not cease until the full conclusion of the operations.' *Re Limond, Limond v Cunliffe* [1915] 2 Ch 240 at 246, per Sargant J

'A review of the cases dealing with privileged wills has made it clear that there has been some doubt whether any soldier could be said to be "in actual military service" unless this country was at war. Section 11 of the Wills Act 1837, provides: "Any soldier being in actual military service . . . may dispose of his personal estate" without the formalities required by the Act. . . . The decision in *Drummond v Parish* [supra], and subsequent decisions in this court, have made it clear that some limitation must be placed on what might otherwise have been considered to be the ordinary meaning of the words "in actual military service". Attributing to those words their ordinary and natural meaning, I should have had little hesitation in saying that an officer in command of a battery who is ordered to rejoin his battery immediately because the competent military authority considers that his presence with his battery is urgently required to ensure preparedness against aerial attack or invasion is in "actual military service". I am, moreover, of opinion that there is nothing in any case in which the meaning of these words has been considered which precludes me from so finding.' *In the Estate of Rippon* [1943] P 61 at 62, 63, 66, per Pilcher J

[A section officer in the Women's Auxiliary Air Force sent instructions in her own handwriting to her solicitors, requiring them to draw up her will. She died before its execution, and while still in the service of the Force. The question was whether she was 'in actual military service' within the Wills Act 1837, s 11 (supra).] 'In view of the fact that this lady was mentioned in despatches and she was in the balloon command, at another time in Bomber Command, at several stations had been in charge of the Women's Auxiliary Air Force, and even at the date of her death was still on the strength of that Force at the depot at Innsworth in Gloucestershire, it seems to me, having regard to the circumstances in which this war was and is being carried on and to the activities she was quite plainly engaged in from time to time, it would be wrong to say she was not in actual military service.' *In the Estate of Rowson* [1944] 2 All ER 36 at 36, per Wallington J

'The first meaning given to the word "actual" is "active" in the Oxford, the Century and Webster's English Dictionaries. The question, therefore, seems to me to be whether Roy Wingham at the time when he made this will was "on active military service". . . . If the presence of danger arising from enemy activity is not essential in order that a man may be properly described as being on active military service, what is the test of such service? In my opinion, the tests are (a) Was the testator "on military service"? (b) Was such service "active"? In my opinion the adjective "active" in this connection confines military service to such service as is directly concerned with operations in a war which is or has been in progress or is imminent.' *Re Wingham, Andrews v Wingham* [1949] 187 at 191, 192, CA, per Bucknill LJ

[The deceased, while on patrol in Northern Ireland, was shot and mortally wounded by an unknown gunman. Whilst dying he made an oral declaration leaving his property to his fiancée.] 'When the deceased in the present case was ordered to go out on his patrol, the fatal patrol, he was obliged, by the conditions of his service in accordance with the discipline which prevailed in his military unit, so to do. That the service was military, that the service was active, seems to me to be beyond contest. The fact that the enemy was not a uniformed force engaged in regular warfare, or even an insurgent force organised on conventional military lines, but rather a conjuration of clandestine assassins and arsonists, cannot in my judgment affect any of those questions and I have no hesitation in pronouncing for this will as a valid nuncupative will. It is not the state of the opponent, or the character of the opponent's operations, in my judgment, which affect the answers to the questions which arise. They must be answered by reference to the activities of the deceased and those with whom he is associated; and it is *nihil ad rem* in relation to the answers to the questions whether there is service, whether it is active and whether it is military that the context in which it occurs is that of foreign expedition, foreign invasion, or local insurrection.' *Re Jones (deceased)* [1981] 1 All ER 1 at 5, 6, per Arnold P

Australia 'There has been a recent comprehensive review of the law and the cases relating to the meaning of the words "in actual military service". The case is *Re the Estate of Wingham* [see supra], and the test evolved in that case as to what persons of the services personnel in time of war are on actual military service within the meaning of the Act is that they are confined at least to those who are actually engaged upon a campaign, or are proceeding or are under orders to proceed, or hold themselves in readiness to proceed upon a campaign, or are situated in what can properly be called a beleaguered fortress, or a war base from which active defensive or offensive operations are being conducted.' *Re Will of NFK Gillett* (1948) 48 NSWSR 477 at 477, per Roper CJ (Eq)

Australia [The National Service Act 1951–1986 (Cth), s 29A(1) provides that a person whose conscientious beliefs do not allow him to engage in any form of 'military service' is, so long as he holds those beliefs, exempt from liability to render service under the Act.] '"In any form of military service" means "in military service at all, whether combatant or non-combatant".' *R v District Court of the State of Queensland* [1968] ALR 509 at 512, per Barwick CJ

New Zealand [The deceased, though not a member of the New Zealand Expeditionary Force, was a member of the Territorial Force, and as such was at all times subject to military law as established by the provisions of the Army Act and the King's Regulations; and such force was called out by Proclamation 'for military service for purposes of defence in New Zealand', on the entry of Japan into the war. At the time of the making of the deceased's will while he was in a military camp, it was considered by the authorities that the Dominion was in peril of bombardment by Japanese forces from both the air and the sea and of invasion by either air-borne or sea-borne forces.] '"Actual military service" for the purposes of the Wills Act 1837 [see now the Wills Amendment Act 1955 (NZ), s 4] is not synonymous with "active service" for the purposes of the Army Act. Any camp in which soldiers were established, whether already trained or in the course of being trained, was a military objective, and if while the deceased was in camp at any time up to his death he had been killed by a bomb dropped from hostile aircraft, can it be doubted that he would have been regarded for the purposes of s 11 of the Wills Act as a soldier "in actual military service"? In the event of invasion or other hostilities he was liable so long as he was in camp to be required at a moment's notice to go to any place in New Zealand which it might have been necessary to defend. In these circumstances, while the position might have been altogether different but for the entry of Japan into the war, I think that the deceased while he was in camp at Trentham was a soldier *in expeditione*, or in "actual military service", within the meaning of s 11 of the Wills Act as interpreted by modern authority.' *Re Rumble* [1944] NZLR 94 at 103, per Myers CJ; also reported [1944] GLR 94 at 97

MILITARY STORES

The expression 'military stores' means any chattel of any description belonging to Her Majesty, which has been issued for use for military purposes or is held in store for the purpose of being so issued when required, and includes any chattel which had belonged, and had been issued or held, as aforesaid at some past time. (Army Act 1955, s 195(5); cf Air Force Act 1955, s 195(5))

MILK

'Milk' [for the purposes of ss 39–46 of the Act] means cows' milk, excluding not only condensed milk and dried milk, but also cream and separated, skimmed and evaporated milk, and butter milk. (Food Act 1984, s 47)

'Milk' includes cream and separated milk, but does not include dried milk or condensed milk. (Food Act 1984, s 132(1))

Raw milk

'Raw milk' means milk which has not been treated by heat. (Food Act 1984, s 132(1))

MILK PRODUCT

'Milk product' means any article of food or drink wholly or partly manufactured or derived from milk. (Agricultural Marketing Act 1958, s 42(1))

MILL

'Mill' includes any erection for the purpose of developing water power, and 'milling' has a corresponding meaning. (Salmon and Freshwater Fisheries Act 1975, s 4(1))

'A mill is a building where goods are subjected to treatment or processing of some sort, and where machinery is used for that purpose. The miller in his cornmill grinds wheat into flour, or oats into oatmeal. So, too, at a scutching-mill, the miller scutches the flax, to prepare it for spinning. The saw-mill, the rolling-mill, the flatting-mill, the puffing-mill, and the cotton-mill are all buildings where goods are treated or subjected to some process.' *Ellerker v Union Cold Storage Co Ltd* [1939] 1 All ER 23 at 28, per Macnaghten J

'The essential of a mill is a process, carried on by machinery, by which the material subjected to it is made suitable for further treatment in a factory or another mill or for use.' *Inland Revenue v Leith Harbour & Docks Comrs* 1942 SC 101 at 109, per the Lord President (Lord Normand)

Canada 'Various types of mills come to mind, such as rolling mills, steel mills, plating mills and stamping mills. And while it could be argued that some change in the product occurs in each of these, the same can hardly be said with respect to "windmills" or "sawmills" . . . I am satisfied that any premises fitted with machinery for the purpose of either mixing, separating, treating or cleaning grain is properly described as a "mill" and specifically that a building equipped to clean grain comes within the term "seed cleaning mill" as used in s 45 of the Canadian Wheat Board Act [RSC 1952, c 44].' *Ammeter v Slywchuk* [1971] 4 WWR 70 at 73, (Sask), per Maher DCJ

MIND *See* MENTAL DISORDER; SOUND MIND

MINE

The word 'mine' is not a definite term, but is susceptible of limitation or expansion according to the intention with which it is used. 'Mine' originally meant an underground excavation made for the purpose of getting minerals, but in particular contexts the word has been given differing meanings. Thus, it has been interpreted so as to include a place where minerals commonly worked underground are in the particular case being worked on the surface, as in opencast coal workings and in certain ironstone mines.

It may also denote a stratum, vein or seam of mineral, as in the phrase 'all that mine, vein, or seam of coal'. If, in such a case, the mine is unopened, it is clear that the word is used in the sense of a stratum of mineral. Where so used, the primary meaning of 'mine' is that of a vein or seam, but it may be used in a wider sense to denote a number of veins or seams, or in a narrower sense to denote only that part of a vein or seam which is within a particular tenement.

A further meaning of 'mine' includes not only the mineral deposits but also so much of the adjoining strata, whether above or below, as it may be necessary to remove for the purpose of working the mineral in a proper manner. The word has also been given, in some cases, a meaning which includes, in addition to the mineral itself, the space created as the mineral is being worked, and the space left when the mineral has been worked out. (31 Halsbury's Laws (4th edn) para 1)

(1) In this Act the expression 'mine' means an excavation or system of excavations made for the purpose of, or in connection with, the getting, wholly or substantially by means involving the employment of persons below ground, of minerals (whether in their natural state or in solution or suspension) or products of minerals. . . .

(3) For the purposes of this Act—

(a) there shall be deemed to form part of a mine so much of the surface (including buildings, structures and works thereon) surrounding or adjacent to the shafts or outlets of the mine as is occupied together with the mine for the purpose of, or in connection with, the working of the mine, the treatment, preparation for sale, consumption or use, storage or removal from the mine of the minerals or products thereof gotten from the mine or the removal from the mine of the refuse thereof; . . .

Provided that there shall not, for the said purposes, be deemed to form part of a mine . . . premises in which a manufacturing process is carried on otherwise than for the purpose of the working of the mine . . . or the preparation for sale of minerals gotten therefrom.

(4) For the purposes of this Act premises for the time being used for depositing refuse from a single mine . . ., being premises exclusively occupied by the owner of that mine . . ., shall be deemed to form part of that mine . . ., and premises for the time being used for depositing refuse from two or more mines . . ., being premises occupied by the owner of one of those mines . . . (either exclusively or jointly with the owner of the other or any of the others) shall be deemed to form part of such one of those mines . . . as the Health and Safety Executive may direct.

(5) For the purposes of this Act a railway line serving a single mine . . . (not being a railway line falling within sub-s (3) of this section or a railway line belonging to a railway company) shall be deemed to form part of that mine . . . and a railway line jointly serving two or more mines . . . (not being a railway line falling within sub-s (3) of this section or a railway line belonging to a railway company) shall be deemed to form part of such one of them as the Health and Safety Executive may direct.

(6) For the purposes of this Act a conveyor or aerial ropeway provided for the removal from a mine . . . of minerals gotten therefrom or refuse therefrom shall be deemed to form part of the mine. . . . (Mines and Quarries Act 1954, s 180, as amended by SI 1974/2013)

[The omitted parts of the section refer to the meaning of 'quarry' (qv).]

'There can be no doubt that the term "mines" may be used in several different senses. . . . Is a mine and a quarry the same thing? According to the ordinary sense of the term mine, does it mean a quarry? I apprehend clearly not. The meaning of the term does not depend upon the nature of the fossil body obtained, it depends on the nature of the mode of working it. Some mines may be worked by means of mining, others by means of quarrying. . . . That which is worked by mines is by a means of working in which the surface is not disturbed, and when limestone is so worked then it is a limestone mine. It is clear that in the popular, and I think in the just and accurate sense, of the distinction between mines and quarries, the question is, whether you are working so as to remove the surface, including perhaps portions of the lateral surfaces so as not to leave a roof. Mining is when you begin only on the surface, and, by sinking shafts, or driving lateral drifts, you are working so that you make a pit or a tunnel, leaving a roof overhead.' *Darvill v Roper* (1855) 3 Drew 294 at 298, per Kindersley V-C

'If there be one shaft by which you can work five seams, and which are all let, but only one is worked at first, I am of opinion, that when the lessee begins to work the other seams it cannot be said to be opening a new mine. I have no doubt that it is substantially and practically the old mine. I agree, that if a man has opened a shaft for winning coal, and he finds in another part of his estate mines of lead or ironstone, which could not be got by means of the old shaft or opening, this would be opening a new mine; but here the lessees were at liberty to open other shafts, and to work all coal and ironstone, and I think that this is only a repetition of the working of the old mine.' *Spencer v Scurr* (1862) 31 Beav 334 at 337, per Romilly MR

'By a quarry I understand a work from which stone or other material is obtained by excavation from the surface only. Directly you cease to excavate from the surface, and carry on a subterranean work, it is no longer a quarry, but becomes something else—whether or not it be a mine, in the strict sense of the word, it ceases to be a quarry. . . . What then is the criterion of a mine and a quarry? The authorities cited put it beyond all doubt. The case of *R v The Inhabitants of Sedgley* [(1831) 2 B & Ad 65] decided by the Court of Queen's Bench puts this very distinctly. . . . That case is valuable as deciding that an operation which is ordinarily a quarrying operation, may, by the particular mode in which it is conducted, become a mine. If it is conducted by underground working, it becomes a mine and not a quarry. . . . I find that the authorities both at law and in equity concur in this, that if the operations carried on are in fact mining operations, and not surface operations, whatever may be the material gained, whether it be slate, as in the present case—limestone, as in *R v The Inhabitants of Sedgley*,—or clay, as in *R v Brettell* [(1831) 3 B & Ad 424] the criterion is not the material obtained, but the mode in which it is obtained.' *Cleveland (Dowager Duchess) v Meyrick* (1867) 37 LJ Ch 125 at 127, 128, per Malins V-C

'The meaning of the word "mines" is not, I think, open to doubt. In its primary signification it means underground excavations or underground workings. From that it has come to mean things found in mines or to be got by mining, with the chamber in which they are contained. When used of unopened mines in connection with a particular mineral it means little more than veins or seams or strata of that mineral. But however the word may be used, when we speak of mines in this country, there is always some reference more or less direct to underground working.' *Glasgow Corpn v Farie* (1888) 13 App Cas 657 at 687, per Lord Macnaghten

'I think in all the cases you find that it is laid down that the question of what constitutes a mine may be properly said to be partly a question of law and partly a question of fact, but it is always largely a question of fact, and what I think is accepted as a very good test, if not a conclusive test, is whether the mineral, be it what it may, is worked underground or not so as to leave the surface untouched, and also, I think, one has to consider the nature of the mineral. Here it is coal, approached by means of a shaft, coal worked by an underground working, and in my opinion it is impossible successfully to contend that this mineral—these 100,000 tons of coal—was not got by mining operations, and by mining operations which constituted the place where the operations took place a mine.' *South Staffordshire Mines Drainage Comrs v Elwell & Sons* (1927) 97 LJKB 13 at 14, 15, CA, per Bankes LJ

Australia 'The primary meaning of the word "mine" is a subterranean excavation for the purpose of getting minerals.' *Federal Comr of Taxation v Henderson* (1943) 68 CLR 29 at 44, per Latham CJ

Australia 'There are certain metals, minerals and substances which have been traditionally recovered by underground workings. They have thus become associated in idea with the concept of a mine and the association of ideas has made it inevitable that whatever the form of the excavation that is made for the purpose of winning them, whether underground or opencast, it will be called a mine and the operations will be called mining. This may be an extension of the primary meaning of mining, but it must we think be recognised that, where the context or subject matter does not otherwise require, it forms today one of the natural applications of the words "mine" and "mining". In this sense it is part of the prima facie meaning.' *Waratah Gypsum Pty Ltd v Federal Comr of Taxation* [1966] ALR 19 at 24, per McTiernan J

Canada [Recovery of capital cost allowance was based on proceeds of disposition of depreciable property, including 'mines'.] 'There can be no doubt that when appellant, or its predecessor, acquired each of the five mines with which we are concerned, what it bought was land with mineral deposits included. This is clearly shown to be the usual method of operation in that business, and it is also what Schedule E [to the Income Tax Act] contemplates. There would be no residual value if mineral rights only were acquired. While it is true that such residual value must be deducted from the cost of the property in establishing the rate of capital cost allowance, this allowance is not expressed to be granted in respect of anything but the "property", that is an "industrial mineral mine".' *Avril Holdings Ltd v Minister of National Revenue* [1971] SCR 601 at 604, SCC, per Pigeon J

Mine of coal

'Mine of coal' means a space which is occupied by coal or which has been excavated underground for a coal-mining purpose, and includes a shaft and an adit made for a coal-mining purpose. (Coal Act 1938, s 44)

'Mine of coal' means a space occupied by unworked coal or excavated underground for the purposes of colliery activities, and includes a shaft or adit made for those purposes, a coal quarry and opencast workings of coal. (Coal Industry Nationalisation Act 1946, s 63)

Open mine

A mine is said to be open when it has been devoted by a person lawfully entitled to do so to the purpose of making a profit by the working and sale of the minerals in it. (31 Halsbury's Laws (4th edn) para 3)

'In order to constitute an opened mine it is sufficient if you find that a shaft or other works have been carried out or erected which serve and are intended to serve the purpose of getting coal. If that is so, and it can properly be said "This coal is served by that shaft, or those works", the coal so served by that shaft or by those works is an opened mine. It is equally, in my judgment, an opened mine if the shaft in question serves one seam or serves half a dozen seams. The moment you get to the fact that the work which has been done is not experimental work but is work which is intended for the purpose of working coal, and it is made obvious by the position and depth of the shaft and machinery themselves that it is adapted to the working of a certain extent of coal—to that extent that coal constitutes an opened mine.' *Chaytor v Trotter* (1902) 87 LT 33 at 37, CA, per Vaughan Williams LJ

'From the observations made by the Court of Appeal in *Chaytor v Trotter* [supra], and especially from what was said by Stirling LJ, it seems to me that an open mine means a mine which is "in course of being worked", and that a mine may fall within that description if a shaft has been sunk down to the same seams and the mine is capable of being worked through that shaft whenever opportunity arises.' *Re Morgan, Vachell v Morgan* [1914] 1 Ch 910 at 918, CA, per Sargant J

MINER

The term 'miners' includes all artisans, labourers, and other persons working in and about a mine, except the purser, secretary, agent, or manager. (Stannaries Act 1887, s 2)

'The applicant was mining barytes [barium sulphate] under a lease from the owner of the soil, and the question is whether the fact of his working for barytes under the authority of the landowner, and not for lead ore under the customs of the district, prevents him from being a miner if in the course of working the barytes he in fact takes lead ore away. . . . In my opinion, if a man in the course of mining, whatever he may be mining for, digs and carries away lead ore he is a miner, and it is immaterial that he did not start his mining operations with the intention of taking lead ore.' *R v Sanders* [1917] 2 KB 390 at 392, DC, per Viscount Reading CJ

MINERAL DEPOSITS

'Mineral deposits' includes any natural deposits capable of being lifted or extracted from the earth. (Capital Allowances Act 1968, s 87)

MINERAL UNDERTAKING

'Mineral undertaking' means an undertaking for the working and getting of minerals, whether by underground or by surface working. (Opencast Coal Act 1958, s 51(1))

MINERALS

'Minerals' admits of a variety of meanings, and has no general definition. Whether in a particular case a substance is a mineral or not is primarily a question of fact. The test is what 'minerals' meant at the date of the instrument concerned in the vernacular of the mining world, the commercial world and among landowners, and in case of conflict this meaning must prevail over the purely scientific meaning. Nevertheless 'mineral' is capable of limitation or expansion according to the intention with which it is used, and this intention may be inferred from the document itself or from consideration of the circumstances in which it was made. In the case of the document itself, the inference may be drawn from a comparison with other parts of the document or from the immediate context. In a reservation of minerals out of a grant of land, the rules of construction describing the substances reserved are the same whether the grant is made by instrument inter partes or by statute. In looking at the circumstances in which the document was made, regard must be had to the relative position of the parties interested, and to the substance of the transaction or arrangement which the instrument or statute embodies. The fact that the owner of minerals is not entitled to get them by surface workings is not sufficient to restrict the meaning of 'minerals'; but the meaning may be restricted by proof of a custom the existence of which is incompatible with the prima facie meaning, or by particular circumstances showing that not all the minerals were intended to be referred to.

'Mines' is frequently found in collocation with 'minerals', as in the term 'mines and minerals' or its equivalents. As so used 'mines' does not narrow the meaning of 'minerals', and the term is wide enough prima facie to include even those minerals which can only be got by surface workings. 'Minerals' does not comprise the space occupied or formerly occupied by mineral substances, even though 'mines' may do so. (31 Halsbury's Laws (4th edn) para 8)

'Minerals' includes all substances obtained or obtainable from the soil by underground or surface working. (Atomic Energy Act 1946, s 18)

'Minerals' includes stone, slate, clay, gravel, sand and other natural deposits except peat. (Mines and Quarries Act 1954, s 182)

'Minerals' includes stone, slate, clay, gravel, sand and similar deposits. (Opencast Coal Act 1958, s 51(1))

'Minerals' means all minerals and substances in or under land which are ordinarily worked for removal by underground or surface working, but excluding water, peat, top-soil and vegetation. (Finance Act 1970, s 29(7))

'The term "minerals", . . . though more frequently applied to substances containing metals, in its proper sense includes all fossil bodies or matters dug out of mines; and Dr Johnson says, that "all metals are minerals, but all minerals are not metals"; and mines, according to Jacob's Law Dictionary, are "quarries or places where anything is digged"; and in the Year Book, 17th Edw 3, c 7, "*mineræ de pierre*" and "*de charbon*" are spoken of. Beds of stone, which may be dug by winning or quarrying, are therefore properly minerals. . . . The word "fossils", in a strict sense, may apply to stones dug or quarried.' *Rosse (Earl) v Wainman* (1845) 14 M & W 859 at 872, 873, per Parke B; affirmed sub nom *Wainman v Rosse (Earl)* (1848) 2 Exch 800

'A mineral is etymologically, properly a substance dug out of the earth by means of a mine.' *Darvill v Roper* (1855) 3 Drew 294 at 299, 301, per Kindersley V-C

'Stone is, in my opinion, clearly a mineral; and in fact everything except the mere surface, which is used for agricultural purposes; anything beyond that which is useful for any purpose whatever, whether it is gravel, marble, fire-clay, or the like, comes within the word mineral, when there is a reservation of the mines and minerals from a grant of land; every species of stone, whether marble, limestone, or ironstone, comes, in my opinion, within the same category.' *Midland Rly Co v Checkley* (1867) LR 4 Eq 19 at 25, per Lord Romilly MR

'Many authorities, some at law and some in equity, have been brought before us to shew what is the meaning of the word "minerals". But the result of the authorities, without going through them, appears to be this: that a reservation of "minerals" includes every substance which can be got from underneath the surface of the earth for the purpose of profit, unless there is something in the context or in the nature of the transaction to induce the court to give it a more limited meaning.' *Hext v Gill* (1872) 7 Ch App 699 at 712, per Mellish LJ

[A prehistoric boat was discovered embedded in soil on land in which the mineral rights were reserved to a lessor. The wood had not become petrified or fossilised, but retained the characteristics of wood.] 'A discussion took place at the Bar whether the boat, just previously to its discovery, ought in point of law to be considered as a mineral, or as part of the soil in which it was embedded, or as still retaining the character of a chattel. It was one or other of these three things. . . . In support of the contention that it was a mineral, reference was made to the case of *Hext v Gill* [supra] and to the statement in the judgment of Lord Justice Mellish (with which Lord Justice James concurred), that the term "minerals" includes every substance which can be got from underneath the earth for the purpose of profit. The terms of this definition are wide enough to include the boat; but I am not aware that the term "minerals" has ever been held to include anything except that which is part of the natural soil. Unquestionably coal is deemed in law a part of the natural soil, without regard to what geologists may show to have been its origin. In law the natural processes by which the trees of a forest have become coal are not investigated: the result only is considered. But the boat has not become petrified or fossilised; it always has been distinguishable from the natural soil itself. If, therefore, I were required to decide the question, I should hold that it is not a mineral.' *Elwes v Brigg Gas Co* (1886) 33 Ch D 562 at 566, 567, per Chitty J

'It is evident . . . that "minerals" mean substances which can be got from beneath the surface not by mining only, but also by quarrying for the purposes of profit.' *A-G v Welsh Granite Co* (1887) 35 WR 617 at 618, CA, per Lord Esher MR

'There is no doubt that more accurate scientific investigation of the substances of the earth and different modes of extracting them have contributed to render the sense of the word "minerals" less certain than when it originally was used in relation to mining operations. I should think that there could be no doubt that the word "minerals" in old times meant the substances got by mining, and I think mining in old times meant subterranean excavation. I doubt whether in the present state of the authorities it is accurate to say that in every deed or in every statute the word "minerals" has acquired a meaning of its own independently of any question as to the manner in which the minerals themselves are gotten.' *Glasgow Corpn v Farie* (1888) 13 App Cas 657 at 669, 670, per Lord Halsbury LC

'To dig out ballast and crushed stone and earth, a mere mixture of heterogeneous portions of the earth's crust, for the purpose of making embankments, where the material goes from one position in the earth's crust to another without modification or being submitted to any process of manufacture, does not seem to me to be making use of minerals, although no doubt the things that you are handling were originally within the earth's crust. Such materials have not a value in use apart from their bulk and weight, and they are only used as being capable of forming a portion of the earth's crust in a new position. On the other hand, everything that has an individual value in use appears to me to be fairly called a mineral. Limestone may vary from a poor quality that is only worth burning into lime up to the very finest Carrara marble, but all those gradations have a value in use, either for building, or statuary, or for the manufacture of lime. Ironstone for the purpose of obtaining the iron, slate for its numerous uses, to which I need not refer—all these things seem to me to be properly called minerals, because from their properties they have a value in use.' *Great Western Rly Co v Carpalla United China Clay Co Ltd* [1909] 1 Ch 218 at 231, CA, per Fletcher Moulton LJ

'Undoubtedly "minerals" is a general term wide enough to include sand and gravel, though it may be controlled so as not to include these substances by the purpose of the statute or instrument in which it is found or by the context in which it occurs.' *Hamilton and Kinneil Estates Ltd v Assessor for Lanarkshire* 1955 SLT 257 at 264, per Lord Patrick

Canada 'The grant from the Crown . . . contained the following clause: "Saving and reserving unto us, our successors and assigns, all mines and minerals which may be found to exist within, upon, or under such lands". In Halsbury's Laws of England [see now 31 Halsbury's Laws (4th edn) para 8], the term "minerals" is defined as follows: "Minerals comprise all substances lying on the strata of the land which are commonly worked for profit and have a value independent of the surface". In *Lord Provost v Farie* [supra, sub nom *Glasgow Corpn v Farie*] Lord Macnaghten laid it down that the word "minerals", when used in a legal document or an Act of Parliament, must be understood in its widest signification, unless there was something in the context or the nature of the case to control the meaning. In the present case there is nothing in the context of the original grant from the Crown which would limit or restrict the meaning of the word "minerals" contained in the reservation therein set out. I am, therefore, bound to give the word when used in the patent its widest signification. In *Ontario Natural Gas Co v Gosfield* 19 OR 591, after a review of all the authorities, it was held that natural gas was a mineral. Under the above definition, and the cases cited in support thereof, and the decision in *Ontario Natural Gas Co v Gosfield*, I think it must be held that "mineral oils" come within the reservation of "minerals" contained in the original grant from the Crown.' *Re Mackenzie & Mann Ltd v Foley* (1909) 10 WLR 668 at 669, Sask KB, per Lamont J

Canada [A grant reserving 'minerals' in 1899 was alleged to include petroleum.] 'Dictionaries in use at the time the grants were made and at the time of the trial may be referred to in determining the commonly accepted meaning of the term. Murray's New English Dictionary, publication of which commenced in 1893, defines "petroleum" as a mineral oil occurring in rocks or on the surface of the water in various parts of the globe. The current New Oxford Dictionary defines "mineral oil" as a general name for petroleum and the various oils distilled from it. Webster's New International Dictionary describes "mineral oil" as any oil of mineral origin such as petroleum. In Soule's Dictionary of Synonyms, petroleum, rock oil, and mineral oil are said to be synonyms. That the word "minerals" was considered by the legislature to include petroleum in the year 1892 is shown by s 2 of the Coal Mines Amendment Act, c 31, of that year to which the learned trial judge has referred. This Act apparently contained the first reference to petroleum by name in the statutes and authorised the issue of prospecting licences for coal or petroleum. So far as relevant the section reads: "Any person desirous of prospecting for coal or petroleum, and acquiring a lease of any lands held by the Crown for the benefit of the province, under which coal measures or petroleum are believed to exist, or wishing to procure a licence for the purpose of prospecting for coal or petroleum upon lands under lease from the Crown in which the mines and minerals, and power to work, carry away, and dispose of the same, is excepted or reserved . . .". The reservation of minerals was thus assumed to reserve petroleum. The word "minerals" standing alone in the grant should, in my opinion, be construed as meaning mineral substances and, as these authorities and references indicate, petroleum and natural gas were prior to and at the time the grants were made and now are regarded as such.' *Crow's Nest Pass Coal Co Ltd v R* [1961] SCR 750 at 760, 761, SCC, per Locke J

New Zealand 'I think the one point that is clear is that, while the word "minerals" is wide enough to include stone, gravel and rock, its meaning in any particular statute depends upon an examination of the purpose of the enactment and the context in which the word appears.' *Taranaki County v A-G* [1967] NZLR 580 at 587, per Wild CJ

MINES AND MINERALS

'Mines and minerals' include any strata or seam of minerals or substances in or under any land, and powers of working and getting the same, but not an undivided share thereof. (Land Registration Act 1925, s 3)

'Mines and minerals' mean mines and minerals whether already opened or in work or not, and include all minerals and substances in, on, or under the land, obtainable by underground or by surface working. (Settled Land Act 1925, s 117)

MINING EFFECTS

The term 'mining effects' includes machinery, materials, goods, and chattels, and all ores and halvans, and all other personal property appertaining to a mine, or used or intended to be used for mining purposes. (Stannaries Act 1887, s 2)

MINING INDUSTRY

Australia 'Expressions such as the "mining industry", the "gold-mining industry", the "coal-mining industry", the "shale-mining industry", the "shale-oil industry" (see Encyclopaedia Britannica), the "iron industry", the "iron and steel industry" and so forth, are not technical expressions, but popular general descriptions without any definite or clear boundary lines. The character of the operations, their connected processes and usage must, in the end, determine the industrial classification under which the operations should be placed. Thus the very general description, "the mining industry" would include not only mining for gold, silver and the base metals, but the various processes by which those metals are recovered. So the gold-mining industry would include not only mining for gold and the processes by which the gold is recovered, e.g. crushing, the use of tables, or the cyanide or any other process. Again, if we take the iron and steel industry, the multitude of processes used in that industry would all be included in the general description of the industry. But it was said that the coal-mining industry does not include the making of gas. Ordinarily that is quite true, because coal is ordinarily produced and sold as a commodity for various uses. If a coal-mining company produced gas from coal for its mining or other operations, then that operation might rightly be described as part of the coal-mining industry. Indeed, a shift of industrial operations might well bring the production of gas into coal-mining industry.' *R v Drake-Brockman, ex p National Oil Pty Ltd* (1943) 68 CLR 51 at 59, 60, per Starke J

MINING LEASE *See* LEASE

MINING OPERATIONS *See also* MINE

Australia 'The expression "mining operations" is not a term of art; it is popular and not technical (*Australian Slate Quarries Ltd v Federal Comr of Taxation* [(1923) 33 CLR at 424]). The common understanding of those words is not a question of law but of fact (*Girls Public Day School Trust v Ereaut* [[1931] AC 12]; *A-G for the Isle of Man v Moore* [[1938] 3 All ER 263 at 267]).' *Federal Comrs of Taxation v Broken Hill South Ltd* (1941) 65 CLR 150 at 155, per Starke J

'The Commissioner [of Taxation] contends that the mine was closed down, or, in other words, the company was not engaged in extracting ore from its mine and was consequently not engaged in mining operations. But the majority of the Board [of Review] took the view that the common understanding of the expression "mining operations" covered activities in connection with a mine additional to the mere extraction of ore or metals such, for instance, as the provision and maintenance of plant both above and below the surface and work connected with the protection and safety of the mine and mining rights. In my opinion this was a conclusion which the Board might reasonably adopt in point of fact, and, if so, there was material before the Board upon which it could reasonably find that the Willyama Mining Pty Ltd was during the years in question here carrying on mining operations.' Ibid at 156

Australia 'In its primary sense the word "mining" relates to the extraction of something from the ground, as distinct from any process of manufacture which may subsequently be exercised upon that which is extracted. When the term "mining" is associated with the name of a particular product according to the ordinary use of the word it relates to the production of that product (e.g. coal) beginning with the actual removal of either the product itself, or that which contains it (e.g. gold-bearing quartz), from the soil, and ending with the production of the product itself.' *R v Drake-Brockman, ex p National Oil Pty Ltd* (1943), 68 CLR 51 at 56, per Latham CJ

Australia 'The expression "mining operations" is not the same as "the working of a mining property". The former is plainly wider and the latter is directed to a different point. Mining operations means operations pertaining to mining and operations is a very large expression. The phrase "the working of a mining property" looks to the exploitation of a mining lease or other form of interest in the soil.' *Parker v Federal Comr of Taxation* (1953) 90 CLR 489 at 494, per Dixon CJ

MINING PROPERTY

Australia 'The word "property" seems here to be used in its popular sense of land considered as subject to private rights, and accordingly "a mining property" may be defined as land which a person is mining in exercise of a private right, either his own right or (by licence) a right vested in someone else. I do not find in the section [Income Tax Assessment Act 1936–1964 (Cth, s 122(1)] anything to confine the expression, as the respondent submits it should be confined, to land which is being mined by a person in exercise of a legally enforceable right to mine as owner or adversely to the owner. I see no reason why land which belongs, for example, to the Crown should not be considered a mining property if it is in fact being mined by a person by permission of the Crown.' *Federal Comr of Taxation v Broken Hill Pty Co Ltd* (1969) 120 CLR 240 at 245, per Kitto J

MINING PURPOSES

'Mining purposes' include the sinking and searching for, winning, working, getting, making merchantable, smelting or otherwise converting or working for the purposes of any manufacture, carrying away, and disposing of mines and minerals, in or under the settled land, or any other land, and the erection of buildings, and the execution of engineering and other works suitable for those purposes. (Settled Land Act 1925, s 117)

MINING TIMBER

[A policy of marine insurance contained a warranty that no 'mining timber' would be carried.] 'I think that mining timber or mining lumber must mean timber used in the direct operation of mining, that is to say, for propping and securing the passages which are made in the course of mining, and not timber which is used, e.g., as sleepers for narrow-gauge tramways, which happen to be in a mine. Such timber is "tramway timber". As regards the smaller lengths of the sleepers, these were adapted for use in the construction of small tramways, such as those used in collieries, and are therefore called colliery sleepers, but I do not think that they are mining timber.' *Akt Grenland v Janson* (1918) 35 TLR 135 at 136, per Rowlatt J

MINING WORKS

In this Part [Part I: regional development grants] of this Act, unless the context otherwise requires . . . 'mining works' means works, or part of any works, constructed for the carrying on of any process for or incidental to the searching for, or extracting or getting of, coal, oil, natural gas or other minerals, brine (but not water) or peat, but excluding any road, tract, pipe or other works for conveying minerals, or bine or peat, from the site at which they have been extracted or got. (Industry Act 1972, s 6(2))

MINISTER

'Minister of a parish' includes a curate licensed under seal by the bishop to the charge of a parish, and the powers exercisable by the minister of a parish shall also be exercisable by an assistant curate or other clergyman assisting the minister. (Extra-Parochial Ministry Measure 1967, s 3)

In this section [s 2: registration of baptisms] 'minister', in relation to a parish, means the incumbent of the benefice to which the parish belongs, a vicar in a team ministry for the area of that benefice, the priest in charge of the parish and any curate licensed to officiate in the parish. (Parochial Registers and Records Measure 1978, s 2(5))

'By the 91st of the canons of 1603, which were regularly adopted by the province of York, the parish clerk is to be appointed "by the parson or vicar; or, where there is no parson or vicar, by the minister of that place for the time being: which choice shall be signified by the said minister, vicar, or parson, to the parishioners the next Sunday following, in the time of divine service". This canon was appealed to on both sides as determining the right of appointment: and the question, therefore, is upon the proper construction of it. It appears to us that, by the words "parson", "vicar", "minister", the canon intends to describe the functionary, whatever title he may bear, who for the time being has the cure of the parish as principal. In some senses, a mere stipendiary or assistant curate might be described as the minister: but, being so only as representing another person who is the real incumbent, he is not properly the minister of the parish. In the four immediately preceding canons the term "minister" is used in this sense.' *Pinder v Barr* (1854) 4 E & B 105 at 115, per cur.

'In the absence of a custom to the contrary, the minister appoints [churchwardens] jointly with the parishioners in accordance with the 89th canon; and I think it is clear that a perpetual curate is a minister within that; he is practically and to all intents and purposes just as much incumbent as a vicar.' *R v Allen* (1872) LR 8 QB 69 at 76, per Quain J

[The Bishop of Lincoln was cited to appear before the Court of the Archbishop of Canterbury to answer charges relating to his failure to celebrate the service of the Holy Communion in the manner laid down in the Book of Common Prayer. He objected on the ground that he had conducted the service in his capacity as bishop and was not therefore a 'minister' within the contemplation of the rubrics of the Church and of the Acts of Uniformity.] 'When a bishop ministers in any office prescribed by the Prayer Book he is a minister bound to observe the directions given to the minister in the rubrics of such office.' *Read v Lincoln (Bp)* (1889) 14 PD 148 at 150, per Archbishop of Canterbury

See, generally, 14 Halsbury's Laws (4th edn) para 432.

Canada 'The words "ministers", "priests" or "ecclesiastics" are not defined in the Act [Election Act, RSM 1970, c E30] and in the absence of statutory definition to the contrary the above-quoted words must have been intended to be used in accordance with their generally accepted definitions. Although the word "ministers" might mean a variety of things to different people in Manitoba when used by itself, it must have been intended to denote persons who occupy positions similar to "priests" and "ecclesiastics" when used jointly with the words "priests" and "ecclesiastics" in s 6(1)(c) of the Act. I agree with the respondents' submission that this court should interpret "ministers" to mean what it means to a Manitoban of ordinary education. If it means to an average Manitoban persons who discharge the duties of a pastor or spiritual leader of a congregation then the legislature must have intended to give it the same meaning in the Act.' *Penner v Schreyer* [1974] 5 WWR 500 at 507, Man QB, per Solomon J

MINOR CANON *See* CANON

MINORITY

[A testator left his real estate and the residue of his personal estate to his daughter for life, subject to an annuity, and after her death to pay the income for the maintenance of her children during their 'minority', and when the youngest should have attained the age of twenty-five years, the principal and income were to be shared equally between all the children.] 'My opinion is that the word "minority", means the time that would elapse before the youngest child attained twenty-five: I say so, because the testator has made a distinction between the word "minority", and the words "under age". For, in two of the passages subsequent to that which contains the word "minority", we have, first, the expression: "In case it shall happen that any or either of my daughter's children shall die leaving a child or children who shall live to attain the age of twenty-one years": and, afterwards, we have the expression: "under age and unmarried". . . . And it appears to me that the proper construction of the sentence with which the disposition to the children commences, is that the trustees were to pay the rents and profits to the children during their minority, that is, until they attained twenty-five, for one purpose, and, when they came to that age, to them generally; that is: "I give my property to them; but, until the youngest attains twenty-five, the rents are to be paid to them for the purposes merely of maintenance and education". So that the whole meaning is made reasonably clear.' *Milroy v Milroy* (1844) 14 Sim 48 at 55, per Shadwell V-C

'In this case, I find the testator making a careful separation between the period of minority and that of full age. In one case I find him providing for the maintenance and education of his children "during their minority, or the minority of either of them". In another that the allowances for pocket-money shall continue "during their minority, or until such division of the property is made", as he had before described. And, looking to these circumstances, I do not feel at liberty to give to the word "minority", when it occurs in the codicil, any other than its strict interpretation, viz "under twenty-one years of age".' *Maddison v Chapman* (1858) 4 K & J 709 at 724, per Page Wood V-C

[As to the reduction of the age of majority from twenty-one years to eighteen years, and the consequent adaptation (in statutes, deeds, wills, and other instruments) of such terms as 'full age', 'infant', 'infancy', 'minor', 'minority', and similar expressions, see now the Family Law Reform Act 1969, s 1]

MISADVENTURE

New Zealand [The Accident Compensation Act 1982 uses the word 'misadventure' in relation to the adverse consequences of an accident.] 'If the risk of an adverse consequence is considered slight but nevertheless the patient suffers that adverse consequence, it can be said that such an unlikely occurrence is injury by misadventure as having the factor of mischance or bad fortune. Similarly, if the risk of some minor adverse consequence is likely but in the event the consequence proves to be grave, it can be said that such a grave consequence is injury by misadventure for the same reason. An adverse consequence not foreseen at all would clearly be injury by misadventure. An adverse consequence from a known risk which might well have been avoided had certain damage been detected (without negligence or medical error) could also be injury by misadventure, as the patient is either the worse for some mishap or has been the victim of "a piece of bad fortune".' *MacDonald v Accident Compensation Corporation* (1985) 5 NZAR 276 at 281, per Bisson J

MISAPPROPRIATION

Australia 'It seems to me that in plain language the words "misappropriation of moneys" means stealing.' *Gladstone CC v Local Government Superannuation Board* [1980] Qd R 48 at 56, per Demack J

MISCARRIAGE

[The Statute of Frauds 1677, s 4 provides that no action shall be brought upon a special promise to answer for the debt, default, or 'miscarriage' of another person, unless the agreement upon which the action is brought, or some note or memorandum thereof, is in writing and signed by the party to be charged therewith.] 'This case is clearly within the mischief intended to be remedied by the Statute of Frauds: that mischief being the frequent fraudulent practices which were too commonly endeavoured to be upheld by perjury; and if it be within the mischief, I think the words of the statute are sufficiently large to comprehend the case. The words are these: "No action shall be brought to charge a defendant upon any special promise to answer for the debt, default, or miscarriage of another person". Now the word "miscarriage" has not the same meaning as the word "debt" or "default"; it seems to me to comprehend that species of wrongful act, for the consequences of which the law would make the party civilly responsible. The wrongful riding the horse of another, without his leave and licence, and thereby causing its death, is clearly an act for which the party is responsible in damages; and, therefore, in my judgment, falls within the meaning of the word "miscarriage".' *Kirkham v Marter* (1819) 2 B & Ald 613 at 616, per Abbott CJ

See, generally 20 Halsbury's Laws (4th edn) para 119.

Of child

Australia [The Crimes Act 1928 (Vic), s 62 (repealed; see now Crimes Act 1958–1986, s 65) provided that the use of any instrument 'with intent to procure the miscarriage of any woman' constituted a felony.] 'It was contended in the first place that the word "miscarriage" in s 62 refers only to the expulsion from the womb of a live fœtus, and does not include the case of the removal or attempted removal of a dead fœtus. . . . We were not referred to any dictionary nor to authority of any kind which suggested that the word "miscarriage" was confined to the bringing about the death of a living fœtus, and I can see no reason why the meaning should be so restricted.' *R v Trim* [1943] VLR 109 at 115, 116, per Martin J

MISCARRIAGE OF JUSTICE

Australia 'What will constitute a miscarriage of justice may vary, not only in relation to the particular facts, but also with regard to the jurisdiction which has been invoked by the proceedings in question; and to reach the conclusion that a miscarriage of justice has taken place does not require a finding that a different result necessarily would have been reached in the proceedings said to be affected by the miscarriage. It is enough if what is done is not justice according to law.' *Wilson v Wilson* [1969] ALR 191 at 200, CA, per Asprey J

MISCONDUCT

Australia 'It appears . . . that a solicitor will not be struck off the roll for professional misconduct, apart from the statutory provisions, unless he has been personally implicated so that he can be said to have been guilty of conduct which other solicitors in good repute would regard as disgraceful or dishonourable.' *Re a Solicitor* [1960] VR 617 at 620, per Dean J

Australia [A police officer was charged with a breach of the Police Regulations 1958 (Tas), reg 41 (repealed) (see now Police Regulations 1974–1986, s 47) which prohibits 'misconduct' against the discipline of the police force.] 'I cannot doubt that misconduct in his private life by a police officer of a nature which tends to destroy his authority and influence in his relations with the public amounts to "misconduct against the discipline of the police force". A police officer must be above suspicion if the public are to accept his authority.' *Henry v Ryan* [1963] Tas SR 90 at 92, per Burbury CJ

New Zealand 'In the context of this present Act [Motor Vehicle Dealers Act 1975], particularly in s 112 with which I am concerned, the misconduct which is required to justify a suspension or cancellation [of a vehicle dealer's licence] must be something which is in my view wilful. It must be more than negligence, mistake—it must be something where there is a wrong motive, something which would cause the public whose interests are concerned to feel that the dealer has in fact been guilty of misconduct.' *NZ Classic Car Co Ltd v Motor Vehicle Dealers Licensing Board* (1985) 5 NZAR 170 at 174, per Davison CJ

Of midwife

[The Midwives Act 1902, s 3(5) (repealed; see now the Nurses, Midwives and Health Visitors Act 1979, s 12) empowered the governing body to remove from the roll the name of any midwife for disobeying the rules and regulations laid down, or for other 'misconduct'.] 'In my view the misconduct dealt with by the section is not limited to misconduct in the discharge of the duties of the midwife. If it is misconduct in the opinion of the Board which tends to unfit her for the discharge of the duties of a midwife then the Board has the right to treat it as misconduct under the statute.' *Stock v Central Midwives Board* [1915] 3 KB 756 at 763, per Lord Reading CJ

Wilful misconduct *See* WILFUL

MISCONVEYANCE

[Goods were consigned at owner's risk under a railway company's consignment note which relieved the company of liability for loss, damage, 'misconveyance', etc, except that arising from the wilful misconduct of the company's servants.] 'There remains the consideration of the word "misconveyance". I share . . . an inability to give this word a plain meaning, but as I regard conveyance as conveyance along the agreed route, misconveyance must equally mean a failure along that route, due, it may be, to accident or even to negligence, if it were not wilful.' *London & North Western Rly Co v Neilson* [1922] 2 AC 263 at 269, per Lord Buckmaster

MISDELIVERY

'Misdelivery means a delivery to a wrong person, and if you keep the goods yourself you do not deliver them at all.' *Neilson v London & North Western Rly Co* [1922] 1 KB 192 at 202, CA, per Scrutton LJ; affirmed sub nom, *London & North Western Rly Co v Neilson* [1922] 2 AC 263

'"Misdelivery" seems to me to mean misdelivery, and not delay or detention.' *Hartstroke Fruiterers Ltd v London, Midland & Scottish Rly Co* [1943] 1 KB 362 at 364, 365, CA, per Lord Greene MR

[It was submitted that 'misdelivery' in the conditions relating to the deposit of baggage at a railway station included *deliberate* delivery to a wrong person, and not only accidental delivery.] 'I am disposed to think that while in certain contexts the word "misdelivery" may bear the wider meaning, in its more natural and popular meaning it is restricted to a wrong delivery involving some form of mistake or inadvertence, and that it is intended to cover the sort of situation where a package is delivered to the wrong person or address by error or inadvertence, or where the wrong article is handed out over a counter or in a cloakroom.' *Alexander v Railway Executive* [1951] 2 All ER 442 at 447, per Devlin J; [1951] 2 KB 882

[A written contract, under the terms of which the plaintiff garaged his car with the defendants contained a condition exempting the defendants from liability for loss or 'misdelivery' of the vehicle. A man who pretended to have been sent by the plaintiff was allowed to drive the car away, and stole it.] 'A number of authorities were cited as to the meaning of the word "misdelivery", and it is thus as well to start any consideration of its meaning in the present contract with reminding oneself that here it is to be construed in relation to a specific subject-matter, cars in the care of a garage proprietor. Before a car can be said to be misdelivered it is, of course, first necessary to establish that there was a delivery. Both counsel, for widely differing reasons, argued the case on the basis that there had here been a delivery to the thief. I will deal with the matter on that footing which, indeed, in relation to the specific subject-matter under consideration seems to me to be correct. . . . What, on that footing, is the meaning of the word "misdelivery" in condition (B)? To my mind, a reasonable man reading it in this contract would interpret it as referring to any delivery made in error to a wrong person or to a wrong place. Equally, he would exclude from its meaning deliveries to a wrong person or a wrong place made deliberately.' *Hollins v Davy (J) Ltd* [1963] 1 All ER 370 at 375, per Sachs J; also reported in [1963] 1 QB 844 at 854

MISDEMEANOUR

'The word "misdemeanour" in its ordinary sense, as appears in all the text books relating to the subject, means all those crimes and offences for which the law has not provided a particular name and which are punishable, according to the degree of the offence, by fine or imprisonment.' *Pickup v United Kingdom Dental Board* [1928] 2 KB 459 at 462, DC, per Shearman J

[The distinction between felony and misdemeanour was abolished by the Criminal Law Act 1967, s 1, and on all matters on which a distinction was previously made between felony and misdemeanour, including mode of trial, the law and practice in relation to all offences cognisable under the law of England and Wales is that formerly applicable only to misdemeanour.]

Australia 'It seems clear enough that at common law the primary meaning of misdemeanour connotes that the offence is indictable, but that a wider secondary meaning is recognised in which the word is sometimes employed covering all offences below the degree of felony whether indictable or not.' *Reynolds v Stacy* (1957) 96 CLR 454 at 462, per Dixon CJ and McTiernan J

MISFEASANCE

'Goods were lawfully with the defendant's licence in their ship, and they tortiously so dealt with them that the goods were injured. It was found, as a fact, that the loading of . . . oxide was negligent. It was therefore wrongful, not as a breach of contract, but as a wrongful act in itself. If the defendants had done what was done wilfully, that is to say intentionally, that it would injure the plaintiff's goods, it is clear they would be liable. But what difference does it make, that they did it ignorantly? It may be asked where is the duty of care? I answer that duty that exists in all men not to injure the property of others. This is not a mere nonfeasance which is complained of, it is a misfeasance; an act and wrongful. Suppose A lets B a horse, B, with C's licence, puts up at C's stables for reward to C from B, C turns into the stables loose a vicious horse, known to be so, not to injure A's horse, but not thinking of the matter; there cannot be a doubt that C would be liable to A if the horse was injured. So if he gave the horse bad oats which injured the horse he would be liable, though he would not be to A if he omitted to feed him.' *Hayn v Culliford* (1879) 4 CPD 182 at 185, CA, per Bramwell LJ

In Companies Acts

[The Companies Act 1862, s 165 (repealed; see now the Companies Act 1985, s 631), enacted (inter alia) that where in the course of the winding-up of a company it appeared that any past or present director of a company had been guilty of 'misfeasance' in relation to the company, he could be compelled to pay money by way of compensation into the assets of the company.] 'I am of opinion . . . that the word "misfeasance" in that section means misfeasance in the nature of a breach of trust, that is to say, it refers to something which the officer of such company has done wrongly by misapplying or retaining in his own hands any moneys of the company, or by which the company's property has been wasted, or the company's credit improperly pledged. It must be some act resulting in some actual loss to the company. Now, it appears to me that a person nominated as director in violation of the articles without proper qualification, and accepting that nomination and acting as a director, has not thereby been guilty of any such misfeasance or breach of trust in relation to the company.' *Re Canadian Land Reclaiming & Colonizing Co, Coventry & Dixon's Case* (1880) 14 Ch D 660 at 670, CA, per James LJ

'This is an application under s 165 of the Companies Act 1862 [repealed; see supra]. . . . The Act . . . applies in the first instance to cases in which a director has misapplied, or retained, or become liable, or accountable for any moneys of the company, that is to say, it applies to moneys misapplied, retained, or received by a director; but does not apply to moneys which he ought to have received but has not. The next words refer to the case of a director who has been guilty of a misfeasance or breach of trust in relation to the company. There is, however, a difference, which the law recognises, between "misfeasance" and "nonfeasance"; in other words, between sins of commission and sins of omission, and I think therefore that the legislature plainly did not refer to cases of mere nonfeasance, except, of course, where there has in fact been a breach of trust.' *Re Wedgwood Coal & Iron Co* (1882) 47 LT 612 at 613, per Fry LJ

'It was urged that a misfeasance does not include nonfeasance, and that no complaint can be made under the statute [Companies Act 1862 (repealed; see supra)] of a sin of omission, as distinguished from one of commission, and in support of this reference was made to a decision of Lord Justice Fry in *Re The Wedgwood Coal & Iron Co* [supra]. . . . He says "that the legislature did not refer to cases of mere nonfeasance, except, of course where there has, in fact, been a breach of trust". The whole point lies in the exception which recognises all breaches of trust as coming, which they expressly do, within the provisions of the statute. What neglect, what omission, constitutes a breach of trust is another question.' *Re Liverpool Household Stores Assocn Ltd* (1890), 59 LJ Ch 616 at 617, per Kekewich J

See, generally, 7 Halsbury's Laws (4th edn) para 1692.

MISMANAGEMENT

[In an action for libel the defamatory statement, as set out in the record, imputed to the plaintiff 'mismanagement' or ignorance.] 'The libel, as stated upon the record, imputes to the plaintiff "mismanagement or ignorance". The words, according to the evidence of one of the witnesses, were, that, "from his ignorance or inattention", etc. It has been argued by the counsel for the plaintiff, that mismanagement and inattention are necessarily identical; but I am of opinion that they are not identical. Mismanagement goes farther than inattention, and may include many cases which inattention would not include. Mismanagement may be wilful; and many cases might be put where you would draw the distinction between the two, and say this is not a case of inattention, but of gross mismanagement. Upon the ground that mismanagement goes higher than inattention, and includes cases which inattention does not, I am of opinion that the evidence did not support the declaration.' *Brooks v Blanshard* (1833) 1 Cr & M 779 at 791, per Bayley B

MISPRISION *See also* ACCESSORY AFTER THE FACT

[The offence of misprision of felony no longer exists in England, the distinction between felony and misdemeanour having been abolished by the Criminal Law Act 1967, s 1.]

'Most lawyers know, roughly speaking, what "misprision of felony" means. It means that a man knows that a felony has been committed and neglects to disclose it [but see note, supra]. But many laymen are perplexed by the word "misprision". What does it mean? Whence its derivation? Lord Coke attempted to fit it in with present notions when he said that "Misprisio commeth of the French word mespris, which properly signifieth neglect or contempt"; but the authors of the Oxford English Dictionary, who included Sir Frederick Pollock, in a very learned article say that the word "misprision" is derived from the old French word "mesprendre" which means to act wrongly; and in early times it meant simply a wrong action or omission. This is borne out by the old law books, where it is used almost as synonymous with misdemeanour, that is to say, something less than felony which did not carry the death penalty. One of the earliest records of its use is in the Year Book in 1484 (2 Richard III case 22 pp 9 (et seq), where a man called Mundy had falsified a writ. It was a felony and, if charged as such, would carry the death penalty; but for mercy's sake, and may be for convenience also, the judges said he could be indicted for a misprision. "It was allowed it was felony and so included misprision, etc." As a result of this case, it was held that every treason or felony included a misprision. The King used to take advantage of this rule in cases of treason, so that, if the man did not deserve the death penalty, he was indicted only with "misprision of treason". Now concealment of treason was itself treason. If anyone knew that another was guilty or in any way incriminated in treason, he was bound at once to go to the King or to anyone in his immediate circle and tell him all that happened; see Bracton, De Legibus, Book III, fol 118, 119. If he did not do so, he could be indicted either for treason which carried the death penalty, or misprision of treason which did not. But this alternative was taken away in 1555. By the statute of 1554 [Treason Act 1554 (repealed by the Criminal Law Act 1967), c 10], s 8 it was enacted that "conceylement or keping secrett of any highe treason be demed and taken onely misprision of treason". . . . From this time forward the phrase "misprision of treason" was taken to denote only the concealment or keeping secret of treason. And by a natural sequence "misprision of felony" denoted only the concealment or keeping secret of felony.' *Sykes v Director of Public Prosecutions* [1961] 3 All ER 33 at 36, HL, per Lord Denning

Australia 'Misprision of felony has certainly come to us from the earliest times in the development of the common law. Apparently the royal judges then assumed jurisdiction to enforce the public duties of the citizen and one of such duties was to disclose any treason or felony of which he had knowledge. See Professor Holdsworth's History of English Law Vol 3, pp 388–389. Professor Holdworth there points out that a citizen, who did not perform such duty, was guilty of a misprision of treason or felony. Now it may be that in the times of which he was speaking, long before the creation of any criminal investigation department, the detection of offenders very largely depended upon citizens performing this duty. And no doubt today, with modern methods of detection, its performance may not appear of such importance. This may be the reason why prosecutions for misprision of felony have been somewhat rare in recent years. In our opinion, however, the citizen's duty to disclose to the appropriate authorities any treason or felony, of which he has knowledge, remains the same and is still as binding upon him as it was in the early days of the common law. And no doubt cases will arise from time to time when the public interest will be best served by the citizen, who fails in this duty, being prosecuted for misprision of felony. There is certainly no justification for the view that such a prosecution is no longer available to the Crown.' *R v Crimmins* [1959] VR 270 at 272, 273, cur

MISREPRESENTATION

A representation is deemed to have been false, and therefore a misrepresentation, if it was at the material date false in substance and in fact. For the purpose of determining whether there has or has not been a misrepresentation at all, the representor's knowledge, belief or other state of mind is immaterial, save in cases where the representation relates to the representor's state of mind, although his state of mind is of the utmost importance for the purpose of considering whether the misrepresentation was fraudulent.

The standard by which the truth or falsity of a representation is to be judged is that if material circumstances are incorrectly stated, that is to say, if the discrepancy between the facts as represented and the actual facts is such as would be considered material by a reasonable representee, the representation is false; if otherwise, it is not. Another way of stating the rule is to say that substantial falsity is, on the one hand, necessary, and, on the other, adequate, to establish a misrepresentation. It results from the foregoing statement that where the entire representation is a faithful picture or transcript of the essential facts, no falsity is established, even though there may have been any number of inaccuracies in unimportant details. Conversely, if the general impression conveyed is false, the most punctilious and scrupulous accuracy in immaterial minutiae will not render the representation true. (31 Halsbury's Laws (4th edn) paras 1044, 1045)

[By the Misrepresentation Act 1967, s 1 a

contract may be rescinded because of innocent misrepresentation notwithstanding that the misrepresentation has become a term of the contract or that the contract has been performed. Section 2 also enables a person who suffers loss by being induced to enter into a contract by a misrepresentation made by another party to the contract to recover damages unless the other party proves that he reasonably believed that the facts represented were true. See also s 3, as to the avoidance of provisions excluding liability for misrepresentation.]

'Misrepresentation, either by word of mouth or otherwise, in my opinion requires something more than a mere entry in a book by the person who is alleged to have made the misrepresentation. I think the expression "make any misrepresentation" [in the Sale of Food (Weights and Measures) Act 1926, s 3 (repealed; see now the Weights and Measures Act 1985, s 29(1))] is equivalent to "misrepresenting" and, using the word as an ordinary English word and giving to it the ordinary meaning, one does not speak of a person "misrepresenting" something if all that he has done is to conceive in his mind an intention to misrepresent to somebody.' *Preston v Coventry & District Co-operative Society Ltd* [1946] 1 All ER 694 at 695, per Humphreys J

[The plaintiff took a dress to a firm of cleaners for cleaning, and signed a document exempting the defendants from liability for damage.] 'In my opinion any behaviour, by words or conduct, is sufficient to be a misrepresentation if it is such as to mislead the other party about the existence or extent of the exemption. If it conveys a false impression, that is enough. If the false impression is created knowingly, it is a fraudulent misrepresentation; if it is created unwittingly, it is an innocent misrepresentation; but either is sufficient to disentitle the creator of it to the benefit of the exemption.' *Curtis v Chemical Cleaning & Dyeing Co Ltd* [1951] 1 KB 805 at 808, 809, CA, per Denning LJ

New Zealand 'The term "misrepresentation" is not defined in the Act [Contractual Remedies Act 1979]. [It was] submitted that there was no misrepresentation in the ECI budget forecasts given to NZMB because they were not a statement of existing fact, but rather, they were an expression of opinion of future fact. I reject this somewhat simplistic approach. I consider that if the budget forecasts were as wildly inaccurate as they have been described and I have found them to be, then they are actionable if the plaintiffs acted in reliance on them. A false forecast is a misrepresentation in that it is saying that present facts are such that the future forecast follows logically.' *New Zealand Motor Bodies Ltd v Emslie* [1985] 2 NZLR 569 at 593, per Barker J

Fraudulent misrepresentation

Fraud, in connection with representations upon which it is sought to base an action of deceit, has the same meaning in all the courts whose province it is to consider it. In this connection there is no distinction between legal and equitable fraud, or between legal fraud and moral fraud, and no such thing as imputed or constructive fraud, if and so far as these expressions serve to suggest that any statement may be construed as fraudulent for the purposes of founding an action for deceit, although the statement is not characterised by actual fraud, as the law has defined it for this purpose.

By the mid-nineteenth century it had been established that not only a misrepresentation known or believed by the representor to be false when made was fraudulent, but that mere non-belief in the truth was also indicative of fraud. Thus, whenever a person makes a false statement which he does not actually and honestly believe to be true, for purposes of civil liability, that statement is as fraudulent as if he had stated that which he did not know to be true, or knew or believed to be false. Proof of absence of actual and honest belief is all that is necessary to satisfy the requirements of the law, whether the representation has been made recklessly or deliberately; indifference or recklessness on the part of the representor as to the truth or falsity of the representation affords merely an instance of absence of such a belief.

A representor will not, however, be fraudulent if he believed the statement to be true in the sense in which he understood it, provided that was a meaning which might reasonably be attached to it, even though the court later holds that the statement objectively bears another meaning, which the representor did not believe. (31 Halsbury's Laws (4th edn) paras 1058, 1059)

Innocent misrepresentation

A misrepresentation must be either fraudulent or innocent. It cannot be both. Fraud and innocence, like falsity and truth, are mutually exclusive categories. It follows from the definition . . . of a fraudulent misrepresentation [supra], that is a misrepresentation made in the absence of actual honest belief in its truth, that the essential characteristic of an innocent misrepresentation is the presence of such actual honest belief; and that, in neither case, is anything more than this absence, or presence, required to constitute fraud or innocence respectively. (31 Halsbury's Laws (4th edn) para 1064)

[*See* note as to the effect of the Misrepresentation Act 1967, supra]

MISSING

'What is the natural and uncontrolled meaning of the word "missing"? I understand the word as expressing a state of things in which a vessel, having started from some known port on some known voyage, has never arrived at her destination, and has not been reported or sighted for so long that the only reasonable conclusion is that she has been lost, and has been lost in circumstances which make it impossible to say what has been the cause of the loss or how it occurred.' *Zachariessen v Importers & Exporters Marine Insurance Co Ltd* (1924) 29 Com Cas 202 at 203, 204, CA, per Bankes LJ

MISSIONARY

[A testatrix by her will left money to be applied to 'missionary' objects.] 'It is suggested that the words of the gift are too vague, as the words "missionary objects" are not necessarily confined to Christian missions. But there is a widely spread use of the word "missionary" as one engaged in the work of religious, and particularly Christian missions. . . . I think that the testatrix used the word "missionary" in its ordinary and popular sense, and I hold that the gift was a valid charitable gift.' *Re Kenny, Clode v Andrews* (1907) 97 LT 130 at 130, per Warrington J

Australia [The question was whether 'missionary' activities were religious purposes and thus a deductible gift for probate duty purposes.] 'Religious missionary activities may be taken to involve religious teaching, worship and service. There is a dictum of Barton J sitting in the Irish Chancery Division which would support that view if support for it be required [*Jackson v A-G* (1917) 1 IR 332]. The question was whether a gift by will "to Presbyterian missions and orphans" was a valid charitable gift. Responding to an argument that the word "mission" does not import charity, Barton J observed [at p 336] that: "There may be 'Presbyterian purposes' which are not religious in the charitable sense, and there may be 'missionary purposes' which are not religious in the charitable sense, e.g., when connected with diplomatic or political missions. But here we have the word 'missions' qualified and defined by the adjective 'Presbyterian'; and it would, in my opinion, be fantastic to give any other meaning to the words than one which would connote religious teaching, worship, or service". It does not follow conversely, however, that all religious teaching, worship or service (being for the advancement of religion and therefore charitable in the legal sense) will involve missionary activities. Barton J was not concerned to define religious missions but to recognise particular missions as religious.' *Meaney v Probate Duties Comr* (1983) 13 ATR 759 at 762–763, Vic, per Tadgell J

MISTAKE

At common law, mistake was admitted as a foundation of relief in three cases only, namely, (1) in actions for money had and received to recover money paid under a mistake of fact; (2) in actions of deceit to recover damages in respect of a mistake induced by fraudulent misrepresentation; and (3) as a defence in actions of contract where the mistake of fact was of such a nature as to preclude the formation of any contract in law, for example, where there was a mutual mistake as to the subject matter of the contract, and, therefore, no consensus ad idem by the parties, or where the mistake was made as to the identity of one of the parties and such identity was an inducement to the other to enter into the contract, or where the mistake related to the nature of the contract under such circumstances as would, if the contract were embodied in a deed, justify a plea of non est factum.

In equity, mistake gives title to relief in a much wider range of cases than at common law, although it must be borne in mind that 'mistake', as a legal term on which a right to relief may be founded, has a much narrower meaning than it has in popular use.

The court has power to grant relief to a plaintiff whose election between two alternative claims is due to a mistake in the manner of making use of the machinery of the court.

The distinction between mistake at common law and equity is also important because of its effect on the rights of third parties. At law mistake renders a contract void ab initio; third parties cannot acquire title to property dealt with under it. However, in equity the contract is merely voidable and third party rights may be acquired.

If the relationship between the parties to a transaction imposes a duty on one party to inform the other of all the material facts and the party owing such a duty fails to do so, the transaction may be set aside on the ground of mistake.

Mistake may also be made a ground for relief by statute.

Mistakes may be divided into (1) those which prevent there being a binding consent to a particular transaction, and (2) those which consist in a failure to express correctly in a written document the intention of the parties with regard to a particular transaction.

Mistakes within head (1) may be further subdivided according to whether they are mistakes as to general law, or mistakes as to fact. Mistakes as to private rights are to be classed rather among instances of error in fact than among instances of error in law, even where there are no circumstances of circumvention or fraud. (32 Halsbury's Laws (4th edn) paras 3, 4)

'I can find no definition of what "mistake" is; but if you treat mistake in its ordinary sense in the English language, is mere forgetfulness mistake? Can you, in English, say "I forgot", and is that the same thing as saying "I was mistaken"? I think not. . . . I cannot find any decision in Courts of Equity which has ever stated that mere forgetfulness is mistake against which equity would relieve.' *Barrow v Isaacs & Son* [1891] 1 QB 417 at 420, 421, CA, per Lord Esher MR

'There are few words in the English language susceptible to more meanings than the word "mistake" and the word is frequently misused. To take but three examples, which are far from being exhaustive. A shoots at a pigeon and kills a crow "by mistake": A shoots at a crow believing it to be a pigeon and kills it "by mistake": A, not intending to fire his gun, lets the gun off "by mistake". In the first case, the mistake was simply a bad shot, in the second, a failure to distinguish a crow from a pigeon, and in the third, gross carelessness.' *Moynes v Cooper* [1956] 1 All ER 450 at 453, per Stable J

New Zealand 'The word appears in the expression "mistake or any other reasonable cause", and clearly the explicit need for the reasonableness of "any other reasonable cause" reflects what is implicit in the concept of "mistake". In this regard, moreover, I think the mistake must not only appear to be reasonably based, but in itself provide a reasonable explanation for what has followed. Mistake in this sense cannot be equated with forgetfulness or ignorance. It must necessarily involve an erroneous conclusion following advertence to the subject matter.' *Caldow v Wall* [1964] NZLR 65 at 68, per Woodhouse J

New Zealand 'A "mistake" is an error or misconception. At the time the contract was entered into the profitability of the contracts and the fees were not errors of fact. They were future prospects and expectations. What the defendant is trying to do is to escape from a bargain which he entered of his own volition. It is his own fault that he was not as careful or informed as he might have been. I do not think that the purpose of the Act [Contractual Mistakes Act 1977] was to remedy this kind of "mistake"—mistake of judgement.' *Clement v Mitchell* [1982] 1 BCR 447 at 456, per O'Regan J

In Lands Clauses Consolidation Act

[The Lands Clauses Consolidation Act 1845, s 124 (see also the Compulsory Purchase Act 1965, s 22) makes provision for cases in which the promoters of an undertaking have entered upon lands which they are authorised to purchase but which they have in fact failed to purchase through 'mistake' or inadvertence.]

'The corporation must show, in order to bring themselves within the 124th section, that it was through mistake or inadvertence that they had failed or omitted duly to purchase or pay compensation for that land. . . . It appears to me perfectly clear, not only that it was through mistake or inadvertence, but that it was through mistake or inadvertence into which they had been led by the imperfect information of [the plaintiff], and the way in which he communicated it to them. It appears to me, therefore, that they are clearly within the position of being parties who have failed to purchase the land within proper time through mistake or inadvertence.' *Hyde v Manchester Corpn* (1852) 5 De G & Sm 249 at 262, per Parker V-C

MISTRESS *See also* COMMON LAW WIFE

'"Mistress", having lost its respectable if not reverential significance, came to mean a woman installed, in a clandestine way, by someone of substance, normally married, for his intermittent sexual enjoyment. This class of woman, if indeed she still exists, is not dealt with by the 1976 [Domestic Violence and Matrimonial Proceedings] Act at all.' *Davis v Johnson* [1978] 1 All ER 1132 at 1148, HL, per Lord Kilbrandon

MOBILIA SEQUUNTUR PERSONAM

'The maxim of the general law, *mobilia sequuntur personam* . . . depends upon a principle which is expressed in the Latin words; and that is the only principle of the whole of our law as to domicil when applicable to the succession of what we call personal estate. . . . Domicil is allowed in this country to have the same influence as in other countries in determining the succession of movable estate; but the maxim of the law of the civilised world is *mobilia sequuntur personam*, and is founded on the nature of things. When "mobilia" are in places other than that of the person to whom they belong, their accidental *situs* is disregarded, and they are held to go with the person. But land, whether held for a chattel interest or held for a freehold interest, is in nature, as a matter of fact, immovable and not movable. The doctrine is inapplicable to it.' *Freke v Carbery (Lord)* (1873) LR 16 Eq 461 at 466, per Lord Selborne

MOCK AUCTION *See* AUCTION

MODEL

The expression 'model' includes design, pattern, and specimen. (Official Secrets Act 1911, s 12)

MODERATE

Moderate means

[A testator made a bequest of residue to institutions which provided for persons of 'moderate means', such as clerks, governesses and others, who might not be able or eligible to benefit under the National Health Insurance Act or other Acts, to have surgical operations, etc., performed on payment of some moderate contribution.] '"Moderate means" . . . are presumably means so moderate as to necessitate some contribution from the bounty of the testator before the recipient would be able to procure the surgical operation or medical treatment of which the recipient might stand in need.' *Re Clarke, Bracey v Royal National Lifeboat Institution* [1923] 2 Ch 407 at 412, 413, per Romer J

MODIFY

[By a debenture-holders' covering deed a majority of the debenture-holders had power by extraordinary general resolution to sanction any 'modification' or compromise of the rights of the debenture-holders against the company or against its property.] 'Lord Justice Lindley [in *Mercantile Investment & General Trust Co v International Co of Mexico* (1891) 7 TLR 616, CA], said: ". . . The power to modify the rights of the debenture-holders against the company does not include a power to extinguish all their rights". . . . What is proposed to be done here is not to extinguish the rights of the debenture-holders at all, but what has been done is to create a mortgage having priority over the charge contained in the debenture-holders' deed which expressly stipulates that the debentures should be the first charge on the property and undertaking of the company. And the question is, whether such a resolution falls within the power to sanction any modification of the rights of the debenture-holders against the company. . . . The conclusion I come to is that . . . this resolution was valid under the power given to the general meeting to sanction "a modification of the rights of the debenture-holders against the company or against its property".' *Follit v Eddystone Granite Quarries* [1892] 3 Ch 75 at 83, 84, 86, per Stirling J

New Zealand 'He [counsel for the plaintiff] relies mainly upon the introductory words of the codicil, "this codicil is to modify and alter my said will in so far as the matters contained therein affect it". . . . I do not think the words "modify" and "alter" are sufficient to justify me in holding that the testatrix intended to revoke the provisions made by her in the will. . . . One of the primary meanings of the word "modify" is, no doubt, "to limit" or "restrict", but it also means "to vary", and there is authority that it may even mean "to extend" or "enlarge".' *Souter v Souter* [1921] NZLR 716 at 724, 725, per Cooper J; also reported [1919] GLR 368 at 372

New Zealand 'The power to modify is given to the [Local Government] Commission as a power to be exercised in consequence of the upholding of an objection. The right of objection must cover the right to object either to the exclusion or the inclusion of land in a scheme. Prima facie therefore "modify" is used in a sense applicable to both classes of objection—in other words as having the meaning "to make partial changes in" (whether restrictive or extensive).' *Waitemata County v Local Government Commission* [1964] NZLR 689 at 696, per Richmond J

MOIETY

[A testator by his will gave the 'moiety' of his property, after his wife had received her *jus relictae* (provision for the widow of a person dying domiciled in Scotland), to trustees upon certain trusts.] 'If one looks in the Shorter Oxford Dictionary the meanings that are given for "moiety" are: "(1) A half, especially in legal or quasi-legal use; (2) loosely one of two (or more) parts into which something is divided". Then there are several meanings set out which I do not think are appropriate to the present case. An example of the loose meaning of the words which is given is "The southern and greater moiety of this island: Fuller". No doubt in the appropriate context one can come to the conclusion that the word "moiety" does not mean an equal half part. If the lady was entitled to *jus relictae*, what she would have been entitled to would have been one-half of the testator's property and the other half would have been left to him to dispose of. I do not find anything here which enables me to put on the word "moiety" anything other than what I think is its primary meaning of "equal half part".' *Re Angus's Will Trusts, Hall v Angus* [1960] 3 All ER 835 at 838, 839, per Buckley J

MOLEST *See also* ANNOYANCE

[A deed of separation contained a covenant by the wife not to 'molest' the husband. After the execution of the deed the wife had been living in adultery, and had given birth to a male child, of whom the husband was not the father.] 'Now in order to determine this point of molestation, I think that I am bound to consider what would be molestation, or what would entitle a jury to say that within the meaning of such a covenant as this in a separation deed there had been molestation by the wife. Now first of all it seems to me that it must be an act done either by the wife herself or by some agent authorised by her tc do it. No act done by any one else can be a breach of the covenant that she will not molest. What kind of act must be done in order to constitute a molestation? I am of opinion that the act done by the wife or by her authority must be an act which is done with intent to annoy, and does in fact annoy; or which is in fact an annoyance; or, to put the latter proposition into another shape, that it must be an act done by her with a knowledge that what she is so doing must of itself without more annoy her husband, or annoy a husband with ordinary and reasonable feeling. . . . Then can adultery come within the principle, that the wife is doing an act with a knowledge that what she is doing must of itself without more annoy her husband? Certainly not. The utmost that can be said, is that she must know that if it comes to the knowledge of her husband it will annoy him; but that is to introduce another circumstance which does not come within the proposition, that circumstance being that her adultery shall be brought to his knowledge; and therefore the mere fact of the adultery does not come within either proposition, and something else must be relied upon to constitute molestation. If that is not within either proposition, the mere fact of having a child afterwards is not. Then it has been urged that, however great her distance may be from her husband, if she commits adultery publicly so that people know that she is doing it, that must molest him. But again the molestation will depend upon whether the people who know it, will go and tell her husband. Another and a particular circumstance must be introduced, for which the wife is not responsible, and which does not necessarily follow, and therefore in no view can it be molestation.' *Fearon v Aylesford (Earl)* (1884) 14 QBD 792 at 801–803, CA, per Brett MR

'The question as to what is molestation is dealt with in *Fearon v Aylesford* [supra], and, without reading the judgments at length, I may say that they amount to this—that to constitute a breach of such a covenant there must be in fact molestation and an intention to annoy.' *Hunt v Hunt* [1897] 2 QB 547 at 549, per A L Smith LJ

' "Molest" is a wide, plain word which I should be reluctant to define or paraphrase. If I had to find one synonym for it, I should select "pester".' *Vaughan v Vaughan* [1973] 3 All ER 449 at 454, CA, per Stephenson LJ

'Violence is a form of molestation but molestation may take place without the threat or use of violence and still be serious and inimical to mental and physical health.' *Davis v*

Johnson [1978] 1 All ER 1132 at 1144, HL, per Viscount Dilhorne

'In divorce proceedings the court, in its inherent jurisdiction, has for years been granting injunctions restraining molestation and/or interference of one party to the marriage by the other. For my part I have no doubt that the word "molesting" in s 1(1)(a) of the 1976 Act [Domestic Violence and Matrimonial Proceedings Act 1976] does not imply necessarily either violence or threats of violence. It applies to any conduct which can properly be regarded as such a degree of harassment as to call for the intervention of the court.' *Horner v Horner* [1982] 2 All ER 495 at 497, CA, per Ormrod LJ

New Zealand 'It is said that the respondent has failed to comply with a condition that she should not "molest, disturb, or annoy" her husband. . . . In my opinion . . . in order to bring an act within the covenant not to molest, disturb, or annoy, it must be shown that there was a personal molestation, done deliberately, with the intention of molesting, disturbing, or annoying.' *Williams v Williams* [1934] NZLR 165 at 176, 178, CA, per Reed J; also reported [1934] GLR 197 at 202

MONEY *See also* CASH; LEGAL TENDER; READY MONEY

General meaning

The primary function of money is to serve as a medium of exchange, and as such it is accepted without question in final discharge of debts or payment for goods or services. Money also serves as a common standard of value by reference to which the comparative values of different commodities are ascertained, as a unit of account in which debts and liabilities are expressed, and as a store of value or purchasing power.

The term 'money' generally includes banknotes as well as coins, although it may be limited to such of each as are legal tender at the time and place in question. The term is sometimes used to include not only actual cash but also a right to receive cash, as, for example, sums standing to the credit of a bank account or invested in securities; and the term may in some cases be used in a popular sense to include all personal or even, exceptionally, all real and personal property. Where the term 'money' is used in relation to the payment of money into court it is to be construed in its ordinary and natural meaning as including money in foreign currency.

The precise meaning of the term depends upon the context in which it is used so that, for example, it is usually given a wide meaning when used in a will and when that meaning gives effect to the intention of the testator, an intermediate meaning in connection with actions for money paid or for money had and received, and a narrow meaning in the criminal law and in relation to execution. (32 Halsbury's Laws (4th edn) paras 101, 102)

'Money' includes a cheque, banknote, postal order or money order. (Lotteries and Amusements Act 1976, s 23(1))

'Consistently with the ordinary mode of expression, an extended meaning may be given to the word "money". We hear persons daily talking of their money in the funds, meaning thereby perpetual government annuities; and the term money has acquired a popular meaning in many other like cases. I agree, that if you take the word "money" by itself, it means money in its strict sense, and nothing else; but when used in connection with other words, it may have a much more extended signification. There is nothing new in that construction of the word, for in the old Roman law, the word "*pecunia*" was held to pass property of every description.' *Glendening v Glendening* (1846) 9 Beav 324 at 326, 327, per Lord Langdale MR

'The exchanging of a coin for other coins is not conclusive proof that the exchanging was that of dealing with current coin on both sides. Many coins, which yet have not been formally withdrawn from currency, have a price far beyond their denominated value, by reason of their antiquity or rarity, or for their beauty of design or execution (though this last is perhaps merely to say again by reason of the coins being struck in another age and mint than ours). Money as currency, and not as medals, seems to me to have been well defined by Mr Walker in "Money, Trade, and Industry" as "that which passes freely from hand to hand throughout the community in final discharge of debts and full payment for commodities being accepted equally without reference to the character or credit of the person who offers it and without the intention of the person who receives it to consume it or apply it to any other use than in turn to tender it to others in discharge of debts or payment for commodities".' *Moss v Hancock* [1899] 2 QB 111 at 116, per Darling J

'The cases seem to establish this: (1) "Money" can (albeit by a process of extension justified by the context) include money on deposit; so can, rather more easily, "money in the bank". (2) "Ready money" or "ready money in the bank" does not normally pass as money for which a substantial period of notice is required. As regards "cash" the question would seem to be whether the testator is using it in the sense of ready money or merely as synonymous with money without any implication of readiness, and in the normal case the conclusion would probably be the former.' *Re Stonham (decd), Lloyd's Bank Ltd v Maynard* [1963] 1 All ER 377 at 382, per Wilberforce J

United States 'Money' means a medium of exchange authorised or adopted by a domestic or foreign government as a part of its currency. (Uniform Commercial Code 1978, s 1–201(24))

In bank

'With regard to the balance standing to the testator's credit at his bankers, which did not bear interest, that balance as well as the money in his house at the time of his death must unquestionably be considered as passing under the term "moneys".' *Manning v Purcell* (1855) 7 De GM & G 55 at 64, 65, per Knight Bruce LJ

'There is no doubt that money on deposit is money in a bank. . . . When money is deposited in a bank it is not intended that the individual sovereigns or notes deposited shall be kept for the depositor, but that the bank shall become his debtor for the amount deposited, and although that debt may not be payable until the expiry of a specified period it still remains money deposited in a bank.' *Harper's Trustees v Bain* (1903) 5 F (Ct of Sess) 716 at 717, per Lord Kinross, Lord President

[By a codicil to his will a testator gave and bequeathed all his 'monies at the bank' to his wife absolutely.] 'I think that . . . money on deposit passes under the bequest of "all my monies at the bank". It must be admitted that the expression "monies at the bank" does not describe with legal accuracy either a current or a deposit account. . . . I do not think that there is any substantial difference between money on a current account and money on deposit account, by reason merely of the fact that for the withdrawal of money on deposit the bank is strictly entitled to seven days' notice.' *Re Glendinning, Steel v Glendinning* (1918) 88 LJ Ch 87 at 88, per Younger J

[A testator by his will gave to the plaintiff and another all 'money in the bank'.] 'In my judgment it cannot be said that the claim which the testator had against the executors of his late wife's will to part of the sum standing to the credit of his late wife in some branch of the Westminster Bank was the testator's money in the bank. It is plain, I think, that by those words he was intending to dispose of money in a bank, over which he has control. He had no control over the sum standing to the credit of the account in his wife's name.' *Re Lowe's Estate, Swann v Rockley* [1938] 2 All ER 774 at 776, per Bennett J

Canada [In a will, the testator's personal estate was described as all 'money in the bank', promissory notes and cash on hand.] 'In view of the fact that the testator clearly stated that he was disposing of all his personal estate. I think it is perfectly clear that "money in the bank" was not intended by the testator to be used in a narrow sense so as to refer only to money on deposit in the bank, but was to include the money he had invested in Dominion of Canada bonds which were in his safety deposit box in the bank. The use of the words "all money in bank, promissory notes and cash on hand" was the testator's method of describing his personal estate as distinct from his real estate.' *Re Swindlehurst* [1952] OR 392 at 396, Ont SC, per McRuer CJHC

In will

'Money' in a will has no strict technical meaning. It was formerly construed strictly as comprehending only cash under the testator's immediate control unless there was a context to extend its meaning, but it has now been judicially recognised that it is a word which in popular usage has a diversity of meanings, and the rule now is that, in construing any particular will, the court must determine the meaning attached to the word by the testator without any presumption that it bears any one of its possible meanings. 'Money' ordinarily includes cash and notes in hand, money immediately payable to the testator at call and money at a bank on current or deposit account. It may include money in the hands of trustees awaiting investment, and investments readily able to be turned into money; it may also include the whole of the testator's personal estate, and even his real estate. On the other hand, the fact that a specific gift comes after the gift in question may prevent it from being residuary, but it is not conclusive against its being a residuary gift, and the fact that there is a residuary gift elsewhere in the will may rebut the inference that a gift of money is of a residuary nature. 'Money' has in particular received a wide meaning where the court has been influenced by the presumption against intestacy. (50 Halsbury's Laws (4th edn) para 478)

'A great number of cases have been cited and a great number more might be cited; but, after all, the whole of the cases upon the subject as to the interpretation of the term "money" profess to proceed on the general rule of law and equity, that, in interpreting written instruments, you give to every word its primary and natural signification, unless you find, on reading the whole will, there is reason to hold that the testator used the term in some secondary sense. Now, no doubt, the natural and primary sense of the word "money" is cash or coin of the realm. It is not necessary to go into the derivation of the word, for that sort of reasoning would not assist in the administration of justice; but the word "money", in the strict signification, means cash or coin of the realm. Still, in the common acceptation of the word, there is a more extensive meaning given to it. For instance, the word certainly implies bank notes as well as cash. Every one would speak of bank notes as money, and there may be many other meanings given to the term. One of the most usual significations is, that personal property which a man possesses, and which he distinguishes from plate, furniture, horses, and carriages, and other things of that nature. It is a common thing to say, that a man possesses a great deal of money; the meaning of which is, that he has great wealth or a large annual income to spend; but a person would never speak of his plate, furniture, horses, etc., as money. Still, if the term "money" is used in the sense of personal property, it might be applied even to such articles as plate, furniture, etc. . . . In trying the question, whether the term "money" is used as general residue or in its strict sense, as distinguished from other property, it is material to consider whether there is any other clause which operates as a gift of the residuary property, because if there were another general residuary clause in the will, that would be a strong reason for confining the word "money" to its primary signification.' *Barrett v White* (1855) 24 LJ Ch 724 at 726, 727, per Kindersley V-C

'There is a well settled rule, that in the absence of anything in the will to indicate a clear intention to the contrary, a gift of "all my money" must be taken to mean "money" in the strict sense, and nothing else; you cannot, in the absence of anything in the will showing a different intention conclude that the testator meant to give more than "money".' *Larner v Larner* (1857) 3 Drew 704 at 707, per Kindersley V-C

'The rule of construction is, that the word "money" does not extend beyond what is literally "money", unless the context requires it; and that the burden of proof lies on those who contend the contrary to show that its signification is to be extended. But I think there are circumstances in this case which show that "money" includes the whole of the property of the testatrix, and the cases cited confirm that view. In the first place, the testatrix professes to "leave everything of which she dies possessed in trust for the following purposes". That is an express desire, on her part, to dispose of the whole of her property for the purposes afterwards mentioned, and if she has not disposed of the whole afterwards, it was clearly by inadvertence. The strong and conclusive thing is this . . . : If a person gives the whole of the residue of his money to A B, and he afterwards gives specific chattels, it is clear that they are not to be treated as money, and therefore the word "money" is not to be treated as the whole of the residuary estate.' *Montagu v Sandwich (Earl)* (1863) 33 Beav 324 at 325, 326, per Romilly MR

[A testatrix died leaving several testamentary instruments. In the second of them were the following words: 'When all my just debts and legacies are paid, without the smallest deduction arising from any sort of taxes, I give the residue of all my *money*, either in my bankers' hands or elsewhere, if any such *cash* be remaining, in trust, etc.'] 'On the question of the construction of the word "money", in the second testamentary paper, there is no doubt, that though the word "money", standing by itself, is confined to the proper meaning of that word, yet, if it be given after a direction to pay debts, legacies, and funeral and testamentary expenses, or with any other words which denote an intention, on the part of the testatrix to dispose of the whole of her estate, it will be construed to be synonymous with "property", and in the popular and inaccurate sense of the word "money". Here, if this testamentary instrument stood alone, I should be disposed to think that the word money, standing alone, meant a general residuary bequest, and that this codicil disposed of all the personal estate of the testatrix. But the interposition of the word "cash", which was wholly unnecessary if the testatrix intended to dispose of all her personal estate, and which, even in loose popular language, is never employed to mean property generally, throws great doubt on the propriety of extending the word "money" to include all her personal estate. It is, therefore, necessary to look at all the rest of the will and examine the scope and effect of the instruments taken collectively. . . . The result that I have arrived at, from taking all these instruments together, and making them, as far as possible, consistent, with each other, is, that the word "money" coupled with the word "cash" in the second testamentary instrument must be confined to money, strictly and properly so called, and not be extended so as to include all the personal property of the testatrix.' *Nevinson v Lennard (Lady)* (1865) 34 Beav 487 at 490–492, per Romilly MR

'I concur in this: that if a testator, by his will, gives matters, which are not money in the ordinary acceptation of the term, and afterwards gives all "other my moneys whatsoever and wheresoever", he applies that expression to things which are not strictly money and consequently that things not of that character pass under the gift. Thus if a testator gives Whiteacre and all the rest of my money to A B, he means all this property, for he treats Whiteacre as "money", although land or real estate and personal chattels are not properly speaking "money".' *Stooke v Stooke* (1866) 35 Beav 396 at 397, per Romilly MR

[A testator, after bequeathing a specific amount to his brother, left 'the rest of my money' as he expressed it, to six named persons.] 'I am of opinion that the use of the term "money" in the will before me was intended by the testator to cover all his personal estate.' *In the Goods of Bramley* [1902] P 106 at 107, per Jeune P

[A testator by his will left a bequest of 'money'.] 'On the principle laid down in the cases the word must be treated as having prima facie a limited meaning and on the construction of this will it cannot extend to items which are only popularly described as money. The word "money", therefore, applies only to cash in the house, money at the bank, or in the hands of agents, and to any other ready money at call at the date of the testator's death.' *Re Hunter Northey v Northey* (1908) 25 TLR 19 at 19, per Eve J

'In this will the testator after directing payment of his debts makes a limited gift of his freehold residence and other specific gifts. He then gives "the remainder of any monies" to nine persons including his housekeeper and his two children. As far as intention is concerned he certainly meant to include the whole of his property in this gift. Under Wood V-C's rule a gift of the remainder of money remaining after payment of debts, in the absence of any other residuary gift, passes the whole property liable to the payment of debts, and that now includes real estate. But, in the present case it is not necessary to call in aid the recent legislation [Administration of Estates Act 1925]. A testator's language may show that he is not using "money" in the strict sense, but intends it to include the whole of his property, whether real or personal. Here he is obviously not using "money" in the strict sense, and his manifest intention to include the whole of his property may be given effect to: *Re Taylor* [1923] 1 Ch 99 at 108, 110. The whole of his property therefore, both real and personal, not specifically disposed of passes under the gift of "the remainder of any monies".' *Re Mellor, Porter v Hindsley* [1929] 1 Ch 446 at 448, 449, per Astbury J

'Looking at all the authorities, and endeavouring to reconcile them as far as possible, the result would appear to be this: The primary meaning of the word "money" is the strict legal meaning in the sense that it is the meaning adopted by lawyers in drafting legal documents, and it is the meaning in which the word must be taken to have been used in any document which the court holds is a document that should be presumed to adopt legal language, unless such construction leads "to some absurdity or some repugnance or inconsistency with the rest of the instrument". But in the case of a layman's will there is no presumption that the word "money" has been used in the clear and unambiguous sense in which it is used by lawyers, and the court may look at once both to the context and to the surrounding circumstances without being compelled before doing so to find some pretext or justification in the context alone. If, however, the result of such a complete survey is entirely negative, then the court, which must make a selection on some ground, can do nothing but decide in favour of the primary or legal meaning, for the simple reason that it is the primary or legal meaning, and is at least *a* reason.' *Re Jennings, Caldbeck v Stafford & Lindemere* [1930] IR 196 at 203, per Meredith J

'My lords, this appeal raises the interesting and important question whether, when the word "money" appears in an English will as the description of that of which the testator is disposing, the word, in the absence of any context or other circumstances proper to be considered as varying its meaning, must be interpreted according to an alleged fixed "rule of construction" which has been regarded by our courts as established and binding for many generations past, and which is said to be traced back to a pronouncement of Gilbert CB in 1725; *Shelmer's Case* [(1725) Gilb Ch 200]. . . . In the case of an ordinary English word like "money", which is not always employed in the same sense, I can see no possible justification for fixing on it, as the result of a series of judicial decisions about a series of different wills, a cast-iron meaning which must not be departed from unless special circumstances exist, with the result that this special meaning must be presumed to be the meaning of every testator in every case unless the contrary is shown. I agree, of course, that, if a word has only one natural meaning, it is right to attribute that meaning to the word when used in a will unless the context or other circumstances which may be properly considered show that an unusual meaning is intended, but the word "money" has not got one natural or usual meaning. It has several meanings, each of which in appropriate circumstances may be regarded as natural. In its original sense, which is also its narrowest sense, the word means "coin". Moneta was an appellation of Juno, and the Temple of Moneta at Rome was the mint. Phrases like "false money" or "clipped money" show the original use in English, but the conception very quickly broadens into the equivalent of "cash" of any sort. The question: "Have you any money in your purse?" refers presumably to bank notes or Treasury notes, as well as to shillings and pence. A further extension would include not only coin and currency in the possession of an individual, but debts owing to him, and cheques which he could pay into his banking account, or postal orders, or the like. Again, going further, it is a matter of common speech to refer to one's "money at the bank", although in a stricter sense the bank is not holding one's own money and what one possesses is a chose in action which represents the right to require the bank to pay out sums held at the call of its customer. Sums on deposit, whether with a bank or otherwise, may be included by a further extension, but this is by no means the limit to the senses in which the word "money" is frequently and quite naturally used in English speech. The statement: "I have my money invested on mortgage, or in debentures, or in stocks and shares, or in savings certificates", is not an illegitimate use of the word "money" on which the courts are bound to frown, though it is a great extension from its original meaning to interpret it as covering securities, and, in considering the various meanings of the word "money" in common speech, one must go even further, as any dictionary will show. The word may be used to cover the whole of an individual's personal property—sometimes, indeed, all of a person's property, whether real or personal. "What has he done with his money?" may well be an inquiry as to the general contents of a rich man's will. Horace's satire at the expense of the fortune-hunter who attached himself to childless Roman matrons, has its modern equivalent in the saying: "It's her money he's after". When St Paul wrote to Timothy that the love of money is the root of evil, he was not warning him of the risks attaching to one particular kind of wealth, but was pointing to the dangers of avarice in general. When Tennyson's Northern Farmer counselled his son not to marry for money, but to go where money is, he was not excluding the attractiveness of private property in land. These wider meanings of "money" are referred to in some of the reported cases as "popular" meanings, in contrast to the "legal" meaning of the term, but for the purpose of construing a will, and especially a home-made will, a popular meaning may be the more important of the two. The circumstance that a skilled draftsman would avoid the use of so ambiguous a word only confirms the view that, when it is used in a will, the popular as opposed to the technical use of the word "money" may be important. I protest against the idea that, in interpreting the language of a will, there can be some fixed meaning of the word "money", which the courts must adopt as being the "legal" meaning as opposed to the "popular" meaning. The proper meaning is the correct meaning in the case of the particular will, and there is no necessary opposition between that meaning and the popular meaning. The duty of the court, in the case of an ordinary English word which has several quite usual meanings which differ from one another is not to assume that one out of several meanings holds the field as the correct meaning until it is ousted by some other meaning regarded as "non-legal", but to ascertain without prejudice as between various usual meanings which is the correct interpretation of the particular document. . . . As Meredith J, in his pungent and entertaining judgment in *Re Jennings, Caldbeck v Stafford* [supra] observes, the judiciary has waged a long fight to teach testators that "money" means "cash", but as the ordinary testator who makes his own will does not study the law reports, he persists in constantly using the word in a wider sense, and it is time that in such cases a "popular" meaning prevailed over the "legal" one.' *Perrin v Morgan* [1943] AC 399 at 405–408, 414, per Lord Simon LC

'In contending that the expression "what money is left over" did not include the heritable property of Broom House and its furniture counsel for the heirs did not go the length of maintaining that the word "money" could never be held to include property of this type. He admitted that the term was an elastic one, and that it might readily be interpreted to cover more than money in the strict sense, but argued that to interpret the term as covering heritage was a very wide stretch and something that a court should not do unless driven to it by the context. Now it is true that to read the word as including heritage is to go a long way from its primary meaning, but, while this consideration is not necessarily without weight, I do not think that it affects the approach to the question of construction. The decisions seem to show that it is wrong to begin with the presumption that the word is, or is not, used in a particular sense, which must prevail unless displaced by the context, and that the right method is to treat the word simply as a word capable of various meanings (one of them including heritage) and to ascertain according to the ordinary rules of construction with what meaning the maker of the deed must be deemed to have used it [*Perrin v Morgan* [1943] AC 399 (supra)].' *Mairs' Trustees v Aberdeen Royal Infirmary & Mental Hospital* 1946 SLT 88 at 89, per Lord Sorn

Canada 'It has already been noted that the ordinary meaning of the words "money" or "monies" has been extended (where the context permitted) to include stocks, bonds, mortgages, agreements for sale, in fact the entire personal estate. The word "money" has come to be regarded as "investments in" and having been judicially held to include personalty I am of the opinion in a proper case it can include realty. This possible construction was raised as far back as 1860 for in *Chaplin v Reynolds* (1860) 28 Beav 221, the Master of the Rolls said: "Stock is not money, but rather the produce of money invested, the same as land purchased is the produce of money invested in it, still it is a common though an inaccurate expression to say, 'I have so much money in the funds', or 'what money had he in the funds', and the like". . . . Notwithstanding the use of the words "devise" and "all my real . . . property" there is no specific gift of realty unless it can be included in the words "any monies". The language used is "any monies left after paying my debts" and in my opinion those words are sufficiently wide and comprehensive to include land and I believe that it was the testator's intention to thereby dispose of all that was left.' *Re Ruller Estate* [1945] 3 WWR 133 at 137, 138, Sask KB, per MacNiven J

New Zealand 'The expression "all money" [in a seaman's will within the Wills Act 1837, s 11 (as extended by the Wills (Soldiers and Sailors) Act 1918)], having regard to the circumstances in which it was used, clearly indicates that it was so used in a popular sense as a description of all his [the testator's] personal estate.' *Re Mackie, Public Trustee v Brown* [1922] NZLR 651 at 655, per Stringer J

New Zealand 'There remains for consideration the claim made by the plaintiff that under the term "moneys" the life insurance policy and shares pass. As to this, the authorities make it quite clear that the term "money" when used in a will means money in the strict sense, unless there is a context which is sufficient to show that the testator used the word in a more extended sense.' *Re Suisted, Suisted v Suisted* [1933] NZLR 119 at 123, per Herdman J; also reported [1933] GLR 142 at 144

Securities passing under bequest of

'I find the authorities confirm the impression I had at the hearing of the cause, that the term "money" will not pass stock, unless there is in the will some explanatory context.' *Gosden v Dotterill* (1832) 1 My & K 56 at 59, 60, per Leach MR

'Although a simple bequest of "money" will not of itself pass stock, yet the word "money" may be so used in a will as from the whole context to show that the testator meant it to pass stock and other personal estate.' *In the Goods of Rebecca Hand* (1849) 7 Notes of Cases 59 at 60, per Sir H Jenner Fust

'There is no doubt upon the authorities that the word "monies" may pass stock in the funds, it being a question of construction upon the whole will whether the testator meant to use the word in that sense or not. I cannot doubt that the words "take and receive all monies in my possession, or due to me at the time of my decease", looking at the general scope of the will and the authorities on the subject, were sufficient to pass this stock.' *Waite v Combes* (1852) 5 De G & Sm 676 at 679, 680, per Parker V-C

'Money on deposit in the Post Office Savings Bank passes under a gift in a will of "money invested in Consols or other securities".' *Re Saxby, Saxby v Kiddell* [1890] WN 171 at 171, per Chitty J

'"Money in the strict sense" means, as I understand, money actually in hand as cash or at a bank on drawing account.' *Re Taylor, Taylor v Tweedie* [1923] 1 Ch 99 at 108, per Warrington LJ

MONEY AND VALUABLES

Australia 'The words of the gift are: "I further bequeath all the remainder of money and valuables that I possess to the aforesaid Elizabeth Martin". . . . The question . . . remains whether the deposits with the two building societies I have mentioned, and the cash balance at one of them, will pass under the words "money and valuables". In my opinion no valid distinction can be drawn between a deposit at interest with a bank and such a deposit with a building society, many of whom as we know carry on a quasi-banking business. . . . I therefore hold that on the true construction of this will the deposits and cash balance at the building societies . . . passed to Elizabeth Martin.' *Cameron v Hunter* (1891) 17 VLR 217 at 220, 221, per Webb J

MONEY BILL

A Money Bill means a Public Bill which in the opinion of the Speaker of the House of Commons contains only provisions dealing with all or any of the following subjects, namely, the imposition, repeal, remission, alteration, or regulation of taxation; the imposition for the payment of debt or other financial purposes of charges on the Consolidated Fund, or on money provided by Parliament, or the variation or repeal of any such charges; supply; the appropriation, receipt, custody, issue or audit of accounts of public money; the raising or guarantee of any loan or the repayment thereof; or subordinate matters incidental to those subjects or any of them. In this subsection the expressions 'taxation', 'public money', and 'loan' respectively do not include any taxation, money, or loan raised by local authorities or bodies for local purposes. (Parliament Act 1911, s 1(2))

MONEY-LENDER

New Zealand 'In none of the authorities is it questioned that the decision whether a person is a moneylender is always one of fact. Their general tendency, however, is to display a reluctance to hold a person to be a "moneylender" who makes a series of loans to a single borrower for the purpose of financing the borrower's business. I share that reluctance, and on the facts of the present case I think that the dealings between the applicants and the bankrupt amount to an isolated transaction or series of transactions which do not, because they are isolated and linked together, display a sufficient degree of system and continuity to establish a business of moneylending.' *Re Austin, ex p Smith* [1965] NZLR 179 at 182, per Richmond J

MONEY'S WORTH

'The taxpayer draws attention to the reference to "money's worth", and he might also, perhaps, have drawn attention to the use of the words "value of the consideration". The expression "consideration, in . . . money's worth" is, of course, one which is very familiar to lawyers as being a way of expressing the price or consideration given for property where property is acquired in return for something other than money, such as services or other property, where the price or consideration which the acquirer gives for the property has got to be turned into money before it can be expressed in terms of money. The use here of the words "money's worth" does not, I think, indicate that Parliament had any idea in mind, when enacting this part of the Act, relating to a change in the value of money in the course of the passage of time. Nor, I think, does the reference to "value of the consideration" indicate that any such idea was in mind.' *Secretan v Hart* [1969] 3 All ER 1196 at 1199, per Buckley J

MONITION

A censure of monition is an order to do or refrain from doing a specified act the omission or commission of which constitutes an ecclesiastical offence or to rectify some previous act the commission of which was an ecclesiastical offence, and is usually accompanied by an order for costs against the accused. It may prohibit not merely the continuance or repetition of the same act but also the commission of acts of the same or a similar nature. (14 Halsbury's Laws (4th edn) para 1382)

The censures to which a person found guilty of an offence under this Measure renders himself liable are the following, namely . . . (d) monition, that is to say an order to do or refrain from doing a specified act. (Ecclesiastical Jurisdiction Measure 1963, s 49)

'The ecclesiastical law . . . even in those proceedings which are called (and in some sense are) criminal and penal, has for its object, not the punishment of individual offenders, but the correction of manners, and the discipline of the Church. "Monition" (which is sometimes itself called an ecclesiastical censure) is described in the books as of a "preparatory" nature, . . . i.e. (as I understand the term) as a warning or command, to be followed in case of disobedience by some coercive sanction. It appears to have been a general (though not an invariable) rule of the canon law, that monition ought to precede suspension or excommunication. . . . It might be, and in practice it often was, issued (for various purposes) at the beginning, or during the progress, of an ecclesiastical cause; it also might be and sometimes was (as in the present case) the sentence or part of a sentence upon the merits, pronounced at the end of such a cause.' *Mackonochnie v Penzance (Lord)* (1881) 6 App Cas 424 at 433, per Lord Selborne LC

MONOPOLY

It is a monopoly, and against the policy of the law, for any person or group of persons to secure the sole exercise of any known trade throughout the country.

A monopoly may come into being by Crown grant or by statute, or from the activities of private persons or combinations of private persons.

There are now a number of monopolies in existence which are authorised by statute, as, for example, that of the Post Office with respect to the carrying of letters and performing incidental services, that of British Telecommunications with regard to running telecommunications systems, that of the Bank of England with respect to the issue of banknotes in England and Wales, that of the National Coal Board with respect to the working and getting of coal in Great Britain, that of the British Gas Corporation to supply gas through pipes to premises, and that of the London Transport Executive with regard to the provision of a London bus service. In other fields of activity virtual monopolies exist in large areas of the country as the result of the transfer of existing undertakings to public ownership, as in the case of the railways. (47 Halsbury's Laws (4th edn) paras 68, 71)

[*See* now the Fair Trading Act 1973, s 4 of which established the Monopolies and Mergers Commission, and ss 6, 7 of which define monopoly situations in relation to goods and services—e.g. in the case of goods, where at least one quarter of all the goods of any description which are supplied in the United Kingdom are supplied by, or to, one and the same person. See also the Competition Act 1980, ss 11, 12.]

MONTH

'Month' is used in several senses. It may mean one of the twelve unequal parts into which the calendar year is divided; it may mean the period which, beginning on any day of a calendar month other than the first, ends on the day next before the corresponding day of the next month; or it may denote a lunar month, that is to say, a period consisting of twenty-eight days.

As a general rule, and in the absence of anything to indicate an intention to the contrary, where the term 'month' is used in a contract made and coming into operation before 1926, or in a statute enacted before the year 1851, it is taken to mean a lunar month. The question whether it was intended to use the word in another sense must be decided according to the ordinary rules of construction; it may be shown that in a particular place, business or trade the word has acquired a secondary meaning.

In the construction of statutes passed after 1850, unless the contrary intention appears, 'month' means calendar month.

In all deeds, contracts, wills, orders, and other instruments executed, made or coming into operation after 31st December 1925 unless the context otherwise requires, 'month' means calendar month. In mortgage transactions a month has always been taken to mean a calendar month; and according to the custom in the City of London a month in a mercantile transaction has always been deemed to be a calendar month.

In ecclesiastical matters the computation has to be made according to the calendar, and thus a six months' notice has always been taken to mean six calendar months.

When the period prescribed is a calendar month running from any arbitrary date the period expires with the day in the succeeding month corresponding to the date upon which the period starts, save that, if the period starts at the end of a calendar month which contains more days than the next succeeding month, the period expires at the end of that succeeding month.

If a period of one calendar month includes the last day of February there must be twenty-nine or twenty-eight days, according as the year is or is not a leap year. (45 Halsbury's Laws (4th edn) paras 1107–1111)

'Month' means calendar month. (Interpretation Act 1978, Sch I)

In a contract of sale 'month' prima facie means calendar month. (Sale of Goods Act 1979, s 10(3))

'Reference to a "month" in a statute is to be understood as a calendar month. The Interpretation Act 1978 says so. It is also clear under a rule that has been consistently applied by the courts since *Lester v Garland*, [(1808) 15 Ves 248] that, in calculating the period that has elapsed after the occurrence of the specified event such as the giving of a notice, the day on which the event occurs is excluded from the reckoning. It is equally well established . . . that when the relevant period is a month or a specified number of months after the giving of a notice the general rule is that the period ends on the corresponding date in the appropriate subsequent month, i.e. the day of that month that bears the same number as the day of the earlier month on which the notice was given.' *Dodds v Walker* [1981] 2 All ER 609 at 610, HL, per Lord Diplock

Australia 'At common law "month" means "lunar month", and whilst it may be that by reference to context this meaning will, particularly because the period more often than not in the everyday use of it has reference to calendar month, readily give way to modern usage, there is nothing [in the present case] . . . to displace the common law meaning. In Queensland "month", when used in statutes, means "calendar month", and in some other States of the Commonwealth and in Great Britain legislative action has given the word a similar meaning in deeds, contracts and other instruments but in this State and outside statutory provision the common law meaning persists.' *Development Underwriting (Queensland) Pty Ltd v Weaber* [1971] Qd R 182 at 188, per Matthews J

New Zealand 'For many purposes, no doubt, "month" means prima facie a lunar month; but in England since the year 1850 and in New Zealand since the year 1858, the term, when used in a statute, has meant a calendar month by virtue of legislative enactment. The term is used in a number of sections in the Land Act 1908 [repealed; see now Land Act 1948] and in all these sections it means a calendar month. Where in a statute the term "month" means a calendar month, prima facie the same meaning ought to be given, I think, to the term when used in connection with any transactions or proceedings effected or taken under the authority of that statute.' *King v Southland Land Board* [1917] NZLR 825 at 827, 828, per Sim J

New Zealand [The defendant was convicted of a driving offence and such conviction entitled the court to disqualify him from driving 'for such period as the Court thinks fit'. The court disqualified him for a period of two months, and the question was whether this meant two calendar or two lunar months.] 'According to the rule of the common law applicable to all legal instruments (contractual and otherwise) a month means lunar month, unless the contrary is indicated by the context, by statutory provision or by recognised exceptions. This rule has been referred to in several New Zealand cases: see for example *Liddle v Rolleston* [[1919] NZLR 408, 416, per Edwards J] and *Sewell v Donald & Sons Ltd* [[1917] NZLR 760, 765, per Chapman J]. But in *Phipps & Co v Rogers*, [[1925] 1 KB 14, 26] Atkin LJ said this about it: "The rule is fortunately almost destroyed by exceptions. It does not apply to mercantile documents, or to statutes, or to mortgages or to cases where the contract requires the meaning of calendar months. It never did apply in ecclesiastical law." In the present case I am concerned to interpret an order initially pronounced by the magistrate in court on 19th March 1970 and later on the same day perfected by entry in the criminal record book. The terms of the order thus perfected are that the defendant was disqualified from driving for a period of two months. It is clear of course that the statutory definition of the word "month" does not apply directly to that order of disqualification. But by reason of the statutory definition the word "month" means calendar month throughout the Transport Act 1962, and it has that meaning both in reference to periods of imprisonment and in reference to the minimum period of disqualification for breach of various traffic regulations. When the magistrate made the order in the present case he did so under the powers conferred upon him by the same Act. That being so, I think that the same meaning should be given to the words "two months" in that order as if the order had been made in pursuance of a provision in the Act expressly prescribing term. In my opinion those words mean two calendar months.' *Police v Maindonald* [1971] NZLR 417 at 419, per MacArthur J

Calendar month

'The term a calendar month is a legal and technical term. . . . The meaning of the phrase is that, in computing time by calendar months, the time must be reckoned by looking at the calendar and not by counting days; and that one calendar month's imprisonment is to be calculated from the day of imprisonment to the day numerically corresponding to that day in the following month less one.' *Migotti v Colvill* (1879) 4 CPD 233 at 238, CA, per Brett LJ

See, generally, 45 Halsbury's Laws (4th edn) paras 1107–1111 supra.

MONUMENT *See also* ANCIENT MONUMENT

'Monument' means (subject to subsection (8), below)—

(a) any building, structure or work, whether above or below the surface of the land, and any cave or excavation;
(b) any site comprising the remains of any such building, structure or work or of any excavation; and
(c) any site comprising, or comprising the remains of, any vehicle, vessel, aircraft or other movable structure or part thereof which neither constitutes nor forms part of any work which is a monument within paragraph (a) above;

and any machinery attached to a monument shall be regarded as part of the monument if it could not be detached without being dismantled. (Ancient Monuments and Archaeological Areas Act 1979, s 61(7))

[Subsection (8) exempts ecclesiastical buildings still in use, and deals further with protection of wrecks.]

MOORING (Of vessel)

'In this case at a particular part of the River Thames, where it is navigable, fishermen and owners of other vessels have put down moorings to which they attach their vessels. The moorings are fixed and are marked with buoys, and all the person navigating has to do is to slip the attachment when he takes his vessel away, and to pick it up again when he returns to the mooring. These moorings are the property of the person who puts them down—at all events, at the time when they are put down. . . . What is the meaning of a mooring? It is such a mode of anchoring a vessel by means of a fastening in the ground, either an anchor or something heavy, and a chain and buoy, as will allow of the vessel picking up the buoy when she returns to it, and so coming to rest. The owner of the vessel takes possession of his mooring when he returns to it. He does not assume to take possession of the land, for he only claims to come back to and use his own mooring, and that no one has the right to remove or destroy the moorings; and I should say that no one has the right to use them in order to anchor his own ship. Now, is that mode of anchoring a ship a common incident of the navigation of ships? It seems to me that it is the duty of judges to bring into force the knowledge that they have in common with all who are engaged in a particular business, and that they should not shut their eyes and affect not to know what everybody conversant with the particular business with which they have to deal knows. In this particular case everyone knows who knows anything about navigation that there are two ways of anchoring a ship. There is the temporary anchoring by means of an anchor, which is lifted when necessary, and there is the more permanent mode by means of moorings. For an example of this latter, there is the *Victory* when she lay in Portsmouth Harbour, where she was at moorings. So the yachts in Cowes Road have moorings, which they take up whenever they return thereto, passing a chain or rope through the ring of the buoy which indicates the mooring. There is, therefore, this mode of bringing a ship to rest and keeping her so for a time, which is within the ordinary course of navigation. This is not a right of any individual: it is a general right to use the waters for navigation in any ordinary way, and to anchor in either of the two well-known ways, either by means of an anchor or of a mooring.' *A-G v Wright* [1897] 2 QB 318 at 320, 321, CA, per Lord Esher MR

[By a provisional order authorising the construction of a pier it was provided that no vessel should be moored alongside the pier without the consent of the pier company, and rates for 'mooring' were specified.] 'The questions is what is meant by the word "mooring". Does it, as used here, include the case of a boat merely coming alongside to embark or disembark passengers? Evidence has been called on both sides which has satisfied me that "mooring" has no technical meaning other than its general meaning in the English language, and that some seafaring persons would apply it to every case in which a boat is made fast in any way, while others would not. If boats simply calling to land and embark passengers are "moored" within the meaning of the Provisional Order, then by clause 38 of the Provisional Order the company could exclude such passengers at will, whereas by clause 28 the company are prohibited from excluding them, even at times when they are entitled to "close the pier against the public". No persons could safely land or embark from the pier without in some manner making fast. I think, therefore, that the mooring or anchoring mentioned in clause 38, which is, I think, the mooring or anchoring for which the rates are payable, cannot include the making fast of boats for the purpose merely of landing or embarking passengers.' *Liverpool & North Wales SS Co Ltd v Mersey Trading Co Ltd & Horton* (1908) 99 LT 863 at 867, 868, per Neville J; affirmed on appeal on another point, 99 LT 868 CA

'I do not think this vessel was under way. . . . In my view, she was none the less moored because she had cast off part of her moorings. Her aft moorings were gone. Her forward moorings still remained, and in my view she was none the less moored, because in consequence of loosening some of her moorings the tide had begun to operate on her. A vessel at anchor is none the less at anchor because she is swinging, and a vessel moored to anything is none the less moored because she is swinging.' *The Dagmar* (1929) 141 LT 271 at 274, per Hill J

Moored in good safety

In the Lloyd's policy and in all common voyage policies the risk on ship is expressed to continue 'until she hath moored at anchor twenty-four hours in good safety', and the ship is not deemed to have been moored for twenty-four hours in good safety unless she has been moored for that space of time under the three following conditions:

(1) She must have been moored in such a state of physical safety that she can keep afloat while the cargo is being unloaded. This condition is not satisfied when the vessel arrives as a mere wreck and is in a sinking state when she is moored, but it is satisfied if she arrives at the ordinary place of discharge, and, even though seriously damaged, is able there to keep afloat, and is kept afloat more than twenty-four hours after being so moored.

(2) The ship must have been for the twenty-four hours in a state of political safety. This condition is not satisfied if, for instance, she has been laid under an embargo, or if steps have been taken to seize her so that she is no longer in her owner's possession and control.

(3) She must have been moored for more than twenty-four hours in such circumstances that she has an opportunity of unloading and discharging at the place where she in fact intends to discharge. This condition is not satisfied if, for instance, she has been ordered into quarantine during the twenty-four hours.

If, however, the ship is moored in such a place and in such circumstances that she has only to wait until her turn for unloading comes without again unmooring, this is held to be a mooring in good safety. (25 Halsbury's Laws (4th edn) para 137)

[The ship *Success* was insured at and from Leghorn to the port of London, and till there 'moored' twenty-four hours 'in good safety'.] 'Though the ship was so long at her moorings, yet she could not be said to be there in good safety, which must mean the opportunity of unloading and discharging, whereas here she was arrested within the twenty-four hours.' *Waples v Eames* (1745) 2 Stra 1243 at 1244, per cur.

[By a Lloyd's policy on a ship, the risk was described in writing to be 'at and from London to Calcutta, upon the said ship, etc, until she hath moored at anchor twenty-four hours in good safety'. The ship, which had been considerably damaged by striking a reef, and which was brought into harbour in a state which necessitated constant pumping, thereafter remained afloat for thirty days. The question was whether the thirty days were to be reckoned from the time of arrival at Calcutta or from the expiration of the twenty-four hours after she had been 'moored in good safety'.] 'Assuming . . . that the thirty days are to be reckoned from the time of the ship being moored for twenty-four hours in good safety, the question arises, what is the meaning of those words in such a policy? We are of opinion that the meaning is not, as has been contended, that the moorings are safe, but that the words refer to the ship being in safety. The words cannot mean that the vessel is to arrive without any damage or injury whatever from the effects of the voyage; otherwise, the loss of a mast, or even a spar, a sail, or a rope, though the vessel was perfectly fit to keep not only the river but the sea, would, contrary to all the ordinary meaning of language, prevent her from being considered as in safety. So, on the other hand, the words would not in our opinion be satisfied by the vessel arriving and being moored in a sinking state, or as a mere wreck, or by a mere temporary mooring. . . . The extension of the period of risk for twenty-four hours after having moored in good safety clearly implies that, notwithstanding the safety intended, the ship is liable to partial or total loss by the occurrence of a peril insured against.' *Lidgett v Secretan* (1870) LR 5 CP 190 at 198, 199, per cur.

MORAL

[Land was conveyed to trustees for the promotion (inter alia) of the 'moral' well-being of persons resident in certain county boroughs.] 'I think the "promotion of well-being" is equivalent to "improvement". . . . Moral improvement, I think, would, undoubtedly, include religious improvement, but it is a wider term, and would also extend to the inculcation of a desirable code of secular ethics, e.g. the secular (though also Christian) virtues of honesty, fair play, unselfishness and so on.' *Baddeley v Inland Revenue Comrs* [1953] 2 All ER 233 at 244, CA, per Jenkins LJ (also reported in [1953] Ch 504 at 525)

MORAL CERTAINTY

Australia 'The expression "moral certainty" has been sanctioned by long-standing usage in the criminal courts as synonymous with the expression "beyond reasonable doubt". . . . My personal view is that it is better to adhere to the expression "beyond reasonable doubt" and to avoid alternative expressions. The expression "moral certainty" is not now used in common speech and writing as perhaps it was in former times and its meaning may not be apparent to jurors. If the expression "moral certainty" is used, I think that it is desirable to explain to the jury that it is used as another way of expressing the notion of satisfaction beyond reasonable doubt. Although the authorities show that there is no prescribed formula which must be followed I think that it is advisable to adhere to the well-known, and in my view easily comprehensible formula "beyond reasonable doubt". The expression "moral certainty", however, is not a watering-down or qualification of the "beyond reasonable doubt" standard, and it would be impossible on the authorities to hold that the use of the expression "moral certainty" in conjunction with the expression "beyond reasonable doubt" amounts to a misdirection.' *R v Conley* (1982) 30 SASR 226 at 232, per King CJ

MORAL TURPITUDE

Canada 'I find very little merit in the applicant's claim that the admitted offences of issuing false cheques and being the operator of worthless cheques are not crimes of moral turpitude. These are acts of baseness in the duties which a man owes to his fellow men contrary to the accepted rule of right and duty between man and his fellow men. . . . I agree entirely with the American decisions that the word "moral", preceding the word "turpitude", adds nothing to it; it is a pleonasm which has been used only for the sake of emphasis.' *King v Brooks* (1960) 129 C CC 239 at 248, Man QB, per Monnin J

MORALLY WRONG

New Zealand [The Crimes Act 1961, s 23(2) (dealing with the defence of insanity) provides that no person shall be convicted of an offence by reason of an act done or omitted by him when labouring under natural imbecility or disease of the mind to such an extent as to render him incapable (a) of understanding the nature and quality of the act or omission; or (b) of knowing that the act or omission was 'morally wrong', having regard to the commonly accepted standards of right and wrong.] 'We are left in no doubt that what was intended by s 23(2)(b) of the New Zealand Act of 1961 was to adopt Dixon J's direction [in *R v*

Porter (1933) 55 CLR 182] as appropriate in future trials in this country. . . . and if the further inquiry is superadded, "but what is meant by 'morally wrong'" then the answer is, as proposed by Dixon J that the meaning to be given to that phrase is the meaning which is commonly accepted [namely, wrong having regard to the everyday standards of reasonable people].' *R v Macmillan* [1966] NZLR 616 at 622, CA, per cur.

MORE OR LESS

'In the lease there are but ten acres demised, and these words (more or less) cannot in judgment of the law extend to thirty or forty acres, for it is impossible by common intendment, and the rather because the land demanded by the declaration is of another nature than that which is mentioned in the *per nomen*.' *Anon* (1609) Yelv 166 at 166, per cur.

[A lessor possessed of a large piece of ground let it on building leases in different lots. One part was described in a lease by proper abuttals and as containing fifty-nine feet 'more or less'. The tenant erected a house sixty-two feet in length, but which corresponded with the abuttals.] 'The words "more or less' in the lease, being indeterminate, and the space covered, in fact corresponding with the abuttals, the tenant has a fair title to insist that it was meant that so much should pass by the demise.' *Neale d Leroux v Parkin* (1794) 1 Esp 229 at 230, per Lord Kenyon

'As to the expression "more or less", I do not say, those words in a contract will not include a few additional acres: but if the parties are contending about three acres, it would be very singular upon those words to add twenty-four map acres.' *Townshend (Marquis) v Stangroom* (1801) 6 Ves 328 at 340, 341, per Lord Eldon LC

'The effect of the words "more or less", added to the statement of quantity, has never been yet absolutely fixed by decision (*Hill v Buckley* (1811) 17 Ves 394); being considered, sometimes as extending only to cover a small difference, the one way, or the other; sometimes, as leaving the quantity altogether uncertain, and throwing upon the purchaser the necessity of satisfying himself with regard to it.' *Winch v Winchester* (1812) 1 Ves & B 375 at 376, 377, per Grant MR

[A contract was drawn up for the sale and shipment of 'about 300 quarters, more or less' of foreign rye.] 'The contract is to take the cargo, or a part of the cargo, shipped on board a particular vessel coming from Hamburgh. As the precise quantity is not mentioned in the agreement, the parties must have contemplated some other criterion of the amount that was to be purchased. If this criterion could be ascertained, the words "more or less", and "about", would merely leave the question between the parties where it was. . . . I cannot help thinking that the whole amount of the cargo must have been the criterion intended; for the parties would otherwise have described the quantity more precisely. But they may have meant the whole that the defendants were authorised to sell, or had of their own, or that had not been sold to other persons. The quantity intended should have been clearly expressed: here, by the terms used, it is left in obscurity; and on that ground I think the defendants cannot succeed.' *Cross v Eglin* (1831) 2 B & Ad 106 at 111, per Lord Tenterden CJ

'It is said that the instrument contains within it the admeasurement of the quantity of acres, etc, comprised within the stated boundaries, and therefore that the conveyance is adapted to pass, and does pass, no more than the exact quantity of land that there is within the fence, and therefore could not convey the strip which is over the fence, and which, moreover, cannot pass as appurtenant to the close; but the parcels are always put down with the saving expression "more or less", in the conveyances of skilful conveyancers, and that part of the deed is so worded in this conveyance; so that the form of the conveyance by no means, as was contended, favours the presumption that the strips belong to the owner of the inclosed land. But, in fact, the words used in the indenture seem to me entirely sufficient to convey the estate in the strips of land to the grantee.' *Simpson v Dendy* (1860) 6 Jur NS 1197 at 1207, per Erle CJ

'The plaintiff's claim is founded on this, that he is the owner of the soil of a part of the passage coloured pink, and that it was not conveyed to the defendant. There is some ambiguity in the defendant's conveyance, but its meaning is explained by the plan. It describes the land conveyed to the defendant as eighty-seven feet six inches, of which five feet six inches consist of part of the passage. According to that measurement the conveyance is substantially correct, and there is a mere inaccuracy which is obviated by the words "be the same a little more or less".' *Dodd v Burchell* (1862) 1 H & C 113 at 121, 122, per Channell B

'I regard the words "more or less" as the ordinary words which one meets with in a contract, where they are equivalent to "about so much", and where the contract is not to be rendered void in respect of either of the parties because either a little more or a little less than the amount contracted for has been supplied. I am rather disposed to agree . . . that the word "estimated" would probably have had the very same operation if the words "more or less" had not been there.' *Tancred, Arrol & Co v Steel Co of Scotland Ltd* (1890) 15 App Cas 125 at 136, per Lord Halsbury LC

Australia 'The contract sued upon in this case . . . begins with a statement that the appellants (by their agents) "have this day sold" to the respondent "the undermentioned stock, more or less". . . . A statement of a number with the words "about" or "more or less", or both, may, in my opinion, in some cases operate as a warranty, especially if the price is a lump sum.' *Goldsbrough, Mort & Co v Carter* (1914) 19 CLR 429 at 434, 438, per Griffith CJ

Australia [A property was described in a contract as comprising 280 acres more or less. After accurate measurement it was found to be 262 acres 2 roods 6 perches.] 'I am not suggesting that the words "more or less" are in every case to be limited to a deficiency arising from errors in measurement, but I think that that is primarily what those words are intended to cover; and I also think that nowadays, when the facilities for accurate measurement are so much greater than formerly in all parts of the country, a smaller discrepancy should be held to be outside the words, "more or less" than in earlier times. But in the present case I have no doubt in my own mind—and I do not think any authority compels me to decide otherwise—that a discrepancy of eighteen acres in an area of 280 acres is outside the qualifying words "more or less". . . . Both parties have concurred in asking me also to indicate to what extent the variation would be covered by the words "more or less". I am asked, in effect, to fix the limits which would be covered by those words. I think it is impossible to do so with accuracy, but, fixing an outside limit, I should think five acres short of 280 acres would be the proper figure to take. . . . I think I have taken a fairly liberal margin.' *Belfrage v McNaughton* [1924] VLR 441 at 443, 444, per Macfarlan J

New Zealand 'The phrase "more or less" in mercantile contracts is well understood to cover only a small variation either way. . . . I do not think that these words when they occur in a shipping receipt are to receive a construction different from that applied to them in the construction of mercantile contracts and which would be placed upon them by business men.' *Carson v Union SS Co* [1922] NZLR 778 at 782, 783, per Adams J

MORTALITY

[A clause in a policy of insurance on mules, asses, and oxen from Cork for the West Indies contained the words 'warranted free of mortality and jettison'.] 'The words "warranted free from mortality", are introduced into this policy by the underwriter for his benefit. It is his duty, therefore, to take care to frame his exception in words sufficiently large and extensive to meet all those descriptions of loss against which he intends to protect himself. The word "mortality" may, under certain circumstances, include every description of death, every termination of life to which mortals are subject. It applies generally, however, to that description of death which is not occasioned by violent means.' *Lawrence v Aberdein* (1821) 5 B & Ald 107 at 112, per Bayley J

MORTGAGE

A mortgage is a disposition of property as security for a debt. It may be effected by a demise or sub-demise of land, by a transfer of a chattel, by an assignment of a chose in action, by a charge on any interest in real or personal property or by an agreement to create a charge, for securing money or money's worth, the security being redeemable on repayment or discharge of the debt or other obligation. Generally, whenever a disposition of an estate or interest is originally intended as a security for money, whether this intention appears from the deed itself or from any other instrument or from parol evidence, it is considered as a mortgage and redeemable.

A mortgage consists of two things, namely a personal contract for payment of a debt and a disposition or charge of the mortgagor's estate or interest as security for the repayment of the debt; in equity the estate or interest so transferred is no more than a pledge or security. Every mortgage implies a debt and a personal obligation by the mortgagor to pay it. If there is a covenant or bond for its payment it is a specialty debt; if not, it is a simple contract debt. A mortgagee has an insurable interest. Covenants in a mortgage are subject to the doctrine against restraint of trade. (32 Halsbury's Laws (4th edn) paras 401, 402)

A mortgage is sometimes called a conditional sale, but a sale subject to a condition for resale to the original seller is distinguishable from a mortgage. The essence of a mortgage of goods is the transfer of the general property in the goods from mortgagor to mortgagee in order to secure a debt. It is a question of substance and not of form whether a given transaction is really a mortgage or a sale. (41 Halsbury's Laws (4th edn) para 602)

Mortgage includes any charge on any property for securing money or money's worth; and mortgage money means money, or money's worth, secured by a mortgage; and mortgagor includes any person from time to time deriving title under the original mortgagor, or entitled to redeem a mortgage, according to his estate, interest, or right, in the mortgage property; and mortgagee includes any person from time to time deriving title under the original mortgagee; and mortgagee in possession is, for the purposes of this Act, a mortgagee who, in right of the mortgage, has entered into and is in possession of the mortgaged property. (Conveyancing Act 1881, s 2)

'Mortgage' includes any charge or lien on any property for securing money or money's worth; 'legal mortgage' means a mortgage by demise or subdemise or a charge by way of legal mortgage and 'legal mortgagee' has a corresponding meaning; 'mortgage money' means money or money's worth secured by a mortgage; 'mortgagor' includes any person from time to time deriving title under the original mortgagor or entitled to redeem a mortgage according to his estate interest or right in the mortgaged property; 'mortgagee' includes a chargee by way of legal mortgage and any person from time to time deriving title under the original mortgagee; and 'mortgagee in possession' is, for the purposes of this Act, a mortgagee who, in right of the mortgage, has entered into and is in possession of the mortgaged property; and 'right of redemption' includes an option to repurchase only if the option in effect creates a right of redemption. (Law of Property Act 1925, s 205)

'Mortgage' includes any charge or lien on any property for securing money or money's worth. (Town and Country Planning Act 1971, s 290)

'A mortgage is a conveyance of land or an assignment of chattels as a security for the payment of a debt or the discharge of some other obligation for which it is given. This is the idea of a mortgage; and the security is redeemable on the payment or discharge of such debt or obligation, any provision to the contrary notwithstanding. That, in my opinion, is the law. Any provision inserted to prevent redemption on payment or performance of the debt or obligation for which the security was given is what is meant by a clog or fetter on the equity of redemption and is, therefore, void. It follows from this, that "once a mortgage always a mortgage"; but I do not understand that this principle involves the further proposition that the amount or nature of the further debt or obligation the payment or performance of which is to be secured is a clog or fetter within the rule.' *Santley v Wilde* [1899] 2 Ch 474 at 474, 475, CA, per Lindley MR

'The doctrine "Once a mortgage always a mortgage" means that no contract between a mortgagor and a mortgagee, made at the time of the mortgage and as part of the mortgage transaction, or, in other words, as one of the terms of the loan, can be valid if it prevents the mortgagor from getting back his property on paying off what is due on his security. Any bargain which has that effect is invalid, and is inconsistent with the transaction being a mortgage.' *Samuel v Jarrah Timber & Wood Paving Corpn Ltd* [1904] AC 323 at 329, per Lord Lindley

'In my opinion, a mortgage . . . covers not only legal mortgages but also equitable mortgages of all kinds, that is to say, all charges created by contract to secure debts or engagements, even although not evidenced by deed or even by writing, as e.g., a charge created by deposit of title deeds. . . . Nevertheless, whilst fully recognising that the word "mortgage" has in modern times received a wider meaning than was formerly given to it, I am clearly of opinion that even according to its extended meaning it does not include a vendor's lien, and that unpaid purchase money owing to a vendor cannot properly be called money secured to him on mortgage.' *Re Beirnstein, Barnett v Beirnstein* [1925] Ch 12 at 18, per Lawrence J

Australia 'Under the general law "a mortgage is a conveyance of land or an assignment of chattels as a security for the payment of a debt or the discharge of some other obligation for which it is given" [*Santley v Wilde*, supra]. Consequently, under the general law a mortgage of land is appropriate to secure the performance of any kind of obligation. However, it is most frequently used to secure a money debt, in particular a money loan. Australian Torrens title legislation draws a distinction between a mortgage and an encumbrance and in so doing uses the word "mortgage" to describe a form of security which is significantly different from the conception of a mortgage at common law and in equity. The statutory mortgage under the Real Property Acts is not a conveyance or transfer of the mortgagor's estate or interest in the land; it is a charge on that estate or interest, as indeed is an incumbrance. What is more important for present purposes is that the statutory definitions of "mortgage" in the real property statutes in Australia restrict it in accordance with its more common exemplifications, to cases in which security is taken for a debt or a loan. Thus, in s 3 of the Real Property Act 1900 (NSW), as amended, "mortgage" is defined so as to mean "any charge on land created merely for securing a debt" and "encumbrance" is defined to mean "any charge on land created for the purpose of securing the payment of an annuity or sum of money other than a debt."' *Cambridge Credit Corpn Ltd v Lombard Australia Ltd* (1977) 136 CLR 608 at 615, per cur.

Charge by way of legal mortgage

'Charge by way of legal mortgage' means a mortgage created by charge under which, by virtue of the Law of Property Act 1925, the mortgagee is to be treated as an estate owner in like manner as if a mortgage term by demise or subdemise were vested in him, and 'legal mortgage' has the same meaning as in that Act. (Land Registration Act 1925, s 3)

Consolidation of mortgage *See* CONSOLIDATION

Equitable mortgage

An equitable mortgage is a contract which creates a charge on the property but does not convey any legal estate or interest to the creditor; such a charge amounts to an equitable interest. Its operation is that of an executory assurance which, as between the parties, and so far as equitable rights and remedies are concerned, is equivalent to an actual assurance. and is enforceable under the court's equitable jurisdiction. (32 Halsbury's Laws (4th edn) para 405)

Legal mortgage

A legal mortgage of personal property is a conditional assignment to the mortgagee of the mortgagor's legal interest in it. A legal mortgage of land or an interest in land must be by deed. A legal mortgage of an estate in fee simple in land or a term of years absolute is effected by a demise or sub-demise for a term of years absolute, or is a charge by deed expressed to be by way of legal mortgage. (32 Halsbury's Laws (4th edn) para 404)

'Legal mortgage' means a mortgage by demise or sub-demise or a charge by way of legal mortgage, and 'legal mortgagee' has a corresponding meaning. (Settled Land Act 1925, s 117)

'I . . . think that a "legal mortgage" means a "first mortgage" for a second mortgage is not, properly speaking, a "legal mortgage" as it conveys no legal interest.' *Thompson v Clark* (1862) 3 F & F 181 at 183, per Cockburn CJ

Puisne mortgage

A legal mortgage which is not protected by a deposit of documents relating to the legal estate affected. (32 Halsbury's Laws (4th edn) para 544)

'Puisne mortgage' means a legal mortgage not protected by a deposit of documents relating to the legal estate affected. (Law of Property Act 1969, s 30(1))

MOTION *See* IN MOTION

MOTION PICTURES *See also* CINEMATOGRAPH FILM; FILM

United States 'Motion pictures' are audiovisual works consisting of a series of related images which, when shown in succession, impart an impression of motion, together with accompanying sound, if any. (Copyright Act of 1976, s 101)

MOTIVE *See also* INTENTION

'On this question of what amounts to an actionable conspiracy "to injure" (I am assuming that damage results from it), I would first observe that some confusion may arise from the use of such words as "motive" and "intention". Lord Dunedin in *Sorrell v Smith*, [[1925] AC 700 at 724], appears to use the two words interchangeably. There is the further difficulty that, in some branches of the law, "intention" may be understood to cover results which may reasonably flow from what is deliberately done, on the principle that a man is to be treated as intending the reasonable consequence of his acts. Nothing of the sort appears to be involved here. It is much safer to use a word like "purpose" or "object". The question to be answered, in determining whether a combination to do an act which damages others is actionable, even though it would not be actionable if done by a single person, is not "did the combiners appreciate, or should they be treated as appreciating, that others would suffer from their action", but "what is the real reason why the combiners did it?" Or, as Lord Cave puts it, "what is the real purpose of the combination?" The test is not what is the natural result to the plaintiffs of such combined action, or what is the resulting damage which the defendants realise or should realise will follow, but what is in truth the object in the minds of the combiners when they acted as they did. . . . The analysis of human impulses soon leads us into the quagmire of mixed motives, and even if we avoid the word "motive" there may be more than a single purpose or object. It is enough to say that if there is more than one purpose actuating a combination, liability must depend on ascertaining the predominant purpose. If that predominant purpose is to damage another person and damage results, that is tortious conspiracy.' *Crofter Hand Woven Harris Tweed Co Ltd v Veitch* [1942] AC 435 at 444, 445, per Lord Simon LC

'I should add that "motive" is clearly not the same thing as "intention", but in many cases the one is the parent of the other, and they are so closely related that they cannot be separated.' Ibid at 452, per Lord Maugham

'The words "motive", "object", "purpose", are in application to practical matters difficult strictly to define or distinguish. Sometimes mere animus, such as spite or ill-will, malevolence or a wanton desire to harm without any view to personal benefit is meant. But motive is often used as meaning purpose, something objective and external, as contrasted with a mere mental state.' Ibid at 469, per Lord Wright

'It has been pointed out more than once that "motive" has two distinct but related meanings. I do not claim to say which sense is correct. Both are used but it is important to realise that they are not the same. In the first sense "motive" means an emotion prompting an act. . . . The motive for murder in this sense may be jealousy, fear, hatred, desire for money, perverted lust, or even, as in so called "mercy killings", compassion or love. In this sense motive is entirely distinct from intention or purpose. It is the emotion which gives rise to the intention and it is the latter and not the former which converts an actus reus into a criminal act. . . . On the other hand "motive" can mean a "kind of intention" [Glanville Williams, Criminal Law (1961), p 48]. . . . It is however, important to realise that in the second sense too, motive, which in that sense is to be equated with the ultimate "end" of a course of action, often described as its "purpose" or "object", although "a kind of intention", is not co-extensive with intention, which embraces, in addition to the end, all the necessary consequences of an action including the means to the end and any consequences intended along with the end.' *Hyam v Director of Public Prosecutions* [1974] 2 All ER 41 at 51, HL, per Lord Hailsham of St Marylebone

Canada 'In ordinary parlance the words "intent" and "motive" are frequently used interchangeably, but in the criminal law they are distinct. In most criminal trials, the mental element, the mens rea with which the court is concerned relates to "intent", i.e. the exercise of a free will to use particular means to produce a particular result, rather than with "motive", i.e. that which precedes and induces the exercise of the will. The mental element of a crime ordinarily involves no reference to motive: [11 Halsbury's Laws (4th edn) para 11]. Difficulty arises, however, from the vagueness in law of the notion of "motive". There would appear to be substantial agreement amongst textwriters that there are two possible meanings to be ascribed to the term. Glanville Williams in his Criminal Law, The General Part (2nd edn, 1961) distinguishes between these meanings: (I) It sometimes refers to the emotion prompting an act, e.g. "D killed P, his wife's lover, from a motive of jealousy." (2) It sometimes means a kind of intention, e.g., "D killed P with the motive (intention desire) of stopping him from paying attentions to D's wife." (p 48) It is this second sense, according to Williams, which is employed in criminal law: Motive is ulterior intention—the intention with which an intentional act is done (or, more clearly, the intention with which an intentional consequence is brought about). Intention, when distinguished from motive, relates to the means, motive to the end (p 48). . . . In the case at bar, the parties have employed the notion of "motive" in the second of Williams' senses. Accepting the term "motive" in a criminal law sense as meaning "ulterior intention" . . .' *Lewis v R* [1979] 2 SCR 821 at 831–832, SCC, per Dickson J

MOTOR CAR *See also* VEHICLE

In this Act 'motor car' means a mechanically propelled vehicle, not being a motorcycle or an invalid carriage, which is constructed itself to carry a load or passengers and the weight of which unladen—

(a) if it is constructed solely for the carriage of passengers and their effects, is adapted to carry not more than 7 passengers exclusive of the driver and is fitted with tyres of such type as may be specified in regulations made by the Secretary of State, does not exceed 3,050 kilograms:

(b) if it is constructed or adapted for use for the conveyance of goods or burden of any description, does not exceed 3,050 kilograms or 3,500 kilograms if the vehicle carries a container or containers for holding for the purposes of its propulsion any fuel which is wholly gaseous at 17.5 degrees Celsius under a pressure of 1.013 bar or plant and materials for producing such fuel or

(c) does not exceed 2,540 kilograms in a case not falling within sub-paragraph (a) or (b) above.

(Road Traffic Act 1988, s 185(1))

'The term "motor car" . . . suggests to the mind of anyone the idea of a vehicle that is mounted on wheels upon which it runs over the surface of land—a vehicle which is guided and controlled by a person riding upon or in it; is designed and intended to carry one or more persons, and is propelled by power, not supplied from any source external to itself, but which is for the time being stored or generated within it. It is a self-moving vehicle. Its French name, automobile, denotes this quality. The terms "motor waggon" and "motor lorry" connote vehicles of much the same character, save that both are specially designed, intended, and fashioned for the carriage of goods, the latter for the carriage of very heavy goods, and the former for that of goods of a lighter description; each of the three having this characteristic, that it is designed and intended to carry as a load something in addition to its own equipment.' *Falkiner v Whitton* [1917] AC 106 at 110, PC, per cur.

Automobile

Canada 'In *Ross Southward Tire Ltd v Pyrotech Products Ltd* [1976] 2 SCR 35 at 39, 57 DLR (3d) 248, Laskin CJC applied to the construction of the terms of a lease "the ordinary test of reading it reasonably and in a business sense." Applying this test, I am of the view that in common understanding a motorcycle is not equated with an automobile. Let us consider the case of a man who receives a telephone call from a friend to invite him to have a ride in his new automobile. He accepts the invitation. The friend arrives with a motorcycle provided with a pillion. I think the man would be considerably startled and might well reconsider his acceptance of the invitation. A motorcycle, having two wheels, is a much different means of conveyance of a passenger than an automobile, and many would consider the risks to a passenger were greater and the comfort considerably less. Further, a motorcycle is not designed primarily to carry more than one passenger, whereas the word in the phrase in the insuring agreement defining "automobile" is in the plural, i.e. "passengers", a word inapplicable to the passenger-carrying capacity of a motorcycle. This internal definition can be neither ignored nor amended.' *Thomeus v Mutual of Omaha Insurance Co* (1978) 5 Alta LR (2d) 168 at 172, Alta CA, per Clement JA

Heavy motor car

In this Act 'heavy motor car' means a mechanically propelled vehicle, not being a motor car, which is constructed itself to carry a load or passengers and the weight of which unladen exceeds 2,540 kilograms. (Road Traffic Act 1988, s 185(1))

MOTOR CYCLE

In this Act . . . 'motor cycle' means a mechanically propelled vehicle not being an invalid carriage with less than four wheels, and the weight of which unladen does not exceed 410 kilograms. (Road Traffic Act 1988, s 185(1))

MOTOR DEALER *See* DEAL–DEALER

MOTOR INSURANCE *See* INSURANCE

MOTOR TRACTOR

In this Act 'motor tractor' means a mechanically propelled vehicle which is not constructed itself to carry a load, other than the excepted articles [e.g. water, fuel, tools etc], and the weight of which unladen does not exceed 7,370 kilograms. (Road Traffic Act 1988, s 185(1))

MOTOR VEHICLE *See* MOTOR CAR; VEHICLE

MOVABLE DWELLING

The expression 'movable dwelling' includes any tent, any van or other conveyance whether on wheels or not, and, subject as hereinafter provided, any shed or similar structure, being a tent, conveyance or structure which is used regularly, or at certain seasons only, or intermittently, for human habitation.

Provided that it does not include a structure to which the building regulations apply. (Public Health Act 1936, s 269(8)(i), as amended by the Building Act 1984, s 133(1), Sch 6)

MOVABLE PROPERTY

'Moveables' means any moveable tangible property, other than the ship, and includes money, valuable securities, and other documents. (Marine Insurance Act 1906, s 90)

'I am of opinion that the word movables in this will comprehends only corporeal movables, though if there was nothing to restrain the meaning of it in this clause or in the other parts of the will, the word would take in the whole purely personal estate: The words plate, jewels, pictures, linen, will not confine the generality of the word, though they are only corporeal things, for etc must signify *et ceteræ mobilia*; nor is the sense of it restrained by the exception: But the testator, by saying that his wife should have £6,000 South Sea stock, besides all his movables shows that in his understanding of the word, movables would not comprehend stock.' *Steignes v Steignes* (1730) Mos 296 at 297, per Varny MR

'Their lordships . . . hold the words "movable property" to include money.' *Asghar Ali Khan v Kurshed Ali Khan* (1901) 17 TLR 715 at 716, PC per cur.

'The terms "movable" and "immovable" are not technical terms in English law, though they are often used, and conveniently used, in considering questions arising between our law and foreign systems which differ from our law. . . . Dicey (2nd edn, pp 76, 496) states that "immovable property includes all rights over things which cannot be moved, whatever be the nature of such rights or interests".' *Re Hoyles, Row v Jagg* [1911] 1 Ch 179 at 183, CA, per Cozens-Hardy MR

'The division into movable and immovable is only called into operation here when the English courts have to determine rights between domiciled Englishmen and persons domiciled in countries which do not adopt our division into real and personal property. In such cases, out of international comity and in order to arrive at a common basis on which to determine questions between the inhabitants of two countries living under different systems of jurisprudence, our courts recognise and act on a division otherwise unknown to our law into movable and immovable. But when there is no such difficulty there is no ground for attempting any such division.' Ibid at 185, per Farwell LJ

'In *Steignes v Steignes* [supra] it was held that the word "movables" in its full sense takes in all personal chattels. That was a decision given at the Rolls on 17th of February, 1730, and, so far as I am aware that word has never been construed in these courts from that date to this. I think, however, that that case is still authority that the word "movables", apart from any context and standing alone, would be sufficient to cover the whole of the personal estate.' *Re Walsh, Walsh v Walsh* [1953] 1 All ER 982 at 983, 984, per Vaisey J; also reported in [1953] Ch 473 at 478, 479

MULTIPLE LEASE *See* LEASE

MUNICIPAL CORPORATION

'Municipal corporation' means the body corporate constituted by the incorporation of the inhabitants of a borough. (Municipal Corporations Act 1882, s 7)

MUNITIONS OF WAR

The expression 'munitions of war' includes the whole or any part of any ship, submarine, aircraft, tank or similar engine, arms and ammunition, torpedo, or mine, intended or adapted for use in war, and any other article, material, or device, whether actual or proposed, intended for such use. (Official Secrets Act 1911, s 12, as amended by the Official Secrets Act 1920)

MURDER

It is murder for a person of sound memory and of the age of discretion, unlawfully to kill any human creature in being and under the Queen's peace, with malice aforethought, either express or implied by law, provided the victim dies of the injury inflicted within a year and a day of the injury. (11 Halsbury's Laws (4th edn) para 1152)

[The Homicide Act 1957 made amendments to the law of murder. It abolished the doctrine of constructive malice and introduced into English law the doctrine of diminished responsibility.

The death penalty for murder was abolished by the Murder (Abolition of Death Penalty) Act 1965, which Act, at first in force for a trial period only, was made permanent by virtue of an affirmative resolution of both Houses of Parliament in December 1969.]

'We have no doubt that when the word "murder" is found in a statute it has the meaning which has always been attached to it throughout the ages, namely, an unlawful killing with malice aforethought.' *R v Page* [1953] 2 All ER 1355 at 1357, per Lord Goddard CJ

'Killing with the intention [either] to kill or to do some grievous bodily harm.' *R v Vickers* [1957] 2 All ER 741 at 744, CAA, per Lord Goddard CJ

'Murder is the taking of human life by a person who either (a) has a malicious and wilful intent to kill or do grievous bodily harm, or (b) is wickedly reckless as to the consequences of his act upon his victim. For murder there must be an evil intent, that is a criminal intent, although it is not necessary that there should be an intent to kill.' *HM Advocate v Kidd* 1960 SLT 82 at 86, per Lord Strachan

[The following point of law was certified by the Court of Appeal as being of general public importance: 'Is malice aforethought in the crime of murder established by proof beyond reasonable doubt that when doing that act which led to the death of another the accused knew that it was highly probable that the act would result in death or serious bodily harm'] '. . . The one point in this case is the intention which it is necessary to impute to an accused person in order to find him guilty of the crime of murder. . . . I therefore propose the following propositions in answer to the question of general public importance. (1) Before an act can be murder it must be "aimed at someone" as explained in *Director of Public Prosecutions v Smith* [[1960] 3 All ER 161], and must in addition be an act committed with one of the following intentions, the test of which is always subjective to the actual defendant: (i) The intention to cause death; (ii) the intention to cause grievous bodily harm in the sense of that term explained in *Director of Public Prosecutions v Smith*, i.e. really serious injury; (iii) where the defendant knows that there is a serious risk that death or grievous bodily harm will ensue from his acts, and commits those acts deliberately and without lawful excuse, the intention to expose a potential victim to that risk as the result of those acts. It does not matter in such circumstances whether the defendant desires those consequences to ensue or not and in none of these cases does it matter that the act and the intention were aimed at a potential victim other than the one who succumbed. (2) Without an intention of one of these three types the mere fact that the defendant's conduct is done in the knowledge that grievous bodily harm is likely or highly likely to ensue from his conduct is not by itself enough to convert a homicide into the crime of murder.' *Hyam v Director of Public Prosecution* [1974] 2 All ER 41 at 43, 56, HL, per Lord Hailsham of St Marylebone

Australia 'Murder is committed when one human being intentionally kills another human being or inflicts grievous bodily harm on him resulting in that person's death in circumstances which the law does not recognise as affording just cause or excuse for the killing or the infliction of grievous bodily harm. Where you have a killing it may, depending on the circumstances, be murder or manslaughter, or it may be no crime at all.' *R v Newman* [1948] ALR 109 at 110, per Barry J

MUSEUM

'Museum' includes any place permanently used for the exhibition of sculpture, casts, models, or other similar objects. (Sunday Entertainments Act 1932, s 5)

MUSHROOM

For the purposes of this subsection [which deals with picking mushrooms growing wild] 'mushroom' includes any fungus. (Theft Act 1968, s 4(3))

MUSICAL ENTERTAINMENT

'Musical entertainment' means a concert or similar entertainment consisting of the performance of music, with or without singing or recitation. (Sunday Entertainments Act 1932, s 5)

'If a music hall artist appears on the stage and gives an entertainment consisting of patter, that cannot by any stretch of imagination be called a musical entertainment [within the Sunday Entertainments Act 1932, s 5 (supra)] in the nature of a concert merely because there is somebody at the back of the stage playing a piano or even an orchestra which plays so softly that the artist's words can be heard above the music.' *Barnes v Jarvis* [1953] 1 All ER 1061 at 1063, per Lord Goddard CJ

MUST

Australia 'Section 56 of the Justices Act 1902–1986 (WA) requires, with certain immaterial exceptions, that the summons *must* be served on the defendant personally. "Must" is a word of absolute obligation and occurs in a section which is concerned with a fundamental principle of justice. It is not merely directory.' *Posner v Collector for Inter-State Destitute Persons (Victoria)* (1947) 74 CLR 461 at 490, per Williams J

MUTINY

In this Act the expression 'mutiny' means a combination between two or more persons subject to service law, or between persons two at least of whom are subject to service law—

(a) to overthrow or resist lawful authority in Her Majesty's forces or any forces cooperating therewith or in any part of any of the said forces,
(b) to disobey such authority in such circumstances as to make the disobedience subversive of discipline, or with the object of avoiding any duty or service against, or in connection with operations against, the enemy, or
(c) to impede the performance of any duty or service in Her Majesty's forces or in any forces co-operating therewith or in any part of any of the said forces.

(Air Force Act 1955, s 31(3); Army Act 1955, s 31(3) Naval Discipline Act 1957, s 8)

'If, as the witness says, Waugh, in liquor, held up his fists to strike his captain, it is so near an act of mutiny, that it was justifiable at once to quell it by striking the first blow.' *The Lima* (1837) 3 Hag Adm 346 at 353, per Sir John Nicholl

'I cannot understand the argument that because there may have been a mutiny therefore it was not a riot. The two words "mutiny" and "riot" do not seem to me to be mutually exclusive. I do not say that all mutiny is riot, and I do not say that all riot is mutiny, but it is impossible to say that mutiny can never be riot.' *Pitchers v Surrey County Council* [1923] 2 KB 57 at 71, CA, per Lord Sterndale MR

'What is mutiny? There is no doubt that mutiny is a collective offence, that is to say, it cannot be committed by one man. There seem to be cases referred to in text-books of some degree of authority showing that in the Peninsular War soldiers were executed for mutiny though the acts were the acts of individuals and not a combination of individuals, but, whatever may have been thought in the days of the Peninsular War, there is no doubt now that mutiny is an offence which deals with collective insubordination, collective defiance or disregard of authority or refusal to obey authority.' *R v Grant* [1957] 2 All ER 694 at 696, per cur.

N

NAME

'Name' includes any designation. (Plant Varieties and Seeds Act 1964, s 20)

'Name' includes any abbreviation of a name. (Trade Descriptions Act 1972, s 1(6))

'The place in a corporation may well be resembled to the surname of a man, and as a grant made by any person's christian name, as John, Thomas, etc, is not good, so in a corporation it is not good to say, Dean and Chapter, Mayor and Comminalty, and the like, without saying, of what place: And anciently men took most commonly their surnames from their places of habitation, especially men of estate, and artizans often took their names from their arts, but yet the law is not so precise in the case of surnames, and therefore a grant made by, or to John, son and heir of IC or *Filio juniori IS* is good: But for the christian name, this always ought to be perfect. So in the case of a corporation, it sufficeth to have a sufficient demonstration of the place where the corporation is, albeit it be not by the precise words comprised in the Charter: as in naming *Accademia Oxon pro Villa Oxon*, and it is common, of which I have seen divers Charters, where a town was incorporated by the name of Mayor, and Comminalty of such a town, as Bristol, Exeter, and others, which afterwards have been made cities, and yet Charters made to them, and grants made by them, by the name of Mayor and Comminalty of the city is good, but more preciseness is used in the body of the name of a corporation before the place to which they are annexed, and yet in them, that which is but an ornament to the name comprehended in the Charter, shall not hurt the grant, as of Chapiter, of St George of Windsor, if it be of St George the Martyr, and the like, the grant by such a name is good, because the Martyr is but an addition of ornament to the name comprised in the Charter, and it is no other but the same in *re vera*. So here, if it had been *Domini nostri Jesu Christi*, because it is the same, and is but an ornament to the word Christ comprised in the Charter, and so should it be also if it had been *Christi filii Dei Salvatoris nostri*, because it is but a true addition of the same.' *Button v Wrightman* (1594) Poph 56 at 56, 57, per Popham CJ

'The Master of the Rolls, Sir Joseph Jekyll . . . in the case of *Barlow v Bateman* [(1730) 3 P Wms 65], lays down, certainly in very unequivocal terms,—that anyone may take upon him what surname, and as many surnames, as he pleases; and for the term during which he uses such a surname, if he has a right to use it, it is what cannot be denominated an untrue name. I am far from meaning to trench upon the reverance due to any assertion of that great man, when I say, that the solid grounds, upon which this proposition of law is stated, do not appear to have occurred to him just at the moment of the delivery of that judgment—because the reasons stated in that report, can hardly, I think, be deemed satisfactory to produce such a conclusion. It is stated that the reasons are, first, that surnames are not of very great antiquity. It is pretty well now established, that surnames were fully in use, even among the common people, by the reign of Edward the Second, which is now five hundred years ago, a pretty reasonable period for the establishment of any legal usage. It is likewise observed, that, in ancient times, the appellation was by the christian name, and place of habitation—as Thomas of Dale, but which of Dale is of itself merely a surname, a local surname certainly,—but not less a surname on that account; for surnames were local, either taken from places of habitation, or descriptive from other circumstances, that belonged to the individuals, to distinguish men who were not at all distinguished by christian names. They are, many of them, general appellatives. Christian names are scattered about among the mass of the people, with such profusion, that convey little or no distinction, and the very introduction of the surname was to discriminate that, which was not before discriminated. It is observed too by Sir Joseph Jekyll, that the usage of an Act of Parliament for a name is but modern. Certainly it is; and so are Acts for many other private family concerns. They are of modern introduction. But there has been a practice of great antiquity, that is, the grant of a licence, for the assumption of a name, by the Crown, passing through one of its public offices. Certainly, the ancient style of the ancient offices of the Crown is of great authority upon such a subject. However, I would observe likewise upon the confusion that must be produced, to a degree that would compel a legislative correction; if the practice at all followed this rule, that everyone might take what surnames he pleased, and when he pleased. The whole world would be at hide and seek about identity, in the concerns of almost every individual.' *Wakefield v Mackay* (1807) 1 Hag Con 394 at 399–401, per Sir William Scott

[The Patents, Designs and Trade Marks Act 1883, s 64 (repealed; see now the Trade Marks Act 1938, s 9), provided that a trade mark must contain at least one of certain essential particulars, amongst which was the 'name' of an individual or firm printed, impressed or woven in some particular and distinctive manner.] 'I have held that the whole name in the case of a single person need not be placed on the trade-mark. It seems to me that equally the whole name of each partner or the whole name of the firm need not appear on the trade-mark, and that it is sufficient as before if we find that the name is used fairly and bona fide on the face of the trade-mark in such a way that it cannot be mistaken for anything else than the name of the owner of the trade-mark and the manufacturer of the goods to which that mark relates.' *Re Colman's Trade-Mark Application* [1894] 2 Ch 115 at 124, 125, 132, per Stirling J

'The controversy between the parties is . . . reduced to a dispute about the use of a name as distinguished from a dignity. Speaking generally, the law of this country allows any person to assume and use any name, provided its use is not calculated to deceive and to inflict pecuniary loss. Your lordships will find the law on this subject examined in a very instructive note from the pen of the late Mr Waley in 3 Davidson's Conveyancing, Pt I, p 283, 2nd ed. The judgment of Tindal CJ in *Davies v Lowndes* [(1835) 1 Bing NC 597] and of the Privy Council delivered by Lord Chelmsford in *Du Boulay v Du Boulay* [(1869) LR 2 PC 430, PC] leave no doubt about it. Lord Chelmsford in *Du Boulay v Du Boulay* stated that "in this country we do not recognise the absolute right of a person to a particular name to the extent of entitling him to prevent the assumption of that name by a stranger." Then, after alluding to trade names, the judgment continues: "The mere assumption of a name which is the patronymic of a family by a stranger who has never before been called by that name, whatever cause of annoyance it may be to a family, is a grievance for which our law affords no redress".' *Cowley (Earl) v Cowley (Countess)* [1901] AC 450 at 460, per Lord Lindley

See, generally, 30 Halsbury's Laws (4th edn) paras 796–800.

Geographical name *See* GEOGRAPHICAL NAME

'Name and blood'

[A testator devised his estates with ultimate remainder to the first and nearest of his kindred being male and of his 'name and blood'.] 'In a general sense the being of a man's kindred is being of his blood; as the word "consanguinity", which is the same as "kindred", imports; but when, in addition to being of his kindred a testator requires, that the object of his bounty shall be of his blood, he must be understood as speaking of that blood, which with some propriety may be called his; namely that, which in tracing an heir is considered as the blood of the most dignity and worth. Such in this case is the blood of the Leighs in contradistinction to that of any other of the testator's ancestors. When therefore he required, that the remainderman should be of his blood, in addition to his being of his kindred, his object was, as I conceive, to ascertain, that stock or family, to which the devisee should belong. . . . The next thing to be considered is, what did the testator mean by requiring, that the remainderman should be of his name; and I do not think, that this testator by the words "of my name" meant the stock or family of Leigh; for according to the common rule of interpretation, which requires, especially in wills, that every word shall have some effect given to it, if it may be, and none rejected, or considered as tautologous, if a distinct and consistent meaning can be put upon it, the testator must be taken to have intended something beyond what was expressed and contained in the other words, which he had used; and, I think, a very obvious meaning may be put upon the word "name" different from, and consistent with that, which, I think, belongs to the word blood; and that it must be understood as intended to exclude the female line of the stock or family of the Leighs; which stock he may be understood as marking with the word "blood" and as intended to narrow the number of persons of that family or stock, from among whom a remainderman was to be sought for; by requiring, that the family name of such person should be Leigh; or, in other words, that he should be a person having the name of Leigh from his agnation to the testator; thereby excluding any person, who could only claim to be of kin with the testator by descent from a female of his family.' *Leigh v Leigh* (1808) 15 Ves 92 at 107, 108, per Lawrence J

NAMED

'It cannot be denied that the word "named" although its primary signification may be "mentioned by name" is also used, and used in no unnatural sense, as synonymous with "specified" or "mentioned"; and I do not think that there is any hard and fast rule to be laid down that in construing a will you are always to give to any particular word that is used what is called its primary meaning.' *Seale-Hayne v Jodrell* [1891] AC 304 at 306, per Lord Herschell

[The articles of association of a company provided that no person might vote or act as a proxy unless the instrument appointing him had been deposited at the registered office of the company not less than a specified period before the meeting at which the person 'named' in the instrument proposed to vote.] 'The objections taken to the proxy are . . . that Mr Macaulay is not named in it. . . . Although not named in it, in the strict literal sense of the word "named", he was sufficiently described in the proxy for all business purposes, and in their Lordships' opinion the articles require nothing more.' *Bombay-Burmah Trading Corpn v Dorabji Cursetji Shroff* [1905] AC 213 at 218, PC, per cur.

NARROW CHANNEL *See* CHANNEL

NATIONAL DEBT

The National Debt of the United Kingdom in its present form had its origin in a loan of £1,200,000 at 8 per cent made to the Crown in 1694 on the security of the public funds, the subscribers being incorporated as the Bank of England. Now an account, known as the National Loans Fund, exists at the Bank of England for which the Treasury is responsible. Money paid into this account forms one general fund to meet all outgoings. Excess of payments out of the National Loans Fund over receipts into it are provided for by money being raised in such manner and on such terms and conditions as the Treasury thinks fit.

The National Debt of the United Kingdom is divided into the External Debt, consisting of money borrowed from the governments of Canada, the United States of America and other overseas countries, and the Internal Debt, consisting of the Funded Debt and the Unfunded Debt.

The Funded Debt is debt the principal of which the government need not repay until it wishes. It consists of the debts to the Banks of England and Ireland and, for the greater part, of undated government securities, that is to say securities not redeemable at any fixed date, for example, 2½ per cent Consols, 2¾ and 2½ per cent perpetual annuities, and 3½ per cent War Loan and 3 per cent Treasury stock issued in exchange for Bank of England stock. The process of reborrowing for a longer period, thus moving towards having no fixed date of redemption, is usually described as funding.

The Unfunded Debt is debt the principal of which must be repaid at a definite date. It consists of all government internal borrowing apart from the Funded Debt, including, for example, savings bonds and defence bonds, funding stocks, premium savings bonds, savings certificates, and certificates of tax deposit, and what is often referred to as the Floating Debt which is made up of Treasury bills and Ways and Means advances from the Bank of England, the Paymaster General, the National Debt Commissioners and certain other departments. Government stocks issued to the former owners of certain nationalised industries, that is to say the coal industry, Cable and Wireless Limited and the iron and steel industry, are included in the Unfunded Debt. (32 Halsbury's Laws (4th edn) paras 218–220)

NATIONALITY

'Whether a person is a national of a country must be determined by the municipal law of that country. Upon this I think all text writers are agreed. It would be strange were it otherwise. How could the municipal law of England determine that a person *is* a national of Germany? It might determine that for the purposes of English municipal law a person shall be deemed to be a national of Germany, or shall be treated as if he were a national of Germany; but that would not constitute him a national of

Germany, if he were not such according to the municipal law of Germany. In truth there is not and cannot be such an individual as a German national according to English law.' *Stoeck v Public Trustee* [1921] 2 Ch 67 at 82, per Russell J

'A person who was a Hungarian national in the days when Hungary was a kingdom does not cease to be a Hungarian national merely because Hungary ceases to be a kingdom or merely because she is dispossessed of part of her former territories. A person, for instance, who was residing in South America at the outbreak of the war and was then a Hungarian national has not, in the absence of other circumstances, lost his nationality. It would not be true to say that whereas he was formerly a national of the kingdom of Hungary he is now a national of the Hungarian Republic. He was, and he remains, a Hungarian national.' *Groedel v Hungarian Property Administrator* (1927) 44 TLR 65 at 66, per Romer J

'"Nationality", in the sense of citizenship of a certain state, must not be confused with "nationality" as meaning membership of a certain nation in the sense of race. Thus, according to international law, Englishmen and Scotsmen are, despite their different nationality as regards race, all of British nationality as regards citizenship. Thus further, although all Polish individuals are of Polish nationality qua race, for many generations there were no Poles qua "citizenship". Just as "nationality" can be used in these two senses, so can the word "national". Bearing in mind the racial objects of the 1965 and 1968 [Race Relations] Acts [see now Race Relations Act 1976], and that the words "national origins" with the other words with which it appears explain what is meant by the word "racial" in the long title, I think that the word "national" in "national origins" means national in the sense of race and not citizenship.' *London Borough of Ealing v Race Relations Board* [1972] 1 All ER 104 at 112, HL, per Viscount Dilhorne

[*See* generally, as to nationality and citizenship the British Nationality Acts 1981 and 1983. The former amends the Immigration Act 1971 as regards the right of abode in the United Kingdom.]

NATURAL

'Their lordships must now make their own examination of the case law [on nuisance]. They find the most striking feature to be the variety of words used: and that is not very surprising because in the great majority of cases the facts were such that it made no difference whether the damage was said to be the direct or the natural or probable or foreseeable result of the nuisance. The word "natural" is found very often, and it is peculiarly ambiguous. It can and often does mean a result which one would naturally expect, i.e. which would not be surprising: or it can mean the result at the end of a chain of causation unbroken by any conscious act, the result produced by so-called natural laws however surprising or even unforeseeable in the particular case.' *The Wagon Mound (No 2), Overseas Tankship (UK) Ltd v Miller Steamship Co Pty Ltd* [1966] 2 All ER 709 at 713, PC, per Lord Reid

Natural children

[A testatrix by her will left a life interest in her property to Edward Bentley, with remainder to his 'natural children'.] 'The well established doctrine is, that where there is a gift to children as a class, then, unless there are words so clear as necessarily to apply to and include illegitimate children, or clearly to exclude any but such children, I must hold that the description will include legitimate children only. Now, in this case the gift is so expressed as clearly to exclude all but illegitimate children. The testatrix was living with the plaintiff, and if I find, when she talked of illegitimate children, persons in existence to answer the description as objects of her bounty, I cannot do less than give the property to them. The law will not contemplate the notion that there can be future illegitimate children, and therefore I must consider that the testatrix meant to give her property to the children which she had had by the plaintiff; but if they died in his lifetime, then there will be an intestacy. I shall declare that the defendants, the children of Mrs Blizard, are the persons described as the natural children of Edward Bourne Bentley.' *Bentley v Blizard* (1858) 4 Jur NS 652 at 652, per Stuart V-C

Natural consequences

'It is argued that the respondent is liable for any damage, which is "a natural consequence" or "a natural and necessary consequence" of his breach of duty. . . . What are "natural, probable, and necessary" consequences? Everything that happens, happens in the order of nature and is therefore "natural". Nothing that happens by the free choice of a thinking man is "necessary", except in the sense of predestination. To speak of "probable" consequence is to throw everything upon the jury. It is tautologous to speak of "effective" cause or to say that damages too remote from the cause are irrecoverable, for an effective cause is simply that which causes, and in law what is ineffective or too remote is not a cause at all. I still venture to think that direct cause is the best expression. Proximate cause has acquired a special connotation through its use in reference to contracts of insurance. Direct cause excludes what is indirect, conveys the essential distinction, which *causa causans* and *causa sine qua non* rather cumbrously indicate, and is consistent with the possibility of the concurrence of more direct causes than one, operating at the same time and leading to a common result.' *Weld-Blundell v Stephens* [1920] AC 956 at 983, 984, per Lord Sumner

Natural representatives

'The testator gives the residue of his personal estate "upon trust to pay and divide the same unto and equally between and among all and every my children, whether sons or daughters who shall then be living or their natural representatives, if dead, according to the statute rule of distribution". Now the primary meaning of the word "representatives" is, of course, "executors or administrators". No one, however, suggests such a meaning here. Indeed, it would be impossible to read it so here in conjunction with the word "natural". There are two other constructions which are open. Representatives may mean the persons who represent the estate of the testator . . . or the persons who are called . . . representatives, being lineal descendants of the intestate. In my opinion, the whole key to this case depends on the meaning of the word "natural". Now, it is not an uncommon thing to speak of lawful and natural children, but it is not a usual phrase to speak of a lawful and natural wife. The wife's position is a contractual one, and that of children, owing to nature, is one by affinity of blood. The testator therefore meant such persons as by nature represented the children, and he intended to exclude contractual relations. . . . In my opinion, therefore, the widow here is excluded.' *Re Bromley, Wilson v Bromley* (1900) 83 LT 315 at 316, per Farwell J

Natural stream or watercourse

'If there is a natural flow of water in a defined channel for a certain distance, I cannot see that it is less a natural stream or watercourse [within the Public Health Act 1875, s 17 (repealed; see now Public Health Act 1936, s 30)] because lower down the physical or geological conditions may be such that the stream burrows into the land or is gradually absorbed by it.' *Maxwell Willshire v Bromley Rural Council* (1917) 87 LJ Ch 241 at 243, per Sargant J

Natural water

[Certain water in bottles was sold by the defendant company under the description 'natural' mineral water. A summons was issued against the company for applying a false trade description.] 'I think it was not false in a material particular to describe this Apollinaris water as a "natural mineral water". To begin with, it was a natural mineral water in the ordinary sense as distinguished from a manufactured mineral water, but it was not of the exact constitution of the water as it came from the spring. The evidence appears to be that it could not be preserved in the exact condition in which it was, and that it went through some processes which preserved it as nearly as possible.' *Davenport v Apollinaris Co Ltd* (1903) 89 LT 19 at 21, DC, per Channell J

NATURAL GAS

'Natural gas' means any gas derived from natural strata (including gas originating outside the United Kingdom). (Gas Act 1965, s 28)

[*See also* the Gas Act 1972, s 48(1).]

NATURAL JUSTICE

[The General Medical Council, having refused to hear certain evidence tendered by a medical practitioner, directed that his name should be erased from the register. The practitioner contended that the due inquiry required by the Medical Act 1858, s 29 (repealed; cf now the Medicines Act 1983, ss 1, 43, Sch 4) had not been held, and that there had been a failure of 'natural justice'.] '"Natural justice" seems to be used in contrast with any formal or technical rule of law or procedure. Some light on what it connotes may be got from the authorities, to certain of which I now refer. Thus *Spackman v Plumstead Board of Works* [(1885) 10 App Cas 229] was a case of administrative decision in a matter of local government. Under the relevant Act an architect's certificate was made conclusive for fixing a general line for buildings. The Earl of Selborne, at p 240, made some general observations, and said: "No doubt in the absence of special provision as to how the person who is to decide is to proceed, the law will imply no more than that *the substantial requirements of justice* shall not be violated. He is not a judge in the proper sense of the word; but he must give the parties an opportunity of being heard before him and stating their case and their view. He must give notice that he will proceed with the matter, and he must act honestly and impartially and not under the dictation of some other person or persons to whom the authority is not given by law. There must be no malversation of any kind. There could be no decision within the meaning of the statute if there were anything of that sort done contrary to *the essence of justice*." I have italicised the two phrases which the Earl of Selborne seems to me to use as meaning what is generally meant by "natural justice". . . . I ought at least to quote what was said by Bowen LJ, in *Leeson's* case [*Leeson v General Medical Council* (1889) 43 Ch D 366, CA], at p 383. He said: ". . . The substantial elements of natural justice must be found to have been present at the inquiry. There must be due inquiry. The accused person must have notice of what he is accused. He must have an opportunity of being heard, and the decision must be honestly arrived at after he has had a full opportunity of being heard. . . ." In *Arlidge's* case [*Local Government Board v Arlidge* [1915] AC 120], Hamilton LJ, is quoted at p 130, as describing the phrase "contrary to natural justice" as "an expression sadly lacking in precision". So it may be and perhaps it is not desirable to attempt to force it into any procrustean bed. But the statements which I have quoted may at least be taken to emphasise the essential requirements that the tribunal should be impartial and that the medical practitioner who is impugned should be given a full and fair opportunity of being heard.' *General Medical Council v Spackman* [1943] 2 All ER 337 at 343, HL, per Lord Wright

'If one accepts that "natural justice" is a flexible term which imposes different requirements in different cases, it is capable of applying appropriately to the whole range of situations indicated by terms such as "judicial", "quasi-judicial" and "administrative". Nevertheless, the further the situation is away from anything that resembles a judicial or quasi-judicial situation, and the further the question is removed from what may reasonably be called a justiciable question, the more appropriate it is to reject an expression which includes the word "justice" and to use instead terms such as "fairness", or "the duty to act fairly". The suitability of the term "fairness" in such cases is increased by the curiosities of the expression "natural justice". Justice is far from being a "natural" concept. The closer one goes to a state of nature the less justice does one find. Justice, and with it "natural justice", is in truth an elaborate and artificial product of civilisation which varies with different civilisations.' *McInnes v Onslow Fane* [1978] 3 All ER 211 at 219, per Megarry V-C

'The phrase "the requirements of natural justice" seems to be mesmerising people at the moment. This must, I think, be due to the apposition of the words "natural" and "justice". It has been pointed out many times that the word "natural" adds nothing except perhaps a hint of nostalgia for the good old days when nasty things did not happen. If, instead, we omit it and put the question in the form stated in *Fisher v Keane* [(1878) 11 Ch D 353]: have the ordinary principles of justice been complied with? it at once becomes much more realistic and even mundane. It is just possible that the pleader in the present case might have hesitated a little longer if he had been deprived of the use of that romantic word "natural". Another source of confusion is the automatic identification of the phrase "natural justice" with giving the person concerned an opportunity of stating his side of the story, and so on. In many cases, of course, the two are synonymous but not by any means in all.' *Norwest Holst Ltd v Department of Trade* [1978] 3 All ER 280 at 294, CA, per Ormrod LJ

NATURE

Of voyage

[Statute (1835) 5 & 6 Will. 4, c 19 (repealed), provided that the 'nature of the voyage' must be stated in a ship's articles.] 'In interpreting the Act of Parliament the words "nature of the voyage" must have such a rational construction as to answer the main and leading purpose for which they were framed, namely, to give the mariner a fair intimation of the nature of the service in which he was about to engage himself when he signed the ship's articles.' *The Westmorland* (1841) 1 Wm Rob 216 at 228, per Dr Lushington

NATURE CONSERVATION *See* CONSERVATION

NATURE RESERVE

In this Part [Part III: nature conservation] of this Act the expression 'nature reserve' means land managed for the purpose—

(a) of providing, under suitable conditions and control, special opportunities for the study of, and research into, matters relating to the fauna and flora of Great Britain and the physical conditions in which they live, and for the study of geological and physiographical features of special interest in the area, or

(b) of preserving flora, fauna or geological or physiographical features of special interest in the area,

or for both those purposes. (National Parks and Access to the Countryside Act 1949, s 15)

NAVAL PROPERTY

'Naval property' means any chattel of any description belonging to Her Majesty, which has been issued for use for naval purposes or is held in store for the purpose of being so issued when required, and includes any chattel which had belonged, and had been issued or held, as aforesaid at some past time. (Naval Discipline Act 1957, s 98(3))

NAVAL SERVICE

'Naval service' shall, as respects a person, include service as a marine, employment as a pilot in piloting or directing the course of a ship of war or other ship when such ship of war or other ship is being used in any military or naval operation, and any employment whatever on board a ship of war, transport, store ship, privateer or ship under letters of marque; and as respects a ship, include any user of a ship as a transport, store ship, privateer or ship under letters of marque. (Foreign Enlistment Act 1870, s 30)

NAVIGABLE RIVER

'The test of a navigable river is its navigability and the flux and reflux of the sea. No river was ever held to be navigable so as to vest the soil in the Crown, and to vest in the public the right to fish, merely because the river became a "public highway". . . . "Navigable" and "tidal", as applied to a river, are synonymous in law, though the former has a popular as well as a legal meaning. I adopt the statement of Chancellor Kent, which will be found to be supported by authority. "In the common law sense of the term, those [rivers] only were deemed navigable in which the tide ebbed and flowed," 3 Kent Com 11th ed 520.' *Murphy v Ryan* (1868) 16 WR 678 at 680, per cur.

'As stated in *Murphy v Ryan* [supra] . . . the word navigable has a popular and also a legal and technical meaning, and . . . this legal and technical meaning, although no doubt essentially requiring navigation to be possible, requires also something more—namely, the ebb and flow of the tide. The history of this limit of distinction between waters which are technically navigable and those which are not is far too long and intricate for examination here. Such an examination would involve reference to many ancient writers, such as Lord Coke and Lord Hale, supplemented by others who have contributed much learning on those and other curious branches of law—as, for instance, Mr Angell, the 13th Chapter of whose work on watercourses, contrasting, as it does the laws of England and America, deserves more attention than I have been able to give to it, and Chancellor Kent, whose Commentaries have often been quoted in connection with this subject. He devotes a section in the second part of his Commentaries to the division line, which has exercised the minds of many writers, between the jurisdiction of the Admiralty and of courts of common law. That division line has had something to do with the matter in hand, and so has also the broad common sense which so often underlies the principles of English law and their application to the affairs of daily life. I am far from saying that the legal and technical meaning of "navigable" has been plainly rested upon any such practical reason as that navigation is impossible for any useful purpose of trade or commerce except where the tide ebbs and flows; but yet I cannot read any of the numerous treatises, whether in text-books or judicial decisions on the subject, without concluding that this practical reason is at the bottom of it.' *Ilchester (Earl) v Raishleigh* (1889) 61 LT 477 at 479, per Kekewich J

'"The flowing and re-flowing of the tide does not make it so," i.e., a navigable river, "for there are many places into which the tide flows which are not navigable rivers; and the place in question may be a creek in their own private estate": per Lord Mansfield in *Mayor of Lynn v Turner* [(1774) 1 Cowp 86]. . . . The flowing of the tide is strong prima facie evidence of the existence of a public navigable river, but whether it is one or not depends upon the situation and nature of the channel. Not every ditch or cutting which is reached by the tide forms part of the public navigable river, even though it be large enough to admit of the passage of a boat. The question is one of degree, and is for the jury, having regard to all the facts.' *Sim E Bak v Ang Yong Huat* [1923] AC 429 at 433, 434, per cur.

NAVIGATION

'*Good v London Steam-Ship Owners' Assocn* [(1871) LR 6 CP 563] was relied on, in which it was held that an injury which happened to a ship moored at a quay where she was lying, having put back to coal, and which injury was owing to the negligent leaving open of a sea-cock, was "damage caused by reason of improper navigation", within the meaning of a deed by which an association of ship-owners agreed to indemnify each other against "loss or damage which by reason of the improper navigation of any such ship may be caused to any goods on board." In that case Willes J said: "Improper navigation, within the meaning of this deed, is, something improperly done . . . in the course of the voyage." I do not think that the case assists the decision of that before me, beyond being an authority for the proposition that the ship need not be in a state of motion in order to be in a state of navigation, within the meaning of that word as used in the deed there in question. Other cases have decided that the word "navigation" for some purposes includes a period when the ship is not in motion; as, for instance, when she is at anchor.' *Hayn v Culliford* (1878) 3 CPD 410 at 417, per Denman J; affirmed (1879) 4 CPD 182, CA

'We have in this case to construe a bye-law. . . . The words are these: "That if any person when . . . navigating any steamboat on the river . . . shall at the same time tow more than six barges, . . . the person . . . navigating the same, shall incur a penalty." . . . All that the tug did was to haul the barges . . . through the gates into the dock. . . . No doubt, as an abstract proposition, the word "navigate" if used in the widest sense of the term, would include such an operation as was conducted here, but I do not think that that operation was a navigation of the tug within the meaning of the bye-law, having regard to the object with which it was framed.' *Rolles v Newell* (1890) 25 QBD 335 at 337–339, DC, per Lord Coleridge CJ

[A vessel, on arriving in London, went into the Victoria Dock to discharge her cargo. During discharge the cargo was damaged by water through negligence in the removal of a bilge-pump.] 'The damage was caused . . . by two combined acts of negligence of the chief engineer and of the workmen from the shore. As regards the latter, it is impossible to say that they were in any sense engaged in the navigation of the ship.' *The Accomac* (1890) 15 PD 208 at 211, per Lord Esher MR

'Without attempting to give an exhaustive definition of navigation, I think that there should in ordinary circumstances at least be an intention to navigate the river as a channel leading from one place to another. Apart from authority, I think that pulling a barge out of dock by a rope, intending that it should be made fast to another barge or to a bollard a little way along the dock wall, there to remain until it is taken away to its destination, . . . is not navigation.' *Gardner, Locket & Hinton Ltd v Doe, Buck v Smith, Keen v Adams* [1906] 2 KB 171 at 184, 185, per Lord Alverstone CJ

[Clause 14 of a charterparty exempted the owners from liability from loss or damage caused by the pilot, master or crew 'in the management or navigation' of the ship.] 'In my opinion the word "navigation" as used in cl 14 refers to a ship which is in motion, a ship which is being navigated. The pilot can hardly make an error in navigation . . . save when the ship is in motion or is being cast off. The word "management" may well be applied to a ship while she is in harbour and also while she is in motion, and the two words taken together denote something done in the user or control of the ship while in harbour or on her voyage. Things done of that nature come within the terms "navigation arrangement", but the deliberate choice, while in harbour, of one of two routes to be pursued cannot, I think, be an error in the "management" or in the "navigation".' *Lord SS (Owners) v Newsum, Sons & Co Ltd* [1920] 1 KB 846 at 849, per Bailhache J

Danger or accident of *See* DANGER

Improper navigation

[An association of steamship owners agreed by deed to indemnify each other against loss of life or personal injury caused by reason of 'improper navigation'.] 'Improper navigation within the meaning of this deed is something improperly done with the ship . . . in the course of the voyage.' *Good v London Steam Ship Owners' Assocn* (1871) LR 6 CP 563 at 569, per Willes J

'Dr Phillimore has referred us to the dictionary for the meaning of the word "navigation"; one of the definitions there given is that navigation is the science or art of conducting a ship from place to place through the water; if that be true it includes the supply of such instruments as are proper for the ship, and such men as are properly skilled in their calling. Skilful mariners, if the ship is not supplied with proper instruments necessary for her locomotion, cannot efficiently and properly conduct her. So also all proper instruments are useless without skilful sailors. If either of these are wanting, and a collision happens, then we have a case of improper navigation.' *The Warkworth* (1884) 9 PD 145 at 148, CA, per Fry LJ

[By the articles of a mutual insurance association the members agreed to indemnify each other against losses, damages, and expenses arising from any loss, etc, caused by 'improper navigation' of the ship carrying goods.] 'Without attempting to define all the cases which may come within the words "improper navigation", I think those words as used in this rule do include every case where something is omitted to be done which ought to be done before the departure of the ship in order to enable the ship to carry the cargo safely from the port of departure to the port of arrival, and where that omission leads to the cargo not being safely and properly so carried.' *Carmichael v Liverpool Sailing Ship Owners' Mutual Indemnity Assocn* (1887) 19 QBD 242 at 249, CA, per Fry LJ

[The rules of an association protected shipowners in respect of loss of or damage to goods caused by the 'improper navigation' of the ship in which the goods were loaded. A cargo of wheat was put into a ship's hold which had not been effectually cleaned, the bottom of the hold being so saturated with creosote that the whole cargo was tainted and spoilt.] 'I should have thought it clear that "damage caused by improper navigation" was equivalent to damage caused by navigation of an improper kind, and consequently that damage, caused by something which was not navigation at all, was not caused by improper navigation. Navigation must mean something having to do with the sailing of the ship; that is, of course, the sailing of the ship having regard to the fact that she is a cargo-carrying ship. Here the damage was caused by something which had nothing to do with the sailing of the ship.' *Canada Shipping Co v British Shipowner's Mutual Protection Assocn* (1889) 23 QBD 342 at 344, CA, per Bowen LJ

'I think that confusion of thought arises when one discusses the negligence of individuals as distinct from improper navigation. Individual negligence does not seem to me to have anything to do with the section, which allows the relief for improper navigation of the ship. Of course the navigation of a ship must be done by individuals, but it is the navigation of the ship which gives a right to limitation of liability, and not the negligence of individuals.' *The Alde* [1926] P 211 at 215, per Bateson J

Navigation authority

'Navigation authority' means any person or body of persons having powers under any enactment or statutory order to work or maintain a canal or other inland navigation, including a navigation in tidal water. (Coast Protection Act 1949, s 49)

'Navigation authority' means a person or body of persons (whether corporate or unincorporate) having a duty or power imposed or conferred by or under an enactment to manage or maintain a canal, whether navigable or not, or to manage or maintain an inland navigation other than a canal, whether natural or artificial and whether tidal or not. (Water Resources Act 1963, s 135)

'Navigation authority' means any person or body having powers under any Act of Parliament to work or maintain a canal or other inland navigation (including a navigation in tidal water). (Land Drainage Act 1976, s 116(1))

'Navigation authority' means persons authorised by any enactment to work, maintain, conserve, improve or control any canal or other inland navigation, navigable river, estuary, harbour or dock. (Highways Act 1980, s 329(1))

[The following comments were made in considering the nature and extent of the common law rights of navigation.] 'So far as these rights are concerned, it must always be remembered that they are rights attached to navigation and that the rights of navigation are analogous to the rights of the public on a highway on land; that is to say, the right of coming and going and doing those things incidental thereto. On a highway I may stand still for a reasonably short time, but I must not put my bed upon the highway and permanently occupy a portion of it. I may stoop to tie up my shoelace, but I may not occupy a pitch and invite people to come upon it and have their hair cut. I may let my van stand long enough to deliver and load goods, but I must not turn my van into a permanent stall. In the same way, so far as navigation is concerned, I may have to wait for a favourable wind; I may have to load or discharge cargo, and I may have to do repairs necessary or desirable before again setting out to sea, but I may not permanently occupy a part of the water over a foreshore even if I am doing something which incidentally assists the navigation of others.' *Iveagh (Earl) v Martin* [1960] 2 All ER 668 at 683, 684, per Paull J

Navigation services

'Navigation services' includes information, directions and other facilities furnished, issued or provided for the purpopses of or in connection with the navigation or movement of aircraft and also the control of movement of vehicles in any part of an aerodrome used for the movement of aircraft. (Airports Authority Act 1975, s 23)

'Air navigation services' includes information, directions and other facilities furnished, issued or provided in connection with the navigation or movement of aircraft, and includes the control of movement of vehicles in any part of an aerodrome used for the movement of aircraft. (Civil Aviation Act 1982, s 105)

NEAR

[A local Act empowered a body of persons to levy tolls from the owners and lessees of collieries 'near' the river Tyne which sold or delivered coal to be exported from or out of the river. The question was whether a colliery ten miles from the river Tyne was within the Act.] 'The word "near" is not a restraining, but an expanding word,—to be extended so far as to give effect to the intention of the legislature. Railways have brought places in one sense near to each other which were not so before the discovery of that rapid mode of transit. It is enough to say that I agree with the rest of the court in thinking that this colliery is near the river Tyne within the meaning of the act.' *Tyne Keelmen v Davison* (1864) 16 CBNS 612 at 622, per Byles J

[The Attorney-General brought an action against the respondent claiming an injunction to restrain him from exercising market rights over certain streets in Stepney. The respondent claimed that by letters patent granted in 1682 the King granted to one Balch, his heirs and assigns the right to hold a market on Thursdays and Saturdays in every week in or 'near' a certain place called Spittle Square. The land called Spittle Square was laid out by Balch or his successors as a market place intersected by four streets, now referred to as the four inner streets; and the land immediately surrounding it was afterwards laid out as Lamb, Commercial, Brushfield and Crispin streets, now referred to as the four outer streets. It was agreed that the respondent held title from Balch's successors.] 'It seems to me that nothing can be more cogent than this, that . . . a charter creating this market in the year 1682, . . . speaking of the limited area to which the appellant wants to confine the market rights, distinctly authorises the holding of a market *in sive juxta* that area. To me it seems perfectly clear, whether you look at the Latin words *in sive juxta* or at their English equivalent, "in or near", that the charter contemplates the extention of the market, if the owner of the market rights should so think fit, and should have the means of so doing, beyond that particular area into the area which surrounds it. *Juxta* will at least include all the four external streets which are now in question.' *A-G v Horner* (1885) 11 App Cas 66 at 75, 76, per Earl of Selborne

'I entirely agree that . . . the question whether one place is near another is entirely a question of circumstances, entirely a question of fact, and entirely a question for the tribunal which determines the claim.' *McMillan v Barclay Curle & Co Ltd* (1899) 2 F (Ct of Sess) 91 at 93, per Lord Adam

'The *Fox* was chartered to carry a cargo of flour, about 170 tons in sacks or bags, and to proceed to "London as ordered or so near thereunto as she may safely get", and there deliver the same. . . . I think the words "to proceed to it, or so near as she can safely get, and there deliver", imply that the alternative place is one of reasonably possible delivery. I do not think the place need be a usual place of delivery. The circumstances, on the assumption of obstruction, are unusual, and may justify an unusual place and method of discharge; but I think place and method must be reasonably possible, having regard to the cargo and surrounding circumstances.' *The Fox* (1914) 83 LJP 89 at 99, 102, CA, per Scrutton J

NEAR RELATIONS

'A devise to the nearest relation is good, and such shall be so accounted as are next by the Statute of Distributions [1670; see now Administration of Estates Act 1925].' *Anon* (1712) 2 Eq Cas Abr 291 at 291, per Lord Harcourt LC

[A testatrix by her will bequeathed property to all and every person or persons who were 'near relations' to her.] 'Such relations only, as would be entitled to a distributive share of her personal estate according to the statute for settling intestate estates, are within the description of near relations entitled to it.' *Whithorne v Harris* (1754) 2 Ves Sen 527 at 527, per Hardwicke LC

Australia 'The testatrix, by her will, bequeathed three-fourths of her estate to her trustees in trust to be distributed by them in their absolute discretion and judgment amongst her "near relatives". . . . Dealing first with the word "relatives", one contention was that this word meant, or rather included within its meaning, those persons related to the testatrix by marriage only. That is not the natural meaning of the word, and I can find nothing whatever in the will to constrain me into giving it that meaning. I think, therefore, that the word "relatives" means here what it naturally and primarily means: those related by blood to the testatrix. . . . I have now to consider what is the effect of the word "near"; and it is in connection with this word that I have found most difficulty in regard to this summons. The solution of the difficulty at which I have arrived is that which was pressed upon me by counsel, and which may be expressed in this way: When the court, in pursuance of the practice to which I have referred, was administering a trust in favour of relatives by distribution amongst next of kin, it apparently would pay no regard to the word "near" at all as occurring in the phrase "near relatives". . . . The proposition seems to be based on *Whithorne v Harris* [supra], and the implication of that decision seems to be this: that, notwithstanding that the testator has created a trust in favour of near relatives, the court will distribute the fund amongst the next of kin, although those next of kin may obviously be very remote relatives indeed. The second implication is that the word "near" will not be construed as if it were "nearest", but rather as in contradistinction to "nearest". . . . If, then, the word "near" is of too vague and uncertain a meaning to affect the discretion of the court in the administration of a trust, I think that there is reasonable ground for holding that it is also too vague and uncertain in meaning to affect the field of selection which would be afforded by use of the word "relatives" alone or to limit in any way the power of selection otherwise given to the trustees.' *Re Griffiths, Griffiths v Griffiths* [1926] VLR 212 at 216–218, per Mann J

NEAR SIDE

[A bye-law required drivers to keep their carriages on the left or 'near side' of the street.] 'The near side of the road means the left side of the centre of the roadway, and this bye-law means that a driver must not go on the right side of the centre of the road unless he has occasion to pass another carriage or actual necessity or some sufficient reason for deviation. The justices were wrong in construing this bye-law to mean that on the near side means as close to the kerb as possible.' *Bolton v Everett* (1911) 105 LT 830 at 831, DC, per Lord Alverstone CJ

NEAREST

Of kin

'The words "nearest and next of kin", are perfectly exempt from ambiguity, and in their general sense unquestionably denote the persons nearest in proximity of consanguinity.' *Brandon v Brandon* (1819) 3 Swan 312 at 317, 318, 324, per Plumer MR

'So long as the old law governing the descent of personal estate remained unaltered, the term "nearest of kin", and equivalent expressions, were used to designate the class of blood-relations entitled to the moveable succession of an intestate. That succession belonged, as stated by Lord Stair "to the nearest of kin, who are the defunct's whole agnates, male or female, being the kinsmen of the father's side, of the nearest degree, without primogeniture or right of representation; wherein those joined to the defunct by both bloods do exclude the agnates by one blood". In the common law of Scotland, next of kin and heirs *in mobilibus* meant one and the same thing; but another meaning might, of course, be impressed upon the term "next of kin", occurring in a written instrument, if the context showed, either expressly or by reasonable implication, that the testator or settlor used it in a different sense. . . . The expression is no longer equivalent to legal heirs *in mobilibus*, inasmuch as it does not include all the members of that class.' *Hood v Murray* (1889) 14 App Cas 124 at 134, 135, per Lord Watson

NECESSARIES

Of bankrupt

Canada [Debts incurred for 'necessaries of life' survive discharge in bankruptcy; Bankruptcy Act, RSC 1970, c-B-3, s 148(1)(g).] 'There is very little authority to give aid and guidance in connection with the meaning of the phrase "necessaries of life" as it is used in the aforementioned section of the Bankruptcy Act. It is clear in general terms that the phrase includes all things necessary to a person or appropriate to a person in his particular circumstances and social situation; that the scope of the phrase with respect to any particular person depends upon his mode of life and that the phrase includes many of the conveniences of refined society and depends to a large degree on the circumstances and conditions of the particular person involved. . . . It is true that some of the gasoline supplied to the defendant was used by him in driving his car around for business activities but it does not strike me that in the context of the facts as I understand them that should mean that the gasoline thereby ceased to have all the attributes of "necessaries of life" for the now discharged bankrupt. He obviously drove a car around because it suited him and was consistent with his station in life and suited his personal tastes. He presumably wore suits, perhaps some of them only on business activities but I somehow doubt that it ought logically to be argued that any suits worn only to the office thereby lost what would otherwise very probably have been their proper legal description as "necessaries of life". I do not see how in the present day and age it can forcefully be argued that the use of a car is somehow something beyond a necessary and something of a luxury. I conclude that the gasoline used in cars available to the defendant constituted a necessary of life to the defendant and that the use thereof by the defendant was consistent and in accord with his station in life and that the mere fact that he burned some of the gas on business activities should not in this case change the categorization of the gasoline as a necessary.' *Texaco Canada Ltd v Minnis* (1974) 52 DLR (3d) 346 at 349, 350, Ont Co Ct

Canada [The Bankruptcy Act, RSC 1970, c B-3, s 148(1)(g) states that an order of discharge does not release the bankrupt from any debt or liability for goods supplied as 'necessaries of life.'] 'Unfortunately there is no definition of the term "necessaries of life" in the Bankruptcy Act. Rarely has the judicial mind placed so many and varied interpretations on a particular phrase in its attempts to determine the intention of the legislators. The legion of cases in no way restricts the term to mean the basic necessaries of life, such as food, shelter, clothing and and the like, but would stretch its coverage to such things as "gas for the family Cadillac". Perhaps this is a reflection of the regional disparity that exists in this country of ours. In any event the general judicial consensus appears to be that the term envisions all goods appropriate to a person according to his or her particular lifestyle.' *Amherst Central Charge Ltd v Hicks* (1979) 29 CBR (NS) 313 at 314, 315, NSSC, per MacIntosh J

Of infant

The law considers it to be clearly for the benefit of an infant that he should be capable of binding himself to pay for the supply of the necessaries of life to himself and members of his household. In order to maintain an action against an infant in respect of necessaries it must be shown that they were of a nature suitable to his condition in life and actually required by him at the time and that he was not at the time otherwise sufficiently provided with them. The burden of proof is on the plaintiff, and the plaintiff's absence of knowledge as to the infant's existing supplies is irrelevant. . . .

Certain things are clearly necessaries, such as food, clothing, medicine and lodging. Articles suitable to and proper for an infant's position in life, though not actually necessary to his existence, are recognised as necessaries. The cost of the funeral of a member of the infant's family is a necessary expenditure. Education suitable to the infant's prospects in life is a necessary for which he can bind himself. The protection of an infant from legal proceedings and the protection of his interests by legal instruments or legal proceedings have been held to be necessaries. Articles which are mere luxuries, as distinguished from luxurious articles of utility, are not recognised as necessaries, even for an infant in a position in which they are commonly enjoyed. (24 Halsbury's Laws (4th edn) paras 416, 417)

Where necessaries are sold and delivered to a minor, or to a person who by reason of mental incapacity or drunkenness is incompetent to contract, he must pay a reasonable price for them. In relation to sales to minors or other incompetent persons, 'necessaries' means goods suitable to his condition in life and to his actual requirements at the time of the sale and delivery.

Mere luxuries can never be necessaries, but luxurious articles of utility may come under the definition of 'necessaries' in the special circumstances of a particular case. The standard is always relative. (41 Halsbury's Laws (4th edn) para 642)

[By the Family Law Reform Act 1969, s 1 the age of majority was reduced from twenty-one years to eighteen years and all statutory references to minority and infancy are to be construed accordingly. Section 9 of the Act of 1969 further provides that the time at which a person attains a particular age expressed in years shall be the commencement of the relevant anniversary of the date of his birth. The old common law rule that a person was deemed to attain a particular age at the first moment of the day immediately preceding the relevant anniversary of his birth has thus been abolished.]

In subsection (2) above [sale and delivery of 'necessaries' to a minor, etc] 'necessaries' means goods suitable to the condition in life of the minor or other person concerned and to his actual requirements at the time of the sale and delivery. (Sale of Goods Act 1979, s 3(3))

[An action was brought to recover the price of certain articles of jewellery, comprising five rings, a pair of pins, and a gold watch chain, bought, though not paid for, by a minor.] 'It is perfectly clear, that from the earliest time down to the present, the word "necessaries" was not confined, in its strict sense, to such articles as were necessary to the support of life, but extended to articles fit to maintain the particular person in the state, station, and degree in life in which he is; and therefore we must not take the word "necessaries" in its unqualified sense, but with the qualification above pointed out. Then the question in this case is, whether there was any evidence to go to the jury that any of these articles were of that description. I think there are two that might fall under that description, viz, the breast-pin and the watch-chain. The former might be a matter either of necessity or of ornament: the usefulness of the other might depend on this, whether the watch was necessary; if it was, then the chain might become necessary itself. Now it is impossible for us to say that a judge could withdraw it from the consideration of the jury, whether a watch was not a necessary thing for a young man at college, and of the age of eighteen or nineteen, to have. That being so, it is equally, as far as the chain is concerned, a question for the jury: there was, therefore, evidence to go to the jury. The true rule I take to be this—that all such articles as are purely ornamental are not necessary, and are to be rejected, because they cannot be requisite for any one; and for such matters, therefore, an infant cannot be made responsible. But if they are not strictly of this description, then the question arises, whether they were bought for the necessary use of the party, in order to support himself properly in the degree, state, and station of life in which he moved; if they were, for such articles the infant may be responsible.' *Peters v Fleming* (1840) 6 M & W 42 at 46, 47, per Parke B

'If it were laid down strictly that an infant can make no contract except for articles that would be necessary to keep him from famishing, that would be a rule which would press very hardly indeed in many cases. But that is not the rule; for a party may make contracts for necessary clothes, and for necessary education. It has been ruled that an infant may be liable for schooling, and if it become a question how much schooling is necessary, then you must inquire what situation in life he is required to fill. A knowledge of the learned languages may be necessary for one, a mere knowledge of reading and writing may be sufficient for another. The real question would be, whether or not what he has contracted for be such as a person in his station and rank in life would require. The articles must be for real use, and such as would be necessary and suitable to the degree and station in life of the infant. The question in these cases is this—Were the articles bought for mere ornament? if so, they cannot be necessaries for any one. If, however, they are bought for real use, then they may be necessaries, provided they are suitable to the infant's age, state, and degree. The jury then must say, whether they are such as reasonable persons, of the age and station of the infant, would require for real use. If so, they will be necessaries, for which an infant will be liable.' Ibid at 47, 48, per Alderson B

'Things necessary are those without which an individual cannot reasonably exist. In the first place, food, raiment, lodging, and the like.

About these there is no doubt. Again, as the proper cultivation of the mind is as expedient as the support of the body, instruction in art or trade, or intellectual, moral, and religious information may be a necesssary also. Again, as man lives in society, the assistance and attendance of others may be a necessary to his well-being. Hence attendance may be the subject of an infant's contract. Then the classes being established, the subject-matter and extent of the contract may vary according to the state and condition of the infant himself. His clothes may be fine or coarse according to his rank; his education may vary according to the station he is to fill; and the medicines will depend on the illness with which he is afflicted, and the extent of his probable means when of age. So, again, the nature and extent of the attendance will depend on his position in society; and a servant in livery may be allowed to a rich infant, because such attendance is commonly appropriated to persons in his rank of life. But in all these cases, it must first be made out that the class itself is one in which the things furnished are essential to the existence and reasonable advantage and comfort of the infant contractor. Thus, articles of mere luxury are always excluded, though luxurious articles of utility are in some cases allowed. So, contracts for charitable assistance to others, though highly to be praised, cannot be allowed to be binding, because they do not relate to his own personal advantage. In all cases there must be personal advantage from the contract derived to the infant himself.' *Chapple v Cooper* (1844) 13 M & W 252 at 258, per cur.

[The defendant, an undergraduate at Oxford, was supplied with goods including fruit, confectionery, marmalade, ices, soda-water, tongues, and sausages.] 'For a young man in some situations of life, not only clothes may be considered necessaries, but a watch, and the like articles, which he is expected to wear in that condition of life: but, with respect to the articles here supplied, it is an outrage to common sense to say that they can possibly be necessaries.' *Wharton v Mackenzie, Cripps v Hills* (1844) 5 QB 606 at 611, 612, per Lord Denman CJ

'Suppose the son of the richest man in the kingdom to have been supplied with diamonds and racehorses, the judge ought to tell the jury that such articles cannot possibly be necessaries. . . . It is said that we are to look at the circumstances of each defendant. True: we must do so. But the articles supplied must be necessaries, and not merely comforts or conveniences. Then we shall arrive at the principle acted on in *Brooker v Scott* [(1843) 11 M & W 67] where the court decided that it could not be necessary for an undergraduate to have dinners at his own lodgings, unless under circumstances furnishing an explanation.' Ibid at 612, 613, per Coleridge J

'A contract by an infant for the supply of goods to him cannot be enforced unless the articles be necessaries, the policy of the law being directed to the protection of infants. In point of fact, a tradesman dealing on credit with an infant does so at his peril, and must lose his money (that is, if the infant does not voluntarily pay him) unless he can prove that the goods supplied were necessaries for the infant according to his station in life. That being the law we come to the question. What are necessaries? To determine this, we must take into account what the infant had at the time of giving the order. For example: a watch may be prima facie in some cases a necessary, but if it turned out that the infant was already supplied with a watch or watches, the one ordered could not be a necessary.' *Barnes & Co v Toye* (1884) 13 QBD 410 at 413, 414, DC, per Lopes J

'What are necessaries for an infant? Food and clothing always are necessaries, if the infant cannot obtain them in any other way. Is education a necessary for an infant? Looking at it independently of authority, I should say that education in a trade with a view to making an infant a useful citizen must always in this working country have been thought of the greatest importance, and must always have been considered a necessary for an infant.' *Walter v Everard* [1891] 2 QB 369 at 374, CA, per Lord Esher MR

'The rule as regards liability for necessaries may, I think, be thus stated: an infant may contract for the supply at a reasonable price of articles reasonably necessary for his support in his station in life if he has not already a sufficient supply. To render an infant's contract for necessaries an enforceable contract two conditions must be satisfied, namely, (1) the contract must be for goods reasonably necessary for his support in his station in life, and (2) he must not have already a sufficient supply of these necessaries'. *Nash v Inman* [1908] 2 KB 1 at 11–13, CA, per Buckley LJ

Of ship

[The Admiralty Court Act 1840 (repealed), s 6 provided that the court could, in certain cases, adjudicate on claims for services and 'necessaries' supplied to any foreign ship or sea-going vessel, although not on the high seas.] 'It is absolutely necessary, when the owner is abroad, to prove not only that the articles supplied were necessaries, but that they were actually wanting for the service of the ship at the time when they were made. The technical meaning of the term necessaries I have already explained, as strictly applying to anchors, cables, rigging, and matters of that description; at the same time, I consider myself at liberty to enlarge the term necessaries so as to include money expended upon necessaries; but in such cases, I must be satisfied that the necessaries were wanting, and that the money was bona fide advanced for the purpose of procuring them.' *The Sophie* (1842) 1 Wm Rob 368 at 369, per cur.

'The first question is, whether copper sheathing is or is not a "necessary" to a ship within the meaning of the statute [Admiralty Court Act 1840 (repealed), s 6]. I am of opinion that it is. It may not be always indispensable, but it is very customary for sea-going vessels to be coppered, and the court will not put a restricted meaning on the term necessaries in this very beneficial statute, so as to confine it to things absolutely and unconditionally necessary for a ship in order to put to sea.' *The Perta* (1858) Sw 353 at 354, per Dr Lushington

'Three objections have been taken to this claim. First, that the coals, as supplied, were not necessaries. . . . As to the statute [Admiralty Court Act 1840 (repealed), s 6] the words used are "necessaries supplied". I am aware that the main reason for passing the Act was to enable foreign vessels in distress off the coast to obtain the necessary articles to enable them to keep the sea, but it may well be that the Legislature intentionally used terms beyond the original grievance to be remedied, and at any rate I have to construe the terms as they stand. The coals that were supplied by Messrs Sack, Bremer & Co were, I think, "necessaries" to the steamer; without them, the steamer could not have left the port of London.' *The West Friesland* (1859) Sw 454 at 455, per Dr Lushington

'I . . . hold that "necessaries" [within the Admiralty Court Act 1840 (repealed), s 6] means primarily indispensable repairs,—anchors, cables, sails, when immediately necessary; and also provisions: but, on the other hand, does not include things required for the voyage, as contradistinguished from necessaries for the ship.' *The Comtesse de Fregeville* (1861) Lush 329 at 332, per Dr Lushington

'This is a motion to reject a petition in a cause of necessaries instituted by a London shipbroker against the Norwegian vessel *Riga* and her freight. The ground of the motion is, that the items set forth by the plaintiff in the petition do not fall under the legal category of "necessaries", according to the construction put upon that term by my predecessor in this court. . . . I must come to the conclusion that there is no distinction as to necessaries between the cases in which by the common law a master has been holden to bind his owner and suits for necessaries instituted in this court. . . . I am unable to draw any solid distinction (especially since the last statute [Admiralty Court Act 1840 (repealed), s 6]) between necessaries for the ship and necessaries for the voyage; and I shall follow the doctrine of the common law as laid down by the high authority of Lord Tenterden in the case of *Webster v Seekamp* [(1821) 4 B & Ald 352]. In that case he says: "The general rule is, that the master may bind his owners for necessary repairs done or supplies provided for the ship. It was contended at the trial that this liability of the owners was confined to what was absolutely necessary. I think that rule too narrow, for it would be extremely difficult to decide, and often impossible, in many cases, what is absolutely necessary. If, however, the jury are to inquire only what is necessary, there is no better rule to ascertain that than by considering what a prudent man, if present, would do under circumstances in which the agent, in his absence, is called upon to act. I am of opinion that whatever is fit and proper for the service on which a vessel is engaged, whatever the owner of the vessel, as a prudent man, would have ordered if present at the time, comes within the meaning of the term 'necessaries', as applied to those repairs done or things provided for the ship by the order of the master, for which the owners are liable".' *The Riga* (1872) LR 3 A & E 516 at 519, 522, per Sir Robert Phillimore

'For a century or more it has been common knowledge that the master is only authorised to pledge his owners' credit for what may be called "things necessary" for the ship; that is to say, he can pledge his owners' credit if he is in a position where it is necessary, for the purposes of his duty, that these things should be supplied, and he cannot have recourse to his owners before ordering them.' *The Orienta* [1895] P 49 at 54, CA, per Lord Esher MR

[For the present law as to Admiralty jurisdiction in the High Court and county courts, see Supreme Court Act 1981, s 20(2)(m) and the County Courts Act 1984, s 27. The word 'necessaries' is no longer used in these Acts but the cases on the meaning of 'necessaries', above, may still be useful in determining whether goods or materials were supplied to a ship 'for her operation or maintenance'.]

New Zealand 'The primary meaning of the word "necessaries" in Admiralty law is that of goods supplied to a ship which are necessary for the purposes either of the ship or the voyage. Into this category would come items such as anchors, cables, rigging, coal, fuel, oil, provisions and the like. A claim for "equipping or repairing" is based, by contrast, on work done on the ship as opposed to goods delivered to the ship. Sometimes the distinction between the two classes of claim with their different consequences has become blurred. One finds, for example, that in *The Mogileff* [[1921] P 236] it was held by Hill J that a claim for necessaries included not only a long list of goods supplied but also payments made for alterations and repairs. In other cases, however, items strictly nominated as necessaries had been segregated and dealt with separately. For myself, I am not impressed with the theory which seems to have prevailed with Hill J in *The Mogileff* that the cost of repairs might be classified as a "necessary" because the ship would be unable to proceed without such repairs being effected. It is to be presumed that all repairs are a matter of necessity for they would not otherwise be ordered and paid for by the shipowners, and yet there has always been a distinction in Admiralty law between those who claim the cost of building, equipping and repairs, and those who claim the cost of supplying necessaries.' *The Lorena* [1973] 1 NZLR 507 at 512, per Mahon J

Of wife

[The power of a wife to pledge her husband's credit, as agent of necessity, in respect of either household necessaries or legal costs, was abolished by the Matrimonial Proceedings and Property Act 1970, s 41, itself now repealed by the Matrimonial Causes Act 1973. The authority which a wife has while still running her husband's household is not affected; nor is any authority which she may have been held out by the husband as having. The Matrimonial Causes Act 1965, s 20(4) (which made the husband liable for necessaries where there had been a judicial separation and where maintenance had not yet been paid) was repealed by s 41, supra.]

'The defendant forced his wife from his house, with circumstances of cruelty; he was divorced from her for adultery committed by himself; and he has complied very little with the decree of alimony. But he is bound to provide for his wife; and all the cases show that the alimony must not only be secured but paid. In this the text writers all concur. Bacon's Abridgment [Bac Abr Baron and Feme, 488] contains the whole of the judgment of Hale CJ, in *Manby v Scott* [(1663) 1 Keb 482], and the summary which the learned compiler extracts from it is as follows:—"It is clear that a husband is obliged to maintain his wife, and may be compelled to find her necessaries, as meat, drink, clothes, physic, etc, suitable to the husband's degree, estate, or circumstances.' . . . No answer has been given to *Ozard v Darnford* [(1779) 1 Selwyn's NP 13th Edn 229, at 260] where Lord Mansfield expressly draws the distinction between an allowance agreed for and an allowance paid. In his charge to the jury in that case, he laid it down, as clear and decided law, "That when husband and wife live together, the husband is liable for all such necessaries wherewith the wife may have been furnished; but that what are or are not necessaries must depend on the rank and situation of the husband".' *Hunt v De Blaquiere* (1829) 5 Bing 550 at 559, 561, per Park J

'The rule as to necessaries for which a husband is liable, means such things as are necessary for the sustenance or protection of the wife.' *Ladd v Lynn* (1837) 2 M & W 265 at 267, per Lord Abinger CB

'It would be difficult and dangerous to attempt to lay down any precise rule as governing the conduct of a husband in his mode or rate of living, so far as concerns his wife. The court has no authority to decide thereon, save so far as it may fall within its jurisdiction, and its jurisdiction is limited to cases of cruelty. Even, however, within this very limited range it is obvious that the means and rank of the parties must raise some distinctions. The denial of necessaries and comforts, even of medical assistance, when there are no pecuniary resources, never can be construed into acts of cruelty; but no one could, I think, entertain a reasonable doubt that such a denial when the fortune was ample, might probably, under circumstances, be considered differently. It also appears to me equally clear that necessaries and comforts must have some relation to the rank and station of the parties; where they are in totally different ranks of life the words "necessaries and comforts" imply not the same things; the want of some would operate altogether differently. A wife brought up as a gentlewoman would suffer in her health and constitution, nay even her life might be endangered by a mode of living which would be comfortable to a female in a different mode of life. This, I think is quite apparent, and such must be the mode of viewing these cases when they occur. Let there, however, be no mistake. I speak of necessaries and comforts, not of luxuries or enjoyments. Whether the question relate to house, furniture, carriage, or provisions, the court abjures all right to enter upon it beyond ascertaining that the health and ordinary comforts of the wife are preserved. As to everything beyond this, the husband, so far as the law is concerned, is the sole judge, and to his will the wife is bound to submit. No human tribunal has authority to interfere, and none could interfere with real benefit to the public interest.' *Dysart (Earl) v Dysart (Countess)* (1844) 1 Rob Eccl 106 at 111, 112, per Dr Lushington

[The plaintiff, a professional rubber and shampooer, sued the defendant for her charges for shampooing the defendant's wife's hair on numerous occasions. The question was raised as to whether the shampooing or rubbing was a 'necessary'.] 'For a thing to be a "necessary" it must be in its nature necessary; it must be necessary in itself, and it must be necessary that the wife should have it. It must be necessary under the circumstances in which the wife was placed. In this case it was said that the rubbing was necessary. It might be so, though there was little evidence of it. The only evidence of it was by the plaintiff, a "professed shampooer", who said a doctor had told her to attend Lady Howard to "rub" her. It might have been some luxury, not in the legal sense a "necessary".' *Canham v Howard* (1887) 3 TLR 458 at 459, DC, per Day J

'It is an undoubted principle of law that where a wife is living apart from her husband and the husband wrongfully refuses to maintain her she has a right to pledge his credit for necessaries, and one of the matters always regarded as included in the terms "necessaries" is the power of the wife to instruct a solicitor to defend her from proceedings taken against her by her husband, to appear for her in proceedings taken by her against her husband, and also, it may be, to appear for her in proceedings which she has taken to protect her interests when living apart from her husband. However that may be, there is a well established exception to that rule—namely, that where the wife has committed adultery she is not entitled to pledge her husband's credit, nor entitled to apply for alimony against her husband in a court of summary jurisdiction.' *Wright (HS) & Webb v Annandale* [1930] 2 KB 8 at 13, 14, CA, per Greer LJ

See, generally, 22 Halsbury's Laws (4th edn) para 1006.

NECESSARY

In conveyance or lease

[In a conveyance to a railway company, the company covenanted to construct on the land thereby conveyed a station-house and other works and conveniences 'necessary and convenient' for passenger and goods traffic.] 'What I have to consider is, whether these are pieces of land which the company are bound to reconvey within the meaning of the covenant of this deed. The company thereby covenanted with the plaintiff, their vendor, to construct on the said pieces of land a "station-house"—a tolerably large phrase—"and other works and conveniences necessary and convenient for passenger and goods traffic" on the company's railway. Mr Wood has pointed out that the words are "necessary and convenient". I am not sure that I know why the two words were put in, because I should have thought either one or the other would have been quite sufficient to express the intention of the parties. It is quite obvious that "necessary" cannot mean that without which the passenger and goods traffic cannot be carried on. . . . It must mean that which is reasonably necessary for passenger and goods traffic as carried on on a railway of this kind, and as from time to time required. When you have got that meaning for "necessary" it seems to me that there is no occasion to consider what "convenient" means.' *Harris v London & South-Western Rly Co* (1889) 60 LT 392 at 392, 393, per Kekewich J

New Zealand [A covenant in a lease provided that a lessee should and would at his own cost and expense do all things 'necessary' to obtain for and on behalf of the lessor a perpetual registrable water easement for the continuance of the water-supply for the premises.] 'Prima facie, he (the lessee) was required, as a condition of his lease, to ensure that another person, who had not then agreed to give him an easement, would agree to do so. This might well impose an impossible obligation. In my opinion, the words "do all things necessary" should be construed to mean that the defendant would take all reasonable steps to obtain the water-supply. If he took those steps, but failed to obtain the easement, he would not have committed a breach of the covenant.' *Skinner v Scott* [1947] NZLR 878 at 881, 882, per Smith J

In regulations

[The Building (Safety, Health and Welfare) Regulations 1948, reg 79(7) (revoked; see now the Construction (Working Places) Regulations 1966, as amended by SI 1984/1593), provided that, where demolition work was being carried out, precautions should, where 'necessary', be taken by shoring, etc.] 'It is urged on behalf of the defendants that "where necessary" means only where found necessary by experience, as opposed to being found necessary, for example, in the light of after events as a result of some latent defect not reasonably anticipated. I do not think I need go further than to hold that it must, at any rate, cover a case where, if the dangers had been appreciated, as I have held they should have been, any reasonable person would say that precautions were necessary.' *Knight v Demolition and Construction Co Ltd* [1953] 2 All ER 508 at 511, per Parker J

[The above regulations will eventually be replaced by new regulations under the Health and Safety at Work etc Act 1974.]

In various statutes

[The Companies Act 1862, s 95 (repealed; see now the Companies Act 1985, s 539(1)(b)), provided that a liquidator should have power to carry on the business of a company as far as might be 'necessary' for the beneficial winding up of the same.] 'I think that the section should be construed in a liberal sense; and I agree with the Master of the Rolls that we are not to take the word "necessary" as importing an absolutely compelling force, but what may be called a mercantile necessity, something which would be highly expedient under all the circumstances of the case for the beneficial winding-up of the company.' *Re Wreck Recovery & Salvage Co* (1880) 15 Ch D 353 at 362, CA, per Thesiger LJ

[A railway company was empowered by a special Act to make and maintain a line and subway, with all 'necessary' approaches, tunnels, shafts, works, etc., connected therewith.] 'The question is . . . what is the meaning there of the word "necessary". . . . It appears to me . . . that necessary works mean works necessary for the purposes of the undertaking, without reference to any particular position of those works, provided they are within the lines shown on the deposited plans. Within those lines they have power to make all works which are necessary for the purposes of their undertaking.' *City & South London Rly Co v London County Council* [1891] 2 QB 513 at 521, 522, CA, per Lindley LJ

[The Pluralities Act 1838, s 59 enacts that any agreement for the letting of a residence or the buildings, etc, 'necessary' for the convenient occupation of the same, belonging to any benefice, shall be made in writing and shall contain a condition for avoiding the same.] 'When the Pluralities Act 1838 was passed most parsonage houses were very large buildings, as indeed some still are; and at that time the incumbent was expected to exercise much hospitality and often had many persons staying with him in his house of residence. *Tempora mutantur*. Today these large buildings not being required for the exercise of lavish hospitality, are not convenient for their purpose and, indeed, owing to the altered financial position of most incumbents, constitute a great burden on them. This aspect cannot be forgotten in construing the words "buildings . . . necessary for the convenient occupation" of the house of residence in s 59 of the Pluralities Act 1838. In my opinion the word "necessary" in that section must be construed in relation to the particular circumstances of the present time and of the particular rectory or vicarage under consideration.' *Neale v Jennings* [1946] KB 238 at 242, CA, per Scott LJ

NECESSARY IMPLICATION *See* IMPLICATION

NECESSITOUS

[A hospital was founded in 1834 for feeble or old men and women so long as they were 'necessitous'. The property from which the revenues were derived was granted to the master, brethren, and sisters and their successors for ever.] 'Here the funds are to be distributed to feeble, old, or necessitous persons—necessitous not necessarily meaning persons in extreme poverty.' *Cowen v Kingston-upon-Hull Town Clerk* [1897] 1 QB 273 at 279, per Hawkins J

NECESSITY

Agency of

Agency of necessity is said to arise in a limited number of cases where, by reason of an emergency (1) the relation of principal and agent is deemed to exist between persons not otherwise in contractual relations or (2) authority to act on behalf of another is implied as between persons already in contractual relations. The term was formerly used to describe the right of a deserted wife who was in need to pledge her husband's credit for necessaries. (1 Halsbury's Laws (4th edn) para 724)

'The object of the common law is to solve difficulties and adjust relations in social and commercial life. It must meet, so far as it can, sets of fact abnormal as well as usual. It must grow with the development of the nation. It must face and deal with changing or novel circumstances. Unless it can do that it fails in its function and declines in its dignity and value. An expanding society demands an expanding common law. A dozen decisions could be cited to illustrate the remarks I have just made. I mention only the words of Bankes LJ in *Rex v Electricity Commissioners* [(1923) 39 TLR 715] when he said: "It has, however, always been the boast of our common law that it will, whenever possible, and where necessary, apply existing principles to new sets of circumstances." I respectfully agree, and I venture to add that it would be well if those words were more often remembered and applied. In my view there is nothing in the existing decisions which confines the agency of necessity to carriers whether by land or sea, or to the acceptors of bills of exchange.' *Prager v Blatspiel, Stamp & Heacock Ltd* [1924] 1 KB 566 at 570, per McCardie J

[The agency of necessity of a wife was abolished by the Matrimonial Proceedings and Property Act 1970, s 41. *See also* AGENT-AGENCY; NECESSARIES.]

Way of *See* RIGHTS OF WAY

NEED

Canada 'One of the essential conditions precedent to the enrolment of the respondent as a notary public under s 5 of the Notaries Act, RSBC 1936, c 205 [now RSBC 1979, c 299, s 5] is that the court shall be satisfied ". . . that there is need of a Notary Public in the place where the applicant desires to practise. . . ." . . . The court is of opinion that the need to which s 5 refers is a public need in the nature of a public necessity as distinguished from an individual need occasioned by the personal or commercial considerations of an applicant.' *Re Law Soc of BC and Gallagher* [1946] 2 WWR 409 at 410, BCCA, per O'Halloran JA

NEEDS

[The Housing Act 1936, s 71 (repealed; see now the Housing Act 1985, s 8(1)) provided that it should be the duty of every local authority to consider the housing 'needs' of the district.] 'It seems to me that a local authority must, when considering the needs of their district, look at the districts immediately adjacent. The Act speaks not of the needs of the people in the district, but of the needs of the district, and I think that that is a deliberate and sensible distinction.' *Watson v Minister of Local Government and Planning* [1951] 2 KB 779 at 783, per Devlin J

New Zealand [The Tenancy Act 1948 (NZ), s 25(4) (repealed) provided that in any proceedings to which the section applied, where the court was satisfied that any alternative accommodation was or would be available for the tenant, that accommodation should be deemed to be suitable unless the court was satisfied that it was inadequate for the 'needs' of the tenant, or was of an unreasonably low standard, or was for any special reason unsuitable for the tenant.] 'The word "needs" is a wide word and is wide enough to cover not only structural needs and space needs but also situational needs. In my view, therefore, unsuitability of situation, if sufficiently serious, constitutes inadequacy for the needs of a tenant within the meaning of sub-s (4) of s 25. Inadequacy is, however, always a question of degrees. . . . A tenant certainly cannot expect his business to remain unscathed by the move. The matter must be looked at reasonably; and, broadly stated, the test is whether the unsuitability of the situation of the alternative premises is such that the tenant will be unable to carry on his business in them in substantially the same way as before, that is to say, without substantial detriment to it.' *Goodman v Furniture Fashions Ltd* [1953] NZLR 547 at 548, per Cooke J

NEEDY

[A testatrix by her will left part of her estate for the benefit of certain persons in 'needy' circumstances.] 'I have on the whole come to the conclusion that the primary intention of the testatrix was the relief of poverty properly so called . . . the phrase "in needy circumstances" is to my mind merely periphrastic for "poor".' *Scarisbrick in re Cockshott v Public Trustee* [1951] 1 Ch 622 at 634, per Evershed MR

NEGLECT *See also* WILFUL

'The word neglect imports culpability.' *Ex p Matson* (1822) 2 Dow & Ry KB 238 at 239, per Abbott CJ

[The Companies Act 1862, s 80 (repealed; see now the Companies Act 1985, s 518(1)(a)) provided that whenever a creditor to whom a company was indebted in a sum exceeding £50 (now £750) had served on such company a demand for payment, and the company for the succeeding period of three weeks 'neglected to pay', etc, such demand, then the company should be deemed to be unable to pay its debts.] 'It is very obvious, on reading that enactment, that the word "neglected" is not necessarily equivalent to the word "omitted". Negligence is a term which is well known to the law. Negligence in paying a debt on demand, as I understand it, is omitting to pay without reasonable excuse. Mere omission by itself does not amount to negligence. Therefore, I should hold, upon the words of the statute, that where a debt is bona fide disputed by the debtor, and the debtor alleges, for example, that the demand for goods sold and delivered is excessive, and says that he, the debtor, is willing to pay such sum as he is either advised by competent valuers to pay, or as he himself considers a fair sum for the goods, then in that case he has not neglected to pay, and is not within the wording of the statute.' *Re London & Paris Banking Corpn* (1874) LR 19 Eq 444 at 445, 446, per Jessel MR

'Lord Campbell's Act [Fatal Accidents Act 1846, s 1 (repealed; see now the Fatal Accidents Act 1976, s 1(1), as substituted by the Administration of Justice Act 1983, s 3(1))] provides as follows: . . . "Whensoever the death of a person shall be caused by wrongful act, neglect or default, and the act, neglect or default is such as would (if death had not ensued) have entitled the party injured to maintain an action and recover damages in respect thereof, then and in every such case the person who would have been liable if death had not ensued shall be liable to an action for damages, notwithstanding the death of the person injured . . ." In my judgment the liability arises where the wrongful act is a breach of contract to exercise reasonable care, and if the death of a passenger is occasioned thereby an action lies under Lord Campbell's Act on behalf of the dependants there mentioned. A failure to exercise reasonable care is a "neglect", whether the duty to exercise such care arises from contract or as the result of a tort. It is a wrongful neglect if it be a breach of contract, even though the contract prohibits an action of tort.' *Grein v Imperial Airways Ltd* [1937] 1 KB 50 at 69, 70, CA, per Greer LJ

'To "neglect" a child is to omit to act, to fail to provide adequately for its needs, and, in the context of s 1 of the 1933 Act [Children and Young Persons Act 1933], its physical needs rather than its spiritual, educational, moral or emotional needs. These are dealt with by other legislation. . . . The use of the verb "neglect" cannot, in my view, of itself import into the criminal law the civil law concept of negligence. The actus reus in a case of wilful neglect is simply a failure, for whatever reason, to provide the child whenever it in fact needs medical aid with the medical aid it needs. Such a failure as it seems to me could not be properly described as "wilful" unless the parent *either* (1) had directed his mind to the question whether there was some risk (though it might fall short of a probability) that the child's health might suffer unless he was examined by a doctor and provided with such curative treatment as the examination might reveal as necessary, and had made a conscious decision, for whatever reason, to refrain from arranging for such medical examination, *or* (2) had so refrained because he did not care whether the child might be in need of medical treatment or not.' *R v Sheppard* [1980] 3 All ER 899 at 904, HL, per Lord Diplock

In name and arms clause

'By his will the testator directed that the freehold lands that should be purchased by his trustees with his residuary estate as therein mentioned should be held to the use of his sister during her life, and after her death to the use of various persons and their male issue in strict settlement. The will contains a name and arms clause in the words following: "I do hereby order and direct and declare it to be my will and meaning that every person who shall be entitled to the possession and enjoyment of the said hereditaments or of my residuary estate . . . shall and do within three months after he shall become entitled to the same as aforesaid take upon him, and use in all writings and on all occasions whatsoever the surname of Dick only, and use the arms of Dick only, and I do hereby direct that in case any person or persons so entitled as aforesaid shall refuse or neglect to take my said surname and arms and to use or take the proper means for so doing within the said period of three months then the limitations in this my will contained to him or them so refusing or neglecting as aforesaid shall cease, determine, and be utterly void." . . . The question that I have to determine is whether a person of the name of Barrett, who is alleged to have become entitled in the year 1923 to the possession of the settled property as tenant in tail male, in complete ignorance not only of the fact that he had so become entitled, but even of the very existence of the will and its contents, and who remained in such ignorance for a year or two thereafter, can be said to have "refused or neglected" to take the name and arms of Dick within the meaning of the clause. . . . The testator might . . . very naturally add the word "neglect" to cover the case of a refusal that was not express. But I cannot think that it would be natural or in accordance with the ordinary use of language to add the word "neglect" in order to cover every case of failure. Although, therefore, as will presently appear, the word "neglect", when used by itself, may in certain contexts mean no more than the word "fail", I should not, in the absence of authority to the contrary, come to the conclusion that it has that wide meaning in the clause with which I have to deal. But my attention has been directed to certain authorities which I must now consider. Some of them certainly seem to establish the proposition that the word "neglect" may cover every form of omission. In others, however, the word has been treated as covering only omissions that are negligent. Amongst the former class are included *In re Hodges' Legacy* [(1873) LR 16 Eq 92] and *Hawkes v Baldwin* [(1838) 9 Sim 355]. But in the first of these cases Wickens V-C did not in terms deal with the meaning of the word "neglect", though he undoubtedly was of the opinion that the word, even in a condition, included an omission due to ignorance. . . . In *Hawkes v Baldwin* . . . it was quite clear, looking at the will as a whole, that in that case the words "neglect to claim" were used as being equivalent to "shall not claim". . . . Having regard to these authorities it may well be that, if in the present case the gift over were directed to take effect if the person becoming entitled to the estate should neglect to take the name and arms within the defined period, the word "neglect" ought to be construed as including a mere omission or failure. . . . If the word "neglect" connotes the exercise of the will it cannot include a failure or omission which is due to ignorance of the provisions of the document, and which therefore does not result from any operation of the mind.' *Re Quintin Dick, Cloncurry (Lord) v Fenton* [1926] Ch 992 at 999–1003, 1006, per Romer J

[A testator by his will settled his real estate and directed that, if any person should for twelve months after becoming entitled in possession to the property 'neglect' to assume and take the name and arms of the testator, his estate, and interest should determine.] 'The question is one which I do not find it possible to decide without reference to authority. If I had been free to follow my own inclination, I should have had no hesitation in saying that neglect, in its legal connotation, implies failure to perform a duty of which the person knows or ought to know. So in a document of this kind "neglect" imports failure to do something which the person knows or ought to know was a condition. Am I at liberty to adopt that view? In *re Quintin Dick* [supra], Romer J had to consider a name and arms clause and he reviewed the authorities. It was insisted on here that, in that case, Romer J had to consider the words "refuse or neglect" and that the case is a binding decision only where "refuse" and "neglect" are in conjunction. However, I cannot ignore the justice of the words of Romer J where after referring to the decision of Warrington J, he says at p 1006: "If the word 'neglect' connotes the exercise of the will it cannot include a failure or omission which is due to ignorance of the provisions of the document, and which therefore does not result from any operation of the mind." As I read that passage, Romer J, was not founding his interpretation of the word "neglect" solely upon its collocation with the word "refuse". I think he was considering what the word "neglect" would mean if it stood by itself. That view of the decision is, I think, correctly adopted in Halsbury, Laws of England [see now 4th edn, vol 42, para 745], where it is said: "If a condition is expressed to take effect if the donee shall 'omit' or 'fail' to take the name and arms, this will cover every case of non-compliance. The word 'refuse', however, implies a conscious act of volition, so that a person who was ignorant of the condition or was under disability cannot be said to have refused to comply with it; but if a person knows of the existence of the condition, a refusal need not be express. 'Neglect', when used alone, prima facie covers only omissions that are negligent, but when used in certain contexts it may mean no more than 'fail'. The expression 'neglect or refuse' also implies a conscious act of volition." The statement there, I think, is a correct one; the relevant part is: "neglect, when used alone, prima facie covers only omissions that are negligent." There is nothing in the context here which, in my judgment, enlarges that prima facie meaning.' *Re Hughes, Rea v Black* [1943] 2 All ER 269 at 271, per Simonds J

Of mentally disordered person

[The Mental Deficiency Act 1913, s 2(1)(b) (repealed; see now the Mental Health Act 1983, s 135) provided that a mental defective might be placed in an institution, etc, if he were 'found neglected'.] 'True the expression "found neglected" connotes a sin or sins of omission rather than of commission but when one finds that the expression "found neglected" is used and coupled with these two expressions "abandoned" and "cruelly treated" to describe the only circumstances which will render a defective person subject to be dealt with under the Act, the word "neglected" must at least be construed as meaning physically suffering from a lack of essentials through want of reasonable care.' *R v Board of Control, ex p Rutty* [1956] 1 All ER 769 at 774, per Hilbery J (also reported in [1956] 2 QB 109 at 123)

'It seems to me reasonable to hold—or at least that a reasonable person might hold—that a feeble-minded person is "neglected" if he is not given the care which he ought to have, or is not under the control which he ought to be, both for his own good and for the good of others.' *Richardson v London County Council* [1957] 2 All ER 330 at 336, CA, per Denning LJ

NEGLIGENCE *See also* NUISANCE

Negligence is a specific tort and in any given circumstances is the failure to exercise that care which the circumstances demand. What amounts to negligence depends on the facts of each particular case. It may consist in omitting to do something which ought to be done or in doing something which ought to be done either in a different manner or not at all. Where there is no duty to exercise care, negligence in the popular sense has no legal consequence. Where there is a duty to exercise care, reasonable care must be taken to avoid acts or omissions which can be reasonably foreseen to be likely to cause physical injury to persons or property. The degree of care required in the particular case depends on the accompanying circumstances, and may vary according to the amount of the risk to be encountered and to the magnitude of the prospective injury. The duty of care is owed only to those persons who are in the area of foreseeable danger; the fact that the act of the defendant violated his duty of care to a third person does not enable the plaintiff who is also injured by the same act to claim unless he is also within the area of foreseeable danger. The same act or omission may accordingly in some circumstances involve liability as being negligent, although in other circumstances it will not do so. The material considerations are the absence of care which is on the part of the defendant owed to the plaintiff in the circumstances of the case and damage suffered by the plaintiff, together with a demonstrable relation of cause and effect between the two.

An act of negligence may also constitute a nuisance where it occasions a dangerous state of affairs and satisfies the other requirements of that tort. Equally it may also be a breach of the rule in *Rylands v Fletcher* if it allows the escape of a dangerous thing which the defendant has brought onto his land.

Under the Congenital Disabilities (Civil Liability) Act 1976 a woman owes a duty of care in respect of the safety of her unborn child in one circumstance only: if she is driving a motor vehicle when she knows or ought reasonably to know herself to be pregnant and in consequence of her breach of duty her child is born with disabilities which would not otherwise have been present, those disabilities are to be regarded as damage resulting from her wrongful act and actionable accordingly at the suit of the child. (34 Halsbury's Laws (4th edn) para 1)

Negligence is a specific tort and in any given circumstances is the failure to exercise that care which the circumstances demand. Where there is a duty to exercise care, reasonable care must be taken to avoid acts or omissions which can be reasonably foreseen to be likely to cause physical injury to persons or property. The plaintiff must prove that the defendant's negligence was a cause of his injuries. In a limited set of circumstances there is a duty to take care to avoid economic loss and liability in negligence for economic loss which results from breach of such duty. (45 Halsbury's Laws (4th edn) para 1278)

For the purposes of this Part [Part I] of this Act, 'negligence' means the breach—

(a) of any obligation, arising from the expression or implied terms of a contract, to take reasonable care or exercise reasonable skill in the performance of the contract;
(b) of any common law duty to take reasonable care or exercise reasonable skill (but not any stricter duty);
(c) of the common duty of care imposed by the Occupiers' Liability Act 1957 or the Occupiers' Liability Act (Northern Ireland) 1957.

(Unfair Contract Terms Act 1977, s 1(1))

'Negligence is the omission to do something which a reasonable man, guided upon those considerations which ordinarily regulate the conduct of human affairs, would do, or doing something which a prudent and reasonable man would not do.' *Blyth v Birmingham Waterworks Co* (1856) 11 Exch 781 at 784, per Alderson B

'The definition of negligence is the absence of care, according to the circumstances.' *Vaughan v Taff Vale Rly Co* (1860) 5 H & N 679 at 688, per Willes J

'In this case the question is, whether the statement of claim upon the face of it, assuming that facts stated in it are true, shows any cause of action against the defendants. It shows no cause of action unless it shows negligence on the part of the defendants towards the plaintiff which makes them liable according to law. In order to show that there is such negligence the statement of claim must show, either expressly or impliedly, that there was a duty from the defendants to the plaintiff to take reasonable care in respect of the matter charged against them, and that there was a breach of that duty. In the statement of claim there is an allegation of negligence, and therefore the question is, whether there are sufficient circumstances disclosed to raise a duty on the part of the defendants to use reasonable care towards the plaintiff in respect of the negligence charged. Now, I myself am prepared to say that, wherever the circumstances disclosed are such that, if the person charged with negligence thought of what he was about to do, or to omit to do, he must see that, unless he used reasonable care, there must be at least a great probability of injury to the person charging negligence against him, either as to his person or property, then there is a duty shown to use reasonable care.' *Cunnington v Great Northern Rly Co* (1883) 49 LT 392 at 392, 393, CA, per Brett MR

'Actionable negligence consists in the neglect of the use of ordinary care or skill towards a person to whom the defendant owes the duty of observing ordinary care and skill, by which neglect the plaintiff, without contributory negligence on his part, has suffered injury to his person or property.' *Heaven v Pender* (1883) 11 QBD 503 at 507, CA, per Brett MR

'By negligence is meant substantially the doing by a person of some act which a reasonable and prudent man would not have done under the circumstances of the case in question, or the omission to do everything that could be fairly and reasonably expected of such a man under such circumstances.' *Snook v Grand Junction Waterworks Co Ltd* (1886) 2 TLR 308 at 309, per Huddleston B

'It is said you cannot have liability for negligence except it is founded on a duty. The duty, however, is that you are bound not to do anything negligently so as to hurt a person near you, and the whole duty arises from the knowledge of that proximity. Whether the negligence is your personal act, or arises from using your property in a particular way, the rule equally applies, and you must so use your personal powers or property as not to injure any other person if by the exercise of reasonable care you can avoid so doing.' *Thomas v Quartermaine* (1887) 18 QBD 685 at 688, CA, per Lord Esher MR

'There may be culpable negligence in omitting to consider whether a proposed act is ultra vires or not, but there cannot be such a thing as negligence ultra vires. The nearest approach to it would be the omission to perform a positive command; but even thus directors could not properly be said to have exceeded their powers in omitting to fulfil them. Charges of negligence, therefore, do not fall within the ambit of an inquiry what acts are intra and what are ultra vires, or what is the liability in respect of breach of duty in this particular. I therefore propose to consider the nature and consequences of negligence and acts ultra vires separately. On behalf of the respondents here it was argued, and, having regard to the principles applicable and the authorities cited, I think successfully argued, that liability for negligence cannot properly be imputed to directors unless the court is satisfied that such negligence was "crass". The Latin word is more often used, but I prefer the vulgar tongue, and there is classical authority for it. What is crass negligence? In the first place, I apprehend, there must be a plain duty to do, or abstain from doing, a particular thing; and next, there must be such abstention from action, or such action as the court would be justified in holding to be mischievous or reckless.' *Re Liverpool Household Stores Assocn* (1890) 59 LJ Ch 616 at 618, per Kekewich J

'I must explain what in law we mean by "negligence". In the ordinary case which does not involve any special skill, negligence in law means this: Some failure to do some act which a reasonable man in the circumstances would do, or doing some act which a reasonable man in the circumstances would not do; and if that failure or doing of that act results in injury, then there is a cause of action. How do you test whether this act or failure is negligent? In an ordinary case it is generally said, that you judge that by the action of the man in the street. He is the ordinary man. In one case it has been said that you judge it by the conduct of the man on the top of a Clapham omnibus. He is the ordinary man. But where you get a situation which involves the use of some special skill or competence, then the test whether there has been negligence or not is not the test of the man on the top of a Clapham omnibus, because he has not got this special skill. The test is the standard of the ordinary skilled man exercising and professing to have that special skill. A man need not possess the highest expert skill at the risk of being found negligent. It is well-established law that it is sufficient if he exercises the ordinary skill of an ordinary competent man exercising that particular art.' *Bolam v Friern Hospital Management Committee* [1957] 2 All ER 118 at 121, per McNair J

Australia 'Whenever anyone does anything of such a kind or in such circumstances that a reasonable man ought to realise that other persons or their property are likely to be exposed to its consequences and that there is a risk of its injuring them or their property unless it is done carefully, and would therefore take care to prevent such injury, he owes them a legal duty to take all reasonable precautions to prevent what he is doing from injuring them, and is negligent if he does not. A breach of this legal duty does not vest in a person to whom it was owed a cause of action for damages at common law unless the breach caused him some damage; but the legal duty none the less exists. Negligence may take the form of an act or an omission, doing what a reasonable man would not do, or omitting to do what he would do.' *Taylor v Comr for Main Roads* (1945) 46 NSWSR 117 at 119, per Jordan CJ

Australia 'Negligence is a failure to attain to the standard of care which a reasonable man would consider appropriate in the particular circumstances.' *R v Newman* [1948] ALR 109 at 112, per Barry J

Australia 'Negligence is the breach of a duty owed by one person to another, a duty to take care, to do the things that a reasonably prudent man would do in the circumstances and not to do the things he would not do.' *Tucker v McCann* [1948] WVLR 322 at 225, per Herring CJ

Canada 'It may be convenient to use a phraseology which has been current for some time in the Canadian courts, especially in Ontario, though it is not precise. The negligence which the plaintiff proves to launch his case is called "primary" or "original" negligence. The defendant may answer that by proving against the plaintiff "contributory negligence". If the defendant fails to avoid the consequences of that contributory negligence, and so brings about the injury, which he could and ought to have avoided, this is called "ultimate" or "resultant" negligence. The opinion has been several times expressed, in various forms, that "original" negligence and "ultimate" negligence are mutually exclusive, and that conduct which has once been relied on to prove the first cannot in any shape constitute proof of the second. The whole law of negligence in accident cases is now very well settled, and, beyond the difficulty of explaining it to a jury in terms of the decided cases, its application is plain enough. Many persons are apt to think that, in a case of contributory negligence like the present, the injured man deserved to be hurt, but the question is not one of desert or the lack of it, but of the cause legally responsible for the injury. However, when once the steps are followed the jury can see what they have to do, for the good sense of the rules is apparent. The inquiry is a judicial inquiry. It does not always follow the historical method and begin at the beginning. Very often it is more convenient to begin at the end, that is at the accident, and work back along the line of events which led up to it. The object of the inquiry is to fix upon some wrong-doer the responsibility for the wrongful act which has caused the damage. It is in search not merely of a casual agency but of the responsible agent. When that has been done, it is not necessary to pursue the matter into its origins; for judicial purposes they are remote. Till that has been done there may be a considerable sequence of physical events, and even of acts of responsible human beings, between the damage done and the conduct which is tortious and is its cause. It is surprising how many epithets eminent judges have applied to the cause, which has to be ascertained for this judicial purpose of determining liability, and how many more to other acts and incidents, which for this purpose are not the cause at all. "Efficient or effective cause", "real cause", "proximate cause", "direct cause", "decisive cause", "immediate cause", "*causa causans*", on the one hand, as against, on the other, "*causa sine qua non*", "occasional cause", "remote cause", "contributory cause", "inducing cause", "condition", and so on. No doubt in the particular cases in which they occur they were thought to be useful or they would not have been used, but the repetition of terms without examination in other cases has often led to confusion, and it might be better, after pointing out that the inquiry is an investigation into responsibility, to be content with speaking of the cause of the injury simply and without qualification.' *British Columbia Electric Rly Co Ltd v Loach* [1916] 1 AC 719 at 725, 727, 728, PC, per cur.

Canada 'It is to be remembered that s 294, sub-s 4 [of the Railway Act (RSC) 1906 (see now RSC 1970, c R 2, s 337)], places liability upon the railway company [for injury to animals at large] even if it has the best possible fence unless it establishes negligence. . . . "Negligence" in s 294 is apparently not used in the full sense generally attributed to it in the common law. Negligence is generally defined as a breach of duty to take reasonable care with reference to the rights of another party giving rise to a right to sue for damages in that other party. Here the owner's negligence, even if existing, does not give a right of action to the railway company. The negligence of the owner referred to in the section is rather a negligence of his own interests, a failure to take reasonable care of his own property.' *Quast v Grand Trunk Pacific Rly Co* (1916) 28 DLR 343 at 343, 344, Alta CA, per Stuart J

Canada 'Negligence is the failure, in certain circumstances, to exercise that degree of foresight which a court, in its aftersight, thinks ought to have been exercised. The proper standards of foresight and care are those attributed by a court to a reasonably careful, skilful person. The ideal of that person exists only in the minds of men, and exists in different forms in the minds of different men. The standard is therefore far from fixed as stable. But it is the best all-round guide that the law can devise, and the degree of correctness with which it is applied in deciding cases depends on the ability, astuteness and wisdom of the court that makes use of that guide.' *Carlson v Chochinov* [1947] 1 WWR 755 at 759, Man KB, per Dysart J; affirmed [1948] 2 WWR 273, Man CA

Contributory negligence

In an action for injuries arising from negligence it was a complete defence at common law if the defendant proved that the plaintiff, by some negligence on his own part, directly contributed to the injury. However, the Law Reform (Contributory Negligence) Act 1945 provides that where any person suffers damage as the result partly of his own fault and partly of the fault of any other person or persons, a claim in respect of that damage is not to be defeated by reasons of the fault of the person suffering the damage, but the damages recoverable in respect thereof are to be reduced to such extent as the court thinks just and equitable having regard to the claimant's share in the responsibility for the damage. (34 Halsbury's Laws (4th edn) para 68)

'Contributory negligence in such a case as the present seems to me to consist of the absence of that ordinary care which a sentient being ought reasonably to have taken for his own safety, and which had it been exercised would have enabled him to avoid the injury of which he complains, or the doing of some act which he ought not to have done and but for which the calamity would not have occurred.' *Wakelin v London & South Western Rly Co* (1886) 12 App Cas 41 at 51, per Lord Fitzgerald

'When a man steps into the road he owes a duty to himself to take care for his own safety, but he does not owe any duty to a motorist who is going at an excessive speed to avoid being run down. Nevertheless, if he does not keep a good lookout, he is guilty of contributory negligence. The real question is not whether the plaintiff was neglecting some legal duty, but whether he was acting as a reasonable man and with reasonable care.' *Davies v Swan Motor Co (Swansea) Ltd, James, Third Party* [1949] 2 KB 291 at 324, 325, CA, per Denning LJ

'Just as actionable negligence requires the foreseeability of harm to others, so contributory negligence requires the foreseeability of harm to oneself. A person is guilty of contributory negligence if he ought reasonably to have foreseen that, if he did not act as a reasonable, prudent man, he might be hurt himself; and in his reckonings he must take into account the possibility of others being careless.' *Jones v Livox Quarries Ltd* [1952] 2 QB 608 at 615, per Denning LJ

Australia 'Two points of importance as to the legal significance of the expression "contributory negligence" are involved. . . . The first is that "negligence" . . . really means unreasonable "conduct". "Negligence" is usually employed to denote absence of care towards others, but in this connection the conduct of a plaintiff which disentitles him to recover notwithstanding the true "negligence" of the defendant has, to some extent at all events, caused him damage, may be either want of care for another, that is, negligence strictly so called, or want of care or caution for his own safety, more properly called "neglect". The issue as to his own conduct is not whether he is responsible to another, but whether he is really the author or an author of his own misfortune. The other point involved is the meaning of "contributory". It is technical. It is not satisfied by a contribution in fact as a sine qua non, and it is more than possible that in the present case the jury may not have had this in mind. No negligence on the part of the plaintiff is in law "deemed" (Lord Birkenhead [in *Admiralty Comrs v SS Volute* [1922] 1 AC 129 at 136] was careful to use the word "deemed") "contributory" unless, where the initial negligence is that of the defendant, the plaintiff by exercising the care and caution reasonably to be expected of him in the circumstances would have avoided the damage, or unless, where the initial negligence is that of the plaintiff, the defendant, even by the exercise of such care and caution as he reasonably should have exercised in the whole circumstances, could not in the result have avoided the consequences of the plaintiff's negligence or carelessness. Only in those cases can the plaintiff's conduct be considered a causa causans, or, in other words, a proximate cause.' *Symons v Stacey* (1922) 30 CLR 169 at 177, 178, per Isaacs J

Australia 'The term "contributory negligence" can properly only be applied to a case where both parties, the plaintiff and the defendant, are each guilty of negligence so connected with the injury as to be a cause materially contributing to it. If the negligence of either party falls short of that test, it is an irrelevant matter.' *Pilloni v Doyle* (1949) 49 NSWSR 13 at 19, per Davidson J

Canada 'It is perhaps unfortunate that the phrase "contributory negligence" uses the word "negligence" in a sense somewhat different from that which the latter word would bear when negligence is the cause of action. It may be pointed out that in the Law Reform (Contributory Negligence) Act 1945 of the United Kingdom Parliament the contrast between the two meanings is recognised, for that Act, which provides for a sharing of responsibility for damage where a person suffers damage as a result partly of his own fault and partly of the fault of any other person or persons, defines "fault" as "negligence, breach of statutory duty or other act or omission which gives rise to a liability in tort or would, apart from this Act, give rise to the defences of contributory negligence". The Contributory Negligence Act of British Columbia [1936] which was passed before the United Kingdom Act, does not contain a definition of "fault", but there is no doubt that in British Columbia the conception of contributory negligence, which is part of the common law, is the same as in this country. Such a plea should be treated as setting up want of care by the plaintiff for his own safety, whether in the circumstances of the accident the plaintiff owed a duty to the defendant or not.' *Nance v British Columbia Electric Rly Co Ltd* [1951] AC 601 at 612, PC, per Viscount Simon

Criminal negligence

'In *R v Bateman* [(1925) 19 Cr App Rep 8] . . . the Lord Chief Justice . . . said . . . "In explaining to juries the test which they should apply to determine whether the negligence . . . amounted . . . to a crime, judges have used many epithets such as 'culpable', 'gross', 'wicked', 'clear', 'complete'. But whatever epithet be used and whether an epithet be used or not, in order to establish criminal liability the facts must be such that, in the opinion of the jury, the negligence of the accused went beyond a mere matter of compensation between subjects and showed such a disregard for the life and safety of others as to amount to a crime against the State and conduct deserving punishment". . . . The substance of the judgment . . . in my opinion is correct. . . . For purposes of the criminal law there are degrees of negligence: and a very high degree of negligence is required to be proved before the felony [of homicide] is established. Probably of all the epithets that can be applied "reckless" most nearly covers the case: . . . but it is probably not all-embracing, for "reckless" suggests an indifference to risk whereas the accused may have appreciated the risk and intended to avoid it and yet shown such a high degree of negligence in the means adopted to avoid the risk as would justify a conviction.' *Andrews v Director of Public Prosecutions* [1937] AC 576 at 582, 583, per Lord Atkin

See, generally, 11 Halsbury's Laws (4th edn) para 1171.

Gross negligence

'The term gross negligence is found in many of the reported cases on this subject; and it is manifest that no uniform meaning has been ascribed to those words, which are more correctly used in describing the sort of negligence for which a gratuitous bailee is responsible, and have been somewhat loosely used with reference to carriers for hire: and in *Hinton v Dibber* [(1842) 2 QB 646]—a case depending on the Carriers Act [1830]—Lord Denman, in giving judgment, observed, with much truth: "It may well be doubted whether between gross negligence, and negligence merely, any intelligible distinction exists". In *Owen v Burnett*, [(1834) 2 Cr & M 353] Bayley B says: "As for the cases of what is called gross negligence, which throws upon the carrier the responsibility from which but for that he would have been exempt, I believe, that, in the greater number of them, it will be found that the carrier was guilty of misfeasance". . . . There is nothing in this declaration amounting to a charge of misfeasance, or renunciation of the character in which the defendants received the goods. The charge is, that they ought to have taken precautions to guard against the consequences of friction of wheels and axles; and that they did not do so; and were guilty of gross negligence, in not doing it. The terms gross negligence, and culpable negligence, cannot alter the nature of the thing omitted; nor can they exaggerate such omission into an act of misfeasance, or renunciation of the character in which the defendants received the horses to be carried.' *Austin v Manchester, Sheffield & Lincolnshire Rly Co* (1852) 10 CB 454 at 474, 475, per cur.

[The plaintiff had passed a night at an inn, as a guest: and, in the course of the night, a watch and some sovereigns, his property, and which he had at the inn, were stolen by a person who was afterwards tried for the theft and convicted. The defence was, that the loss had been occasioned by the 'negligence' of the owner, who had shown some money in the commercial room of the inn, and had afterwards placed his watch on the table in his bedroom, leaving the door of the bedroom ajar. The sovereigns which were lost were in a paper in a pocket of the plaintiff's trousers, which lay on a chair in the room.] 'It does not appear that there was any information given to the jury as to what they were to understand by gross negligence. If they were told to understand by gross negligence the absence of that ordinary care which, under the circumstances, a prudent man ought to have taken, as seems to have been the meaning given to gross negligence in some of the modern cases cited before us, the direction as to the degree of negligence might not have been objectionable: but the legal meaning of gross negligence is greater negligence than the absence of such ordinary care. It is such a degree of negligence as excludes the loosest degree of care, and is said to amount to *dolus*. We think that the rule of law resulting from all the authorities is that, in a case like the present, the goods remain under the charge of the innkeeper, and the protection of the inn, so as to make the innkeeper liable as for breach of duty unless the negligence of the guest occasions the loss in such a way as that the loss would not have happened if the guest had used the ordinary care that a prudent man may be reasonably expected to have taken under the circumstances.' *Cashill v Wright* (1856) 6 E & B 891 at 899, 900, per cur.

'The authorities are numerous, and the language of the judgments various, but for all practical purposes the rule may be stated to be, that the failure to exercise reasonable care, skill and diligence is gross negligence.' *Beal v South Devon Rly* (1864) 3 H & C 337 at 341, 342, per Crompton J

'I entirely agree with the dictum of Lord Cranworth in *Wilson v Brett* [(1843) 11 M & W 113] that gross negligence is ordinary negligence with a vituperative epithet. . . . The confusion seems to have arisen in using the word "negligence" as if it was an affirmative word, whereas, in truth, it is a negative word; it is the absence of such care, skill and diligence as it was the duty of the person to bring to the performance of the work which he is said not to have performed.' *Grill v General Iron Screw Collier Co* (1866) 35 LJCP 321 at 330, per Willes J

'If they [the defendants] were gratuitous bailees, it is clear that they would only be liable for that degree of negligence which would earn the epithet of "gross". I do not know whether that degree of negligence can be accurately defined, but it must be some sort of carelessness which would appear to the plain man of common sense as being gross.' *Martin v London County Council* [1947] KB 628 at 631, per Henn Collins J

'Epithets applied to negligence, so far as the common law is concerned, are meaningless. Negligence is well known and well defined. A man is either guilty of negligence or he is not. Gross negligence is not known to the English common law so far as civil proceedings are concerned, and one has only to consider the phrase in criminal cases, particularly in cases of manslaughter.' *Pentecost v London District Auditor* [1951] 2 All ER 330 at 332, per Lynskey J

'The use of the expression "gross negligence" is always misleading. Except in the one case when the law relating to manslaughter is being considered, the words "gross negligence" should never be used in connection with any matter to which the common law relates because negligence is a breach of duty, and, if there is a duty and there has been a breach of it which causes loss, it matters not whether it is a venial breach or a serious breach. A breach of legal duty in any degree which causes loss is actionable.' Ibid at 333, per Lord Goddard

'In relation . . . to professional negligence I regard the phrase "gross negligence" only as indicating so marked a departure from the normal standard of conduct of a professional man as to infer a lack of that ordinary care which a man of ordinary skill would display.' *Hunter v Hanley* 1955 SLT 213 at 217, per the Lord President (Clyde)

'It appears to me that in civil cases based on negligence . . . there is, as recognised in recent precedents and practice, only one standard, viz the absence of reasonable care in the circumstances of ordinary *culpa*. It is however recognised that in relation to criminal responsibility flowing from negligence, the words "gross negligence" are not uncommonly used to denote the very high standard of negligence or recklessness required to establish criminal responsibility—a degree of negligence which goes beyond a mere case of compensation between subjects in a civil claim, and is higher than ordinary negligence or *culpa*.' Ibid at 218, per Lord Russell

Canada 'The term "gross negligence" involves a combination of inconsistent elements and when used as it is in conjunction with "wilful and wanton misconduct" it implies a certain mens rea, an intentional disregard of danger, a recklessness.' *Osmond v McColl-Frontenac Oil Co Ltd* (1939) 47 Man LR 176 at 178, Man KB, per Dysart J

Canada 'I think that "gross negligence" and "wilful and wanton misconduct" connote different mental attitudes, presumably of similar gravity; and that the intention of the statute is to express a standard of care in negative and positive terms, each of which may include the other. That being so, inadvertence, or mistake or error of judgment by the driver of an automobile would not, in an ordinary case, be gross negligence. I would not attempt to make an exhaustive statement of the elements necessary to constitute gross negligence; but when, instead of taking reasonable care, the driver, in circumstances which showed neither necessity nor excuse, intentionally took great risks, which he knew to be dangerous and in so doing endangered the lives and severely injured the persons of those with him in the automobile, the jury might reasonably find him grossly negligent. It was a question for them, which they established by their finding: "Reckless driving".' *Murray v McCulloch* [1941] 3 DLR 42 at 57, per Graham J; affirmed [1942] SCR 141

Canada 'The meaning of the term "gross negligence" has been considered in many cases. . . . These cases, it seems, acknowledge that the term "gross negligence" is not susceptible of definition but that it may be paraphrased as "very great negligence". When so stated, the term suggests that a defendant is not held up to the ordinary level of duty in respect of care, and is liable only if it falls very far below that level.' *Paul v Dauphin* [1941] 1 WWR 43 at 46, Man KB; affirmed [1941] 2 WWR 224, Man CA

Canada 'All these phrases, gross negligence, wilful misconduct, wanton misconduct, imply conduct in which, if there is not conscious wrong doing, there is a very marked departure from the standards by which responsible and competent people in charge of motor cars habitually govern themselves.' *McCulloch v Murray* [1942] SCR 141 at 145, SCC, per Duff CJ

Canada 'As I understand the recent decisions of the courts interpreting the term "gross negligence" the expression must be taken to import conduct which in terms of the surrounding circumstances has aggravated flagrant or extreme characteristics.' *Scardina v LaRoche* [1951] 1 DLR 117 at 127, BCCA, per Bird JA

Canada 'What exactly is meant by "gross negligence"? Now, courts have repeatedly declined to give any general, or abstract, definition of the expression: whether conduct is negligent at all, or grossly negligent, must depend upon the circumstances of each case. What all the authorities seem to agree upon is that the words connote something going beyond ordinary actionable negligence. Some judges translate them as "great negligence"; others, as "very great negligence". Without joining in the dispute at all, I will only give it as my opinion, having regard to all the arguments I have advanced above, that the best view is that . . . the word gross, which seems to have become a term of reproach and usually to suggest something opprobrious, is used in its simple and original sense of denoting something large.' *Drake v Power* (1961) 46 at 104, 105, Nfld SC, per Winter J

Canada 'Sedgewick J in *City of Kingston v Drennan* [(1896) 27 SCR 46], defined gross negligence as "very great negligence". This paraphrase has generally been accepted and while it is probably not too satisfactory, it clearly indicates that in any given case the factual situation, in order to form a basis for gross negligence, must indicate conduct that is a marked departure from the standard by which ordinary responsible persons govern themselves.' *Jackson v Millar* [1973] 1 OR 399 at 404, Ont CA, per Evans JA

NEGOTIABLE INSTRUMENT

'Wherever we find words which have no accurately fixed meaning, we are bound to give them the ordinary sense; and I am sure it would startle every member of the mercantile community were they to hear that it had been decided that a bank-note was not a negotiable instrument. . . . It is said that the words "negotiable instrument" are to be confined to . . . bills of exchange. . . . If this narrow mode of construction is adopted, it is absurd; for then a promissory note, which is really *ejusdem generis* with a bill of exchange, is excluded.' *M'Donnell v Murray* (1860) 1 LT 498 at 500, per Pigot CB

'In the notes of *Miller v Race* [(1758) 1 Burr 452] where all the authorities are collected, the very learned author [of 1 Smith, LC (12th edn), at p 533] says: "It may therefore be laid down as a safe rule that where an instrument is by the custom of trade transferable, like cash, by delivery, and is also capable of being sued upon by the person holding it pro tempore, then it is entitled to the name of a *negotiable instrument*, and the property in it passes to a bona fide transferee for value, though the transfer may not have taken place in market overt. But that if either of the above requisites be wanting, i.e. if it be either not accustomably transferable, or, though it be accustomably transferable, yet, if its nature be such as to render it incapable of being put in suit by the party holding it pro tempore, it is not a *negotiable instrument*, nor will delivery of it pass the property of it to a vendee, however bona fide, if the transferor himself have not a good title to it, and the transfer be made out of market overt." Bills of exchange and promissory notes, whether payable to order or to bearer, are by the law merchant negotiable in both senses of the word. The person who, by a genuine indorsement, or, where it is payable to bearer, by a delivery, becomes holder, may sue in his own name on the contract, and if he is a bona fide holder for value, he has a good title notwithstanding any defect of title in the party (whether indorser or deliverer) from whom he took it.' *Crouch v Credit Foncier of England Ltd* (1873) LR 8 QB 374 at 381, 382, per Blackburn J

United States Any writing to be a negotiable instrument within this Article must (a) be signed by the maker or drawer; and (b) contain an unconditional promise or order to pay a sum certain in money and no other promise, order, obligation or power given by the maker or drawer except as authorised in this Article; and (c) be payable on demand or at a definite time; and (d) be payable to order or to bearer. (Uniform Commercial Code 1978, s 3–104(1))

NEGOTIATE

[The Bills of Exchange Act 1882, s 20 provides that if a blank paper after completion is 'negotiated' to a holder in due course, it shall be valid and effectual for all purposes in his hands, and he may enforce it as if it had been filled up within a reasonable time and strictly in accordance with the authority given.] 'Can we hold that this note was "negotiated" to the plaintiff within the meaning with which the words are used in the proviso to the 20th section? . . . As to this, we certainly have the opinion of the late Lord Chief Justice that a delivery to a payee for value is not a "negotiating" within the meaning of the Act. In the 31st section it is said "a bill is negotiated when it is transferred from one person to another in such a manner as to constitute the transferee the holder of the bill". . . . We have come to the conclusion that we should be unfairly straining the words if we did not hold that "negotiated" in the proviso at the end of the 20th section meant transferred by one holder to another.' *Herdman v Wheeler* [1902] 1 KB 361 at 372, 373, 376, per cur.

NEGOTIATION

'Negotiation . . . is that which passes between parties or their agents in the course of or incident to the making of the contract; and if the negotiation is brought to such a close as leaves the principal at liberty to say, "I accept the offer"—then the agent has done all that a negotiating agent can do, and within the meaning of the rule he has arranged the sale, the sale afterwards being effected.' *Re Macgowan, Macgowan v Murray* [1891] 1 Ch 105 at 115, 116, CA, per Bowen LJ

Of commercial paper

United States Negotiation is the transfer of an instrument in such form that the transferee becomes a holder. If the instrument is payable to order it is negotiated by delivery with any necessary indorsement; if payable to bearer it is negotiated by delivery. (Uniform Commercial Code 1978, s 3–202(1))

NEIGHBOUR

'What is the right of the adjoining owner? . . . It is to the support of his land in its natural state—support by whom? The judges have said, "Support by his neighbour". What does that mean? Who is his neighbour? It was contended that all the landowners in England however distant, were neighbours for this purpose if their operations in any remote degree injured the land. But surely that cannot be the meaning of it. The neighbouring landowner to me for this purpose must be the owner of that portion of land, whether a wider or narrower strip of land, the existence of which in its natural state is necessary for the support of my land. As long as that land remains in its natural state, and it supports my land, I have no rights beyond it, and therefore it seems to me that he is my neighbour for this purpose. There might be land of so solid a character, consisting of solid stone, that a foot of it would be enough to support the land. There might be other land so friable and of such an unsolid character that you would want a quarter of a mile of it. But whatever it is, as long as you have got enough land on your boundary, which left untouched will support your land, you have got your neighbour's land whose support you are entitled to.' *Birmingham Corpn v Allen* (1877) 6 Ch D 284 at 289, CA, per Jessel MR

'Who, then, in law is my neighbour? The answer seems to be persons who are so closely and directly affected by my act that I ought reasonably to have them in contemplation as being so affected when I am directing my mind to the acts or omissions which are called in question.' *M'Alister (or Donoghue) v Stevenson* [1932] AC 562 at 580, per Lord Atkin

NEIGHBOURHOOD

[An agreement for the sale of a retail milk business contained a covenant by the vendor not to employ anyone or to retail milk on his own account in the 'neighbourhood' of Southampton or Norham.] 'The word neighbourhood equals in this case a distance to stop competition. We are asked to say that because an agreement has the word "neighbourhood" in it, you cannot enforce it by injunction. It is not too wide.' *Stride v Martin* (1897) 77 LT 600 at 601, DC, per Channell J

[A section of a repealed Act empowered the court to authorise the conversion of a house into several tenements, where it was proved that, owing to changes in the character of the 'neighbourhood' in which such house was situate, the house could not readily be let as a ingle tenement but could readily be let for ccupation if converted into tenements.] 'I ass now to consider what is indicated by the xpression "neighbourhood". In this conection it is impossible to lay down any genral rule. In country districts people are said o be neighbours, that is, to live in the same eighbourhood, who live many miles apart. 'he same cannot be said of dwellers in a town vhere a single street or a single square may onstitute a neighbourhood within the neaning of the section. Again, physical conitions may determine the boundary or oundaries of a neighbourhood, as, for nstance, a range of hills, a river, a railway, r the line which separates a high-class esidential district from a district consisting nly of artisans' or workmen's dwellings. Again, I think that the physical conditions f some particular area may entitle it to be onsidered as a matter of law as neighbourhood within the meaning of he section. The circumstances must be xceptional, but I think that they may exist.' *lliance Economic Investment Co v Berton* (1923) 92 LJKB 750 at 752, CA, per Bankes LJ

ustralia 'What constitutes "the neighourhood" in any given case is related to he nature of the proposed development, ts potential consequences and the area over vhich they may extend, and the particular spect of amenity which is liable to be ffected thereby. Similarly, the ambit of "the ocality" is related to the character of the roposed development and of the surroundng development, and to the particular lement of conformity or disconformity, harnony or inharmony, of one with the other, vhich are in question. Although it has a lependence on geographical considerations, he ambit of these expressions is not necesarily governed entirely thereby. Other actors may be material in delimiting a 'locality" or a "neighbourhood", such as an xisting homogeneity of development whether the product of restrictions or the esult of spontaneous growth) or a planning cheme or planning proposals. It is impos-ible to attach to these expressions a greater recision of definition than they themselves, ead in their context, or the inherent diffiulties of the subject matter, permit.' *Shellcove Gardens Pty Ltd v North Sydney Municipal Council* [1960] NSWR 237 at 244, per Sugerman J

NEIGHBOURING

'The lease . . . contained a power in case of non-payment of the rent to distrain upon and sell the goods and chattels of the company "in or about any of the premises hereby demised or any adjoining or neighbouring collieries". These last words give rise to the difficulty which has arisen. . . . The words "neighbouring colliery" are large enough to apply to collieries in the neighbourhood not worked with the seam of coal demised. I am, however, of opinion that to construe those words in that wide sense would be unreasonable and extravagant. The power of distress must, in my opinion, be construed to apply to those neighbouring mines only which, though not actually adjoining the seam of coal demised, might be or become connected with it by underground workings.' *Re Roundwood Colliery Co, Lee v Roundwood Colliery Co* [1897] 1 Ch 373 at 389, CA, per Lindley LJ

NEPHEW—NIECE

'According to the ordinary rule of construction the word nieces as used in this will must be taken in its natural sense, which beyond all doubt means the children of a brother or sister. The word is derived from the Latin *nepos*, signifying a grandchild, but it is clear that such an interpretation could not now be given to the word nephew or niece. . . . Here the word nieces might doubtless be construed as grandnieces, but when there is no evidence that the testatrix has used the word in any other sense than that of niece proper, it would be contrary to all precedent to give the term a more extended signification. . . . The testatrix must have known that there had been more than one niece, though she may have believed that there were some deceased. The doubt has arisen from the fact of there being only one such niece at the date of the will. It was not contended that she meant to exclude that one, but that she must be understood to have meant to include grandnieces also. I think that it cannot be so understood.' *Crook v Whitley* (1857) 7 De GM & G 490 at 494, 495, per Lord Cranworth LC

'Looking at the will, and at such parts of the evidence as are plainly admissible, I think that the plaintiff's title is established. There was, when the will was made, a person who answered sufficiently the description of "my niece Elizabeth Stringer". It is true that her name was Elizabeth Jane, but it is hardly to be called error of description to leave out one of her christian names and designate her simply by the other. She was a great-grandniece; still she was a niece, and there being no other person of any similar name who answered the description of niece at all, she was naturally described simply as "niece".' *Stringer v Gardiner* (1859) 4 De G & J 468 at 471, per Lord Campbell LC

'Here there is a gift in these terms, "Unto all my nephews and nieces". Have these words a primary signification? The Court of Appeal has so decided in two cases. In the case of *Re Blower's Trusts* [(1871) 6 Ch App 351 at 355], Lord Justice Mellish observed: "It is clear that the words 'nephews and nieces' prima facie mean the children of brothers and sisters'; and in *Sherratt v Mountford* [(1873) 8 Ch App 928] the same learned judge observed: "There is no doubt a man's nephews and nieces are primarily his nephews and nieces, but I am of opinion that his wife's nephews and nieces are his nephews and nieces according to the ordinary meaning of the words in a secondary sense.' If that is so, the words "my nephews and nieces" must, according to these decisions, mean nephews and nieces in the primary sense, unless there is something in the context to give the words a different meaning.' *Wells v Wells* (1874) LR 18 Eq 504 at 505, 506, per Jessel MR

[A testator by his will gave his property to his wife for life and after her death to all his 'nephews and nieces' living at her death.] 'The nephews and nieces of the half-blood are included in the gift; the question is covered by the authority of the case *Reeves v Rawley* [*Grieves v Rawley* (1852) 10 Hare 63].' *Re Hammersley, Kitchen v Myers* (1886) 2 TLR 459 at 459, per Chitty J

'The question is whether under the gift to the children of the testator's sister Jane Weightman, Richard H Weightman [an illegitimate child of Jane Weightman], who is called "nephew" in the early part of the will, is to be included. . . . In *Bagley v Mollard* [(1830) 1 Russ & M 581] . . . the Master of the Rolls (Sir John Leach) . . . following the opinion of Lord Eldon in *Wilkinson v Adam* [(1813) 1 Ves & B 422] put the case on the broad ground that whenever the general description of children will include legitimate children, it cannot also be extended to illegitimate children. . . . Here there is nothing whatever in the will to include Richard H Weightman among the children of Jane Weightman except the description of him in the earlier part of the will by the word "nephew". . . . On the whole . . . I must hol that he does not take as one of the children c Jane Weightman under the general gift t children contained in the later part of the will *Re Hall, Branston v Weightman* (1887) 35 Ch 551 at 555–557, per Kay J

'I find . . . a gift to "all the nephews and niece living at my death". That, beyond all questior if it stood alone, means "my legitimat nephews and nieces living at my death"; but, c course, there may be something in the will t show that it is not confined to legitimat nephews and nieces, and that it include illegitimate nephews and nieces—or, possibly that it includes an illegitimate nephew or niece But there must be something in the will to lea one to that conclusion, and enable one to pu upon the words "nephew and nieces living a my death" some other than their natural an proper prima facie meaning, which is "m legitimate nephews and nieces".' *Re Brown Brown v Brown* (1889) 58 LJ Ch 420 at 423, pe North J

'The testator gave his residuary estate to hi "niece Eliza Waterhouse". There was no pe son accurately answering to that descriptior Neither the testator nor his wife had any niece but his wife had two grandnieces, named Eliz Waterhouse, of whom one was legitimate an the other was illegitimate. . . . The perso most nearly answering the description is th legitimate grandniece of the testator's wife and . . . no evidence can be admitted to prov that her illegitimate grandniece was intended *Re Fish Ingham v Rayner* [1894] 2 Ch 83 at 8 CA, per Lindley LJ

'The sole question for decision is whether th defendant James William Robinson, who take a legacy under the title of "my wife's nephe James William Robinson" can share th residue given to "all and every the nephew an niece and the nephews and nieces of my sai wife", he being in truth not a nephew but a illegitimate child of a deceased brother of th testator's wife. . . . The term "nephew" c "niece" . . . postulates the marriage of th brother or sister. . . . Therefore Jame William Robinson cannot take under the gift c residue standing alone, and what I have t decide is whether the language in which a leg acy is given to him alters this interpreta tion. . . . It being permissible to enlarge th class of nephews and nieces so as to includ those who are illegitimate, if the testator ha indicated his intention that this should b done, and especially if he has furnished dictionary by means of which his language may be interpreted, I cannot hesitate to say that, as regards James William Robinson, the indication is here and the dictionary is forthcoming. . . . I now decide . . . that James William Robinson, notwithstanding his illegitimacy, is included in the class of "my wife's nephews and nieces".' *Re Parker, Parker v Osborne* [1897] 2 Ch 208 at 210, 211, 213, per Kekewich J

'The words "nephews and nieces" mean prima facie the children of brothers and sisters, including those of the half-blood. . . . The expression "my own nephews and nieces" in this will restricts the class to persons who are the lawful nephews and nieces of the testatrix, of the whole or half-blood, to the exclusion of great-nephews or great-nieces of the testatrix, nephews or nieces of her husband, a daughter of an illegitimate son of a sister of the testatrix, and all other persons, though some of them may have been inaccurately referred to in some other part of the will as "my nephew" or "my niece".' *Re Cozens, Miles v Wilson* [1903] 1 Ch 138 at 141, 144, per Swinfen Eady J

'The question . . . is whether there are included amongst the class to take not only the two persons expressly included, namely, the illegitimate son of the testator's legitimate brother and the illegitimate son of the testator's natural sister Mary, but also the legitimate descendants of the testator's natural sister Sarah. . . . It is, I think, fairly clear that the testator . . . is obviously using both the word "sister" in relation to the parent of a nephew, and the word "nephew" itself, in a sense going beyond the strict legal meaning of the word, and as including in the case of the word . . . "nephew" a son of a natural sister.' *Re Helliwell, Pickles v Helliwell* [1916] 2 Ch 580 at 585, 586, per Sargant J

'The problem to be decided in this case is what the testatrix meant by the residuary devise when she used the words "nephews and nieces". . . . I have come to the conclusion regarding the residuary devise in this will which is in these words: subject to the payment of funeral and testamentary expenses she gives her residue "Upon trust that my trustees shall divide the same equally between all or any my nephews and nieces living at my death". If one looks at those words alone it is absolutely clear to demonstration that the words mean nephews and nieces in the ordinary sense in which those words are used in the English language: sons and daughters of brothers or sisters, and if another meaning is to be attached to them one must find somewhere in the will what is called a dictionary whereby you can draw the conclusion that the testatrix did not mean what she says but meant to put on the words of her will a special meaning which they would not have in the absence of that alleged dictionary; and the effort is made to find a dictionary in the third clause of the will, which is in these terms: "I give free of duty to my nephew Clifford Rich the infant child of my late niece Annie Gertrude Rich the sum of one thousand pounds". So far from inducing me to give a special meaning to the residuary devise to the nephews, that seems to indicate to me that she was in this clause providing for that person whom she described as "the infant child of my late niece Annie Gertrude Rich", and refers affectionately to as her nephew, providing for him because his mother was dead; she would take no part of the residuary devise, and therefore the testatrix designated to put that individual in some kind of position of benefit which would put him more or less in the same position as if he were one of the children of somebody who took part of the residuary devise. It does not seem to me to indicate in the least degree that when she was dealing with her residuary property and providing for her nephews and nieces living at her death, she meant any persons except those who really were, in the true sense of the word, her nephews and nieces at her death.' *Re Ridge, Hancock v Dutton* (1933) 149 LT 266 at 270, 271, CA, per Greer LJ

'The testatrix . . . directed a division of her residuary estate: ". . . in equal shares per capita between such of my nephews and nieces and descendants of nephews and nieces as shall be living at the date of my death and shall attain the age of twenty-one years or being female marry under that age". The question is who are the nephews and nieces of the testatrix to whom she was referring in the words I have quoted. I have, in the first place, to consider what is in contemporary English the proper meaning of the word "nephew" and of the word "niece". There seems no doubt at all that the strict and proper meaning of the word "nephew" is "son of a brother or sister"; and, similarly, "niece" means, in the strict sense, "daughter of a brother or sister". But the meaning of each of these words is, in my judgment, susceptible of extension, having regard to the context and circumstances of the case, in two directions. First of all, the word may describe the child of a brother-in-law or of a sister-in-law; and, in the second place, I think that "nephew" is often used to indicate a niece's husband and "niece" is often used to describe the wife of a nephew. There are, of course, other extensions of meaning which may have to be made in special cases, such as, for exampe, in the case of an adopted child. Unless compelled by context or circumstances, the court will always construe a class gift to nephews and nieces as a gift confined to children of a brother or sister, and the mere fact that the testator or testatrix has chosen elsewhere in the will erroneously to describe as a nephew or a niece some person not strictly and properly so related to him or her will not affect the general rule by admitting that person into the class.' *Re Daoust, Dobell v Dobell* [1944] 1 All ER 443 at 444, per Vaisey J

Australia 'There is not here [in a will] a context sufficient to deprive the word "nieces" of its legal signification as meaning nieces by blood and not by affinity.' *Re Davis, Douglass v McPhee* (1933) 33 NSWSR 330 at 332, per Long Innes J

Australia 'By what often may be a technical rule, gifts to children, and, of course, gifts to nephews and nieces, in a will are construed as gifts to those born in wedlock or to those who according to the law which governs the construction of a will, are legitimate.' *Re James, Equity Trustees Executors & Agency Co Ltd v James* [1942] VLR 12 at 15, per Gavan Duffy J

Canada 'With respect to the words "lawful nephews and nieces of the first blood" [in a will] I do not think the word "lawful" can have any special significance under the circumstances involved here. The phrase "of the first blood" does not appear to have any definite meaning in legal terminology. But I am not able to give these words any meaning which would have the effect of enlarging or extending the usual and ordinary meaning of the words "nephews and nieces". If they are disregarded as meaningless or treated as mere surplusage, then the residuary estate goes to the nephews and nieces of the testator and prima facie nephews and nieces mean children of brothers or sisters of the testator.' *Re Waines Estate* [1944] 4 DLR 149 at 154, Alta SC, per Macdonald J; affirmed [1947] 1 WWR 880

NERVOUS

'We must . . . take it as proved that the negligent driving of the defendants' servant reasonably and naturally caused a nervous or mental shock to the plaintiff by her reasonable apprehension of immediate bodily hurt, and that the premature childbirth, with the physical pain and suffering which accompanied it, was a natural and a direct consequence of the shock. I may just say in passing that I use the words "nervous" and "mental" as interchangeable epithets on the authority of the judgment of the Privy Council in *Victorian Railways Comrs v Coultas* [(1888) 13 App Cas 222], but I venture to think "nervous" is probably the more correct epithet where terror operates through parts of the physical organism to produce bodily illness, as in the present case.' *Dulieu v White & Sons* [1901] 2 KB 669 at 672, 673, per Kennedy J

NET

'The accounts which the defendants rendered to the plaintiff have charged him every fortnight a certain sum (say) "8½*d*. net". That was a sum which exceeded the amount they were paying to the jobber and was a sum charged to cover both the payment made to the jobber and the services of the brokers in carrying over the shares. I understand the word "net" to mean "neat" or exact. . . . According to the language of the Stock Exchange it seems that the word "net" is used to mean "I am not going to charge you any more than this; this is the total amount of my charge".' *Stubbs v Slater* [1910] 1 Ch 632 at 643, 644, CA, per Buckley LJ

'In my opinion no distinction can be drawn . . . between a "clear" yearly sum, and a "net" yearly sum.' *Re Waller, Margarison v Waller* [1916] 1 Ch 153 at 159, per Sargant J

'I think that when the testator uses the words "net annual proceeds" . . . he means the free income of the estate after paying income tax.' *Smith's Trustees v Gaydon* 1919 SC 95 at 98, per Lord Cullen

Net estate

'Net estate', in relation to a deceased person, means—

(a) all property of which the deceased had power to dispose by his will (otherwise than by virtue of a special power of appointment) less the amount of his funeral, testamentary and administration expenses, debts and liabilities, including any capital transfer tax payable out of his estate on his death;

(b) any property in respect of which the deceased held a general power of appointment (not being a power exercisable by will) which has not been exercised;
(c) any sum of money or other property which is treated for the purposes of this Act as part of the net estate of the deceased . . .;
(d) any property which is treated for the purposes of this Act as part of the net estate of the deceased by virtue of an order. . . .;
(e) any sum of money or other property which is by reason of a disposition or contract made by the deceased, ordered . . . to be provided for the purpose of the making of financial premium under the Act.

(Inheritance (Provision for Family and Dependants) Act 1975, s 25(1))

Net profits

'There is no occasion to lay down any general rule as to the effect of the expression "net profit". It is preposterous to speak of such an expression as having an inflexible sense. There may be cases in which the use of such words would not exclude the interest of capital from the calculation of profit.' *Kirkby v Wright* (1833) Coop *temp*. Brough 215 at 218, per Lord Brougham LC

'In the course of the argument upon this present case I think that we have arrived at a very clear perception of the principle upon which the directors and the company were bound to act in ascertaining . . . net profits. The first step would be to make good the capital by taking stock and putting a value upon all the assets of the company, of whatever nature, and deducting therefrom all the liabilities (including amongst those liabilities the amount of contributed capital), and the surplus, if any, then remaining of the gross receipts would be net profit.' *Binney v Ince Hall Coal & Cannel Co* (1866) 35 LJ Ch 363 at 367, per Kindersley V-C

[Article 57 of the articles of association of a company provided that the directors, as remuneration for their services, should be paid in each year out of the funds of the company either a sum of £300 or a sum equal to 3 per cent of the 'net profits' of the company for such year.] 'The plaintiff alleges . . . that a large profit was made by the company on this sale—a profit of some £600,000 . . . and on this profit, whatever it may actually be, the plaintiff claims one-fifth of 3 per cent as being "net profits" of the year. In my opinion article 57 is addressed to the state of things existing while the company is a going concern, and does not apply to a winding-up or to any profit made by the sale of the whole undertaking.' *Frames v Bultfontein Mining Co* [1891] 1 Ch 140 at 142, per Chitty J

[A testator bequeathed to a legatee one fifth share of the 'net profits' in three undertakings. The first two undertakings were limited companies in each of which the testator held shares and to each of which he had made advances. The third was a verbal partnership, two third shares in which belonged to the testator.] 'It is an undoubted rule of law, or rather perhaps of construction, that a gift unlimited in point of time of the income of a fund is a gift of the fund itself, and the reason is obvious, for it would be absurd to say that the income arising from a fund was for all time to be paid to one person while the corpus of the fund was to belong to someone else. What I have to consider is whether the rule is applicable to the case of dividends derived by a shareholder from shares in a limited company. I can see no reason why it should not be. Dividends arising from a share in a limited company are the fruit of the share, and therefore a gift unlimited in time of the dividends on a share in a company is as much a gift of the share as a gift of the income of a sum of Consols is a gift of the sum itself. . . . What can a gift of "net profits" in a limited company mean except a gift of that which the testator was entitled to receive on his shares in the company? A shareholder is entitled to the dividends which are duly declared according to the articles of association of the company, and therefore a gift of the profits of shares amounts to a gift of the dividends on them, and that amounts to a gift of the corpus of the shares. . . . I cannot see how the net profits of a share in a partnership can come under the rule to which I have referred. The net profits of a partnership business are not the fruit of the capital employed in the business alone, but are the result of the employment of the capital and of the exertions of the partners as well; moreover, a partner's share of the profits may, and often does, bear no relation to the share in which he is interested in the capital of the partnership. In my opinion, therefore, the rule does not apply to a gift of a share of the net profits of a partnership, and such a gift does not entitle the legatee to a share in the corpus of the assets; but the words of the gift must have some meaning and effect given to them, and in my opinion the true meaning is that the legatee, his executors, administrators, or assigns, are entitled to receive one fifth share of that part of the net profits which would otherwise have been payable to the executors of the testator so long as the partnership business is being carried on.' *Re Lawes-Wittewronge, Maurice v Bennett* [1915] 1 Ch 408 at 412, 413, per Warrington J

'"Net profits" . . . signify the excess of receipts over current expenses and outgoings of a business, the fund which in any year is capable of being applied to the payment of a dividend or capable of being divided between partners as the fruit of the year's operations.' *Re Condran, Condran v Stark* [1917] 1 Ch 639 at 645, per Peterson J

'If a company having made an apparent net profit of £10,000, has then to pay £1,000 to directors or managers as the contractual recompense for their services during the year, it is plain that the real net profit is only £9,000. A contract to pay a commission at 10 per cent. on the net profits of the year must necessarily be held to mean on the net profits before the deduction of the commission, that is, in the case supposed, a commission on the £10,000.' *Indian Radio & Cable Communications Co v Income Tax Comr, Bombay Presidency & Aden* [1937] 3 All ER 709 at 714, PC, per Lord Maugham; applied by Greene MR in *British Sugar Manufacturers Ltd v Harris* [1938] 2 KB 220 at 236, 237, CA

NEW

'It is perfectly clear from the plaintiffs' documents that they regard and hold out to their distributors and to the public that a car ceases to be a new car once it is sold retail. That appears to me to be the only safe course to take. Once a car becomes the subject-matter of a sale or purchase, once it is registered with the local county council, once the number plates have been affixed and it has been driven out of the distributor's or the dealer's premises, that car, in my judgment, ceases to be a new car.' *Morris Motors Ltd v Lilley* [1959] 3 All ER 737 at 739, per Wynn-Parry J

'The heart of this case really turns on . . . the suggestion that a car ceases to be new as soon as it sustains any significant damage and irrespective of the quality of the repairs. This is a test which we do not find it possible to accept. It seems to us that in this respect the questions to be asked when a car has sustained damage which has thereafter been repaired, both events having occurred away from the manufacturer's premises, are first: what is the extent and nature of the damage? and second: what is the quality of the repairs which have been effected? If the damage which a new car after leaving the factory has sustained is, although perhaps extensive, either superficial in character or limited to certain defined parts of the vehicle which can be simply replaced by new parts, then provided that such damage is in practical terms perfectly repaired so that it can in truth be said after repairs have been effected that the vehicle is as good as new, in our judgment it would not be a false trade description to describe such a vehicle as new.' *R v Ford Motor Co Ltd* [1974] 3 All ER 489 at 495, CA, per cur.

Australia 'It is always difficult to define the simple words of common use; but I think the primary meaning of "new" is "not old" or "of recent origin", and I think that the onus is upon those who contend that a word like this is used in any secondary sense to show that it was so intended. New and old are relative terms, but it seems to me that there are various ways in which an article of commerce may lose the quality of newness. A thing is no longer "new" when it has been used for a comparatively short period—*Andrews Brothers (Bournemouth) Ltd v Singer & Co Ltd* [[1934] 1 KB 17, CA]—but when things become old they are no longer new, and if the mere lapse of time results in deterioration in quality, or depreciation in value, I think that the thing is no longer new according to the ordinary use of the English language.' *Anderson v Scrutton* [1934] SASR 10 at 11, per Napier J

Australia 'The meaning of the word "new" particularly in relation to motor vehicles has been considered several times in the courts. It seems there are at least five possible meanings which the word may bear when used to describe a vehicle. They are: 1. That the vehicle has not been previously sold by retail, that is, that it is not a secondhand vehicle; 2. That the vehicle is a current and not a superseded model; 3. That the vehicle has not suffered significant deterioration or been used to any significant extent; 4. That the vehicle is of recent origin; 5. That the vehicle is one which has suffered a measure of damage but this damage has been quite effectively repaired or any damaged part replaced and the vehicle is otherwise new in every respect.' *Annand & Thompson Pty Ltd v Trade Practices Commission* (1979) 40 FLR 165 at 168, per Franki J

Australia 'It is not easy to define simple words of common use; but in my opinion the word "new" as used in s 53(b) of the Act [Trade Practices Act 1974–1986 (Cth)] does not have a fixed and inflexible meaning for the purposes of the section applying to all cases irrespective of the context in which the representation is made. . . . Depending on the context in which the word appears, it may mean "not secondhand", "not old", "of recent origin", or "not excessively used". . . . For goods to be new they do not necessarily have to be in "mint condition" and the mere fact that goods are damaged, irrespective of the nature or quality of the repairs, does not mean that they have ceased to be new.' *Hollis v ABE Copiers Pty Ltd* (1979) 41 FLR 141 at 147, 148, per Lockhart J

NEW OR ORIGINAL

[The Patents and Designs Act 1907, s 49 (repealed; see now the Registered Designs Act 1949, ss 1, 3) provided for the registration of any 'new or original' design not previously published in the United Kingdom.] 'The words "new or original" involve the idea of novelty either in the pattern, shape, or ornament itself or in the way in which an old pattern, shape, or ornament is to be applied to some special subject-matter. There must be the exercise of intellectual activity so as to originate, that is to say suggest for the first time, something which had not occurred to any one before as to applying by some manual, mechanical, or chemical means some pattern, shape, or ornament to some special subject-matter to which it had not been applied before.' *Dover Ltd v Nürnberger Celluloidwaren Fabrik Gebrüder Wolff* [1910] 2 Ch 25 at 29, 30, CA, per Buckley LJ

NEWSPAPER

The word 'newspaper' shall mean any paper containing public news, intelligence, or occurrences, or any remarks or observations therein printed for sale, and published in England or Ireland periodically, or in parts or numbers at intervals not exceeding twenty-six days between the publication of any two such papers, parts, or numbers.

Also any paper printed in order to be dispersed, and made public weekly or oftener, or at intervals not exceeding twenty-six days, containing only or principally advertisements. (Newspaper Libel and Registration Act 1881, s 1)

In this section [which deals with qualified privilege in respect of newspapers] the expression 'newspaper' means any paper containing public news or observations thereon, or consisting wholly or mainly of advertisements, which is printed for sale and published in the United Kingdom either periodically or in parts or numbers at intervals not exceeding thirty-six days. (Defamation Act 1952, s 7(5))

'Newspaper' includes any periodical or magazine. (Accommodation Agencies Act 1953, s 1(6))

'Newspaper' includes any journal magazine or other periodical publication. (Lotteries and Amusements Act 1976, s 23(1))

NEWSPAPER PROPRIETOR

The word 'proprietor' shall mean and include as well the sole proprietor of any newspaper, as also in the case of a divided proprietorship the persons who, as partners or otherwise, represent and are responsible for any share or interest in the newspaper as between themselves and the persons in like manner representing or responsible for the other shares or interests therein, and no other person. (Newspaper Libel and Registration Act 1881, s 1)

NEWSREEL

Special provisions apply where a film consisting wholly or mainly of photographs which, at the time when they were taken, were means of communicating news, satisfies the following requirements: (1) that the maker was, throughout the time of its making, either a British subject or a citizen of the Republic of Ireland or of any country that is a member state or a qualified company; (2) that the film was edited in the United Kingdom and its commentary was written and recorded there; and (3) that each of the persons who edited it or spoke the commentary was a British subject or citizen of the Republic of Ireland. Where these conditions are satisfied, the Secretary of State must, on written application, by its maker or renter in the prescribed form and accompanied by the prescribed fee, certain statutory declarations and an undertaking as to its origin, register it as a British film and as a quota film. Where the film is so registered, the Films Act 1960 applies to it subject to certain modifications. Films which are so eligible for registration or which have been so registered are called 'newsreels'. (45 Halsbury's Laws (4th edn) para 1038)

NEXT

[Where a bill is returned for nonpayment to a party residing in the country, notice to the drawer, or other party, on the bill ought to be sent by the 'next post'.] 'I am of opinion that by "the next post" you must understand the next reasonably convenient post; otherwise the holder of the bill would have less time to give notice in the country or to his correspondent abroad, than he would if the drawer lived in the same town. . . . It cannot be understood, that, let the next post go out when it may, you are to send it, at all events by that conveyance. If it were so, every man must be nailed, as it were, to the post-house to open the letters immediately as they arrive, and must lay aside all other business in order to answer them, or dispatch a notice to his indorser or the drawer immediately.' *Darbyshire v Parker* (1805) 2 Smith KB 195 at 198, per Lord Ellenborough CJ.

[See now, as to notice of dishonour, the Bills of Exchange Act 1882, ss 48–50.]

'The next sessions [for appeals] has always been considered the next practicable sessions.' *R v Suffolk JJ* (1840) 8 Dowl 618 at 620, per Williams J

[A testator by his will directed his trustees to present his son to the living on the 'next' avoidance thereof.] 'The expression "next avoidance" . . . must mean the next over which the testator's will could operate.' *Hatch v Hatch* (1855) 20 Beav 105 at 109, per Romilly MR

'The word "next" means nearest or nighest; not in the sense of propinquity alone, as, for example, three persons on three chairs, one in the midst, those on each side of the middle one are equally near, each "next" to the centre one. But it signifies also order or succession or relation, as well as propinquity'. *Southgate v Clinch* (1858) 27 LJR Ch 651 at 654, per Kindersley V-C

[A testator by his will provided that in certain events the share of any child should go to his 'next' surviving son according to seniority of age and priority of birth.] 'When you speak of the next in order of things, you must have regard to the person exhibiting the order to you; if he arranges the objects in a given way, placing this one first, that one second, and so on, and then says "the next", the word "next" must mean the next according to his own demonstration and arrangement.' *Eastwood v Lockwood* (1867) LR 3 Eq 487 at 495, per Page Wood V-C

[Conditions of sale, drawn up at the beginning of December, provided that the outstanding balance of the purchase money was to be paid on the 28th day of December 'next'.] 'Having regard to the other conditions of sale by which, though no time was fixed for the delivery of the abstract of title, a very short time, seven days only, was allowed for sending in objections and requisitions, it is not a reasonable contention to hold that the meaning of the condition as to completing the purchase by "the 28th day of December next" is that completion should be deferred for more than a year. . . . I am of opinion, therefore that by the words "the 28th day of December next" the 28th of December in the same month in which the conditions were issued was meant, and not the 28th day of the next month of December.' *Dawes v Charsley* (1886) 2 TLR 530 at 530, 531, CA, per Cotton LJ

'In my opinion, the "next eldest", when we speak of sons in succession, must mean the next in order of age, beginning at the top, and going down, step by step, in order of birth.' *Crofts v Beamish* [1905] 2 IR 349 at 365, CA, per Fitzgibbon LJ

[The plaintiffs entered into a written agreement with the defendant, an authoress, for the publication of a novel already written by her, and by the same agreement secured an option to publish her 'next' three books upon certain royalty terms therein contained.] 'That Mrs Eyles was right in saying in her letter of 28th of November, 1919, to Mr Flower, who was acting for Messrs Cassell & Co, that the scheme which her literary agent had evolved and which she had adopted was not a "nice way" of treating the plaintiffs no one can doubt. She was conscious that she and the plaintiffs intended in clause 10 of the agreement of 10th of May, 1919, to refer to the next three novels which she should write, and that neither party contemplated that she would be at liberty to satisfy her obligations to the plaintiffs by collecting and offering to the plaintiffs a number of short stories or verses which she had already published in a variety of periodicals. Whether this scheme was honourable or dishonourable is not the question in this action. Mrs Eyles had already expressed her view of it in phraseology which is less vigorous than that which I should use if I were called upon to say what I thought of the moral aspect of this part of the case. Now the question is whether by offering these relics of her literary efforts in the past she has complied with her obligation to offer the plaintiffs "her next three books". Mrs Eyles and her literary agent acted on the supposition that any compilation by Mrs Eyles of literary material provided by her would if offered to the plaintiffs for the purpose of being published as a book satisfy the requirements of clause 10 of the agreement. In my opinion this is an erroneous view of the meaning of that clause. Clause 10 relates to work which Mrs Eyles may produce after "Margaret Protests", and does not relate to past products. The words "her next three books" mean the first three books which she shall write after "Margaret Protests".' *Macdonald v Eyles* [1921] 1 Ch 631 at 637, per Peterson J

NEXT FRIEND

Subject to special rules of procedure an infant may sue and be sued; but he may not in person assert his rights in a court of law as plaintiff or applicant nor make himself liable to a defendant or respondent for costs, with the single exception that he may sue in a county court for a sum not exceeding £2,000 due to him for wages, or piecework, or for work as a servant, in the same manner as if he were of full age [*see* MINORITY]. Consequently, if an infant is to institute and carry on proceedings he must do so by his guardian or some other person, who is called his next friend, and is for most purposes *dominus litis*.

Application may be made on behalf of an infant for legal aid. . . .

Any person within the jurisdiction who is not an accounting party or connected with the defendant or otherwise interested adversely to the infant may be next friend. Preference will be given to the father or mother or guardian or some other of the relatives or connections of the infant or their nominee, but he must be a substantial or proper person. . . .

The next friend is an officer of the court appointed to look after the infant's interests and has the conduct of the proceedings in his hands but he is not actually a party to the proceedings and is not, as next friend entitled to appear in them in person. (24 Halsbury's Laws (4th edn) paras 895:1, 895:3, 895:5).

[As to the next friend of a mentally disordered person, *see* 30 Halsbury's Laws (4th edn) paras 1017–1019.]

NEXT OF KIN *See also* NEAREST

Under a gift to the next of kin of any person simply and without reference either to intestacy or to the Statutes of Distribution, now replaced by the provisions as to succession on intestacy contained in the Administration of Estates Act 1925, the donees are considered to be the nearest kindred in blood, including the half-blood, and not to be the statutory next of kin; and prima facie they take as joint tenants. The same meaning is attached prima facie to descriptions similar to next of kin. In a gift to the next of kin of two persons, prima facie the donees are a class composed of the next of kin of one together with the next of kin of the other, but, according to the context, may be such persons as are common to the two classes of next of kin.

If a will describes the doness by reference to the statutory rules, either expressly or impliedly (where, for instance, the distribution is to be as on an intestacy), the distribution may be under either the former law or the new law. References to any Statutes of Distribution in a will coming into operation after 1925 are to be construed as references to the provisions for the distribution of residuary estates of intestates [i.e. to the Administration of Estates Act 1925, Part IV, as amended (in relation to deaths after 1952) by the Intestates' Estates Act 1952, s 4], and references in such a will to statutory next of kin are to be construed, unless the context otherwise requires, as referring to the persons who would take beneficially under those provisions. Trusts declared in a will which came into operation before 1926 by reference to the Statutes of Distribution are, unless the contrary thereby appears, to be construed by reference to those former statutes. (50 Halsbury's Laws (4th edn) paras 526, 527)

'The authorities which up to a certain point are distinctly applicable to this case, have settled that the words "next of kin", without more, mean the nearest blood relations of the *propositus*. The words here "next of kin in blood", are not less strong. I do not say stronger, for the words "in blood" appear only to indicate an intention to exclude affinity in favour of consanguinity.' *Halton v Foster* (1868) 3 Ch App 505 at 506, per Wood LJ

'The persons who are to take under the ultimate limitation in the settlement are "the next of kin in blood" of the settlor, and the widow is not one of the next of kin in blood. . . . No doubt if the settlor had died intestate the widow would . . . have taken a share of his effects; but I cannot take the additional words as enlarging the meaning of the words "next of kin in blood" so as to let in a person who was not one of the next of kin in blood. I think the result would have been the same if the words had been "next of kin" simply; but the additional words, "in blood", made the case stronger against the widow.' *Re Fitzgerald* (1889) 58 LJ Ch 662 at 663, per North J

Australia 'It is not, and I think cannot be, disputed that the primary meaning of the expression "next of kin" used *simpliciter* in a will is "the nearest blood relations of the testator at the date of his death", [*Elmsley v Young* (1835) 2 My & K 780]. I think it also true that the expression "my next of kin" so used is a technical expression or at any rate an expression of known legal import.' *Gutheil v Ballarat Trustees, Executors & Agency Co Ltd* (1922) 30 CLR 293 at 299, 300, per Knox CJ

New Zealand [A will directed the executors to divide the residue of the estate equally among the 'next-of-kin' of a named person.] 'The word [next-of-kin] has, by virtue of decisions of long standing and high authority, acquired a definite and precise meaning, when used *simpliciter*, and without qualification by the context or the scheme of the will read as a whole. It is, in a sense, a "technical" word or word of art, and means "nearest in blood": *Gutheil v Ballarat Trustees, Executors & Agency Co Ltd* [supra]'. *Re Goldie, Goldie v Goldie* [1952] NZLR 928 at 934, per Fair J; also reported [1952] GLR 331 at 333

NICKING

'Nicking' means the deliberate severing of any tendon or muscle in the tail of a horse and the expression 'nicked' shall be construed accordingly. (Docking and Nicking of Horses Act 1949, s 3)

NIECE *See* NEPHEW—NIECE

NIGHT *See also* DAY; HOURS OF DARKNESS

As to what is reckoned night, and what day, for this purpose [the former law as to burglary]: antiently the day was accounted to begin only at sunrising, and to end immediately upon sunset; but the better opinion seems to be, that if there be daylight or *crepusculum* enough, begun or left, to discern a man's face withal, it is no burglary. But this does not extend to moonlight; for then many midnight burglaries would go unpunished; and besides the malignity of the offence does not so properly arise from its being done in the dark, as at the dead of night; when all creation, except beasts of prey, are at rest; when sleep has disarmed the owner, and rendered his castle defenceless. (4 Bl Com 224)

[Night-time is no longer an ingredient of the offence of burglary. See now the Theft Act 1968, s 9.]

For the purposes of this Act the night shall be considered and is hereby declared to commence at the expiration of the first hour of sunset, and to conclude at the beginning of the last hour before sunrise. (Night Poaching Act 1828, s 12)

'Night' signifies a period of at least eleven consecutive hours, including the interval between ten o'clock in the evening and five o'clock in the morning. (Employment of Women, Young Persons and Children Act 1920, Sch, Pt II, art 3)

'Night' means the period between 11 pm and 5 am. (Customs and Excise Management Act 1979, s 1(1))

[The National Insurance (Old Persons' and Widows' Pensions and Attendance Allowance) Act 1970, s 4(2) (repealed; see now the Social Security Act 1975, s 61) entitled a disabled person to an attendance allowance if he required (inter alia) prolonged or repeated attention during the 'night.'] 'We are told that dictionaries describe "night" as being the period between sunset and sunrise, and no doubt for many purposes that is its only true meaning. It would not be a misuse of language however to say a particular public house closed at ten o'clock "last night" even though by reason of the latitude and the time of the year the sun was shining at that time. The word "night" is used loosely to describe the latter part of the day. It would be entirely wrong . . . to give "night" the sort of "sunset to sunrise" meaning to which I have referred. The purpose of the Act and the provision it seeks to make is not related to whether the sun is shining or not; it is related to the domestic routine of the house, and the distinction between day and night in s 4 is no doubt made because the giving of attention to a sick or disabled person may be far more onerous at night, when the attendant has to get out of bed in the middle of his sleep, than it would be in the middle of the day when the house is alive and people are about and ready to respond to the call of the sufferer. That is why I think this section distinguishes service by night from service by day. Therefore one must give a meaning to the words "night" and "day" which is consistent with that background. . . . I am not going to attempt to give any single definition of "night" for present purposes for the very good reason I do not think it can be done. The argument before us has been at one in a number of respects; both counsel invite us to regard the night for the purpose of the section as being that period of inactivity, or that principal period of inactivity through which each household goes in the dark hours, and to measure the beginning of the night from the time at which the household, as it were, closed down for the night. I would commend to boards dealing with this difficult question in future that they should look at the matter in that way. It was fairly suggested in argument that the night begins at the time when in a hospital or an army barracks "lights out" is ordered; the night begins when everything closes down, people put the lights out and go to sleep. It has been suggested also that night for this purpose begins when a child who having run about during the day is eventually put to bed, kissed by his mother, told to go to sleep, the light is put out and the door is shut. For that child it is perfectly sensible to describe "night" as beginning when the child was settled down for the night in that way. In future when these matters come before attendance boards, I would recommend them first to instruct themselves as a matter of law in the meaning of "night" which I have given to it, namely the coming of night according to the domestic routine of the household. When they have done that there is no more law to bother about; from then onwards it is for them to decide, using their good sense and medical knowledge what services are fairly to be described as rendered at night and what are fairly to be described as rendered by day.' *R v National Insurance Comr, ex p Secretary of State for Social Services* [1974] 3 All ER 522 at 526, 527, per Lord Widgery CJ

NIGHTCAP

With respect to the covering or cap called a 'biretta", which Mr Purchas was proved to have carried in his hand, and a clergyman to have worn in a procession, it appears to me as innocent an ornament as a hat or a wig, or as a velvet cap, which latter is not uncommonly worn by bishops, clergy, and laity as a protection to the head when needed. The 74th Canon, which is still in force, and which enjoins decency of apparel to ministers when out of their houses, provides that "no ecclesiastical persons shall weare any coife or wrought nightcaps, but onely plaine night-caps of blacke silke, sattin, or velvet". And the 18th Canon provided that "no man shall cover his head in the church or chappell in the time of divine service, except he have some infirmity, in which case let him wear a night-cap or coife", which word "night-cap" is not to be understood as a covering worn in bed, but as a kind of close-fitting cap, as is shown by the words in the Latin canons, *pileolo aut ricâ*. And I do not pronounce this particular kind of black cap, called a biretta, so worn, to be unlawful.' *Elphinstone v Purchas* (1870) LR 3 A & E 66 at 94, 95, per Sir Robert Phillimore; reversed on other grounds (1871) LR 3 PC 605, PC

NO ARRIVAL, NO SALE

United States Under a term 'no arrival, no sale' or terms of like meaning, unless otherwise agreed, (a) the seller must properly ship conforming goods and if they arrive by any means he must tender them on arrival but he assumes no obligation that the goods will arrive unless he has caused the non-arrival; and (b) where without fault of the seller the goods are in part lost or have so deteriorated as no longer to conform to the contract or arrive after the contract time, the buyer may proceed as if there had been casualty to identified goods (s 2–613). (Uniform Commercial Code 1978, s 2–324)

NO CURE, NO PAY

'The services were rendered on Lloyd's standard form of salvage agreement, "No cure, no pay"; that is to say, it is a salvage contract, and provides for security being given by the owners of the ship and cargo. Clause 5 provides that "pending the completion of the security as aforesaid the contractor shall have a maritime lien on the property salved for his remuneration. . . . In the event of security not being provided as aforesaid or in the event of any attempt being made to remove the property salved contrary to his agreement, the contractor may take steps to enforce his aforesaid lien". . . . In the present case the contract was a contract to salve "No cure, no pay", with all the attending consequences, if salving services are performed, of there being a maritime lien on the property in favour of the salvors; and that maritime lien on the property has never been put an end to by any action of a competent court or by any bargain which has been fulfilled between the parties. . . . It is true that Lloyd's "No cure, no pay" form is an agreement to go to arbitration and have the matter settled by an arbitrator out of court; but it seems to me that the basis of the contract, by clause 1 and clause 5 together, is that the owner of the salved property shall provide security in the terms of the contract, and if he does not provide security then the contractor may take steps to enforce his lien through the court.' *The Goulandris* [1927] P 182 at 186, 191, 192, per Bateson J

NOISE *See also* NUISANCE

Australia [The Local Government Act 1919–1986 (NSW) s 289, provides inter alia that a council may control and regulate the use of premises so as to prevent objectionable 'noises' thereon or noises thereon at unreasonable hours.] 'There is no precise or exact definition of the word "noise". It is sometimes referred to as "sound out of place". Noise can be measured by a sound level meter but the legislature did not intend to bind a local governing body in the exercise of this power to the niceties of ascertaining the intensity level and expressing it in decibels or of measuring the loudness level of the noise in phons. Leaving aside all technicalities, there are various noise sources in this city and in its environs; for example, the rustle of leaves in a gentle breeze, a speeding motor truck on a suburban thoroughfare, very busy traffic in the centre of the city, a pneumatic drill used in preparing foundations for a large building, an aeroplane motor on the ground revolving at 2,000 rpm and hammer blows on steel plate. Of the illustrations the first is barely above the threshold of hearing but they increase in volume and the last is at or close to the threshold of painful sound. Mr Ellicott referred me to a decision of the full court of Victoria, *Leslie v City of Essendon* [[1952] VLR 222] and to the definition of noise appearing in the judgment of Sholl J, who said: "Volume amounting to loudness, I think, is alone involved in the conception of 'noise', once one limits it so as not to include all audible sounds". I adopted that view since the law recognises that noises due to some of the sources to which I have referred must be accepted in a large city, but has recognised the necessity of controlling the use of a pneumatic drill at unreasonable hours. In my opinion hammer blows on steel plate produce noises which are nearer to the threshold of painful sound than noise produced by a pneumatic drill. The test is whether noises from rivetting, hammering, chipping and cutting of iron and steel products are sufficiently near to the threshold of painful sound as to amount to a nuisance. In my opinion they are and I regard them as noises which the legislature intended to be controlled or regulated at unreasonable hours.' *Williams v Storey* (1957) 2 LGRA 226 at 232, 233, per Richardson J

Australia [The Local Government Act 1919 (NSW) s 289(c), as amended, provides that a council may control and regulate the use of premises so as to prevent objectionable noises thereon or noises thereon at unreasonable hours.] 'In considering whether there has in fact been a breach, and bearing in mind that the word "noise" is not synonymous with sound, it seems to have been established that the word "noises" where used in the section involves the noise of a substantial degree of loudness [*Leslie v City of Essendon* [1952] VLR 222] and that they are of a nature which would materially interfere with the ordinary comfort and convenience of residents of the neighbourhood [*Williams v Storey* (supra)].' *Bankstown Municipal Council v Berzins* [1962] NSWR 641 at 644, per Manning J

NOMINAL CAPITAL *See* CAPITAL

NOMINAL DAMAGES *See* DAMAGES

NOMINAL PLAINTIFF *See* PLAINTIFF

NOMINAL VALUE

'Macnaghten J appears to have been influenced by a misapprehension into which he was led by an item in the earlier balance sheets of the company. In those balance sheets there appears on the asset side a sum of £29,99[illegible] under the description "Nominal value o shares issued". This, Macnaghten J thought, was the same thing as entering the shares themselves as an asset as well as a liability. This could not be so, since from the accountancy point of view shares can only be a liability and can never appear on the asset side of the balance sheet. In truth the description "Nominal value of shares issued" is a slovenly and inaccurate expression intended to describe the value of the assets acquired by the issue of the shares. If an accurate expression had been used, it would have been "Value of rights acquired by the company under the contract of 15th October, 1932". The appellant company later wrote down this item to nothing on a revaluation of its assets, a thing which it was perfectly entitled to do.' *Osborne v Steel Barrel Co Ltd* [1942] 1 All ER 634 at 638, CA, per cur.

NON COMPOS MENTIS *See* MENTAL DISORDER

NON-CONTENTIOUS *See also* CONTENTIOUS BUSINESS

'Non-contentious or common form probate business' means the business of obtaining probate and administration where there is no contention as to the right thereto, including (a) the passing of probates and administrations through the High Court in contentious cases where the contest has been terminated, (b) all business of a non-contentious nature in matters of testacy and intestacy not being proceedings in any action, and (c) the business of lodging caveats against the grant of probate or administration. (Supreme Court Act 1981, s 128)

NON-DELIVERY *See* DELIVERY

NON EST FACTUM

The plea of *non est factum*, or *nient son fait*, is that by which a man sought to be charged in some action or proceeding upon a writing alleged to have been sealed and delivered by him avers that it is not his deed. This plea is only available where the party sued can show either that there never has been, or that there is not existing at the time of the plea, any valid execution of the deed on his part. (12 Halsbury's Laws (4th edn) para 1365)

'Was not the effect of the deeds which the defendants signed, misrepresented to them? If their execution was obtained by fraud, cannot that be given in evidence on a plea of *non est factum*? . . . Now I do not intend to advert to the form of pleading such a plea. . . . The rule of law is that if a person who seals and delivers a deed is misled by the misstatements or misrepresentations of the persons procuring the execution of the deeds, so that he does not know what is the instrument to which he puts his hand, the deed is not his deed at all, because he was neither minded not intended to sign a document of that character or class, as, for instance, a release while intending to execute a lease. Such a deed is void.' *National Provincial Bank of England v Jackson* (1886) 33 Ch D 1 at 6, 10, CA, per Cotton LJ

'I come . . . to the plea which is the most important . . . the plea of *non est factum*, that is, that the deed is void. . . . If the plea of *non est factum* is to succeed, the deed must be wholly, and not partly, void.' *Howatson v Webb* [1907] 1 Ch 537 at 543, 548, 549, per Warrington J

'In an action upon a deed, the defendant may say by way of defence that it is not his deed, *non est factum*. If it is found to be his deed, the plaintiff gets judgment and there is an end of the case. But suppose that it is found not to be his deed, and he succeeds on *non est factum*, the case is not necessarily over, because the plaintiff may say "True you have established that this is not in fact your deed, but you are estopped by your conduct from saying that it is not your deed, and I can recover against you, although it is not your deed" . . . The true way of ascertaining whether a deed is a man's deed, is, I conceive, to see whether he attached his signature with the intention that that which preceded his signature should be taken to be his act and deed. It is not necessarily essential that he should know what the document contains; he may have been content to make it his act and deed, whatever it contained. . . . If, on the other hand, he is materially misled as to the contents of the document, then his mind does not go with his pen. In that case it is not his deed.' *Carlisle & Cumberland Banking Co v Bragg* [1911] 1 KB 489 at 495, 496, per Buckley LJ

'The plea of *non est factum* obviously applies when the person sought to be held liable did not in fact sign a document. But at least since the sixteenth century it has also been held to apply in certain cases so as to enable a person who in fact signed a document to say that it is not his deed. Obviously any such extension must be kept within narrow limits if it is not to shake the confidence of those who habitually and rightly rely on signatures when there is no obvious reason to doubt their validity. Originally this extension appears to have been made in favour of those who were unable to read owing to blindness or illiteracy and who therefore had to trust someone to tell them what they were signing. I think that it must also apply in favour of those who are permanently or temporarily unable through no fault of their own to have without explanation any real understanding of the purport of a particular document, whether that be from defective education, illness or innate incapacity.' *Sanders v Anglia Building Society* [1970] 3 All ER 961 at 963, HL, per Lord Reid

'She [a child of fourteen] had not the least understanding . . . of the documents which she signed; and those who put them before her must have known it. In these circumstances the law will say: *non est factum*—it is not her deed. It is not her settlement. It is not her contract. This doctrine, on recent authority, applies not only to the blind or illiterate, but also to those who are unable, through innate incapacity, or through dotage or non-age, without any fault of their own, to have any real understanding of the purport of the particular document.' *Mills v Inland Revenue Comrs* [1972] 3 All ER 977 at 987, CA per Lord Denning MR; reversed [1974] 1 All ER 722, HL

Australia 'In the case of an action on a deed the plea of *non est factum* is made out when it is proved that there was an ignorance of the nature and contents of the document, brought about by the misstatements of the person who induced the defendant to sign that deed, but the plea of *non est factum* is not made out when the defendant so induced to append his signature to the deed is aware that he is signing a document affecting his property, but is misled as to the extent to which that document affected his property.' *Cansdell v O'Donnell* (1924) 24 NSWSR 596 at 602, per Gordon J

NON-MONETARY PRIZE

In this section [use of machines for gaming by way of amusement with prizes] 'non-monetary prize' means a prize which does not consist of or include any money and does not consist of or include any token which can be exchanged for money or money's worth or use for playing a game by means of the machine; and for the purposes of subsection (3)(d) of this section a token or tokens shall be taken to be exchanged for a non-monetary prize or prizes at the appropriate rate if either—

(a) the value or aggregate value of the prize or prizes does not exceed [£4] and the token or tokens exchanged represent the maximum number of tokens which can be won by playing a game once by means of the machine, or

(b) in any other case, the value or aggregate value of the prize or prizes does not exceed [£4] and bears to [£4] a proportion not exceeding that which the number of tokens exchanged bears to the maximum number of tokens which can be won by playing a game once by means of the machine.

(Gaming Act 1968, s 34(8)).

[The prize limits are variable: the amounts in square brackets were substituted by the Gaming Act (Variation of Monetary Limits) 1986, SI 1986/1981.]

NON-RESIDENT

A 'non-resident group' of companies—

(i) in the case of a group, none of the members of which are resident in the United Kingdom, means that group, and

(ii) in the case of a group, two or more members of which are not resident in the United Kingdom, means the members which are not resident in the United Kingdom. (Capital Gains Tax Act 1979, s 16(2))

NONSUIT

Where the plaintiff appears at the hearing of an action or matter [in the county court] but does not prove his claim to the satisfaction of the court it may either nonsuit him or give judgment for the defendant. . . . The court has no power to nonsuit a plaintiff at the end of his opening address without hearing the evidence tendered by him.

Subject to his direction to direct judgment to be entered for the defendant, the judge should nonsuit the plaintiff when there is no evidence to support the plaintiff's case, and he may hold that there is for this purpose no evidence when there is no substantial evidence (a mere scintilla of evidence not being sufficient to preclude a nonsuit), and in the case of a jury when there is no evidence on which it may reasonably and properly conclude the facts necessary to maintain the plaintiff's case. If a judge declines to nonsuit at the end of the plaintiff's case and the defendant appeals, the court will consider the whole of the evidence given in the county court, including that given on behalf of the defendant. Where from the plaintiff's evidence it appears that the defendant is not the person liable, the defendant is entitled to judgment and the judge should not enter a nonsuit.

After being nonsuited the plaintiff may bring another action for the same or substantially the same cause of action, but the court may stay the subsequent action until any costs awarded to the defendant upon the nonsuit have been paid. (10 Halsbury's Laws (4th edn) paras 416–418)

NOR

[A testator gave a life interest to his daughter, and after his death to any children she might have; and in the event of her not marrying 'nor' having children, the property was to be at her disposal.] 'The testator directing that the money should be at her disposal in the event of her not marrying nor having children must be understood to mean that it should be at her disposal if she did not marry or if she should not leave children. "Nor" must be read "or not".' *Mackenzie v King* (1848) 17 LJ Ch 448 at 448, 449, per Knight Bruce V-C

NORMALLY

'In my view the word "normally" has a perfectly ordinary meaning which would be given to it by ordinary people in everyday use as a man might say "I normally get to the office every morning at nine-thirty but this morning I was delayed by fog and only arrived at ten o'clock". In using the word "normally", one is referring to something which is in contradistinction to abnormal or exceptional.' *Peak Trailer & Chassis Ltd v Jackson* [1967] 1 All ER 172 at 176, per Widgery J

NOT EARLIER THAN

New Zealand 'In ordinary English, not earlier than a particular day does not necessarily mean later than such a day. If the act, whatever it is, is done on the day itself, it is done not earlier than the day.' *Ward v Berndston* (1889) 8 NZLR 21 at 24, 26–28, per Williams J

NOT NEGOTIABLE

'I think it is very important that every one should know that people who take a cheque which is upon its face "not negotiable" and treat it as a negotiable security must recognise the fact that if they do so they take the risk of the person for whom they negotiate it having no title to it. . . . I do not understand what additional security is supposed to be given to a cheque by putting the words "not negotiable" upon it, if the fact of its being negotiated can give a title to any one.' *Great Western Rly Co v London & County Banking Co Ltd* [1901] AC 414 at 418, per Lord Halsbury LC

[A bill was drawn 'to the order of the Irish Casing Co only' and was crossed 'not negotiable.'] 'I think that the words "not negotiable" are affirmative and govern the whole tenour of the instrument. . . . In so far as this bill is not negotiable, it is not a bill payable to order within the meaning of the Bills of Exchange Act [1882] and must have some lesser and more conditional effect. I think that that effect may be carried out by limiting it to cases where the order is merely for money to be paid to someone as agent for, or for the purposes of, the Irish Casing Co, and no more. In that view, the instrument does not become irreconcilable or impossible of interpretation. It remains a non-negotiable instrument drawn by the Irish Casing Co Ltd and accepted by the defendants, but limited as to its effect as between those two parties. It is not transferable.' *Hibernian Bank Ltd v Gysin & Hanson* [1939] 1 KB 483 at 488, 489, CA, per Slesser LJ

'In the present case the cheque was on its face expressed to be "not negotiable", the result of which was that it was deprived of the peculiar characteristic that makes it possible for a transferor of a negotiable instrument to confer a better title than he has himself. The consequence of marking the cheque not negotiable is to be found in s 81 of the Bills of Exchange Act 1882, which provides as follows: "Where a person takes a crossed cheque which bears on it the words 'Not Negotiable', he shall not have and shall not be capable of giving a better title to the cheque than that which the person from whom he took it had".' *Wilson & Meeson v Pickering* [1946] KB 422 at 428, CA, per Lord Greene MR

NOTABLE CRIME

'Without attempting in this judgment to give an exhaustive enumeration of what may be regarded as "notable crimes" or "impediments" [within the meaning of the Ordination Service] there is not a trace to be found in any of the authorities that a mere allegation that a candidate has been a party to, or taken part in, the service in a church in which breaches of prescribed ritual have taken place comes within those words.' *Kensit v St Paul's (Dean & Chapter)* [1905] 2 KB 249 at 257, per Lord Alverstone CJ

NOTARY (Public)

A notary public is a duly appointed officer whose public office it is, among other matters, to draw, attest or certify, usually under his official seal, deeds and other documents, including conveyances of real and personal property, and powers of attorney relating to real and personal property situate in England and Wales, other countries in the Commonwealth or in foreign countries; to note or certify transactions relating to negotiable instruments; to prepare wills or other testamentary documents; to draw up protests or other formal papers relating to occurrences on the voyages of ships and their navigation as well as the carriage of cargo in ships.

His office, which is one of great antiquity, is recognised in all civilised countries, and by the law of nations his acts have credit everywhere. (34 Halsbury's Laws (4th edn) para 201)

NOTATION CREDIT

United States A [letter of] credit which specifies that any person purchasing or paying drafts drawn or demands for payment made under it must note the amount of the draft or demand on the letter or advice of credit is a 'notation credit'. (Uniform Commercial Code 1978, s 5–108(1))

NOTED

Canada 'In my view the legislature in using the words "noted on" [a bye-law] must have contemplated, as one possible method of deemed amendment of the bye-law, the attachment thereto of a written memorandum. Had the legislature intended to restrict the manner of annotation to endorsement or inscription directly on the bye-law, they could readily have used the more precise words "endorsed on".' *Pales v Surrey District Corpn* [1975] 2 WWR 668 at 671, BCCA, per Carrothers JA

NOTICE *See also* CONSTRUCTIVE NOTICE; DUE NOTICE

'The word "notice" to a lawyer, in my judgment, means something less than full knowledge. It means, no doubt, that the thing of which a man must have notice must be brought clearly to his attention. What, in different cases, may be sufficient notice is a matter which will be decided when those cases come before the courts.' *Goodyear Tyre and Rubber Co (Great Britain) Ltd v Lancashire Batteries Ltd* [1958] 3 All ER 7 at 12, CA, per Lord Evershed MR

'I do not myself regard the word "notice" as a synonym for the word "knowledge". Notice is a word which involves that knowledge may be imparted by notice, but "notice" and "knowledge" are not the same thing, although loosely one sometimes talks as if to act with notice and to act with knowledge were indeed the same.' *Cresta Holdings Ltd v Karlin* [1959] 3 All ER 656 at 657, CA, per Hodson J

United States A person has 'notice' of a fact when (a) he has actual knowledge of it; or (b) he has received a notice or notification of it; or (c) from all the facts and circumstances known to him at the time in question he has reason to know that it exists. (Uniform Commercial Code 1978, s 1–201(25))

In Bankruptcy Acts

'The first question is, what is the meaning of a debtor's "giving notice" that he has suspended, or is about to suspend, payment of his debts? I think it does not mean mere casual talk; it must be something formal and deliberate, something done by the debtor with a consciousness that he is "giving notice", and ıtended to be understood in that sense.' *Re 'riedlander, ex p Oastler* (1884) 13 QBD 471 t 475, CA, per Lindley J

n Food Act

The Sale of Food and Drugs Act 1875, s 8 repealed; see now Food Act 1984, s 3(1)(ii)) rovided that no person selling an article of ɔod mixed with an ingredient not injurious to ealth should be guilty of an offence under the ιct, if he supplied to the person receiving the rticle of food a 'notice', by a label written or rinted on or with such article, to the effect ıat the same was mixed.] 'Where, as here, the eller relies on written notice he must prove ıat notice of any circumstance which he was equired to make known was in fact conveyed ɔ the purchaser. He must prove that the urchaser understood the notice. If the notice 'as conspicuous, the justices would be more kely to hold that the purchaser saw it, but ere they have found as a fact that he did not ee it, and for that reason the defence fails.' *'reston v Grant* [1925] 1 KB 177 at 184, 185, er Salter J

[Under the 1984 Act the notice must be of dequate size, distinctly and legibly printed nd conspicuously visible.]

)f dishonour

[t seems to me to be perfectly clear . . . that, nder the allegation that a party has received otice of the dishonour of a bill, after the ishonour has taken place, an actual notice to ıat effect must be proved; and that showing ıe party's knowledge of the fact that it will not e paid at maturity, is not sufficient. There ıust be proof of a notice given from some arty entitled to call for payment of the bill, nd conveying in its terms intelligence of the resentment, dishonour, and parties to be held able in consequence. That is the true meaning f the word "notice" when used in declarations f this kind, and the mere knowledge of a party not enough.' *Burgh v Legge* (1839) 5 M & W 18 at 420, per Parke B

[think we ought to construe the word "notice" s meaning notification of the fact of the bill aving been dishonoured after the present-ıent took place; and it is far better, for the dvancement of justice, to adhere to this imple meaning, than to confound notice with nowledge. The real question before the jury ı such cases is, not whether a certain fact occurred, but whether it was notified to a certain party.' Ibid at 422, per Alderson B

[*See* now, as to notice of dishonour, the Bills of Exchange Act 1882, ss 48–50.]

Of intended prosecution

'Notice' includes an announcement, whether or not in writing and any other communication or pretended communication. (Unfair Contract Terms Act 1977, s 14)

[The Road Traffic Act 1930, s 21(c) (repealed; see now Road Traffic Offenders Act 1988, s 1(1)(c)) provided that a person should not be convicted upon a prosecution for reckless or dangerous driving unless within fourteen days a 'notice of the intended prosecution' specifying the nature of the alleged offence was served on him.] 'I do not and cannot assent to the argument . . . that the words in para (c) of s 21, "a notice of the intended prosecution specifying the nature of the alleged offence" necessarily mean that the notice must be a notice of the particular section of the Act under which the prosecution is contemplated. . . . I do not think that the appellant can be heard to complain, even if the notice did suggest that he might be charged under s 11, that in point of fact he was only summoned for an offence less serious than that under s 11.' *Milner v Allen* [1933] 1 KB 698 at 702, 703, DC, per Avory J

See, generally, 40 Halsbury's Laws (4th edn) para 532.

NOTICE TO QUIT

'Notice to quit' means a notice to terminate a tenancy (whether a periodical tenancy or a tenancy for a term of years certain) given in accordance with the provisions (whether express or implied) of that tenancy. (Landlord and Tenant Act 1954, s 69(1))

'In my opinion . . . a notice to quit is a notice given by an existing landlord to an existing tenant; from which it follows, if that view be right, that a person cannot give a valid notice to quit before he has become a landlord, and the recipient of the notice his tenant, or before legal relations exist between them which otherwise permit such a notice.' *Lower v Sorrell* [1962] 3 All ER 1074 at 1083, CA, per Donovan LJ; also reported in [1963] 1 QB 959 at 975

NOTIFIABLE DISEASE *See* DISEASE

NOTIFY

United States A person 'notifies' or 'gives' a notice or notification to another by taking such steps as may be reasonably required to inform the other in the ordinary course whether or not such other actually comes to know of it. A person 'receives' a notice or notification when (a) it comes to his attention; or (b) it is duly delivered at the place of business through which the contract was made or at any other place held out by him as the place for receipt of such communications. (Uniform Commercial Code 1978, s 1–201(26))

NOTORIETY

Every usage must have acquired such notoriety in the particular market or branch of trade or in the department of business or amongst the class of persons who are affected by it, that any person in that branch or department or class who enters into a contract of a nature affected by the usage must be taken to have done so with the intention that the usage should form part of the contract. Notoriety in this connection does not mean that it must be known to all the world, nor even that it should be known to the person against whom it is asserted; but it means that it must be well known at the place to which it applies, and be capable of ready ascertainment by any person who proposes to enter into a contract of which that usage would form part. (12 Halsbury's Laws (4th edn) para 451)

NOVATION

Contractual rights, but not liabilities, may, as a general rule, be transferred by assignment without the consent of the promisor. Novation, however, is an act whereby, with the consent of all parties, a new contract is substituted for an existing contract and the latter discharged. Usually, but not necessarily, a novation takes the form of the introduction of a new party to the new contract and the discharge of a person who was a party to the old contract. At common law novation was the only known method of assigning a contractual right. (9 Halsbury's Laws (4th edn) para 580)

Specific performance is refused where the contract has been rescinded by novation; that is, where the parties have come to a fresh agre ment for good consideration which from i nature must be presumed to be in substitutic for the former agreement. (44 Halsbury's Lav (4th edn) para 496)

'A novation (if I am obliged to use that wor has been completely effected. T Institutes—the oldest law upon the subject have been referred to, and they say that tv things must concur: there must be the *anim novandi*, and the substitution of some oth thing for that original obligation out of whi the debt arose. . . . The *animus novandi* . . . a thing which is not to be proved as a fact, but an inference from the facts which are provec *Wilson v Lloyd* (1873) LR 16 Eq 60 at 74, p Bacon V-C

'Novation . . . as I understand it means . . that there being a contract in existence, son new contract is substituted for it, eith between the same parties (for that might be) between different parties; the consideratic mutually being the discharge of the old co tract.' *Scarf v Jardine* (1882) 7 App Cas 345 351, per Lord Selborne LC

'Counsel for the trustee . . . submitted th novation comprises two distinct elements, v the annulment of one debt and the creation o substituted debt in its place. . . . No expre judicial authority was cited to us in support counsel for the trustee's suggested dichotom but in our view it is right in principle. T discharge of the original debtor must preced and is distinct from, the acceptance by imposition on the creditor of a substitut debtor. It follows from this that although t elements of a statutory novation may, a usually will, be comprised in one statute decree and, for practical purposes, opera simultaneously, each has nevertheless separate and distinct legal identity.' *Re Unit Railways of Havana and Regla Warehouses L* [1959] 1 All ER 214 at 229, CA, per Jenkins

NOVUS ACTUS INTERVENIENS

'There are invoked certain well-knov formulae, such as that the chain of causati was broken, that there was a *novus actus int veniens*. These somewhat august phrase sanctified as they are by standing authorit only mean that there was not such a dire relationship between the act of negligence a the injury that the one could be treated flowing directly from the other.' *Lord v Paci Steam Navigation Co, The Oropesa* [1943] 1 A

ER 211 at 213, CA, per Lord Wright; also reported in [1943] P 32 at 36

NOW

[A testator devised to All Souls College, Oxford, 'my library of books now in the custody of Mr Carswell', together with a gift of £4,000 to augment the college library. The court decreed that new books should pass with old, the word 'now' relating not to specific books, but to the place where the library should be found.] 'Where I devises all the corn now in my barn, if that corn be afterwards spent, and new corn put in, such new corn will not pass: But if I devise all my flock of sheep now on such a hill, or in such a pasture; in that case, because sheep are in their nature fluctuating, some must die, some be killed, and some lambs be produced which will afterwards breed, and it being the case of a collective body, the sheep produced afterwards shall pass; and this is within the reason of a devise of a personal estate, which, because always fluctuating, shall therefore relate to the time of the testator's death; besides the will, as to personals, does not speak till after the testator's death. It is natural to think that the testator did not in the principal case intend his executor should be garbling the library after his death, by picking out the books bought since the making the will, which appears more plainly from the subsequent devise of £4,000 to the college to buy books, so that his design manifestly was to increase rather than diminish. As to the cases that have been put of a devise of all the leases which I now have, or of all the horses now in my stable and afterwards I purchase more of each, the new leases or horses will not pass; the reason is, because these are particular chattels, and not part of a collective body as a flock of sheep, or library of books. Indeed a flock of sheep differs somewhat from a library of books; for the former must by necessity fluctuate as above; but there is no necessity that books should be changed.' *All Souls College v Coddrington* (1719) 1 P Wms 597 at 598, 599, per cur.

'I have not any doubt whatever on this will what was the testator's intention. . . . I find a will with a date to it, showing the period when it was executed; and I find that he gives "all the estates of which I am now seised or possessed". "Now" has no meaning in itself; and if there is no date to construe it, you must ascertain something to which it can refer, where the date of the execution does not appear. But here the date does appear, and the word "now" can only have reference to the time specified in the will. The time specified in the will is the date of it, namely, the 29th of April, 1843; and it appears to me to be just the same as if he had said, "all the freehold and leasehold estates of which I am, on this 29th of April, 1843, seised and entitled". If those had been the words, of course there could not have been a doubt. Are they not, in effect, the same words? What is the difference whether he repeats the date, or whether the word "now" shows he refers to the date? That is one view of it, in which I merely refer to the very words to be found in this particular clause. But the testator does not stop there; for he uses the word "now" in two other parts of the will, in each of which he evidently and clearly alludes, not to the time at which it may come into operation by his death, but to the particular time at which he is making the will. Am I, then, in taking a fair view of the expressions used, in order to see what he intended, and in trying to put a fair construction on the word "now", which you find in the particular clause, to disregard the same word used with reference to other gifts in other parts of the will? It would be departing from the ordinary rule of construction to do so; and it appears to me beyond all doubt and question, that, in using the word "now", he meant the day on which he made his will, and no other time.' *Cole v Scott* (1849) 1 H & Tw 477 at 484, 485, per Cottenham LC

[The Wills Act 1837, s 24 enacts that every will shall be construed, with reference to the real estate and personal estate comprised in it, to speak and take effect as if it had been executed immediately before the death of the testator, unless a contrary intention shall appear by the will.] 'The Act is imperative that the word "now" is to be understood as spoken at the time of death, and unless a distinction is made by the testator and it can be shown that he meant to refer to after-acquired property, the word "now" must refer to the time of his death. In this case there was a gift by the testator of the property which he possessed in the hand and under the management of a certain individual and in the company's funds, and there was a direction that interest should be paid, and this property was given with whatever might be found due thereon. I am asked to construe that which referred to the time of his death as following a direction that the gift should apply to what the testator then at the date of his will possessed, and as showing a sufficiently contrary intention. That is the only way in which the argument in favour of an intestacy can be supported. In the view which I take I cannot reconcile to myself that this is a case in which the language of the Act of Parliament has been controlled by any manifestation by the testator of a contrary intention, and therefore I shall declare that the whole of the property passes under the will.' *Hepburn v Skirving* (1858) 32 LTOS 26 at 26, per Stuart V-C

[A testator by his will made a gift of 'all the real and personal estate which I now possess'.] 'I may compare the expressions which the testator has made use of with two other forms of expression. If the testator had said "I give all my real and personal estate" there can be no doubt that after-acquired property would have passed. So again, if he had said "I give all the real and personal estate I possess". Does it make any difference when he puts in the word "now"? The words "I possess" mean the same thing as "I now possess". In all these cases the law says that you must read the will as if it had been written on the day of the testator's death, and you must have distinct words, as there were in *Cole v Scott* [supra] in order to show that the property acquired subsequently to the date of the will is not intended to pass.' *Wagstaff v Wagstaff* (1869) LR 8 Eq 229 at 230, per Lord Romilly MR

[A testator gave all his leasehold properties to his son absolutely, charged nevertheless with payment of all mortgage debts thereon, and with payment of an annuity described as 'now' charged thereon.] 'All the testator says is that the property given to the son is to bear the charges upon it, whether mortgages or annuity. He speaks of the annuity "now charged". It was an existing annuity at the date of the will, but it might come to an end before the death of the testator by the death of the sister. The words are merely an indication of the particular charge.' *Re Ord, Dickinson v Dickinson* (1879) 12 Ch D 22 at 25, CA, per Beggallay LJ

'The devise I have to construe is in these terms: "I devise all my copyhold messuages . . . and parts and shares of copyhold messuages . . . now held by me as a customary tenant" . . . unto trustees, upon the trusts there mentioned. The first question is . . . does that devise extend to the whole of the testator's copyholds . . . or is it limited to those of which he was customary tenant at the date of the will. . . . The question . . . is whether, by reason of any context, or any other of the provisions of this will, I ought to hold that the testator intended by the use of the word "now" to exclude the after-acquired interest from his devise. . . . In the will before me I can discover no context, or other indications from which I can conclude that the testator intended the word "now" to refer to any moment of time other than the moment immediately preceding his death. . . . I come to the conclusion that on the true construction of the will all the testator's interests in the copyholds passed under the devise.' *Re Horton, Lloyd v Hatchett* [1920] 2 Ch 1 at 8, 10, 11, per Eve J

[By a codicil to his will a testator excluded from a bequest of residue certain articles of jewellery and other chattels 'now' deposited for safe custody at a named safe deposit.] 'However rightly it may have been held in other cases, where "now" appeared in quite different contexts, that the word was not an essential part of the description, the question we have to decide is whether in this codicil and in this context it is an essential part of the description. Speaking for myself I find it impossible to construe these words in any other sense. It seems to me that the testator was thinking of a particular time, namely, the date of his codicil, just as he was thinking of a particular place.' *Re Whitby, Public Trustee v Whitby* [1944] Ch 210 at 215, CA, per Lord Greene MR

NOW PAID

[The Bills of Sale Act (1878) Amendment Act 1882, s 8 provides that every bill of sale shall be duly attested, etc, and shall truly set forth the consideration for which it was given, or else it shall be void in respect of the personal chattels comprised therein.] 'There was an agreement that the grantor should have a present advance of £1,500, and should give a bill of sale as security for it. He got the money, and he gave the bill of sale. It was afterwards found to be worthless, and it was replaced by the present bill of sale, which states the consideration as money "now paid". In my opinion that does properly describe the consideration. The deed was given, not to secure a past debt, but for a present advance. In my opinion, if the consideration had been stated in any other way it would have been wrongly stated.' *Re Munday, ex p Allam* (1884) 14 QBD 43 at 47, DC, per Cave J

[A debtor borrowed money on his promise to give security, but no security was actually given until three weeks later. The security then took the form of a bill of sale, the consideration being stated (as required by the Bills of Sale Act (1878) Amendment Act 1882, s 8 (see supra)) as money 'now paid'.] 'The principle is this—that in these bills of salė cases the statement of the consideration must be looked at broadly, and not in a narrow spirit. In this case we have to determine whether it is true to say that the consideration is "now paid". If a bill of sale is being given to secure now a debt incurred in the past, that is not "now paid". Again, if the money was advanced upon an executory promise to give a bill of sale, I should not think it would be right to say "now paid". But if the bill of sale is given against the money, I think the matter can be looked at broadly, and that it can properly be said that the consideration was money "now paid".' *Re Rouard, ex p Trustee* (1915) 85 LJKB 393 at 395, DC per Rowlatt J

[The plaintiff borrowed £400 from the defendants on the security of a bill of sale. The money was repayable by instalments, of which £325 was unpaid. A further transaction was entered into by which the plaintiff gave another bill of sale for £450 of which £100 went to another creditor, £25 was handed to the plaintiff and the defendants retained £325 to meet their claim of that amount. The consideration was stated to be £450 'now paid'.] 'The transaction seems to me to have been a perfectly honest and straightforward one, entered into by the plaintiff with a full knowledge of what she was doing and without deception or compulsion on the part of the defendants. . . . The consideration was stated as £450 "now paid", and the question is if that is correct. In order to make it so the money must either have been handed over to her under such circumstances that she had a real control and power of disposition over it, or if she had not such a control and power, and what happened amounted to a retention of part of it by the defendants, the retention must have been under such circumstances as to amount to payment.' *Parsons v Equitable Investment Co Ltd* [1916] 2 Ch 527 at 531, CA, per Pickford LJ

'This is an appeal from Rotherham County Court in an action which was followed by interpleader proceedings. The plaintiff, Henshall, obtained judgment against the defendant, Widdison, for £692 10*s* and thereupon wanted to put in execution. When the plaintiff had levied execution on some furniture, the claimant, Mrs Widdison, the wife of the judgment debtor, came forward and told the plaintiff that he could not sell the goods as they belonged to her because her husband had given her a bill of sale covering them. "I advanced £600 or so", she said, "and he gave me this bill of sale. The goods are not his." The plaintiff, however, maintained that the bill was bad for several reasons, but on appeal, only one reason has been urged—namely, that it is said that the bill does not truly state the consideration. The bill is in statutory form and reads "In consideration of a sum of £600 now paid. . . ." Evidence was given as to the drawing up of the bill and that it was all in order. Also that the defendant's wife, Mrs Widdison, had borrowed the money from her mother to help her husband, that her mother had lent her £600 which she handed over to her husband to pay his debts at 6 pm on the same day as the bill was executed. The real point of the appeal, therefore, is this—Was there any evidence for the judge that the money was "now paid"? In my opinion this is merely a question of fact, and if there was such evidence that the money was "now paid", the finding cannot be disturbed. I do not wish to embarrass my successors by putting analogies by way of illustration, but, obviously, if the money were not paid for a period of say, ten days, there would be no evidence that the money was "now paid". It may well be, however, that although the money may not have been paid at the very moment of the execution of the bill, there is evidence that it was "now paid", and that to say that it was "now paid" would be substantially correct, and that the bill is not invalid. . . . In my opinion in the present case there was evidence for the county court judge that the money was now paid.' *Henshall v Widdison* (1923) 130 LT 607 at 608, DC, per Sankey J

NOXIOUS

'The word "noxious" not only means "hurtful and offensive to the smell"; but it is also the translation of the very technical term *nocivus*. . . . It is not necessary that the smell should be unwholesome: it is enough, if it renders the enjoyment of life and property uncomfortable.' *R v White & Ward* (1757) 1 Burr 333 at 337, per Lord Mansfield CJ

[The Offences Against the Person Act 1861, ss 23, 24, make it an offence to administer unlawfully and maliciously any poison or other destructive or 'noxious thing', either so as to endanger the life of a person or inflict grievous bodily harm, or with intent to injure, aggrieve, or annoy a person.] 'The statute requires, in order to constitute an offence, that there shall have been the administration of a noxious thing, and we think, in order to make out an offence, the thing administered must be of such a character as to satisfy rigorously the requirement of the law, namely, that it must be a noxious thing. I think there must be a distinction between a thing only noxious when given in excess, and a thing which is a recognised poison and is known to be a thing noxious and pernicious in effect.' *R v Hennah* (1877) 13 Cox CC 547 at 549, per Cockburn CJ

[The Offences Against the Person Act 1861, s 58 enacts (inter alia) that it shall be a felony to administer any 'noxious thing' with intent to procure a miscarriage.] 'The statute speaks first, of poisons, secondly, of other things. If the thing administered is a recognised poison the offence may be committed, though the quantity given is so small as to be incapable of doing harm. What was the thing administered in the present case? So much oil of juniper. Was this proved to be noxious? It was, consequently it was a "noxious thing".' *R v Cramp* (1880) 5 QBD 307 at 309, 310, CCR, per Field J

[The Offences against the Person Act 1861, s 23 makes it an offence for a person unlawfully and maliciously to administer, etc, to any other person any 'noxious' thing.] 'What is a noxious thing, and in particular is heroin a noxious thing? The authorities show that an article is not to be described as noxious for present purposes merely because it has a potentiality for harm if taken in an overdose. There are many articles of value in common use which may be harmful in overdose, and it is clear on the authorities when looking at them that one cannot describe an article as noxious merely because it has that aptitude. On the other hand, if an article is liable to injure in common use, not when an overdose in the sense of an accidental excess is used, but is liable to cause injury in common use, should it then not be regarded as a noxious thing for present purposes? When one has regard to the potentiality of heroin in the circumstances which we read about and hear about in our courts today we have no hesitation in saying that heroin is a noxious thing.' *R v Cato* [1976] 1 All ER 260 at 268, CA, per cur.

NUCLEAR

Nuclear matter

'Nuclear matter' means, subject to any exceptions which may be prescribed—

(a) any fissile material in the form of uranium metal, alloy or chemical compound (including natural uranium), or of plutonium metal, alloy or chemical compound, and any other fissile material which may be prescribed; and
(b) any radioactive material produced in, or made radioactive by exposure to the radiation incidental to, the process of producing or utilising any such fissile material as aforesaid.

(Nuclear Installations Act 1965, s 26)

Nuclear reactor

'Nuclear reactor' means any plant (including any machinery, equipment or appliance, whether affixed to land or not) designed or adapted for the production of atomic energy by a fission process in which a controlled chain reaction can be maintained without an additional source of neutrons. (Nuclear Installations Act 1965, s 26)

[*See also* s 44(8) of the Health and Safety at Work etc Act 1974.]

NUISANCE *See also* ANNOYANCE

The term 'nuisance' as used in law is not capable of exact definition. Although most nuisances arise from a long continuing condition, a single isolated happening is sufficient if it arises from a continuing condition on land in the control of the defendant.

Nuisances may be broadly divided into (1) acts not warranted by law or omissions to discharge a legal duty, which obstruct or cause inconvenience or damage to the public in the exercise of rights common to all the Queen's subjects; (2) acts or omissions which have been designated or treated by statute as nuisances; and (3) acts or omissions generally connected with the user or occupation of land which cause damage to another person in connection with that other's user of land or interference with the enjoyment of land or some right connected with the land.

Some varieties of nuisance closely resemble acts classed under the head of trespass. The distinction between the two is that in trespass the immediate act which constitutes the wrong causes an injury to the sufferer's person or damage to his property or amounts to dispossession, whereas in nuisance the act itself often does not directly affect the person or property of another, but has consequences which become or are prejudicial to his person or property. Nuisance must also be distinguished from negligence although many acts which constitute a nuisance involve an element of negligence and may also be actionable as such.

The word 'nuisance', when used in a covenant between a lessee and a lessor, should perhaps be construed prima facie in the same sense as in the general law of nuisance, but a covenant against committing acts of nuisance is commonly joined with a prohibition against doing other acts such as causing annoyance and inconvenience, and this will extend the scope of the obligation.

Nuisances are divisible into common law and statutory nuisances.

A common law nuisance is one which, apart from statute, violates the principles which the common law lays down for the protection of the public and of individuals in the exercise and enjoyment of their rights.

A statutory nuisance is one which, whether or not it constitutes a nuisance at common law. is made a nuisance by statute either in express terms or by implication.

Nuisances may be divided into those which are public and those which are private.

A public nuisance is one which inflicts damage, injury or inconvenience on all the Queen's subjects or on all members of a class who come within the sphere or neighbourhood of its operation. However, it may affect some to a greater extent than others. The question whether the number of persons affected is sufficient to constitute a class is one of fact.

There are many statutory provisions which impose penalties for nuisances affecting public health, morals and comfort. However, the common law liability remains, and any person who by any act unwarranted by law or by any omission to carry out a legal duty endangers the life, health, property, morals or comfort of the public commits an offence known as public nuisance.

A private nuisance is one which interferes with a person's use or enjoyment of land or of some right connected with land. It is thus a violation of a person's private rights as opposed to a violation of rights which he enjoys in common with all members of the public. The ground of the responsibility is ordinarily the possession and control of land from which the nuisance proceeds.

The importance of the division of nuisances into public and private lies partly in the difference of the remedies and defences applicable to each, and partly in the fact that a private individual has no right of action in respect of a public nuisance unless he can show that he has sustained some special damage over and above that inflicted on the community at large.

Whereas a private nuisance may be justified on the ground that the right to commit it has been acquired by prescription, no amount of time will afford a like defence to an allegation of a public nuisance. Moreover, the Crown cannot grant to a person a right to commit a public nuisance.

In order to constitute a nuisance there must be both (1) an unlawful act, and (2) damage, actual or presumed. Damage alone gives no right of action; the mere fact that an act causes loss to another does not make that act a nuisance.

For the purposes of the law of nuisance, an unlawful act is the interference by act or omission with a person's use or enjoyment of land or some right over or in connection with land. (34 Halsbury's Laws (4th edn) paras 301–309)

Nuisance, *nocumentum*, or annoyance, signifies any thing that worketh hurt, inconvenience, or damage. And nuisances are of two kinds; public or common nuisances, which affect the public, and are an annoyance to all the king's subjects; . . . and private nuisances; which . . . may be defined, any thing done to the hurt or annoyance of the lands, tenements, or hereditaments of another. (3 Bl Com 216)

'I do not think that the nuisance for which an action will lie is capable of any legal definition which will be applicable to all cases and useful in deciding them. The question so entirely depends on the surrounding circumstances—the place where, the time when, the alleged nuisance, what, the mode of committing it, how, and the duration of it, whether temporary or permanent, occasional or continual,—as to make it impossible to lay down any rule of law applicable to every case, and which will also be useful in assisting a jury to come to a satisfactory conclusion: it must at all times be a question of fact with reference to all circumstances of the case. Most certainly in my judgment it cannot be laid down as a legal proposition or doctrine, that anything which, under any circumstances, lessens the comfort or endangers the health or safety of a neighbour, must necessarily be an actionable nuisance. That may be a nuisance in Grosvenor Square which would be none in Smithfield Market, that may be a nuisance at midday which would not be so at midnight, that may be a nuisance which is permanent and continual which would be no nuisance if temporary or occasional only. A clock striking the hour, or a bell ringing for some domestic purpose, may be a nuisance, if unreasonably loud and discordant, of which the jury alone must judge; but although not unreasonably loud, if the owner, from some whim or caprice, made the clock strike the hour every ten minutes, or the bell ring continually, I think a jury would be justified in considering it to be a very great nuisance. In general, a kitchen chimney, suitable to the establishment to which it belonged, could not be deemed a nuisance, but if built in an inconvenient place or manner, on purpose to annoy the neighbours, it might, I think, very properly be treated as one. The compromises that belong to social life, and upon which the peace and comfort of it mainly depend, furnish an indefinite number of examples where some apparent natural right is invaded, or some enjoyment abridged, to provide for the more general convenience or necessities of the whole community.' *Bamford v Turnley* (1862) 3 B & S 66 at 79, 80, per Pollock CB

'The defendant has infringed the maxim *Sic utere tuo ut alienum non laedas*. Then, what principle or rule of law can he rely on to defend himself? It is clear to my mind that there is some exception to the general application of the maxim mentioned. The instances put during the argument, of burning weeds, emptying cess-pools, making noises during repairs, and other instances which would be nuisances if done wantonly or maliciously, nevertheless may be lawfully done. It cannot be said that such acts are not nuisances, because, by the hypothesis, they are; and it cannot be doubted that, if a person maliciously and without cause made close to a dwelling-house the same offensive smells as may be made in emptying a cess-pool, an action would lie.' Ibid at 82, 83, per Bramwell B

[The plaintiff was the tenant of a basement and three rooms, which he occupied as a restaurant. The defendants carried on the business of printing and publishing newspapers on land adjoining the plaintiff's premises. The plaintiff alleged that the noise and vibration caused by the printing of the newspapers, which were printed at various hours of the day and night, were very great and caused a substantial 'nuisance' and serious injury.] 'A nuisance must be something which diminishes the value of the plaintiffs' property or interferes with their use or enjoyment of it. The question is one of difficulty and is necessarily one of degree. In a large city like Birmingham there must be a great deal of noise. For myself, if I had to determine the question, certainly I should be disposed very favourably for the plaintiffs; for I have no doubt that if I had to listen to these noises for a few hours I should be in the position of Hogarth's "enraged musician". . . . A certain amount of noise and many discordant sounds are necessarily incident to the business of a crowded and busy town, and it is a question for a jury to determine, as practical men.' *Smith v Jaffray* (1886) 2 TLR 480 at 482, DC, per Grove J

[A covenant in a building lease was directed against any act which might be to the annoyance, 'nuisance', grievance, or damage of the lessor, his heirs or assigns, or the inhabitants of the neighbouring or adjoining houses.] 'The question which arises is, what is the meaning of the expression "shall or may be or grow to the annoyance, nuisance, or damage" of the persons named. Certainly that string of words is introduced in order to give the covenantee a greater protection than he would have had without any such words at all, or if only one of those words were used. There is no use in putting in the words "any grievance or damage" as additions to nuisance except for the very purpose of giving some greater protection than he would have had if the word "nuisance" alone were used and included in the covenant. When Bacon V-C held, as he did in *Harrison v Good* [(1871) LR 11 Eq 338] that the word "nuisance" in the covenant meant only that which would be an actionable nuisance without the covenant, I doubt whether he gave sufficient weight to the consideration that the whole object of having a covenant against nuisance is to give the covenantee some protection in addition to what he would have had without the covenant; but for a nuisance in the strict sense there would be an action, covenant or no covenant. I am not by any means sure that the Vice-Chancellor did not put on the word "nuisance" in that covenant too restricted an interpretation. But be that as it may, I cannot at all agree with the contention that these words "annoyance or grievance to the inhabitants" mean that which would be according to law a nuisance, or that the covenant is only against such acts as would produce pecuniary damage.' *Tod-Heatly v Benham* (1888) 40 Ch D 80 at 95, 96, CA, per Lindley LJ

'Any material interference with the ordinary comfort of existence: that would be a nuisance. The law, in thus defining "nuisance", has stopped short, I will not say of protecting the fancies of people, because the mere fancies of people I do not think can in any view be an element in the definition, but has stopped short, according to what is said in *Aldred's Case* [(1610) 9 Co Rep 57b] of giving an action in respect of that which is a matter only of delight, and not of necessity. "Annoyance" is a wider term than nuisance, and if you find a thing which reasonably troubles the mind and pleasure, not of a fanciful person or of a skilled person who knows the truth, but of the ordinary sensible English inhabitants of a house— if you find there is anything which disturbs his reasonable peace of mind, that seems to me to be an annoyance, although it may not appear to amount to physical detriment to comfort. You must take sensible people, you must not take fanciful people on the one side or skilled people on the other; and that is the key as it seems to me of this case. Doctors may be able to say, and, for anything I know, to say with certainty, that there is no sort of danger from this hospital to the surrounding neighbourhood. But the fact that some doctors think there is makes it evident at all events that it is not a very unreasonable thing for persons of ordinary apprehension to be troubled in their minds about it. And if it is not an unreasonable thing for an ordinary person who lives in the neighbourhood to be troubled in his mind by the apprehension of such risk, it seems to me there is danger of annoyance, though there may not be a nuisance.' Ibid at 98, per Bowen LJ

'A nuisance is complained of on two grounds—(1) the interference with personal comfort; (2) injury to property. . . . What sort of interference with personal comfort was it necessary for the plaintiffs to show? To use the words of Knight-Bruce V-C in *Walter v Selfe* [(1851) 4 De G & Sm 315], it must be "an inconvenience materially interfering with the ordinary comfort physically of human existence—not merely according to elegant or dainty modes and habits of living, but according to plain and sober and simple notions among the English people". . . . A supply of milk in large quantities must take place in a place like London. Necessarily a good deal of noise is created and some inconvenience is caused to sensitive people; but, on the evidence, I hold that there is no nuisance materially interfering with the comfort of the plaintiff.' *Fanshawe v London & Provincial Dairy Co* (1888) 4 TLR 694 at 694, per Kekewich J

'The only question I have to decide is purely one of fact, namely, whether or not what the defendants have done has created or occasioned a public nuisance within the neighbourhood of their brickfields. Now, in law, a public nuisance need not be injurious to health. It is not necessary to show that people have been made ill by what has been done. It is sufficient to show that there has been what is called injury to their comfort, a material interference with the comfort and convenience of life of the persons residing in or coming within the sphere of the influence of that which has been done by the defendants on their works.' *A-G v Keymer Brick & Tile Co Ltd* (1903) 67 JP 434 at 435, per Joyce J

'Apart from any right which may have been acquired against him by contract, grant or prescription, every person is entitled as against his neighbour to the comfortable and healthful enjoyment of the premises occupied by him, and in deciding whether, in any particular case, his right has been interfered with and a nuisance thereby caused, it is necessary to determine whether the act complained of is an inconvenience materially interfering with the ordinary physical comfort of human existence, not merely according to elegant or dainty modes and habits of living, but according to plain and sober and simple notions obtaining among English people: see *Walter v Selfe* [(1851) 4 De G & Sm 315] and the remarks of Knight Bruce V-C. It is also necessary to take into account the circumstances and character of the locality in which the complainant is living. The making or causing of such a noise as materially interferes with the comfort of a neighbour when judged by the standard to which I have just referred, constitutes an actionable nuisance, and it is no answer to say that the best known means have been taken to reduce or prevent the noise complained of, or that the cause of the nuisance is the exercise of a business or trade in a reasonable and proper manner. Again, the question of the existence of a nuisance is one of degree and depends on the circumstances of the case.' *Vanderpant v Mayfair Hotel Co Ltd* [1930] 1 Ch 138 at 165, 166, per Luxmoore J

'I can think of no better definition of nuisance than this, given in Winfield's Textbook on the Law of Tort, 3rd edn, p 426: "Nuisance is the unlawful interference with a person's use or enjoyment of land, or of some right over, or in connection with it". If a person's right of free passage over a highway is subject to interference he has an action, just as he would have if a private right of way of which he was the grantee was obstructed.' *Howard v Walker* [1947] 2 All ER 197 at 199, per Lord Goddard CJ

[A nuisance order was issued against the owners

of premises which had been allowed to fall into a state of disrepair.] 'A public nuisance at common law has been expressed to be an act or omission which materially effects the material comfort and quality of life of a class of Her Majesty's subjects. A private nuisance has often been defined in this way: private nuisances, at least in the vast majority of cases, are interferences for a substantial length of time by owners or occupiers of property with the use or enjoyment of neighbouring property.' [*Held:*—A nuisance could not be said to have arisen on premises if what had taken place only affected the person or persons occupying the premises.] *National Coal Board v Neath Borough Council* [1976] 2 All ER 478 at 481, per Watkins J

Australia 'To constitute a nuisance, noise must be unusual or excessive. It must be such as materially to interfere with the ordinary comfort of those living in the neighbourhood, according to plain and sober and simple notions. The persistent noise of woodsawing at high speed is sufficiently loud to carry some distance, and discordant and shrill enough to be difficult for persons, not enured to it, or without the special quality of being capable to enure themselves to it, or who are unable to concentrate on their immediate task, whether laborious or pleasurable, to the exclusion of such competitive distraction. When that noise occurs daily for long periods, I think it becomes a menace to reasonable comfort. It may be true that some people can readily adapt themselves to it without effort, others can with the exercise of determination adapt themselves to it, something like the inhabitants of London towards bombing, but that does not necessarily mean, because that is so, if it is, that the law requires all persons to enure themselves to the unpleasantness or quit.' *Spencer v Silva* [1942] SASR 213 at 219, 220, per Mayo J

New Zealand [The Tenancy Act 1948 (NZ), s 24(1)(c) (repealed) permitted the court to make an order for possession on the ground that the tenant had been guilty of conduct that was a 'nuisance or annoyance' to adjoining or neighbouring occupiers.] 'It can scarcely be doubted that by "nuisance" the legislature meant, not a nuisance in a technical sense, but a nuisance in fact. Secondly, the word "nuisance" in the subsection cannot, I think, be disassociated from the phrase "to adjoining or neighbouring occupiers". Only a nuisance in fact could affect such occupiers. The conclusion, therefore, seems to me inescapable that sub-s (1) of s 24 has application only to nuisances in fact, and not to nuisances merely deemed to be such by law. That every nuisance in fact is also an annoyance to adjoining, if not neighbouring, occupiers may well be true, but the word "annoyance" seems to me to have been used in a sense extending to circumstances which might not amount to what the Act defines as a nuisance. There is nothing inconsistent, therefore, in the use by the legislature of the two terms in the alternative, even if nuisance means, as I think it does, a de facto nuisance, and not merely a nuisance declared such by statute.' *Angelo v Kean Clarke Bros* [1950] NZLR at 7, per Finlay J; also reported [1949] GLR 591 at 594

Highway to *See* BARBED WIRE

In Acts relating to public health

[The Nuisances Removal Act 1855, s 8 (repealed; see now the Public Health Act 1936, s 141) provided that the word 'nuisances' should include any drain, sewer, etc, or premises in such a state as to be a nuisance or injurious to health.] 'I think it clear the words used in s 8 are not used in their ordinary legal sense as denoting everything which is the subject of an indictment at common law. But they must receive some limitation. Instances may be put of nuisances which are clearly beyond the province of this Act, as obstructing a highway or keeping an unruly bull in a field in which there is a public footpath; then if the word nuisance in the Act must be limited, I can see no other guide to its construction than by referring to those wrongful acts spoken of by the statute, viz injuries to health.' *Great Western Rly Co v Bishop* (1872) LR 7 QB 500 at 553, per Lush J

'In my opinion the decision of the justices was right, and must be affirmed. It has been contended before us that, as the appellants have a right to drain into the sewer, they may lawfully send into it liquids innocuous when kept separate, although upon combination they may create a nuisance: for the appellants are liable only in respect of what happens in their own drains. It would be a singular result of the legislation as to the removal of nuisances, if the appellants could send from their works matter which, upon reaching a public sewer, is dangerous to the health of the inhabitants of the borough. I certainly think that the appellants are persons 'by whose act, default, permission, or sufferance the nuisance arises" within the meaning of 18 & 19 Vict c 121, s 12 [Nuisances Removal Act 1855 (repealed; see now Public Health Act 1936, s 141)]. The escape of a noxious gas like sulphuretted hydrogen is clearly a nuisance in ordinary language.' *St Helens Chemical Co v St Helens Corpn* (1876) 1 Ex D 196 at 201, 202, per Grove J

[The Public Health Act 1875, s 47 (repealed; see now the Public Health Act 1936, s 50), made it an offence to keep swine so as to be a 'nuisance'.] 'This section contains a specific provision against keeping swine in a dwelling-house or so as to be a nuisance to any person. There is nothing said about injury to health. . . . It appears to me that the word "nuisance" here is used in the ordinary and legal sense, and includes, in addition to matters injurious to health, matters substantially offensive to the senses.' *Banbury Urban Sanitary Authority v Page* (1881) 8 QBD 97 at 98, per Grove J

Negligence compared

'Comparing nuisance with negligence the main argument for the respondent was that in negligence foreseeability is an essential element in determining liability, and therefore it is logical that foreseeability should also be an essential element in determining the amount of damages: but negligence is not an essential element in determining liability for nuisance, and therefore it is illogical to bring in foreseeability when determining the amount of damages. It is quite true that negligence is not an essential element in nuisance. Nuisance is a term used to cover a wide variety of tortious acts or omissions, and in many negligence in the narrow sense is not essential. An occupier may incur liability for the emission of noxious fumes or noise, although he has used the utmost care in building and using his premises. The amount of fumes or noise which he can lawfully emit is a question of degree, and he or his advisers may have miscalculated what can be justified. Or he may deliberately obstruct the highway adjoining his premises to a greater degree than is permissible hoping that no one will object. On the other hand the emission of fumes or noise or the obstruction of the adjoining highway may often be the result of pure negligence on his part: there are many cases . . . where precisely the same facts will establish liability both in nuisance and in negligence.' *The Wagon Mound (No 2), Overseas Tankship (UK) Ltd v Miller Steamship Co Pty Ltd* [1966] 2 All ER 709 at 716, PC, per Lord Reid

Private nuisance

'It is the very essence of a private nuisance that it is the unreasonable use by a man of his land to the detriment of his neighbour. He must have been guilty of the fault, not necessarily of negligence, but of the unreasonable use of the land.' *Miller v Jackson* [1977] 3 All ER 338 at 344, CA, per Lord Denning MR

See, generally, 34 Halsbury's Laws (4th edn) para 307.

Public nuisance

'It is . . . clear, in my opinion, that any nuisance is "public" which materially affects the reasonable comfort and convenience of life of a class of Her Majesty's subjects. The sphere of the nuisance may be described generally as "the neighbourhood"; but the question whether the local community within that sphere comprises a sufficient number of persons to constitute a class of the public is a question of fact in every case. It is not necessary, in my judgment, to prove that every member of the class has been injuriously affected; it is sufficient to show that a representative cross-section of the class has been so affected for an injunction to issue.' *A-G v P Y A Quarries Ltd* [1957] 1 All ER 894 at 902, CA, per Romer LJ; also reported in [1957] 2 QB 169 at 184

'Counsel for the defendants raised at the outset this question: What is the difference between a public nuisance and a private nuisance? He is right to raise it because it affects his clients greatly. The order against them restrains them from committing a public nuisance, not a private one. The classic statement of the difference is that a public nuisance affects Her Majesty's subjects generally, whereas a private nuisance only affects particular individuals. But this does not help much. The question: when do a number of individuals become Her Majesty's subjects generally? is as difficult to answer as the question: when does a group of people become a crowd? Everyone has his own views. Even the answer "Two's company, three's a crowd" will not command the assent of those present unless they first agree on "which two". So here I decline to answer the question how many people are necessary to make up Her Majesty's subjects generally. I prefer to look to the reason of the thing and to say that a public nuisance is a nuisance which is so widespread in its range or so indiscriminate in its effect that it would not be reasonable to expect one person to take proceedings on his own responsibility to put a stop to it, but that it should be taken on the responsibility of the community at large.' Ibid at 908, 909, per Denning LJ

See, generally, 34 Halsbury's Laws (4th edn) para 305.

Australia 'As regards nuisance, any wrongful or negligent act or omission in a highway which interferes with the full, safe and convenient use by the public of their right of passage is a public nuisance.' *Taylor v Comr for Main Roads* (1945) 46 NSWSR 117 at 120, per Jordan CJ

Statutory nuisance

For the purposes of the provisions respecting statutory nuisances, a nuisance must affect the public health. However, it is not necessary to prove injury to health; a matter which interferes with personal comfort, if it is found to be a nuisance, may be a statutory nuisance. Defects in premises which affect only the occupants cannot amount to a nuisance.

The nuisance may be a private nuisance as well as a public nuisance; it is not necessary to prove annoyance to any particular person or injury to any particular property. Statutory nuisances were thought to be confined to nuisances from private sources or nuisances caused on private property and not to comprise nuisances arising from public works such as sewers or sewage works constructed by local authorities when they were sewerage authorities. Public authorities do not now possess any special immunity.

Whether there is a nuisance or not is a question of fact for the magistrates; they may take into consideration the fact that the matter complained of continued for a period of several days. (38 Halsbury's Laws (4th edn) para 403)

See also 34 Halsbury's Laws (4th edn) para 304.

To highway

It is a nuisance at common law either to obstruct a highway or to render it dangerous. Obstruction or hindrance may be justifiable as an exercise of rights reserved by the dedicating owner, or as an ordinary and reasonable exercise of the rights of a frontager, or under statutory powers. Whether an obstruction, encroachment or other act or omission amounts to a nuisance is a question of fact, and it may be that an obstruction is so inappreciable or so temporary as not to amount to a nuisance. Causing danger in a highway is a different form of wrongful interference whic need not necessarily involve obstruction. Gen erally, however, it is a nuisance to interfer with any part of a highway. It is no defence t show that, although the act complained of is nuisance with regard to the highway, it is i other respects beneficial to the public. Th principles applicable to highway nuisances d not apply in respect of private roads. (2 Halsbury's Laws (4th edn) para 419)

NULLITY *See also* MARRIAGE (void and voidable)

Where a marriage is void the courts regard th marriage as never having taken place and n status of matrimony as ever having bee conferred.

Where a marriage is void in law, the purpos of a nullity suit is to place the fact on record b a judgment equivalent to a judgment in rem but there is no need for such a decree, an nothing in the provisions of the Matrimonia Causes Act 1973 restating additional ground for a decree of nullity in respect of voidabl marriages celebrated before 1st August 1971 i to be construed as validating any marriag which is by law void but with respect to which decree of nullity has not been granted.

In cases of void marriages neither delay no conduct constitutes a bar to a decree.

A voidable marriage is regarded as valid an subsisting until a decree of nullity has bee obtained during the lifetime of the parties.

Before 1st August 1971 the form of th decree purported to put the parties retro spectively in the position of never having bee married to each other at all but, nevertheless, i was held that transactions which had take place during the marriage on the footing that i was subsisting, or in direct contemplation of marriage which afterwards took place, wer not affected by the subsequent decree o annulment.

A decree of nullity after 31st July in respec of a voidable marriage operates to annul th marriage only as respects any time after th decree has been made absolute and notwith standing the decree, the marriage is treated a if it had existed up to that time.

The court has power to order maintenanc for either party to the marriage and to var settlements. (13 Halsbury's Laws (4th edn paras 540–542)

[The grounds on which a marriage is void o voidable are codified by the Matrimonia Causes Act 1973, ss 11–16. Section 13 has bee amended by the Matrimonial and Family Proceedings Act 1984, s 2.]

NUMBER *See also* GENDER AND NUMBER

Words importing the singular number shall include the plural number, and words importing the plural number shall include the singular number. (Town Police Clauses Act 1847, s 3)

NURSE

'Nurse' means a nurse for the sick. (Nurses Agencies Act 1957, s 8, as amended).

NURSERY GROUNDS

'The point which has been raised is whether this land can be regarded as "nursery grounds" within the meaning of s 2(2) of the Rating and Valuation (Apportionment) Act 1928 [repealed], so that it is exempt from rating as agricultural land by virtue of s 67(1) of the Local Government Act 1929. It appears that it is a pasture field which is rolled and fertilised with artificial fertilisers, and that the weeds are removed. When that operation has been carried on for a certain length of time (which depends on whether the turf is to be sold as first class turf or as second class turf) the turf is cut and sold for golf links, lawns, and so forth. In our opinion, we cannot hold that this field is a nursery ground. It is old turf being put into good condition by fertilising and weeding, but it is in no sense a rearing or tending of young plants for the purpose of transplanting.' *Butser Turf & Timber Co Ltd v Petersfield Rating Authority* [1950] 1 All ER 288 at 289, 290, per Lord Goddard CJ

See, generally, 1 Halsbury's Laws (4th edn) para 1002.

NURSERY SCHOOL *See* SCHOOL

NURSERY STOCK

Canada 'The question shortly is, whether or not the phrase "nursery stock", as used in sub-s 4 of s 19BBB of c 8 of 5 Geo 5 [Special War Revenue Act 1915 (see now the Excise Tax Act RSC 1970, c E-13, Sch III)], includes cut flowers and potted plants. . . . It seems perfectly clear to us that cut flowers cannot be brought within the term "nursery stock". As to potted plants—"nursery" implies a place devoted to the cultivation of trees, shrubs, and plants—for the purpose of transplantation; bringing them to a degree of maturity in which that is practicable. . . . Potted plants, in our view, are not within the ordinary meaning of the phrase "nursery stock".' *Bradshaw v Minister of Customs & Excise* [1928] SCR 54 at 56, 57, per cur.

NURSING HOME

(1) In this Act 'nursing home' means, subject to subsection (3) below—

(a) any premises used, or intended to be used, for the reception of, and the provision of nursing for, persons suffering from any sickness, injury or infirmity;
(b) any premises used, or intended to be used, for the reception of pregnant women, or of women immediately after childbirth (in this Act referred to as a 'maternity home'); and
(c) any premises not falling within either of the preceding paragraphs which are used, or intended to be used, for the provision of all or any of the following services, namely—
  (i) the carrying out of surgical procedures under anaesthesia;
  (ii) the termination of pregnancies;
  (iii) endoscopy;
  (iv) haemodialysis or peritoneal dialysis.
  (v) treatment by specially controlled techniques.

(2) In subsection (1) above 'specially controlled techniques' means techniques specified under subsection (4) below as subject to control for the purposes of this Part [Part II: mental homes and mental nursing homes] of this Act.

(3) The definition in subsection (1) above does not include—

(a) any hospital or other premises maintained or controlled by a government department or local authority or any other authority or body instituted by special Act of Parliament or incorporated by Royal Charter;
(b) any mental nursing home;
(c) any sanatorium provided at a school or educational establishment and used or intended to be used solely by persons in attendance at, or members of the staff of, that school or establishment or members of their families;

(d) any first aid treatment room provided at factory premises, at premises to which the Offices, Shops and Railway Premises Act 1963 applies or at a sports ground, show ground or place of public entertainment;

(e) any premises used or intended to be used, wholly or mainly—

 (i) by a medical practitioner for the purpose of consultations with his patients;

 (ii) by a dental practitioner or chiropodist for the purpose of treating his patients; or

 (iii) for the provision of occupational health facilities, unless they are used, or intended to be used, for the provision of treatment by specially controlled techniques and are not excepted by regulations under paragraph (g) below;

(f) any premises used, or intended to be used, wholly or mainly as a private dwelling; or

(g) any other premises excepted from that definition by regulations made by the Secretary of State.

(Registered Homes Act 1984, s 21(1)–(3))

Mental nursing home

(1) In this Act 'mental nursing home' means, subject to subsection (2) below, any premises used, or intended to be used, for the reception of, and the provision of nursing or other medical treatment (including care, habilitation and rehabilitation under medical supervision) for one or more mentally disordered patients (meaning persons suffering, or appearing to be suffering, from mental disorder), whether exclusively or in common with other persons.

(2) In this Act 'mental nursing home' does not include any hospital as defined in subsection (3) below, or any other premises managed by a government department or provided by a local authority. (Registered Homes Act 1984, s 22)

[Subsection (3) of the above section defines 'hospital' for the above purpose.]

NURTURE

'Under seven is sometimes called the age of nurture; but this is the peculiar nurture required by a child from its mother, and is entirely different from guardianship for nurture, which belongs to the father in his life time, even from the birth of the child. We can find no distinction in the books as to the rights and incidents of this species of guardianship from the time when it commences till the time when it expires. One of these incidents is that the guardian shall be entitled to the custody of the person of the child. Without such right he could not possibly perform the duties cast upon him as a guardian. He is to nurture the child; the legal sense of the word is its natural and common sense in the English language, which, Dr Johnson says, is "to educate; to train; to bring up".' *R v Clarke, Re Race* (1857) 7 E & B 186 at 192, 193, per cur.

O

OK

'Each document was considered, altered by agreement, with each alteration initialled, and then the whole document was initialled as agreed by each side, or . . . OK'd, the court being informed by evidence that OK means "Orl Korrect".' *British Russian Gazette and Trade Outlook Ltd v Associated Newspapers Ltd* [1933] 2 KB 616 at 641, CA, per Scrutton LJ

'The judgments of the courts below ultimately depend on the meaning of the letters "OK", on the delivery orders. . . . The origin of this commercial barbarism (which, according to the Oxford Dictionary, was already in use as far back as 1847) is variously assigned in different works of authority. The general view seems to be that the letters hail from the United States and represent a spelling, humorous or uneducated, of the words "all correct". Another view is that they represent the Choctaw word *okeh*, which signifies "so be it". . . . The only conclusion at which, in our opinion, it is possible to arrive, is that the letters OK on . . . delivery notes and bills mean . . . that the details in those documents are correctly given.' *Dawsons Bank Ltd v Japan Cotton Trading Co Ltd* (1935) 79 Sol Jo 213 at 214, PC, per Lord Russell of Killowen.

:**anada** 'The supposed agreement consists of n offer in writing dated 3rd June, 1941, ddressed by the respondent to Empire Realty :o Ltd, who were negotiating on behalf of the ppellant, to rent the premises for a term of ve years at a rental of $125 per month, with he privilege of renewing same for a further eriod of five years at an appraisal rental. Vhen this offer was presented to the appellant e wrote on it "OK Kenneth Drury". . . . I annot agree with the conclusion that the vords written by the appellant . . . constitute r were intended to constitute an acceptance of he offer. The learned Judge held that the ppellant by writing the letters "OK" and igning them thereby accepted the offer. I vould not so hold. These letters have been the ubject of judicial interpretation in *British ?ussian Gazette, etc, Ltd v Associated Newsapers Ltd* [supra]. While they may be used as vidence that the terms set out in a contract are atisfactory to the parties, nevertheless they nay be explained. In the case mentioned there vere, aside from the "OK", definite words of ffer and acceptance. Here I feel no doubt pon the evidence that the appellant knew he ad no authority to bind his co-owners, that the espondent knew it, and that when the appelant wrote the letters "OK" he intended to say, nd respondent knew he intended to say, that he terms, in so far as they were expressed, vould be satisfactory to the appellant if they urned out, upon inquiry, to be equally satisactory to the other owners. In my opinion here was no concluded agreement on 3rd June, 941.' *Saperstein v Drury* [1943] 3 WWR 193 t 195, 196, CA, per McDonald CJBC

)ATH

Vith certain exceptions no evidence is dmissible in any court unless it is given upon ath or affirmation. By statute, an oath may be dministered as follows: the person taking the ath holds the New Testament or, in the case of Jew, the Old Testament, in his uplifted hand, nd says or repeats after the officer dministering the oath the words 'I swear by Almighty God . . .' followed by the words of he oath prescribed by law. The officer must dminister the oath in that form and manner vithout question unless the witness objects to, r is physically incapable of, so taking it; but a vitness who is neither a Christian nor a Jew nay take the oath in any other lawful manner.

If a witness desires to take the oath in the cottish manner with uplifed hand he must be ermitted to do so without further question.

If a witness takes the oath, in whatever form, without objection, or has declared it to be binding on him, or has affirmed, then if he gives false evidence he may be convicted of perjury.

A witness may object to be sworn on the ground that he has no religious belief, or that the taking of an oath is contrary to his religious belief; and he may be permitted to make a solemn affirmation instead of taking an oath, and this has the same force and effect in law as though the oath had been taken in the ordinary form. A witness may also affirm, and he may be required to do so, where it is not reasonably practicable without inconvenience or delay to administer an oath in the manner appropriate to his religious belief. It is for the court to decide by questioning the witness whether he is entitled to affirm, but where the witness has taken the oath without objection the fact the he had at the time no religious belief does not affect its validity in any way.

A special form of affirmation has long been permitted to members of the religious bodies of Quakers and Moravians, and to persons who have ceased to belong to those bodies but who retain their religious objection to the taking of oaths.

With regard to certain oaths required to be taken out of court and such voluntary declarations as may be required in confirmation of written instruments, proofs of debts, or other matters, any person may make a solemn declaration in place of an oath. (17 Halsbury's Laws (4th edn) paras 264–266)

[The number of peremptory challenges which may be made without cause on a trial on indictment was reduced from seven to three by the Criminal Law Act 1977, s 43.

Any person who objects to being sworn may make a solemn affirmation, instead of taking an oath. See the Oaths Act 1978, s 5. The Oaths Act 1838 and the Oaths Acts 1888 to 1977 were consolidated in the Oaths Act 1978.

A new form of giving oath was introduced with effect from 3 December 1984, the wording being: 'I swear by Almighty God that I will faithfully try the defendant and give a true verdict according to the evidence.' Direction of Court of Appeal (Criminal Division) given by Lord Lane CJ on 12 October 1984.

In relation to any oath administered to and taken by any person before a juvenile court or administered to and taken by any child or young person before any other court the words 'I promise before Almighty God' are substituted by the Children and Young Persons Act 1963, s 28(1).]

The expression 'oath' in the case of persons for the time being allowed by law to affirm or declare instead of swearing, includes 'affirmation' and 'declaration', and the expression 'swear' in the like case includes 'affirm' and 'declare'. (Perjury Act 1911, s 15)

'Oath' and 'affidavit' include affirmation and declaration, and 'swear' includes affirm and declare. (Interpretation Act 1978, Sch 1)

'An oath is a religious asseveration, by which a person renounces the mercy, and imprecates the vengeance of heaven, if he do not speak the truth; and therefore a person who has no idea of the sanction which this appeal to heaven creates, ought not to be sworn as a witness in any Court of Justice.' *R v White* (1786) 1 Leach 430 at 430, 431, per cur.

Canada 'The word "oath", now finding itself in a statute [Canada Evidence Act, RSC 1970, c E-10], must be given its ordinary meaning unless, as a matter of statutory construction, it can be concluded a legal meaning was intended by the legislature. In any event, the ordinary meaning and the legal meaning are the same in this case. The Shorter Oxford English Dictionary defines oath as "a solemn appeal to God (or to something sacred) in witness that a statement is true". Jowitt's Dictionary of English Usage gives the meaning, "an appeal to God to witness the truth of a statement".' *R v Budin* (1981) 120 DLR (3d) 536 at 539, Ont CA, per Jessup JA

OBITER DICTUM *See also* DICTUM

'It is of course perfectly familiar doctrine that obiter dicta, though they may have great weight as such, are not conclusive authority. Obiter dicta in this context means what the words literally signify—namely, statements by the way. If a judge thinks it desirable to give his opinion on some point which is not necessary for the decision of the case, that of course has not the binding weight of the decision of the case, and the reasons for the decision.' *Flower v Ebbw Vale Steel, Iron & Coal Co Ltd* [1934] 2 KB 132 at 154, per Talbot J

OBJECT OF VERTU *See* VERTU

OBJECTS (Of company) *See also* MOTIVE

[The plaintiff company (limited by guarantee claimed to be entitled to the benefit of th provisions of the Rating and Valuation (Mis cellaneous Provisions) Act 1955, s 8 (repealed because its 'main objects' were non-prof making and educational.] 'The expressio "main objects" is nowhere defined, as far as know. There is a fairly simple answer to thi problem, because in my view there are tw kinds of "objects" in this kind of documen [the memorandum of association of the com pany], i.e. objects which are properly so called as distinguished from objects which are not i fact objects so much as powers. That is th point which is dealt with in *Cotman Brougham* [[1918] AC 514], in the speech o Lord Wrenbury—than whom no greate authority on companies and the law of com panies can be found—where he says: "Ther has grown up a pernicious practice of regis tering memoranda of association which, unde the clause relating to objects, contain par agraph after paragraph not specifying o delimiting the proposed trade or purpose, bu confusing power with purpose and indicatin every class of act which the corporation is t have power to do." I may perhaps mention tha the same comment was made by myself som years ago in *Re Cole Ltd* [[1945] 1 All EI 521 n]. In that case I called attention to th importance of not inserting a clause which ha become so common, making every sub-clause heading or objects clause, independent of th other objects and therefore to be construed i isolation. Lord Wrenbury's speech gives m the requisite clue to the proper significance t be attached to that phrase, "main objects" What is meant by "main objects" in s 8 of th Act of 1955 is, those objects which are reall objects, excluding those so-called object which are, in fact, nothing more or less tha powers.' *North of England Zoological Societ v Chester Rural District Council* [1958] 3 A ER 535 at 537, per Vaisey J; affirmed [1959] All ER 116

[Generally, see now the Companies Act 1985 ss 2(1)(c), 4.]

OBLIGATION *See also* BOND

The ordinary form of bond came to be on accompanied by a condition in the nature of defeasance, the performance of the conditio nerally being secured by a penalty. This rm of bond is called a double or conditional nd, and consists of two parts: first, the ligation, and secondly, the condition. The ndition, which may be contained in the me or another instrument, or may be dorsed on the back, specifies the real agreeent between the parties, that is to say, the oney to be paid or acts or duties to be performed or observed, the payment, performce, or observance of which is intended to be cured by the bond, and it provides that on e performance of the condition the bond all be void. The obligation, as in the case of single bond, simply binds the obligor to the yment of a certain sum of money, such sum money being usually, though not necesrily, a penalty, and does not in terms refer the condition. On breach of the condition e bond is said to become forfeited or absote, though . . . it does not follow that the ligee is entitled to recover the sum entioned in the obligation. (12 Halsbury's aws (4th edn) para 1387)

here are two terms by which English lawrs designate bonds, both well known terms. ne is bond, and the other is obligation. ddly enough, we generally use the term nd to distinguish the instrument, and the rms derived from obligation or from oblige distinguish the parties to it. We speak of a nd, and of the obligor and the obligee of a nd. But still the word "obligation" denotes bond as well as the word "bond".' *Norton v orence Land & Public Works Co* (1877) 7 h D 332 at 337, per Jessel MR

anada 'The Act [Canadian Broadcasting ct 1936 (Can) c 24 s 4 (now the Broadcastg Act RSC 1970, c B-11, s 40(4))] now says at an action, suit or other legal proceeding respect of any obligation incurred, may be ought or taken against the [Canadian roadcasting] Corporation. "Any obligation curred" may not be very apt language to scribe a liability in tort. The very words iability in tort" could have been used and en there would have been no question. But I n not going to stop this action at this stage by stricting the meaning of the word "obligan" in this legislation to a duty arising out of ntract. I think it also includes a duty or bility arising from an actionable tort.' *Smith Canadian Broadcasting Corpn* [1953] 1 DLR 0 at 512, per Judson J

OBLIGATORY

'I can see no difference at all between enacting that certain words shall be valid and obligatory and saying that the agreement is to be confirmed and made binding on the several parties. . . . I do not understand how an agreement which is not made binding can be made obligatory; the only meaning that I can attach to the word "obligatory" when so used is that the parties to the agreement are bound by its contents; just as the meaning of a contract being binding is that its various clauses are binding upon the parties to the contract.' *R v Midland Rly Co* (1887) 19 QBD 540 at 547, DC, per Stephen J

OBLIGEE—OBLIGOR

A bond is an instrument under seal, usually a deed poll, whereby one person binds himself to another for the payment of a specified sum of money either immediately or at a fixed future date. The person who so binds himself is called the obligor, and the person to whom he is bound the obligee; and the instrument itself is sometimes called an obligation. (Shep Touch 367; 12 Halsbury's Laws (4th edn) para 1385)

OBLITERATION

[The Wills Act 1837, s 21 provides that 'obliterations', interlineations or other alterations in a will after execution are void, if not affirmed in the margin, or otherwise, by the signature of the testator, and the attestation of witnesses.] 'It is not a mere difference of ink or handwriting, which would constitute any of the acts done according to the true meaning of the statute. The mere circumstance of the amount or name of the legatee, inserted in a different handwriting and in different ink, would not alone constitute an obliteration, interlineation, or other alteration. Blanks may be supplied, and in a different ink, because the will may very probably be brought with blanks to the testator, and then filled up; no presumption could arise in such a case against the will having been executed as it appears. But the case is different when there is an erasure apparent on the face of the will, and when that erasure has been superinduced by other writing. In such a case there is an obliteration and something more, which constitutes an alteration, and then the question arises, whether this was done before the execution of the will or not? We apprehend it to be now settled, that whoever alleges such alteration to have been done before the execution of the will, is bound to take upon himself the *onus probandi.*' *Greville v Tylee* (1851) 7 Moo PCC 320 at 327, 328, PC, per Dr Lushington

'For the purposes of this case I must hold that a pasting over a piece of paper is an obliteration within the meaning of the Act [Wills Act 1837, s 21 (supra)]. It is not, perhaps, an exact use of the word according to ordinary parlance in a case where, as on this codicil, and no doubt on this will, the piece of paper could with perfect ease be removed, leaving the document intact. Parts of a document sealed up under an order for discovery can hardly be said to be obliterated. A picture would rather be said to be concealed than obliterated if a curtain is drawn before it, or a letter if placed in an envelope. If the pasting on of pieces of paper in this case were not an obliteration within the meaning of the Act, then all difficulty would be removed by the very simple process of their removal. But I cannot hold that they did not constitute such an obliteration. In the original sense of the Latin word from which obliteration is derived—in Facciolati's Lexicon "*oblitterare*" is defined as "*aliquid literis superducere*"—a placing of a piece of paper over writing would be an obliteration.' *Ffinch v Combe* [1894] P 191 at 201, 202, per Jeune P

See, generally, 50 Halsbury's Laws (4th edn) para 273.

OBSCENE

For the purposes of this Act an article shall be deemed to be obscene if its effect or (where the article comprises two or more distinct items) the effect of any one of its items is, if taken as a whole, such as to tend to deprave and corrupt persons who are likely, having regard to all relevant circumstances, to read, see or hear the matter contained or embodied in it. (Obscene Publications Act 1959, s 1(1))

[As to the interpretation of the Obscene Publications Act 1959, s 1(1), with particular reference to the words 'read, see or hear,' see *A-G's Reference* (*No 2 of 1975*) [1975] 2 All ER 753 at 769, CA, per James LJ

For the purposes of this section [prohibition of presentation of obscene performances and plays] a performance of a play shall be deemed to be obscene if, taken as a whole, its effect was such as to tend to deprave and corrupt persons who were likely, having regard to all relevant circumstances, to attend it. (Theatres A 1968, s 2(1))

'It is quite clear that the publishing an obsce book is an offence against the law of the land. is perfectly true . . . that there are a gre many publications of high repute in the litera productions of this country the tendency which is immodest, and, if you pleas immoral. . . . But it is not to be said, becau there are in many standard and establish works objectionable passages, that therefo the law is not as alleged on the part of t prosecution, namely, that obscene works a the subject-matter of indictment; and I thi the test of obscenity is this, whether the te dency of the matter charged as obscenity is deprave and corrupt those whose minds a open to such immoral influences, and in whose hands a publication of this sort may fal *R v Hicklin* (1868) LR 3 QB 360 at 371, p Cockburn CJ

'The classic definition, delivered by Cockbu CJ, in the Queen's Bench in 1868, in *R v Hic lin* [supra], was: ". . . the test of obscenity this, whether the tendency of the matt charged as obscenity is to deprave and corru those whose minds are open to such immo influences, and into whose hands a publicati of this sort may fall." We are being asked upset these convictions because something w not said about the standards of today. T learned recorder said, and this court entire agrees with him, that the law is the same now it was in 1868, and, indeed, counsel for t appellants . . . has not sought to s differently. If that is the test, the jury tod have to consider whether, today, these boo have a tendency to deprave and corrupt the whose minds are open to such immoral infl ences, and into whose hands a publication this sort may fall. When considering wheth books have a tendency to deprave and corru everybody's mind goes to the depraving corrupting of young people into whose han they may fall. There may be dirty-mind elderly people, no doubt, but it is not to expected that many elderly people would re this stuff. Younger people would, howeve and we are told that these books circulate in t armed forces. The jury have to consid whether or not, looking at these books as whole, people would be corrupted. I can w understand that, nowadays, novelists a other writers mention things which they wou not have mentioned in the reign of Queen V toria, but it is one thing to discuss a subject a quite another to discuss it and write about it the way in which these books deal with it. It seems to me idle to contend that these books are not of the tendency which Cockburn CJ described in 1868.' *R v Reiter* [1954] 1 All ER 741 at 742, CCA, per Lord Goddard CJ; see also [1954] 2 QB 16

The test today is extracted from a decision of 1868, and the test of obscenity is this [*R v Hicklin*, supra]: ". . . whether the tendency of the matter charged as obscenity is to deprave and corrupt those whose minds are open to such immoral influences, and into whose hands a publication of this sort may fall". Because that is a test laid down in 1868, that does not mean that what you have to consider is, supposing this book had been published in 1868 and the publishers had been prosecuted in 1868, whether the court or a jury, nearly a century ago, would have reached the conclusion that the book was an obscene book. Your task is to decide whether you think that the tendency of the book is to deprave those whose minds today are open to such immoral influences and into whose hands the book may fall in this year, or last year when it was published in this country, or next year or the year after that.' *R v Martin Secker Warburg* [1954] 2 All ER 683 at 685, CCA, per Stable J

'In my judgment, there is no reason whatever to confine obscenity and depravity to sex.' *John Calder (Publications) Ltd v Powell* [1965] 1 All ER 159 at 162, per Lord Parker CJ; also reported [1965] 1 QB 509

'The test of obscenity is now laid down in s 1 of the Act of 1959 [Obscene Publications Act 1959 (supra)] which, in so far as it is material, reads as follows: "(1) For the purposes of this Act an article shall be deemed to be obscene if its effect . . . is, if taken as a whole, such as to tend to deprave and corrupt persons who are likely, having regard to all relevant circumstances, to read . . . it." The learned judge read out this section to the jury, laying emphasis on the words "if taken as a whole". He then went on to say: "Those other vital words 'tend to deprave and corrupt' really mean just what they say. You have heard several efforts to define them. 'Tend' obviously means 'have a tendency to' or 'be inclined to'. 'Deprave' is defined in some dictionaries . . . as 'to make morally bad; to pervert or corrupt morally'. . . . The essence of the matter, you may think, is moral corruption." The appellants contend that this direction as to the meaning of obscenity does not go far enough; the learned judge should have gone on, so they say, to explain that the essence of moral corruption is to make a person behave badly or worse than he otherwise would have done, or to blur his perception of the difference between good and bad. The court cannot accept that contention. Were it sound, it would perhaps be difficult to know where the judge ought to stop. When, as here, a statute lays down the definition of a word or phrase in plain English, it is rarely necessary and often unwise for the judge to attempt to improve on or redefine the definition. Certainly, in the circumstances of the present case he cannot be blamed for saying no more than he did about the words "deprave and corrupt".' *R v Calder & Boyars Ltd* [1968] 3 All ER 644 at 647, per Salmon LJ

[The Post Office Act 1953, s 11 makes it an offence to send a postal packet which encloses any indecent or 'obscene' article.] 'So far as the Post Office Act count is concerned, there is no doubt in our judgment but that "obscene" in its context as an alternative to indecent has its ordinary or as it is sometimes called dictionary meaning. It includes things which are shocking, lewd, indecent and so on. On the other hand, in the Obscene Publications Act 1959, there is a specific test of obscenity [a tendency to deprave or corrupt] and in charges under that Act it is this test and this test alone which is to be applied.' *R v Anderson* [1971] 3 All ER 1152 at 1158, CA, per cur.

'It is well known that the words (deprave and corrupt) are derived from the judgment of Cockburn CJ in *R v Hicklin* [supra] where he said: ". . . I think the test of obscenity is this, whether the tendency of the matter charged as obscenity is to deprave and corrupt those whose minds are open to such immoral influences, and into whose hands a publication of this sort may fall." The Obscene Publications Act 1959 adopted the expression "deprave and corrupt" but gave a new turn to it. Previously, although appearing in Cockburn CJ's formula, the words had in fact been largely disregarded; the courts simply considered whether the publication was obscene and the tendency to deprave and corrupt was presumed. But the Act of 1959 changed all this. Instead of a presumed consequence of obscenity, a tendency to deprave and corrupt became the test of obscenity and became what had to be proved. One consequence appears to be that the section does not hit "articles" which merely shock however many people. It can only have been the pressure of Parliamentary compromise which can have produced a test so difficult for the courts. No definition of "deprave and corrupt" is offered—no guideline as to what kind of influence is meant. Is it criminal conduct, general or sexual, that is feared (and we may note that the articles here treated are of sadistic and violent behaviour) or departure from some code of morality, sexual or otherwise, and if so whose code, or from accepted or other beliefs, or the arousing of erotic desires "normal" or "abnormal", or as the justices have said "fantasies in the mind". Some, perhaps most, of these alternatives involve deep questions of psychology and ethics; how are the courts to deal with them? Well might they have said that such words provide a formula which cannot in practice be applied. What they have said is first, that no definition of "deprave and corrupt" can be provided, though the words are meant to be strong and emphatic; secondly, that judges or juries must decide for or against a tendency to deprave and corrupt as a question of fact and must do so without expert, i.e. psychological or sociological or medical, advice. I simply state this attitude as a fact; it is not appropriate to endorse or to disapprove it on this present occasion. I have serious doubts whether the Act will continue to be workable in this way, or whether it will produce tolerable results. The present is, or in any rational system ought to be, a simple case, yet the illogical and unscientific character of the Act has forced the justices into untenable positions. . . . The Act's purpose is to prevent the depraving and corrupting of men's minds by certain types of writing; it could never have been intended to except from the legislative protection a large body of citizens merely because, in different degrees, they had previously been exposed, or exposed themselves, to the "obscene" material. The Act is not merely concerned with the once for all corruption of the wholly innocent, it equally protects the less innocent from further corruption, the addict from feeding or increasing his addiction. To say this is not to negate the principle of relative "obscenity"; certainly the tendency to deprave and corrupt is not to be estimated in relation to some assumed standard of purity of some reasonable average man. It is the likely reader.' *Director of Public Prosecutions v Whyte* [1972] 3 All ER 12 at 18, 19, HL, per Lord Wilberforce

Australia 'The offence is one against public morality. It is for convenience generally known as "obscene libel", but the gist of it is publishing matter to deprave or corrupt the public with the intention of depraving and corrupting them. It does not depend on th exact meaning of "obscene" any more tha on the exact meaning of "lewd" or "bawdy" epithets which generally kept company wit "obscene" in the common law indictmen The substantial requirement is that th matter published and the manner of its publ cation establish the guilt of the accused i accordance with the test.' *R v Close* [194 VLR 445 at 453, per Gavan Duffy J

'The first thing, I think, that strikes one, i considering a "tendency to corrupt" as th characteristic of obscenity, is that it does n at all reproduce the ordinary popul meaning of the word "obscene". There probably no exact synonym, but the wor "indecent", "filthy", "disgusting", "offe sive", all readily occur to one's mind an express more or less fully and clearly th popular meaning. . . . Perhaps "filthy" today a stronger word than "obscene", b this is not true, I think, of "indecent", c "disgusting" or of "offensive". Th derivation of the word seems obscure. Wh seems important is that the word "obscene in its ordinary sense denotes today somethin which is indecent or disgusting. The notion of that which offends good taste or decenc it could be quite properly used of somethin which has no sexual significance, and c something which is not likely to corrupt c deprave anybody. No doubt most thin which are "obscene" in the ordinary sens could be said to have a tendency to depra or corrupt, but such a tendency is, I think, n part of the ordinary meaning of the word Ibid at 463, per Fullagar J

New Zealand 'By what standard . . . shoul a court determine whether . . . particul language is sufficiently offensive to decency The standard which must be taken is th current standard of the community. Th statute [Police Offences Act 1927, s 48] is n concerned with morality; it is directed towar public behaviour; it prohibits the use of obscen or indecent language as a breach of decoru when that language offends against the co temporary standards of propriety in the com munity. In any particular case whether it do so offend is not to be decided in the abstrac but must be viewed against the circumstanc and the setting in which the words were used *Police v Drummond* [1973] 2 NZLR 263 at 26 per McCarthy J. [See also per Turner P at 26 and per Richmond J at 268.]

OBSERVE

[A landlord failed to 'observe' the covenants contained in a lease.] 'The word "observe" is not a purely negative word. It cannot, I think, mean that the covenantor may simply sit by noticing what is happening and doing nothing. What it means, I think, is "to comply with the obligation" and therefore it has a positive and not merely a negative meaning.' *Ayling v Wade* [1961] 2 All ER 399 at 402, CA, per Danckwerts LJ

OBSOLETE

[The question was whether a covenant was 'obsolete' within the meaning of the Law of Property Act 1925, s 84(1)(a).] 'Counsel for the applicants referred us to the Shorter Oxford English Dictionary, and, out of the many meanings of "obsolete" which are to be found there, he selected as being appropriate to this case such definitions as "fallen into disuse", or "out of date", and submitted that that was the proper interpretation to apply to "obsolete" in s 84(1)(a). Counsel submitted that such an interpretation was quite distinct from the interpretation which, he said, the tribunal inferentially put on the word, namely, "valueless". The meaning of the term "obsolete" may well vary according to the subject-matter to which the term is applied. Many things have some value, even though they are out of date in kind or in form—for example, motor cars, or bicycles. Here, however, we are concerned with the application of the term to restrictive covenants as to user, and these covenants are imposed when a building estate is laid out, as was the case with this estate which was laid out in 1898, for the purpose of preserving the character of the estate as a residential area for the mutual benefit of all those who build houses on the estate or subsequently buy them. If, as sometimes happens, the character of an estate as a whole, or of a particular part of it, gradually changes, a time will come when the purpose to which I have referred can no longer be achieved, for what was intended at first to be a residential area has become, either through express or tacit waiver of the covenants, substantially a commercial area. When that time comes, it may be said that the covenants have become obsolete, because their original purpose can no longer be served and, in my opinion, it is in that sense that the word "obsolete" is used in s 84(1)(a).' *Re Truman, Hanbury, Buxton & Co Ltd's Application* [1955] 3 All ER 559 at 563, 564; see also [1956] 1 QB 261

New Zealand '"Obsolete" does not mean merely suspended or reserved for special aggravated cases, but means wholly and entirely out of date, unsuited to existing conditions, existing in theory but inapplicable in practice. It is not only obsolescent (growing out of use), but obsolete (disused). The long bow was formerly the weapon of Englishmen. It is still in use in some countries "consisting principally of coloured populations", but it is obsolete in England.' *A-G v Bloomfield, A-G v Geddis* (1913) 33 NZLR 545 at 568, per Denniston J; also reported 16 GLR 218 at 229

New Zealand 'An obsolete process or jurisdiction is one which is no longer used, not necessarily one that is no longer capable of being used.' Ibid at 581; 235, per Chapman J

New Zealand [The Property Law Act 1952, s 127(1) (repealed) authorised the court to modify or extinguish easements which ought to be deemed 'obsolete'.] 'The first ground requires it to be shewn that the easements "ought to be deemed obsolete" because of some change in the user of any land to which the easements are annexed. For convenience I shall refer to such land as a "dominant tenement". "Obsolete" usually means "gone out of use", "discarded" or "out of date" but in this context I think it means "no longer relevant to the circumstances presently obtaining". I also think that the points of time which require to be considered in order to ascertain whether or not there has been a change of user, and the extent of any such change, are the time when the easement was created and the time when the application for its extinguishment comes before the Court. For that reason I do not think it proper under this head to have regard to future user of the dominant tenements, however probable, or even the projected use of some of them. . . . My duty, as I see it, is to compare the existing user of the dominant tenements with the user contemplated when the rights of way were granted nearly 110 years ago.' *Hunton (C) Ltd v Swire* [1969] NZLR 232 at 234, per Wilson J

OBSTRUCT

In Malicious Damage Act

[The Malicious Damage Act 1861, s 35 makes it a felony unlawfully and maliciously to do certain acts with intent to 'obstruct' any engine, tender, carriage or truck using a railway, and s 36 makes it a misdemeanour to 'obstruct' any engine or carriage by any unlawful act or wilful omission or neglect.] 'The offence, under s 36 is the unlawfully obstructing a train, not in obstructing it unlawfully with a malicious intent, as required by s 35. In this case a drunken man unlawfully changed the signals. The natural result of this would be to stop the train, and to cause derangement of the whole machinery of the railway. If this is the natural result of the prisoner's act, is it not causing a train to be obstructed? There is nothing in s 36 to show that the obstruction must be a physical one. It is sufficient if a train is in fact obstructed.' *R v Hadfield* (1870) LR 1 CCR 253 at 256, CCR, per Blackburn J

'There can be no doubt in this case that the prisoner did in fact make a signal, namely, by holding up his arms in the mode used by inspectors of the line when desirous of stopping a train between two stations; or that he did thus obstruct the train, for the driver shut off steam and diminished the speed of the train from twenty to four miles an hour; or that the prisoner did what he did with the intention of producing this result. We have to consider whether this is such an obstruction as is contemplated by s 36 [of the Malicious Damage Act 1861 (see supra)]. . . . The first question is whether the section applies to anything except a mere physical obstruction. If it had spoken of obstructing the line of railway, it might have been limited to physical obstructions. But the words are "obstruct any engine or carriage". And further the section speaks not only of obstruction "by any unlawful act", but also of obstruction "by any wilful omission or default". These latter words are probably directed to the case of a servant of the company delaying a train by wilfully omitting some act which it is his duty to do; and they must include something beyond mere physical obstruction. But all doubt is removed when we refer to s 35. That section makes it felony to do certain acts maliciously and with intent to obstruct. It enumerates first a number of acts which would no doubt amount to a physical obstruction of the line itself, such as placing wood or stones across the railway, displacing the rails, or altering the points. Then follow the words "shall unlawfully and maliciously make or show hide or remove any signal or light upon or near to any railway"; and then the general words "shall unlawfully and maliciously do or cause to be done any other matter or thing with intent, etc." Now it is quite clear that the making or altering of a signal need not necessarily create any physical obstruction; and it is therefore clear that the word obstruct in s 35 is not limited to physical obstruction. I should have said the same of s 36, even if it had stood alone. But plainly the same word must have the same meaning in both sections; and therefore s 36 applies to other than physical obstructions.' *R v Hardy* (1871) LR 1 CCR 278 at 280, 281, CCR, per Bovill CJ

[All distinctions between felonies and misdemeanours were abolished by the Criminal Law Act 1967, s 1(1).]

See, generally, 11 Halsbury's Laws (4th edn) para 1314.

Local government officer

Australia [The Local Government Act 1919–1986 (NSW), s 635 makes it an offence for any person wilfully to 'obstruct' a servant of a municipal council in the execution of his duty under the Act.] 'The verb "obstructs" of course can, in various contexts, have different shades of meaning, but a common and natural meaning of the verb "to obstruct" is to impede or hinder, to retard or to oppose the activities of, or to oppose the course of conduct of a person who is seeking to achieve a particular purpose. Those meanings which I have suggested seem to me to be perfectly natural and straightforward synonyms, as it were, of the verb "to obstruct" and if they are to be regarded as indicating the meaning of the word "obstructs" as used in s 635, then I think the evidence before the magistrate did indeed disclose a prima facie case in support of the offence charged against the present respondent. What does or does not amount to obstruction of course depends upon the particular facts and circumstances of the case. It is clear that it is not even necessary in all cases that there should be any physical interference with the activities of the person said to have been obstructed.' *Auburn Municipal Council v Ivanoff* (1964) 10 LGRA 258 at 260, per Maguire J

Police obstructed in execution of duty

[The Prevention of Crimes Amendment Act 1885, s 2 (repealed) extended the Prevention of Crimes Act 1871, s 12 (also repealed; see now the Police Act 1964, s 51(3)) (under which a person convicted of an assault on a constable was guilty of an offence under that Act), to all cases of resisting or wilfully 'obstructing' any constable or police officer when in the execution of his duty.] 'In my opinion a man who, finding that a car is breaking the law, warns the driver, so that the speed of the car is slackened, and the police are thereby prevented from ascertaining the speed and so are prevented from obtaining the only evidence upon which, according to our experience, courts will act with confidence, is obstructing the police in the execution of their duty. . . . However, nothing that I now say must be construed to mean that the mere giving of a warning to a passing car that the driver must look out as there is a police trap ahead will amount to an obstruction of the police in the execution of their duty in the absence of evidence that the car was going at an illegal speed at the time of the warning given.' *Betts v Stevens* [1910] 1 KB 1 at 6, 7, DC, per Lord Alverstone CJ

'I think that the police, in the execution of their duty, intended to get into the inn. They wanted to get in before anybody in the inn had an opportunity of putting things away, and if they had knocked at the door and the licensee had not opened the door for several minutes, the justices could have found that the licensee was obstructing the police. "Obstructing" . . . means, for this purpose, making it more difficult for the police to carry out their duties.' *Hinchliffe v Sheldon* [1955] 3 All ER 406 at 408, per Lord Goddard CJ

'It is an offence by statute wilfully to obstruct any constable or peace officer when in the execution of his duty. This offence is not confined to physical obstruction. If a policeman was investigating a crime, and someone wilfully misled him by false information, he might well be guilty of this offence. But it is one thing to obstruct a policeman. It is another thing to refuse to help him. Take the case in Australia where a man, who was shot and wounded in an affray, refused to disclose to the police the name of the person who had shot him. It would seem that he was engaged in gang warfare, for he said that he would "cop it sweet" if he did disclose the name. He said he would attend to the matter himself, that is, take his own revenge. No civilised community can tolerate such behaviour. But his offence is not obstructing the police. It is misprision of felony: see *R v Crimmins* [[1959] VLR 270].' *Sykes v Director of Public Prosecutions* [1961] 3 All ER 33 at 41, HL, per Lord Denning

'What the prosecution have to prove is that there was an obstructing of a constable; that the constable at the time was acting in the execution of his duty and that the person obstructing did so wilfully. To carry the matter a little further, it is in my view clear that "obstruct" under s 51(3) of the Police Act 1964, is the doing of any act which makes it more difficult for the police to carry out their duty. That description of obstructing I take from *Hinchliffe v Sheldon*, [supra]. It is also in my judgment clear that it is part of the obligations and duties of a police constable to take all steps which appear to him necessary for keeping the peace, for preventing crime or for protecting property from criminal injury. There is no exhaustive definition of the powers and obligations of the police, but they are at least those, and they would further include the duty to detect crime and to bring an offender to justice. Pausing there, it seems to me quite clear that the defendant was making it more difficult for the police to carry out their duties, and that the police at the time and throughout were acting in accordance with their duties. The only remaining ingredient, and the one upon which in my judgment this case revolves, is whether the obstructing of which the defendant was guilty was a wilful obstruction. "Wilful" in this context not only in my judgment means "intentional" but something which is done without lawful excuse.' *Rice v Connolly* [1966] 2 All ER 649 at 651, per Lord Parker CJ

OBSTRUCTION *See also* WILFUL

Of floor

[The Factories Act 1961, s 28(1) provides that factory floors shall be kept free from any 'obstruction'. The plaintiff was injured while taking a reel of paper from a rack.] 'The word "obstruction" is not capable of precise definition, and I do not think it wise to attempt it. In one sense anything that is on a floor is an obstruction. If you want to walk straight across a room, even a table or a chair may be an obstruction in your path. If you carried it thus far, you might say that a machine on a factory floor was an obstruction. Even one of these racks in this storeroom would be an obstruction. That would be absurd. In this section, an "obstruction" is something on the floor that has no business to be there, and which is a source of risk to persons ordinarily using the floor.' *Pengelley v Bell Punch Co Ltd* [1964] 2 All ER 945 at 946, CA, per Lord Denning MR

'My Lords, when considering whether something is an "obstruction" or not it is no use trying to define by further language what is meant by that word for it is a word in common and everyday use in the English language and is, in my opinion, thus incapable of further definition. Everyone is agreed that some limitation must be put on the word but that limitation is itself incapable of definition. All one can do is to suggest tests by which to measure whether something is an obstruction or not. Lord Denning MR, in *Pengelley v Bell Punch Co Ltd* [supra] laid down as a test: "In this section, an 'obstruction' is something on the floor that has no business to be there, and which is a source of risk to persons ordinarily using the floor." That in many cases will be a most useful guide but like all tests can be no more than a guide and as such must be applied with caution and bend to the particular facts and cases of each case; its slavish application may, and, in my opinion in this case would, fail to give any satisfactory answer or might even point to the wrong answer.' *Jenkins v Allied Ironfounders Ltd* [1969] 3 All ER 1609 at 1619, HL, per Lord Upjohn

Of highway

The placing of an obstacle on or such an improper use of a highway as amounts to an obstruction of the traffic on it constitutes a nuisance at common law. In some cases obstruction of the highway may be authorised by law or agreement. It may be either temporary or permanent. Where it is temporary, there is a duty, breach of which is an act of negligence, to remove the obstruction as soon as possible, and to see that it is so guarded that the risk to persons using the highway is reduced as far as possible. Where it is permanent, there is a duty, breach of which is an act of negligence, to maintain it in such a state of security as persons using the highway have become accustomed to expect. The duty of care extends to blind persons on city streets, even though in the circumstances a sighted person would not have been injured, because the presence of blind persons there is foreseeable. (34 Halsbury's Laws (4th edn) para 42)

'I am bound to administer the law according to the legal rights of the public as they now exist, and which are thus aptly defined in the language of pleading—to pass and repass, on foot and with horses and carriages, at their free will and pleasure, over the said highway, i.e. over every part of it at their free will and pleasure. Every obstruction which, to a substantial degree, renders the exercise of that right unsafe or inconvenient, is a violation of that right. And I think the authority of parliament is necessary to legalise such a dealing with the highway, as deprives any class of passengers, whether on foot or with horses and carriages, of use of any part of it.' *R v Train* (1862) 3 F & F 22 at 27, per Erle CJ

'For a person merely to stand still, or to cause his horse and cart to stand still, in the roadway is not causing an obstruction. An obstruction will only be caused if there is an unreasonable use of the road by stopping.' *Gill v Carson & Nield* [1917] 2 KB 674 at 677, 678, DC, per Lord Reading CJ

'The law as regards obstructions to highways is conveniently stated in a passage in Salmond on Torts (11th edn), at p 303: "A nuisance to a highway consists either in obstructing it or in rendering it dangerous", and then a number of examples are given. I will not take up time reading them, but a reference to these examples seems to me to show that prima facie, at any rate, when one speaks of an obstruction to a highway one means something which permanently or temporarily removes the whole or part of the highway from public use altogether. To take the simplest and most obvious case, if I erect a fence or a wall halfway across the road, I obstruct it, because to that extent the road ceases to be usable at that point as such. The alternative in the text which I read "or in rendering it dangerous", adds a different conception of wrongful interference, viz, the putting on a highway of something which, though it does not obstruct, that is, bar the highway in the sense that I have already mentioned, yet is liable to make it dangerous. Again, one example will suffice: if I make a small hole in the highway difficult to see, or put some greasy substance on it, so that treading in the hole or on the substance is liable to cause a man as a natural consequence to fall, then it may be that I have caused a nuisance to the highway, not by obstructing it, but by rendering it dangerous.' *Trevett v Lee* [1955] 1 All ER 406 at 409, CA, per Evershed MR

'In my judgment . . . the word "obstruction" falls to be construed in a purely objective sense. The motive or purpose underlying the act alleged to constitute an obstruction is irrelevant. An act which in fact causes an obstruction cannot be justified by the motive or purpose which inspires or induces its commission and, conversely, a lawful act cannot amount to an obstruction merely because the motive or purpose which leads to its commission is one which does not commend itself to the court.' *Anderson (WR) (Motors) Ltd v Hargreaves* [1962] 1 All ER 129 at 132, per Slade J

'An "obstruction" to a highway occurs when it is rendered impassable, or more difficult to pass along it by reason of some physical obstacle. It may be obstructed without it being out of repair at all. If a tree falls across the road, it may not injure the surface at all, it may even straddle it without touching the surface, the road is then "obstructed" but it is not out of repair. If a barbed-wire fence is across a footpath or if bushes and branches overhang it the footpath is "obstructed" but it is not out of repair. . . . So also if a highway is blocked by a fall of snow, or by a landslide without injuring the surface of the road the highway is "obstructed" but it is not out of repair.' *Haydon v Kent County Council* [1978] 2 All ER 97 at 102, 103, CA, per Lord Denning MR

Australia '"Obstruction" . . . is not a term of art nor has it acquired any special meaning, but it is always used in describing a particular kind of nuisance, viz the obstruction of a highway. What is obstruction of a highway? It is not only an obstruction which actually prevents someone from exercising his right on the highway; it is any obstruction which interferes to an appreciable practical extent with the right which every member of the public has to use the highway, and to use it at all times and under all circumstances. The right of each person is not restricted to the particular part of the highway which may happen not to be in use by others at the time; it extends to the whole of the highway. Everybody has the right to use the whole of the highway at any time he thinks fit for the purpose of passing and repassing, and anything which appreciably and practically interferes with that right is an obstruction of the highway.' *Haywood v Mumford* (1908) 7 CLR 133 at 140, 141, per O'Connor J

Of police

'What the prosecution have to prove is that there was an obstructing of a constable; that the constable at the time was acting in the execution of his duty and that the person obstructing did so wilfully. To carry the matter a little further, it is in my view clear that "obstruct" under s 51(3) of the Police Act 1964, is the doing of any act which makes it more difficult for the police to carry out their duty. That description of obstructing I take from *Hinchliffe v Sheldon* [1955] 1 WLR 1207. It is also in my judgment clear that it is part of the obligations and duties of a police constable to take all steps which appear to him necessary for keeping the peace, for preventing crime or for protecting property from criminal injury. There is no exhaustive definition of the powers and obligations of the police, but they are at least those, and they would further include the duty to detect crime and to bring an offender to justice. Pausing there, it seems to me quite clear that the defendant was making it more difficult for the police to carry out their duties, and that the police at the time and throughout were acting in accordance with their duties. The only remaining ingredient, and the one upon which in my judgment this case revolves, is whether the obstructing of which the defendant was guilty was a wilful obstruction. "Wilful" in this context not only in my judgment means "intentional" but something which is done without lawful excuse.' *Rice v Connolly* [1966] 2 All ER 649 at 651, per Lord Parker CJ

Of road in mine

[In an action by a dependant of one of the deceased, it was contended by the plaintiff that the death of two repairers had been caused by a breach of the statutory duty imposed on the defendants by the Coal Mines Act 1911, s 47 (repealed; see now the Mines and Quarries Act 1954, s 34(1)(b)), which required that every haulage road should be kept clear as far as possible of pieces of coal and other 'obstruction'.] 'In our opinion, the argument of counsel for the defendants that the section is not a traffic regulation is right; it is intended to deal with the condition or state of the haulage way. A truck left on or across the line, either negligently or deliberately, would, we think, fairly come within the meaning of obstruction as used in the section. It would then be as much an obstruction as a piece of coal or a baulk of timber. But a section which requires the way to be left clear of pieces of coal or other obstruction does not appear to us to be intended to deal with the case of a truck, or line of trucks, which is being legitimately moved along the rails, but owing to a failure to signal, or to a disregard of signals, causes a collision.' *Alexander v Tredegar Iron & Coal Co Ltd* [1944] 1 All ER 451 at 452, CA, per Goddard LJ

OBSTRUCTIVE BUILDING *See* BUILDING

OBTAIN

For purposes of this section [which deals with the obtaining of property by deception] a person is to be treated as obtaining property if he obtains ownership, possession or control of it, and 'obtain' includes obtaining for another or enabling another to obtain or to retain. (Theft Act 1968, s 15(2))

[The Larceny Act 1916, s 33 (repealed; cf now the Theft Act 1968, s 15 (supra)) made a person, who received any property knowing the same to have been 'obtained' in any way whatsoever under circumstances which amounted to an offence under the Act, guilty of an offence of the like degree.] 'The word "obtained" in s 33, sub-s 1 of the Larceny Act 1916, is sought to be construed as if it were wide enough to apply to a particular change of intention on the part of a person into whose hands goods have lawfully come. But by "obtained" an actual and physical obtaining is meant, and what is referred to is such obtaining as occurs in the case of an obtaining by false pretences.' *R v Missell, Ringle & Errington* (1926) 19 Cr App Rep 109 at 111, CCA, per Lord Hewart CJ

Australia 'According to the Oxford Dictionary "obtain" means primarily to come into possession or enjoyment of (something) by one's own effort or by request; to procure or gain as the result of purpose and effort, hence generally to acquire or get.' *Re Woods, Woods v Woods* [1941] St R Qd 129 at 137, per Philp J

Australia [A contract was expressed to be subject to the purchaser 'obtaining' a loan of not less than a certain sum from a building society.] 'The expression "obtaining a loan" means obtaining a loan in the sense of procuring the moneys and not in the sense of obtaining approval of the loan. That appears to me to be the ordinary meaning of the words. One does not obtain a loan until one has the actual moneys available and until the moneys are available the prospective lender might change its mind. One cannot be said to have obtained a loan until one actually has the money.' *Tait v Bonnice* [1975] VR 102 at 106, per Menhennitt J

Canada [An action for real estate commission could only be brought where an agent had 'obtained' an offer in writing that was accepted.] 'I am of the opinion that the plaintiff broker "has obtained an offer in writing" which the vendor accepted, when he obtained a draft offer from the purchaser's solicitor arranged a meeting of the parties to discuss th draft, and thereafter delivered this draft in th company of the two principals to the vendor' solicitor, who made certain technica adjustments thereto and added some terms t the lengthy first draft prepared by th purchaser's solicitor.' *Cash v George Dunda Realty Ltd* (1973) 40 DLR (3d) 31 at 37, 38 Ont CA, per Estey JA

OBVIOUS

'In my judgment "obvious" means somethin which, as soon as you look at it, strikes one a once as being so like the original design, th registered design, as to be almost unmistake able. I think an obvious imitation is somethin which is very close to the original design, th resemblance to the original design bein immediately apparent to the eye looking a the two.' *Dunlop Rubber Co Ltd v Golf Ba Developments Ltd* (1931) 48 RPC 268 at 279 per Farwell J

Canada 'In order that a thing shall b "obvious" it must be something that woul directly occur to some one who was searchin for something novel, a new manufacture o whatever it might be, without the necessity o his having to do any experimenting o research, whether the research be in th laboratory or amongst literature.' *J R Shor Milling Co (Canada) Ltd v Geo Western Brea & Cakes Ltd* [1941] Ex CR 69 at 86, Ex Ct, pe Maclean J; affirmed 2 Fox Pat C 103

OCCASION

'The expression "on the occasion of" . . . i not equivalent in meaning to the phrase "o the same date as". An "occasion" is not period of twenty-four hours. If we say that man took out an assurance policy on the occa sion of his marriage, we do not mean "on th day of his marriage", but rather "at or abou the time of his marriage", with the implicatio that the coincidence in time was designed an not accidental.' *Ideal Life Assurance Co Ltd Hirschfield (H J) & Hirschfield (A H)* [1943] KB 442 at 446, CA, per cur

'As occasion may require'

'One of the most important of these question relates to the validity of r 32 [of a benefi building society], which gives the director power, from time to time, as occasion ma require, to borrow money from the society's banker or from any other banker or person. In both the courts below it was assumed to be settled law that the rule was invalid, because it does not impose any limit upon the amount which the directors are authorised to borrow. It cannot with strict accuracy be said that the power conferred is absolutely without limit, seeing that it is only to be exercised "as occasion may require" which plainly implies that it is not to be exercised at all except in the case of a loan being needed for the purposes of the society in the course of its legitimate transactions as a benefit building society.' *Murray v Scott, Agnew v Murray, Brimelow v Murray* (1884) 9 App Cas 519 at 556, 557, per Lord Watson

OCCUPANCY *See also* OWNER

Ownership may be acquired by occupancy of a thing without an owner, for example the capture of wild animals, the appropriation of free natural elements, such as air and water, the lawful severance of a thing, for example corn or other emblements, from the soil, and, perhaps, the finding of a thing absolutely abandoned or irretrievably lost.

It has been said that when the species of a thing is changed, as by making wine, oil, bread or malt out of another person's grapes, olives, wheat or barley, the owner's title is destroyed and the operator, although liable in damages, acquires title by virtue of this possession; but it appears that, in modern law, alterations to a chattel divest the owner's title only when the chattel has been worked into the property of another, or is no longer identifiable. (35 Halsbury's Laws (4th edn) para 1136)

OCCUPATION (Calling)

[The Bills of Sale Act 1854, s 1 (repealed; see now the Bills of Sale Act 1878, s 12) required a bill of sale to be filed together with an affidavit stating (inter alia) the 'occupation' of the maker. An affidavit described the maker of a bill as 'gentleman'.] 'The Act says that the bill of sale shall not be valid unless there be filed with it an affidavit containing a description of the residence and occupation of the person making or giving the same. Here the person making it had an occupation, being employed by a certain house to buy silk for them. He thereby earned his living, and it was therefore clearly his occupation within the ordinary meaning of that word, and the definitions of it given by the dictionaries.' *Adams v Graham* (1864) 3 New Rep 372 at 373, per Cockburn CJ

'This is a question of the meaning to be put upon the word "occupation" in the Act of Parliament [Bills of Sale Act 1854 (repealed; see supra)]. In my opinion, it means the trade or calling by which the maker of the bill of sale ordinarily seeks to get his livelihood. In this case the maker of the bill of sale had been married a short time to the master of the workhouse, who, a month or so before his death, had taken a farm, and who died leaving the farm as part of his assets. It thus came into her hands as executrix of his will, and she was put to the alternative of abandoning it altogether or sowing it with seed and cultivating it till disposed of. She did not do this personally, her previous life and habits rendering her incapable of so doing; but she employed a bailiff to carry on the farm for her. I do not think she could be, with the least propriety, described as a farmer; she did not carry on the business of farming as her ordinary means of livelihood, and that, I think, is what the Act means by the term "occupation".' *Luckin v Hamlyn* (1869) 21 LT 366 at 366, per Kelly CB

'The word "occupation" in this Act means the business in which a man is usually engaged to the knowledge of his neighbours. The intention is, that such a description should be given that if inquiry be made in the place where the person resides, he may be easily identified.' Ibid at 366, per Martin B

[The lease of a house contained a covenant not to use the premises thereby demised, or any part thereof, or permit the same or any part thereof to be used in the exercise or carrying on of any art, trade, or business, 'occupation', or calling whatsoever.] 'The question is what is the meaning of "any occupation or calling whatsoever". It is suggested on the part of the defendants that that means where you get a profit. I cannot accede to that. I do not think profit is the test, but the use of the house for the purpose. A man may have an occupation from which he does not get any profit, and never intends to get any profit. He may have as an occupation the printing and publishing of papers, or books, or pamphlets, for a charitable society for which he charges nothing. It may be carried on, as it is in some cases, by an officer of the society who is not paid, and who does it from charitable and benevolent motives. Can that make any difference? The using of the house for that purpose is a using it for some occupation or calling.' *Portman v*

Home Hospital Assocn (1879) 27 Ch D 81 n at 82, 83, per Jessel MR

Canada 'It is suggested here that the duties of a housewife do not amount to an "occupation". The term "occupation" has not as far as I can find any technical meaning. It ordinarily means that which engages the time and attention. I think no housewife would be prepared to admit that her housewifely duties do not engage her time and attention.' *Northern Trusts Co v Eckert* [1942] 2 WWR 382 at 387, Alta CA, per Ewing JA

OCCUPATION (Of property) *See also* ACTUAL OCCUPATION; BENEFICIAL OCCUPATION; EXCLUSIVE OCCUPATION

Generally

'There is a material difference between a holding and an occupation. A person may hold though he does not occupy. A tenant of a freehold is a person who holds of another: he does not necessarily occupy. In order to occupy, a party must be personally resident by himself or his family.' *R v Ditcheat (Inhabitants)* (1829) 9 B & C 176 at 183, 184, per Littledale J

'The first question is, what is the meaning of a person being in possession of property under a lease? Is it to be said that a man is not in occupation of property comprised in that lease unless he be actively using and enjoying it? I apprehend the true meaning of the words "occupation under a lease" is not actual personal use and occupation, but occupation to which he is entitled under the instrument by which the right of possession was granted.' *Whittington v Corder* (1852) 20 LTOS 175 at 175, per Turner V-C

[A testator, after providing for the upkeep of his house and its contents and grounds as a residence for his family until the youngest came of age, gave to his eldest son, as soon as that event took place, the option to 'occupy and enjoy the use of' the house, rent-free, for life.] 'I am not disposed to agree that this was a gift of an option to the son to reside only; the words used are an option "to occupy and enjoy the use of", and unless there be something to show that the meaning of those words is restricted, they extend to something beyond residence, as has been decided in many cases. In this case I do not myself see anything to limit the words. I agree that the idea in the testator's mind was probably that his children should reside in the house. The difference between the words "reside" and "occupy and enjoy the use of" is perfectly well known. If he meant it to restrict it to residence I do not see the reason for his not using the appropriate word "reside".' *Re Gibbons, Gibbons v Gibbons* [1920] 1 Ch 372 at 379, CA, per Lord Sterndale MR

'Occupation' means that the owner is in actual physical enjoyment of the house, property or estate by himself, his agents or servants. Strictly speaking "occupation" by the owner cannot include the case of sub-tenants for the actual occupation is in them. A limited form of occupation is "residence" which involves the dwelling for some period of the year on the premises personally of the owner or his family, or alternatively, at least, of his domestic servants.' *Martin Estates Co Ltd v Watt & Hunter* [1925] NI 79 at 85, per Moore LJ

'It is never true to say that a mere intention to occupy, in hypothetical circumstances which may never come into existence, is equivalent to occupation.' *Hampstead Borough Council v Associated Cinema Properties Ltd* [1944] 1 All ER 436 at 438, CA, per cur.

'Legal possession is not the same as occupation. Occupation is a matter of fact and only exists where there is sufficient measure of control to prevent strangers from interfering. . . . There must be something actually done on the land, not necessarily on the whole but on part in respect of the whole. No one would describe a bombed site or an empty unlocked house as "occupied" by anyone; but everyone would say that a farmer "occupies" the whole of his farm even though he does not set foot on the woodlands within it from one year's end to another.' *Newcastle City Council v Royal Newcastle Hospital* [1959] 1 All ER 734 at 736, PC, per Lord Denning; also reported [1959] AC 248 at 255

'"Occupiers" have been entered in the valuation roll since 1854 in virtue of the first section of the Valuation Act of that year, but the Lands Valuation Acts have provided no definition of the term. Section 379 of the Act [Local Government (Scotland) Act 1947] defines "occupier" as meaning the tenant or sub-tenant or any person in the actual occupation of the land. The words "actual occupation of land" seem to me to have been used to make plain that the occupation which is necessary to make the occupier liable to pay rates is de facto occupation as opposed to de jure occupation, the kind of constructive occupation which might be held to flow from mere ownership of land in as much as the right to possess is a cardinal attribute of the ownership of land. It would appear that for the purposes of the Act of 1947 an owner of land must have made some actual use of the premises during the relevant year before he had been called on to pay the occupier's rates leviable in respect of the land.' *Greenock Corpn v Arbuckle Smith & Co Ltd* 1960 SLT 49 at 52, per Lord Patrick; reversed on appeal, but above dictum approved: *see* 1960 SLT 123 at 124, HL, per Viscount Kilmuir LC

Australia 'The word "occupation" has been several times defined, but I do not think its meaning is more clearly set out anywhere than in the passage . . . in the judgment of Lush J in the case of *The Queen v St Pancras Assessment Committee* [(1877) 2 QBD 581], where he says: "Occupation includes possession as its primary element, but it also includes something more. Legal possession does not of itself constitute an occupation. The owner of a vacant house is in possession, and may maintain trespass against anyone who invades it, but as long as he leaves it vacant he is not rateable for it as an occupier. If, however, he furnishes it, and keeps it ready for habitation whenever he pleases to go into it, he is an occupier, though he may not reside in it one day in a year. On the other hand, a person who, without having any title, takes actual possession of a house or piece of land whether by leave of the owner or against his will, is the occupier of it." It is of course a question of fact in each case. If a man is merely there for a night or two, as in the case of a tramp sleeping in an outhouse—he is not in occupation. But if he is living on the land for a continuous period of time the magistrates may properly draw the conclusion that he is in occupation of it.' *Poowong Shire v Gillen* [1907] VLR 37 at 40, per Hood J

Canada 'Apart from cases involving questions of the building being occupied for some other purpose or some other character, which do not arise here, a dwelling-house may be said to be "occupied" while it is dwelt in, and unoccupied when no person is dwelling therein.' *Lambert v Wawanesa Mutual Fire Ins Co* [1945] 1 DLR 694 at 695, Ont CA, per Gillanders JA

Canada 'The words "occupy" and "occupant" have a variety of shades of meaning. No doubt, we commonly speak of the "occupants" of a dwelling-house, meaning thereby all persons who, at the time, live there. We use the word in even a wider sense when we speak of the "occupants" of premises, meaning thereby all the persons who happen to be within them at the particular time. Primarily, however, "to occupy" means "to take possession", and such wider meanings, while no doubt now well recognised by usage, and proper enough in the right context, are not the only meanings, according even to present common use.' *R v Lon Hay Hung* (1946) 85 CCC 308 at 313, Ont CA, per Robertson CJO

Canada 'The word "occupy", like many English words, has various meanings, depending on how it is used. . . . In one context, therefore, the word "occupy" may suggest some measure of control, but when it is used in relation to the seat of a motor car, its proper meaning, in my view, is simply "to fill the dimensions of" the seat; similarly, a person may occupy a pew in a church or a seat in a theatre. So used, the word "occupy" certainly does not suggest any measure of control.' *R v Wilson* [1957] OWN 19 at 21, Ont SC, per Aylen J

New Zealand [The Tenancy Act 1955 (NZ), s 36(e) (repealed; see now the Residential Tenancies Act 1986, s 51) provides as a ground for the recovery of possession that the premises are reasonably required by the landlord or by one or more of several joint landlords for his or their own 'occupation'.] 'The word "occupation" as used in this legislation is one which has given rise to difficulty, and little help can be gained from a consideration of the meaning ascribed to the word in other statutes. In *J R McKenzie Ltd v Gianoutsos and Booleris* [[1957] NZLR 309 at 392], McGregor J, in a judgment which had the concurrence of Gresson J, expressed the opinion that the word "occupation" was used in the Act in a physical or personal sense and that it should not be given any technical meaning. The word was used in a popular sense *uti loquitur vulgus*, and the question of occupation was to some extent a question of fact. Very much the same view was expressed by Turner J in the judgment of this Court in *McKenna v Porter Motors Ltd* [[1955] NZLR 832 at 847], where he pointed out that, whereas in the case of a dwelling-house the landlord was required to establish that the premises were reasonably required by him for his occupation as a dwelling-house, no such limitation was imposed in the case of urban property.' *Kerry v*

Hughes [1957] NZLR 850 at 852, 853, CA, per McCarthy J

Lawful occupation

New Zealand 'The phrase "in lawful occupation" where used in s 2(1) of the Trespass Act 1980 is appropriate to describe the status of a person who has the right for the time being to control the place or land.' *Polly v Polly* [1985] 1 NZLR 445 at 448

'Occupied' for insurance purposes

[A proposal form for insurance contained a question whether the premises proposed to be insured were 'occupied' at night. The assured answered this in the affirmative. The policy was issued on this proposal. Later, during an air raid, the assured went to a shelter, and during this temporary absence his premises were burgled.] 'I am clearly of opinion that the mere going away from the premises to an air raid shelter for an hour or two during an air raid at night did not make the premises unoccupied by night within the meaning of the declaration.' *Winicofsky v Army & Navy General Assurance Assocn Ltd* (1919) 88 LJKB 1111 at 1112, per Bray J

'The question is what is the meaning of the clause in this policy: "Warranted that the said premises are always occupied". If that means, as the defendant contends, that the premises are never to be left unattended, then there has undoubtedly been a breach of the warranty for both the plaintiff and his wife were absent from the premises for some hours on the day in question. But in my judgment that is not the meaning of the warranty. I think it means that the premises are to be used, continuously and without interruption, for occupation, that is to say, as a residence, and not merely used as a lock-up shop which is left unoccupied after business hours.' *Simmonds v Cockell* [1920] 1 KB 843 at 844, per Roche J

'Occupier'

The expression 'occupier' includes any number of persons and a body corporate; and in the case of any manufacture or trade, includes any person carrying on such manufacture or trade. (Explosives Act 1875, s 108)

'Occupier' means, in the case of land not occupied by any tenant or other person, the owner of the land. (Destructive Imported Animals Act 1932, s 12)

'Occupier' in relation to a public institution, includes the governor, keeper, master, matron, superintendent, or other chief resident officer, and, in relation to a house let in separate apartments or lodgings, includes any person residing in the house who is the person under whom the lodgings or separate apartments are immediately held, or his agent. (Births and Deaths Registration Act 1953, s 41)

In this Part of this Act [Part I: prohibition of use of land as caravan site without site licence] the expression 'occupier' means, in relation to any land, the person who, by virtue of an estate or interest therein held by him, is entitled to possession thereof or would be so entitled but for the rights of any other person under any licence granted in respect of the land:

Provided that where land amounting to not more than four hundred square yards in area is let under a tenancy entered into with a view to the use of the land as a caravan site, the expression 'occupier' means in relation to that land the person who would be entitled to possession of the land but for the rights of any person under that tenancy. (Caravan Sites and Control of Development Act 1960, s 1(3); see also the Caravan Sites Act 1968, s 1(1))

'Occupier', in relation to any stall, vehicle, ship or aircraft or in relation to the use of any place for any purpose, means the person for the time being in charge of the stall, vehicle, ship or aircraft or, as the case may be, the person for the time being using that place for that purpose. (Weights and Measures Act 1985, s 94(1))

'It is not easy to give an accurate and exhaustive definition of the word "occupier". Occupation includes possession as its primary element, but it also includes something more. Legal possession does not of itself constitute an occupation. The owner of a vacant house is in possession, and may maintain trespass against any one who invades it. . . . If, however, he furnishes it, and keeps it ready for habitation whenever he pleases to go to it, he is an occupier, though he may not reside in it one day in a year. On the other hand, a person who, without having any title, takes actual possession of a house or a piece of land, whether by leave of the owner or against his will, is the occupier of it. . . . A transient, temporary holding of land is not enough to make the holding rateable. It must be an occupation which has in it the character of permanence; a holding as a settler not as a wayfarer. These I take to be the essential elements of what is called a beneficial or rateable occupation.' *R v St Pancras Assessment Committee* (1877) 2 QBD 581 at 588, 589, per Lush J

'The term "occupier" is ambiguous. In one sense a caretaker is an occupier, but in another sense his occupation is that of some other person.' *Paterson v Gas Light & Coke Co* [1896] 2 Ch 476 at 482, 483, per Lindley LJ

[A testator bequeathed to his wife any house of which he might be in occupation at the time of his death. At the time of his death the wife was in occupation of a house which contained the testator's furniture, but in which he had never resided as he had been removed to a mental hospital.] 'There is no question but that the testator was the owner of the house at the time of his death. The question is whether he was also the occupier. In order that the widow might take the house under the terms of the devise two conditions had to be fulfilled. The testator had to be the owner and also the occupier. . . . The house was furnished in August 1930, and thereafter until the time when the testator died it was ready for the testator to go into whenever he recovered. I think that, on these facts, . . . I am able to come to the conclusion that the testator was not only the owner of the house in question but also the occupier.' *Re Garland, Eve v Garland* [1934] Ch 620 at 622, per Bennett J

'To my mind, it is placing a most artificial limitation on the ordinary meaning of the word "occupier" to exclude from its scope persons in the position of statutory tenants under the Rent Restrictions Acts [see now the Rent Act 1977]. I need only refer to the words of Greer LJ in *Abbey v Barnstyn* [[1930] 1 KB 660 at 670]. Again and again in his judgment in that case Greer LJ used the word "occupier" to describe the position of a statutory tenant. He says: "The use of the word 'tenant' for such an occupier does however create some difficulty when we have to interpret the word 'tenant' when used in other parts of the Act. . . ." Whatever criticism he and the other lords justices in that case and many other cases may have made of the word "tenant", no one has suggested, so far as I am aware (and counsel has been unable to draw my attention to any case which might even suggest) that persons living in premises—occupying them by virtue of the provisions of the Rent Restrictions Acts—are not occupiers of those premises in the ordinary and reasonable sense of that term.' *Brown v Ministry of Housing and Local Government* [1953] 2 All ER 1385 at 1391, per Barry J

'Wherever a person has a sufficient degree of control over premises that he ought to realise that any failure on his part to use care may result in injury to a person coming lawfully there, then he is an "occupier" [for the purposes of the Occupiers' Liability Act 1957, s 1(2)] and the person coming lawfully there is his "visitor"; and the "occupier" is under a duty to his "visitor" to use reasonable care. In order to be an "occupier" it is not necessary for a person to have entire control over the premises. He need not have exclusive occupation. Suffice it that he has some degree of control. He may share the control with others. Two or more may be "occupiers". And whenever this happens, each is under a duty to use care towards persons coming lawfully on to the premises, dependent on his degree of control. If each fails in his duty, each is liable to a visitor who is injured in consequence of his failure, but each may have a claim to contribution from the other.' *Wheat v Lacon (E) & Co Ltd* [1966] 1 All ER 582 at 593, 594, HL, per Lord Denning

[The Misuse of Drugs Act 1971, s 8 makes it an offence for the 'occupier' of premises to permit (inter alia) the smoking of cannabis. The appellant, a student, lived in a room in a university hostel.] 'It seems to us that the correct legal analysis of the appellant's right of occupation of that room in the K College Hostel was this: he had an exclusive contractual licence from the college to use that room. He was entitled to retain the use of that room to live in, to sleep in, to eat in and to work in: he paid the college for the use of that room. It was, in our view, clearly a licence which gave him not merely a right to use but a sufficient exclusivity of possession, so that he can fairly be said to be "the occupier" of that room for the purpose of s 8. He does not have to be a tenant or to have an estate in land before he can be "the occupier" within that section. It is in every case a question of fact and degree, whether someone can fairly be said to be "the occupier" for the purpose of that section.' *R v Tao* [1976] 3 All ER 65 at 69, CA, per cur.

New Zealand 'It is in the nature of the powers of a person who occupies a managerial role (whether as manager or sub-manager or acting manager) that he should control matters of access to his employer's property and in a sense he is the alter ego of the corporate occupier. It does not strain the definition of occupier under the Trespass Act 1980 to treat such a person as being in lawful occupation of corporate premises.' *Polly v Police* [1985] 1 NZLR 443 at 448, per McMullin J

OCCURRENCE

'Occurrence' in sections 16(1), 17(3) and 18 of this Act [occurrences incurring liability to pay compensation]

(a) in the case of a continuing occurrence, means the whole of that occurrence; and

(b) in the case of an occurrence which is one of a succession of occurences all attributable to a particular happening on a particular relevant site or to the carrying out from time to time on a particular relevant site of a particular operation, means all those occurrences collectively.

(Nuclear Installations Act 1965, s 26)

ODD LOT

Australia [This was a case stated by a judge of the Workers' Compensation Commission (NSW) for the opinion of the Supreme Court. The appeal was heard by the Full Court.] 'The expression "odd lot" refers to that expression used in a number of cases decided under Workers' Compensation legislation, and it is used to describe a situation of a worker who has been so injured that he is incapable of becoming an ordinary worker of average capacity in any well-known branch of the labour market, so that the capacities for work left to him fit him only for special uses and do not make his powers of labour a merchantable article in some of the well-known lines of the labour market. The cases show that if a man is an "odd lot", the onus is upon the employer to show that special employment is available to him, and if that is not shown, the worker is entitled to receive compensation on the basis of total incapacity.' *Wheatley v John Herford & Sons Ltd* (1954) 54 NSWSR 232 at 237, per Roper CJ in Eq

ODDS *See* FIXED ODDS

OF

[A maintenance order, after reciting the complaint of the churchwardens against A, 'of' the parish of C, proceeded to an adjudication against him without showing in any more direct manner what was the place of his residence.] 'The word "of" certainly in general imports dwelling, therefore it may fairly mean prima facie in such an order as this that the party did reside in the place he is described as being of, and the only question is, whether this is the description of the justices, whether they have adopted the word of the churchwardens: if they have not, then the order can be good only by intendment. I think "of" does import dwelling, and that the justices have adopted the word of the churchwardens, and, consequently, the order is good without resorting to the doctrine of intendment.' *R v Stokes Kent JJ* (1838) 2 Jur 564 at 565, per Patteson J

'When you speak of "a bishop of the province of Canterbury", you mean a bishop who is beneficed in that province.' *Day v Peacock* (1865) 18 CBNS 702 at 722, per Byles J

OFFENCE *See also* AUTREFOIS ACQUIT

'Offence' as used in this Act means an act neglect or default of such a description as would, if committed within the body of a county in England, be punishable on indictment according to the law of England for the time being in force. (Territorial Waters Jurisdiction Act 1878, s 7)

New Zealand '"Offence" generally is regarded as an action which offends against some statutory provision or involves some crime or misdemeanour known to the common law. *Re Derbyshire County Council and Derby Corporation* [[1896] 2 QB 53, and on appeal to the House of Lords [1897] AC 550], is authority for the proposition that, while the use of the word "offence" is not conclusive in creating a misdemeanour, none the less the criterion is whether it is followed by a penalty.' *Zimmerman v Inland Revenue Comr* [1960] NZLR 8 at 13, per Hardie Boys J

In Sheriffs Act

[The Sheriffs Act 1887, s 29 imposes a penalty upon any sheriff's officer who inter alia is guilty of any 'offence' against the provisions of the Act.] 'What is the reasonable construction of the Act? It cannot be doubted that it is a penal statute. It ought not, therefore, to be pressed further against those who are hit by it than we are compelled to press it within reason. When, therefore, we see that there is to be a punishment by summary process, it seems to me immaterial whether the act is called a crime or not. It is at any rate an offence in the nature of a crime. And, in order to constitute an offence in the nature of a crime, there must be what is called a mens rea; the thing must be done with a bad mind. The words used are "offence" and "offender", and in Tomlin's Dictionary of Law Terms, 4th edn, I find this definition of "offence". "The term 'offence' is usually" (that is, if there is nothing in the context to the contrary) "by itself understood to be a crime not indictable, but punishable summarily or by the forfeiture of a penalty." This is an exact description of the words which are used in s 29. The act referred to is called an "offence", and it is a crime not indictable, but punishable summarily or by the forfeiture of a penalty. It does not signify whether it is strictly speaking a crime; it is an offence in the nature of a crime, and a man who does a thing of that kind merely unguardedly or accidentally, without any evil mind, cannot be said to have committed an offence.' *Lee v Dangar, Grant & Co* [1892] 2 QB 337 at 347, 348, CA, per Lord Esher MR

'The persons who do certain acts are not declared to be guilty of an offence, but are spoken of as persons who have committed an offence. The legislature considered that persons who do these things fall within the natural description of "offenders". They are not made offenders, but are treated as being offenders, according to the natural meaning of the word in the English language. Therefore, I think the legislature must be dealing with a case in which there is a criminal mind or some criminal negligence. Then not only is the act spoken of as an "offence", but the person who commits it is spoken of as an "offender", he is spoken of as being "guilty", and he is made subject to "punishment". All those words seem to me inapplicable to the doing of an act by that kind of innocent mistake which is inherent to the human mind in human business, or negligence of that venial kind which is not criminal. I cannot bring myself to think that the very heavy penalty and the very heavy punishment which the court is authorised to inflict could have been intended to be inflicted on a person who acts without criminal mind and without criminal laches, and I think that the section must be so read.' Ibid at 351, per Fry LJ

Motoring offence

[The Motor Car Act 1903, s 4 (repealed; see now, as to disqualification for certain motoring offences, the Road Traffic Offenders Act 1988, s 34) empowered the Court, before whom a person was convicted of an 'offence' in connection with the driving of a motor car, to disqualify the offender from obtaining a driving licence.] 'The words "any offence in connection with the driving of a motor car" when read with their context in s 4 of the Motor Car Act 1903, point to offences connected with the handling or manipulation of the car in the process of driving it. Inasmuch as a person wilfully obstructing the free passage of a highway may be convicted under other statutes independently of the Motor Car Acts and the regulations made under them, there is no reason for construing the words in question so as to include that offence. It seems more reasonable to take them as applying to offences in respect of the actual locomotion of the car, and not as including the mere leaving of the car at rest in the highway, which cannot properly be said to be an offence in connection with the driving of the car.' *R v Yorkshire (West Riding) JJ, ex p Shackleton* [1910] 1 KB 439 at 441, 442, DC, per Lord Alverstone CJ

'The only question we are called upon to decide is whether there was an offence committed "in connection with the driving of a motor car" within the meaning of s 4, sub-s 1 of the Motor Car Act 1903 [repealed; see supra], which would render necessary the production of the licence for indorsement. In my view it is not enough that the offence should be committed whilst the person charged is driving the motor car. There must be a connection between the offence charged and the driving of the car, but the statute clearly contemplates a class of offences which are connected with the driving of a motor car, but are not created by the Act itself.' *Simmonds v Pond* (1918) 88 LJKB 857 at 859, DC, per Slater J

See, generally, 40 Halsbury's Laws (4th edn) para 479.

Political offence

[The Extradition Act 1870, s 3 provides that no fugitive criminal shall be surrendered if the 'offence' in respect of which his surrender is demanded is one 'of a political character'.] 'The language . . . which . . . I entirely adopt . . . is the expression of my brother Stephen in his History of the Criminal Law of England in vol ii, pp 70, 71. . . . "If a civil war were to take place, it would be high treason by levying war against the Queen. Every case in which a man was shot in action would be murder. Whenever a house was burnt for military purposes arson would be committed. To take cattle etc, by requisition would be robbery. According to the common use of language, however, all such acts would be political offences, because they would be incidents in carrying on a civil war. I think, therefore, that the expression in the Extradition Act ought . . . to be interpreted to mean that fugitive criminals are not to be surrendered for extradition crimes, if those crimes were incidental to and formed a part of political disturbances." I cannot help thinking that everybody knows there are many acts of a political character done without reason, done against all reason; but at the same time one cannot look too hardly and weigh in golden scales the acts of men hot in their political excitement.' *Re Castioni* [1891] 1 QB 149 at 165, 166, DC, per Hawkins J

[Some Polish seamen mutinied, brought their trawler to an English port, and asked for political asylum. The seamen claimed that their 'offence' was of a political character, and that they were therefore protected by the Extradition Act 1870, s 3(1).] 'The words "offence of a political character" must always be considered according to the circumstances existing at the time when they have to be considered. The present time is very different from 1890 when *Castioni*'s case [supra] was decided. It was not then treason for a citizen to leave his country and start a fresh life in another. Countries were not regarded as enemy countries when no war was in progress. Now a state of totalitarianism prevails in some parts of the world and it is a crime for citizens in such places to take steps to leave. In this case, the members of the crew of a small trawler engaged in fishing were under political supervision. The applicants revolted by the only means open to them. They committed an offence of a political character and if they were surrendered there could be no doubt that, while they would be tried for the particular offence mentioned, they would be punished as for a political crime. Thus they have brought themselves within s 3(1) and made good their claim to have the restriction referred to observed." *Re Kolczynski* [1955] 1 All ER 31 at 35, per Cassels J

See, generally, 18 Halsbury's Laws (4th edn) para 259.

OFFENDER

'The fact is that the word "offender" has both a narrower and a wider meaning (rather like the word "*reus*" in Latin). It may have the stricter meaning of one who is guilty of an offence, but it also sometimes has the meaning of a person who is under accusation of having committed an offence. I do not think it would be an abuse of language for a magistrate engaged in a juvenile court to describe his work as that of trying "young offenders", but that would not mean that every boy and girl who came before him was guilty.' *Barnard v Gorman* [1941] AC 378 at 383–386, per Lord Simon LC

OFFENSIVE TRADE

[The question was whether the carrying on of a fried fish business amounted to a breach of a covenant not to carry on a noxious or "offensive" trade or business.] 'The words with which I have to deal are, "and also shall not, nor will at any time hereafter", without the consent of the Duke of Devonshire, "use the said premises as a public-house or beer-shop or for carrying on any offensive trade or business whatsoever". The forms with which I am better acquainted specify some of the offensive trades intended to be prohibited. This form does not, so I have to construe the words without the aid of any context. . . . The question I have to determine is whether, having regard to the nature of the business, and the locality in which it is situated, and the manner in which it is carried on, this is an offensive trade or business. Now I have sufficient to show that this business is so carried on as to be an offence to some of the neighbours. I have the evidence of several people who have lost lodgers, and have their houses unlet for this reason. Therefore, I have it proved as a fact that the business as carried on offends many persons, and so far as I can judge from seeing them in the box the witnesses are not persons or extraordinary delicacy in the nostrils or elsewhere. I therefore think it is proved that the business is an offence to them. Then I have evidence on the other side that certain persons are not offended; but you can always meet people like these, they are the plaintiff's friends, perhaps determined not to be offended, not wishing to be offended, or having some reason for saying so. The business must be more or less offensive even to these witnesses, but they have all got some reason for saying they do not mind the smell, the existence of which they know. It is said that the defendant is doing his best to prevent the offence, but that is a double-edged argument. I assume that he is doing his very best, but unfortunately that shows that the business is offensive, and how bad it would be if he did not take these precautions.' *Devonshire (Duke) v Brookshaw* (1899) 81 LT 83 at 84, per Kekewich J

[The plan and conditions of sale of a residential estate provided that lots should be subject to certain restrictive covenants for the benefit of the estate, and (inter alia) that the purchasers were not to erect any building for manufacturing purposes or for the carrying on of any noisy, noisome, 'offensive' or dangerous trade or calling. A lessee from one of the purchasers of two lots had erected along the boundary of the land where it adjoined the plaintiff's plot a hoarding covered with advertisements.] 'I think this hoarding is both a "fence" and an "offence", or, to put it more accurately, that the hoarding is a fence and that the carrying on upon it the trade of bill-posting is a use of the hoarding for an offensive trade or calling. . . . Upon callings and upon trades otherwise permitted there is a veto expressed in the words upon which the question arises. The relevant provision is that they shall not be "offensive". The context in which that word occurs shows that the condition forbids (1) noisy trades or callings which offend the ear, (2) noisome trades or callings which offend the nose, (3) trades or callings which expose a man to danger, and (4) trades or callings which are "offensive". In this context this may mean offensive not to the ear, not to the nose, nor by way of danger, leaving as an obvious meaning offensive to the eye. It is not confined to this, but I see no reason why it should not extend to it. Further, the word "offensive" is, I think, to be construed relatively to the person contemplated as enjoying the benefit of the stipulation, that is to say, relative to such a person as would be the purchaser of such a plot upon such an estate as this estate is by the conditions and plan shown to be. The question, therefore, is whether the trade or calling of a bill-poster carried on upon a hoarding 156 feet long and 15 feet high, carrying with it such disfigurement and such litter by waste-paper and so on as would result from the employment of the site for such a purpose, can properly be called offensive, that is as legitimately furnishing ground of offence to a reasonable person who became a purchaser of a lot on this estate. A man may be legitimately offended by an annoyance which does not amount to a legal nuisance. The evidence here is not strong, but it is sufficient, I think, to show that this plaintiff and the other residents on the estate are actuated by considerations founded not in aesthetic sensitiveness, but in reasonable good sense in regarding such a hoarding as this occupied under an agreement for seven years for the purpose of posting bills as a legitimate ground of offence to them as owners of adjoining plots.' *Nussey v Provincial Bill Posting Co & Eddison* [1909] 1 Ch 734 at 738, 739, CA, per Cozens-Hardy MR

'We have no right to say because offensive is an adjectival derivative from the verb offend that therefore whatever offends is rightly termed offensive. A man by tactless language in a speech may give just offence, but that would not justify one in saying that he was guilty of using offensive language. The word "offensive" as applied to trades has a fairly defined meaning of its own, though it would no doubt be interpreted more widely in a high-class residential neighbourhood than in a case like the present, where at the time of the sale there were no houses, and which it was not intended to restrict to residential purposes.' Ibid at 742, per Fletcher Moulton LJ (dissenting)

Australia 'In my opinion, s 94(1) [of the Health Act 1958 (Vic)] ("offensive trade", para (b)) applies to any trade which is shown in fact to cause effluvia or offensive fumes or vapours or gases which discharge dust or foul liquid or blood or other impurity, and it is not necessary to show that the trade causes effluvia, etc to a substantial degree and for a substantial part of the time when the trade is being carried on the offence is established.' *Hicks v Nufarm Chemicals Pty Ltd* [1972] VR 583 at 591, per Pape J

New Zealand [In the Food and Drugs Act 1969, s 6(4)(b), consolidated by Food Act 1981, see s 9(4)(b), it is an offence to sell food containing any 'offensive' extraneous thing.] 'The correct test . . . is whether or not an ordinary person, neither hypersensitive nor insensitive, would find the extraneous thing to be disgusting, nauseous or repulsive.' *Flint v Hellaby Peach Products Ltd* [1974] 1 NZLR 718 at 721, per Wilson J

OFFENSIVE WEAPON

In this section . . . 'offensive weapon' means any article made or adapted for use for causing injury to the person, or intended by the person having it with him for such use by him. (Prevention of Crime Act 1953, s 1)

'Weapon of offence' means any article made or adapted for use for causing injury to or incapacitating a person, or intended by the person having it with him for such use. (Theft Act 1968, s 10(1)(b); Criminal Law Act 1977, s 8(2))

[Penalties are imposed for offences in connection with certain dangerous weapons by the Restriction of Offensive Weapons Act 1959. These weapons are defined by s 1(1) as '(a) any knife which has a blade which opens automatically by hand pressure applied to a button, spring or other device in or attached to the handle of the knife, sometimes known as a "flick knife" or "flick gun"; or (b) any knife which has a blade which is released by the force of gravity or the application of centrifugal force and which, when released, is locked in place by means of a button, spring, lever, or other device, sometimes known as a "gravity knife".']

In this Part [Part I: powers to stop and search] of this Act 'offensive weapon' means any article (a) made or adapted for use for causing injury to persons; or (b) intended by the person having it with him for such use by him or by some other person. (Police and Criminal Evidence Act 1984, s 1(9))

[Statute (1746) 19 Geo 2, c 34 (repealed), was an Act for the further punishment of persons going armed with firearms or other 'offensive weapons', in defiance of the laws of custom or excise.] 'A person catching up a hatchet accidentally, during the hurry and heat of an affray, is not being armed with an offensive weapon within the meaning of this Act.' *R v Rose* (1784) 1 Leach 342 n at 342, per cur.

'Although it is difficult to say what should or should not be called an offensive weapon, it would be going a great deal too far to say, that nothing but guns, pistols, daggers, and instruments of wars should be so considered; . . . bludgeons, properly so called, clubs, and any thing that is not in common use for any other purpose but a weapon, are clearly offensive weapons within the meaning of the legislature.' *R v Hutchinson* (1784) 1 Leach 339 at 343 n per cur.

[Statute (1734) 7 Geo 2, c 21 (repealed), provided that a person convicted of assaulting another with any 'offensive weapon' or instrument, with intent to rob, should be transported for seven years.] 'If the prisoner used his stick by way of attack for the purpose of effecting . . . robbery, it might, I think, be considered as an offensive weapon within the meaning of the statute.' *R v Johnson* (1822) Russ & Ry 492 at 493, per Holroyd J

[The Night Poaching Act 1828, s 9 makes it a misdemeanour for three or more persons to enter land at night for the purpose of taking or destroying game or rabbits, any of such persons being armed with any gun, crossbow, firearms, bludgeon, or any other 'offensive weapon'.] 'If a man goes out with a common walking stick, and there are circumstances to shew he intended to use it for purposes of offence, it may perhaps be called an offensive weapon within the statute; but if he has it in the ordinary way, and upon some unexpected attack or collision is provoked to use it in his own defence, it would be carrying the statute somewhat too far to say it is an offensive weapon within the meaning of the Act.' *R v Fry & Webb* (1837) 2 Mood & R 42 at 43, per Gurney B

'The sticks which were taken from the prisoners could hardly be called bludgeons, though they certainly might be termed offensive weapons; it was clear that the men did not use them to defend themselves, . . . for they did not attempt any violence. In fact, the only use to which they put the sticks, was to hang . . . hares on, and so carry them home over their shoulders. If the jury should think that the prisoners brought out their sticks with them merely for that purpose, then they were not armed within the Act [Night Poaching Act 1828 (see supra)].' *R v Turner* (1849) 3 Cox CC 304 at 306, per Rolfe B

[The Prevention of Crime Act 1953, s 1(4) defines 'offensive weapon' as any article made or adapted for use for causing injury to the person, or intended by the person having it with him for such use by him.] 'It is clear that the definition section of the Act contemplates offensive weapons of, at any rate, two classes, namely, (a) an article which per se is an offensive weapon, that is to say, an article made or adapted for use for causing injury to the person; and (b) an article which, though it is not made or adapted for such use, is carried with the intent so to use it. A cosh, a knuckle-duster, and a revolver are examples of articles in the first class. A sandbag and a razor are examples of articles in the second class. No jury could find that a sandbag was in the first class because there would be no evidence to support such a finding. It seems to this court that the same is true about an ordinary razor. There are some articles which are equivocal, for example, knives. It would always be for a jury to say whether a knife was made or adapted for use for causing injury to the person. It would depend on the view the jury took of the knife.' *R v Petrie* [1961] 1 All ER 466 at 468, CCA, per cur.

'Section 1(4) [of the Prevention of Crime Act 1953] contains a definition of "offensive weapon", and it is in these terms: "'offensive weapon' means any article made or adapted for use for causing injury to the person, or intended by the person having it with him for such use by him." If one analyses the words of the definition, there are three possible categories of offensive weapon. First of all the weapon made for causing injury to the person, that is a weapon offensive per se as it is called, for instance, a bayonet, a stilleto or a handgun. The second category is the weapon which is adapted for such a purpose; the example usually given is the bottle deliberately broken in order that the jagged end may be inserted into the victim's face. The third category is an object not so made or adapted, but one which the person carrying intends to use for the purpose of causing injury to the person.' *R v Simpson* [1983] 3 All ER 789 at 791, per cur.

Australia 'An "offensive weapon" is defined in The Macquarie Dictionary as "any weapon made or adapted for use for causing injury to a person, or intended for such use by the person having it" and "dangerous" as "full of danger or risk; careless, hazardous or unsafe". What should or should not be classified as an offensive weapon is not an easy matter. It was said by the court in an early English decision—*Cosans' case* (1785)—that "although it was difficult to say what should or should not be called an offensive weapon, it would be going too far to say, that nothing but guns, pistols, daggers and weapons of war should be so considered' and that bludgeons, clubs and anything not in common use for any other purpose than a weapon are clearly offensive weapons. But to my mind, it cannot be said that to be armed with a short section of a .22 rifle barrel—three to four inches in length—is to be armed with a weapon made or adapted for use for causing injury to the person. Patently, such an instrument is not, per se, a dangerous weapon.' *Van den Berg v R* (1984) WAR 162 at 169

OFFER *See also* AGREE

An offer is an expression by one person or group of persons, or by agents on his behalf, made to another, of his willingness to be bound to a contract with that other on terms either certain or capable of being rendered certain.

An offer may be made to an individual or to a group of persons or to the world at large. It may be made expressly by words, or it may be implied from the conduct of the offeror.

An offer must be distinguished from a mere invitation to treat. (9 Halsbury's Laws (4th edn) para 227)

A person exposing goods for supply or having goods in his possession for supply shall be deemed to offer to supply them. (Trade Descriptions Act 1968, s 6)

[A firm of estate agents sought to recover commission from a client for having secured an 'offer' for his property, this phrase having been used in a letter confirming the client's instructions in the matter.] 'Applying the proper test of construction, viz what is the ordinary, straightforward meaning of the language, it seems to me reasonably clear that the answer here is that by "offer" is meant a firm offer. In the ordinary sense of the term in business matters an offer is something which by acceptance creates a bargain. An offer subject to contract lacks that essential characteristic, for its acceptance does not create a contract. Prima facie when the word "offer" in such a document as this is used, what is meant is something, which, if accepted, gives rise to a contractual relationship.' *Bennett, Walden & Co v Wood* [1950] 2 All ER 134 at 137, CA, per Evershed MR

'It is clear that, according to the ordinary law of contract, the display of an article with a price on it in a shop window is merely an invitation to treat. It is in no sense an offer for sale the acceptance of which constitutes a contract.' *Fisher v Bell* [1960] 3 All ER 731 at 733, per Lord Parker CJ

Of shares to public

[The Companies Act 1900, s 8(1) (repealed; see now Companies Act 1985, ss 59, 60) empowered a company, under certain conditions, to pay commission upon any 'offer of shares to the public'.] 'An offer is not the less made to the public because it is sent to shareholders or debenture-holders as well as to other persons, or because it is not advertised in the public newspapers. But if it is sent solely to the shareholders or debenture-holders of the company, there is no offer to the public.' *Burrows v Matabele Gold Reefs & Estates Co Ltd* [1901] 2 Ch 23 at 27, CA, per Farwell J

[The Companies Act 1900, s 4 (repealed; see now the Companies Act 1985, s 83(1)), enacted that no allotment should be made of any share capital of a company 'offered to the public' for subscription, unless certain conditions were complied with.] 'What the section means by an offer of shares to the public for subscription is that there should be an offer of share capital by the company, and not an offer by some individual. It means, in my judgment, an offer of shares to anyone who should choose to come in. . . . The result of the evidence is that there is nothing but an intention on the part of the existing members of the company to keep the share capital to themselves and a few other persons whom they may like to bring in. The plaintiff has not made out that there has been any share capital offered to the public for subscription within the meaning of the Act.' *Sherwell v Combined Incandescent Mantles Syndicate Ltd* (1907) 23 TLR 482 at 483, per Warrington J

United States The term 'offer to sell', 'offer for sale', or 'offer' shall include every attempt or offer to dispose of, or solicitation of an offer to buy, a security or interest in a security, for value. (Securities Act 1933, s 2(3))

See, generally, 7 Halsbury's Laws (4th edn) paras 190, 293

OFFERTORY

'A collection made during Mattins or Evensong—I exclude an offertory during the Communion service because that is expressly provided for by rubric, and may therefore perhaps be regarded as a part of the service—is not provided for in the Prayer Book. It is an incident occurring during a service or interposed between different portions of it, but it is no more part of the service than a voluntary played on the organ or the action of a verger closing windows or lighting the gas while the service is in progress. Though of course varying in degree of importance, they are all alike in being matters, not in themselves irreverent or unseemly, but outside the rites and ceremonies of public worship. Such a collection is an interlude entirely at the option of the minister, and has its sole justification in the sanction of long custom. It is quite impossible to treat the action of the minister in ordering a collection to be made during morning or evening service as an ecclesiastical offence.' *Marson v Unmack* [1923] P 163 at 167, 168, CA, per the Dean of the Arches

OFFICE (Building)

'Office premises' means a building or part of a building, being a building or part the sole or principal use of which is as an office or for office purposes. (Offices, Shops and Railway Premises Act 1963, s 1(2)(a))

[The Betting Act 1853, s 3 (repealed; see now the Betting, Gaming and Lotteries Act 1963, s 1) made it an offence for the owner or occupier of (inter alia) an 'office' to keep or use the same for the purpose of betting. A temporary wooden structure was placed upon a racecourse and used for the business of betting during race meetings.] 'This structure was clearly a place and an office opened, kept, and used for the purpose of carrying on the business of which the appellant had the care and management, or which he assisted in conducting. . . . It is no matter whether there is a roof or none, or whether the structure is movable or fastened to the earth; it is clearly an office within the meaning of the Act.' *Shaw v Morley* (1868) LR 3 Exch 137 at 139, 140, per Kelly CB

Canada [MR 963 provides that where the time for doing any act, etc, expires on a day on which the 'offices' are closed, such act, etc, shall be held to be duly done if done on the day when the offices shall next be open.] 'It has been suggested that "offices" may refer both to court registry and lawyers' offices. I find however that the reference can only be to registry offices since otherwise delivery of pleadings could be made to depend on the caprice of counsel for one of the litigants who might choose to close his office on some normal working days.' *Active Construction Ltd v Routledge Gravel Ltd* (No 2) (1961) 34 WWR 421 at 423, BCSC, per Ruttan J

OFFICE (Employment)

'The first point to consider is whether trusteeship is within the ordinary sense of the word an "office", and on this I can only say that "office" is an apt word to describe a trustee's position, or any position in which services are due by the holder and in which the holder has no employer.' *Dale v Inland Revenue Comrs* [1953] 2 All ER 671 at 673, HL, per Lord Normand (also reported in [1954] AC 11 at p 26)

Australia 'We do not think it is necessary to decide whether a member of Parliament or a Minister of State for the Commonwealth holds an office in the strict common-law sense of the term, though it seems probable that the latter position, at all events, involves the holding of an office in that strict sense. . . . There is either an office in the strict sense or something analogous to such an office, and in respect of both there may be a diminution of reputation.' *Pratten v The Labour Daily Ltd* [1926] VLR 115 at 125, per Cussen J

In Income Tax Acts

'The Commissioners have found what Mr Hall's position is in fact. He . . . is about thirty-nine years of age. He receives a "salary" . . . which in the year in question was altogether £175. . . . In plain language he is in a situation as a clerk at a modest salary. . . . To say that Mr Hall holds an "office" seems to me to be an abuse of language. . . . Mr Hall . . . is in no sense a public character, nor does he hold any office at all. He merely sits in one.' *Great Western Rly Co v Bater* [1922] 2 AC 1 at 25, 27, per Lord Sumner

'If any meaning is to be given to "office" in this [income tax] legislation, as distinguished from "employment" or "profession" or "trade" or "vocation" (these are the various words used in order to tax people on their earnings), the word must involve a degree of continuance (not necessarily continuity) and of independent existence: it must connote a post to which a person can be appointed, which he can vacate and to which a successor can be appointed.' *Edwards (Inspector of Taxes) v Clinch* [1981] 3 All ER 543 at 546, HL, per Lord Wilberforce

In Local Government Acts

[Statute (1835) 5 & 6 Will 4, c 76 (repealed), enabled the justices of every borough, to which a separate commission of the peace was granted, to appoint a fit person to the 'office' of clerk to the justices.] 'It is not necessary that there should be an office, strictly speaking. Looking at the words of s 102, where the words are "office of clerk to the justices", it is clear that the word is not used there in the strict sense in which we find it employed in our law books, but in the general and liberal sense of a place to which duties and profits are attached.' *R v Bridgwater Corpn* (1837) 6 Ad & El 339 at 348, per Coleridge J

[The Local Government Act 1888, s 100 provides that the expression 'office' includes any place, situation, or employment.] 'In my opinion the term "office" does not extend to an employment which, like that in the present case, is casual in its nature. If the employment is of such a nature that the person employed is employed on each occasion, as it occurs, for the particular matter that may arise on that occasion, in my opinion it does not come within the term "office". . . . as used in the section.' *Re Carpenter & Bristol Corpn* [1907] 2 KB 617 at 622, per Vaughan Williams LJ

Public office

The meanings of 'public office' and 'public officer' vary according to the context in which the terms are used. In general, a public officer may be said to be one who discharges a duty in the performance of which the public are interested; a person is more likely to be such an officer if he is paid out of a fund provided by the public but it does not necessarily follow that the fund must belong to the central government. Tenure of a public office is not inconsistent with a relationship between master and servant; but the occupants of certain public offices, such as that of a police officer, are not regarded as having the status of servants of any authority. (1 Halsbury's Laws (4th edn) para 9)

OFFICE OF PROFIT

[The Income Tax Act 1853, s 2, Sch E (repealed) imposed taxation in respect of every public 'office or employment of profit'.] 'In my view if a profit does accrue to the holder of an office or employment by reason of his office or employment, such office or employment is an office or employment of profit.' *Cowan v Seymour* [1920] 1 KB 500 at 511, CA, per Atkin LJ

'"Office of profit" is not a thing particularly easy to define; everybody, I think, has a good idea of what it means, but certainly it is not easy of exact definition. . . . It is, of course, and must be an office, and no doubt it must be an office to which remuneration is in some way or other attached. You cannot have an office of profit unless you have got the remuneration attached to it. That does not, of course, mean that in any particular year there must necessarily be any remuneration. It is, I should think, clear beyond any controversy—indeed, it was not controverted—that if you take the case, the perfectly possible case, of a holder of an office remunerated by share of profits, and by reason of the fact that in difficult times there are no profits so that there is no remuneration, it is not questioned, I think, and could not be questioned, that that would none the less be an office of profit and would continue to be an office of profit even though for one year or for more than one year no remuneration accrued.' *Henry v Galloway* (1933) 148 LT 453 at 455, per Finlay J

'An "office or employment of profit" . . . necessarily involves service over a period of time during which the office is held or the employment continues. The ordinary way of remunerating the holder or the person employed is to make payments to him periodically, but I cannot think that such payments can escape the quality of income which is necessary to attract income tax because an arrangement is made to reduce for the future the annual payments while paying a lump sum down to represent the difference.' *Tilley v Wales* [1943] AC 386 at 393, per Lord Simon LC

'To my mind, an "office of profit", in the ordinary sense of the words, is an office which carries with it remuneration, as distinct from an honorary office.' *Dale v Inland Revenue Comrs* [1953] 2 All ER 671 at 677, HL, per Lord Morton of Henryton (also reported in [1954] AC 11 at 26)

OFFICE PURPOSES

'Office purposes' includes the purposes of administration, clerical work, handling money and telephone and telegraph operating. (Offices, Shops and Railway Premises Act 1963, s 1(2)(b))

'When there is imported this definition [in the Offices, Shops and Railway Premises Act 1963, s 1 (supra)] by reference "for office purposes", it seems to me quite clear that the matters which are included for office purposes must be read as activities, and these activities include here clerical work and handling of money.' *Minister of Labour v Morgan* [1967] 2 All ER 732 at 735, per Lord Parker CJ

OFFICER *See also* MANAGER

'Officer' includes employee. (Parliamentary Commissioner Act 1967, s 12)

'Officer', in relation to a building society, means any director, chief executive, secretary or manager of the society; and, in relation to any offence, 'officer' also includes any person who purports to act as an officer of the society; and in relation to any other body corporate means the corresponding officers of that body. (Building Societies Act 1986, s 119(1))

Of company

'Officer', in relation to a body corporate, includes a director, manager or secretary. (Companies Act 1985, s 744)

[The Companies (Winding up) Act 1890, s 10 (repealed; see now the Companies Act 1985, s 631) empowered the court to assess damages against any past or present director, manager, liquidator, or other 'officer' of the company, who had misapplied or retained any moneys or property of the company, or been guilty of any misfeasance or breach of trust in relation to the company.] 'It seems to me that merely because he was appointed solicitor to the society, without more, the solicitor does not become an officer of the society any more than it has been held that a banker does if he is appointed banker to the society, or a broker if he is appointed broker to the society, or the auditor if he is appointed auditor to the society. All these persons render services to the society, but they cannot be said to be in the employment of the society so as to make them officials.' *Re Liberator Permanent Benefit Building Society* (1894) 71 LT 406 at 407, DC, per Cave J

Of court

The expression 'officer of a court of summary jurisdiction' means the constable, officer, or person to whom any process issued by the court is directed, or who is by law required or authorised to serve or execute any process issued by the court. (Summary Jurisdiction (Process) Act 1881, s 8)

'Officer', in relation to a court, means any registrar, deputy registrar or assistant registrar of that court, and any clerk, bailiff, usher or messenger in the service of that court. (County Courts Act 1984, s 147(1))

Of Crown

'Officer', in relation to the Crown, includes any servant of [Her] Majesty, and accordingly (but without prejudice to the generality of the foregoing provision) includes a Minister of the Crown. (Crown Proceedings Act 1947, s 38(2))

Of friendly society

'Officer' includes any trustee, treasurer, secretary, or member of the committee of management of a society or branch or any person appointed by the society or branch to sue and be sued on its behalf. (Friendly Societies Act 1974, s 111(1))

Naval officer

The term 'officers and crew' includes all flag officers, commanders, and other officers, engineers, seamen, marines, soldiers, and others on board any of Her Majesty's ships of war. (Naval Agency and Distribution Act 1864, s 2)

The term 'officer' means a commissioned officer in Her Majesty's naval or marine force. (Navy and Marines (Property of Deceased) Act 1865 s 2, as amended by the Armed Forces Act 1971, s 77(1), Sch 4)

In this Act 'officer', in relation to any of Her Majesty's naval forces, means a person of or above the rank of cadet, and in relation to any other forces means an officer of rank corresponding to the said rank or any superior rank. (Naval Discipline Act 1957, s 133(1))

Superior officer

In the foregoing provisions of this section the expression 'superior officer', in relation to any person, means an officer, warrant officer or non-commissioned officer of the regular air force [*or* forces] of superior rank, and includes an officer, warrant officer or non-commissioned officer of that force [*or* those forces] of equal rank but greater seniority while exercising authority as the said person's superior. (Air Force Act 1955, s 33(2); Army Act 1955, s 33(2))

In this Act 'superior officer', in relation to any person means an officer or a rating not below the rate of leading seaman who is of rank or rate higher than that person, or senior to that person in the same rank or rate. (Naval Discipline Act 1957, s 133(3), as amended by the Armed Forces Act 1971, s 43, Sch 1)

OFFICIAL

'Official', in relation to a trade union, means any person who is an officer of the union or of a branch or section of the union or who (not being such an officer) is a person elected or appointed in accordance with the rules of the union to be a representative of its members or of some of them, including any person so elected or appointed who is an employee of the same employer as the members, or one or more of the members, whom he is to represent. (Trade Union and Labour Relations Act 1974, s 30(1); Employment Protection (Consolidation) Act 1978, s 153(1))

Canada 'What then is an "official" mark within the meaning of s 9(1)(n)(iii) [of the Trade Marks Act, RSC 1970, c T-10]. An official mark is not defined in the statute. The Registrar in his reasons dated 14 April 1978 resorted to a dictionary meaning of the word "official". One such definition was "derived from the proper office or officer or authority".' *Insurance Corp of British Columbia v Registrar of Trade Marks* [1980] 1 FCR 669 at 678, FCTD, per Cattanach J

OFFICIAL CAPACITY

United States 'Official capacity' means: (i) when used with respect to a director, the office of director in a corporation; and (ii) when used with respect to an individual other than a director, as contemplated in s 8.56, the office in a corporation held by the officer or the employment or agency relationship undertaken by the employee or agent on behalf of the corporation. 'Official capacity' does not include service for any other foreign or domestic corporation or any partnership, joint venture, trust, employee benefit plan, or other enterprise. (Revised Model Business Corporation Act 1984, s 8.50(5))

OFFICIAL RECEIVER

Attached to each bankruptcy court is an officer called 'the official receiver of the district' of the particular court, whose duties are (1) to assume control over the estate of a debtor against whom a receiving order has been made,

(2) to take a leading part in the investigation of the debtor's conduct, (3) to report to the court on the debtor's conduct, and (4) to act as trustee when no trustee is appointed by the creditors, or if there is a vacancy in the trusteeship or when the trustee appointed by the creditors is released. (3 Halsbury's Laws (4th edn) para 483)

OFFICIAL SECRETS

[The Official Secrets Act 1911, s 2 enacts that if any person having in his possession or control any sketch, plan, model, article, note, document, or information, which he has obtained owing to his position as a person who holds or has held office under Her Majesty, communicates it to any person, other than a person to whom he is authorised to communicate it, or a person to whom it is in the interest of the State his duty to communicate it, he is guilty of a misdemeanour.] 'In my opinion there is evidence in this case that the defendant Crisp, having in his possession information which he had obtained owing to his position as a person who held office under His Majesty, communicated that information to a person other than a person to whom he was authorised to communicate it. If there was evidence that he did that, that brings him within the words of s 2 of this statute. . . . The next point is that this is not information of a confidential character and is not within the description of "official secrets". It is a well-known proposition in the construction of a statute that the enacting words of it are not to be cut down or limited by the title of the Act, although where there is any ambiguity the title of the Act may assist to construe it. But when there is no ambiguity in the enacting part of the statute the words cannot be altered or limited merely by the title "Official Secrets". Even if it could I think there is evidence that these documents were official secrets. Certainly there can be no question that these documents contained information which had been obtained by Crisp owing to his position. It seems to me that s 2 applies to any document or information of an official character which has been obtained by a person holding office under His Majesty, provided, of course, that he communicates it to some person to whom he was not authorised to communicate it. Again, it is suggested that it was not prejudicial to the interests of the State to communicate it. That argument overlooks the fact that it is in the alternative—"If he communicates it to a person other than a person to whom he is authorised to communicate it or other than a person to whom it is in the interest of the State his duty to communicate it." I will only say, with reference to these documents and the argument that they are not confidential and cannot be regarded as official secrets, that there appear to me to be many grounds, which I need not specify, on which the jury might properly come to the conclusion that this information was or might be useful to the person to whom it was communicated.' *R v Crisp & Homewood* (1919) 83 JP 121 at 122, 123, CCA, per Avory J

OFF-LICENCE

In this Act 'justices' on-licence' and 'justices' off-licence' mean respectively—

(a) a justices' licence authorising sale for consumption either on or off the premises for which the licence is granted; and
(b) a justices' licence authorising sale for consumption off those premises only.

(Licensing Act 1964, s 1(2), as amended by the Finance Act 1967)

OFFSHORE INSTALLATION

'Offshore installation' means any installation which is intended for underwater exploitation of mineral resources or exploration with a view to such exploitation. (Health and Safety at Work etc Act 1974, s 53(1))

[See also the Mineral Workings (Offshore Installations) Act 1971, s 1, as substituted by the Oil and Gas (Enterprise) Act 1982, s 24.]

OFFSPRING *See also* ISSUE

[A testator by his will gave personal estate to A for life and after her death to her children; but if there should be no child or 'offspring' left the gift was to be otherwise disposed of.] 'It is clear that the word offspring is a general word; it may mean children. But the testator has said if there are not any children, which is sufficient to provide for that event, and then he adds, "or offspring". He must have meant something more than children, otherwise the language would be absurd; it would be as if he had said, "if there shall not be any child or child". What I think the testator meant was, that at the death of the tenant for life, if there were no children, or other offspring beyond children, then the plaintiff was to have £20, but not otherwise.' *Thompson v Beasley* (1854) 3 Drew 7 at 9, per Kindersley V-C

[A testator by his will gave personalty to A and at his death to his surviving daughters and their lawful 'offspring'.] 'The word "off spring", like the words "issue" and "descendants", may be used in different senses. It may mean children only, or it may include more remote descendants. If this testator had intended children only, I cannot help thinking he might have used the simple and obvious term "children". In my opinion the term "offspring", in its proper and natural sense, extends to every degree of lineal descendants, and has the same meaning as the word "issue".' *Young v Davies* (1863) 2 Drew & Sm 167 at 171, 172, per Kindersley V-C

[A testator bequeathed a legacy to the 'offspring' of his brother.] 'Offspring may have two meanings, children or issue. So far as the dictionaries are concerned children is the meaning first given. The cases cited are not of much assistance, depending as they do on the construction to be placed upon the particular wills. In the present case I am of opinion that the word should be construed as children.' *Tabuteau v Nixon* (1899) 15 TLR 485 at 485, per Byrne J

See, generally, 50 Halsbury's Laws (4th edn) para 518.

OFF-STREET PARKING *See* PARKING PLACE

OIL

'Oil' means oil of any description and includes spirit produced from oil of any description, and also includes coal tar. (Prevention of Oil Pollution Act 1971, s 29(1))

Oil installations

'Oil installations' means any works for the storage or transmission of oil (including oil pipe-lines and works accessory to oil pipe-lines) and any works for giving access to, or otherwise required in connection with, any such works. (Land Powers (Defence) Act 1958, s 25(1))

Oil pipe-line

'Oil pipe-line' means any main or pipe for the transmission of oil, or for the transmission of water or any other substance in connection with the storage or transmission of oil, or any part of such a main or pipe (Land Powers (Defence) Act 1958, s 25(1))

Oil residues

'Oil residues' means any waste consisting of, or arising from, oil or a mixture containing oil. (Prevention of Oil Pollution Act 1971, s 29(1))

OLD BEERHOUSE LICENCE *See* BEERHOUSE

OMISSION *See also* ACCIDENTAL SLIP OR OMISSION

'An accidental slip occurs when something is wrongly put in by accident, and an accidental omission occurs when something is left out by accident.' *Sutherland & Co v Hannevig Brothers Ltd* [1921] 1 KB 336 at 341, DC per Rowlatt J

Australia [The Motor Vehicles Insurance Act 1936–1986 (Qld), s 4F(4)(b) authorises the court to extend the time for giving notice of intention to claim to the Nominal Defendant if it is satisfied that the failure to give notice was not due to any act or 'omission' of the claimant. The applicant, though wishing to recover damages for his injuries, did not seek legal advice for some four months, by which time the period for giving notice had expired. Until his solicitor told him about it, the applicant was ignorant of the requirement for notice.] 'It is desirable to consider whether such ignorance was an "omission" within s 4F(4)(b). A labourer is ignorant of the population of Mexico. This is not an omission or due to an omission on his part. He simply does not know the fact. He had no interest to inquire as to it and no one had told him of it. A traveller in Brisbane wishes to reach Thursday Island on the following day. He makes no inquiry as to whether transport by air is available, and remains ignorant that it is. I think that this ignorance was occasioned by an omission on his part. He had an interest in knowing what the position was. I think that a person who has an interest in knowing his legal position and who does not make appropriate inquiries to ascertain it, has "omitted" to ascertain it. But a time factor must enter into the question: he must have a reasonable time to act. This will vary with circumstances.' *Moon v Nominal Defendant (Queensland)* [1966] Qd R 59 at 64, per Hanger J

OMNIA PRÆSUMUNTUR CONTRA SPOLIATOREM

'In *Morison v Walton* [unreported] . . . the House of Lords held that the man who had, by breaking his contract, destroyed the possibility of any evidence on the subject, could not be heard to say that there was no evidence that his breach of contract caused the loss. It was his duty as bailee to prove that his breach of duty did not cause the loss, not the plaintiff's duty to show that it did. This appears to be merely an application of the principle *omnia præsumuntur contra spoliatorem*, under which a man who, having converted property, refuses to produce it that its exact value may be known, is liable for the greatest value that such an article could have.' *Coldman v Hill* [1919] 1 KB 443 at 457, 458, CA, per Scrutton LJ

OMNIA PRÆSUMUNTUR RITE ESSE ACTA

'It is a maxim of the law of England to give effect to everything which appears to have been established for a considerable course of time, and to presume that what has been done was done of right, and not in wrong.' *Gibson v Doeg* (1857) 2 H & N 615 at 623, per Pollock CB

'The maxim, *Omnia præsumuntur rite esse acta*, is an expression, in a short form, of a reasonable probability, and of the propriety in point of law of acting on such probability. The maxim expresses an inference which may reasonably be drawn when an intention to do some formal act is established; when the evidence is consistent with that intention having been carried into effect in a proper way; but when the actual observance of all due formalities can only be inferred as a matter of probability. The maxim is not wanted where such observance is proved, nor has it any place where such observance is disproved. The maxim only comes into operation where there is no proof one way or the other; but where it is more probable that what was intended to be done was done as it ought to have been done to render it valid; rather than that it was done in some other manner which would defeat the intention proved to exist, and would render what is proved to have been done of no effect.' *Harris v Knight* (1890) 15 PD 170 at 179, per Lindley LJ

ON *See also* AT

[An agreement to issue shares provided for the payment of commission 'on allotment'.] 'It is said on behalf of the plaintiffs that the words 'on allotment' means if the company were put into such a position that they could go to allotment. That long paraphrase of the words cannot be found in the letter. I read "on allotment" in its ordinary sense, meaning as and when allotted.' *Browne v Pickering & Co* (1888) 4 TLR 726 at 726, CA, per Lord Esher MR

'When considering the validity of a notice to quit given in time and expiring on the anniversary of the commencement of a tenancy, I can find no distinction ever drawn between tenancies commencing "at" a particular time, or "on" a particular day, and "from" the same day. "At", "on", "from", and "on and from" are for this purpose equivalent expressions.' *Sidebotham v Holland* [1895] 1 QB 378 at 384, CA, per Lindley LJ

'It seems perfectly clear to this court, quite apart from authority, that, where s 21 of the Act of 1907 [Criminal Appeal Act 1907 (repealed; cf now Part I of the Criminal Appeal Act 1968)], says "any order of the court made on conviction", it must mean "made as a consequence of conviction".' *R v Harman* [1959] 2 All ER 738 at 739, CCA, per cur; also reported [1959] 2 QB 134 at 135

ON ACCOUNT

'A payment "on account" imports an acknowledgment of a liability for a larger sum (see *Friend v Young* [[1897] 2 Ch 421 at 436, per Stirling J]). When a payment is merely stated to be "on account" without the liability on account of which it is made being specified, one must first inquire what liabilities on the part of the payer to the recipient exist. If, on inquiry, it is found that the only liability is in respect of a balance due on current account, the natural conclusion to reach is, in my judgment, that the payment is made on account of that balance generally, not on account of any particular items contributing to that balance.' *Re Footman Bower & Co Ltd* [1961] 2 All ER 161 at 165, per Buckley J; also reported [1961] Ch 443 at 451

New Zealand [A testator, by his will, provided that his trustees should pay the annual income of his estate to his widow quarterly, and that pending the realisation and investment of his property they might pay to his widow out of any moneys in their hands such sums as might be needful for her suitable maintenance and support 'on account' of her said annual income.] 'This clause is a charge upon the corpus of any moneys which might be paid to the plaintiff under its authority. The clause then declares that any moneys so paid are to be paid to the plaintiff "on account of her said annual income". These words recognise and, we think, declare that sooner or later the plaintiff's annual income shall be paid to her in full. The direction to pay "on account" is a direction to pay in respect of the plaintiff's annual income a sum which is to be brought into account in a future accounting. No such accounting could take place except in connection with the corpus, for the necessity to make payments to the plaintiff out of the corpus of the estate could arise only in the event of the income of the estate in its unconverted condition being insufficient to satisfy the plaintiff's annuity, and, inasmuch as upon realisation of the estate the whole income was thereafter disposed of in a different way, there could be no accounting except in connection with the corpus of the estate or with moneys directed to be added to the corpus. We think, therefore, that the period which the testator contemplated for the accounting was upon the realisation of the estate. There can be no doubt that moneys paid by the trustees under this power were a charge upon the corpus. The charge is, in our opinion, created by the testator, not by the act of the trustees, and if created by the testator it extends to the entirety of the plaintiff's annuity, not merely to such part of it as the trustees of the will thought fit to pay on account of it.' *Fantham v Public Trustee* (1913) 33 NZLR 447 at 461, per cur; 16 GLR 63, 71

ON BEHALF OF

'I cannot perceive a difference between the words "for behoof of" and "in trust for". I hold the expression "for behoof of" to mean exactly the same as if the words used had been "on behalf of" or "for the benefit of", or any of those other words, of which many might be suggested, which indicate that although to the bank you are the absolute owner of the shares, yet as regards a third person, with whom you have entered into an arrangement, you are not that owner.' *Gillespie v City of Glasgow Bank* (1879) 4 App Cas 632 at 642, per Lord Hatherley

'It seems to me that a man cannot be said to make a photograph for or on behalf of another, when that other is not entitled to have the negative of the photograph when made.' *Melville v Mirror of Life Co* [1895] 2 Ch 531 at 536, per Kekewich J

'In my opinion the statement at the head of the note that the plaintiffs are acting "for and on behalf of" a foreign principal does not get rid of the prima facie presumption that a person signing a contract in his own name is personally liable on it. There is not sufficient to show that the foreign principal is the contracting party.' *Brandt (H O) & Co v Morris (H N) & Co* [1917] 2 KB 784 CA, per Lord Reading CJ

Australia 'The phrase "on behalf of" is, as Latham CJ observed in *R v Portus, ex p Federated Clerks' Union of Australia* [(1949) 79 CLR 428 at 435] "not an expression which has a strict legal meaning", it bears no single and constant significance. Instead it may be used in conjunction with a wide range of relationships, all however in some way concerned with the standing of one person as auxiliary to or representative of another person or thing.' *Re Ross, ex p A-G for Northern Territory* (1980) 54 ALJR 145 at 149, Stephen, Mason, Murphy and Aickin JJ

ON DEMAND

'In general, where money is made payable on demand, the law holds that the debtor is bound to find out the creditor and pay him. But where, by the express terms of the instrument, time is given up to the time of notice in writing, a reasonable time at least must be meant by "immediately"; and this agrees with what is said in Com Dig tit "Condition" (G5): "Where a condition is to be performed immediately, he shall have a reasonable time to perform it, according to the nature of the thing to be done. So if it be to be performed upon demand." And by a "reasonable time" must be meant time enough to seek the creditor, or a person authorised from him to receive the money.' *Toms v Wilson* (1862) 32 LJQB 33 at 37, per Blackburn J

'A promissory note payable on demand is payable at once without any demand, and may be sued upon accordingly.' *Edwards v Walters* [1896] 2 Ch 157 at 166, CA per Lindley LJ

'In my judgment, where there is the relationship of banker and customer and the banker permits his customer to overdraw on the terms of entering into a legal charge which provides that the money which is then due or is thereafter to become due is to be paid "on demand", that means what it says. As between the customer and banker, who are dealing on a running account, it seems to me impossible to assume that the bank were to be entitled to sue on the deed on the very day after it was executed without making a demand and giving the customer a reasonable time to pay.' *Lloyds Bank Ltd v Margolis* [1954] 1 All ER 734 at 738, per Upjohn J

ON-LICENCE *See* OFF-LICENCE

ON OR ABOUT

'If the words "on or about the date" are used in an indictment then, provided that the offence is shown to have been committed within some period that has a reasonable approximation to the date mentioned in the indictment, the fact that the date is not correctly stated does not preclude a valid verdict of guilty.' *R v Hartley* [1972] 1 All ER 599 at 603, CA, per Sachs LJ

Australia [A stipulation in a contract was that certain machinery was to be delivered 'on or about' October 1922. It was held that delivery on 2 September did not necessarily imply a delivery pursuant to that stipulation.] 'Delivery on 2nd September could not . . . be a reasonable performance of an order asking for delivery "on or about" the 1st day of October. . . . The words "on or about" in the context in which they are used, do not . . . allow of much latitude. If the expression had been "in or about the first week in October" possibly a week on either side would be included but I should have no hesitation in holding that twenty-nine days would not. . . . A day or two on either side or perhaps three . . . would . . . be the most that could reasonably be held to be covered by the expression.' *Blackett v Clutterbuck Brothers (Adelaide) Ltd* [1923] SASR 301 at 306, 307, per Murray CJ

ON OR BEFORE

'The use of the phrase "on or before" some fixed date is to-day by no means uncommon, particularly in covenants or demands for payment of money, and in such a context it cannot, in our judgment, be open to serious doubt that it means, and would be understood to mean, that the covenantor or debtor is under obligation to pay the debt on (but not earlier than) the date fixed but has the option of discharging it at any earlier time selected by him: see per Parker J in *Re Tewkesbury Gas Co* [[1911] 2 Ch 279, 284]. In our judgment that reasoning is equally applicable to a notice to quit and to a covenant or demand for the payment of money.' *Dagger v Shepherd* [1946] KB 215 at 223, CA per cur.

ON-COURSE BET *See* BET

ONEROUS

[The terms of an insurance policy provided that the suicide of the assured should not affect the interests of bona fide 'onerous' holders.] 'The primary meaning of "onerous" is burdensome, or troublesome, or inconvenient, or difficult. You may talk about an onerous property, meaning a white elephant. You may talk about an onerous task, meaning one which requires great effort to perform. You may talk about an onerous obligation – namely, an obligation which imposes a serious burden upon the person upon whom it falls. But with regard to the holder of a policy, none of those meanings . . . would be available. . . . "Onerous holder" is, according to our English terms, an assignee for valuable consideration.' *Rowett, Leakey & Co Ltd v Scottish Provident Institution* [1927] 1 Ch 55 at 71, 72, CA per Warrington LJ

OPEN COUNTRY

In this Part [Part 5] of this Act the expression 'open country' means any area appearing to the authority with whom an access agreement is made or to the authority by whom an access order is made or by whom the area is acquired, as the case may be, to consist wholly or predominantly of mountain, moor, heath, down, cliff or foreshore (including any bank, barrier, dune, beach, flat or other land adjacent to the foreshore). (National Parks and Access to the Countryside Act 1949, s 59(2); but see infra)

(1) The definition of 'open country' in s 59(2) of the Act of 1949 [supra] shall include, if in the countryside, any woodlands.

(2) Subject to sub-s (6) below, the said definition shall include, if in the countryside—

(a) any river or canal, and
(b) any expanse of water through which a river, or some part of the flow of a river, runs, and
(c) a strip of the adjacent land on both sides of any river or canal, or of any such expanse of water, of reasonable width, and where a highway crosses or comes close to the river, canal or other water, so much of any

land connecting the highway with the strip of land as would, if included together with the strip in an access agreement or order, afford access from the highway to some convenient launching place for small boats.

(3) The strip of adjacent land comprised in any access order shall be wide enough to allow passage on foot along the water and wide enough to allow the public to picnic at convenient places and, where practicable, to embark or disembark, and shall include—

(a) the banks, walls or embankments along the water, and

(b) any towpath or other way or track beside the water. . . .

(6) Subsections (2) and (3) above shall not apply as respects, or as respects land held with,—

(a) a reservoir owned or managed by statutory undertakers,

(b) a reservoir owned or managed by a river authority, or

(c) a canal, or a part of a canal, owned or managed by the British Waterways Board. . . .

(9) In this section 'river' includes a stream and the tidal part of a river or stream.

(10) The provisions of this section shall not be construed as restricting in any way the definition of 'open country' in the said s 59(2) as originally enacted.

(Countryside Act 1968, s 16)

See, generally, 34 Halsbury's Laws (4th edn) para 470.

OPEN COURT

'Open court is what any one would take to be a court, with the usual accompaniments of the jury-box, the witness-box, the Judge's seat, and seats for solicitors and counsel and others—in fact, with all those external signs which people are accustomed to suppose necessary for it to be a court.' *Kenyon v Eastwood* (1888) 57 LJQB 455 at 456, per Lord Coleridge CJ

'The use of the term "open court" is customarily designed to emphasise the publicity of English judicial proceedings. These things must be done in open court, they must be done publicly and they must be done for all men to see. That, I think, is the usual use of the words "open court".' *Hawksley v Fewtrill* [1953] 2 All ER 1486 at 1495, CA, per Birkett LJ

'Although it is easy enough to say that a hearing must be in open court, and although the conception of an open court as opposed to one which is in camera is easy enough to understand, it is not altogether easy to define in terms the characteristics which make a court open, as opposed to one which is conducted in private. I get assistance from two authorities to which counsel for the respondents has referred, giving some observations on this question. The first is *Daubney v Cooper* [(1829) 10 B & C 237] . . . Bayley J, dealing with the question which is before us, said: ". . . we are all of opinion, that it is one of the essential qualities of a court of justice that its proceedings should be in public, and that all the parties who may be desirous of hearing what is going on, if there be room in the place for the purpose—provided they do not interrupt the proceedings, and provided there is no specific reason why they should be removed—have a right to be present for the purpose of hearing what is going on." I would commend those words to any presiding judge or magistrate who is asking himself what was his duty with regard to keeping the court open to the public for present purposes. There is a transatlantic authority which counsel for the respondents put before us, *People v Hartman*, a case in the Supreme Court of California in 1894. Again the facts do not matter and I refer to it for the statement of principle which appears in this observation of the judge: 'The trial should be "public", in the ordinary commonsense acceptation of the term. The doors of the court room are expected to be kept open, the public are entitled to be admitted, and the trial is to be public in all respects . . . with due regard to the size of the court room, the conveniences of the court, the right to exclude objectionable characters and youth of tender years, and to do other things which may facilitate the proper conduct of the trial." Again, one may say, the injunction to the presiding judge or magistrate is: do your best to enable the public to come in and see what is happening, having a proper common sense regard for the facilities available and the facility for keeping order, security and the like. I start by accepting those two explanations of the significance of the phrase "open court", but I would at once add to them a comment based on the fact that since those cases were decided, the press has assumed a very much greater importance in these matters. Today, as everybody knows, the great body of the British public get their news of how justice is administered through the press or other mass media, and the presence or absence of the press is a vital factor in deciding whether a particular hearing was or was not in open court. I find it difficult to imagine a case which can be said to be held publicly if the press have been actively excluded. On the other hand, the fact that the press is present is not conclusive the other way, because one must not overlook the other factor of an open and public proceeding, namely one to which individual members of the public can come if they have sufficient interest in the proceedings to make it worth their while so to do.' *R v Denbigh Justices, ex p Williams* [1974] 2 All ER 1052 at 1055, 1056, per Lord Widgery CJ

Australia 'The hearing took place . . . [in] a small room in the police building. . . . There was little, if any, accommodation provided for the public. . . . There was no public intimation outside the building . . . that a court was being held. . . . There was no intimation at the main court that the defendant's case or any case would be taken at the police office. . . . It seems that what happened on this occasion was in accordance with a long-standing practice. . . . Persons resorting to the main court for the purpose of hearing the proceedings in the defendant's case would be completely unaware that the case was being heard somewhere else. The approach and entrance to the room in question were not of a kind likely to lead to the belief that a court was being held and that the public might enter and remain. There were a number of things calculated to lead the public to be ignorant of the fact that a court was being held and to believe they had no right to enter and view the proceedings. The character and situation of the building, the purpose it normally served, the equipment and lay-out of the room, the size of the room, the small portion of it devoted to the administration of justice, the absence of reasonable facilities for public accommodation are all inconsistent with the view that it was an "open court". Against these facts, the long continued practice of hearing cases in this way has little significance. . . . If a court were to sit in an empty building in a remote part of the town, with no public intimation of any kind, it could hardly be an open court merely because the doors were kept open.' *Dando v Anastassiou* [1951] VLR 235 at 236–238, per Dean J

OPEN-END CREDIT

United States 'Open-end credit' means consumer credit extended by a creditor under a plan in which:

(i) The creditor reasonably contemplates repeated transactions;

(ii) The creditor may impose a finance charge from time to time on an outstanding unpaid balance; and

(iii) The amount of credit that may be extended to the consumer during the term of the plan (up to any limit set by the creditor) is generally made available to the extent that any outstanding balance is repaid. (Truth in Lending Regulations 1982, 12 CFR, s 226.2(a)(20))

OPEN LAND

The Town and Country Planning Act 1947, s 33 (repealed; see now the Town and Country Planning Act 1971, s 65) empowered a local planning authority to require the owner of any garden, vacant site or other 'open land' to abate any injury to the area of the authority.] 'The words of the section . . . seem to me to be very wide. The section applies to any "garden, vacant site or other open land", and it seems to me that those three phrases taken together are describing in the widest possible terms any land on which there is no building, land which is not built up. The reason, no doubt, for the use of the words "open land" in that way is to make it perfectly clear that the draftsman is departing from the definition of "land" in s 119 of the Act of 1947, where "land" is described as including buildings. That, of course, is subject to the provision that the context should not otherwise require, and it seems to me that s 33 is dealing with any land which has not got a building on it. That as it seems to me, is the literal interpretation.' *Stephens v Cuckfield Rural District Council* [1959] 1 All ER 635 at 637, per Lord Parker CJ; also reported [1959] 1 QB 516 at 524

OPEN MARKET

[The Finance (1909–10) Act 1910, s 25 (repealed; but see now Leasehold Reform Act 1967, s 9) provided that the gross value of land for the purposes of the Act should be the amount which the fee simple of the land might be expected to realise if sold by a willing seller in its then condition in the 'open market'.] 'A value, ascertained by reference to the amount obtainable in an open market shews an intention to include every possible purchaser. The market is to be the open market, as distinguished from an offer to a limited class only, such as the members of the family. The market is not necessarily an auction sale. The section means such amount as the land might be expected to realise if offered under conditions enabling every person desirous of purchasing to come in and make an offer, and if proper steps were taken to advertise the property and let all likely purchasers know that the land is in the market for sale.' *Inland Revenue Comrs v Clay, Inland Revenue Comrs v Buchanan* [1914] 3 KB 466 at 475, CA, per Swinfen Eady LJ

OPEN-MARKET PRICE

'Open-market price', in relation to any machinery or plant, means the price which the machinery or plant would have fetched if sold in the open market at the time of the event in question. (Capital Allowances Act 1968, s 33(2))

OPEN MINE *See* MINE

OPEN SPACE

The expression 'open space' means any land, whether inclosed or not, on which there are no buildings or of which not more than one-twentieth part is covered with buildings, and the whole or the remainder of which is laid out as a garden or is used for purposes of recreation, or lies waste and unoccupied. (Open Spaces Act 1906, s 20)

'Open space' means any land laid out as a public garden, or used for the purposes of public recreation, or land which is a disused burial ground. (Town and Country Planning Act 1971, s 290(1); Housing Act 1985, s 581(4))

'Open space' includes any public park, heath, common, recreation ground, pleasure ground, garden, walk, ornamental enclosure or disused burial ground under the control and management of a local authority. (Ministry of Housing and Local Government Provisional Order Confirmation (Greater London Parks and Open Spaces) Act 1967, s 6)

'It seems to me that the essential quality which is connoted by an "open space of land" is the quality of being unbuilt upon.' *Re Bradford City Premises* [1928] Ch 138 at 143, per Tomlin J

Public open space

'Public open space' means land laid out as a public garden or used (otherwise than in pursuance of s 193 of the Law of Property Act 1925 [rights of the public over common and waste land] or of Part V of the National Parks and Access to the Countryside Act 1949 [access to open country]) for the purpose of public recreation, or land being a disused burial ground. (Forestry Act 1967, s 9(6); Agriculture Act 1967, s 52(15))

The definition of 'public open space' in s 9(6) of the Forestry Act 1967 [supra] shall not include a country park provided under s 7 of this Act, or a park or pleasure ground in the Lee Valley Regional Park which in the opinion of the Minister serves the purpose set out in s 6(1) of this Act when the considerations in paras (a) and (b) of that subsection are taken into account. (Countryside Act 1968, s 24(4))

[Section 6(1)(a), (b) provides that a local authority shall have regard to the location of an area in the countryside in relation to an urban or built-up area; and to the availability and adequacy of existing facilities for the enjoyment of the countryside by the public. Section 7 gives general powers to provide country parks.]

OPERATE

Australia 'The defendant . . . covenanted "not to operate as a land agent" in the municipality. This appears to me to be not so wide as "not to do any work as a land agent", but rather to mean "not to carry on the business of a land agent".' *Lawrence v Lloyd* [1930] SASR 194 at 198, per Richards J

Australia [The State Transport (Co-ordination) Act 1931–1986 (NSW), s 28 (see now s 28(1)) provides that no person shall, except in pursuance of a permit under the Act or under an exemption granted or declared under the Act, drive or 'operate' or cause or permit to be driven or operated as a public motor vehicle any motor vehicle, unless the motor vehicle is licensed as a public motor vehicle and is used in conformity with the licence.] 'The word "operate" where it occurs in s 28 includes a person who employs a driver to drive the particular public motor vehicle, and if in fact that vehicle is then driven or used in breach of the terms of the licence or the conditions annexed to it, then an offence is committed, whether the owner was aware of the way in which it was being used or not. . . . I think there is clearly to be found in the Act a prohibition against the use of a public vehicle in contravention of the terms and conditions of the licence, and it is no answer for the licensee to say what while it was being driven for him by his employee he was not aware of the breach of those terms. . . . It is the licensee who must answer for the acts of his driver.' *Ex p Thompson , Re Maxwell* (1953) 53 NSWSR 91 at 93, per Street CJ

Australia [The Transport Act 1930–1986 (NSW), s 158 deals, inter alia, with the 'operation' of a bus route.] 'What does s 158 mean when it speaks of a route being "operated" by the respondent? I cannot think that there is much difficulty in understanding the word, inelegant though its use in the context may be. If a route is the line of travel established for an omnibus service between two termini, to "operate" a route must be to provide the omnibus service, that is the whole omnibus service, for that line of travel. What is referred to is the operation, that is to say the complete and not a part of the operation, of the route.' *Gilbert v Government Transport Comr* [1960] ALR 673 at 679, 680, per Kitto J

OPERATION *See* ASSOCIATED OPERATIONS

OPERATIONAL LAND

In this Act 'operational land' means, in relation to statutory undertakers—

(a) land which is used for the purpose of carrying on their undertaking; and
(b) land in which an interest is held for that purpose,

not being land which, in respect of its nature and situation, is comparable rather with land in general than with land which is used, or in which interests are held, for the purpose of the carrying on of statutory undertakings. (Town and Country Planning Act 1971, s 222)

OPERATIONS *See* BUILDING OPERATIONS

OPERATIVE *See* MACHINERY

OPERATOR *See also* DRIVE—DRIVER

'Operator', in relation to an aircraft, means the person having the management of the aircraft for the time being or, in relation to a time, at that time. (Civil Aviation Act 1982, s 105(1))

[The Factories Act 1937, s 14(1) (repealed; see now the Factories Act 1961, s 14(2)) required machinery to be securely fenced, and the proviso thereto required a device which automatically prevented the 'operator' from coming into contact with a dangerous part.] 'Contact between a body and moving machinery will in all probability always result in serious injury. Contact between a tool and such machinery is unlikely to result in serious injury provided the body is properly guarded; and it would be a strong thing without clear words to construe the statute as completely prohibiting all such contact. The section is to be read in the light of the common law principle that in any particular case in which the employer ought to anticipate danger, he will be liable unless he guards against it. I cannot hold that the word 'operator' by itself clearly includes the tools the man is working with: and I am not therefore willing to conclude that in guarding against this sort of contact the statute goes further than the common law.' *Sparrow v Fairey Aviation Co Ltd* [1961] 3 All ER 452 at 458, CA, per Devlin LJ; also reported [1962] 1 QB 161 at 173

Canada [Insurable persons for crop insurance were limited to 'operators' of farms.] 'Webster's Third New International Dictionary, to which I resorted for assistance, gives this relevant definition to the word "operator": "a person that actively operates a business (as a mine, a farm, or a store) whether as owner, lessor or employee." Consistent with that definition the Oxford Dictionary defines "operator" as: "one who operates. (1) one who does or effects something. (2) one who performs the practical or mechanical operations belonging to any process, business, or investigation."

The term "operator of a farm" means precisely what those words suggest in the circumstances. The farm operator is the person in charge of the farming process.' *Alberta Hail & Crop Insurance Corp v Sarafinchan* (1979) 96 DLR (3d) 106 at 111, Alta CA, per Haddad JA

OPIUM

Medicinal opium

'Medicinal opium' means raw opium which has undergone the process necessary to adopt it for medicinal use in accordance with the requirements of the British Pharmacopœia, whether it is in the form of powder or is granulated or is in any other form, and whether it is or is not mixed with neutral substances. (Misuse of Drugs Act 1971, Sch 2, Part IV)

Opium poppy

'Opium poppy' means the plant of the species *Papaver somniferum* L. (Misuse of Drugs Act 1971, Sch 2, Part IV)

Prepared opium

In this Act . . . 'prepared opium' means opium prepared for smoking and includes dross and any other residues remaining after opium has been smoked. (Misuse of Drugs Act 1971, s 37(1))

Raw opium

'Raw opium' includes powdered or granulated opium, but does not include medicinal opium. (Misuse of Drugs Act 1971, Sch 2, Part IV)

OPPRESSION

A public officer commits the common law offence of oppression if while exercising, or under colour of exercising, his office he inflicts upon any person from an improper motive any bodily harm, imprisonment or injury other than extortion. The offence is not committed if the officer acted in good faith, in the belief that he had the legal right to do the act in question, and without any intention to act corruptly or oppressively.

Oppression is an indictable offence punishable by imprisonment and fine at the discretion of the court. (11 Halsbury's Laws (4th edn) para 930)

Oppression means that there has been a disregard of the essentials of justice and the infliction of a penalty which is not properly related to the crime of which the party stands convicted, but is either to be regarded as merely vindictive or as having proceeded upon some improper or irregular consideration, or, it may be, upon some misleading statement of facts put before the Sheriff by the prosecutor, or the like.' *Stewart v Cormack* 1941 SC(J) 73 at 77, per the Lord Justice-General (Lord Normand)

'Whether or not there is oppression [of an accused] in an individual case depends upon many elements. I am not going into all of them. They include such things as the length of time of any individual period of questioning, the length of time intervening between periods of questioning, whether the accused person had been given proper refreshment or not, and the characteristics of the person who makes the statement. What may be oppressive as regards a child, an invalid or an old man or somebody inexperienced in the ways of this world may turn out not to be oppressive when one finds that the accused person is of a tough character and an experienced man of the world.' *R v Priestly* (1965) 51 Cr App Rep 1, per Sachs J

'In an address to the Bentham Club in 1968, Lord MacDermott described "oppressive questioning" as—"questioning which by its nature, duration or other attendant circumstances (including the fact of custody) excites hopes (such as the hope of release) or fears, or so affects the mind of the suspect that his will crumbles and he speaks when otherwise he would have stayed silent." We adopt these definitions or descriptions and apply them to the present case.' *R v Prager* [1972] 1 All ER 1114 at 1119

New Zealand 'Oppressive conduct seems to me to begin when directors, or officers, or a group of shareholders, use powers expressly or impliedly given to them by [Act of Parliament] or by the constitution of the company, as to the use of which they have a discretion, in a way which is unjust to other shareholders.' *Re Empire Building Ltd* [1973] 1 NZLR 214 at 220 per Turner P

New Zealand [The Companies Amendment Act 1980, s 11 provides that any member of a company who complains that the affairs of the company have been or are being or are likely to be conducted in a manner that is, or any act or acts of the company have been or are likely to be, 'oppressive', unfairly discriminatory, or unfairly prejudicial . . . may make an application to the court for relief.] 'Having regard to . . . the wider global expression "oppressive, unfairly discriminatory or unfairly prejudicial", it would I think be wrong to assume that the new section was intended to adopt the meaning accorded to "oppressive" under the old English provision by Viscount Simonds in *Scottish Co-operative Wholesale Society Ltd v Meyer* [[1958] 3 All ER 66, HL] . . . In employing the words "oppressive, unfairly discriminatory or unfairly prejudicial" Parliament has afforded petitioners a wider base on which to found a complaint. Taking the ordinary dictionary definition of the words from the Shorter Oxford English Dictionary: oppressive is 'unjustly burdensome"; unfair is "not fair or equitable; unjust"; discriminate is "to make or constitute a difference in or between; to differentiate"; and prejudicial, "causing prejudice, detrimental, damaging (to rights, interests, etc)". I do not read the subsection as referring to three distinct alternatives which are to be considered separately in watertight compartments. The three expressions overlap, each in a sense helps to explain the other, and read together they reflect the underlying concern of the subsection that conduct of the company which is unjustly detrimental to any member of the company whatever form it takes and whether it adversely affects all members alike or discriminates against some only is a legitimate foundation for a complaint.' *Thomas v HW Thomas Ltd* [1984] 1 NZLR 686 at 691, 692, 693, CA, per Richardson J

New Zealand [The Credit Contracts Act 1981, s 10(1)(a) empowers the court to re-open a credit contract where it considers that the contract or any term thereof is 'oppressive'.] 'The word "oppressive" clearly connotes that some real detriment or hardship is involved'. *Italian Holdings (Properties) Ltd v Lonsdale Holdings (Auckland) Ltd* [1984] 2 NZLR 1 at 15, per Vautier J

OPTION

A traditional option is the right to elect on declaration dates until the end of a specified period whether or not to call for delivery or to make delivery or to elect to do either in respect of a definite amount of a particular security at a fixed price, and may be dealt in in the same way as a security. The question whether or not what is ostensibly a genuine option agreement is a contract by way of gaming and wagering is governed by the same principles as apply to an agreement to buy or sell securities, and is dealt with elsewhere in this work.

In addition to the traditional option market, there is also a market in 'London Traded Options'. Such an option takes the form of a contract which is capable of being bought or sold independently of the securities to which it relates at any time until the expiry date of the option, unless during that period the option is exercised. The Council of The Stock Exchange determines which underlying securities it will permit London Traded Options to be dealt in and when new series are to be created. All bargains in London Traded Options must be fulfilled in accordance with the rules, regulations and usages of The Stock Exchange and must be done on the trading floor in London in the appropriate crowd by means of open outcry during the trading hours specified from time to time by the council. The council provides a clearing house for London Traded Options. and clearing of bargains must be carried out only by stock exchange firms authorised so to do by the council under such conditions and until such time as it thinks fit. (45 Halsbury's Laws (4th edn) para 14)

'There is no evidence that the contract sued on here was merely a bargain to pay differences without any right given or intended to be given to enforce the contract in its terms. The bargain was an ordinary Stock Exchange transaction. The defendant came to the plaintiffs who were members of the Stock Exchange in Amsterdam, and said he wanted to get a call in these particular shares, and they obtained that option for him on the terms agreed. The defendant, therefore, during the time that the option was exercisable, had a right to call for the delivery of the shares at the fixed price. The defendant was not bound to call; that was the object of the option which gave him the right to call for the shares, or not, as might be best for him at the end October settlement. The learned judge was wrong, therefore, in holding that this bargain, being an option, could not be enforced as being in fact nothing but a "bet" and the appeal must be allowed and judgment entered for the plaintiffs.' *Buitenlandsche Bankvereeniging v Hildesheim* (1903) 47 Sol Jo 707 at 708, CA, per Collins MR

[The owners of freehold property agreed to give the defendants the first 'option' of purchasing any part of the said property that might be designated for dairy purposes.] 'Here people have purported to come to an agreement; but, in fact, have not come to any agreement at all, because the terms of the agreement are not expressed. The words "first option" by themselves have no meaning; there is no mention of price, or time, or anything else.

Ryan v Thomas (1911) 55 Sol Jo 364 at 364, per Warrington J

[Under the terms of a lease, the tenant was given the 'option' of continuing for an extension of seven or fourteen years.] 'The plain meaning of the word "option" is "choice". Reading "choice" for "option", the clause means that the tenant has the choice of continuing his tenancy.' *Gardner v Blaxill* [1960] 2 All ER 457 at 460, per Paull J

'My Lords, "option" in its widest interpretation means simply choice or freedom of choice. An obligation in a contract can frequently be performed in a large number of ways and the party under obligation can choose any one of the ways that he likes. A contract may, for example, provide for September/October shipment and the shipper may then select any one of the sixty-one days which he likes. I doubt if in such a case the shipper would, in the ordinary use of language, be described as having sixty-one options. But when a contract itself limits and enumerates the obligations, as when it obliges the shipper to ship wheat or barley or flour, it is quite sensible and natural to talk of his having an option to ship any one of these three commodities. There is, however, a narrower sense in which the word can be used and that is to confer a right of choice specially granted to the holder of the option and to be used solely for his own benefit. It is in this sense, I think, that the word is generally used in the business world.' *Reardon Smith Line Ltd v Ministry of Agriculture, Fisheries and Food* [1963] 1 All ER 545 at 559, HL, per Lord Devlin; also reported in [1963] AC 691 at 729

'It was conceded by counsel for the plaintiffs that an option on a proper analysis is no more than an ordinary offer coupled with a promise not to withdraw the offer during the period of the option. Indeed, an option was analysed on this basis by Danckwerts J in *Stromdale & Ball Ltd v Burden* [[1952] 1 All ER 59].' *Mountford v Scott* [1974] 1 All ER 248 at 254, per Brightman J

Australia 'The plaintiff's counsel contended . . . that the use of the word "option" in itself implies an exclusive right. Now, the word is not a term of art, and neither in my own recollection of contemporary use, nor in any of the dictionaries to which I have referred . . . have I found any such usage of the word. The word by itself does not mean an option to purchase or to call for a grant of the whole of the interest of the person giving the option in the subject-matter. It defines in itself neither the quality nor quantity of the interest with regard to which the "option" is given. Its meaning depends on the context.' *Nicholls v Lovell* [1923] SASR 542 at 545, per Poole J

Australia [The rules of a trade union provided for 'optional preferential voting' in elections for certain positions.] 'An election by optional preferential voting means an election in which the voter has the choice to take part in the election as though it were a preferential election or to cast a vote as though the election had no preferential features.' *Re Vehicle Builders Employees Federation of Australia* [1975] 6 ALR 653 at 656, per Smithers J

Canada 'An option is defined in *Paterson v Houghton* (1909) 19 Man R 168, 12 WLR 330 as follows: "An option is defined to be a right acquired by contract to accept or reject a present offer within a limited, or, it may be a reasonable, time in the future".' *Yanik v Conibear & Northern Transportation Co Ltd* (No 2) [1945] 1 WWR 33 at 42, Alta CA, per Ewing JA

New Zealand '"Option", in its legal sense, implies that the giver of the option is to be taken as making a continuing offer which the other party may at any time during an agreed period convert into a contract by notifying his acceptance.' *Adaras Developments Ltd v Marcona Corpn* [1975] 1 NZLR 324 at 332, per O'Regan J

OR *See also* AND

'S. Burrill surrendered the estate to the use of himself for life, then to his wife during her widowhood; then, that is, in case her estate for life is put an end to by doing this act, which he meant to guard against, to his son W Wallis for life, and after his decease to the issue of his body. . . . The surrender then proceeds to state a proviso, that, in case W Wallis should die in the life-time of the surrenderor, or without issue of his body, the estate should go to the right heirs of the surrenderor; and here the question arises on the word "or". Now there is no doubt on the intention of the parties: and where sense requires it, there are many cases to shew that we may construe the word "or" into "and", and "and" into "or", . . . in order to effectuate the intent of the parties. Here, therefore, in order to give effect to the intention of the surrenderor, we must say, that, when he used the word "or", he meant "and".' *Wright d Burrill v Kemp* (1789) 3 Term Rep 470 at 473, per Lord Kenyon CJ

[A testator by his will gave a bequest to Hugh Brown to be applied for such religious "or" charitable purposes as he should think fit.] 'It is contended that when both words are used and connected by the word "or", the gift must fail; that the use of the word "charitable" shows that the word "religious" means something distinct from charitable; and that, as this would permit Mr Brown to apply the whole or part of the money to purposes not charitable, the whole gift must fail . . . The word "or" does not necessarily imply that an alternative is given to the legatee. It may of course connect alternative objects on which the legatee may expend the sum bequeathed, but not necessarily. It is often used by the best English authors, not to connect real alternatives, but merely to connect different words expressing the same or a cognate idea. . . . I . . . hold the gift . . . to be valid.' *Rickerby v Nicholson* [1912] 1 IR 343 at 347, 348, per Ross J

'In logic, there is no rule which requires that "or" should carry an exclusive force. Whether it does so depends on the context. So one must ask what, in a legal context, is the meaning of an assertion that "A or B" is to be guilty of an offence? The law is supposed to be certain: the subject is entitled, and presumptively bound, to know what laws, particularly what criminal laws, apply to him. To say that a law which fails to satisfy these demands is void for uncertainty, is certainly a last resort, but if that conclusion is to be avoided, some intelligible meaning must be found by supplying, or substituting, words within the limits of what courts may legitimately do. It seems clear enough that where the law says that something is to happen to "A or B", if what is intended is an exclusionary alternative (i.e. one, but not the other), the law must state either some qualification by which the affected person may be determined, or must name a third person by whom the choice may be made.' *Federal Steam Navigation Co Ltd v Department of Trade & Industry* [1974] 2 All ER 97 at 110, HL, per Lord Wilberforce

Canada 'A separate offence is not created by the mere use of the disjunctive "or", which is employed frequently to convey a descriptive meaning, to amplify, to escape from verbal rigidity, and sometimes to explain a situation or combination of circumstances more flexibly and comprehensively through the use of words as if they were pictures or symbols. Some things may be more easily described than defined. For example, Code s 115 [now RSC 1970, c C-34, s 82] provides that everyone is guilty of an offence who "has in his custody or possession, or carries any offensive weapon". . . . I think it must be clear that that section does not create three distinct offences. "Custody", "possession" and "carrying" appear there disjunctively, not to create separate offences as such, but to better describe one offence, which may be composed of one or more or all of the acts pictured by any distinctive meaning of which those three words may be capable.' *R v Clarke and Tomkins* [1948] 1 WWR 75 at 76, BCCA, per O'Halloran J

Read as 'and'

'The rule of construction is quite clear, that in a deed as well as a will the court may, in favour of the intention, read "or" for "and", or "and" for "or".' *White v Supple* (1842) 2 Dr & War 471 at 474, 475, per Sugden LC

[Under the terms of a marriage settlement property was vested in trustees upon trust for such child or children 'or' their issue in such shares as the wife should appoint.] 'I think the words "or their issue" must be read "and their issue". Read strictly, "or their issue" makes some sense of a sort. It would mean that the appointment had to be made either to the children or only to their issue. . . . I think the words must be construed as a gift to the children and their issue as the wife may appoint, with a limitation that the children can only take if they attain twenty-one or in the case of daughters marry with consent, followed by a provision that if there is only one child who shall comply with the conditions that one child shall take.' *Re Llewellyn's Settlement, Official Solicitor v Evans* [1921] 2 Ch 281 at 284, 285, per Russell J

'The question to be determined is what is the meaning and effect of a gift over in the will of one Joseph Hayden relating to freehold property at Pinner after the death of a named person to be equally divided "between her sisters or their issue". . . . One sister had issue, the others had no issue; the testator does not say that the issue are to take such shares as their parents would have taken. . . . It seems to me that there is, in the present case, an obvious reason why "or" should be read as "and", for by so doing you make sense of the words.' *Re Hayden, Pask v Perry* [1931] 2 Ch 333 at 336, 339, 340, per Luxmoore J

Refusal to read as 'and'

[A testator bequeathed to Mary Tattershall a yearly sum of £40 during the term of her natural life, and immediately after her decease to his (the testator's) nephew 'or' his heirs.] 'It appears to me that "or" must be construed disjunctively here, as the context requires it; and that the testator contemplated that his nephew might not be alive at the death of Mary Tattershall; and therefore I think that the nephew did not take an absolute interest in the annuity.' *Girdlestone v Doe* (1928) 2 Sim 225 at 226, per Shadwell V-C

'I have looked at the will in this case, and . . . I am of opinion that it is not possible to accede to the argument with respect to the annuity . . . and change the word "or" into "and". The words are:—"Then after the death of my mother, Hannah Hawksworth, or the second marriage, death or forfeiture of my wife Hannah Hawksworth, then I give and bequeath to my daughter Emma Green" an annuity of £40 for life, etc, with reversion to her daughters. The argument has not induced me to come to the conclusion that the word "or" ought to be read "and", and that both the death of the mother and the failure of interest of the wife ought to occur before the annuity to the daughter takes effect. It would be to alter the gift, which is in the disjunctive form, and is to take effect whichever of the events specified may occur first.' *Hawksworth v Hawksworth* (1858) 27 Beav 1 at 4, per Romilly MR

[A marriage settlement provided that on default of issue of the marriage certain of the settled property should, on the death of the survivor of the husband and wife, go to 'every child and children or grandchild' of A.] 'The word "or" in this settlement, I think, must be construed as "or", and I think that the class of grandchildren is a substitutional class. . . . I think that Mr Theobald has accurately summed up the result of them in the 5th edition of his work at page 592. He there says "When the gift is to a class or their issue, the further question arises whether the original and substituted legatees form two mutually exclusive classes, so that no substituted legatees can take if there are any members of the original class to take, or whether the issue of members of the original class dying can take with the surviving members of the original class. It is clear that if all the original class survive the time of distribution, they alone take".' *Re Coley, Gibson v Gibson* [1901] 1 Ch 40 at 42, 43, per Byrne J

'The income of . . . two-thirds of the fund is to be applied "in charity or works of public utility". The real question is as to the meaning of that phrase. In my judgment, the word "or" is there used disjunctively, and the word "charity" is used in contradistinction to the "works of public utility". . . . I am unable to distinguish the case from that of *Blair v Duncan* [[1902] AC 37], which has been referred to. There the House of Lords held that the words "charitable or public" in a gift for "such charitable or public purposes as my trustee thinks proper" were used disjunctively, and that the gift, therefore, failed for uncertainty.' *Langham v Peterson* (1903) 19 TLR 157 at 157, 158, per Swinfen Eady J

'You do sometimes read "or" as "and" in a statute. In *Brown & Co v Harrison* [(1927) 43 TLR 394], MacKinnon J read "or" as "and" in the Carriage of Goods by Sea Act 1924, and his decision was confirmed by this Court. But you do not do it unless you are obliged, because "or" does not generally mean "and", and "and" does not generally mean "or".' *Green v Premier Glynrhonwy Slate Co Ltd* [1928] 1 KB 561 at 568, CA, per Scrutton LJ

'In the present case the testator . . . gives the residue of his property to his executors who are to apply it "for such charitable institution or institutions or other charitable or benevolent object or objects in England as my acting executors or executor may, in their or his absolute discretion select, and to be paid to or for such institutions and objects if more than one, in such proportions as my executors or executor may think proper". . . . Taking that language and reading it in its natural and grammatical meaning, it does not seem to me to be open to doubt that the testator is giving to his trustees an option to apply his residue either, first to a charitable institution or institutions, or, secondly, to some other charitable object, or thirdly, to some benevolent object or objects. The word "or" is prima facie, and in the absence of some restraining context, to be read as disjunctive, and if a testator wishes to give his trustees a discretion to apply his property either to charitable or to benevolent objects. I do not myself know what word in the English language he can more suitably use than the word "or". I approach this question therefore on the view that the word "or" is prima facie to be read as meaning what it says. Mr Harman, as one of the arguments which he put before us, invited us to construe the word "or" as meaning "and", or as meaning "*id est*", or, he said, it should be omitted altogether. I am quite unable to understand on what principle of construction, or indeed of common sense, it would be justifiable to apply such violence to the language of a testator. That words may be omitted, that they may even be changed in their meaning, or read in a meaning which is far from their natural meaning, if the context so requires it, is a truism; but I can find no vestige of a context in this will which would justify the court in reading the word "or" in that way.' *Re Diplock, Wintle v Diplock* [1941] Ch 253 at 260, 261, CA, per Greene MR; affirmed sub nom *Chichester Diocesan Fund and Board of Finance (Incorp) v Simpson* [1944] AC 341, HL

ORDER

'The promissory note was made payable to the testator "or order"; that means order in writing.' *Bromage v Lloyd* (1847) 1 Exch 32 at 35, per Alderson B

'The difference between a request and an order is this, the former purports to be made without authority, the latter with authority to command.' *R v Snelling* (1853) Dears CC 219 at 223, CCR, per Jervis CJ

'Mr Hollins has directed my attention to Murray's *Oxford Dictionary*, from which it is quite clear, as I should myself have supposed, that in certain contexts "order" and "direction" are interchangeable terms. A "direction" is said to be "an order to be carried out", and "order", for example, so far as the Supreme Court is concerned, is said to be "a direction other than final judgment".' *Benson v Benson* [1941] P 90 at 97, per Lord Merriman P

'An order is an order, and to draw a distinction between an order made on an originating summons and any other order for costs appears to me in principle to be unjustifiable. Mr Myles [counsel for the respondent] says a proceeding by originating summons is not like a case of "hostile litigation", but originating summonses are often extremely hostile, and I find it impossible to draw any such distinction as that contended for.' *Re Blake, Clutterbuck v Bradford* [1945] Ch 61 at 67, CA, per Lord Greene MR

'The word "order" in relation to legal proceedings in itself is ambiguous; clearly it may mean, perhaps, a linguistic purist would say that its most accurate connotation was to indicate, an order requiring an affirmative course of action to be taken in pursuance of the order, but it is equally clear that the word may have a much wider meaning covering in effect all decisions of courts.' *R v Recorder of Oxford, ex p Brasenose College* [1969] 3 All ER 428 at 431, per Bridge J

Commercial paper

United States An 'order' is a direction to pay and must be more than an authorisation or request. It must identify the person to pay with reasonable certainty. It may be addressed to one or more such persons jointly or in the alternative but not in succession. (Uniform Commercial Code 1978, s 3–102(1)(b))

Confirmation of order *See* CONFIRMATION

Final order

'I conceive that an order is "final" only where it is made upon an application or other proceeding which must, whether such application or other proceeding fail or succeed, determine the action.' *Salaman v Warner* [1891] 1 QB 734 at 736, 737, CA, per Fry LJ

'The matter in dispute was simply this: the applicant said the respondents were his solicitors and ought to give him a bill of costs, and that that bill ought to be taxed. The solicitors opposed that, and . . . objected to deliver a bill. That was in substance the matter in dispute between the parties; and what was the order made? It was an order dismissing the application. If the order had been the other way, if an order had been made in favour of the applicant, it would equally have disposed of the matter in dispute. That being so, the order would be a final order within the definition in *Salaman v Warner* [supra], and, following that, I am of opinion that this was a final order.' *Re Reeves (Herbert) & Co* [1902] 1 Ch 29 at 33, CA, per Romer LJ

'It seems to me that the real test for determining this question ought to be this: Does the judgment or order, as made, finally dispose of the rights of the parties? If it does, then I think it ought to be treated as a final order.' *Bozson v Altrincham Urban District Council* [1903] 1 KB 547 at 548, 549, CA, per Lord Alverstone CJ

'Section 164 of the Merchant Shipping Act 1894 [repealed; see now the Merchant Shipping Act 1970, s 16] enables a seaman to recover his wages before a court of summary jurisdiction in or near the place where he is discharged. It gives him a summary tribunal in a convenient place. . . . The section says that "the order made by the court in the matter shall be final". I take that to mean not merely final in the sense that the matter once having been litigated is not to be brought in question again, but final in the sense that no appeal lies from it.' *Wills & Sons v McSherry* [1914] 1 KB 616 at 619, per Channell J

Australia 'In my opinion, under s 52(j) [of the Bankruptcy Act 1924–1950 (Com) (repealed; see now the Bankruptcy Act 1966–1986, s 40(1)(g))], the elements essential to constitute a final judgment are equally essential to constitute a final order. The order must be one which finally determines the rights of the parties in a proceeding which is not an action. It also appears that the final order must be one made in a proceeding in which the party sought to be made liable to pay money to the actor has had the opportunity of setting up a counterclaim, set-off or cross-demand.' *Re Stanton Hayek* (1957) 19 ABC 1 at 4, 5, per Clyne J

In Bankruptcy Acts

[The Bankruptcy Act 1883, s 104 (repealed; see now the Insolvency Act 1986, s 375) enacted that 'orders' in bankruptcy matters should, at the instance of any person aggrieved, be subject to appeal as therein provided.] 'When the High Court makes a declaration of right, and further orders the costs of the application to be paid, . . . and that is drawn up and sealed with the seal of the court, and, I suppose placed on record, as all orders of the High court are, it seems to me that it is clearly an order of the Court.' *Re Lamb, ex p Board of Trade* [1894] 2 QB 805 at 813, CA, per Kay LJ

In Judgments Act

[The Judgments Act 1838, s 18 enacted that all 'orders' of courts of equity, whereby any sum of money was payable to any person, were to have the effect of judgments in the superior courts of common law.] 'It appears to me preposterous to argue that an order upon an officer of the court to ascertain what is due can by any possibility amount to an order to pay. And so again as to the report of that officer, the *allocatur*, stating what is due, it is preposterous to contend that that is an order to pay. They are both proceedings in order to arrive at that which is the ultimate judgment, namely the direction of the court that payment shall be made.' *Shaw v Neale* (1858) 6 HL Cas 581 at 612, per Lord Cranworth

In Supreme Court Act

[The Judicature Act 1873, s 19 (repealed; see now the Supreme Court Act 1981, s 16(1)), gave the Court of Appeal jurisdiction to hear and determine appeals from any judgment or 'order' of the High Court.] 'The agreement to state a special case was entered into pursuant to powers conferred by the legislature; and the order of the judge is an order made under the authority of a statute. The question is put to the Queen's Bench Division pursuant to the statute in order that the point may be decided so as to bind the parties; that is an adjudication or order.' *Peterborough Corpn v Wilsthorpe Overseers* (1883) 12 QBD 1 at 3, CA, per Brett MR

Interlocutory

An order which does not deal with the final rights of the parties, but either (1) is made before judgment, and gives no final decision on the matters in dispute, but is merely on a matter of procedure, or (2) is made after judgment, and merely directs how the declarations of right already given in the final judgment are to be worked out, is termed 'interlocutory'.

An interlocutory order, even though not conclusive of the main dispute, may be conclusive as to the subordinate matter with which it deals.

The phrase 'interlocutory judgment' is also used to describe a judgment for damages to be assessed. (26 Halsbury's Laws (4th edn) para 506)

ORDER CHEQUE *See* CHEQUE

ORDER IN COUNCIL

Proclamations and Orders in Council are instruments made by the Crown. The great majority of powers conferred on the Crown are required to be exercised by Orders in Council which are orders expressed to be made by and with the advice of the Privy Council. (44 Halsbury's Laws (4th edn) para 982)

ORDER OF COUNCIL

Orders of Council are orders made by the Privy Council in pursuance of powers conferred on it alone and, as is normally the case with such powers, expressed to be exercisable by order. (44 Halsbury's Laws (4th edn) para 982)

ORDINANCE

Canada 'The exercise of the power conferred on the Governor in Council to amend Sched J of the Food and Drugs Act [1952–53 (Can) c 38; see now RSC 1970, c F-27] is legislative in nature and equivalent to an Act of Parliament or an Act of a provincial legislature. The fact that it is made by an authority less than the sovereign enacting power distinguishes it from a statute and in my opinion brings it within the class of instrument properly termed an "ordinance".' *R v Whalen* (1971) 15 CRNS 187 at 191, NB, per Hughes JA

ORDINARILY RESIDENT *See also* RESIDE

[The Education Act 1962, s 1(1), as substituted by the Education Act 1980, s 19, Sch 5, imposes a duty on local education authorities to bestow awards for designated courses to students who were 'ordinarily resident' within their areas.] 'There are two, and no more than two, respects in which the mind of the propositus is important in determining ordinary residence. The residence must be voluntarily adopted. Enforced presence by reason of kidnapping or imprisonment, or a Robinson Crusoe existence on a desert island with no opportunity of escape, may be so overwhelming a factor as to negative the will to be where one is. And there must be a degree of settled purpose. The purpose may be one or there may be several. It may be specific or general. All the law requires is that there is a settled purpose. This is not to say that the propositus intends to stay where he is indefinitely; indeed his purpose, while settled, may be for a limited period. Education, business or profession, employment, health, family or merely love of the place spring to mind as common reasons for a choice of regular abode. And there may well be many others. All that is necessary is that the purpose of living where one does has a sufficient degree of continuity to be properly described as settled. Unless, therefore, it can be shown that the statutory framework or the legal context in which the words are used requires a different meaning, I unhesitantly subscribe to the view that "ordinarily resident" refers to a man's abode in a particular place or country which he has adopted voluntarily and for settled purposes as part of the regular order of his life for the time being, whether of short or long duration.' *Shah v Barnet London Borough Council* [1983] 1 All ER 226 at 235, HL, per Lord Scarman

[See also *Eastleigh Borough Council v Betts* [1983] 2 All ER 1111, HL, in which the phrase under consideration was 'normally resident' within the Housing (Homeless Persons) Act 1977.]

Canada 'The appellant contends that he is not ordinarily resident in Canada under s 9(a) [of the Income War Tax Act, RSC 1927, c 97 (see now Income Tax Act, RSC 1970, c I–5, s 203)], but that he merely sojourns in Canada for a period less than 183 days in each year and is therefore not taxable under s 9(b). A reference to the dictionary and judicial comments upon the meaning of these terms indicates that one is "ordinarily resident" in the place where in the settled routine of his life he regularly, normally or customarily lives. One "sojourns" at a place where he unusually, casually or intermittently visits or stays. In the former the element of permanence, in the latter that of the temporary predominates. The difference cannot be stated in precise and definite terms, but each case must be determined after all of the relevant factors are taken into consideration, but the foregoing indicates in a general way the essential difference. It is not the length of the visit or stay that determines the question. Even in this statute under s 9(b) the time of 183 days does not determine whether the party sojourns or not but merely determines whether the tax shall be payable or not by one who sojourns.' *Thomson v Minister of National Revenue* [1946] SCR 209 at 231, SCC, per Estey J

Canada [The Social Services Tax Act, RSBC 1960, s 3(3); see now RSBC 1979, c 388, s 2(4), imposes a tax on persons residing or 'ordinarily resident' or carrying on business in British Columbia.] 'It is my view that . . . the word 'ordinarily' used in sub-s (3) does not qualify the phrase "carrying on business". It is in my opinion used to designate two types of residents, the one those residing in the province, the other those ordinarily residing in the province. I think its function is then exhausted leaving as the third class of persons who come under the section those "carrying on business in the Province".' *Re Social Services Tax Act* (1961) 35 WWR 264 at 270, 271, BCSC, per Hutcheson J

ORDINARY

[To constitute an actionable obstruction of ancient lights there must be a substantial interference with the 'ordinary' user of light, and, if in respect of business premises, with the ordinary user required for an 'ordinary' business.] 'What is meant by the expressions which are to be found in the special case and in the judgment in *Colls Case* [*Colls v Home & Colonial Stores Ltd* [1904] AC 179], "ordinary user" or "ordinary business" or "ordinary purposes"? I think that the word "ordinary" is used solely with reference to light; and an ordinary user, or an ordinary business means a user or business which in fact requires only an ordinary amount of light. Is this a question of law or fact? In my opinion it is a question of fact. It must depend upon the evidence in each case, and it cannot be adjudicated as a matter of law whether an architects' business or any other business is an ordinary business.' *Ambler v Leeds* (*Bp*) (1905) 53 WR 300 at 301, per Bray J

ORDINARY (Ecclesiastic) *See* BISHOP

ORDINARY COURSE OF BUSINESS

[The Factors Act 1889, s 2 enacts that where a mercantile agent is, with the consent of the owner, in possession of goods or of the documents of title to goods, any sale, pledge or other disposition of the goods made by him when acting in the 'ordinary course of business' of a mercantile agent is, subject to the provisions of the Act, as valid as if he were expressly authorised by the owner of the goods to make the same.] 'The question is whether Moss can possibly be said to be acting in the ordinary course of business as a mercantile agent. He is clearly a mercantile agent. But the ordinary course of business of a mercantile agent is to raise money either by going himself or by sending his clerk, who in the ordinary course of business raises money on his behalf, not be going to somebody else and asking him to do it. It is not in the ordinary course of business of a mercantile agent to go to some friend and ask him to pledge goods.' *De Gorter v Attenborough & Son* (1904) 21 TLR 19 at 19, per Channell J

[This phrase in the Factors Act 1889, s 2(1)] 'means "acting in such a way as a mercantile agent acting in the ordinary course of business of a mercantile agent would act"; that is to say, within business hours, at a proper place of business, and in other respects in the ordinary way in which a mercantile agent would act, so that there is nothing to lead the pledgee to suppose that anything wrong is being done, or to give him notice that the disposition is one which the mercantile agent had no authority to make.' *Oppenheimer v Attenborough & Son* [1908] 1 KB 221, at 230, 231, per Buckley LJ

Australia [The Bankruptcy Act 1924–1930, s 95 (repealed; see now the Bankruptcy Act 1966–1986 (Cth), s 123) provided that every conveyance or transfer of property by any person unable to pay his debts as they became due from his own money, in favour of any creditor and having the effect of giving that creditor a preference over the other creditors, should be void as against the trustee in bankruptcy; but nothing in the section was to affect the rights of a purchaser, payee or encumbrancer in good faith and for valuable consideration and in the 'ordinary course of business'.] 'The "ordinary course of business" is not, I think, to be related to any special business carried on by either debtor or creditor but is concerned with the character of the impeached transaction itself.' *Robertson v Grigg* (1932) 47 CLR 257 at 273, per Evatt J

Australia 'As was pointed out in *Burns v McFarlane* (1940) 64 CLR 108, at p 125, the issues in sub-s 2(b) of s 95 of the Bankruptcy Act 1924–1933 [see now Bankruptcy Act 1966–1986 (Cth), s 123(3)] are "(1) good faith; (2) valuable consideration; and (3) ordinary course of business". This last expression, it was said, "does not require an investigation of the course pursued in any particular trade or vocation and it does not refer to what is normal or usual in the business of the debtor or that of the creditor". It is an additional requirement and is cumulative upon good faith and valuable consideration. It is, therefore, not so much a question of fairness and absence of symptoms of bankruptcy as of the everyday usual or normal character of the transaction. The provision does not require that the transaction shall be in the course of any particular trade vocation or business. It speaks of the course of business in general. But it does suppose that according to the ordinary and common flow of transactions in affairs of business there is a course, an ordinary course. It means that the transaction must fall into place as part of the undistinguished common flow of business done, that it should form part of the ordinary business as carried on, calling for no remark and arising out of no special or particular situation.' *Downs Distributing Co Pty Ltd v Associated Blue Star Stores Ptd Ltd (In Liquidation)* (1948) 76 CLR 463 at 476, per Rich J

Australia [The Companies Act 1961–1966 (NSW), s 207(1), as amended (see now s 208(1)), prohibits an official manager from disposing of the company's assets save in the 'ordinary course of the company's business'.] 'The transaction must be one of the ordinary day-to-day business activities, having no unusual or special features, and being such as a manager of a business might reasonably be expected to be permitted to carry out on his own initiative without making prior reference back or subsequent report to his superior authorities, such as, for example, to his board of directors.' *Re Bradford Roofing Industries Pty Ltd* [1966] 1 NSWR 674, per Street J

ORDINARY RESOLUTION *See* RESOLUTION

ORDINARY SHARES *See* SHARES

ORDNANCE MAP

'The defendant's witnesses are corroborated in their evidence that there never has been a track in fact by the Wellhouse, and certainly no road used by heavy wagons, not only by the nature of the ground, but by two documents or sets of documents, both of which, I think, I am justified in accepting as admissible evidence on this point. The first is the Ordnance map of 1874. Such maps are not evidence on questions of title, or questions whether a road is public or private, but they are prepared by officers appointed under the provisions of the Ordnance Survey Acts, and set out every track visible on the face of the ground, and are in my opinion admissible on the question whether or not there was in fact a visible track at the time of the survey. The map of 1874 shews no trace of the alleged Wellhouse track.' *A-G v Antrobus* [1905] 2 Ch 188 at 203, per Farwell J

ORGANISATION

In this section [which deals with proscribed organisations under the Act] 'organisation' includes an association or combination of persons. (Prevention of Terrorism (Temporary Provisions) Act 1986, s 1(6))

Industrial organisation

In this section [exemptions from provisions regulating hours of employment] 'organisation' includes—

(a) in relation to workers, an association of trade unions, and
(b) in relation to employers, an association of organisations of employers and also any body established by or under any enactment for the purpose of carrying on under national ownership any industry or part of any industry or undertaking.

(Factories Act 1961, s 117(3))

'Organisation', in relation to workers, means a trade union and, in relation to employers, means an employers' association. (Wages Councils Act 1979, s 28)

United States 'Organisation' includes a corporation, government or governmental subdivision or agency, business trust, estate, trust, partnership or association, two or more persons having a joint or common interest, or any other legal or commercial entity. (Uniform Commercial Code 1978, s 1–201(28))

ORGANISE

'The question here is whether there was evidence that the defendant organised the procession. "Organised" is not a term of art. When a person organises a procession, what does he do? A procession is not a mere body of persons; it is a body of persons moving along a route. Therefore the person who organises the route is the person who organises the procession. . . . It seems to me clear that, at any rate from the time when these people reached Piccadilly Circus, the defendant was organising the route for the procession to follow, and that they followed it. Therefore I think there was evidence on which the magistrate could find that he organised a procession. . . . By indicating or planning the route a person is in my opinion organising a procession.' *Flockhart v Robertson* [1950] 2 KB 498 at 502, 503, per Lord Goddard CJ

ORIGIN

'The fundamental idea of the function of a trade mark . . . was to indicate the origin of the goods. . . . There is a fundamental difference between the "origin" of goods, that is between that which gives them their permanent and essential character before they leave their source of origin, and a mere repair or processing which may be done at any subsequent time and is merely partial and evanescent, like the repair of "ladders" in stockings or the processing or servicing of goods which does not affect their essential character. The word "origin" is no doubt used in a special and almost technical sense in this connection, but it denotes at least that the goods are issued as vendible goods under the ægis of the proprietor of the trade mark, who thus assumes responsibility for them, even though the responsibility is limited to selection like that of the salesman of carrots on commission in *Major Bros v Franklin & Son* [[1908] 1 KB 712]. By putting them on the market under his trade mark he vouched his responsibility, and the carrots were "his goods" by selection, though he was neither the owner nor grower of them.' *Aristoc Ltd v Rysta Ltd* [1945] AC 68 at 101, 102, HL, per Lord Wright

ORIGINAL *See also* LITERARY WORK; NEW OR ORIGINAL

'Where there are a great number of persons who produce the same article, "original" means that the article so called is that made by the first inventor. That is the meaning of the word "original" which the Court of Chancery has always recognised.' *Cocks v Chandler* (1871) LR 11 Eq 446 at 449, per Lord Romilly MR

'The word "original" does not in this connection mean that the work must be the expression of original or inventive thought. Copyright Acts are not concerned with the originality of ideas, but with the expression of thought. . . . The originality which is required relates to the expression of the thought. But the Act does not require that the expression must be in an original or novel form, but that the work must not be copied from another work—that it should originate from the author.' *University of London Press Ltd v University Tutorial Press Ltd* [1916] 2 Ch 601 at 608, 609, per Peterson J

Canada 'For a work to be "original" it must originate from the author; it must be the product of his labour and skill and it must be the expression of his thoughts. Thus, if an artist were to sketch a particular view, the painting is the result of his labours and skill and is an expression of his thoughts. On the other hand, a mere amanuensis who does no more than take down what is dictated to him does not exercise labour or skill of the required character—there is no expression of his thoughts therein and he is not entitled to copyright.' *Canadian Admiral Corpn Ltd v Rediffusion Inc* [1954] Ex CR 382 at 398, 399, Ex Ct, per Cameron J

New Zealand 'It is clear that the engravings were made from photographs of Mr Berry's original designs. But the argument for the plaintiff is that the engraving represents a change of medium in which the original design has been converted into a three-dimensional form. It is said that it was the skill in working out the third dimension which makes the work an original artistic work. For the defendant, on the other hand, it is contended that the work, though three-dimensional, is still only a reproduction of Mr Berry's original design and is therefore not original. Upon consideration I do not think that argument takes due account of the underlying principle of copyright law that it is with physical material and not with ideas that copyright is concerned. Thus it is that copyright protection has been given to the published verbatim report of a speech, a photograph of a picture, a sketch of a piece of machinery, and a translation of a foreign work [8 Halsbury's Laws (4th edn) para 831]. Though each of these is made from existing subject-matter the medium of expression has been changed. Where the author has made use of existing subject-matter in this way the question is whether, in changing the medium, he has himself done sufficient independent labour to justify copyright protection.' *Martin v Polyplas Manufacturers Ltd* [1969] NZLR 1046 at 1049, per Wild CJ

ORIGINATE

[A policy of insurance covered loss or damage 'originating' from any cause whatever except (inter alia) fire. On a fire breaking out in a neighbouring house, the insured, fearing that it would spread, began to remove his goods from his shop. During this process the plate glass window of the shop was broken and some of the goods stolen.] 'The question is, whether the damage here "originated from fire"? The rule which governs in such cases is, that *causa proxima non remota spectatur*. Here it is clear that the fire was not the proximate cause of the damage, nor did the breakage "originate from fire". The expression "originating", etc, in the present case, has no greater effect to prevent the rule, that the proximate and not the ultimate cause is to be looked at, from applying here, than had the word "consequences" in the case of *Ionides v The Universal Marine Insurance Company* [(1863) 8 LT 705].' *Marsden v City & County Assurance Co Ltd* (1865) 13 LT 465 at 468, per Willes J

'The injury here did not originate in fire. The fire here was the remote cause, the *causa sine qua non*. If there had been no fire there would have been no mob, and if there had been no mob there would have been no damage to the plate glass, and so on. The real proximate cause, the efficient cause here was the felonious will and conduct of the mob, who were guilty of burglary. Putting the ordinary construction on the language used here, the fire was not the cause of the loss.' Ibid at 468, per Byles J

ORIGINATING SUMMONS

'The definition in Order LXXI [revoked; see now RSC 1965, Ord 7] of the term "originating summons" is not a very happy one. It would, I think, have been better to say that an "originating summons" is that mode of commencing an action by summons which is now allowed instead of commencing it by a writ. . . . The real meaning of the definition of an "originating summons" is, a summons by which an action may be commenced otherwise than by writ.' *Re Holloway, ex p Pallister* [1894] 2 QB 163 at 166, 167, CA, per Lord Esher MR

ORNAMENTAL TIMBER *See* TIMBER

ORNAMENTS *See also* DESIGN

A distinction must be drawn between those articles which are ornaments of the church in the strict sense of the term and those which are merely decorations, furnishings or fittings. In ecclesiastical law 'ornaments' is not confined, as by modern usage, to articles of decoration or embellishment, but it is used in the larger sense of the word 'ornamentum'; all the several articles used in the performance of the service and rites of the church, including organs and bells, are 'ornaments'.

The term 'ornaments of the church' in the rubric is confined to those articles the use of which in the services and ministrations of the church is prescribed by the First Prayer Book of Edward VI. Thus, the rubric provides for the use, inter alia, of an English Bible, the new prayer book, a poor man's box, a chalice, a corporas, a paten and a bell.

The canons require the provision, inter alia, of a font (with cover), a holy table, articles of communion plate and linen, a reading desk and pulpit, seats for the use of parishioners and others, at least one church bell, a Bible, a Book of Common Prayer and a service book for use at the communion table, an alms box, and the necessary register books.

Articles not expressly provided for by the rubric or canons may be permitted, subject in the case of ornaments to the condition that their use must be consistent with and subsidiary to the services of the church; in the case of other articles such as decorations, the test of legality is whether or not they are in danger of being used for purposes of veneration or adoration. (14 Halsbury's Laws (4th edn) para 961)

'The term "ornaments" in ecclesiastical law is not confined, as by modern usage, to articles of decoration or embellishment, but it is used in the larger sense of the word *ornamentum* which, according to the interpretation of Forcellini's Dictionary, is used *pro quocumque apparatu, seu instrumento*. All the several articles used in the performance of the services and rites of the Church are "Ornaments". Vestments, Books, Cloths, Chalices, and Patens, are amongst church ornaments. . . . In modern times organs and bells are held to fall under this denomination.' *Liddell v Westerton* (1857) Brod & F 117 at 129, PC, per cur.

ORPHANAGE

Australia 'Whether the particular institution is or is not an orphanage is a question of fact, but in answering the question of fact I am not disposed to treat the rules (i.e. of the Institution) as conclusive or as more than a circumstance to be considered. I think that for the purpose of saying what an institution is it is rather more important to see what it does than to see what it can or ought to do. The rules may show what the institution can or ought to do; but—particularly in view of the limits placed upon the powers of statutory corporations—the objects are normally stated in comprehensive rather than restrictive terms. Any competent draftsman is therefore inclined to incorporate the institution with capacity to do things which it may decide to do, but does not necessarily intend to do, and even if the intention exists it does not follow that it is effectuated. I agree with the Deputy Master firstly that it is not enough that some of the inmates are orphans, and secondly, that an institution does not cease to be an orphanage merely because it extends charity in some cases to neglected children who are not orphans. I think that an institution is an orphanage when the main or primary purpose which it is actually fulfilling is to provide and care for orphaned children.' *Re Dodson* [1931] SASR 387 at 390, 391, per Napier J

OSTENSIBLE

'An "actual" authority is a legal relationship between principal and agent created by a consensual agreement to which they alone are parties. Its scope is to be ascertained by applying ordinary principles of construction of contracts, including any proper implications from the express words used, the usages of the trade, or the course of business between the parties. To this agreement the contractor is a stranger; he may be totally ignorant of the existence of any authority on the part of the agent. Nevertheless, if the agent does enter into a contract pursuant to the "actual" authority, it does create contractual rights and liabilities between the principal and the contractor. It may be that this rule relating to "undisclosed principals", which is peculiar to English law, can be rationalised as avoiding circuity of action, for the principal could in equity compel the agent to lend his name in an action to enforce the contract against the contractor, and would at common law be liable to indemnify the agent in respect of the performance of the obligations assumed by the agent under the contract. An "apparent" or "ostensible" authority, on the other hand, is a legal relationship between the principal and the contractor created by a representation, made by the principal to the contractor, intended to be and in fact acted on by the contractor, that the agent has authority to enter on behalf of the principal into a contract of a kind within the scope of the "apparent" authority, so as to render the principal liable to perform any obligations imposed on him by such contract. To the relationship so created the agent is a stranger. He need not be (although he generally is) aware of the existence of the representation. The representation, when acted on by the contractor by entering into a contract with the agent, operates as an estoppel, preventing the principal from asserting that he is not bound by the contract. It is irrelevant whether the agent had actual authority to enter into the contract.' *Freeman v Buckhurst Park Properties (Mangal) Ltd* [1964] 1 All ER 630 at 644, CA, per Diplock LJ

Canada '"Ostensibly" is defined as "open to view; open to public view; conspicuous". An ostensible occupation, therefore, is the employment of a person's time in a certain calling or pursuit so openly and conspicuously that the members of the public coming in contact with such person would know that he was following that calling or pursuit. It does not, to my mind, import an exclusive occupation, nor yet a chief occupation, but it must be in the general way of business and not an intermittent or spasmodic employment.' *Re Dunlop, Quinn v Guernsey* [1927] SCR 512 at 518, 519, SCC, per Lamont J

OTHER

Ejusdem generis rule *See also* EJUSDEM GENERIS

[The words 'where general words follow particular ones, the rule is to construe them as applicable to persons *ejusdem generis*' is sometimes called Lord Tenterden's Rule. Some examples of the application of the rule follow.]

[The Metropolitan Building Act 1855, s 108 (repealed), enacted that no writ or process should be sued out against any district surveyor or 'other person' for anything done until the expiration of one month next after written notice had been delivered to him stating the cause of action.] 'I think . . . some limitation must be put upon those words. . . . Here the protection is confined to any "district-surveyor or other" person, which to my mind shews that it was intended to restrict it to a class of persons *ejusdem generis* with the district-surveyor, and that a tradesman who is employed by the building-owner in doing work on his own premises . . . is not an "other person" of the same class as the district-surveyor.' *Williams v Golding* (1865) LR1CP 69 at 77, 78, per Erle CJ

[A member of an equitable society mortgaged to the society a property to secure principal, interest, his subscription, and 'other moneys' becoming due from the mortgagor to the society.] 'The first covenant, the covenant for payment (which is the first material part on which reliance is placed by the defendants), is a covenant to pay the money advanced by instalments, and also to pay all subscriptions, and other moneys becoming due from the mortgagor to the society. Upon that this observation arises, that the words "all other moneys", following moneys which are particularly described and specified, would prima facie be read as being moneys of a similar kind to those particularly specified. The ordinary rule would, I think, apply, and they would be moneys of a similar kind, debts of a similar kind becoming due from the mortgagor to the society. . . . I see nothing . . . upon the face of the deed, or in the circumstances of the case, to take it out of the ordinary rule, that these other moneys must be *ejusdem generis* with the principal moneys or subscriptions, and it is to be observed that that gives a perfectly sensible and rational construction of the deed, for there are other moneys *ejusdem generis* both with the principal money advanced under the deed and with the subscriptions, which would be covered by that construction.' *Bailes v Sunderland Equitable Industrial Society Ltd* (1886) 55 LT 808 at 810, per Stirling J

[The Railways Clauses Consolidation Act 1845, s 77 enacts that a railway company shall not be entitled to any mines of coal, ironstone, slate, or 'other minerals' unless they are expressly purchased.] 'Questions of nicety have arisen, and may yet arise, as to the particular substances meant to be included in the general words "or other minerals" as these occur in s 77 of the . . . Railways Clauses Act of 1845. . . . The substances to which the argument at the bar has been confined are "ironstone", which is one of the minerals specially excepted in these clauses, and "limestone" which appears to me to be so much *ejusdem generis* with the minerals enumerated that it must necessarily be held to come within the description of "other minerals".' *Midland Rly Co & Kettering, Thrapston & Huntingdon Rly Co v Robinson* (1889) 15 App Cas 19 at 33, per Lord Watson

'I am of opinion that the words, "port charges, pilotages, and other expenses at those ports" which are to be found in the latter of the two parts of the charterparty which have been adverted to, mean that the owners have only to bear port charges, pilotages, and other expenses *ejusdem generis*, and have not to pay for coals, which the charterers by a previous clause have undertaken to provide and pay for.' *The Durham City* (1889) 14 PD 85 at 87, 88, per Brett J

[A charterparty excepted (inter alia) strikes, lock-outs, accidents to railway, and 'other causes beyond charterer's control'.] 'In my opinion this clause must be read as covering exceptions *ejusdem generis* with those that precede it. . . . The contention that because . . . delay arose from the loading of . . . ships in the port in the order of their arrival the charterer is exempt cannot prevail, for it is impossible to treat delay arising from such a cause as due to accident to the railways or as coming within the term "other causes beyond the charterer's control".' *Re Richardsons & Samuel (M) & Co* [1898] 1 QB 261 at 267, CA, per AL Smith LJ

[In *Chandris v Isbrandtesn-Moller Co Inc* [1951] 1 KB 240, CA, Devlin J said: 'If the *ejusdem generis* principle is a rule of automatic application, it becomes of the first importance to determine exactly what the rule is. If it is merely, as I think, an aid to ascertaining the intention of the parties, no point of controversy need arise at all. If there is something to show that the literal meaning of the words is too wide, then they will be given such other meaning as seems best to consort with the intention of the parties. In some cases it may be that they will seem to indicate a genus; in other that they perform the simpler office of expanding the meaning of each enumerated item. If a genus cannot be found, doubtless that is one factor indicating that the parties did not intend to restrict the meaning of the words. But I do not take it to be universally true that whenever a genus cannot be found the words must have been intended to have their literal meaning, whatever other indications there may be to the contrary.']

Canada 'In my judgment the familiar rule that where there are general words following particular and specific words all of one genus, the general words are presumed to be restricted to the same *genus* as the particular words,—applies to the words "grant, subsidy or other assistance" as used in section 20(6)(h) of the Income Tax Act. In this section there are the specific words "grant" and "subsidy" followed by the general words "or other assistance". *GTE Sylvania Canada Ltd v R* [1974] 2 FC 726 at 736, FCTD, per Cattanach J; affirmed [1974] 2 FC 212, FCA

Canada 'Where general words, such as "other bodies of water", are found in a statute immediately following specific words, such as "rivers, streams, watercourses, lakes", which all fall into the same category or genus, the general words should be restricted to the same category or genus of the specific words provided that the specific words do not exhaust the category or genus and provided further that it is not clear from the statute read as a whole that the legislature intended that the general words be given a broad interpretation. If the same category or genus cannot be found for the specific words, the *ejusdem generis* rule does not apply. Also, if the wording of the statute is clear and unambiguous, there is no room for application of the rule.' *Re R in right of Alberta and Very* (1983) 149 DLR (3d) 688 at 706, Alta QB, per Egbert J

In marriage settlement

[A power in a marriage settlement enabled retiring or refusing trustees or the executors or administrators of the last acting trustee to appoint any 'other' person or persons to be a trustee or trustees.] 'The question is what is the meaning of the word "other". Does it mean other than the trustee who is dead? If it does, it is admitted the word is superfluous. Does it mean other than the trustee who is retiring? There again it is quite superfluous, because the retiring trustee would not be appointed; it would not be necessary or possible that he should be appointed. Does it mean other than the trustee residing abroad or becoming incapable? It would have some meaning in those cases, no doubt; a better meaning than if you apply it only to the trustee who is dead or who desires to retire. But why should it not mean other than the person making the appointment as well? I observe that the person making the appointment may be the continuing trustee. The continuing trustee may appoint "any other person or persons to be a trustee or trustees", etc. In that case "other" must mean some other person than the trustee deceased, or going abroad, or retiring, or refusing, or becoming incapable to act, and also other than the trustee making the appointment, that is to say, other than the appointor himself. Or if continuing trustee only refers to the case of a trustee being dead, still "other" must mean other than the continuing trustee himself. He cannot possibly appoint himself. Well, then, take the case of the executors or administrators of the last acting trustee. Can this mean that the executors or administrators of the last acting trustee, who are to appoint any other person or persons to be trustee or trustees, may appoint themselves? The more natural meaning to give to the word "other" is to say that it must be other than the trustee to be replaced, and the person who is replacing him by making the appointment. I have no desire to decide the case simply on this narrow ground, and therefore I have taken the broader question first; but if there be a doubt, or difficulty, or any ambiguity as to whether the word "other" is meant to exclude the appointor as well as the retiring or deceased or other trustee, I am of opinion that the proper mode of construing the word is to say that it does mean to exclude the appointor, because the general practice of conveyancers, the understanding of lawyers, and the purposes of deeds like this are against the notion of a person appointing himself.' *Re Skeats' Settlement, Skeats v Evans* (1889) 42 Ch D 522 at 528, 529, per Kay J

In will

[A testatrix bequeathed a fund upon trust for one of her children for life; and after the death of that child without issue, to the 'others or other' of her children, equally to be divided between or amongst them if more than one.] 'I am asked to hold that the words "others or other" of my children in this will mean the same thing as children surviving at the death of the tenant for life. But I am of opinion that the words must have their ordinary signification. . . . The principal argument in favour of the petitioners' contention is that founded on the words "equally to be divided between or amongst them if more than one", which words, it was said, point to survivorship. But these are the words ordinarily used to give a tenancy in common instead of a joint tenancy, and merely import that an equal distribution is intended, and I cannot merely, because of them, alter the meaning of the words "others or other", and violate the intention of the testatrix. There must be a declaration that the fund in court is divisible in fourths.' *Re Hagen's Trusts* (1877) 46 LJ Ch 665 at 667, per Hall V-C

'Now to look more closely at the words of the codicil. The first part gives clearly an estate to the two sons who were living, . . . and then it proceeds: "and secondly, the eldest son among our grandchildren shall always have the same right thereto",—that must mean the right which had been given to the two sons— . . . "with this understanding, however, that the other heirs who may still be born shall enjoy equal share and right thereto". It is contended that these words, "other heirs", should not be read as applying to children who might be born after the making of the codicil, but that they have reference to grandchildren, and possibly even beyond grandchildren. It appears to their Lordships that the natural construction of these words is, that it was intended to provide for what might have been suggested to the testator and testatrix . . . that another child might possibly be born, and it was necessary to make some provision for that event happening. Their Lordships think they were inserted to provide for that case.' *De Jager v De Jager* (1886) 11 App Cas 411 at 414, PC, per cur.

'I think the true conclusion . . . is that if you find the words "other son" used [in a will], the eldest son not being previously mentioned may take under that description provided there is nothing else in the will which shows a contrary intention. But . . . in no case which I have been able to find, is it laid down that the court is bound necessarily to give that meaning to the word "other" if you find indications of contrary intentions in other parts of the will.' *Locke v Dunlop* (1888) 39 Ch D 387 at 396, per Stirling J; affirmed (1888) 39 Ch D 404

'The question we have to decide is, whether this voluntary settlement included the horses, carriages, harness, and stable furniture which were in the stables and coach-house at the time of the settler's death. . . . In the present case the words are "other goods, chattels, and effects in or upon or belonging to the said leasehold messuage hereinbefore demised, and other goods, chattels, and effects, which shall or may, at any time . . . during the joint lives, be brought into or upon the aforesaid messuage and premises". . . . When you find a man making such a settlement as this upon his wife, and clearly giving her "goods, chattels, and effects" in the coach-house and stables, I think it would be absurd to come to any other conclusion than that he intended to give her all those goods, chattels, and effects which would generally be found in the coach-house and stables, namely, the carriage, horses, and harness.' *Anderson v Anderson* [1895] 1 QB 749 at 752–754, CA, per Lord Esher MR

'The gift over is to "the others and other of my said children". . . . The testator has clearly contemplated that the class to which it is to go over will be or may be a diminishing class, and may consist of one person only, because it is to go to the "others or other". . . . I think . . . that the words "others and other" mean the children other than those upon whose death the gift over is to take effect.' *Re Chaston, Chaston v Seago* (1881) 18 Ch D 218 at 223, per Fry J; applied by Luxmoore J in *Re Crosse, Crosse v Crosse* (1933) 77 Sol Jo 116 at 117

OTHERWISE

[A dog was shipped under a bill of lading which exempted the shipowner from liability for damage arising in providing, dispatching, and navigating the vessel 'or otherwise'. The dog was lost while let loose.] 'For the purposes of my decision I will assume that the loss was caused by the negligence of the shipowner's servants in leaving the dog loose. The shipowners contend that, assuming everything against them, they are protected by the negligence clause. Against that it is said that the dog was not lost from any act, neglect, or default of the defendants' servants in "providing, dispatching, and navigating the vessel", and I think that was so. But the clause goes on "or otherwise", and I think that means "in any other way", and that the clause does apply to the negligence of the butcher in allowing the dog to go loose and be lost.' *Packwood v Union-Castle Mail SS Co Ltd* (1903) 20 TLR 59 at 60, per Walton J

'Under s 10 [of the Private Street Works Act 1892 (repealed; see now the Highways Act 1980, s 207(3)(a))], if the authority thinks it just, and if they are of opinion that the owner of premises benefits by the proposed works, they may apportion the expenses on such owner notwithstanding that the premises do not front or abut on the works, if access thereto from the part of the street upon which the repairs are to be executed is obtained "through a court, passage or otherwise". . . . I have come to the conclusion that the words "or otherwise" must mean some means of access of a similar character to that of a court or passage. . . . It seems to me that what is meant is access through a court or passage or something similar to a court or passage, and not through a street.' *Chatterton v Glanford Rural Council* [1915] 3 KB 707 at 713, per Lord Reading CJ

OUT OF *See also* COURSE OF EMPLOYMENT

[The Workmen's Compensation Act 1906, s 1(1) (repealed; cf now the Social Security Act 1975, s 50) provided for compensation (now benefit for industrial injuries) to be paid in cases of injury arising 'out of' and in the course of employment.] 'In these cases under the

Workmen's Compensation Act a distinction must, I think always be drawn between the doing of a thing recklessly or negligently which the workman is employed to do, and the doing of a thing altogether outside and unconnected with his employment. A peril which arises from the negligent or reckless manner in which an employee does the work he is employed to do may well be held in most cases rightly to be a risk incidental to his employment. Not so in the other cases. For example, if a master employs a servant to carry his (the master's) letters on foot across the fields on a beaten path, or on foot by road to a neighbouring post office, and the servant, having got the letters, went to the stables, mounted his master's horse, and proceeded to ride across country to the post office, was thrown and killed, or went to his master's garage, took out his motor car, and proceeded to drive by road to the post office, came into collision with something and was killed, it could not be held, I think, according to reason or law, that the injury to the servant arose out of his employment, though, in one sense, he was about to do ultimately the thing he was employed to do, namely, to bring his master's letters to the post. In such a case the servant puts himself into a place he was not employed to be in, and had no right to be in—the back of his master's horse, or the seat of his master's motor car. He was doing a thing he was not employed to do, and had no right to attempt to do, namely, to ride his master's horse across country or to drive his motor car. These were altogether outside the scope of his employment. He exposed himself to a risk he was not employed to expose himself to—a risk unconnected with that employment, and which neither of the parties to his contract of service could ever be reasonably supposed to have contemplated as properly belonging or incidental to it. The unfortunate deceased in this case lost his life through the new and added peril to which by his own conduct he exposed himself, not through any peril which his contract of service, directly or indirectly, involved or at all obliged him to encounter. It was not, therefore reasonably incidental to his employment. That is the crucial test. It has been many times adopted. There was not, therefore, to my mind any evidence that the injury the deceased received arose out of his employment.' *Barnes v Nunnery Colliery Co Ltd* [1912] AC 44 at 49, 50, per Lord Atkinson

'In the case of *Conway v Pumpherston Oil Co* [[1911] SC 660] in the Court of Session, I adopted the phrase of Collins LJ and pointed out that there were two sorts of ways of frequent occurrence in which a workman might go outside the sphere of his employment—the first, when he did work which he was not engaged to perform, and the second, when he went into a territory with which he had nothing to do.' *Plumb v Cobden Flour Mills Co Ltd* [1914] AC 62 at 66, per Lord Dunedin

'In inquiring whether or not an injury by accident in fact arises out of the employment, it is surely unnecessary to ask whether such a thing has ever happened before or is likely to happen again within, say, a hundred years, or, for that matter, for ever.' *Trim Joint District School Board of Management v Kelly* [1914] AC 667 at 682, per Lord Loreburn

'In one sense, whenever there is an accident to a drunken man whilst he is in the ambit of his employment it may be said that the accident arose out of the employment because but for his being in the place where the accident occurred the man's drunken condition might have been immaterial. Take for instance the case where a man's work causes him to be close to machinery in motion or in any other dangerous place, it may be said that his employment took him there, and that if he had been at home drunk he would, if he had fallen, have been able to lie on the floor till he was sober. In this way it may be said that this was an additional risk, but in my opinion the accident does not arise out of the employment in such circumstances. It is not sufficient that a drunken man should meet with an accident in the ambit of his employment.' *Nash v Rangatira (Owners)* [1914] 3 KB 978 at 985, CA, per Swinfen Eady LJ

'There may be causes of danger arising to all employees, which causes are not confined to the individual situation, but are general and applicable to the employment as a whole. It may be that that employment is underground, with all the risks attached to underground work. It may be in the air or on the sea, with a special exposure to the dangers relative to such elements; or it may be on the surface of the earth, in surroundings which are those in peril. In all such cases it is quite possible to figure injuries by accident in the course of and arising out of the employment, which are totally disconnected with the nature of the employment upon which the workman was generally or for the moment engaged, but which, without any doubt, sprang from the employment in the sense that it was on account of the obligations or conditions thereof, and on that account alone, that he incurred the danger.' *Thom (or Simpson) v Sinclair* [1917] AC 127 at 142, per Lord Shaw of Dunfermline

'Where the risk is one shared by all men, whether in or out of employment, in order to show that [an] accident arose out of the employment it must be established that special exposure to it is involved. But when a workman is sent into the street on his master's business, whether it be occasionally or habitually, his employment necessarily involves exposure to the risks of the streets and injury from such a cause arises out of his employment.' *Dennis v White (A J) & Co* [1917] AC 479 at 482, 483, per Lord Finlay LC

'The expression "arising out" no doubt imports some kind of causal relation with the employment; but it does not logically necessitate direct or physical causation. . . . The expression "cause" may always be regarded as including an infinity of conditions, but in ordinary life we have to look for those which are relevant to the standpoint of the inquiry. A direct physical cause will, of course, fall among those which are included in s 1 of the Workmen's Compensation Act [1906 (repealed)] but the scope of the Act and the inquiry which it enjoins appear to extend also to the general conditions under which the workman has been directed to act. If he simply dies of heart disease the effect of which has not been aggravated by anything which his employment led to his doing, or if he is struck by lightning in a place where the conditions of his employment rendered him no more exposed to danger than any member of the public not so employed, the injury will not have resulted from the conditions under which he was being employed. But if, for example, he is sent on a message on a bicycle and an ordinary collision which might have happened to anybody takes place, then what has happened would not have done so had he not been engaged in fulfilling his duty, and there is liability. . . . If, in the course of his employment, the workman meets with injury by an accident which has arisen directly out of circumstances encountered because to encounter them fell within the scope of the employment, compensation may be claimed. His own negligence may have been an immediately contributing factor. If, as in the present case, his death has resulted, such negligence is immaterial. The question is whether circumstances such as I have referred to are to be found among the causal conditions of the accident. These may have amounted to no more than passive and inert surroundings, requisite only to provide circumstances which admitted of the accident being occasioned by his own movement. Active physical causation by the surroundings is not required in order to satisfy what is implied by the expression "arising out of the employment".' *Upton v Great Central Rly Co* [1924] AC 302 at 306–308, per Lord Haldane

'The words "out of" connote origin. In matters physical a plant arises "out of" a seed—a vessel may be wrecked "out of" the violence of the waves. In matters metaphysical a motor-car accident may arise "out of" the carelessness or "out of" the inefficiency of the driver. The words indicate an origin, a source or a cause. It has been said that the expression "arising out of the employment" applies to the employment as such—to its nature, its conditions, its obligations, and its incidents. I am disposed to agree with this if the wideness of the language does not lead to uncertainty in the meaning. A first step is to ascertain whether the accident had its origin in the employment and therefore arose out of it.' *St Helens Colliery Co Ltd v Hewitson* [1924] AC 59 at 91, per Lord Wrenbury

Australia 'The proper construction of these words is now fairly well settled. The words "out of" require that the injury had its origin in the employment, whilst the words "in the course of" are not equivalent to "during"; the injury must occur in the course of the employment, that is, whilst the worker is doing something which is part of his service to his employer or master or incidental to the employment, or, in other words, whether the workman was at the time of the injury about his own business or that of his master.' *South Maitland Railways Pty Ltd v James* (1943) 67 CLR 496 at 502, per Starke J

New Zealand [The Workers' Compensation Act 1922 (NZ), s 3(1) (repealed; see now the Accident Compensation Act 1982, s 57) provided that if in any employment to which the Act applied personal injury by accident arising 'out of' and in the course of the employment was caused to a worker, his employer should be liable to pay compensation in accordance with the provisions of the Act.] 'The burden of proof is on the plaintiff to show that the accident arose out of and in the course of the employment. The difficulty is the rule or test to be applied to determine this. . . . The cases cited for the plaintiff are illustrations of how the law has been applied to the facts of those cases. I have examined those cases with a view to extracting an underlying rule or test. . . . These cases all point to the test enunciated by Lord Sumner in *Lancashire and Yorkshire Railway Co v Highley* [[1917] AC 352], and adopted by Viscount Cave in *Bourton v Beauchamp and Beauchamp* [[1920] AC 1001], and by Lord Birkenhead in *AG Moore and Co v Donnelly* [[1921] 1 AC 329], as containing "an admirable summary of the law". Lord Sumner there said: "I doubt if any universal test can be found. Analogies, not always so close as they seem to be at first sight, are often resorted to, but in the last analysis each case is decided on its own facts. There is, however, in my opinion, one test which is always at any rate applicable, because it arises upon the very words of the statute, and it is generally of some real assistance. It is this: Was it part of the injured person's employment to hazard, to suffer, or to do that which caused his injury? If yea, the accident arose out of his employment. If nay, it did not, because, what it was not part of the employment to hazard, to suffer, or to do, cannot well be the cause of an accident arising out of the employment." I adopt that test as the proper test to apply in this case.' *Sadd v New Zealand Co-operative Dairy Co Ltd* [1946] NZLR 249 at 257, 258; per Ongley J; also reported [1946] GLR at 111, 113

OUTER DOOR

[The plaintiffs occupied a warehouse within a courtyard. The defendant, a broker, gained entry to the courtyard for the purposes of levying a distress, and did so without touching the outer gate; but once inside the courtyard he broke open the main door of the warehouse and distrained.] 'The doctrine of the inviolability of the outer doors of a house and its precinct has long been established by English law. The principle is one which carries us back in imagination to wilder times, when the outer door of a house, or the outer gates and enclosures of land, were an essential protection, not merely against fraud, but violence. The proposition that a man's house is his castle, which was crystallised into a maxim by the judgment in *Semayne's Case* [(1604) 5 Co Rep 91] and by Lord Coke, dates back to days far earlier still, when it was recognised as a limitation imposed by law on all process except that which was pursued at the King's suit and in his name. A landlord's right to distrain for arrears of rent is itself only a survival of one among a multitude of distraints, which, both in England and other countries, belonged to a primitive period when legal procedure still retained some of the germs of a semi-barbarous custom of reprisals, of which instances abound in the early English books and in the Irish Senchus Mor. Later, all creditors and all aggrieved persons who respected the king's peace, the sheriff in a civil suit, and the landlord in pursuit of his private remedy for rent and services, were both of them held at bay by a bolted door or barred gate. To break open either was to deprive the owner of protection against the outer world for his family, his goods and furniture, and his cattle. "The law," says the court in *Semayne's Case*, "abhors the destruction or breaking of any house." The landlord (like the sheriff in a civil suit) could only therefore enter by an open door or an open window—*per ostia et fenestras*. The form of plea which he pleaded in his defence, if sued for trespass, was that he had found the house open—*trove la meason ouverte*. . . . This immunity of the outer door extended not merely to dwelling-houses, but to all detached buildings and enclosures. . . . It was indeed contended before me that the law was only that the landlord might not break a door to enter on the demised premises, but that once lawfully on them he might break doors. This contention seems to me one utterly untenable. The doctrine of the law is far stricter. *Lee v Gansel* [(1774) 1 Cowp 1] only shows that an officer, in the execution of mesne process, who has gained peaceable entry through an outer door may break open the inner door of a lodger. The case does not impugn the ancient principle that the outer door of a building may not be broken open either by a landlord or sheriff except at the suit of the King. Finally, it was urged on behalf of the defendants that the broken door of the warehouse was not its outer door within the meaning of the proposition. It was not, it is true, the outer gate of the courtyard. That opened upon the lane. But the fact that it was not one of the outer enclosures of the whole premises demised is nothing if it was the outer door of the building. It protected what was inside the building from persons who were in, or might obtain access to, the courtyard. As to this point the story speaks for itself. It was through this door, and this door only, that the broker entered the warehouse from outside. The plaintiffs, therefore, are entitled to succeed and to recover damages from the defendants.' *American Concentrated Must*

Corpn v Hendry (1893) 62 LJQB 388 at 389–391, CA, per Bowen LJ

OUTFIT

'The question in this case was, whether the alteration of this policy, from a policy upon ship and out-fit to one on ship and goods, required an additional stamp. . . . The policy was "at and from London to the South Seas, during the ship's stay and fishing there, and at and from thence to Great Britain, etc". The alteration was made from ship and out-fit to ship and goods, by consent of the underwriters, after the ship had sailed on the voyage insured, and of course after the policy had fully attached upon what was, at the time of such sailing, the thing or subject insured, viz ship and out-fit. Out-fit, particularly for such a voyage as is described in the policy, differs materially from what is comprehended under the term goods. Out-fit, in a fishing voyage, principally consists in the apparatus and instruments necessary for the taking of fish, seals, etc, and the disposing of them, when taken, in such a manner as to bring home the oil, blubber, bone, skins, and other animal produce of the adventure, with the greatest convenience and advantage. As far as the out-fit consists of provisions put on board for the use of the crew, it is (according to the case of *Brough v Whitmore* [)1791) 4 Term Rep 206]) covered by an insurance on ship, being in effect part of the necessary furniture, stores, and equipment of every ship proceeding on a voyage. But out-fit, though it may in this qualified sense be considered as part of the ship or ship's furniture, yet it cannot be considered as goods in any proper sense of that word; i.e. as part of the wares or cargo for sale, laden on board the ship; still less as part of the homeward bound cargo in this voyage out and home; recollecting that in a fishing voyage the only cargo on board the ship from first to last is, in general, the homeward bound cargo, consisting of the immediate produce and result of the fishing adventure.' *Hill v Patten* (1807) 8 East 373 at 374, 375, per cur.

OUTGOINGS

The term 'outgoings' is of very wide import, and includes not merely rates, rent, repairs and the ordinary expenses of cultivating or managing . . . property, but also expenses, even if of a capital nature, of works executed by local authorities under their public health, highway and other powers which are recoverable from the owner, and which are also, in general, charged on the property. (42 Halsbury's Laws (4th edn) para 131)

Australia 'As to what "outgoings" [in a will which gave the use of premises to testator's housekeeper 'free from payment by her of any rent rates taxes insurance or other outgoings'] does mean, I think its proper interpretation in the will is any annual payment, similar to rates, taxes and insurance premiums which are ordinarily payable by a tenant for life.' *Re Jose* [1941] SASR 26 at 30, per Murray CJ

New Zealand '"Outgoings" is a proper word to use in connection with rent, salaries, and expenses of management.' *Yates v Yates* (1913) 33 NZLR 281 at 285, per Cooper J; also reported 15 GLR 623 at 625

Estate management expenses

'What is meant by the expression "all outgoings of the said hereditaments properly chargeable . . . and not discharged in my life time", which the testator directs to be paid? . . . We are of opinion that the expression "outgoings of the hereditaments" in the clause under consideration, ought to be construed in the larger and popular sense as including every expense relating to the estate which, in the ordinary course of management, would require to be made in order to maintain the estate in a fit state to earn rent, or would be a proper deduction before ascertaining the net rent receivable as income. . . . The result is that in our opinion all such expenses remaining unpaid at the testator's death, as in the ordinary course of management as carried on by the testator would come into charge against the rents due or accruing due at the time of death, treating each estate as a whole, will have to be deducted.' *Re Cleveland's (Duke) Estate, Wolmer (Viscount) v Forester* [1894] 1 Ch 164 at 174, 175, CA, per Davey LJ

Expenses of demolishing dangerous building

[A clause in a contract for the sale of land provided that the purchaser should be entitled, after completion of the purchase, to possession, or to the receipt of rents and profits, from 8 May (the date for completion), all 'outgoings' up to that date being cleared by the vendor.] 'A contract was entered into on 30th of March, 1893, by which the defendant agreed to sell certain land to the plaintiff. The buildings which were on this land had before that date been certified as dangerous . . . and an order to pull down the building was made before 8th of May, . . . the date fixed . . . for the completion of the purchase. . . . What are the rights of the parties? The defendant, the vendor, was, on 8th of May, under an order to pull down the buildings, which order he did not carry out. After 8th of May the county council did the work, and put pressure upon the plaintiff to compel him to pay the expenses. The plaintiff now sues the defendant to recover the amount of the expenses so paid. . . . I am of opinion . . . that the expenses in question are covered by the expression "outgoings". . . . I am of opinion that the plaintiff is entitled to recover in respect of all outgoings up to 8th of May.' *Tubbs v Wynne* [1897] 1 QB 74 at 77, 79, 80, per Collins J

Improvement ordered by local authority

[A lessee covenanted to pay all rates, taxes, assessments, and 'outgoings' of every description, for the time being payable in respect of the premises, as they became due.] 'It is clearly established by the decisions that the word "outgoings" in such a covenant covers expenditure of the kind here in question. These expenses were incurred in obedience to an order made by the local authority for the alteration of the system of drainage on the premises, so as to bring it up to the modern standard. . . . It is every-day experience that local authorities require such improved sanitary arrangements. That being so, if a tenant makes an agreement in perfectly clear and unambiguous terms that he will bear all outgoings, I do not see how we can throw aside the plain meaning of the language used, and introduce some imitation of that meaning, which it would be very difficult, if not impossible, to define.' *Stockdale v Ascherberg* [1904] 1 KB 447 at 449, 450, per Collins MR

Rates and taxes

'The precise meaning of "outgoing" may be open to doubt; but it is certainly a large word and may fairly comprehend rates and taxes.' *R v Shaw* (1848) 12 QB 419 at 427, per Patteson J

OUTHOUSE

'It has been settled from ancient times, that an outhouse must be that which belongs to a dwelling-house, and is in some respects parcel of such dwelling-house. . . . This building being wholly unconnected with the dwelling-house, it is not included in the legal definition of outhouse.' *R v Haughton* (1833) 5 C & P 555 at 559, per Taunton J

OUTPUT

'What is the ordinary meaning of the words "annual output of coal and dross from the mineral field?" . . . I suppose there is no doubt that in their ordinary sense they mean all the coal and dross that is brought to the surface within the field. . . . I find no repugnancy in adopting the primary sense of the words.' *Dalgleish v Fife Coal Co Ltd* (1892) 30 SLR 58 at 59, per the Lord President

OUTPUT TAX *See* INPUT TAX

OUTRAGE

'It should be emphasised that "outrage", like "corrupt", is a very strong word. "Outraging public decency" goes considerably beyond offending the susceptibilities of, or even shocking, reasonable people.' *Knuller (Publishing, Printing & Promotions) Ltd v Director of Public Prosecutions* [1972] 2 All ER 898 at 936, per Lord Simon of Glaisdale

OVEN

'Oven' includes any form of retort or container used to subject solid fuel to any process involving the application of heat. (Clean Air Act 1956, s 34(1))

OVER *See also* ABOVE

'Prima facie, a bridge over a river or over a street means a bridge with an arch which shall clearly span it; and, if I covenant to build a bridge over a river or a road, I must not block up or obstruct any part of it with piers or abutments, but must make an arch which shall span completely over without contracting it.' *Clarke v Manchester, Sheffield & Lincolnshire Rly Co* (1861) 1 John & H 631 at 636, 637, per Page Wood V-C

[Section 67 of a local Act provided that in the borough of Liverpool no projection of any kind should be made in front of any building 'over or upon' the pavement.] 'The 67th section is one of a string of sections having reference to the footways. . . . The object of the string of sections, of which the 67th is one, appears to us to be to keep the pavement clear for the foot passengers, and to prevent obstructions to the passage of the street. The words "over or" appear to have been inserted to prevent the Act being evaded by putting obstructions a little above the pavement but not exactly upon it. . . . The words, as it seems to us, must be read as if they ran "over or upon the pavement so as to obstruct the passage along it".' *Goldstraw v Duckworth* (1880) 5 QBD 275 at 277, per cur.

OVERHAUL *See* SERVICE

OVERSEAS

'Overseas territory' means any territory or country outside the United Kingdom. (Overseas Aid Act 1968, s 4)

United States A shipment by water or by air or a contract contemplating such shipment is 'overseas' insofar as by usage of trade or agreement it is subject to the commercial, financing or shipping practices characteristic of international deep water commerce. (Uniform Commercial Code 1978, s 2–323(3))

OVERSEAS CUSTOMER

For the purposes of this section [limitation of tax deductions in respect of business entertaining expenses] 'overseas customer' means, in relation to any United Kingdom trader—

(a) any person who is not ordinarily resident nor carrying on a trade in the United Kingdom and avails himself, or may be expected to avail himself, in the course of a trade carried on by him outside the United Kingdom, of any goods, services or facilities which it is the trade of the United Kingdom trader to provide; and
(b) any person who is not ordinarily resident in the United Kingdom and is acting, in relation to such goods, services or facilities, on behalf of an overseas customer within paragraph (a) of this sub-section or on behalf of any government or public authority of a country outside the United Kingdom.

(Finance Act 1965, s 15(6))

OVERT ACT *See* MENS REA

OVERTAKE

'Unless one ship is going faster than another it is impossible to say that she is overtaking another. Can we, then, form a definition of the difference between crossing ships and overtaking ships? It seems to me that this may be a very good definition—I will not say that it is exhaustive, or that it may not on some occasion be found to be short of comprising every case, but I think it is a very good rule—that if the ships are in such a position, and are on such courses and at such distances, that if it were night the hinder ship could not see any part of the side lights of the forward ship, then they cannot be said to be crossing ships, although their courses may not be exactly parallel. It would not do, I think, to limit the angle of the crossing too much, but a limit to that extent it seems to me is a very useful and practical rule. And then if the hinder if two such ships is going faster than the other she is an overtaking ship.' *The Franconia* (1876) 2 PD 8 at 12, CA, per cur.

OVERTIME

In this Part of this Act [Part VI: employment of women and young persons (hours and holidays)] 'overtime employment' means, in relation to any woman or young person, any period during which that woman or young person is at work in the factory outside the period of employment fixed for the day for that woman or young person by a notice under this Part of this Act; and for the purposes of this Part of this Act—

(a) in calculating hours of overtime employment any fraction of an hour less than half an hour shall be treated as half an hour and any fraction of an hour greater than half an hour shall be treated as an hour; and
(b) in reckoning for any factory, part of a factory, or set of persons, the aggregate hours of overtime employment or the number of weeks in which overtime employment can take place, account shall be taken of every period during which any woman or young person is employed overtime in that factory, part or set.

(Factories Act 1961, s 89(10))

'The employment of women in factories is permitted [under the Factory and Workshop Act 1901, s 49 (repealed; see now the Factories Act 1961, s 89)] only during specified periods of the day, in all cases limited to twelve hours, which may be from 6 to 6, or from 7 to 7, or from 8 to 8, according to the hour at which the day's work begins; but there is this exception—that on a limited number of days in the year overtime not exceeding two hours may be worked. It is difficult to say whether overtime means the two hours from 6 to 8, or from 7 to 9, or from 8 to 10, for this must vary with the different sets of workers, according to the hour at which they started work, though I think that overtime begins as soon as the twelve hours of the ordinary day are finished.' *Smith v Silbray, Hall & Co* [1903] 2 KB 707 at 712, DC, per Wills J

'For the wages contracted for in the articles the seaman is bound to give his full services, and there is no such thing recognised as overtime or payment in respect of overtime merely because the seaman is called upon to work for longer hours than are expected by the parties when they enter into the contract.' *Harrison v Dodd* (1914) 111 LT 47 at 49, DC, per Channell J

New Zealand '"Overtime" . . . may mean overtime in terms of time or money.' *Bodley v Slaughter* [1916] NZLR 75 at 81, per Hosking J; also reported [1916] GLR 156 at 158

OWING

'The word "indebted" describes the condition of a person when there is a present debt, whether it be payable *in præsenti* or *in futuro*, and I think that the words "all debts owing or accruing" mean the same thing. They describe all *debita in præsenti*, whether *solvenda in futuro*, or *solvenda in præsenti*. The material question which has been argued before us is this: does the meaning go further, and does it include debts which may hereafter arise? If they may hereafter arise, it is possible also they may not hereafter arise, and it would require explicit words to include such future possible debts.' *Webb v Stenton* (1883) 11 QBD 518 at 529, CA, per Fry LJ

Australia [The articles of a company provided that when a member's shares were forfeited he had forthwith to pay what was 'owing'.] 'The call is "owing" as soon as it is made, owing *in præsenti*, although payment thereof cannot be enforced until the date at which it is resolved that it shall be paid: but when a member's shares have been forfeited then he has "forthwith" to pay what is owing: he does not get the benefit of the future day fixed for payment. He has to pay at once all the calls which were then owing.' *Land Mortgage Bank of Victoria Ltd v McConnell* (1902) 28 VLR 19 at 23, per cur.

OWN

'Rule 11 of Order XVI of the Rules [of the Supreme Court] of 1883 [revoked; see now RSC 1965, Ord 15, r 8] . . . is: "No person shall be added as a plaintiff suing without a next friend, or as the next friend of a plaintiff under any disability, without his own consent in writing thereto." What is the meaning of that? But for the word "own" I should have thought that a person whose solicitor consents for him in his presence would be bound; but when the history of the rule is looked at it will be seen that "own" is an abbreviated mode of expressing what is expressed more at length in s 34 [repealed] of the Common Law Procedure Act 1852, where it is provided that persons to be added as plaintiffs must consent either in person or "by writing under his, her, or their hands" to be so joined. The language of that Act makes it plain that the consent must be the consent of the party himself in writing.' *Fricker v Van Grutten* [1896] 2 Ch 649 at 655, 656, CA, per Lindley LJ

[A testator by his will bequeathed certain property to his wife for life, and declared that at her death the property should be divided equally among his 'own brothers and sisters'.] 'The question in this case is whether the gift to the testator's brothers and sisters included those of the half blood as well as of the whole blood. Now, the words are not "my" brothers and sisters, but "my own" brothers and sisters. There is no suggestion that the testator had any brothers-in-law or sisters-in-law, but he had brothers and sisters of the half blood. In this state of things I think the testator intended to refer to his brothers and sisters born of the whole blood—of the same parents. The gift is expressed to be to the own brothers and sisters born "at her" (the wife's) "death". "At her death" indicates, in my opinion, the brothers and sisters then in existence. The natural meaning is that the property was to be divided between the testator's brothers and sisters of the whole blood; and no case has been cited that compels me to come to a different conclusion.' *Re Dowson, Dowson v Beadle* (1909) 101 LT 671 at 672, per Joyce J

OWN (Possess)

Canada 'Does the word "own" have but one meaning in a plain and literal sense? Clearly, in everyday English usage, the word "own" may have different meanings depending upon the context in which it is used. It may have the significance of full and complete legal title to an object as well as possession of the object. It would be totally in accordance with common usage for one who had just purchased a book which was in the purchaser's hand to declare that he or she "owned" the book. On the other hand, a person might, in accordance with ordinary English usage, say that he or she owned the house which, in fact, was mortgaged and was leased, even though the speaker would not have legal title in the sense of *fee simple* to the premises and was neither in possession of nor entitled to possession of the premises. Ownership therefore appears to be a question of mixed fact and law and its meaning in any particular case will depend upon the context in which it is used.' *R v Kentish* (1979) 96 DLR (3d) 706 at 717, Ont Co Ct, per Lyon Co Ct J

OWN RIGHT *See* RIGHT

OWNER

Ownership consists of innumerable rights over property, for example the rights of exclusive enjoyment, of destruction, alteration and alienation, and of maintaining and recovering possession of the property from all other persons. Those rights are conceived not as separately existing, but as merged in one general right of ownership.

The ownership of goods differs from the ownership of land in that the common law did not treat land as the subject of absolute ownership but only of tenure. The common law also did not recognise the possibility of the ownership of goods being split up into lesser successive interests or estates, nor did it contemplate remainders or reversions in chattels.

Ownership is nevertheless divisible to some extent. For example one or more of the collection of rights constituting ownership may be detached. Thus prima facie an owner is entitled to possession or to recover possession of his goods against all the world, a right which a dispossessed owner may exercise by peaceable retaking. He may, however, voluntarily or involuntarily part with possession, for example by the pledging, lending, hiring out, bailment, theft or loss of his goods, in any of which cases he is left with a right of ownership without possession, accompanied or not accompanied, as the case may be, with the right to possess. Ownership is also divorced from possession where the goods are in possession of a person who has a lien on them, or when they are seized under a distress and until a statutory sale is made.

In the case of trusts, the legal ownership is usually in the trustee, and the beneficiary is said to have a beneficial or equitable interest in the trust property. (35 Halsbury's Laws (4th edn) paras 1127, 1128)

'Owner', in relation to a conveyance which is the subject of a hiring agreement or hire-purchase agreement, means the person in possession of the conveyance under that agreement. (Theft Act 1968, s 12(7)(b))

'Owner', in relation to a vehicle which is the subject of a hiring agreement or hire-purchase agreement, means the person in possession of the vehicle under that agreement. (Road Traffic Act 1988, s 192(1))

'Owner' means, in relation to land, a person, other than a mortgagee not in possession, who is for the time being entitled to dispose of the fee simple of the land, and includes also a person holding, or entitled to the rents and profits of, the land under a lease or agreement. (Agricultural Statistics Act 1979, s 6(1))

'Owner', in relation to any premises, means a person, other than a mortgagee not in possession, who, whether in his own right or as trustee or agent for any other person, is entitled to receive the rack rent of the premises or, where the premises are not let at a rack rent, would be so entitled if the premises were so let. (Highways Act 1980, s 325(1))

'Owner', in relation to premises—

(a) means a person (other than a mortgagee not in possession) who is for the time being entitled to dispose of the fee simple in the premises, whether in possession or in reversion, and
(b) includes also a person holding or entitled to the rents and profits of the premises under a lease of which the unexpired term exceeds three years.

(Housing Act 1985, s 56)

[The defendant, as 'owner' or proprietor of a messuage, was charged with not having kept such messuage in a state of repair, as a result of which a neighbouring messuage was damaged.] 'The defendant's counsel justly relied upon the case of *Russell v Shenton* [(1842) 3 QB 449], in which . . . it was held that the duty of cleansing and repairing drains, and preventing them from being a nuisance to neighbours, is prima facie that of the occupier; that the terms "owner and proprietor" do not imply actual occupation; and that if the owner and proprietor of drains as distinguished from the occupier, is charged with neglect to cleanse, and consequent injury to the plaintiff, some special ground of liability ought to be stated in the declaration. . . . The term "owner" , as well as "proprietor", is ambiguous. It may mean that the defendant had the whole legal interest in the house, so that no one also had an estate in possession or reversion, or that he had the subsisting legal interest at the time of the wrong complained of, or that he was owner of the whole or some interest as distinguished from that of the tenant in possession.' *Chauntler v Robinson* (1849) 4 Exch 163 at 169, 170, per cur.

[The Police (Property) Act 1897, s 1(1) provides that where property has come into the possession of the police in connection with their investigation of a suspected offence, a court of summary jurisdiction may make an order for the delivery of the property to the person appearing to be the 'owner'.] 'I have listened to counsel for the appellants' argument and would readily accept that in certain circumstances the word "owner" can have a meaning different from the ordinary popular meaning. The popular meaning of "owner" is a person who is entitled to the goods in question, a person whose goods they are, not simply the person who happens to have them in his hands at any given moment. I have little doubt that in s 1 "owner" is to be given that ordinary popular meaning, which lay justices would naturally give to it, using the word in the ordinary layman's sense. I think that that conclusion is underlined by the fact that the draftsman is distinguishing between "possession" and "ownership" because the section, it will be remembered began with the phrase "where any property has come into the possession of the police".' *Raymond Lyons & Co Ltd v Metropolitan Police Comr* [1975] 1 All ER 335 at 338, per Lord Widgery CJ

Canada 'At common law "owner" is an indefinite expression and may mean anyone who has an interest.' *Zed v Fullerton* (1944) 17 MPR 417 at 419, NSBC, per Baxter CJ

New Zealand [The Oil in Navigable Waters Act 1965, s 2(1) (repealed) defined the term 'owner' as follows:—' "Owner" in relation to any ship, includes any agent in New Zealand of the owner and any charterer to whom the ship may be demised'. The question was whether this definition also included the agent of the charterer of a ship.] 'I hold that the definition of "owner" in this Act includes two categories. The first is the agent in New Zealand of the owner and the second is any charterer to whom the ship may be demised; but the legislature has not seen fit to make the agent of the charterer liable to the penal provisions of s 6(1).' *Russell & Somers Ltd v Auckland Harbour Board* [1973] 2 NZLR 390 at 392, per Wilson J

In Merchant Shipping Acts

'Owner', in relation to a registered ship, means the person registered as its owner, except that in relation to a ship owned by a State which is operated by a person registered as the ship's operator, it means the person registered as its operator. (Merchant Shipping (Oil Pollution) Act 1971, s 20)

Of mine or quarry

(1) Subject to the provisions of this section, in this Act the expression 'owner' means, in relation to a mine or quarry, the person for the time being entitled to work it.

(2) Where the working of a quarry is wholly carried out by a contractor on behalf of the person entitled to work it, the contractor shall, to the exclusion of that person, be taken for the purposes of this Act to be the owner of the quarry.

(3) Where two or more persons are entitled to work a quarry independently, that one of those persons who is the licensor of the others shall, to the exclusion of the others, be taken for the purposes of this Act to be the owner of the quarry.

(4) Where the business of a person who, by virtue of the foregoing provisions of this section is, for the purposes of this Act, to be taken to be owner of a mine or quarry is carried on by a liquidator, receiver or manager, or by some other person authorised to carry it on by an order of a court of competent jurisdiction, the liquidator, receiver, manager or other person shall be taken for the purposes of this Act to be an additional owner of the mine or quarry. (Mines and Quarries Act 1954, s 181)

Of trees

In relation to trees, 'owner' means the owner of the land on which the trees are growing and, in the case of trees which have been felled, means the person who was the owner immediately before the felling. (Forestry Act 1967, s 34(4))

Of vehicle

Canada [The Vehicles and Highway Traffic Act, RSA 1955, c 356, s 130 (now the Highway

Traffic Act, RSA 1980, c H-7, s 181) dealt with the vicarious liability of an 'owner' of a motor vehicle.] 'There is a logical reason why the registered owner should be treated as "owner" within the meaning of the Act because the very purpose of the registration is to give notice to all users of the highway of the identity of an individual to whom they may look as owner in the event of an accident. In the present case, however, the contention that the father was the owner within the meaning of s 130 does not rest upon registration alone. Here the father was the purchaser of the motor vehicle in conformity with the terms of a conditional-sale contract which he had signed and the son had not. It is true that the son made all payments under this contract from his own resources but the contract was obtained on the credit of the father and the payments thereunder were not fully discharged until after the accident had occurred. With all respect to the members of the Appellate Division, I agree with the learned trial judge that a valid sale of this motor vehicle had been made to the defendant Peter Pidoborozny (the father) and that he was the owner at common law, notwithstanding the fact that his son had made the payments under the conditional-sale contract and had had exclusive possession of the vehicle from the date of its purchase.' *Hayduk v Pidoborozny* [1972] 4 WWR 522 at 527, 528, SCC, per Ritchie J

Reputed owner *See* REPUTED OWNER

OWNER-OCCUPIER

(1) Subject to the following provisions of this section, in these provisions 'owner-occupier', in relation to a hereditament, means a person who—

(a) occupies the whole or a substantial part of the hereditament in right of an owner's interest therein, and has so occupied the hereditament or that part thereof during the whole of the period of six months ending with the date of service [of a blight notice]; or

(b) occupied, in right of an owner's interest, the whole or a substantial part of the hereditament during the whole of a period of six months ending not more than twelve months before the date of service, the hereditament, or that part thereof, as the case may be, having been unoccupied since the end of that period.

(2) Subject to the following provisions of this section, in these provisions 'owner-occupier', in relation to an agricultural unit, means a person who—

(a) occupies the whole of that unit, and has occupied it during the whole of the period of six months ending with the date of service; or

(b) occupied the whole of that unit during the whole of a period of six months ending not more than twelve months before the date of service,

and at all times material for the purposes of paragraph (a) or paragraph (b) of this subsection, as the case may be, has been entitled to an owner's interest in the whole or part of that unit. (Town and Country Planning Act 1971, s 203)

[Subsection (3) of the section goes on to define 'resident owner-occupier'; sub-s (4) defines 'owner's interest' and 'date of service'.]

In this section [which deals with the right to compensation for depreciation caused by the use of public works] 'owner-occupier', in relation to land in a hereditament, means the person who owns the whole or a substantial part of the land in right of an owner's interest there in and, in relation to land in an agricultural unit, means a person who occupies the whole of that unit and is entitled, while so occupying it, to an owner's interest in the whole or any part of that land. (Land Compensation Act 1973, s 2(5))

[Cf also s 41(9) of the Act of 1973.]

OWNER'S RISK

'The goods in question, consisting of waxwork figures, were sent by the defendants' railway from Chester to be carried to Halifax, under a special contract which described them as being carried "at owner's risk". The greater part of the goods arrived safely; the remainder, consisting of twenty cases, did not reach their destination until several days afterwards, having been delayed on the journey and damaged in consequence of the negligence of the servants of the company, of which there was abundant evidence for the jury. The court in *Robinson v Great Western Rly Co* [(1865) 35 LJCP 123], determined, upon a contract in terms very similar to those of the contract in the present case, that the words "at owner's risk" only exempted the company from the ordinary risks incurred by goods in going along the railway, and does not cover injury from delay caused by the negligence of the company. That case is directly in point, the only difference being that there the thing carried was live stock, and here goods.' *D'Arc v*

London & North Western Rly Co (1873) LR 9 CP 325 at 330, per Lord Coleridge CJ

'A railway company which holds itself out to carry a particular commodity, say cherries, carries that commodity prima facie as a "common carrier" with all the liability attaching to that calling. It can by a proper special contract within s 7 of 17 & 18 Vict c 31 [Railway and Canal Traffic Act 1854 (repealed)], limit those responsibilities. It is well-established law that the "owner's risk" clause can only be effective in cases in which the railway company affords the consignor an alternative rate below the general rate.' *Gunyon v South Eastern & Chatham Rly Co's Managing Committee* [1915] 2 KB 370 at 375, DC, per Lawrence J

OYSTER LAYING

'The words oyster-layings would not pass the privilege of getting oysters; because those words only import a privilege of laying oysters there, and it might be doubtful whether it would give a right to take them.' *Scratton v Brown* (1825) 4 B & C 485 at 503, 504, per Littledale J

'For a long series of years the plaintiff and his predecessors have been the occupiers of certain oyster beds, which are constructions of the nature of artificial ponds, high up on the foreshore of the locality, into which beds or ponds oysters that have been dredged elsewhere are brought to be laid down in order to fatten, and to be taken from those beds to the market. . . . I have come to the conclusion that an oyster bed of this kind, which I prefer to call by the older and unambiguous term of an "oyster laying", has nothing whatever to do with a several oyster fishery, and can exist quite independently of the existence of such a fishery. If we consider what is the purpose of such a bed, one sees that it has nothing in common with rights of fishing. Rights of fishing signify the right to catch that species of creatures known as *feræ naturæ* which exist in the sea, and there is no doubt that when, as in a several oyster fishery, or in a public oyster fishery, you dredge oysters from their natural beds, you are fishing, you are taking things in respect of which, in the case of a public fishery, nothing in the nature of a proprietory right exists in anyone, and are appropriating them and making them your own property. But an "oyster laying" does not come into operation until the act of appropriation is finished. It exists only for the purpose of being used in connection with chattels the property of which is in some individual. The oysters are first caught or purchased by the owner, they are then laid down in the "oyster laying" for the purpose of improving, and, unless the owner by so laying them down has committed an act of abandonment, the property still remains in him. . . . The position where these "oyster layings" are usually placed is high up on the foreshore, where they are formed in the shape of shallow ponds, covered by the flux and reflux of the tide, but by no means in places where natural beds of oysters exist. It cannot be said that their existence de facto limits any rights of taking oysters from their natural beds; they are usually put in places in ground belonging to some individual, that is to say, on parts of the waste of the manor, quite away from those places in which the fishing for what I may call wild oysters would take place. In my mind, oysters in an "oyster laying" do not differ substantially, as regards legal status, from lobsters that are in a lobster pot. Everyone has a right to take lobsters in the sea, unless he is thereby interfering with the rights of a several fishery; but, if a lobster is in a lobster pot, and a stranger takes it out, that is not fishing, but taking something the property in which has passed to some individual. If we go a little further, and consider the practice which exists in some parts of the coast, I believe, of placing lobsters that have been captured in larger wicker cages where a considerable number of them can be kept till it is convenient to send them to market, we see a still closer analogy to these "oyster layings". It is quite true that in such cages the lobsters are wholly enclosed, but that is because it is impossible in the case of such fish to keep them safely unless they are so enclosed. The fact that the mature oyster has practically no means of locomotion makes it quite unnecessary that you should place oysters in a wholly enclosed space in order to confine them, but the oysters in an "oyster laying" are just as much kept in captivity as would be the lobsters in a wicker construction of the character that I have described. It therefore seems to me that, in the absence of authority that these "oyster layings" are not capable of legal existence except as part of a several fishery, there is no ground in good sense why we should suppose that they must necessarily be parcel of or appurtenant to such a fishery.' *Foster v Warblington Urban Council* [1906] 1 KB 648 at 678, 680–682, CA, per Fletcher Moulton LJ

OYSTER SPAT

'The preservation of the spawn, fry, or brood of fish has been, for centuries, . . . a favourite subject of legislation, and the statutes passed for the purpose are extremely numerous. If the plaintiffs had, in the declaration or in the replication, averred that the oyster spat taken by defendant was the spawn, fry, or brood of fish, the defendant could not have defended himself by stating his immemorial right, as one of the subjects of this realm, to take them in plaintiffs' close, being a navigable river. But the declaration stated that "oyster spat" was taken; and the plea justifies taking it, and only denies the repeated assertion of the same immemorial right; still, however, they have alleged and defendant has not denied, that the oyster spat is the spawn or young brood of oysters; and though the epithet rather applies to fish than spawn, and all the other circumstances in the description, given in the replication, are as consistent with the idea of fish as of spawn, yet it appears to us that the word "spawn" is sufficient.' *Maldon Corpn v Woolvet* (1840) 12 Ad & El 13 at 20, 21, per cur.

[Under the repealed Sea Fisheries Act 1868, 'oysters' were defined to include the brood, ware, half-ware, spat and spawn. There is no corresponding definition in the Sea Fisheries (Shellfish) Act 1967. See FISH.

P

PACKAGE *See also* POSTAL PACKET

'Package', in relation to any medicinal products, means any box, packet or other article in which one or more containers of the products are or are to be enclosed, and, where any such box, packet or other article is or is to be itself enclosed in one or more other boxes, packets or other articles, includes each of the boxes, packets or articles in question. (Medicines Act 1968, s 132(1))

In this part of this Act [Part I: packaged goods] . . . 'package' means . . . a container containing prescribed goods together with the goods in the container in a case where—

(a) the goods are placed for sale in the container otherwise than in the presence of a person purchasing the goods; and
(b) none of the goods can be removed from the container without opening it.

(Weights and Measures Act 1985, s 68(1))

[The Carriers Act 1830, s 1 relieves a common carrier from responsibility for loss or injury to any articles contained in any parcel or 'package' delivered to him above a certain value, unless the value has been declared. In this instance goods were packed into a waggon with wooden sides and no top.] 'I think this waggon with its contents was a "package" within the meaning of the Act. Although one would not commonly describe it in that way, yet, looking at the object and purpose of the Act, I think we are not only entitled, but compelled to say that it was a "package or parcel" within the section. It is to be observed that the plaintiff himself and his foreman authorise us in so describing it, for they say they "packed" the goods in the waggon, and no one would doubt that this expression was rightly used; but if so, then the waggon so packed with goods was a package.' *Whaite v Lancashire & Yorkshire Rly Co* (1874) LR 9 Exch 67 at 69, 70, per Bramwell B

[A clause in a bill of lading stipulated that the liability of the shipowner was to be limited to the agreed value of each 'package'. The question was whether cars put on board a ship without any boxes, crates or coverings could be said to be 'packages' within the meaning of this clause.] 'The goods are expressly stated to be unboxed, and the case was argued before me by both parties, who doubtless want a decision on what are known to be the actual facts, on the footing that the cars were put on board without any covering, or, to state it in another way, just as they came from the works. I confess I do not see how I can hold that there is any package to which the clause can refer. 'Package' must indicate something packed.' *Studebaker Distributors Ltd v Charlton Steam Shipping Co Ltd* [1938] 1 KB 459 at 467, per Goddard J

New Zealand 'It seems that a "package" may consist of a number of different articles packed into a container, such as a box or carton. It may also consist of a number of articles tied together and wrapped in paper or sacking or other covering to help protect and cover the articles in transit. . . . I think the word "package", taken in its ordinary meaning, in relation to goods consigned on the railways, must include articles merely tied together into a single bundle even though not in any container and not packed with any special covering.' *New Zealand Railways v Progressive Engineering Co Ltd* [1968] NZLR 1053 at 1055, per Tompkins J

PACKET *See* INLAND PACKET

PAGE BOY

Canada 'The words "bell boy" and "page boy" are used interchangeably by the public to describe the employment of a youth in a hotel, and who performs such duties as responding to calls from rooms, carrying messages to hotel guests, and carrying out a variety of duties assigned to him.' *Tuckett Tobacco Co Ltd v St Germain* [1940] Ex CR 58 at 63, Ex Ct, per Maclean J

PAID *See* PAY

PAID-UP CAPITAL *See* CAPITAL

PAINTING

[The Carriers Act 1830, s 1 relieves a common carrier from responsibility for loss or injury to (inter alia) 'paintings', engravings, and pictures delivered to him above a certain value, unless the higher value has been declared.] 'The only question in this case was, whether certain painted carpet and rug patterns and painted carpet designs were paintings or pictures within the Carriers Act. . . . The only remark to be made upon the language of the statute, as affecting the meaning to be given to the word "paintings", is that the other matters mentioned in connection with it, "engravings, pictures", show that the statute cannot be construed as meaning everything which has painting done upon it by a workman, it must mean something of value as a painting (value being necessary to make the statute applicable), and something on which skill has been bestowed in producing it. . . . The articles are not paintings in the ordinary meaning of such a word used in connection with the words, "engravings, pictures". I think they are something different. They are rug patterns, and carpet patterns, and working designs. They would not, in my opinion, be described in any transaction relating to them collectively as paintings, but each would be described by its proper description, rug model, or carpet model, or working design.' *Woodward v London & North Western Rly Co* (1878) 3 Ex D 121 at 123, 124, per Cleasby B

PALACE *See* ROYAL RESIDENCE

PALATINE *See* COUNTY PALATINE

PANNAGE

Although swine are not as a rule commonable in a forest, there is in most forests a right to turn out swine during a limited period to feed on the beech mast and acorns. This is known as pannage or pawnage, and is exercisable either by the persons having rights of common of pasture or by agistment. (6 Halsbury's Laws (4th edn) para 515)

In the Queen's woods pannage begins on Holyrood Day, which is fifteen days before Michaelmas, and ends forty days after Michaelmas. (Manwood's Forest Laws (5th edn) 230; 6 Halsbury's Laws (4th edn) para 515*n*)

'The right of pannage is simply a right granted to an owner of pigs—the grant was usually to an owner of land of some kind who kept pigs—to go into the wood of the grantor of the right and to allow the pigs to eat the acorns or beech-mast which fell upon the ground. That is what the right has always been defined to be. The pigs have no right to take a single acorn or any beech-mast off the tree, either by themselves or by the hands of those who drive them. There is not even a right to shake the tree. It is only a right to eat what has fallen to the ground.' *Chilton v London Corpn* (1878) 7 Ch D 562 at 565, per Jessel MR

PAPER

[Statute (1839) 2 & 3 Vict c 23 (repealed), by s 66, provided that all 'paper' should be chargeable with duty, and by s 65 defined the term 'paper'.] 'The question was, whether the article manufactured by the defendant on which the duty was claimed was paper within the meaning of the 2 & 3 Vict c 23, ss 65 and

66. . . . It becomes material to know what is paper as generally understood. The leaves of plants are not paper, though the term no doubt has been taken from papyrus, which people formerly used to write upon as paper now is used. The skins of animals are not paper. Perhaps paper may be described fairly as a manufactured substance composed of fibres adhering together, in form consisting of sheets of various sizes and of different thicknesses, used for writing or printing or other purposes to which flexible sheets are applicable.' *A-G v Barry* (1859) 4 H & N 470 at 475, 476, per cur.

PARAMOUNT

Australia 'The fact that the interests of the child are to be the paramount consideration does not mean that his welfare is to be the only consideration. The very use of the word "paramount" shows that other considerations are not excluded. They are only subordinated.' *Priest v Priest* [1966] ALR 40 at 47, per Herring CJ

PARAPHERNALIA

The term 'paraphernalia' comprises jewels and ornaments, exclusive of old family jewels, which belong to the husband but which the wife is permitted to wear. It is extremely doubtful whether the doctrine of paraphernalia is applicable at the present day, but it cannot be treated as definitely obsolete, and the relevant law would appear to be as follows.

Jewels and trinkets given to the wife by relatives or friends are generally considered her property, and not paraphernalia. In case of gifts by the husband, there is a presumption that they are intended as absolute gifts, and not as gifts of paraphernalia, if they are given to the wife at Christmas, or on her birthday, or in order to settle differences. During the lifetime of the husband, paraphernalia cannot be disposed of by the wife, they may, however, be sold, pledged or given away by him. On the death of the husband, paraphernalia belong to the wife, subject to liability for the husband's debts on failure of other assets, and the husband cannot, therefore, dispose of them by will; they are not liable to satisfy his legacies, and, if he has pledged them during his life, his widow is entitled to have them redeemed out of his personalty, to the prejudice of legatees. (22 Halsbury's Laws (4th edn) para 1082)

'The law of paraphernalia and the practice of constituting paraphernalia are unfamiliar, if not antiquated. But, no doubt, before the Married Women's Property Act 1882, if a husband expressly indicated his intention to make a gift of paraphernalia, he could do so; and, even if he had never heard of paraphernalia, but the intention were made manifest that . . . jewels were given to the wife not absolutely, but for her use as a wife, this peculiar kind of property might be created. . . . It was suggested to me that the Married Women's Property Act 1882 [see now Law Reform (Married Women and Tortfeasors) Act 1935] had abolished paraphernalia. I do not think that Act affects a gift of paraphernalia, although some text writers have taken a different view.' *Tasker v Tasker* [1895] P 1 at 4, per Jeune P

'The whole difficulty has arisen from a misconception of the meaning of paraphernalia: it was a right given by the common law to a widow; it was not a right of the husband's at all, but was a limitation of the legal rights of his executors or administrators after his death. At common law all the wife's personal chattels were the property of the husband; the marriage made them *unica caro*, "so that the very being and existence of the woman is suspended during the coverture or entirely merged or incorporated in that of the husband" and the wife had no separate rights at common law to any personal chattel at all. The idea of her asserting any right to paraphernalia against her husband during his life is out of the question, and any claim by him of his wife's personal chattels as paraphernalia is equally out of the question; such chattels were his own property, and if he claimed them, he claimed them as such. But, in mitigation of this extreme severity, the common law, borrowing to some extent from the civil law, gave to the widow a right to keep certain personal chattels, of which she had the use during coverture, as her own property after her husband's death. It is thus put by Richardson CJ and Croke J in *Hastings v Douglas* [(1632) Cro Car 343 at 345]: "Of all chattels personal, although the wife had them before marriage, the absolute property by the marriage is vested in the husband and he may give them in his life, or dispose of them by his will: so of those goods which are termed paraphernalia the absolute property is in the husband." So in Comyn's Digest, Baron and Feme, F (i). What goes to the wife if she survives. Paraphernalia "so the wife shall have after the death of the husband as her paraphernalia, a necessary bed and apparel agreeable to the quality of her husband. The property of the paraphernalia is vested in the wife presently upon the death of her husband." So too in Blackstone's Commentaries, Vol 2, 435 (1766): "And as the husband may thus, generally, acquire a property in all the personal substance of his wife, so in one particular instance the wife may acquire a property in some of her husband's goods: which shall remain to her after his death and shall not go to his executors. These are called her paraphernalia; which is a term borrowed from the civil law, and is derived from the Greek language, signifying something over and above her dower. Our law uses it to signify the apparel and ornaments of the wife, suitable to her rank and degree; which she becomes entitled to at the death of her husband over and above her jointure or dower, and preferably to all other representatives." To the same effect are Godolphin's Orphan's Legacy, p 130, and Noy's Legal Maxims (Blythewood's edition), p 241: "Widow. The widow shall have all her apparel, her bed, her copher, her chains, borders, and jewels by the honourable custom of the realm, except her husband unkindly give any of them away or be so in debt that it cannot be paid without her bed, etc, yet even in that case she shall have her necessary apparel," for (as it is put in Comyn's Digest) "she ought not to be naked or exposed to shame or cold".' *Masson, Templier & Co v De Fries* [1909] 2 KB 831 at 836–838, CA, per Farwell LJ

PARCEL *See* PACKAGE

'No doubt the word "parcel" in ordinary usage conveys the idea of something enclosed in a wrapper. But this is not the original meaning of the word, which obtains in many legal phrases, such as "part and parcel", and the "parcels" of a conveyance. Here the word is clearly synonymous with "portion".' *Maguire v Porter* [1905] 2 IR 147 at 153, per Madden J

PARCEL OF LAND

Australia 'A "parcel of land" means a piece of land which can be distinguished from adjoining pieces or areas.' *Russell v Brisbane City Council* [1955] St R Qd 419 at 435, per Macrossan CJ

Canada 'It was urged that the idea of a parcel connotes not only a part of something but a comparatively small part. While the word is not used in the Land Titles Act or in its forms, the words being "piece", "tract", or merely "land", I have no doubt that parcel is used in the Dower Act simply as "piece" or "tract", and has no necessary connection with any other portion of land. To hold otherwise would mean that the Act does not apply to an isolated parcel.' *Lawson v Lawson* (1959) 29 WWR 432 at 434, Alta SC, per Riley J

PARENT

'Parent', in relation to any child or young person, includes a guardian and every person who has the actual custody of the child or young person. (Education Act 1944, s 114(1))

'Parent' means a parent or guardian of, or person having the legal custody of, or the control over, a young person, and includes, in relation to any young person, a person having direct benefit from his wages. (Mines and Quarries Act 1954, s 182(1))

'Parent' means a parent or guardian of, or person having a legal custody of, or the control over, a child or young person, and includes, in relation to any child or young person, any person having direct benefit from his wages. (Factories Act 1961, s 176(1))

'Parent', in relation to a child who is illegitimate, means his mother, to the exclusion of his father. (Child Care Act 1980, s 87(1))

'The question is . . . whether the parties in this case are parents. There was one child born, which died on the day of its birth. Suppose a person had had a child which died twenty years ago, I could not say he is still a parent. It seems to me the same *ratio decidendi* affects this case as that of *Thomas v Thomas* [(1860) 2 Sw & Tr 89], and I must decide the parties are not parents.' *Bird v Bird* (1866) 35 LJP & M 102 at 103, per the Judge Ordinary

[The Education Act 1921, s 87 (repealed; see now the Education Act 1944, s 54(2)) enabled a local education authority, if its medical authority reported that a child attending a public elementary school was in a verminous state, to give written notice to the 'parent' of the child requiring him to cleanse the child within twenty-four hours.] 'The justices were clearly right. They came to the conclusion that the "parent" referred to in s 87 of the Education Act 1921, where the father and mother were living together and the child was living with both of them, was the father.'

London County Council v Stansell (1935) 154 LT 241 at 242, DC, per Lord Heward CJ

'It is perfectly clear from a number of authorities that, if the context is sufficient, the use of the word "parent" in connection with "issue", does not necessarily have the effect of cutting down the word "issue" so as to mean "children". As Sargant J put it in *Re Burnham* [*Carrick v Carrick* [1918] 2 Ch 196 at 204]: ". . . such a clause is quite susceptible of being construed so as to provide for representation in each successive generation. . . . In other words, the reference to "parent's share" can, if the context is sufficient, be construed as merely a stirpital direction and not as assuming that the parent in question would necessarily have to take a share.' *Re Hipwell, Hipwell v Hewitt* [1945] 2 All ER 476 at 477, CA, per Lord Greene MR

'The word "parent" is defined in s 114(1) [of the Education Act 1944 (supra)] as follows: "'Parent', in relation to any child or young person, includes a guardian and every person who has the actual custody of the child or young person." That sub-section does not say that the mother is not a parent, and I take it that if a child is living with, say, an aunt or grandparent so that that person has the actual custody of the child, that person might be answerable [for the cleanliness of the child] under s 54(6). I think it is at least a reasonable interpretation of those words in s 114(1) that the legislature is drawing a distinction between actual and legal custody, and that the words "actual custody" show that the person responsible is that person who at the time of the summons really has the child in his or her custody. We have also to remember that, unless the contrary intention appears, the Interpretation Act [1978, s 6], requires us to read the singular as including the plural. Therefore, the word "parent" must be construed as "parents" unless the contrary intention appears.' *Plunkett v Alker* [1954] 1 All ER 396 at 397, per Lord Goddard CJ

'In my opinion the word "parent" in an Act of Parliament does not include the father of an illegitimate child, unless the context otherwise requires.' *Re M (an Infant)* [1955] 2 All ER 911 at 912, CA, per Denning LJ

Australia 'The English legislation under consideration in *Re M (an Infant)* [[1955] 2 All ER 911] is markedly different from that now in question. It seems to me to be reasonably clear that in the Adoption of Children Ordinance 1965–1986 (ACT), s 25(2) the word "parent" includes the father of an illegitimate child.' *Re an Adoption* (1972) 20 FLR 330 at 331, per Fox J

Canada 'I have been unable to find any judicial consideration of the meaning of "parent" in either s 250.2(1) [of the Criminal Code] or in any of the nearby sections where it has a longer history, e.g. s 249. At common law, its meaning prima facie is confined to the lawful mother and father of the party spoken of. . . . In exceptional circumstances, the common law apparently recognised the rights of a father of a child born out of wedlock to custody after the mother and the Family Maintenance Act [of Nova Scotia] now puts them on an equal plane.' *R v Levesque* (1984) 15 CCC (3rd) 413 at 414, NS Co Ct, per O'Hearn Co Ct J

PARENT COUNTRY

'Parent Country', in relation to a ship, means the country or territory in which the ship is registered, or, if the ship is not registered anywhere, means the country or territory whose flag the ship flies. (Merchant Shipping (Load Lines) Act 1967, s 32)

PARI PASSU

Australia 'This clause provides in clear terms that payment is to be made pari passu [lit on an equal footing] of all moneys owing in respect of the issued stock. It does not provide that payment is to be made pari passu in proportion to the stock held. The natural meaning of its words is that all stockholders were to be treated equally and all were to receive payment, at the same rate, of moneys owing to them.' *Merchant Bills Corpn Ltd v Permanent Nominees (Australia) Ltd* [1972–3] ALR 565 at 572, per Gibbs J

PARISH

Ecclesiastical

According to the general definition of the term an ecclesiastical parish is a district committed to the charge of one incumbent having the cure of souls in it. For certain purposes, however, a special statutory definition may be applicable. Thus, in the Church Representation Rules 'parish' is defined as including also a district which is constituted a conventional district for the cure of souls and has a separate curate licensed to it. In the Pastoral Measure 1968 'parish' means a parish constituted for ecclesiastical purposes, and does not include a conventional district.

The ancient parishes appear to have been gradually formed between the seventh and twelfth or thirteenth centuries. Their boundaries seem to have been originally identical with or determined by those of manors, as a manor very seldom extends over more than one of these parishes, although in many cases one parish contains two or more manors. Besides being ecclesiastical units, ancient parishes have been at different periods, and in many cases still are, administrative areas for various civil purposes, although the boundaries of parishes for civil purposes have in many cases been altered under statutory authority. (14 Halsbury's Laws (4th edn) paras 534, 535)

'Parish' means any ecclesiastical parish or district, parochial chapelry or other place the incumbent or minister whereof either is entitled to retain for his own benefit or is under a duty to pay over to another clerk in holy orders the fees chargeable in respect of the performance of church offices. (Ecclesiastical Fees Measure 1962, s 7)

'Parish' means an ecclesiastical parish or district the Minister of which has a separate cure of souls, and includes a conventional district to the charge of which a separate curate is licensed. (Extra-Parochial Ministry Measure 1967, s 3)

'Parish' means a parish constituted for ecclesiastical purposes, and does not include a conventional district. (Pastoral Measure 1983, s 86(1))

'A parish is a place having a known or defined boundary.' *R v Hardy* (1868) LR 4 QB 117 at 120, per Cockburn CJ

[Under a private Act property was vested in trustees upon trust to apply the income in aid of specified charitable purposes for the benefit of the inhabitants and parishioners of the 'parish'.] 'The question . . . turns on the meaning of the word "parish" as used in the Act. . . . It has been said that "parish" here may mean one of three things. It may mean either the ecclesiastical parish, or the area which is separately rated, or so much of the ecclesiastical parish as on the evidence has contributed towards church-rates, and to repairs of the old parish church. In my opinion . . . the first and the larger sense is the only possible one; the ecclesiastical parish is, properly speaking, the whole parish and parish proper.' *Re Sandbach School & Almshouse Foundation, A-G v Crewe (Earl)* [1901] 2 Ch 317 at 322, per Farwell J

PARISH CHURCH

'The question is whether . . . the trust income is applicable (inter alia) for the repair of the chancel as well as the rest of the church. . . . There may be considerable doubt as to what the donors really intended, but the trust as it stands is for the expenditure of the . . . fund "about the parish church" or, as stated in another part of the deed, "in upon or about the said parish church". I see no ground for holding that the donors by the use of the expression "parish church" did not mean the church as a whole . . . there is no sufficient certainty that those general and wide words were intended to be limited to parochial expenditure as distinct from general expenditure in and about the church. . . . I am of opinion that the income of the trust funds under . . . the scheme is applicable inter alia for the repair of the fabric of the church, including the chancel.' *A-G v Parr* [1920] 1 Ch 399 at 345–347, per Astbury J

PARISH COUNCIL

A parish council is a body corporate consisting of the chairman and of such number of parish councillors, not being less than five, as the district council may from time to time fix. It is styled 'the Parish Council' with the addition of the name of the particular parish. A parish council has all such functions as are vested in it by the Local Government Act 1972 or otherwise. Notwithstanding anything in any rule of law, a parish council need have no common seal, but where it has no seal an act of the council which is required to be signified by an instrument under seal may be signified by an instrument signed and sealed by two members of the council. (28 Halsbury's Laws (4th edn) para 1039)

[Powers of parish councils to provide public amenities, e.g. seats and shelters, public clocks and street lighting, are to be found in Part I of the Parish Councils Act 1957. The constitution and powers of parish meetings and parish councils, as from 1 April 1974, are now set out in the Local Government Act 1972 ss 9–16, as amended by the Representation of the People Act 1983.]

PARISH MEETING

The parish meeting of a parish consists of the local government electors for the parish. The acts of the parish meeting may be signified by an instrument signed by the person presiding and two other electors present at the meeting. Where there is no separate parish council the chairman of the parish meeting and the proper officer of the district council are a body corporate by the name of the 'The Parish Trustees' with the addition of the name of the parish. The parish trustees act in accordance with the directions of the parish meeting. (28 Halsbury's Laws (4th edn) para 1042)

[See note to PARISH COUNCIL, above.]

PARISH VESTRY *See* VESTRY

PARISH WORK

'The question is, what is the meaning of the words [which describe the beneficiaries under a will] "the Vicar and Churchwardens of St Columba's Church, Hoxton (for parish work)"? . . . "Parish work" seems to me to be of such vague import as to go far beyond the ordinary meaning of charity, in this case in the sense of being a religious purpose. The expression covers the whole of the ordinary activities of the parish, some of which no doubt fall within the definition of religious purposes, and all of which no doubt are religious from the point of view of the person who is responsible for the spiritual care of the parish in the sense that they are conducive, perhaps, to the moral and spiritual good of his congregation. But that, I think, quite plainly is not enough; and the words are so wide that I am afraid that on no construction can they be brought within the limited meaning of "charitable" as used in the law. I find myself in entire accord with what was said by the Master of the Rolls in the Court of Appeal, in a passage which I will read. "To my mind," he said "the whole question in this case turns on whether or not the words "for parish work" can in some way be limited, either by their own inherent meaning or by reference to the character and quality of the trustees. I have come to the conclusion, and I do so with regret, that that limitation cannot be imposed upon the words. . . . It appears to me that, taking them as words of ordinary English they cover any activity in the parish, any work in the parish which trustees of that character may be expected to perform, whether that work be strictly a religious purpose or strictly a charitable purpose, or whether it be a work considered to be conducive to the good of religion, or considered to be benevolent or generally useful to the inhabitants of the parish or the congregation of the church".' *Farley v Westminster Bank* [1939] AC 430 at 434–436 per Lord Atkin

PARISHIONER

'Parishioner is a very large word, takes in, not only inhabitants of the parish, but persons who are occupiers of lands, that pay the several rates and duties, tho' they are not resiant, nor do contribute to the ornaments of the church. Inhabitants is still a larger word, takes in housekeepers, tho' not rated to the poor, takes in also persons who are not housekeepers; as for instance, such who have gained a settlement and by that means become inhabitants.' *A-G v Parker* (1747) 3 Atk 576 at 577, per Lord Hardwicke LC

'Prior to the passing of the Vestries Act 1818 [repealed] . . . there can be no doubt that, if the minister and the parishioners of a parish did not agree as to the appointment of the churchwardens, the minister appointed his churchwarden, and the parishioners appointed their churchwarden—that is, the people's churchwarden. The 89th canon of the Canons of 1603, which is declaratory of the common law, makes this abundantly plain. The canon is as follows: "All churchwardens or questmen in every parish shall be chosen by the joint consent of the minister and the parishioners, if it may be; but if they cannot agree upon such a choice, then the minister shall choose one and the parishioners another; and without such a joint or several choice none shall take upon them to be churchwardens." I agree with my brothers Wills and Channell that in this canon the parishioners are mentioned in such a way as to shew that, in case the vestry cannot agree the minister is to choose his own churchwarden, and the parishioners, as opposed to and distinguished from him, are to choose their churchwarden. The term "parishioners" in the canon means, in fact, the minister's parishioners, and would not include the minister himself.' *R v Salisbury (Bp)*

[1901] 2 KB 225 at 226, 227, CA, per A L Smith MR

PARK

A legal park differs from a chase (q.v.) in being confined to land of the grantee, which must also be enclosed with a wall or paling. (2 Bl Com (14th edn) 38)

[Franchises of forest, free chase, park and free warren were abolished by the Wild Creatures and Forest Laws Act 1971, s 1.]

The Parks Regulation Act 1872 . . . shall apply to all parks, gardens, recreation grounds, open spaces and other land for the time being vested in, or under the control or management of, the Commissioners of Works, and accordingly in that Act the expression 'park' shall include all such parks, gardens, recreation grounds, open spaces and land as aforesaid. (Parks Regulation Amendment Act 1926, s 1)

[The Settled Land Act 1890, s 10 (repealed; see now the Settled Land Act 1925, s 65) imposed restrictions on the power of a tenant for life to dispose of the principal mansion house, and the pleasure grounds and 'park' and lands, if any, usually occupied therewith.] 'In my opinion . . . it is abundantly clear that the Settled Land Acts do not use the word park in its legal or technical sense, but according to its ordinary and natural meaning in common parlance. In addition to the legal meaning, the Imperial Dictionary gives (inter alia) the following meanings: "(2) A considerable extent of pasture and woodland, surrounding or adjoining a mansion-house, devoted to purposes of recreation or enjoyment, but chiefly to the support of a herd of deer, though sometimes to cattle and sheep. (3) Any piece of public ground, generally in or near a large town, laid out and cultivated for the sole purpose of pleasure and recreation, without any regard to the size of the ground or the style of the arrangement." The Settled Land Acts evidently use the word in the former sense, namely, an ordinary private park.' *Pease v Courtney* [1904] 2 Ch 503 at 509, 510, per Swinfen Eady J

[The Housing Act 1936, s 75 (repealed; cf now the Compulsory Purchase Act 1965, s 8, as substituted by the Highways Act 1980, s 250) provided that nothing in the Act should authorise the compulsory purchase of any land which formed part of any 'park', garden or pleasure ground.] 'The Oxford English Dictionary defines a park as follows: "1. Law. An enclosed tract of land held by royal grant or prescription for keeping beasts of the chase. 2. Hence extended to a large ornamental piece of ground, usually comprising woodland and pasture, attached to or surrounding a country house or mansion, and used for recreation, and often for keeping deer, cattle or sheep. (In these the name has either come down from a time when the ground was legally a park in sense 1, or has been more recently given to a ground laid out in imitation of such as were originally parks.) . . ." It is true that thirty-five acres is not a very large piece of ground. But I see no reason why it should not be a park, if perhaps a small one.' *Re Ripon (Highfield) Housing Confirmation Order* 1938, *White & Collins v Minister of Health* [1939] 2 KB 838 at 843, 847, CA, per MacKinnon LJ

Canada 'Golf is a form of recreation, and it is, therefore, within the powers of the board [a public parks board] to provide facilities therefor. A golf course requires so much space, and the danger of injury from flying balls is so great, that it is not practically feasible to include a golf course in an ordinary park. . . . In my opinion a parks board is permitted to exercise common sense in carrying out its statutory powers; and, in working out a scheme of public parks, it may elect to devote one of its parks exclusively to golf, without thereby depriving it of its character as a public park. . . . The best and most comprehensive definition of "park" which I have found, and the one which I adopt as my own, is contained in *Northport Wesleyan Grove Camp Meeting Assn v Andrews* (1908) 71 Atl 1027 at 1030 (Maine), and is as follows: "A 'park' may be defined as a piece of ground set apart to be used by the public as a place for rest, recreation, exercise, pleasure, amusement, and enjoyment." Applying this definition I hold that the Windsor Park Golf Course is land used for public park purposes within the meaning of s 4 of the 1918 Charter [Winnipeg Charter 1918, ch 120 (see now Winnipeg Charter 1956 (Man) c 87, s 470)] and as such exempt from taxation by the rural municipality of St. Vital.' *Winnipeg City v St Vital Rural Municipality* [1945] 1 WWR 161 at 177–179, Man CA, per Bergman JA; affirmed [1946] SCR 101

'The term "public park" or "park" generally connotes a portion of land of considerable extent, provided with the means and facilities of recreation and pleasure for the public at large without fee or charge. It may conceivably—and often does—include within its borders, baseball grounds, lawn bowling grounds, tennis courts, and even golf courses.' Ibid at 180, per Dysard J

PARK CONSTABLE

'Park constable' shall mean any person who, previously to the passing of this Act, has been or may hereafter be appointed keeper of a park as defined by this Act. (Parks Regulation Act 1872, s 3, as amended by the Parks Regulation (Amendment) Act 1974, s 2)

[The definition of 'park' is now to be found in the Parks Regulation (Amendment) Act 1926. *See* PARK.]

PARKING

'You take a car park ticket in order to obtain permission to park your car at a particular place, and parking your car means, I should have thought, leaving your car in the place. If you park your car in the street you are liable to get into trouble with the police. On the other hand, you are entitled to park your car in places indicated by the police or the appropriate authorities for the purpose. Parking a car is leaving a car and, I should have thought, nothing else.' *Ashby v Tolhurst* [1937] 2 KB 242 at 249, CA, per Greene MR

PARKING PLACE

'Parking place' means a place where vehicles, or vehicles of any class, may wait; and . . . an underground parking place shall not be deemed to be part of a road by reason only of its being situate under a road. (Road Traffic Regulation Act 1984, s 32(4)(b))

'Street parking place' and 'off-street parking place' refer respectively to parking places on land which does, and on land which does not, form part of a road. (Road Traffic Regulation Act 1984, s 142(1))

PARLIAMENT *See also* PEERAGE

The Parliament of the United Kingdom of Great Britain and Northern Ireland consists of the Sovereign and the three Estates of the Realm, namely the lords spiritual and the lords temporal, who sit together in the House of Lords, and the elected representatives of the people, who sit in the House of Commons.

The House of Lords is composed of the lords spiritual and the lords temporal, who sit together in one chamber.

The lords spiritual are the archbishops and such of the bishops of the Church of England as have seats in the House of Lords.

Bishops are appointed by the Crown and their right to sit and vote in the House of Lords is established by ancient usage and by statute.

The lords temporal comprise (1) the hereditary peers of England, Scotland, Great Britain and the United Kingdom; and (2) life peers, being peers created under (a) the Appellate Jurisdiction Act 1876; and (b) the Life Peerages Act 1958. (34 Halsbury's Laws (4th edn) paras 1001, 1029, 1030, 1035)

The constituent parts of a parliament . . . are, the King's majesty, sitting there in his royal political capacity, and the three estates of the realm; the lords spiritual, the lords temporal, (who sit, together with the King, in one house) and the Commons, who sit by themselves in another. And the King and these three estates, together, form the Great Corporation or body politic of the Kingdom, of which the King is said to be *Caput, principium et finis*. (1 Bl Com 149)

'According to our modern ideas, no doubt, the word "Parliament" is used to denote an assembly in which the third estate of the realm is represented on settled principles in fixed numbers and according to positive laws; but nothing could be more misleading than to apply those notions to assemblies called into existence over six centuries ago. The creation of peers of Parliament is effected by the will of the Sovereign in the exercise of his Royal prerogative. He may express that will through Letters Patent or by the issue of a writ of summons to the person named to attend and act in an assembly in which peers of Parliament, and only peers of Parliament, can take part under the authority of writs of summons of this kind. Representatives of the third estate are returned to that assembly, under writs addressed not to them, but to the sheriffs or other returning officers. It does not appear to me that it necessarily follows that the will of the Sovereign is exercised less effectively because those other persons are not returned to serve in that assembly by an entirely different process, and by virtue of an entirely different right, if only it be clear that the intention of the Sovereign was to summon to an assembly which he designed and intended to act and be regarded as a Parliament, with the full rights and power of a true Parliament.' *St John*

Peerage Claim [1915] AC 282 at 301, HL, per Lord Atkinson

PARLIAMENTARY ELECTION *See* ELECTION

PAROCHIAL CHARITY *See* CHARITY

PAROCHIAL CHURCH COUNCIL

The council is a body corporate by the name of the parochial church council of the parish for which it is appointed, and has perpetual succession. It consists of (1) all clerks in holy orders beneficed in or licensed to the parish, including in the case of a team ministry all vicars in the team; (2) any deaconess or woman worker licensed to the parish or any male lay worker licensed to the parish and receiving a stipend in respect of work for the cure of souls in the parish; (3) the churchwardens, being actual communicant members of the Church of England whose names are on the church electoral roll of the parish; (4) such, if any, of the readers whose names are on the church electoral roll of the parish as the annual meeting may determine; (5) all persons whose names are on the church electoral roll of the parish and who are lay members of the General Synod or any diocesan or deanery synod; (6) such number of representatives of the laity as the annual meeting may decide; and (7) co-opted members, if the parochial church council so decides, not exceeding in number one-fifth of the representatives of the laity elected to the council, and being either clerks in holy orders or actual lay communicant members of the Church of England of seventeen years of age or upwards. (14 Halsbury's Law (4th edn) para 569)

PAROL

'All contracts are, by the laws of England, distinguished into agreements by specialty, and agreements by parol; nor is there any such third class as some of the counsel have endeavoured to maintain, as contracts in writing. If they be merely written and not specialties, they are parol, and a consideration must be proved.' *Rann v Hughes* (c 1764) 7 TR 351n

[The word 'parol' literally means 'by word of mouth', as in the term 'parol evidence'; but, as the above extract shows, it is also used to denote agreements in writing not under seal.]

PARSON

A parson, *persona ecclesiae*, is one that hath full possession of all the rights of a parochial church. He is called parson, *persona*, because by his person the church, which is an invisible body, is represented; and he is in himself a body corporate, in order to protect and defend the rights of the church (which he personates) by a perpetual succession. He is sometimes called the rector, or governor, of the church: but the appellation of *parson* (however it may be depreciated by familiar, clownish, and indiscriminate use) is the most legal, most beneficial, and most honourable title that a parish priest can enjoy. (1 Bl Com 372)

PARSONAGE *See also* GLEBE

'By the parsonage is meant the endowments of the benefice. It is thus defined in Degge's Parson's Counsellor (Ed 1703) 190: "A parsonage, or rectory, is a certain portion of land, tythes and offerings, established by the laws of this Kingdom, for the maintenance of the minister that hath the cure of souls within the parish where he is rector, or patron".' *Re Alms Corn Charity, Charity Comrs v Bode* [1901] 2 Ch 750 at 758, per Stirling LJ

PARSONAGE HOUSE

'Parsonage house' means the house or other dwelling vested in the incumbent of a benefice (when the benefice is full) and being his official residence, and includes any out-buildings or land included in the curtilage of any such house or dwelling and any rights appurtenant thereto. (Pastoral Measure 1983, s 87(1))

[Cf the definition in the Repair of Benefice Buildings Measure 1972, s 31(1).]

PART

Of estate

[The Vendor and Purchaser Act 1874, s 2(5) (repealed; see now the Law of Property Act 1925, s 45(9)) provided that where the vendor retained any 'part' of an estate to which any documents of title related he was entitled to retain such documents.] 'In my opinion r 5 of s 2, when it speaks of the vendor retaining "part of an estate" clearly refers to part of an estate in land, that is, "land" with the enlarged meaning given to the word by s 3 of the Interpretation Act [1889 (repealed)], namely, a freehold, copyhold or leasehold estate in land.' *Re Williams & Newcastle's (Duchess) Contract* [1897] 2 Ch 144 at 148, per North J

Of house

[The Lands Clauses Consolidation Act 1845, s 92 (cf now the Compulsory Purchase Act 1965, s 8) enacted that no person should be required to sell or convey a 'part' only of any house, or other building or manufactory, if such party were willing and able to sell and convey the whole thereof.] 'The construction of the word "house" in the Act of Parliament has been clearly settled by authority to comprise all that would pass by a grant of a house; and this, according to the old authorities, would include not only the curtilage, but also a garden attached to the house; a fortiori, therefore, any buildings forming part of or appertaining to the messuage would also be included. . . . It would be impossible to say that the theatre of a hospital could be separately taken, even if it happened to have no internal communication with the wards of the hospital; nor can I doubt that this north wing, standing as it does within the garden, though at a little distance from the other buildings, is part of St Thomas's Hospital. If I held otherwise, I might with almost as much reason say that the kitchen of a mansion was no part of the house, if it happened to be a separate building approached only by a covered way. So far, therefore, as the case turns on the nature of the locality, I am of opinion that the garden and the north wing form part of the hospital within the meaning of the Act of Parliament.' *St Thomas's Hospital (Governors) v Charing Cross Rly Co* (1861) 1 John & H 400 at 404–406, per Page Wood V-C

Of income

'The relevant part of the subsection [Finance Act 1939, s 15(2) (repealed; see now the Finance Act 1972, Sch 16)] runs as follows: "The Special Commissioners may apportion to him [a member of an investment company] such part of the income of the company as appears to them to be appropriate and may adjust the apportionment of the remainder of the company's income as they may consider necessary." No stress was laid on the word "apportion", a word which though embracing fractional division does not import it. Emphasis was, for the purposes of this argument, laid on the use of the word "part" as necessarily implying a fraction only, and the use of the word "remainder" as necessarily implying the existence of something which remains. . . . In our view, the language used does not demand the construction suggested and the topic to which the subsection is addressed excludes its acceptance. The words "such part of the income" are in our opinion capable of being read and ought to be read as "such part, it may be the whole" of the income—in the same way as the word "some" in formal logic means "some, it may be all"—and the words "the remainder" as "the remainder if any", and so on.' *Chamberlain v Inland Revenue Comrs* [1945] 2 All ER 351 at 355, 356, CA, per Uthwatt J

Of ship

'I think it may fairly be said that a vessel comes into collision with another vessel if it comes into contact with any portion of that other vessel. There are many moveable things about a ship which may be treated as appurtenances of the ship. In a narrow view it may be said that the hull, masts, yards, standing rigging, bridge (in the case of a steamer) form the ship, and that these alone are parts of the ship; but if there be a collision with projecting booms, or boats at the side, or with the anchor at the bows, no one could doubt that in the fair use of language it is a collision with the ship. A ship often extends her area by swinging boats over her side, or casting out her anchor, and, in my opinion, a collision with the anchor belonging and attached to the ship, although it be at a distance from her, is a collision with an extended portion of the ship.' *Re Margetts & Ocean Accident & Guarantee Corpn* [1901] 2 KB 792 at 796, 797, DC, per Phillimore J

PART PERFORMANCE

'There is no conflict of judicial opinion, and in my mind no ground for reasonable controversy as to the essential character of the act which shall amount to a part performance, in one particular. It must be unequivocal. It must have relation to the one agreement relied upon, and to no other. It must be such, in Lord Hardwicke's words [*Gunter v Halsey* (1739) Amb 587] "as could be done with no other view or design than to perform that agreement". It must be sufficient of itself, and without any other information or evidence, to satisfy a court, from the circumstances it has created and the relations it has formed, that they are only consistent with the assumption of the existence of a contract the terms of which equity requires, if possible, to be ascertained and enforced.' *Maddison v Alderson* (1883) 8 App Cas 467 at 485, per Lord O'Hagan

PART WITH

[A lessee covenanted not to 'part with' the possession of the demised premises or any part thereof without the previous consent in writing of the lessor.] 'In my view a lessee cannot be said to part with the possession of any part of the premises unless his agreement with his licensee wholly ousts him from the legal possession of that part. If there is anything in the nature of a right to concurrent user there is no parting with possession.' *Stening v Abrahams*, [1931] 1 Ch 470 at 473, 474, per Farwell J

PARTIAL

New Zealand 'If two persons have an interest in the same piece of land it is impossible to assert that either of them has a total interest. Each must have only a partial interest; for the interest of either subtracts from the totality of the interests of the other. That must be so in any popular understanding of the terms "total" and "partial".' *R v Evans* [1957] NZLR 1128 at 1130, 1131, CA, per Barrowclough CJ and McGregor J

PARTIAL ACCEPTANCE

An acceptance [of a bill of exchange] is qualified which is . . . partial, that is to say, an acceptance to pay part only of the amount for which the bill is drawn. (Bills of Exchange Act 1882, s 19(2))

PARTIAL LOSS *See* LOSS

PARTICIPATE

'It is necessary to affix some meaning to the words which express the wish and desire of the settlor, that his other children should be allowed to participate with his eldest son in the trust property. It is a distinct direction, which must either be struck out of the deed, or it must be interpreted in a clear and reasonable manner. The direction to convey is executory, to be carried into effect on the eldest son attaining twenty-one. The property is then to be conveyed to him, but in such a manner, that the plaintiffs and any future born children of the settlor may be allowed to come in and participate. Suppose the deed had gone on to say, "in equal shares", as tenants in common or as joint tenants, it would then have been impossible for the defendant to resist the fair inference, that the conveyance should be made to effectuate that object. But the direction is, that the children are to participate, without saying in what shares. The absence of such direction does not make the clause void for uncertainty. If a testator had left the property so that all the children should participate, the court could not have held the gift void for uncertainty; it holds equality to be equity, and, therefore, if a testator leaves property to children in such shares and proportions as trustees shall direct, and the trustees refuse to exercise any discretion, the court does not hold the gift void for uncertainty, but it distributes the property equally among all the children.' *Liddard v Liddard* (1860) 29 LJ Ch 619 at 621, per Romilly MR

[A testator, by his will, appointed A and B his executors and trustees and gave his residuary estate to his trustees for their absolute use and benefit. By a codicil C was appointed an additional executor and trustee, and the testator declared that the will should be read as if in the bequest of the residuary estate the names of A, B and C were inserted, instead of A and B, so that C might 'participate' in the bequest with A and B.] 'I have . . . no doubt that the word "participate" is sufficient to indicate an intention to divide, and to create a tenancy in common.' *Robertson v Fraser* (1871) 6 Ch App 696 at 699, per Lord Hatherley LC

'I cannot hold, as a proposition of law, that the mere looking on is ipso facto a participation in or encouragement of a prize-fight. I think there must be more than that to justify a conviction for assault. If, for instance, it was proved that a person went to a prize-fight, knowing it was to take place, and remained there for some time looking on, I think that would be evidence from which a jury might infer that such person encouraged, and intended to encourage, the fight by his presence.' *R v Coney* (1882) 8 QBD 534 at 552, per Lopes J

PARTICIPATING POLICY *See* POLICY OF INSURANCE

PARTICIPATOR

For the purposes of this Part [Pt XI, close companies], a 'participator' is, in relation to any company, a person having a share or interest in the capital or income of the company, and, without prejudice to the generality of the preceding words, includes—

(a) any person who possesses, or is entitled to acquire, share capital or voting rights in the company,
(b) any loan creditor of the company,
(c) any person who possesses, or is entitled to acquire, a right to receive or participate in distributions of the company (construing 'distributions' without regard to s 418) or any amounts payable by the company (in cash or in kind) to loan creditors by way of premium on redemption, and
(d) any person who is entitled to secure that income or assets (whether present or future) of the company will be applied directly or indirectly for his benefit.

(Income and Corporation Taxes Act 1988, s 417(1))

PARTICULAR

'The agreement and contract are contained in the memorandum on the back of the paper, and the paper is entitled, "Particulars and Conditions of Sale". By that agreement the parties bind themselves to fulfil the said conditions of sale; that is to say, the within conditions, to which reference had been immediately before made in these words: "Lot one, mentioned and comprised in the within particulars and conditions of sale". The ninth condition provides that "if, through any mistake, the said lots, or either of them, shall be improperly described, or any error or misstatement be made in this particular, etc". It is not very clear that "in this particular" may not mean "in this respect"; that is, in respect of misdescription; the paper being called "Particulars", and "particular" being a word afterwards used with reference to the tenements within the manor. But I incline to think that we may take the word as applying to the particulars which follow.' *White v Cuddon* (1842) 8 Cl & F 766 at 783, 784, HL, per Lord Brougham

PARTICULAR AVERAGE LOSS *See also* AVERAGE

A particular average loss is a partial loss of the subject-matter insured, caused by a peril insured against, and which is not a general average loss.

Expenses incurred by or on behalf of the assured for the safety or preservation of the subject-matter insured, other than general average and salvage charges, are called particular charges. Particular charges are not included in particular average. (Marine Insurance Act 1906, s 64)

'It is . . . contended on behalf of the defendant that as the policy under which all these goods were insured was warranted free of particular average, and as only a portion of these goods was stolen, there has not been a total loss of the whole or any severable part of the goods, and therefore that there can be no claim under the policy. The law by which it is determined whether or not a loss is a particular average loss seems to me to be clear both on authority and under the Marine Insurance Act 1906. Where perishable goods are insured for a lump sum and in bulk which is all of the same description, then the total loss of part of the bulk is a particular average loss and gives no claim under a policy which is free of particular average. To this rule, however, there are exceptions in three instances. First, it very often happens that there are express words in the policy which make each package a separate insurance, and in that case the loss of one package is a total loss of that particular package, and even although the policy contains a f.p.a. clause the underwriters are liable for the loss of that particular package. Secondly, there is sometimes an insurance in one lump sum of goods of actually distinct kinds. The instance was given in which the master of a ship insured for one sum all his effects, including things of such different kinds as a feather bed and a chronometer, and it was held that the effects were so distinguishable in kind that the loss of one particular article was a total loss of that article and not a particular average loss of the whole, and that the assured was entitled to recover: see *Duff v Mackenzie* [(1857) 3 CB (NS) 16]. Another instance given was that in which an emigrant going to Natal effected one general insurance of the whole of his equipment, including a wagon, a tent, and many other things equally diverse, in separate packages, and it was held that the packages were so distinct in character that the loss of one package was a total loss of that package and not a particular average loss of the whole, and that the assured could recover: see *Wilkinson v Hyde* [(1858) 3 CB (NS) 30]. Thirdly, even where the goods insured are all of the same species, yet if they are contained in cases or packages which are themselves separately valued, the loss of one of those packages is a total loss of that package and not a particular average loss of the whole.' *Fabrique de Produits Chimiques SA v Large* [1923] 1 KB 203 at 209, per Bailhache J

PARTISAN

Canada [The Broadcasting Act, RSC 1970, c B-11, s 28(1), prohibited broadcasts of a 'partisan' character on the day of an election or referendum or the immediately preceding day.] 'In my view, a partisan broadcast is one intended to favour one candidate over the other or others, in an election, or to favour one point of view over another, in a referendum. The broadcast need not have a political sponsor, nor need there be a connection between the speaker and any political party or recognisable faction.' *R v CFRB Ltd* (1976) 30 CCC (2d) 386 at 390, 391, Ont CA, per Arnup JA

PARTITION

The legal term 'partition' is applied to the division of land, tenements and hereditaments belonging to co-owners and the allotment among them of the parts so as to put an end to community of ownership between some or all of them. (39 Halsbury's Laws (4th edn) para 552)

PARTNERSHIP *See also* ASSOCIATION; COMPANY

Partnership involves a contract between the partners to engage in a business with a view to profit. As a rule, each partner contributes either property, skill or labour, but this is not essential. A person who contributes property without labour, and has the rights of a partner, is usually termed a sleeping or dormant partner. A sleeping partner may, however, contribute nothing. (35 Halsbury's Laws (4th edn) para 2)

(1) Partnership is the relation which subsists between persons carrying on a business in common with a view of profit.

(2) But the relation between members of any company or association which is—

(a) Registered as a company under the Companies Act 1862, or any other Act of Parliament for the time being in force and relating to the registration of joint stock companies [see now Companies Act 1985]; or

(b) Formed or incorporated by or in pursuance of any other Act of Parliament or letters patent, or Royal Charter; or

(c) A company engaged in working mines within and subject to the jurisdiction of the Stannaries:

is not a partnership within the meaning of this Act. (Partnership Act 1890, s 1)

[By section 2 of the Act of 1890, regard must also be had to the following rules in determining whether or not a partnership exists:

(1) Joint tenancy, tenancy in common, joint property, common property, or part ownership does not of itself create a partnership as to anything so held or owned, whether the tenants or owners do or do not share any profits made by the use thereof.

(2) The sharing of gross returns does not of itself create a partnership, whether the persons sharing such returns have or have not a joint or common right or interest in any property from which or from the use of which the returns are derived.

(3) The receipt by a person of a share of the profits of a business is prima facie evidence that he is a partner in the business, but receipt of such a share, or of a payment contingent on or varying with the profits of a business, does not of itself make him a partner in the business; and in particular—

(a) The receipt by a person of a debt or other liquidated amount by instalments or otherwise out of the accruing profits of a business does not of itself make him a partner in the business or liable as such:

(b) A contract for the remuneration of a servant or agent of a person engaged in a business by a share of the profits of the business does not of itself make the servant or agent a partner in the business or liable as such:

(c) A person being the widow or child of a deceased partner, and receiving by way of annuity a portion of the profits made in the business in which the deceased person was a partner, is not by reason only of such receipt a partner in the business or liable as such:

(d) The advance of money by way of loan to a person engaged or about to engage in any business on a contract with that person that the lender shall receive a rate of interest varying with the profits, or shall receive a share of the profits arising from carrying on the business, does not of itself make the lender a partner with the person or persons carrying on the business or liable as such. Provided that the contract is in writing, and signed by or on behalf of all the parties thereto:

(e) A person receiving by way of annuity or otherwise a portion of the profits of a business in consideration of the sale by him of the goodwill of the business is not by reason only of such receipt a partner in the business or liable as such.]

'An ordinary partnership is a partnership composed of definite individuals bound together by contract between themselves to continue combined for some joint object, either during pleasure or during a limited time, and is essentially composed of the persons originally entering into the contract with one another.' *Smith v Anderson* (1880) 15 Ch D 247 at 273, CA, per James LJ

'I cannot find any authority throwing any doubt on the accuracy of the passage in Lindley on Partnership, which makes the participation in profits essential to the English idea of partnership, and states that, although in former times the word "copartnership" was used in the sense of "co-ownership" the modern usage has been to confine the meaning of the term to societies formed for gain. A number of definitions given by writers from all parts of the world are appended to the passage, and in all of them the idea involved appears to be that of joint operation for the sake of gain.' *R v Robson* (1885) 16 QBD 137 at 140, CCR, per Lord Coleridge

United States A partnership is an association of two or more persons to carry on as co-owners a business for profit. (Uniform Partnership Act 1914, s 6(1))

Limited partnership

United States 'Limited partner' means a person who has been admitted to a limited partnership as a limited partner in accordance with the partnership agreement and named in the certificate of limited partnership as a limited partner. (Revised Uniform Limited Partnership Act 1976, s 101(6))

PARTY

'Party', in relation to any proceedings, includes any person who pursuant to or by virtue of rules of court or any other statutory provision has been served with notice of, or has intervened in, those proceedings. (Supreme Court Act 1981, s 151)

'Party' includes every person served with notice of, or attending, any proceeding, whether named as a party to that proceeding or not. (County Courts Act 1984, s 1)

'The first objection which has been raised against this award, namely, that the arbitrator has exceeded his authority, would, if it were well founded, be destructive of it. But that is answered by reading the terms of the reference; by which it appears that "all matters in difference between the parties in the cause" were referred. "The parties in the cause" is merely a description of the persons, and not of the subject-matter in dispute." *Malcolm v Fullerton* (1788) 2 Term Rep 645 at 646, per Lord Kenyon CJ

United States 'Party' includes an individual who was, is, or is threatened to be made a named defendant or respondent in a proceeding. (Revised Model Business Corporation Act 1984, s 8.50(6))

PARTY ARCH

'Party arch' means an arch separating adjoining buildings storeys or rooms belonging to different owners or occupied or constructed or adapted to be occupied by different persons or separating a building from a public way or a private way leading to premises in other occupation. (London Building Act 1930, s 5)

PARTY FENCE WALL

'Party fence wall' means a wall (not being part of a building) which stands on lands of different owners and is used or constructed to be used for separating such adjoining lands but does not include a wall constructed on the land of one owner the artificially formed support of which projects into the land of another owner. (London Building Acts (Amendment) Act 1939, s 4)

PARTY STRUCTURE

'Party structure' means a party wall and also a floor partition or other structure separating buildings or parts of buildings approached solely by separate staircases or separate entrances from without. (London Building Acts (Amendment) Act 1939, s 4)

PARTY-WALL

Subject to the change as regards tenancy in common made by the Law of Property Act 1925, the term 'party-wall' may be used in four different senses, as meaning (1) a wall of which two adjoining owners are tenants in common; (2) a wall divided vertically into two strips one belonging to each of the adjoining owners; (3) a wall which belongs entirely to one of the adjoining owners, but is subject to an easement or right in the other to have it maintained as a dividing wall between the two tenements; (4) a wall divided vertically into halves, each half being subject to a cross easement in favour of the owner of the other half. . . . The effect of the Law of Property Act 1925 is to substitute for the first of the above meanings of 'party-wall' a holding in which the wall is severed vertically as in the second and fourth cases, but the owners have rights corresponding to those under the former law. (4 Halsbury's Laws (4th edn) para 889)

'Party-wall' (except in Part VI (Rights etc of building and adjoining owners) of this Act) means so much of a wall which forms part of a building as is used or constructed to be used for separating adjoining buildings belonging to different owners or occupied or constructed or adapted to be occupied by different persons together with the remainder (if any) of the wall vertically above such before-mentioned portion of the wall. (London Building Acts (Amendment) Act 1939, s 4)

'What is the meaning of the term "party-wall"? . . . The words appear to me to express a meaning rather popular than legal, and they may, I think, be used in four different senses. They may mean, first, a wall of which the two adjoining owners are tenants in common, as in *Wiltshire v Sidford* [(1827) 1 Man & Ry KB 404] and *Cubitt v Porter* [(1828) 8 B & C 257]. I think that the judgments in those cases shew that that is the most common and the primary meaning of the term. In the next place the term may be used to signify a wall divided longitudinally into two strips, one belonging to each of the neighbouring owners, as in *Matts v Hawkins* [(1813) 5 Taunt 20]. Then, thirdly, the term may mean a wall which belongs entirely to one of the adjoining owners, but is subject to an easement or right in the other to have it maintained as a dividing wall between the two tenements. . . . Lastly, the term may designate a wall divided longitudinally into two moieties, each moiety being subject to a cross easement in favour of the owner of the other moiety.' *Watson v Gray* (1880) 14 Ch D 192 at 194, 195, per Fry J

PASS

Of property

Canada 'Property which "passes on the death of any person" means property which changes hands at the death. It vests in the executor though he has no beneficial interest in it: *Re Bennett, Provincial Treasurer v Bennett* [1936] 2 DLR 291, 44 Man R 63. It only actually "passes" to the beneficiary when it reaches him.' *Re Jost* [1941] 1 DLR 642 at 643, NSSC, per Graham J; reversed on other grounds, [1942] SCR 54, SCC

Pass and repass

[A local turnpike Act enacted that no horse should 'pass' without paying a toll, provided that if the toll should have been paid it should be permitted to 'repass' toll free unless it had a different load.] 'I think that the word "repass" is used in contradistinction to the word "pass". The case appears to me to be clear on the construction of the Act. . . . It seems to me that the word "pass" and "repass" mean no more than "going" and "returning".' *Hill v Browning* (1870) 22 LT 712, per Mellor J

Upon highway

[The Highway Act 1835, s 78 makes it an offence for the driver of a carriage to leave it unattended whilst it is 'passing' upon a highway.] 'The words in the section "whilst it shall be passing upon such highway" mean, whilst it is on its way or journey, and apply equally whether the driver leaves his horses while they are moving, or first stops them and then leaves them.' *Phythian v Baxendale* [1895] 1 QB 768 at 770, per Cave J

PASS BOOK

'Considering that this pass-book (as its name indicates) is a book which passes between the bankers and their customer, being alternately in the custody of each party, on proof of its having been in the custody of the customer, and returned by him to the bankers without objection being made to any of the entries by which the bankers are credited, I think such entries may be prima facie evidence for the bankers as those on the other side prima facie evidence against them.' *Commercial Bank of Scotland v Rhind* (1860) 3 Macq 643 at 651, 652, DC, per Lord Campbell LC

[Under modern banking practice the majority of customers, as regards their current accounts, are now issued with periodical bank statements instead of pass books. Pass books are however still used in respect of deposit accounts.]

PASSABLE

Canada [The Highway Traffic Act, RSM 1940, c 93, s 71 (now RSM 1970, c H60, s 134) provided that pedestrians should walk on the sidewalk unless it was not 'passable'.] 'There is room for argument as to what the section means in using "passable". Perhaps it is "not passable in safety", "not fit to walk on" or "without undue difficulty or inconvenience", or something similar; but I am quite certain the words do not mean "utterly impassable".' *Gard v Slobodian* [1952] 1 DLR 575 at 578, Man CA per Coyne JA

PASSAGE

[The Street Betting Act 1906, s 1(4) (repealed; see now the Betting, Gaming and Lotteries Act 1963, s 8) enacted that for the purposes of the section, which imposed a penalty on persons frequenting or loitering in streets for the purpose of betting, the word 'street' should include any 'public passage'. Section 3 of the Act contained a definition of the word 'passage' in the application of the Act to Scotland.] 'It is . . . necessary to consider s 3, which gives a special definition of the word "passage" in the application of this Act to Scotland. The provision is that "In Scotland 'passage' includes common close or common stair, or passage leading thereto." I am inclined to agree . . . that the world "passage" which is there defined must be read as meaning "public" passage.' *Hasson v Neilson* 1908 SC(J) 57 at 59, 60, per Lord Low

'The words "access to which is obtained . . . through a . . . passage" [in the Private Street Works Act 1892, s 10 (repealed; cf now Highways Act 1980, s 207)] cannot be construed in their widest and most literal meaning. It is not desirable, nor do we propose, to lay down any definition of the words. We are not prepared to hold, as suggested, that a passage to be within the Act must be the only means of approaching the street to be made up, but we are of opinion that it means something in the nature of a feeder of the street.' *Oakley v Merthyr Tydfil Corpn* [1922] 1 KB 409 at 421, per Lord Trevethin CJ

[A local authority served a notice on a property company, requiring the company to 'flag, asphalt or pave' a path under the Public Health Act 1936, s 56(1) (repealed: see now the Building Act 1984, s 84(1)) The section required 'courts', 'yards' and 'passages' to be so treated; this, however, was a pathway running through a front garden and round the side of a house.] 'It has not been suggested here, and counsel for the council does not contend, that "a court or a yard" would include a garden and there is no reason why it should. If a court or yard where cars may be washed is appurtenant to a house it is, no doubt, very desirable that the water should be made to drain away, especially if the court or yard is flagged or made hard in some way. Different considerations might apply to a mere path, but these words are not, "if any court or yard or passage appurtenant to a house"; they are "any passage giving access to a house". I think that the section aims at a passage in the nature of a court. One knows perfectly well that in towns there are passages down which people go to get to houses. I do not think the word "passage" is apt in this context to describe what the council want to have paved in the present case, viz the way a man may walk from his front gate to his front door and round the side of the house to the back door.' *Denton Urban District Council v Bursted Properties Ltd* [1955] 1 All ER 273 at 274, per Lord Goddard CJ

'Counsel for the plaintiff has called our attention to the definitions given in the Oxford English Dictionary, which are these. "Passage" is defined there apparently as: "That by which a person or thing passes or may pass, way, road, path or channel especially when serving as an entrance or exit." The definition of gangway is: "A road, thoroughfare or passage of any kind, a passage in a building." Notwithstanding the definition of the words in the dictionary, certainly in common language I should not have said that this roadway thirty feet wide, with a pavement running along it, was a "gangway". We are told that "gangway" is derived from a Scottish or other term meaning a "going-way", a way in which you go. That seems to me a bit archaic in the circumstances, and I should not have expected the draftsman of the Act of 1961 to use it in that way. "Passage" is perhaps more easy because "passage" may well mean something on which people pass; but I should have thought that the ordinary common-place use of "passage" is not usually used in connection with a roadway thirty feet wide. "Passage" in ordinary use, I should have thought, suggested something narrower, in the same way as the description with which one is quite familiar, narrow passages going through various places, or between walls or between other bits of land, as the case may be.' *Thornton v Fisher & Ludlow Ltd* [1968] 2 All ER 241 at 244, CA, per Danckwerts LJ

Right of passage

'The only "dedication" in the legal sense that we are aware of is that of a public right of passage, of which the legal description is a "right for all her Majesty's subjects at all seasons of the year freely and at their will to pass and repass without let or hindrance". A claim on the part of persons so minded to assemble in any numbers, and for so long a time as they please to remain assembled, upon a highway, to the detriment of others having equal rights, is in its nature irreconcilable with the right of free passage, and there is, so far as we have been able to ascertain, no authority whatever in favour of it.' *Ex p Lewis* (1888) 21 QBD 191 at 197, DC, per Wills J

'The legitimate use of a highway is generally described as a "right of passage" or "a right of passing and repassing". In 1 Rolle's Abridg 392 B, pl 1, 2, referred to and adopted by Lord Mansfield in *Goodtitle v Alker* [(1757) 1 Burr 133], the law as to highways is thus stated: "The King has nothing but the passage for himself and his people, but the freehold and all profits belong to the owner of the soil." . . . The plaintiff went upon the highway, not for the purpose of exercising as one of the public his right of passage, but of interfering with the grouse drive by placing himself upon the soil of the highway so as to prevent the grouse from flying over the butts. . . . I am unable to agree that this was a use of the right of passing along the highway. I think it was an abuse of that right.' *Harrison v Rutland (Duke)* [1893] 1 QB 142 at 155, 160, CA, per Kay LJ

'Primarily the purpose for which a highway is dedicated is that of passage, as is shewn by the case of *Dovaston v Payne* [(1795) 2 Hy Bl 527]; and, although in modern times a reasonable extension has been given to the use of the highway as such, the authorities shew that the primary purposes of the dedication must always be kept in view. The right of the public to pass and repass on a highway is subject to all those reasonable extensions which may from time to time be recognised as necessary to its exercise in accordance with the enlarged notions of people in a country becoming more populous and highly civilised, but they must be such as are not inconsistent with the maintenance of the paramount idea that the right of the public is that of passage.' *Hickman v Maisey* [1900] 1 QB 752 at 757, 758, CA, per Collins LJ

PASSENGER

[The question was whether lorry drivers, who travelled free with their lorries on ships travelling between England and Denmark, were 'passengers' for the purpose of the Pilotage Act 1913, s 11(1) (repealed; see now the Pilotage Act 1983, s 31(1)).] 'For the purposes of the Pilotage Act 1913 only three possible categories have been suggested into which people carried in ships can fall. The two main categories are crew and passengers, but there is a third category of people described in some of the authorities as "nondescript". So far as the authorities cited to us go, these "nondescript" people seem to be either shipwrecked people picked up in distress, or relations or friends of the master who have sometimes been carried without the owners' authority and sometimes I think with it. I find it impossible to find any common factor in these nondescript people which would enable one to identify a clearly defined class. . . . These lorry drivers were clearly not crew. I cannot find any analogy between them and any of the people who have been held in the earlier authorities to fall into the "nondescript" class. My own impression is quite clear that they are passengers.' *Clayton v Albertson* [1972] 3 All ER 364 at 372, per Browne J

[The taxpayer company, who operated an amusement device known as 'the Big Dipper', claimed to be zero-rated for the purpose of value added tax, since their services constituted the 'transport of passengers'.] 'Counsel for the commissioners . . . has referred us to two meanings in the Oxford English Dictionary, which for my part I find helpful, if not more. "Transport" according to that dictionary contains amongst its meanings "the action of carrying or conveying a thing or person from one place to another; conveyance". I attach importance to the phrase "from one place to another". Furthermore, in the definition of "passenger" in the same dictionary we find that a "passenger" includes "a passenger by or through; a traveller; a wayfarer". Again I think myself that the element of travelling is a factor in the ordinary meaning of the word "passenger".... I cannot accept that a person who in effect remains on one spot all the time is on any view to be considered under the head of being transported as a passenger, and I think as a matter of reality and common sense the movement of patrons on the Big Dipper, or any of its associated installations, is in effect movement on one spot. None of those who patronise these entertainments desire that the track should be constructed so that they shall visit a particular point. The actual construction of the track is a matter of indifference to them as long as it contains the necessary gradients and corners. In no kind of sense is the patron, in my view, being taken from one place to another, and I think that using the words [transport of passengers] in their ordinary meaning it must necessarily exclude movement which in effect is confined to a single point and does not involve the deliberate movement or transfer of a passenger from one point to another.' *Customs & Excise Comrs v Blackpool Pleasure Beach Co* [1974] 1 All ER 1011 at 1013, 1014, per Lord Widgery

'As it seems to us, in the definition of "passenger" in s 26(1)(a) of the 1949 Act [Merchant Shipping (Safety Convention) Act 1949], which is determinative for present purposes, in the exception of "a person . . . engaged in any capacity on board the ship on the business of the ship", the word "engaged" must properly be construed against the background of these statutory provisions and authorities. It has a technical meaning relating to the terms of the engagement of the person in question to render services on board in some capacity, and it cannot properly be interpreted to refer merely to his activities while on board and to the question whether or not these happen to have been carried out "on the business of the ship". For instance, if a person comes on board as a fare-paying passenger, but renders assistance to the crew during the voyage, he does not thereby cease to be a passenger or become "engaged on the business of the ship" for the purposes of this provision.' *Secretary of State for Trade and Industry v Booth, The Biche* [1984] 1 All ER 464 at 469, per cur.

In motor vehicle

'The contention was that she [a pupil having a driving lesson] could not fairly be regarded as a passenger, because the word "passenger" properly understood meant a person who exercises no control and takes no part in the management of the car. It was suggested that there is the clearest possible division into two classes, those who are driving or taking part in the management of cars, on the one hand, and those who are carried, on the other hand. I cannot help thinking that that contrast is somewhat unreal. A person who is conveyed for the purpose of receiving instruction seems to me capable of being included in the class of passengers.' *Green v Dynes* (1938) 159 LT 168 at 169, DC, per Lord Hewart CJ

[A policy of motor insurance provided that the assured was to be indemnified against payment of (inter alia) all sums which he should become legally liable to pay in respect of a claim by any person, including 'passengers' in the automobile, for loss of life or accidental bodily injury.] 'In my view, a driver is clearly not a "passenger".' *Digby v General Accident Fire & Life Assurance Corpn Ltd* [1943] AC 121 at 133, per Lord Maugham

On ship

In Part III of the principal Act [Merchant Shipping Act 1894], in the Merchant Shipping (Safety and Load Line Conventions) Act 1932, and in this Act the expression 'passenger' means any person carried in a ship, except—

(a) a person employed or engaged in any capacity on board the ship on the business of the ship,
(b) a person on board the ship either in pursuance of the obligation laid upon the master to carry shipwrecked, distressed or other persons, or by reason of any circumstance that neither the master nor the owner nor the charterer (if any) could have prevented or forestalled, and
(c) a child under one year of age.

(Merchant Shipping (Safety Convention) Act 1949, s 26)

PASSENGER SHIP *See* SHIP

PASSENGER STEAMER

References in the Merchant Shipping Acts to a passenger steamer shall be construed as including any ship while on or about to proceed on a voyage or excursion in any case where a passenger steamer's certificate is required to be in force in respect of her. (Merchant Shipping Act 1964, s 17(2))

'I have come to the conclusion without any hesitation that it is not possible to make sense of s 271 [of the Merchant Shipping Act 1894; amended by the Merchant Shipping Act 1964; s 17] unless the words "every passenger steamer which carries more than twelve passengers" are read as meaning that the steamer must first be a passenger steamer, that is to say, one that is used either habitually, or at any rate substantially, for carrying passengers or is constructed as a passenger steamer.' *Duncan v Graham* [1951] 1 KB 68 at 76, per Lord Goddard CJ

PASSENGER TRAIN

'One knows perfectly well what is meant in practice by an excursion train. It is a train which like others goes from one place to another, it may or may not stop and pick up passengers on the road. I believe it commonly picks them up, but it is a train which goes from one place to another with a view to people getting to that other place on cheap terms and very frequently upon the condition that the railway company are not to be delayed or inconvenienced by people taking luggage with them. But why is that not a "passenger train"? Passengers go by it, and they go by it from one place to the other in order that they may get to the other place. It is not the less a passenger train because they pay a small fare; nor is it the less a passenger train because by agreement with the company they do not carry luggage with them. It seems to me really that the substance of the thing is that, as I said before, passenger train is not a term of art, it is a popular expression, and these popularly speaking are passenger trains, and no reason has been given why the words should have any other than their natural meaning.' *Burnett v Great North of Scotland Rly Co* (1885) 10 App Cas 147 at 167, HL, per Lord Bramwell

'What is a passenger train? It would seem to me that every train of the company over which the company retains its general control and dominion, and by which the company professes or offers to carry for hire in ordinary course such travellers as may take advantage of it on payment of their fares, is within the meaning of the stipulation in controversy a passenger train. It may be a special, or it may be an express train, it may carry the mail, or a Queen's messenger, or even excursionists, but its does not follow that it is not also a passenger train.' Ibid at 169, per Lord FitzGerald

[A consignment note provided that certain goods were to be carried by 'passenger train' at owner's risk.] 'While the railway company may provide a train which is fitted for passenger traffic, and which may convey passengers if they turn up, it cannot find them if they do not come, and therefore a train may be a "passenger train" though there are no passengers in it. I think a reasonable construction of the words "passenger train" is this—a train which has all the equipment of a passenger train and all the privileges of a passenger train.' *Caledonian Rly Co v Muirhead's Trawlers Ltd* (1904) 6 F 605 at 607, per Lord Trayner

PASSENGER VEHICLE *See* VEHICLE

PASSING

'I am of opinion that . . . the words "the date of the passing [of an Act of Parliament]" mean what they say. They are English words, common words, and words which have a fixed meaning in our language and law. They mean the time when the Royal Assent is given to a bill which has passed both Houses of Parliament.' *Ex p Rashleigh, Re Dalzell* (1875) 2 Ch D 9 at 12, 13, CA, per James LJ

PASSING OFF

'The well-established action for "passing off" involves the use of a name or get-up which is calculated to cause confusion with the goods of a particular rival trader, and I think that it would be fair to say that the law in this respect has been concerned with unfair competition between traders rather than with the deception of the public which may be caused by the defendant's conduct, for the right of action known as a "passing-off" action is not an action brought by the member of the public who is deceived but by the trader whose trade is likely to suffer from the deception practised on the public but who is not himself deceived at all.' *Bollinger v Costa Brava Wine Co Ltd* [1959] 3 All ER 800 at 805, per Danckwerts J

PASSPORT

'It will be well to consider what a passport really is. It is a document issued in the name of the Sovereign on the responsibility of a Minister of the Crown to a named individual, intended to be presented to the Governments of foreign nations and to be used for that individual's protection as a British subject in foreign countries, and it depends for its validity upon the fact that the Foreign Office in an official document vouches the respectability of the person named.' *R v Brailsford* [1905] 2 KB 730 at 745, per Lord Alverstone CJ

PASTIME

[The Gaming Act 1845, s 17 makes it an offence to win money from a person in wagering on the event of any game, sport, 'pastime' or exercise. The prosecutor was induced by the accused to toss with coins for wagers, and staked his watch and chain upon the result of a toss, which he lost.] 'The case is clearly within the words of the statute. This was undoubtedly a pastime or exercise, if not a game, within the meaning of the statute.' *R v O'Connor & Brown* (1881) 45 LT 512 at 513, CCR, per Lord Coleridge CJ

PASTURE

'Pasture' includes meadow. (Agricultural Holdings Act 1986, s 96).

[The Land Law (Ireland) Act 1881, s 58(3) (repealed) provided that the Act should not apply to certain holdings let to be used wholly or mainly for the purpose of 'pasture'.] 'I entertain no doubt that "pasture" in this place means feeding cattle or other live stock upon the land. This is both the etymological sense of the word and its sense according to ordinary agricultural use.' *Westropp v Elligott* (1884) 9 App Cas 815 at 819, 820, per Lord Selborne LC

[By a tenancy agreement, the tenant covenanted (inter alia) not to plough or break up any of the 'pasture lands'.] 'I think the expression "the pasture lands" in the agreement refers solely to those portions of the farm which were meadow land, or laid down permanently to grass at the date of the agreement, and that it would be straining the language beyond all reasonable limits were I to hold that a field tilled to corn at the date of the agreement and for at least thirteen years previous thereto had become pasture land within the meaning of the covenant because the tenant had in subsequent years left it for a considerable period in grass.' *Rush v Lucas* [1910] 1 Ch 437 at 441, 442, per Eve J

Common of pasture

The right of feeding cattle, horses, sheep, or other animals on the land of another, which may exist either as appendant, as appurtenant, in gross, or by reason of vicinage. (6 Halsbury's Laws (4th edn) para 509)

See, generally, 6 Halsbury's Laws (4th edn) paras 547–575

[The Inclosure Act 1845, s 27 (repealed), enacted that in making a provisional order the commissioners, if the lord of the manor was entitled to the soil of the land proposed to be enclosed, should specify the share or proportion of the residue of the land which should be allotted to the lord in respect of his right and interest in the soil, either exclusively or inclusively of his right to the mines, etc, under such land, or inclusively or exclusively of any 'right of pasturage' which might have been usually enjoyed by such lord or his tenants.] 'I cannot construe the Act of Parliament, when it says "right of pasturage which may have been usually enjoyed by such lord or his tenants" as meaning anything else than rights of pasturage and common which have been enjoyed by the lord and his tenants in such a manner as . . . would prove an established right beyond the memory of man to common over the waste in question.' *Musgrave v Inclosure Comrs* (1874) LR 9 QB 162 at 175, per Blackburn J

'It is clear from the pleadings . . . that the defendants . . . claimed nothing but a well-known right, namely, the right of common of pasturage and herbage; that is to say, a right in respect of their tenements to feed upon this waste by the mouths of their cattle; not merely the grass, but whatever the cattle would eat, which I take to be included under the word "herbage".' *De La Warr (Earl) v Miles* (1881) 17 Ch D 535 at 589, CA, per Brett LJ

PATENT

The word 'patent' . . . denotes a monopoly right in respect of an invention. The coming into force of the Patents Act 1977 necessitates a distinction between 'old patents' and 'new patents'. The terms 'old patents' and 'old application' are used . . . to denote letters patent granted and applications made under the Patents Act 1949. Such a patent is a grant from the Crown of a monopoly and is a matter of the Sovereign's grace. The patent was granted in a form authorised by rules made under statutory power, and was sealed with the seal of the Patent Office, which has the same effect as if the patent were sealed, as patents used to be, with the Great Seal of the United Kingdom. An old patent has effect throughout the United Kingdom and the Isle of Man.

The term 'new patent' is used in this title to denote patents granted pursuant to the Patents Act 1977. Unlike an old patent, a new patent is not a royal grant of monopoly but is a collection of rights conferred by the Patents Act 1977 in respect of a patentable invention. A certificate that a new patent has been granted is in a form authorised by rules made pursuant to the Act and is signed by the Comptroller-General of Patents, Designs and Trade Marks. A new patent has effect throughout the United Kingdom and the Isle of Man.

Both old and new patents and applications for them are personal property but without being things in action. (35 Halsbury's Laws (4th edn) para 303)

'The truth is that letters patent do not give the patentee any right to use the invention—they do not confer upon him a right to manufacture according to his invention. That is a right which he would have equally effectually if there were no letters patent at all; only in that case all the world would equally have the right. What the letters patent confer is the right to exclude others from manufacturing in a particular way, and using a particular invention.' *Steers v Rogers* [1893] AC 232 at 235, per Lord Herschell LC

'A patent right is a privilege granted by the Crown in the exercise of its prerogative to a first inventor, and is described in Stephen's Commentaries, 11th edn, vol ii, p 8, as an incorporeal chattel. I should be disposed to classify it myself as a chose in action, which has been defined to be a "right to be asserted or property reducible into possession either by action at law or suit in equity": see *Fleet v Perrins* [(1869) LR 4 QB 500, 505]. I refer to the common form of a patent: "Know ye therefore, that we . . . do by these presents . . . give and grant unto the said patentee our special licence, full power, sole privilege, and authority, that the said patentee by himself, his agents, or licencees, and no others, may . . . make, use, exercise, and vend the said invention . . . and that the said patentee shall have and enjoy the whole profit and advantage from time to time accruing by reason of the said invention. . . . And to the end that the said patentee may have and enjoy the sole use and exercise and the full benefit of the said invention, we do by these presents . . . strictly command all our subjects whatsoever . . . that they do not at any time during the continuance of the said term of fourteen years, either directly or indirectly, make use of or put in practice the said invention, or any part of the same, nor in anywise imitate the same nor make or cause to be made any addition thereto or subtraction therefrom . . . without the consent, licence, or agreement of the said patentee. . . ." Now this confers necessarily a right to bring an action to restrain infringement and to recover damages—at any rate, it is not a chose in possession.' *British Mutoscope & Biograph Co Ltd v Homer* [1901] 1 Ch 671 at 675, 676, per Farwell J

'It would be difficult to frame a complete or comprehensive definition of what falls under the term "patented article". . . . The term "patented article" would imply to most people any article protected by the patent. . . . The real test I think is—Does the article in question contain or embody the patentee's invention?' *Re Wardwell's Patent* (1913) 30 RPC 408 at 410, per cur.

PATENT AMBIGUITY *See* AMBIGUITY

PATENT DEFECT *See* DEFECT

PATIENT

'Patient' includes an expectant or nursing mother and a lying-in woman. (National Health Service Act 1977, s 128)

The functions of the judge under this Part of this Act [Part VIII: management of property and affairs of patients] shall be exercisable where, after considering medical evidence, he is satisfied that a person is incapable, by reason of mental disorder, of managing and administering his property and affairs; and a person as to whom a judge is so satisfied is in this part of this Act referred to as a patient. (Mental Health Act 1983, s 94(2))

'Patient' (except in Part VIII of this Act [see supra]) means a person suffering or appearing to be suffering from mental disorder. (Mental Health Act 1983, s 145(1))

[The Road Traffic Act 1972, s 8(2) (repealed; see now the Road Traffic Act 1988, s 7(2))

allows, in certain circumstances, a breath test to be taken from a person who was a 'patient' at a hospital.] 'A "patient" in our judgment, for this purpose, is someone who is at the hospital for the purpose of being treated. The essence of being a patient, as opposed to any other person coming to the hospital premises, is that the patient comes for treatment, and it seems to us, as a matter of plain English, that a person who comes to a hospital as a patient because he seeks treatment, will cease to be a patient as soon as the treatment contemplated for that visit is over.' *A-G's Reference (No 1 of 1976)* [1977] 3 All ER 557 at 559, CA, per cur.

PATRIAL

In the following provisions of this Act the word 'patrial' is used of persons having the right of abode in the United Kingdom. (Immigration Act 1971, s 2(6))

PATRIOTIC

Australia 'The words [in a will] are "to set apart a sum of £1,000 to be expended by my trustees from time to time and at their discretion for any patriotic purposes they may approve of". Mr Thompson [counsel] has been good enough to supply me with the definition of the word "patriotic" from Murray's English Dictionary on Historical Principles; that is as follows:—"Patriotic: Of or belonging to one's country; having the character of a patriot; marked by devotion to the well-being or interest of one's country." . . . It comes to this—that the testator directed that the money in question should be expended by the trustees for such purposes of general public utility as they might from time to time in their discretion approve. . . . The gift is not a good charitable bequest, and the bequest fails.' *Re Tyson, Tyson v Webb* (1906) 7 NSWSR 91 at 94, 95, per Street J

PATRON *See also* ADVOWSON

The expression 'the patron' with reference to any benefice means the person or persons for the time being entitled otherwise than by lapse to present or collate to such benefice upon a vacancy. (Benefices (Exercise of Rights of Presentation) Measure 1931 (No 3), s 9)

The expression 'the patron' means the person or body of persons or corporation for the time being entitled to a right of patronage, including a trustee, whether for sale or otherwise, and the incumbent of a benefice in whom a right of patronage is vested by virtue of his office. (Benefices (Purchase of Rights of Patronage) Measure 1933, s 1)

The expression 'right of patronage' means the perpetual right of presentation to a benefice on a vacancy, including an alternate right, and 'presentation' includes in the case of a non-presentative benefice nomination. (Benefices (Purchase of Rights of Patronage) Measure 1933, s 1)

'Patron', in relation to any benefice, means the person or persons for the time being entitled, otherwise than by lapse, to present to that benefice upon a vacancy, including—

(a) in any case where the right to present is vested in different persons jointly, every person whose concurrence would be required for the exercise of the joint right, and
(b) in any case where the patronage is vested in different persons by way of alternate or successive right of presentation, every person who is for the time being the person who would be entitled to present on the next or any subsequent turn,

and 'right of patronage' shall be construed accordingly:

Provided that, in the application of these definitions, the fact that any person is a Roman Catholic shall be disregarded. (Pastoral Measure 1983, s 87(1))

PATTERN *See* DESIGN

PAUPER *See* INDIGENT

PAWN

A 'pawn' or 'pledge' is a bailment of personal property as a security for some debt or engagement. A 'pawnor' is one who, being liable to an engagement, gives to the person to whom he is liable a thing to be held as a security for the payment of his debt or the fulfilment of his liability. A 'pawnee' is one who receives a pawn or pledge. . . .

The contract of pawn or pledge is one of the five classes of bailment. It is distinguishable from a transaction of mortgage in two main ways. In the first place it is essential to the contract of pawn that the property pledged should be actually or constructively delivered to the pawnee, whereas on a mortgage the property passes by assignment, and possession by the mortgagee is not essential in every case. Secondly, whereas on a legal mortage of personal property the mortgagee acquires by assignment an absolute interest in the property subject to a right of redemption, in pawn the pawnee has only a special property in the pledge, while the general property in it remains in the pawnor and wholly reverts to him on discharge of the debt or engagement.

Pawn has been described as a security where, by contract, a deposit of goods is made a security for a debt and the right to the property vests in the pawnee so far as is necessary to secure the debt; in this sense it is intermediate between a simple lien and a mortgage which wholly passes the property in the thing conveyed. (36 Halsbury's Laws (4th edn) paras 101, 103)

A mortgage conveys the whole legal interest in the chattels; a pawn conveys only a special property, leaving the general property in the pawnor: a pawn is subject in law to a right of redemption, and no higher or different right of redemption exists in equity than at law; a mortgage is subject, not only to the legal condition for redemption, but to the superadded equity. A pawn involves transfer of the possession from the pawnor to the pawnee. A mortgage may be made without any transfer of possession. In my opinion, the two transactions of pawn and mortgage are in their nature distinct, and I think that, except by new agreement between the parties, what was originally a pawn never becomes a mortgage, and what was originally a mortgage never becomes a pawn.' *Re Morritt, ex p Official Receiver* (1886) 18 QBD 222 at 234, 235, CA, per Fry LJ

PAWNBROKER

A 'pawnbroker' is one whose business is to lend money, usually in small sums, upon pawn or pledge, and includes, for statutory purposes, every person who carries on the business of taking goods and chattels in pawn. (36 Halsbury's Laws (4th edn) para 101)

PAY (Remuneration)

[An award provided that the amount of permanent maintenance to be paid by the defendant should be adjusted according to the amount of his army 'pay'.] 'First, as to the meaning of the word "pay". . . . From the total amount received by the defendant he seeks to deduct two main items on the ground that they do not fall within the meaning of the word "pay". The two items are (1) command pay and (2) allowances. . . . I shall not deal . . . with "allowances" because I am satisfied that these are not "pay" within the meaning of the award. . . . In my opinion "command pay" is distinct in substance and fact from mere allowances. It is "pay" in the true sense. It is a definite financial remuneration for discharging the duties of a definite rank. I think that it falls within the fair meaning of the word "pay".' *Bayley v Bayley* [1922] 2 KB 227 at 228–231, per McCardie J

PAY (Verb) *See also* PAYABLE; PAYMENT

'I apprehend, where a person writes under a bill the word paid, with the name of the tradesman, it will be difficult to say that it does not purport to be a receipt for the money.' *R v Houseman* (1837) 8 C & P 180 at 182, per Lord Denman CJ

'The trustee is to "pay such money"; but he is to "deliver over such property". "Money" and "property" are clearly distinguished; and I confess that, to my mind, the word "property" here does not include "money". The words are, to "pay" money and to "deliver" property. If it had been necessary to identify the actual money which had been received, I cannot think that the phraseology used would have been to "pay" the money. Other words, such as "to pay over the money", would, I think, have been used. But the words used are, "pay such money". That is the phraseology ordinarily used when speaking of the payment of a debt. To "pay" money is to pay it in respect of a right which some person has to receive it—not to pay over any particular money or hand over any particular coins.' *Re Miller, ex p Official Receiver* [1893] 1 QB 327 at 334, CA, per Lord Esher MR

Canada '"Pay" may mean many things. Usually money is not paid until the debtor seeks out his creditor and puts it in the hands of the creditor, but it does not necessarily mean that; under some circumstances and some contracts, or in the course of practice adopted by the debtor and the creditor, the money may be paid as soon as it is mailed by post, properly addressed to the creditor. In that case the responsibility for its loss or delay lies not upon the shoulders of the debtor but upon the shoulders of the creditor.' *R v Kern's Motor Town Sales Ltd* [1968] CTC 221 at 222, BCCA, per Davey CJBC

In Companies Acts

For the purposes of this subsection [prohibition of allotment of share capital unless minimum subscription received], a sum is deemed paid to the company and received by it, if a cheque for that sum has been received in good faith by the company and the directors have no reason for suspecting that the cheque will not be paid. (Companies Act 1985, s 83(2))

In Gaming Act

[The Gaming Act 1892, s 1 provides that any promise to pay a person any sum of money 'paid' by him under or in respect of any contract or agreement rendered null and void by the Gaming Act 1845 is null and void, and no action may be brought or maintained to recover any such sum of money. The question was whether a sum of money deposited with a stakeholder was within the section.] 'I think that the word "paid" in the connection in which it is used by the Act of 1892, and having regard to the stage in the history of the law at which it was so used, ought not, upon the true construction of the Act, to be read as covering a deposit such as this, i.e. a sum handed to a person with a mandate that in a particular event it is to be paid to a particular person.' *Burge v Ashley & Smith Ltd* [1900] 1 QB 744 at 750, 751, CA, per Collins LJ

'It would be unreasonable to limit the words [in s 1] of the [Gaming] Act [1892], "any sum of money paid", to sums of money actually paid. . . . Those words mean money "to be paid" equally with money "actually paid".' *Levy v Warburton* (1901) 70 LJKB 708 at 709, per Kennedy J

In Income Tax Acts

Canada '"Pay" may mean many things. Usually money is not paid until the debtor seeks out his creditor and puts it in the hands of the creditor, but it does not necessarily mean that; under some circumstances and some contracts, or in the course of practice adopted by the debtor and the creditor, the money may be paid as soon as it is mailed by post, properly addressed to the creditor. In that case the responsibility for its loss or delay lies not upon the shoulders of the debtor but upon the shoulders of the creditor.' *R v Kern's Motor Town Sales Ltd* [1968] CTC 221 at 222, per Davey CJBC

In Insolvency Acts

[The Bankruptcy Act 1883, s 35 (repealed; see now the Insolvency Act 1986, s 129) enabled the court to annul the adjudication of a bankrupt on proof to the satisfaction of the court that his debts were 'paid' in full.] 'I cannot agree . . . that the release of a debt is equivalent to or the same as "payment in full", which, by s 35 of the Bankruptcy Act 1883 is the condition precedent to the exercise of the jurisdiction to annul. . . . The section is not very clear, but I think that in practice it has always been construed as meaning that the condition of annulment is payment in full of all debts which have been admitted to proof, unless the proof has been expunged on the ground that it never ought to have been admitted.' *Re Keet* [1905] 2 KB 666 at 672–674, CA, per Vaughan Williams LJ

PAY CASH *See* CHEQUE

PAYABLE

'Words, accompanying an acceptance, "payable at a particular place", or the words "accepted, payable at, etc" are not words restricting or qualifying the acceptor's liability, but rendering him generally and universally liable, and it is not necessary to prove a demand at the particular place in an action against such acceptor.' *Smith v De la Fontaine* (1785) Holt NP 366, n at 366, 367, per Lord Mansfield CJ

'Whatever cases may be adduced in favour of, or against, the doctrine laid down by KB in *Fenton v Goundry* [(1811) 13 East 459], an invincible argument with me for the opinion there given is, the constant and undeviating usage of merchants; who never consider such an acceptance to be a restrictive acceptance; that it is mere matter of convenient arrangement, and does not raise any obligation, on the part of the holder, to demand payment at the particular place.' Ibid at 367, per Lord Ellenborough

'In an action against the acceptor, where the bill is accepted "payable at a particular place", as in the present case, it is not necessary to prove a demand at that place. He is generally and universally liable upon such an acceptance.' *Head v Sewell* (1816) Holt NP 363 at 363, 364, per Gibbs CJ

'The main argument . . . presented to your Lordships was centred on the words "payable to". It was said that those words necessitated the existence of a payer and a payee, and that income could not become "payable" out of partnership funds to a company which was a member of the partnership. A partner, it was contended, was already the owner, among other things, of his share of the partnership profits and could no more pay himself out of those profits than an individual could pay himself out of the profits of his own business. No doubt, it is true to say that an individual cannot pay himself, if "pay" be used in its strict sense, but no question of an individual's ability to do so arises here. The only question is whether income can be said to be payable to a partner out of the partnership assets. I think it can. "Payable" is not a term of art, and, though a partner cannot sue the partnership or the partners individually for the purposes of recovering partnership assets, yet . . . he has at his disposal means whereby he can ensure that his share reaches his hands. In such circumstances it seems to me that the word "payable" is appropriately used and accurately conveys the process by which the income finds its way into the pocket of the individual. It would, I think, not inaccurately be described as having been paid to him out of the partnership funds.' *Latilla v Inland Revenue Comrs* [1943] AC 377 at 384, 385, per Lord Porter

Instalments

United States 'Payable in instalments' means that payment is required or permitted by agreement to be made in (a) two or more periodic payments, excluding a down payment, with respect to a debt arising from a consumer credit sale pursuant to which a credit service charge is made, (b) four or more periodic payments, excluding a down payment, with respect to a debt arising from a consumer credit sale pursuant to which no credit service charge is made, or (c) two or more periodic payments with respect to a debt arising from a consumer loan. If any periodic payment other than a down payment under an agreement requiring or permitting two or more periodic payments is more than twice the amount of any other periodic payment, excluding the down payment, the consumer credit sale, consumer lease, or consumer loan is 'payable in instalments'. (Uniform Consumer Credit Code 1969, s 1.301(12))

In settlement

'A portion is not properly said to be payable by trustees until two things have occurred, viz when the time appointed for raising it has arrived, and the person entitled is able to give a discharge for it; but a portion is often said to be payable to a child so soon as the event has happened which gives the child a vested interest in it; and in the latter case, the word "payable" denotes only that the child is entitled or enabled to receive such share or portion.' *Massy v Lloyd* (1863) 10 HL Cas 248 at 268, per Lord Westbury LC

[By the terms of a settlement, the income of a trust fund was to be paid to certain children, at twenty-one if male, at twenty-one or on marriage if female; and the issue of any of the said children whose parent or parents were to die before his, her or their share or shares became 'payable' were to be entitled to the share or shares which his, her or their parent or parents would have been entitled to if living.] 'Can there be a doubt, independently of authority, that the words "before his, her or their share or shares become payable" mean before the period of distribution? One remark which strongly tends to shew this to be the meaning is, that if you read "payable" as "vested" as I am asked to do, then the provision in favour of issue can never take effect as regards daughters, for a daughter cannot have children until she is married, and if she marries her share becomes vested.' *Day v Radcliffe* (1876) 3 Ch D 654 at 657, per Jessel MR

'The question arises entirely upon the construction of a very few words in a marriage settlement. . . . The words are "as tenants in common and not as joint tenants, the share of such child or children as shall be a son or sons to be paid to him or them upon his or their respectively arriving at the full age of twenty-one years, and the share or shares of such of them as shall be daughters to be paid upon their respectively arriving at their full age of twenty-one years or day or days of marriage, whichever shall first happen." . . . Then it goes on "with benefit of survivorship to the survivor or survivors of such children if any of such children shall die before his, her, or their share or shares shall become payable." If it had stopped there, there could not have been a doubt upon it that "payable" would have meant "shall become vested whether the time for distribution has come or not". Then come the words "unmarried and without leaving issue as aforesaid" and the . . . only question, is, Have these words such a meaning as to shew that there is something which prevents the words "paid" and "payable" being construed not in their primary meaning, but in the meaning which I have already mentioned? It seems to me that there is nothing.' *Wakefield v Maffet* (1885) 10 App Cas 422 at 429, 430, per Lord Blackburn

'"Paid and payable" means no more than payable, . . . and "payable" in reference to portions is a very elastic word, capable of meaning "vested" if the context requires it, but primarily referring to the time of actual payment, whether the portion is or is not antecedently vested.' *Haverty v Curtis* [1895] 1 IR 23 at 32, per Porter MR

In will

[A testator by his will gave his estate, subject to a life interest, to trustees to hold in trust for his nephew and nieces, and to pay it to them equally at their respective ages of twenty-one years; with survivorship in case any one should die before his or their shares became 'payable'.] 'The bequest in this case being absolute in the first instance, and not depending upon the contingency of surviving the testator's mother, the question is, whether it is qualified by the subsequent words; and made to depend upon that contingency. The introduction of a period of payment by itself, would have had no effect upon the right. A trust being already declared for the benefit of the nephew and nieces, those additional words would only postpone the payment; but then the testator does not mean, that any nephew or niece, who should die under the age of twenty-one, should take a vested interest; and my opinion is, that all he intended by the subsequent words was to give to those, who should attain the age of twenty-one, the shares of those who should die under that age. He has, however, used the word "payable", a word of ambiguous import: in one sense and with reference to the capacity of the persons to take, he had just before declared, that the age of twenty-one was the period, at which their shares were to be payable; in another sense, with reference to the interest of the tenant for life, they could not be payable until her death; but then it is with the direction to pay at the age of twenty-one that the bequest over is immediately connected; and it is to that period of payment as it seems to me, that the subsequent words, are most naturally to be referred. . . . In the cases referred to the difficulty did not merely consist in finding a restricted meaning for the word "payable", though it was necessary in most of them so to do, but in getting the better of other words; which seemed almost expressly to postpone the vesting until after the death of the parent. Whereas here the whole turns upon the meaning of the word "payable". There is no other difficulty: that word is determined in almost all those cases to be capable of a double construction; and the construction, which I am inclined to put upon it, is that, which seems to me to be most consistent with the testator's intention.' *Hallifax v Wilson* (1809) 16 Ves 168 at 171–173, per Grant MR

'The first gift is to the children . . . when and as they shall attain the age of twenty-one years; and if any of them happen to die before their shares become payable, leaving issue, their shares are to go to their issue; but, if they die before their shares become payable, leaving no lawful issue, their shares are to go to the survivors or survivor of them. . . . The question is whether "payable" does not mean on attaining twenty-one? I think that it does.' *Jones v Jones* (1843) 13 Sim 561 at 568, per Shadwell V-C

'The testator . . . gives shares of his residue to each of his two daughters during their lives, and after their deaths to their children; that is a vested gift to the children. He then directs these shares to be paid to the children at the age of twenty-one, and this is distinct from the period of vesting. To be paid to them does not mean it to be paid to them at twenty-one, although the mother should be alive, but it means that they shall be entitled to payment at twenty-one if the mother be dead. He then says, with benefit of survivorship amongst such children if either of them shall die before his or her share shall become payable. In that event, the share is to go over to the others. The testator then directs, that in case the last-named daughters or either of them shall happen to die without issue, or having issue if all of them shall die without becoming entitled to the receipt of the trust money, it shall go to the daughter's next of kin. How can the words "entitled to the receipt" differ from the word "payable"? Whenever there is money payable, there is somebody entitled to the receipt of the money to be paid, and I am unable to distinguish between the expression, that there is money payable to a person, and that there is a person entitled to the receipt of that money which is to be paid. In neither case does it mean the actual receipt of the money, because if it did, it would be unmeaning, for if so, until the money has been received, no right could accrue; nor could it mean, that any formal or accidental delay in payment after the right to the receipt had accrued would give the next of kin a right to the money. But it means, "before the money becomes payable", that is to say, before there are persons in existence who are entitled to receive the money, provided it could be paid at that period.' *Hayward v James* (1860) 28 Beav 523 at 528, 529, per Sir John Romilly MR

'The language used here is so rational and consistent that the court can do nothing less than carry it out in its literal sense. It is this: "A gift of £2,000 to David Maxwell Aitken, and in case of his death before the same should be actually paid or payable to him, then the trustees for the time being are directed to stand possessed thereof, or the securities whereon the same should be invested, in trust for all of his children." The word "paid" points so distinctly to an event which the testator intended should happen, that there can be no doubt about it. "Payable" would seem only to refer to the legatee's death in the lifetime of the testator. In one of the cases referred to in the course of the argument, the words "due and payable" are made use of, and in another "payable and divisible". These are such doubtful expressions that they might well give rise to considerable argument. But in the present case nothing can be more rational and explicit than the language used; it provides that in case of the legatee dying before the legacy shall have been paid to him, his children are to have the benefit of it.' *Whitman v Aitken* (1866) 14 LT 248 at 248, per Stuart V-C

[A testator by his will bequeathed property to A for life, with remainder to B, and with a gift over in case of death before the original gift became 'payable'.] 'Unquestionably, in the ordinary use of language, the words "before it becomes payable" would mean before it comes to the hands of the person who is to receive it; but the inconvenience of such a construction, leading as it does to the postponement of the time at which an absolute interest is taken, is so great that the court has held, in a very long series of decisions, that "payable" shall mean "vested".' *Haydon v Rose* (1970) LR 10 Eq 224 at 227, 228, per Lord Romilly MR

'I am entirely inclined to give the natural meaning to the words of a will whenever I can, and I should have been disposed to give to the word "payable" in the present case its natural meaning—i.e. as referring to the time of actual payment—but for the existence of a class of authorities which shew that it may be construed differently, and for the particular words of this will. . . . I think there are indications of intention in the will which lead to an inference that the rule in *Hallifax v Wilson* [supra] ought to be applied. In the first place, the words of the gift over are "payable as aforesaid", and the words of the previous trust for payment are "as and when they shall severally and respectively attain their respective age or ages of twenty-one years". I think the words "as aforesaid" must be taken to refer to that direction to pay, so that the gift over in the event of the death of a child before its share becomes payable is equivalent to a gift over in the event of its death under twenty-one. Again, the power of maintenance given to the trustees is limited to the minorities of the children, and this, though a small point, looks in the same direction. Again, the ultimate gift over is in the event of the death of all the children under twenty-one without leaving a child, and the inference is that the gift over in the event of the death of all the children and the gift over in the event of the death of some of them were intended to apply in a similar state of circumstances, which they would not do, unless I read the words "payable as aforesaid" as meaning the attainment of twenty-one, so that both the gifts over may apply to death without issue under twenty-one.' *Partridge v Baylis* (1881) 17 Ch D 835 at 837, 838, per Fry J

PAYABLE ON DEMAND

New Zealand 'What is meant by "payable on demand" in the debentures? It was submitted that "upon demand" cannot in the context mean instantaneously upon service of a demand without regard to the surrounding circumstances but must mean within a reasonable period of service of the demand having regard to all the surrounding circumstances. I am satisfied that such a submission is sound.' *ANZ Banking Group (NZ) Ltd v Gibson* [1981] 2 NZLR 513 at 526, per Holland J

PAYING GUEST

'I do not think that "paying guest" is an accurate description when the "paying guest" has to do all her own work in connection with the accommodatioon which she has and the only thing with which she is provided is a little food.' *R v Battersea Rent Tribunal, ex p Parikh* [1957] 1 All ER 352 at 355, per Cassels J

PAYMENT *See also* ADVANCE; ANNUAL PAYMENT; PAY; PAYABLE; REPAYMENT

'Payment' includes any pecuniary or other reward. (Representation of the People Act 1983, s 118)

[The Statute of Frauds 1677, s 4 provides that any promise to pay for the debt, default or miscarriage of another shall be void, unless some note or memorandum thereof is in writing and signed by the party to be charged.] 'If two come to a shop, and one buys, and the other, to gain him credit, promises the seller, if he does not pay you, I will; this a collateral undertaking, and void without writing, by the Statute of Frauds: But if he says, let him have the goods, I will be your paymaster, or I will see you paid, this is an undertaking as for himself, and he shall be intended to be the very buyer, and the other to act but as his servant.' *Birkmyr v Darnell* (1704) 1 Salk 27 at 28, per cur.

'The words, "I will see you paid", as it seems to me, may mean either one thing or the other. "I will see you paid", that is, "I will pay you", or "You shall be paid". But I do not think these words are necessarily to be taken . . . as meaning, "I will see that somebody else pays you", or that "your principal debtor pays you; and if he does not, I will be the surety for payment". I do not think that phrase, "I will see you paid", has any hard and fast meaning of that kind; it must depend on the other facts of the case.' *Mountstephen v Lakeman* (1871) LR 7 QB 196 at 205, per Pigott B

'Nothing is clearer than that if parties account with each other, and sums are stated to be due on one side, and sums to an equal amount due on the other side on that account, and those accounts are settled by both parties, it is exactly the same thing as if the sums due on both sides had been paid. Indeed, it is a general rule of law, that in every case where a transaction resolves itself into paying money by A to B, and then handing it back again by B to A, if the parties meet together and agree to set one demand against the other, they need not go through the form and ceremony of handing the money backwards and forwards.' *Re Harmony & Montague Tin & Copper Mining Co, Spargo's Case* (1873) LR 8 Ch App 407 at 414, per Mellish LJ

[The Real Property Limitation Act 1874, s 8 (repealed; see now the Limitation Act 1980, s 15) provided that no action to recover money secured by mortgage, or otherwise charged upon or payable out of land, should be brought but within twelve years after the last 'payment' of principal or interest.] 'It appears to me clear that the payment to take the case out of the statute must not be a payment by a stranger, but must be a payment by a person who is entitled to pay the principal or interest of the mortgage money.' *Re Clifden (Lord), Annaly v Agar-Ellis* [1900] 1 Ch 774 at 780, per Byrne J

'The word "fund" may mean actual cash resources of a particular kind (e.g. money in a drawer or a bank), or it may be a mere accountancy expression used to describe a particular category which a person uses in making up his accounts. The words "payment out of" when used in connection with the word "fund" in its first meaning connote actual payment, e.g. by taking the money out of the drawer or drawing a cheque on the bank. When used in connection with the word "fund" in its second meaning they connote that, for the purposes of the account in which the fund finds a place, the payment is debited to that fund, an operation which, of course, has no relation to the actual method of payment or the particular cash resources out of which the payment is made. Thus, if a company makes a payment out of its reserve fund—an example of the second meaning of the word "fund"—the actual payment is made by cheque drawn on the company's banking account, the money in which may have been derived from a number of sources. The phrase "reserve fund" only has a meaning as indicating the item in the company's accounts to which it decides to debit the payment. It will be seen, therefore, that to speak of an actual payment being made out of a fund in the second sense is really a misuse of language. A fund in the second sense is merely an accountancy category. It has a real existence in that sense, but not in the sense that a real payment can be made out of it as distinct from being debited to it. Unless these two meanings of the phrase "payment out of a fund" are kept distinct, much confusion of thought must ensue. A real payment cannot be made out of an imaginary fund; per Lord Macmillan in the *Central London Railway* case [*Central London Rly Co v Inland Revenue Comrs* [1937] AC 77].' *Allchin v Coulthard* [1942] 2 KB 228 at 234, 235, CA, per Lord Greene MR; affirmed [1943] AC 607, HL

'The word "payment" in itself is one which, in an appropriate context, may cover many ways of discharging obligations. It may even . . . include a discharge, not by money payment at all, but by what is called "payment in kind".'

White v Elmdene Estates Ltd [1959] 2 All ER 605 at 610, 611, CA, per Lord Evershed MR; affirmed [1960] 1 All ER 306, HL

PEACE

'I think the learned counsel for the respondent was right in saying that the law recognises a state of peace and a state of war, but that it knows nothing of an intermediate state which is neither the one thing nor the other—neither peace nor war. In every community it must be for the supreme power, whatever it is, to determine the policy of the community in regard to peace and war. It is not, I think, for private individuals to pronounce upon the foreign relations of their Sovereign or their country and to measure their own responsibilities arising out of civil contracts with foreigners by a standard of public policy which they set up for themselves, even though their views may be right in the abstract and might possibly find acceptance with a jury of their countrymen if such a question were within the competence of such a tribunal. Public policy, in my opinion, requires a good citizen in matters of this sort to conform to the rule and guidance of the State. However critical may be the condition of affairs, however imminent war may be, if and so long as the Government of the State abstains from declaring or making war or accepting a hostile challenge there is peace—peace with all attendant consequences—for all its subjects.' *Janson v Driefontein Consolidated Mines Ltd* [1902] AC 484 at 497, 498, per Lord Macnaghten

'The authorities shew that, in the absence of any specific statutory or contractual provision to the contrary, the general rule of international law is that as between civilised Powers who have been at war, peace is not concluded until a treaty of peace is finally binding upon the belligerents, and that that stage is not reached until ratifications of the treaty of peace have been exchanged between them.' *Kotzias v Tyser* [1920] 2 KB 69 at 76, 77, per Roche J

Canada '"Public peace" may be taken as equivalent to "the King's Peace", in its broader and later signification. The King's Peace is "the legal name of the normal state of society" (Stephens' History of the Criminal Law, Vol 1, p 185). "The Peace" is defined in Murray's New English Dictionary as being "the King's Peace in its widest sense, the general peace and order of the realm as provided for by law." "Peace", particularly connotes "a quiet and harmless behaviour towards the King and his people".' *R (Wilbur) v Magee* [1923] 3 WWR 55 at 57, Sask CA, per Haultain CJS

New Zealand [A lease provided that the term should expire 'twelve calendar months after the date of declaration of peace between the British Empire and Germany in respect of the present state of war'.] 'The words of the lease are "the date of the *declaration* of peace". There has been no actual "declaration of peace", and it therefore becomes necessary to consider what can be gathered as to the intention of the parties from the use of such words. "The law recognises a state of peace and a state of war, but it knows nothing of an intermediate state which is neither the one thing nor the other—neither peace nor war": per Lord Macnaghten, in *Janson v Driefontein Consolidated Mines Ltd* [supra]. "The authorities show that . . . the general rule of international law is that . . . peace is not concluded until a treaty of peace is finally binding upon the belligerents, and that that stage is not reached until ratifications of the treaty of peace have been exchanged between them": per Roche J in *Kotzias v Tyser* [supra]. In that case . . . the defendant agreed to pay to the plaintiff a certain sum 'in the event of peace between Great Britain and Germany not being concluded on or before June 30th, 1919". Although the Treaty of Peace was signed on June 28th, 1919, it was held that peace had not been *concluded* "on or before June 30th, 1919". . . . In *Lloyd v Bowring* [(1920) 36 TLR 397] Mr Justice Sankey held, as regards a contract in which the words were "if peace is not declared", that the case was concluded by the judgment in *Kotzias v Tyser*. He said, "in that case the word used was 'concluded'; here the word was 'declared'; and he thought that the present was the stronger case of the two, for a thing could not be 'declared to exist' until it had actually come into existence." These cases appear to conclude the matter. Peace did not exist between the British Empire and Germany until the ratification of the treaty on the 10th January, 1920; therefore there could not be any state of affairs before that date which could be interpreted to be a declaration of peace.' *Thompson v Mason* [1921] NZLR 973 at 976, 977, per Reed J; also reported [1921] GLR 563 at 564, 565

PEACEABLY AND QUIETLY *See*

QUIET ENJOYMENT

PEACEFUL PICKETING *See* PICKETING

PEAT

'Peat is the vegetable and the soil of which it has become a part.' *Wilkinson v Haygarth* (1847) 12 QB 837 at 845, per Lord Denman CJ

PECULIAR

Some places, called 'peculiars', are exempt from the visitation of the customary Ordinary [bishop], and in the case of royal peculiars are visitable only by the Crown. Most of the peculiars which once existed were abolished by statute, but royal residences and certain other places still remain as peculiars [e.g. Westminster Abbey, St. George's Windsor, and the Chapels Royal]. The Temple Church is extra-diocesan.

The powers of the archbishops and bishops may, however, in certain cases be exercised over peculiars by virtue of express statutory provisions. (14 Halsbury's Laws (4th edn) para 492)

[Section 2 of Stat (1531–2) 23 Hen 8, c 9 (repealed) enacted that no person should be summoned before (inter alia) any commissary, or any other judge spiritual, out of the diocese, or 'peculiar' jurisdiction where the person summoned was inhabiting at the time of the summons, except in certain cases.] 'Another objection arising on stat 23 Hen 8, c 9, assumed that the appointment of a commissary constituted the district a peculiar; but we are clearly of opinion, that the word "peculiar" is there employed in the ordinary sense of some district exempt from the diocesan's jurisdiction, and that the commission appointing Dr Lushington judge for a particular part of the diocese within the bishop's jurisdiction does not make a peculiar.' *R v Thorogood* (1840) 12 Ad & El 183 at 197, 198, per Lord Denman CJ

[Statute (1531–2) 23 Hen 8, c 9, was repealed by the Ecclesiastical Jurisdiction Measure 1963; but by s 83(3) of the latter Measure, nothing therein authorises proceedings against a holder of an office in a Royal Peculiar.]

PECUNIARY ADVANTAGE

(1) A person who by any deception dishonestly obtains for himself or another any pecuniary advantage shall on conviction on indictment be liable to imprisonment for a term not exceeding five years.

(2) The cases in which a pecuniary advantage within the meaning of this section is to be regarded as obtained for a person are cases where—

(a) . . .

(b) he is allowed to borrow by way of overdraft, or to take out any policy of insurance or annuity contract, or obtains an improvement of the terms on which he is allowed to do so; or

(c) he is given the opportunity to earn remuneration or greater remuneration in an office or employment, or to win money by betting.

(Theft Act 1968, s 16, as amended by the Theft Act 1978, s 5(5))

PECUNIARY CONSIDERATION

[The Landlord and Tenant (Rent Control) Act 1949, s 18(1) (repealed; see now the Rent Act 1977, s 128(1)) provides that the expression 'premium' in the Act includes any fine or other like sum and any other 'pecuniary consideration' in addition to rent.] 'Of the real nature of this transaction no doubt can be entertained. It was born of the determination of the landlords to obtain a considerable sum of money in addition to the rent as a condition of the grant of a tenancy. It was carried out by requiring the sale of a house at an undervalue of £500. The respondent suffered a pecuniary detriment of that amount; the appellant company (or a third party to whom it surrendered that advantage) obtained a comparable benefit. If this is not a pecuniary consideration moving from the respondent, I do not know what those words mean. That there was consideration cannot be denied. Was it not pecuniary? That word is defined as meaning "of, belonging to or having relation to money". There may be transactions in which it is difficult to say whether the consideration is pecuniary. The line dividing valuable consideration which is pecuniary from that which is not is a twilight line, but on one side of it in broad noonday is the transaction in which one party says to the other: "I will not grant you a tenancy unless you sell me a house for £500 below its value". It is in substance, and I would be inclined to say in form also, a consideration stated in terms of money and it is not disguised by the cloak of a sale of property at an undervalue.' *Elmdene Estates Ltd v White* [1960] 1 All ER 306 at 309, HL, per Viscount Simonds

'Can a tenant be said to have *paid* a premium if he has agreed to discharge a debt due to him by the landlord? I would say "Yes". If such discharge is a pecuniary consideration, he has satisfied the landlord's demand for a premium by agreeing to the discharge and such satisfaction in the context of this Act is, in my opinion, equivalent to payment.' Ibid at 312, per Lord Keith of Avonholme

Australia [A testator by his will directed his trustee to hold his residuary estate on trust to pay one-third of the income to his widow, and subject thereto, on trust as to capital and income for his children. He empowered the trustee to use the residuary estate for the purchase or lease of a dwelling for the use of the widow and also to sell or dispose of such dwelling at any time. By an instrument executed by the widow, the children and the trustee, it was agreed that the income from the real estate should be paid to the widow and any deficiency below a certain amount charged upon the realty whilst the residue of the estate should be forthwith distributed amongst the children. The Third Schedule to the Stamps Act 1946–1949 (Vic) (repealed) see now the Stamps Act 1958–1986, Sch 3 Pt IX(a), includes amongst dutiable instruments, any instrument, whether voluntary or upon any good or valuable consideration other than a bona fide adequate 'pecuniary consideration', whereby any property is settled or agreed to be given or directed to be given in any manner whatsoever.] 'A pecuniary consideration is a consideration in money, not in money's worth. The widow gave up the chance of obtaining a larger income . . and acquired the greater degree of security which has already been mentioned. What she acquired did not amount to a pecuniary consideration. Similarly the children for what they gave up obtained an immediate right to the distribution of the residue of personalty instead of a postponed right. The consideration, however, was not pecuniary in the sense of money moving from a beneficiary under a settlement or an agreement for a settlement to a settlor, accordingly, the indenture is not within the exception as being made for a bona fide pecuniary consideration.' *Buzza v Comptroller of Stamps (Victoria)* (1951) 83 CLR 286 at 294, per Latham CJ

PECUNIARY DAMAGES *See* DAMAGES

PECUNIARY GAIN

New Zealand 'The words "pecuniary gain" are ordinary English words used in their ordinary sense. "Pecuniary" means no more than monetary or financial and its presence there [in the Industrial Relations Act 1973] excludes any argument that personal satisfaction or private convenience to the employer would be sufficient. It has been remarked judicially that gain is not susceptible of precise or scientific definition (*Armour v Liverpool Corporation* [1939] Ch 422, 437 per Simonds J). While in association with pecuniary it may be taken to mean an increase in or augmenting of financial resources, it does not follow that the undertaking must be intended to show an overall commercial profit before an employee can be regarded as employed for the pecuniary gain of the employer. If the services performed by the employee are allowed for in the charge which is made the employer's intention or purpose is to acquire gain from that employment whether he budgeted for an overall surplus or a loss.' *Salvation Army v Canterbury Hotel Union* [1985] 2 NZLR 366 at 370, per Richardson J

PECUNIARY INTEREST

[The Local Government Act 1933, s 76(1) (repealed; see now the Local Government Act 1972, ss 94–98) made it necessary for any member of a local authority who had a 'pecuniary interest' in a contract or proposed contract to disclose the fact in certain circumstances.] 'The object of s 76(1) is clearly to prevent councillors from voting on a matter which may affect their own pockets and, therefore, may affect their judgment, and a councillor's judgment may be affected by a proposal to preserve his liability just as much as by a proposal to terminate it, particularly where other persons in a like situation are being relieved from the same liability. In those circumstances, no narrow construction ought to be put on the words "pecuniary interest" in their context in s 76(1); in particular they ought not to be construed . . . as meaning pecuniary advantage. The appellants had a pecuniary interest in the sense that an existing liability in the case of some, and a possible future liability in the case of others, was going to be maintained, and in that way their pockets were or might be affected.' *Brown v Director of Public Prosecutions* [1956] 2 All ER 189 at 192, per Donovan J (also reported in [1956] 2 QB 369 at 378)

PECUNIARY LEGACY *See also* LEGACY

'If you find simply the word "legacy" used, and a direction to apportion the property amongst the legatees, unless there be something apparent on the face of the will which shows that the testator has not used the word in its ordinary legal signification, it will include annuitants. The expression "pecuniary legatees" in itself, I do not think, would go further than this—it would exclude specific legatees, that is, legatees of mere chattels, but it would have no effect in excluding, prima facie, annuitants from taking the same benefit as they would have taken if the word had been "legatees" instead of "pecuniary legatees". All these rules of construction are open to the general and cardinal principle of considering what you can collect from the testator's whole will, as to words which themselves are not of such clear and definite import as certain other words which have their established and fixed meaning in law.' *Gaskin v Rogers* (1866) LR 2 Eq 284 at 291, per Page Wood V-C

PECUNIARY LOSS INSURANCE *See* INSURANCE

PECUNIARY REWARD

'Money' and 'pecuniary reward' shall be deemed to include—

(a) any office, place or employment, and
(b) any valuable security or other equivalent of money, and
(c) any valuable consideration,

and expressions referring to money shall be construed accordingly. (Representation of the People Act 1983, s 185)

PEDESTRIAN SUBWAY *See* SUBWAY

PEDIGREE

Reputation or family tradition is admissible in certain circumstances for the purposes of proving or disproving pedigree or the existence of a marriage.

In matters of pedigree there must be a genealogical question in issue in the proceedings; the rule does not apply to proof of the facts which constitute a pedigree when they have to be proved for other purposes. The reputation must relate either directly or to some incident of family history required for the proof of such an issue. The declaration must have been made before the onset of the dispute by a person who has since died, and the declarant must have been related to the person whose pedigree is in question. A person related must be either a blood relative, or the spouse of one. (17 Halsbury's Laws (4th edn) para 82)

PEDIGREE ANIMAL *See* ANIMAL

PEDLAR *See also* HAWKER

The term 'pedlar' means any hawker, pedlar, petty chapman, tinker, caster of metals, mender of chairs, or other person who, without any horse or other beast bearing or drawing burden, travels and trades on foot and goes from town to town or to other men's houses, carrying to sell or exposing for sale any goods, wares, or merchandise, or procuring orders for goods, wares, or merchandise immediately to be delivered, or selling or offering for sale his skill in handicraft. (Pedlars Act 1871, s 3)

[Twelve ladies, of whom the respondent was one, purchased materials and made them up into articles of wearing apparel. Each in turn, for one month, carried these articles about in a basket, called a missionary basket, from house to house for sale. The ladies did not find the money to purchase the materials, but the money derived from the sales was applied towards the purchase, and the profits of the sales were devoted to a school and religious purposes. The question was whether the respondent came within the definition of a 'pedlar' in s 3 of the Pedlars Act 1871 (supra) and was liable under s 4 to a penalty for acting as a pedlar without a certificate.] 'It is quite clear that these ladies do not come within the mischief of the Act, and it is equally clear that they do not come within the definition of pedlar in s 3. The definition says that person is a pedlar who travels and trades on foot. The Act talks of the person licenced carrying on the trade of a pedlar. It is impossible to say that the chief officer of police, who is to grant these certificates under s 5, could be satisfied that these ladies "in good faith intended to carry on the trade of a pedlar". Again, the form of application for a pedlar's certificate is given in the second schedule, and on it the person applying is to state his trade and occupation, e.g. that he is a hawker, pedlar, etc. How is it possible for these ladies so to describe themselves? To say, therefore, that these ladies act as pedlars would be an abuse of language and common sense.' *Gregg v Smith* (1873) LR 8 QB 302 at 304, per Blackburn J

See, generally, 29 Halsbury's Laws (4th edn) paras 711 et seq.

PEERAGE

'Peerage' may be defined as a dignity to which is attached the right to a summons by name to sit and vote in Parliament. . . . The right to a peerage is distinct from a title of honour conferring a particular rank in the peerage, which is a merely collateral matter. There are today five degrees of peerage, namely, duke, marquess, earl, viscount and baron. Lords of Appeal in Ordinary and life peers are entitled to rank as barons.

The following are the five classes of peers:—

(1) Peers of England. They are all entitled to a summons to the Parliament of the United Kingdom.

(2) Peers of Scotland. From 1707 until 1963 they were represented in the Parliament of the United Kingdom by sixteen representative peers of Scotland. Since 1963 they have all been entitled to writs of summons to the Parliament of the United Kingdom.

(3) Peers of Great Britain. These are peers created between the dates of the Union with Scotland and the Union with Ireland. They are entitled to a writ of summons to the Parliament of the United Kingdom. . . .

(5) Peers of the United Kingdom. These are peers created since the Union with Ireland other than peers of Scotland or Ireland. They are entitled to a writ of summons to sit in Parliament.

In addition to peers there are peeresses in their own right of England, of Scotland and of the United Kingdom. Most of them have inherited their peerages, although hereditary peerages have occasionally been conferred upon women. Peeresses in their own right possess all the privileges of peerage including the right of sitting and voting in the House of Lords. A life peerage may be conferred on a woman, who thereby becomes entitled to a writ of summons and to sit and vote in the House of Lords. (35 Halsbury's Laws (4th edn) paras 802–805)

[The power of Her Majesty to confer life peerages by letters patent (other than spiritual peers and Lords of Appeal in Ordinary) is given by the Life Peerages Act 1958. Such life peers rank as barons and are entitled to writs of summons to attend the House of Lords.

Hereditary peerages may be disclaimed under the provisions of the Peerage Act 1963.

The right to elect Irish representative peers no longer exists. See *Petition of the Earl of Antrim* [1967] 1 AC 691, HL.]

'I did not hear any reply given by Sir F Thesiger, who was counsel in this case, when he was asked what in point of fact was the interpretation to be given to the word "peerage"—I did not hear any answer given to that question, though it was given by some of the learned judges, namely, that the plain and simple interpretation of the word "peerage" and that which puts the different parts of this Act [Union with Ireland Act 1800] in perfect unison together, was, that peerage was the status and condition of a peer, and although one peer might hold together many titles, yet that he had by virtue of his titles but one peerage, and that consequently so long as one of those titles remained in him or his descendants, there was not an extinction of a peerage, although the peerage was robbed of one, two, or three of the titles appertaining to it. I think that is the fair and reasonable construction of the word "peerage".' *Fermoy Peerage Case* (1856) 28 LTOS 15 at 18, per Lord Derby

'A peerage is an inalienable incorporeal hereditament created by the act of the Sovereign which, if and when he creates it, carries with it certain attributes which attach to it not by reason of any grant of those attributes by the Crown, but as essentially existing at common law by reason of the enoblement created by the grant of the peerage. The right to sit in Parliament is such an attribute. It is a right residing at common law in the person ennobled and exercisable by him unless for some reason he is disqualified from exercising it. The right to ennoble, which resides solely in the Crown, can be exercised only consistently with the common law, so that, for instance, the dignity cannot be made descendible in a course not known to the law. By parity of reasoning I think the dignity cannot be created so as not to carry with it attributes which the common law annexes to it. One of these is the right to sit in Parliament. This is not a right existent to-day and not existent tomorrow, ceasing to exist when an adult peer dies and is succeeded by a minor, coming again into existence when the minor attains his majority. The right exists during the minority, but is in abeyance because the minor has not attained his majority.'

Rhondda (Viscountess's) Claim [1922] 2 AC 339 at 393, 394, per Lord Wrenbury

PENAL

'A penal law is a statute which imposes a penalty.' *Spencer (Earl) v Swannell* (1838) 7 LJ Ex 73 at 74, per cur.

'Their Lordships have already indicated that, in their opinion, the phrase "penal actions", which is so frequently used to designate that class of actions which, by the law of nations, are exclusively assigned to their domestic forum, does not afford an accurate definition. In its ordinary acceptation, the word "penal" may embrace penalties for infractions of general law which do not constitute offences against the State; it may for many legal purposes be applied with perfect propriety to penalties created by contract; and it therefore, when taken by itself, fails to mark that distinction between civil rights and criminal wrongs which is the very essence of the international rule. The phrase was used by Lord Loughborough and by Mr Justice Buller in a well-known case (*Folliott v Ogden* [(1789) 1 H Bl 135], and *Ogden v Folliott* [(1789) 3 TR 734]), and also by Chief Justice Marshall, who, in *The Antelope* [10 Wheaton 123 (USA)], thus stated the rule with no less brevity than force: "The Courts of no country execute the penal laws of another". Read in the light of the context, the language used by these eminent lawyers is quite intelligible, because they were dealing with the consequences of violations of public law and order, which were unmistakably of a criminal complexion. But the expressions "penal" and "penalty", when employed without qualification, express or implied, are calculated to mislead, because they are capable of being construed so as to extend the rule to all proceedings for the recovery of penalties, whether exigible by the State in the interest of the community, or by private persons in their own interest.' *Huntington v Attrill* [1893] AC 150 at 186, PC, per Lord Watson

PENALISE

Australia 'To penalise a person means to punish, or subject him to some penalty, detriment or disadvantage, because of a real or supposed dereliction on his part.' *Wells v English Electric Company of Australia Ltd* (1926) 38 CLR 295 at 299, per Knox CJ, Gavan Duffy and Starke JJ

'Though the word "penalise", as a matter of origin, comes from the Latin for punishment, it is habitually used in a much wider sense—*uti loquitur vulgus*; and that is the sense which we must give to such non-technical words. According to the Oxford Dictionary, there is a general meaning as well as the meaning of origin—the meaning "to subject to comparative disadvantage, to handicap".' Ibid at 305, per Higgins J

PENALTY *See also* DAMAGES

Liquidated damages distinguished

'Where a sum is payable as a punishment for a default, or by way of security, and the realisation of that sum is not within the original intention of the parties, the sum is a penalty; but when it forms part of the original intention, that upon default a sum otherwise payable at a future period, shall become forthwith payable, it is no longer a penalty.' *Protector Loan Co v Grice* (1880) 5 QBD 592 at 596, CA, per Bramwell LJ

'In this case, although there is a substantial difference between the damages which would arise on two events, the same sum is made payable in either event. Under those circumstances I think that this sum is a penalty and not liquidated damages.' *Willson v Love* [1896] 1 QB 626 at 630, 631, CA, per Lord Esher MR

'I believe that from the time of *Kemble v Farren* [(1829) 6 Bing 141] down to the present day it has been the recognised opinion of the legal profession that, where a sum is made payable by a contract to secure performance of several stipulations, the damages for the breach of which respectively must be substantially different, or, in other words, the performance of stipulations of varying degrees of importance, that sum is prima facie to be regarded as a penalty and not as liquidated damages.' Ibid at 631, per Smith LJ

'There was another class of actions as to which there was no definite limitation of time, namely, "actions for penalties, damages or sums of money given to the party grieved" by various Acts of Parliament, by way of penalty or punishment; not by way of compensation to the person injured, but where, as was pointed out by Lord Esher MR, when commenting in *Saunders v Wiel* [[1892] 2 QB 321] upon *Adams v Batley* [(1887) 18 QBD 625], punishment was the object; and where the money to be paid, whether it was called penalty, or damage or sum of money, was not assessed with the view of compensating the plaintiff, although he might put some of it in his pocket. That is the class of action which . . . are popularly called "penal actions".' *Thomson v Clanmorris (Lord)* [1900] 1 Ch 718 at 725, CA, per Lindley MR

'Though the parties to a contract who use the words "penalty" or "liquidated damages" may prima facie be supposed to mean what they say, yet the expression used is not conclusive. . . . The essence of a penalty is a payment of money stipulated as *in terrorem* of the offending party.' *Dunlop Pneumatic Tyre Co Ltd v New Garage & Motor Co Ltd* [1915] AC 79 at 86, 87, per Lord Dunedin

'The only question that has to be determined in the present case is whether the sum that the parties have mentioned in the agreement is obviously larger than any damage that could possibly be sustained by the plaintiffs by reason of any particular breach of the contract. If it is larger than any such damage then we must hold that the sum is a penalty and not liquidated damages: if it is not larger, then . . . it seems to me that we are driven to the conclusion that these sums constitute liquidated damages and not a penalty.' *Imperial Tobacco Co (of Great Britain & Ireland) Ltd v Parslay* [1936] 2 All ER 515 at 526, CA, per Romer LJ

'My Lords, when a question arises whether a sum stipulated to be payable under a contract is liquidated damages for a breach of that contract or some part of it or is a penalty attached to the breach, I think that, by this date, there is ample guidance in the authorities how to decide between the two alternatives. The appropriate tests have been worked out in a number of leading cases and, as we know, they are conveniently brought together in the speech of Lord Dunedin in *Dunlop Pneumatic Tyre Co Ltd v New Garage & Motor Co Ltd* [supra]. I believe that the line of demarcation is drawn in its simplest form (as Lord Dunedin himself said in *Public Works Comr v Hills* [[1906] AC 368]) if one says that a sum cannot be legally exacted as liquidated damages unless it is found to amount to "a genuine pre-estimate of" damages (to use the phrase originated by Lord Robertson in *Clydebank Engineering & Shipbuilding Co v Yzquierdo y Castaneda (Don Jose Ramos)* [[1905] AC 6]). If it does not amount to such a pre-estimate, then it is to be regarded as a penalty, and I do not myself think that it helps to identify a penalty to describe it as in the nature of a threat "enforced *in terrorem*" (to use Lord Halsbury's phrase in *Lord Elphinstone v Monkland Iron & Coal Co* [(1886) 11 App Cas 332]). I do not find that that description adds anything of substance to the idea conveyed by the word "penalty" itself, and it obscures the fact that penalties may quite readily be undertaken by parties who are not in the least terrorised by the prospect of having to pay them and are, as I understand it, entitled to claim the protection of the court when they are called on to make good their promises.' *Bridge v Campbell Discount Co Ltd* [1962] 1 All ER 385 at 395, HL, per Lord Radcliffe

Canada 'A penalty is the payment of a stipulated sum on breach of the contract, irrespective of the damage sustained. The essence of liquidated damages is a genuine covenanted pre-estimate of damage.' *Canadian General Electric Co v Canadian Rubber Co* (1915) 52 SCR 349 at 351, SCC, per Fitzpatrick CJ

Punishment

'I am clearly of opinion that the word "penalty" is large enough to mean, is intended to mean, and does mean, any punishment, whether by imprisonment or otherwise.' *R v Smith* (1862) Le & Ca 131 at 138, CCR, per Blackburn J

[The question was whether disqualification from holding or obtaining a driving licence under the Road Traffic Act 1930 (repealed; see now as to the prosecution and punishment of motoring offences the Road Traffic Offenders Act 1988) was a 'penalty' within the meaning of the Criminal Justice (Scotland) Act 1949, Sch VII.] 'I consider that the word "penalty" falls to be read in a wide popular sense, . . . and I select two definitions adequately conveying that sense. The late Mr Roberton Christie [The Encyclopaedia, Vol 11, p 204] said: "Penalty in the broad sense may be defined as any suffering in person or property by way of forfeiture, deprivation or disability, imposed as a punishment by law or judicial authority in respect of . . . an act prohibited by statute." The Oxford Dictionary echoes the same wide conception by referring to "a loss, disability or disadvantage of some kind . . . fixed by law for some offence". If, as I think, this is the sense in which the Act of 1949 must be read, it necessarily follows that a disqualification from holding or applying for a licence imposed on conviction for an offence under the Road Traffic Acts is a "penalty".']

Coogans v Macdonald 1954 SLT 279 at 281, per the Lord Justice-General (Cooper)

PENDENTE LITE

'The absence of . . . provisions to meet the case of an innocent wife who has succeeded in obtaining a decree nisi strongly indicates that the order for alimony pendante lite was intended to include the period between decree nisi and decree absolute. As Cotton LJ said in *Ellis v Ellis* [(1883) 8 PD 188, 189], until the decree becomes absolute the parties are still husband and wife". In that case the Court of Appeal upheld the decision of Sir James Hannen that the court had power to order alimony pendente lite after a decree nisi had been made dissolving the marriage. Lord Herschell in *Foden v Foden* [[1894] P 307, 312] also made it clear that a petition continues until decree absolute. "It was said," Lord Herschell remarked, "that there was no pending suit, because a decree nisi had been made. That argument is, in my opinion, quite untenable. Till the decree nisi has been made absolute, the suit is clearly pending." If, then, the suit is pending and the order is to pay alimony pending suit, prima facie the order continues in force until the suit is finally determined by decree absolute.' *Stevenson (otherwise Bowerbank) v Stevenson* [1944] P 52 at 53, per Bucknill J

PENDING

'A cause is still pending [within the Judicature Act 1873, s 24(7) (repealed; cf now the Supreme Court Act 1981, s 49)] even though there has been final judgment given, and the Court has very large powers in dealing with a judgment until it is fully satisfied. It may stay proceedings on the judgment, either wholly or partially, and the cause is still pending, therefore, for this purpose, as it appears to me, and must be considered as pending, although there may have been final judgment given in the action, provided that judgment has not been satisfied.' *Salt v Cooper* (1880) 16 Ch D 544 at 551, CA, per Jessel MR

'There is ample authority for saying that during the time between the conviction of an accused person on indictment and his appeal to the Court of Criminal Appeal the case is not ended at all; the case is still *sub judice*. The case is pending, to use the expression which has been used in many cases and in many judgments, and the publication of improper matter may amount to a contempt of court. . . . Newspapers which choose to publish or editors of newspapers who choose to publish comments upon a criminal case while it is still pending, and a criminal case is still pending while the time for appealing has not run out at least, and most assuredly in the case of a man who is appealing or is proposing to appeal—if they choose to comment on the facts of the case other than upon matters which have been given in evidence in open court, they do so at their peril.' *Delbert-Evans v Davies & Watson* [1945] 2 All ER 167 at 172, 173, DC, per Humphreys J

Canada '"Litigation pending", as here used [in a statutory provision that the provisions of an enactment do not affect "litigation pending" at the time of the enactment, unless expressly stated], means any legal proceeding, suit or action remaining undecided or awaiting decision or settlement.' *Garnham v Tessier* (1959) 27 WWR 682 at 688, Man CA, per Schultz JA

New Zealand 'I can find nothing in the many definitions of "pending" . . . to suggest that "pending" as applied to the legal proceedings means anything more than that which remains undecided, or is awaiting decision, or settlement, and I have no doubt that it is in this sense that the word "pending" is used in s 9(1) [of the Adoption Act 1955].' *A v B* [1969] NZLR 534 at 535, per Roper J

New Zealand '"Litigation pending" means any legal proceeding, suit or action remaining undecided or awaiting decision or settlement [*Garnham v Taylor* (1959) 27 WWR 682]. A legal proceeding can be said to be "pending" as soon as it has been commenced and it remains pending until it has been concluded that is, so long as the court having original cognisance of it can make an order on the matters in issue, or to be dealt with, therein.' *National Bank of New Zealand Ltd v Chapman* [1975] 1 NZLR 480 at 482, per McMullin J

New Zealand 'I am of the view that, except in special cases, proceedings under the Matrimonial Property Act 1976 should be regarded as "pending" for the purposes of s 5(3) from the time of filing until finally determined.' *Levy v Levy* (1985) 3 NZFLR 698 at 704, per Prichard J

PENNAGE *See* STALLAGE

PENSION

'Pension', in relation to any person, means a pension, whether contributory or not, of any kind whatever payable to or in respect of him, and includes a lump sum or a gratuity so payable and a return of contributions to a pension fund, with or without interest thereon or any other addition thereto. (Superannuation (Miscellaneous Provisions) Act 1948, s 17)

In this Act 'pension' includes—

(a) any allowance or other benefit payable (either in respect of the services of the recipient or in respect of the services of any other person) by virtue of any superannuation scheme, whether contained in any enactment or otherwise, including any superannuation scheme providing benefits in the case of injury or death; and

(b) any compensation payable in respect of retirement from any office or employment in pursuance of the provisions of any enactment, any compensation payable in respect of the loss, abolition or relinquishment of any office or employment occasioned by any alteration in the organisation of any department or service or by any transfer or other reorganisation of the functions of local authorities, and any compensation payable in respect of any diminution in the emoluments of any office or employment which has been occasioned as aforesaid.

(Pensions (Increase) Act 1971, s 8)

Canada 'One of the definitions of a pension in the New Oxford Dictionary is this: "An annuity or other periodical payment made, especially by a government, a company or an employer of labour, in consideration of past services." Here it is true a lump sum was voted but it was made payable in instalments, that is periodically. I would not like to tie myself to the pronouncement that a pension, to attract . . . tax, need always be paid in instalments. As one of the old examples in the Greater Oxford Dictionary says, "They who are maimed in the wars have to them a pension for life or the value of the pension in ready money".' *Re Nelson* (1971) 22 DLR (3d) 603 at 605, BCSC, per Wilson CJ

PENTHOUSE

Canada [In an application for an order to strike out the trade mark registration of the word 'Penthouse'.] 'Counsel for the parties furnished me with a great number of definitions of the word "penthouse" extracted from standard and recognised dictionaries and other sources. It is apparent therefrom that the word originally referred to, and still refers to, any subsidiary or added structure attached to a larger building and covered by a roof sloping down and away from the main wall of a building. It also describes any bracketed, sloping roof projecting from a wall of a building to give shelter to a door, window or outside stair. In modern usage the term is applied to any subsidiary roof construction and in particular to structures built above the main roof line and recessed behind the exterior wall line, to house water tanks, elevator machinery (which are now referred to as mechanical penthouses) and, in more recent times, living quarters often of a luxurious nature. With the advent of the plethora of highrise apartment houses in urban centres, the landlords have taken liberties with the precise technical meaning of the word "penthouse" and have adopted it to refer to apartments on the topmost floor of the building with the implication that such apartments are more desirable and command a correspondingly higher rental. The word "penthouse" is now accepted as referring to premises located upon the roof of a building, or on the topmost floor thereof.' *Great Lakes Hotels Ltd v Noshery Ltd* (1968) 56 CPR 165 at 169, Fed Ct, per Cattanach J

PEOPLE *See also* ARRESTS, RESTRAINTS AND DETAINMENTS

[A ship was insured against (inter alia) arrests, restraints and detainments of kings, princes and 'people'. During her voyage she was forced by stress of weather to put into an Irish port, where her cargo of corn was looted by a mob.] 'That which happened in this case does not fall within the meaning of "arrests, restraints, and detainments of kings, princes, and people". The meaning of the word "people", may be discovered here by the accompanying words: *noscitur a sociis*; it means "the ruling power of the country".' *Nesbitt v Lushington* (1792) 4 Term Rep 738 at 787, per Lord Kenyon CJ

'The words "my people" are not words of art.

According to the Imperial Dictionary they may mean those who are closely connected with a person as attendants, domestics, or followers; sometimes relatives or ancestors. In the Oxford English Dictionary the word is said to mean: "Those to whom anyone belongs; the members of one's tribe, clan, family, community, association, church, etc, collectively; one's parents, brothers and sisters, or other relatives at home." One of the illustrations given is taken from Carlyle's Sterling: "Mrs Sterling and the family had lived with his father's people through the winter." The word does not appear to me to be confined to persons who are strictly relatives, thus it may, I think, include a stepfather or stepmother. In this will it was in my view used to denote the family to which the testatrix belonged, or persons who were connected with the testatrix by family ties. . . . The words "my people" do not appear to me to have a more restricted, or less flexible signification than the words "my family".' *Re Keighley, Keighley v Keighley* [1919] 2 Ch 388 at 390, 391, per Peterson J

PER CENT

'It is really beyond dispute, I should have thought, that, in the ordinary common sense use of words, unless there be something in the context to suggest that there is a possibility of some different meaning attaching, if a rate "per cent" is expressed without any further indication, that rate means "per cent per annum" just as much as if the words "per annum" were written in. It is, of course, true that there can be a context which would either indicate that the percentage was to be something other than "per cent per annum", or that it might be so. But, in the absence of some context which leads to that possibility, I have no doubt that "per cent" would be taken, by any reasonable, sensible, person, as being "per cent per annum".' *London and Harrogate Securities Ltd v Pitts* [1796] 3 All ER 184 at 185, CA, per Megaw LJ

PER INCURIAM

'What is meant by giving a decision per incuriam is giving a decision when a case or statute has not been brought to the attention of the court and they have given the decision in ignorance or forgetfulness of the existence of that case or that statute.' *Huddersfield Police Authority v Watson* [1947] 2 All ER 193 at 196, per Lord Goddard CJ

'As a general rule the only cases in which decisions should be held to have been given per incuriam are those decisions given in ignorance or forgetfulness of some inconsistent statutory provision or of some authority binding on the court concerned: so that in such cases some part of the decision or some step in the reasoning on which it is based is found, on that account, to be demonstrably wrong. This definition is not necessarily exhaustive, but cases not strictly within it which can properly be held to have been decided per incuriam must, in our judgment, consistently with the *stare decisis* rule which is an essential feature of our law, be . . . of the rarest occurrence.' *Morelle Ltd v Wakeling* [1955] 1 All ER 708 at 718, CA, per Evershed MR; see also [1955] 2 QB 379

PER PROCURATION

A signature by procuration operates as notice that the agent has but a limited authority to sign, and the principal is only bound by such signature if the agent in so signing was acting within the actual limits of his authority. (Bills of Exchange Act 1882, s 25)

'It makes no difference whatever whether the agent professes to act in the name of his principal as if he were the principal, or whether he professes to act as the agent signing as AB, agent for CD, or whether he professes to act under a power of attorney. The term "procuration" does not appear to me altogether necessarily to imply that it is under procuration. I believe that expression is frequently used by persons who are in employment, and who have no power of doing it at all. All that the expression "Per procuration" means is this—"I am an agent, not acting on any authority of my own in the case, but authorised by my principal to enter into this contract".' *Smith v M'Guire* (1858) 27 LJ Ex 465 at 468, per Pollock CB

'A simple "p", "pro", or "for", expresses an authority generally, and "per pro" or "pp" expresses an authority erected by procuration or power of attorney. Except in cases where the law requires an agent to have authority in writing, I do not see how using one form instead of the other can be material.' *Ulster Bank v Synnott* (1871) IR 5 Eq 595 at 612, per Chatterton V-C

PERAMBULATION

Rights incident to the perambulation of a district by inhabitants at certain times of the year for the purpose of preserving the notoriety of the boundaries of the district form a distinct class of customary rights of way. These rights of perambulation are pecular in themselves, inasmuch as they are only exercised on rare occasions, sometimes only once a year or once in many years. Like other customary rights they must be shown to have existed either actually or presumptively from time immemorial, and may exist in favour of the inhabitants of a parish, manor, liberty, hundred, or other similar district. The right to perambulate parochial boundaries and to enter private property for that purpose, and to remove obstructions which might prevent this from being done, was, at one time, custom in all parts of England, but a customary right to perambulate boundaries cannot confer a right to enter any house in the particular district the boundaries of which are being perambulated under a customary right, unless it is necessary to enter for any purpose connected with the perambulation. (12 Halsbury's Laws (4th edn) para 440)

PEREMPTORY

'Peremptory' is often used in regard to judicial proceedings, as, for instance, a peremptory plea as distinguished from a plea in abatement and a peremptory order or a peremptory mandamus. A peremptory order is an order by which a person is required to do something within a fixed time or suffer the consequences. (45 Halsbury's Laws (4th edn) para 1149)

[The question was whether a 'peremptory' order for time to plead precluded the defendant from applying again for a summons for further time.] 'The peremptory order is only the expression of the then opinion of the judge; but it is not absolutely final; neither does it import any undertaking or contract on the part of the defendant. The meaning of the word is only that the judge makes an absolute order,—but, like all other orders, liable to be varied if he thinks fit.' *Beazley v Bailey* (1846) 16 M & W 58 at 59, per Parke B

[An order made by a Master gave the defendant a month 'peremptory' as extension of time for delivering his defence.] 'With regard to the meaning of the word "peremptory" in the order, I take it to mean that the order for extension of time is given on the footing that it is to be final unless some very special and urgent circumstances are brought forward as a reason for altering it.' *Falck v Axthelm* (1889) 24 QBD 174 at 177, CA, per Lopes LJ

PERFORM

[Under the Building (Safety, Health and Welfare) Regulations 1948, reg 4 (see now Building Regulation 1985) it was the duty of every contractor and employer of workmen who was undertaking certain operations to comply with the requirements of specified regulations which related to any work, act or operation 'performed' or about to be performed.] 'There is . . . an argument for the construction of the word "perform" so as to extend to cover a contractor who is not actually doing any works but had agreed with the building owners to do the work. On the other hand, manifestly inconvenience and possibility of injustice may arise, especially where there is a chain of contractors and sub-contractors, each of whom had undertaken to do the work. These considerations suggest a narrower construction of the word "perform" as being appropriately applied to the person who is physically performing the work. The employer, not the contractor, unless he is involved in the performance, must take the precautions. The wide construction of "perform" involves that every person who enters into a contract and undertakes to do any part of the work is deemed to be performing it although he sub-contracts it. This construction is not, I think, consistent with the division of duties set out in reg 4. I am of opinion . . . that the only person liable under para (ii) is he who physically "performs" the operation.' *Donaghey v Boulton & Paul Ltd* [1967] 2 All ER 1014 at 1027, HL, per Lord Hodson

PERFORMANCE *See also* PART PERFORMANCE; PUBLIC PERFORMANCE; SPECIFIC PERFORMANCE; THEATRE

Of copyright work

In this Part [Pt I. Copyright] 'performance', in relation to a work—

(a) includes delivery in the case of lectures, addresses, speeches and sermons, and
(b) in general, includes any mode of visual or acoustic presentation, including presentation by means of a sound recording, film, broadcast or cable programme.

(Copyright, Designs and Patents Act 1988, s 19(2))

In this Part [Pt II. Rights in performances] 'performance' means—

(a) a dramatic performance (which includes dance and mime),
(b) a musical performance,

(c) a reading or recitation of a literary work, or
(d) a performance of a variety act or any similar presentation, which is, or so far as it is, a live performance given by one or more individuals.

(Copyright, Designs and Patents Act 1988, s 180(2))

[The Copyright Act 1911, s 1(2) (repealed; see now Copyright, Designs and Patents Act 1988, s 1) enacted that, for the purposes of the Act, 'copyright' meant the sole right to produce or reproduce a work or any substantial part thereof in any material form whatsoever, or to 'perform', or in the case of a lecture to deliver, the work or any substantial part thereof, 'in public'.] 'The defendants' hotel . . . has accommodation for about 175 guests, and regularly, for the four past years, on Sunday evenings the trio . . . has played in the lounge. In addition to playing on Sunday evenings it plays at tea time during the Christmas and Easter holidays. On 20th of November, 1932, a number of guests were sleeping at the hotel. Some of them were in the lounge on the occasion in question. . . . I think that it is quite plain, on the evidence, that any member of the public who had given notice to the defendants of his desire to dine at the hotel on 20th of November, 1932, or on any other Sunday, would have been allowed to have dinner there. . . . No doubt he would also have been at liberty to go into the lounge and listen to the music performed by the trio. . . . In my judgment the performance by the defendants in these circumstances was a performance "in public".' *Performing Right Society Ltd v Hawthorns Hotel (Bournemouth) Ltd* [1933] Ch 855 at 856, 857, per Bennett J

'By s 35 of the Copyright Act 1911 [repealed; see now Copyright, Designs and Patents Act 1988, s 1 (supra)], the term "performance" is defined as meaning "any acoustic representation of a work". The question therefore resolves itself into whether the defendants, by operating their wireless set, were causing an acoustic representation of the works to be given at their hotel. In my judgment that question must be answered in the affirmative. The wireless receiving set by means of which alone the sounds were produced at the hotel belonged to and was under the control of, the defendants, who operated it for the purpose of giving to their customers at the hotel an acoustic representation of the musical works which were being performed at Hammersmith. . . . I find it impossible to escape from the conclusion that the owner of a receiving set who puts it into operation causes an acoustic representation of a musical work which is being broadcast to be given at the place where the receiving set is installed, and is therefore himself performing or authorising the performance of the musical work within the meaning of the Copyright Act 1911.' *Performing Right Society Ltd v Hammond's Bradford Brewery Co* [1934] Ch 121 at 136, 137, CA, per Lawrence LJ

'I take the view that when the wireless set reproduces the music within the area in which that wireless set stands, the performance which ensues seems to me to take place wherever that music is audible as music to a person hearing it as a musical piece.' *Performing Right Society Ltd v Camelo* [1936] 3 All ER 557 at 559, 560, per Clauson J

[A dramatic society performed a play at a Women's Institute. The question was whether this was a 'performance in public' within the Copyright Act 1911, s 1(2) (repealed; see supra).] 'No one would question that the performance was in public if the audience, other circumstances being the same, had been, not sixty-two, but 600, as I suppose in one of the larger villages it might have been. If that were not a performance in public, and might be repeated indefinitely all over the country, the performing right would not be of much value. The quality of domesticity or quasi-domesticity seems to me to be absent. I think such performances are in public within the meaning of the statute.' *Jennings v Stephens* [1936] Ch 469 at 480, 481, CA, per Lord Wright MR

United States To 'perform' a work means to recite, render, play, dance, or act it, either directly or by means of any device or process or, in the case of a motion picture or other audiovisual work, to show its images in any sequence or to make sounds accompanying it audible. (Copyright Act of 1976, s 101))

See, generally, 9 Halsbury's Laws (4th edn) para 917.

Of dramatic or musical work

'Performance of a dramatic or musical work' includes any performance, mechanical or otherwise, of any such work, being a performance rendered or intended to be rendered audible by mechanical or electrical means. (Dramatic and Musical Performers' Protection Act 1958, s 8(1))

Of vessel

[A contract for the building of a yacht provided that construction was to be deemed to have been completed at the conclusion of a trial run provided that the 'performance' of the craft during such trial run was satisfactory.] 'In my view, the effect of cll 5 and 6 of the contract is to entitle the buyer to refuse delivery if he is not reasonably satisfied of the performance of the craft when tendered by the seller for delivery at the conclusion of the acceptance trials; and in the context of cl 6 I construe the expression "performance" widely and as including the standard of workmanship and materials and the compliance of the craft with the specification. To read the words "performance of the craft" in a narrower sense would result in the seller being deemed to have fulfilled his contract even if the interior fittings were incomplete or different from those specified, so long as the vessel sailed well.' *McDougall v Aeromarine of Emsworth Ltd* [1958] 3 All ER 431 at 438, per Diplock J

PERIL *See* ACCIDENT

PERILS OF THE SEAS *See also* DANGER; MARITIME PERILS

The term 'perils of the seas', as used in a marine policy, does not include every casualty which may happen to the subject matter of the insurance on the sea; it must be a peril of or due to the sea. It does not, for instance, cover fire or capture at sea, nor any loss proximately caused by insects, or the wilful throwing away of a ship. . . . Moreover, the purpose of a marine policy is to secure an indemnity against accidents which may happen, not against events which in the ordinary course of things must happen. Therefore, in general, the term 'perils of the seas' refers only to fortuitous accident or casualties of the seas, and does not include the ordinary action of the winds and waves. (25 Halsbury's Laws (4th edn) para 153)

The exception [in a charter-party] of loss or damage by perils of the seas covers losses of a marine character incident to a ship as such, that is, as a means of transportation by sea. It is not confined to the violent action of the winds or waves or to damage due to contact with sea water or occurring while the ship is afloat. However, it does not include accidents on rivers or canals, or accidents which, although they occur at sea, are in no way due to the fact that the ship is at sea and might equally well be encountered on land. As the phrase is 'perils of' not 'perils on' the sea, it does not include every misfortune that may befall the ship or cargo on the sea or every loss or damage of which the sea is the immediate cause. Thus, it does not include the natural and inevitable action of the winds and waves which results in wear and tear; there must be some casualty, something which could not be foreseen as one of the necessary incidents of the adventure.' [*Wilson, Sons & Co v Xantho* (infra)]. (43 Halsbury's Laws (4th edn) para 454)

The term 'perils of the seas' refers only to fortuitous accidents or casualties of the seas. It does not include the ordinary action of the winds and waves. (Marine Insurance Act 1906, Sch 1)

'The taking by pirates are accompted perils of the sea.' *Pickering v Barkley* (1648) Sty 132 at 132, per cur.

[Slaves on a voyage died from starvation caused by a prolongation of the voyage due to bad weather. The question was whether this loss was amongst the 'perils of the seas' against which the plaintiff had insured.] 'I do not know that it was ever decided that a loss arising from a mistake of the captain was a loss within the perils of the seas. There was a case [*Gregson v Gilbert* (1783) 3 Doug (KB) 232], where a ship mistook Jamaica for Domingo, and it was decided not to be a loss within the perils of the seas. In this case it is impossible to decide that the plaintiff can recover, without saying that the slaves did not die natural deaths. If they had died of fevers or other illness occasioned by the length of the voyage, the plaintiff certainly could not have recovered. Now the length of the voyage occasioned the want of provisions, and that occasioned the illness of which they died: but that is a natural death.' *Tatham v Hodgson* (1796) 6 Term Rep 656 at 659, per Lawrence J

[A loss was caused by two ships running foul of one another, the accident occuring without negligence in either party.] 'If the defendants have been guilty of any degree of negligence, and it could have been proved that the accident could have been prevented, they would certainly have been liable; but they are exempt by the condition of the charterparty from misfortunes happening during the voyage, which human prudence could not guard against,—against accidents happening without fault in either party. I am of opinion, that neither ship could be deemed to be in fault: and that the misfortune must be taken to be within the exception of the perils of the sea.' *Buller v Fisher* (1799) 3 Esp 67 at 67, 68, per Lord Kenyon

'I am of opinion that the loss in this case was not a loss by perils of the sea, but a damage falling within the description of ordinary wear and tear. No doubt that the question is one of importance; but I think it has been very unnecessarily brought before the court; for, the matter seems to have been perfectly understood and settled by all the text-writers upon this branch of the law. To make the underwriters liable, the injury must be the result of something fortuitous or accidental occurring in the course of the voyage. Here, the vessel, upon her arrival at Sunderland, goes up the river, and, in consequence of the rising and falling of the tide, rests upon the river's bed, and receives damage. There was nothing unusual, no peril, no accident. To hold that the assured were covered in such a case, would be virtually making the policy a warranty against the wear and tear and ordinary repairs of the vessel.' *Magnus v Buttemer* (1852) 11 CB 876 at 881, per Jervis CJ

'The injury, so far as the damage occasioned by the sea is concerned was the inevitable consequence of the immersion of the cable in its then state in the sea water. But the purpose of insurance is to afford protection against contingencies and dangers which may or may not occur; it cannot properly apply to a case where the loss or injury must inevitably take place in the ordinary course of things. The wear and tear of a ship, the decay of her sheathing, the action of worms on her bottom, have been properly held not to be included in the insurance against perils of the seas, as being the unavoidable consequences of the service to which the vessel is exposed. The insurer cannot be understood as undertaking to indemnify against losses which, in the nature of things, must necessarily happen.' *Paterson v Harris* (1861) 1 B & S 336 at 352, 353, per cur.

'I cannot see how, if there was no peril from sea or wind, and an accident is caused by the negligent act of one of the two ships which comes into collision, that can be said to be a peril at sea. In my opinion that which results, not from difficulty of navigation in itself, but from the negligent act of man without any difficulty of waves or wind contributing to the accident is not a peril of the sea.' *Woodley v Michell* (1883) 11 QBD 47 at 53, CA, per Cotton LJ

'I think the definition of Lopes LJ in *Pandorf v Hamilton* [(1886) 17 QBD 670, CA] very good: "In a seaworthy ship damage to goods caused by the action of the sea during transit, not attributable to the fault of anybody, is a damage from a peril of the sea." I have thought that the following might suffice: "All perils, losses or misfortune of a marine character, or of a character incident to a ship as such".' *Thames & Mersey Marine Insurance Co Ltd v Hamilton, Fraser & Co* (1887) 12 App Cas 484 at 492, per Lord Bramwell

'I think it clear that the term "perils of the sea" does not cover every accident or casualty which may happen to the subject-matter of the insurance on the sea. It must be a peril "of" the sea. Again, it is well settled that it is not every loss or damage of which the sea is the immediate cause that is covered by these words. They do not protect, for example, against that natural and inevitable action of the winds and waves, which results in what may be described as wear and tear. There must be some casualty, something which could not be foreseen as one of the necessary incidents of the adventure. It was contended that those losses only were losses by perils of the sea, which were occasioned by extraordinary violence of the winds or waves. I think this is too narrow a construction of the words. . . . It is beyond question, that if a vessel strikes upon a sunken rock in fair weather and sinks, this is a loss by perils of the sea. And a loss by foundering, owing to a vessel coming into collision with another vessel, even when the collision results from the negligence of that other vessel, falls within the same category. . . . I am unable to concur in the view that a disaster which happens from the fault of somebody can never be an accident or peril of the sea; and I think it would give rise to distinctions resting on no sound basis, if it were to be held that the exception of perils of the seas in a bill of lading was always excluded when the inroad of the sea which occasioned the loss was induced by some intervention of human agency.' *Wilson, Sons & Co v Xantho (Cargo Owners)* (1887) 12 App Cas 503 at 511, per Lord Herschell

'Some effect must be given to the words "perils of the sea". A rat eating a cheese in the hold of a vessel is not a peril of the sea; the sea, or the vessel being on the sea, has nothing to do with the destruction of the cheese. . . . I think the idea of something fortuitous and unexpected is involved in both words "peril" or "accident".' *Hamilton, Fraser & Co v Pandorf & Co*

(1887) 12 App Cas 518 at 523–525, per Lord Halsbury LC

'This is the third case in which this House has had to consider whether a peril of the sea or other peril within the general words was shewn. . . . As I have said elsewhere, I think the definition of Lopes LJ very good: "It is a sea damage, occurring at sea, and nobody's fault." What is the "peril"? It is that the ship or goods will be lost or damaged; but it must be "of the sea". Fire would not be a peril of the sea; or loss or damage from it would not be insured against by the general words. So of lightning. In the present case the sea has damaged the goods. That it might do so was a peril that the ship encountered. It is true that rats made the hole through which the water got in, and if the question were whether rats making a hole was a peril of the sea, I should say certainly not. If we could suppose that no water got in, but that the insured sued the underwriter for the damage done to the pipe, I should say clearly that he could not recover. But I should equally say that the underwriters on goods would be liable for the damage shewn in this case.' Ibid at 526, 527, per Lord Bramwell

'The only question is whether the loss was occasioned by a "peril of the seas or navigation". If it was, then the shipowner is protected . . . although the loss was caused by the negligence of his servant. . . . If by some accident the ship is not kept tight and the water comes in and damages the cargo, that is damage by an accident or peril of the seas. In my opinion, these considerations afford a simple answer to the question in this case. The engineer intentionally opened the sea-cock, but the vessel still remained perfectly tight. The sea-water could not come into the carrying part of the vessel, nor sink the vessel; it was the same as if the water had been let into the ballast tank, in which case the ship would have remained perfectly tight. That being the position of things, the engineer, entirely by a mistake which was probably an act of negligence, opened a valve by which the sea-water was let into the carrying part of the ship, and then the ship was no longer tight. The sea-water then damaged the cargo which was in the carrying part of the ship. I cannot distinguish this case from the case in which a port was accidentally left open by negligence and the sea-water was thereby let into the ship. . . . It seems to me that in either case the ship by negligence, by an accident, was exposed to the peril that, if the ship was not kept tight, the sea-water would come in; and that is essentially a peril of the seas, and a peril to which every ship is exposed while she is afloat.' *Blackburn v Liverpool, Brazil & River Plate Steam Navigation Co* [1902] 1 KB 290 at 294–296, per Walton J

'It is not desirable to attempt to define too exactly a . . . "peril of the sea", but it can at least be said that it is some condition of sea or weather or accident of navigation producing a result which but for these conditions would not have occurred.' *Grant, Smith & Co & McDonnell Ltd v Seattle Construction & Dry Dock Co* [1920] AC 162 at 171, per cur.

'When the vessel is unseaworthy, and the water consequently gets into the vessel and sinks her, it would never be said that the loss was due to the perils of the sea. It is true that the vessel sank in consequence of the inrush of water, but this inrush was due simply to the unseaworthiness. The unseaworthiness was the proximate cause of the loss. Exactly the same reasoning applies to the case of scuttling; the hole is there made in order to let in the water. The water comes in and the vessel sinks. The proximate cause of the loss is the scuttling, as in the other case the unseaworthiness. The entrance of the water cannot be divorced from the act which occasioned it.' *Samuel (P) & Co v Dumas* [1924] AC 431 at 455, per Lord Finlay

'Where there is an accidental incursion of sea-water into a vessel, at a part of the vessel, and in a manner, where sea-water is not expected to enter in the ordinary course of things, and there is a consequent damage to the thing insured, there is prima facie a loss by perils of the sea. The accident may consist in some negligent act, such as improper opening of a valve, or a hole made in a pipe by mischance, or it may be that sea-water is admitted by stress of weather or some like cause bringing the sea over openings ordinarily not exposed to the sea or, even without stress of weather, by the vessel heeling over owing to some accident, or by the breaking of hatches or other coverings. These are merely a few amongst many possible instances in which there may be a fortuitous incursion of sea-water. It is the fortuitous entry of the sea-water which is the peril of the sea in such cases.' *Canada Rice Mills Ltd v Union Marine & General Insurance Co Ltd* [1941] AC 55 at 68, 69, PC, per cur.

'The expression "ordinary perils" has long been associated with investigations as to seaworthiness, but it is not to be limited, in this connexion, to hazards that are commonplace or that lurk only in usual conditions. It also comprehends those worse than average blows and whims of the sea which may be expected of that element in conditions of wind and weather that are known or might reasonably be anticipated.' *The Princess Victoria* [1954] NI 172 at 175, per Lord MacDermott LCJ

Australia 'It is not an essential element of a peril of the sea that it cannot be foreseen or guarded against. . . . The question whether an alleged peril of the sea might reasonably have been anticipated and guarded against has no bearing on the question whether it is or is not a peril of the sea, but is material only on the question of negligence or no negligence.' *Vacuum Oil Co Pty Ltd v Commonwealth & Dominion Line Ltd* [1922] VLR 693 at 698, per McArthur J

Canada 'It is clear that to constitute a peril of the sea, the accident need not be of an extraordinary nature or arise from irresistible force. It is sufficient that it be the cause of damage to goods at sea by the violent action of the wind and waves, when such damage cannot be attributed to someone's negligence." *Keystone Transports Ltd v Dominion Steel & Coal Corpn Ltd* [1942] SCR 495 at 505, SCC, per Taschereau J

PERIOD OF ACCOUNT *See* ACCOUNTING DATE

PERIOD OF EMPLOYMENT

'Period of employment' means the period (inclusive of the time allowed for meals and rest) within which persons may be employed on any day. (Factories Act 1961, s 176)

PERIODIC TENANCY *See* TENANCY

PERIODICAL

[The Copyright Act 1842, s 18 (repealed) dealt with the question of copyright in (inter alia) articles, etc, published in 'periodicals.'] 'The object of the Act of Parliament plainly was to give a new species of copyright in periodical works: by which I mean to have it once and for all understood, a work that comes out from time to time and is miscellaneous in its articles.' *Brown v Cooke* (1846) 16 LJ Ch 140 at 142, per Shadwell V-C

'The words of the 18th section [of the Copyright Act 1842 (repealed)] are of the most comprehensive kind—any "periodical work" —a term which certainly includes a newspaper.' *Walter v Howe* (1881) 50 LJ Ch 621 at 622, per Jessel MR

PERISHABLE

Australia 'Perishable product is not an exact expression, but I notice that the Oxford English Dictionary gives the word "perishable" as meaning especially, naturally subject to speedy decay, as organic substances, minerals which rapidly weaken or become decomposed, and the like. Unprotected wheat would qualify under this definition.' *Nelungaloo Pty Ltd v Commonwealth* (1948) 75 CLR 495 at 577, per Dixon J

PERJURY

If any person lawfully sworn as a witness or as an interpreter in a judicial proceeding wilfully makes a statement material in that proceeding, which he knows to be false or does not believe to be true, he shall be guilty of perjury. . . . (Perjury Act 1911, s 1)

'It is not enough to say that a man suborned another to commit a perjury, but he must shew what perjury it is, which cannot be without an oath; for an indictment cannot be framed for such an offence, unless it appear that the thing was false which he was persuaded to swear. The question therefore is, If the person had sworn what the defendants had persuaded him to do, whether that had been perjury? There is a difference when a man swears a thing which is true in fact, and yet he doth not know it to be so, and to swear a thing to be true which is really false; the first is perjury before God, and the other is an offence of which the law takes notice.' *R v Hinton & Brown* (1687) 3 Mod Rep 122 at 122, per cur.

'It is necessary in every crime that the indictment charge it with certainty and precision to be understood by everybody; alleging all the requisites which constitute the offence: but every crime stands on its own circumstances, and has peculiar rules. In the case of perjury, I take the circumstances requisite to be these; the oath must be taken in a judicial proceeding, before a competent jurisdiction; and it must be material to the question depending. If there be any doubt on the words of the oath, which can be made more clear and precise by a reference to former matter, that may be supplied by an innuendo. There must be an allegation of time and place, which are sometimes material and necessary, and sometimes not.' *R v Aylett* (1785) 1 Term Rep 63 at 69, per Lord Mansfield CJ

See, generally, 11 Halsbury's Laws (4th edn) para 938 et seq.

PERMANENT

[A company appointed a solicitor to be 'permanent' attorney.] 'I . . . think the plaintiff has failed to prove the promise in the first count in the terms in which it must be understood. It states, that, in consideration that the plaintiff, at the request of the company, had agreed to become the permanent attorney and solicitor of the company, they, the said company, promised to retain and employ him as such permanent attorney and solicitor. It then alleges that the company did in fact retain and employ the plaintiff as such permanent attorney and solicitor; but that the company, disregarding their promise, refused to permit him to continue to be or to act as such attorney and solicitor. This must be understood to mean a promise to employ the plaintiff for some certain time. But the evidence does not support such a promise; it does not shew any contract on the part of the company to retain and employ him as their attorney any longer than they should think proper. In fact, "permanent attorney" means no more an enduring engagement than "standing counsel".' *Elderton v Emmens* (1847) 4 CB 479 at 495, 496, per Maule J

[Under a charterparty, a ship was to deliver goods at a port or so near thereto as she could safely get. The question was whether a physical cause preventing a ship from reaching port need only be temporary or need be 'permanent' before the ship can claim to be as near thereto as she can get.] 'I should say that subject, means that it is an obstacle which cannot be overcome by the shipowner by any reasonable means, except within such a time as, having regard to the objects of the adventure of both charterer and shipowner, is as a matter of business wholly unreasonable.' *Nelson v Dahl* (1879) 12 Ch D 568 at 592, CA, per Brett LJ

'"Permanent" is indeed a relative term, and is not synonymous with "everlasting".' *Henriksen v Grafton Hotel Ltd* [1942] 2 KB 184 at 196, CA, per Du Parcq LJ

[By her will a testatrix directed that her residuary estate should be held on trust for various people in succession. She further provided that every person who, under the trusts, should become entitled in possession of her residuary estate as tenant for life or in tail male or in tail should within six months from the date of becoming so entitled take up 'permanent' residence in England.] 'The use of the word "permanent" inevitably, I think, imports into the phrase the notion of the intention of the person concerned. One cannot take up a permanent residence at any particular point of time unless, at the time when one takes up residence, one intends that it should be permanent, i.e., that one should go on living there for one's natural days.' *Re Gape's Will Trusts, Verey v Gape* [1952] 2 All ER 579 at 582, CA, per Evershed MR (also reported in [1952] Ch 743 at 749)

'I do not for my part think that, in a contract of service, use of the word "permanent" would be of itself sufficient to import the notion of a life appointment. The word is clearly capable, according to the context, of many shades of meaning; and it seems to me of considerable importance, in interpreting its use in a contract of service, that such a contract cannot be specifically enforced.' *McClelland v Northern Ireland General Health Service Board* [1957] 2 All ER 129 at 140, HL, per Lord Evershed

Australia [The specification of a patent set out (inter alia) that the invention had reference to an improved process of sterilising cheese to render it 'permanently keeping'.] 'The expression "permanently keeping" cannot be given a very precise connotation. "Permanent" does not mean perpetual or eternal. But it is difficult to resist the view that in the specification the expression describes the freedom of the cheese from all liability to that destruction or deterioration which arises from bacterial agents contained in the cheese itself. The degree of "permanence" is that which results from the complete absence from the cheese of the agent which formerly made it a perishable commodity. The specification cannot be interpreted as if the expression "permanently keeping" were to be construed and applied without regard to the description of the process, and to the statements that the cheese is to be completely sterilised. Any attempt to restrict its meaning or application by reference to the course of trade in cheese or to commercial purposes must fail.' *Kraft v McAnulty* [1932] St R Qd 139 at 179, per Dixon J; affirmed [1932] St R Qd 183, PC

Australia [The Income Tax Assessment Act 1936–1986 (Cth), s 6(1)(a)(i) provides (inter alia) that a 'resident' includes a person whose domicile is in Australia, unless the Commissioner is satisfied that his 'permanent' place of abode is outside Australia.] 'The word "permanent" as used in para (a)(i) of the extended definition of "resident", must be construed as having a shade of meaning applicable to the particular year of income under consideration. In this context it is unreal to consider whether a taxpayer has formed the intention to live or reside or to have a place of abode outside of Australia indefinitely, without any definite intention of ever returning to Australia in the foreseeable future. The Act is not concerned with domicile except to the extent necessary to show whether a taxpayer has an Australian domicile. What is of importance is whether the taxpayer has abandoned any residence or place of abode he may have had in Australia. Each year of income must be looked at separately. If in that year a taxpayer does not reside in Australia in the sense in which that word has been interpreted, but has formed the intention to, and in fact has, resided outside Australia, then truly it can be said that his permanent place of abode is outside Australia during that year of income.' *Federal Comr of Taxation v Applegate* (1979) 38 FLR 1 at 12, per Northrop J

New Zealand 'A thing cannot be permanent *stricto sensu* if it's "permanency" can be brought to an end at will.' *Long v Graham* [1967] NZLR 1030 at 1033, per Hardie Boys J

New Zealand 'I can find nothing, even if I read the advertisement [offering "permanent employment"] as part of the contract, to make it inevitable that I should reach the conclusion that the plaintiff's employment was ever intended to be for life. . . . This contract means no more than that the plaintiff's employment was . . . "general as distinct from merely temporary" . . . that the plaintiff would be "on the regular established staff" of the defendant.' *Clark v Independent Broadcasting Co Ltd* [1974] NZLR 587 at 594, per Moller J

PERMANENT WAY

'It was said that the expression "permanent way" was a term of art in railway parlance and evidence was adduced by the appellant company to the effect that in the vernacular of railway men the permanent way comprises only the ballast and sleepers, chairs, rails and fastenings of which the track is composed, while the apparatus for working the signals and points with which the system is equipped is never referred to as part of the permanent way, except in the case of points operated by hand levers and unconnected with any signals. . . . Assuming that evidence was admissible as to the meaning of "permanent way" I am not satisfied, on the evidence adduced in this case, which was largely based on administrative practice and convenience, that the expression "permanent way" as used in the statute and rule ought to be read in the limited sense for which the appellant company contended. The movable tapering rails which form the points are as much part of the running track as the immovable rails and the apparatus of rods attached to these movable rails for the purpose of actuating them is a necessary part of the equipment of the running track. The relaying or repairing of this apparatus is an operation attended with the same danger as the relaying or repairing of the rails themselves and, having regard to the purpose of the statute and rule, I can see no adequate reason for providing protection in the one case and not in the other. I do not, however, find it necessary to pronounce finally on this matter for in my opinion, even if the system of connecting rods forms part of the permanent way, the deceased was not engaged in relaying or repairing these rods.' *London & North Eastern Rly Co v Berriman* [1946] AC 278 at 293, 294, HL, per Lord Macmillan

'"Permanent way" in my opinion includes not only the track itself but also all the equipment for guiding a train on its proper course and on to its proper track as well as the metals on which it runs and the ground or structure supporting them, and I feel great difficulty in saying that the point lines are part of the permanent way whereas the point rods which move them and are permanently fastened to them for that purpose are not.' Ibid at 306, per Lord Porter

PERMISSION *See also* PERMIT

[A policy of insurance insured any person driving a car with the 'permission' of the insured. The insured gave his son permission to drive the car, but subsequently died. The son was involved in an accident whilst driving the car after his father's death.] 'In the majority of cases the question whether a person is driving a car with the permission of the insured is simply a question of fact. In this case it was argued that as a matter of law it was not possible for Michael Kelly [the appellant's father] to give permission to drive his car which would be effective eight months after his death. It was argued that it was inherent in the grant of permission, that the permittor should have power during the period covered by the permission to revoke or to cancel it. On this basis, it was contended that any permission given by Michael Kelly during his lifetime ceased on his death, or alternatively within a reasonable time thereafter, or in the further alternative when the person to whom permission had been given had notice of the death. No authority was cited to your lordships in support of this proposition. There is, in my view, nothing in the policy which supports the argument that the word "permission" in the policy means and only meant permission which during its currency the insured had power to revoke. The word "permission" by itself cannot be construed as implying that the permission must be one which there is power to revoke, or can endure only so long as the grantor is in a position to revoke it.' *Kelly v Cornhill Insurance Co Ltd* [1964] 1 All ER 321 at 323, HL, per Lord Dilhorne LC

'I cannot accept the argument that the meanings of the ordinary English words "order" and "permission" are so rigid that they cannot in any context refer to a period after the death of the person giving the order or permission.' Ibid at 326, per Lord Reid

PERMISSIVE

'It was solemnly decided by the Court of Error, . . . in a case in which the judgment was delivered . . . by the late Chief Justice Jervis [*York & North Midland Rly Co v R* (1853) 1 E & B 858], that permissive words in an Act of Parliament are not obligatory.' *Edinburgh, Perth & Dundee Rly Co v Philip* (1857) Macq 514 at 526, per Lord Wensleydale

'When a statute confers powers upon a public body there may be duties which arise out of the powers when they are exercised, but the mere fact that such powers are conferred involves no implication, when the statute is silent upon the point, that the powers must be exercised. Permissive words are not compulsory.' *R v Great Western Rly Co* (1893) 62 LJQB 572 at 580, CA, per Bowen LJ

PERMISSIVE WASTE *See* WASTE

PERMIT *See also* CAUSE OR PERMIT; PERMISSION

[The Licensing Act 1872, s 13 (repealed; see now the Licensing Act 1964, s 172) imposed penalties for 'permitting' drunkenness on licensed premises.] 'In a case where the defendant does not know that the person who was on his premises was in fact drunk, he cannot be said to permit drunkenness.' *Somerset v Wade* [1894] 1 QB 574 at 576, 577, DC, per Mathew J

'To my mind the word "permit" means one of two things, either to give leave for an act which without that leave could not be legally done, or to abstain from taking reasonable steps to prevent the act where it is within a man's power to prevent it.' *Berton v Alliance Economic Investment Co* [1922] 1 KB 742 at 759, CA, per Atkin LJ

'I am inclined to think that in certain circumstances a man may permit the continuance of an act if he can prevent it by taking legal proceedings and refrains from doing so. I can imagine a simple case, where a bailee, having agreed with the owner of a chattel not to permit any third person to have possession of it, is deprived of it by a third person; where he knows the third person is in possession of the chattel, and that a writ claiming a specific return to it could have but one result; if he refrained from taking proceedings I suggest that he might be held to have permitted the third person to have possession.' *Barton v Reed* [1932] 1 Ch 362 at 377, per Luxmoore J

'If a man permits a thing to be done, it means that he gives permission for it to be done, and if a man gives permission for a thing to be done, he knows what is to be done or is being done.' *Lomas v Peek* [1947] 2 All ER 574 at 575, per Lord Goddard CJ

'"Permit" is a word open to construction and permission may sometimes even be inferred from an unfettered handing over for use without a knowledge of the particular use.' *Vettraino v Grosset* 1948 SC(J) 49 at 55, per Lord Carmont

'Apart altogether from authority I would think that outside the sphere of purely polite social language, the word "permit", used even between laymen bent on serious business or other affairs intended to have legal consequences, would be used as a word connoting on the part of the one whose permission is asked the right effectively to refuse and on the part of the applicant the necessity to ask for and obtain permission, so as lawfully to undertake his proposed course of action. This, in my view, is its legal meaning.' *Tophams Ltd v Sefton (Earl)* [1966] 1 All ER 1030 at 1044, HL, per Lord Guest

'The offence under para (a) [Dangerous Drugs Act 1965, s 5 (repealed; see now the Misuse of Drugs Act 1971, s 8)], with which the appellant was not charged, can only be committed by the occupier of premises. The act of the occupier which is prohibited is to "permit" those premises to be used for the purpose of smoking cannabis or cannabis resin or of dealing in cannabis or cannabis resin. Here the word "permits" used to define the prohibited act in itself connotes as a mental element of the prohibited conduct knowledge or grounds for reasonable suspicion on the part of the occupier that the premises will be used by someone for that purpose and an unwillingness on his part to take means available to him to prevent it.' *Sweet v Parsley* [1969] 1 All ER 347 at 363, per Lord Diplock

Australia 'As a matter of English, and apart from any arbitrary definition, it [the word permit] connotes an authorisation by a person who has at least a de facto control.' *Broad v Parish* (1941) 64 CLR 588 at 594, per Rich ACJ

Australia 'What . . . of the word "permit"? Its primary meaning, according to the Oxford Dictionary, is "to allow, suffer, give leave, not to prevent". And it seems to me that when a section is addressed . . . to persons in control of others, and makes it unlawful for them to permit those others to contravene the section, it should be read as making it unlawful for them "to allow" or "not to prevent" their contravening it.' *Broadhurst v Larkin* [1954] VLR 541 at 544, 545, per Herring CJ

Australia 'I think the result of the English cases may be sufficiently well described by saying that a person cannot "suffer" or "permit" an act unless he knows it is or is to be done. If he does so know, however, he may suffer or permit it by not exercising the power or authority he possesses to prevent it.' *Bond v Reynolds* [1960] VR 601 at 602, per Gavan Duffy J

Canada 'It was urged on behalf of defendant that . . . the term "letting" or "permitting" involved the idea of action or abstaining from action. . . . If a person kindles a fire on his own land and does not properly watch it to see that it does not get away, and it does get away, he lets or permits it to do so; that is, he abstains from taking the action that he ought to have taken to have prevented it so getting away, and therefore he is guilty of an offence [against the Prairie Fires Ordinance].' *Macartney v Miller* (1905) 2 WLR 87 at 89, NWTSC, per Wetmore J

Canada 'I am cited . . . as laying down [in *Macartney v Miller* (supra)] that the term, "letting" or "permitting" involves the idea of action or abstaining from action. I am inclined to think that I only intended to concede that for the purposes of that case. . . . I will not say anything further on that subject than to refer to a definition given for the word "permit" in Murray's Dictionary, namely, "not to prevent".' *Moseley v Ketchum* (1910) 12 WLR 721 at 725, NWTSC, per Wetmore J

PERPETUAL INJUNCTION *See* INJUNCTION

PERPETUITIES

Rule against

'It is a general rule—too firmly established to be controverted, that an executory devise to be valid must be so framed that the estate devised *must* vest, if at all, within a life or lives in being and twenty-one years after; it is not sufficient that it *may* vest within that period; it must be good in its creation; and unless it is created in such terms that it cannot vest after the expiration of a life or lives in being, and twenty-one years, and the period allowed for gestation, it is not valid, and subsequent events cannot make it so.' *Dungannon (Lord) v Smith* (1845) 12 Cl & Fin 546 at 563, HL, per Creswell J

[Since 16 July 1964 a period of eighty years, instead of any other period, may be chosen as the perpetuity period applicable to a disposition under the rule against perpetuities. *See*, generally, the Perpetuities and Accumulations Act 1964.]

PERQUISITES

'The respondent, as general manager of Nobel's Explosives Ltd under an agreement to which in a moment I will more particularly refer, received during the years 1914 to 1917 a fixed salary and commission or bonus on the company's revenue. During those years, and for a series of years prior thereto, he was assessed under Sch E upon the amount of the salary received by him during the year of assessment, together with an amount equal to the average of the bonuses received by him during the three years preceding the year of assessment. Then additional assessments were made, which are the subject of the present appeal, under which it was proposed to assess both salary and bonus upon the amounts received or receivable by the respondent in respect of each year of assessment. Only one point, and that within the briefest possible compass, requires determination by your Lordships, and that is whether the bonuses under discussion are to be assessed under r 1 or under r 4 of s 146 of the Income Tax Act 1842, Sch E [repealed; cf Part V of the Income and Corporation Taxes Act]. . . . The first rule is intended, as I read it, to define the extent of the charge, and it accordingly uses wide words in order to bring within the charge all profits whatsoever accruing by reason of the office. The object of the fourth rule, on the contrary, is to deal in a more specific manner with profits which vary, and here the important words from the point of view of the subject matter of the present appeal are those which supply the definition of "perquisites". It is at first sight not altogether easy to see what in the definition of "perquisites" in the fourth rule is added to the definition of "perquisites" in the first rule; but the words about which an observation falls to be made in the definition of "perquisites" in the later rule are "such profits of offices and employments as arise from fees or other emoluments, and payable in the course of executing such offices or employments". My Lords, what is the purpose of the definition? It surely must be to ascertain what are the profits which are to be assessed either by reference to the receipts of the year preceding the year of assessment, or by reference to the average of the three preceding years. The words that are used are "such profits of offices and employments as arise from fees or other emoluments". Is it possible to contend with success that a bonus payable under the circumstances provided for by the clause of the agreement I have read is not a "perquisite" in the sense in which "perquisite" is explained by the words that follow it in r 4?' *M'Donald v Shand* [1923] AC 337 at 339, 341, 342, per Lord Birkenhead

PERSISTENT

[The appellant had been convicted of 'persistently' importuning in a public place for immoral purposes, contrary to the Sexual Offences Act 1956, s 32.] 'The sole point taken by counsel for the appellant is that there must be a persistent importunity, and whatever the word "persistent" means, it must, so he says and I think rightly, mean a degree of repetition, of either more than one invitation to one person or a series of invitations to different people.' *Dale v Smith* [1967] 2 All ER 1133 at 1136, per Lord Parker CJ

[The Adoption Act 1958, s 5(2) (repealed) provided that the court might dispense with consent to an adoption where any person whose consent would normally be required had 'persistently' failed to discharge the obligations of a parent or guardian.] 'It is not helpful to attempt to give a meaning to the adverb "persistently" by reference to its use in other Acts, e.g. "persistently importuning" or "persistent cruelty". A black eye in each of two consecutive weeks might well justify a finding of persistent cruelty; but a father who failed to send two weekly instalments of child maintenance could never be said to have persistently failed to discharge his obligations as a parent. I think that in the subsection the word is to be understood in the sense (see the Shorter Oxford English Dictionary) of "permanently", which is consistent with the few reported decisions.' *Re D (Minors)* [1973] 3 All ER 1001 at 1005, per Sir George Baker P

[Under the Adoption Act 1976, s 16, parental agreement to the making of an adoption order will be able to be dispensed with on various grounds, including the parent or guardian having 'persistently' failed without reasonable cause to discharge the parental duties in relation to the child.]

PERSON *See also* ANY PERSON

For the purpose of subscribing to the memorandum of association 'persons' includes aliens (although residing abroad, even when the company is formed to own a British ship, which cannot be owned by aliens), persons who are trustees for other subscribers, and persons who sign by agents, although only orally appointed. It also includes corporations and limited companies, and it may perhaps also include minors. (7 Halsbury's Laws (4th edn) para 80)

In this Act 'person' does not include a body of persons corporate or unincorporate which is not concerned in a representative, fiduciary or official capacity so as to authorise advice, assistance or representation to be granted to such a body. (Legal Aid Act 1988, s 2(10))

'Person' includes a body of persons corporate or unincorporate. (Interpretation Act 1978, Sch 1)

'"Person" when used in a legal sense, is an apt word to describe a corporation as well as a natural person.' *Royal Mail Steam Packet Co v Braham* (1877) 2 App Cas 381 at 386, PC, per cur.

[The Pharmacy Act 1868, s 1 (repealed; cf the Misuse of Drugs Act 1971, s 4 and the Poisons Act 1972, s 3) made it unlawful for any 'person' to sell or compound poisons (now 'non-medicinal' poisons), or to assume the title of chemist and druggist unless such person was qualified. Section 15 made any 'person', who failed to comply with that provision, liable to a penalty.] 'The word "person" may very well include both a natural person, a human being, and an artificial person, a corporation. I think that in an Act of Parliament, unless there be something to the contrary, probably (but that I should not like to pledge myself to) it ought to be held to include both. I have equally no doubt that in common talk, the language of men not speaking technically, a "person" does not include an artificial person, that is to say, a corporation. . . . My view of the matter is that it is the question of what the word "person" means in this particular Act that gives rise to the whole difficulty in the present case. . . . My conclusion, looking at this Act is that it is clear to my mind that the word "person" here is so used as to show that it does not include a corporation.' *Pharmaceutical Society v London & Provincial Supply Assocn Ltd* (1880) 5 App Cas 857 at 869, 870, per Lord Blackburn

[A testator by his will gave power to trustees to grant leases to any 'person' or persons they thought fit.] 'I think the trustees have power to grant this lease, which appears to be one beneficial to their trust estate. Lord Blackburn, in the case that has been cited [*Pharmaceutical Society v London & Provincial Supply Assocn* (1880) 5 App Cas at 869], said, "I am quite clear about this, that whenever you can see that the object of the Act requires that the word 'person' shall have the more extended or the less extended sense, then, whichever sense it requires, you should apply the word in that sense, and construe the Act accordingly". That principle appears to me to apply to the case of a power in a will also, and since the object of the will appears to require that the word "person" should include a corporation, I answer the question in the affirmative.' *Re Jeffcock's Trusts* (1882) 51 LJ Ch 507 at 507, per Chitty J

[The Companies Act 1862, s 6 (repealed; see now the Companies Act 1985, s 1) enacted that any seven (now two) or more 'persons' associated for any lawful purpose, might, by subscribing their names to a memorandum of association, form a company.] 'An infant at the time of signing is a "person" within the meaning of that section. It is quite true that he may afterwards avoid the contract which arises on his signature; but it seems to me that unless and until he does so, he is a "person".' *Re Laxon & Co (No 2)* [1892] 3 Ch 555 at 562, per Vaughan Williams J

'The question, whether the word "person" in Lord Tenterden's Act [Statute of Frauds Amendment Act 1828] includes a corporation, must be judged of by considering the context and the object of the enactment. Section 6 of that Act provides that "no action shall be brought whereby to charge any person upon or by reason of any representation . . . concerning or relating to the character . . . of any other person, to the intent . . . that such other person may obtain credit . . . unless such representation . . . be made in writing signed by the party to be charged therewith." . . . It is . . . argued that the protection given by this enactment must be taken to be limited to "persons" who are capable of signing a representation. . . . That argument is based on the context: but I do not think that the true construction of the enactment supports it. . . . Nor do I think that there is anything in the object of the Act to exclude a corporation from the benefit of it.' *Hirst v West Riding Union Banking Co Ltd* [1901] 2 KB 560 at 563, CA, per Stirling LJ

'The appellant was convicted on a count framed under s 4 of the Offences against the Person Act 1861, which makes it an offence to solicit any person to murder "any other person". The appellant undoubtedly did solicit the woman Shephard to murder her child if and when it should be born, and the question is whether the case falls within the section having regard to the fact that at the date when the letter containing the solicitation was written the child was unborn and therefore could not be the subject of murder. . . . All that is essential to bring a case within the section is that there should be a person capable of being murdered at the time when the act of murder is to be committed. If there is such a person then in existence it is quite immaterial that that person was not in existence at the date of the incitement. Here the child was in fact born alive, so that the event happened upon which the act was to be done. That is enough to satisfy the section.' *R v Shephard* [1919] 2 KB 125 at 126, CCA, per cur.

'The important thing to ascertain is the meaning of the word "person" in the vocabulary of the Income Tax Acts. The word constantly occurs throughout the Acts, and I think that it is most generally used to denote what may be termed an entity of assessment, i.e., the possessor or recipient of an income which the Acts require to be separately assessed for tax purposes.' *Income Tax Comrs v Gibbs* [1942] AC 402 at 418, 419, per Lord Macmillan

'On examining the provisions of s 2 [of the policy] it will be found that the first subsection deals with the policy-holder. Starting from the body of the policy, "will indemnify the policy-holder in respect of the [scheduled] automobile against . . . s 2(1) all sums which the policy-holder shall become legally liable to pay in respect of any claim by any person (including passengers in the automobile), for loss of life or accidental bodily injury or damage to property . . . caused by, through, or in connexion with such automobile". "Any person" should surely receive its ordinary meaning of any member of the public. The policy-holder himself cannot come within the term, not because he is not a person, but because the clause only relates to a claim by any person which the policy-holder is legally liable to pay, and such a liability cannot exist on a supposed claim at the same time by and against himself. It would appear also that for similar reasons a claim by any person would not include a claim by the wife or husband of the policy-holder. Put in another way, the words "any person" do not bear a restricted meaning, but the policy-holder is excluded from the scope of the indemnity by the very description of the liability insured. Apart from this it includes any member of the family, child, parent, relative, fiancé, liabilities towards whom have often been established. . . .' *Digby v General Accident, Fire & Life Assurance Corpn Ltd* [1943] AC 121 at 136, 137, per Lord Atkin

'In the present instance it seems to me that para 1 and r 11(2) of Sch D [to the Income Tax Act 1918 (repealed; see now Income and Corporation Taxes Act 1988, s 18)] are so different in their subject-matter and purpose that the word "person" must be given a different connotation in each. Paragraph 1 is intended to impose a tax and, in conformity with the rule of construction I have mentioned, the Crown is not included in the general word "person" because, if it were, it would be bound to its prejudice. Rule 11(2), on the other hand, is not intended to impose a tax or to do anything prejudicial to any of the persons to whom it refers. It may work now one way and now another, but its object is not to add to the liabilities of the taxpayer but to provide for terminal computations in the case of a trade changing hands. It does not purport to tax those who were not taxable before, and I am unable to see how its provisions can prejudice the Crown so as to justify its exclusion from the word "person" as used therein.' *Madras Electric Supply Corpn Ltd v Boarland* [1955] 1 All ER 753 at 760, HL, per Lord MacDermott; see also [1955] AC 667

[The Factories Act 1937, s 26 (repealed; see now the Factories Act 1961, s 29) provided, by sub-s (1), that safe means of access should be provided and maintained to every place at which 'any person' had at any time to work; and, by sub-s (2), that certain safety precautions, e.g. by the provision of fencing, should be taken where 'any person' had to work at a place from which he would be liable to fall a distance more than ten feet. An independent contractor employed as a window cleaner fell from his ladder and was killed.] 'The real question is what is meant by the words "any person" which appear in both sub-sections? They cannot be of entirely general application: I agree that a policeman who enters a factory in pursuit of a felon, or a fireman who enters to put out a fire, is not within the section, although he is a "person" and he is "working". I think one must exclude, for example, the film actor who enters the factory where a scene in which he is playing is to be shot, though he again is a "person" and the factory is a place in which he is to work. In my view, the true distinction is between those who are to work for the purposes of the factory and those who are not. Clearly, maintenance of the factory is work for the purpose of the factory, while the arrest of a felon or the putting out of a fire is not, though it may benefit the factory indirectly. Window cleaning is part of the maintenance of the factory and in my view the deceased was within the protection afforded by s 26.' *Wigley v British Vinegars Ltd* [1962] 3 All ER 161 at 164, HL, per Viscount Kilmuir; also reported in [1964] AC 307 at 324

Australia 'The time has passed for supposing that the legislature would use the word "person" only to signify a natural person in dealing with a class of business in which the utility of the proprietary company has long been made manifest. Indeed, it may be said that in modern business, as elsewhere, few persons remain natural.' *Leske v SA Real Estate Investment Co Ltd* (1930) 45 CLR 22 at 25, per Rich and Dixon JJ

Australia 'It has been long established, by undoubted judicial authority and now by statute, that the word "person", occurring in a written contract such as the policy before us [a comprehensive motor car policy] is to be read as including a corporation unless a contrary intention appears. . . . This is a technical rule of convenience limited to the construction of written documents, and is quite contrary to all practice in spoken language, as was pointed out by Lord Blackburn in *Pharmaceutical Society v London & Provincial Supply Association* [(1880) 5 App Cas 857 at 868].' *Bennett-Hullin v Clark (T P) & Co* [1944] VLR 45 at 46, per Mann CJ

Australia 'We think it clear that, as a matter of necessary implication, the word "person" where first used in s 64 [of the Workers' Compensation Act 1926–1986 NSW (see now s 64(1))] includes the Crown or any statutory instrumentality and we think it equally clear that this word has the same meaning when later used throughout the whole of the section.' *Government Transport Comr v Gumley* [1964–5] NSWR 1564 at 1567, per cur.

Australia 'I should have thought for myself that you must regard the court here as one of the arms of government set up under the Constitution by direct royal authority, and it does seem to me to be very difficult in those circumstances to say that a provision in an Act [Land Tax Act [1958–1986 (as amended)], s 4 (see now s 4(5) (Vic)] which says that an officer shall not disclose information to any person is intended to apply to a court.' *Cowan v Stanhill* [1966] VR 604 at 609, per Pape J

Juristic person

United States The term 'juristic person' includes a firm, corporation, union, association, or other organisation capable of suing and being sued in a court of law. (Lanham Act 1946, s 45)

PERSON AGGRIEVED

Generally

'If one came to the expression "person aggrieved by the decision" without reference to judicial authority one would say that the words meant no more than a person who had the decision given against him; but the courts have decided that the words mean more than that and have held that the word "aggrieved" is not synonymous in this context with the word "dissatisfied". The word "aggrieved" connotes some legal grievance, for example, a deprivation of something, an adverse effect on the title to something.' *Ealing Borough Council v Jones* [1959] 1 All ER 286 at 289, per Donovan J; also reported [1959] 1 QB 384 at 392

'The words "person aggrieved" are of wide import and should not be subject to a restrictive interpretation. They do not include, of course, a mere busybody who is interfering in things which do not concern him; but they do include a person who has a genuine grievance because an order has been made which prejudicially affects his interests.' *A-G of the Gambia v N'Jie* [1961] 2 All ER 504 at 511, PC, per cur.; also reported [1961] AC 617 at 634

Canada 'The question of who is an aggrieved person has been the topic of numerous decisions and I take it to mean a person who has had his legal rights infringed or one who has a substantial interest in overturning [an] order.' *Re Prince Edward Island Health Services Commission and Appeal Board* (1979) 95 DLR (3d) 684 at 689, PEI, per MacDonald J

Canada 'One general principle, leaving aside for the moment the significance of the statutory context in which the words are used, is that the words "person aggrieved" in a statute generally connote some legal grievance or signify someone whose legal rights have been infringed. Another general principle is that the words "person aggrieved" includes one with a genuine grievance because an order has been made which prejudicially affects his or her interests. The starting point is that grievance, right, or interest must be a legal grievance, right or interest. It is, of course, easier to say what will not constitute a "person aggrieved" than it is to say what a "person aggrieved" includes, and that will be, in the final analysis, my approach. Another somewhat generalisation is that to be a "person aggrieved" the grievance must be an immediate and direct result of the order to be appealed against. A "person aggrieved" must be aggrieved by the order alone, and not by the order combined with extraneous circumstances. . . . A "person aggrieved" is not merely a stranger, dissatisfied person or disappointed person. A "person aggrieved" is not merely a person who is frustrated in taking some course of action desired to be taken. A "person aggrieved" is not merely one who claims prejudice in a secondary sense, not being directly or immediately aggrieved or affected by a decision or order.' *Re Yulka and Minister of Social Services* (1982) 138 DLR (3d) 574 at 575, Sask QB, per Walker J

In Licensing Act

[The Licensing Act 1872, s 52 (repealed; see now the Licensing Act 1964, s 21), enacted that if any 'person' felt 'aggrieved' by any order or conviction made by a court of summary jurisdiction the 'person so aggrieved' might appeal therefrom.] 'It appears to me that a person to be a person aggrieved within s 52 of this Act must be a person who has a *locus standi* in the proceedings when they are first taken before the justices.' *R v Andover JJ* (1886) 16 QBD 711 at 717, DC, per Smith J

In Local Government Act

'A "person aggrieved" [within the Rating and Valuation Act 1925, s 37(1) (repealed)] for the purpose of this Act, that is to say, a person who is entitled to make a proposal either for increasing or decreasing the amount of the valuation, must mean a person who considers that he is aggrieved and may be able to show that he is aggrieved because until the decision is given either by the assessment committee . . . if there is an appeal, no one can say whether the person is aggrieved.' *R v Surrey (Mid-Eastern Area) Assessment Committee, ex p Merton and Morden Urban District Council* [1948] 1 All ER 856 at 858, per Lord Goddard CJ

In Patents Act

'Lord Justice Bowen says [in *Re Powell's Trade Mark* (1894) 62 LJ Ch 848 at 853]: "Persons who are aggrieved [within the Patents, Designs and Trade Marks Act 1883 (repealed; see now the Patents Act 1977, s 34(1))] are persons who are in some way or other substantially interested in having the mark removed from the register, or persons who would be substantially damaged if the mark remained." It is very difficult to frame a nearer definition than that.' *Re Talbot's Trade Mark* (1894) 63 LJ Ch 264 at 268, per Stirling J

[The Trade Marks Act 1905, s 35 (repealed; see now the Trade Marks Act 1938, s 33), provided for the rectification of the Register of Trade Marks, on the application of any 'person aggrieved'.] 'I think a trade mark, the infringement of which no person is in a position to prevent, is very much like an abandoned ship; it is a danger to the community so long as it is allowed to remain afloat, and any trader who may desire in the course of his trade to adopt a mark which in the circumstances he is honestly entitled to adopt, but which might be an infringement of the registered mark were there anybody entitled to sue in respect of the registered mark, is in my opinion an aggrieved person and as such has a right to come to the court and ask to have the derelict and abandoned mark removed.' *Pink v Sharwood (JA) & Co Ltd, Re Ord (Sidney) & Co's Trade Mark* (1913) 109 LT 594 at 599, per Eve J

Canada [In the trade mark legislation dealing with the right to bring an application to have a mark expunged] 'The words [a person aggrieved] are construed to mean . . .:—Any person who is in any way hampered in his trade by the presence of the marks or who can show any real interest in having them removed.' *Crean & Co v Dobbs & Co* [1930] SCR 307 at 313, SCC, per Lamont J; see now 48 Halsbury's Laws (4th edn) para 220

Canada 'Where proceedings are attacked on certiorari as being without jurisdiction or in excess of jurisdiction, the court very properly inquires whether the applicant has some interest in quashing the proceedings over and above the interest which any member of the public has in seeing that justice is properly administered. Is he in some manner adversely affected by the proceedings? Or is he simply a stranger off the street seeking to right a wrong? The former qualifies as a person aggrieved within the meaning of the law of certiorari. The latter does not.' *Young v A-G of Manitoba* (1961) 33 WWR 3 at 17, Man CA, per Freedman J

PERSON OF UNSOUND MIND *See* MENTAL DISORDER

PERSONAL

'I have come to the conclusion that the word "personal" cannot be limited to the person of the testator. I think that personal jewellery is a phrase which is used to describe jewellery appropriate for wearing on the person as distinct from jewellery which is ornamental to a chattel or a place.' *Re Resch (decd)* [1966] 2 NSWR 232 at 242, per Jacobs J

PERSONAL ACCIDENT INSURANCE *See* INSURANCE

PERSONAL ACTION *See* ACTION

PERSONAL BELONGINGS

Canada [A deceased left her 'personal belongings' to M in her will but provided no guidance as to what that encompassed. The court was asked for directions concerning the interpretation of the words.] 'To assist in determining the intention of the testatrix in using the words she did, their context in the rest of the words in the will is important. . . . I find this context to be compelling in favour of the testatrix intending a narrow, rather than a broad, meaning of the word "belongings". . . . In these circumstances I have concluded that the bequest of personal belongings carries clothes, jewellery, personal effects, household furnishings and the like, but no more. The van, the trailer, the motor club insurance, cash bank accounts and any debt or payment due to the estate falls to be divided . . . with the bequest of residue.' *Re Stanner's Estate, Jansen v Stanner's Estate* (1984) 28 Man R (2d) 64 at 65, 66, Man QB, per Scollin J

PERSONAL CHATTELS *See* CHATTELS

PERSONAL EFFECTS *See* EFFECTS

PERSONAL ESTATE *See also* EFFECTS; REAL ESTATE

'The distinction between personal estate which a man can bequeath and personal estate which he can appoint by will as he pleases is an extremely subtle one, and, although for certain purposes it is necessary to bear the distinction between the two in mind, for practical purposes it does not seem an unlikely use of words that both classes of property should be referred to as "his personal estate". In the connexion in which these words "his personal estate" are found in the Wills Act I think that they may well be construed as referring to both characters of property, both personal estate which a man may bequeath and personal estate which he may appoint.' *Re Wernher, Wernher v Beit* [1918] 2 Ch 82 at 95, CA, per Neville J

PERSONAL EVIDENCE *See* EVIDENCE

PERSONAL GIFT *See* GIFT

PERSONAL INJURY *See* INJURY

PERSONAL LUGGAGE *See* LUGGAGE

PERSONAL POSSESSIONS

Australia [A testator by his will left his 'personal possessions' to his father and mother.] 'In the context "personal possessions" means "personal effects", that is, physical chattels having some personal connection with the testator such as articles of personal or domestic use or ornament, clothing and furniture but not the testator's motor car and motor truck.' Headnote to *Re Leury (deceased)* [1975] VR 601

PERSONAL PROPERTY

Personal property or personalty may be roughly described as comprising all forms of property, movable or immovable, corporeal or incorporeal, other than freehold estates and interests in land (which may include chattels affixed to land) and its appurtenances. Moreover, by the equitable doctrine of conversion, equitable interests in freehold property are sometimes treated as personal property, for example where the freehold is held by trustees upon trust for sale. The distinction in English law between personal and real (or freehold) property was manifested in the early rule that freehold estates and interests in land were specifically recoverable, by a 'real' action, from a wrongful taker, whereas no action lay to compel restitution of other forms of property, the appropriate remedy for such cases being a mere 'personal' action for damages; and, although the later law provided remedies for the recovery of some forms of personal property, such innovations did not remove them from the sphere of personal property or from those other rules that had become characteristic of it. At common law the rules applicable to personal property differed in many important respects from those applicable to real property, but the removal of many of these differences by legislation during the nineteenth and twentieth centuries has deprived the distinction between realty and personalty of much of its former importance. When the question of the application of a foreign system of law arises a more important distinction is that to be drawn between movables and immovables.

Personal property is divisible into two classes: chattels personal and chattels real. Chattels personal have retained much of their former individuality; in particular, the rules that govern the acquisition and alienation inter vivos of chattels personal differ from those applicable to real property. . . .

'Personalty' or 'personal property' includes many kinds of property unknown to the common law, such as bills of exchange, bank notes and cheques, land improvement charges, copyrights, patents, shares in joint stock companies, debentures, government annuities and stock in the public funds, goodwill, and the exclusive right of burial in any particular place; but does not include title deeds relating to real estate, heirlooms in the strict sense, fixtures or wild animals, and it does not always include growing crops or trees. (35 Halsbury's Laws (4th edn) paras 1101, 1104)

New Zealand 'The testator devised and bequeathed to three legatees "the whole of my real and personal estate in Oamaru and Dunedin". The will contained no residuary devise or bequest, nor any other devise or bequest whatever. The great bulk of his estate consisted of two sums of £1,700 each which had been placed by the testator on deposit in two banks in Oamaru, and of £113 on current account at one bank there. There was some real estate in Oamaru and Dunedin worth about £820, and personal estate in Oamaru, consisting of furniture, personal effects, shares, and debts due from persons in Oamaru, of the total value of about £150. The question is what the testator meant by "the whole" of the "personal estate in Oamaru". . . . The term "personal estate" includes money. A man's money is part of his personal estate. If the testator, instead of bequeathing the whole of his personal estate in Oamaru, had bequeathed the whole of his money in Oamaru, it is certain that the amounts to his credit at the banks, both in current and deposit accounts, would have passed, although he might have had other money in Oamaru: *Manning v Purcell* [(1855) 7 De GM&G 55]. The reason as stated in that case is that although the amount is properly only a debt due from the bankers, the ordinary usage of mankind treats it as money. And more than that, the ordinary usage and language of mankind treats it as money locally situated at the bank where it has been deposited. If a person were estimating the amount of his personal property at a particular place he would certainly take into account sums of money deposited to his credit at a bank at that place. And if he spoke or wrote of his personal property or estate at a particular place he would be understood, taking the ordinary and popular meaning of such language, to include in the term "property or estate" sums so deposited. As was said by Mr Justice Chitty and Lord Halsbury in *In re Prater* [*Re Prater, Desinge v Beare* (1888) 37 Ch D 481, CA], in order to interpret the will you must take the ordinary and popular meaning of the words used by the testator. I think, therefore, that the term "personal property in Oamaru" includes the sums in question.' *Young v Bain, Re Young* (1902) 21 NZLR 503 at 504–506, per Williams J; also reported 4 GLR 484 at 485

United States The term 'personal property' means any property which is not real property under the laws of the State where situated at the time offered or otherwise made available for lease. (Truth in Lending Act 1968, s 181(4))

PERSONAL REPRESENTATIVE *See also* ADMINISTRATION; REPRESENTATIVES

The expression 'personal representative' is used to describe either an executor (whether he has proved the will or not) or an administrator, and is defined by the Administration of Estates Act 1925, for the purposes of that Act, to mean the executor, original or by representation, or administrator for the time being of a deceased person. It includes a special executor and, as regards liability for capital transfer tax, an executor de son tort. The personal representatives represent the deceased both in regard to his real and his personal estate and are deemed in law to be his heirs and assigns within the meaning of all trusts and powers. (17 Halsbury's Laws (4th edn) para 704)

'Personal representative' means the executor, original or by representation, or administrator for the time being of a deceased person, and as regards any liability for the payment of death duties includes any person who takes possession of or intermeddles with the property of a deceased person without the authority of the personal representatives or the court. (Law of Property Act 1925, s 205)

'Personal representative' means the executor, original or by representation, or administrator for the time being of a deceased person, and as regards any liability for the payment of death duties includes any person who takes possession of or intermeddles with the property of a deceased person without the authority of the personal representatives or the court, and "executor" includes a person deemed to be appointed executor as respects settled land. (Administration of Estates Act 1925, s 55(1))

'Personal representative' means the executor, original or by representation, or administrator, for the time being of a deceased person, and where there are special personal representatives for the purposes of settled land means those personal representatives. (Settled Land Act 1925, s 117)

'The ordinary sense of legal representatives, is executors or administrators.' *Price v Strange* (1820) 6 Madd 159 at 163, per Leach V-C

In settlement inter vivos

[A settlement made by Ellis Duckworth provided that in certain circumstances the trustees were to pay and apply the principal trust moneys to his (the settlor's) 'personal representatives'.] 'I think . . . that the expression "personal representatives", occurring where it does . . . means consanguinity. I also think that the terms of this instrument render it necessary for me to decide that the persons intended to be benefited were the next-of-kin living at the death of Ellis Duckworth.' *Wilson v Pilkington* (1847) 16 LJ Ch 169 at 170, per Knight Bruce V-C

'I take it to be clear that I must construe the words "such persons or person as shall be her personal representatives or representative" according to their ordinary meaning, and that ordinary meaning is "executors and administrators"; that the words being in a marriage settlement as distinguished from a will are not to be taken as having other than their ordinary meaning, unless there is something in the nature of the settlement or the context to give them a different meaning.' *Re Best's Settlement Trusts* (1874) LR 18 Eq 686 at 691, per Hall V-C

In will

'It was . . . contended, that the words "legal personal representatives" import in this will kindred or representation in blood, and are, therefore, words of purchase, not meaning merely representation in estate. . . . That it is impossible to suppose a will so worded, as that the expression "legal personal representatives" should mean "kindred" or representatives in blood, I will not say; but certainly, it would require a context strongly and clearly denoting such an intention in order to justify a departure so wide from the proper meaning of the phrase.' *Taylor v Beverley* (1844) 1 Coll 108 at 116, per Knight Bruce V-C

'I apprehend that the words "personal representative", or the words "legal personal representative", mean ordinarily, and must prima facie be taken to intend, an executor or administrator, that is, a representative in law as to personal estate; not a kinsman or kinswoman, not a wife or husband, not a person entitled by statute to claim distribution. Generally, also, and prima facie, as I suppose, a bequest made to a "personal representative", when the expression is so interpreted, must be understood as made to that representative not for his or her own benefit necessarily, but for the purposes, whatever they may be, for which he or she holds, or would hold, the general personal estate of the individual whom he or she is described as personally representing.' *Smith v Barneby* (1846) 2 Coll 728 at 735, 736, per Shadwell V-C

'It may be said that the words "personal representatives" or "legal representatives", or "legal personal representatives" when applied to personal estate as is frequently said of the word "issue" when applied to real estate, are words of limitation or words of purchase as will best effectuate the intention. But I think it may now be considered as settled that any of those words when applied to personal estate, unaccompanied by explanatory or controlling words are to be construed as being equivalent to "executors and administrators", and, consequently, as words of limitation, when they follow a limitation for life to the person to whose representative the property is given, and as a gift to the "executors and administrators" in that capacity when there is no such limitation.' *Stockdale v Nicholson* (1867) LR 4 Eq 359 at 365, per Malins V-C

'The . . . term "personal representatives", standing alone, ordinarily means executors and administrators.' *Wing v Wing* (1876) 34 LT 941 at 941, per Jessel MR

[A testator made a gift of the residue of his estate to his four nephews and nieces, the children of his sister, or their respective 'personal representatives' equally.] 'The reference to the number of the children being equivalent to the insertion of their names, . . . the residuary gift was to designated persons and not to a class; . . . there is no lapse; and . . . "personal representatives" must be taken to mean next of kin, who take by substitution.' *Jacob v Catling* [1881] WN 105 at 105, per Hall V-C

'Although, prima facie, legal personal representative means executor or administrator, it may under certain circumstances mean the person beneficially entitled.' *Surman v Wharton* [1891] 1 QB 491 at 495, DC, per Charles J

'It is apparently not disputed that the primary meaning of the word "personal representatives" is "executors or administrators", nor that the rule of construction is that words must be given their primary meaning unless there be found something in the context inconsistent with that primary meaning.' *Re Brooks, Public Trustee v White* [1928] Ch 214 at 222, CA, per Lawrence LJ

PERSONAL USE

New Zealand [A testatrix by her will bequeathed jewellery and articles of 'personal use.'] 'There is inherent in the phrase "personal use" . . . a connotation of some measure of exclusiveness of use by the testatrix; such an exclusiveness, in fact, as would provoke the recognition in the family circle of an association so intimate, and so far exceeding the merely proprietary or familiar, that the existence of any right of use by anyone else would be regarded as untenable.' *Re McFetridge, Speakman v McFetridge* [1950] NZLR 176 at 178, per Finlay J; also reported [1949] GLR 598, at 599

PERSONALTY *See* PERSONAL PROPERTY

PERSONATION

A person shall be deemed to be guilty of personation at a parliamentary or local government election if he—

(a) votes in person or by post as some other person, whether as an elector or as proxy, and whether that other person is living or dead or is a fictitious person; or
(b) votes in person or by post as proxy—
    (i) for a person whom he knows or has reasonable grounds for supposing to be dead or to be a fictitious person; or
    (ii) when he knows or has reasonable grounds for supposing that his appointment as proxy is no longer in force

(Representation of the People Act 1983, s 60(2))

'As soon as by word or act a man professes to be the person who is entitled to vote, with the object of passing himself off as that person, he is guilty of personation, and it is entirely immaterial, as far as this offence is concerned, that he abstained from going beyond tendering the voting-paper, and did not go so far as actually to hand it in.' *R v Hague* (1864) 33 LJMC 81 at 83, per Blackburn J

'When a man presents a voting-paper to the officer, the personation is complete. It is true he does not persist when the question is put to him, but he has not the less been guilty of personation, though unsuccessful.' Ibid at 83, per Mellor J

PERSUADE

[The Offences against the Person Act 1861, s 4 makes it a misdemeanour for any person (inter alia) to 'persuade' or endeavour to persuade any person to murder another person.] 'I think that the words "endeavour to persuade" in the statute are descriptive of the character of the offence which involves direction to a particular person and in my opinion the words have the same meaning as the words "encourage", "solicit", "persuade" and "propose to". Therefore, I think there must be some communication to the person in order to constitute the statutory offence.' *R v Krause*

(1902) 66 JP 121 at 121, CCA, per Lord Alverstone CJ

PERTAINING TO

Australia [The Commonwealth Conciliation and Arbitration Act 1904 (Cth), s 4 [see now Conciliation and Arbitration Act 1904–1986] defines the term 'industrial matters' as 'all matters pertaining to the relations of employers and employees'.] 'The words "pertaining to" mean "belonging to" or "within the sphere of", and the expression "the relations of employers and employees" must refer to the relation of an employer as employer with an employee.' *R v Kelly, ex p State of Victoria* (1950) 81 CLR 64 at 84

PETITIONER

[The Parliamentary Costs Act 1865, s 1 provides (inter alia) that where the parliamentary committee on a private Bill decides that the preamble is not proved, the 'petitioners' are, in certain circumstances, to be entitled to recover costs.] 'The question before us is, what is the statutory jurisdiction as to costs conferred by the Act. This turns on what is the meaning of the word "petitioner". There has been no alteration as to this since the passing of the Act, and it appears to me that in 1865 the word "petitioner" had a definite and ascertained meaning: petitioners are persons who properly subscribe a written petition and appear before the committee to support its prayer.' *Mallet v Hanley* (1887) 18 QBD 787 at 794, 795, CA, per Fry LJ

PETTY SESSIONS

'Petty-sessional court-house' means any of the following, that is to say—

(a) a court-house or place at which justices are accustomed to assemble for holding special or petty sessions or for the time being appointed as a substitute for such a court-house or place (including, where justices are accustomed to assemble for either special or petty sessions at more than one court-house or place in a petty sessional division, any such court-house or place);

(b) a court-house or place at which a stipendiary magistrate is authorised by law to do alone any act authorised to be done by more than one justice of the peace.

(Magistrates' Courts Act 1980, s 150(1))

PETTY SESSIONS AREA

'Petty sessions area' means any of the following areas, that is to say, a non-metropolitan county which is not divided into petty sessional divisions, a petty sessional division of a non-metropolitan county, a metropolitan district which is not divided into petty sessional divisions, a petty sessional division of a metropolitan district, a London commission area which is not divided into petty sessional divisions, a petty sessional division of a London commission area and the City of London. (Magistrates' Courts Act 1980, s 150(1))

PEW

'The word "pew" is said to be derived from the Dutch "puye" and to signify "a seat inclosed in a church" (Johnson's Dictionary.) An obvious inconvenience would arise if it were lightly held that . . . [the] owner of a pew or seat was owner of so much of the site of a church as is comprised within the area of such pew or seat.' *Brumfitt v Roberts* (1870) LR 5 CP 224 at 232, per cur.

PHILANTHROPIC

'The question . . . arises whether a bequest for "charitable or philanthropic purposes" is valid according to the law of England. . . . The question is whether philanthropic purposes can be effectively distinguished from benevolent purposes or purposes of general utility. "Philanthropic" is, no doubt, a word of narrower meaning than "benevolent". An act may be benevolent if it indicates goodwill to a particular individual only; whereas an act cannot be said to be philanthropic unless it indicate goodwill to mankind at large. . . . The word "philanthropic" is wide enough to comprise purposes which are not charitable in the technical sense.' *Re Macduff, Macduff v Macduff* [1896] 2 Ch 451 at 455–457, CA, per Stirling J

'What is the meaning of the word "philanthropic"? He [the testator] means by that something distinguished from charitable in the ordinary sense; but I cannot put any definite meaning on the word. All I can say is that a philanthropic purpose must be a purpose which indicates goodwill to mankind in general.' Ibid at 464, 467, per Lindley LJ

'The present case . . . is a gift to charitable or philanthropic purposes. . . . I do not think it is very different from a gift for philanthropic purposes. There may be an argument that, "philanthropic" being joined with "charitable", the philanthropic purposes must also be charitable; but then there is also another argument that as philanthropic purposes are distinguished from charitable purposes by "or", that shows that philanthropic purposes are something different from charitable purposes. I think the one argument may be set off against the other, and that we get very little assistance from the fact that there is a word "charitable" used along with the word "philanthropic". Now, suppose the word "philanthropic" stood alone. . . . The word "philanthropy" may include—not cases of a totally exceptional character, but cases of a very wide class indeed, and numerous cases which would be within the popular meaning of philanthropic, and would have nothing to do with charity. That appears to me sufficient to decide the case. . . . The promotion of the happiness of mankind is undoubtedly a philanthropic purpose . . . the expression "for promoting the happiness of mankind" is nearer in its meaning to that of the word "philanthropic" than any other expression dealt with in the cases.' Ibid at 470–475, per Rigby LJ

PHONORECORDS

United States 'Phonorecords' are material objects in which sounds, other than those accompanying a motion picture or other audiovisual work, are fixed by any method now known or later developed, and from which the sounds can be perceived, reproduced, or otherwise communicated, either directly or with the aid of a machine or device. The term 'phonorecords' includes the material object in which the sounds are first fixed. (Copyright Act of 1976, s 101)

PHOTOGRAPH

'Photograph' means a recording of light or other radiation on any medium on which an image is produced or from which an image may by any means be produced, and which is not part of a film. (Copyright, Designs and Patents Act 1988, s 4(2))

[The Fine Arts Copyright Act 1862, s 1 (repealed; see now the Copyright, Designs and Patents Act 1988, s 4(2) supra), gave copyright to the author of every original painting, drawing or 'photograph', for the term of his natural life and seven years after his death.] 'We can understand the difference between an original painting or design and a copy of it, but it is hard to say what an original photograph is. All photographs are copies of some object, either picture, statue, piece of architecture, or the like. And I think that the photograph of a picture is an original photograph so far as this, that the copying of it is an infringement of the statute.' *Re Graves, ex p Walker* (1869) 10 B&S 680 at 691, per Blackburn J

Author of *See* AUTHOR

PHYSICAL INJURY *See* INJURY

PHYSICIAN *See* MEDICAL PRACTITIONER

PICCAGE *See also* STALLAGE

'Though every person has of common right a liberty of coming into a publick market for the purpose of buying and selling; yet he has not of common right a liberty of placing a stall there, but he must acquire that by a compensation, which is called stallage; and in Blunt's Law Dictionary, Minsheu's, Boyer verbo Estallage, and Spelman's Glossary, is defined to be a satisfaction to the owner of the soil, for the liberty of placing a stall upon it; and if in the erecting one the soil is broke, it is called piccage.' *Northampton Corpn v Ward* (1745) 2 Stra 1238 at 1239, per cur.

PICK

'Pick', in relation to a plant, means gather or pluck any part of the plant without uprooting it. (Wildlife and Countryside Act 1981, s 27(1))

PICKETING

(1) It shall be lawful for a person in contemplation or furtherance of a trade dispute to attend—

(a) at or near his own place of work, or
(b) if he is an official of a trade union, at or near the place of work of a member of that union whom he is accompanying and whom he represents,

for the purpose only of peacefully obtaining or communicating information, or peacefully persuading any person to work or abstain from working.

(2) If a person works or normally works—
(a) otherwise than at any one place, or
(b) at a place the location of which is such that attendance there for a purpose mentioned in subsection (1) above is impracticable,

his place of work for the purposes of that subsection shall be any premises of his employer from which he works or from which his work is administered.

(3) In the case of a worker who is not in employment and whose last employment was terminated in connection with a trade dispute, subsection (1) above shall in relation to that dispute have effect as if any reference to his place of work were a reference to his former place of work.

(4) A person who is an official of a trade union by virtue only of having been elected or appointed to be a representative of some of the members of the union shall be regarded for the purposes of subsection (1) above as representing only those members; but otherwise an official of a trade union shall be regarded for those purposes as representing all its members. (Trade Union and Labour Relations Act 1974, s 15, as substituted by the Employment Act 1980, s 16(1))

'"Picketing" . . . really means watching and besetting and stationing men outside a place where a strike has taken place, and where the workmen have been called out, to compel persons not to go into that place to work for the owner of it as long as the strike lasts. That is the meaning of picketing pure and simple.' *Lyons (J) & Sons v Wilkins* [1896] 1 Ch 811 at 834, 835, CA, per A L Smith LJ

[On an interlocutory appeal for the discharge of an interim injunction, Lord Denning MR (dissenting on the question of the injunction being discharged) made the following observations on 'picketing'.] 'Picketing is not a nuisance in itself. Nor is it a nuisance for a group of people to attend at or near the plaintiffs' premises in order to obtain or to communicate information or in order peacefully to persuade. It does not become a nuisance unless it is associated with obstruction, violence, intimidation, molestation or threats. . . . I see no valid reason for distinguishing between picketing in furtherance of a trade dispute and picketing in furtherance of other causes. Why should workers be allowed to picket and other people not? I do not think there is any distinction drawn by the law save that, in the case of a trade dispute, picketing is governed by statutory provisions; and, in the case of the other causes, it is left to the common law. But, broadly speaking, they are in line the one with the other. Picketing is lawful so long as it is done merely to obtain or communicate information, or peacefully to persuade; and is not such as to submit any other person to any kind of constraint or restriction of his personal freedom.' *Hubbard v Pitt* [1975] 3 All ER 1 at 9, CA, per Lord Denning (diss)

Canada 'Throughout the argument the appellants have adhered to the term "peaceful picketing". Before discussing the legality of what was done, it should be said at once that in my view at least the term "peaceful picketing" has no place in the law of this province. It is a negation in terms, for "picketing" as conducted here cannot be described as peaceful. While violence did not occur, it was not due to lack of provocation; the display of organised labour strength and the atmosphere of labour power cowed active opposition and discouraged retaliatory or protective measures which would have led inevitably to violence. Without intimidation, obstruction and moral coercion it was useless for the purposes employed; with them it was provocative. Professor Dicey in the introductory chapter to "The Law of the Constitution" (8th Edn) 1931, at p 40, wrote: "Hence the invention of that self-contradictory idea of 'peaceful picketing', which is no more capable of real existence than would be 'peaceful war' or 'unoppressive oppression'."' *Hollywood Theatres Ltd v Tenney* [1940] 1 WWR 337 at 346, 347, CA, per O'Halloran JA

PICTORIAL, GRAPHIC, AND SCULPTURAL WORKS

United States 'Pictorial, graphic, and sculptural works' include two-dimensional and three-dimensional works of fine, graphic, and applied art, photographs, prints and art reproductions, maps, globes, charts, technical drawings, diagrams, and models. Such works shall include works or artistic craftsmanship insofar as their form but not their mechanical or utilitarian aspects are concerned; the design of a useful article . . . shall be considered a pictorial, graphic, or sculptural work only if, and only to the extent that, such design incorporates pictorial, graphic, or sculptural features that can be identified separately from, and are capable of existing independently of, the utilitarian aspects of the article. (Copyright Act of 1976, s 101)

PICTURE

[A testatrix, by her will, bequeathed her plate, linen, china, glass, books, 'pictures', plated articles, prints, and her household furniture and effects, which at the time of her decease should be in and about her house.] 'The only question . . . upon which any doubt could arise, would be concerning the pictures [portraits framed in jewels], which it appears are adorned in a costly manner, and are very valuable; and without determining whether or not they would pass under the word "pictures", as to which, I think, there may be some doubt, I should wish to see them before I decide; because, if they were not articles ordinarily worn, but more resembling miniatures not intended to be worn, they might pass under this bequest. I propose, therefore, to make a declaration, that, by this bequest, none of the articles mentioned in the schedule passed, which were articles exclusively of personal ornament, and not adapted for the use or ornament of the house.' *Tempest v Tempest* (1856) 2 K&J 635 at 644, 645, per Page Wood V-C

'Pictures are, in general, encompassed with frames; and the frame not only forms part of the picture, but is ordinarily as necessary for its security as the outside package in which it is sent.' *Henderson v London & North Western Rly Co* (1870) LR 5 Exch 90 at 91, per Kelly CB

'In common language, it would be said that a picture, consisting of the canvas, the painting, and the frame, is one entire thing; and it might as well be contended that the plaintiff could recover for the canvas alone, or that if jewelry were sent in jewel cases, the owner could recover for the cases, though not for the jewels, as that the plaintiff can here recover for the frames of the pictures apart from the pictures themselves. In the common sense and understanding of mankind the whole is one thing.' Ibid at 91, per Martin B

'It was argued that miniatures would not pass [under a bequest of pictures]; but, in my opinion, they do. They are clearly small pictures as appears from the list produced, some being copies of pictures and others portraits; but in saying this I do not mean to include those that are only accessory to some other object, such as an ivory mirror with a miniature on the back.' *Re Craven, Crewdson v Craven* (1908) 24 TLR 750 at 751, per Swinfen Eady J

PIE POWDER

'All the Judges conceived, that the court being stiled "a Court of Pypowders" (which is a court incident to fairs and markets, and for causes only arising within them), shall not be intended a court unless it be shewn to be held by charter or prescription.' *Hodges v Moyse & Scriven* (1626) Cro Car 46 at 46, per cur.

[The Tolzey and Pie Poudre Courts of the City and County of Bristol were abolished by the Courts Act 1971, s 43.]

PIECE

[A testator devised to his son his messuage or dwelling-house and premises, with the 'piece of land' thereto adjoining, and their respective appurtenances.] 'We think that the question is not so much what might have been meant by the word "piece", standing alone, as what is meant by the expression "piece of land" used in the will. The expressions "piece of land" or "bit of land" are so familiar as to be almost colloquial. In ordinary language they mean a small portion of land. Nor is the primary meaning of the word "piece" departed from, when the expression "piece of land" is thus understood; for, "piece of land", in this sense, still imports a portion of land, as separated or distinguished from other land, not indeed, of the same owner, but of other owners. It may be added, that this sense of the word "piece" itself seems at least as consistent with the testator's language as the other, if not more so; for, he does not say, "the piece of my land", but simply "the piece of land".' *Josh v Josh* (1858) 5 CBNS 454 at 466, per cur.

PIED-A-TERRE

'Counsel for the landlord has justly pointed out that the phrase "pied-a-terre" is in itself ambiguous. It is sometimes used to mean simply a convenient resort. In another context a man may refer to his home as a pied-a-terre, particularly if it is of small dimensions.' *Beck v Scholz* [1953] 1 All ER 814 at 815, 816, CA, per Evershed MR (also reported in [1953] 1 QB 570 at 575)

PIER

'The clause [in a contract of reinsurance] in question here . . . refers to collision with a floating substance on the one hand, and to collision with a permanent structure on the other hand. It then proceeds to include collision with harbours, wharves, piers, stages, or similar structures. The words of the clause which are applicable to the present case are the words "piers or similar structures". The evidence shows that both these vessels struck and were wrecked on the toe of the breakwater outside the harbour at Holyhead. The breakwater in question was made by the deposit of a number of large boulders, forming the toe of the breakwater, behind which the wall of the breakwater itself is built. I am of opinion that the words "pier", "breakwater", and "toe" all denote one and the same structure, and therefore that the expression "collision with piers . . . or stages or similar structures" covers the present case.' *Union Marine Insurance Co v Borwick* [1895] 2 QB 279 at 281, per Mathew J

PIG

'Pig' includes any boar, hog or sow. (Protection of Animals Act 1911, s 15)

PILFERAGE

'Counsel for the plaintiffs submits that at some stage, and probably when the goods were discharged at Hong Kong, there was a loss by theft. He does not rely on "pilferage" [within the standard form of Lloyd's marine policy] which he says, and I think rightly says, refers to a furtive theft and probably to the taking of a small part of the goods rather than of the whole.' *Nishina Trading Co Ltd v Chiyoda Fire & Marine Insurance Co Ltd* [1968] 3 All ER 712 at 719, per Donaldson J; reversed on other grounds, [1969] 2 All ER 776, CA

PILOT

Of aircraft

'Pilot in command' in relation to an aircraft means a person who for the time being is in charge of the piloting of the aircraft without being under the direction of any other pilot in the aircraft. (Civil Aviation Act 1982, s 94(7))

Of ship

'Pilot' means any person not belonging to a ship who has the conduct thereof. (Merchant Shipping Act 1894, s 742)

PIN MONEY

Pin money was an allowance made by a husband to his wife for her separate personal expenses and was usually provided for in a settlement by a yearly rent charge on the husband's real estate: see *Howard v Earl of Digby* (1834) 2 Cl & Fin 634, HL, where the nature of pin money and the legal principles applying to it are discussed. It was not assignable: *Jodrell v Jodrell* (1845) 15 LJ Ch 17. Provision for pin money is now rarely included in settlements. (22 Halsbury's Laws (4th edn) para 1083n)

'It is a very material fact, in a case where authority is so little to be had, that the general opinion of all those who give pin-money, either to their own wives, or to the wives of their sons, upon marriage, should be entirely coincident with the view to which the argument had led; namely, that it is a sum allowed to save the trouble of a constant recurrence by the wife to the husband upon every occasion of a milliner's bill, upon every occasion of a jeweller's account coming in,—I mean not the jeweller's account for the jewels, because that is a very different question,—but I mean for the repair and the wear and tear of trinkets and for pocket money, and things of that sort; I do not of course mean the carriage, and the house, and the gardens, but the ordinary personal expenses. It is in order to avoid the necessity of perpetual recurrence by the wife to the husband, that a sum of money is settled at the marriage, which is to be set apart to the use of the wife, for the purpose of bearing those personal expenses.' *Howard v Digby* (1934) 8 Bli NS 224 at 265, per Lord Lyndhurst LC

PIOUS

'So far as I am able to discover, "godly" and "pious" as applied to trusts or uses, had, in early times much the same significance in Scotland as in England. Their meaning was not limited to objects of a religious or eleemosynary character, but embraced all objects which a well-disposed person might promote from motives of philanthropy.' *Income Tax Special Purposes Comrs v Pemsel* [1891] AC 531 at 558, per Lord Watson

PIPE-LINE

In this Act 'pipe-line' (except where the context otherwise requires) means a pipe

(together with any apparatus and works associated therewith), or system of pipes (together with any apparatus and works associated therewith), for the conveyance of any thing other than air, water, water vapour or steam, not being—
(a) a drain or sewer; or
(b) a pipe or system of pipes constituting or comprised in apparatus for heating or cooling or for domestic purposes; or
(c) a pipe or system of pipes on the site of any operations or works to which certain provisions of the Factories Act 1961, apply by virtue of subsection (1) of section one hundred and twenty-seven (building operations and works of engineering construction) of that Act; or
(d) a pipe or system of pipes wholly situate within the boundaries of an agricultural unit and designed for use for purposes of agriculture; or
(e) a pipe or system of pipes wholly situate in premises used for the purposes of education or research; or
(f) a pneumatic dispatch-tube.

(2) For the purposes of the foregoing subsection, the following apparatus and works, and none other, shall be treated as being associated with a pipe, or system of pipes, namely,—
(a) apparatus for inducing or facilitating the flow of any thing through the pipe or, as the case may be, through the system or any part thereof;
(b) valves, valve chambers, manholes, inspection pits and similar works, being works annexed to, or incorporated in the course of, the pipe or system;
(c) apparatus for supplying energy for the operation of any such apparatus as is mentioned in paragraph (a) of this subsection or of any such works as are mentioned in paragraph (b) thereof;
(d) apparatus for the transmission of information for the operation of the pipe or system;
(e) apparatus for affording cathodic protection to the pipe or system;
(f) a structure for the exclusive support of a part of the line or system.

(Pipelines Act 1962, s 65)

'Pipe-line works' means works of any of the following kinds, that is to say,—
(a) placing a pipe-line or a length of pipeline; inspecting, maintaining, adjusting, repairing, altering or renewing a pipe-line or a length of pipe-line; changing the position of a pipe-line or a length of pipe-line or removing a pipe-line or a length of pipe-line;
(b) breaking up or opening land for the purposes of works mentioned in the foregoing paragraph and tunnelling or boring for those purposes and other works requisite for or incidental to those purposes.

(Pipe-Lines Act 1962, s 65)

[See also s 33(1) of the Petroleum and Submarine Pipe-Lines Act 1975, as extended by the Oil and Gas (Enterprise) Act 1982, s 25.]

PIRACY *See also* REVOLT

Piracy in international law (piracy jure gentium) was defined by the Convention on the High Seas, and this definition forms part of the law of England. According to the convention, piracy consists of the following acts: (1) any illegal act of violence, detention or depredation committed for private ends by the crew or the passengers of a private ship or a private aircraft, and directed (a) on the high seas against another ship or aircraft, or against persons or property on board such ship or aircraft, or (b) against a ship, aircraft, persons or property in a place outside the jurisdiction of any state; (2) any act of voluntary participation in the operation of a ship or of an aircraft with the knowledge of facts making it a pirate ship or aircraft; or (3) any act of inciting or intentionally facilitating an act described in head (1) or (2). The acts described in head (1), (2) or (3), if committed by a warship whose crew has mutinied and taken control of the ship or aircraft, are assimilated to acts committed by a private ship. A ship or aircraft is considered a pirate ship or aircraft if it is intended by the persons in dominant control to be used for any of the acts which constitute piracy. The same applies if the ship or aircraft has been used to commit any such act, so long as it remains under the control of the persons guilty of that act. (18 Halsbury's Laws (4th edn) para 1536)

The term 'pirates' in the Lloyd's policy includes passengers who mutiny and rioters who attack the ship from the shore. Revolutionaries organising and carrying out an armed expedition against the government, however, are not pirates within the meaning of that term in the policy. (25 Halsbury's Laws (4th edn) para 162)

The term 'pirates' includes passengers who

mutiny and rioters who attack the ship from the shore. (Marine Insurance Act 1906, Sch 1)

'Now piracy is only a sea-term for robbery, piracy being a robbery committed within the jurisdiction of the Admiralty. If any man be assaulted within that jurisdiction and his ship or goods violently taken away without legal authority,—this is robbery and piracy. If the mariners of any ship shall violently dispossess the master, and afterwards carry away the ship itself or any of the goods, or tackle, apparel or furniture, with a felonious intention, in any place where the lord Admiral hath, or pretends to have jurisdiction, this also is robbery and piracy. The intention will, in these cases, appear by considering the end for which the fact was committed; and the end will be known, if the evidence shall shew you what hath been done.' *R v Dawson* (1696) 13 State Tr 451 at 454, 455, per Hedges J

'How am I to determine who are pirates, except by the acts that they have committed? I apprehend that, in the administration of our criminal law, generally speaking, all persons are held to be pirates who are found guilty of piratical acts; and piratical acts are robbery and murder upon the high seas. I do not believe that, even where human life was at stake, our Courts of Common Law ever thought it necessary to extend their inquiries further, if it was clearly proved against the accused that they had committed robbery and murder upon the high seas. In that case they were adjudged to be pirates, and suffered accordingly. Whatever may have been the definition in some of the books . . . it was never, so far as I am able to find, deemed necessary to inquire whether parties so convicted of these crimes had intended to rob on the high seas, or to murder on the high seas indiscriminately. Though the municipal law of different countries may and does differ, in many respects, as to its definition of piracy, yet I apprehend that all nations agree in this: that acts, such as those which I have mentioned, when committed on the high seas, are piratical acts, and contrary to the law of nations. It is true, that where the subjects of one country may rebel against the ruling power, and commit divers acts of violence with regard to that ruling power, that other nations may not think fit to consider them as acts of piracy. But, however this may be, I do not think it necessary to follow up that disquisition on the present occasion. I think it does not follow that, because persons who are rebels or insurgents may commit against the ruling power of their own country acts of violence, they may not be, as well as insurgents and rebels, pirates also; pirates for other acts committed towards other persons. It does not follow that rebels or insurgents may not commit piratical acts against the subjects of other states, especially if such acts were in no degree connected with the insurrection or rebellion. Even an independent state may, in my opinion, be guilty of piratical acts. What were the Barbary pirates of olden times? What many of the African tribes at this moment? It is, I believe, notorious, that tribes now inhabiting the African coast of the Mediterranean will send out their boats and capture any ships becalmed upon their coasts. Are they not pirates, because, perhaps, their whole livelihood may not depend on piratical acts? I am well aware that it has been said that a state cannot be piratical; but I am not disposed to assent to such dictum as a universal proposition. . . . I refer to Russell on Crimes, where we find the result of many older authorities. He commences in these words: "The offence of piracy, at Common Law, consists in committing those acts of robbery and depredation upon the high seas, which, if committed upon land, would have amounted to felony there": and in a subsequent part I find the following: "If a robbery be committed in creeks, harbours, ports, etc, in foreign countries, the Court of Admiralty indisputably has jurisdiction of it, and such offence is consequently piracy." There is a case also stated here which I think applies: "Where a prisoner was indicted for stealing three chests of tea out of the *Aurora*, of London, on the high seas, and it was proved that the larceny was committed while the vessel lay off Wampa, in the river, twenty or thirty miles from sea, but there was no evidence as to the tide flowing or otherwise, at the place where the vessel lay; it was held, from the circumstance that the tea was stolen on board the vessel which had crossed the ocean, that there was sufficient evidence that the larceny was committed on the high seas." Again, it was decided in another case, that where A, standing on the shore of a harbour, fired a loaded musket at a revenue cutter which had struck upon a sand-bank in the sea, about 100 yards from the shore, by which firing a person was maliciously killed on board the vessel, it was piracy.' *The Magellan Pirates* (1853) 1 Ecc & Ad 81 at 83, 84, per Dr Lushington

[A policy of marine insurance covered the assured against (inter alia) 'pirates'.] 'It cannot be contended that the loss . . . was not attributable to the perils stated in the declaration, if it is to be considered that the acts of the Chinese emigrants or coolies were the proximate, and not merely the remote cause of such loss. The admitted seizure of the vessel by them, the taking her out of the possession and control of the master and crew, and the diverting her from the voyage insured, were either direct acts of piracy or acts so entirely *ejusdem generis*, that, if not reducible to the special words of the policy, they are clearly included within the general words at the end of the peril clause.' *Palmer v Naylor* (1854) 10 Exch 382 at 389, per cur.

[Section 1 of Stat (1843) 6 & 7 Vict c 76 (repealed) provided for the extradition of persons charged with the crime (inter alia) of 'piracy' committed within the jurisdiction of the United States of America.] 'It appears clearly enough, both from the American authorities and our own, that there are offences called piracy by the laws of those respective countries which are not piracy by the law of nations. It does not follow from thence that piracy jure gentium need be excluded; but when we come to the question, whether it is within the jurisdiction of either country, the taking piracy in this treaty to mean piracy jure gentium is not satisfactory. Those words in the treaty are followed in the Act, which, by sect 1, provides for the extradition of persons charged with the crime of murder, etc, or with the crime of piracy, etc. "committed within the jurisdiction of the United States." Then comes the question, does that mean within the jurisdiction of one party exclusively? I do not say how that would be in the case of a murder committed within the United States by a British subject, over whom we have a personal jurisdiction. It is enough to say Mr Lush convinced me that much might be said on that subject and if the case turned upon it I should have wished for time to consider. But this is a question of piracy which does not depend on any personal, but on general, jurisdiction. In proof of this, I take the following from 1 Kent Comm 186 (10th Edn.):—"It is of no importance, for the purpose of giving jurisdiction, on whom or where a piratical offence has been committed. A pirate, who is one by the law of nations, may be tried and punished in any country where he may be found, for he is reputed to be out of the protection of all laws and privileges. The statute of any government may declare an offence committed on board its own vessels to be piracy"; and I may add, though Kent does not say it, "on other vessels". He goes on, "And such an offence will be punishable exclusively by the nation which passes the statute. But piracy, under the law of nations, is an offence against all nations, and punishable by all".' *Re Tivnan* (1864) 5 B&S 645 at 687, 688, per Blackburn J

[A policy of marine insurance contained a clause by which the underwriters were freed from liability from capture, seizure and detention, 'piracy' excepted, etc.] 'I adopt what Pickford J says as to the meaning of "piracy" in the following passage of his judgment: "I do not think that can be better expressed than it is in Hall's International Law, 5th ed, p 259, where it is said: 'Besides, though the absence of competent authority is the test of piracy, its essence consists in the pursuit of private as contrasted with public ends. Primarily the pirate is a man who satisfies his personal greed or his personal vengeance by robbery or murder in places beyond the jurisdiction of a State. The man who acts with a public object may do like acts to a certain extent, but his moral attitude is different, and the acts themselves will be kept within well-marked bounds. He is not only not the enemy of the human race, but he is the enemy solely of a particular State.'" That I think expresses what I have called the popular or business meaning of the word "private", and I find that several, though not all, of the definitions cited in the note on p 260 of the same work bear out that idea. No doubt there are definitions which do not embody that idea, but that I think is the common and ordinary meaning; a man who is plundering indiscriminately for his own ends, and not a man who is simply operating against the property of a particular State for a public end, the end of establishing a government, although that act may be illegal and even criminal, and although he may not be acting on behalf of a society which is, to use the expression in Hall on International Law, politically organised. Such an act may be piracy by international law, but it is not, I think, piracy within the meaning of a policy of insurance; because, as I have already said, I think you have to attach to "piracy" a popular or business meaning, and I do not think, therefore, that this was a loss by piracy.' *Bolivia Republic v Indemnity Mutual Marine Assurance Co Ltd* [1909] 1 KB 785 at 796, 797, CA, per Vaughan Williams LJ

'All that their Lordships propose to do is to answer the question put to them, and having examined all the various cases, all the various statutes and all the opinions of the various juriconsults cited to them, they have come to the conclusion that the better view and the proper answer to give to the question addressed to them is that stated at the beginning—namely, that actual robbery is not an essential element in the crime of piracy jure gentium, and that a frustrated attempt to commit piratical robbery is equally piracy jure gentium.' *Re Piracy Jure Gentium* [1934] AC 586 at 600, PC, per cur.

'I have to consider whether force or a threat of force is an essential element of piracy. . . . The only case to which I was referred that bears directly on the point was *Re Piracy Jure Gentium* [[1934] AC 586], and that went no further than holding that an attempt at robbery would amount to piracy, even if the substantive offence were not achieved. But the general tenor of the authorities supports the conclusion that theft without force or a threat of force cannot be piracy. . . . The very notion of piracy is inconsistent with clandestine theft. . . . It is not necessary that the thieves must raise the pirate flag and fire a shot across the victim's bows before they can be called pirates. But piracy is not committed by stealth.' *Athens Maritime Enterprises Corpn v Hellenic Mutual War Risks Association (Bermuda) Ltd, The Andreas Lemos* [1983] 1 All ER 590 at 598, 599, 600, per Staughton J

PISCARY

Common of piscary is a right of fishing with other persons in another man's water, and does not differ from other rights of common. It may be either appurtenant or in gross. It may be annexed to lands formerly copyhold of a manor, and in that case may be claimed by custom, but in all other cases it must be based on grant or prescription. The right may exist in common not only with other persons, but also with the owner of the soil. (6 Halsbury's Laws (4th edn) para 581)

'There are three sorts of fisheries. 1 *Seperalis piscaria*, and there, he who has the fishery is owner of the soil, and therefore it is a good plea in an action brought by him, that it is *liberum tenementum* of another. 2 *Libera piscaria*, which is where the right of fishing is granted to the grantee, and such a grantee hath a property in the fish, and may bring a possessory action for them, without making any title. 3 *Communis piscaria*, and this is to be resembled to the case of other common.' *Smith v Kemp* (1693) 2 Salk 637 at 637, per Holt CJ

PISTOL

'It has been urged . . . that after the repeal of the Pistols Act 1903, by the Firearms Act 1920 [repealed in part; see now Firearms Act 1968], the omission from the latter Act of any express reference to the word "pistol" ought to be taken as showing that it is not included in the word "gun". No doubt there is some force in the contention that while a smoothbore bore shot gun or air gun or air rifle is, subject to some exceptions, saved from the definition of "firearm", there is no saving for a pistol, which is more portable and more easily concealed. But when one reflects that it is under the Gun Licence Act 1870 [repealed], that a licence for a revolver must be obtained, one inclines to the opposite view.' *Saint v Hockley* (1925) 41 TLR 555 at 555, DC, per Lord Hewart CJ

PIT

'Pit' has no precise meaning. In reference to underground workings it can denote not only the shafts but also the underground workings to which they give access. It can also describe workings on the surface, whether the mineral is taken from the bottom or the sides of the workings. (31 Halsbury's Laws (4th edn) para 14)

'The question of construction is the sense in which the word 'pits' is used in the learned chairman's award. The plaintiffs called a number of witnesses, the joint effect of whose evidence was that the word "pits" is commonly and properly used in three senses—first, to denote the underground workings and the shafts; secondly, to denote the underground workings only; and thirdly, to denote the shafts only. The defendant called witnesses, the joint effect of whose evidence was that the primary meaning of the word "pits" is the shaft, though they agreed that the word is frequently used in the wider sense spoken to by the defendant's witnesses. They also referred to certain Acts of Parliament, and conveyancing precedents, and to the rules of the plaintiffs' colliery. Upon the whole of the evidence on both sides I find as a fact that the word "pits" is used to denote A, the shaft, B, the underground workings with or without the shafts, and C, the colliery as a whole. The primary meaning of "pits" is the shafts. When the word "pits" is used to mean either the underground workings or the colliery as a whole, it derives such meaning from the fact that in the connexion in which or the circumstances under which it is being used, it is obvious that something other than the shafts is referred to, as for instance, when a miner speaks of working in the pit, or a buyer of coal speaks of his coal coming from a particular pit. In considering, therefore, the sense in which the learned chairman used the word "pits" here, it is necessary to ascertain whether there was anything in the context or in the circumstances under which the word was used by him to lead one to the conclusion that it was so used in any other than its primary meaning. . . . I see no reason for giving the word "pits" here anything but its primary meaning. . . . The learned chairman says the pits. Surely that must mean the shafts by which the men go down and come up, and through which the coal is raised to the surface. They are obvious. The men know where they are and inquiry and dispute are alike excluded.' *Lofthouse Colliery Ltd v Ogden* (1912) 107 LT 827 at 828, 829, per Bailache J

Canada '"Pit" is not defined in the Act [Mines Act, RSM 1940, c 41 (now RSM 170 c M160)] or regulations, nor is "hole". Neither word has a restricted meaning. The dictionaries use "pit", "hole" and "excavation" as generally synonymous and define each by using the others, the mean feature in common being that in each case the pit, hole or excavation begins at the surface and is open to air and sight as it goes down. Each of these words is distinct from a well, usually a cylindrical hole of, at most, a few feet cross-section or a drill hole or boring with a cross-section measured in inches; and distinct from a shaft, larger than a well, and perpendicular or nearly so into the earth, used in underground mining for ingress and egress and facilities therefor and ventilation.' *Clark v Chutorian* (1955) 14 WWR 1 at 13, Man CA, per Coyne JA

PITCH

'Justices for the borough of Hythe convicted the appellant under s 72 of the Highway Act 1835 [repealed; see now the Highways Act 1980, s 148] which provides that: "if any hawker, higgler, gipsy or other person travelling shall pitch any tent, booth, stall, or stand, or encamp upon any part of any highway he shall be guilty of an offence." . . . I can imagine no English active verb less appropriate to the stopping of a motor van than to say that it is thereby "pitched" on the highway.' *Divito v Stickings* [1948] 1 All ER 207 at 207, per Humphreys J

PLACE *See also* PUBLIC PLACE

In betting legislation

[The Betting Act 1853, s 1 (repealed) enacted that no house, office, room or other 'place' should be opened, kept or used for the purpose of the owner, occupier or keeper thereof, or any person using the same, etc, betting with persons resorting thereto. Section 3 of the Act imposed penalties for opening, keeping or using such a 'place'.

The provisions of the Betting, Gaming and Lotteries Act 1963 are somewhat different, the emphasis being on the use of 'premises' rather than 'places'. Section 1 of the Act of 1963 does, however, restrict the use of premises as a 'place' where persons resorting thereto may effect pool betting transactions; whilst s 8 prohibits betting in streets or 'public places'.

A selection of cases under the former repealed Act is accordingly included to illustrate the judicial view of what, under that Act, was or was not a 'place' for the purposes of betting.]

'There are two questions; first, whether this is a "place" within the meaning of 16 & 17 Vict c 119 [Betting Act 1853, s 1 (repealed; see supra)]; and, secondly, whether there is evidence that it was permitted to be used for the purpose of betting. . . . There may be a "place" although it is open to the air; there may be a "place" without any kind of erection; and of course it must depend upon the circumstances of each particular case whether it is brought within the description of "place". Upon the facts as they appear here, the magistrates were justified in holding that this was a "place". The area is of three or four acres in extent. The "place" is one inclosed, having a gateway. Persons were admitted by ticket, and on payment of a price for entrance. The appellant is the occupier of this inclosed land, and received money from the persons for admission into it. I think that, under those circumstances, it cannot be doubted that this was a "place" within the meaning of the Act.' *Eastwood v Miller* (1874) LR 9 QB 440 at 445, per Archibald J

'The real question is whether the facts in the case constituted a "place" within the meaning of 16 & 17 Vict c 119, s 3 [Betting Act 1853, s 3 (repealed; see supra)]. The facts are that the respondent and his companion had a small wooden box, not attached to the ground, but defining a certain spot in a certain limited railed inclosure, and there, standing on and at the box, they advertised by their voices their willingness to bet, and took and made bets . . . during the races. Were they within the Act? I am of opinion that they were. . . . I think all the cases shew that a "place" to be within the statute must be a fixed ascertained place, occupied or used so far permanently that people may know that there is a person who stands in a particular spot indicated by a certain definite mark with whom they may bet. . . . Here . . . there was, in my opinion, a place within the meaning of the Act.' *Gallaway v Maries* (1881) 8 QBD 275 at 278, 281, DC, per Grove J

'I cannot find anything in the Act [Betting Act 1853 (repealed; see supra)] requiring the place to be defined by metes and bounds. In my opinion, the fact that the expression is not defined in the Act shews that it was intended that justices should have a discretion to say whether the ground in question was "a place" or not. As it seems to me, if a man were to use the ground at the foot of the statue at Charing Cross for the purpose of habitually betting with persons resorting to him there, that, although the space used was entirely undefined, would be "a place" within the meaning of the statute.' *Liddell v Lofthouse* [1896] 1 QB 295 at 299, DC, per Kay LJ

'I have arrived at the conclusion that any area of inclosed ground (expressing no opinion as to unenclosed areas) covered or uncovered, which is known by a name, or is capable of reasonably accurate description, to which persons from time to time or upon any particular occasions resort, and who may very properly be described as resorting thereto, used by a professional betting-man for the purpose of exercising his calling, and betting with such persons, or for the purpose of carrying on a ready-money betting business, may be a place, within the meaning of the statute [Betting Act 1853 (repealed; see supra)].' *Hawke v Dunn* [1897] 1 QB 579 at 598, DC, per cur.

'It was admitted that the appellant was a professional bookmaker, and that on the day and at the place above mentioned he was making bets on the Lincolnshire Handicap. . . . The magistrates found that the spot where the appellant stood was a "place" [within the Betting Act 1853, ss 1, 3 (repealed; see supra)]. . . . On the argument before us all the authorities bearing on the subject of what is a place were fully discussed. . . . In this case the appellant evidently went to that particular spot on the Pit Heap to bet with those who had been brought together there in the expectation of finding him there to bet with. . . . Would it have made any difference if he had stood on a box, interposed a layer of wood between his feet and the ground, or had sat on a high porter's chair, carrying on that kind of betting which most of all the legislature meant to suppress? . . . Can anybody seriously suppose the legislature meant to exclude from the operation of the Act such betting, on such a place? . . . This conviction ought to be affirmed.' *McInaney v Hildreth* [1897] 1 QB 600 at 603–606, DC, per cur.

'Any place which is sufficiently definite, and in which a betting establishment might be conducted, would satisfy the words of the statute [Betting Act 1853, s 1 (repealed; see supra)].' *Powell v Kempton Park Racecourse Co* [1899] AC 143 at 162, per Lord Halsbury LC

'Whilst the place mentioned in the Act must be to some extent *ejusdem generis* with house, room or office, I do not think it need possess the same characteristics; for instance, it need not be covered in or roofed. It may be, to some extent, an open space. But certain conditions must exist in order to bring such space within the word "place". There must be a defined area so marked out that it can be found and recognised as "the place" where the business is carried on and wherein the bettor can be found. . . . Directly a definite localisation of the business of betting is effected, be it under a tent or even movable umbrella, it may be well held that a "place" exists for the purposes of a conviction under the Act.' Ibid at 194, per Lord James of Hereford

'The Act of Parliament [Betting Act 1853 (repealed; see supra)] has been fruitful in litigation. It can be best construed by considering its policy. The object of the Act was not to make pariahs of betting men, but to put difficulties in the way of professional betting men. You will do well to consider whether the prisoner was habitually in one spot, and whether that spot, if the case were so, were such a "place" as the Act contemplated. The yard might be a place, though it was not roofed over. All that is necessary is that the area should be so defined and marked out that it could be found and recognised.' *R v Cranny* (1899) 63 JP Jo 826 at 826, per Phillimore J

'If members of a club, which is nothing but a social club, bet with other members of the club, and the betting is merely incidental to their meeting in the club . . . no offence would be committed [under the Betting Act 1853, s 1 (repealed; see supra)]. . . . The magistrate . . .

seems to have thought that if a club is an honest social club there may be apparatus for betting on the club premises, and that bookmakers, so long as they are members of the club, can go there and carry on their business. That is not the law. Even though a club be a bona fide social club, none the less a portion of the club premises may be kept and used for the purposes of betting; and if that is the case it does not matter whether the people with whom the bets are made are members of the club or bookmakers.' *Jackson v Roth* [1919] 1 KB 102 at 114, per Darling J

'The main question is whether a certain shed situated in a shipbuilding yard was a "place" . . . within the meaning of section 1 of the Betting Act 1853 [repealed; see supra]. . . . The shed covered a punching machine, and enclosed a space sufficient to afford accommodation to employees in the yard during meal hours. That is all we know about the shed. . . . I think the Sheriff-substitute was wrong in saying that the shed was not a "place" within the meaning of section 1.' *Young v Darrah* 1929 SC(J) 17 at 20, 21, per the Lord Justice-General (Lord Clyde)

[As to the licensing and conduct of betting offices, see now the Betting, Gaming and Lotteries Act 1963, ss 9, 10]

Australia [Certain statutes relating to betting in the various Australian States make it an offence for persons to open, keep or use, etc, any house, office, room or 'place' for purposes of betting.] 'The term "use" having regard to the context, involves as an element of the offence that the place in question is in the occupation or possession of some person, by whom or by whose permission use is or might be made of it for the prohibited purpose. It follows that the place used, if it is not a house, office, or room, must be some specific area of land which is in the actual occupation of the defendant or some person by whose permission he makes use of it. If the area alleged to be used for the prohibited purpose forms part of a larger area, to which other persons are entitled to access, and the whole of which is not in the actual occupation of the defendant the character of his occupation of the specific area must be such that it is differentiated from that of other persons present either by the existence of some extrinsic object, which is itself of such a nature that its use involves the actual exclusive occupation of some specific portion of land (however small) of which the defendant has the use, or else by the existence of some structural or natural features which delimit a specific area of which he is, and they are not, in actual occupation. If these conditions do not exist, there is no user of the place within the meaning of the Statute.' *Prior v Sherwood* (1906) 3 CLR 1054 at 1070, per Griffith CJ

In marine insurance policy

[By a policy of marine insurance a ship was insured whilst at 'port or ports, place or places', in New Caledonia.] 'I think the words "place or places" are used in order to add something to the meaning of "port or ports". . . . I think that, used as they are in connection with the words "port or ports" the words "place or places" have a meaning somewhat wider than that attributed to them by the witnesses. They seem to me to mean place or places at which the vessel arrives in the course of her voyage for the purpose of loading, discharging, coaling, repairing, or even of taking shelter–in other words, a place to which she has come for some purpose and with some object other than that of merely passing through it without stopping on her way to some other point.' *Maritime Insurance Co Ltd v Alianza Insurance Co of Santander* [1907] 2 KB 660 at 663, 664 per Walton J

In various statutes

[The Conspiracy and Protection of Property Act 1875, s 7(4) imposes a penalty on every person who watches or besets the house or other 'place' where a person resides, works, carries on business, or happens to be.] 'The . . . question is whether the case is within sub-s 4, which prohibits watching or besetting the house, or the place where a person resides, or where he happens to be. . . . The words "place where he happens to be" seem to me to embrace any place where the workman is found, however casually.' *Charnock v Court* [1899] 2 Ch 35 at 38, 39, per Stirling J

[The Factory and Workshop Act 1901, s 149(4) (repealed; see now the Factories Act 1961, s 175(6)) provided that where a 'place' situate within the close, curtilage or precincts forming a factory or workshop was solely used for some purpose other than the manufacturing process or handicraft carried on in the factory or workshop, that 'place' should not be deemed to form part of the factory or workshop for the purposes of the Act, but should, if otherwise it would be a factory or workshop, be deemed to be a separate factory or workshop.] 'I think that the question really depends upon what the

Act of Parliament means by a place, because this spot certainly is situate within the close, curtilage and precincts of the factory, and is solely used for purposes other than the manufacturing process carried on within the factory. At the same time if this was an area, for instance, of twenty, or thirty, or forty feet square in the middle of a factory under a roof where the common work of a factory was being carried on, and not separated from it by any physical demarcation, I should feel that it was exceedingly improbable that the Act of Parliament could have meant to exempt from its operation such a place as that, where every danger which is intended to be guarded against by this Act would be present. Therefore we are driven to ask ourselves what is meant by "place". Obviously it is not necessary that the place should be inclosed on all sides. If it had been necessary the Act of Parliament would have said so; and, therefore, the absence of fencing on all four sides we cannot take as a test. But this place seems to be a place so entirely outside the factory altogether where the manufacturing processes are carried on, and to be so distinctly separated from it, that it may very fairly be considered to be a place—a definite spot, an area which is marked and defined and ascertainable, and which is dedicated, so to speak, to purposes quite other than those which are contemplated as a factory. This appears to me to be a spot which was marked out for the creation of a new building, and nothing else, and it would certainly, to my mind, be a very strained construction of this sub-section to say that that was the sort of place which was contemplated by this Act.' *Lewis v Gilbertson & Co Ltd* (1904) 91 LT 377 at 380, DC, per Wills J

[The Merchant Shipping Act 1894, s 742 provides that unless the context otherwise requires, the word 'port' includes 'place'.] 'Spurn appears to be a very good place for a rest cure; it is at the extreme end of a spit of sand with no road but with a trolley line to it, with four inhabitants, a Lloyd's signalling station and a lighthouse, and it has been argued that, whatever else it is, it is a "place", and as "port" includes "place", the *Maud Llewellyn*, when she received signals from it, was making use of a "place" which is the same as "port". In my view that is putting much too wide a meaning on the word "place". I think that "place" following "port" must be interpreted as *ejusdem generis* with "port", as a locality having some or many of the characteristics of a port, though by reason of the absence of charter or other reasons one would not speak of it as a port.' *Humber Conservancy Board v Federated Coal & Shipping Co* [1928] 1 KB 492 at 495, DC, per Scrutton LJ

[The Shops (Sunday Trading Restriction) Act 1936, s 13 (repealed; see now Shops Act 1950, s 23) enacted that the provisions of the Act should extend to any 'place' where any retail trade or business was carried on as if that place were a shop.] 'The Act of 1936 begins with a provision about the closing of shops and the serving of customers in shops, and s 11 contains the words: 'No person shall be employed on Sunday about the business of a shop which is open for the serving of customers on that day" unless certain requires are complied with. It becomes clear, when one looks at the whole scheme and purpose of the Act, that it is essential that the place where the employment is carried on, to be a "place" within s 13, must be either a shop or premises akin to a shop.' *Eldorado Ice Cream Co Ltd v Clark, Eldorado Ice Cream Co Ltd v Keating* [1938] 1 KB 715 at 721, DC, per Lord Hewart CJ

[The appellants were charged with an offence under the Sunday Observance Act 1780, s 1 in that they had used on Sunday a 'place' for public entertainment to which persons were admitted by the payment of money, whereby the place was deemed to be a disorderly place.] 'The Sunday Observance Act 1780 and the Disorderly Houses Act 1751, show plainly that there can be not only disorderly houses, but also disorderly places. A "disorderly house" indicates something within four walls and a roof, and a "disorderly place" means a place set aside for public entertainment, or music, or dancing, or whatever the particular Act prohibits. . . . To my mind, it is perfectly clear that the word "place" is meant deliberately to be wider than the words "house, room", and, therefore, the justices were justified in finding that the part of Cuerdon Park used for [a] motor cycle scramble was a "place" within the meaning of the Act.' *Culley v Harrison* [1956] 2 All ER 254 at 256, per Lord Goddard CJ (also reported in [1956] 2 QB 71 at 76, 77)

[The Sunday Observance Act 1780, s 1 is no longer applicable to licensed theatres: see the Sunday Theatre Act 1972, s 1.]

PLACE (Verb)

Canada 'With respect to "placed", I do not think it is used in the statute [Assessment Act, RSO 1937, c 272, s 1(i)(iv) (now RSO 1980, c 31, s 1(k)(v))] as equivalent merely to "brought upon" so as to take in mere personal property which is intended to be shift about at will. It involves the idea of setting a thing in a particular position with some idea of permanency.' *Northern Broadcasting Co v District of Mountjoy* [1950] SCR 502 at 510, SCC, per Kellock J

PLACE OF ABODE *See* ABODE

PLACE OF EMPLOYMENT *See* EMPLOYMENT

PLACE OF PUBLIC ENTERTAINMENT *See* ENTERTAINMENT

PLACE OF PUBLIC RESORT

In local Act

'Does "other place of public resort" [in a local Act] mean a place to which the public are entitled to go as of right, or a place to which the public do go as a matter of fact? I am of opinion that the latter is the true meaning.' *Kitson v Ashe* [1899] 1 QB 425 at 429, DC, per Channell J

In Vagrancy Act

The Vagrancy Act 1824, s 4 (repealed in part; but cf s 35 of the Act) enacted (inter alia) that every suspected person or reputed thief frequenting any 'place of public resort' or any avenue leading thereto, with intent to commit an offence should be deemed a rogue and vagabond within the meaning of the Act.] 'It seems to me that the magistrates were quite right in their decision, and that, at the time when the appellant was apprehended, the place he was found in was "a place of public resort" within the meaning of the Statute. I see nothing in the language of the Act to require that the place shall be a permanent place of resort all the year round. The object of the provision is the protection of large assemblies of persons from the depredations of thieves and pickpockets; and the permanent character of the assembly appears to me to be quite immaterial. The places are made protected places whilst being used for public resort. I take that to be the test. Suppose a race or a cricket-match to take place in a meadow, to which the public were invited to come, would not that be for the time a place of public resort? I think it would, and that the streets immediately adjoining would be "streets, highways, or places adjacent thereto" within the fair meaning of the Act, and therefore for the time being protected places. It would, as it seems to me, be a very narrow construction of the Act to hold that it is confined to places which are permanently open to the public. If that were the true construction of the Act, it might be said that a theatre which is only open to the public at certain hours in the evening, or a church which is only open during divine service, is not a "place of public resort" within it. Nobody would ever venture to suggest that. I think it quite clear that this place was at the time a place of public resort, and therefore that the conviction was right.' *Sewell v Taylor* (1859) 7 CBNS 160 at 163, 164, per Erle CJ

'It is no offence within the Act [Vagrancy Act 1824, s 4 (see supra)], to frequent a public highway with intent to commit a felony. A public highway is merely a place where people have a right to go; it is not necessarily a place of public resort. If it were so, and were thus included in the term "place of public resort", the Statute would speak of frequenting a highway, and then again of frequenting a highway adjacent to a highway. It is suggested that it may be a place of public resort, and that the magistrates would be justified in so finding. It might well be that they would be so justified, as for instance, if the highway were one where things were exposed for sale, as in *Re Davis* [(1857) 2 H & N 149] and the justices might if the circumstances warranted it, have so described the place which the defendant was found frequenting. but we must take the commitment as it stands, and cannot extend the words. Unless, therefore, we are satisfied that a highway must be a place of public resort, we must discharge the prisoner.' *Re Timson* (1870) LR 5 Exch 257 at 262, per Cleasby B

[The distinction between felony and misdemeanour was abolished by the Criminal Law Act 1967, s 1(1).]

[The appellants were convicted of being suspected persons, having frequented a 'place of public resort' (namely, Tattersall's enclosure at Goodwood) within the meaning of the Vagrancy Act 1824, s 4 (see supra).] 'A place does not cease to be a place of public resort because the public have to pay to go there. An exhibition is obviously a place of public resort. The Zoological Gardens are, no doubt, a place of public resort because the public are invited to go there, and they enter the gardens on payment of a sum of money. So is a racecourse—not an open course like Nemarket, Brighton or Ascot, but a course in a park. They are all places of public resort because the owners or occupiers invite the public to go there, but it is said that because a person who has been warned off, or any other undesirable character, will not be allowed into Tattersalls or into a racecourse, that prevents it from being a place of public resort. It must be to some extent a question of degree, but I cannot see that property to which the owner invites the public to resort becomes any the less a place of public resort because he refuses to allow a particular individual or individuals to enter. If he limits admission to a certain category of people, for instance, if he allows only members of the universities of Oxford or Cambridge to go to a stand or a window he has got at the Boat Race, it may be said that that stand or window is not a place of public resort. It has been suggested to us that a good analogy is the Royal Enclosure at Ascot, but that is not a place of public resort because the public are not invited to go to the Royal Enclosure. Those who wish to go to the Royal Enclosure have to apply for permission. Everybody is invited to Tattersall's enclosure, subject to his paying 30*s*. and subject to the right of the keeper of the gate to say he will not be allowed to enter. The justices have found that the enclosure was a place of public resort, and, in my opinion, they had no option since it did not cease to be a place of public resort because a payment for entry was demanded, nor, in my judgment, did it cease to be a place of public resort because the occupier reserved the right to refuse admission to some particular individual or individuals.' *Glynn v Simmonds*, [1952] 2 All ER 47 at 48, per Lord Goddard CJ

PLACE OF WORSHIP *See* WORSHIP

PLAINTIFF

The expression 'plaintiff' shall include pursuer, complainer, or any person at whose instance any action or proceeding in an inferior court is instituted; and the expression 'defendant' shall include defender, respondent, or other person against whom any such action or proceeding is directed. (Inferior Courts Judgments Extension Act 1882, s 2)

Nominal plaintiff

[The Stannaries Act 1869, s 13 provides that the purser of a cost-book mining company can sue as the 'nominal plaintiff' for the company in respect of unpaid calls on shares.] 'The right to sue for the debt is given in express terms, not to the purser but to the company. . . . How are they to sue? "In the name of the purser as the nominal plaintiff for the company." . . . The section does not say that the action is to be by the purser as plaintiff, but that the company are to sue in the name of the purser, as the nominal plaintiff. The company are to sue, and the company are to recover the amount. The debt is not due to the purser. . . . The judgment is not in his favour; it is in the favour of the company. The purser is not the judgment creditor. . . . So far as the bankruptcy law is concerned, he is nothing but a name. . . . When an Act confers a limited power upon a company to sue in the name of their officer, it does not thereby make that officer a good petitioning creditor in bankruptcy on behalf of the company.' *Re Nance, ex p Ashmead* [1893] 1 QB 590 at 593, 594, CA, per Lord Esher MR

PLANT

'Plant' includes any machinery, equipment or appliance, whether affixed to land or not. (Atomic Energy Act 1946, s 18)

'Electrical plant' means any plant, equipment, apparatus and appliances used for the purposes of generating, transmitting and distributing electricity, but not including any electrical fittings. (Electricity Act 1947, s 67(1))

'Plant or equipment' includes vessels, (Harbours Act 1964, s 57)

'I am clearly of opinion that plant cannot be held to mean stock in trade. There is no special reason in this will why I should so hold. When a testator gives the goodwill of his business and £1,000 to his foreman, it may well be imagined that the object of this bounty will be able to carry on the business and obtain the necessary capital for the purpose. In most cases the word "plant" is used to describe something which, if not in direct contrast to stock, is at any rate of an entirely different nature. All the matters permanently used for the purposes of a trade, as distinguished from the fluctuating stock, are commonly included in the term "plant". It consists sometimes of things which are fixed, as, for example, counters, heating, gas, and other apparatus and things of that kind, and in other cases of horses, locomotives, and the like, which are in this sense only fixed that they form a part of the permanent establishment intended to be replaced when dead or worn out, as the case may be. Therefore, I cannot treat either the stock or the household furniture as part of the plant.' *Blake v Shaw* (1860) John 732 at 734, per Page Wood V-C

'There is no definition of plant in the Act [Employers' Liability Act 1880 (repealed)]: but, in its ordinary sense, it includes whatever apparatus is used by a business man for carrying on his business,—not his stock-in-trade which he buys or makes for sale; but all goods and chattels, fixed or moveable, live or dead, which he keeps for permanent employment in his business.' *Yarmouth v France* (1887) 19 QBD 647 at 658, per Lindley LJ

'I think that as, speaking generally, "machinery" includes everything which by its action produces or assists in production, so "plant" may be regarded as that without which production cannot go on. It is, so to speak, dead stock; it does not itself act, but is that through and by means of and in which action takes place, and includes such things as brewers' pipes, vats, and the like.' *Re Nutley & Finn* [1894] WN 64 at 64, per Kekewich J

'When attention is paid to s 5 of the Bills of Sale Act 1878, and it is read with s 8 of the Bills of Sale Act 1882, it is plain that the word "plant" was intended to prefer to things more or less similar in kind to trade fixtures or trade machinery.' *London & Eastern Counties Loan & Discount Co v Creasey* [1897] 1 QB 442 at 443, 444, per Wright J

'A machine does not cease to be plant in the interval between the giving in order that it shall be repaired and the completion of the repair.' *Thompson v City Glass Bottle Co* [1902] 1 KB 233 at 235, CA, per Collins MR

'It is quite impossible to say that the taxpayer's own body is a thing which is subject to wear and tear, and that the taxpayer is entitled to deduct medical expenses because they relate to wear and tear. It is wear and tear of plant or machinery. Your own body is not plant. Your horse conceivably may be. I do not know what it is under the Income Tax Acts. It certainly has, under the Employers' Liability Acts [repealed], been held to be plant in a suitable case, but I have never heard it suggested by anybody that the taxpayer's own body could be regarded as plant.' *Norman v Golder* [1945] 1 All ER 352 at 354, CA, per Lord Greene MR

'Clearly land in its natural state is not plant although its configuration may be such that its use is an essential element in a trading operation. The soil on a farm is not plant although cultivation has greatly improved it. So a loch which impounds water is not plant although a trader uses it as the source of the water he needs. And a dam is generally simply an improvement of the loch giving a better supply. But I could imagine circumstances in which a dam would be such an integral part of the means required for a trading operation that it should be regarded as plant.' *Inland Revenue Comrs v Barclay Curle & Co Ltd* [1969] 1 All ER 732 at 741, HL, per Lord Reid

'In the context of an Act which deals with what goes on in factories, "plant" is an ordinary English word in common usage whose meaning is well understood. To quote the Shorter Oxford English Dictionary it means "The fixtures, implements and apparatus used in carrying on any industrial process". As such it is to be distinguished from the products of the process or the objects on which the process is carried out. Save in its restriction to "industrial" processes, which is appropriate to an Act in which the definition of "factory" is confined to premises in which processes which would ordinarily be called "industrial" are carried on, this definition is substantially the same as that stated by Lindley LJ in *Yarmouth v France* [supra]. . . . It was this ordinary meaning which he ascribed to the word "plant" as used in the Employers Liability Act 1880, in a context in which it was not confined to plant of employers whose business consisted of carrying on industrial processes. The marked preference which courts habitually show for citing judicial in preference to lexicographers' definitions of ordinary English words, even when they are not legal terms of art, has led to the acceptance of Lindley LJ's definition as being the meaning of the word "plant" where it has been used without any express statutory definition in a variety of enactments, particularly those dealing with taxation of industrial enterprises. It is a definition of a physical object by reference to the use to which it is being put. Where, as in the Factories Act 1961, all references to "plant" are to plant within a factory in which an industrial process is carried on, the only relevant use, in my opinion, is that to which the physical object is being put in that factory. If it is there as part of the apparatus for use in carrying on the industrial process undertaken on those premises, it is "plant" within the meaning of the Act even though it may be temporarily out of use or in the course of installation, repair or removal. If it is there for the purpose of being subjected to that industrial process it is an "article" . . . on which are carried out those industrial processes which qualify the premises where they are undertaken as a "factory" within the meaning of the Act; it is not "plant", whatever may be the use to which it has been previously put or may be subsequently put elsewhere.' *Haigh v Ireland (Charles W) Ltd* [1973] 3 All ER 1137 at 1147, 1148, HL, per Lord Diplock

'Counsel for the Crown . . . would confine a professional man's "plant" to things used physically like a dentist's chair or an architect's table or, I suppose the typewriter in a barrister's chambers; but, for myself, I do not think "plant" should be confined to things which are used physically. It seems to me that on principle it extends to the intellectual storehouse which a barrister or a solicitor or any other professional man has in the course of carrying on his profession. The difficulty has arisen because the legislature, when it extended this provision [Finance Act 1971, ss 41(1)(a), 47(1)] to professions, did not make clear the scope of the word "plant" in that context. It seems to me, in the context of a profession, the provision of "plant" should be so interpreted that a lawyer's books, his set of law reports and his textbooks, are "plant".' *Munby v Furlong (Inspector of Taxes)* [1977] 2 All ER 953 at 956, CA, per Lord Denning MR

'A characteristic of plant appears to me to be that it is an adjunct to the carryng on of a business and not the essential site or core of the business itself.' *Benson (Inspector of Taxes) v Yard Arm Club Ltd* [1979] 2 All ER 336 at 346, CA, per Shaw LJ

Australia 'The conveyor belt, the railway trucks and sleepers, the workshops, the fuel store and the office, must be regarded as "plant" rather than as "development". "Plant" is the fixtures, implements and machinery used in an industrial process. Although the introduction of these fixtures and pieces of equipment into the mining operations could possibly be regarded as "development" I think that "plant" is a more apt nomenclature in the circumstances.' *Waratah Gypsum Pty Ltd v Federal Comr of Taxation* [1966] ALR 19 at 24, per McTiernan J

Australia 'However far the meaning of the word "plant" may be stretched, it does not in its ordinary meaning include land or the buildings thereon which are merely the general setting of a business.' *Re Jacobson* [1970] VR 180 at 184, per Gowans J

PLANT VARIETY

'Plant variety' includes any clone, line, hybrid or genetic variant. (Plant Varieties and Seeds Act 1964, s 38, as amended by the Plant Varieties Act 1983)

PLATE

Gold and silverware

[A testator by his will made a bequest of household furniture, 'plate', china, and other household effects. At his death he was possessed of forty-two snuff-boxes made of gold, silver, china, tortoiseshell and agate.] 'In the first place, "household furniture" and "household effects" will ordinarily pass plate and household ornaments, and these were really used for ornament, just as much so as any of the other things about the room. But in addition to that, the testator uses the words "plate" and "china", which I think would by themselves carry all the snuff-boxes made of gold, silver or china, so that in both ways they would pass.' *Field v Peckett (No 2)* (1861) 29 Beav 573 at 574, per Romilly MR

[A testator made a gift of all his furniture, with the exception of 'plate'.] 'It is to be observed that the gift is of all the furniture in the said house, and that it is from this particular furniture that the testator excepts the plate and pictures. It is admitted that if the exception had not been made every article of plate would have passed under the description of furniture. The single question seems to be, whether there is enough to authorise the Court to hold that the testator used the word in any other than its proper sense; and my opinion is, that there is nothing in the context of the will or in the evidence as to the situation of the testator with regard to the time of gift, legitimately to show that the word was not used in its proper sense. Therefore the exception applies to the word "plate", properly does not include plated articles.' *Holden v Ramsbottom* (1863) 4 Giff 205 at 206, per Stuart V-C

'The words "gold and silver plate", especially, of course, the word "plate", are words which are used in the English language in very many different senses. . . . I cannot help saying at starting that in ordinary language as it is usually used, such an expression as gold and silver plate would not, I think, be understood to include a gold or silver watch. It is not an ordinary expression to use for the thing, and if it appeared in a will or anything of that sort I should think it would be fairly clear that plate would not include a gold or silver watch. . . . I do not think in order to make a thing come within the term of gold and silver plate it would be necessary that the thing should be entirely gold or entirely silver, but it must be something of which that is the main element or constituent part, anything added to it being accessory to the thing which is the gold or silver plate. But where the gold or the silver which forms part of the article really is only part and not the main thing, accessory rather to the main thing, then I think that article, unless it should be something that in all common acceptations would be gold or silver plate, does not come within the word "plate".' *Goldsmiths' Co v Wyatt* (1905) 93 LT 515 at 516, 518, 519, per Channell J

'It was argued, on the authority of *Holden v Ramsbottom* [supra] that nothing but silver passed under the description "plate". . . . That is the only relevant authority. It was decided in 1863, and, although the "sixties" have been described as the age of stucco and electro plate, I find myself unable to accept this limitation on the proper meaning of the word "plate" in a will made in the year 1934. . . . To my mind, at the present day the ordinary person using the word "plate" or reading the word "plate" as it appears in such a document as that before me, would not have in mind only articles composed of silver or gold, and would understand the word "plate" in the extended sense attributed to it by the makers of the Oxford English Dictionary as including plated articles. It is not uncommon for a word to change its meaning and in the case of the word "plate" it is clear that this has happened. Reasons may be suggested for this change. Plated ware in many forms has become available to the whole mass of the population; there is a settled habit of applying to new articles of secondary worth a name which properly belongs to superior articles of the same general character and serving the same purpose as the new articles; and, lastly, the new articles, serving the purpose of "plate", as formerly understood, are produced by "plating". To some, indeed, the word "plate" if used in ordinary conversation would suggest electroplate as distinct from silver or Sheffield plate. In my opinion therefore no article is excluded from the category of "plate" in this will by reason that it is Sheffield plate or electro plate.' *Re Grimwood, Trewhella v Grimwood* [1946] Ch 54 at 55, 56, per Uthwatt J

PLATFORM *See* WORKING PLATFORM

PLAY

'Play' means—

(a) any dramatic piece, whether involving improvisation or not, which is given wholly or in part by one or more persons actually present and performing and in which the whole or a major proportion of what is done by the person or persons performing, whether by way of speech, singing or acting, involves the playing of a role; and

(b) any ballet given wholly or in part by one or more persons actually present and performing, whether or not it falls within paragraph (a) of this definition.

(Theatres Act 1968, s 18(1))

PLAYER

'Player', in relation to a game of chance, includes any person taking part in the game against whom other persons taking part in the game stake, play or bet. (Betting, Gaming and Lotteries Act 1963, s 55)

'The meaning of "player" in relation to a game of chance includes any person taking part in the game against whom other persons taking part in the game stake, play or bet. Players must, therefore, be persons who take part in one and the same game.' *Adcock v Wilson* [1968] 1 All ER 929 at 930, HL, per Lord Morris of Borth-y-Gest

PLEADING

The term 'a pleading' is used in civil cases to denote a document in which a party to a proceeding in a court of first instance is required by law to formulate in writing his case or part of his case in preparation for the hearing. In legislation concerning procedure of the Supreme Court, 'pleading' includes . . . the statements in writing of the claim or demand of any plaintiff, and of the defence of any defendant to it, and of the reply of the plaintiff to any counterclaim of a defendant, but in the Rules of the Supreme Court 'pleading' does not include a petition, summons of preliminary act. Documents directed to be served in third party and similar proceedings are, however, pleadings. 'Pleading' also denotes the act of drafting or settling any such document or part thereof. (36 Halsbury's Laws (4th edn) para 1)

[In the rules of the Supreme Court, 'pleading' does not include a petition, summons or preliminary act. (RSC 1965, Ord 1, r 4(1))]

'Pleadings continue to play an essential part in civil actions, and although there has been since the Civil Procedure Act 1833 a wide power to permit amendments, circumstances may arise when the grant of permission would work injustice or, at least, necessitate an adjournment which may prove particularly unfortunate in trials with a jury. To shrug off a criticism as "a mere pleading point" is therefore bad law and bad practice. For the primary purpose of pleadings remains, and it can still prove of vital importance. That purpose is to define the issues and thereby to inform the parties in advance of the case they have to meet and so enable them to take steps to deal with it.' *Farrell v Secretary of State for Defence* [1980] 1 All ER 166 at 173, HL, per Lord Edmund-Davies

PLEASURE

[The insured under a policy of insurance was covered in respect of accidental injury to any person, subject to the following exception: 'Loss, damage, or other liability caused when the motor car is being used for other than private pleasure.'] 'In my judgment, the word "pleasure" is used in this policy in contradistinction to "business".' *Piddington v Co-operative Insurance Society Ltd* [1934] 2 KB 236 at 238, per Lawrence J

Canada [A policy of insurance on a motor yacht contained a warranty that it should be used solely for 'private pleasure purposes'. The yacht was destroyed by fire while being used by Racicot, a friend fo the insured, without his knowledge, to take his uncle across a lake to inspect a mine.] 'The question is whether Racicot, who "took his uncle up to another part of the lake, without remuneration, to a dam where the uncle was to inspect a mine for his own benefit" was using the yacht solely for private pleasure purposes. That question, in my view, must be answered in the affirmative. . . . The word "pleasure" has various meanings, depending upon the context in which it is used, and I think that on the occasion in question, it must be held that Racicot experienced "enjoyment, delight, gratification" (Oxford Dictionary), in transporting his uncle from one part of the lake to another, equally as well as if he had taken his uncle as a matter of friendship to a part of the lake in order to board a train or bus.' *Staples v Great American Insurance Co New York* [1941] SCR 213 at 223, SCC, per cur.

PLEASURE FAIR *See* FAIR

PLEASURE GROUND

'A pleasure ground, I think, ought to have some equipment of a more or less permanent character that would be of service to persons frequenting it for the purpose of recreation.' *Stevens v National Telephone Co Ltd, Lee (Edward) & Co Ltd v National Telephone Co Ltd* [1914] 1 IR 9 at 12, per Ross J

'I do not propose to attempt any definition of the words "pleasure ground". It is enough to say that the mere fact that a vacant piece of land in the neighbourhood of a house is sometimes used to procure amusement for neighbours, be they schoolchildren or others, is not enough to constitute it a pleasure ground, according to the ordinary use of the English language.' *Re Newhill Compulsory Purchase Order* 1937, *Re Payne's Application* [1938] 2 All ER 163 at 164–166, per Du Parcq J

[The plaintiff board proposed to erect overhead electric lines across ground, consisting of moorland and pasture, used by a gliding club. The club objected on the ground that the club was using the land as a 'pleasure ground' within an exception contained in the Electricity (Supply) Act 1919, s 22.] 'In my judgment, the words "pleasure ground" import the conception that it is the ground which gives pleasure to people. It does not mean ground on which a person carries on an activity which is pleasurable to him or her. If the latter were true Twickenham, Wembley and Ascot would be pleasure grounds. I cannot think that the legislature, in 1919, thought that a sports stadium or a racecourse was a pleasure ground. I think that it also imports the conception that the ground is not completely natural but that some planting, cultivation or planning has been carried out in producing the ground so that it gives pleasure to people. When one speaks of persons using a pleasure ground for rest and recreation one is thinking of a person going for a walk in the ground and gaining pleasure from its appearance. . . . If then in this case the general considerations which I have mentioned are applied to the club's land, can it be described as "a pleasure ground"? In my judgment it cannot, since it consists of pasture land and moor in Yorkshire to which the only work which has been carried out is the levelling of the ground and the removal of stones to permit the taking-off and landing of gliders and to which the members go to enjoy gliding and not to enjoy the ground as a ground. In my judgment, therefore, the club's land is not a "pleasure ground" within the exception contained in s 22.' *Central Electricity Generating Board v Dunning* [1970] 1 All ER 897 at 902, 903, per Foster J

New Zealand 'I think a motor-camping site is clearly a pleasure ground. A pleasure ground is a place to which the public resort for the purpose of taking their pleasure, and it is unimportant whether they go for the purpose of playing games, as in grounds specially prepared for football or cricket, or to grounds with special amenities for those who take their pleasure there as campers.' *Napier Borough v Napier Harbour Board* [1942] NZLR 435 at 438, per Northcroft J; also reported [1942] GLR 311 at 313

PLEDGE *See also* PAWN

'Pledge' shall include any contract pledging, or giving a lien or security on goods, whether in consideration of an original advance or of any further or continuing advance or of any pecuniary liability. (Factors Act 1889, s 1)

'Pledge' means the pawnee's rights over an article taken in pawn. (Consumer Credit Act 1974, s 189(1))

PLUMAGE

Plumage, that is to say, any feather or feathers, or any skin or any other part with any feather or feathers on it, of any bird or birds, other than excepted plumage. (Endangered Species (Import and Export) Act 1976, Sch 3, para 19).

[The paragraph goes on to list excepted varieties of plumage, which include ostrich feathers and the feathers of domestic fowls, etc.]

PLURALITY

'By his will the testator bequeathed "the sum of £1,000 to the Ecclesiastical Commissioners for England and their successors (thereinafter called the Ecclesiastical Commissioners), as an augmentation fund for the benefice or rectory of Kingston, Isle of Wight". So far there is a good charitable legacy, nor can any doubt be raised as to the testator's meaning. Then the will goes on "upon condition that the said benefice or rectory never be held in plurality by any neighbouring clergyman". . . . "Plurality" is "where one and the same clergyman is possessed of two or more ecclesiastical benefices with cure of souls at one and the same time". It involves, therefore, the holding of a benefice by some clergyman who at the same time holds one or more other benefices. That is the state of things which on coming into existence brings into operation the condition of defeasance in the testator's will. Has that condition of things come about? I think not. What has happened is that this benefice has been amalgamated with or merged into two other benefices, and the three now constitute one united parish or benefice, and are no longer three distinct benefices. The rector is rector of the united single parish, not the holder in plurality of the three benefices out of which it has been formed, and there is therefore no holding in plurality in the sense in which the testator used the expression.' *Re Macnamara, Hewitt v Jeans* (1911) 104 LT 771 at 773, per Eve J

PLY

[Section 1 of Stat (1856) 19 & 20 Vict c 107 (repealed) enacted that all steam vessels 'plying' to and fro between London Bridge and any place on the River Thames to the westward of the Nore Light should be subject to penalties for not consuming their own smoke.] 'We are all of opinion that this vessel is within the class to which the statutes in question were intended to apply. There was an intention, no doubt, to make a distinction between sea going vessels and vessels plying between London Bridge and any place westward of the Nore Light; and the legislature, for the general convenience and comfort of persons living near the river within those boundaries, has enacted that all vessels so plying shall consume their own smoke. The only question is, whether this steam tug, though she sometimes goes beyond those boundaries, is, while she is travelling between them, a vessel "plying" between those boundaries within the meaning of the Act. The appellant contends that she is not, because those boundaries are not the fixed limits of her voyages: but she is nevertheless, within the mischief of the statute, if she is passing to or fro, for the time, within those limits. She does, it is true, go occasionally beyond them; but that does not make her a sea going vessel.' *Walker v Evans* (1859) 2 E & E 356 at 359, DC, per Cockburn CJ

[The Merchant Shipping Act 1854, s 318 (repealed; see now the Merchant Shipping Act 1894, s 271) provided that if a passenger steamer should 'ply' or to go sea without a certificate the owner thereof should incur a penalty.] 'This vessel did not proceed to sea, and I do not think she can be said to have plied. The word "ply", as defined in Johnson's Dictionary would not include this case. No doubt the ordinary meaning of the word contains the notion of plying for hire, and I agree that it is the first and natural meaning of the word, but it does not exhaust it.' *Hedges v Hooker* (1889) 60 LT 822 at 823, DC, per Lord Coleridge CJ

'It is not alleged in this case that this was a passenger steamer, whereas s 318 of the Merchant Shipping Act 1854, under which the respondent was charged, says: "If any passenger steamer plies or goes to sea with any passengers on board without having one of the duplicates of such certificate so put up as aforesaid in some conspicuous part of the ship, the owner thereof shall for such offence incur a penalty not exceeding £100." But, even assuming that it was a passenger steamer, and that persons were on it, and going down the Orwell, could it be said to be "plying" within the meaning of the Act? The justices came to the conclusion that there was no evidence that it was plying, and I cannot think that having persons on board for the purpose of this pleasure trip was "plying".' Ibid at 824, per Hawkins J

PLY FOR HIRE

In London Hackney Carriage Act

[The London Hackney Carriage Act 1831, s 4 defines a hackney carriage to be every carriage with two or more wheels which shall be used for the purpose of standing or 'plying for hire' in any public street or road at any place within the distance of five miles from the General Post Office in the City of London.] 'Was the carriage in this case "standing or plying for hire"? Those words must mean that the carriage is to be at the disposal of any one of the public who may think fit to hire it. I think, therefore, that they are not applicable here. The railway company, it appears, allow a number of cabs to come upon their premises, and there await the arrival of the trains in order to provide accommodation for the arriving passengers. In one sense, these cabs are undoubtedly plying for hire, but they are not so plying in a general sense, but only to such an extent and subject to such regulations as the license given to them by the railway company may admit. "Standing or plying for hire" . . . must mean ready at any moment to be hired by any one of the public.' *Case v Storey* (1869) LR 4 Exch 319 at 322, 323, per Kelly CB

In Metropolitan Public Carriage Act

[The Metropolitan Public Carriage Act 1869, s 4 (repealed as to public service vehicles) defines a hackney carriage as being a carriage for the conveyance of passengers which 'plies for hire' within the limits of the Act, and is not a stage carriage. Section 7 of the Act imposes a penalty upon the owner of a stage carriage or hackney carriage which 'plies for hire' without a licence.] 'Where a person has a carriage ready for the conveyance of passengers, in a place frequented by the public, he is plying for hire, although the place is private property.' *Clarke v Stanford* (1871) LR 6 QB 357 at 359, per Cockburn CJ

'In my judgment a carriage cannot accurately be said to ply for hire [within the Metropolitan Public Carriage Act 1869 (see supra)] unless two conditions are satisfied. (1) There must be a soliciting or waiting to secure passengers by the driver or other person in control without any previous contract with them, and (2) the owner of person in control who is engaged in or authorises the soliciting or waiting must be in possession of a carriage for which he is soliciting or waiting to obtain passengers. If I may so express myself he must have appropriated, or be able at the time to appropriate, a carriage to the soliciting or waiting. Unless there is a carriage so appropriated or capable of appropriation it is in my opinion a misuse of words to say that it is plying for hire; the proper phrase would be that a man is soliciting or waiting for persons to make a contract with him which he proposes to fulfil by providing the necessary carriage. No doubt in popular language a cab is sometimes said to ply for hire when the process of soliciting or waiting is over, and the passenger obtained by this process is being driven on his journey. In my opinion that is an inaccurate expression, natural enough, since, before the journey began, the carriage was plying for hire, and as soon as the journey is over it will in the normal course be plying for hire again. But it is to be observed that even in this loose application of the phrase the idea of soliciting passengers is present; the phrase would not be used unless the speaker thought that the passenger had been obtained in this way, and that the process of soliciting or waiting for passengers would in due course be renewed as soon as the journey was over.' *Sales v Lake* [1922] 1 KB 553 at 557, 558, DC, per Lord Trevethin CJ

'As Montague Smith J said in the latter case [*Allen v Tunbridge* (1871) LR 6 CP 481] "plying for hire" is very different from a customer going to a job-master to hire a carriage, and I think Mr Meadows White [counsel] was right in his argument in that case when he said "plying for hire" means soliciting customer without any previous contract.' Ibid at 562, per Avory J

'The expression "plying for hire" is not defined in the statute [Metropolitan Public Carriage Act 1869 [see supra], and I would respectfully concur in the justices' finding that no comprehensive definition is to be found in the decided cases; but the term does connote in my view some exhibition of the vehicle to potential hirers as a vehicle which may be hired. One can perhaps best explain the reason by taking an example. It is a fairly common sight today to see in smaller towns and villages a notice in the window of a private house "Car for Hire". If the car in question is locked up in the owner's garage adjacent to the house, it could not in my view reasonably be said that at that moment the car was "plying for hire". If a customer wishes to hire it he comes and makes his terms with the owner. On the return journey the owner might exhibit a sign on its windscreen, as some of them do, "Taxi" and then clearly he would be plying for hire. Similarly, if he left the car outside his house, the same notice on the car would involve, I think, that the car was then plying for hire, and the notice in the window might also then have the same effect. The essential difference in the circumstances that I have compared is that in the one the car is not exhibited at all, whereas in the other it is, coupled with the notification that it may be hired.' *Cogley v Sherwood* [1959] 2 All ER 313 at 319, per Donovan J (also reported [1959] 2 QB 311 at 317)

PNEUMOCONIOSIS

'Pneumoconiosis' means fibrosis of the lungs due to silica dust, asbestos dust or other dust, and includes the condition of the lungs known as dust-reticulation; and . . . in the case of a person who suffers from pneumoconiosis accompanied by tuberculosis, the effects of the tuberculosis may be treated . . . as if they were effects of the pneumoconiosis. (Industrial Injuries and Diseases (Old Cases) Act 1975, s 14(1))

POINT

Australia [The Superannuation Act 1916–1986 (NSW), s 85 (see now s 85(1)) provides that any dispute under the Act may be determined in the first place by a Board: provided that any person aggrieved by a decision of the Board may within a period of six months from the date of such decision appeal to the Minister who shall thereupon refer the matter for opinion to a judge of the Supreme Court and shall decide the 'point' in accordance with such opinion.] 'The "matter" is intended to have a wider ambit than the "point". The "point" I think means the question in dispute, the answer to which will emerge from the judge's opinion upon the matter. . . . To my mind the "matter" means the whole of the matter which involves the dispute, the Board's decision and the appeal.' *Re Brereton* [1975] 1 NSWLR 667 at 670, 671, per Samuels J

POISON

[The prisoner was indicted for the murder of an infant child, by administering to her a certain deadly 'poison', called spirits of hartshorn.] 'The word "deadly" appears to me to be used merely in pursuance of an ancient form, and not to be essential to the validity of the indictment. It would be sufficient to describe it simply as a poison, and under that term would fall any thing calculated to destroy life. Substances harmless in themselves might become poison by the time or manner of their administration. This seems to me the view most accordant with common sense, and therefore I hold this indictment to be good, even though it describes spirits of hartshorn as a deadly poison.' *R v Haydon* (1845) 1 Cox CC 184 at 184, per Erle J

See, generally, 30 Halsbury's Laws (4th edn) paras 782 et seq.

POLICY HOLDER

'Policy holder' means the person who for the time being is the legal holder of the policy for securing the contract with the insurance company, or, in relation to capital redemption business, means the person who for the time being is the legal holder of the policy, bond, certificate, receipt or other instrument evidencing the contract with the company, and—

(a) in relation to such ordinary long-term insurance business or industrial assurance business as consists in the granting of annuities upon human life, includes an annuitant; and
(b) in relation to insurance business of any kind other than such as is mentioned in the foregoing paragraph or capital redemption business, includes a person to whom, under a policy, a sum is due or a periodic payment is payable.

(Insurance Companies Act 1982, s 96(1))

POLICY OF INSURANCE

'Policy' normally denotes the document containing a contract of assurance, but in relation to industrial assurance may include any contract of assurance. Where there is no policy in the ordinary sense of the term, the date of the making of the contract is deemed to be the date of the issue of a policy. (24 Halsbury's Laws (4th edn) para 215).

Therefore, any document which contains the terms of the contract [of non-marine insurance] may be treated as, or even called, a policy. Historically, the word 'policy' came into existence as the term applied by those carrying on the business of insurance to the formal document in which they set out the terms of their obligations in consideration of the stipulated premium; and it is in this sense that the word is still normally used. (25 Halsbury's Laws (4th edn) para 405)

'Policy'—

(a) in relation to ordinary long-term insurance business and industrial assurance business, includes an instrument evidencing a contract to pay an annuity upon human life;
(b) in relation to insurance business of any other class includes any policy under which there is for the time being an existing liability already accrued or under which a liability may accrue; and
(c) in relation to capital redemption business, includes any policy, bond, certificate, receipt or other instrument evidencing the contract with the company.

(Insurance Companies Act 1982, s 96(1))

'Policies of insurance against fire or marine risk are contracts to recoup the loss which parties may sustain from particular causes. When such loss is made good *aliunde* the companies are not liable for a loss which has not occurred; but in a life policy there is no such provision. The policy never refers to the reason for effecting it. It is simply a contract, that, in consideration of a certain annual payment, the company will pay at a future time a fixed sum, calculated by them with reference to the value of the premiums which are to be paid, in order to purchase the postponed payment. Whatever event may happen meanwhile, is a matter of indifference to the company.' *Law v London Indisputable Life Policy Co* (1855) 1 K & J 223 at 228, 229, per Page-Wood V-C

'A policy is, property speaking, a contract to indemnify the insured in respect of some interest which he has against the perils which he contemplates it will be liable to.' *Wilson v Jones* (1867) LR 2 Exch 139 at 150, per Blackburn J

'This note is not a policy of insurance in the common understanding of that word, and was certainly not understood to be so by the parties to it. It is expressly a contract with a view to a policy, making interim provision until a policy is prepared and delivered. It contains a proposal for insurance, which, if accepted by the company, would result in a policy to be based on the terms of the proposal, and issued by the company to the respondent. . . . Their Lordships, therefore, are disposed to come to the conclusion that the interim note in question is not a policy of insurance.' *Citizens Insurance Co of Canada v Parsons* (1881) 7 App Cas 96 at 214, PC, per cur.

'It is my opinion, any contract of insurance comes within the word "policy". There is no statutory or formal document necessary to make a contract of insurance. If a contract of insurance is created by any binding means, that is a policy to all intents and purposes.' *Re Norwich Equitable Fire Assurance Society* (1887) 57 LT 241 at 246, per Kay J

[The Road Traffic Act 1930, s 36(4) (repealed; see now the Road Traffic Act 1988, s 148) conferred statutory rights upon persons specified in a 'policy' issued under the section.] 'A policy, it is said, is none the less a "policy issued under the section" because it has been obtained by misrepresentation or fraud, and the statutory right to indemnity arising, by force of the statute, on the issue of the policy, and not of the contract contained in the policy, remains in force, though the contract may be voidable—or, indeed, avoided or rescinded—by mutual consent of the parties. Apart from authority, I cannot so construe the subsection.' *Guardian Assurance Co Ltd v Sutherland* [1939] 2 All ER 246 at 249, 250, per Branson J

Floating policy

(1) A floating policy is a policy which describes the insurance in general terms, and leaves the name of the ship or ships and other particulars to be defined by subsequent declaration.

(2) The subsequent declaration or declarations may be made by indorsement on the policy, or in other customary manner. (Marine Insurance Act 1906, s 29)

Honour policy

'I respectfully agree with the statement in Arnould on Marine Insurance (10th edn), s 311, that "a wager (or honour) policy may be defined to be one in which the parties, by express terms, disclaim, on the face of it, the intention of making a contract of indemnity". This statement, I think, puts the point forcibly and well. It matters not in what way the disclaimer be expressed, whether by the words "Production of this policy to be deemed full and sufficient proof of interest", or by any like phrase.' *Edwards (John) & Co v Motor Union Insurance Co Ltd* [1922] 2 KB 249 at 255, per McCardie J

Life policy

In the construction and for the purposes of this Act the expression 'policy of life assurance' or 'policy' shall mean any instrument by which the payment of monies by or out of the funds of an assurance company, on the happening of any contingency depending on the duration of human life, is assured or secured; and the expression 'assurance company' shall mean and include every corporation, association, society, or company now or hereafter carrying on the business of assuring lives, or survivorships, either alone or in conjunction with any other object or objects. (Policies of Assurance Act 1867, s 7)

'Life policy' means any instrument by which the payment of money is assured on death (except death by accident only) or the happening of any contingency dependent on human life, or any instrument evidencing a contract which is subject to payment of premiums for a term dependent on human life. (Insurance Companies Act 1982, s 96(1))

Participating policy

'The participating policy is in the ordinary form with nothing too indicate its special character, but the true agreement is to be found in the printed prospectus of the company under the head of "life department". "Division of profits. Two-thirds of the gross profits of the participating series of policies are allotted every five years to the assured, every policy in force at the date of the valuation being entitled to participate. The assured have the option of receiving their share of the profits in cash, or of appropriating it in increase of the sum assured, or in reduction of the future annual premiums." In the preceding page of the prospectus, but under the same heading, the following passage occurs:—"The bonus to the assured is increased owing to the arrangement by which, in consideration of a fixed percentage of the gross profits of the life assurance business, the corporation bears all the expenses of management".' *Last v London Assurance Corpn* (1885) 10 App Cas 438 at 449, per Lord Fitzgerald

'Let us see what is the difference between the two classes of insurance, the participating and non-participating. The ordinary insured, i.e. the one not entitled to any return or benefit beyond the sum insured, pays at fixed intervals during his life a sum which, it is calculated, if laid out at compound interest, will produce such a sum as after paying expenses and the sum insured, will leave a fair profit to the shareholders. The insured entitled to a return of premium or benefit beyond the sum insured does precisely the same thing. He pays at fixed intervals during the life a sum which it is calculated, if laid out at compound interest, will produce such a sum, as, after paying expenses and the sum insured, and two-thirds of what, but for the obligation to pay it, would all go to the shareholders, will leave a fair profit to them.' Ibid at 446, per Lord Bramwell

Unvalued policy

An unvalued policy is a policy which does not specify the value of the subject matter insured, but, subject to the limit of the sum insured, leaves the insurable value to be subsequently ascertained. . . . (Marine Insurance Act 1906, s 28)

Valued policy

A valued policy is a policy which specifies the agreed value of the subject-matter insured. (Marine Insurance Act 1906, s 27(2))

'The . . . question is what is the actual property at stake (for insurance is a contract of indemnity), and that in an ordinary policy, if nothing appears to the contrary, depends on the real value of the stake. But it is open to the parties to dispense with this; and if they state on the face of the policy that as between them it shall be taken at such a value, it becomes all one as if it were of that value, and then the policy is called a valued policy.' *Wilson v Nelson* (1864) 5 B & S 354 at 356, 357, per Blackburn J

Voyage and time policies

Where the contract is to insure the subject-matter 'at and from', or from one place to another or others, the policy is called a 'voyage policy', and where the contract is to insure the subject-matter for a definite period of time the policy is called a 'time policy'. A contract for both voyage and time may be included in the same policy. (Marine Insurance Act 1906, s 25(1))

POLITICAL

[The Extradition Act 1870, s 3(1) provides that a fugitive criminal shall not be surrendered if the offence in respect of which his surrender is demanded is one of a 'political character'.] 'It appears to me that, in order to constitute an offence of a political character, there must be two or more parties in the State, each seeking to impose the Government of their own choice on the other, and that, if the offence is committed by one side or the other in pursuance of that object, it is a political offence, otherwise not.' *Re Meunier* [1894] 2 QB 415 at 419, DC, per Cave J

'In my opinion the idea that lies behind the phrase "offence of a political character" is that the fugitive is at odds with the state that applies for his extradition on some issue connected with the political control or government of the country. The analogy of "political" in this contract is with "political" in such phrases as "political refugee", "political asylum" or "political prisoner". It does indicate, I think, that the requesting state is after him for reasons other than the enforcement of the criminal law in its ordinary, what I may call its common or international, aspect. It is this idea that the judges were seeking to express in the two early cases of *Re Castioni* [[1891] 1 QB 149] and *Re Meunier* [supra] when they connected the political offence with an uprising, a disturbance, an insurrection, a civil war or struggle for power: and in my opinion it is still necessary to maintain the idea of that connection. It is not departed from by taking a liberal view as to what is meant by disturbance or these other words, provided that the idea of political opposition as between fugitive and requesting state is not lost sight of: but it would be lost sight of, I think, if one were to say that all offences were political offences, so long as they could be shown to have been committed for a political object or with a political motive or for the furtherance of some political cause or campaign. There may, for instance, be all sorts of contending political organisations or forces in a country, and members of them may commit all sorts of infractions of the criminal law in the belief that by so doing they will further their political ends: but if the central government stands apart and is concerned only to enforce the criminal law that has been violated by these contestants, I see no reason why fugitives should be protected by this country from its jurisdiction on the ground that they are political offenders.' *Schtraks v Government of Israel* [1962] 3 All ER 529 at 540, HL, per Viscount Radcliffe

'Policies are about government. "Political" as descriptive of an object to be achieved must, in my view, be confined to the object of overthrowing or changing the government of a state or inducing it to change its policy or escaping from its territory the better so to do. No doubt any act done with any of these objects would be a "political act", whether or not it was done within the territory of the government against whom it was aimed.' *Cheng v Pentonville Prison (Governor)* [1973] 2 All ER 204 at 209, HL, per Lord Diplock

'One reaches the stage now on the weight of authority, and a considerable weight it is, that an offence may be of a political character, either because the wrongdoer had some direct ulterior motive of a political kind when he committed the offence, or because the requesting state is anxious to obtain possession of the wrongdoer's person in order to punish him for his politics rather than for the simple criminal offence referred to in the extradition proceedings.' *R v Governor of Winson Green Prison, Birmingham, ex p Littlejohn* [1975] 3 All ER 208 at 211, 212, per Lord Widgery CJ

See, generally, 18 Halsbury's Laws (4th edn) para 217. *See also* OFFENCE

POLITICAL PARTY

In this section 'political party' means a political party which qualifies for exemption [from capital gains tax] under para 11 of Sch 6 to the Finance Act 1975 (gifts to political parties). (Finance (No 2) Act 1983, s 7(8))

[Under the provisions of the Act of 1975, a party, in order to qualify for exemption, in certain circumstances, from capital gains tax, must have had, at the last general election, at least two members elected to the House of Commons, or one member elected and at least 150,000 votes cast for its candidates.]

POLL

'A poll must prima facie mean a poll of all entitled to vote, i.e. those who are or may be present during the poll.' *R v Southampton Water-Works Comrs* (1845) 5 LTOS 216 at 216, per Lord Denman CJ

PONY

'Pony' means any horse not more than 147 centimetres in height, except a foal travelling with its dam if the dam is over 147 centimetres. (Animal Health Act 1981, s 89(1))

Registered pony

For the purposes of this section [restriction on export of registered ponies] the expression 'registered pony' means a pony registered in—
(a) the Arab Horse Society Stud Book,
(b) the National Pony Society Stud Book,
(c) the British Palomino Society Stud Book, or
(d) the British Spotted Horse and Pony Society Stud Book

or in the stud book of any of the following native breed societies, namely, English Connemara, Dales, Dartmoor, Exmoor, Fell, Highland, New Forest, Shetland and Welsh. (Animal Health Act 1981, s 42)

POOL

Canada 'The definitions of the word "pool" show that in order to constitute a "pool" there must be an "aggregation of interest or property" or a throwing of revenue of property into one common fund or a sharing of interest in that fund by all on an equal or previously agreed basis.' *Canadian Fur Auction Sales Co (Quebec) Ltd v Neely* (1954) 11 WWR (NS) 254 at 265, Man CA, per Beaubien JA

POOL BETTING *See* BET

POOR

'The expression "poor person" in a trust for the benefit of poor persons does not mean the very poorest, the absolutely destitute; the word "poor" is more or less relative.' *Mary Clark Home (Trustees) v Anderson* [1904] 2 KB 645 at 655, per Channell J

'It is true that ladies of limited means are not destitute, and that the expression "limited means" [in a gift for the maintenance of a home for ladies of limited means] may vary in its signification according to the standard by which the means are measured, but these arguments provoke the rejoinder that there are degrees of poverty less acute than abject poverty or destitution, but poverty nevertheless, and further that in this case the limitation of means contemplated is presumably a limitation such as will necessitate some contribution from the bounty of the testatrix before the recipient would be able to defray the expense of a temporary sojourn in the home. In other words the objects to be benefited by the bequest are ladies too poor to provide themselves with a temporary home without outside assistance.' *Re Gardom, Le Page v A-G* [1914] 1 Ch 662 at 667, 668, per Eve J

Canada 'I read "poor and needy" [in a will] as meaning persons who are really poor and indeed so poor that they are in need of assistance.' *Re Cohn* [1952] 3 DLR 833 at 836, NSSC, per Doull J

Canada [The Assessment Act RSO 1960, c 23, s 4, para 12, exempts from taxation 'land of an incorporated charitable institution organised for the relief of the poor . . . or any similar incorporated institution. . . .'] 'To my mind the respondent institution [which maintained a home for the aged] is essentially similar to a charitable institution organised for the relief of the poor. The corporate purpose the respondent is effecting through the home in question is "the care and security of the aged".

Both the poor and the aged are classes of mankind which are the subject of special bibilical injunction, the obedience to which can be expressed best by care. Moreover, "poor" is a word of relative meaning and it does not include only the destitute [*Re Clarke* [1923] 2 Ch 407]. The respondent provides food and lodging for an aged person for $165 or $175 a month. Clearly its purpose in providing such necessities at bare cost is to relieve those who, if they are not poor, are in very similar circumstances. I do not think it affects such obvious and controlling purpose that it is possible, though improbable, some individuals of affluence might avail themselves of the charitable bounty of the respondent.' *Re Mennonite Home Association of York County and Village of Stouffville* [1970] 2 OR 753 at 760, Ont CA, per Jessup JA; affirmed sub nom, *Assessment Comr of Village of Stouffville v Mennonite Home Assocn of York County* [1973] SCR 237, SCC

POPPY-STRAW

'Poppy-straw' means all parts, except the seeds, of the opium poppy after mowing. (Misuse of Drugs Act 1971, Sch 2, Part IV)

PORT *See also* HAVEN

Where the terminus 'at and from' which the voyage is to commence is a port named in the policy [of marine insurance], the name is, as a general rule, presumed to mean that place which in the ordinary commercial sense is considered the port, and not to extend to all the different places it may comprise for purposes of revenue, or which may be included in the technical legal meaning of the word 'port'.

Where the policy is 'at and from' an island or other district containing several ports, the risk on ship commences as soon as the ship has arrived in good safety at the first port at which she touches on the island, for the purpose of discharging her outward cargo. Thus a ship insured for a homeward voyage 'at and from' any of the islands of the West Indies is protected by the word 'at' in going from port to port of the island. (25 Halsbury's Laws (4th edn) para 135)

A port may be natural, consisting of a haven or access of the sea by which ships conveniently come, a safe situation against winds where they may safely lie, and a good shore where they may conveniently unload; or it may be artificial, containing such facilities as quays, wharfs, cranes and warehouses. It has a town as its head for the receipt of sailors and merchants. 'Port' may bear different meanings in different contexts. The Commissioners of Customs and Excise have power to appoint and name any area as a port for customs and excise purposes. (36 Halsbury's Laws (4th edn) para 401)

'Port' includes any place at which ships are loaded or unloaded. (Dock Workers (Regulation of Employment) Act 1946, s 6)

'Port' means any port, harbour, river, estuary, haven, dock, canal or other place so long as a person or body of persons is empowered by or under an Act to make charges in respect of ships entering it or using the facilities therein, and 'limits of a port' means the limits thereof as fixed by or under the Act in question or, as the case may be, by the relevant charter or custom. (County Courts Act 1984, s 30(3))

'*Portus est locus inclusus*, and that for safety from pyrates, and the King is at the charge of this, and ports are as the gates of the kingdom, and none is owner of them but the King onely.' *R & Waller v Hanger* (1615) 3 Bulst 1 at 9, per Fleming CJ

[A ship insured by a policy of insurance was warranted free from capture in 'port'.] 'If you would protect yourself by the warranty, you must show that the ship was in some port at the time of the capture. . . . You must make the place where she lay at anchor a "port". . . . You only show the spot to be within the headlands of a river; but this is greatly too loose.' *Baring v Vaux* (1810) 2 Camp 541 at 542, per Lord Ellenborough CJ

'The stipulation that the vessel should be "free of capture and seizure in her port or ports of discharge", meant to take away from the underwriters any risk of land capture, and leave them only liable to sea-risks: and the word port ought to receive a construction co-extensive with that meaning. Port is here used in contra-distinction to the high seas. If this were otherwise, the ship would have been secured by this policy while sailing up and down every river on the continent, watching for an opportunity of landing her cargo; which was manifestly contrary to the intention of the parties. Unless therefore we read the word port in contra-distinction to the high seas, the contracting parties will not be put in the same situation in which they meant to put themselves.' *Jarman v Coape* (1811) 13 East 394 at 398, per Bayley J

'The policy extends to cover an adventure to all

ports and places in the Baltic; with liberty to touch, stay, and trade at all places, etc. and take in and charge goods wheresoever the ship might touch at, etc in the most extensive terms; but warranted free from capture or seizure in the ship's port of discharge. And now, after the arrival of the ship in Pillau Roads, where she came to an anchor for the purpose of discharging her cargo, and where she was seized, we are desired to put the narrowest sense possible upon the words port of discharge, and to confine it to the very place where the customhouse is situated, and where the usual conveniences for landing exist only in greater abundance. But with reference to this policy and the adventure thereby meant to be insured, the word port is not to be taken in its narrow or strict legal sense. . . . Now here the parties meant a port in its natural, and not merely in its technical or artificial sense. . . . The meaning of the parties was, that if the assured chose to come for the purpose of discharging his cargo within the danger of a land risk; if he came within a haven, in the large sense of the word, as his elected port of discharge, the underwriter was not to be liable to the risk of seizure there. It is asked, where else in this case can the line be drawn than at the bar which divides the harbour from the road, so called? I answer, that in a large sense the word port will include the haven of the port, into which the ship came to anchor for the purpose.' *Dalgleish v Brooke* (1812) 15 East 295 at 303–305, per Lord Ellenborough CJ

'It is cited by the defendants' counsel as the doctrine of the Court of King's Bench in *Jarman v Coape* [supra] that that Court has extended the term "port" so widely as to cover all land risks. To what extent that Court would extend the principle, the defendants do not say, but I do not apprehend the Court of King's Bench have gone so far, as to hold that to be the port, where vessels do not unload.' *Levy v Vaughan, Levy v Buck* (1812) 4 Taunt 387 at 398, per Gibbs J

'The question is, whether the words "port of Kingston-upon-Hull" are to be understood in the sense of locality, as denoting the particular place so named, or in a more enlarged and extensive sense, as comprising all the places and the whole district that, for some purposes of control, management, or superintendence, are within the limits of, and dependent upon or members of, a port whereof Kingston-upon-Hull is the head and chief. . . . In the argument at the bar on behalf of the defendants, reference was made to . . . two acts passed for enabling the Dock Company to make additional docks or basins; and it is manifest that the name "port of Kingston-upon-Hull" is there used in the limited sense of locality, and as designating that port as a port on the river Hull, according to the popular meaning and acceptation of that word, which is in general the meaning of words used in an Act of Parliament not relating to matters of science, whether of law or any other science or to matters of art on any particular subject of practical performance.' *Kingston-upon-Hull Dock Co v Browne* (1831) 2 B & Ad 43 at 54, 62, 63, per cur.

[A policy of marine insurance covered a ship and cargo at and from her 'port of lading'.] 'We cannot construe the words "at and from her port of lading", as if they were "at and from her ports", the expression used points out one single place. Nor can we adopt the technical meaning which may be ascribed to "port", as signifying all that is subject to one customhouse, or one port jurisdiction; the result of which would be that a ship, under such a policy as this, might sail to every part of a district so situated.' *Brown v Tayleur* (1835) 4 Ad & El 241 at 247–249, per Patteson J

[A new trial was ordered of a case on the ground that the judge had improperly rejected evidence to show that 'arrival in the port of ——' might by custom of certain ports mean arrival at a certain spot in the port.] 'Now it is plain upon principle, and upon authority also, if authority were wanted, that, where the laydays are to commence running "on arrival" at the ship's port of discharge, evidence may be given to show what is commonly understood to be the port. Some ports are of large area, and by custom "arrival" is understood to mean arriving at a particular spot in the port. That has been held as to the ports of London, Hull, Antwerp, and many others. The port of Liverpool, as we all know, is of many miles extent, with a series of docks for different classes of ships and trades. . . . It would be perfectly legitimate to receive evidence to show that arrival "in the port of Liverpool" did not mean arriving at the mouth of the Mersey.' *Norden SS Co v Dempsey* (1876) 1 CPD 654 at 658, 659, DC, per Lord Coleridge CJ

[A charterparty provided that a vessel should proceed with cargo to a safe 'port' as ordered, or as near thereunto as she could safely get and always lay and discharge afloat.] 'The question here is what was the sort of port to which, when the ship arrived at Falmouth or Queenstown for orders, the charterers or the person representing the charterer had a right to order the ship to go. It seems to me the first necessity was that that should order her to go to a port, to something which is known in seafaring language as a port. Secondly, it should be a port in which she might always lay and discharge afloat, and, according to my view, the meaning of that is that it should be a port in which from the moment she went into it, in the condition in which she was entitled to go into it, she should be able to lay afloat, and that she should be able to lay afloat until the time when she was fairly discharged. The condition in which she was entitled to go into this port was as fully loaded, and she was not bound to unload before she got into that port. Therefore the meaning of it is that she was entitled to be ordered to a port in which when she was fully loaded she would be able to lay afloat, and a port which would remain in such a condition that she would be able to lay afloat from that moment until she was discharged in a reasonable way.' *The Alhambra* (1881) 6 PD 68 at 72, CA, per Brett LJ

'The question . . . is, what is meant by sailing from the last port. The word "port" must be understood in its ordinary commercial sense. There are ports which, like the port of Cardiff, extend to miles for fiscal purposes, but they are not for commercial purposes to be treated as having that extent.' *Price v Livingstone* (1882) 9 QBD 679 at 681, CA, per Jessel MR

'The word "port" in a charterparty does not necessarily mean an Act of Parliament pilotage port. . . . Therefore, when you are trying to define the port with regard to which persons who enter into a charterparty, are contracting, you endeavour to find words which will shut out those things which you know they do not intend. . . . What do you go to a port for? Because you want either to load or to unload goods. . . . It is a place of safety for the ship and the goods, whilst the goods are being loaded or unloaded. . . . Now what will constitute a port as regards the loading and unloading of goods, and the safety of the ship during the process? . . . If you can see with your eyes that the land is so shaped that there is protected water within a certain space. You may be almost sure that that will be the port which is spoken of by business men under a certain name—a place where there is protected water by reason of the natural lie of the land and water.' *Garston Sailing Ship Co v Hickie* (1885) 15 QBD 580 at 587–589, CA, per Brett MR

'In determining the limits of a port we must take into consideration what are held to be its limits by merchants, sailors, shipowners, and underwriters—in short, . . . we should not give any technical meaning to the term, but should adopt the popular idea of what it comprehends.' *Afton (Owners) v Northern Marine Insurance Co Ltd* (1887) 14 544 at 553, 554, per the Lord President (Lord Inglis)

'A port is a place where a vessel can lie in a position of more or less shelter from the elements, with a view to the loading or discharge of cargo. The natural configuration of the land is, therefore, often a most important element in determining what are the limits of a port. All the waters within given boundaries which possess the common character of safety and protection would be generally admitted to be within its ambit.' *Hunter v Northern Marine Insurance Co Ltd* (1888) 13 App Cas 717 at 726, per Lord Herschell

'The parties agreed to the clause giving the vessel "liberty to call at any ports in any order". The intention was that she should call at other places for the purpose of loading and discharging such other goods as in the exercise of the right reserved the defendant contracted to carry for other shippers. But then it was argued that the defendant could not rely upon that clause, for that what the vessel did was to call, not at any other ports, either for loading or discharging, but at different places in the same ports. But, according to my view, the word "ports" in this contract was not intended to be used in any technical sense, but meant nothing more than any customary and proper places for loading and discharging cargo whether in different ports or in the same port.' *Caffin v Aldridge* [1895] 2 QB 366 at 370, per Lord Russell CJ

'If . . . we find a charterparty naming a "port" simply, and without further particularity or qualification, as the destination for the purpose of loading or unloading, we must construe it in regard to the "arrival" of the ship at that destination as meaning that port in its commercial sense, that is to say, as it would be understood by persons engaged in shipping business, and in regard to the arrival of a ship there for the purposes of the charterparty. In the case of a small port, "port" may or may not mean the whole of the geographical port. In the case of a widely extended area, such as London, Liverpool or Hull, it certainly signifies some area which is less than the geographical port, and which may, I think, not unfitly be called the commercial area.' *Leonis SS Co Ltd v Rank Ltd* [1908] 1 KB 499 at 520, CA, per Kennedy LJ

'In my opinion the term "port" in a charterparty is to be taken in its commercial sense, and is not to be defined by the meaning given to it by the legislature in Acts passed for such entirely different objects as pilotage or revenue. Any doubt or controversy on the point must now be taken as settled in *Leonis Steamship Company Limited v Rank Limited* [supra], where Buckley and Kennedy LJJ discuss all the cases. Founding myself on their judgments, I come to the conclusion that the port of King's Lynn in a commercial sense is the dock at that place.' *Hall Brothers SS Co Ltd v Paul (R & W) Ltd* (1914) 111 LT 811 at 812, per Sankey J

[By the Hague Convention 1907 an enemy ship seized in 'port' was not confiscable but only liable to be detained during hostilities.] 'In this Convention, I am of opinion that the word "port" must be construed in its usual and limited popular or commercial sense as a place where ships are in the habit of coming for the purpose of loading or unloading, embarking or disembarking. It does not mean the fiscal port.' *The Mowe* [1915] P 1 at 15, per Evans P

'The word "port" may bear different meanings in different connections. In relation to enemy goods—by their nature the subject of naval prize when at sea after the commencement of the war—I think the word "port" has a meaning extended beyond the part covered with water in which a ship carrying the goods would be afloat. Indeed, counsel for the German owners conceded that a wharf alongside would come within the "port" in this sense, although it would be strictly "on land". I fail to see what difference the 100 yards from the edge of the wharf ought to make.' *The Roumanian* [1915] P 26 at 43, 44, per Evans P

'A port denotes a place to which merchant vessels are in the habit of going to load or discharge cargo, and not a place in an open roadstead at which no cargoes are ever discharged or unloaded.' *The Belgia* [1916] 2 AC 183 at 185, PC, per cur.

Dockyard port

A dockyard port is any port, harbour, haven, roadstead, sound, channel, creek, bay, or navigable river of the United Kingdom in, on or near to which Her Majesty has any dock, dockyard, steam factory yard, victualling yard, arsenal, wharf or mooring. (36 Halsbury's Laws (4th edn) para 401)

In this Act the term 'dockyard port' means any port, harbour, haven, roadstead, sound, channel, creek, bay, or navigable river of the United Kingdom in, on, or near to which Her Majesty now or at any time hereafter has any dock, dockyard, steam factory, yard, victualling yard, arsenal, wharf, or mooring. (Dockyard Ports Regulation Act 1865, s 2)

Final port *See* FINAL PORT

Franchise port

A franchise port is a complex entity consisting of (1) something that is natural, namely a haven or access of the sea by which ships may conveniently come, a safe situation against winds where they may safely lie, and a good shore where they may conveniently unload; (2) something that is artificial, such as quays, wharfs, cranes and warehouses, and customs houses; and (3) something that is civil, namely privileges and franchises such as the right to moor a ship and to trade, and several other characteristic given to it by civil authority.

It has a town as its head for the receipt of sailors and merchants, and may include more than the bare place where ships unload, and sometimes extends many miles. (Hale's *De Partibus Maris*, c 2; 8 Halsbury's Laws (4th edn) para 1008)

Port charges

'There is no suggestion that the expression "port charges" has any special or customary meaning. The ordinary meaing of the phrase seems to me to be those charges which a vessel must pay before she leaves a port. . . . It appears to me that there is nothing unreasonable in holding that the words should have their ordinary and natural meaning, namely, that if the charterers chose to take the vessel to Deptford they must pay all the charges which would have to be paid by the vessel before she could leave that port. . . . The words must be given their ordinary and natural meaning.' *Newman & Dale v Lamport & Holt* [1986] 1 QB 20 at 23, per Mathew J

'The last point to be decided is as regards the port charges claimed in the defendant's counterclaim. These port charges are sums paid for pilotage. The captain thought it reasonably to employ a pilot, and he accordingly made a contract with a pilot. In my opinion, expenses so incurred do not fall within what is usually meant by the term "port charges". That term means some charge made by an outside authority, and does not include a special expense which the captain thought right to incur under the circumstances.' *Whittall & Co v Rahtkens Shipping Co Ltd* (1907) 76 LJKB 538 at 541, per Bray J

PORTER

'In the English language "porter" is not one word, but two distinct words—two words of the same sound and spelling, but of different meaning and derivation, which may be confused. Sometimes "porter" means a doorkeeper or janitor, and is derived through mediaeval French from the Latin noun *porta*. The Porter in Macbeth, or Cerberus as the Porter of Hades, was a porter in this sense. The second word means someone who carries things (e.g. a railway porter) and is derived from the Latin verb *portare*. There can be no doubt that the "porter" often to be found at the entrance of a block of flats is a porter with the first meaning, in the absence of a special covenant by the landlord that the porter shall carry things.' *Palser v Grinling, Property Holding Co Ltd v Mischeff* [1948] AC 291 at 311, per Viscount Simon

PORTION *See also* ADVANCEMENT

Since the principal trusts of a strict settlement were traditionally framed so as to carry the settled land in its entirety to one son of the settlor and his descendants, further provisions are commonly inserted for the purpose of providing sums of money for the benefit of the other, and generally younger, children of the settlor who did not succeed to the land. Such sums are known as portions. Formerly, such sums were secured by limiting the settled land to trustees for a long term upon trust by mortgage or sasle of the land or otherwise to raise such sums. However, after 1925 it became usual to declare trusts for raising portions without limiting a term of years. The portions were generally directed to be held in trust for such children on their attaining the age of twenty-one, or, if female, marrying under that age, in such shares and proportions as the husband and wife might jointly appoint by deed, and subject to any such appointment as the survivor might by deed or will appoint and in default of any such appointment for the qualified children in equal shares. (42 Halsbury's Laws (4th edn) para 725)

'The word portion, to be sure, may imply a fortune out of the father's estate; but, on the other hand, it relates likewise to what the wife brings with her in marriage, and answers to the word *dos* in Latin; so that it is as properly and naturally applied to this sense as the other, and no argument in favour of the plaintiff is to be drawn merely from the term portion being made use of in the marriage-settlement.' *Wood v Briant* (1742) 2 Atk 521 at 522, per Lord Hardwicke LC

[The Accumulations (Thellusson) Act 1800, s 2 (repealed; see now the Law of Property Act 1925, s 164(2)), enacted that nothing in the Act should extend to any provision for raising 'portions' for children.] 'I see no reason for putting a strained interpretation upon the expression "portions for children", used in this Act. It would be contrary to the policy of the Act to do so, and would afford a ready means of escaping form its provisions. Is this then a provision for raising portions within the fair meaning of the words of the Act? I think not. Portions for children are, I think, generally understood to be sums of money secured to them out of property springing from or settled upon their parents; and although there may, no doubt, be cases in which provisions for children out of property in which the parents take no interest may well be called portions, I think that such provisions would only receive that designation where the nature or context of the instrument gives them that character. Where there is a gift to children both of capital and income, and there is nothing in the nature or context of the instrument to impress upon the gift the character of a portion, I do not think it would be called a portion in the ordinary sense of the word, or ought to be so considered within the meaning of this Act of Parliament.' *Jones v Maggs* (1852) 9 Hare 605 at 607, per Turner V-C

'The meaning of the word "portion" as generally understood, is a sum of money secured to a child out of property either coming from or settled upon its parents. The benefit is none the less a portion because it is given to all the children, including the eldest child , and not to younger children only.' *Re Stephen, Kilby v Betts* [1904] 1 Ch 322 at 327, per Buckley J

'I may state as the unquestionable doctrine of the court, that, where a parent gives a legacy to a child, not stating the purpose, with reference to which he gives it, the court understands him as giving a portion; and by a sort of artificial rule, in the application of which legitimate children have been very harshly treated, upon an artificial notion, that the father is paying a debt of nature, and a sort of feeling upon what is called a leaning against double portions, if the father afterwards advances a portion on the marriage of that child, though of less amount, it is a satisfaction of the whole or in part.' *Ex p Pye* (1811) Ves 140 at 151, per Lord Eldon LC

'To establish a case for the application of this rule as to double portions, there must be two matters, I think, made out, and . . . there are two presumptions. . . . In the first place, both of the suggested gifts . . . must be gifts in the nature of a portion. The first presumption here comes under discussion: it is said that, whatever gifts are made by the father, which it may be supposed will have to be distributed among the children, or which are given by the father to one child with a view to establishing him in life, are presumed to be portions. . . . Then comes a further question, for the solution of which a further presumption is invoked. That question is, whether it was intended that the former gift or portion should take the place of an advancement of the gift which is given by the will, and there the second presumption . . . has to be dealt with—a presumption to the effect that the former gift, the gift inver vivos, was intended as an advancement pro tanto of the gift under the bequest. . . . This, like the former, is a presumption which may be rebutted.' *Re Lacon, Lacon v Lacon* [1891] 2 Ch 482 at 497, 498, CA, per Bowen LJ

PORTRAIT *See also* PICTURE

'Various passages were cited from the works of Fuseli, from his Lectures on Painting, and from the admirable lectures of Sir Joshua Reynolds. Now, what is the scope and object of those passages? I have read them with attention. The object of them is not to define what is a portrait and what is not a portrait, but to show what a portrait ought to be. The head is the great object—the countenance, the resemblance of the living individual; these are the great objects, to which everything else must be subordinate. That is the scope and object of the celebrated writers to whom I have referred. If you introduce anything, you must take care to introduce it as accessory, and make it subordinate. If you look at the picture, the first thing that arrests your attention is the countenance of the individual. There are rules of art, and if those rules are violated, still the picture is not less a portrait. Suppose a man paints a picture of a knight in the Garter robes, a very splendid dress, and calculated to attract the eye. If he is a good artist, in spite of the richness of that dress, he will take care so to manage and conduct it, either in colour or disposition, as to make it subordinate to the countenance. That is what is meant by the writers to whom I have referred: they mean nothing more than that. A clumsy artist will so manage such a dress, that when you look at the picture, the first thing that will strike you will be the dress. Still the picture will be equally a portrait, though a picture of a different description from one which is painted by an eminent artist; but if that be a bad portrait, still it is a portrait.' *Leeds (Duke) v Amherst (Earl)* (1844) 14 LJ Ch 73 at 82, per Lord Lyndhurst LC

'The question in this case turns on the construction of two gifts contained in the will of Sir H A Layard—one of certain pictures to the National Gallery, and the other of certain portraits to his nephew, Major Layard. The question is whether fifteen pictures, which are portraits in the sense that they were primarily intended to represent the features of particular persons, pass to the National Gallery under a gift of pictures "except portraits"; and if they do not, then whether they pass to Major Layard under a gift of "family and other portraits". . . . I think, in the first place, the expression "family and other portraits" refers to, and includes, the same pictures, whatever they may be as the "portraits" excepted from the preceding bequest. The result, then, is that the testator divides his pictures into two categories—those which he calls "portraits" and the rest. In order to understand the meaning of his will it is necessary to ascertain whether his pictures did in fact fall into two such categories, and of what particulars they respectively consisted. The facts I have stated seem to me to answer the question. There were in his possession two classes of pictures—first, those of which the substantial characteristic was that they were portraits of himself and his wife and members of his family and friends; and secondly, those of which the substantial characteristic was that they were the works of particular artists or of particular schools, and as to which the fact that some of them happened to be the pictorial representations of certain persons was a merely accidental quality. I think the will ought to be construed accordingly, and that by "portraits" the testator meant to describe only those pictures which are included in the first class above mentioned. This construction is assisted to some extent by the express mention in the gift to the nephew of "family portraits". I do not think it is a case in which "other portraits" can be confined to those *ejusdem generis* with "family" portraits; but at the same time the expressions used, taken with the facts as to the nature of the testator's collections, indicate the kind of thing he had in his mind when he spoke of "portraits".' *Re Layard, Layard v Bessborough (Earl)* (1916) 85 LJ Ch 505 at 518, CA, per Warrington LJ

'The word "portrait" has been judicially considered in an interesting case, which, however, does not help very much, namely, *Leeds (Duke) v Amherst (Earl)* [supra]. "Engraving, photograph or portrait" [within the Copyright Act 1911 (repealed; cf now the Copyright Act 1965)] is a curious collocation of words: one would have expected the third word in that grouping to be something like "painting", because engraving is a method of production, and so is photography; and it would seem that "portrait" covers all kinds of pictorial representation, however produced. I am not sure that it is necessary to express a concluded view about the matter, but I should have thought that on the whole this [a sketch made of a person after his death] was a portrait, a portrait produced by the mental process of the artist, and intended to represent a deceased person as that person was when living; and that it is none the less a portrait because the materials that the artist used were entirely subjective.' *Leah v Two Worlds Publishing Co Ltd* [1951] 1 Ch 393 at 398, 399, per Vaisey J

POSITION

'Position', in relation to an employee, means the following matters taken as a whole, that is to say, his status as an employee, the nature of his work and his terms and conditions of employment. (Employment Protection (Consolidation) Act 1978, s 153(1))

POSSESSION *See also* SUPPLY

'Possession' is a word of ambiguous meaning, and its legal senses do not coincide with the popular sense. In English law it may be treated not merely as a physical condition protected by ownership, but as a right in itself. The word 'possession' may mean effective, physical or manual control, or occupation, evidenced by some outward act, sometimes called de facto possession or detention as distinct from a legal right to possession. This is as question of fact rather than of law.

'Possession' may mean legal possession: that possession which is recognised and protected as such by law. The elements normally characteristic of legal possession are an intention of possessing together with that amount of occupation or control of the entire subject matter of which it is practically capable and which is sufficient for practical purposes to exclude strangers from interfering. Thus, legal possession is ordinarily associated with de facto possession; but legal possession may exist without de facto possession, and de facto possession is not always regarded as possession in law. A person who, though having no de facto possession, is deemed to have possession in law, is sometimes said to have consecutive possession.

The normal case of legal possession is where the true owner has de facto possession and intends to exclude unauthorised interference. In this instance de facto and legal possession are associated in the same person. A bailee also has de facto and legal possession during the bailment.

Legal possession of an article may remain in the owner even where he has lost or abandoned physical possession of it or otherwise ceased to exercise effective control over it, for example where he has lost a jewel in his house, left his implements of husbandry in a field with the intention of returning, or even, perhaps, where he has abandoned the article altogether, provided that no one else has taken de facto possession.

The owner has legal possession of an article temporarily in the custody of his employee, except where the employee receives an article from a third person to hold for his employer in which case the employee holds as bailee and has legal possession. In the same way the owner retains the legal possession where the article is in the custody of a guest or licensee.

A thief, however, may have legal possession of stolen goods, the true owner having merely the right to possession, on the principle that possession in fact with the manifest intention to exercise sole dominion imports possession in law.

The word 'possession' is sometimes used inaccurately as synonymous with the right to possession. This right to possess is a normal incident of ownership but an owner's right to possess may be temporarily suspended, for example, where he has bailed the goods to a bailee for a term, and, conversely, the right to possess may exist temporarily in one who is not the owner, for example a bailee. Moreover, a right to possess may be subject to the superior right of one who has a better title. For example a finder's right to possess does not avail against that of the true owner.

The word 'possession' is used in various contexts and phrases, for example in the phrase 'actual possession', or 'to take possession', or 'interest in possession', or 'estate in possession', or 'entitled in possession', although it is inaccurate to describe an interest in expectancy as falling into possession. (35 Halsbury's Laws (4th edn) paras 1111–1114)

'Possession does not consist merely in manual detention. Suppose I request a bystander to hold anything for me, it still remains in my possession. So also possession may be required or retained over goods which are in the manual detention of a third person.' *R v Sleep* (1861) Le & Ca 44 at 57, per Willes J

'Suppose five men went down together to a river to take fish, and caught two, and were met when on their way up with the fish. Would not all five men be in possession of the fish although some of them may never have touched them? They certainly would.' *M'Attee v Hogg* (1903) 5 F 67 at 69, per the Lord Justice-Clerk (Lord MacDonald)

'"Possession" as enjoyed by the owner of a house, property, or estate may mean either the user of it by someone else who is a sub-tenant, the rents and profits being received by the owner; or it may equally mean that the user may be exercised by the owner in whole or in part and in lieu of or in addition to mere receipt of profits.' *Martin Estates Co Ltd v Watt & Hunter* [1925] NI 79 at 85, per Moore LJ

'Actual possession of empty premises, or of chattels which are locked up within a building or in a package of some sort, is retained by retaining the key. Possession of the key gives actual possession.' *Thomas v Metropolitan Housing Corpn Ltd* [1936] 1 All ER 210 at 216, CA, per Scott LJ

[The Factors Act 1889, s 1(2) enacts that a person is deemed to be in 'possession' of goods, or of the documents of title to goods, where the goods or documents are in his actual custody or are held by any other person subject to his control or for him or on his behalf. The Sale of Goods Act 1893, s 25(1) (repealed; see now the Sale of Goods Act 1979, s 24) deals with the delivery or transfer of goods by a person who has sold the goods, but continues or is in 'possession' of the goods.] 'I think it is perfectly plain by a reference to the Factors Act 1889, s 1(2), that it is sufficient in that Act that possession is possession by another person on behalf of the person whose possession is material, and I see no reason why the same kind of construction should not be put upon the words "in possession of the goods" in s 25(1) of the Act of 1893. Possession by an agent, possession by a warehouseman or mercantile agent, is a perfectly well known form of possession in the business world, and I can see no reason for confining the meaning of it to personal possession or actual possession of the person who has sold the goods.' *City Fur Manufacturing Co Ltd v Fureenbond (Brokers) London Ltd* [1937] 1 All ER 799 at 802, per Branson J

'Handing over a key is a symbolic act, which at common law carried with it possession of that to which the key is the means of access. . . . If the symbolic act is one which, on the facts of the case in evidence, is shown quite clearly to be an act in which the key is intended to carry possession, then it is impossible to treat the handing over of the key as anything but the handing over of possession.' *Holt v Dawson* [1939] 3 All ER 635 at 637, 638, CA, per Scott LJ

'If a man buys an empty house, though he never goes inside it, he is in actual possession of it. Nobody else can be. If there is a tramp sleeping in it without his permission, the new owner is still in possession of it. If there is somebody there whom he allows to be there, not as a tenant, but merely as a licensee, still it may be said that there are facts on which it can reasonably be found that the new owner is in possession of it. . . . All that Scrutton LJ decided [in *Goudge v Broughton* [1929] 1 KB 103 at 130, CA] . . . was that, where a man who must be held to be the landlord had been in possession of a house, and there was nothing to show that he was not in possession except that he allowed a gardener to live in it, as a tenant at will, then, through the gardener, or licensee, he could be said to have not only possession, but actual possession. . . . If one is once in actual possession, nothing can happen to show that one has not been in actual possession.' *Mouser v Major* [1941] 1 KB 477 at 485–487, CA, per du Parcq LJ

'"Possession" is a word that, perhaps like a great many words, is incapable of an entirely precise and satisfactory definition. Possession of a house is essentially different from possession of a gold watch. One has to look at the property possessed.' *Bank View Mill Ltd v Nelson Corpn & Fryer & Co (Nelson) Ltd* [1942] 2 All ER 477 at 486, per Stable J; reversed on other grounds [1943] 1 KB 337, CA

'It is quite clear, without referring to authority, that for a man to be found to have possession, actual or constructive, of goods, something more must be proved than that the goods have been found on his premises. It must be shown either, if he was absent, that on his return he has become aware of them and exercised some control over them or . . . that the goods had come, albeit in his absence, at his invitation or by arrangement. It is also clear that a man cannot be convicted of receiving goods of which delivery has been taken by his servant unless there is evidence that he, the employer, had given the servant authority or instructions to take the goods.' *R v Cavendish* [1961] 2 All ER 856 at 858, CCA, per cur.

[The appellant, who sold scent as a side-line, went to a café, where on inquiry whether anything had been left for him the proprietor told him that there was something for him under the counter. The appellant found two boxes there which, according to his evidence, he took without looking inside the smaller box, assuming that it also contained scent. A police officer stopped the appellant when driving his van. In the smaller of two boxes were found twenty thousand tablets containing amphetamine sulphate, a prohibited drug specified in the schedule to the Drugs (Prevention of Misuse) Act 1964, (repealed; see now the Misuse of Drugs Act 1971, Sch 2). The larger box contained scent. The appellant was charged with having in his possession drugs contrary to s 1 of the Act of 1964.] 'The question resolves itself into one as to the nature and extent of the mental element which is involved in "possession", as that word is used in the section now being considered. In my view, in order to establish possession the prosecution must prove that an accused was knowingly in control of something in circumstances which showed that he was assenting to being in control of it. They need not prove that in fact he had actual knowledge of the nature of that which he had. In *Lockyer v Gibb* [[1966] 2 All ER 653], Lord Parker CJ gave the illustration of something being slipped into a person's basket. While the person was unaware of what had happened there would be no possession. But in such circumstances on becoming aware of the presence of the newly discovered article there would be opportunity to see what the article was: whether the opportunity was availed of or not, if the article was deliberately retained there would be possession of it. So also in the illustration given by Alderson B in 1846 in *R v Woodrow* [(1846) 15 M & W 404]. Something is placed in a man's stable without his knowledge. He is not in possession of it. If he goes to his stable and sees the unexpected presence of the article then, according to the particular circumstances, he might with knowledge so act as to assume control of it. He would then be in possession of the article.' *Warner v Metropolitan Police Comr* [1968] 2 All ER 356 at 375, HL, per Lord Morris of Borth-y-Gest

'Counsel for the appellant has said that there may be cases where a man, as it were, consumes something, puts it in his mouth or swallows it, such as a diamond or a gold ring, in order to conceal it, when he may well be in possession of it. I entirely agree but when, as here, something [i.e. a drug] is literally consumed and changed in character, it seems to me impossible to say that a man is in possession of it within the meaning of this Act [Drugs (Prevention of Misuse) Act 1964 (repealed: see supra)]. *Hambleton v Callinan* [1968] 2 All ER 943 at 945, per Lord Parker CJ

'Having something in one's possession does not mean of necessity that one must actually have it on one's person.' *R v Purdy* [1974] 3 All ER 465 at 473, CA, per cur.

[The Firearms Act 1968, s 1(1) makes it an offence for a person to have a firearm in his 'possession' without a certificate.] 'Looking at the context of the word "possession" in s 1 of the 1968 Act in the present case, I have no doubt that one can be in possession of a firearm even though one is at a place other than that at which the firearm physically is. To agree with the justice's decision in the present case would in my view effectively be to equate the word "possession" in s 1 with custody, and this I am satisfied would be wrong.' *Sullivan v Earl of Caithness* [1976] 1 All ER 844 at 847, per May J

'Possession is a deceptively simple concept. It denotes a physical control or custody of a thing plus knowledge that you have it in your custody or control. You may possess a thing without knowing or comprehending its nature; but you do not possess it unless you know you have it.' *R v Boyesen* [1892] 2 All ER 161 at 163, HL, per Lord Scarman

Australia 'The ambiguity of the word "possess" in all its forms need not be emphasised. In criminal law the word "possession" connotes an exclusive dominion over the subject matter. . . . The prohibition is stated in the Order as "an alien shall not possess another car". Many of the authorities which illustrate the criminal law on the subject deal with the expression "in possession". Here the verb "to possess" is used. In my opinion it has a different shade of meaning from the verbal expression "to have in possession". Its concept seems to be nearer the realm of proprietary right. If I say I am "in possession" of a thing, that seems to indicate that I have it in my custody, control or power, while if I say I "possess" a thing, something more than a mere right of custody or control seems to be intended.' *McCaskill v Marzo* (1944) 46 WALR 64 at 71, 72, per Wolff J

Australia 'Possession as defined by the Act [Firearms Act 1958 (Vic) s 3] embraces the factual situation of a person, unendowed with any propriety or exclusive possessory rights, having the physical custody or control of a firearm, and to the factual situation of a person who has and exercises access to a weapon, whether alone or shared with others. There is no warrant for qualifying either the words "custody" or "control" or "access" with any legal doctrine of possessory rights.' *Yeates v Hoare* [1981] VR 1034 at 1038, per Kaye J

Canada 'If any meaning is given to a literal reading of s 5(2) of the Criminal Code, RSC, 1927, ch 36 [see now 1953–54 (Can) c 51, s 3(4)] It must apply to this case. . . . The issue in this case is whether or not in law the facts bring it within the purview of s 5, sub-s 2. It reads as follows: "2 If there are two or more persons, and any one or more of them, with the knowledge and consent of the rest, has or have anything in his or their custody or possession, it shall be deemed and taken to be in the custody and possession of each and all of them." We have here two persons, one of them, namely, the runner, with the knowledge and consent of the accused (because of the previous arrangement) had in his "custody or possession" a deck of opium. The section provides that on that state of facts "it shall be deemed and taken to be in the custody and possession of each and all of them." Custody or possession in the hands of the runner "with the knowledge and consent" of the accused is by virtue of this section the latter's custody and possession.' *R v Lee Chew* [1940] 3 WWR 285 at 286, 287, BCCA, CA, per Macdonald CJBC

Canada 'I think that the word "possession" as used in s 4 of the Opium and Narcotic Drug Act [see now the Narcotic Control Act, RSC 1970, c N-1, s 3] and amendments thereto, should be given the meaning it had at common law. It was there used in relation to movable things in three different senses; firstly, to signify mere physical possession; secondly, to signify possession in the legal sense; and thirdly, to signify the right to possession. Physical possession has been sometimes described as "actual", "manual" or "de facto" possession. Possession in the legal sense may exist without physical possession. It is possession attributed in law to a person and describes his or her legal relation to a thing with respect to other persons. It has sometimes been called constructive possession. The right to possession has also been called "possession" and "constructive possession". . . . I conclude that by giving to the word "possession" the meaning and sense given to it at common law, and independent of s 5(1)(b) (ii) of the Criminal Code [see RSC 1970, c C-34, s 3(4)] it includes, as therein expressly provided, "having in any place, whether belonging to or occupied by one's self or not, for the use or benefit of one's self or of any other person". But "having" a thing means "possessing" a thing, and thus before it can be held that a person is one "having possession" there must be evidence to establish physical possession, possession in the legal sense or the right to possession." *R v Martin*]1948] OR 963 at 966, 967, per Laidlaw JA

Canada 'To constitute "possession" within the meaning of the criminal law it is my judgment that where, as here, there is manual handling of a thing, it must be co-existent with knowledge of what the thing is, and both these elements must be co-existent with some act of control (outside public duty).' *R v Hess* (No 1) [1949] 1 WWR 577 at 579, BCCA, per O'Halloran JA

Canada [The Vehicles Act 1945 (Sask) c 98, s 141(1) (now RSS 1965, c 377, s 168), concerned the liability of the owner of a motor vehicle for damage done by it unless it had been stolen or otherwise wrongfully taken out of his 'possession'.] 'The word "possession" in English law is, as has often been pointed out, a most ambiguous word. As most often used, however, it imparts actual physical possession. . . . When a motor car is stolen from the owner, the thief takes actual physical possession, and thus takes it out of the possession of the owner, although the right to possession remains with the latter. That this is the idea in contemplation of the statute is shown by the use of the phrase "or otherwise . . . taken out of his possession".' *Marsh v Kulchar* [1952] 1 DLR 593 at 595, per Kellock J

Canada 'It is apparent from the portion of the charge above set out [of possession of drugs for trafficking] that the learned trial judge distinguished the incidence of "possession" used in the Opium and Narcotic Drug Act [RSC 1952 (see now Narcotic Control Act, RSC 1970, c N-1)] from its incidence when used as in other criminal charges to the prejudice of the accused. I am of the opinion that "possession" under the Opium and Narcotic Drug Act is not something different to possession in other criminal cases in which mens rea is a material element of the offence.' *R v Larier* (1960) 129 Can CC 297 at 301, per Procter JA

Canada [Rule 464(1) of the Federal Court Rules authorises the Federal Court to make an order for production and inspection of documents in the 'possession' of persons not parties to the action.] 'What is involved is simply the meaning of "possession" in Rule 464. No case was cited in which the meaning is discussed and, in the absence of any expression of opinion on it, I think it means what is referred to as "legal possession" by Lord Cottenham in *Reid v Langlois* (1849) 1 Mac & G 627 at 636; 41 ER 1408 at 1411, when he said: "In one sense it [the document] is in his possession; but when possession for the purpose of production is spoken of, that is to say a right and power to deal with it, actual corporeal possession is not meant, but legal possession in respect of which the party is authorised to deal with the property in question." The word plainly includes the situation where the owner of a document has physical possession of it. It includes as well, in my view, the situation where the document is not physically in the possession of its owner but is in the possession or custody of an agent or bailee from whom the owner is entitled to obtain it. I do not think, however, that it includes bare custody or possession held by one who does not own the document for, as I see it, the purpose of the notice of the application required by the rule to be given to the person in possession is to give the person entitled to it an opportunity to object to its production and that purpose would not be served if a mere custodian without title were the only person entitled to be heard.' *Bowlen v R*]1977] CTC 531 at 533, (Fed Ct), per Thurlow ACJ

New Zealand 'The term "possession" when used with reference to land, includes the receipt of income thereof: s 2 of the Property Law Act 1952. Apart from this reference, no express guide is provided by the Act as to whether "possession" in s 50 means physical occupation or merely the legal right to such. During the course of the trial I ruled that the latter was the true meaning. There seems to be no direct authority on this point. Further consideration has not changed my mind. . . . I think that, reading s 50 of the Property Law Act in conjunction with the definition in s 2, a purchaser is in possession of land for the purposes of the former section if he is entitled to the actual or physical occupation thereof or has put another into such occupation on terms requiring that other to make to the possessor payments in the nature of income in respect of that occupation. It follows that, in order to relinquish possession so as to exclude the operation of s 50, there must be an actual abandonment of the possessor's right.' *Woods v Tomlinson* [1964] NZLR 399 at 405, per Wilson J

Adverse possession *See* ADVERSE

Apparent possession

Personal chattels shall be deemed to be in the 'apparent possession' of the person making or giving a bill of sale, so long as they remain or are in or upon any house, mill, warehouse, building, works, yard, land, or other premises occupied by him, or are used and enjoyed by him in any place whatsoever, notwithstanding that formal possession thereof may have been taken by or given to any other person. (Bills of Sale Act 1878, s 4)

'In my opinion the expression "in the apparent possession of" [in the Bills of Sale Act 1878, s 8 (but see the Bills of Sale Act (1878) Amendment Act 1882, s 3)] is equivalent to "apparently in the possession of", and I think the interpretation clause [s 4 (supra)] does no more than declare that the mere giving or receiving formal possession shall not have the legal effect of taking the goods out of the apparent possession of the grantor where they are in a house or on premises in his occupation, or where they are in his actual use at the time. . . . In my opinion the true meaning of "apparent possession" in this statute is, "apparently in possession", as distinguished from "actually in possession", and goods may be in the true and actual possession of one, and in the apparent possession of another.' *Robinson v Tucker* (1883) Cab & El 173 at 178, 179, per Williams J

Australia [The Bills of Sale Act 1899–1986 (WA), s 25, provides that an unregistered bill of sale is void so far as the property in or right to the possession of any chattels comprised in such bill of sale which at any time within three months before the passing of an effective resolution for winding up shall have been in the possession or 'apparent possession' of the grantee.] 'What then is meant by the words "possession or apparent possession" in s 25? As regards tangible chattels, it means actual possession or the appearance of dominion over the thing, and in a narrow sense it might be argued that there can be no possession of or dominion over an obligation to pay, and the right to receive, an instalment which has not yet come into existence. This would lead to a curious result, which we do not think was intended by the Act, one of the main purposes of which is to prevent the mischief of traders and others obtaining credit on assets which are apparently their own, but are not so in fact.' *Plunketts Ltd v Harrods Ltd* (1942) 44 WALR 1 at 6, Wolff J.

Estate in possession

Australia 'The essential element of an "estate in possession" is, in my opinion, that the owner of it has a present right of beneficial enjoyment, whether accompanied by physical possession of the land or not.' *Glenn v Federal Comr of Land Tax* (1915) 20 CLR 490 at 498, per Griffith CJ

Of land

An owner in possession for an estate of freehold is said to be 'seised' of the land, and his possession is called 'seisin'. 'Possession', as applied to land, denotes in its narrowest meaning, possession for a chattel interest; thus as between the freeholder and the lessee, the freeholder is seised and the lessee possessed of the land. The possession of the lessee supports the seisin of the lessor. In a wider sense, 'possession' denotes occupation under any title, whether of freehold or leasehold, or even without title, and it may include receipt of rent. (39 Halsbury's Laws (4th edn) para 487).

Actual possession is a question of fact. It consists of two elements: the intention to possess the land and the exercise of control over it to the exclusion of other persons. The extent of the control which should be exercised in order to constitute possession varies with the nature of the land; possession means possession of that character of which the land is capable. Thus, a person may be in possession of minerals even though he is not in possession of the surface and has no actual occupation of the minerals. (45 Halsbury's Laws (4th edn) para 1394)

'Possessed of'

'The words used in the covenant in this case are, that all the estate, etc, which Mrs Home shall become seised, possessed of, or entitled to: the word "possessed" in this covenant has been principally relied on: and the word "entitled" has also been relied on, though not so much. The word "seised" has not; and indeed, that word being properly applicable to real estate, it is plain that the covenant of the husband could not operate on the wife's real estate of which she should be seised; and it is admitted that in fact all her interest was personalty. Now it so happened, that at the time of the marriage, Mr Paterson's affairs were not wound up; by reason of some entanglement, there was difficulty as to the settlement of his property, and it was not till 1814 that it was brought about, and then it was brought about by compromise between the parties interested; but the interest which Mrs Home had at the time when the marriage took place was the same that she had in 1814. It was not ascertained, it is true, what was its value or extent; it was not ascertained whether, by reason of debts of Mr Paterson, the property might not turn out to be of no value; but the interest of Mrs Home in the residuary estate of Mr Paterson was an interest in possession; she was entitled in possession, and the interest remained the same, though it was not till long after that it was realised. In what sense then is the word "possessed" used in the covenant? The word may have three different meanings. In connection with the word "seised", it is often used as meaning to embrace all that the party is entitled to, both in realty and personalty; to embrace all interests which the party has or may have at any time, whether in possession, remainder or reversion; and vested or contingent. Another sense in which the term is used, is to describe an estate in possession, as distinguished from an estate in reversion or remainder. A third sense is that of reduction into actual, into manual possession. These are the three senses in which the word "possessed" may be used; I am not aware of any other in which it can be used.' *Wilton v Colvin* (1856) 3 Drew 617 at 622, 623, per Kindersley V-C

Possession and enjoyment

Australia [The Stamp Duties Act 1920–1986 (NSW), s 102 [see now s 102(d)] provides for the inclusion for purposes of death duty as part of the estate of a deceased person any property comprised in any gift made by the deceased of which bona fide possession and enjoyment has not been assumed by the donee immediately upon the gift.] 'The phrase "possession and enjoyment" is a composite one, and means in this case beneficial possession and enjoyment.' *Perpetual Trustee Co Ltd v Comr of Stamp Duties of New South Wales* (1941) 64 CLR 492 at 500, per Rich ACJ

Writ of possession

A judgment or order for the giving of possession of land is enforced by a writ of possession, and, in cases where the defendant is required to do or abstain from doing any act, by an order of committal or a writ of sequestration. Except in certain cases, a writ of possession must not issue without the leave of the court, which will not be granted unless it is shown (1) that every person in actual possession of the whole or any part of the land has received such notice of the proceedings as appears to the court sufficient to enable him to apply to the court for any relief to which he may be entitled, and (2) if the operation of the judgment or order is suspended under the Landlord and Tenant Act 1954, that the applicant has not received notice in writing from the tenant that he desires that certain provisions of that Act shall have effect. . . .

A writ of possession may include provision for enforcing the payment of any money adjudged or ordered to be paid by the judgment or order which is to be enforced by the writ. At the plaintiff's election there may be either one writ or separate writs of execution for the possession and for the costs. (17 Halsbury's Laws (4th edn) para 500)

POST (Mail)

'In my view, the word "post", construed in its ordinary and natural meaning, is wide enough to cover both registered post and ordinary post. I do not think that as a matter of construction it is possible to limit it to one or the other. . . . I think it is clear that the words which the legislature has used in earlier Acts and repeated in 1948 [in the Companies Act 1948 (repealed; see now the Companies Act 1985, s 695)], refer to "post" in the ordinary sense of the term and are not limited either to registered post or to ordinary prepaid post. That view is supported to some extent by the provisions in the Post Office Act 1908, s 12 and s 13 [repealed], which touch on registration. They do not create any real difference of genus between ordinary post and registered post.' *T O Supplies (London) Ltd v Jerry Creighton Ltd* [1951] 2 All ER 992 at 993, 994, per Devlin J

Post office

'Post office' includes any house, building room, vehicle or place used for the purposes of the Post Office, and any post office letter box. (Post Office Act 1953, s 87)

Post office letter box

'Post office letter box' includes any pillar box, wall box, or other box or receptacle provided by the permission or under the authority of the Postmaster-General for the purpose of receiving postal packets, or any class of postal packets, for transmission by or under the authority of the Postmaster-General. (Post Office Act 1953, s 87)

Postal packet

'Postal packet' means a letter, postcard, reply postcard, newspaper, printed packet, sample packet, or parcel, and every packet or article transmissible by post, and includes a telegram. (Post Office Act 1953, s 87)

Return of post

[An offer was made subject to acceptance by 'return of post'.] 'That does not mean exclusively a reply by letter by return of post, but you may reply by telegram or by verbal message, or by any means not later than a letter written and sent by return of post would reach us.' *Tinn v Hoffmann & Co* (1873) 29 LT 271 at 274, Ex Ch, per Honyman J

'The words "your reply by return of post" fixes the time for acceptance and not the manner of accepting.' Ibid at 278, per Brett J

'The words on the [order] form "orders to be acknowledged by return" are not intended to be words of contract. . . . On the authority of *Tinn v Hoffmann & Co* [supra], I hold that the words "by return" only relate to the time within which, and not to the method by which, acknowledgement is to be made.' *Willis v Baggs & Salt* (1925) 41 TLR 453 at 454, per Roche J

Service by post *See* SERVICE

POST NUPTIAL SETTLEMENT *See* SETTLEMENT

POST OBIT

A *post obit* bond is a bond conditioned for the payment of a sum of money after the death of a specified person, and is usually given in respect of a loan for a sum greater than that advanced. Such bonds are of two kinds: (1) where the payment depends on a contingency, as for instance in the event of the obligor surviving a relative in regard to whom he has expectations; (2) where the payment is certain, but the time of payment uncertain, as in the case of a bond conditioned for payment of a certain sum on the death of the obligor. (12 Halsbury's Laws (4th edn) para 1393)

POST OFFICE *See* POST

POSTAGE STAMP *See* STAMP

POSTHUMOUS CHILD

Australia 'It is clear that the ordinary meaning of the words "posthumous child" is a child born after the death of the father.' *Re Goodwin* (1904) 4 SRNSW 682 at 698, per Darley LJ

POULTRY *See also* LIVESTOCK

'Poultry' means domestic fowls, turkeys, geese, ducks, guinea-fowls, pigeons, pheasants and partridges. (Medicines Act 1968, s 132(1))

'Poultry' means the domestic varieties of the following, that is to say, fowls, turkeys, geese, ducks, guinea-fowls, pigeons, peacocks and quails. (Animals Act 1971, s 11)

In this Act . . . poultry means birds of the following species—
(a) domestic fowls, turkeys, geese, ducks, guinea-fowls, and pigeons, and
(b) pheasants and partridges.
(Animal Health Act 1981, s 87(4))

[By subs (5) the definition may be extended or restricted by order.]

'I do not think that these pheasants were poultry. They were reared for the purpose of being released to serve as targets for sportsmen, and pheasants which have never been in captivity are clearly not poultry. It may well be that, if it should prove profitable to rear and keep pheasants in captivity until killed for human consumption, such pheasants should be regarded as poultry. The mere fact, however, that these pheasants like other game will come to the table after they have been shot seems to me to be immaterial. It would not in my view be in accordance with the ordinary use of language to say that they were poultry until released and then became game. They were game throughout, and the farm where they were reared was properly called a game farm.' *Kendall (Henry) & Sons v Lillico (William) & Sons Ltd* [1968] 2 All ER 444 at 458, HL, per Lord Reid

POUND (Enclosure) *See also* POUNDBREACH

The expression 'pound', used in relation to the impounding or confining of animals, includes any receptacle of a like nature. (Protection of Animals Act 1911, s 15)

POUND (Money)

'I remember a case, in which Sir William Fish was obliged by debt to pay on a certain day fifty pounds (without saying of money). And for this, on that day, when the gentlemen were at supper, he came and offered fifty pounds weight of stone, which was adjudged no offer.' *Hookes v Swaine* (1663) 1 Sid 151 at 151, per Twisden J

'Where there is a common unit of account, to which the same denomination applies, as is the case with the word "pound" here, the debt expressed in the common unit of account must, in the absence of contrary evidence of actual intention, be discharged by payment in the currency of the place of payment.' *Auckland Corpn v Alliance Assurance Co Ltd* [1937] AC 587 at 606, PC, per cur.

POUNDBREACH

At common law poundbreach is an indictable offence, though it may perhaps be regarded as virtually obsolete. It consists in the forcible release of cattle or other animals lawfully placed in a proper pound, or in forcibly damaging or destroying the pound with that object. (2 Halsbury's Laws (4th edn) para 438)

Pound breach is an indictable offence at common law consisting in the removal of goods impounded upon a distress for rent or damage feasant from the pound against the will of the person impounding them or in forcibly releasing cattle or other animals lawfully placed in a proper pound or forcibly damaging or destroying the pound with that object. (11 Halsbury's Laws (4th edn) para 972)

Poundbreach is the retaking from the custody of the law of a chattel which has been impounded. A person cannot be guilty of poundbreach unless he knows that the goods have been impounded or otherwise secured. Where the goods have been impounded on the premises and left in their existing position under a walking possession agreement between the tenant and the distrainor, the tenant will be guilty of poundbreach if he removes the goods, but not so a stranger if he removes the goods in ignorance of the impounding. Furniture removers who in the ordinary course of their business remove goods which have already been brought outside the premises where they were impounded are not guilty of poundbreach. A person who removes impounded goods may be guilty of poundbreach even though the tenant has been given permission to use the goods temporarily. Where goods are impounded or otherwise secured, and either the tenant or a stranger knowing of the impounding does that which, if the goods were the property of or in the possession of the landlord, would as against him amount to conversion, then, it seems, the offender is guilty of poundbreach. (13 Halsbury's Laws (4th edn) para 363)

'In order to "impound or otherwise secure" the goods there must be some distinct act manifesting it. Words alone are not enough. To prove the point, it is as well to remember the offence of poundbreach. As soon as the distress is impounded, whether on or off the premises, it is in the custody of the law: and anyone who breaks the pound (as by forcing the lock) or takes the goods out of the pound, is guilty of poundbreach. He is indictable for a misdemeanour for which he can be sent to prison, and is also liable to an action which carries penal consequences, namely, for treble damages [under Stat 2 Will & M c 5 (1689), s 3]. On principle, a man is not to be held guilty of this offence unless he has a guilty mind. He must know what the goods have been impounded or otherwise secured, on or off the premises. How can a stranger be expected to know this unless there is some open and manifest act so as to show it? I am prepared to hold, therefore, that, as against strangers, goods are not validly impounded unless they are locked up in a room or otherwise secured in such a way that it is manifest that they are not to be taken away. "Walking possession" may be sufficient as against the tenant who agrees to it, but not as against a stranger who knows nothing of it.' *Abingdon RDC v O'Gorman* [1968] 3 All ER 79 at 83, CA, per Lord Denning MR

POVERTY

'It is clear from the cases which have been cited to me that a gift may be a good charitable gift, as in relief of poverty, although the recipients of the gift are not in destitution, or even on the borderline of destitution. "Poverty", it has been said, is a relative term.' *Re Central Employment Bureau for Women & Students' Careers Association Incorporated* [1942] 1 All ER 232 at 233, per Simmonds J

'Poverty, of course, does not mean destitution. It is a word of wide and somewhat indefinite import, and, perhaps, it is not unfairly paraphrased for present purposes as meaning persons who have to "go short" in the ordinary acceptation of that term, due regard being had to their status in life and so forth.' *Re Coulthurst's Will Tusts* [1951] 1 All ER 774 at 776, per Evershed MR

'"Poverty" is not confined to destitution, but extends to those who have small means and so have to "go short".' *Re Niyazi's Will Trusts*, [1978] 3 All ER 785 at 787, per Megarry V-C

POWER

'Power' is a term of art, denoting an authority vested in a person, called 'the donee' to deal with or dispose of property not his own. A power may be created by reservation or limitation; the dealing or disposition may be total or partial, and for the benefit either of the donee or of others; and the property may be real or personal. A power is distinct from the dominion that a man has over his own property.

Powers are usually classified (1) in relation to the donee's interest in the property; (2) in relation to the interest conveyed or created; and (3) in relation to the purpose for which the power was created.

Classification as to donee's interest

There are three categories in the classification in relation to the donee's interest, namely, (1) powers simply collateral, (2) powers in gross, and (3) powers appendant or appurtenant.

A power simply collateral is a bare power, given to a mere stranger who has no interest in the property to which the power relates.

A power in gross is a power given to a person having an estate or interest in the property to which the power relates but where the estate or interest created by the power is subsequent to and does not affect the estate or interest of the donee of the power. An example is a power given to a tenant for life to jointure and to appoint the estate in remainder to his children.

A power appendant is a power given to a person having an estate or interest in the property to which the power relates such that the exercise of the power overrides and affects the estate or interest of the donee of the power. An example is a power of leasing in possession.

This classification was formerly important for determining whether a donee could release the power, but is now of little value.

Classification as to interest conveyed or created

There are three heads in the classification of powers in relation to the interest conveyed or created, namely (1) common law powers, (2) statutory powers and (3) equitable powers.

Under a common law power the common law enables the donee to convey or create a legal estate. A power of attorney may confer a common law power.

A statutory power is a power conferred by statute to convey or create a legal estate. Instances are the power of a legal mortgagee to convey the estate vested in the mortgagor, and the power of a receiver of a person suffering from a mental disorder to make or concur in making all requisite dispositions for conveying or creating a legal estate in his name and on his behalf. Since 1925 the only powers over land, whether created by statute or other instrument or implied by law, and whenever created, which can operate at law are the powers vested in a legal mortgagee or in an estate owner in right of his estate, and exercisable by him or by another person in his name and on his behalf. All other powers of appointment over, or powers to convey or charge land, or any interest in land, operate only in equity.

An equitable power is a power which affects the equitable and not the legal estate or interest; no legal estate passes by the execution of the power. However, the legal owner must give effect to the equitable estate or interest of the appointee, and equity will so compel him. Where the appointee is entitled to call for the transfer of a legal estate, the legal owner must complete the appointee's title by such a transfer, as on the exercise of an ordinary power to appoint absolute interests to children in a marriage settlement by which personalty is vested in trustees.

Classification as to purpose

There are two heads in the classification of powers in relation to their purpose, namely (1) administrative or managerial powers, and (2) dispositive powers or powers of appointment.

Administrative or managerial powers are powers given to a person for the purpose of managing either his own or another person's property, such as powers of sale or leasing. The powers of management conferred by statute upon a tenant for life or the trustees of a settlement, upon trustees for sale of land, and upon personal representatives, are dealt with elsewhere. This category also includes powers to appoint to various offices, of which the power of appointing new trustees is of the most general importance.

Dispositive powers, commonly known as powers of appointment, are powers authorising a person to create or dispose of beneficial interests in property. Such powers are usually sub-divided into general powers and special powers, but this division is neither precise nor exhaustive, for there are some powers which may be general for some purposes and not for others, or may be regarded as neither general nor special, but as hybrid or intermediate powers. A classification for one purpose is not necessarily decisive or even a guide to the classification for another purpose. A power to appoint by deed or will really constitutes two distinct powers, one exercisable by each type of instrument.

General and special powers

A general power is a power that the donee may exercise in favour of such person or persons as he pleases, including himself or his executors and administrators. What appears to be a general beneficial power may, as a matter of construction, be a power given by virtue of his office which may only be exercised in a fiduciary capacity. A special power may be exercised only in favour of certain specified persons or classes, such as the donee's children or relations and friends. It is a question of construction whether a power is general or special. (36 Halsbury's Laws (4th edn) paras 801–806)

Fraud on power *See* FRAUD

Generally

'Legal powers' include the powers vested in a

chargee by way of legal mortgage or in an estate owner under which a legal estate can be transferred or created; and 'equitable powers' mean all the powers in or over land under which equitable interests or powers only can be transferred or created. (Law of Property Act 1925, s 205)

'Power' includes any right or power exercisable by virtue of the holding of shares in or debentures of a company, and any right or power to procure an issue of shares in or debentures of a company. (Finance Act 1940, s 59)

'It appears that the plaintiffs had a power of sale under their mortgage securities. If they had put the property up to auction in pursuance of such power, they would have been bound to sell it on the usual terms. The defendants wished to get possession of the property which they could not obtain by purchase under the power of sale, without paying the price of the whole estate. . . . It is . . . objected that the allegation of the plaintiffs being about to sell their interest under a power, is repugnant and inconsistent, inasmuch as conveyancers understand a power as being a very different thing from an interest in an estate. I do not think we are bound to construe this record in such a narrow sense; but that we ought to give to the word "power" its ordinary signification, and read the allegation as averring that the plaintiffs were about to sell the property by virtue of some authority which they possessed. Moreover, as the agreement includes both real and personal property, we may, if we choose to give the word its strict technical meaning, understand it to refer only to such property as might be sold under a power of sale.' *Hallewell v Morrell* (1840) 1 Man & G 367 at 387, 388, per Maule J

'A "power" is an individual personal capacity of the donee of the power to do something. That it may result in property becoming vested in him is immaterial; the general nature of the power does not make it property. The power of a person to appoint an estate to himself is, in my judgment, no more his "property" than the power to write a book or to sing a song. The exercise of any one of those three powers may result in property, but in no sense which the law recognises are they "property". In one sense no doubt they may be called the "property" of the person in whom they are vested, because every special capacity of a person may be said to be his property; but they are not "property" within the meaning of that word as used in law. . . . That being so, have the Courts of Equity ever said that such powers are "property"? . . . They have always recognised the distinction between "power" and "property".' *Re Armstrong, Ex p Gilchrist* (1886) 17 QBD 521 at 531, 532, CA, per Fry LJ

POWERS OR DUTIES

Australia [The Traffic Act 1949–1986 (Qld) s 36 provides that a person shall not obstruct or hinder any member of the police force in the exercise of his 'powers or duties' under the Act.] 'It is not necessary here to determine the difference between "powers" and "duties" as used in that section. As at present advised, I incline to the view that a duty is an express or implied obligation to do something; and a power is at least a capacity conferred by the Act to do something for the purpose of fufilling a duty under the Act.' *Patch v Ebbage, ex p Patch* [1952] St R Qd 32 at 41, per Stanley J

PRACTICABLE

'Practicable' means reasonably practicable having regard, amongst other things, to local conditions and circumstances, to the financial implications and to the current state of technical knowledge, and 'practicable means' includes the provision and maintenance of plant and the proper use thereof. (Clean Air Act 1956, s 34(1))

[The Factories Act 1937, s 47(1) (repealed; see now the Factories Act 1961, s 63) required all 'practicable' measures to be taken to protect persons employed against the inhalation of dust.] 'What does "practicable" mean? In Webster's Dictionary "practicable" is defined as "possible to be accomplished with known means or resources", and, though dealing with a different point, Lord Goddard, in *Lee v Nursery Furnishings Ltd* [[1945] 1 All ER 387], adopted a definition in the Oxford Dictionary of "capable of being carried out in action" or "feasible". It seems to me that "practicable" must impose a stricter standard than "reasonably practicable". Questions of cost might be eliminated under "practicable", but the measures must be possible in the light of current knowledge and invention.' *Adsett v K and L Steelfounders and Engineers Ltd* [1953] 1 All ER 97n at 98n, per Parker J; affirmed [1953] 2 All ER 320, CA

'What is meant by the phrase "all practicable

measures" [within the Factories Act 1937, s 47(1) (repealed; see supra)]? . . . The nature of the obligation [to protect employees from the inhalation of dust] has been epigrammatically expressed as being that the measures taken must be possible in the light of current knowledge and according to known means and resources. It is clear then, in my judgment, that the matter must be judged in the light of the state of the relevant knowledge at the time of the alleged breach. Thus the fact that at some later date some method of protection has been discovered which was not dreamed of at the date of the alleged breach, even though all the individual materials therefore were known and available, will not suffice. On the other hand, I must not be taken to be saying that the state of knowledge, or absence of knowledge, within the limited scope of a particular industry, or branch of an industry, is by any means necessarily conclusive. It must be a question of fact and of the weight of all the material evidence in any particular case to assess what was in truth known, or what ought to have been known, by the employers charged at the relevant dates.' *Richards v Highway Ironfounders (West Bromwich) Ltd* [1955] 3 All ER 205 at 209, 210, CA, per Evershed MR

[The question was whether the defendants had taken all 'practicable' measures to protect employees against the inhalation of dust under the Factories Act 1937, s 47(1) (repealed; see supra)]. 'The meaning of the word "practicable" has been discussed in several recent cases. The introduction of the word, as qualifying the measures to be taken, clearly negatives an absolute duty to protect against inhalation, since only measures which, in the light of current knowledge, are feasible can be regarded as practicable. Nevertheless, it seems to me that the words "practicable measures", as opposed to the other expression to be found in the Act "so far as is reasonably practicable", import a high duty.' *Gregson v Hick Hargreaves & Co Ltd* [1955] 3 All ER 507 at 515, 516, CA, per Parker LJ

PRACTICABLE ASSISTANCE *See* ASSISTANCE

PRACTICAL

[The plaintiff, a member of a trade union, having attained the retiring age, was entitled to a superannuation benefit, provided he was not 'practically working' at the trade.] 'It was urged before us that "practically working" necessarily involved "manual" labour. I think this is too narrow a construction. Almost every trade, if carried on to any extent, involves the employment of supervisors, who do not necessarily do manual work but are still practically working.' *McCord v Sproat* [1931] NI 119 at 126, per Moore CJ

PRACTICE—PRACTISE

'In my opinion, the phrase "practising as a solicitor" connotes a person who is a principal; it connotes a person who has clients; it connotes a person, in short, who has a practice, and the words are not apt words to describe the position of a person [in this case the managing clerk of a solicitor] who is acting as the servant of another who is a practising solicitor.' *Way v Bishop* [1928] Ch 647 at 660, CA, per Russell LJ

Australia 'The common conception of a practising barrister or solicitor is that of a legally qualified barrister and solicitor who holds himself out to the public in general as willing to act as a direct and responsible personal confidential legal adviser, and to do, and be directly responsible for, legal work generally and who has clients for whom he does legal work in that way. . . . We think that it is not fatal to that conception that the barrister and solicitor holds a position under the public service for which he is paid as such and that the only persons for whom he acts are either the Crown or State instrumentalities, or a fellow servant of the Crown. . . . There are a number of things which are marks or characteristics of a practising solicitor. The most important of these is an independence of any superior control in the conduct of his professional work and a direct responsibility to the client or person who stands in an analogous relationship to that of client; another is the extent and volume of the legal business conducted by him; of less importance is the control of an office and a staff trained and versed in legal business and also the manner in which "the other side" in a bilateral transaction commonly treats him.' *Downey v O'Connell* [1951] VLR 117 at 122, 123, per Gavan Duffy and O'Bryan JJ

Canada 'The "practice" of a profession or calling has a well-defined meaning as being the exercise of that profession or calling frequently, customarily or habitually.' *R v Mills* [1964] 1 OR 74 at 76, Ont CA, per McLennan J

New Zealand [A clause in a partnership deed between medical practitioners contained a covenant that in the event of retirement or expulsion from the partnership no partner would 'practise privately' within a certain radius and period.] 'In our opinion, the words "practising privately" mean a practice which is personal to the practitioner, which he is at liberty to carry on or discontinue as he may elect, and which he may conduct free from the control of a superior as to how and when he works and whom he examines and whom he employs, and in which he is free to fix the fees for his services and to receive them for his own benefit. These, we think, are the criteria to be applied in determining whether there is a "practising privately".' *Blakely v de Lambert* [1959] NZLR 356 at 390, CA, per cur.

PRACTICE AND PROCEDURE

[The Judicature (Procedure) Act 1894, s 1(4) (repealed; see now Part III of the Supreme Court Act 1981) provided that in matters of 'practice and procedure' every appeal from a judge should be to the Court of Appeal.] 'In my opinion, a summons for taxation [of costs] is within the words "practice and procedure" in sub-s 4, and, therefore, this Court has jurisdiction to hear this appeal.' *Re Oddy* [1895] 1 QB 392 at 394, CA, per A L Smith LJ

'The action is an action for an injunction, and the order sought by the appellant is an interlocutory order in that action; it is not in any sense a final order unless it is so treated by consent of the parties, and there is no such consent in the present case. It seems, therefore, that this summons was simply a step in the cause, a part of the machinery by which the action was to be worked out to its final determination. I am quite unable to see why such a summons should not be a matter of practice and procedure. I am far from saying that all interlocutory applications are matters of practice and procedure [within the Judicature (Procedure) Act 1894, s 1(4) (repealed; see supra)]; they certainly are not; but in my judgment such an application as the present clearly is.' *McHarg v Universal Stock Exchange Ltd* [1895] 2 QB 81 at 82, CA, per Charles J

'The "practice and procedure" mentioned in the section [the Judicature (Procedure) Act 1894, s 1(4) (repealed; see supra)] cover matters of practice and procedure in connection with a cause or matter in the High Court, and not a matter in which a county court judge is sought to be prohibited from exceeding his jurisdiction in his court. . . . The judge of the High Court before whom the application [for a prohibition] came has made an order, and the appeal against that order must go to the Divisional Court, because the appeal is not embraced by the words "practice or procedure" in the Act of 1894.' *Watson v Petts* [1899] 1 QB 54 at 55, CA, per cur.

'This is not a matter of practice and procedure within the meaning of the statute [the Judicature (Procedure) Act 1894, s 1(4) (repealed; see supra)]. Generally speaking, a matter of practice or procedure arises in the course of an action. . . . The present proceeding was an originating summons, which raised the question whether an order ought to be made upon a solicitor to pay a sum of money. It is plain that the judgment on this originating summons is final. . . . Under those circumstances it is prima facie not a matter of practice or procedure.' *Re Marchant* [1908] 1 KB 998 at 999, 1000, CA, per Vaughan Williams LJ

'The words practice and procedure [in the Judicature (Procedure) Act 1894, s 1(4) (repealed; see supra)] are now generally understood to refer to interlocutory matters arising in proceedings in the High Court and most of the decisions are, I think, consistent with that view.' *Re Jackson* [1915] 1 KB 371 at 376, DC per Rowlatt J

'[RSC] Order LIV, r 23 [revoked; see now RSC 1965, Ord 58 r 7] . . . is in the following terms: "In the King's Bench Division, except in matters of practice and procedure, the appeal from a decision of a judge at chambers shall be to a Divisional Court." . . . After an order for an injunction has been made and there is a disobedience of it followed by a committal, is that order for committal a part of the practice or procedure? In my opinion, it clearly is. I think the matter is stated sufficiently in . . . *Poyser v Minors* [(1881) 7 QBD 329 at 333], where Lush LJ . . . speaking of the word "practice" which occurs in s 32 of the County Courts Act 1856 [repealed; see now the County Courts Act 1984, s 75], which authorises county court judges, with the approval of the Lord Chancellor, to frame rules and orders for regulating the practice of the courts and forms of proceedings therein, says "'Practice' in its larger sense . . . denotes the mode of proceeding by which a legal right is enforced, as distinguished from the law which gives or defines the right, and which by means of the proceeding the court is to administer the machinery as distinguished from its product. 'Practice' and 'procedure' . . . I take to be convertible terms." The language of the section, which I read in the Act of 1856, is not exactly the same as that of the order we have here to consider, but I think the definition of "practice" which is there stated is one which can properly be applied here, and I ask myself . . . whether . . . this order for committal, is not a mode of proceeding by which a legal right is enforced. It appears to me clearly that it is so.' *Lever Brothers Ltd v Kneale & Bagnall* [1937] 2 KB 87 at 92, 93, CA, per Slesser LJ

Australia 'In *Payser v Minors* [(1881) 7 QBD 329 at 334] Lush LJ said that the term "practice" denoted the mode of proceeding to enforce a right as distinguished from the law which gives or defines the right, and that he took "practice" and "procedure", as applied to that subject, to be convertible terms. "Practice" in the common or ordinary sense of the word denotes 'the rules that make or guide the *cursus curiæ*, and regulate the proceedings in a cause within the walls or limits of the court itself' (*Attorney-General v Sillem* [(1864) 10 HLC 704 at 723, per Lord Westbury]). *Minister for Army v Parbury Henty & Co Pty Ltd* (1945) 70 CLR 459 at 489, per Latham CJ

Australia 'The words "practice" and "procedure" are commonly used in juxtaposition and, so used, have at times been regarded as a complete phrase. . . . Strictly speaking, however, practice is not completely synonymous with "procedure" but is a word of less comprehensive meaning. According to Lord Westbury LC in *Attorney-General v Sillem* (1862–1864) 10 HLC 704 at p 723, the common and ordinary sense of "practice" is "the rules that make or guide the *cursus curiæ* and regulate the proceedings of a cause within the walls of the court itself". "Procedure" has a wider meaning. "Procedure in a suit includes the whole course of practice, from the issuing of the first process by which the suitors are brought before the court to the execution of the last process on the final judgment"—per Erle CJ in *Attorney-General v Sillem* (1863) 2 H&C 431 at p 627. In the appropriate context it comprehends all steps necessary to be taken in litigation for the establishment of a right in order that the right may be judicially recognised and declared in such manner as will enable the party asserting the right legally to enjoy it; it covers not only the acts of the judges of the court, but also the acts of the officers of the court which are necessary to give effect to judicial pronouncements.' *White v White* [1947] ALR 342 at 344, per cur.

PRACTITIONER *See* MEDICAL PRACTITIONER; PRACTICE-PRACTISE

PREAMBLE

A preamble to a statute is a preliminary statement of the facts or reasons which have made the passing of a statute desirable. It is placed immediately after the title and the date of the royal assent. Preambles have also been used to introduce a particular section or group of sections. (44 Halsbury's Laws (4th edn) para 814)

PRECARIOUS

'As stated by Lord Coke, Co Litt 113 b, quoting Bracton, 222 b, the possession or *seisina* necessary for an easement must be *nec per vim nec clam nec precario*. What is precarious? That which depends, not on right, but on the will of another person.' *Burrows v Lang* [1901] 2 Ch 502 at 510, per Farwell J

PRECATORY TRUST *See* TRUST

PRECAUTION

[An allegation was made against a railway company that a house fell when the company was making its railway in consequence of its not taking due 'precautions' to prevent such an accident.] 'The word "precaution" here is little more than expanding the words "care and skill".' *Davis v London & Blackwall Rly Co* (1840) 2 Ry & Can Cas 308 at 312, per Tindal CJ

PRECINCTS *See* CLOSE

PREDECESSOR IN TITLE

The expression 'predecessor in title' in relation to a tenant or landlord means any person through whom the tenant or landlord has derived title, whether by assignment, by will, by intestacy, or by operation of law. (Landlord and Tenant Act 1927, s 25(1))

'By s 25(1) of the Act of 1927 [Landlord and

Tenant Act 1927 (supra)]: "The expression 'predecessor in title' in relation to a tenant or landlord means any person through whom the tenant or landlord has derived title, whether by assignment, by will, by intestacy, or by operation of law." It seems to me that the expression must mean the same in relation to a tenant as it does in relation to a landlord. In relation to a landlord it clearly means predecessor in title to the property, not to the business. So, also, in relation to the tenant it must mean, and its natural meaning is, predecessor in title to the property and to the legal interest which the tenant holds.' *Pasmore v Whitbread & Co Ltd* [1953] 1 All ER 361 at 363, CA, per Denning LJ (also reported in [1953] 2 QB 226 at 229)

PREDISPOSED

'The certificate starts with the implication that the man is no longer suffering from nystagmus. It then goes on to say that he is predisposed to that particular disease. I should have thought myself that the word "predisposed" in the context meant predisposed by nature and not made more susceptible as the result of a previous disease. . . . But the word "predisposed" may mean either predisposed by nature, or predisposed by reason of the previous attack. At best the word appears to me to be ambiguous.' *Astbury v William Harrison Ltd* (1942) 35 BWCC 85 at 93, CA, per Lord Greene MR

PRE-EMPTION *See* FIRST REFUSAL

PREFERENCE *See also* DISCRIMINATION; FRAUDULENT PREFERENCE

'A preference, by definition, seems to me to be the payment of one creditor to the exclusion, in whole or in part, of another and it postulates, in its very nature, a deficiency of assets to pay all creditors. A payment "with intent to prefer" or with a view to preferring necessarily, therefore, presupposes a knowledge on the part of the payer that his assets are insufficient to pay all.' *Re Sarflax Ltd* [1979] 1 All ER 529 at 537, per Oliver J

Australia 'The decision of this court in the present case depends upon the true construction of the Federal Bankruptcy Act 1924–1930 [repealed; see now the Bankruptcy Act 1966–1986 (Cth), s 122(1)]. Now that Act says nothing about the view or intention of the debtor, nor about any choice or selection by him. It simply declares that a conveyance, transfer or assignment, made within a certain time before bankruptcy, having the effect of giving the creditor a preference, shall be void. It looks to the effect of the transaction and not to the intent, or state of mind, of the debtor.' *Richards (S) & Co Ltd v Lloyd* (1933) 49 CLR 49 at 62, per Starke J

Australia [The Re-Establishment and Employment Act 1945–1986 (Cth), s 27(1) provides that 'an employer shall, in the engagement of any person for employment, engage, in preference to any other person, a person entitled to preference, unless he has reasonable and substantial cause for not doing so'.] 'In my view s 27(1) imposes a primary duty on an intending employer to engage a person entitled to preference unless he can show reasonable and substantial cause for not doing so. I think the words "in preference to any other person" are inserted to secure to the preferred person an absolute preference over all persons even though they be entitled under any other law or award to a preference (see s 24), and that those words are not intended to cut down the primary duty of the intending employer and make his duty arise only when there are contending applicants to him for a particular engagement. In my view, an employer who engages a non-preferred person does so at his peril, i.e. he has the onus cast on him of proving the prescribed excuse. . . . It was argued that the other sub-section of s 27 shows in effect that the words "in preference to any other person" mean "in preference to any other applicant". . . . In my view the preference accorded in s 27(1) is over all other persons, and not only over all other applicants.' *Retallack v Hodda, ex p Hodda* [1947] St R Qd 105 at 111, 112, per Philp J

PREFERENCE DIVIDEND *See* DIVIDEND

PREFERENCE SHARES *See* SHARES

PREFERMENT *See also* CATHEDRAL

'Preferment' includes an archbishopric, a bishopric, archdeaconry, dignity or office in a cathedral or collegiate church, and a benefice, and every curacy, lectureship, readership, chaplaincy, office or place which requires the discharge of any spiritual duty. (Ecclesiastical Jurisdiction Measure 1963, s 66)

PREMATURE

Canada '"Premature" as used in clause (b) of the Planning Act 1955 (Ont) c 61, s 26(4) (now RSO 1980, c 379, s 28(4)(b))] means that a proposed subdivision may be premature in the sense that it is presented too soon for any real need or demand for housing of the type contemplated or is perhaps being put forward before finalisation of a pending official plan as defined by the Act or before final determination of zoning provision under current consideration in a municipality.' *Re Highbury Estates and Highbury Developments Ltd* [1957] OWN 198 at 202, Ont CA, per Aylesworth JA; affirmed 12 DLR (2d) 145, SCC

PREMISES *See also* BUSINESS PREMISES; DOMESTIC PREMISES; OFFICE PREMISES; RAILWAY; SHOP

'Premises', in relation to any school, includes any detached playing fields, but except where otherwise expressly provided, does not include a teacher's dwelling-house. (Education Act 1944, s 114(1))

'Premises' includes any land, whether covered by buildings or not, including any place underground and any land covered by water. (Radioactive Substances Act 1960, s 19(1))

'Premises' includes any place. (Private Places of Entertainment (Licensing) Act 1967, s 7)

'Premises' includes any place and any stall, vehicle, ship or aircraft. (Trade Descriptions Act 1968, s 39(1))

'Premises' includes any place and, in particular, includes—(a) any vehicle, vessel, aircraft or hovercraft, (b) any installation on land (including the foreshore and other land intermittently covered by water), any offshore installation, and any other installation (whether floating, or resting on the seabed or the subsoil thereof, or resting on other land covered with water or the subsoil thereof), and (c) any tent or movable structure. (Heath and Safety at Work etc Act 1974, s 53(1))

'Premises' means a building or part of a building, and any forecourt, yard or place of storage used in connection with a building or part of a building, and includes, in relation to dairies and dairy farms, and the trade of diaryman or dairy farmer, any land other than buildings. (Food Act 1984, s 132(1))

[The Leasehold Reform Act 1967, s 3(6) deals with separate tenancies, with the same landlord and the same tenant, of two or more parts of a house, or a house or part of it and land or other 'premises' occupied therewith.] 'The word "premises" in s 3(6) is not used in a wide sense, such as to include another house. It is used in a narrow sense to denote a garage or outbuilding, or such like, ancillary to the house. That is the meaning of "premises" when used in the combined phrase "house and premises".' *Wolf v Crutchley* [1971] 1 All ER 520 at 521, CA, per Lord Denning MR

'"Premises" is an ordinary word of the English language which takes colour and content from the context in which it is used. . . . It has, in my opinion, no recognised and established primary meaning. Frequently it is used in relation to structures of one kind or another. No one would, I think, in the ordinary use of the English language refer to ordinary use of the English language refer to farm land as "premises" though farm buildings may often be referred to as "farm premises".' *Maunsell v Olins* [1975] 1 All ER 16 at 19, HL, per Viscount Dilhorne

Land and buildings

'The word "premises" is commonly used as comprising land and houses and other matters.' *Doe d Hemming v Willetts* (1849) 7 CB 709 at 715, per Wilde CJ

[A covenant in a lease referred to 'the demised premises'. Held, that this included the demised building as altered after the date of the lease.] 'The word "premises" in the lease is, I think, a vague, loose term, meaning the subject-matter of the demise, even though under the terms of the lease it might be subsequently altered.' *Horner v Franklin* [1904] 2 KB 877 at 881, 882, per Darling J; affirmed on other grounds [1905] 1 KB 479, CA

'I can see no reason why a room separately occupied should cease to be "premises" because it is contained within the structure of a larger building which is also "premises". My view is that expressed in Fraser's Representation of the People Acts, 2nd edn, where it is said (p 50) that "the words 'any land or premises' are very wide, and will include any piece of land or any kind of structure or building of whatsoever kind, or any part thereof, provided it is capable of being 'occupied'".' *Frost v*

Caslon, Frost v Wilkins [1929] 2 KB 138 at 147, CA, per Scrutton LJ

'When we look at s 17 [of the Landlord and Tenant Act 1927] the definition section, and we find the reference to "any premises held under a lease", I see no sufficient reason for supposing that the legislature did not there include not merely the actual buildings in which a trade is carried on, but also the land surrounding them, the easements granted as appurtenant to them, and any other incorporeal hereditaments which may form part of the premises in the strict legal sense of the term which are the subject-matter of the habendum.' *Whitley v Stumbles* [1930] AC 544 at 547, per Lord Hailsham

' "Premises" is, no doubt, a word which is capable of many meanings. How it originally became applied to property is, I think, generally known. It was from the habit of conveyancers when they were drawing deeds of conveyance referring to property and speaking of "parcels". They set out the parcels in the early part of the deed, and later they would refer to "the said premises", meaning strictly that which had gone before, and gradually by common acceptance "premises" became applied, as it generally is now, to houses, land, shops, or whatever it may be, so that the word has come to mean generally real property of one sort or another.' *Gardiner v Sevenoaks RDC* [1950] 2 All ER 84 at 85, per Lord Goddard CJ

'There is no definition of the word "premises" in the Act [Water Act 1945], but it is stated in s 59 that it includes land. The fact that it does so does not mean that it is defined as land. The word "premises" as used in the Act is obviously not a term of art: it means some form of property used as domestic premises; and . . . before the undertakers can be required to provide water to any particular premises there must be a site—some degree of permanency.' *West Mersea Urban District Council v Fraser* [1950] 2 KB 119 at 123, 124, per Lord Goddard CJ

'The word "premises" is not defined in the Act [Landlord and Tenant Act 1954]. Its strict legal meaning is the subject-matter of the habendum in a lease, and it would cover any sort of property of which a lease is granted; but no doubt the word is used sometimes in a popular sense which is considerably more restricted, in the sense of buildings, or buildings with land immediately adjoining them, and I do not think that in the popular sense anybody would call some gallops on a downland, with no building on or near them, "premises".' [It was held, however, that 'premises' in s 23(1) of the Act was not to be construed in this popular sense, and that the gallops in question were 'premises' within the section.] *Bracey v Read* [1962] 3 All ER 472 at 475, per Cross J; also reported in [1963] Ch 88 at 92

[The Petroleum (Consolidation) Act 1928, s 2 provided that a local authority might attach to any petroleum-spirit licence such conditions as they thought expedient as to the mode of storage and the nature and situation of the 'premises' in which the petroleum-spirit was to be stored.] 'In the context of this legislation, I see no basis whatsoever for extending the meaning of the word "premises" beyond its ordinary and natural meaning, namely, that it connotes land or buildings on land.' *Grandi v Milburn* [1966] 2 All ER 816 at 821, per James J

[The Copyright Act 1956, s 12(7) (repealed) afforded protection from infringement of copyright in cases (inter alia) where sound recordings were caused to be heard in public at any 'premises' where persons reside or sleep as part of the amenities provided exclusively or mainly for such residents, etc.] 'Counsel for the plaintiffs has put his submissions under a number of headings. The first centres on the words "at any premises". He says that in this case one cannot take the camp [a holiday camp], as a whole as being "premises" at which a sound recording is caused to be heard but that here there are a number of different premises the chalets, the amenity hall, and so on which are quite separate. It is as though there was a village of small houses or cottages with a central inn or public-house where the dwellers in the village could resort for the purpose of getting meals, dancing, listening to music, and so on. On the other hand, it is said that that is not the right way of looking at it, and that there is no distinction between this camp and a seaside hotel standing in its own grounds. It really makes no difference that the bedrooms instead of being vertically above the reception rooms, the dining-room, the bar, and so on are spread about the grounds in the form of bungalows. Of those two contentions I myself prefer the second. I cannot draw any distinction for the purpose of the application of the subsection between this camp and a seaside hotel. In my judgment the camp as a whole can properly be regarded as the premises.' *Phonographic Performance Ltd v Pontin's Ltd* [1967] 3 All ER 736 at 738, per Cross J

'In my judgment, the only true inference to be drawn from the facts is plainly this, that, when the respondent first occupied the caravan on this piece of land ten years ago, the appellant agreed that he might live and reside in the caravan on that land. That is a clear inference because he has been allowed by the appellant to do so continuously ever since. The premises on which he was allowed to reside are the composite unit of the caravan and the land on which it stands. Looked at in that way, the fact that the caravan is not attached to the land so as to become part of the realty is quite unimportant. The land and caravan together are the premises in which the respondent resided with the agreement of the appellant.' *Norton v Knowles* [1967] 3 All ER 1061 at 1063, per Salmon LJ

'It seems to me that it is quite clear that where "premises" is used in the Act of 1964 [Licensing Act], though it is not defined, it clearly refers to "buildings".' *R v Hastings Licensing Justices* [1968] 2 All ER 270 at 271, per Lord Parker CJ

Australia 'It [i.e. the word 'premises'] includes at common law houses or lands, the definition being probably derived from reference to lands or houses, or both, recited in deeds and grants as being sold or conveyed, and afterwards referred to in the conveyance or deed of grant as "premises".' *Mowling v Hawthorn JJ* (1891) 17 VLR 150 at 154, per Higinbotham CJ

Australia [The Police Act (Amendment) Act 1902 (WA), s 2 [see now Police Act 1892–1986, s 76B] relates to charges against a person having gold in his possession on any premises of which he is the tenant or occupier.] 'I am inclined to think that the interpretation contended for by Mr Curran is correct, that "premises" means something in the nature of a building or enclosure; it may be a bush shed or some sort of restricted area; and that in this case the place where the articles were found is not the type of place contemplated by the 1902 Act. I arrive at that conclusion not only because of the word "premises" but because of the presence of the words . . . "tenant or occupier". I think there must necessarily be something definite and quasi-continuous about the tenancy or occupation, and it seems a misuse of words to talk about an unknown uninhabited and undefined spot in the bush being the subject of a tenancy or occupation in the sense those words are used.' *Egan & Egan v Kevan* (1941) 44 WALR 14 at 19, per Dwyer J

Australia [The appellant had been leased certain vacant land by the respondent, and upon ejectment action being brought against him, contended that such land was prescribed 'premises' within the meaning of the Landlord and Tenant (Amendment) Act 1948–1986 (NSW), s 8.] 'The word "premises" is no doubt a vague one but in legislation of this sort there are great advantages in a test of its application which is objective and consists in a readily ascertainable physical fact. Having regard to the history of the provision and the dictionary meaning of the word "premises", I think that we should adhere to the rule laid down that bare land without buildings, if let for the purpose of occupation as bare land, does not constitute premises. If land is let upon terms that the tenant shall or may erect buildings which are not removable by him but will pass with the freehold, then I should say that the land and buildings when erected would form premises.' *Turner v York Motors Pty Ltd* (1951) 85 CLR 55 at 75, per Dixon J

New Zealand 'The words "the 'premises' of a man engaged in business" signify the place in which he carries on his business. Such premises may be wholly buildings, as in the case of many shopkeepers; or wholly land, as in the case of a timber-yard; or partly buildings and partly land, as in the case of a timber-yard used in conjunction with a large joinery business; or, more aptly as applied to the present case, large stables erected upon land part of which is used as a paddock. No one, I venture to think, would refer to the stock of a farmer or grazier as stock "in, or at, or upon his premises". These words appear to me to have been intentionally used to cover stock which are not depastured upon a farm or station.' *Re Alloway* [1916] NZLR 433 at 443, 444, per Edwards J; also reported [1916] GLR 327 at 331

New Zealand [The Tenancy Act 1948 (NZ), s 24(1)(e) (repealed: see now the Residential Tenancies Act 1986, s 51) provided that an order for the recovery of possession of any dwelling-house or urban property, or for the ejectment of a tenant, might be made (h) in the case of an urban property, where the 'premises' were reasonably required by the landlord for his own occupation; or (m) where the 'premises' were reasonably required by the landlord for demolition or reconstruction or for removal to another site.] 'In para (m) "premises" can mean only the *buildings* on the land, since it is clear that only buildings can be demolished or reconstructed. . . . In para (h), however, "premises" must mean the land with any buildings thereon, since para (h) can undoubtedly have reference to urban land upon which no buildings are erected of which possession is sought. . . . "Premises"—i.e. land and the buildings upon it—may be required by the landlord for his own occupation when it is the intention of that landlord, upon obtaining possession, to demolish or reconstruct the "premises"—i.e. the buildings situate upon the land.' *McKenna v Porter Motors Ltd* [1955] NZLR 832 at 847, CA, per cur.

Things before mentioned

'The word premises in the first clause [of a will] meant the several things before mentioned; and according to the same sense in the last clause, it comprehends all that was then before described.' *Doe d Biddulph v Meakin* (1801) 1 East 456 at 459, per Lawrence J

[A testator by his will devised and bequeathed all his freehold messuage or tenement, together with the household effects and furniture therein, to his wife, and after her decease he devised and bequeathed the same messuage or tenement and 'premises' to his son.] 'The . . . question regards the bequest of the furniture in the house in Cavendish Square. My opinion is, that the word premises is sufficient to comprehend every thing which was described in the prior part of the clause. That term in its strict sense refers to what has been previously mentioned, without regard to the nature of the thing; and though it is in popular language often used to denote particularly land and houses, there is no reason for taking it in that restricted sense here.' *Sanford v Irby* (1825) 4 LJOS Ch 23 at 28, per Lord Gifford MR

'The word "premises", although in popular language it is applied to buildings, in legal language means, the subject or thing previously expressed.' *Beacon Life & Fire Assurance Co v Gibb* (1862) 1 Moo PCCNS 73 at 97–99, PC, per cur.

'As stated in Sheppard's Touchstone, 7th edn, p 74 . . . the word "premises" may sometimes mean all the foreparts of the deed antecedent to the habendum, that is, the *premissa* or preceding parts of the deed. . . . Or it may mean the thing demised or granted by the deed. The meaning of the word must depend on the language actually employed in the deed and the relevant context.' *County Hotel & Wine Co Ltd v London & North Western Rly Co* [1918] 2 KB 251 at 257, per McCardie J; on appeal [1919] 2 KB 29, CA; [1921] 1 AC 85

PREMIUM *See also* FINE

Insurance

The consideration required of an assured for any form of insurance is a money payment universally referred to as a premium. There may be a single lump sum premium, but more commonly the premium is payable either at specified intervals, as in the case of life insurance, or as consideration for successive renewals of the policy. The amount of the premium appropriate to the risk involved is essentially a matter for the insurers, as experts in the business, to assess, but their assessment is not binding unless the assured prospectively or retrospectively agrees that it should be so. In making their assessment insurers normally work on the basis of an average of their previous experience of comparable risks, increasing or perhaps reducing the figure according to their estimate as to whether the graph of the risk is tending or likely to rise or fall. The rate of premium in fact charged may give rise to important inferences. Thus the materiality of a representation which has been made may be inferred from a reduced rate of premium being charged. Similarly, ignorance on the part of the insurers of some matter supposed to be well known may be inferred if they charge no more than the ordinary rate of premium, while an exceptionally high rate of premium may be indicative of their acceptance of the risk as hazardous without requiring disclosure of the precise facts making it so. (25 Halsbury's Laws (4th edn) para 458)

'"Premium" in the context of insurance law is a term of art. It means a sum of money paid by an assured to an insurer in consideration of his indemnifying the assured for loss sustained in consequence of the risk insured against.' *Swain v Law Society* [1982] 2 All ER 827 at 832, HL, per Lord Diplock

Rent

'Premium' includes (1) any fine or other like sum, (2) any other pecuniary consideration in addition to rent, and (3) any sum paid by way of a deposit, other than one which does not exceed one-sixth of the annual rent and is reasonable in relation to the potential liability in respect of which it is paid. 'Premium' has been judicially defined as a cash payment made to the lessor, and representing, or supposed to represent, the capital value of the difference between the actual rent and the best rent that might otherwise be obtained. It is now settled, however, that a payment made to a third person to the order of the landlord is a premium for these purposes. 'Pecuniary consideration' includes any consideration sounding or expressed in terms of money by which there is a benefit to the landlord or a detriment to the tenant; the particular means adopted of passing the consideration is not significant. It would seem that a requirement by a landlord that a tenant should contribute to repairs for which the tenant is not responsible or that he should buy the goodwill of a business would constitute a premium. It is sometimes difficult to distinguish between a payment of a premium and a payment of rent in advance. Each case must be decided on its own facts and the substance of the transaction must be regarded, not the name given to the payment. (27 Halsbury's Laws (4th edn) para 759)

' "Premium" includes—
(a) any fine or other like sum;
(b) any other pecuniary consideration in addition to rent; and
(c) any sum paid by way of a deposit, other than one which does not exceed one-sixth of the annual rent and is reasonable in relation to the potential liability in respect of which it is paid.

(Rent Act 1977, s 128, as substituted by the Housing Act 1980, s 79)

'There is no magic in the use of the word "premium"; it merely means a lump sum paid as a consideration for the acquisition of the lease. So also, if the premium or lump sum is paid by instalments spread over the term of the lease, it still remains of a capital nature; it may be very difficult as a practical matter in a particular case to ascertain whether, on the true construction of the document, such periodical payments are rent or payment of a lump sum by instalments, but once that question has been answered the distinction is clear. If it is a premium, that is to say, a lump sum payable by instalments it is capital. If it is rent or royalty it is an outgoing deductible for the purposes of tax.' *Regent Oil Co Ltd v Strick* [1965] 3 All ER 174 at 197, HL, per Lord Upjohn

[The Protection of Depositors Act 1963, s 26(1) defines 'deposit' to mean (with certain exceptions) a loan of money at interest, or repayable at a 'premium'.] 'We have to construe the word "premium" as it appears in s 26 of the Act of 1963. It has a wide and imprecise meaning. This court cannot derive any assistance from other cases in which the word has been construed in the sense in which it appears in other Acts. In considering the sense in which it is used in the Act of 1963 it is perhaps helpful to look at the short title to the Act which is: "An Act to penalise fraudulent inducements to invest on deposit. . .'. Ought we to give the word "premium" the very narrow meaning for which counsel for the appellant contends, namely, ought we to confine it to the payment of some ascertained capital sum on the repayment of the loan; or ought we to give it a more liberal and wider meaning? This court has no doubt particularly having regard to the manifest purpose of the Act, that the word "premium" truly has a much wider meaning than that contended for on behalf of the appellant. Any advertisement that invites the deposit of money as a loan on the basis that if one deposits £x one will in fact receive in return not £x but £$x+y$, is an invitation within the meaning of this Act to make a deposit or a loan repayable at a premium.' *R v Delmayne* [1969] 2 All ER 980 at 983, CA, per cur.

' "Premium" in the context of insurance law is a term of art. It means a sum of money paid by an assured to an insurer in consideration of his indemnifying the assured for loss sustained in consequence of the risk insured against.' *Swain v Law Society* [1982] 2 All ER 827 at 832, HL, per Lord Diplock

PRE-PACKED

'Pre-packed' means made up in advance ready for retail sale in or on a container. (Weights and Measures Act 1985, s 94(1))

PREPARATION

'Preparation', in relation to food, includes manufacture and any form of treatment, and 'preparation for sale' includes packaging; and 'prepare' and 'prepare for sale' shall be construed accordingly. (Food Act 1984, s 132(1))

Australia [The Narcotic and Psychotropic Drugs Act 1934 (SA), s 5(2) provides that a person who produces, 'prepares' or manufacturers a drug to which the Act applies shall be guilty of an indictable offence.] 'Prepare is a word in common use and means "to make ready", or "to bring into proper state for use by some special or technical process", although it can also mean "to manufacture, to make up or compound": Shorter Oxford English Dictionary. The process of drying may be called special even if it is not technical, and it conforms to ordinary usage to say that a person who dries, e.g. fish or fruit or coffee to bring it into a state in which it is fit for consumption in a particular way takes part in its preparation. Thus in the ordinary sense of the word, one who dries Indian hemp, in order to make it fit for use, "prepares" it.' *Calabria v R* (1983) 151 CLR 670 at 675, per cur.

PREROGATIVE

The royal prerogative may be defined as being that pre-eminence which the Sovereign enjoys over and above all other persons by virtue of the common law, but out of its ordinary course, in right of her regal dignity, and comprehends all the special dignities, liberties, privileges, powers, and royalties allowed by the common law to the Crown of England.

The prerogative is thus created and limited by the common law, and the Sovereign can claim no prerogatives except such as the law allows, nor such as are contrary to Magna Carta, or any other statute, or to the liberties of the subject.

The courts have jurisdiction, therefore, to inquire into the existence or extent of any alleged prerogative, it being a maxim of the common law that the King ought to be under no man, but under God and the law, because the law makes the King. If any prerogative is disputed, the courts must decide the question whether or not it exists in the same way as they decide any other question of law. If a prerogative is clearly established, they must take the same judicial notice of it as they take of any other rule of law. (8 Halsbury's Laws (4th edn) paras 889, 890)

'The prerogative is defined by a learned constitutional writer as "The residue of discretionary or arbitrary authority which at any given time is legally left in the hands of the Crown". Inasmuch as the Crown is a party to every Act of Parliament it is logical enough to consider that when the Act deals with something which before the Act could be effected by the prerogative, and specially empowers the Crown to do the same thing, but subject to conditions, the Crown assents to that, and by that Act, to the prerogative being curtailed.' *A-G v De Keyser's Royal Hotel Ltd* [1920] AC 508 at 526, per Lord Dunedin

'Starting with Blackstone Commentaries (1 Bl Com (15th edn) 251) and Chitty A Treatise on the Law of the Prerogatives of the Crown (1820), pp 6–7, they [the authorities] are at one in stating that, within the sphere of its prerogative powers, the Crown has an absolute discretion. In more recent times the best known definition of the prerogative is that given in Dicey Introduction to the Study of the Law of the Constitution (8th edn, 1915), p 421, which is as follows: "The prerogative is the name for the remaining portion of the Crown's original authority, and is therefore, as already pointed out, the name for the residue of discretionary power left at any moment in the hands of the Crown, whether such power be in fact exercised by the King himself or by his Ministers."' *Council of Civil Service Unions v Minister for Civil Service* [1984] 3 All ER 935 at 941, HL, per Lord Fraser of Tullybelton

PRESCRIBE

'The Registrar contends that the word "prescribe" in the first line of this clause [in an agreement for the distribution and sale of motor vehicles] bears its ordinary natural meaning recorded in the Concise Oxford English Dictionary as being: "To lay down or impose authoritatively", or in the Shorter Oxford English Dictionary as being: "To lay down as a rule or direction to be followed", and that the expression "the retail prices of his products" means the prices at which his products shall be sold by retail. Accordingly, the provision that "Each signatory shall prescribe and may at any time vary as he shall in his own unfettered discretion decide the retail prices of his products . . ." places on each signatory the obligation to lay down authoritatively (i.e. as a rule or direction to be followed) prices at which his products shall be sold by retail, but reserves to him the liberty from time to time to lay down authoritatively other prices in their stead; that is to say, he is placed under an obligation when selling his products to the trade for re-sale to sell them subject to a condition that they may only be re-sold retail at prices fixed by him. This seems to us to be the plain meaning of the words and it is, in our view, confirmed by a detailed examination of the language of the agreement as a whole.' *Re The Motor Vehicles Distribution Scheme Agreement* [1961] 1 All ER 161 at 174, RPC, per cur.

PRESCRIPTION

An easement may be established by a court of law sanctioning and upholding under the doctrine of prescription a claim to the right founded upon its enjoyment. Inasmuch as the court's sanction is given solely upon the presumption that the easement has in fact validly existed before the claim is made, it is not strictly accurate to regard the doctrine of prescription as a mode of creating an easement; it is rather a mode of establishing an easement.

A title may be established by prescription in any one of three ways: first, prescription at common law; secondly, prescription under the doctrine of a lost modern grant; and thirdly, prescription as governed by the provisions of the Prescription Act 1832.

Prescription at common law is based upon a presumed grant which the law assumed to have been made prior to 1189, the first year of the reign of Richard I. By the ancient rule of the common law, enjoyment of an easement has to be proved from time 'whereof the memory of man runneth not to the contrary', that is to say, during legal memory or since the commencement of the reign of Richard I. (14 Halsbury's Laws (4th edn) paras 72, 73, 79)

PRESENCE *See* IN THE PRESENCE OF

PRESENT

[A repealed Act enacted that the provisions of the Act should take effect in a parish, if, at a meeting of ratepayers, it should be so determined by a majority consisting of two-thirds of the votes of the ratepayers 'present' at such meeting.] 'All are present who are in the room.' *Eynsham Case* (1849) 12 QB 398n at 400n, per Erle J

'When articles say that a quorum is to consist of so many members "present" I think the word has to be given the meaning of present in person. That is the primary meaning of the word, and if a second and wider meaning is desired, this must be provided for expressly.' *Harris (M) Ltd, Petitioners* 1956 SLT 367 at 368, 369, per Lord Sorn

PRESENT AGAIN

New Zealand 'To my mind, the answer "Present Again" marked on a cheque conveys the meaning, inter alia, that the customer has insufficient credit in his account to meet the cheque on original presentation. . . . Whatever the answer "Present Again" may imply as to prospects of future or later payment, it surely imports the clear intimation that the maker of the cheque so answered has defaulted as to time for performance of the legal and ethical obligation to provide for payment by the bank on presentation of a cheque issued for immediate payment. Written words which convey such meaning must, to my mind, tend to lower a person in the estimation of right-minded members of society generally. Accordingly, I hold that the answers made "Present Again" are as a matter of law reasonably capable of conveying a defamatory meaning.' *Baker v Australia and New Zealand Bank Ltd* [1958] NZLR 907 at 910, 911, per Shorland J

PRESENTATION

Of document

[A document stated that a certain firm held at the disposal of the plaintiff a quantity of pig-iron, which the firm would deliver to his order, free of all charge, into boats, on the 'presentation' of the document, duly indorsed.] 'I am of opinion that the word "presentation" in that document means, that, before the iron, or any part of it, is to be delivered to the person by whom it is presented, it must be handed over into keeping and control of the persons who are to deliver the iron.' *Bartlett v Holmes* (1853) 13 CB 630 at 637, per Jervis CJ

[The question was whether a complaint of unfair dismissal had been 'presented' within time under the Employment Protection (Consolidation) Act 1978, s 67(2).] 'The Shorter Oxford English Dictionary defines "present" as "to deliver a document to the proper quarter for acceptance" or "to bring a thing before or into the presence of a person or put it into his hands for acceptance". And Donaldson P in *Hammond v Haigh Castle & Co Ltd* [[1973] 2 All ER 289] said: "Although it is immaterial to the present appeal, we have been asked to express our opinion on the meaning of the word 'presented'. In our judgment, a claim is presented to a tribunal when it is received by the tribunal, whether or not it is dealt with immediately on receipt. Thus a claim delivered to the tribunal office by post on a Saturday is presented on that day, even if not registered before the following Monday. A claim is not, however, presented by the act of posting it addressed to the tribunal." In my opinion it is difficult to say that presentation requires any action on the part of the body to which presentation is made. Delivery of a document to the proper quarter does not require action on the part of anybody at that proper quarter.' *Swainston v Hetton Victory Club Ltd* [1983] 1 All ER 1179 at 1184, CA, per Waller LJ

Of petition

I must decide that a petition is presented when it is filed with the court.' *Alston v Alston* [1946] P 203 at 204, 205, per Willmer J

To benefice

'Presentation' includes nomination and any other manner of filling vacant benefices except collation, and 'present' shall be construed accordingly. (Reorganisation Areas Measure 1944, s 53; Pastoral Reorganisation Measure 1949, s 19)

PRESENTLY ENTITLED

Australia 'The words "presently entitled to a share of the income" refer to a right to income "presently" existing—i.e. a right of such a kind that a beneficiary may demand payment of the income from the trustee. . . . A beneficiary who has a vested right to income . . . but who may never receive any payment by reason of such right, is entitled to income, but cannot be said to be "presently entitled" as distinct from merely entitled.' *Federal Comr of Taxation v Whiting* (1943) 68 CLR 199 at 215, 216, per Latham CJ and Williams J

'My brother Rich thought it "reasonably plain that in the case of a beneficiary who is *sui juris* all that is necessary . . . is that he should be presently entitled to income of the estate. By this . . . is meant entitled for an interest in possession as contrasted with an interest in expectancy. It is not necessary that he should have received his share of the income." The last mentioned proposition is true enough, but a beneficiary is not, I think, presently entitled to income unless it can be established that there is income which he is presently entitled to receive: that he is entitled to obtain payment thereof from the trustee.' Ibid at 219, per Starke J

PRESSURE *See* DURESS

PRESUMPTION

Certain presumptions are peculiar to criminal proceedings, while others, although common to both civil and criminal proceedings, are more commonly applied in the latter.

Presumptions may be classified as (1) conclusive and irrebuttable presumptions of law, (2) rebuttable presumptions of law, that is inference recognised by law, which stand until the contrary is proved, and (3) so-called presumptions of fact, which are ordinary inferences of fact, having no special significance in law.

There are three irrebuttable presumptions of law which are peculiar to the criminal law, namely that a child under the age of ten is incapable of committing an offence; that a boy under the age of fourteen is incapable of committing rape; and, in a law relating to homicide, that if death does not follow until after the expiration of a year and a day from the date when the injury was inflicted it is attributable to some other cause. These presumptions are conclusive in favour of the defendant.

Although classed as presumptions, these exonerating principles may be said to belong rather to the substantive law of crime, than to the law of evidence. There is no irrebuttable presumption of law in criminal cases which is conclusive against the defendant.

A rebuttable presumption of law is one which at first sight leads to a decision on a particular issue in favour of the party who establishes it or relies upon it. Such a presumption may be rebutted. Where a presumption operates against a defendant in a criminal trial its effect is that in the absence of some evidence giving rise to a reasonable doubt as to the presumed fact, a jury may regard that fact as established. The presumption of sanity may be rebutted by proof on a balance of probabilities; the presumption of innocence can only be rebutted by proof beyond a reasonable doubt of the guilt of a defendant.

The presumption that a child between the ages of ten and fourteen years is incapable of forming a criminal intention is peculiar to the criminal law. In offences of bigamy, an actual marriage must be proved, for although a presumption of marriage from evidence of reputation and cohabitation is common both to criminal and civil proceedings, it does not apply to bigamy. If the celebration of the first marriage is proved, there is a presumption in favour of the validity of the marriage; but there is no such presumption in the case of foreign marriages. There is no presumption that the first husband or wife was alive at the date of the second or subsequent marriage; this must be proved. The presumption that everything has been done according to due form is common to both criminal and civil proceedings.

There are certain statutory presumptions which are peculiar to the criminal law, for example the presumption of innocence, on a charge of bigamy, from the fact that the other party to the marriage has been continuously absent for seven years before the subsequent marriage and was not known by the defendant to be living within that time. There are also statutory presumptions of guilt from the possession of public stores; from acting or behaving as the master or mistress of a disorderly house; and from living with, or being habitually in the company of a prostitute, or exercising control, direction or influence over her movements in a way which shows that one is aiding, abetting or compelling her prostitution. (11 Halsbury's Laws (4th edn) paras 401–404)

'There are presumptions of several sorts, some are violent, and some probable: A violent presumption, that such a man hath done such a fact, must be when a fact is done, and no other can be thought of to have done it: As if a man be kill'd in a room, and another man comes out of the room with a sword bloody in his hand, and no body else was in the room. Here is a plain fact done, and tho' no body can swear they saw this man do the fact, that he killed him, yet from this evidence there is a very strong proof. But a probable presumption alone is no proof to rely upon; where indeed there is some proof of witness positive, and the presumption is probable that is added thereto, it may be a good fortifying evidence, but it signifies very little of itself for a foundation.' *Bath & Mountague's Case* (1693) 3 Cas in Ch 55 at 105, per Holt CJ

Of fact

Presumptions of fact are inferences logically drawn from one fact as to the existence of other facts. There is no obligation upon a tribunal of fact to draw such inferences, and presumptions of fact are rebuttable by evidence to the contrary. In the law of negligence the doctrine of res ipsa loquitur is a particular application of the effect of inferences of fact. (17 Halsbury's Laws (4th edn) para 111)

United States 'Presumption' or 'presumed' means that the trier of fact must find the existence of the fact presumed unless and until evidence is introduced which would support a finding of its non-existence. (Uniform Commercial Code 1978, s 1–201(31))

Of innocence

'The ordinary rule is that a man is not held guilty of fault unless fault is established and found by the court. This rule, which is sometimes described as the presumption of innocence, is no doubt peculiarly important in criminal cases or matters, but it is also true in civil disputes.' *Joseph Constantine SS Line Ltd v Imperial Smelting Corpn Ltd* [1942] AC 154 at 192, per Lord Wright

Of law

Presumptions of law may be either irrebuttable, so that no evidence to the contrary may be given, or rebuttable. A rebuttable presumption of law is a legal rule to be applied by the court in the absence of conflicting evidence. Where two inconsistent rebuttable presumptions arise they neutralise each other, and the issue must be decided upon the evidence actually adduced.

The classification of many presumptions is uncertain. In some cases the same rule has, at different periods in its history, been treated as a presumption of fact, a rebuttable presumption of law, an irrebuttable presumption, or a rule of substantive law. (17 Halsbury's Laws (4th edn) para 12)

PRESUMPTIVE

[A testator by his will empowered his trustees to apply in or towards the advancement in life of each child of the testator a sum not exceeding £500 of his or her 'presumptive share'.] 'The cases cited shew that, in the opinion of the learned judges who decided them, the word "advancement" if standing by itself without the addition of larger words, has a narrow and restricted meaning. Here I have the words "advancement in life" alone, and there is further the limitation that the advance is not to exceed "£500 of his or her presumptive share". It seems to me that the word "presumptive" refers to the period when the share is not vested. . . . Looking at it as a matter of construction, I am of opinion that the word "presumptive", unless it is to be neglected altogether, limits the power of advancement to the time at which the share is presumptive.'

Molyneux v Fletcher [1898] 1 QB 648 at 653, per Kennedy J

PRETENCE

'The word "pretence" in itself implies that something has been done with a false and sinister design.' *R v King* (1844) 1 Cox CC 36 at 37, per Tindal CJ

'A pretender is one who claims to be what is not. A pretence involves a claim that something or somebody exists which or who does not exist.' *R v Kemp* [1964] 1 All ER 649 at 653, CCA, per Paull J

PREVALENT

New Zealand [The Wildlife Act 1953, s 61(1) provides that in any prosecution for an offence against the Act or against any regulations under the Act, proof that any person found in any area where any species of wildlife is usually 'prevalent' had with him or under his control any firearm, net, trap, decoy, or other instrument or device capable of being used for the purpose of hunting or killing any such species shall be evidence from which the Court may infer that that person was in pursuit of that species.] 'The word "prevalent" is used in the subsection in the sense of having a presence which can be established in the area under review, and . . . any necessary protection to hunters or others in regard to inferences which might be drawn is afforded by the qualification of the word "prevalent" by the preceding word "usually".' *Kingi v Kehoe* [1966] NZLR 788 at 789, per Woodhouse J

PREVENTION

'"Preventing" delivery, means in my view, rendering delivery impossible; and "hindering" delivery means something less than this, namely rendering delivery more or less difficult, but not impossible.' *Tennants (Lancashire) Ltd v Wilson (CS) & Co Ltd* [1917] AC 495 at 518, per Lord Atkinson

'If upon ordinary occasions I have three alternative means of reaching this building, and on a particular occasion I find that two of such means have been suddenly suspended, by reason of a sympathetic strike, or for some other cause, and the third is so overcrowded as to preclude my using it, I should say that those facts would amount to a hindrance of my arrival here; none the less so, if by reason of some gratuitous lift in a motor car I ultimately reach my destination. . . . The mere fact that there was a possibility of surmounting the hindrance does not do away with or remove the hindrance. If the hindrance is insurmountable then it become prevention, and no longer hindrance.' *Dixon (Peter) & Sons Ltd v Henderson, Craig & Co* [1919] 2 KB 778 at 788, 789 CA, per Eve J

'As to the prevention of shipment by hostilities [a condition terminating a contract for the purchase of goods] it is remarkable that the arbitrators, who find this as a fact, also find that the sellers shipped all the goods under their contracts in accordance with their tenders. They have obviously in my view put a very wide and erroneous meaning on the word "prevention". Economic unprofitableness is not "prevention", though a very high price for the article sold may be evidence of such a physical scarcity due to hostilities as amounts to prevention by hostilities. They have not considered whether the ships in which the contract goods were placed could physically go to the contract ports, but have rested themselves on the fact that the voyage might be financially unprofitable for the sellers, if they were not insured against war risk, and financed from shipment till payment. I agree with the judge below that no facts are found which amount to prevention by hostilities in the true meaning of that term.' *Re Comptoir Commercial Anversois & Power, Son & Co* [1920] 1 KB 868 at 898, per Scrutton LJ

PREVENTIVE JUSTICE

'I am not prepared to assent . . . that there can be no binding over of a person to be of good behaviour unless he has done something which tends to a breach of the peace in the sense of something which is calculated to lead to violence, that is, to personal violence. . . . I think the passage from Blackstone, Vol IV, p 251, shows that the scope of this remedy is what is called preventive justice. The passage reads: "This preventive justice consists in obliging those persons, whom there is probable ground to suspect of future misbehaviour, to stipulate with and to give full assurance to the public, that such offence as is apprehended shall not happen; by finding pledges or securities for keeping the peace, or for their good behaviour."' *R v Sandbach, ex p* Williams [1935] 2 KB 192 at 196, DC, per Avory J

PRICE *See also* MARKET PRICE

'Price' includes a charge of any description. (Resale Prices Act 1976, s 8(1))

'The words [in a charter-party] to be construed are "If and when the price of good class bunker coals . . . is reduced to 80*s*. per ton." There is no one price of coals which is the same to every buyer and in every place. The price at the pit head will be one figure, the price of the same coal delivered at a port some miles distant will be another. The price to a broker or middleman will be one figure, the price of the same coal to a consumer who buys through a broker or middleman will be another. In this contract I think that . . . "the price" means the price which this shipowner under the circumstances disclosed by his contract would have to pay, and that his freight is reducible if and when the market is such that his expenses of performing the contract are reduced.' *Hansen v Wade & English* (1924) 93 LJKB 1089 at 1096, HL, per Lord Wrenbury

Australia 'Price is the sum of money or its equivalent at which a thing is valued.' *Johnston, Fear & Kingham and the Offset Printing Co Pty Ltd v Cph* (1943) 67 CLR 314 at 327, per Starke J

Invoice price

Canada [The defendants agreed to purchase from the plaintiffs merchandise at the rate of one hundred and ten cents on the dollar 'invoice price'.] 'This was a purchase on a basis of price ascertainable either by the production of the original invoice, or such satisfactory evidence as would convince fairminded business men skilled in such business of the truth of what the original invoice had, or of necessity must have, exhibited if correctly made out.' *Periard v Bergeron* (1912) 47 SCR 289 at 294, SCC, per Idington J

Resale price

In this section 'the resale price', in relation to a sale of any description, means (a) any price notified to the dealer or otherwise published by or on behalf of a supplier of the goods in question (whether lawfully or not) as the price or minimum price which is to be charged on or is recommended, as appropriate for a sale of that description, or (b) any price prescribed or purporting to be prescribed for that purpose by any contract or agreement between the dealer and any such supplier. (Resales Price Act 1976, s 11(2))

PRIMAGE

In addition to the freight, the bill of lading may provide for the payment of primage and average accustomed. Primage is, strictly speaking, payable to the master as his remuneration for looking after the cargo, and may therefore be recovered by him from the consignee. A contract between the shipowner and the consignor by which no primage is payable binds the master if brought to his knowledge. In practice, the master agrees with the shipowner to forgo primage in return for a regular salary, and in this case any primage which may have been reserved belongs to the shipowner. (43 Halsbury's Laws (4th edn) para 735)

'From the earliest periods of commerce, primage, which is sometimes called the master's hat-money, has been paid to the captain. It was originally a gratuity, and a reward for his care and attention to the interests of those who shipped goods on board his vessel. By degrees it became an established practice, and though at first uncertain in amount, it was by custom reduced to certainty. Prima facie, therefore, primage is the right of the captain, and we must see whether any thing has taken place in this instance to divest him of that right. There are, it is true, different ways of stipulating for the payment of primage; it may be given for the benefit of the owner, and not the captain; but this can only be by a special arrangement among the parties.' *Best v Saunders* (1828) Dan & Ll 183 at 185, 186, per Lord Tenterden CJ

PRIMARILY

Australia [A testator by his will directed that all his just debts, funeral and testamentary expenses, which should include all probate and succession duty both State and Federal, should be paid by his executors 'primarily' out of his personal estate.] 'The word "primarily" to my mind clearly shows that it is only in the first instance that the payment is to be made out of the personal estate, and implies that ultimately the liability may rest elsewhere, it is to rest ultimately where the law places it.' *Re Richardson* [1920] SALR 24 at 35, per Poole J

Australia [The Motor Car Act 1958–1986 (Vic), s 33(2)(a)(ii) (see now s 33(2)(a)) makes it an offence for a motor car constructed 'primarily' to carry goods to travel above a specified speed.] 'In my opinion . . . the language under consideration plainly imports "purpose" and the word "primarily" means that the purpose of carrying goods is the principal purpose—the principal purpose it was constructed to serve as distinct from a subsidiary purpose.' *Barnes v Deveson* [1960] VR 604 at 605, 606, per Little J

PRIMARY EDUCATION *See* EDUCATION

PRIMARY SCHOOL *See* SCHOOL

PRIME COST

[The Marine Insurance Act 1906, s 16 enacts (inter alia) that, in insurance on goods or merchandise, the insurable value is the 'prime cost' of the property insured, plus the expenses of and incidental to shipping and the charges of insurance upon the whole.] 'In my opinion s 16 of the Marine Insurance Act 1906 is to be construed in the light of the consideration that the object of all insurance is indemnity. . . . I think the words "prime cost" in that section mean the prime cost to the assured at or about the time of shipment, or at any rate at some time when the prime cost can be reasonably deemed to represent their value to their owner at the date of shipment. To hold that the prime cost at a period of boom long past must by statute be taken to be the value at a time when values had become diminished by 50 per cent would have the effect of enabling the assured to recover under his right to indemnity for loss during the voyage a sum which would represent a loss incurred long before the voyage started.' *Williams v Atlantic Assurance Co Ltd* [1933] 1 KB 81 at 102, 103, CA, per Greer LJ

PRIME MOVER

'Prime mover' means every engine, motor or other appliance which provides mechanical energy derived from steam, water, wind, electricity, the combustion of fuel or other source. (Factories Act 1961, s 176)

PRINCIPAL

Principal office

[The Companies Clauses Consolidation Act 1845, s 135 provides that any proceeding required to be served upon a company may be left at or posted to the 'principal office' of the company, or one of their principal offices when there shall be more than one.] 'We have a Scotch company to be served with a writ, and the question is whether Carlisle is the principal office or one of the principal offices, of the company. I should have thought, without any authority, that the principal office of the company must be the place at which the business of the company is controlled and managed. The only office that answers this description is the company's office at Glasgow. No part of the business of the company is controlled or managed, in the sense that it is independently controlled or managed, at Carlisle. The directors meet at Glasgow, and the office from which and through which they manage the business of the company is at Glasgow. If the expression "principal office" means the office at which the business of the company is managed, it does not apply to Carlisle; and the service of the writ at the office there was not a service at the principal office of the company, and must be set aside.' *Palmer v Caledonian Rly Co* [1892] 1 QB 823 at 827, 828, per Lord Esher MR

Principal value *See* VALUE

PRINCIPLE

'A "principle" means a general guiding rule, and does not include specific directions, which vary according to the subject matter.' *M'Creagh v Frearson* [1922] WN 37 at 37, 38, per Shearman J

PRINTING

Australia [The question was whether a document produced by an offset process was 'printed' within the meaning of ss 154, 154A of the Electoral Act 1907 (Tas), ss 154, 154A (repealed; see now Electoral Act 1985–1986, ss 154, 154A)]. 'It is printing because it is produced by pressing one thing against another so as to produce a facsimile. The first typing, through the typewriter ribbon, produces a positive. Although it was not fully explained I infer that the use of the particular typewriter ribbon has a chemical effect. Water and ink are used. The paper on which the operator has typed is pressed against a roller which produces the negative. This in turn is pressed against the paper to be used and produces another positive image. To my mind this is "printing".' *Re Baker's Election, ex p Clemente* [1965] Tas SR 152 at 170, per Crawford

PRIOR

Canada 'As to the dictionary definitions I do not find that in them the learned editors are saying that "prior", "preceding", "antecedent" or other synonyms involved, necessarily connote that the event or other thing concerned must occur immediately prior to the matter in question—here, the accident.' *Adamson v Insurance Corp of British Columbia* (1978) 90 DLR (3d) 540 at 541, BCSC, per Fulton J

PRIORITY

Of legacies

'In case of a deficiency, all the annuities and legacies abate rateably, for since they cannot all be paid in full, they shall all abate rateably on the principle of the maxim, "equality is equity", or "equity delighteth in equality". This rule is indeed subject to exceptions, for there are cases in which some annuities or legacies are to be paid in priority to others; but it is settled that the onus lies on the party seeking priority, to make out that such priority was intended by the testator, and that the proof of this must be clear and conclusive. The reason is, that a testator, in the absence of clear and conclusive proof to the contrary, must be deemed to have considered that his estate would be sufficient, and consequently not to have thought it necessary to provide against a deficiency by giving a priority, in case of a deficiency, to some of the objects of his bounty. It is true that the testator does in many cases contemplate the possibility of a deficiency, and provide against it; but I think it may be safely affirmed that, in the absence of all indication to the contrary, it is generally to be assumed that the testator considers that his estate may be sufficient to answer the purposes to which he has devoted it, and consequently makes no provision against a deficiency; and such being the general rule, the Court would not be right in saying, without clear and conclusive reasons, that he intended to provide against an event which in general it is not to be supposed that he ever contemplated.' *Miller v Huddlestone* (1851) 3 Mac & G 513 at 523, 524, per Lord Truro LC

PRISON *See also* IMPRISONMENT

'The prison of the king's bench is not any local prison confined only to one place, and . . . every place where any person is restrained of his liberty is a prison; as if one take sanctuary and depart thence, he shall be said to break prison.' *Hobert & Stroud's Case* (1630) Cro Car 209 at 210, per cur.

Civil prison

'Civil prison' means a prison in the United Kingdom in which a person sentenced by a civil court to imprisonment can for the time being be confirmed. (Army Act 1955, s 143(1); Air Force Act 1955, s 143(1))

Military prison

'Military prison' means separate premises under the control of the Secretary of State and primarily allocated for persons serving military sentences of imprisonment. (Army Act 1955, s 143(1))

PRIVATE ACT *See* STATUTE

PRIVATE CARRIER *See* CARRIER

PRIVATE DWELLING *See also* DWELLING; DWELLING-HOUSE

In this Act, except so far as the context otherwise requires, 'private dwelling' means any building or part of a building used or intended to be used as such, and a building or part of a building shall not be deemed for the purposes of this Act to be used or intended to be used otherwise than as a private dwelling by reason that a person who resides or is to reside therein is or is to be required or permitted to reside therein in consequence of his employment or of holding an office; and 'dwelling' shall be construed accordingly. (Clear Air Act 1956, s 34(4))

[An agreement for a lease contained a covenant by the defendants to use a garage for standing a 'private' car only.] 'It seems to me that in conjunction with the sentence which follows it, which refers to the use of the flat as a "private" dwelling-house, "private" there must mean used for some personal or domestic purpose; not merely a car which is constructed for such purpose, but which is indeed used for such purpose. A dwelling-house, of course, is a house which people normally dwell in. A "private" dwelling-house is one actually used for domestic purposes. So construing that agreement, one has got to take note of the conjunction of the use of that word in two different aspects, one relating to the flat, No 9. It would follow that use of the word "private" there means for private purposes.' *Bell v Alfred Franks & Bartlett Co Ltd* [1980] 1 All ER 356 at 359, 360, per Shaw LJ

PRIVATE GAIN *See* GAIN

PRIVATE HIRE *See* HIRE

PRIVATE HOUSE *See* HOUSE

PRIVATE INTERNATIONAL LAW *See* CONFLICT OF LAWS

PRIVATE LOTTERY *See* LOTTERY

PRIVATE NUISANCE *See* NUISANCE

PRIVATE PAPERS

'Two questions of construction . . . arise on the will of Charles Dickens, . . . who died some sixty-four years ago. He bequeathed to his sister-in-law, Georgina Hogarth "all his private papers whatsoever and wheresoever", and the first question is whether there is included in this bequest the manuscript of an unpublished work, being an account of the Life of Christ. . . . I am of opinion that, like letters, diaries and memoranda, it comes fairly within the description of private papers. The manuscript, that is the pieces of papers with the writing on them, therefore passed on the death of the author to Miss Hogarth. I can see no sound ground for doubting whether, if Charles Dickens had finished some novel or story but had not published it at the date of his death, it would have passed under the bequest of his copyrights. Nor can I see that any different conclusion should be arrived at in the present case because of the bequest to Miss Hogarth of "all his private papers whatsoever".' *Re Dickens, Dickens v Hawksley* [1935] Ch 267 at 301, 306, CA, per Maughham LJ

PRIVATE PREMISES

'Private premises' means premises to which the public have access (whether on payment or otherwise) only be permission of the owner, occupier, or lessee of the premises. (Public Order Act 1936, s 9)

PRIVATE RELATIONS

The three great relations in private life are, 1 That of master and servant; which is founded in convenience, whereby a man is directed to call in the assistance of others, where his own skill and labour will not be sufficient to answer the cares incumbent upon him. 2 That of husband and wife; which founded in nature, but modified by civil society: the one directing man to continue and multiply his species, the other prescribing the manner in which that natural impulse must be confined and regulated. 3 That of parent and child, which is consequential to that of marriage, being its principal end and design: and it is by virtue of this relation that infants are protected, maintained, and educated. But, since the parents, on whom this care is primarily incumbent, may be snatched away by death or otherwise, before they have completed their duty, the law has therefore provided a fourth relation; 4 That of guardian and ward, which is a kind of artificial parentage, in order to supply the deficiency, whenever it happens, of the natural. (1 Bl Com 410)

PRIVATE RESIDENCE *See* RESIDE; RESIDENCE

PRIVATE ROAD *See* ROAD

PRIVATE TRUST *See* TRUST

PRIVILEGE

'A "privilege" describes some advantage to an individual or group of individuals, a right enjoyed by a few as opposed to a right enjoyed by all.' *Le Strange v Pettefar* (1939) 161 LT 300 at 301, per Luxmoore LJ

Australia 'A privilege afforded to a prisoner seems [under the Prisons Act 1952 (NSW), s 23A (now repealed)] to me to connote some advantage given to him which is in addition to his basic rights as a prisoner—an indulgence granted to a prisoner suggests a diminution in the rigours of imprisonment.' *Bromley v Dawes* (1983) 34 SASR 73 at 106, per Mitchell ACJ

Absolute privilege

If the occasion of the publication of a defamatory and untrue statement concerning the plaintiff is privileged, the statement may be protected by either absolute or qualified privilege depending on the nature of the occasion. If the occasion is absolutely privileged no action for defamation lies, whether or not the defendant was actuated by malice.

The occasions of absolute privilege may be classified as the administration of justice, proceedings in Parliament, certain aspects of local government administration and advising the Sovereign in affairs of state. The last mentioned category extends to communications between officers of state in relation to state affairs. (28 Halsbury's Laws (4th edn) paras 95, 97)

Privileged occasion

'The present case is not, strictly speaking, one of "privileged occasion". In a legal sense that term is used with reference to a case in which one or more members of the public are clothed with a greater immunity than the rest.' *Merivale v Carson* (1887) 20 QBD 275 at 282, CA, per Bowen LJ

Qualified privilege

On grounds of public policy the law affords protection on certain occasions to a person acting in good faith and without any improper motive who makes a statement about another person which is in fact untrue and defamatory. Such occasions are called occasions of qualified privilege. It is not possible to set out all the occasions at common law which will be held to be privileged but, as a general rule, there must be a common and corresponding duty or interest between the person who makes the communication and the person who receives it. (28 Halsbury's Laws (4th edn) para 108)

PRIVITY

Privies are of three classes: (1) privies in blood, for example, ancestor and heir; (2) privies in law, for example (formerly) tenant by the curtesy or in dower, and others that come in by act in law, for example testator and executor, intestate and administrator; bankrupt and trustee in bankruptcy; (3) privies in estate, for example testator and devisee, vendor and purchaser, lessor and lessee, a husband and his wife claiming under his title and *e converso*; successive incumbents of the same benefice, assignor and assignee of a bond, the employee of a corporation defending an action of trespass at the cost of his employers and justifying under their title, and the corporation itself. (16 Halsbury's Laws (4th edn) para 1543)

The term 'privity' implies mutual or successive relationship to the same interests, and the admissions of privies are receivable because they are identified in interest with the party against whom they are tendered. (17 Halsbury's Laws (4th edn) para 68)

'There are three manner of privities, *scil* privity in respect of estate only, privity in respect of contract only, and privity in respect of estate and contract together: privity of estate only; as if the lessor grants over his reversion (or if the reversion escheat) between the grantee (or the lord by escheat) and the lessee is privity in estate only, so between the lessor and the assignee of the lessee, for no contract was made between them. Privity of contract only, is personal privity, and extends only to the person of the lessor and to the person of the lessee, as in the case at bar, when the lessee assigned over his interest, notwithstanding his assignment the privity of contract remained between them, although the privity of estate be removed by the act of the lessee himself. . . . The third privity is of contract and estate together, as between the lessor and the lessee himself.' *Walker's Case* (1587) 3 Co Rep 22a at 23a, per cur.

'When the old common lawyers spoke of a man being "privy" to something being done, or of an act being done "with his privity", they meant that he knew of it beforehand and concurred in it being done. If it was a wrongful act done by his servant, then he was liable for it if it was done "by his command or privity", that is with his express authority or with his knowledge and concurrence. "Privity" did not mean that there was any wilful misconduct by him, but only that he knew of the act beforehand and concurred in it being done. Moreover, "privity" did not mean that he himself personally did the act, but only that someone else did it and that he knowingly concurred in it. Hence, in the later Merchant Shipping Acts, the owner was entitled to limit his liability if the act was done without his "actual fault or privity". Without his "actual fault" meant without any actual fault by the owner personally. Without his "privity" meant without his knowledge or concurrence.' *Companía Martitime San Basilio SA v Oceanus Mutual Underwriting Assocn (Bermuda) Ltd* [1976] 3 All ER 243 at 251, CA, per Lord Denning MR

PRIZE

Admiralty

'Prize' is the term applied to a ship or goods captured by the maritime force of a belligerent at sea or seized in port. The term has been extended by statute to aircraft and goods carried in them; and save for certain exceptions, the law relating to prize applies in relation to aircraft and goods carried in them as it applies in relation to ships and goods carried in them, and it so applies notwithstanding that the aircraft is on or over land.

Enemy ships or goods, and in certain circumstances neutral ships or goods, when captured at sea by one of her Majesty's ships are droits of the Crown.

If ships or goods which are liable to condemnation are seized in a port they will be condemned as droits of Admiralty. It is an essential condition to such a decree of condemnation that the ship should have entered the port voluntarily, or by stress of weather and not from a cause connected with warlike operations or knowledge that a state of war existed.

Ships or goods captured by a ship other than a ship of war, or by a force on land, are also droits of Admiralty. (37 Halsbury's Laws (4th edn) paras 1301–1303)

'It is plain . . . that the Prize Court has jurisdiction in every case of seizure or capture of a ship alleged to have belonged to the enemy and to decide "according to the course of Admiralty and to the law of nations" whether it should be condemned as true and lawful prize. "Prize", in this connection, means nothing more than "taking" or seizure. "Capture in prize" or "as prize" is not one species of capture. If a ship is captured, she thereby becomes a prize subject to the jurisdiction of the Prize Court. The French equivalent for our "Prize Court" is "Cours des Prises", and "prise" means "taking".' *Schiffart-Treuhand v Procurator-General* [1953] 1 All ER 364 at 370, PC, per cur. (also reported in [1953] AC 232 at 258)

Lottery

[The question at issue was whether a football pool was a competition in which 'prizes' were offered for forecasts of the result of a future event within the Betting and Lotteries Act 1934, s 26(1) (repealed; see now the Lotteries and Amusements Act 1976, s 14). 'It is said that the word "prize" is not applicable to the division of a pool, as is provided by this scheme. In our opinion, the word is used in the Act to indicate the reward to be given to successful competitors, whether in money or in kind, and it matters not that the reward is provided not by the promoters, but out of the fund subscribed by the participators. The scheme has some of the features of a sweepstake, in connection with which the word "prize" is always used to describe that which the winner will receive.' *Bretherton v United Kingdom Totalisator Co Ltd* [1945] KB 555 at 560, DC, per Lord Goddard

PROBABLE

'Their lordships must now make their own examination of the case law [on nuisance]. They find the most striking feature to be the variety of words used: and that is not very surprising because in the great majority of cases the facts were such that it made no difference whether the damage was said to be the direct or the natural or probable or foreseeable result of the nuisance. . . . Another word frequently used is "probable". It is used with various shades of meaning. Sometimes it appears to mean more probable than not, sometimes it appears to include events likely but not very likely to occur, sometimes it has a still wider meaning and refers to events the chance of which is anything more than a bare possibility, and sometimes, when used in conjunction with other adjectives, it appears to serve no purpose beyond rounding off a phrase.' *The Wagon Mound (No 2), Overseas Tankship (UK) Ltd v Miller Steamship Co Pty Ltd* [1966] 2 All ER 709 at 713, PC, per Lord Reid

[The rule in *Hadley v Baxendale* (1854) 9 Exch 341, is as follows: 'Where two parties have made a contract with one of them has broken, the damages which the other party ought to receive in respect of such breach of contract should be such as may fairly and reasonably be considered either arising naturally, i.e., according to the usual course of things, from such breach of contract itself, or such as may reasonably be supposed to have been in the contemplation of both parties, at the time they made the contract, as the probable result of the breach of it.'] 'The word "probable" in *Hadley v Baxendale* covers both parts of the rule, and it is of vital importance in applying the rule to consider what the court meant by using this word in its context. The common use of this word is no doubt to imply that something is more likely to happen than not. In conversation, if one says to another "If you go out in this weather you will probably catch a cold" this is, I think, equivalent to saying that one believes there is an odds on chance that the other will catch a cold. The word "probable" need not, however, bear this narrow meaning. . . . A close study of the rule was made by the Court of Appeal in the case of *Victoria Laundry (Windsor) Ltd v Newman Industries Ltd* [[1949] 1 All ER 997]. The judgment of the court was delivered by Asquith LJ who suggested the phrase "liable to result" as appropriate to describe the degree of probability required. This may be a colourless expression, but I do not find it possible to improve on it. If the word "likelihood" is used, it may convey the impression that the chances are all in favour of the thing happening, an idea which I would reject.' *The Heron II, Konfos v Czarnikow (C) Ltd* [1967] 3 All ER 686 at 707, 708, HL, per Lord Hodson

'The word "probable" is a common enough word. I understand it to mean that something is likely to happen.' *Goldman v Thai Airways International Ltd*, [1983] 3 All ER 693 at 700, CA, per Eveleigh LJ

PROBATION HOSTEL

'Probation hostel' means premises for the accommodation of persons who may be required to reside there by a probation order. (Powers of Criminal Courts Act 1973, s 57(1), as amended by the Criminal Law Act 1977, s 65, Sch 13)

PROCEDURE *See* PRACTICE AND PROCEDURE

PROCEED

'By art 20 of the regulations for preventing collisions at sea (steering and sailing rules) it is provided that "When a steam vessel and a sailing vessel are proceeding in such directions as to involve risk of collision, the steam vessel shall keep out of the way of the sailing vessel." But in applying this rule the facts of the case must be kept in mind. The trawler had her trawl still out, though she was engaged in the operation of hauling it in. She was thereby rendered stationary, and was as if she were an anchored ship. The evidence shews that in this condition she could neither go ahead nor astern. The trawl being close aboard, she could not have moved her engines ahead without risk of fouling her propeller, and if her engines had been moved astern, she would probably have fallen off head on to her trawl in an unmanageable position. She was an incumbered vessel and practically, until her trawl was up, immovable. In my opinion a vessel so placed cannot properly be said to be "proceeding" within the meaning of art 20.' *The Gladys* [1910] P 13 at 16, per Bigham P

Canada 'The substantive verbal definition of proceeding is, indeed, . . . "the action of going onward: advance onward". That definition, [the plaintiff] argues, means that when something is stationary it is not proceeding. . . . The cases . . . seem to suggest that a vessel—or as here a vehicle—is "proceeding" so long as there is no "discontinuance" of the intended journey. Halting for a proper and reasonable act such as awaiting tides, loading coal or turning left safely does not discontinue a journey. It appears therefore that a vehicle that is halted on a roadway for the purpose of turning left, in law would still be "proceeding" since the journey has not been discontinued.' *Wigton v Ratke* (1984) 9 DLR (4th) 464 at 466, 467, Alta QB, per Wachewich J

PROCEEDINGS *See also* ACTION

A summons upon which no order has been made is not deemed to be a proceeding for the purpose of the rule requiring notice of intention to proceed after a year's delay. For this purpose 'proceedings' means an interlocutory proceeding before and not after final judgment, and it has no reference to execution. (37 Halsbury's Laws (4th edn) para 35)

[By RSC 1883, Ord LXX, r 1 (revoked; see now RSC 1965, Ord 2, r 1), non-compliance with any of the rules, or with any rule of practice for the time being in force, did not render any 'proceedings' void, but they might be set aside, etc. Rule 2 dealt with applications to set aside for irregularity.] '"Proceedings" are intended by these rules to be the day-to-day steps in the action, and not merely the cause of action on which they rest. The wording of RSC Ord 70, r 2, confirms me in the view that "proceedings" means the day-to-day steps in the action, since that provides that proceedings can cure themselves of irregularity by delay, in the sense that the other party cannot rely on an irregularity unless making complaint within reasonable time.' *Smalley v Robey & Co Ltd* [1962] 1 All ER 133 at 135, CA, per Holroyd Pearce LJ

'The word "proceedings" is not defined in the Act [Rent Act 1968 (repealed)], but I think it covers any proceedings of a legal nature, even though they do not take place in a court of law.' *R v Westminster (City) London Borough Rent Officer, ex p Rendall* [1973] 3 All ER 119 at 121, CA, per Lord Denning MR

'The ordinary or natural meaning or meanings of the word "proceedings" standing by itself, without any adjectival description, are so general and imprecise that the dictionary definition do not carry the matter any further. The phrase "judicial proceedings" implies some form of adjudication and some kind of order of a court or of some other person or body acting in a judicial capacity.' *Quazi v Quazi* [1979] 3 All ER 424 at 429, 430, HL, per Ormrod LJ

Australia [The Service and Execution of Process Act (Cth) 1901–1986, s 16(1) provides (inter alia) that when a summons has been issued by any Court or Judge in any State, requiring any person to appear and give evidence, or to produce books or documents in any civil 'proceeding', such summons may be served in any other part of the Commonwealth.] 'A "proceeding", used broadly as it is used in section 16 of the Federal Service and Execution of Process Act, is merely some method permitted by law for moving a Court or judicial officer to some authorized act, or some act of the Court or judicial officer.' *Cheney v Spooner* (1929) 41 CLR 532 at 536, 537, per Isaacs and Gavan Duffy JJ

Australia 'The word [proceedings] is not limited merely to applications to the court, or to any proceedings that must be brought to the court under the Act [Companies Act 1961; now Companies Act 1981 (Cth)] in relation to a winding-up. In my opinion, all the matters that flow directly from or are invoked by the making of an order as a part of the process of winding-up under the provisions of the Companies Act 1961 are "proceedings in relation to the winding-up". It is the performance or observance of all the statutory powers and duties . . . which are comprehended within the expression "all proceedings in relation to the winding-up".' *Krextile Holdings Pty Ltd v Widdows* [1974] VR 689 at 693, per Gillard J

New Zealand 'The word "proceedings" is a word which covers not only those steps taken on an information up to the moment of conviction but also includes steps taken on that information after conviction to the point where sentence is imposed.' *Elliott v Auckland City* [1971] NZLR 824 at 828, per McMullin J

United States 'Proceeding' means any threatened, pending, or completed action, suit, or proceeding, whether civil, criminal, administrative, or investigative and whether formal or informal. (Revised Model Business Corporation Act 1984, s 8.50(7))

Civil proceedings

'Civil proceedings' includes proceedings by . . . proceedings by the Crown in the High Court or a county court for the recovery of fines or penalties, and references to proceedings to which the Crown is a party include references to proceedings to which the Attorney-General or any Government department or any officer of the Crown as such is a party, so, however, that the Crown shall not be deemed to be a party to any proceedings by reason only that the proceedings are proceedings by the Attorney-General on the relation of some other person. (Administration of Justice (Miscellaneous Provisions) Act 1933, s 7(2))

'Civil proceedings' includes proceedings in the High Court or the county court for the recovery of fines or penalties, but does not include proceedings on the Crown side of the King's Bench Division. (Crown Proceedings Act 1947, s 38(2))

New Zealand 'The fact that a proceeding has elements of inquiry or inquisition and that the public interest is involved are not at all inconsistent with describing the proceeding as civil. These features are present to some degree in many cases concerning, for instance, paternity, custody or guardianship—proceedings which are clearly civil.' *Pallin v Department of Social Welfare* [1983] NZLR 266 at 269, CA, per Cooke J

Judicial proceedings

'The ordinary or natural meaning or meanings of the word "proceedings" standing by itself, without any adjectival description, are so general and imprecise that the dictionary definitions do not carry the matter any further. The phrase "judicial proceedings" implies some form of adjudication and some kind of order of a court or of some other person or body acting in a judicial capacity.' *Quazi v Quazi* [1979] 3 All ER 424 at 429, 430, HL, per Ormrod LJ

Legal proceedings

'Legal proceeding' means any civil or criminal proceeding or inquiry in which evidence is or may be given, and includes an arbitration. (Bankers' Books Evidence Act 1879, s 10)

[The Merchant Shipping Act 1894, s 496 contains provisions as to the deposit of money with a wharfinger by the owner of goods, the payment thereout of sums due to the shipowner, and the repayment of the balance to the owner of the goods at the expiration of a specified period, unless 'legal proceedings' have in the meantime been instituted by the shipowner against the owner of the goods.]

'"Legal proceedings" mean prima facie that which the words would naturally import—i.e., legal process taken to enforce the rights of the shipowner.' *Runciman & Co v Smyth & Co* (1904) 20 TLR 625 at 626, DC, per Lord Alverstone CJ

'The words "legal proceedings" are, in my opinion, wide enough to cover criminal as well as civil process; "instituting legal proceedings", however, seems to me a phrase much more appropriate to civil than to criminal process.' *Re Vexatious Actions Act* 1896, *Re Boaler* [1915] 1 KB 21 at 37, CA, per Scrutton J

PROCEEDS

[The Law of Property Act 1925, s 28(1) provides that trustees for sale shall, in relation to land or to manorial incidents and to the 'proceeds of sale', have all the powers of a tenant for life and the trustees of a settlement under the Settled Land Act 1925.] 'It is clear, and I think it is common ground that the phrase "the proceeds of sale" in that context means the proceeds of a sale for which the trustees are trustees for sale.' *Re Wellsted's Will Trusts, Wellsted v Hanson* [1949] 1 All ER 577 at 579, CA, per Lord Greene MR; [1949] Ch 296

PROCESS

United States The term 'process' means process, art or method, and includes a new use of a known process, machine, manufacture, composition of matter, or material. (Act of July 19, 1952, c 950(b))

PROCESS (Manufacture)

'An operation may amount to a "process", even though it is merely incidental to the main purpose which is being served.' *Forster v Llanelly Steel Co* (1907) *Ltd* [1941] 1 All ER 1 at 3, per Lord Simon LC

'A process which is incidental to a manufacturing process is not necessarily itself a manufacturing process. In *Joyce v Boots Cash Chemists (Southern) Ltd* [[1950] 2 All ER 719] Slade J said, following a Scottish decision, that a "process" was an "activity".' *Powley v Bristol Siddeley Engines Ltd* [1965] 3 All ER 612 at 617, per Megaw J

'In my view, "process' connotes a substantial measure of uniformity of treatment or system of treatment.' *Vibroplant Ltd v Holland (Inspector of Taxes)* [1981] 1 All ER 526 at 532, per Dillon J

PROCESS OF LAW

In this Act, unless the context otherwise requires,— . . . The expression 'process' includes any summons or warrant of citation to appear either to answer any information or complaint, or as a witness; also any warrant of commitment, any warrant of imprisonment, any warrant of distress, any warrant of poinding and sale, also any order or minute of a court of summary jurisdiction or copy of such order or minute, also an extract decree, and any other document or process, other than a warrant of arrestment, required for any purpose connected with a court of summary jurisdiction to be served or executed. (Summary Jurisdiction (Process) Act 1881, s 8)

Canada 'The word "process" viewed as a legal term is a word of comprehensive signification. In its broadest sense it is equivalent to "proceedings" or "procedure" and may be said to embrace all the steps and proceedings in a case from its commencement to its conclusion. "Process" may signify the means whereby a Court compels a compliance with its demands. Every writ is, of course, a process, and in its narrowest sense the term "process' is limited to writs or writings issued from out of a court under the seal of the court and returnable to the court. . . . As there used [in the Bankruptcy act, RSC 1970, c B-3, s 2] I take it to extend to a formal writing issued under authority of law by an official having the authority to issue it as a means of enforcing the judgment of the court.' *Re Selkirk* [1961] QR 391 at 397, Ont CA, per Schroeder JA

PROCESSING

'Processing', in relation to fish, includes preserving or preparing fish, or producing any substance or article wholly or partly from fish, by any method for human or animal consumption. (Sea Fish Industry Act 1970, s 27(1))

PROCLAMATION *See* ORDER IN COUNCIL

PROCURATION *See* PER PROCURATION

PROCURE

Obtain

[By a conveyance, a theatre company covenanted to 'procure' that a theatre retained by the company as vendors should not be open save for certain types of performance. The restriction was registered as a land charge. Subsequently the theatre company was wound up.] 'The word "procure" is defined in the Oxford English Dictionary as meaning "obtain by care or effort", and can be more simply paraphrased as "see to it". The obligation undertaken by Thanet Theatrical is to see to it that a certain state of affairs prevails during the specified term. It seems to me that a covenant so expressed is naturally to be regarded as of a purely personal character. The tenant of property is in a position to ensure that during his tenancy the property is not to be used in a specified manner either by himself or by persons claiming under him, whether as licensees under-lessees or assignees, and the word "procure" is appropriate to denote a personal obligation so to ensure. So here, the covenant regarded as purely a personal covenant would have been perfectly sensible and workable had Thanet Theatrical remained in existence. On the other hand, it seems to me that a covenant so expressed is not naturally to be regarded as a covenant on behalf of the covenantor and his successors in title so as to run with the land. The causative verb "procure" is not appropriate where successors in title are themselves to be bound. The covenantor under a covenant intended to run with the land would not sensibly be expressed as procuring his successors to abstain from doing whatever is covenanted not to be done.' *Re Royal Victoria Pavilion, Ramsgate, Whelan v FTS (Great Britain) Ltd* [1961] 3 All ER 83 at 86, per Pennycuick J; also reported [1961] Ch 581 at 587, 588

[The Offences against the Person Act 1861, s 59 provides that whosoever shall unlawfully supply or 'procure' any poison or other noxious thing, or any instrument or thing whatsoever, knowing that the same is intended to be unlawfully used or employed with intent to procure the miscarriage of any woman whether she be or be not with child, shall be guilty of a misdemeanor.] 'Counsel for the appellant . . . says that the natural meaning, at any rate, of the word "procure" is to get possession of from someone else and that the word is quite inapt to cover the case of a man who has instruments in his possession and goes to the cupboard, or whatever it may be, and produces them in order to sterilise them. He says that that meaning is made all the more natural by the juxtaposition of the words "supply or procure", "supply" denoting the passing of possession from one person to another, and he suggests that "procure" should mean the obtaining of possession of something which one has not already got. . . . The court has come to the conclusion that counsel for the appellant's argument is correct. . . . As has already been said, "supply" must denote the passing of possession from one person to another and, in those circumstances, there seems no reason to give the word "procure" anything but its ordinary meaning of getting possession thereof from another person.' *R v Mills* [1963] 1 All ER 202 at 203, 204, CCA, per cur.

[The question was whether the accused had 'procured' the commission of a misdemeanour within the Accessories and Abettors Act 1861, s 8] 'To procure means to produce by endeavour. You procure a thing by setting out to see that it happens and taking the appropriate steps to produce that happening. We think that there are plenty of instances in which a person may be said to procure the commission of a crime by another even though there is no sort of conspiracy between the two, even though there is no attempt at agreement or discussion as to the form which the offence should take.' *A-G's Reference (No 1 of 1975)* [1975] 2 All ER 684 at 686, CA, per cur.

Sexual offences

[The Criminal Law Amendment Act 1885, s 11 (repealed; see now the Sexual Offences Act 1956, s 13) enacted that any male person who, in public or private, committed, or was a party to the commission of, or 'procured' or attempted to procure the commission of, any act of gross indecency with another male person, should be guilty of a misdemeanour.] 'It is said that because the Act uses the expression "another male person" that person cannot be the person who procures the commission of the offence, but must be some third person. That does not seem to me to be the proper construction of the section. I think that the person who procures the commission of the offence may himself be the person with whom it is committed.' *R v Jones* [1896] 1 QB 4 at 6, CCR, per Lord Russell of Killowen CJ

[The Criminal Law Amendment Act 1885, s 2(1) (repealed; see now the Sexual Offences Act 1956, s 23) provided that any person who (inter alia) 'procured' or attempted to procure any girl or woman under twenty-one years of age, not being a common prostitute, or of known immoral character, to have unlawful carnal connexion with any other person or person, should be guilty of a misdemeanour. The appellant Mackenzie, a woman, issued advertisements in Scotland for a lady's maid. X, who answered an advertisement, was engaged by Mackenzie and brought to London, where the appellant Higginson seduced her.] 'It was said that the act of procuration was complete in Scotland, outside the jurisdiction. . . . We think, though the attempt might be completed before, that the full offence is not brought about until the procurer has gained his or her object, and the carnal knowledge has been obtained.' *R v Mackenzie & Higginson* (1910) 75 JP 159 at 160, CCA, per Lord Alverstone CJ

'No one could have sat in this court so long as I have without knowing that there are girls who do not want procuring at all. There is no need to stretch this statute [Criminal Law Amendment Act 1885 (repealed; see now the Sexual Offences Act 1956, s 22)]; if you have got facts to meet it, well and good. This girl says she went of her own free will. The Act is not aimed at brothel keepers who give girls an opportunity, if they come in there, of carrying on that trade. It is aimed at people who get girls by some fraud or persuasion, or by inviting them to it if they cannot get money in any other way—turning them on to the streets. It would be absurd to stretch this Act to meet the case described by the girl herself. It is a bad enough case in all parts, but that is no reason why we should stretch the Act.' *R v Christian* (1913) 78 JP 112 at 112, per Bosanquet, Common Serjeant

[The Sexual Offences Act 1956, s 23(1) makes it an offence to 'procure' a girl under the age of twenty-one to have unlawful sexual intercourse with a third person.] 'The real question here is: does the section provide on its true construction that an offence is committed only if the girl actually has unlawful sexual intercourse, or is it sufficient that he procures the girl for the purposes of unlawful sexual intercourse with another. This court has come to the clear conclusion that, before a man can be found guilty of that offence, it is necessary to prove that unlawful sexual intercourse did take place.' *R v Johnson* [1963] 3 All ER 577 at 578, CCA, per cur.

'It is essential . . . that the interpretation of the word should be a matter of common sense for the jury concerned, and this court can see nothing wrong in the judge having suggested to the jury the word "recruited" as being a useful expression to consider in deciding what they thought on this particular issue.' *R v Broadfoot* [1976] 3 All ER 753 at 755, 757, CA, per cur.

Australia 'There is very little reported authority on what is necessary to constitute a procuring [within the Crimes Act 1900 (NSW), s 91A]. Such as there is suggests that some element of persuasion or inducement or influencing is essential. . . . This accords with the meaning in general of the word "procure", which imports effort, care, management or contrivance towards the obtaining of a desired end; and this, too, is involved in the performance of the functions of a "procurer" or "pander".' *R v Castiglione* [1963] NSWR 1 at 6, per Sugerman J

New Zealand [Under the Crimes Act 1961, s 149 it is an offence for gain or reward to agree to 'procure' a woman to have intercourse with a male person other than her husband.] 'In our opinion it is plain that the word "procures" is used in its ordinary meaning, namely, "obtains, arranges, or agrees to supply", all of which are meanings to be found in dictionaries where the phrase "procures a woman" is involved.' *R v Johnston* [1963] NZLR 92 at 94, per cur.

PRODUCE *See also* CONSUMABLE PRODUCE; HORTICULTURE

'Produce' includes anything (whether live or dead) produced in the course of agriculture. (Agriculture Act 1947, s 109; Agriculture Act 1957, s 11)

For the purposes of this section 'produce' includes anything (whether live or dead) produced in the course of agriculture or, as the case may be, horticulture. (Agriculture and Horticulture Act 1964, s 1)

'Produce' in relation to the production of minerals or other substances, includes getting them, and, in relation to the production of animals or fish, includes taking them. (Fair Trading Act 1973, s 137(2))

[The Betting, Gaming and Lotteries Act 1963, s 52(4) empowers the court to make an order for the forfeiture of anything 'produced'.] 'In my view, the requirement that some thing must be produced to the court does not mean that it must be physically produced in the court-room where the court happens to be sitting. Quite obviously in many cases . . . it would be very difficult to do so and perhaps sometimes impossible to do so. In my view, what it does mean is that the objects to which the order is going to be related must be properly identified as being the objects which were concerned in the offence and they must be available for the court to look at, if it wishes to do so.' *R v Edmonton JJ, ex p Stannite Automatics Ltd* [1965] 2 All ER 750 at 752, per Browne J

Australia [Under the Extradition (Commonwealth Countries) Act 1966–1986 (Cth), s 15(6), certain documents may be 'produced' to the magistrate hearing an application.] 'Does [this] mean "produced in evidence" or does it mean merely produced in the sense that he can view it visually without it being admitted to evidence? For myself I doubt strongly whether it means simply production in the latter sense. I think it means produced in evidence, although the words "in evidence" do not appear in this particular sub-section.' *Watson v Superintendent, Metropolitan Reception Centre* [1971] 1 NSWLR 67 at 69, per Isaacs J

PRODUCTION

'Production' includes repair, maintenance, testing and development. (Defence Contracts Act 1958, s 6(1))

Australia [The Local Government Act 1919–1986 (NSW), s 618 provides that the 'production' of a copy of the Gazette containing any proclamation shall be prima facie evidence of the due making, existence, confirmation and approval of such proclamation and of its contents.] '"Production" in s 618, I think, means produced to the court so as to make it evidence in the case. This is the equivalent of tendering it. . . . I think . . . that "production" means, in effect, "put in evidence".' *Ex p Normanby, Re Britliff* (1954) 54 SR (NSW) 299 at 306, 307, per Herron J

PROFESSION *See also* BUSINESS

'The term profession involves the idea of an occupation requiring either purely intellectual skill, or of manual skill controlled, as in painting and sculpture, or surgery, by the intellectual skill of the operator, as distinguished from an operation which is substantially the production or sale or arrangements for the production or sale of commodities.' *Inland Revenue Comrs v Maxse* [1919] 1 KB 647 at 657, per Scrutton LJ

'In my view it is impossible to lay down any strict legal definition of what is a profession, because persons carry on such infinite varieties of trades and businesses that it is a question of degree in nearly every case whether the form of business that a particular person carries on is, or is not, a profession. Accountancy is of every degree of skill or simplicity. I should certainly not assent to the proposition that as a matter of law every accountant carries on a profession or that every accountant does not. The fact that a person may have some knowledge of law does not, in my view, determine whether or not the particular business carried on by him is a profession. Take the case that I put during the argument, of a forwarding agent. From the nature of his business he has to know something about railway Acts, about the classes of risk that are run in sending goods in a particular way, and under particular forms of contract. That may or may not be sufficient to make his business a profession. Other persons may require rather more knowledge of law, and it must be a question of degree in each case. Take the case before Rowlatt J of a photographer: *Cecil v Inland Revenue Commissioners* [(1919) 36 TLR 164]. Art is a matter of degree, and to determine whether an artist is a professional man again depends, in my view, on the degree of artistic work that he is doing. All these cases which involve questions of degree seem to me to be eminently questions of fact, which the legislature has thought fit to entrust to the commissioners, who have, at any rate, from their very varied experience, at least as much knowledge, if not considerably more, of the various modes of carrying on trade than any judge on the bench.' *Currie v Inland Revenue Comrs, Durant v Inland Revenue Comrs* [1921] 2 KB 332 at 340, 341, CA, per Scrutton LJ

'It seems to me to be dangerous to try to define the word "profession". . . . There are a good many cases about which almost everybody would agree. Everybody would agree, I should think, that when you find a business, however extensive and however distinguished in some ways it may be, which consists merely of selling property, whether real or personal, that is not a profession. It is necessary to add the word "merely", since a sculptor, for instance, may be said to be selling goods. I know there may be a question whether one can regard the contract in that case as a contract for sale, but, if it is not a contract for sale, it may be described as a contract to do work and labour, and there, again, everybody would agree as a general rule that a man who earns his money merely by doing work and labour, without more, is carrying on a trade and not a profession. Again the word "merely" has to be inserted to guard against it being thought that many people are not carrying on a profession who at the same time may be said to be doing work or labour. I think that everybody would agree that, before one can say that a man is carrying on a profession, one must see that he has some special skill or ability, or some special qualifications derived from training or experience. Even there one has to be very careful, because there are many people whose work demands great skill and ability and long experience and many qualifications who would not be said by anybody to be carrying on a profession. Ultimately one has to answer this question: Would the ordinary man, the ordinary reasonable man—the man, if you like to refer to an old friend, on the Clapham omnibus—say now, in the time in which we live, of any particular occupation, that it is properly described as a profession? I do not believe one can escape from that very practical way of putting the question; in other words, I think it would be in a proper case a question for a jury, and I think in a case like this it is eminently one for the Commissioners. Times have changed. There are professions to-day which nobody would have considered to be professions in times past. Our forefathers restricted the professions to a very small number; the work of the surgeon used to be carried on by the barber, whom nobody would have considered a professional man. The profession of the chartered accountant has grown up in comparatively recent times, and other trades, or vocations, I care not what word you use in relation to them, may in future years acquire the status of professions. It must be the intention of the legislature, when it refers to a profession, to indicate what the ordinary intelligent subject, taking down the volume of the statutes and reading the section, will think that "profession" means. I do not think that the lawyer as such can help him very much.' *Carr v Inland Revenue Comrs* [1944] 2 All ER 163 at 166, 167, CA, per du Parcq LJ

Australia 'The word [i.e. profession] implies . . . professed attainments in special knowledge as distinguished from mere skill, "knowledge" which is "to be acquired only after patient study and application" (see *United States v Laws* [(1896) 163 US 258]). Thus many vocations may fall within the accepted and ordinary use of the word; such, for instance, as those of architects, accountants, engineers, journalists, bankers, and so forth. But whether a person in any given case carried on a profession is a question of degree and always of fact.' *Robbins Herbal Institute v Federal Taxation Comr* (1923) 32 CLR 457 at 461, per Starke J

Australia 'The word "profession" is not one which is rigid or static in its signification; it is undoubtedly progressive with the general progress of the community, but at the present time and according to the present understanding of people, the business of a horse-trainer is not included in the word "profession".' *Bradfield v Federal Taxation Comr* (1924) 34 CLR 1 at 7, per Isaacs J

Canada 'Reference to standard dictionaries discloses that the word "profession" in its broadest sense was first applied to the three learned professions of divinity, law and medicine and subsequently to the military profession. During the centuries those broad categories have been expanded and subdivided and the word "profession" now is used more widely to refer to "a vocation in which a professed knowledge of some department of learning is used in its application to the affairs of others, or in the practice of an act founded upon it" (Shorter Oxford Dictionary, 3rd edn).' *R v Chemical Institute of Canada* [1974] FC 247 at 251, Fed Ct, per Urie J

United States The term 'professional employee' means (a) any employee engaged in work (i) predominantly intellectual and varied in character as opposed to routine mental, manual, mechanical, or physical work; (ii) involving the consistent exercise of discretion and judgment in its performance; (iii) of such a character that the output produced or the result accomplished cannot be standardized in relation to a given period of time; (iv) requiring knowledge of an advanced type in a field of science or learning customarily acquired by a prolonged course of specialized intellectual instruction and study in an institution of higher learning or a hospital, as distinguished from a general academic education or from an apprenticeship or from training in the performance of routine mental, manual, or physical processes; or (b) any employee, who (1) has completed the courses of specialized intellectual instruction and study described in clause (iv) of paragraph (a), and (ii) is performing related work under the supervision of a professional person to qualify himself to become a professional employee as defined in paragraph (a). (Labour Management Relations Act of 1947, s 2(12))

PROFIT *See also* ADVANTAGE; OFFICE OF PROFIT

'I propose to declare in substance that the profits, according to the true construction of the deed, are the gross returns, less the working expenses, and that in such working expenses are to be included just allowances in respect of interest on the capital expended, in respect of bad debts and in respect of wear and tear of machinery.' *Rokeby (Lord) v Elliot* (1878) 47 LJ Ch 764 at 767, 768, per Fry J; on appeal (1879) 13 ChD 277, CA, sub nom *Elliot v Rokeby (Lord)* (1881) 7 App Cas 43

'The present question is a very simple one. There is a bargain made with the company that certain persons will advance the money as preference shareholders—that is, that they shall be entitled to a preferential dividend of 6 per cent over the ordinary shares of the company "dependent on the profits of the particular year only". That means, that the preference shareholders only take a dividend if there are profits for that year sufficient to pay their dividend. If there are no profits for that year sufficient to pay their dividends, they do not get it; they lose it for ever; and if there are no profits in one year and 12 per cent profit the next year, they would only get 6 per cent, and the other 6 per cent would go to the ordinary shareholders; so that they are, so to say, co-adventurers for each particular year, and can only look to the profits of that year. . . . "Profits for the year" mean of course the surplus of the receipts after paying expenses and restoring the capital to the position it was in on the 1st Jan in that year.' *Dent v London Tramways Co* (1880) 44 LT 91 at 93, 94, per Jessel MR

'The difference between what a thing costs and the larger sum it sells for is not profit if the buying and selling are attended with expense to the trader.' *Dobbs v Grand Junction Waterworks Co* (1883) 9 App Cas 49 at 55, per Lord Bramwell

[Article 117 of the articles of association of a company provided that no dividend should be payable except out of 'profits' arising out of the business of the company.] 'Apart from the use of the word "profits" in art 117 . . . art 126 seems to me to shew that what was contemplated by the word "profits" was the excess of receipts over all expenditure properly attributable to the year.' *Wilmer v McNamara & Co Ltd* [1895] 2 Ch 245 at 254, per Stirling J

'The word "profits" like many other words in the English language, and even some of a technical character, is capable of more than one meaning, and it is often, and properly, used in more than one sense; and it seems to me that the two different senses of the word "profits" afford the key to the solution of the difficulty which I have now to deal with. In ordinary parlance among mercantile men and lawyers, "profits" mean that sum which periodically, at the end of the half-year, or year, or other time fixed by agreement, is divisible among the partners—a term which, of course, includes members of a company—as income. It is sometimes called "net profits", only to distinguish it from what are called "gross profits". It is the sum which is ascertained by the taking of a proper account of what has been made by trading and is therefore distributable between the parties entitled. But the word "profits" is also used properly in this sense: when you come to wind up a concern, you have to pay all the debts; you have to repay to each partner what he has brought in as capital; and after that has all been done, if the concern has been a successful one, there is a balance, and that balance is "profit": it cannot properly be called anything else.' *Bishop v Smyrna & Cassaba Rly Co* [1895] 2 Ch 265 at 269, 270, per Kekewich J

'In my opinion a solicitor's "profit" is that which he receives from his bill of costs beyond his disbursements out of pocket in the particular business.' *Re Gallard, ex p Gallard* [1896] 1 QB 68 at 71, CA, per Lord Esher MR

'There is no hard and fast rule by which the Court can determine what is capital and what is profit. 'The mode and manner in which a business is carried on, and what is usual or the reverse, may have a considerable influence in determining the question"; per Earl Halsbury LC in *Dovey v Cory* [[1901] AC 477 at 486]. "It may be safely said that what losses can be properly charged to capital, and what to income, is a matter for business men to determine, and it is often a matter on which the opinions of honest and competent men will differ"; see *Gregory v Patchett* [(1864) 33 Beav 595]. . . . There is no single definition of the word 'profits' which will fit all cases.' *Bond v Barrow Haematite Steel Co* [1902] 1 Ch 353 at 364–366, per Farwell J

'There have been many learned discussions lately, and I suppose there are likely to be more, as to what may fairly be brought into account in that way for the purpose of division of profits, but, in the absence of anything of that kind, if it is a mere question what were the profits made in a particular year, it seems to me that the duty is to ascertain what cash has been received and what cash has been expended, and, if that is fairly done, you know the profits of the year. If there is a large outstanding liability which cannot be settled, the partners will estimate that, and it will not be considered as part of the profits. If there is a large outstanding possible loss, and there is a large sum due to a client, then you would provide for that. But in ascertaining what is really actually divisible for the year fairly, you take the cash account as it stands, and really that is the principle, of course, of income tax returns. The income tax return is a return of the actual receipts less such expenditure as is properly chargeable against those receipts.' *Badham v Williams* (1902) 86 LT 191 at 193, per Kekewich J

'The word "profit" has in my opinion a well-defined legal meaning, and this meaning coincides with the fundamental conception of profits in general parlance, although in mercantile phraseology the word may at times bear meanings indicated by the special context which deviate in some respects from this fundamental signification. "Profits" implies a comparison between the state of a business at two specific dates usually separated by an interval of a year. The fundamental meaning is the amount of gain made by the business during the year. This can only be ascertained by a comparison of the assets of the business at the two dates. . . . We start therefore with this fundamental definition of profits, namely, if the total assets of the business at the two dates be compared, the increase which they shew at the later date as compared with the earlier date (due allowance of course being made for any capital introduced into or taken out of the business in the meanwhile) represents in strictness the profits of the business during the period in question. But the periodical ascertainment of profits in a business is an operation of such practical importance as to be essential to the safe conduct of the business itself. To follow out the strict consequences of the legal conception in making out the accounts of the year would often be very difficult in practice. Hence the strict meaning of the word "profits" is rarely observed in drawing up the accounts of firms or companies. . . . In the absence of special stipulations to the contrary, "profits" in cases where the rights of third parties come in mean actual profits, and they must be calculated as closely as possible in accordance with the fundamental conception or definition to which I have referred.' *Re Spanish Prospecting Co Ltd* [1911] 1 Ch 92 at 98, 99, 101, CA, per Fletcher Moulton LJ

[A sum of £45,000 was paid to the appellant, who had intimated to his fellow directors his intention of resigning his directorship, in consideration of his agreeing not to cease giving his services as such.] 'If a sum is paid by a company to a man who has long been and still is director of the company and whose services are greatly valued, and if the consideration is that he will not resign but will continue to act as a director, I cannot myself doubt that in such a case the sum is a profit of his office and that it is liable to tax, and none the less that the time during which he will continue to be a director is not fixed.' *Cameron v Prendergast* [1940] AC 549 at 559, per Lord Maugham

'The word "profit" generally speaking, means the excess of returns over outlay, but in commercial agreements its meaning may be and often is restricted to annual pecuniary profits or such profits as would ordinarily appear in a profit and loss account.'

McClelland v Hyde [1942] NI 1 at 12 per Babington LJ

'Profits, as it seems to me, must not be confused with receipts. Profits consist of a sum arrived at by adding up the receipts of a business and by deducting all the expenses and losses, including depreciation and the like, incurred in carrying on the business.' *Rushden Heel Co Ltd v Keene, Rushden Heel Co Ltd v Inland Revenue Comrs* [1946] 2 All ER 141 at 144, per Atkinson J

Australia 'In my view net profit is the only true profit. The term "gross profit" is a manufactured term which does not mean profit at all, but merely money received, part of which may or may not be a profit. Indeed, the term may be applied to receipts in transactions which show a loss. In ordinary parlance profit means financial gain, that is to say money received over and above the money expended. In the Oxford Dictionary the following meanings are given: "pecuniary gain in any transaction; the amount by which value acquired exceeds value expended; the excess of returns over outlay of capital".' *Brandt v WG Tatham Pty Ltd* [1965] NSWR 126 at 127, per Ferguson J

Net profit *See* NET

Profits or gains

'The Carlisle and Silloth Golf Club is not in a position to assert that its receipts from visitors, not being members of the club, cannot constitute annual "profits and gains" in respect of which income tax is assessable. It has entered into an agreement with . . . the lessor of the club ground, under which the club is bound to allow visitors, who are not members of the club, to use the club-house and play on the club's links, upon payment of fees. . . . The club retains no right of discrimination; the use of its club-house and ground is open to anyone who presents himself and is willing to pay the prescribed fee. . . . Upon the facts . . . it appears to me that this club is really carrying on the business of supplying to the public for reward a recreation ground fitted for the enjoyment of the game of golf, and that the receipts derived from this business are in the nature of profits and gains in respect of which it is liable to assessment for income tax.' *Carlisle & Silloth Golf Club v Smith* [1913] 3 KB 75 at 82, 83, CA, per Kennedy LJ

'I am of opinion that copyright must be comprised within the word "property"; lawyers have spoken of copyright as property, and it can, of course, be transferred. I think that copyright itself is property. If that is so, it seems to me that the royalties which are to be secured are annual profits or gains within the scope of the income tax. If that is the right way to look at it, the owner of the copyright in this country would be taxable exactly in the same way as the agents were taxed on his behalf in the present case.' *Curtis Brown Ltd v Jarvis* (1929) 73 Sol Jo 819 at 819, per Rowlatt J

'"Profits" and "profits and gains" are terms often used interchangeably in the Income Tax Acts with the meaning "assessable" or "taxable profits" [*London County Council v A-G* [1901] AC 26 at 45, HL, per Lord Davey]. In my opinion, that is the meaning of the word "profits" standing alone in s 27(1) [of the Finance Act 1927 (repealed; see now the Income and Corporation Taxes Act 1988, ss 18(1), 348, 392)] as it is also the meaning of the words "profits and gains" lower down in the section, and it is impossible to draw a distinction which would assign to the words "profits and gains" the ordinary meaning in income tax law and to "profits" the meaning of commercial profits.' *Barron (Inspector of Taxes) v Littman* [1952] 2 All ER 548 at 555, HL, per Lord Normand (also reported in [1953] AC 96 at 113)

'"Profits and gains" include remuneration for work done, services rendered, or facilities provided. They do not include gratuitous payments which are given for nothing in return. Nor do they include profits in the nature of capital gains. So they do not include gains made on purchase and sale of an asset. Such gains (except for recent legislation) are only taxable if the transaction was an adventure in the nature of trade.' *Scott v Ricketts* [1967] 2 All ER 1009 at 1011, CA, per Lord Denning MR

PROFIT À PRENDRE

The chief distinction between an easement and a profit à prendre is that whereas an easement only confers a right to utilise the servient tenement in a particular manner or to prevent the commission of some act on that tenement, a profit à prendre confers a right to take from the servient tenement some part of the soil of that tenement or minerals under it or some part of its natural produce, or the animals ferae naturae existing upon it. (14 Halsbury's Laws (4th edn) para 43)

A profit à prendre is a right to take something off another person's land. It may be more fully defined as a right to enter another's land and to take some profit of the soil, or a portion of the soil itself, for the use of the owner of the right. The term 'profit à prendre' is used in contradistinction to the term 'profit à rendre', which signified a benefit which had to be rendered by the possessor of land after it had come into his possession. A profit à prendre is a servitude. (14 Halsbury's Laws (4th edn) para 240)

The right to enter upon another person's land and extract minerals, as distinguished from the ownership of a stratum of minerals in another person's land, is a profit à prendre and may be created by grant, statute or prescription. A common case of a profit à prendre in respect of minerals is a right for freehold tenants of a manor to cut turf and dig loam, sand and gravel out of the waste. (31 Halsbury's Laws (4th edn) para 19)

'It appears to us, that the liberties to hawk, hunt, fish and fowl, granted to one, his heirs and assigns, are interests, or profits à prendre.' *Wickham v Hawker* (1840) 7 M & W 63 at 79, per cur.

'The property in animals, *ferae naturae*, while they are on the soil, belongs to the owner of the soil, and he may grant a right to others to come and take them by a grant of hunting, shooting, fowling and so forth; that right may be granted by the owner of the fee simple, and such a grant is a licence of a profit à prendre.' *Ewart v Graham* (1859) 7 HL Cas 331 at 344, 345, per Lord Campbell LC

'I do not think it is disputed that the law was accurately stated by Willes J in *Constable v Nicholson* [(1863) 14 CBNS 240] where he says:—"The distinction is well established that by custom you may claim an easement to be enjoyed over the land of another, but you cannot claim a profit out of the land. The only difficulty in these cases is to ascertain what is a profit à prendre, and what an easement." And I think it was not disputed that a license to take and carry away fish for sale or otherwise is a license of a profit à prendre, which may at this day be created by a grant to a grantee, capable of taking an interest in the land.' *Goodman v Saltash Corpn* (1882) 7 App Cas 633 at 654, per Lord Blackburn

'A profit à prendre is a right to take something off another persons land; such a right does not prevent the owner from taking the same sort of thing from off his own land; the first right may limit, but does not exclude, the second. An exclusive right to all the profit of a particular kind can, no doubt, be granted; but such a right cannot be inferred from language which is not clear and explicit.' *Sutherland (Duke) v Heathcote* [1892] 1 Ch 475 at 484, 485, CA, per cur.

'Lindley LJ in *Duke of Sutherland v Heathcote* [[1892] 1 Ch 475, supra], defines a profit as a right to take something off another person's land, . . . but it appears from the case of *Rigg v Earl of Lonsdale* [(1857) 1 H & N 923] that if a man shoots grouse on his neighbour's land, trover will lie for the birds killed, though grouse had long before been decided not to be birds of warren—see *Duke of Devonshire v Lodge* [(1857) 7 B & C 36]—and certainly a right to fish in another man's stream is a profit.' *Fitzhardinge (Lord) v Purcell* [1908] 2 Ch 139 at 163, per Parker J

Appendant

A profit à prendre appendant is a right which arose at common law upon the grant of arable land prior to the Statute of Quia Emptores. Before the passing of this statute, when a lord of the manor enfeoffed a person of some parcels of arable land the feofee thereby became entitled to certain ancillary rights with respect to other lands in the manor; after the statute was passed these rights no longer arose upon a grant of the land. Consequently all profit à prendre appendant must have come into existence prior to 1290. Profits à prendre appendant are therefore said to be 'of common right'. (14 Halsbury's Laws (4th edn) para 246)

Appurtenant

Profit à prendre appurtenant are 'against common right': they are rights attached to the ownership of a particular piece of land, not as the necessary consequence of the original tenure, but because of a grant, prescription or other extraneous means. They cannot be severed or enjoyed apart from the dominant tenement, and they pass with the dominant tenement into the hands of each successive owner. The general words which by statute are implied as included in a conveyance or disposition of the dominant tenement include such a profit à prendre. (14 Halsbury's Laws (4th edn) para 247)

In gross

Where a profit à prendre exists as a right in gross it may be assigned and dealt with as a valuable interest, according to the ordinary rules of property. In default of any disposition inter vivos or by will a profit à prendre in gross descends as an ordinary incorporeal hereditament. (14 Halsbury's Laws (4th edn) para 248)

PROFIT AND LOSS ACCOUNT

Australia 'No definite guidance has been afforded by the Court as to the meaning of the words "carried forward in a profit and loss account". A profit and loss account, strictly so called, relates only to receipts and expenditure during a definite period: a profit and loss appropriation account is an account showing disposition of profit or method of dealing with a loss.' *Comr of Taxation v Miller Anderson Ltd* [1946] ALR 150 at 154, 155, per Latham CJ

PROFITABLE *See* BENEFICIAL OCCUPATION

PROHIBITED WEAPON *See* FIREMAN

PROHIBITION

The order of prohibition is an order issuing out of the High Court of Justice and directed to an ecclesiastical or inferior temporal court, or to the Crown Court, which forbids that court to continue proceedings therein in excess of its jurisdiction or in contravention of the laws of the land.

Besides the ordinary order of prohibition an order may also be granted *quousque*, that is until the inferior court alters its decision. (1 Halsbury's Laws (4th edn) paras 128, 129)

PROLONGATION

'What he [the assured under a policy of marine insurance] is entitled to recover is: "Expenses incurred by reason of the prolongation of the voyage". If those words stood by themselves, "prolongation" might conceivably be construed in a geographical sense, although this is not the primary sense in which I would read it. Alternatively, it might be construed as meaning that the assured could recover the difference between the expenses actually incurred by him during the whole of the prolonged voyage and those which would have been incurred if the voyage had been carried out as originally contemplated. These words, however, do not stand alone. That "prolongation" is used in a purely temporal sense appears from the reference to "period of prolongation" in the last part of the clause.' *Union Castle Mail Steamship Co Ltd v United Kingdom Mutual War Risks Assocn Ltd* [1958] 1 All ER 431 at 440, per Diplock J (also reported in [1958] 1 QB 380 at 402)

PROMISE

A promise is in the nature of a verbal covenant, and wants nothing but the solemnity of writing and sealing to make it absolutely the same. If therefore it be to do any explicit act, it is an express contract, as much as any convenant; and the breach of it is an equal injury. (3 Bl Com 157)

[The Corrupt and Illegal Practices Prevention Act 1883, s 17(1) (repealed; but see now the Representation of the People Act 1983, s 111) enacted that no person should, for the purpose of promoting or procuring the election of a candidate at any election, be engaged or employed for payment or 'promise' of payment for any purpose or in any capacity whatever, except as authorised by the Act.] 'I think that when the word "promise" of payment is used in s 17 of the Act of 1883, it means an actual express promise, and not that the promise may be inferred by the conduct of the parties, which would entitle a man to recover in a civil action.' *Stafford (County) Lichfield Division Case, Wolseley, Levitt, Alkin & Shaw v Fulford, Sadler's Case* (1895) 5 O'M & H 27 at 29, 30, per Pollock B

Australia 'Promise is a term of art which has been elaborated in the law of contract. The basis of the decision in *Greene v King* (1949) 79 CLR 353 was that a promise cannot be a pretence because a pretence relates to the past or present and a promise relates to the future. But a contractual promise as to the future is not limited to the conduct of the promissor but may relate to the conduct of other persons or to a future state of affairs not dependent on human conduct. The promissor engages that "acts will be done . . . or . . . facts . . . will exist in the future"; *Lowe v Lombank Ltd* [1960] 1 All ER 611 at 615. By his guarantee given to a mortgage the guarantor promises that the borrower will repay principal and perform other covenants. *Trade Credits Ltd v Burnes* [1979] 1 NSWLR 630. A vendor of a machine can be held liable on a promise that it will perform in a particular way: *Ross v Allis-Chalmers Australia Pty Ltd* (1980) 55 ALJR 8. I see no reason why the term promise used as an element in the description of a statutory offence should bear its established meaning in the law of contract.' *R v Freeman* [1981] 2 NSWLR 686 at 691, per Glass JA

United States A 'promise' is an undertaking to pay and must be more than an acknowledgement. (Uniform Commercial Code 1978, s 3–102(1)(c))

PROMISSORY ESTOPPEL *See* ESTOPPEL

PROMISSORY NOTE

A promissory note is an unconditional promise in writing made by one person to another signed by the maker, engaging to pay, on demand or at a fixed or determinable future time, a sum certain in money, to, or to the order of, a specified person or to bearer. (Bills of Exchange Act 1882, s 83)

(1) For the purposes of this Act the expression 'promissory note' includes any document or writing (except a bank note) containing a promise to pay any sum of money.

(2) A note promising the payment of any sum of money out of any particular fund which may or may not be available, or upon any condition or contingency which may or may not be performed or happen, is to be deemed a promissory note for that sum of money. (Stamp Act 1891, s 33)

[A gold coupon Treasury note contained a promise to pay principal and interest to bearer at fixed dates, either abroad or in London at the option of the holder.] 'If the plain man conversant with business were asked to describe this instrument I think he would call it a foreign Government security. It is found as a matter of fact that the thing is marketable. It is therefore marketable security. Now it is true that from the point of view of legal analysis it contains a promise to pay, and is therefore in legal phraseology a promissory note.' *Speyer Brothers v Inland Revenue Comrs* [1908] AC 92 at 96, per Lord Robertson

PROMOTER

The term 'promoter' is not a term of law, but of business. It is a short and convenient way of designating those who set in motion the machinery of which the Companies Act 1985 enables them to create an incorporated company. It involves the idea of exertion for the purpose of getting up and starting a company, or what is called 'floating' it, and also the idea of some duty towards the company imposed by, or arising from, the position which the so-called promoter assumes towards it. (7 Halsbury's Laws (4th edn) para 37)

'Promoter' means a promoter who was a party to the preparation of the prospectus, or of the portion thereof containing the untrue statement, but does not include any person by reason of this acting in a professional capacity for persons engaged in procuring the formation of the company. (Companies Act 1985, s 67(3))

In this Part [Part 1: betting duties] of, and in Sch 1 to, this Act . . . 'promoter', in relation to any betting, means the person to whom the persons making the bets look for the payment of their winnings, if any. (Betting and Gaming Duties Act 1981, s 12(4))

In ss 17 to 19 of, and in Sch 3 to, this Act [bingo duty] . . . 'the promoter', in relation to bingo, means the person to whom the players look for the payment of prizes, and 'promote' and 'promotion' shall be construed accordingly. (Ibid, s 20(2))

'With respect to the word promoters, we are of opinion that it has no very definite meaning. . . . As used in connexion with companies, the term promoter involves the idea of exertion for the purpose of getting up and starting a company (or what is called floating it), and also the idea of some duty towards the company imposed by, or arising from the position which the so-called promoter assumed towards it. It is now clearly settled that persons who get up and form a company have duties towards it before it comes into existence. . . . Moreover, it is in our opinion an entire mistake to suppose that after a company is registered, its directors are the only persons who are in such a position towards it as to be under fiduciary obligations to it. A person, not a director, may be a promoter of a company which is already incorporated, but the capital of which has not been taken up, and which is not yet in a position to perform the obligations imposed upon it by its creators.' *Emma Silver Mining Co v Lewis & Son* (1879) 40 LT 749 at 750, per Lindley J

'The term "promoter" is a term not of law, but of business, usefully summing up in a single word a number of business operations familiar to the commercial world by which a company is generally brought into existence. In every case the relief granted must depend on the establishment of such relations between the promoter and the birth, formation, and floating of the company, as render it contrary to good faith that the promoter should derive a secret profit from the promotion. A man who carries about an advertising board in one sense promotes a company, but in order to see whether relief is obtainable by the company what is to be looked to is not a word or name, but the acts and the relations of the parties.' *Whaley Bridge Calico Printing Co v Green* (1880) 5 QBD 109 at 111, per Bowen J

[The Companies Act 1862, s 165 (repealed; see now the Companies Act 1985, s 631), empowered the court to order repayment of any moneys misappropriated by any officer of a company.] 'It becomes of the utmost importance in this case and all others to know whether a man who acts as solicitor, and only as solicitor, thereby comes within the 165th section and is to be called a promoter. That a banker is not an officer of the company, though his name is in the list of persons engaged in carrying on the company, has been very plainly decided. Why should I hold that because a solicitor's name is printed in the body of the prospectus he becomes a promoter? It seems to me to be a conclusion that I cannot for a moment draw. Suppose a company the object of which is to construct buildings or works, canals, or anything else, where it would be necessary that a contract should be entered into with builders and other persons. It is very reasonable that their names should be inserted in the prospectus to give confidence in the affair. Can it therefore be said that they are promoters, or that they were officers, because they were employed in the business of the company?" *Re Great Wheal Polgooth Co Ltd* (1883) 53 LJ Ch 42 at 47, per Bacon V-C

Australia [One of the matters in issue was whether, on the facts, certain parties, who were interested in business dealings involving two companies, including the respondent company, were company 'promoters'.] 'The word "promoter" has been said on many occasions to be a word which has no very definite meaning . . . It is not only the persons who take an active part in the formation of a company and the raising of the necessary share capital to enable it to carry on business who are promoters. . . . Persons who leave it to others to get up the company upon the understanding that they also will profit from the operation may become promoters.' *Tracy v Mandalay Pty Ltd* (1953) 88 CLR 215 at 241, 242, per Dixon CJ, Williams and Taylor JJ

PROMOTION

[The Representation of the People Act 1949, s 63(1) (repealed; see now the Representation of the People Act 1983, s 75) limited the amount of money which a candidate and his supporters might spend with a view to 'promoting' or procuring the candidate's election.] 'In my view, promoting as distinct from procuring the election of a candidate means improving his chances of being elected.' *Director of Public Prosecutions v Luft* [1976] 2 All ER 569 at 574, HL, per Lord Diplock

PROMPT

Where . . . an act is required to be performed 'promptly', it shall be performed within as short a period as possible, in the circumstances, from the moment when the act could reasonably be performed. (Uniform Laws on International Sales Act 1967, Sch 1)

PRO-MUTUUM

Whenever a person, acting under a misapprehension as to an existing fact or state of facts, delivers to another a chattel which cannot be restored in specie, there arises the quasi-contract of *pro-mutuum*, which imposes upon the recipient the obligation to restore its equivalent. *Pro-mutuum* differs from *mutuum* (q.v.) in that this obligation is imposed by law, whereas in *mutuum* it arises out of the voluntary agreement between the lender and the borrower; it resembles *mutuum* in that the subject-matter to which it relates must always consist of money or fungibles, that is, chattels which, owing to their being consumed in the using, cannot be restored in specie. (2 Halsbury's Laws (4th edn) para 1536)

PROOF

'It is said . . . that by s 18 of the Prevention of Crimes Act 1871, under which these convictions were proved, there must be "proof of the identity of the person against whom the conviction is sought to be proved with the person appearing in the record or extract of conviction to have been convicted", and that there was no "proof" in this case. In my opinion "proof" does not mean conclusive proof. It means evidence upon which a jury may find that the identity is proved. No doubt in most criminal cases the prosecution calls a warder or a police officer who was present at the previous trial to prove that the prisoner is the same person, and for a good reason, because in many cases the prisoner was passing under a different name when he committed the previous offence, and therefore his identity has to be proved. But the cases of *Simpson v Dismore* [(1842) 9 M & W 47] and *Russell v Smyth* [(1842) 9 M & W 810] are authorities to shew that the Court may act upon identity of name and address as evidence of the identity of the individual.' *Martin v White* [1910] 1 KB 665 at 681, per Lord Alverstone CJ

Of debt in bankruptcy

[The Bankruptcy Act 1883, s 168 (repealed; cf now the Insolvency Act 1986, s 322), provided that unless the context otherwise required, 'debt provable in bankruptcy', or 'provable debt', included any debt or liability by the Act made provable in bankruptcy.] 'In order that a debt may be proved in bankruptcy, two things must concur. There must be a provable debt, and the person who seeks to prove it must not be under a personal incapacity for doing so. It seems to me clear that the construction which we are adopting is the true meaning of the Act. The question whether the debt in the particular case may or may not be proved no doubt depends on whether the creditor had or had not notice of an act of bankruptcy when the debt was incurred. But the existence of such notice cannot alter the quality of the debt itself, which is provable. There is merely a personal incapacity for proving the debt which arises from the fact of the creditor having had notice of an act of bankruptcy.' *Buckwell v Norman* [1898] 1 QB 622 at 626, CA, per Collins LJ

Of service

[The County Courts Act 1846, s 80 (repealed; see now the County Courts Act 1984, s 133) enabled the judge to proceed, in the absence of the defendant, to the hearing of the cause upon 'due proof of service' of the summons; see now CCR 1981, Ord 7.] 'The words, in the 80th section, "the judge, upon due proof of the service of the summons" do not require to be understood as meaning that such service has been "absolutely proved". but that there has been such proof as satisfied the mind of the judge that service of the process has been made.' *Robinson v Lenaghan* (1848) 2 Exch 333 at 337, per Pollock CB

PROPAGANDA

'Propaganda writing' means any writing letter device or sign intended or appearing to be intended for the purpose of propagating advancing or supporting any principles or views or the dissemination of information or for any like purpose. (London County Council (General Powers) Act 1954, s 20)

PROPER

[A testator directed an annuity to be paid by the trustees appointed by his will, into the 'proper' hands of his daughter for her own 'proper' use and benefit.] 'Admitting . . . that a direction to pay into the proper hands of a woman would not be a gift to her separate use, and that I am only to try whether the super-added words are to have any effect; the first thing which, independently of authority, I should have to consider is, the meaning of the word "proper", according to the ordinary use of the English language. Now the word "proper" is defined as meaning "peculiar"—"not belonging to other persons"—"not common to other persons". And the ordinary rule of construction is to give, where it is possible, some effects to all the words. Now, if, in *Margetts v Barringer* [(1835) 7 Sim 482] a declaration, that the property was to be held by the lady "independently of any other person", created a separate use, it is difficult to see why the same effect should not be given to a direction (superadded to the direction to pay into her hands) that she shall hold it—for her "peculiar use"—so as not to belong to any other—or so as not to be enjoyed by others "in common" with her. If the words are to have any operation, they must make it a gift to her separate use, as in *Margetts v Barringer* and other cases. Lord Brougham, however, rejecting or not relying upon the Vice-Chancellor's reasoning, goes (I might almost say) out of his way to decide that the word "proper" is mere repetition or surplusage, and means nothing more than "own", overruling a decision in which Lord Alvanley [in *Hartley v Hurle* (1800) 5 Ves 545] held, that the use of the word "proper" would create a separate use. And I cannot, in the face of a decision of Lord Brougham, so recently given, and the remarks of Lord Cottenham on the same point, act on any impression of my own as to the word "proper", when applied as in this case.' *Blacklow v Laws* (1842) 2 Hare 40 at 52, 53, per Shadwell V-C

'The words in RSC Ord 65, r 27(29) [now replaced by the Supreme Court Costs Rules 1959, r 28(2)] are "necessary or proper"; and "proper" has always been construed as "reasonably incurred". . . . Indeed "reasonable", "proper" and "reasonable and proper" . . . are obviously interchangeable expressions in the context under consideration, and all include something beyond what is meant by "necessary". . . . When considering whether or not an item in a bill is "proper" the correct viewpoint to be adopted by a taxing officer is that of a sensible solicitor sitting in his chair and considering what in the light of his then knowledge is reasonable in the interests of his lay client.' *Francis v Francis* [1955] 3 All ER 836 at 840, per Sachs J

Australia [The Testator's Family Maintenance and Guardianship of Infants Act 1916–1986 of NSW, s 3(1) provides that if any person dying disposes of or has disposed of his property by will, in such a manner that the widow, husband or children or any of them are left without adequate provision for their 'proper' maintenance, education or advancement in life, the Court may order that such provision be made out of the estate.] 'It will be convenient to consider carefully the language and effect of the sub-section with which the appeal is concerned. The use of the word "proper" in this connexion is of considerable importance. It connotes something different from the word "adequate". A small sum may be sufficient for the "adequate" maintenance of a child, for instance, but, having regard to the child's station in life and the fortune of his father, it may be wholly insufficient for his "proper" maintenance. So, too, a sum may be quite insufficient for the "adequate" maintenance of a child and yet may be sufficient for his maintenance on a scale that is "proper" in all the circumstances. A father with a large family and a small fortune can often only afford to leave each of his children a sum insufficient for his "adequate" maintenance. Nevertheless, such sum cannot be described as not providing for his "proper" maintenance, taking into consideration "all the circumstances of the case" as the sub-section requires shall be done.' *Bosch v Perpetual Trustee Co Ltd* [1938] AC 463 at 476, per cur.

Proper law

'The words "proper law" are well understood when applied to a contract. In such a context they mean the law which the contracting parties intend to govern their contractual obligations, wherever performed; but they have a less natural significance where applied to a will.' *Philipson-Stow v Inland Revenue Comrs* [1959] 3 All ER 879 at 883, CA, per Lord Evershed MR

Proper lease

'I am of opinion that the words in this case, "a proper lease with all proper clauses, to be approved of by me and my solicitor", are not at all stronger than the words, "subject to the title being approved by our solicitors"; and that any lease which was to contain "all proper clauses" would be subject to the jurisdiction of this Court as to whether or not the clause objected to was proper or improper.' *Eadie v Addison* (1883) 52 LJ 80 at 82, per Pearson J

PROPERLY

'The natural and ordinary meaning of "properly" in antithesis to "carefully" in the phrase "properly and carefully load, handle, stow, carry, keep, care for and discharge" [in Art III, r 2 of the Hague Rules] is, in accordance with a sound system. It has not a geographical significance.' *Renton (G H) & Co Ltd v Palmyra Trading Corpn of Panama* [1956] 3 All ER 957 at 963, HL, per Viscount Kilmuir LC (also reported in [1957] AC 149 at 166)

Properly brought

'The application is made under Order XI, r 1(g), of the Rules of the Supreme Court (revoked; see now RSC 1965, Ord 11, r 1] which says that where "any person out of the jurisdiction is a necessary or proper party to an action properly brought against some other person duly served within the jurisdiction", service out of the jurisdiction may be allowed; and the real question is whether the action is one which is properly brought against some other person duly served within the jurisdiction. . . . I think that "properly brought" refers to something more than the mere fact that one of the parties has been served, and in that way jurisdiction has been obtained over that person. It seems to me by its context to imply considerations affecting the other person out of the jurisdiction as well as the person out of the jurisdiction who has been served by leave. . . . Now the action was brought when the writ was issued, and the writ was marked, as Swinfen Eady LJ in his judgment . . . points out as "Not for service out of the jurisdiction"; consequently there was no action "properly brought" against anybody out of the jurisdiction at that time.' *Russell (John) & Co Ltd v Cayzer, Irvine & Co Ltd* [1916] 2 AC 298 at 302–304, per Lord Haldane

'I do not think it is part of the function of the court, in considering whether an action is "properly brought" against a party within the jurisdiction, to arrive at a conclusion as to whether the plaintiff will or will not succeed against that party. It is enough if the court is satisfied and that party which the plaintiff may reasonably ask the court to try.' *Ellinger v Guinness, Mahon & Co, Frankfurter Bank A-G & Metall Gesellschaft A-G* [1939] 4 All ER 16 at 22, per Morton J

Properly incurred

'A trustee can only be indemnified out of the pockets of his *cestuis que trust* against costs, charges and expenses properly incurred for the benefit of the trust—a proposition in which the word "properly" means reasonably as well as honestly incurred.' *Re Beddoe, Downes v Cottam* [1893] 1 Ch 547 at 562, CA, per Bowen LJ

Properly maintained

[The plaintiff claimed damages under the Factories Act 1937, s 25(1) (repealed; see now the Factories Act 1961, s 28(1)) for failure of the employers to see that a floor was 'properly maintained'. 'Maintained' was defined by s 152(1) of the Act (see now s 176(1) of the Act of 1961) as meaning 'maintained in an efficient state, in efficient working order, and in good repair'.] 'While the question must be approached in the light of the definition of the word "maintained", I think this definition must involve a consideration of safety. "Properly maintained", to my mind, means properly in relation to safety; "efficient" connotes safety in achieving the result which is intended, and the words "in good repair" also, I think, connote safety. That construction is supported by the placing of this section in a group of sections in Part 2 of the Act which are headed: "Safety (General Provisions)". They are provisions inserted in the Act for the safety of the workman, and one can only consider efficient maintenance and good repair against a background of safety.' *Payne v Weldless Steel Tube Co Ltd* [1955] 3 All ER 612 at 614, 615, CA, Hodson LJ; see also [1956] 1 QB 196

[The Mines and Quarries Act 1954, s 81(1) provides that the gear and machinery forming part of the equipment of a mine shall be 'properly maintained'.] ' "Maintain" may be a word of ambiguous import, but ambiguity may disappear in the context in which the word is used. Looking to what is one, if not the main, object of this legislation, namely, to safeguard the workman in the performance of his duties, and having regard to the context in which the words "shall be properly maintained" appear in s 81, I think they should be construed as meaning to keep in proper order by acts of maintenance before the thing to be maintained falls out of condition. To construe the words as covering the restoration of the thing to be maintained to a proper condition by acts of maintenance after it has fallen out of condition would greatly lessen the protection afforded to the workman. . . . In this case, I would read the words "and shall be properly maintained" in s 81(1) of the Act of 1954 as imposing an absolute obligation to keep the equipment in question at all times in a sound state of repair and fit for use. I would make one reservation. This obligation may not involve a higher measure of obligation than would be involved in the initial obligation of providing the parts of the machinery and apparatus referred to in the section.' *Hamilton v National Coal Board* [1960] 1 All ER 76 at 83, 85, HL, per Lord Keith of Avonholme

PROPERTY *See also* PERSONAL PROPERTY; REAL PROPERTY

'Property' is that which belongs to a person exclusively of others, and can be the subject of bargain and sale. It includes goodwill, trade marks, licences to use a patent, book debts, options to purchase, life policies, and other rights under a contract. An annuity secured only by a personal undertaking is not, however, treated as property; nor is a revocable licence. An owner of unworked minerals who gives an undertaking to the surface owner not to work them does not thereby convey property, and a grant of a purported exclusive right to carry on a certain business in an area when the grantor has no such right is not a conveyance of property. (44 Halsbury's Laws (4th edn) para 657)

Property, unless a contrary intention appears,

includes real and personal property, and any estate or interest in any property, real or personal, and any debt, and any thing in action, and any othe right or interest. (Conveyancing Act 1881, s 2)

(1) 'Property' includes money and all other property, real or personal, including things in action and other intangible property.

(2) A person cannot steal land, or things forming part of land and severed from it by him or by his directions, except in the following cases, that is to say—

(a) when he is a trustee or personal representative, or is authorised by power of attorney, or as liquidator of a company, or otherwise, to sell or dispose of land belonging to another, and he appropriates the land or anything forming part of it by dealing with it in breach of the confidence reposed in him; or
(b) when he is not in possession of the land and appropriates anything forming part of the land by severing it or causing it to be severed, or after it has been severed; or
(c) when, being in possession of the land under a tenancy, he appropriates the whole or part of any fixture or structure let to be used with the land.

For purposes of this subsection 'land' does not include incorporeal hereditaments; 'tenancy' means a tenancy for years or any less period and includes an agreement of such a tenancy, but a person who after the end of a tenancy remains in possession as statutory tenant or otherwise is to be treated as having possession under the tenancy. and 'let' shall be construed accordingly.

(3) A person who picks mushrooms growing wild on any land, or who picks flowers, fruit or foliage from a plant growing wild on any land, does not (although not in possession of the land) steal what he picks, unless he does it for reward or for sale or other commercial purpose.

For purposes of this subsection 'mushroom' includes any fungus, and 'plant' includes any shrub or tree.

(4) Wild creatures, tamed or untamed, shall be regarded as property; but a person cannot steal a wild creature not tamed nor ordinarily kept in captivity, or the carcase of any such creature, unless either it has been reduced into possession by or on behalf of another person and possession of it has not since been lost or abandoned, or another person is in course of reducing it into possession. (Theft Act 1968, s 4)

In this Act 'property' means property of a tangible nature, whether real or personal, including money and—

(a) including wild creatures which have been tamed or are ordinarily kept in captivity, and any other wild creatures or their carcases if, but only if, they have been reduced into possession which has not been lost or abandoned or are in the course of being reduced into possession; but
(b) not including mushrooms growing wild on any land or flowers, fruit or foliage of a plant growing wild on any land.

For the purposes of this subsection 'mushroom' includes any fungus and 'plant' includes shrub or tree. (Criminal Damage Act 1971, s 10(1))

'Property' means the general property in goods, and not merely a special property. (Sale of Goods Act 1979, s 61(1))

'Property' includes any land, buildings or works, any aircraft or vehicle and any baggage, cargo or other article of any description. (Aviation Security Act 1982, s 38(1))

'The testatrix has used the expression "property in and about my dwelling-house", and the question is whether, whatever may be the meaning of those words in common parlance, securities for money can, in a court of law, be said to be property in a particular place. . . . If a person were to give all the property in his house, and certain title deeds happened to be in it, it never could be contended that the land to which those title deeds related, would pass to the legatee, nor could it be contended that the title-deeds of land devised to another person or allowed to descend to the heir, would pass. . . . Therefore I am not at liberty to say that either the country bank-notes, promissory notes, accountable memorandum, deposit notes or mortgage passed to the testatrix' niece; but . . . I am of opinion that, in this case the Bank of England notes as well as the coins passed under the clause in question to the testatrix' niece.' *Brooke v Turner* (1836) 7 Sim 671 at 681, 682, per Shadwell V-C

'The word "property", when used with respect to an author's right to the productions of his brain, is used in a sense very different from what is meant by it when applied to a house or a watch. It means no more than that the author has the sole right of printing or otherwise multiplying copies of his work. The right which a manufacturer has in his trade mark is the exclusive right to use it for the purpose of indicating where, or by whom, or at what manufactory, the article to which it is affixed was manufactured. If the word "property" is aptly used with reference to copyright, I see no reason for doubting that it may with equal propriety be applied to trade marks.' *Leather Cloth Co Ltd v American Leather Cloth Co Ltd* (1865) 11 HL Cas 523 at 533, 534, per Lord Cranworth

'Property is not a term of art, but a common English word, which must be taken in an ordinary sense, and any ordinary person would certainly think it strange, if he were told that a debt due to him was not part of his property.' *Queensbury Industrial Society v Pickles* (1865) LR 1 Exch 1 at 4, per Bramwell B

'The testator having in the earlier part of his will given pecuniary legacies, gives . . . a legacy of £500, "also half of"—not my money, not my cash balance, but "half of my property at Rothschilds' Bank". On the most ordinary principles of construction there is nothing to cut down the wide general term "property" and . . . I come to the conclusion that when he said "property at Rothschilds' Bank" he meant everything belonging to him with which the bank was concerned.' *Re Prater, Desinge v Beare* (1888) 37 Ch D 481 at 484, 485, CA, per Lord Halsbury LC

'It is admitted that upon the authorities, . . . the word "property" used as a word of reference, cannot be treated as explaining a previous gift which prima facie carries only a life estate.' *Hill v Brown* [1894] AC 125 at 128, PC, per cur.

'A vested interest in reversion is plainly property, and . . . I am unable to see how the reversionary interest in a valuable estate, dependant on the falling in of one life, namely, that of the defendant's mother, can be described as anything but "property"—a description used in contrast to "money", the term by which it is immediately proceded.' *Cannon v Hartley*, [1949] 1 All ER 50 at 53, per Romer J

'Where there is a tenancy, whether it be a weekly tenancy or any other tenancy, that tenancy is property; and, if there is no contractual or statutory provision which prevents its being transferred by the tenant himself, the court has power in an appropriate case to make an order for that transfer, which the tenant himself could have made without consulting or obtaining the consent of the landlord.' *Hale v Hale* [1975] 2 All ER 1090 at 1094, CA, per Megaw LJ

Australia 'The Constitution [Commonwealth of Australia Constitution Act 1901–1986] . . . s 51(xxxi) provides: "The Parliament shall, subject to this Constitution, have power to make laws for the peace, order, and good government of the Commonwealth, with respect to:—The acquisition of property on just terms from any State or person for any purpose in respect of which the Parliament has power to make laws"; and s 85 provides: "When any department of the public service of a State is transferred to the Commonwealth—I. All property of the State, of any kind, used exclusively in connexion with the department, shall become vested in the Commonwealth. . . . II. The Commonwealth . . . may acquire any property of the State, of any kind, used, but not exclusively used in connexion with the department. . . ."] "No implied limitation can be placed on the fullest meaning that can be given to the word 'property' in ss 51(xxxi) and 85 of the Constitution." . . . If that be so, then, by force of the very words of s 85, the whole physical mass of the soil from the surface contained within the metres and bounds of the land actually used to the centre of the earth, that mass, including all minerals, royal or otherwise, passed directly to the Commonwealth on the transfer of the respective Departments.' *Commonwealth of Australia v State of New South Wales* (1923) 33 CLR 1 at 37, 38, per Isaacs J

Australia 'It has often been explained by writers upon jurisprudence that the term "property" is ambiguous. As applied to land it may mean the land itself in relation to which rights of ownership exist, or it may refer to the rights of ownership which exist in relation to the land. . . . In the former sense a man may say that his property consists of land. In the latter sense a man's property would consist not of land, but of rights in respect of land which were rights of ownership. I can see no reason why, so far as land is concerned, "property" in s 51(xxxi) of the Constitution [supra] should not be interpreted so as to include land itself and also proprietary rights in respect of land. The provision in the Constitution [Commonwealth of Australia Constitution Act 1901–1986] is plainly intended for the protection of the subject, and should be liberally interpreted.' *Minister of State for the Army v Dalziel* (1944) 68 CLR 261 at 276, per Latham CJ

'The word "property" in s 51(xxxi) is a

general term. It means any tangible or intangible thing which the law protects under the name of property.' Ibid at 295, per McTiernan J

Australia 'The word "property" is used in different senses. It may denote either objects of proprietary rights, such as pieces of land, domesticated animals, and machines; or the proprietary rights themselves (*In re Earnshaw Wall* [[1894] 3 Ch 156]). In common parlance it is usually employed in the former sense, but in the language of jurisprudence in the latter. Property, in the sense of proprietary rights, may exist in relation to physical objects, or to intangible things such as debts or patent rights.' *McCaughey v Comr of Stamp Duties* (1945) 46 NSWSR 192 at 201, per Jordan CJ

Australia [The Family Law Act 1975 (Cth), s 79 empowers the court to alter the interests of the parties in any property; the issue in this case being whether shares constituted property.] 'It seems unnecessary to attempt to set out a catalogue of what "property" may include in the content of s 79. It is sufficient for the purposes of this case to say that "property" means property both real and personal and includes choses in action.' *In the Marriage of D L and E J Duff* (1977) 3 Fam LR 11, 211 at 11, 217, per cur.

Australia 'Divorced from the context of taxing statutes, the word property, standing by itself, has been said to "include property, rights and powers of any description"; *Nokes v Doncaster Amalgamated Collieries Limited* [1940] AC 1015, 1033, per Lord Atkin; and cf *O'Brien v Benson's Hosiery (Holdings) Ltd* [1980] AC 562. It includes a claim or right of action: see *Re United Pacific Transport Pty Ltd* [1968] QdR 517, 524–525. "Property" was long ago said to be "the most comprehensive of all terms which can be used, inasmuch as it is indicative and descriptive of every possible interest that a party can have: *Jones v Skinner* (1836) 5 LJ Ch 90. Insofar as "property" includes "right" . . . the word "right" is said to mean "a capacity residing in one man of controlling, with the assent and assistance of the State, the actions of others". *Bailey v Uniting Church in Australia Property Trust (Qld)* (1984) 1 QdR 42 at 58, per McPherson J

In bill of lading

[The Bills of Lading Act 1855, s 1 provides that every consignee of goods named in a bill of lading, and every indorsee of a bill of lading to whom the 'property' in the goods therein mentioned shall pass, shall have transferred to and vested in him all rights of suit, and be subject to the same liabilities in respect of such goods as if the contract contained in the bill of lading had been made with himself.] 'The question in the present case resolves itself into whether the security was intended to operate, or . . . did operate, in the same way as an assignment by bill of sale or as a mere pledge. If the former, the whole and entire property would pass, and as a consequence the liability to freight would be transferred to the defendants. . . . On the other hand, if the contract, although carried out by the indorsement of the bill of lading, remained merely a pledge, I think it clear that "the property" as expressed in the Act did not pass, for by those words I understand the whole and entire legal property, and not merely the limited interest which is transferred by the contract of pledge.' *Burdick v Sewell* (1883) 10 QBD 363 at 367, 368, per Field J

In debentures

'I quite assent to the general proposition that where the word "property" is used in debentures it will not prima facie cover uncalled capital.' *Holme v Drachenfels Banket Gold Mining Syndicate* (1895) 2 Mans 146 at 147, per Vaughan Williams J

'This company, by its memorandum and articles, had authority to borrow on a charge of its uncalled capital, and I have to consider whether it has exercised that power to its fullest extent by means of these debentures . . . which purport to charge "the undertaking and all the property whatsoever and wheresoever both present and future" with payment of the sums advanced. . . . When one considers that according to the decision of Jessel MR in *Re Colonial Trusts Corporation* [(1879) 15 Ch D 465] the word "property" in debentures of this kind includes present and future property of the company down to the commencement of the winding-up, but not capital then uncalled, it seems to me to be an extraordinary proposition to say that because you find the words "present and future property" in the deed creating the charge you must make it include that which by force of the term "property" itself is not included: to do this would be altering the meaning of the word "property". I hold, therefore, that the addition of the word "future" does not in any way extend the meaning of the word "property" as defined by the authorities.' *Re Streatham & General Estates Co* [1897] 1 Ch 15 at 17, 18, per Chitty J

'We have all come to the conclusion that although, in a sense, uncalled capital may be called property, yet it is property of a very peculiar description. After all, it is not a debt. It is a right to make a call and create a debt; and it is rather stretching the meaning of the word "property" to make it include such a right as that. When we look at the decisions we see that for years past, and in all the text-books to which professional men have recourse, it has been considered that in this class of document, namely, debentures of limited companies, the word "property" will not include uncalled capital.' *Re Russian Spratts Patent Ltd Johnson v Russian Spratts Patent Ltd* [1898] 2 Ch 149 at 152, CA, per Lindley MR

'The question whether I have jurisdiction to appoint a manager depends entirely on the question whether the goodwill or business of the company is charged by the debentures. The words of the debentures are these: "The company" thereby charges "all its lands, buildings, property . . . and effects whatsoever, both present and future." . . . Here the words are "all property and effects whatsoever". If as regards a partnership the words "partnership assets" or "effects" cover goodwill, it would seem that the word "property" must also cover "goodwill".' *Re Leas Hotel Co, Salter v Leas Hotel Co* [1902] 1 Ch 332 at 333, 334, per Kekewich J

In will

'It is well known, that the word "property" is the most comprehensive of all the terms which can be used, inasmuch as it is indicative and descriptive of every possible interest which the party can have. The question, in these cases, is, whether the terms used are descriptive of the interest which the testator had, or descriptive of a particular estate. If they are descriptive of the particular estate, one construction would prevail; but if they are descriptive of the interest which he has in that estate, then another construction would prevail. But when we find the word, "property" used, nothing can be more strong, for the purpose of adopting that construction, which would carry any interest the testator might have in any property, or over which he had any control.' *Jones v Skinner* (1836) 5 LJ Ch 87 at 90, per Langdale MR

Of company

[The memorandum and articles of association of a company empowered the directors to borrow by way of mortgage or otherwise on any of the 'property' of the company.] 'Book debts are property of the company.' *Bloomer v Union Coal & Iron Co* (1873) LR 16 Eq 383 at 385, per Bacon V-C

'The question in this appeal is, whether a power in a deed of settlement of a joint stock company authorising the directors to mortgage or charge the property of the company, gives them authority to include in such mortgage or charge future calls, or, in other words, the unpaid capital of the company. There was a difference of opinion amongst the Judges of the Supreme Court. . . . The majority were of opinion that the word "property" included future calls. . . . It is much to be regretted that the attention of the Judges was not called to *Stanley's Case* [(1864) 4 De G J & S 407]. . . . In that case the words of the power were "property and funds" and it was held that a charge on future calls was ultra vires and void. It is impossible to distinguish that case from the one under appeal. . . . The right of the company is, strictly speaking, more in the nature of power than of property; and, although that which a man has power to make his own may be charged, as well as that which is actually his, it requires apt and proper words, or a sufficient context, to have this effect.' *Bank of South Australia v Abrahams* (1875) LR 6 PC 265 at 269–271, PC, per cur.

PROPRIETARY CLUB *See* CLUB

PROPRIETARY INTEREST

In this section the expression 'proprietary interest', in relation to a patent, means the interest of a person whose name is for the time being entered or required to be entered in the register of patents as the grantee or proprietor of the patent or as one of two or more grantees or proprietors thereof and, in relation to a registered design, means the interest of a person whose name is for the time being entered or required to be entered in the register of designs as the proprietor of the design or as one of two or more proprietors thereof. (Coal Industry Nationalisation Act 1946, s 6(8))

PROPRIETOR

'Proprietor', in relation to any school, means the person or body of persons responsible for the management of the school, and for the purposes of the provisions of this Act relating to applications for the registration of independent schools, includes any person or body of persons proposing to be so responsible. (Education Act 1944, s 114(1))

PROSCRIBE

[The Clergy Discipline Act 1892, s 2(12) (repealed; but see now Ecclesiastical Jurisdiction Measure 1963, s 14) declared that the expressions 'immoral act', 'immoral conduct', and 'immoral habit' included such acts, conduct and habits as were 'proscribed' by the 75th and 109th Canons of 1603.] 'The 109th canon is entitled "Notorious crimes and scandals to be certified unto Ecclesiastical Courts by presentment'. . . . Now, what are the offences "proscribed" by this canon. To proscribe means to condemn capitally. Strictly speaking, nothing is condemned by the canon. It merely provides that certain offences are to be reported to the authorities with a view to some subsequent proceedings. But I suppose we ought to read the section as if "described" or "mentioned" had been substituted for "proscribed".' *Rochester (Bp) v Harris* [1893] P 137 at 142, per the Chancellor (Dibdin)

PROSECUTION *See also* MALICIOUS PROSECUTION

A prosecution exists where a criminal charge is made before a judicial officer or tribunal, and any person who makes or is actively instrumental in the making or prosecuting of the charge is deemed to prosecute it, and is called the prosecutor. (45 Halsbury's Laws (4th edn) para 1342)

Want of

'The power to dismiss for want of prosecution should be exercised only where the court is satisfied that either: A the default has been intentional and contumelious, e.g. disobedience to a peremptory order of the court or conduct amounting to an abuse of the process of the court; or B (i) there has been inordinate and inexcusable delay on the part of the plaintiff or his lawyers, and (ii) such delay (a) either will give rise to a substantial risk that it is not possible to have a fair trial of the issues in the action, or (b) is such as is likely to cause or to have caused serious prejudice to the defendants either as between themselves and the plaintiff or between each other or between them and a third party.' *Bremer Vulkan Schiffbau und Maschinenfabrik v South India Shipping Corpn* [1979] 3 All ER 195 at 197, per Donaldson J

PROSPECTIVE DAMAGES *See* DAMAGES

PROSPECTIVE PURCHASER

'As far as I know, there is no authority on what is meant by "a prospective purchaser". . . . It appears to me, however, that the word "prospective" does not connote necessarily either the term "ready" or "willing" or "able"; it means a man who has the question of buying this property in prospect or in contemplation and is prepared to make an offer with regard to it.' *Drewery v Ware-Lane* [1960] 3 All ER 529 at 532, CA, per Ormerod LJ

PROSPECTUS

'Prospectus' means any prospectus, notice, circular, advertisement, or other invitation, offering to the public for subscription or purchase any share in or debentures of a company. (Companies Act 1985, s 744)

[The Companies Act 1900, s 4 (repealed; see now the Companies Act 1985, s 83) made it unlawful for a company to proceed to allotment unless (inter alia) the amount of the minimum subscription was stated in the 'prospectus'. The term 'prospectus' was defined by s 30 (see now s 744 of the Act of 1985, supra).] 'A prospectus is defined in s 30 to mean "any prospectus, notice, circular, advertisement, or other invitation, offering to the public for subscription or purchase any shares or debentures of a company", and it appears to me to be a reasonable interpretation of the term "the prospectus" used in s 4 to hold that although as regards every invitation issued to the public the statutory provisions, apply, yet, when we come to the remedy, "the prospectus" is that document offering capital to the public upon the basis of which the applicant has actually subscribed.' *Rousell v Burnham* [1909] 1 Ch 127 at 130, 131, per Parker J

'A document is not a prospectus unless it is an invitation to the public, but if it satisfies this condition it is not the less a prospectus because it is issued to a defined class of the public.' *Nash v Lynde* [1929] AC 158 at 171, per Lord Buckmaster

United States The term 'prospectus' means any prospectus, notice, circular, advertisement, letter, or communication, written or by radio or television, which offers any security for sale or confirms the sale of any security. . . . (Securities Act 1933, s 2(10))

PROSTITUTION

'The respondent was a prostitute who occupied premises in Manchester, and who was prosecuted under s 13, sub-s 2 of the Criminal Law Amendment Act 1885 [repealed; see now Sexual Offences Act 1956, s 36], for knowingly permitting the premises to be used for the purpose of habitual prostitution. The magistrate dismissed the information, and the question is whether he was right in so doing. In my opinion he was quite right. The respondent had committed no offence, and his view that she was not permitting her premises to be used for the purpose of habitual prostitution was the right one. The effect of the argument for the appellant is that it would be an offence for a woman to use premises occupied by her alone for the purposes of her own habitual prostitution. Supposing that men resort to her premises for those purposes, can it be said that the woman is knowingly permitting the premises to be used for the purposes of habitual prostitution? This is not a case of another person letting the premises to her with knowledge that they were to be used for such purposes. It is a case where the woman herself commits the acts which, it is said, must not be knowingly permitted. I feel no doubt about this case. We have only to construe the language of the section and endeavour to ascertain the intention of the legislature, and it would certainly be odd to make it an offence for a woman to commit acts of prostitution on premises which she rents. If Parliament meant that, they could easily have said so in plain terms.' *Mattison v Johnson* (1916) 85 LJKB 741 at 742, 743, DC, per Lord Reading CJ

[The Criminal Law Amendment Act 1885, s 2(2) (repealed; see now the Sexual Offences Act 1956, s 22) made it a misdemeanour to procure or attempt to procure any woman or girl to become a common 'prostitute'.] 'The argument advanced on behalf of the appellant practically was that the offering by a woman of her body for the gratification of the sexual passions of men, even if it is done as a regular trade, indiscriminately and for gain, is not prostitution unless the men's passions are gratified by the act of sexual connexion and not otherwise. We have come to the conclusion that that contention is not well-founded. . . . The Court is of opinion that the term "common prostitute" in the statute is not limited so as to mean only one who permits acts of lewdness with all the sundry, or with such as hire her, when such acts are in the nature of ordinary sexual connexion. We are of opinion that prostitution is proved if it be shown that a woman offers her body commonly for lewdness for payment in return.' *R v De Munck* [1918] 1 KB 635 at 637, 638, CCA, per cur.

[The Criminal Law Amendment Act 1885, s 13 (repealed; see supra) imposed penalties upon any person who (inter alia), being the tenant, lessee or occupier or person in charge of any premises, knowingly permitted such premises or any part thereof to be used as a brothel or for the purposes of habitual 'prostitution'.] 'In my opinion the magistrates here have given too restricted a meaning to the words "brothel" and "prostitution" as used in this section. It is not disputed that they have dismissed the information on the ground that there was no evidence that the women resorting to the premises were known to the police as prostitutes, and no evidence that they were resorting to the premises for fornication and receiving payment therefore. There was evidence before them from which the necessary inference was that a number of women were resorting to the premises habitually for the purpose of fornication with men who resorted there. There is a significant piece of evidence in the case from which it appears that a motor-car with four men and two girls arrived at these premises. The respondent came to the door and said, "Have you been here before to-night?" and a girl replied, "The men have not, but we girls have". The only inference is that the girls had already resorted to these premises on previous occasions for unlawful purposes with other men. That is sufficient to constitute these particular girls prostitutes in the ordinary sense.' *Winter v Woolfe* (1930) 47 TLR 145 at 147, per Avory J

'The words used by Darling J [in *R v De Munck*, supra] . . . that "prostitution" means "the offering of a woman of her body for purposes amounting to common lewdness for payment" may well have been taken from the dictionary meaning; indeed, in the Shorter Oxford English Dictionary, under "Prostitution", the first meaning given is "The offering of the body to indiscriminate lewdness for hire". The court in *de Munck's* case were clearly treating lewdness in the expression they used as not confined to the gratification of normal sexual appetite. It appears from cases to which we have been referred that, in the United States, it has been held that while "lewdness" may include obscene acts, yet "prostitution" is confined to the exposure by a woman of her body for sexual intercourse. So far as this court is concerned, however, we see no reason to depart in any way from the decision of this court in *de Munck's* case.' *R v Webb* [1963] 3 All ER 177 at 179, CCA, per cur.; also reported in [1964] 1 QB 357 at 365, 366

'A common prostitute is any woman who offers herself commonly for lewdness for reward. This appellant on his own version plainly attempted to persuade the woman . . . to offer herself for lewdness for reward. What about the word "common", or its adverbial form? Is it a meaningless word which adds nothing to the word "prostitute", or does it have some effect? That really is the only point in this appeal. It is clear to us that the word is not mere surplusage. We do not pause to consider whether the performance by a woman or a single act of lewdness with a man on one occasion for reward constitutes the woman a prostitute. But we are of the view that it does not make her a woman who offers herself commonly for lewdness. That must be someone who is prepared for reward to engage in acts of lewdness with all and sundry, or with anyone who may hire her for that purpose.' *R v Morris-Lowe* [1985] 1 All ER 400 at 402, CA, per cur.

Australia 'The ordinary meaning of "prostitution" is "the offering of the body to indiscriminate lewdness for hire". The same or a similar meaning has been applied to the word "prostitution" in criminal statutes.' *Samuels v Bosch* (1972) 127 CLR 517 at 524, per Gibbs J

Canada [As defence to a charge of keeping a bawdy house, counsel for the accused asserted that the absence of proof of payment for the services rendered by the inmates vitiated the charge.] 'It is not more illicit for a woman to give herself up for payment to a man who is not her husband than to do so solely to satisfy her own passion or that of her partner. Neither the one nor the other of these acts is prohibited by the criminal law; both are in the moral domain. But what the law intended to repress, according to my opinion, is the keeping of establishments destined to encourage immoral relations between men and women. If the appellant's allegation were fair it would be necessary to say that a keeper who admitted to her establishment only girls who gave themselves up solely through passion, or to satisfy the passion of another, could not be found guilty of keeping a house of prostitution. It seems impossible to me to interpret the word "prostitution" in a sense that would lead to such a result. I therefore believe that the word prostitution must be understood in a much larger sense and in a manner to include relations between unmarried men and women, whether these relations take place for payment or not.' *Dube v R* (1948) 94 Can CC 164 at 171, Que CA, per Pratte J

Living on earnings of

For the purposes of this section [which makes it an offence for a man to live on the earnings of prostitution] a man who lives with or is habitually in the company of a prostitute, or who exercises control, direction or influence over a prostitute's movements in a way which shows he is aiding, abetting or compelling her prostitution with others, shall be presumed to be knowingly living on the earnings of prostitution, unless he proves the contrary. (Sexual Offences Act 1956, s 30(2))

'What . . . is meant by living in whole or in part on the earnings of prostitution? It was not contended by the Crown that these words in their context [the Sexual Offences Act 1956, s 30(1)] bear the very wide meaning which might possibly be ascribed to them. The subsection does not cover every person whose livelihood depends in whole or in part on payment to him by prostitutes for services rendered or goods supplied, clear though it may be that payment is made out of the earnings of prostitution. The grocer who supplies groceries, the doctor or lawyer who renders professional service, to a prostitute do not commit an offence under the Act. It is not to be supposed that it is its policy to deny to her the necessities or even the luxuries of life if she can pay for them. I would say, however, that, though a person who is paid for goods or services out of the earnings of prostitution does not necessarily commit an offence under the Act, yet a person does not necessarily escape from its provisions by receiving payment for the goods or services that he supplies to a prostitute. The argument that such a person lives on his own earnings not on hers is inconclusive. To give effect to it would be to exclude from the operation of the Act the very persons, the tout, the bully or protector, whom it was designed to catch. For they would surely claim that they served the prostitute, however despicable their service might seem to others. Somewhere the line must be drawn, and I do not find it easy to draw it. It is not enough to say that here are plain English words and that it must be left to a jury to say in regard to any particular conduct whether the statutory offence has been committed. I have said enough, for instance, to show that the wider meaning of which the words are clearly capable is admissible. The jury should be directed that some limitation must be put on the words. What is the limitation? My Lords, I think that (apart from the operation of sub-s (2) [which provides that a man who lives with or who is habitually in the company of a prostitute, etc, shall be presumed to be living on her earnings]) a person may fairly be said to be living in whole or in part on the earnings of prostitution if he is paid by prostitutes for goods or services supplied by him to them for the purpose of their prostitution which he would not supply but for the fact that they were prostitutes. I emphasise the negative part of this proposition, for I wish to distinguish beyond all misconception such a case from that in which the service supplied could be supplied to a woman whether a prostitute or not. It may be that circumstances will be equivocal, though no example readily occurs to me. But a case which is beyond all doubt is one where the service is of its nature referable to prostitution and to nothing else. No better example of this could be found than payment by a prostitute for advertisement of her readiness to prostitute herself.' *Shaw v Director of Public Prosecutions*, [1961] 2 All ER 446 at 449, 450, HL, per Viscount Simonds

'"Living on" normally, I think, connotes living parasitically.' Ibid at 454, per Lord Reid

PROTECTED SITE

For the purpose of this Part of this Act [Part I; provisions for protection of residential occupiers] a protected site is any land in respect of which a site licence is required under Part I of the Caravan Sites and Control of Development Act 1960 or would be so required if paragraph 11 of Schedule 1 to that Act (exemption of land occupied by local authorities) were omitted, not being land in respect of which the relevant planning permission or site licence—

(a) is expressed to be granted for holiday use only; or
(b) is otherwise so expressed or subject to such conditions that there are times of the year when no caravan may be stationed on the land for human habitation.

(Caravan Sites Act 1968, s 1(2))

Commercial paper

United States A protest is a certificate of dishonour made under the hand and seal of a United States consul or vice consul or a notary public or other person authorised to certify dishonour by the law of the place where dishonour occurs. It may be made upon information satisfactory to such person. (Uniform Commercial Code 1978, s 3–509(1))

PROTEST

Ship's protest

The object of the protest is to exonerate the master and mariners or person making the protest from any charge of improper, illegal or negligent conduct when damage or injury has happened to a ship or her cargo during a voyage, and to record formally any facts or circumstances relating to disputes or other matters which it is thought desirable to authenticate formally in order to exculpate the master or mariners from any charge or complaint of illegal or improper action. (34 Halsbury's Laws (4th edn) para 226)

A protestd is a declaration by the master when damage has been caused to a ship or her cargo, and is made before a notary or British consul at the first port of call. The object of a protest is to record promptly in an authentic form the circumstances in which loss or damage occurred so as to exonerate the master and his crew from blame. Thus, a protest would record details of an accident or heavy weather encountered on a voyage which might have caused loss of deck cargo or which might have prevented the ventilation of cargo or which might have delayed the voyage, or caused the vessel to put into a port of refuge. Although protests are not compulsory or essential in England, they are often made in practice to support insurance claims by foreign cargo owners in countries where protests are required. In English courts they are not receivable in evidence, although they may be used in cross-examination. (43 Halsbury's Laws (4th edn) para 193)

'Under protest'

'It is said, that the money was received by the petitioner, and the receipt given "under protest". These words are often used on these occasions, but they have no distinct technical meaning, unless accompanied with a statement of circumstances, shewing that they were used by way of notice or protest, reserving to the party, by reason of such circumstances, a right to a taxation, notwithstanding such payment. The words have no distinct meaning by themselves, and amount to nothing, unless explained by the proceedings and circumstances.' *Re Massey* (1845) 8 Beav 458 at 462, per Langdale MR

PROTESTANT

Australia 'A meaning given by the Oxford Dictionary to the word "Protestant" is: "A member or adherent of any of the Christian churches or bodies which repudiated the papal authority, and separated or were severed from the Roman communion in the Reformation of the sixteenth century, and generally of any of the bodies of Christian descended from them; hence in general language applied to any Western Christian or member of a Christian church outside the Roman communion." I do not see any difficulty in determining, of anyone who professes a religious faith, whether that faith is Protestant or not.' *Re Cross, Law v Cross* [1938] VLR 221 at 226, 227, per Martin J

New Zealand 'The first condition of the present codicil raises the question whether the phrase "the Protestant faith" as it is there used is ambiguous. That the word "Protestant" may have a special meaning in relation to the Church of England is shewn by the definitions of "Protestant" in the standard dictionaries of Murray, Webster, and Funk and Wagnall. The Church of England is, in the ordinary sense, a Protestant Church, but a section of it, the Anglo-Catholics, maintain that the method of Church government and the doctrine of the Church remain unchanged by the Reformation of the sixteenth century. Nevertheless, I assume that to-day the term "Protestant faith" indicates generally the faith of Christians of the Western World who are not Roman Catholics. The distinctive doctrine of that faith is the denial of the authority of the Pope in matters of religion. That, however, is by no means the only doctrine of the Protestant faith. It contains, as well, the other doctrines which make the content of the Christian religion as it is understood by Protestants. The sum of these doctrines is only to be found in the doctrines of all the various Protestant Churches. Yet the testator can never have intended that his grandson should adhere, or attempt to adhere, to all those doctrines even though they all include an article of faith denying the authority of the Pope in religious matters. If one asks whether the testator intended his grandson to adhere to the Protestant faith according to the creeds and articles of the Church of England or according to the Catechisms of the Church of Scotland or according to the tenets and rules of any Non-conformist Church or of any Church of Christian Science, the answer is that it is impossible to say. The testator has therefore failed to define the particular kind or degree of Protestant faith, which is to constitute "the Protestant faith" of his grandson, and the term is void for uncertainty.' *Re Lockie, Guardian, Trust, & Executors Co of New Zealand Ltd* [1945] NZLR 230 at 244, 245, per Smith J; also reported [1944] GLR 464 at 468

PROVIDE

[The Factories Act 1937, s 49 (repealed; see now the Factories Act 1961, s 65) imposed a duty on employers to 'provide' suitable goggles or effective screens where processes were used involving special risk of injury to the eyes.] 'Goggles would be "provided" if they were given to each man individually. I do not think that is the only way in which they could be "provided", but, in my view, in order to "provide" them within the meaning of the Act it would be necessary either that they should be put in a place where they come easily and obviously to the hand of the workman who is about to grind, or, at the very least, that he should be given clear directions where he is to get them.' *Finch v Telegraph Construction and Maintenance Co Ltd* [1949] 1 All ER 452 at 454, per Devlin J

'A butcher does not "provide" or "supply" his customer with meat if he leaves it at the roadside a mile away from the customer's house.' *Norris v Syndi Manufacturing Co Ltd* [1952] 1 All ER 935 at 941, CA, per Romer LJ

[The plaintiff was working upon a roof which was defective, and the defendants, noticing that he was working without using boards, brought two duckboards from their own builder's yard and left them close by where the workman could see them. The question was whether they had 'provided' boards within reg 31(3) (a) of the Building (Safety, Health and Welfare) Regulations 1948 (revoked; see now the Construction (Working Places) Regulations 1966, SI 1966/94).] 'I do not think that there is any hard and fast meaning of the word "provided"; it must depend on the circumstances of the case as to what is "provided" and how what is "provided" is going to be used. It is a very material circumstance here that the boards had to be used in different places. They must be nearby; they must be shown to the person requiring them and placed at his disposal; he must know that they are there for him to use, and he must know that he can put them where he wants. No doubt it should be added that they must not be far away, but *Farquhar v Chance Bros Ltd* [(1951) 115 JP 469] decides that fifty yards is not too far away, and there is a much shorter distance in the present case. In these circumstances, therefore, I find that there was a sufficient "providing" of the boards in this case to satisfy reg 31(3)(a), and, accordingly, there was no breach in that respect by the Belmont company.' *Ginty v Belmont Building Supplies Ltd* [1959] 1 All ER 414 at 422, per Pearson J

PROVIDED THAT

'It was pointed out by Lord Clauson during the argument, I think with coherent reason, that the phrase "provided always" does not really introduce a proviso to what has gone before. It is really a shortened form of saying: "Provided always and it is hereby agreed". That is to say, that it adds a substantive provision for the protection of the defendants and is not merely importing a proviso to that which has been provided for the protection of the plaintiffs before.' *Egham & Stains Electricity Co Ltd v Egham Urban District Council* [1942] 2 All ER 154 at 156, CA, per MacKinnon LJ; on appeal, [1944] 1 All ER 107

Australia 'The words "provided that" are ordinarily used to introduce an exception from, or qualification of, a general rule to which it is added, and, when that rule is an enactment granting a privilege, suggest, prima facie, that the privilege is to be limited or qualified, and not that a larger privilege is to be conferred, although the context may compel the latter construction.' *Emmerton v Federal Land Tax Comr* (1916) 22 CLR 40 at 49, per Griffith CJ, Barton, Gavan Duffy and Rich JJ

PROVINCIAL

Canada [An Ontario corporation took assignment of interests in Yukon with intent to carry on provincial business there.] 'Provincial' means, I think, provincial as to the incorporating province; and although it is perhaps conceivable that as regards companies formed for some communal or governmental purpose, the word 'provincial' might be read as having reference to the province as a political entity, I think that as regards companies formed for the purpose of carrying on some business for private gain it must be read as having reference to the province as a geographical area.' *Bonanza Creek Gold Mining Co v R* (1914) 50 SCR 534 at 574, 575, SCC, per Duff J

PROVISION

'Provision' in relation to a building, includes, in addition to the construction or erection thereof, the acquisition of a site and the provision of necessary fittings, installations, outbuildings, fences, paths and drives, and 'provide' shall be construed accordingly. (Pastoral Measure 1983, s 87(1)).

PROVISIONS

'The word "provisions", I suppose, in the broad sense means consumable articles; all that you eat and drink. If you speak of providing an army in the field with "provisions", you certainly would not mean exclusively that which is in the trade supplied by a "provision merchant". It would be a very much larger supply.' *Lovell & Christmas Ltd v Wall* (1911) 104 LT 85 at 93, 94, CA, per Buckley LJ

[A harbour order exempted from rates all ships' 'provisions' necessary for the voyage.] 'I think . . . that bunker coals cannot be held to fall within the terms "ships' provisions—necessary for the voyage". . . . The words "ships' provisions", however, in their ordinary use, refer to the victualling of the ship.' *Fraserburgh Harbour Comrs v Will* 1916, SC 107 at 119, per the Lord Justice Clerk (Lord Scott Dickson)

PROVISO

'Now, the ordinary and proper function of a proviso coming after a general enactment is to limit the general enactment in certain instances. No doubt sometimes a proviso has been used in Acts of Parliament and in other documents to enlarge a previously given discretion; but that is not its proper function.'

Re Barker, Ex Constable [1890] 25 QB 285 at 292, per Lord Esher MR

'I decline to read into any enactment words which are not to be found there, and which would alter its operative effect because of provisions to be found in any proviso. Of course a proviso may be used to guide you in the selection of one or other of two possible constructions of the words to be found in the enactment, and shew when there is doubt about its scope, when it may reasonably admit of doubt as to its having this scope or that, which is the proper view to take of it; but to find in it an enacting provision which enables something to be done which is not to be found in the enactment itself on any reasonable construction of it, simply because otherwise the proviso would be meaningless and senseless, would, as I have said, be in the highest degree dangerous. And for this reason: one knows perfectly well that it not unfrequently happens that persons are unreasonably apprehensive as to the effect of an enactment when there is really no question of its application to their case; they nevertheless think that some Court may possibly hold that it will apply to their case, and they suggest if it is not intended to be applicable no harm would be done by inserting a proviso to protect them; and, accordingly, a proviso is inserted to guard against the particular case of which a particular person was apprehensive, although the enactment was never intended to apply to his case, or to any other similar cases at all. If the construction contended for were adopted the result would be this: Having put in a proviso which was thought to be needless in order to satisfy certain persons, or a particular class of persons, and allay their fears, you would have the enactment so construed against the intention of the Legislature as to impose a liability upon a number of people who were not so apprehensive, or perhaps were not present, and therefore either did not think it necessary or were not in a position to protect their own interests by a proviso. My Lords, I am satisfied that many instances might be given where provisos could be found in legislation that are meaningless because they have been put in to allay fears when those fears were absolutely unfounded, and when no proviso at all was necessary to protect the persons at whose instance they were inserted.' *West Derby Guardians v Metropolitan Life Assurance Society* [1897] AC 647 at 655, 656, HL, per Lord Herschell

'It is said that where there is a proviso, the former part, which is described as the enacting part, must be construed without reference to the proviso. No doubt there may be cases in which the first part is so clear and unambiguous as not to admit in regard to the matters which are there clear any reference to any other part of the section; the proviso may simply be an exception out of what is clearly defined in the first part, or it may be some qualification not inconsistent with what is expressed in the first part. . . . The proper course is to apply the broad general rule of construction, which is that a section or enactment must be construed as a whole, each portion throwing light, if need be, on the rest.' *Jennings v Kelly* [1940] AC 206 at 229, per Lord Wright

PROVOCATION

Where on a charge of murder there is evidence on which the jury can find that the person charged was provoked (whether by things done or by things said or by both together) to lose his self-control, the question whether the provocation was enough to make a reasonable man do as he did shall be left to be determined by the jury; and in determining that question the jury shall take into account everything both done and said according to the effect which, in their opinion, it would have on a reasonable man. (Homicide Act 1957, s 3)

'The possibility of a verdict of manslaughter instead of murder only arises when the evidence given before the jury is such as might satisfy them as the judges of fact that the elements were present which would reduce the crime to manslaughter, or, at any rate, might induce a reasonable doubt whether this was, or was not, the case. Murder by secret poisoning, for example, does not give room for the defence that, owing to provocation received, the administration of the poison should be treated as manslaughter. . . . It is not all provocation that will reduce the crime of murder to manslaughter. Provocation, to have that result, must be such as temporarily deprives the person provoked of the power of self control, as the result of which he commits the unlawful act which causes death. "In deciding the question whether this was or was not the case, regard must be had to the nature of the act by which the offender causes death, to the time which elapsed between the provocation and the act which caused death, to the offender's conduct during that interval, and to all other circumstances tending to show the state of his mind." Stephen's Digest of the Criminal Law, art 317. The test to be applied is that of the effect of the provocation on a reasonable man, as was laid down by the Court of Criminal Appeal in *Rex v Lesbini* [[1914] 3 KB 1116], so that an unusually excitable or pugnacious individual is not entitled to rely on provocation which would not have led an ordinary person to act as he did. In applying the test, it is of particular importance (a) to consider whether a sufficient interval has elapsed since the provocation to allow a reasonable man time to cool, and (b) to take into account the instrument with which the homicide was effected, for to retort, in the heat of passion induced by provocation, by a simple blow, is a very different thing from making use of a deadly instrument like a concealed dagger. In short, the mode of resentment must bear a reasonable relationship to the provocation if the offence is to be reduced to manslaughter.' *Mancini v Director of Public Prosecutions* [1942] AC 1 at 8, 9, per Lord Simon LC

'What are the suggested elements of provocation in this case which, according to the contentions put forward on behalf of the appellant, should have been left to the jury? That the appellant's reason was dethroned (a not unfamiliar phrase in the forensic arena) because the woman whom he had adulterously known for two months desired to resume intimate companionship with another man whom, for that night at any rate, she preferred to the appellant. That annoyed the appellant; that made him angry and that aroused the feeling of jealousy. What is jealousy? It has been defined as "apprehension of being displaced in the love of another", and "fear of being supplanted in the affection of a lover". It is not an unknown motive for murder, but motive is not provocation. A man may conjure up a motive or reasons sufficient for himself to cause him to kill, but it does not follow that that provides evidence of provocation. Motive is not provocation, and it only creates confusion if it is sought to establish provocation merely on a foundation of motive. Provocation in this connexion has a very precise meaning in law. The incidents upon which the contention of provocation is based must be contemporaneous with the killing, or, at any rate, closely related to the killing in point of time. A man cannot receive what he contends is provocation, go for a walk, think it over, deliberate upon killing the person whom he thinks has provoked him, find a deadly weapon, carry it to the scene and use it with fatal results hours after the start of the incident giving rise to the resentment, and they say: "There is evidence that I was provoked within the meaning of that word in law." There may be evidence of provocation if there is evidence of assault and battery of serious nature and then a sudden killing, if there is a fight, if there is unlawful imprisonment, or if a husband observes an act of adultery on the part of the wife. There may be other circumstances which may provide evidence of provocation within the meaning of the law, but such things as those that I have mentioned indicate the general nature of the evidence to be looked for.' *R v Gauthier* (1943) 29 Cr App Rep 113 at 118, 119, per cur.

'The whole doctrine relating to provision depends on the fact that it causes, or may cause, a sudden and temporary loss of self-control whereby malice, which is the formation of an intention to kill or to inflict grievous bodily harm, is negatived. Consequently, where the provocation inspires an actual intention to kill (such as Holmes admitted in the present case), or to inflict grievous bodily harm, the doctrine that provocation may reduce murder to manslaughter seldom applies. Only one very special exception has been recognised, viz, the actual finding of a spouse in the act of adultery. . . . A sudden confession of adultery without more can never constitute provocation of a sort which might reduce murder to manslaughter.' *Holmes v Director of Public Prosecutions* [1946] AC 588 at 598, 600, HL, per Lord Simon

'The only possible defence that could be set up was that the appellant acted under such provocation as to reduce the crime to manslaughter, and on this point the summing up of the learned judge [Devlin J], in the opinion of this court, was impeccable. I am going to read a passage from his summing-up, because I think it deserves to be remembered as a clear and accurate charge to a jury when provocation is pleaded as can well be made. He said: "Provocation is some act, or series of acts, done by the dead man to the accused which would cause in any reasonable person, and actually causes in the accused, a sudden and temporary loss of self-control, rendering the accused so subject to passion as to make him or her for the moment not master of his mind. Let me distinguish for you some of the things which provocation in law is not. Circumstances which merely predispose to a violent act are not enough. Severe nervous exasperation or a long course of conduct causing suffering and anxiety are not by themselves sufficient to constitute provocation in law. Indeed, the further removed an incident is from the crime, the less it counts. A long course of cruel conduct may be more blameworthy than a sudden act provoking retaliation, but you are not concerned with blame here—the blame attaching to the dead man. You are not standing in judgment on him. He has not been heard in this court. He cannot now ever be heard. He has no defender here to argue for him. . . . It does not matter how cruel he was, how much or how little he was to blame, except in so far as it resulted in the final act of the appellant. What matters is whether this girl had the time to say: 'Whatever I have suffered, whatever I have endured, I know that thou shalt not kill.' That is what matters. Similarly, as counsel for the prosecution has told you, circumstances which induce a desire for revenge, or a sudden passion of anger, are not enough. Indeed, circumstances which induce a desire for revenge are inconsistent with provocation, since the conscious formulation of a desire for revenge means that a person has had time to think, to reflect, and that would negative a sudden temporary loss of self-control which is of the essence of provocation. . . . Provocation being, therefore, as I have defined it, there are two things, in considering it, to which the law attaches great importance. The first of them is whether there was what is sometimes called time for cooling, that is, for passion to cool and for reason to regain dominion over the mind. That is why most acts of provocation are cases of sudden quarrels, sudden blows inflicted with an implement already in the hand, perhaps being used, or being picked up, where there has been no time for reflection. Secondly, in considering whether provocation has or has not been made out, you must consider the retaliation in provocation—that is to say, whether the mode of resentment bears some proper and reasonable relationship to the sort of provocation that has been given. Fists might be answered with fists, but not with a deadly weapon, and that is a factor you have to bear in mind when you are considering the question of provocation." That is as good a definition of the doctrine of provocation as it has ever been my lot to read, and I think it might well stand as a classic direction given to a jury in a case in which the sympathy of everyone would be with the accused person and against the dead man and it was essential that the judge should see that the jury had an opportunity of vindicating the law, whatever the consequences might be.' *R v Duffy* [1949] 1 All ER 932 at 932, 933, CCA, per Lord Goddard

'Provocation in law consists mainly of three elements—the act of provocation, the loss of self-control, both actual and reasonable, and the retaliation proportionate to the provocation. The defence cannot require the issue to be left to the jury unless there has been produced a credible narrative of events suggesting the presence of these three elements. They are not detached. Their relationship to each other—particularly in point of time, whether there was time for passion to cool—is of the first importance. The point that their Lordships wish to emphasise is that provocation in law means something more than a provocative incident. That is only one of the constituent elements.' *Lee Chun-Chuen v R* [1963] 1 All ER 73 at 79, PC, per Lord Devlin; also reported in [1963] AC 220 at 231

'The court desires to say for general application, that wherever there has been a killing, or indeed the infliction of violence not proving fatal, in circumstances where the defendant puts forward a justification such as self-defence, such as provocation, such as resistance to a violent felony, it is very important and is essential that the matter should be so put before the jury that there is no danger of their failing to understand that none of those issues of justification is properly to be regarded as a defence: unfortunately there is sometimes a regrettable habit of referring to them as, for example, the defence of self-defence. Where a judge does slip into the error or quasi-error of referring to such explanations as defences, it is particularly important that he should use language which suffices to make it clear to the jury that they are not defences in respect of which any onus rests on the accused, but are matters which the prosecution must disprove as an essential part of the prosecution case before a verdict of guilty is justified.' *R v Wheeler* [1967] 3 All ER 829 at 830, CA, per cur.

[The cases *Mancini v Director of Public Prosecutions and Holmes v Director of Public Prosecutions* were explained in *Director of Public Prosecutions v Camplin* from which the extract below is taken.]

'A crucial factor in the defence of provocation from earliest times has been the relationship between the gravity of provocation and the way in which the accused retaliated, both being judged by the social standards of the day. When Hale was writing in the 17th century pulling a man's nose was thought to justify retaliation with a sword; when *Mancini* [[1941] 3 All ER 272] was decided by this House a blow with a fist would not justify retaliation with a deadly weapon. But so long as words unaccompanied by violence could not in common law amount to provocation the relevant proportionality between provocation and retaliation was primarily one of degrees of violence. Words spoken to the accused before the violence started were not normally to be included in the proportion sum. But now that the law has been changed [by the Homicide Act 1957, supra] so as to permit of words being treated as provocation, even though unaccompanied by any other acts, the gravity of verbal provocation may well depend on the particular characteristics or circumstances of the person to whom a taunt or insult is addressed. To taunt a person because of his race, his physical infirmities or some shameful incident in his past may well be considered by the jury to be more offensive to the person addressed, however equable his temperament, if the facts on which the taunt is founded are true than it would be if they were not. It would stultify much of the mitigation of the previous harshness of the common law in ruling out verbal provocation as capable of reducing murder to manslaughter if the jury could not take into consideration all those factors which in their opinion would affect the gravity of taunts and insults when applied to the person to whom they are addressed.' *Director of Public Prosecutions v Camplin* [1978] 2 All ER 168, HL, per Lord Diplock

Australia 'The defence of provocation is dependent upon this: that the act which is charged as the wrongful act must be done under the influence of the provocation, and common sense suggests that, however resentful he may be of the loss, a man could not be still lacking in self-control at 7 o'clock at night in respect of a matter which had happened at 2 o'clock in the morning. Similarly, words of gross abuse and threatening words . . . do not in law constitute provocation.' *R v Newman* [1948] ALR 109 at 111, per Barry J

PROXIMATE CAUSE

It is a fundamental principle of marine insurance that *causa proxima non remota spectatur*, and that the underwriter is not liable for any loss which is not proximately caused by a peril insured against. This principle is embodied in the Marine Insurance Act 1906, but certain decisions of the House of Lords have to some extent modified the previous application of the principle. Subject to the provisions of that Act, and unless the policy otherwise provides, the insurer is liable for any loss proximately caused by a peril insured against, but, subject as aforesaid, he is not liable for any loss which is not proximately caused by a peril insured against. For this purpose the word 'proximate' means proximate in efficiency, rather than proximate in time. 'Proximate cause' in fact means the same thing as 'dominant' or 'effective' or 'direct' cause. (25 Halsbury's Laws (4th edn) para 180)

'In cases of marine insurance the liability of the underwriters depends upon the proximate cause of the loss. . . . Only the *causa proxima* can be regarded. This question can only arise where there is a succession of causes, which must have existed in order to produce the result. Where that is the case, according to the law of marine insurance, the last cause only must be looked to and the others rejected, although the result would not have been produced without them.' *Pink v Fleming* (1890) 25 QBD 396 at 397, 398, CA, per Lord Esher MR

'In using the word "proximate" one must be careful not to mix up the question of time with the question of causation. You may have a proximate cause, although something has intervened after the act which has caused the mischief.' *Cory & Son v France, Fenwick & Co* [1911] 1 KB 114 at 133, per Kennedy LJ

PROXY

'What is meant by a proxy? A person representative of the shareholder who may be described as his agent to carry out a course which the shareholder himself has decided upon.' *Cousins v International Brick Co Ltd* [1931] 2 Ch 90 at 100, per Lord Hanworth MR

'Every proxy is subject to an implied condition that it should only be used if the shareholder is unable or finds it inconvenient to attend the meeting. The proxy is merely the agent of the shareholder, and as between himself and his principal is not entitled to act contrary to the instructions of the latter. As between these persons and the company, the shareholder is under article 74 [of the articles of association of the company] entitled to exercise his option to vote in person or by proxy at the time when the occasion for its exercise arises, that is to say, when the vote is taken and if the proxy insists on voting notwithstanding that the shareholder himself attends and votes and thus a double vote is given at the meeting in respect of the same shares, it is the duty of the chairman to reject the vote of the proxy as the personal vote is an unequivocal exercise on the part of the shareholder of his option to vote in person.' Ibid at 102, per Lawrence LJ

[As to proxies at parliamentary and local government elections, see the Representation of the People Act 1983, ss 21, 34.]

PSEUDONYMOUS WORK

United States A 'pseudonymous work' is a work on the copies or phonorecords of which the author is identified under a fictitious name. (Copyright Act of 1976, s 101)

PSYCHOPATHIC DISORDER

In this Act 'psychopathic disorder' means a persistent disorder or disability of mind (whether or not including significant impairment of intelligence) which results in abnormally aggressive or seriously irresponsible conduct on the part of the patient, and requires or is susceptible to medical treatment (Mental Health Act 1983, s 1(2))

See, generally, 30 Halsbury's Laws (4th edn) para 1002

PUBLIC *See also* OPEN COURT

[The Copyright Act 1911, s 1(2) (repealed; see now the Copyright, Designs and Patents Act 1988, s 19) defined copyright in a dramatic work as the sole right to produce the work 'in public'.] 'Such authorities as there are do not seem very precise in defining the meaning of the words "in public"; it is certainly difficult and perhaps impossible to define the precise borders of the territory which they cover. "The public" is a term of uncertain import; it must be limited in every case by the context in which it is used. It does not generally mean the inhabitants of the world or even the inhabitants of this country. In any specific context it may mean for practical purposes only the inhabitants of a village or such members of the community as particular advertisements would reach, or who would be interested in any particular matter, professional, political, social, artistic, or local. In the case of a dramatic work the public may be regarded as including persons to whom the drama appeals, but that again must be limited by local and other conditions. Thus it is clear that by "public" is meant in the words of Bowen LJ, "a portion of the public". . . . The presence or absence of visitors is thus not the decisive factor, nor does it matter whether the performance is paid or gratuitous, nor is it conclusive that admission is free or for payment, nor is the number of the audience decisive. It may be observed that in this country actions are in general tried in public, and the Court is public, though the number of the public present at any hearing may not be more than half a dozen. Again, an unsuccessful dramatic performance, though freely advertised to the relevant public, may not attract an audience of more than ten or twenty, but is still a public performance. The antithesis adopted by the cases between performances in public and performances domestic or quasi-domestic cannot be said necessarily to depend on these factors either separately or in combination. The true criterion seems to be the character of the audience.' *Jennings v Stephens* [1936] 1 Ch 469 at 476, 479, CA, per Lord Wright MR

'It cannot, in my opinion, be said that the common, natural meaning of the expression "the public" is restricted to signifying nothing more and nothing less than the ordinary run of humanity, taken as it comes and without special attribute or qualification of any kind. No doubt, the requirement of particular attributes or qualifications may reach a point when one can say that a process of discrimination has produced a class which is not "the public". But, according to everyday parlance, payment alone need not involve this result. There is nothing incongruous or exceptional about referring to 'buses, trains, museums, and picture galleries, for example, as being accessible to the public despite a charge of admission; and the same might be said of many places of entertainment.' *Russell v Thompson* [1953] NI 51 at 56, CA, per Lord MacDermott LCJ

'One would not, on any ordinary use of the word, describe a man's child or partner, and above all his wife, as being a member of the public in relation to himself.' *Morrisons Holdings Ltd v Inland Revenue Comrs* [1966] 1 All ER 789 at 798, per Pennycuick J

Australia 'It should be pointed out that the public [within the Registration of Business Names of Act 1928–1961 (SA), s 4a (repealed; see now the Business Names Act 1963–1986, s 26)] whom it invites, must not be confused with the amorphous mass of the general public. The invitees are the members of the public who (1) happen to see or hear the advertisement, and

(2) are sufficiently interested to read or listen to it. It may be quite impracticable to enumerate them, but they must, in the nature of things, be people with names and faces. It follows that an invitation "to the public" cannot mean anything but an invitation to "members of the public".' *Evans v Lee* [1964] SASR 210 at 214, per Napier, CJ, Chamberlain and Bright JJ

Australia [The Legal Practitioners Ordinance (No 2) 1970–1986 (ACT) , s 30(3), as amended, provides that an inquiry under the Ordinance shall not be open to the 'public'.] 'In my opinion it is a natural construction of the words "the public" to say that they include all persons except those who are parties to the inquiry or necessary for the conduct of the inquiry—that is to say, the members of the disciplinary committee, counsel and solicitors representing the barrister and solicitor and the Law Society respectively, witnesses while they are in the course of giving evidence, and those persons who are required to be present for the purpose of producing a transcript of the proceedings in accordance with s 34 of the Ordinance; this list is possibly not exhaustive. There is in my opinion no justification for excluding a person from the category of "the public" on the ground that he has made the original complaint to the Law Society and thus has a natural personal interest in the proceedings.' *Re A Barrister and Solicitor* (1979) 40 FLR 316 at 318, per Blackburn CJ

Canada 'It was urged before me that in fact the *public* had not been excluded in any way, shape or form because the record shows that the *press* were allowed to remain in attendance; I am not prepared to equate "public" to "the press", even if "press" is defined as including representatives from each and every of the mass media.' *Re Armstrong and State of Winconsin* [1972] 3 OR 229 at 235, per O'Driscoll

In public

'It is established that in deciding whether a performance is "in public" [within the Copyright Act 1956, s 2(5)(c) (repealed; see now the Copyright, Designs and Patents Act 1988, s 19)] the character of the audience is the decisive factor. The authorities relied on by the defendants were cases in which the court had to decide whether a performance was properly called "public" when given to an audience which had certain features pointing to the performance being public and other features pointing to the performance being private, for example performances given to members of clubs and performances given by employers to employees. In such cases there is a relationship between the giver of the performance and the audience which raises the possibility of the performance being treated as being in private and the court has to decide whether the public or private features are to prevail. But in my judgment it is not a correct use of authority to lift passages from judgments dealing with performances capable of being described as being either public or private and to rely on them as authority for treating the words "in public" as not extending to a performance which on any normal meaning of the words could not be treated as anything but "public". In my judgment a performance given to an audience consisting of the persons present in a shop which the public at large are permitted, and indeed encouraged, to enter without payment or invitation with a view to increasing the shopowner's profit can only properly be described as a performance in public.' *Performing Right Society Ltd v Harlequin Record Shops Ltd* [1979] 2 All ER 828 at 833, 834, per Browne-Wilkinson J

Public demonstration

'The justices appear to have thought that "public . . . demonstration" [in an airport byelaw] meant a demonstration involving the public. We cannot agree to such a construction. It is one which would lead to a curious consequence in that a demonstration in public by numerous members of a society or organisation would not constitute a "public . . . demonstration" within the meaning of the byelaw. In our view the prefatory word "public" is to be construed as indicating that the demonstration must be one which occurs in public. In that sense what the respondents did was "public". Was it, however, a "demonstration"? The researches of counsel did not reveal any decision on that word. We were referred to the Shorter Oxford English Dictionary (3rd edn), which gives as the seventh variant of the word the meaning "public manifestation of feeling; often taking the form of a procession and mass meeting". We find this an acceptable description in the present context.' *British Airports Authority v Ashton* [1983] 3 All ER 6 at 12, per cur.

PUBLIC AUTHORITY

A public authority may be described as a person or administrative body entrusted with functions to perform for the benefit of the public and not for private profit. Not every such person or body is expressly defined as a public authority or body, and the meaning of a public authority or body may vary according to the statutory context. The problem of definition became less important with the abolition of the special period of limitation for actions against public authorities. (1 Halsbury's Laws (4th edn) para 6)

PUBLIC BAR *See* BAR; PUBLIC HOUSE

PUBLIC BENEVOLENT INSTITUTION *See also* BENEVOLENT

Australia 'The description "public benevolent institution" has received an interpretation by this Court (*Perpetual Trustee Co v Federal Commissioner of Taxation* [(1931) 45 CLR 224]). It is to be treated as a compound expression referring to institutions "organized for the relief of poverty, sickness, destitution, or helplessness" (per Starke J at p 232). The phrase I used was "the relief of poverty, distress, suffering or misfortune" (p 233). Evatt J said (at pp 235, 236):—'Such bodies vary greatly in scope and character. But they have one thing in common: they give relief freely to those who are in need of it and who are unable to care for themselves. Those who receive aid or comfort in this way are the poor, the sick, the aged, and the young. Their disability or distress arouses pity, and the institutions are designed to give them protection. They are very numerous—'the nobler a soul is the more objects of compassion it hath'—and they have come to be known as 'benevolent institutions'." . . . Conceding that a gift to an institution benefiting young children in a way which makes it a charitable or benevolent object may be a valid disposition for charitable purposes. I nevertheless do not think that the institutions it covers are confined to public benevolent institutions of the required description. Institutions connected with the health, upbringing, welfare, and education of young children coming within the legal conception of "charitable" may be imagined to which no one would apply the term "public benevolent institution".' *Public Trustee (NSW) v Federal Taxation Comr* (1934) 51 CLR 75 at 103, 104 per Dixon J

PUBLIC BODY

The expression 'public body' means any council of a county or county of a city or town, any council of a municipal borough, also any board, commissioners, select vestry, or other body which has power to act under and for the purposes of any Act relating to local government, or the public health, or to poor law or otherwise to administer money raised by rates in pursuance of any public general Act, but does not include any public body as above defined existing elsewhere than in the United Kingdom. (Public Bodies Corrupt Practices Act 1889, s 7)

'Public body' includes any local authority or statutory undertaker, and any trustees, commissioners, board or other persons, who, as a public body and not for their own profit, act under any enactment for the improvement of any place or the production or supply of any commodity or service. (Countryside Act 1968, s 49(2))

'Public body' includes

(a) a local authority and a joint board on which, and a joint committee on which, a local authority or parish meeting are represented;
(b) any trustees, commissioners or other persons who, for public purposes and not for their own profit, act under any enactment or instrument for the improvement of any place, for the supply of water to any place, or for providing or maintaining a cemetery or market in any place; and
(c) any other authority having powers of levying or issuing a precept for any rate for public purposes.

(Local Government Act 1972, s 270)

PUBLIC BUILDING

'Public building' means—

(a) a building used wholly or partly as a church chapel or other place of public worship (not being a dwelling-house so used) or as a public assistance institution or public library or as a place for public entertainments public balls public dances public lectures or public exhibitions or otherwise as a place of public assembly; or
(b) a building of a cubical extent exceeding two hundred and fifty thousand cubic feet which is used wholly or partly as an hotel or hospital or as a school college or other place of instruction;

and includes the buildings and premises of the

Stock Exchange within the city. (London Building Act (Amendment) Act 1939, s 4)

PUBLIC CHARITY *See* CHARITY—CHARITABLE PURPOSES

PUBLIC COMPANY *See* COMPANY

PUBLIC DUTY

Canada 'The question before me, briefly stated, is this: Is a police constable, employed by a municipality, executing a "public duty or authority" [for the purpose of the limitation provision in the Public Officers Act, RSM 1970, c P-230, s 21] when engaged on a radar patrol? What is "a public duty or authority"? A public duty is, in my view, one in the discharge of which the public, the community at large, has an interest, as affecting their legal rights or liabilities. The duties of a police constable concern all citizens, they relate to and affect the whole body of people.' *Koshurba v Rural Municipality of North Kildonan* (1965) 52 DLR (2d) 84 at 87, Man QB, per Dickson J

PUBLIC ENTERTAINMENT *See* ENTERTAINMENT

PUBLIC FUNDS

'The testator has directed that all his estate should be converted, with the exception of monies in the public funds. That is not a very accurate description of any particular species of public security, but it is sufficient to describe some portion of some one or other of the public stocks or securities. . . . The direction here must be considered to mean a sale of his property, except such part thereof as consists of consols, reduced annuities, long annuities, or any other public funds, and the monies to arise therefrom to be invested in public stocks or funds.' *Howard v Kay* (1858) 27 LJ Ch 448 at 448, per Kindersley V-C

[A testatrix left to her brother everything she might be possessed of at her decease, for his life, and if he married and had children of his own, then to those children; but if he were to die a bachelor, the whole of her fortune then standing in 'the Funds' to ES] 'I think the words "the Funds" must be taken to mean the same as the "Government Funds" or "Public Funds". . . . I think clearly the legitimate meaning of the expression "the Public Funds", is that portion of the public debt which is paid out of the funds appropriate to that purpose by Parliament.' *Slingsby v Grainger* (1859) 7 HL Cas 273 at 280, per Lord Cranworth

Canada 'Counsel for the plaintiff argues that the words "public funds" [in the Assessment Act, RSO 1950, c 24, s 4(12) (now RSO 1980, c 31, s 3, para 12) exempting from assessment charitable institutions supported by 'public funds'] are to be given a very wide significance so as to include all moneys paid to the plaintiff by members of the public as voluntary donations. I cannot agree that the words are to be so broadly interpreted. These words have a well-recognised meaning in the public statutes of this Province and must be limited to money provided from the treasuries of either the federal or provincial or municipal Governments.' *Les Soeurs de la Visitation d'Ottawa v Ottawa* [1952] OR 61 at 71, 72, per Schroeder J

PUBLIC HOUSE

A 'public house' may be a hotel within the statutory definition [in the Hotel Proprietors Act 1956, s 1], but is not to be assumed to be one. As the term is ordinarily used, a public house differs from a hotel, in respect of which a licence is held for the sale of intoxicating liquor in that the public house does not provide for the reception of travellers desirous of sleeping and staying there as guests. A private hotel is not a public house by reason merely that intoxicating liquors are sold to guests and travellers staying in the house and to no other persons. (24 Halsbury's Laws (4th edn) para 1209)

[A purchaser of land covenanted with the vendors not to carry on upon the property certain offensive trades or any business which was or might be deemed a public or private nuisance, nor to use any building which should be erected thereon as a 'public house' for the sale of beer, wine, malt liquors, or spirits.] 'It is curious enough to observe how little one finds in the way of authority upon this word "public house", which seems to be a word of quite modern introduction, the word "alehouse" being that originally used in the earlier editions of the works relating to the subject; the word "public house" being placed in the margin of the last edition of Burn's Justice against the title "alehouse", while the word "inn" is used with this observation, "or, as it is now more generally called, a 'public house'". Nor is much assistance to be derived from the various Licensing Acts. . . . I approach the question, therefore, without much assistance from the Acts of Parliament, and what little indications are to be found in them seem adverse to the contention of the Plaintiffs. The point that has most weighed with me is, that if I construed the covenant as the Plaintiffs ask me to do, I should have, this convenant being disjunctive, to strike out the word "public" altogether. I must apply it to every grocer's shop, such as Fortnum & Mason, or Hedges & Butler, where wine is sold by retail, and all meaning of the word "public" would thus be destroyed. Moreover, the deed of covenant is dated after all these Acts of Parliament; and if it had been intended to introduce a restriction against the sale of beer *simpliciter*, it would have been easy to have done so. Further than this, the covenant is directed against nuisances of a local character, arising from offensive smells, and the noise and disturbance that would be occasioned by a parcel of tipplers congregating about any of the houses or the property. I cannot, therefore, hold the sale of beer under a license not to be drunk on the premises to be within the restriction contained in the covenant.' *Pease v Coats* (1866) LR 2 Eq 688 at 690, 691, per Page Wood V-C

'I assume . . . that we are here dealing with the demolished site of what was an ordinary public house as that term is commonly understood: a place, resort to which would primarily be had for obtaining alcoholic refreshment but in which there would also be sold as ancillary to the main business and in the same part of the premises, non-alcoholic drinks and also some light refreshments, that is, perhaps bread and cheese or biscuits.' *Central Land Board v Saxone Shoe Co Ltd* [1955] 3 All ER 415 at 418, CA, per Evershed MR; see also [1956] 1 QB 288

PUBLIC IMPROVEMENT

Canada 'Section 449 [of the Municipal Act 1933 (Man) (now RSM 1954, c 173, s 468)] adds that "If a municipal corporation make default in keeping in reasonable repair that portion of a highway on which work has been performed or public improvements made by the corporation, it shall, besides being subject to any punishment provided by law, be civilly responsible for all damages sustained by any person by reason of such default". The vehicular crossing over the sidewalk in question was a "public improvement" and, although not actually made by the defendant, it was prescribed as to design by the defendant's engineer and constructed with its sanction and approval. The crossing therefore seems to me to be a "public improvement made by" the defendant within the meaning of this section.' *Paul v Dauphin (Town)* [1941] 1 WWR 43 at 45, 46, Man KB, per Dysart J; affirmed [1941] 2 WWR 224

PUBLIC INTEREST

'It is fallacious to say that a condition [attached to a justices' licence] is not in the public interest, or may not be in the public interest, if it is the case that a great many of those persons who constitute the public are not directly affected by it; and it is equally fallacious to say that a condition cannot be in the public interest if a great many members of the public neither know nor care anything about it.' *R v Sussex Confirming Authority, ex p Tamplin & Sons' Brewery (Brighton) Ltd* [1937] 4 All ER 106 at 112, DC, per Du Parcq J

'When the press [in a case relating to the publication of confidential documents] raise the defence of public interest, the court must appraise it critically, but, if convinced that a strong case has been made out, the press should be free to publish, leaving the plaintiff to his remedy in damages. I end with one word of caution. There is a world of difference between what is in the public interest and what is of interest to the public. This judgment is not intended to be a mole's charter.' *Lim Laboratories Ltd v Evans* [1984] 2 All ER 417 at 435, CA, per Griffiths LJ

PUBLIC MEETING *See* MEETING

PUBLIC NUISANCE *See* NUISANCE

PUBLIC OFFICE

(1) In the last foregoing section [employment in more than one public office] references to employment in a public office shall be construed as references to employment of the following kinds, and 'public office' shall be construed accordingly—

1. Employment in the civil service (whether or not in an established capacity).

2. Employment in any other capacity remunerated out of moneys provided by Parliament or the Consolidated Fund or the Post Office Fund or the revenue of the Isle of Man, but not including employment in the armed forces of the Crown.
3. . . . employment in the civil service of the Government of Northern Ireland (whether or not in an established capacity).
4. . . . employment in any other capacity remunerated out of moneys provided by the Parliament of Northern Ireland or the Consolidated Fund of Northern Ireland.
5. Employment in the civil service of the government of any colony, or of any country or place outside Her Majesty's dominions in which for the time being Her Majesty has jurisdiction, or of any territory consisting partly of one or more colonies and partly of one or more such countries or places.
6. Employment as an officer to whom the Overseas Service Act 1958 applies (if not employment within any of the other paragraphs in this subsection).
7. Employment which is remunerated out of any of the following funds, or out of the revenues of any of the following bodies—

The Agricultural Research Council.
The Church Commissioners.
. . .
The Development Fund.
The Forestry Fund.
The funds of Branches of the Royal Mint at Melbourne and Perth.
The General Lighthouse Fund.
The Greenwich Hospital Fund.
The land revenues managed by the Crown Estate Commissioners.
The Metropolitan Police Fund.
The Nature Conservancy Council.
The Overseas Audit Department.

(2) The Treasury may by order—

(a) designate any employment as employment in a public office for the purposes of this section, and
(b) add to, amend or repeal any of the provisions of subsection (1) of this section . . .

(Superannuation Act 1965, s 39, as amended)

'Public office' means any office—

(a) under the Crown, or
(b) under the charter of a city or borough, or
(c) under the Acts relating to local government or public health or public education,

where the office is that—

(i) of mayor, provost, chief magistrate, chairman, alderman, councillor, member of a board, commission or other local authority in any local government or other areas; or
(ii) of proper officer or other officer under a council, board, commission or other authority; or
(iii) of any other office to which a person is elected or appointed under any such charter or enactment as is mentioned above including any other municipal or parochial office.

(Representation of the People Act 1983, s 185)

'What is the test of a public office. Is it not, that the officer may be indicted for negligence or breach of duty?' *R v Mersham (Inhabitants)* (1806) 3 Smith KB 151 at 153, per Ellenborough CJ

'To make the office a public office, the pay must come out of national and not out of local funds, and the office must be public in the strict sense of that term. It is not enough that the due discharge of the duties of the office should be for the public benefit in a secondary and remote sense.' *Re Mirams* [1891] 1 QB 594 at 596, 597, per Cave J

'A public office includes the holding of a commission in the Territorial Army, or in any other of the armed forces of the Crown.' *Re Edgar, Cohen v Edgar* [1939] 1 All ER 635 at 637, per Bennett J

PUBLIC OFFICER

'A public officer is an officer who discharges any duty in the discharge of which the public are interested, more clearly so if he is paid out of a fund provided by the public. If taxes go to supply his payment, and the public have an interest in the duties he discharges, he is a public officer.' *R v Whitaker* [1914] 3 KB 1283 at 1296, 1297, CCA, per cur.

'To the words "public officer" different meanings can be given according to the statute in which they occur. For instance, I called attention in the course of the argument to the expression "public officer" which is to be found in the Country Bankers Act [1826 (repealed)]. Under that Act country bankers who were carrying on business in partnership had to appoint for certain purposes certain members of the partnership who were to be known as "public officers". The public officer under that Act was appointed for a particular purpose under a particular Act; he was not paid out of public funds. We have to consider whether in this Act [Solicitors Act] of 1932 [repealed; see now the Solicitors Act 1974] the expression "public officer" refers to any clerk of a local authority or whether it must not be given a stricter interpretation, that is to say, a public officer who is an officer of a public department. . . . The words "public officer" in s 47, sub-s 3(a), of the Act of 1932 [see now the Solicitors Act 1974, s 22(2)(b)] should be limited to a public officer in the strict sense, that is to say, to an officer of a public department, whose salary is charged on national and not local funds.' *Beeston and Stapleford Urban District Council v Smith* [1949] 1 KB 656 at 663, 665, per Lord Goddard CJ

PUBLIC PERFORMANCE *See also* PUBLIC; PUBLIC PLACE

The question whether a work is performed, or a sound recording, film or television broadcast seen or heard in public is solely one of fact, but certain considerations and tests have been applied; among them the question whether there has been any admission, with or without payment of any portion of the public to the injury of the author, that is to say, of the class of persons who would be likely to go to a performance if there was a performance at a public theatre for profit, or whether the performance was private and domestic, a matter of family and household concern only.

Any performance which is not domestic or quasi-domestic will be regarded as in public notwithstanding that only a few members of the public are present or that no charge for admission is made. A performance may be in public notwithstanding that it is given in a place not habitually used for dramatic entertainments. Persons who are responsible for broadcasting a performance and who grant licences which entitle listeners to perform the broadcast in public are liable for infringement as persons who have authorised a public performance, and there are grounds for saying that in any case a broadcast to private listeners only is in public although the audience is not in one place. Performances by teachers or pupils in schools are, in general, not performances in public. (9 Halsbury's Laws (4th edn) para 918)

In this section [prohibition of certain public contests, performances, and exhibitions with animals] . . . the expression 'public performance' does not include a performance presented to the public by means of the cinematograph. (Protection of Animals Act 1934, s 1(3))

'Public performance' includes any performance in a public place within the meaning of the Public Order Act 1936 and any performance which the public or any section thereof are permitted to attend, whether on payment or otherwise. (Theatres Act 1968, s 18(1))

[The Copyright Act 1911, s 1(2) (repealed; see now the Copyright, Designs and Patents Act 1988, s 19(2)) provided that the term 'copyright' meant (inter alia) the sole right to 'perform' a work 'in public'.] 'The plaintiff . . . is the composer of the well known comic opera called 'The Little Michus'. . . . He alleges that the defendants, the British Broadcasting Company, infringed his musical copyright in that opera by a wireless performance given by them. . . . The actual performance . . . was given in the defendants' private studio at Savoy Hill, London, by the orchestra and performers engaged by the defendants. The public were not admitted to the studio. Officials and a few friends only were present apart from those who rendered the opera. It was by means of electrical instruments that the defendants, by modulating the waves in the ether, were able to affect, as they intended to affect, a vast number of electrical instruments possessed by members of the public and thereby to render audible to the public the performance given within the walls of the defendants' studio. . . . The defendants, in doing what they did, clearly gave a public performance. Instead of gathering the public into a vast assembly room, they set in motion certain ether waves knowing that millions of receiving instruments in houses and flats were tuned to the waves sent forth, and knowing and intending also that acoustic representation of the opera would thereby be given to an enormous number of listeners. If I did not hold this to be a public performance by the defendants I should fail to recognise the substance and reality of the matter and also the object and intent of the Copyright Act.' *Messager v British Broadcasting Co* [1927] 2 KB 543 at 544, 548, 549, per McCardie J

'In the present case the nature of the audience, when properly understood, in my opinion, puts the matter beyond doubt. In each case the audience constitutes a substantial part of the working population of the district. It is collected from different households in the district. It is an audience which obviously is fond of music. In one case . . . the practice of performing music in the way in which it has been performed was initiated at the request of the workpeople themselves. From time to time groups of workpeople or individual workmen or women asked for a particular song to be played by the gramophone record. It is quite obvious, therefore, that the whole object of these performances is to supply to the workpeople something which they like. So far as regards the music, the workpeople are an audience. The fact that it assists their work appears to me to be entirely irrelevant. While the performances are being given and the workpeople are doing their work, they are doing two things at once. They are working and they are enjoying music, which normally is a thing they would enjoy in their leisure hours. Instead of having the music in their leisure hours, they have it while they are working. None the less they are, so far as the music is concerned, an audience listening to music, and the fact that they are working at the same time does not alter that, any more than it alters the fact that a housewife who turns on her radio set while she is doing her housework is listening to the music at the same time as she is doing that work. . . . In the present case, having regard to the character of the audience and all the relevant facts which bear upon that matter, I have no doubt that those performances were performances in public.' *Ernest Turner Electrical Instruments Ltd v Performining Right Society Ltd, Performing Right Society Ltd v Gillette Industries Ltd* [1943] 1 All ER 413 at 415, 416, CA, per Lord Greene MR

Of new play

In this section 'public performance of a new play' means a public performance of a play of which no previous public performance has ever been given in Great Britain, but does not include a public performance of a play which—
(a) is based on a script substantially the same as that on which a previous public performance of a play given there was based; or
(b) is based substantially on the text of the play which has been published in the United Kingdom.
(Theatres Act 1968, s 11(3))

PUBLIC PLACE *See also* PLACE OF PUBLIC RESORT

'Public place' includes any highway and any other premises or place to which at the material time the public have or are permitted to have access, whether on payment or otherwise. (Public Order Act 1936, s 9(1), as substituted by the Criminal Justice Act 1972, s 33; see also the Prevention of Terrorism (Temporary Provisions) Act 1984, s 2(3))

In this section 'public place' includes any highway and any other premises or place to which at the material time the public have or are permitted to have access, whether on payment or otherwise. (Prevention of Crime Act 1953, s 1; Criminal Justice Act 1967, s 91(4))

'Public place' includes any highway and any other premises or place to which at the material time the public have or are permitted to have access, whether on payment or otherwise. (Firearms Act 1968, s 574)

'Public place', in relation to the display of any matter, means any place to which the public have or are permitted to have access (whether on payment or otherwise) while that matter is displayed except—
(a) a place to which the public are permitted to have access only on payment which is or includes payment for that display; or
(b) a shop or any part of a shop to which the public can only gain access by passing beyond an adequate warning notice . . . (Indecent Displays (Control) Act 1981, s 1(3))

[The question was whether an omnibus was a 'public place', for the purposes of an indictment for indecent exposure to the great scandal of divers liege subjects of the Queen.] 'I think that this omnibus was a public place, and that an exposure there to more than one person is an offence.' *R v Holmes* (1853) Dears CC 207 at 209, CCR, per Parke B

[The prisoner indecently exposed himself on the roof of a house in view of the windows of several other houses, but could not be seen from any public highway.] 'Surely, if the people in twenty or thirty houses round could see it, it is a sufficiently public place.' *R v Thallman* (1863) Le & Ca 326 at 329, CCR, per Martin B

'"Public place" does not mean a public highway.' Ibid at 329, per Erle CJ

'It is clear to me that railway stations are not either public streets or public roads. They are private property; and although it is true they are places of public resort, that does not of itself make them public places. The public only resort there upon railway business, and the railway company might exclude them at any moment they liked, except when a train was actually arriving or departing.' *Case v Storey*

(1869) LR 4 Exch. 319 at 322, 323, per Kelly CB

'A public place is one where the public go, no matter whether they have a right to go or not. The right is not the question. Many shows are exhibited to the public on private property, yet they are frequented by the public—the public go there.' *R v Wellard* (1884) 14 QBD 63 at 66, 67, per Grove J

[A bye-law made by a local authority provided that no person should in any 'public place' use any profane, obscene or indecent language to the annoyance of passengers.] 'I express no opinion as to whether the appellant's language was indecent, but I am clearly of opinion that it was not used in a public place to the annoyance of passengers within this bye-law. It may be that a public house is a public place for some purposes and under some statutes, but it is impossible to say that it is a public place within this bye-law, having regard to the words "to the annoyance of passengers". The words "public place" are not defined in these bye-laws, but in later bye-laws made by the same council they are defined as including "any common, part, pleasure ground, or roadside waste to which the public have access", I think that the words "public place" are used in the same sense in these bye-laws.' *Russon v Dutton (No 2)* (1911) 104 LT 601 at 602, DC, per Avory J

'I think it is clear that a public house is not a public place under any of the words used in sub-s 4 of s 1 [of the Street Betting Act 1906 (repealed; see now the Betting, Gaming and Lotteries Act 1963, s 8)]. The justices may have been misled by the fact that in common parlance licensed premises are called a public house. There is no finding here that the premises were a common inn. If they were, the case might require some further consideration because travellers have a right to be taken into an inn if there is room in the house. But a public house is only a place where a person holding a justices' licence is entitled to sell drink, and it is no more a public place than a draper's shop. The public, it may be, are invited to enter, as they may be invited to enter any other place, but that does not give a right of access, because the invitation may be withdrawn at any moment. . . . As a rule, of course, any person who desires refreshment is welcomed as a guest. He is invited to enter as long as the doors are open, unless the publican refuses to have him in his house, as he has a perfect right to do. The publican can close the doors of the house at any time, and the fact that the licensing justices might interfere if they thought the publican was acting unreasonably is neither here nor there. There is no right of entry into a public house, restricted or otherwise.' *Brannan v Peek* [1948] 1 KB 68 at 71, per Lord Goddard CJ

'At common law, "a public place" is a place to which the public can, and do, have access. I direct you as a matter of law that it matters not whether they come to that place at the invitation of the occupier or whether they come to it merely with his permission; also, that it matters not whether some payment, or, indeed, the performance of some small formality such as the signing of a visitors' book, is required before they are allowed access.' *R v Kane* [1965] 1 All ER 705 at 709, per Barry J

Australia [The defendant was charged with offensive behaviour in a public place contrary to the provisions of the Police Act 1936 (SA), s 75 (repealed; see now Summary Offences Act 1953–1986, s 22). It was proved that he was found in a women's lavatory in a city office building.] 'In the case of the corridor on the street level, it may well be that the public are tacitly invited in, and that the number who do actually go in, for one reason or another, is sufficient to constitute a use by the public, and to justify a finding that the corridor is a public place. But this lavatory is in the basement . . . is shut off by a door and there is nothing to suggest that it is open to the public. . . . It may be that, from time to time, people who know the lay-out of the building, or are shown there by the tenants, have been allowed to use the convenience, but I cannot agree that a use of that sort would make it a public place within the meaning of the Act.' *O'Sullivan v Brady* [1954] SASR 140 at 142, per Napier CJ

Australia 'In the case of a man who is found drunk and disorderly in the front seat of a motor car in a public place I can see no reason to doubt that he is found in the public place [within the Summary Offences Act 1966 (Vic), s 13 (see now Summary Offences Act 1966–1986, s 14)]. Whether the motor car is itself a public place is in those circumstances immaterial.' *McKenzie v Stratton* [1971] VR 848 at 851, per Nelson J

Australia 'It appears to me that . . . it is helpful to set out three different categories of circumstances in which, as I understand the authorities, a place will ordinarily be a "public place" at common law or within . . . the definition [in the Summary Offences Act 1966–1986 (Vic), s 3]. In my opinion, a place will ordinarily be a "public place" . . . (1) If at the relevant time members of the public are lawfully entitled, invited or permitted to be there in their capacity as members of the public, whether or not subject to payment for admission or to other conditions, and irrespective of the number of persons in fact present at the relevant time. . . . (2) If the place is one to which significant numbers of the public in their capacity as such are in the habit of going, whether or not by legal right or authority, either at all hours or during hours which include the relevant time, and even if at the relevant time none or only a few persons are present. . . . (3) If at the relevant time a large number of persons are in fact there, whether or not by legal right or authority.' *McIvor v Garlick* [1972] VR 129 at 133, 134, per Newton J

Australia 'Special questions might arise as to the applicability of s 13 [of the Summary Offences Act 1966–1986 (Vic)] to persons found drunk in caravans, tents or the like in cases where the caravan, tent or other habitat or receptacle is itself in a public place. It may be that a person so found could not be said to be found drunk in a public place because of the degree of his insulation therefrom. . . . But no such questions arise in the present case, and we express no views upon them. An ordinary motor car is not in the same category as a caravan or tent. Its occupants are readily visible to outside observers.' *Mansfield v Kelly* [1972] VR 744 at 745, per cur.

Canada '"Public place" is a fluctuating term, and the meaning varies with the context, but as a general thing the words of Grove J in *Regina v Wellard* (1884) (supra) are suggestive: "A public place is one where the public go, no matter whether they have a right to go or not".' *R v Leitch* (1916) 36 OLR 1 at 2, Ont SC, per Boyd C

Canada [The Criminal Code, 1953–54 (Can), c 51, s 160a(1), deals with causing a disturbance in a 'public place'.] 'To constitute a "public place" does not, in my view, require that all segments of the public have a right of access thereto. The word "public" is capable of being broken down into groups or divisions, some examples of which immediately come to mind , being the "buying public", the "book-reading public", the "travelling public" and, without attempting to be facetious, the "drinking public". Many groups that can be identified by habits, or pursuits or other things that distinguish them, are often described as "public", the only qualifications appearing to be that the number constituting the group is substantial and that all possessing the same common interest are included. It follows that a segment of the public interested in partaking of alcoholic beverages may logically be described as "public", even though certain portions of the public at large may be excluded either by choice or otherwise.' *Teqstrom v R* [1971] 1 WWR 147 at 149, 150, Sask Dist Ct, per Maher DCJ

Canada [The accused, who was sitting in his car which was parked in a public lot with the doors closed and the driver's window open, called a child over to his car and indecently exposed himself to her when she was standing beside the car. The accused was charged under the Criminal Code, RSC 1970, c C-34, s 169(a), with committing an indecent act in a public place.] 'Without attempting to enunciate any exclusive test which will apply in all circumstances in determining whether a place is a public place for the purpose of a prosecution under s 169(a) of the Criminal Code, I am satisfied that in this instance the indecent act did occur in a public place, for two reasons. Firstly, even though the respondent's automobile was his private property, it lost its character of a private place because of the manner in which he made use of it on the day in question. He drove his private car to the public parking lot and located it in that public place. When he did the indecent act inside his car he was not screened from public view as though the windows of the car were curtained. He invited the little girl to approach his open car, so that she was within range to observe his indecent act and exposure. The car was thereby made accessible to her, by the express or implied invitation of the respondent. Secondly, and that apart, I consider that the site of the indecent act in this case was the public parking lot. I think that the object of s 169(a) is to proscribe the wilful doing of an indecent act in a public place within the sight of a member or members of the public. The fourth definition of the word "in" appearing in the Shorter Oxford English Dictionary includes the following: "I. Of position or location . . . Within the limits or bounds of . . . any place or thing". and "II. (b) Situation within the range of sensuous observation or the sphere of action of another". Applying those definitions to the facts, and having regard to the object of the section, I hold that the indecent act was done in the public parking lot and therefore, in a public place.' *R v Wise* [1982] 4 WWR 658 at 671, 672, BC Co Ct, per Perry Co Ct J

PUBLIC POLICY

'I, for one, protest . . . against arguing too strongly upon public policy;—it is a very unruly horse, and when once you get astride it you never know where it will carry you. It may lead you from the sound law. It is never argued at all but when other points fail.' *Richardson v Mellish* (1824) 2 Bing 229 at 252, DC, per Burrough J

'Exceptions have been made to the expression of "public policy", and it has been confounded with what may be called political policy; such as whether it is politically wise to have a sinking fund or a paper circulation, or the degree and nature of interference with foreign States; with all which, as applied to the present subject, it has nothing whatever to do. Public policy, in relation to this question, is that principle of the law which holds that no subject can lawfully do that which has a tendency to be injurious to the public, or against the public good, which may be termed, as it sometimes has been, the policy of the law, or public policy in relation to the administration of the law.' *Egerton v Brownlow (Earl)* (1853) 4 HL Cas 1 at 196, per Lord Truro

'In treating of various branches of the law learned persons have analysed the sources of the law, and have sometimes expressed their opinion that such a provision is bad because it is contrary to public policy; but I deny that any Court can invent a new head of public policy; so a contract for marriage brokerage, the creation of a perpetuity, a contract in restraint of trade, a gaming or wagering contract, or, what is relevant here, the assisting of the King's enemies, are all undoubtedly unlawful things; and you may say that it is because they are contrary to public policy they are unlawful; but it is because these things have been either enacted or assumed to be by the common law unlawful, and not because a judge or Court have a right to declare that such and such things are in his or their view contrary to public policy. Of course, in the application of the principles here insisted on, it is inevitable that the particular case must be decided by a judge; he must find the facts, and he must decide whether the facts so found do or do not come within the principles which I have endeavoured to describe—that is, a principle of public policy, recognised by the law, which the suggested contract is infringing, or is supposed to infringe.' *Janson v Driefontein Consolidated Mines Ltd* [1902] AC 484 at 491, 492, HL, per Lord Halsbury LC

'When questions arise as to conditions or provisions being void as being against the public good or against public policy, great caution is necessary in considering them. . . . In my opinion, however, there can be few, if any, provision more against the public good and the welfare of the State than one tending to deter persons from entering the naval or military services of the country. . . . If conditions imposed be really and in principle against the public good, and clearly and directly opposed to the public welfare, they are certainly void. . . . It is manifest that any condition divesting property on a devisee or legatee becoming a member of those (naval or military) forces which Parliament considers necessary for the safety of the kingdom has a tendency to deter persons from entering those forces, and is, therefore, against the welfare of, and injurious to, the community, and absolutely void.' *Re Beard, Reversionary & General Securities Co Ltd v Hall, Re Beard v Hall* [1908] 1 Ch 383 at 386–388, per Swinfen Eady J

'You do not look for public policy, in the sense in which that expression is used, in an Act of Parliament. It is something which is really part of the common law of the land and does not depend upon statute.' *In the Estate of Hall, Hall v Knight & Baxter* [1914] P 1 at 5, CA, per Cozens-Hardy MR

'The question of public policy may well give rise to a difference of judicial opinion. Public policy, it was said by Burrough J in *Richardson v Mellish* [supra], "is a very unruly horse, and when once you get astride it you never know where it will carry you". But the Courts have not hesitated in the past to apply the doctrine whenever the facts demanded its application. In *Janson v Driefontein Consolidated Mines* [supra], Lord Halsbury LC said: "I deny that any Court can invent a new head of public policy." I very respectfully doubt if this dictum be consistent with the history of our law or with many modern decisions. In *Wilson v Carnley* [[1908] 1 KB 729] the Court of Appeal held that a promise of marriage made by a man who to the knowledge of the promisee was at the time of making the promise married is void as being against public policy. This decision marked a new application or head of public policy. In *Nevill v Dominion of Canada News Co* [[1915] 3 KB 556] the Court of Appeal held, affirming Atkin J, that an agreement by a journalist not to comment upon the plaintiff's company or its directors or business was void as against public policy. This decision created, I think, a wholly new head of public policy. In *Horwood v Millar's Timber and Trading Co* [[1917] 1 KB 305] the Court of Appeal held that an agreement which unduly fettered a man's liberty of action and the free disposal of his property was void as against public policy. This decision also, I think, created in substance a new head of public policy. The truth of the matter seems to be that public policy is a variable thing. It must fluctuate with the circumstances of the time.' *Naylor, Benzon & Co Ltd v Krainische Industrie Gesellschaft* [1918] 1 KB 331 at 342, per McCardie J

Australia 'The phrase "public policy" appears to mean the ideas which for the time being prevail in a community as to the conditions necessary to ensure its welfare; so that anything is treated as against public policy if it is generally regarded as injurious to the public interest. . . . It is well settled that a contract is not enforceable if its enforcement would be opposed to public policy. . . . Public policy is not, however, fixed and stable. From generation to generation ideas change as to what is necessary or injurious, so that "public policy" is a variable thing. It must fluctuate with the circumstances of the time: *Naylor, Benzon & Co v Krainische Industrie Gesellschaft* [supra]. New heads of public policy come into being, and old heads undergo modification.' *Re Jacob Morris (deceased)* [1943] NSW SR 352 at 355, 356, per Jordan CJ

See, generally, 9 Halsbury's Laws (4th edn) paras 391 et seq.

PUBLIC PURPOSES

'The question . . . is whether the purpose to which the profits in the hands of the custodian [of enemy property] were applicable were public purposes or not. As a preliminary to this inquiry, it must, of course, be ascertained what is meant by the phrase "public purposes". As to this, the following criteria were laid down by Lord Westbury LC in the cases of *Mersey Docks and Harbour Board Trustees v Cameron* [(1865) 11 HL Cas 443] and *Greig v University of Edinburgh* [(1868) LR 1 Sc & D 348]. In the former he said that public purposes "must be such as are required and created by the government of the country, and are therefore deemed part of the use and service of the Crown". In the second case he somewhat amplified this definition by saying that such purposes are "the purposes of the administration of the government of the country".' *Bank voor Handel en Scheepvaart NV v Slatford* [1953] 1 QB 248 at 298, CA, per Romer LJ

New Zealand [Certain houses were let by the Army Department to provide housing accommodation for army personnel. The tenancy agreement provided that if at any time the whole premises were required for 'public purposes' the tenancy might be determined by the Department.] 'The very fact that the high purposes of State for which the Army exists are essentially the province of Government is sufficient to show that all property that it holds to enable it to carry out those high purposes, including property held by it for the purpose of being let as living-quarters to its servicing personnel, is property that is held by it for public purposes. I think, too, that, in letting to its serving members as living-quarters property that is held by it for that purpose, the Army is acting in the pursuit of and for public purposes.' *R v James, R v King* [1952] NZLR 596 at 599, per Cooke J, also reported [1952] GLR 588 at 589; affirmed [1953] NZLR 137, CA

PUBLIC RECREATION

Australia 'To my mind the dedication of land "for purposes of public recreation" necessarily involves the use of such land *by the public* for their recreation; land used by an individual or a council to manufacture or provide entertainment media for subsequent enjoyment by the public or to disseminate information as to where recreation may be found is not land used for public recreation. It is obviously not necessary that the public must at all times have access to all parts of the land; indeed the type of recreation provided on it may require the exclusion of the public from parts of it, but any restriction upon the public's access to the whole of the area for the purpose of recreation can be justified only on the basis that it is in the interest of the public and to provide for their recreation *within the area* that they are so excluded from part of it.' *A-G for NSW v Cooma Municipal Council* [1963] NSWR 1657 at 1663, per Brereton J

PUBLIC RELIGIOUS WORSHIP *See* WORSHIP

PUBLIC RESORT *See* PLACE OF PUBLIC RESORT

PUBLIC REVENUE *See* REVENUE

PUBLIC SCHOOL *See* SCHOOL

PUBLIC SERVICE

'Articles required for the public service' means—
(a) articles required for the purpose of the discharge of its functions by any government department, the United Kingdom Atomic Energy Authority, the Civil Aviation Authority, or any Research Council within the meaning of the Science and Technology Act 1965;
(b) articles required for the defence of any part of the Commonwealth, including any territory under Her Majesty's protection or in which She has jurisdiction, or for the maintenance or restoration of peace and security in any part of the world or for any measures arising out of a breach of apprehended breach of peace in any part of the world;
(c) articles required by any international organisation of which the United Kingdom is a member or (where the relevant international agreement so provides) by any other member of such an organisation;
(d) articles which in the opinion of the Secretary of State would be essential for the needs of the community in the event of war;
(e) articles for supply to a person carrying on an undertaking which includes the production of articles of that or any other description where that person requests the Secretary of State to supply those articles and the Secreary of State is satisfied that the supply will serve the interests of the community;
(f) anything which, in the opinion of the Secretary of State, is or is likely to be necessary for or in connection with the production of any such articles as are mentioned in paragraphs (a) to (e) above

and 'works required for the public service' shall be construed accordingly. (Supply Powers Act 1975, s 7)

[A railway Act provided that if at any time it should be made to appear to the Board of Trade to be requisite for the 'public service', the company should lay down additional rails.] 'It was argued . . . that the expression "requisite for the public service" means requisite for the public service of the government or of her Majesty. But we see no reason for taking public service to mean no more than the government public service or the service of government acting for the public, and we think any service which would supply wants felt by the public or which the public might reasonably be desirous of having on its own behalf is included.' *Re Launceston (Inhabitants) Application* (1877) 3 Ry & Can Tr Cas 137 at 139, per cur.

PUBLIC SERVICE VEHICLE

'Foreign public service vehicle' means a public service vehicle which has been brought into Great Britain and is not registered in the United Kingdom. (Road Traffic (Foreign Vehicles) Act 1972, s 7(1)

[See also the Transport Act 1980, s 43.]

(1) Subject to the provisions of this section, in this Act 'public service vehicle' means a motor vehicle (other than a tramcar) which—
(a) being a vehicle adapted to carry more than eight passengers, is used for carrying passengers for hire or reward; or
(b) being a vehicle not so adapted, is used for carrying passengers for hire or reward at separate fares in the course of a business of carrying passengers

(Public Passenger Vehicles Act 1981, s 1(1))

PUBLIC TRUST *See* TRUST

PUBLIC UTILITY

Australia 'Literally the word "utility" means usefulness but it is commonly used to refer to a corporation that performs a public service and so is a public utility. Hence railroads, airlines, bus lines, gas and electricity corporations are known as 'public utilities'. Webster defines a public utility as a business organisation performing some public service and, hence, subject to special governmental regulations such as fixing of rates and requirements of incidental facilities. The Shorter Oxford Dictionary defines "public utilities" as the services or supplies commonly available in large towns such as omnibuses, electricity, water etc. The expression "of public utility" could mean of usefulness for or in the service of the public and so on undertaking for the general utility of the public.' *Top of the Cross Pty Ltd v Federal Commr of Taxation* (1980) 50 FLR 19 at 40, per Woodward J

PUBLIC WORK

New Zealand 'The term "public work" conveys the sense of community benefit or community utility, something done for the common good: and done by a body charged with furthering the common good in one or more particular aspects.' *Invercargill Licensing Trust v Invercargill City Council* [1985] 10 NZTPA 426 at 431, per Hardie Boys J

PUBLIC WORSHIP *See* WORSHIP

PUBLICATION—PUBLISH

The Contempt of Court Act 1981, s 1 provides that, in the Act, 'the strict liability' means the rule of law whereby conduct may be treated as a contempt of court as tending to interfere with the course of justice in particular legal proceedings regardless of intent to do so. The strict liability rule applies only to publications, and for this purpose 'publication' includes any speech, writing, broadcast or other communication in whatever form, which is addressed to the public at large or any section of the public ibid, s 2(1)).]

'In relation to copyright, whether under common law or statute, "publishing" and "publications" are fundamental expressions meaning making available to the public, and it would take a great deal of contextual restraint to force them into a narrower and special meaning.' *Infabrics, Ltd v Jaytex Ltd* [1981] 1 All ER 1057 at 1061, HL, per Lord Wilberforce

Canada The Criminal Code, RSC 1970, c C–34, s 159, regarding obscenity, uses the word 'publication'.] 'When a published play is performed in public it is a publication in the sense that the written word is being made "publicly known" and communicated "to a limited number regarded as representing the public".' *R v Smith* [1973] 4 WWR 563 at 576, BCCA, per Nemetz JA

Agricultural charge

For the purpose of this section [which restricts the publication of agricultural charges], 'publication' means the issue of copies to the public, and 'publish' has a corresponding meaning, and without prejudice to the generality of the foregoing definition the confidential notification by an association representative of a particular trade to its members trading or carrying on business in the district in which property subject to an agricultural charge is situate of the creation of the charge shall not be deemed to be publication for the purposes of this section. (Agricultural Credits Act 1928, s 10(4))

Award

'I am of opinion that this award was sufficiently published, for the purpose of making it valid, in the lifetime of the plaintiff. For that purpose it is only necessary that the act should be complete, so far as the arbitrator is concerned; that he should have done some act whereby he becomes *functus officio*, and has declared his final mind. That is the rule to be collected from the cases of *Brown v Vawser* [(1804) 4 East 584], and *Henfree v Bromley* [(1805) 6 East 309]; and that is the meaning of the term "publication". Here the instrument was complete as an award, and the umpire could make no alteration to it, after the execution of it; he was then *functus officio*, having declared his final mind.' *Brooke v Mitchell* (1840) 6 M & W 473 at 476, 477, per Parke B

Commercial publication

'Commercial publication', in relation to a literary, dramatic, musical or artistic work means—

(a) issuing copies of the work to the public at a time when copies made in advance of the receipt of orders are generally available to the public, or
(b) making the work available to the public by means of an electronic retrieval system;

and related expressions shall be construed accordingly. (Copyright Designs and Patents Act 1988, s 175)

Copyright *See also* RECORDING

'Publication', in relation to a work—

(a) means the issue of copies to the public, and
(b) includes, in the case of a literary, dramatic, musical or artistic work, making it available to the public by means of an electronic retrieval system;

and related expressions shall be construed accordingly. (Copyright, Designs and Patents Act 1988, s 175)

The International Copyright Act 1844, s 19 (repealed; see now the Copyright, Designs and Patents Act 1988, s 159) deprived the author of a dramatic work of any exclusive right of representation or performance in this country if the work in question had first been 'published' abroad.] 'I see nothing contrary to reason or justice in saying that if an English author chooses to go abroad and there represent, or allow to be represented, his composition for the first time, he shall be in the same position as a foreigner who has done the same thing. If that be so, the word "published" must have its natural construction, whether it is applied to the compositions of Englishmen or of foreigners. That ordinary meaning is "made public", and a dramatic composition is made public the moment it is represented or acted.' *Boucicault v Chatterton* (1876) 5 Ch D 267 at 281, CA, per Brett LJ

'What is the meaning of "publishing" a newspaper? It is plainly something different from printing it. I see no reason why a newspaper should not be published in more than one place. . . . It seems to me that a paper is published when and where it is offered to the public by the proprietor. Webster's definition of the word is as follows:—"To send forth as a book, newspaper, musical piece or other printed work, either for sale or for general distribution".' *McFarlane v Hulton* [1899] 1 Ch 88 at 888. 889, per Cozens-Hardy J

United States 'Publication' is the distribution of copies or phonorecords of a work to the public by sale or other transfer of ownership, or by rental, lease, or lending. The offering to distribute copies or phonorecords to a group of persons for purposes of further distribution, public performance, or public display, constitutes publication. A public performance or display of work does not of itself constitute publication. (Copyright Act of 1976, s 101)

Defamation

Merely to write down defamatory words is not to publish a libel. Even to deliver a defamatory statement to another is not to publish it to him if he does not become aware of the defamatory words. Publication consists in making known the defamatory statement after it has been reduced into some permanent form. (28 Halsbury's Laws (4th edn) para 60)

A person publishes a slander who speaks words defamatory of the plaintiff to or in the presence of a third person who hears them and understands them in a defamatory sense. (28 Halsbury's Laws (4th edn) para 78)

For the purposes of the law of libel and slander, the broadcasting of words by means of wireless telegraphy shall be treated as publication in permanent form. (Defamation Act 1952, s 1)

'The first question is, whether, assuming the letter to contain defamatory matter, there has been a publication of it. What is the meaning of "publication"? The making known the defamatory matter after it has been written to some person other than the person of whom it is written. If the statement is sent straight to the person of whom it is written, there is no publication of it; for you cannot publish a libel of a man to himself. If there was no publication, the question whether the occasion was privileged does not arise. If a letter is not communicated to any one but the person to whom it is written, there is no publication of it. And, if the writer of a letter locks it up in his own desk, and a thief comes and breaks open the desk and takes away the letter and makes its contents known. I should say that would not be a publication. If the writer of a letter shews it to his own clerk in order that the clerk may copy it for him, is that a publication of the letter? Certainly it is shewing it to a third person; the writer cannot say to the person to whom the letter is addressed, 'I have shewn it to you and to no one else'. I cannot, therefore, feel any doubt that, if the writer of a letter shews it to any person other than the person to whom it is written, he publishes it. If he wishes not to publish it, he must, so far as he possibly can, keep it to himself, or he must send it himself straight to the person to whom it is written.' *Pullman v Hill & Co* [1891] 1 QB 524 at 527, CA, per Lord Esher MR

Australia 'To publish a libel is to convey by some means to the mind of another the defamatory sense embodied in the vehicle.' *Webb v Bloch* (1928) 41 CLR 331 at 363, per Isaacs J

New Zealand '"Publication" as applied to actions for defamation is the communication of the defamatory matter to some person or persons other than the person defamed. That covers both spoken and written defamation. The dictation of defamatory matter to another is a publication of such matter. But such dictation is slander, and not libel.' *Angelini v Antico* (1912) 31 NZLR 841 at 848, CA, per cur; also reported 14 GLR 654 at p 657

See, generally, 28 Halsbury's Laws (4th edn) para 60.

Incitement by

Australia [The defendant had handed out to members of the public a pamphlet urging persons not to register for military service. He was charged under the Crimes Act 1914–1986 (Cth), s 7A which provides that a person is guilty of an offence who 'publishes' any writing which incites to the commission of offences against the law of the Commonwealth.] 'It seems to me that the conduct of the defendant in handing the pamphlet to a member of the public is clearly a publication within the meaning of the section.' *Sullivan v Hamel-Green* [1970] VR 156 at 158, per Starke J

Obscene publications

For the purposes of this Act a person publishes an article who—
(a) distributes, circulates, sells, lets on hire, gives, or lends it, or who offers it for sale or for letting on hire; or
(b) in the case of an article containing or embodying matter to be looked at or a record, shows, plays or projects it

Provided that paragraph (b) of this subsection shall not apply to anything done in the course of . . . television or sound broadcasting. (Obscene Publications Act 1959, s 1(3), as amended by the Criminal Law Act 1977, s 53(1))

'Although the actual [photographic] negative may not be sold or distributed or lent within the meaning of s 1 of the Act [Obscene Publications Act] of 1857 (repealed; see now the Obscene Publications Act 1959, as amended by the Obscene Publications Act 1964, s 2), it is, in my view, "otherwise published" when the picture that is taken from it is published, because publication of the positive is publication of the negative.' *Cox v Stinton* [1951] 2 All ER 637 at 640, per Lord Goddard CJ; [1951] 2 KB 1021

[It was held in *Straker v Director of Public Prosecutions* [1963] 1 All ER 697, that photographic negatives were not articles capable of publication within the meaning of the Obscene Publications Act 1959. The Obscence Publications Act 1964, s 2, overcame this defect by providing that the Act of 1959 should apply to anything intended for use for the reproduction of obscene articles.]

Patents

'Published', except in relation to a complete specification, means made available to the public; and without prejudice to the generality of the foregoing provision a document shall be deemed for the purposes of this Act to be published if it can be inspected as of right at any place in the United Kingdom by members of the public, whether upon payment of a fee or otherwise. (Patents Act 1949, s 101)

[See also the similar definition in the Patents Act 1977, s 130)1).]

Race relations

References in this Part [Part III: racial hatred] to the publication or distribution of written material are to its publication or distribution to the public or a section of the public. (Public Order Act 1986, s 19(3))

Report of proceedings

In this section . . . 'publish', in relation to a report [of committal proceedings], means publish the report, either by itself or as part of a newspaper or periodical, for distribution to the public. (Magistrates' Courts Act 1980, s 8(10))

PUFFING

Representation of fact as to the quality of the subject matter of a contract must be distinguished from such expressions of opinion as to its value or desirability as do not involve any representation of fact. A purchaser cannot avoid liability to perform his contract on the ground that he has been misled by statements which are mere puffing. It has been held to be puffing to describe property as a desirable residence for a family of distinction, when in fact it is a small farmhouse, or (formerly) to describe renewable leaseholds as nearly equal to freehold, or to describe a house as substantial and convenient, or well built, or eligible. (42 Halsbury's Laws (4th edn) para 49)

'Puffer' shall mean a person appointed to bid on the part of the owner. (Sale of Land by Auction Act 1867, s 3)

PUISNE MORTGAGE *See* MORTGAGE

PUNCTUAL

'All we have to do is to look at the mortgage deed. There is a covenant by the mortgagor to pay the mortgagees on August 15 next £7,000, with interest at 5 per cent. . . . 'Lastly, it is hereby agreed that payment of the principal money . . . shall not be required . . . until the expiration of three years . . . if in the meantime every half-yearly payment of interest shall be punctually paid." That surely means if . . . every half-yearly payment of interest is paid on the days specified in the covenant. I do not think you want authority to shew that 'punctually' means punctually on the day fixed for payment; and I am not aware of any authority which shews it does not.' *Leeds & Hanley Theatre of Varieties v Broadbent* [1898] 1 Ch 343 at 348, 349, CA, per Lindley MR

'Where a party has contracted that he will make a payment punctually upon a day specified, can he be heard to say that that payment is a payment punctually made if in fact it is made at a later day? . . . I am of opinion that where an instrument clearly expresses that payment is to be made punctually on a day specified, such a payment is not so made unless it is made upon that day.' *Maclaine v Gatty* [1921] 1 AC 376 at 283, 383, per Lord Birkenhead LC

A promissory note contained a provision that, should any instalment not be paid 'punctually', the whole of the balance should immediately become due.] 'The note provides inter alia, that in default of the punctual payment of each instalment the whole of the balance shall become immediately payable. The defendant contends that three days of grace were allowed for the payment of each instalment, and that if one added the days of grace, the second instalment would not have become payable until December 24. It is not denied that if the word "punctually" had been omitted the defendant would have had until December 24 to pay; but the plaintiff said that the insertion of the word in the instrument showed that the parties intended that the three days of grace should not be allowed, and reference was made to s 14 of the Bills of Exchange Act 1882, which was as follows:— "Where a bill is not payable on demand, the day on which it falls due is determined as follows:—(1) Three days, called days of grace, are, in every case where the bill itself does not otherwise provide, added to the time of payment, as fixed by the bill, and the bill is due and payable on the last day of grace." . . . I have come to the conclusion that the note did not otherwise provide within the meaning of the section. I think that it meant that the maker had his attention drawn to the fact that, if he was not prompt in payment, he would lose the benefit of paying by instalments, and would have to pay the whole of the balance. I cannot think that it was intended that the maker should be deprived of the usual concession as to the three days of grace. It was only intended to emphasize the necessity, on the part of the maker, of not being dilatory in paying his instalments.' *Schaverien v Morris* (1921) 37 TLR 366 at 366, 367, per Lush J

'The authorities show that 'punctual' payment is to be construed strictly. It is stronger than payment "on or before" a certain day, as to which see *Hawley v Simpson* [(1583) Cro Eliz 14]. Punctual payment means payment on the very day. Not on the day before: see *Lord Cromwell v Andrews* [(1583) Cro Eliz 15]; nor the day after: see *Maclaine v Gatty* [[1921] 1 AC 376]; but the very day itself. 'Punctual payment', said Viscount Finlay [in the latter case], "emphasises the necessity of payment being made on that day, not on a subsequent day". But if payment cannot be made on the very day, because the banks are closed, what is the position? In the parallel case of the courts of law, when anything is to be done on a Sunday, or the last day is a Sunday, when the offices of the courts are closed, it is done in time if done on the next day on which the offices are open that is, on the Monday: see RSC Ord 3, r 4. . . . If such be the rule when the offices of the courts are closed, it should be the same when the banks are closed. There should be a definite rule throughout the law—as to the effect of closure of offices—so that people should know where they stand.' *Mardorf Peach & Co Ltd v Attica Sea Carriers Corpn of Liberia, The Laconia* [1976] 2 All ER 249 at 254, CA, per Lord Denning MR

PUNISHMENT *See also* TREATMENT

Legal punishment is punishment awarded in a process instituted at the suit of the Crown standing forward as prosecutor on behalf of the subject on public grounds; such process, once instituted, may be stayed only at the instance of the Attorney General acting on behalf of the Crown, and the punishment, when imposed, may be remitted only by the Crown or by Parliament. (11 Halsbury's Laws (4th edn) para 3)

Canada 'When a sentence is suspended and a person is ordered to be released on conditions,

I am satisfied that that would not come into the ambit of being "punishment" because it is a suspension of punishment. But when an accused is ordered or directed to obey and comply with certain conditions under s 663(1)(b) [of the Criminal Code, RSC 1970, c C-34 (amended 1972, c 13), respecting probation orders], I think that that is a form of punishment within the meaning of the Code. I can see no difference in principle between a convicted accused being ordered to pay a sum of money as a fine and being ordered to perform certain actions or abide by certain conditions of conduct. In either case the accused is sentenced by the court to a penalty, because of his conviction of an offence, and hence is being sentenced to a "punishment" in the sense that I think that word is used in the Code.' *R v Johnson* [1972] 2 WWR 145 at 146, 147, BCCA, per Bull JA

Canada 'One characteristic of "punishment", obviously not illustrated by the imposition of a fine but certainly illustrated by the imposition of a term of imprisonment, is that the accused is deprived of his liberty—his freedom to associate with his family and friends and to carry on his normal employment and other activities. . . . A second characteristic of "punishment" is . . . "It must involve pain or other consequences normally considered unpleasant." . . . Involuntary confinement in a prison or jail, and even the payment of a fine, are illustrations of consequences normally considered unpleasant. A third characteristic of "punishment" is that the penalty, like the conviction itself, carries with it a degree of stigmatization. This is inherent in the public nature of the adult criminal adjudicatory process.' *R v TR (No 2)* 1984 7 DLR (4th) 262 at 269, Alta QB, per McDonald J

PUNITIVE DAMAGES *See* DAMAGES

PUPIL

'Pupil', where used without qualification, means a person of any age for whom education is required to be provided, under this Act but includes a junior pupil who has not attained the age of five years. (Education Act 1944, s 114(1), as amended by the Education Act 1980, s 24(3))

Junior pupil

'Junior pupil' means a child who has not attained the age of twelve years. (Education Act 1944, s 114(1))

Registered pupil

'Registered pupil' means, in relation to any school, a pupil registered as such in the register kept in accordance with the requirements of this Act. (Education Act 1944, s 114(1))

Senior pupil

'Senior pupil' means a person who has attained the age of twelve years but has not attained the age of nineteen years. (Education Act 1944, s 114(1))

PURCHASE

'The question is, whether the lands which the testator had obtained by exchange passed under this devise of his sisters? and we are of opinion that they did. The devise is in these terms: "I give and devise all and every my several messuages, tenements, mill, lands, rents, hereditaments, and real estates whatsoever, situate in the several parishes of Llanfechell, etc, or elsewhere, in the county of Anglesey, which I have heretofore from time to time purchased from different persons in the several deeds of conveyances thereof named, and which are now vested in me in fee simple, or in some other person or persons to and for my use and benefits, unto and to the use and behoof of my sisters, Ann Meyrick and Elizabeth Meyrick.' Whether we consider the word "purchased" in its general or its legal sense, the lands so acquired are comprehended within it. They were purchased, not indeed with money, but with other lands which were given for them; and we are bound to give the word its usual interpretation, unless there is some circumstance to shew, and to shew clearly, that the testator intended to use it in a different sense. No such circumstance appears in the will, or was suggested at the bar; and we are of opinion, therefore, that the land in question passed by the devise.' *Doe d Meyrick v Meyrick* (1833) 1 Cr & M 820 at 826, 827, per Lord Lyndhurst CB

[A testator in his marriage settlement covenanted that if at any time during the marriage he should become possessed of or entitled by devise, bequest, 'purchase', or otherwise, of or to any property or estate, real or personal, he would convey or assign it to the trustees of the marriage settlement.] 'Policies [of insurance on the testator's life] come with the class of property acquired 'by purchase' during his life. It was contended that they did not come within the meaning of this term; but in my opinion they may properly be considered as acquired by purchase during his life. They are contracts under which the policy-holder has a right to recover certain sums of money from the insurance office in certain events, and the premiums which he pays may be regarded as money paid as an investment, so as to obtain for him the benefit of the policies.' *Re Turcan* (1888) 40 Ch D 5 at 8–10, CA, per Cotton LJ

'The father originally effected these fifteen policies on his own life, and, after maintaining them for some time, assigned them to his son under a family arrangement . . . necessitated by his (the father's) pecuniary difficulties. In substance, it came to this, that the son mortgaged his inheritance in the family estates to save his father, and the father in return assigned these policies, together with an annual sum out of his life interest . . . sufficient to pay the premium, and also to pay an annuity during their joint lives. . . . Did the son give in money or money's worth full consideration for the policies and the other advantages he acquired under the arrangement? . . . He gave full value and more. . . . The fact that the transaction was a family arrangement is not inconsistent with its being also a purchase for full consideration in money or money's worth.' *Lethbridge v A-G* [1907] AC 19 at 22–24, per Lord Loreburn LC

'Speaking for myself, I . . . agree with what has been said by Lord Herschell in *Helby v Matthews* [[1895] AC 471 at 475], that if the defendant agreed to buy the car she could not, "by calling it a hiring, or by any mere juggling with words, escape from the consequences of the contract into which she had entered". But that is not the case here. It is not disputed that the defendant had seen a car and was minded to have it, and had got it on the terms of an agreement. Mr Salter [counsel] argued that taking possession under the agreement amounted to a purchase. But it is impossible to treat hiring with an option to purchase as a purchase. With regard to the hire purchase agreement, down to clause 13 there is no difficulty about it. There are the usual clauses and the hirer may determine the agreement by delivering up the car at any time. But then it is said by clause 13 the car became the property of the defendant. That clause was as follows:— "In the event of the hiring being determined under clauses 8 and 9 hereof the owners shall be at liberty to sell the motorcar and to reimburse themselves in respect of all expenses incurred in consequence of such seizure and sale or otherwise under this agreement, and shall carry the balance of the proceeds of such sale to the credit of the hirer in addition to the sum paid by her on the signing of this agreement. The hirer shall then be entitled to receive any surplus which such aggregation shall show over the agreed price of the motor-car—namely, eight hundred and six pounds five shillings. In the event of the owners preferring to retain the car instead of selling it the hirer shall be credited with an amount to be agreed between the parties or in case of dispute an amount to be settled by one indifferent person selected by mutual consent, and failing mutual consent, by a person selected by the town clerk of Newcastle-upon-Tyne upon the application of either party." That clause, however, is really supplemental to and not inconsistent with the previous clauses of the agreement, which are not sufficient to establish a purchase. The effect of the agreement throughout is that it amounts to a hiring of a car and not to a purchase, giving only an option to purchase in certain events. I cannot see that the defendant has purchased a new motor-car within the meaning of the arrangement between the parties.' *Grande Maison d'Automobiles Ltd v Beresford* (1909) 25 TLR 522 at 522, CA, per Lord Alverstone CJ

'I am well aware that the word "purchaser" and the words "by purchase" have in certain contexts a technical meaning which is well-known to all lawyers, but I am not aware of any case in which the words "by purchasing a dwelling-house" have been given any technical meaning. For my part I feel no doubt that they simply refer to a transaction of purchase or buying.' *Baker v Lewis* [1946] 2 All ER 592 at 594, per Morton LJ

[*See* now the Rent Act 1977, Sch 15, Part I, case 9] any means of acquisition for money or money's worth, whether or not the interest acquired had any previous existence; or should it be confined to "buying" some interest already in existence? It is, in our judgment, not open to doubt that the ordinary meaning of the word 'purchasing' in the context in which it appears in para (h) of the schedule—the meaning which first strikes the mind on reading the formula used—is . . . equivalent to "buying".' *Powell v Cleland* [1948] 1 KB 262 at 269, CA, per Evershed LJ

[The Landlord and Tenant Act 1954, s 30(2) prevents a landlord from resisting the grant of a new tenency if his interest was 'purchased' or created after the beginning of the period of five years which ends with the termination of the tenancy.] '"Purchased" in this Act . . . has its popular meaning of buying for money, and not the technical legal meaning of acquisition otherwise than by descent of escheat.' *Bolton (HL) (Engineering) Co Ltd v Graham (TJ) & Sons Ltd* [1956] 3 All ER 624 at 628, CA, per Denning LJ (also reported in [1957] 1 QB 159 at 170)

Australia 'I have no doubt that the phrase "by purchase" has its popular meaning, and envisages a person acquiring a dwelling-house by way of bargain and sale for money or other valuable consideration.' *Hollingsworth v Lee* [1949] VLR 140 at 144, per Barry

Canada 'In the case at bar we are dealing with chattels under the Conditional Sales Act [1961 (BC), c 9] and consequently I feel there is even greater reason for holding that the word "purchase" in s 10(2) [amended, 1972, c 14] should be given the ordinary and commercial and businesslike meaning of the word, viz, ('Acquisition by payment of money or an equivalent" and refusing to apply to it ('the technicalities of real property law."' *Re Frontier Construction and Development Ltd* (1970) 14 CBR (NS) 291 at 295, BC, per Dryer J

United States 'Purchase' includes taking by sale, discount, negotiation, mortgage, pledge, lien, issue or re-issue, gift or any other voluntary transaction creating an interest in property. (Uniform Commercial Code 1978, s 1–201(32))

PURCHASE MONEY

[The County Courts Act 1888, s 67(4) (repealed; see now the County Courts Act 1984, s 23(d)) enacted that the county court should have and exercise all the powers and authority of the High Court in actions (inter alia) for the rectification or cancellation of a contract where the 'purchase-money' did not exceed the county court limit.] 'It would not be safe to put an artificial construction on the words "purchase money" in the section, and we must read the words as referring to the actual purchase money of the subject-matter of the contract sought to be reformed or cancelled.' *R v Whitehorne (Judge)* [1904] 1 KB 827 at 829, 830, DC, per Lord Alverstone CJ

'What . . . is meant by the words "purchase money" in the codicil? The words used must be taken as they stand. . . . The trustees were to raise "a sum equal to the purchase money thereof". That involves the idea of two persons, a vendor and purchaser, and the idea that a sum of money is paid by the purchaser in respect of the estate; for purchase money is the money which a purchaser pays to the vendor for the estate which he is buying.' *Re Oliver, Ramsden v Ramsden* (1910) 55 Sol Jo 12 at 13, per Warrington J

[A railway company, by virtue of a private Act of Parliament, acquired running powers over the system of another upon payment of interest on the cost of construction, such cost to include the 'purchase money' of any land.] 'On the question whether the 'purchase money' of the land embraces also the expenses incurred in connexion with its acquisition I agree with the Lord Ordinary. It was pointed out in the argument that he speaks of the "purchase price", whereas the statutory expression is "purchase money". . . . The two expressions "money" and "price" seem to me in this connexion to mean the same thing, and to exclude money not actually paid for the land itself. *Caledonian Rly Co v North British Rly Co* 1916 SC 332 at 335, 336, per the Lord President (Lord Strathclyde)

PURCHASER

'Purchaser' means a lessee, mortgagee or other person who in good faith acquires an interest in property for valuable consideration, also an intending purchaser and 'valuable consideration' includes marriage, but does not include a nominal consideration in money. (Administration of Estates Act 1925, s 55(1))

'Purchaser' means a purchaser in good faith for valuable consideration and includes a lessee, mortgagee or other person who for valuable consideration acquires an interest in property except that in Part I of this Act and elsewhere where so expressly provided 'purchaser' only means a person who acquires an interest in or charge on property for money or money's worth; and in reference to a legal estate includes a chargee by way of legal mortage; and where the context so requires 'purchaser' includes an intending purchaser; 'purchase' has a meaning corresponding with that of 'purchaser'; and 'valuable consideration' includes marriage but does not include a nominal consideration in money. (Law of Property Act 1925, s 205(xxi))

'I think that the observations made in the House of Lords, and particularly those of Lord Russell of Killowen and Lord Romer in *Luxor (Eastbourne) Ltd v Cooper* [[1941] AC 108], show that they were clearly of opinion that if an agent is employed to introduce a purchaser for a house and before the purchaser has entered into a binding and legal contract, the house is withdrawn from the market, the agent cannot say that he has earned his commission. . . . In his speech, Lord Russell of Killowen [at p 129] said: "It is possible that an owner may be willing to bind himself to pay a commission for the mere introduction of one who offers to purchase at the specified or minimum price; but such a construction of the contract would in my opinion require clear and unequivocal language." There, again, having regard to the former passage I have read, the learned lord is drawing a distinction between the case of "introducing a purchaser" and one in which the contract is for the introduction of a person who is "willing to buy". Lord Romer was clearly of the same opinion as Lord Russell of Killowen. He said [at p 154]: "Where an owner of property employs an agent to find a purchaser which must mean at least a person who enters into a binding contract to purchase, is it an implied term of the contract of agency that, after the agent has introduced a person who is ready, willing and able to purchase at a price assented to by the principal, the principal shall enter into a contract with that person to sell at the agreed price subject only to the qualification that he may refuse to do so if he has just cause or reasonable excuse for his refusal?' In that passage Lord Romer is again contrasting the situation of an agent employed to find a purchaser who becomes entitled to his commission on introducing a purchaser who enters into a binding contract with that of an agent who has only got so far as to find someone who is ready, willing and able to purchase, and his observations afford the clearest indication that he was of the same opinion as Lord Russell of Killowen. It seems to me that I should be flying in the face of those high authorities if I were to construe the contract for the payment of commission on the introduction of a purchaser, in the present case as having been performed by the plaintiff by the introduction of a purchaser who was ready, able and willing to purchase, but who did not in fact proceed to the signing of a binding contract.' *Jones v Lowe* [1945] KB 73 at 75–77, per Hilbery J

[The plaintiff who wished to find a purchaser for his house, signed a printed form, supplied by the defendants, instructing them to find a 'purchaser' and to receive any deposit paid by such purchaser and to apply it on the signing of the contract towards payment of their expenses and commission.] 'I think it must be taken that in the ordinary way the meaning of "purchaser" in such a document is a purchaser who is able and willing to complete. This proposed purchaser may well have been willing to complete—he signed two contracts—but he was not able to complete. Dealing with the first point raised by counsel for the defendants, I am satisfied that when the document speaks of a purchaser, it means a purchaser not only willing but also able to complete, and in that sense no such purchaser was found by the agent.' *Poole v Clarke & Co* [1945] 2 All ER 445 at 448, per Singleton J

'The courts have said that to speak of a "purchaser" without any other words, is to speak of one who actually does complete the contract of sale and purchase; but in common parlance one does not always speak of a purchaser in that limited sense of the word. "Buyer" certainly is a word of description in many great firms for a person holding a general office of buying for the firm. . . . Though he does not buy anything for months, he remains a buyer. . . . In ordinary parlance, we do not use the word necessarily as restricted to a person who actually completes a transaction of purchase and sale; and here in this letter, I think, the very fact that they add the words "who is able and willing to complete the transaction" shows that they are speaking of some one who is in the character of a buyer—who is taking the part, if I may borrow an expression from the stage, of a buyer, and is in a position to complete the transaction, that is to say, to become in the full sense of the term as construed by the courts, an actual buyer who has completed the transaction of purchase and sale.' *Bennett & Partners v Millett* [1949] 1 KB 362 at 366, 367, per Hilbery J

For valuable consideration

Australia [The Bankruptcy Act 1966 (Cth), s 120(1) provides that a settlement of property, not being a settlement made in favour of a purchaser in good faith and for valuable consideration is, if the settlor becomes bankrupt within two years after the date of the settlement, void as against the trustee in the bankruptcy.] 'In *Re Abbott* [1983] Ch 45 Vice-Chancellor Sir Robert

Megarry in a short concurring judgment, referred briefly, at p 57, to the meaning of "purchaser . . . for valuable consideration" in s 42 [of the Bankruptcy Act 1914 (UK)]; "Plainly, 'good consideration', in the sense of the natural love and affection that a man has for his wife and children, is not enough. Nor is a merely nominal consideration, even though it would suffice to support a simple contract at common law. In the context of the avoidance of settlements by a trustee in bankruptcy, a 'purchaser . . . for valuable consideration' must be someone who can not only be described as being a 'purchaser' but can also be said to have given a consideration for his purchase which has a real and substantial value, and not one which is merely nominal or trivial or colourable.' Unless there is good reason to the contrary, we believe it to be important in legislation of this kind to maintain a construction of the Australian Act which accords with English authority. We would therefore accept Sir Robert Megarry's formulation and endorse the Full Court's ruling that a "purchaser . . . for valuable consideration" within the meaning of s 120(1) of the Act is one who has given consideration for his purchase "which has a real and substantial value, and not one which is merely nominal or trivial or colourable'. *Barton v Official Receiver* (1986) 66 ALR 355 at 360–362, per cur.

PURE

'I think this case is not entirely free from doubt owing to the difficulty created by the word "pure". . . . In one sense of the word it cannot be contended that this was pure butter, because it has a small percentage of boracic acid added to it, and we know that butter, which is a manufactured article, can be made without this being done. But common salt is always added and yet no one would say that the addition of a little salt to the butter rendered the butter not pure. Then why should the addition of a very small percentage of boracic acid, which is added exactly for the same reason as salt is added, make pure butter thereby impure? Speaking for myself, I think it does not.' *Roose v Perry & Co* (1900) 44 Sol Jo 503 at 503, DC, per Ridley J

'For the purpose of interpreting this warranty the judge should have taken into consideration what was the trade meaning of "pure" butter, as that expression would be used by the plaintiff and the defendants. The judge asked the defendants' counsel where the line was to be drawn if this was held by him to be pure butter and the presence of some preservative was to be admitted as consistent with a warranty that the butter was pure. But I think the line is to be drawn where the added ingredient ceased to be a preservative and became something else. If the decision of the judge was to be upheld in this case it seems to me that the mere introduction of a little salt would render the defendants liable. I cannot believe the parties ever intended that the butter to be supplied should be in the simple state that it left the churn, for the purchaser expected that some preservative would be added so that it should keep good while exposed for sale in her shop. I should myself have had no hesitation in finding that this was pure butter within the meaning of the warranty, but that is a question of fact for the judge and not us to decide. I think that he went wrong in refusing to take into consideration evidence that this expression 'pure butter' had a meaning as used between the plaintiff and the defendants in trade apart from its natural meaning.' Ibid at 503, per Bigham J

New Zealand 'Their Lordships are of opinion that an act empowering local authorities to supply "pure water" should receive a "fair large and liberal" construction as provided by s 5(j) of the Acts Interpretation Act 1924. They are of opinion that as a matter of common sense there is but little difference for the relative purpose between the adjectives "pure" and "wholesome". Their Lordships think it is an unnecessarily restrictive construction to hold . . . that, because the supply of water was already pure there is no power to add to its constituents merely to provide medicated pure water, i.e. water to which an addition is made solely for the health of the consumers. The water of Lower Hutt is no doubt pure in its natural state but it is very deficient in one of the natural constituents normally to be found in water in most parts of the world. The addition of fluoride adds no impurity and the water remains not only water but pure water and it becomes a greatly improved and still natural water containing no foreign elements.' *A-G v Lower Hutt City* [1965] NZLR 116 at 124, PC, per Lord Upjohn

PURPORT

[A marriage settlement provided that property should be disposed of as the wife should direct or appoint by deed will, or codicil, or any writing in the nature of or 'purporting to be a will' or codicil.] 'What is the meaning of the expression "purporting to be" a will or codicil? . . . The question here is whether a document which is in form and substance a will, but which, because it was not duly executed as such, fails to be a will, in a legal sense, is or is not a document which "purports" to be a will. . . . This document . . . is on the face of it a disposition of property made in contemplation of death, and it only fails to be a will because the maker of it did not comply with the requirement of the Wills Act [1837] that the witnesses should be present when she signed it. I think, therefore, that I must hold that this document . . . is one which "purports" to be a will.' *Re Broad, Smith v Draeger* [1901] 2 Ch 86 at 91, 92, per Kekewich J

[The Landlord and Tenant Act 1954, s 38(1) provides that any agreement relating to a tenancy under Part II of the Act (business, professional and other tenants) shall be void in so far as it 'purports' to preclude the tenant from making an application or request under the Act, etc.] 'The word "purports" . . . does not mean "professes". It means "has the effect of".' *Joseph v Joseph* [1966] 3 All ER 486 at 490, CA, per Lord Denning MR

'There was some discussion on the words "purports to". For my part I would not give a narrow construction to that phrase in this context: one meaning I take to be "to have as its effect", and this seems to be a suitable meaning when the statute is avoiding an agreement and, therefore, is presumably aimed at its effect.' Ibid at 493, per Russell LJ

PURPOSE *See also* FOR THE PURPOSE OF; INTENTION; MOTIVE

'The liberty to call at any ports "for bunkering or other purposes" cannot be read as meaning that the ship was to be at liberty to call at any ports for bunkering purposes or any purposes other than bunkering, for that would be tantamount to saying that she might call at any port for any purpose. I read the words as meaning "for the purpose of bunkering or for any similar purpose". What purposes are similar to the purpose of bunkering I shall not attempt to define.' *Stag line Ltd v Foscolo, Mango & Co Ltd* [1932] AC 328 at 348, 349, per Lord Macmillan

[The Official Secrets Act 1911, s 1(1) provides that a person who, for any 'purpose' prejudicial to the safety or interests of the state, enters, etc, any prohibited place, shall be guilty of felony.] 'I shall begin by considering the word "purpose", for both sides have relied on this word in different senses. Broadly, the appellants contend that it is to be given a subjective meaning and the Crown an objective one. I have no doubt that it is subjective. A purpose must exist in the mind. It cannot exist anywhere else. The word can be used to designate either the main object which a man wants or hopes to achieve by the contemplated act, or it can be used to designate those objects which he knowns will probably be achieved by the act, whether he wants them or not. I am satisfied that in the criminal law in general, and in this statute in particular, its ordinary sense is the latter one. In the former sense it cannot in practice be distinguished from motive which is normally irrelevant in criminal law. Its use in that sense would make this statute quite inept. As my noble and learned friend Lord Reid pointed out during the argument, a spy could secure an acquittal by satisfying the jury that his purpose was to make money for himself, a purpose not in itself prejudicial to the state, and that he was indifferent to all other consequences of his acts. Accordingly, all the results which a man appreciates will probably flow from his act are classifiable as "purposes" within the meaning of s 1: and since the statute refers to "any purpose", the prosecution is entitled to rely on any of them.' *Chandler v Director of Public Prosecutions* [1962] 3 All ER 142 at 155, HL, per Lord Devlin

'The word "purpose" although it has some subjective content is used in an objective sense. If the purpose was in fact prejudicial, the offence is committed, no matter how benevolent the motives of the spy or saboteur that led him to essay the purpose.' Ibid at 160, per Lord Pearce

'It seems to me . . . that the words [in the Dangerous Drugs Act 1965, s 5 (see now the Misuse of Drugs Act 1971, s 8)] "premises . . . used for the purpose of smoking cannabis" are not happily chosen if they were intended to denote premises in which at any time cannabis is smoked. In my opinion, the words "premises used for any such purpose . . ." denote a purpose, which is other than quite incidental or casual or fortuitous; they denote a purpose which is or has become either a significant one or a recognised one though certainly not necesssarily an only one. There is no difficulty in appreciating what is meant if it is said that premises are used for the purposes of a dance hall or a billiard hall or a bowling alley or a hairdressing saloon or a café. A new or additional use might, however, arise. It might happen that a house let as a private dwelling might come to be used as a brothel or for the purposes of prostitution. A room let for private occupation might come to be the resort of a number of people who wished to smoke opium so that the time would come when the room could rationally be described as a room used for the purpose of smoking opium.' *Sweet v Parsley* [1969] 1 All ER 347 at 355, per Lord Morris of Borth-y-Gest

'"Purpose" connotes an intention by some person to achieve a result desired by him.' Ibid at 363, 364, per Lord Diplock

Australia 'When a person applies for a permit, subjectively he has some end or object to achieve. That is the purpose of his application. On the other hand, the "effect" caused by the permit when granted will be the result of achieving the end or object, and not necessarily the achievement of the end or object in itself.' *SS Constructions Pty Ltd v Ventura Motors Pty Ltd* [1964] VR 229 at 241, per Gillard J

PURSUANT TO

Australia 'Conduct may be said to be "pursuant to" a specified course if that course is followed by compulsion, or by voluntary adoption or perhaps by accident. . . . "Pursuant to" may, as it were, link up the reason for what is carried out, or may describe objectively the nature or character of the acts, or may include both these features.' *Groves v Groves* [1944] SASR 187 at 189, 190, per Mayo J

Australia 'The respondent's further submission, and this was accepted by the learned magistrate, was that the drawing of water from the well could not be said to be "pursuant to a licence" [within the Rights in Water and Irrigation Act 1914–1986 (WA)] because the appellants had broken an essential condition of their licence in refusing to permit meters to be fixed to their wells. "Pursuant to" is defined by the Oxford Dictionary to mean, inter alia, "in accordance with", "consequent and conformable to". The respondent maintains that the licence was clearly conditional on meters being fixed if so required by him, and that by their refusal to allow this condition to be fulfilled, the appellants were really drawing water in a manner not authorised by the licence and in fact in disregard of its provisions and, therefore, the water was drawn otherwise than "pursuant to a licence" and the appellants were in breach of s 15(2) [see now s 11]. We agree with this contention.' *Garbin v Wild* [1965] WAR 72 at 76, per Wolff CJ and Jackson J

PURSUIVANT *See* ARMS

PURVEYOR

'Purveyor', in relation to milk, includes any person who sells milk, whether wholesale or by retail. (Food Act 1984, s 132(1))

PUT OFF

'I must confess, if I were a juryman, I should have little doubt what was the meaning of the term "put off". . . . The meaning appears to be . . . postponed.' *Thornton v Charles* (1842) 9 M & W 802 at 809, per Rolfe B

Q

QUACK

'Unfortunately the learned judge told the jury more than once that the term ('quack') means a pretender to skill which the pretender did not possess. If that were a sound direction, and really it was put as a direction, there could not be a verdict on this point against the plaintiff, for admittedly he possessed skill. But there are other meanings of the word "quack", such as a person who, however skilled, lends himself to a medical imposture.' *Dakhyl v Labouchere* [1908] 77 LJKB 728 at 729, per Lord Loreburn LC

QUALIFIED

[The memorandum of association of a company provided that a director should be a 'qualified' person.] 'What does a "qualified person" postulate? Table A, art 70, provides that the qualification of a director shall be "the holding of at least one share". . . . It looks at first sight difficult to decide what the expression "qualified person" in special art 20 really means. . . . I think it means a person actually "holding" the necessary share qualification.' *Spencer v Kennedy* [1926] Ch 125 at 133, 134, per Astbury J

[As to the share qualification of directors see now the Companies Act 1985, s 291.]

Canada 'It is a matter of fact whether anyone may or may not be qualified [to drive a motor vehicle], in other words, qualified is synonymous with competent or being capable of driving. . . . In my view, the principle established . . . is not that "qualified" goes to the matter of obtaining a permit, but qualified means exactly what it says, that is, whether a person is or is not capable of operating a motor vehicle, and if he is so the policy is not voided.' *Schauerte v Wawanesa Mutual Insurance Co* (1959) 27 WWR 618 at 620, Alta SC, per Cairns J; affirmed 29 WWR 560, Alta SC

QUALITY *See also* CONDITION; MERCHANTABLE QUALITY

'Quality', in relation to any articles, includes the state and condition of those articles. (Agricultural Produce (Grading and Marketing) Act 1928, s 7)

'Quality', in relation to goods, includes their state or condition. (Sale of Goods Act 1979, s 61(1))

'It seems to me that while in reference to some things and to some defects in them "condition" and "quality" may mean the same thing, yet that they do not either necessarily or even usually do so. I think that "condition" refers to external and apparent condition, and "quality" to something which is usually not apparent, at all events to an unskilled person. I think a captain is expected to notice the apparent condition of the goods, though not the quality.' *Compania Naviera Vasconzada v Churchill & Sim, Compania Naviera Vasconzada v Burton & Co* [1906] 1 KB 237 at 245, per Channell J

[The Sale of Food and Drugs Act 1875, s 6 (repealed; see now the Food Act 1984, s 2(1)) enacted that no person should sell to the prejudice of the purchaser any article of food which was not of the nature, substance and 'quality' of the article demanded by the purchaser.] 'There has been some argument with reference to the meaning of the word "quality" in the section, and there has been a suggestion, that "quality" is equivalent in the section to "description". I do not think that is so. In my judgment quality means commercial quality, and not the commercial description of the article.' *Anness v Grivell* [1915] 3 KB 685 at 691, per Lord Reading CJ

'If a commodity has various qualities, an expensive and good quality and a cheap inferior quality, if a person demanding the article pays the price which is known to be the price of the most expensive and the best quality, and the vendor palms off upon him an article of the cheapest and inferior quality, it seems to me that it is perfectly competent to the justices . . . to take into consideration the price that the purchaser paid and infer from that that when the cheaper article or the cheaper quality of that article was given to him, but he was paying the price known to be the price of the higher quality, he was getting something not of the quality demanded.' Ibid at 694, per Lush J

'I should take it to be an offence [under the Sale of Food and Drugs Act 1875, s 6 (repealed; see supra)] to supply under a demand for milk or cows' milk asses' or goats' milk, and I notice that Darling J in *Smithies v Bridge* [[1902] 2 KB 13] said: "I understand by the word 'milk' cows' milk, and I do not think that a person asking for milk would expect to get asses' milk, or that of any other animals." I gather that the learned judge would have convicted a vendor of milk who supplied asses' milk of supplying goods not of the nature demanded, though he had added nothing to and subtracted nothing from the natural product. The same view would apply to a man supplying chicory in answer to a demand for coffee, plaice in answer to a demand for soles, margarine with no butter in it in answer to a demand for butter. He has not supplied goods of the nature demanded, whether he has adulterated the goods or not. It is not necessary to consider here what meaning "substance" has as distinct from "nature". Perhaps Reginald Picard, of Stamford, who was convicted at the fair of St Ives in 1275 of selling a ring of brass for 5½d, "saying that the ring was of the purest gold and that he and a one-eyed man found it on the last

Sunday in the church of St Ives near the cross", could be convicted at the present day, amongst other offences, of selling an article not of the "substance" demanded. There remains the word "quality". Again it appears that a vendor commits an offence who sells an article not of the quality demanded whether he has or has not added anything to or taken anything from the article he sells. Where natural products are sold as "firsts" or "seconds" according to quality it would be, in my view, an offence to sell seconds when asked for firsts though nothing had been done to the seconds by the vendor. This would apply to different qualities of coal or of eggs. A man who when asked for new laid eggs supplied cooking eggs, as these terms are understood in the market, could be convicted of supplying goods not of the quality demanded, though he had not adulterated the eggs by addition or abstraction. On the meaning of the word "quality" we have the guidance of the court in *Anness v Grivell* [supra]. Lord Reading CJ said: "Quality means commercial quality, and not the commercial description of the article." Darling J said: "I quite agree that the word 'quality' in s 6 of the Sale of Food and Drugs Act 1875 means the commercial quality, and is not equivalent to such a word as 'kind'. I do not think we can limit it to the sort of use that Mr Barrington-Ward [counsel] suggested, on behalf of the appellant, in the illustration that a purchaser would ask for Scotch or Irish, Lowland or Highland whisky. I think it means quality in the sense which my Lord has indicated." Lush J agreed, and contrasted the most expensive and best quality with the cheapest and inferior quality.' *Hunt v Richardson* [1916] 2 KB 446 at 457, 458, DC per Scrutton J

'There can be no doubt that, if a person orders pills of one grain and gets a pill 75 per cent of that quantity, he is not getting an article of the nature and quality he has demanded, but is getting an article which is sold to his prejudice.' *Breed v British Drug Houses Ltd* [1947] 2 All ER 613 at 614, per Lord Goddard CJ

QUALITY OR FITNESS

(1) Except as provided by this section and section 15 [sale by sample] below and subject to any other enactment, there is no implied condition or warranty about the quality or fitness for any particular purpose of goods supplied under a contract of sale.

(2) Where the seller sells goods in the course of a business, there is an implied condition that the goods supplied under the contract are of merchantable quality, except that there is no such condition—

(a) as regards defects specifically drawn to the buyer's attention before the contract is made; or
(b) if the buyer examines the goods before the contract is made, as regards defects which that examination ought to reveal.

(3) Where the seller sells goods in the course of a business and the buyer, expressly or by implication, makes known—

(a) to the seller, or
(b) where the purchase price or part of it is payable by instalments and the goods were previously sold by a credit-broker to the seller, to that credit broker,

any particular purpose for which the goods are being bought, there is an implied condition that the goods supplied under the contract are reasonably fit for that purpose, whether or not that is a purpose for which such goods are commonly supplied, except where the circumstances show that the buyer does not rely, or that it is unreasonable for him to rely, on the skill or judgment of the seller or credit-broker

(4) An implied condition or warranty about quality or fitness for a particular purpose may be annexed to a contract of sale by usage.

(5) The preceding provisions of this section apply to a sale by a person who in the course of a business is acting as agent for another as they apply to a sale by a principal in the course of a business, except where that other is not selling in the course of a business and either the buyer knows that fact or reasonable steps are taken to bring it to the notice of the buyer before the contract is made.

(6) Goods of any kind are of merchantable quality within the meaning of subsection (2) above if they are as fit for the purpose or purposes for which goods of that kind are commonly bought as it is reasonable to expect having regard to any description applied to them, the price (if relevant) and all the other relevant circumstances. (Sale of Goods Act 1979, s 14)

QUANTITY

In this section 'quantity' includes length, width, height, area, volume, capacity, weight and number. (Trade Descriptions Act 1968, s 2)

QUANTITY RECEIPT

New Zealand 'Counsel for the defendant argued that the words "more or less", and "weight, measure, quality contents, and value unknown", on the shipper's receipt constitute what is known in shipping and railway business as a "quantity receipt", and therefore that the onus of showing that any given quantity was in fact received on board the SS Moeraki lay upon the plaintiff. There was no evidence to support the suggestion that a receipt in this form is recognised as a "quantity receipt", and I do not think it can be so described. The Railway receipts produced admit receipt of a "quantity" only, no number or measurements of pieces being given. They are properly called "quantity receipts", but the term cannot be applied to documents which give both the number of pieces shipped and their measurements.' *Carson v Union SS Co* [1922] NZLR 778 at 782, per Adams J

QUANTUM MERUIT

The terms 'quantum meruit' or 'quantum valebat' are used in three distinct senses at common law, namely as denoting: (1) a claim by one party to a contract, for example on breach of the contract by the other party, for reasonable remuneration for what he has done; (2) a mode of redress on a new contract which has replaced a previous one; (3) a reasonable price of remuneration which will be implied in a contract where no price or remuneration has been fixed for goods sold or work done.

Of these three types of claim, the second and third are clearly contractual, whereas the first is not based on contract and is considered in the following paragraphs. Analogous to this first type are the Admiralty rules of salvage, and the statutory claims for necessaries supplied to persons under a contractual disability and benefits conferred under frustrated contracts. (9 Halsbury's Laws (4th edn) para 692)

QUARRY *See also* MINE

'Quarry' usually implies surface workings of minerals, leaving no roof overhead. The manner in which the minerals are extracted is not, however, a conclusive test in distinguishing a quarry from a mine. Thus in some circumstances surface workings are regarded as mines, while 'quarry' may be used to denote workings for slate even where they are carried on almost exclusively underground, although it has been held that a slate quarry worked by means of underground levels in a mine. A sand or gravel pit may be a quarry; but workings in a heap of furnace slag are not. (31 Halsbury's Laws (4th edn) para 2)

(2) In this Act the expression 'quarry' means an excavation or system of excavations made for the purpose of, or in connexion with, the getting of minerals (whether in their natural state or in solution or suspension) or products of minerals, being neither a mine nor merely a well or bore-hole or a well and bore-hole combined.

(3) For the purposes of this Act—

(a) . . .

(b) there shall be deemed to form part of a quarry so much of the surface (including buildings, structures and works thereon) surrounding or adjacent to the quarry as is occupied together with the quarry for the purpose of, or in connexion with, the working of the quarry, the treatment, preparation for sale, consumption or use, storage or removal from the quarry of the minerals or products thereof gotten from the quarry or the removal from the quarry of the refuse thereof:

Provided that there shall not, for the said purposes, be deemed to form part of a . . . quarry premises in which a manufacturing process is carried on otherwise than for the purpose of the working of the . . . quarry or the preparation for sale of minerals gotten therefrom.

(4) For the purposes of this Act premises for the time being used for depositing refuse from a single . . . quarry, being premises exclusively occupied by the owner of that . . . quarry, shall be deemed to form part of that . . . quarry, and premises for the time being used for depositing premises occupied by the owner of one of those . . . quarries (either exclusively or jointly with the owner of the other or any of the others) shall be deemed to form part of such one of those . . . quarries as the Health and Safety Executive may direct.

(5) For the purposes of this Act a railway line serving a single . . . quarry (not being a railway line falling within subsection (3) of this section or a railway line belonging to a railway company) shall be deemed to form part of that . . . quarry and a railway line jointly serving two or more . . . quarries (not being a railway line falling within subsection (3) of this section or a railway line belonging to a railway company)

shall be deemed to form part of such one of them as the Health and Safety Executive may direct.

(6) For the purposes of this Act a conveyor or aerial ropeway provided for the removal from a . . . quarry of minerals gotten therefrom or refuse therefrom shall be deemed to form part of the . . . quarry. (Mines and Quarries Act 1954, s 180)

[The omitted parts of this section refer to the meaning of 'mine' (qv).]

'Upon reference to the lexicographical part of the Encyclopaedia Metropolitana, I find . . . that the . . . word "quarry" is . . . stated to be derived from the French word "*quarriere*" and the derivation is followed by this description: "In the Latin of the lower ages, *quadratarius* was a stonecutter *qui marmora quadrat*, and hence *quarriere*, the place where he *quadrates* or cuts the stones in squares; the place where the stone is cut in squares; generally, a stone-pit";—clearly, therefore, referring to a place upon or above, and not under, the ground.' *Bell v Wilson* (1866) 1 Ch App 303 at 309, per Turner LJ

'I do not pretend to define exactly what a quarry is; but I think that by that word one generally means a place from which something is cut out in large shapes or blocks, not a place from which the material is got in small quantities, such as lumps of coal, ironstone and the like.' *Jones v Cwmorthen Slate Co Ltd* (1879) 49 LJ QB 110 at 111, CA, per Bramwell LJ

'The conveyance is of all the lands, tenements, and hereditaments mentioned in the schedule, and if there were no reservation, that would carry all the minerals within the ambit; but then there is reserved "all mines of coal culm iron and all other mines and minerals whatsoever except stone quarries. . . ." Now I cannot help thinking that should be read "all mines of coal culm iron and all other mines and all minerals whatsoever", for I do not think the word "other" can be applied to minerals. Then come the words "except stone quarries". Does not that shew that mines must be included which have to be worked by taking away the refuse from two or more . . . quarries, being surface? A quarry is a thing which is worked in that way, and not by sinking a shaft.' *Jersey (Earl) v Neath Poor Law Union Guardians* (1889) 22 QBD 555 at 558, CA, per Lord Esher MR

QUARTER

'We find in a lease made in 1793, a reservation of so many quarters of corn; and in deciding on this lease, we must understand it to be so many quarters according to legal measure.' *St Cross Hospital (Master) v Howard de Walden (Lord)* (1795) 6 Term Rep 338 at 344, per Grose J

QUARTER DAYS

For some purposes, and especially in the relations of landlord and tenant, the year is divided into four quarters, the four usual quarter days being the four feast days, Lady Day (25th March), Midsummer Day (24th June), Michaelmas Day (29th September), and Christmas Day (25th December).

The half-quarter days are 2nd February, 9th May, 11th August, and 11th November (Martinmas). (45 Halsbury's Laws (4th edn) para 1106)

In this Act . . . 'quarter' means a period of three months ending at the end of March, June, September or December. (Value Added Tax Act 1983, s 48(1))

QUARTER SESSIONS

[Quarter sessions were abolished by the Courts Act 1971, and their jurisdiction transferred to the Crown Courts. See now the Supreme Court Act 1981, s 8.]

QUASH

[The Court of Criminal Appeal made an order 'quashing' a sentence and substituting a lesser term of imprisonment.] 'Counsel for the plaintiff has submitted to me cogently that the word "quash" in that order means that the ten-year sentence was thereby rendered null and void and wholly set aside as though it had never been. There would be persuasive force in that argument, and I would be disposed to accept it, had I not found in the very wording of s 4(3) of the Criminal Appeal Act 1907 [repealed; see now the Criminal Appeal Act 1968, s 11(3)(a)] the provision that, wherever the Court of Criminal Appeal finds itself of the opinion that a sentence passed has been too severe, it shall quash that sentence and pass such sentence as the court thinks ought to have been passed in substitution therefor. It seems to me that, when one finds those words in the section and considers the context in which they are used and the subject-matter to which they must be applied, one is inevitably driven to the conclusion that the word "quash" is not there used in the sense in which the Shorter Oxford

Dictionary tells me that it often is used, "to annul, make null or void"; but instead that it is used in the less drastic meaning, that the former sentence is by the order of the court rendered null and void at the moment when the Court of Criminal Appeal decides to substitute for it a different sentence, so as to make that earlier sentence null and void and of no effect from that point of time onwards, but not so as to render it null and void *ab initio*, i.e., as from the date when it was passed.' *Hancock v Prison Comrs* [1959] 3 All ER 513 at 514, per Winn J

[The Court of Criminal Appeal has been abolished and appeals are now heard by the criminal division of the Court of Appeal; see the Supreme Court Act 1981, s 3.]

QUASI CONTRACT

In some cases a contract is said to be implied by law. Such an implied contract is really an obligation imposed by law independently of an actual agreement between the parties, and may be imposed notwithstanding an expressed intention by one of the parties to the contrary. It is not a contract in the true sense of the term at all, but an obligation of the class known as quasi contract, a term derived from the civil law systems. (9 Halsbury's Laws (4th edn) para 212)

QUASI EASEMENT

Quasi easements are rights which are analogous to easements but which are not in strictness easements, because some necessary element is wanting. They are not easements proper, inasmuch as they are generally enjoyed by classes of persons the members of which are continually changing and are continually fluctuating in number, so that they could not in the class name take a grant of such rights; for, unless rights in the land of another are such that they are capable of being granted to and released by the persons enjoying them, they do not amount to easements.

The term quasi easement is not a strict legal term. It is used generally as denoting the accommodation afforded by one tenement to another when both tenements are owned by the same person and where the accommodation thus afforded would in fact be an easement had the tenement affording the accommodation been owned by another person. (12 Halsbury's Laws (4th edn) para 429, 429n)

QUAY

'The question on the first part of the present case is whether that which was occupied by the respondent does properly answer the description in the rate-book. If it was properly described and it did not appear upon the facts, as compared with the description, that certain premises not in occupation of the respondent had been included, then the above-mentioned consequence follows. The description which is in the rate-book and which has to be satisfied is "quay and wharves". No doubt there may be many descriptions containing different terms between which the difference is so great that it is impossible to say that a particular hereditament might appear indifferently to be either the one or the other. No one, for example, except perhaps for a controversial purpose, could suggest that a mansion-house can be mistaken for a stable. But it may be very different with other things, as, for example, boots and shoes, or quays and wharves. . . . I ask myself whether the expression "quay and wharves", is not a generic description which the hereditaments occupied by the respondent satisfied, and I hope that in coming to the conclusion that they did satisfy it, I am not influenced by the complete lack of merits in the respondent's contention. When one looks at the map, it is obvious that while in the printed words a certain portion of what is delineated is described as a "wharf" the very same thing is described on the plan as a "quay". I cannot help thinking that this expression "quay and wharves" is no more a combination of distinct things than would be the expression "quay and (or) wharves", or "quay or wharves", and in this case that which was occupied by the respondent faithfully satisfied the description.' *Vernon v Castle* (1922) 127 LT 748 at 753, per Lord Hewart CJ

'I think that for the purpose of this case no distinction can be made between the words "quay" and "wharf", or "wharves", and the expression "quay and wharves" applies to a quay or wharves.' Ibid at 753, per Salter J

' "Quay" . . . is a water-side structure of solid character for loading or unloading ships.' *Feeney v Pollexfen & Co Ltd* [1931] IR 589 at 597, per Kennedy CJ

See, generally 20 Halsbury's Laws (4th edn) para 428.

QUESTION

'I proceed . . . to consider what is the statutory

duty laid upon the Board of Education in regard to disputes of this kind. Their duties, so far as concerns the present litigation, are twofold. In the first place they are required by s 7, sub-s 3, of the Act of 1902 [Education Act 1902 (repealed; see now Education Act 1944, s 67)] to determine a certain class of questions. The words of the sub-section run as follows: "If any question arises under this section between the local education authority and the managers of a school not provided by the authority, that question shall be determined by the Board of Education." The Attorney-General argued, as I understood him, that the questions here pointed at are only such as arise from the statutory relations between a local education authority and managers, and are not such as arise from the duty of one or other toward the public. He contended that the duty of maintaining and keeping efficient a non-provided school, though it is in terms imposed by s 7 of the Act, is not a matter which can be a "question" between the local education authority and the managers, so as to come within the jurisdiction of the Board. I cannot accept this view. The managers are directly interested in the proper maintenance. They are the persons primarily to call upon the local education authority for such proper maintenance. And I do not understand how it can be held that if they do so call upon the local education authority, and the latter disputes the point, it is not a question arising between them.' *Board of Education v Rice* [1911] AC 179 at 181, per Lord Loreburn LC

[There are now no managers of schools. Questions between local education authorities and governors are to be decided by the Secretary of State for Education and Science.]

QUI PRIOR EST TEMPORE, POTIOR EST JURE

Australia 'In all cases where a claim to enforce an equitable interest in property is opposed on the ground that after the interest is said to have arisen a third party innocently acquired an equitable interest in the same property, the problem, if the facts relied upon as having given rise to the interests be established, is to determine where the better equity lies. If the merits are equal, priority in time of creation is considered to give the better equity. This is the true meaning of the maxim *qui prior est tempore potior est jure*. . . . But where the merits are unequal, as for instance where conduct on the part of the owner of the earlier interest has led the other to acquire his interest on the supposition that the earlier did not exist, the maxim may be displaced and priority accorded to the later interest.' *Latec Investments Ltd v Hotel Terrigal Pty Ltd* [1965] 113 CLR 265 at 276, per Kitto J

QUIET ENJOYMENT

An express covenant for quiet enjoyment may be a qualified covenant, namely a covenant that the tenant is peaceably to hold and enjoy the demised premises during the term without interruption by the landlord or person claiming through or under him; or it may be an absolute covenant, in which case it extends also to interruption by persons claiming by title paramount. The qualified form is usually adopted, and under it the landlord is not liable for acts of persons claiming by title paramount, even though those acts are the consequences of his own default. Hence in the case of a sublease, if the superior landlord evicts the sublessee for non-payment of the head rent, or for non-observance by him of a covenant of which he had received no notice from the sub-lessor, this is not a breach of the covenant for quiet enjoyment; but it is a breach if the sub-lessor submits to judgment in an action for recovery of possession by a person who has no title to sue, and the sub-lessee is in consequence evicted.

The covenant usually provides for quiet enjoyment 'without interruption by the landlord or any persons rightfully claiming under or in trust for him', or 'without any lawful interruption by the landlord or any persons claiming under or in trust for him'. Whichever of these forms is used, the covenant only protects against the acts of persons claiming under the landlord so far as they are successors in title to the landlord, or actually have authority from him to do the acts; and the effect is the same even if the words 'rightfully' or 'lawful' are not inserted. The covenant does not extend to acts of a stranger, notwithstanding that he purports to claim under the landlord, nor does it extend to unlawful acts of persons who in fact derive title under the landlord; but it extends to all acts of the landlord himself which interrupt the enjoyment, whether they are lawful or not. An act may constitute a breach of the covenant even where, apart from the covenant, the landlord has the right to do the act complained of.

Although in general the covenantor is not taken to covenant against the wrongful acts of strangers, it is otherwise if a person is specified in the covenant, as the covenantor then knows against whose acts he covenants.

It follows that it is no breach if the interruption is caused by an adjoining tenant whose lease, although granted by the same landlord, does not authorise the act causing the interruption; and there is no breach, in the case of a lease of sporting rights over a farm with a covenant for quiet enjoyment, if the farm tenant interferes with the sporting rights in breach of the terms of his own lease.

Where a lease granted by the Crown contains an express covenant for quiet enjoyment, the covenant must by necessary implication be read so as to exclude those measures affecting the nation as a whole which the Crown takes for the public good. (27 Halsbury's Laws (4th edn) paras 322, 323)

'The plaintiff rests his case, in the first place, on the covenant for quiet enjoyment, and the point so raised is one of importance. He has a lease, and in that lease there is a covenant in the usual terms. Those terms vary very little in one lease from another, but it is a covenant that he "and his executors, administrators, and assigns shall and may peaceably and quietly possess and enjoy the hereby demised premises during the said term without any eviction or disturbances by the said J E Jackson and C J Jackson", or any persons lawfully claiming under them. It is in the ordinary form; and before passing further let me observe, lest there should be a mistake, that "quietly" does not mean undisturbed by noise. When a man is quietly in possession it has nothing whatever to do with noise, though the word "quiet" is frequently used with reference to noise. "Peaceably and quietly" means without interference—without interruption of the possession.' *Jenkins v Jackson* (1888) 40 Ch D 71 at 73, 74, per Kekewich J

New Zealand 'A breach of a covenant [in a lease] for quiet enjoyment can occur without actual physical interference. It is sufficient if there is substantial interruption which prevents the lessee from enjoying its premises for the very purpose for which they were leased.' *Kalmac Property Consultants Ltd v Delicious Foods Ltd* [1974] 2 NZLR 631 at 637, CA, per Haslam J

QUIT

'The plaintiff might be unable to pay [his creditors], without being guilty of fraud, as imputed by the word "bolting", used in the libel. That expression charged the plaintiff with going away suddenly, . . . leaving debts unpaid, and under such circumstances that the creditors could not find him, and therefore means more than . . . mere "quitting". . . . That would be an innocent departure, and consistent with proof that the plaintiff went out of the town for a day, but then returned and paid his debts.' *O'Brien v Bryant* (1846) 16 M & W 168 at 171, per Parke B

QUIT RENT *See* RENT

QUO WARRANTO

An information in the nature of a *quo warranto* took the place of the obsolete writ of *quo warranto* which lay against a person who claimed or usurped an office, franchise, or liberty, to inquire by what authority he supported his claim, in order that the right to the office or franchise might be determined. It also lay in cases of non-user, abuse, or long neglect of a franchise. Certain limitations were imposed on the scope of the information by statutory provisions to the effect that elections to certain offices should not be questioned on the ground that the person elected was at the time of election disqualified, save by election petition. In 1933 an alternative form of proceedings was substituted for informations in respect of the qualification of persons acting as members of a local authority or as mayors of boroughs, and it was provided that except in the form so substituted no proceedings, whether by way of information in the nature of *quo warranto* or otherwise, should be taken against a person on the ground that he had, while disqualified from acting as a member of a local authority or mayor of a borough, so acted or claimed to be entitled so to act. In 1938 all informations in the nature of *quo warranto* were abolished, and it was provided that, in any case where a person acted in an office in which he was not entitled to act and an information in the nature of *quo warranto* would have lain against him, the High Court may at the instance of any person who would have been entitled to apply for such an information, grant an injunction restraining the former from so acting and may, if the case so required declare the office to be vacant. (1 Halsbury's Laws (4th edn) para 169)

QUORUM

'The word "quorum", in its ordinary signification, has reference to the existence of a complete body of persons, of whom a certain specified number are competent to transact the business of the whole. But a quorum of a board of directors does not constitute the board, though, in the absence of other existing directors, it may legally transact all such business as the whole board is competent to transact.' *Faure Electric Accumulator Co Ltd v Phillipart* (1888) 58 LT 525 at 527, per Hawkins J

New Zealand 'A quorum is "the number of members of an administrative or judicial body whose presence is necessary for the acts of the body to be valid": Wharton's Law Lexicon [10th ed 635]. What is the object of fixing a quorum? Is it enabling, by allowing a statutory body which could otherwise act only by an actual majority to carry out its powers and duties by a majority of a lesser number than its whole members; or is it restrictive, by constituting a fixed minimum of its members as necessary to constitute a valid meeting? If enabling, then it would, in the absence of a fixed quorum, require at least a majority of the whole members to give validity to any action; if restrictive, then, until a quorum was fixed, the business of such statutory body could be done by any two or more members attending a properly called meeting.' *Loughlin v Guinness* (1904) 23 NZLR 748 at 754, per Denniston J; also reported 6 GLR 458 at 461